the
AMERICANA
ANNUAL

1980

GROLIER

AN ENCYCLOPEDIA OF THE EVENTS OF 1979

YEARBOOK OF THE ENCYCLOPEDIA AMERICANA

This annual has been prepared as a yearbook for general encyclopedias. It is also published as *Encyclopedia Year Book*.

CONTENTS

FEATURE ARTICLES OF THE YEAR

THE ALPHABETICAL SECTION

Separate entries on the continents, the major nations of the world, U. S. states, Canadian provinces, and chief cities will be found under their own alphabetically arranged headings.

"WEAPONRY INFLATION"

SUPERPOWER SALT SALES

U.S.-U.S.S.R. ARMS SPECIAL REDUCED INCREASE from what the increase would otherwise be

1979

© 1979 BY HERBLOCK IN "THE WASHINGTON POST"

SALT 2 AGREEMENT

W. EUROPE

© "LONDON SUNDAY TELEGRAPH"/ROTHCO

SALT II

The Embattled Treaty

By Strobe Talbott

Diplomatic Correspondent, Time Magazine
Author, "Endgame: The Inside Story of SALT II"

The two presidents—Jimmy Carter of the United States and Leonid Brezhnev of the Soviet Union—met on a stage in the splendid ballroom of the Hofburg, the Imperial Palace of the Habsburgs, in Vienna, Austria. It was Monday, June 18, 1979. In front of each leader was a leather binder embossed in gold with the seal of his country. The binders contained copies, in English and Russian, of a treaty that would last until 1985, a protocol that would run to the end of 1981, and set of accompanying declarations and agreements relating to the deadliest weapons possessed by the two superpowers. Together, the documents were known as SALT II—the consummation of the second round in the ten-year-old Strategic Arms Limitation Talks.

The first round, SALT I, began in 1969 and culminated in May 1972, when President Richard Nixon met with Brezhnev in Moscow and the two leaders signed an agreement limiting the size of their respective arsenals. Congressional approval for SALT I in 1972 had been a foregone conclusion. Not so with its sequel, SALT II. Much of the American public and many members of Congress had grown fearful of burgeoning Soviet military might and skeptical of arms-control pacts. So when Carter and Brezhnev went through the motions of the signing ceremony beneath the chandeliers of the Hofburg in Vienna, whatever sense of relief, achievement, and celebration they managed to generate was clouded by apprehension, uncertainty, and suspense over the fate of the treaty. That fate did not rest exclusively in the hands of the executive branch of the U. S. government. Before its provisions could be binding on the Soviets it had to be ratified by a two-thirds majority of the Senate. The politics of ratification were destined to be every bit as harrowing as the negotiations that produced the treaty.

It was not the first time that U. S. diplomacy abroad had been complicated by the workings of democracy at home. At the end of World War I, President Woodrow Wilson promoted the creation of the League of Nations to assure a permanent peace. The Senate, however, sought to attach to the legislation an array of amendments and reservations that would have enabled the United States to join the League. Wilson opposed any attempts to amend the Treaty of Versailles. He wanted all or nothing—and got nothing. In November 1919 the Senate rejected the treaty. Six years later, ambassadors from most of the nations in the world met in Geneva to sign a prohibition on the use of poisonous gas and bacteriological weapons. The United States did not become a party to that agreement until 1975—a full 50 years after it was originally enacted. There has always been a deep U. S. suspicion of international covenants that oblige it to forswear weapons and surrender even a modicum of its sovereignty. The reason is not so much pugnacity as prudence: many Americans have worried that other nations, less encumbered by honesty and idealism, might

U. S. President Woodrow Wilson and other leaders gather to draft the constitution of the League of Nations.

THE BETTMANN ARCHIVE, INC.

UPI

To celebrate the 1963 nuclear test ban treaty, Dean Rusk and Nikita Khrushchev enjoy some badminton.

pretend to comply with such agreements while secretly stockpiling the proscribed weapons. This longstanding American mistrust of attempts to regulate the arms race—"What if we play by the rules and the other guy cheats?"—was to become a prominent theme in the domestic political debate over SALT II.

Historically, the Soviet Union has been even less predisposed to arms control than the United States. Centuries of invasions and outside influence have left the Russian people leery of foreign powers. It was therefore not surprising that the Soviets would wait nearly two decades after the explosion of their first nuclear device before seriously considering any limitations on their arsenal of offensive weapons.

Before the Strategic Arms Limitation Talks began in earnest in 1969, there was a series of modest but significant steps along the path to SALT II. In December 1959, toward the end of the Eisenhower administration, the United States and eleven other countries, including the USSR, signed a treaty forbidding the testing and deployment of weapons in Antarctica. Then in August 1963, during the Kennedy administration, the United States, Great Britain, and the Soviet Union signed a treaty that banned the testing of nuclear weapons in the atmosphere, under water, and in outer space; only underground tests were allowed. In the 16 years since that pact, the three signatories sought to extend the treaty to cover underground tests as well. In 1974 they agreed on the Threshold Test Ban Treaty, which limited underground nuclear weapons tests to a maximum explosive force equivalent to 150,000 tons (150 kilotons) of TNT. Two years later they imposed the same limit on the underground testing of nuclear explosives, such as those that might be used for excavating a canal or altering the course of a river. Since that time, the Carter administration has been pressing ahead with the negotiation of a Comprehensive Test Ban that would prohibit *all* testing of nuclear weapons.

Limiting and ultimately banning nuclear explosions is, of course, an important goal of arms control negotiations, since even test explosions wreak havoc on the physical environment and tend to unsettle the political environment as well. But after decades of testing, the genie of compact, reliable, high-yield nuclear warheads is already out of the bottle. Therefore, the more important and more difficult challenge is to restrict the means whereby the superpowers would hurl their warheads at each other: their intercontinental bombers and rockets and their missile-firing submarines. Restrictions on such offensive strategic (i.e. intercontinental) nuclear weapons have been the principal objective of SALT.

The principal achievement of the SALT I negotiations was, however, a treaty of indefinite duration restricting the number of *defensive* weapons allowed to each country. At the Moscow summit meeting of May 1972, Nixon and Brezhnev agreed to limit their respective antiballistic missile (ABM) defenses to two sites—one protecting the nation's capital and the other protecting a single cluster, or field, of silo launchers for intercontinental ballistic missiles (ICBMs). Two years later, they agreed to cut back one ABM site each. Paradoxical as it may seen, it was crucial for both nations to restrict their missile defenses if subsequent negotiations on the limitation of offensive arms were to be meaningful. In the strategy of doomsday, the best offense is a good defense. If one side is able to protect itself against the threat of a nuclear strike; it may be more inclined to throw its political weight around, bullying smaller countries and bluffing larger ones; the other side is then anxious to develop new and better offensive weapons, as well as to improve its own defenses. The ABM Treaty

U. S. President Richard Nixon and Soviet Chairman Leonid Brezhnev sign SALT I in Moscow, May 26, 1972.

UPI

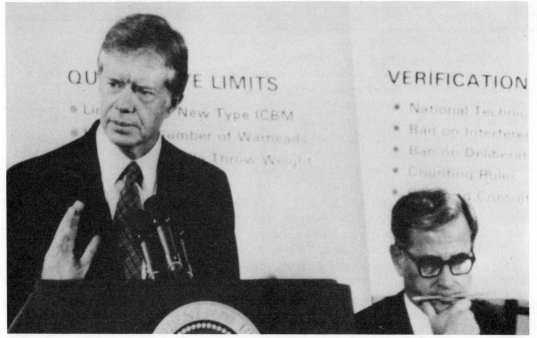

U. S. President Jimmy Carter and Secretary of Defense Harold Brown lobby for Congressional approval of SALT II.

of 1972 was a momentous achievement because it checked the proliferation of defensive weapons.

The accompanying SALT I Interim Agreement of Offensive Arms, also signed in May 1972, was more modest both in duration—it would expire after five years—and in strategic significance. It specified quantitative limitations on launchers for ICBMs and submarine-launched ballistic missiles (SLBMs). A protocol to the agreement allowed each side to deploy a limited number of additional SLBM launchers so long as an equal number of older ICBM or SLBM launchers were taken out of service. For ICBMs, "launchers" referred to underground silos; for SLBMs, it meant tubes aboard submarines. The negotiators agreed to count launchers rather than missiles because the aerial reconnaissance capabilities of each side could keep track of silos and boats more easily than individual rockets. Since the beginning of the negotiations, it has been a cardinal principle that each side must be able to verify independently the compliance of the other. There is no honor system in SALT.

Still, the SALT I Interim Agreement contained some serious defects. First, since it froze the intercontinental missile forces of both sides, and since the Russians had already built up a larger arsenal than the Americans, the pact left the USSR with a numerical advantage in strategic launchers of about 2,400 to 1,700. Second, it left the Russians with a monopoly of so-called heavy ICBMs. These are monstrous rockets twice as tall as the mainstay of the American deterrent force, the Minuteman ICBM. The disparity in size between the two types of ICBMs was the result of long-standing differences in U. S. and Soviet approaches to national defense: in the 1960's, the United States had decided to concentrate on the development of smaller, more accurate ICBMs and to distribute its nuclear firepower three ways—aboard bombers, on submarines, and in underground silos; the Soviets, meanwhile, concentrated on developing heavy ICBMs—blunder-

Soviet and American leaders completed SALT II negotiations in Vienna, Austria, in June 1979.

busses as opposed to sharpshooters' rifles—and kept the preponderance of their missiles on land rather than in the air or at sea.

In approving SALT I, the U. S. Senate attached a proviso in the form of a resolution sponsored by Sen. Henry Jackson (D-WA): future agreements must not contain numerical inequalities like those in SALT I. In negotiating SALT II, former National Security Adviser and Secretary of State Henry Kissinger was therefore under a congressional mandate to equalize any ceilings specified in the new agreement. This was achieved in November 1974, when Brezhnev hosted talks in Vladivostok with Kissinger and President Gerald Ford. The so-called Vladivostok Accord set a framework for SALT II, whereby each side would be limited to 2,400 strategic weapons, of which 1,320 could be armed with multiple, independently targetable reentry vehicles (MIRVs). For the first time Brezhnev also agreed to drop the long-standing Soviet insistence that SALT II restrict U. S. nuclear weapons in Europe, the so-called forward-based systems (FBS). In return, Ford and Kissinger agreed to allow the Soviets to keep their monopoly in heavy ICBMs. The biggest shortcoming at Vladivostok was the negotiators' failure to define two new weapons: the American cruise missile, a highly accurate drone, and the Soviet Backfire bomber. In subsequent months, SALT bogged down over the U. S. claim that the Backfire should count as a strategic weapon and a similar Soviet claim with regard to the cruise missile.

Early in 1976, Kissinger flew to Moscow and worked out a tentative compromise that would have imposed restrictions on the Backfire bomber in exchange for limitations on the cruise missile. But that year's presidential campaign was already heating up, and Ronald Reagan was challenging Ford for the Republican nomination. Détente, SALT, and Kissinger himself were out of favor with the resurgent right wing of the Republican Party, and Ford would not support the deal Kissinger had made in Moscow. SALT was allowed to languish until after the November election.

The new president, Jimmy Carter, came into office brimming with new and ambitious ideas for SALT. In March 1977, he sent Secretary of State Cyrus Vance to Moscow with a proposal that disregarded most of what had been accomplished in the previous five years of SALT II negotiations. The proposal would have required the Soviets to make immediate and drastic cuts in their nuclear arsenal, including a 50% reduction in their heavy ICBMs. In exchange, the United States offered to scrap plans for the development of some new weapons, notably the MX, or "Missile-Experimental," a much larger successor to the Minuteman ICBM. The Soviets rejected the proposal out of hand and insisted that the Vladivostok accord remain the basis for SALT II.

Thus rebuffed, the Carter administration went back to the drawing board. Two months later, in May 1977, Vance carried a new American proposal to Geneva, where he met with Soviet Foreign Minister Andrei Gromyko. The proposal consisted of three parts: a treaty that would run until 1985, a shorter-term protocol, and a statement of principles to govern the next round of negotiations, SALT III. Gromyko accepted the three-tiered framework, but the two sides were far apart on which weapons should be covered in which tier. That disagreement—exacerbated by tensions in U. S.-Soviet relations over the Carter administration's advocacy of human rights, the Soviet and Cuban military involvement in Africa and the Middle East, and the normalization of diplomatic ties between Washington and Peking—dragged out the talks for two more years, until the late spring of 1979. The agreement that Carter and Brezhnev finally signed in Vienna was, as the Soviets had insisted, based largely on the Vladivostok accord and similar in some features to the compromise that Kissinger had hammered out with the Kremlin in early 1976. Relative to its predecessors, however, the SALT II agreement was more complex,

Members of the U. S. Senate Foreign Relations Committee consider the merits of the 1979 arms control agreement.

UPI

TASS FROM SOVFOTO   JAMES K. W. ATHERTON, ''THE WASHINGTON POST''

Soviet missiles (*left*) were a major concern of senators considering SALT II. Sen. Henry Jackson (D-WA) is opposed.

more comprehensive, and in many respects more favorable to the United
States:

> It required the Soviets to reduce their total arsenal of strate-
> gic launchers from the Vladivostok ceiling of 2,400 to 2,250
> by dismantling some of their older intercontinental missiles and
> bombers.

> It established two new limits unforeseen at Vladivostok—a
> combined maximum of 1,200 ICBM and SLBM launchers with
> multiple warheads, and not more than 820 MIRVed ICBMs
> alone. There was also a freeze on the number of multiple war-
> heads per type of ICBM. These provisions—the subceiling on
> MIRVed ICBMs and the MIRVing freeze—were intended to
> slow the rate at which the Soviets could add to their land-based
> multiple warheads, the most powerful, accurate, and threaten-
> ing part of their arsenal.

> It contained limits on the modernization of ICBMs and
> established a variety of rules by which the United States could
> more easily monitor the testing and deployment of Soviet rock-
> ets and thereby verify compliance with the treaty.

Still, the SALT II agreement was immensely controversial in the
United States. Critics of the treaty, such as Senator Jackson and Senate
Republican Party leader Howard Baker (TN), faulted the administration
for failing to force the Soviets to count the Backfire bomber as a strategic
weapon, failing to eliminate the Soviet advantage in heavy ICBMs, and

agreeing to restrictions on cruise missiles. Sen. John Glenn (D-OH) was concerned that the treaty did not go far enough in circumscribing the Soviets' right to use codes or scrambling in the transmission of electronic data during missile tests.

But the most serious doubts about SALT concerned not so much the text of the treaty as its political context—that is, how it fit into what were widely perceived as adverse trends in U. S.-Soviet relations. There was widespread concern that the USSR was embarked on an ominous military buildup and a global political offensive. Many felt that the United States needed a matching arms buildup of its own. Sen. Sam Nunn (D-GA) and Henry Kissinger led a movement to make ratification of the treaty contingent on a substantial increase in the U. S. defense budget. The Carter administration was willing to accept some such "linkage." By the end of summer, however, the Senate seemed to be moving toward ratification, and advocates seemed to be successfully resisting attempts by the opposition to attach "killer" amendments that would require renegotiation.

The progress of SALT II in the Senate was brought to an abrupt stop, however, when in late August the Carter administration belatedly discovered a Soviet combat brigade in Cuba. This touched off a firestorm of controversy about the geopolitical intentions and trustworthiness of the USSR, and SALT was suddenly in grave jeopardy. Sen. Frank Church (D-ID), the chairman of the Senate Foreign Relations Committee and a leading proponent of SALT, declared that the treaty would not be ratified until the issue of the Soviet brigade in Cuba was resolved. The Carter administration proclaimed the "unacceptability" of Soviet combat forces in Cuba; the Kremlin denied that the unit was there for combat purposes, saying its sole function was to train Cubans. Finally the United States warned it would monitor the brigade's maneuvers to make sure that it behaved like a training and not a combat unit. That finesse satisfied enough senators for the ratification debate to resume.

Diplomats and visiting statesmen from allies of the United States joined forces with the administration in lobbying Capitol Hill on behalf of the treaty. They argued that the failure of SALT II would undercut West European confidence in the reliability of the U. S. political system and thereby cast doubt on America's ability to lead the North Atlantic Treaty Organization (NATO). The force of that argument helped restore some of the momentum that had been lost in the Cuban imbroglio. On November 9, after four months of deliberation, the Senate Foreign Relations Committee approved the treaty and sent it to the floor for debate. The Committee's final vote was nine to six—more than the simple majority required to send the treaty to the full chamber but less than the two-thirds majority that would be required for ratification there. The crisis created in November and December by the seizure of the U. S. embassy in Tehran, Iran, threatened further to cloud the atmosphere of the debate with anger and anxiety about America's standing in the world, and the Soviet invasion of Afghanistan in the final days of the year led President Carter to call upon the Senate to delay its consideration of the treaty—possibly until after the presidential election of 1980. Nevertheless, the administration had already established an interagency task force to prepare for SALT III. Whether such preparations were merely wishful thinking would depend on whether the superpowers could, in the course of 1980, salvage détente and SALT from the clear and present danger of a new cold war and a new arms race.

MORLEY SAFER OF CBS
REVIEWS THE 1970's

For journalists there is something extremely reassuring about reviewing a decade. It is a reminder that unlike the petrochemical or elephant-hair bracelet industry, ours will never run out of raw material. Human foolishness, for better or worse, is not an endangered species or declining resource.

One need only browse through a list of events and crazes that possessed us during ten years to confirm that the outlook is very bright indeed. Journalists and undertakers are the only professionals I can think of who can be guaranteed that the future will be as grisly and rewarding as the past. We may not be the most welcome guests at dinner, but at least we know there is in the offing one version or other of war, pestilence, disco dancing, leisure suits, et al, to be first described, and then interred. After all, somebody's got to do it.

To try to extract a theme from the list below is as profitable a pastime as to try to read the next decade through the last one's chicken bones— particularly given that one of the technological breakthroughs of the 1970's was the boneless chicken.

The study of the future, anyway, may be the least precise of the sciences, if it is a science at all. Most of the "futurologists" of 1970, for example, had no inkling of OPEC, an acronym that can shatter the world with a whim. So, as you read the list below, do not try to divine from it some theme or some signpost. It is merely a list. Lots of important items were omitted for no other purpose than to make the list fit its space.

1970

January 12	Civil war in Nigeria ends as secessionist region of Biafra surrenders.
March 18	Cambodia's Norodom Sihanouk is overthrown in a coup led by Lon Nol.
April 1	The U. S. population is up 13.3% from 1960 census.
April 22	Americans observe Earth Day to center concern on the world environment.
April 24	China launches its first space satellite.
May	Demonstrations for and against the Indochina war, including the recent incursion of allied troops in Cambodia, spring up across the United States. Four student protesters are killed by National Guardsmen at Kent State, Kent, OH.
May 22	Leonard Woodcock succeeds, as UAW president, Walter Reuther, who was killed in a May 9 plane crash.
June 19	Conservative Party leader Edward Heath becomes prime minister of Britain.
August 12	An independent U. S. Postal Service replaces the U. S. Post Office.
August 26	American women observe the 50th anniversary of women's suffrage.
September 13	Asia's first world's fair, EXPO '70, closes in Osaka, Japan.
September 27	Jordan's King Hussein and guerrilla leader Yasir Arafat agree to end clashes between Palestinian guerrillas and Jordanian troops. Arab guerrillas had sought to dramatize their cause by staging a series of airline hijackings.
October 13	Canada and Communist China establish diplomatic relations.
October 16	Emergency wartime authority is invoked to combat separatist terrorism in Quebec.

1970 ALSO SAW—*skyjackings; women's pant suits; new industrial pollution controls; magicubes for instamatic cameras; coed campus living; NFL-AFL merger; Soviet spacecraft on Venus.*

October 17	Anwar el-Sadat becomes president of Egypt, succeeding Gamal Abdel Nasser, who died September 28 of a heart attack.
November 13	A massive cyclone and tidal wave strikes East Pakistan, killing thousands.
December 1	Italy's first divorce is approved.
December 20	Edward Gierek succeeds Władysław Gomułka as first secretary of Poland's Communist Party, following a week of riots caused by economic discontent.

1971

January 1	Cigarette advertising on radio and television ceases.
January 15	Egypt's Aswan High Dam is dedicated officially.
January 25	Idi Amin overthrows Uganda's President Milton Obote.
February	Women are given the vote in Switzerland and denied it in Liechtenstein.
February 11	Sixty-seven nations sign treaty banning nuclear weapons from ocean floor.
April 17	U. S. table-tennis team concludes seven-day visit to Communist China.
May 1	The U. S. National Railroad Passenger Corporation (Amtrak) begins to run the nation's intercity railroads.
May 9	West Germany and the Netherlands permit their currencies to float in relation to the U. S. dollar.
June 30	The U. S. Supreme Court rules that *The New York Times* and *The Washington Post* may resume publication of articles based on the Pentagon study of the Vietnam war.
	The 26th Amendment to the U. S. Constitution, lowering the voting age to 18, is ratified.
July	A primitive tribe of Stone Age human beings, the Tasadays, is discovered in the Philippines.
July 3	Indonesia holds its first elections in 16 years.
August 15	U. S. President Richard M. Nixon orders a 90-day freeze on wages and prices.
September 3	The United States, Britain, France, and the USSR sign a treaty regarding the divided city of Berlin.
September 8	The John F. Kennedy Center for the Performing Arts opens in Washington.
October 14	Iran marks the 2,500th anniversary of the Persian Empire.
October 25	The United Nations votes to seat the People's Republic of China and to expel the Republic of China (Taiwan).
November 5	The United States announces the sale of $136 million of feed grain to the Soviet Union—"the first step in an expansion of U. S.-USSR trade."
November 13	Mariner 9 orbits Mars, the first space probe to orbit another planet.
December 2	The White House Conference on Aging ends.
December 10	William H. Rehnquist is the fourth Nixon appointee to the Supreme Court to be confirmed.
December 17	Fifteen-day war between India and Pakistan over Bangladesh ends.
December 22	Austrian diplomat Kurt Waldheim is chosen secretary-general of the UN.

1971 ALSO SAW— snowmobiles and dune buggies; no-fault auto insurance; Hare Krishna and Jesus People; astronomical black holes; war demonstrations; hot pants; Walt Disney World; new off-track betting parlors.

1972

January 12	Sheikh Mujibur Rahman, leader of the new nation of Bangladesh, adopts a provisional constitution and names a cabinet.
February 3–13	Japan is the first Asian nation to host the Winter Olympics.
February 21–28	Richard Nixon is the first U. S. president to visit Communist China.
March 30	Britain suspends provisional government in Northern Ireland and imposes direct rule from London.
April 10	Seventy nations sign UN treaty banning stockpiling of "germ warfare" weapons.
April 15	The United States renews bombing of North Vietnam.

May 3	J. Edgar Hoover dies; L. Patrick Gray is named acting FBI director.
May 15	The United States returns the island of Okinawa to Japan.
	Alabama Gov. George C. Wallace is paralyzed from the waist down by a would-be assassin's bullet while campaigning for the presidency in Maryland.
May 26	Richard Nixon, the first U. S. president to visit Moscow, and Soviet Party Chairman Leonid Brezhnev sign agreement limiting antiballistic missile systems and offensive missile launchers.
June 17	Five men with electronic surveillance equipment are arrested for breaking into the headquarters of the Democratic National Committee in the Watergate complex in Washington.
July 18	President Sadat orders the immediate withdrawal of Soviet "military advisers and experts" from Egypt.
August 11	The last U. S. combat unit in Vietnam is deactivated.
August 26– September 11	At the XX Olympiad in Munich, Germany, Arab terrorists murder 11 Israelis; American swimmer Mark Spitz wins seven gold medals; 17-year-old Soviet gymnast Olga Korbut delights the world.
September 1	Bobby Fischer is the first American to win the world chess title.
September 23	Philippine President Ferdinand Marcos imposes martial law.
September 29	China and Japan establish diplomatic relations.
October 17	South Korea's President Chung Hee Park declares martial law.
November 7	U. S. President Nixon and Vice President Spiro T. Agnew win a second term, defeating Sen. George McGovern and R. Sargent Shriver.
November 14	The Dow-Jones industrial average closes above 1,000 for the first time.
December 19	Apollo 17 lands in the Pacific Ocean, completing the Apollo space program.
December 23	A series of earthquakes destroys Managua, Nicaragua.
December 30	U. S. bombing of North Vietnam north of 20th parallel, which was halted in October and resumed December 18, is stopped again.

1972 ALSO SAW—the 100th anniversary of Yellowstone; a trend toward condominiums and townhouses; U. S.-Soviet space cooperation treaty; the return of pandas to the U. S.; pocket calculators and the Polaroid SX-70; "The Godfather" and "Cabaret"; the ordination of the first woman rabbi; banning of DDT; more health-food stores; renewed curiosity concerning acupuncture.

The Olympic Village, Munich, 1972: West German policemen dressed as athletes attempt to confront Arab guerrillas and to free Israeli hostages. A 1978 treaty turned over the Panama Canal to Panamanian jurisdiction.

WIDE WORLD

RAY HALIN, RAPHO

1973

1973 ALSO SAW—*long gas lines and reduction of speed limits; blue jeans; beginning of Skylab space program; O. J. Simpson's rushing record; new telescope at Kitts Peak, AZ; "The Sting" and "The Way We Were"; Princess Anne marry; Billie Jean King defeat Bobby Riggs; the masses playing tennis.*

April 8, 1974, Hank Aaron hits his 715th homer, surpassing Ruth's record.

BALIOTTI, MOVEMENT CONCEPTS

January 1	Britain, Denmark, and Ireland join the Common Market.
January 22	The U. S. Supreme Court declares unconstitutional all state laws against women's right to abortion during first three months of pregnancy.
January 23	Vietnam cease-fire agreement is initialed in Paris.
January 27	The military draft ends in the United States.
February 12	U. S. prisoners of Vietnam war begin to return home.
February 15	U. S.-Cuban and Canadian-Cuban anti-hijacking agreements are signed.
February 21	The Laotian government and the Communist Pathet Lao agree to end war.
March 29	President Nixon announces price ceiling on beef, pork, and lamb, eight days after the release of report indicating highest monthly increase in Consumer Price Index in 22 years.
April 8	Spanish artist Pablo Picasso dies at 91.
April 30	President Nixon accepts responsibility for Watergate break-in. White House assistants H. R. Haldeman and John D. Ehrlichman and Attorney General Richard G. Kleindienst resign; John Dean is fired as presidential counsel.
May 7	*The Washington Post* wins a Pulitzer for its Watergate investigation.
May 8	The 70-day confrontation between Indians and federal agents at Wounded Knee, SD, ends.
May 17	The U. S. Senate Select Committee on Watergate, chaired by Sen. Sam Ervin (D-NC), opens public hearings.
June 9	Secretariat is the first horse to win racing Triple Crown since 1948.
July 16	The White House confirms that since early 1971 virtually all presidential meetings and conversations have been recorded.
August 12	American golfer Jack Nicklaus wins his 14th major tournament—a record.
August 22	Presidential adviser Henry A. Kissinger is named U. S. secretary of state.
September 11	Salvador Allende, Marxist president of Chile since September 1970, is killed in a coup.
September 18	East and West Germany are admitted to the UN.
October 10	Spiro T. Agnew resigns as U. S. vice president and pleads nolo contendere to one count of income-tax evasion.
October 17	Organization of Petroleum Exporting Countries (OPEC) imposes oil embargo against Western nations.
October 24	The UN adopts a second cease-fire agreement to end Arab-Israeli (Yom Kippur) war which began October 6.
December 3	Pioneer 10 transmits color photos of Jupiter.
December 6	U. S. Rep. Gerald R. Ford becomes the first unelected vice president.

1974

1974 ALSO SAW—*Ella Grasso elected governor of Connecticut; more small cars; Chris Evert win 10 tournaments; streaking; EXPO '74; the managerial debut of Frank Robinson.*

January 15	Six court-appointed experts find 18½ minutes of Watergate tape were erased.
February 13	Aleksandr Solzhenitsyn is deported by USSR.
February 28	Egypt and the United States restore diplomatic relations, cut since 1967.
March 18	Arab oil embargo against the United States ends.
April 25	Group of army officers ends 40 years of dictatorship in Portugal.
May 19	Finance Minister Valéry Giscard d'Estaing becomes president of France.
July 20	Turkish forces invade Cyprus.
August 8	Facing impeachment, President Nixon agrees to resign.
August 9	Gerald Ford takes the oath of office.
September 4	East Germany and the United States establish diplomatic relations.
September 12	Emperor Haile Selassie of Ethiopia is deposed.
October 17	President Ford defends his unconditional pardon of Richard Nixon.

The new decade brought hopes for peace in South Vietnam, but the nation's combat forces faced a continuing struggle for years to come.

A courageous trip to Jerusalem by Egyptian President Anwar el-Sadat in November 1977 ultimately led to normalized relations between two longtime enemies.

President Richard Nixon's state visit to China in February 1972—the first ever by a U.S. chief executive—opened Western eyes to a new part of the world.

August 1974: The Watergate scandal brings Nixon's resignation and the installation of Gerald Ford as president.

A new word in U. S.-Soviet relations—"détente"—is discussed by two of its major proponents, U. S. Secretary of State Henry Kissinger and USSR Foreign Minister Andrei Gromyko.

An aggressive, grass-roots campaign brought the presidency to an unknown peanut farmer and one-term governor from Georgia.

November 8	Former Lt. William Calley, Jr., convicted of murdering 22 civilians at Mylai, Vietnam, is paroled.
November 22	The UN grants the Palestine Liberation Organization observer status.
December 19	Nelson Rockefeller is sworn in as vice president.

1975

January 1	H. R. Haldeman, John D. Ehrlichman, John N. Mitchell, Robert Mardian are convicted of Watergate conspiracy.
February 13	Turkish Cypriots announce a separate state in northern Cyprus.
March 25	Faisal, Saudi Arabian king, is assassinated by a nephew.
April 5	Chiang Kai-shek, leader of Nationalist China, dies in Taiwan.
April 23	President Ford announces the end of American involvement in Vietnam war.
April 30	South Vietnam surrenders to Communists. The U. S. airlift of evacuees ends.
June 5	President Sadat reopens the Suez Canal, closed in 1967 war.
June 17	Mariana Islanders accept U. S. commonwealth status and become citizens.
June 26	India's Prime Minister Indira Gandhi declares a state of emergency.
July 17	The U. S. *Apollo* and USSR *Soyuz* spacecraft meet and link in space.
August 15	President Mujibur Rahman of Bangladesh is assassinated.
September 14	Elizabeth Ann Bayley Seton becomes the first native American saint of the Roman Catholic church.
September 18	After 19 months in hiding with the Symbionese Liberation Army, who kidnapped her, Patricia Hearst is captured.
October 13	Emperor Hirohito ends the first U. S. visit of a reigning Japanese monarch.
November 22	Juan Carlos is proclaimed king of Spain two days after the death of Gen. Francisco Franco.

1975 ALSO SAW—the end of Portuguese rule in Africa; more casual wear; a woman climb Mt. Everest; "Jaws."

© MIGDOLL

Mikhail Baryshnikov

1976

January 21	The Anglo-French *Concorde* supersonic transport enters commercial service.
February 4	More than 25,000 Guatemalans are killed and one fourth the population is made homeless by massive earthquakes.
March 29	General Jorge Videla becomes president of Argentina, following the overthrow of Isabel Peron, who had succeeded her late husband Juan, July 1, 1974.
April 5	James Callaghan becomes Britain's prime minister.
April 7	Hua Guofeng is named prime minister of China, succeeding Zhou Enlai.
April 9	Syrian troops move into Lebanon, as civil war heats up.
April 14	Morocco and Mauritania agree to divide former Spanish Sahara.
May 28	The USSR and U. S. sign a treaty limiting underground nuclear explosions and calling for on-site inspections.
July 2	North and South Vietnam are officially reunited, with Hanoi the capital.
July 3	In a precision raid, Israeli commandos rescue 91 passengers and 12 crew of an Air France flight hijacked to Entebbe airport, Uganda, by Palestinian guerrillas on June 27.
July 4	The United States' celebration of the 200th anniversary of the Declaration of Independence is shared across the land.
July 20	Viking I lands on Mars and begins sending photos to earth.
July 28	Unnumbered thousands die when earthquake registering 8.2 on the Richter scale devastates Tangshan, China, and its environs.
August 1	The Games of the XXI Olympiad close in Montreal, leaving the host city with a billion-dollar debt.
August 7	The United States and Iran sign a pact calling for the sale of $10 billion of arms to Iran.
August 18	Two Americans are killed and 9 U. S. and South Korean soldiers are wounded in DMZ clash with North Korea.

1976 ALSO SAW—record U. S. wheat crop; Barbara Jordan address Democrats; CBs; "Legion disease"; "Mary Hartman"; Barbara Walters at ABC; a swine flu scare.

IMAGE BANK CANADA

Nov. 1976, René Lévesque is Quebec's new premier.

August 24	Britain suffers the worst drought on record.
August 26	Prince Bernhard of the Netherlands is forced to resign almost all his posts, having been guilty of taking unacceptable initiatives.
September 9	Mao Zedong dies in Peking.
October 12	Hua Guofeng is confirmed as Mao's successor.
November 2	Jimmy Carter defeats Gerald Ford for the presidency.
November 26	The Vatican and Italian government revise the concordat that has governed church-state relations since 1929. Roman Catholicism will no longer be the state religion.
December 1	José Lopéz Portillo becomes 60th president of Mexico.

1977

January 17	In Utah, Gary Gilmore, 36-year-old convicted murderer, becomes the first person executed in the United States since 1967.
January 20	Jimmy Carter thanks Gerald Ford for "all he has done to heal our land" as a new administration takes over.
January 21	President Carter signs an unconditional pardon for the vast majority of Vietnam war era draft evaders.
January 23–30	A record television audience views the 12-hour dramatization of Alex Haley's best-selling book, *Roots*.
March 24	Morarji R. Desai succeeds Indira Gandhi as prime minister of India.
March 27	A Pan American 747 and a KLM 747 collide on a runway at the Tenerife airport in the Canary Islands, killing 581 persons.
June 15	Spain holds its first free elections since 1936.
June 20	The Trans-Alaska Pipeline System opens.
June 21	A former Zionist extremist, Menahem Begin, becomes prime minister of Israel as a right wing coalition government displaces the Labor party government, in power since 1948.
August 4	The U. S. Department of Energy is created.
August 20	The appointment of Hua Guofeng as the chairman of the Chinese Communist Party is confirmed. In July Deng Xiaoping was restored to his positions of party deputy chairman and deputy prime minister.
August 31	Spyros Achilles Kyprianou succeeds the late Archbishop Makarios as president of Cyprus.
October 4	Judge John J. Sirica reduces the prison sentences of John D. Ehrlichman, H. R. Haldeman, and John Mitchell.
November 19–21	Egypt's President Sadat is the first Arab leader to visit Israel.
December 5	Five Arab states break diplomatic relations with Egypt.
December 25–26	President Sadat and Israel's Prime Minister Begin meet in Ismailia, Egypt.

OWEN FRANKEN, STOCK BOSTON

The Episcopal Church permits women priests.

1977 ALSO SAW—*Koreagate; concern over human rights; N. Y. C. blackout; FESTAC; T-shirts; TV video games; Freddie Laker and Skytrain; "Rocky."*

1978

January 6	NASA chooses 35 new astronauts, including 6 women, 3 blacks, 1 Oriental.
January 24	Soviet reconnaissance satellite bearing a nuclear reactor breaks up over Canada's Northwest Territories.
February 19	Mix-up at Larnaca airport, Cyprus, has Cypriot National Guard killing 15 Egyptian commandos trying to rescue a Cypriot airliner held by Palestinian terrorists.
March 9	Somalia withdraws from the Ogaden, bested by Ethiopians and Cubans.
March 17	The Amoco *Cadiz,* aground near Brest, France, spills a record amount of oil.
April 6	President Carter signs a bill raising mandatory retirement age to 70.
May 9	Former Italian Prime Minister Aldo Moro, kidnapped March 16, is found murdered in Rome.
June 1	Electronic bugs are found in the U. S. embassy in Moscow.
June 6	California voters approve property-tax-cutting Proposition 13.
June 16	President Carter and Brig. Gen. Omar Torrijos exchange instruments of ratification of the Panama Canal treaties which cede the canal to Panama's jurisdiction.

1978 ALSO SAW—*new FBI head; crown of Stephen return to Hungary; soccer gain American popularity; higher heels; Luciano Pavarotti on TV from the Met; a black Mormon priest; John Travolta and discomania; "Annie Hall" and "Coming Home."*

Rapid customer turnover, self-service operation, and a flexible labor force led to a vast expansion of the fast food industry.

All in the Family revolutionized television entertainment with its open discussion of race, sex, and other delicate issues.

Big Bird of TV's *Sesame Street* brought delight to children, while the show itself was applauded by parents and teachers.

TONY KORODY, SYGMA

Proposition 13 (CA) led to a taxpayer revolt.

	June 28	The U. S. Supreme Court agrees that Allan Bakke was the victim of "reverse discrimination."
	July 25	A baby girl, grown from an egg fertilized in a laboratory, is born in England.
	August 17	Three Americans complete the first transatlantic balloon flight.
	October 16	Karol Cardinal Wojtyla becomes Pope John Paul II, the first non-Italian pope in 456 years, succeeding the late John Paul I, who reigned 33 days. Pope Paul VI died August 6.
	November 13	Mexico announces a new oil find, with possible 100 million barrel reserves.
	November 18	U. S. Rep. Leo Ryan (D-CA) and four companions are killed by members of the Peoples Temple, Jonestown, Guyana. Soon thereafter the cult leader, the Rev. Jim Jones, presides over some 900 murders and suicides.
	December 9	Pioneer Venus II sends back photos and data from Venus.
	December 15	Cleveland becomes the first major U. S. city since the depression to default.
	December 19	Indira Gandhi is expelled by the Indian parliament and ordered to jail.
1979	**January 1**	China and the United States establish full diplomatic relations.
	March 26	Egyptian President Sadat and Israeli Prime Minister Begin sign a formal peace treaty in Washington, DC, ending a 31-year state of war.
	May 4	Conservative Margaret Thatcher becomes the first woman prime minister of Great Britain.
	June 12	Pedaling continuously for 2 hours 49 minutes, Bryan Allen pilots the first man-powered airplane, Gossamer Albatross, across the English Channel.
	July 7	At Wimbledon, American tennis star Billie Jean King wins a record 20th title and Björn Borg is the first player to win 4 consecutive men's singles titles.
	October 17	The Department of Education becomes the 13th cabinet level U. S. agency.
	October 26	The World Health Organization announces the eradication of smallpox from Africa.
	December 8	With its 3,243d performance, *Grease* displaces *Fiddler on the Roof* as the longest running show in Broadway history.

1979 ALSO SAW—*U. S. aid for Chrysler; "Star Trek"; 1980 presidential candidates; record prices for gold and silver; more bottled water; Pinyin; Ann Meyers and women's pro basketball; gas at $1+ a gallon.*

There was very little in the 1970's to give comfort to calm, thoughtful, peaceful people. Americans by and large are a people with high hopes for mankind, a people who believe that the best ways of realizing those hopes are through generosity, strength, and example. Aid the world, be firm while practicing this unique democracy we have, and the world will become a better place. Disengage from the costly and futile blunder of Vietnam and thus prove our essentially decent nature to a justifiably doubting Third World.

It didn't quite work out that way. The withdrawal from Vietnam was taken to be a sign of weakness of American will. Having blundered in and out of Southeast Asia, America in the 1970's was seen to be too weak and uncertain to act decisively anywhere.

It is too early to tell how accurate that assessment is, but the United States was tested a few times in the seventies and it responded with a confused kind of patience. While the Russians and the Cubans and others worked their mischief, Americans felt quite secure repeating that homily of the seventies: "We can't be policemen for the world!"

As the decade ended and Americans were held hostage in their own embassy in Tehran and Soviet troops were overrunning neighboring Afghanistan, many were thinking that it was time for a new homily.

IF I GO UP, AREN'T YOU SUPPOSED TO GO DOWN?

UNEMPLOYMENT

FED TIGHTENS MONEY SUPPLY

INFLATION

AUTH

RECESSION· Causes and Consequences

By Paul A. Samuelson
and
William F. Samuelson

Business conditions never stand still. One year, sales are booming and jobs plentiful. Another year, the stock market collapses and the bankruptcy courts have standing room only. Economic history books chronicle the sequence of recession, expansion, recession. And in the bad old days of ruthless capitalism, there even occurred major depressions when banks failed by the thousands and grass grew in Main Street.

An Extinct Species? In the United States, pure capitalism has gradually given way to a *mixed economy,* in which the government shapes its tax and expenditure policies to stabilize the ups and downs of business. The Federal Reserve Board acts to control the money supply and counteract the business cycle. Is it therefore the case that recessions are a thing of the past—like smallpox, only a bad memory?

No. It is premature to announce the death of the business cycle. From 1973 to 1975 the whole world experienced a recession—the worst and longest in the post-World War II Age of John Maynard Keynes. As the decade of the 1980's begins, the United States shows all the traditional symptoms of a recession, major or mini. Production drops. People get the bad news of job layoffs. Construction of homes, industrial plants, and manufacturing equipment slows down. Red ink begins to show up on corporate annual reports, and families find it harder to make ends meet.

About the authors: Paul A. Samuelson is Institute Professor at the Massachusetts Institute of Technology [M. I. T.]. He is the author of numerous articles and books, including *Economics,* a standard college text. In 1970 he won the Nobel Prize in Economic Science. William F. Samuelson, his son, is Assistant Professor of Economics at Boston University.

Although a final cure for tuberculosis is yet to be found, its occurrence these days is rarer than it used to be and its form less virulent. Similarly, we can take real comfort in the fact that recessions are milder in the mixed economy than they were under pre-New Deal capitalism. They are also shorter and occur less often. Our parents and grandparents grew gray and wrinkled with worries our children will scarcely know.

Stagflation. Alas, when you cure one old disease, you may be brought face-to-face with a new one. At the same time that the mixed economy has alleviated the curse of old-fashioned depression and recession, there has arisen the dread new specter of "stagflation"—the odd fact of stagnation in production and employment *coinciding* with inflation in the cost of living.

The economic challenge that confronts the United States also haunts other nations. In Germany and Japan, Sweden and Switzerland, France and Italy, Britain, Canada, and Australia, voters and government officials are ringing out the 1970's and ringing in the 1980's with anxious concern: Is a worldwide recession brewing? Could it turn into a great depression like that of the 1930's? Can the system enjoy reasonably full employment and essential price stability for the things we buy? Can *humane* distribution of the aggregate economic pie be compatible with *efficiency* and *progress* in the production and growth of the total size of that pie?

These are hard questions. To answer them and throw light on probable economic developments just ahead, we must apply the tools of economic science to current business conditions in the United States and abroad.

Defining the Scourge. Begin with the OPEC energy cartel. In 1973, the mideast oil sheikhdoms succeeded in raising five-fold the real price of energy. The increases came just when food and fiber harvests were at a low point all around the world: in Russia and China, Brazil and Ghana, Burma and Iowa. The inflated price of oil was the one straw too many. The U. S. recession of 1973–75 was declared to have officially begun in the last quarter of 1973.

What is a recession? Who decides? The press and Las Vegas oddsmakers have a simple pragmatic definition:

UPI

Easy credit, lax rules, and a weak U. S. economy led to Black Tuesday, Oct. 29, 1929, the day the stock market crashed. On the fiftieth anniversary of the collapse of stock prices, the Dow Jones industrial average slipped 0.68 point and volume registered the slowest turnover in five months.

Alfred Kahn (*left*), chairman of the Council on Wage and Price Stability, and Charles Schultze, chairman of the Council of Economic Advisers, glumly try to explain a 1.1% rise in U.S. consumer prices during April 1979.

UPI

> When the real Gross National Product (total value of all goods and services, corrected for inflationary price rises) declines for *two quarters* in a row—that is a recession.

This rough definition is adequate for most purposes. The National Bureau of Economic Research, a prestigious nonprofit organization that has kept the official score on business cycles, naturally insists on more refined tests and measurements. Yet, for the most part, it arrives at the same conclusions when it applies its own definition:

> "A recession is a recurring period of decline in total output, income, employment, and trade, usually lasting six months to a year and marked by widespread fluctuations in the economy."

By both these tests, the United States had the following postwar recessions: 1948–49, 1953–54, 1957–58, 1960–61, 1969–70, 1973–75. Japan, however, did not have a postwar recession until 1973. Is Japan, therefore, immune to the pulses of optimism and pessimism in world markets, suffering no fluctuation in its own business economy? Hardly. Because the Japanese economy is growing so rapidly, overheating shows up merely as an extraordinary acceleration of its growth rate. A slowdown merely brings the growth rate below its normal level—and does not necessarily cause an actual drop in absolute levels of income and employment.

Therefore, economists these days want to define a new species of recession—a "mini-" or "growth-recession." In 1966–67 the American people had to live with such a recession when a credit crunch curtailed housing starts and shaved 20% off stock prices. The mini- or growth-recession is defined as follows:

> When output and employment grow for half a year or more at significantly less than their average trend rate of growth, an economy is in a growth recession—even if actual growth rates never turn negative.

Are We? Aren't We? In 1979 no one in the United States could decide whether April Fool's Day marked the beginning of a recession. A drop in real GNP was recorded in the second quarter of the year, but many experts were surprised when the third quarter did not also show a decline. By the crude test of journalists and oddsmakers, a true recession did not occur. But by almost everyone's agreement, 1979 would go down in the history books as a year of growth-recession, at least.

An Old Expansion. Why the slowdown? Again, oil scarcity and OPEC price-hikes provided an immediate threat to U. S. economic stability. Empty gasoline pumps and long service station lines at midyear paralyzed consumer buying of the larger cars produced by the American auto industry. The result was a decline in total retail sales. Rising oil prices and soaring food prices contributed to two-digit inflation—i.e., a rise in consumer prices of more than 10% for the year.

The U. S. economy began to slow in 1979 *because* of its successful expansion after the 1975 upturn, the period when U. S. production grew more vigorously than that of West Germany and Western Europe in general. Millions of new jobs had been provided for women, now dedicated to working outside the home, and the great baby boom of the 1940's and 1950's required millions of jobs for young adults.

Thus, the first reason for the 1979–80 slowdown was the fact that the post-1975 expansion was getting old, as business cycles go. The United States began running short of industrial capacity and spare labor power. Signs of "demand-pull" inflation appeared in late 1978: too much spending on and bidding for a limited supply of produceable goods.

Government Policy. The second reason for the recessionary tone of business has been tight money and credit policies. This is not because a president is cruel. Or because Congressmen don't want to get reelected. Or because members of the Federal Reserve Board are less smart and informed than economists in New York or Cambridge.

The dilemma of stagflation requires that steps be taken by the federal government to cool off the economy. High interest rates on loans—15% for large companies, 20% for less credit-worthy borrowers—are intended to combat inflation. But, one might argue, a high interest rate adds to company costs and thereby leads to inflated prices. Yes, it does so in the shortest run. But if tight money and credit cut down on housing starts, inventory speculation, investment spending, and the purchase of durable goods, this will also chill aggregate spending and cause an easing of the rate of inflation.

That is the theory on which President Jimmy Carter, Secretary of the Treasury G. William Miller, and Federal Reserve Board Chairman Paul Volcker have been operating. Historical experience suggests that this hard-money medicine does eventually help bring down soaring prices. But history also shows that government can overdo the cure, sometimes almost killing the patient in the process. Each advance against inflation comes dear. The poor and unskilled—be they white, black, or brown, on marginal farms or in city slums—take it on the chin when a mixed economy goes on a crusade against stagflation. In the case of stagflation, cures for the "flation" often exacerbate the "stag."

Two Soft Cheers. It is evident that political economy is not yet a perfected science. Fame still awaits the scholar who can find the way to give modern mixed economies real mastery over deep depressions by acquiring a better control over chronic inflation.

Fortunately, the early outlook for the 1980's is not so bleak that only an immediate breakthrough in the cure for stagflation can save us from disorder. Our far-from-perfect economic system has been functioning to make lives longer, healthier, and more secure in a way that the 19th century apologists of capitalism would never have expected.

"There will be a period of slow (economic) growth in our country. I believe that next year we'll see this growth restored to a moderate rate. We will watch this situation very closely. Obviously inflation is not the only factor. I am deeply concerned about the chronic unemployment in some of the types of people in our country. . . . But my judgment now is to maintain our steady course and to dwell as best I can on balanced growth. . . ."
President Carter,
July 25, 1979

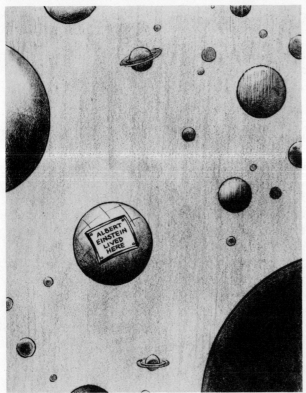

FROM "HERBLOCK'S HERE AND NOW," SIMON AND SCHUSTER, 1955

ALBERT EINSTEIN REMEMBERED

BY JOHN ARCHIBALD WHEELER

Ashbel Smith Professor and Director of the Center for Theoretical Physics

University of Texas, Austin

Albert Einstein was born into a "happy comfortable home" at Ulm, on the Danube, in Germany, on March 14, 1879. The family soon moved to Munich, where Albert spent five years in a good primary school. Then, from his 10th to his 15th years, he was sent to a secondary school so dismayingly authoritarian—apart from a few inspiring teachers—that he advised young people "not to give a damn for what their teachers tell them or think of them." After being expelled from the hated school he spent over a year with his family in and near Milan, Italy. His family wanted him to become an electrical engineer, but he decided to aim at a teacher's degree. He brought his secondary school education up to the mark at an unusual cantonal school at Aarau in Switzerland, where he had friendly and encouraging teachers and opportunity to work with electricity, mechanical devices, and magnets. There the teacher and the student joined, as he put it, in "responsible and happy work such as cannot be achieved by regimentation, however subtle." At seventeen he won admission to the Swiss Federal Institute of Technology (Eidgenösse Technische Hochschule or ETH) at Zürich. Einstein was not at the bottom of his class, but he was next to the bottom. In his laboratory work he was always behind. He tells us that he skipped lectures and depended on his friends' lecture notes to study for the examinations that he hated. One of his professors, the mathematical physicist Hermann Minkowski, who later became one of the leading expounders and defenders of Einstein's ideas, considered the student Einstein a "lazy dog" who "never bothered about mathematics at all."

The young man liked to read, and he loved to walk and talk with a few close student friends. It was not for nothing that, at the Institute for Advanced Study in Princeton, NJ, where Einstein spent the last twenty-two years of his life, tea was defined as "where we explain to each other what we don't understand."

To Einstein's development his few close student colleagues meant much; but even more formative were the older colleagues he met in books. To his visitor in later years he would quote James Clerk Maxwell, the founder of electromagnetic theory, or express his admiration for the courage and judgment of Isaac Newton in adopting what were impossible ideas of absolute space and absolute time as the only way then available to describe and explain planetary motion. From the feeling with which he spoke, Einstein's visitor sensed that his heroes peopled his brain as advisers and friends—Newton and Maxwell, Leibniz and Faraday, Hume and Kant, Boltzmann and Mach. Through their influence he turned from mathematics to physics, from a subject where, as he put it, there are dismayingly multitudinous directions for dizzy man to choose, to a subject where this one and only physical world directs our endeavors.

Of all his heroes, Benedict de Spinoza was Einstein's greatest. No one expressed more strongly a belief in the harmony, the beauty, and, above all, the comprehensibility of nature. As a student Einstein was already beginning to stand for his number one principle, which he stated later as: "The most incomprehensible thing about the world is that it is comprehensible"; or "What really interests me is whether God had any choice in the creation of the world"; or, at the conclusion of one of his books, "All of these endeavors are based on the belief that existence should have a completely harmonious structure. Today we have less ground than ever before for allowing ourselves to be forced away from this wonderful belief."

"This huge world stands before us like a great eternal riddle."

With his unpromising university record Einstein could get only temporary jobs for two years after finishing at Zürich. Then, June 23, 1902, Friedrich Haller, head of the Swiss Patent Office in Bern, took him on as an examining clerk, and there Einstein was to continue for seven formative years. Every morning he faced his quota of patent applications and working models. Haller, a kind man, was exacting and wise. He gave strict instructions: explain very briefly, if possible in a single sentence, why the device would work or why it would not; why the application should be granted or why it should be denied. Day after day Einstein had to distill the central lesson out of objects of the greatest variety that men had the ingenuity to invent. Whoever asks how Einstein won his unsurpassed power of expression need only refer to Einstein's years in the patent office and the boss who "taught me to express myself correctly."

Why did Einstein in later years attend so painstakingly to letters from children and amateurs? Did he not continue to find the simplest of questions the best of ways to the greatest of insights?

Einstein resigned from the Patent Office July 6, 1909. Five years and five jobs later he was in Berlin, with the most distinguished physics professorship in the world. When the advent of Adolf Hitler brought a dark cloud to Germany, Einstein accepted an appointment at the Princeton Institute for Advanced Study, where he took up residence in October 1933. He lived at 112 Mercer Street the rest of his life, and died in Princeton, April 18, 1955.

Two subjects above all others occupied Einstein throughout his life: one, the mystery of the quantum, the backbone principle of 20th century physics; the other, the nature of space and time.

As early as 1900 in Berlin, Max Planck experimented with a black body—a box blackened on the inside and having a small opening to let out radiant light. He had discovered that the energy of light of a given color confined within a box cannot take on any arbitrary value. Instead, this energy, rising or falling from time to time, is never anything but one or another integral multiple of a basic unit that Planck called the quantum.

In Latin this word means "how much" but in German it has more the meaning of "hunk." Energy comes in hunks, and the size of the hunks depends on the color of the light. Violet light has high vibration frequency and comes in quanta each roughly twice as energy-rich as hunks of red light, of lower vibration frequency. Planck could hardly credit his strange finding. Einstein took it seriously, and not only for what it said about luminous energy trapped in a box. What if light winging its way across space and hitting a distant metal surface could deliver its energy to that surface only a hunk at a time? Then, he reasoned, the electron knocked out of that metal by a hunk of violet light would have more energy than the electron thrown out by a quantum of red light. Moreover, the energy of the ejected "photoelectron" would be completely unaffected by the distance from the light source to the metal plate. These predictions agreed impressively with the previously unexplained observations other experimenters had made on this so-called "photoelectric effect." Einstein was forced to conclude that light travels through space in quanta, like bullets, and that it is random in direction and in time of arrival.

Until this discovery about light quanta—for which Einstein was awarded the Nobel Prize in 1922—all physical processes had been thought to be governed by deterministic laws, with the future uniquely fixed by the past. And now Einstein, the adherent of Spinoza and of his belief in a harmonious universe, had, Aladdinlike, disrupted that harmony by loosing on it a genie, chance. That he could not arrest the genie would, in later years, upset Einstein more than anyone else. He would often say, "God does not play dice." Even so, chance remains an inescapable element of modern physics.

The Planck (1900) and Einstein (1905) quantum theory of light opened the door to Niels Bohr's 1913 quantum theory of the atom, with its characteristic "energy levels" or "quantum states." When the electron "jumps" down from a higher level to a lower one the atom emits a quantum of light, but when the atom absorbs a quantum of light the electron jumps from a lower state to a higher one. Einstein discovered in 1916 how, by the laws of chance, to relate to each other these processes of emission and absorption. In 1924 he was the first to encourage the young Louis de Broglie to pursue his idea of the electron as describing a wave. Had not Erwin Schrödinger gone on to develop Broglie's concept into the modern "wave mechanics," it is believed that Einstein would have done it within a month or so. Einstein joined in recommending the Nobel prizes that were awarded to Broglie, Schrödinger, and Werner Heisenberg, who arrived at the same result by another mathematical method. Not otherwise than by modern quantum mechanics would we today understand the structure of everything from atoms to crystals, from elementary particles to superconductors, and from atomic nuclei to molecules.

By 1927 Bohr and Heisenberg in Copenhagen, analyzing the lesson of the new quantum mechanics, showed that it left no escape from chance,

China and the U. S. were among nations that issued stamps in honor of the Einstein centennial.

under whatever name—unpredictability, indeterminism, "complementarity," uncertainty of prediction. This conclusion Einstein was unwilling to accept. He had been convinced since student days that nature at bottom must be deterministic; it was a central teaching of the Spinoza whom he so admired. Thus began a great dialogue between Einstein and Bohr. They had met in 1920, and Einstein had written afterward to Bohr, his junior by six and one-half years: "I am studying your great works and—when I get stuck anywhere—now have the pleasure of seeing your friendly young face before me smiling and explaining." Einstein persisted in trying to prove that quantum theory is logically inconsistent. Bohr overcame every objection on this score that Einstein could raise. Then, after his move to the United States, Einstein argued that quantum mechanics is incompatible with any reasonable concept of reality. To this Bohr replied, in essence, that "your concept of reality is too limited." Einstein, to make his point, had devised—with two colleagues, Boris Podolsky and Nathan Rosen—a by-now famous idealized experiment. It demonstrates clearly what Einstein considered to be the paradoxical and unacceptable consequences of quantum theory. That theory, as applied to a particle or quantum of light, was already known to say that by suitable preparations one can predict the numerical value of some attribute A of the projectile, or by other preparations predict the magnitude of some other attribute B,

A sculpture of Albert Einstein, designed by Robert Berks, was unveiled at Washington's National Academy of Sciences in April 1979. Of the memorial, John Archibald Wheeler, an Einstein colleague and author of the accompanying text, said: "No statue of a scientist ever erected" in the United States "was meant to have more meaning, and has more meaning, than this."

but one is forever denied the possibility simultaneously to predict or know or assign a tangible meaning to two "complementary" attributes, A and B. In the EPR experiment one chooses *which* attribute of the projectile shall be predictable by what one does in the region of launch *after* the projectile has left! This apparently impossible result is not to be rejected, Bohr responded; rather than showing anything wrong with quantum theory the EPR experiment brings into new clarity its absolutely central point. The properties of the projectile in all its long course from launch to reception are undefined and undefinable until the experiment is complete. One can assign neither meaning nor numerical value to those attributes of the particle until, in Bohr's words, the experiment has been "brought to a close by an irreversible act of amplification"; that is, by an act of "registration" or "observation." In other words, *No elementary phenomenon is a phenomenon until it is a registered (observed) phenomenon.*

Half a dozen experimenting groups doing as many variants of the EPR experiment confirmed the predictions of quantum theory. What little support there had been in the physics community for Einstein's position crumbled. Yet he continued for the rest of his life to oppose the view that what happens "out there" depends on any act of "registration" or "observation" here. In his last talk, to the Princeton seminar on relativity, a year before his death, he objected to the quantum description: "It seems to make the world quite nebulous unless somebody, like a mouse, is looking at it."

In all of history it would be difficult to name a dialogue between two greater men than Niels Bohr and Albert Einstein, over a longer period of years, at a higher level of colleagueship, on a deeper issue.

Today quantum theory remains the backbone of physics. To many it is more: a challenge to search out the utterly simple foundation idea from which it can all be derived. No one is a greater inspiration to this endeavor than Einstein himself.

In quantum theory Einstein was one in a galaxy of talents. In elucidating the other great theme of his life work—spacetime geometry and its connection with gravitation—Einstein was unique. In 1905 he distilled out of the complications of electricity and magnetism the simple central lesson. There is no observational means whatsoever to detect, let alone measure—and therefore no way even to define—motion with respect to the "absolute space" postulated by Newton, nor is there any way to define Newton's absolute time. The separation in time between event F and event G depends on the frame of reference, earth-bound or rocket-transported, in which it is recorded, and so does the separation in space between those events. However, there is a new and higher unity, spacetime, that is distinct from frame-dependent "space" and "time." The separation in spacetime between F and G, known as the "interval FG," is recorded by all observers as having the same value. So, if I, in a rocket going at 60% of the speed of light, shoot out ahead of me one flash of radiation at the full speed of light, the flash travels at the speed of light and no more, whether it is measured by me in the rocket or by you, standing on earth and seeing both speeding rocket and light pulse. The speed of light cannot be exceeded. It is the same in all frames of reference.

This 1905 "special relativity" of Einstein, in reducing time from a mystery to one of the four dimensions of spacetime geometry, also showed that all other physical quantities are likewise expressible in geometric

"I suppose it was conscience. He saw things in his own particular way. He believed in the way he saw things. And then, if he believed, he had the feeling he shouldn't be a coward and keep quiet. He should speak out strongly, boldly and without fear."

Banesh Hoffmann, Professor Emeritus, Queens College The City University of New York

language. Energy, it became clear, is the "time component" of mass. In consequence, all previous evaluations of the energy content of matter had to be recognized as far short of the truth. The energy that an object has in virtue of its motion at any everyday speed is negligible in comparison with the energy that resides in it even when it is at rest, an energy summed up by Einstein's famous formula, $E = mc^2$; that is, (energy locked up in mass at rest) = (magnitude of that mass) times (square of the speed of light). This equation inspired many to undertake immense labors to release all or part of the energy inherent in mass at rest. It is the master formula of the uranium fission and hydrogen fusion enterprises of our day.

Is spacetime the ideal mathematical perfection of special relativity? By 1908 Einstein had to answer, "no." If space acts on matter, telling it how to move, then by the principle of action and reaction matter must act back on space, telling it how to curve. Gravitation is viewed not as a foreign and "physical" force acting *through* space, but as a manifestation of the curvature *of* space (or spacetime). By November 1915 Einstein had found the uniquely natural and compelling way to state these ideas in mathematical form. The resulting "general relativity" or curved-space geometric theory of gravitation remains for physicists today an ideal of what any physical theory should be and do. Starting from simple ideas it leads to definite predictive equations. It brings under one explanatory roof physical phenomena of great variety: the already known deviations of the planet Mercury from the Newtonian predictions, the since-observed bending—and delay—of light in passing by the sun, and half a dozen other testable and tested effects in the solar system, as well as gravitational-wave and black-hole phenomena for which tentative evidence has already been found.

Of all the predictions of general relativity the greatest was the simplest. The universe cannot be static. It must be dynamic. Fourteen years after Einstein gave the world his theory Edwin Hubble of Mt. Wilson Observatory in California discovered that the universe is expanding outward from a presumptive "big bang." In 1965 A. A. Penzias and R. W. Wilson of the Bell Telephone Laboratories in New Jersey discovered the primordial cosmic fireball radiation that arose from this big bang. To predict, and predict correctly, and predict against all expectation, a phenomenon so fantastic as the expansion of the universe is the most marvellous sign of hope that we have that we will someday understand how this strange and beautiful universe came to be.

Einstein's power to reach into the unknown, his independence of thought, his conscience, and his gift of expression, made him seem a modern reincarnation of an Old Testament prophet. He spoke out for social justice, social responsibility, the ideals of the Jewish community, and peace. But when it came to a choice between peace or freedom and justice, he spoke for freedom and justice.

"The only way to escape the personal corruption of praise is to go on working."

Albert Einstein

In 1979, scores of Einstein centenary celebrations were held all over the world, shelves of memorial volumes were published, and commemorative postage stamps were issued by dozens of countries. An Einstein memorial sculpture, designed by Robert Berks, was erected on the grounds of the National Academy of Sciences in Washington. Important or trivial, they were all efforts to honor the man who, more closely than any scientist who ever lived, stands for the proposition that this is an *understandable* universe.

International Year of the Child 1979

CHILDREN: Their Needs, Their Promise

Marian Wright Edelman, *Director, Children's Defense Fund*

In 1959, the United Nations adopted a "Declaration of the Rights of the Child," articulating children's most basic needs as goals toward which all the world's nations would work. The right to a name and nationality, to adequate nutrition and medical care, to a free education, to affection, love, and understanding were just some of the needs the world community agreed ought to be entitlements for all children.

The year 1979 marked the twentieth anniversary of that Declaration, and the unfinished business all countries faced in fulfilling children's rights prompted the General Assembly to ask nations to rededicate themselves to surveying the status of children at home and abroad, and to take the necessary steps to prevent their dying, to alleviate their suffering, and to assure their healthy growth and development. The Assembly declared 1979 to be the International Year of the Child (IYC), and in countries around the world, children's accomplishments were praised, their problems highlighted, and their needs assessed.

In the United States, a national commission of people from different

COURTESY, UNITED TELECOM

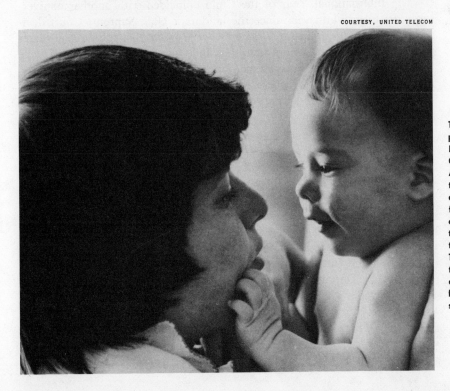

The UN General Assembly proclaimed 1979 as the International Year of the Child. In so doing, the Assembly urged the nations of the world to rededicate themselves to fostering the basic rights of children enunciated in the 1959 Declaration of the Rights of the Child. These rights, illustrated on the following pages, include: the right "to affection, love, and understanding"

". . . to adequate nutrition, housing, medical care, and recreation"

walks of life was appointed by President Jimmy Carter to "plan for and promote the national observance in the United States of the year 1979 as the International Year of the Child." Mrs. Jean Young, wife of the former U. S. ambassador to the United Nations, chaired the commission. Mrs. Young made clear that "during the International Year of the Child, we want to affirm children. . . . If we affirm children, we are on the road to effecting change." Mrs. Young also noted that "children are resilient, tenacious, and adaptable. Many survive in the most deplorable conditions. They are also vulnerable, defenseless, and powerless. With a little help from us, they can develop into the beautiful, loving, confident, contributing human beings they were meant to be."

The International Year of the Child coincided with another anniversary: the twenty-fifth year since the landmark U. S. Supreme Court decision, *Brown v. the Board of Education of Topeka,* that ruled racial segregation illegal in public schools and took the United States farther down the long path toward equal educational opportunity. The year 1979, then, was a time for taking stock of where American children are and assessing what is still needed to ensure an improved future for all children. Areas of special concern include:

EDUCATION

In developing nations, more than half of the school-age children are not in school.

In the United States in 1977, almost one million children over age 6 and under 18 were neither enrolled in school nor high school graduates. More than 800,000 handicapped children did not receive the special educational services they need. During 1976, some 1.8 million students were suspended from school at least once. Experts estimated that 13% of all 17-year-olds in the United States were functionally illiterate, i.e., unable to do basic reading, writing or computations; unable to understand want ads or to make sure that the change given at the supermarket is correct.

"...to free education, to learn to be a useful member of society and develop individual abilities"

Minority children fare even worse. One black child drops out of school for every two who graduate. Black children are more than twice as likely to be suspended from school and to receive corporal punishment in school as white children. They are three times as likely to be placed in classes for the educable mentally retarded, but are less than half as likely to be placed in gifted classes as their white peers.

The work of desegregation remains to be completed. One black public school child in every three attends a school that is at least 90% black. In 1970, that figure was two out of every five. The progress has occurred almost entirely in the South and border states, where segregation was most blatant. Elsewhere, progress has been token or nonexistent. In the Midwest, for example, 39% of all black children attended schools that were 99% black in 1970. A black child who moves from the South—where the *Brown* decision has had some real impact—to the Midwest quadruples his or her chance of being in a 99% black school. An absolute majority of all black children in the Midwest are attending schools that are at least 90% black.

HEALTH

Too many countries have high infant mortality rates and children dying in their early years from preventable diseases and accidents.

In the United States, one out of 65 white infants dies each year. Over 18 million American children under 17 have never seen a dentist, and 9.5 million children under 18 have no known regular source of primary health care. Only one sixth of the children eligible for Medicaid get the services of the Early and Periodic Screening, Diagnosis, and Treatment (EPSDT) program to which they are entitled. When they do, more than 600,000 (40%) of their detected health problems go untreated.

In the United States, nonwhite mothers die in childbirth at three times the rate of white mothers. Today a black American baby has almost twice the chance of dying within the first year of life as a white baby. One of every 43 nonwhite infants dies each year. In the United States capital, one of 33 nonwhite infants dies annually. Many of these deaths are preventable. Minority children aged 1 to 4 die at a rate 70% higher than white children; minority children aged 5 to 9 die at a rate 40% higher than white children. Nonwhite children of all ages from 1 to 19 die from disease and birth defects at rates about 25% higher than whites.

POVERTY

The poverty of the 2.5 billion people in the world's poorest countries is staggering, and the contrast immense between their average $250 per capita income and Americans'.

But many American children are poor. One in 6 children in the United States is poor in any one year. One in 4 is on Aid to Families with Dependent Children (AFDC) at some time in his or her lifetime. In 1977, while 11.6% of the general population lived in poverty, 16.0% of all children did. And the younger children are, the more likely they are to be poor: 18.4% of all those under 3; 17.9% of all those 3 to 5; and 16.0% of all those 6 to 13. In 1977, children 18 and younger accounted for more than 70%—7.6 million of 10.8 million—of those receiving AFDC. In 1975, over 84% of AFDC children were 14 and younger, and over half were 8 and younger. One of every 9 children in the United States depends on welfare for survival each year.

One of every two black preschool children lives in poverty. Black children are four times as likely to grow up in a poor family, twice as likely to grow up in a family with unemployed parents, and almost twice as likely to be on welfare as white children. One black child in two, under age 6, lives in a one-parent household. There is one poor black child for every single black family with children in the United States. One black child in two has a working mother. Although more black than white mothers with young children have to work, the per capita income of intact black households is almost $1,000 less than the per capita income of female-headed white households.

CHILDREN WITHOUT HOMES

Throughout the world, families with young children still bear the brunt of national strife that makes refugees of millions. Children are shifted from their native lands, lose their homes, are split from their families, and fall casualty to the miserable conditions of impermanence and isolation.

"... to an opportunity to develop physically, mentally, and morally in freedom and dignity"

PETER L. GOULD, FPG

"...to a name and nationality"

DAVID STRICKLER, MONKMEYER

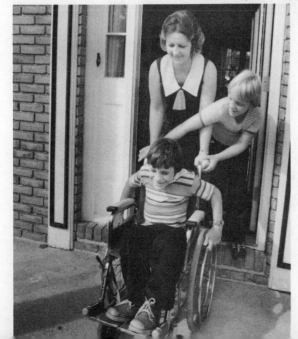

"... to special care, if handicapped"

"... to be among the first to receive relief in times of disaster"

"... to be brought up in a spirit of
peace and universal brotherhood"

"... to protection against neglect,
cruelty, and exploitation"

Although the cause differs, hundreds of thousands of children in the United States suffer rootlessness, too. Between 500,000 and 750,000 American children are removed from their own homes and live in foster and group homes or large institutions. Far too many of these children are unnecessarily or prematurely removed from their homes before attempts have been made to work with or to provide services to their families. Tens of thousands have been placed in inappropriate facilities, for long periods of time, often away from their communities. They languish in a twilight area, neither returned home nor provided a permanent new family through adoption.

A disproportionate number of children in foster care, group homes, and institutions are black.

CHILDREN IN THE CONTEXT OF FAMILIES AND SOCIETY

One of the most serious obstacles to helping children is believing that the typical nuclear family can take care of its problems privately. But the typical family—two parents (a male wage earner and a stay-at-home mother) and two children (healthy and unhandicapped)—represents only

Children are people

International Year of the Child 1979

<u>Every Child has the Right to:</u> enjoy its rights, regardless of race, colour, sex, religion, national, or social origin...

The child shall enjoy all the rights set forth in this Declaration. All children, without any exception whatsoever, shall be entitled to these rights without distinction or discrimination on account of race, colour, sex, language, religion, political or other opinion, national or social origin, property, birth or other status, whether of himself or of his family.

". . . to enjoy these rights, regardless of race, colour, sex, religion, national or social origin."

seven of every 100 families in the United States today. It ignores the reality of the 28.2 million children whose mothers worked outside the home in 1976, the children growing up in 9.7 million single-parent families who are disproportionately poor, and the 5 million families who have at least one child with a physical, mental, or emotional handicap. It ignores the fact that many families lack the money to buy needed health and day care services. And it ignores the millions of young teenage parents, themselves merely children, struggling to raise another generation of young. Each year some 600,000 babies are born to teenage mothers.

We have not yet invented anything better for children than families. The best way to help most children is to help their families. But to focus on parent education and counseling alone will leave unchanged many of the statistics of need described above. It is clear that they stem more from inappropriate public policies than from individual parental failures. When confronted with school, health, mental health, child welfare, and juvenile justice bureaucracies, few parents—however well-educated and resourceful—are a match.

The second major obstacle to helping children lies in the distrust of government to institute programs and to offer services that strengthen families. The rhetoric that says society should stay out of family life matches a growing fiscal conservatism. During the International Year of the Child, when the government and the public were supposed to be paying attention to children's unmet needs, proportionately fewer federal dollars were proposed for children and family services than for the military budget. Some states, including California, voted to reduce taxes and to cut back on such services as education, child care, foster care, and health clinics.

"As we affirm children, enjoy them, listen to voices of concern, seek solutions, we must not forget the most important voice in all, the voice of our children themselves."

Mrs. Andrew Young

Chairperson
U. S. Commission, IYC

But this is a penny wise and dollar foolish approach, since children represent an investment for the future. Preventive health services, preschool programs such as Head Start, adequate employment and income opportunity, and family support services such as homemakers and day care cost little compared to paying for the consequences of disease, disability, educational failure, welfare dependency, and family break-ups later on.

The United States must decide now whether it will honor rather than simply preach equal opportunity for all children. It is long past the time when the nation should have faced up to the fact that the problems of children are problems of national dimension, with national implications, requiring national responses. All levels of government and the private and public sectors must cooperate to improve public policies and strengthen American family life and ensure that the 64 million American children grow up healthy and productive. The American populace must begin to act—individually, corporately, and publicly—as if it honestly cares for all children.

The Chilean poet Gabriela Mistral has written movingly about why it is imperative to take children's needs seriously. "Many of the things we need can wait," she wrote. "But the child cannot. Right now is the time his bones are being created, his senses are being developed. To him we cannot answer, Tomorrow. His name is Now, Right Now."

This article was adapted from publications about the status of children by the Children's Defense Fund. For further information see *America's Children and their Families, Portrait of Inequality: Black and White Children in America,* and *Annual Report: 1978* (Children's Defense Fund, 1520 New Hampshire Ave. NW, Washington, DC 20036).

Mork & Mindy features Pam Dawber as Mindy McConnel and Robin Williams as Mork.

THE SITUATION COMEDY

BY DWIGHT WHITNEY
Chief, Hollywood Bureau, *TV Guide*

What is situation comedy? In a momentary fit of aggravation, author and critic John Mason Brown once suggested that it is "chewing gum for the eyes." It is television's portrayal of little problems, little solutions, life the way it isn't but the way many fervently wish it to be.

Today it is not easy to dismiss television's situation comedy—the sitcom, as it is called by the industry that produces it—as a poor relation among the arts. In the 30-odd years since the first one went on the air, the sitcom has grown steadily in influence and come to resemble a folk art if not an art form. Whatever it is, Americans are hooked on it. The average American household now keeps the television set on for 6.2 hours daily, and according to A. C. Nielsen, the experts of television ratings, the set is most frequently tuned to the situation comedy.

No wonder. From the beginning it seemed as indigenous to the new medium as a cherry nose to Santa Claus. In the early days of TV, producers, faced with endless stretches of empty air time to fill, presented fixed characters in a fixed situation. The procedure eliminated the necessity of inventing new characters and new situations each week. It was a technique borrowed from radio. Audiences were conditioned to believe, for instance, that Jack Benny was cheap. Thus when a stick-up man demanded, "Your money or your life!" all Benny had to do was place a finger to his cheekbone, cast his eyes heavenward, and murmur, "Mmmmm?" and Americans rocked with laughter.

Jack Benny's antics brought on a seemingly endless parade of well-known comedians with strong characteristics—Ed Wynn and his funny hats; Red Skelton and a gallery of photogenic hobos and former pugs; Jimmy Durante and his nose; Gracie Allen and her magnificent sense of the irrational. Programs featuring these great stars were in a very real sense the first sitcoms.

The form really constellated, however, in 1949 when CBS introduced *Mama*. It offered the same anticipation of known quantities played against the joys and sorrows of ordinary family life and set the tone for hundreds of programs to come. *Mama* found fun in unadorned human fallibility. Heavily nostalgic, dripping with sentiment, it made a ritual of the dinner hour, endlessly playing out the symbolic moment when the family sits down together. When Katrin intoned, "I remember my brother, Nels, my little sister, Dagmar, and, of course, Papa, but most of all I remember Mama," millions wiped their eyes and found it all too easy to identify.

But by the mid-1950's, there were literally dozens of family sitcoms. They tended to take a simple-minded, frankly stereotypical view of the family unit. And it was largely matriarchal in character. The variations were endless. In *The Life of Riley*, father (William Bendix) was portrayed as the lovable bumbler. In *Life With Father*, Leon Ames played a stern Victorian who underneath the stiff collar was really a marshmallow. In *Father Knows Best*, an easy-to-manipulate father (Robert Young) only appeared to know best; actually it was mother (Jane Wyatt) who had the clout.

The Adventures of Ozzie and Harriet introduced the first father without visible means of support. Ozzie (Ozzie Nelson) had no known job, slept late in the morning, and spent an inordinate amount of time worrying about whom son Ricky would take to the junior prom. Danny Thomas, a night-club comic himself, added a dash of wry to his show. Millions applauded when, on peering into the carnage that was his son Rusty's room, he turned to his wife (Marjorie Lord) and asked, "Were there any survivors?"

Isabel Sanford, Sherman Hemsley, and Paul Benedict (*right*) star in *The Jeffersons*, a spin-off from *All in the Family*.

CBS

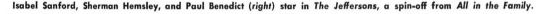

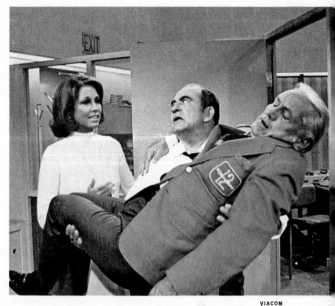

JIM VICTORY COMPANY

VIACOM

The Mary Tyler Moore Show (above), one of the all-time most popular situation comedies, reviewed the careers of Mary, Lou, and Ted. *Rhoda*, a spin-off, told of the unsuccessful marriage of Rhoda (Valerie Harper) and Joe (David Groh).

The Honeymooners, on the other hand, injected some heavy doses of realism into the form. Jackie Gleason's Ralph Kramden was a bus driver with more bluster than sense. The show was a comedy paean to life's colorful losers. It offered a kind of inevitability, as predictable as a Greek tragedy. Ralph kept threatening to belt his wife, Alice, "right in the kisser" (he never did), and 30 million people relished the moment every week.

Then there was Lucy. Lucille Ball, a onetime starlet who had never really made it in films, decided to try television in 1951. With her she took her husband, Desi Arnaz, over the objections of CBS network executives who thought audiences would not like the Cuban Arnaz. Just the opposite occurred. The show was an immediate hit. Lucy proved to be adept at stylized physical comedy and her shows dominated TV sitcom for more than 20 years (later without Arnaz). During this time her programs never dropped out of the top 20 (seldom out of the top 10). Within the deceptively simple framework of the addled wife trying to outsmart a constantly put-upon husband and later as a widow looking for a new husband and as a secretary working for her brother-in-law, she achieved moments that would have done Chaplin proud.

In 1957, a bucolic comedy called *The Real McCoys* hit the air amid predictions of doom. This story of gallus-snapping West Virginia mountain folk newly-moved to California was supposed to be a flop. Corn was not a popular commodity in the big city. But the opposition had not counted on Walter Brennan, the wily character actor who played Grandpa. With *The Real McCoys* ABC had its first big hit and soon *Playhouse 90,* the dramatic success seen one-half hour afterward, was only a memory. This first of the rube operas gave rise to many similar ones, including *The Andy Griffith Show, The Beverly Hillbillies,* and *Petticoat Junction.*

Also in 1957 came the first in a long line of comedies featuring single parents. *Lassie* had substituted the grandfather for the father several years

THE RATING SYSTEM

Nearly 98% of all households in the United States have one or more television sets. Millions of people watch TV every day, often for a significant number of hours. Viewing activity and program preference vary, of course, with the individual. The programming offered for viewer consumption—and equally important, the programming *not* offered—is decided by the broadcasters and networks. As an alternative to a full census, and much like a blood test, a sample of the viewing public is used to determine what people are watching when. The information produced from these viewing samples is called "ratings." Ratings are not, as the term implies, a subjective evaluation of programs. They are statistical estimates of audience size. Ratings are used by the business side of broadcasting as a basis for pricing commercial time and for making programming decisions. They are the counterpart of the circulation figures used by newspapers and magazines in selling their advertisement space.

In 1936, the A. C. Nielsen Company acquired from two MIT professors an ingenious device that monitored radio tuning and produced a detailed record of this activity on a paper tape. This mechanism was called an Audimeter®. With this unique research tool, the Nielsen Radio Index was launched in 1942 to provide the broadcast industry with a national network radio audience measurement service. With the dawn of the age of television, A. C. Nielsen began in 1950 to produce ratings for that medium.

Through a complex procedure of "random sampling," Nielsen selected for study some 1,200 households across the United States. The sampling process is designed to cull a group whose demographic characteristics and tastes reflect those of the entire population. The choices of that group are, in theory at least, projectable to the entire population. If 25% of the sample views a particular program, it can be said that the program was viewed in 25% of all U. S. households with a television. Because a sample and not a census is used, ratings cannot be regarded as precise measurements. They are statistical estimates of audience size, and each rating has a plus or minus tolerance.

Identical in function to the 1936 original, the current generation Audimeter is an electronic device that monitors the tuning status of all TV sets in the sample household. This information is stored in an electronic memory similar to that of a computer. Each Audimeter is attached to a special telephone line, and a computer in Nielsen's production offices "calls" each Audimeter daily to retrieve the stored information. The data are processed along with those from the other sample homes to determine the percentage of TV households tuned to different programs.

WILLIAM R. BEHANNA, *A. C. Nielsen Company*

A. C. Nielsen Television Ratings
As of Dec. 10–16, 1979

Rating	Program	Network	Rating	Program	Network
1.	*60 Minutes*	CBS	6.	*Angie*	ABC
2.	*One Day at a Time*	CBS	7.	*Dallas*	CBS
3.	*Circus of the Stars*	CBS	8.	*M*A*S*H*	CBS
4.	*Three's Company*	ABC	9.	*NFL Monday Night*	
5.	*Archie Bunker's*			*Football*	ABC
	Place	CBS	10.	*Happy Days*	ABC

VIACOM

The Beverly Hillbillies, the story of the Clampett family from the Ozarks who struck it rich, enjoyed a long run.

earlier. But *Bachelor Father* concentrated on the financially well-off Bentley Gregg (John Forsythe) bringing up a teenage girl. *My Three Sons* carried the idea a step further. Fred MacMurray, the onetime saxophone player and movie star, had an all-male contingent. The formula called for surrounding the kids with platoons of lovable old housekeepers, butlers and/or irascible uncles to act as a kind of parental auxiliary. *A Family Affair* placed heavy emphasis on urban life. Its high-living, apartment-dwelling single guardian (Brian Keith) pressed into service Sebastian Cabot, the very embodiment of the loving if snobbish English butler, to take care of his three charges. John Forsythe employed an inscrutable oriental named Peter to take care of his teenage niece.

Not all sitcoms involved the family unit per se. *The Phil Silvers Show* used the army as a showcase for one of the great comedy stylists of our time. Silvers played a fast-talking, conniving master sergeant, Ernie Bilko, the quintessential confidence man-turned-father-figure. The effect was stunning. The other side of that coin was *Mr. Peepers,* played by Wally Cox. As a shy midwestern high school teacher, he was so withdrawn and gentle that he frequently seemed to disappear altogether a fact which did not detract from the show's charm.

Back in 1951, CBS had presented *Amos 'n' Andy,* an ethnically outdated blackface comedy adapted from radio. Seventeen years later the medium passed a milestone of sorts. NBC's *Julia* concerned a young, smartly-attired, widowed nurse (Diahann Carroll) with a small son, portrayed without a trace of the old-fashioned ethnic cliché. In every way it was a breakthrough show. When Julia applies for her nursing job by telephone, she tells the doctor (Lloyd Nolan) that she is black. "Have you always been a Negro or are you just trying to be fashionable?" he replies.

My World and Welcome to It added to the family a touch of Thurberesque sophistication. *Hazel* incorporated the domestic into the sitcom. When Hazel, portrayed by Shirley Booth, declared, "You're a doozey, Mr. B," referring to the head of the household, a tear was shed for a rapidly disappearing occupation. *Leave It To Beaver* (1957–63), was the first and perhaps the only family sitcom to tell a story from the point of view of the kids. Beaver Cleaver (age 7 when the show began) espoused the basic philosophy that frogs are better than girls. When there was a problem, it was he and his older brother, Wally, who talked the matter over.

It was not until 1961 and the introduction of *The Dick Van Dyke Show* that the sitcom began to find its own voice. The show sounded innocuous enough—straight family sitcom with an unobtrusive show business background. Van Dyke played a TV comedy writer. Van Dyke, Mary Tyler Moore, and the show's creator, Carl Reiner, added a new element to the sitcom, wit, and a new dimension, later to be described as ensemble playing, in which the supporting actors played almost as important a role as the stars. Moore became known as "the great re-actor"—it was the people around her who did the heavy acting, she merely reacted.

After a slow start the show went on to become the most important sitcom of the early 1960's; Miss Moore was its most important star. It became evident that in this new type of program an acting quality was called for that was quite different from the ones required for stage or even film acting. That quality was an understated, laid-back one which did not jostle, rattle, or jar. This format was exploited to its fullest in the new *Mary Tyler Moore Show* (1970–77) in which ensemble acting was the key. Each actor performed his or her specialty, to which Moore "reacted."

The effect was electric. It engendered other ensemble shows, most notably *M*A*S*H,* a less manic version of the Robert Altman movie about medics in the Korean War. Through it, the show's producers spoke obliquely of the horrors of war and how one kept one's sanity through humor.

The 1960's also ushered in the age of silliness. *Gilligan's Island,* about a group of inept castaways, set new highs in inanity. *F Troop* added

Television audiences still laugh at reruns of *The Honeymooners,* starring Art Carney, Jackie Gleason, and Audrey Meadows. *Amos 'n' Andy,* a major radio hit, was first presented on television in June 1951.

VIACOM

The antics of Lucille Ball made "Lucy" shows a major television success for more than 20 years.

The *Adventures of Ozzie and Harriet*, a long-running family comedy, was the story of the real-life Nelsons. On the air, however, Ozzie had no visible source of income.

UPI

In many ways, the situation comedy came of age with *The Dick Van Dyke Show*, which starred Dick Van Dyke and introduced Mary Tyler Moore. The show ran for five years (1961–66).

VIACOM

Mack Sennett pratfalls to an Old West in which nobody could ride and nobody could shoot well. From there it was just a step into comedic fantasy—*The Addams Family* (and its clone, *The Munsters*) in which ghoulish behavior became the accepted norm; *I Dream of Jeannie,* in which an astronaut kept a beautiful female genie in a bottle; *Mister Ed,* about an architect with a talking horse; and *The Flying Nun,* about a novice nun with an aerodynamic hat.

Then in 1971 things took a dramatic turn. Norman Lear, until then a filmmaker of only modest accomplishment, came on with *All in the Family.* It was not an easy trick. Indeed, the show was so new, so controversial, so opposed to what was traditionally supposed to be acceptable on commercial television that CBS delayed its debut for more than two years. When it did begin, the network hired extra telephone operators to handle the complaints it was sure would short-circuit the switchboard. But they were not counting on the wile of Lear or on the artfulness of Carroll O'Connor's performance as the lead character. Archie Bunker was a big mouth and a bigot who spoke disparagingly of "spicks, chinks, and hebes," and argued with his liberal son-in-law, Mike Stivic, about the black family next door. He was also funny and human.

The show's success may have been because it played on two levels. If a part of Archie's audience laughed at him, and another part took him seriously, all were exposed to the preposterousness of his attitude. Whatever it was, *All in the Family* soon became the number one show on the air, where it remained for at least five seasons.

From this hit Lear spun off, or originated outright, other shows with varying degrees of success: *Maude,* a horselaugh at the expense of the liberals; *The Jeffersons,* which reversed the stereotype and made the black family the affluent one; *Hot L Baltimore,* life on the big city's seamy side; *Good Times,* an attempt to take a serious look at black ghetto life in Chicago; *One Day at a Time,* the trials and tribulations of a divorced mother of two teenage girls; and *Diff'rent Strokes,* in which an affluent white bachelor adopts two young black children.

As the 1970's wore on, however, Lear had to relinquish his dominance of the ratings to another gifted sitcom maker, Garry Marshall, who had first come to prominence with a series version of Neil Simon's *The Odd Couple.* In January 1974, he was ready for a blockbuster. Not only did *Happy Days* have a popular theme (growing up in the 1950's), but it had an accidental cult hero in Fonzie, a leather-jacketed biker who had been added to the script as an afterthought. Kids went crazy for the Fonz, as played by Henry Winkler, and the ratings went through the roof. Marshall promptly spun off another massive hit, *Laverne and Shirley,* about a couple of scatter-brained bottle-cappers in a Milwaukee brewery. The series was said to have the common touch.

Less common was his *Mork & Mindy,* about a man from another planet who said "Na nu, na nu" and stood on his head a lot, and who, incidentally, set off a search for other comics who could act just like *Mork*'s star, Robin Williams.

There were other challengers, of course. *Soap* was an avant-garde attempt to make satire out of soap opera. *Taxi* took a loving and sometimes literate look at the world of the New York taxi driver. *Three's Company* (one guy living with two girls) was a leading proponent of the new sexual candor in sitcom. None, however, seemed ready to succeed *All in the Family* as the earthshaker of the 1980's.

LAND: The Vast Estate — The American Dream

BY PETER MEYER
Free-lance Writer

Few issues of the last decade have stirred such intense national concern and fostered so much unmitigated confusion as the future of America's land. From New York City to the Alaska tundra, from the swamplands of the bayou to the deserts of the west, from the hallowed halls of Congress to clapboard homes of local governments, a certain kind of battle rages. It is not easy to classify because the thousands of land disputes that have erupted across the United States run the gamut from intricate zoning code and tax loophole arguments to live ammunition, Hatfield-McCoy style vendettas.

American Indians want back much of the east coast. Small farmers and public interest groups in 17 western states are trying to get the federal government to enforce a 1902 law which would mean the redistribution of 1,500,000 acres (607 028 ha) of valuable agricultural land. Corporations, federal officials, state government, and Indians are all haggling over Alaska. In 1979 almost a fifth of America was being disputed in court-rooms, legislative halls, corporate boardrooms, and open fields. In short, the country is up for grabs.

There are 2.2 billion acres (890 308 000 ha) of indisputably beautiful and bountiful land in the vast American estate. Only the Soviet Union, Canada, and China are larger; and perhaps none is richer. Seventeen per-cent of the land is farmed; 30% is used for grass and pasture; and 32% is wooded. Despite the uproar over urban sprawl, only 1.5% of the coun-try is citified: more than 70% of the population still lives on less than 2% of the land.

Without even counting the resources extracted from it—the lettuce and potatoes and wheat, the oil and coal and iron, the pine and oak, and all the rest—the bare, naked land of America is worth more than $1,500,000,-000,000, 15% of the nation's total assets. If divided equally among its 220 million inhabitants, more than 10 acres (4.05 ha) of land could be given to every man, woman, and child in the country: a 100′ × 70′ (30.4 m × 21.3 m) lot in the city, almost 2 acres (.8 ha) of cropland, 3 acres (1.2 ha) of grass and pastureland, more than 3 acres (1.2 ha) of forestland, and almost 2 acres (.8 ha) of mountaintop, desert, quagmire, and mesa.

But the riches are not divided equally, not used equally, not appreciated and cared for equally. It has always been that way. Some believe that fact to be the touchstone of American greatness. Others, more recently, more loudly, have declared it to be its Achilles heel, and eventually its undoing. That land—as a commodity, as a resource, as a wonder, as a political weapon, and an economic sledgehammer—is perhaps America's greatest resource means that, despite the confusion and consternation, one fundamental question will run through all arguments like a lacerated vein: who should control the vast estate and exactly how should its resources be distributed?

UPI

In May 1977, New York Secretary of State Mario Cuomo and Indian spokesman Kakirakeron agreed that the Mohawk Indian nation would receive the rights to 5,700 acres (2-300 ha) of New York State land in Clinton County. Other Indian land claims disputes remain unsettled.

Has the Eagle Landed? After almost two centuries of carving up the continent into millions of bastions of private mini-kingdoms; of protecting the rights to private ownership of land and the individual's claim—no matter how large or small—to his personal retreat, his Walden Pond, his place of business, against the many demands and constraints of the body politic; of pursuing the Jeffersonian ideal that "there are never too many ways to subdivide the land"; of nurturing the American dream; there is now a pressing, unsettling fear that the land is being washed irretrievably into a large, amorphous public estate—or into an equally vast corporate state—and out of the control of the individuals who people it. The lyrics of Woody Guthrie may no longer apply—from New York harbor to the redwood forest Americans are now shouting: if this land isn't *your* land, and it isn't *my* land, then *to whom does it belong?*

There are ample reasons for the concern. And they are increasing with every increase in the price of a barrel of oil and with each new government mandate. On the one hand, much of the country's reaction to such environmental crises as petroleum scarcity, runaway urban growth, the destruction of farmland, forests, rivers, and mountains, is a sign of a new national consciousness, a signal that the American dream of private property in land must be rejected as chimera. But at the same time the inordinate volume of government regulation, the increasing concentration of land in the hands of fewer and fewer people, and the huge information vacuum within which social planners and legislators do their work, are also symptoms of a new national malaise, a growing distrust of, as Adam Smith called them, "those who affect to trade for the public good," a collective soul-searching to figure out if there is, in fact, anything with which to replace the old dream.

The Age of Scarcity: A New Caretaker for the Estate. As late as 1953 a Secretary of the Interior, Douglas McKay, advocated a policy that would turn over all federal lands, almost one third of the country, to individual states and private parties. It seemed to be a proposal eminently suited to the spirit of the American dream; and it might have seen fruition had it not been for the intervention of spaceship earth.

Someone once suggested that the environmental epoch began with a single photograph, began when an orbiting satellite beamed to earth a frightening image of a small blue dot floating helplessly in the black abyss of space. It was graphic evidence for all the earthlings below that they live in a fragile and finite spaceship, and their lives depend on the proper care of its limited resources. But whether or not that one picture was cause or simply vivid evidence, the neo-Malthusian fear—of a population destroying itself by decimating its vital resources—almost overnight transformed what had been a casual concern of an elite few into a loud apocalyptic cry to save the earth, even at the risk of losing civilization itself.

Environmental groups bloomed like cherry blossoms in spring. They represented everything from wolverines to whooping cranes; from one redwood tree, to all trees, to the earth itself. They carried their briefs for salvation to every governmental body that would listen. And many listened. They went earnestly searching for the "invisible hand" which was wreaking so much havoc on the land, passing hundreds of laws and regulations, until in 1976 President Gerald Ford proclaimed that the country was finally achieving "the institutionalizing of environmental values." The president said there was a "consensus that the unrestrained private use of land is not consistent with the public good." That same year Congress put Secretary McKay's proposal in the closet—for good, it thought—by passing the Federal Land Policy and Management Act, expressing its intention of

Wild sunflowers add to the beauty of an undeveloped Colorado desert.

GRANT HEILMAN

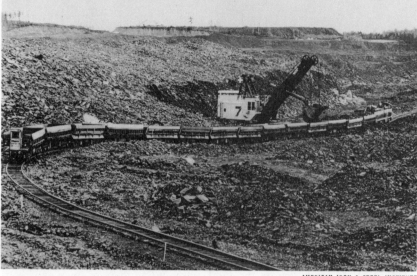

Legislation stipulating that operators of strip mines must restore the mined land to its former state has been enacted in the United States.

holding on to its more than 750 million acres (303.5 million ha) and expressly authorizing the Bureau of Land Management, which managed almost two thirds of the federal fiefdom, to "retain the public domain in perpetuity."

But not content to be caretaker of its 750-million acre (303.5-million ha) estate only, the federal government charged over the rest of America like a herd of wild mustangs. New laws were written at such a dizzying pace—states contributed more than 200 new land-control laws of their own in 1978—that few people bothered to analyze their impact. In the second session of the 94th (1976) and first session of the 95th (1977) Congresses, the Senate passed some 80 land-use bills, two thirds of which were signed into law. Rep. Morris Udall (D-AZ) counted more than 140 different federal programs which had land as their business. Much of it belonged to other people. In 1975 the Office of Land Use and Water Planning made a number of Congressional enemies—who ultimately cut off the Office's funds—when it reported that 12% of the entire federal budget, some $40 billion, had a direct impact on the use of private land.

If nowhere but from the perspective of sheer numbers, it has been, as land-use expert Fred Bosselman has characterized it, ten years of "quiet revolution," a "decade of quiet federalization" of land-use decisions that has shifted dramatically the locus of control over the land. In 1978 a Washington, D. C., consultant, then half-way through a quarter of a million dollar land-use research project for the Council on Environmental Quality, declared that "it no longer matters who owns the land. . . . Government legislation and regulation—not to mention direct dollar expenditures—have pretty much eliminated the meaning of private land ownership." Though few people have doubted the existence of the trend, many of late have bitterly denounced it.

The current disputes would be much more easily resolved were there any sort of consensus about who or what is to blame for the present condition of the land—or even about what the condition is; who or what is responsible for its inequitable distribution—or if indeed it is inequitable. Despite a decade of massive public land planning, the gaps in the information base are still as numerous and yawning as the mountains of proposals are tall. The fear of the consequences of land use operating in the free market must be balanced against the record of a government which handed

FLORIDA STATE NEWS BUREAU

over some 90 million acres (36.4 million ha) of public land to railroad companies in the 19th century. In 1972 the Census Bureau reported that 10 to 12 million Americans suffered because of malnutrition; yet during the decade preceding such dismal news, the Department of Agriculture each year was paying farmers to keep some 50 million acres (20.2 million ha) of agricultural land idle.

There are still only three basic factors—all increasingly interdependent —that determine how land outside the public domain is used—or abused: first, the millions of individuals, collectively referred to as the private sector, who daily make millions of decisions about what to do with their land; second, the thousands of government laws which, like zoning codes, are designed specifically to regulate those market decisions; and finally, another myriad government incentives and disincentives—property and income tax laws, highway and mass transit programs, grants for urban development, pollution regulations, to name but a few—which guide and push individuals toward decisions about the use of their land.

Yet even though some 26 million acres (10.5 million ha) of land—an area the size of Tennessee—are converted from one use to another each year, very little is known about why it happens, how market decisions and government decisions affect one another.

If there had been anything like a nationwide consensus about "public" control of "private" land, such unanimity was not evident in the spring of 1979 when the Carter administration shelved as too controversial its plans to "consolidate all public and private land and land-related resource functions" in a huge new Executive Department of Natural Resources.

That the impact of public regulation has been significant, or at least unsettling, is seen in the numbers of complaints brought to the courts for resolution: more than 400 to state courts in 1978; more than $500 million worth of claims against the federal government in 1978 by people who argued that their property had been "taken" unconstitutionally by the promulgation of any number of different statutes; three zoning cases to the Supreme Court in 1976, more than had been heard in the previous 50 years. The Justice Department's Land and Natural Resources Division said in 1979 that its workload had doubled in the previous five years, and as of October 1978 almost $14 billion worth of land claims—initiated by both government and private parties—were in its files.

That the federal government's charge into the private sector has not gone unchallenged has been proven with the surprising defeat in Congress on numerous occasions of a proposal for a single, comprehensive federal land-use law. Environmental groups, trade associations, labor, and big business have supported such legislation.

By 1979 western states were beginning to react to Congress' 1976 Land Policy and Management Act. The Nevada legislature fired the first dramatic—if only symbolic—shot in what the press was calling the Sagebrush Rebellion and what one Interior Department spokesman said was the most important land-use battle of the decade. In July, Nevada declared 49 million acres (19.8 million ha) of federal land to be, in effect, state property. Then California, using a different tactic, sued the federal government when it proposed opening a national forest to development. The Alaska state government continued to lobby Washington in a desperate attempt to retrieve at least something of its 362 million acres (146.5 million ha) from control of the national capital. By early September the attorneys general of most of the western states gathered in Reno, NV, to plan a common strategy with which to confront their common landlord who then owned some 676 million acres (274 million ha)—half the land—in ten of the western states: 96% of Alaska, 86% of Nevada, 66% of Utah, 63% of Idaho, 52% of Oregon, 47% of Wyoming, 45% of California, 42% of Arizona, 36% of Colorado, and 33% of New Mexico.

And if all were not quiet on the western front, Indian tribes in six eastern seaboard states were still trying to reassert their rights to some 12 million acres (4.9 million ha) of land—most of it now in private hands.

A Rival Caretaker: The Corporate State. One of the bitter ironies faced by those who have objected strenuously to a federal monopoly over land—and one of the principal arguments used to support public ownership—is the growing monopolization of land by private parties.

In 1946 the U.S. Senate published a remarkable study by Walter Goldschmidt, then in the employ of the Department of Agriculture. The study, which has since been characterized by one land-use planner as "an underground classic of rural anthropology," compared two small farming communities in California's San Joaquin valley. The towns were identical in every respect but farm size; and some of Goldschmidt's conclusions were startling:

—The small farm community had more institutions encouraging democratic decision making and a much broader participation in such activities by its citizenry.
—The small farms supported about 20% more people and at a measurably higher level of living.
—The majority of the small farm community population were independent entrepreneurs, as against less than 20% in the large farm community, where nearly two thirds were agricultural wage laborers.
—The small farm community in all instances had better community facilities, more schools, more parks, more newspapers, more civic organizations, and more churches.
—The small farm community had twice as many business establishments as the large farm town and did 60% more retail business.

Despite the dramatic sociological and cultural impacts that Goldschmidt discovered in concentrated land ownership, he was not allowed to expand his research to other areas of the country, and the United States is still plagued by an appalling lack of data about ownership patterns. By 1979, 33 years after Goldschmidt's study, there still had been no survey

A Nebraska farm. American farms have decreased in number but increased in size.

of ownership, and, according to USDA economist Gene Wunderlich, "national censuses, federal agencies, commerce and industry, state land agencies, universities, local governments, and public interest groups produce only interesting fragments of data or inferential information. . . . Nationally, the situation is chaotic."

Even so, the scattered pieces of information that are available have allowed Wunderlich, recognized as one of the country's foremost experts in the field, to make "rationalized estimates" about the patterns of proprietorship so crucial to economic and political power-brokering. His findings are surprising. Even though about a quarter of the population are landowners, most of their holdings are limited to small residential lots which all together comprise a scant 2% of all privately owned land. The overwhelming majority of acres, Wunderlich believes, 95% of all private land, is owned by just 3% of the population. His conclusions are especially sobering when measured against the findings of people like Walter Goldschmidt.

In just the last two decades almost 50% of all American farms have disappeared, 500,000 in the last ten years alone. At the same time there has been no appreciable decrease in the number of acres devoted to farming, and this fact indicates conclusively that farms are not being destroyed by urban sprawl so much as they are being simply swallowed by larger farms. In many cases huge multinational corporations seeking to diversify have purchased vast tracts of agricultural land. Del Monte, which operates 11 farms in the United States and owns 96,400 acres (39 000 ha) of land; IU International, which, through a subsidiary, owns 127,000 acres (51 400 ha) in Hawaii alone; and Tenneco Corporation, which owns almost 86,000 acres (34 800 ha) of irrigated farmland, are just a few examples.

Foreigners are thought to own over 6 million acres (2.4 million ha) of land in the United States, and fears about the increasing speed with which these outside investors are gobbling up American real estate has spawned a number of restrictive laws from both federal and state legislators. For example, in the spring of 1979 Iowa Gov. Robert Ray signed a bill which prohibited foreigners from buying Iowa farmland and limited their purchases of commercial and industrial land in the state to 320 acres (129.5 ha).

But even while farmland ownership has received a greater amount of attention—perhaps because it not only symbolizes most graphically man's ultimate dependence on the earth, but also because the small family farm has always been the epitome of American individualism and pioneer spirit —many people are beginning to see the important link between all types of land and corporate profit. Exxon, for example, the world's largest company, hold interests in more than 40 million acres (16 million ha) in the United States, an area equivalent to 3% of all private land. Such well-known companies as Time Inc., Proctor and Gamble, and ITT, not normally thought of as land resource corporations, together control over 3 million acres (1.2 million ha) of timber, farm, and development land. In Maine, where the federal government owns less land than in almost any other state (only .6 of 1%), a 1974 Ralph Nader study reported that seven "absentee corporations" owned 32% of the state's 20 million acres (8 million ha). And with the value of land increasing at almost double the rate of inflation, most companies find land a worthwhile investment even if they choose to leave it unused.

Most recently, an unpublished random survey completed in 1978 by the Department of Agriculture found that the 568 companies it investigated had interests in 301.7 million acres (122 million ha) of land, a figure that represents 23% of all the land in private hands.** As one official commented, "land ownership is probably more concentrated in the hands of a few in the United States than in those notorious South American countries that you hear so much about."

Few people would disagree that the next decade promises even more intense and bitter struggles than the last. The energy crisis, to cite just one example, will put incredible pressures on the land. Mining interests and agricultural interests will collide over the allocation of scarce water that both of them need, and environmentalists and industrialists will disagree regarding clean air and the millions of yet untapped acres of wilderness.

That these issues will be thought of as national concerns will in turn increase the pressure to devise a *national* solution, a federal land-use plan. Yet at the same time the pressures on the land will also strengthen the resolve of individual landowners—state governments and cities as well as private parties—to hold on to what they have. The Sagebrush Rebellion is one significant sign of that resolve, and already there is a proposal in Congress to bring Douglas McKay's 26-year-old recommendation out of the closet and liquidate the federal estate. In a critical sense, everyone, for reasons both selfish and sublime, will be assiduously and with increasing seriousness heeding the advice of Will Rogers: "Buy land. They ain't makin' any more of it."

** Many of these figures can be misleading if the term "ownership" is confused with "holdings" or "interests." Because of the manner in which various rights to the land are distributed, it is possible, and common, for a number of different parties to have claims on the same parcel of land—e.g., one may be the title holder or "owner"; another, the lessee; another, the "owner" of timber rights only; another, the "owner" of the right to drill for oil; etc. From this point of view, then, the United States really possesses, though it is almost impossible to quantify, many more acres of land than the simple geographical measurement indicates. Though it is instructive to know how many acres the companies had interest in (345 of them owned outright more than 57 million acres—23 million ha), it would be more instructive to compare their "holdings" with the total number of possible holdings in the country.

The Jerry Lewis Telethon has been held annually for 14 years to benefit the Muscular Dystrophy Association.

THE CHARITY BUSINESS

By Sandra Stencel, *Associate Editor, "Editorial Research Reports"*

These are troubling times for American philanthropy. Beset by rising administrative and fund-raising costs, the charitable and religious organizations of the United States are looking for new sources of funds. At the same time, today's double-digit inflation makes it more difficult to convince Americans to part with their money—however worthy the cause. As a result, the charity business has become every bit as competitive as its for-profit counterpart and, some would say, just as bureaucratic and depersonalized. "American charity is very much like America itself," Harvey Katz noted in his 1974 examination of the charity business. According to Katz, the business was "born of a heroic rebellion against an insensitive establishment, but is now an established institution itself—wealthy, powerful, and respectable."

Like other big institutions in America today, the charity business faces an increasingly skeptical public. The educational, scientific, and social projects that private philanthropy pioneered are now largely supported by federal, state, and local governments. The government's incursion into these areas has put charitable institutions in the uncomfortable position of having to justify their continued existence. Evidence of discrepancies in the management of some charities has led to a lessening of confidence toward all of them and increased support for legislation to put charities under tighter controls. At least 35 states have laws directly regulating the solicitation of charitable contributions and the U. S. Congress is considering proposals that would require financial disclosures by charities that use the mails to solicit funds.

Public suspicion of philanthropic motives should not be overemphasized. Americans continue to respond generously to compassionate appeals, donating their time and labor as well as their money to worthy causes. The American Association of Fund-Raising Counsel in New York estimates that 25% of Americans engage in some philanthropic work.

Donations to charitable organizations in 1978, the counsel said in its 1978 annual report, reached a record $39.56 billion, a 9.4% gain over 1977. Although this was slightly above the 9% increase in the cost of living that year, it was considerably below the 11% annual growth rate charities need to continue their work at present levels. The 11% figure was determined by the Commission on Private Philanthropy and Public Needs, the blue-ribbon panel set up in 1973 by John D. Rockefeller 3d, the noted philanthropist who died in July 1978 at the age of 72.

During his lifetime, Rockefeller—the oldest of the five brothers who inherited a fortune that began with the Standard Oil operations of their grandfather, John D. Rockefeller, Sr.—gave an estimated $94 million to philanthropic causes. Although few Americans can afford to be as generous, the bulk of private giving in the United States comes not from big corporations or foundations, but from individuals. Nearly 83% of the money received by charitable organizations in 1978, $32.8 billion, came from individual donors. Bequests accounted for 6.6% ($2.6 billion), foundations for 5.5% ($2.16 billion), and corporations for 5%.

On the receiving end, religious organizations collected the biggest share of the charity dollar in 1978, 46.5%. Education came in second with 14%, more than half of it going to higher education. Health agencies and hospitals came in third with 13.8%. Social welfare organizations received 10% and civic and cultural causes collected 9.2%. The remaining funds went primarily to private foundations and to overseas relief and technical assistance agencies.

Although contributions to charitable organizations have never been higher, this is a time of financial uncertainty for all those involved in philanthropic work. A major cause of the present financial crisis is the increase in fund-raising costs. Much of the increased cost can be attributed to the switch from door-to-door solicitations to direct mail campaigns. Nonprofit groups send out billions of direct mail packages each year. Most of them end up in the recipient's waste paper basket. In recent years the average response rate has dropped from 2% to less than 1%.

Because prices for donor address lists are so high, direct mail campaigns rarely make an immediate profit. The payoff, if any, comes after the first year, when donors renew their contributions. A third of all contributions that nonprofit groups receive comes from direct mail campaigns, according to the Direct Mail/Marketing Association.

The high cost of direct mail fund-raising has prompted charity officials to search for new sources of revenue. A growing number of philanthropic agencies is looking to U. S. businesses for funds. The Commission on Private Philanthropy and Public Needs called corporate giving "the last major undeveloped frontier" in philanthropy. Since the early 1970's corporations have more than doubled their charitable contributions. But business in general does not take full advantage of federal tax law that permits corporations to deduct up to 5% of their pre-tax income for charitable contributions. Corporate giving in 1978 amounted to $2 billion, or just 1.01% of net income for that year.

One of the biggest recipients of corporate donations is the United Way, the largest and most visible charitable fund-raiser in the United States. The United Way is actually a federation of local chapters calling on local citizens to support local services. Nearly 40,000 programs benefited from the more than $1.3 billion that United Way's 2,200 local chapters collected in 1978. Federated fund-raising drives have been popular in the United States since World War I, when war chest programs in some 400 cities demonstrated that large sums could be raised for diversified welfare programs by single, community-wide campaigns. The idea of a federated fund-raising drive appealed to businessmen and labor leaders, who viewed it as a way to reduce the disruption to work schedules that a succession of fund-raising campaigns had created previously.

In time, many companies granted the United Way the sole right to solicit their employees. Today the bulk of United Way's funds comes from employee payroll deduction plans. Participating employers ask their employees to contribute their "fair share"—a sliding amount keyed to salary. The United Way also has devised the corporate equivalent of the fair share —the "corporate guidelines," which are geared to a company's financial and operating record.

In recent years the United Way has been under attack from other charity groups because of its privileged access to payroll-deduction contributions. Several agencies have gone to court to challenge this dominance. So far the courts have supported United Way. Minority groups and social activists also have accused the United Way of favoring safe, uncontroversial causes, such as the Boy Scouts, the Girl Scouts, the American Red Cross, and the Salvation Army. Among those who feel they are not getting their fair share are environmentalists, consumer and community action groups, abortion and birth control services, and blacks and other minorities.

An ad campaign of United Way. With William Aramony as national executive and with 2,200 local chapters, the United Way collected more than $1.3 billion in 1978.

Robert Bothwell, the executive director of the Washington-based National Committee for Responsive Philanthropy, spoke for many of these groups when he said, "The United Way is a very closed-door place." Walter Bremond, executive director of the National Black United Fund in Los Angeles, has called United Way a "racist institution" because of the relatively small number of minority group members in important policy-making positions. William Aramony, United Way's national executive, vigorously defends the agency's choice of beneficiaries as those that meet the broadest range of needs. "By its very nature United Way cannot have extremes of left and right," Aramony said. "It's a consensus system."

The war of words between United Way and its critics underscores a deep philosophical split over the function of charity. "Traditional charity tends to be service oriented," James Joseph, a former National Black United Fund board member and now undersecretary of the Interior, told *Forbes* magazine. "But the black community also needs social activism and the traditional charities have not been interested in supporting potentially controversial social activism."

There are signs that some nonprofit groups are responding to demands for greater equity in the distribution of philanthropic dollars. The Ford Foundation, for example, in January 1979 named Franklin A. Thomas, a black lawyer, as its new president. The choice of Thomas was viewed as a move to strengthen the foundation's involvement in programs aimed at helping the poor and minorities.

Recent changes in U. S. tax law may make it easier for philanthropic organizations to assume a more activist role. Under the old law, public charities were barred from engaging in partisan political activities and from devoting "substantial" effort to "carrying on propaganda or otherwise attempting to influence legislation." Charities judged by the Internal Revenue Service to be engaging in "substantial" lobbying lost their eligibility for tax-deductible contributions. Many charities complained that the substantial test was so vague that even the IRS did not understand it.

The Tax Reform Act of 1976 offered qualifying charities a choice: they could continue to be judged under the old substantial test or they could comply with specific lobbying spending limits contained in section 2503 of the tax revision. The expenditure allowances are rather liberal. For any

DAN MILLER, COURTESY, MARCH OF DIMES

Entertainment personalities, clowns, and the general public participate in the New York March of Dimes Superwalk. Below: an American Cancer Society ad.

Following a nationwide search, the Ford Foundation named Franklin A. Thomas as president. The 44-year-old lawyer had served as a deputy New York City police commissioner (1965–67) and as president and chief executive officer of the Bedford Stuyvesant Restoration Corp., Brooklyn, NY (1967–77).

UPI

one year, they permit a charity to devote to lobbying activities 20% of the first $500,000 of its expenditures for exempt purposes. Declining percentages apply to portions of the organization's budget exceeding $500,000. An overall spending limitation of $1 million is imposed, no matter how large the charity's total budget is. Up to 25% of the total lobbying expenditure can be spent on grassroots legislative activities, that is, efforts to influence public opinion on legislative matters.

Excluded from coverage under the revision are churches, church groups, and private foundations. Many church groups had expressed alarm that the new terms, if applied to them, would violate their constitutional rights guaranteed by the First Amendment. Church spokesmen contended that the IRS had no authority to monitor church activities.

Charitable organizations have been alarmed by recent changes in tax law that make it more attractive for taxpayers to use the standard deduction instead of itemizing their claims. The number of taxpayers who itemize fell from 30% in 1970 to 23% in 1977. The American Association of Fund-Raising Counsel maintains that the trend toward the standard deduction removes the tax incentive for giving and has cost American charities over $6 billion since 1969.

Charitable organizations are supporting a bill, introduced by Reps. Barber B. Conable, Jr. (R-NY) and Joseph Fisher (D-VA), that would allow taxpayers claiming the standard deduction to take a special additional deduction for charitable contributions. A similar bill was rejected by the House Ways and Means Committee in 1978. A companion bill, introduced in the Senate by Daniel P. Moynihan (D-NY) and Bob Packwood (R-OR), was stopped in the Senate Finance Committee. Supporters of the Fisher-Conable proposal believe that if Congress does not do something to encourage more private giving, the government could end up picking up the tab for many of the goods and services charities now provide.

Theoretically, it would be possible for the government to provide all the funds now supplied by private donors. But Americans have taken the view that to abolish private philanthropy would be to destroy their country's long-cherished beliefs in diversity and pluralism.

CHRONOLOGY

JANUARY

1 The United States and China open diplomatic relations, while at the same time formal U. S. ties with Taiwan are severed.

6 On Guadeloupe, leaders of the United States, France, Great Britain, and West Germany end two days of talks with statements generally supporting arms limitation and détente with the Soviet Union.

7 The Cambodian capital of Phnom Penh falls to rebel forces backed by Vietnam, and the government of Prime Minister Pol Pot collapses.

11 The surgeon general of the United States, Dr. Julius B. Richmond, issues a 1,200-page report which offers new and "overwhelming proof" that cigarette smoking causes lung cancer, heart disease, and other serious ailments.

12 Bella Abzug is dismissed by President Jimmy Carter from her post as co-chairman of the National Advisory Committee on Women.

16 Shah Mohammed Reza Pahlavi leaves Iran for a "vacation" abroad, which many observers feel will be permanent exile. A new civilian cabinet, headed by Prime Minister Shahpur Bakhtiar, receives final parliamentary approval and takes over the running of the country.

During his nine-day visit to the United States, China's Deputy Premier Deng Xiaoping is guest at a Texas rodeo.

UPI

21 The Pittsburgh Steelers win the championship of the National Football League by defeating the Dallas Cowboys, 35–31, in Super Bowl XIII.

22 U. S. President Carter submits to Congress his budget for fiscal 1980. Designed to restrain inflation, the budget calls for expenditures of $531.6 billion and revenues of $502.6 billion.

23 In his annual State of the Union message to Congress, President Carter outlines his plans for controlling inflation, reaching an arms control agreement with the Soviet Union, and building a "new foundation" for the future.

26 Former U. S. Vice President Nelson A. Rockefeller dies of a heart attack in New York City.

27 Pope John Paul II opens the third meeting of the Latin American Episcopal Conference in Mexico City.

28 Chinese Deputy Prime Minister Deng Xiaoping arrives in Washington, D. C., for the first official visit by a Chinese Communist leader to the United States. It is the first stop on a nine-day tour.

31 Prime Minister Giulio Andreotti of Italy submits the resignation of his Christian Democrat government after the Communist Party withdrew its support January 26.

Britain's James Callaghan (left), Germany's Helmut Schmidt, United States' Jimmy Carter, and France's Giscard d'Estaing (right) hold a two-day summit on the island of Guadeloupe. The four leaders were accompanied by their wives.

UPI

FEBRUARY

1 Exiled religious leader Ayatollah Ruhollah Khomeini returns to Iran from France in a bid to seize government power and establish an Islamic state.

Heiress Patricia Hearst is released from a federal prison near San Francisco, CA, after her sentence was commuted by President Carter. She had served 22 months of a 7-year sentence for bank robbery.

3 Six soldiers of the United Nations Interim Force in Lebanon (UNIFIL) are killed in a clash with Palestinian guerrillas in southern Lebanon.

5 More than 3,000 protesting farmers drive their tractors, vans, and trucks into Washington, D. C., to dramatize their demands for higher price supports.

7 Algeria's acting Defense Minister Col. Benjedid Chadli is elected president, succeeding the late Houari Boumedienne.

8 The United States severs military ties with Nicaragua after President Anastasio Somoza Debayle rejected mediation of his nation's civil disorders.

11 Following massive demonstrations in support of a provisional government named by Ayatollah Khomeini and headed by Mehdi Bazargan, Iranian Prime Minister Shahpur Bakhtiar resigns, and the army pledges neutrality.

14 The U. S. ambassador to Afghanistan, Adolph Dubs, is abducted and shot to death by Muslim terrorists in Kabul.

As U. S. President Carter arrives in Mexico City for three days of talks, Mexican President José López Portillo is openly critical of the United States. According to Portillo, "it is difficult . . . to maintain cordial and mutually advantageous relations in an atmosphere of mistrust or open hostility."

17 China launches a massive invasion of Vietnam in retaliation against Vietnam's incursion into Cambodia. The action follows months of unresolved border disputes.

18 For the first time in six years, representatives of North and South Korea meet in Panmunjom.

Iranians mark the return of the Ayatollah Khomeini by demonstrating near the Shahyad monumental arch.

UPI

19 Live television coverage of routine sessions of the U. S. House of Representatives begins.

21 St. Lucia, a tiny island in the Caribbean, gains full independence from Great Britain.

26 A total solar eclipse is seen in the northwestern United States; it is the last total eclipse of the sun over the continental United States until the year 2017.

MARCH

1 The United States and China officially open embassies in Peking and Washington, D. C., respectively. The appointment of Leonard Woodcock as the first U. S. ambassador to Communist China was confirmed by the Senate February 26.

U. S. Secretary of the Treasury W. Michael Blumenthal signs an agreement with Chinese officials calling for the repayment, at 41 cents on the dollar, of a $196.6 million claim for property seized by the Chinese in 1949.

2 Queen Elizabeth II of Great Britain returns from a three-week tour of Arab nations in the Persian Gulf.

5 The Chinese government reports the withdrawal of its troops from Vietnam, but Hanoi claims that attacks continue.

The U. S. Voyager I spacecraft conducts the first extensive close-up exploration of Jupiter.

6 South African forces in Namibia launch a military offensive into Angola against guerrillas of South–West Africa People's Organization. The raid comes a day after the South African government rejected a UN cease-fire plan.

9 A U. S. District Court judge in Milwaukee, WI, issues a ten-day temporary restraining order prohibiting *Progressive* magazine from publishing an article describing the workings of the hydrogen bomb.

12 Luis Herrera Campíns is inaugurated president of Venezuela.

13 The European Monetary System officially goes into effect as a two-day summit meeting of European Community (EC) government leaders draws to a close.

UPI

Photographs returned from the U. S. spacecraft Voyager 1 give scientists a closer look at the planet Jupiter.

On the White House lawn, March 26, Prime Minister Menahem Begin and President Anwar el-Sadat (left) signed the Israeli-Egyptian peace treaty. At right, President Carter witnesses the agreement for the United States.

14 Indian Prime Minister Morarji Desai and Soviet Premier Aleksei Kosygin sign accords in New Delhi promising trade, technological, and scientific cooperation for periods of 10 to 15 years.

15 Gen. João Baptista de Oliveira Figueiredo is sworn in as the new president of Brazil.

23 Former President Félix Malloum leaves Chad for Nigeria, and Goukoni Waddaye assumes control of an eight-member provisional government council.

26 In Washington, D. C., Egyptian President Anwar el-Sadat and Israeli Prime Minister Menahem Begin sign a formal peace treaty bringing to an end a 31-year state of war between the two nations. The signing comes after a Mideast trip by U. S. President Carter in which he obtained acceptance of new compromises from Egypt and Israel. Carter signs the treaty as a witness.

Canadian Prime Minister Pierre Elliott Trudeau dissolves parliament and calls for general elections May 22.

Maurice Bishop, who seized power in Grenada in a bloodless coup March 13, announces that he has suspended the country's constitution but will keep the country in the Commonwealth.

27 In Afghanistan, Foreign Minister Hafizullah Amin is named prime minister by the pro-Communist Revolutionary Council.

28 A series of breakdowns in the cooling system of the nuclear power plant at Three Mile Island, PA, leads to a major accident and the release of above-normal amounts of radiation into the atmosphere.

29 After the British Labour Party government loses a parliamentary vote of confidence, Prime Minister James Callaghan submits his resignation and elections are set for May 3.

The presidents of North and South Yemen sign a provisional agreement ending hostilities and uniting the two countries under one government.

31 Ministers of 18 Arab League nations and a representative of the Palestine Liberation Organization (PLO) pass resolutions severing all economic and diplomatic relations with Egypt.

In Ecuador's first free elections in 11 years, voters selected Jaime Roldós Aguilera for the presidency.

APRIL

1 Following a national referendum in which Iranian voters approve the formation of an Islamic republic, Ayatollah Ruhollah Khomeini proclaims "the first day of a government of God."

2 A six-month government crisis in Belgium comes to a close as King Baudouin announces the formation of a five-party coalition headed by Wilfried Martens.

Italian President Sandro Pertini dissolves parliament after the eleven-day-old coalition headed by Giulio Andreotti loses a vote of confidence. National elections are planned for early June.

3 Jane M. Byrne is the first woman to be elected mayor of Chicago.

Israeli Prime Minister Menahem Begin returns from a two-day visit with Egyptian President Anwar el-Sadat in Cairo. This first trip by an Israeli leader to the Egyptian capital is marked by the signing of several accords, including one to set up a "hot line" between Cairo and Jerusalem.

China informs the Soviet Union that it will not extend its 30-year treaty with Moscow when it expires in April 1980.

4 Former Pakistani Prime Minister Zulfikar Ali Bhutto is hanged in Rawalpindi on charges of conspiring to murder a political rival in 1974.

5 U. S. President Carter orders a gradual decontrol of domestic oil prices and asks Congress for a tax on windfall profits by the nation's oil-producing companies.

6 A 24-member cabinet, Spain's first constitutional government in more than 30 years, is sworn in by King Juan Carlos. Parliamentary elections were held March 1.

7 Amin Abbas Hoveida, the former prime minister of Iran, and other officials who served under exiled Shah Mohammed Reza Pahlavi are executed by firing squad in Tehran.

11 Ugandan exiles in Tanzania announce the formation of a new provisional government, headed by Yusufu K. Lule, to replace the eight-year regime of President-for-Life Idi Amin Dada. The announcement comes as an invasionary force of Tanzanian soldiers and Ugandan rebels marches into the capital city of Kampala.

Y. G. BERGES, SYGMA

A portrait of Idi Amin is simply a discarded item following the overthrow of Uganda's president-for-life, April 11.

12 International negotiations sponsored by the General Agreement on Tariffs and Trade (GATT) culminate after 5½ years with the signing in Geneva of a comprehensive agreement that will reduce tariffs by an average of 33% and overcome other obstacles to world trade.

18 A Superior Court judge in Los Angeles, CA, denies a breach of contract claim by Michelle Triola Marvin for half of the $3.6 million earned by actor Lee Marvin during the six-year period in which the couple lived together out of wedlock.

24 Bishop Abel Muzorewa becomes prime minister-elect as his United African National Council wins 51 of 100 parliamentary seats in Rhodesia's first universal suffrage elections.

27 Five leading Soviet dissidents, including Jewish human rights activist Alexandr Ginzburg, arrive at New York's Kennedy International Airport. In exchange, two convicted Soviet spies are released by the United States.

29 Jaime Roldós Aguilera, a 38-year-old lawyer, is elected president of Ecuador in that nation's first free general election since June 2, 1968.

MAY

UPI

Laurence Olivier, now Lord Olivier, receives an honorary Oscar at Hollywood's Academy Award ceremonies.

2 Japanese Prime Minister Masayoshi Ohira meets with U.S. President Carter in Washington. The two leaders issue a communiqué pledging "a more harmonious pattern of international trade and payments."

4 Margaret Thatcher is the first woman to become prime minister of Great Britain, after voters gave her Conservative Party a solid majority over the incumbent Labour Party in parliamentary elections May 3.

5 Spectacular Bid wins the 105th running of the Kentucky Derby.

6 More than 65,000 demonstrators march from the White House to the Capitol in a peaceful protest against the use of nuclear power. It is the largest antinuclear demonstration in the United States to date.

Austrian Chancellor Bruno Kreisky is elected to an unprecedented fourth term, and the Socialist Party increases by two seats its majority representation in parliament.

UPI

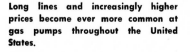

Long lines and increasingly higher prices become ever more common at gas pumps throughout the United States.

9 California institutes gasoline rationing in nine counties. Buying is limited to alternate days, based on an odd or even license plate.

16 Lebanese Prime Minister Selim al-Hoss and his eight-member cabinet resign in an attempt to bring together feuding Muslim and Christian party groups.

18 In a negligence suit against the Kerr-McGee Corp., $10.5 million in damages is awarded to the estate of Karen Silkwood, a laboratory technician who was contaminated by radiation at that company's Cimarron, OK, plutonium plant in 1974.

21 The Montreal Canadiens win their fourth consecutive Stanley Cup.

22 The 11-year tenure of Canadian Prime Minister Pierre Elliott Trudeau comes to an end as the Progressive Conservatives, led by Joe Clark, win a plurality of seats in parliamentary elections.

UPI

To the House of Lords and before Prince Philip, Queen Elizabeth outlines the plans of the new Thatcher government.

23 Karl Carstens, a former member of the Nazi Party, is elected president of West Germany.

25 An American Airlines DC-10 jet loses an engine shortly after takeoff from Chicago's O'Hare International Airport and crashes, killing all 272 persons aboard. The accident sets off an intensive investigation by the Federal Aviation Administration (FAA).

Convicted murderer John A. Spenkelink, 30, is put to death in the electric chair at the Florida State Prison in Starke.

26 A four-party, center-left coalition, headed by Mauno Koivisto, takes office in Finland.

27 The opening of the Egyptian-Israeli border is announced two days after Israel begins its withdrawal from the Sinai Peninsula.

28 Greece becomes the tenth member of the European Community as Prime Minister Constantine Caramanlis signs a treaty with the other members of the Common Market. Full integration will take place Jan. 1, 1981.

JUNE

In May, Abel Muzorewa was installed as prime minister, as Rhodesia became Zimbabwe Rhodesia.

PETER JORDAN, SYGMA

1 After more than 80 years of white rule, Rhodesia's first black government is installed, a new constitution takes effect, and the country's name is officially changed to Zimbabwe Rhodesia.

The Seattle SuperSonics win the championship of the National Basketball Association.

2 Pope John Paul II arrives in his native Poland for a nine-day visit.

4 In Canada's first televised swearing-in ceremony, Joseph Clark becomes the nation's 16th prime minister and youngest head of government.

President John Vorster of South Africa resigns after being implicated in a political scandal involving the spending of government money on secret propaganda projects.

Dissident Ghanaian enlisted men, led by Flight Lt. Jerry Rawlings, take control of the government from Gen. Fred Akuffo and promise a return to civilian rule.

In Italian parliamentary elections, the Christian Democrats suffer a marginal loss but retain their plurality in the 630-seat Chamber of Deputies. The Communist Party loses ground for the first time since the end of World War II.

6 The Federal Aviation Administration grounds indefinitely all 138 U. S.-operated DC-10 airliners after safety investigations disclose a flaw in the plane's engine-mount assembly.

President Anastasio Somoza Debayle of Nicaragua declares a state of siege in response to a general strike and continuing guerrilla attacks.

7 President Antonio Ramalho Eanes of Portugal accepts the resignation of Prime Minister Carlos Mota Pinto's center-right government.

10 The first elections for the newly-expanded European Parliament are completed. The outcome is seen as favorable to center and right-wing parties.

11 Movie actor John Wayne dies at the age of 72.

UPI

Early in June, Canada's Joe Clark and his wife Maureen McTeer took occupancy of the prime minister's residence.

18 Meeting in Vienna, Austria, U. S. President Carter and Soviet President Brezhnev conclude seven years of strategic arms limitation talks by signing the SALT II agreement.

20 Ugandan President Yusufu K. Lule, the successor to Idi Amin Dada, is forced out of office and replaced by 59-year-old Godfrey Binaisa.

22 Jeremy Thorpe, former Liberal Party leader and member of British parliament, is found not guilty of conspiring to murder male model Norman Scott, who had claimed to be Thorpe's lover.

27 The U. S. Supreme Court, in *Kaiser Aluminum & Chemical Corp.* v. *Weber, Weber* v. *U. S.,* and *United Steelworkers of America* v. *Weber,* rules 5–2 that private employers and unions can legally give special preference to minorities and women to help eliminate manifest imbalances, even when there is no evidence of past discrimination by the employer.

28 Meeting in Geneva, Switzerland, the Organization of Petroleum Exporting Countries (OPEC) agrees on a new two-tier price system for crude oil, with per barrel costs ranging from $18 to $23.50. The increase brings to 50% the aggregate price rise for the year to date.

In a Vienna palace, June 18, Soviet President Brezhnev and U. S. President Carter sign the SALT treaty.

UDO SCHREIDER, GAMMA-LIAISON

29 Concluding a two-day summit conference in Tokyo, the leaders of the United States, France, Great Britain, Japan, West Germany, Italy, and Canada agree to set specific, country-by-country ceilings on oil imports through 1985.

30 At a special conference dealing with the rising problem of Indo-Chinese refugees, the foreign ministers of the Association of Southeast Asian Nations (ASEAN) announce in Katu, Indonesia, that they will refuse to accept any more refugees into their countries. The announcement comes two days after President Carter doubled the U. S. refugee quota to 14,000 per month.

JULY

1 William F. Niehous, a U. S. business executive kidnapped in Venezuela in February 1976, is reunited with his family in Toledo, Ohio, after being rescued by Venezuelan policemen in a gun battle with leftist guerrillas.

President Carter concludes a two-day state visit to South Korea.

3 The West German Bundestag (lower house of parliament) votes to abolish the statute of limitations for murder, enabling prosecutions of German Nazi war criminals to continue.

4 U. S. President Carter cancels without explanation a July 5 address to the nation on energy. The cancellation comes just as Carter's approval rating dips to 29%, one of the lowest for a U. S. president ever recorded in the Gallup Poll.

Former president of Algeria Ahmed Ben Bella is freed by President Benjedid Chadli after 14 years under house arrest.

10 President Carter signs a proclamation prohibiting the air conditioning of commercial, government, and most other public buildings to less than 78° F (25.5° C).

Hilla Limann wins a runoff election against Victor Uwusu to become president of Ghana's new civilian government, which is scheduled to take office in October.

11 Skylab, the 77-ton unmanned U. S. space station, breaks up in the Earth's atmosphere and scatters debris over the Indian Ocean and the desert of southwestern Australia.

12 The Gilbert Islands become the independent republic of Kiribati.

UPI

Björn Borg is the first to win four consecutive Wimbledon singles titles.

13 The U. S. Federal Aviation Administration (FAA) lifts its June 6 ban on flights of DC-10 jet airliners.

15 Returning from Camp David, MD, after a ten-day "domestic summit," President Carter cites "a crisis of confidence" in the United States. In his nationally televised address, Carter proposes a six-point, $140 billion energy program to reduce U. S. dependence on foreign oil.

16 Iraqi President Ahmed Hassan al-Bakr resigns, citing ill health, and names Gen. Saddam Hussein as his successor.

17 Simone Veil of France is elected president of the European Parliament.

The U. S. House of Representatives Select Committee on Assassinations releases its final report, which concludes that the murders of former President John F. Kennedy and the Rev. Martin Luther King, Jr., were "likely" the result of conspiracies.

18 The price of gold rises to more than $300 an ounce on the London market.

19 The Nicaraguan Sandinista junta takes control of the capital of Managua, bringing to an end a seven-week civil war. The rebel takeover comes two days after President Anastasio Somoza Debayle and 45 top aides left the country for exile in Miami, FL.

President António Ramalho Eanes of Portugal names Maria de Lurdes Pintassilgo, 49, as caretaker prime minister to preside over the fall parliamentary elections.

21 At the close of a two-day, 65-nation conference in Geneva, U. N. Secretary General Kurt Waldheim announces that Vietnam promised to halt the flow of refugees out of the country and to provide safe and orderly departure for those persons who do leave.

28 Charan Singh is sworn in as prime minister of India following the resignation July 15 of Morarji R. Desai.

31 John J. Riccardo, the chairman of Chrysler Corp., announces that the company lost $207.1 million in the second quarter of 1979. Riccardo asks $1 billion in cash from the federal government as an advance on proposed tax cuts.

Major Changes in Carter Administration

In mid-July all members of President Carter's Cabinet and senior White House staff offered their resignations. Following a "period of evaluation," major changes within the administration occurred. The president expressed the belief that the shake-up would enable him to "be better able to serve" the country.

DEPARTMENT	OUTGOING OFFICIAL	INCOMING OFFICIAL
	The Cabinet	
Defense, deputy secretary	Charles W. Duncan, Jr.	W. Graham Claytor, Jr.
Energy, secretary	James R. Schlesinger, Jr.	Charles W. Duncan, Jr.
HEW, secretary	Joseph A. Califano, Jr.	Patricia Roberts Harris
HUD, secretary	Patricia Roberts Harris	Moon Landrieu
Justice, attorney general	Griffin B. Bell	Benjamin R. Civiletti
Transportation, secretary	Brock Adams	Neil E. Goldschmidt
Treasury, secretary	W. Michael Blumenthal	G. William Miller
	Federal Agencies	
Federal Reserve Board, chairman	G. William Miller	Paul A. Volcker
	White House Staff	
Chief of Staff		Hamilton Jordan
Senior adviser to the President		Hedley W. Donovan
Counsel to the President	Robert J. Lipshutz	Lloyd N. Cutler
Assistant to the President	Timothy E. Kraft	Sarah C. Weddington
Assistant to the President and Director of the White House Staff		Alonzo L. McDonald

Paul A. Volcker

Hamilton Jordan

Charles W. Duncan, Jr.

Neil E. Goldschmidt

AUGUST

In Italy, Francesco Cossiga, a Christian Democrat, formed a new 24-member coalition government.

UPI

1 South Africa's Prime Minister Pieter Botha names Gerrit Viljoen to succeed Marthinus Steyn as administrator general for Namibia (South-West Africa); the action is reportedly to placate conservative whites.

3 Macias Nguema Biyogo is overthrown as president of Equatorial Guinea.

5 In Italy, a three-party coalition government, headed by Francesco Cossiga, a Christian Democrat, is sworn in.

6 Following a deadlock in July 1 popular elections, the Bolivian Congress elects Walter Guevara Arce as provisional president. New elections are to be held in May 1980, with Guevara barred from running.

Meeting in Lusaka, Zambia, delegates from 39 Commonwealth nations endorse a set of proposals for Zimbabwe Rhodesia. The plan includes a new constitution and new elections under British auspices. Zimbabwe's Prime Minister Bishop Abel Muzorewa calls the plan "totally unfair."

10 Jaime Roldós Aguilera is sworn in as president of Ecuador.

13 The U. S. Justice Department files a civil rights suit against the city of Philadelphia, Mayor Frank Rizzo, and high-ranking police and city officials, charging "widespread and severe" police brutality.

15 U. S. ambassador to the UN Andrew Young resigns over an uproar caused by his unauthorized meeting with a representative of the Palestine Liberation Organization (PLO).

16 In Nigeria, Shehu Shagari, a former elementary school teacher, is proclaimed winner of August 11 presidential elections.

19 Soviet cosmonauts Valery Ryumin and Col. Vladimir Lyakhov return safely to earth following a record 175 days in space.

21 Nine rival groups in Chad meet in Nigeria and sign an agreement to form a government of national union, with Goukouni Oueddei, leader of the Chad Liberation Front, as president and Wadal Abdelkadar Kamougue as vice president. The accord provides for free elections within 18 months.

22 President Neelam Sanjiva Reddy of India dissolves parliament and calls for elections within three months. Charan Singh, who had resigned as prime minister August 20, is named to head a caretaker government until the elections.

24 U. S. Vice President Walter Mondale arrives in Peking for a week-long visit.

27 Earl Mountbatten of Burma, a British World War II hero and cousin of Queen Elizabeth, is killed when a bomb explodes aboard his fishing boat about 1 mile (1.6 km) off the northwest Ireland coast; the Irish Republican Army claims responsibility for the explosion.

Soviet ballerina Lyudmila Vlasova returns to the USSR after U. S. State Department officials had delayed for three days her take-off from New York's Kennedy International Airport. Following the August 23 defection to the United States of her husband, Alexander Gudunov of the Bolshoi Ballet company, American State Department officials insisted upon interviewing Ms. Vlasova to ascertain whether she was returning to her homeland of her own volition.

OLIPHANT © 1979, "WASHINGTON STAR," REPRINTED WITH PERMISSION LOS ANGELES TIMES SYNDICATE

MORE BALLERINAS THAN HE NEEDS

A cartoonist's view of the question: Which U. S. diplomat is in charge of U. S. policy regarding Middle East peace negotiations? The issue gained media attention in August.

28 Six days of heavy fighting between Iranian government forces and Kurdish rebels comes to an end as an informal truce takes effect.

31 The U. S. State Department confirms a report of the presence of 2,000 to 3,000 Soviet combat troops in Cuba.

SEPTEMBER

1 The U. S. spacecraft Pioneer 11 takes its first close look at the planet Saturn.

5 Israel's Prime Minister Begin and Egypt's President Sadat agree to joint Israeli-Egyptian patrols in the Sinai Peninsula following withdrawal of the UN Emergency Force.

6 U. S. President Carter commutes the sentences of four Puerto Rican nationalists who had been imprisoned since the 1950's for terrorist activities against U. S. politicians.

7 Hurricane David, a strong Atlantic storm, dwindles to heavy winds as it moves inland from the eastern seaboard of the United States. During an eight-day period, David caused billions of dollars in damage and left more than 1,100 persons dead. The Dominican Republic was particularly affected.

U. S. President Carter announces his approval of a $33 billion plan to base the new long-range MX missile in underground shelters connected by a race-track system in Western desert valleys.

The Right Rev. Robert Runcie is designated as the 102d archbishop of Canterbury.

UPI

In a White House ceremony, September 23, Donald F. McHenry took the oath of office as U. S. ambassador to the UN.

The British royal family leads the mourners at the funeral of Lord Mountbatten at Westminster Abbey, September 5.

UPI

9 The sixth conference of nonaligned nations ends in Havana, Cuba. During the summit, six countries and one guerrilla group were admitted to the movement.

John McEnroe and Tracy Austin win the men's and women's singles titles at the U. S. Open tennis tournament.

10 Agostinho Neto, president of Angola, dies in Moscow.

12 U. S. President Carter announces that he has asked 27 of the largest U. S. oil companies not to raise the price of heating oil for the remainder of 1979.

16 The Israeli cabinet ends a 12-year regulation that inhibited Israeli citizens and business enterprises from buying Arab-owned land in the occupied West Bank and Gaza Strip.

Afghanistan President Noor Mohammad Taraki resigns and turns over the leadership to Prime Minister Hafizullah Amin.

17 Leonid and Valentina Kozlov, members of the Bolshoi Ballet company, are granted political asylum in the United States.

The Cuban government frees the last four U. S. citizens which it had held on political charges.

18 The UN General Assembly opens its 34th session.

20 Sweden's Prime Minister Ola Ullsten resigns in order to negotiate on forming a new government following the non-Socialist political parties' victory, with a majority of one, in September 16 parliamentary elections.

21 France sends troops to Bangui, Central African Empire, following a coup in which Emperor Bokassa I was overthrown. Former president David Dacko is the new chief of state, and the country returns to its former name of Central African Republic.

The United States and Mexico reach agreement on the sale of Mexican natural gas to U. S. companies.

24 Hilla Limann officially becomes president of Ghana's first civilian government since 1966.

28 Denmark's Prime Minister Anker Jørgensen resigns in a dispute within his two-party coalition on means to cut the 1980 budget. Elections are scheduled for October 23.

29 Pope John Paul II begins a nine-day visit to Ireland and the United States.

OCTOBER

1 The first phase of the 1978 Panama Canal treaties is implemented as U. S. control over the Canal Zone ends.

Nigeria's first civilian government in more than 13 years takes office as Shehu Shagari is installed as president.

2 Pope John Paul II addresses the UN General Assembly.

6 The U. S. Federal Reserve System announces that "to dampen inflationary forces" the discount rate is being raised to 12%, an additional reserve requirement of 8% is being established for certain liabilities held by member banks, and a greater emphasis is being placed on "day-to-day operations, on the supply of bank reserves, and less emphasis on continuing short-term fluctuations in the federal fund rate."

7 In Japan's national elections for the House of Representatives the governing Liberal Democratic Party retains its power.

9 In Canada, the Speech from the Throne, outlining the program of the new Clark government, is read as the 31st Canadian Parliament opens.

11 Sweden's parliament confirms the appointment of Thorbjörn Fälldin as head of a new coalition government.

12 Cuba's President Fidel Castro addresses the UN General Assembly.

15 In El Salvador, the military government of President Carlos Humberto Romero is overthrown in a coup.

UPI

Cuba's Prime Minister Fidel Castro was frequently in the news in September–October. Early in September, he hosted the nonaligned nations conference (*right*); in October, he denounced the United States before the UN General Assembly.

Park Chung Hee, president of South Korea since 1963, was assassinated in Seoul, October 26. A state funeral and procession through the capital city (*left*) was held eight days later.

DAVID BURNETT, CONTACT

15 China's Premier Hua Kuo-feng begins a three-week, four-nation tour of Western Europe.

17 U. S. District Judge Oliver H. Gasch rules that President Carter cannot end the Mutual Defense Treaty between the United States and Taiwan without the consent of Congress.

The Pittsburgh Pirates defeat the Baltimore Orioles, 4 games to 3, to win the 1979 World Series.

18 Zimbabwe-Rhodesia's guerrilla organization, the Patriotic Front, accepts Britain's proposals for a new constitution.

21 Moshe Dayan, foreign minister of Israel, resigns effective October 23.

23 In Denmark's parliamentary elections, the Social Democratic Party of Premier Anker Jørgensen retains power.

24 In New York, the disposed Shah of Iran undergoes a gallbladder operation; he is also treated for cancer.

26 South Korea's President Park Chung Hee is fatally shot; Choi Kyu Hah is named acting president.

27 The Caribbean islands of St. Vincent and the Grenadines become an independent nation.

30 U. S. Federal District Judge J. William Ditter dismisses the major portions of a lawsuit against Philadelphia's mayor and other city officials.

The President's Commission on the Accident at Three Mile Island issues its report, urging the creation of a new executive agency to oversee the nuclear-power industry.

Shirley Hufstedler, a court of appeals judge, is named secretary of the newly created U. S. Department of Education.

NOVEMBER

1 Mamie Doud Eisenhower, wife of former U. S. president Dwight Eisenhower, dies in Washington.

3 Four persons are killed and ten others injured in Greensboro, NC, following a gun-shooting outbreak during preparations for an anti-Ku Klux Klan demonstration.

4 Muslim students seize the U. S. embassy in Tehran, Iran, holding approximately 100 persons, including 62 Americans, as hostages.

6 Iran's provisional revolutionary government dissolves; Prime Minister Mehdi Bazargan concedes governmental power to the Ayatollah Ruhollah Khomeini.

In off-year elections across the United States, Democrats John Y. Brown, Jr., and William Winter are elected governors of Kentucky and Mississippi, respectively.

10 U. S. President Carter orders deportation proceedings against Iranian students found to be in the United States illegally.

13 Following Rosalynn Carter's official report of her tour of refugee camps in Thailand, President Carter orders an airlift of food and authorizes $6 million for the purchase of supplies.

19 Turkey's Suleyman Demirel, who succeeded Bulent Ecevit as prime minister, presents his program to the Turkish National Assembly.

20 President Carter orders a second naval task force into the Indian Ocean, south of Iran, and warns that while a peaceful solution to the hostage crisis in Iran is preferred, other "remedies" provided by the UN Charter are available.

21 Former Canadian Prime Minister Pierre Elliott Trudeau announces his resignation as Liberal Party leader.

Hundreds of Pakistanis, enraged by false reports that the United States and Israel were involved in the November 20 seizure of the Great Mosque in Mecca, storm and partly burn the U. S. embassy in Islamabad.

22 Thirteen hostages freed by Iran from the U. S. embassy in Tehran arrive in the United States.

23 Lydia Gueiler Tejada, who was declared interim president of Bolivia on November 16, orders Army commander Gen. Luis Garcia Meza to step down, but he refuses, stating that the government "failed to keep its word." He is supported by the Tarapaca Regiment, the primary backer of Col. Alberto Natusch Busch. The colonel overthrew Bolivia's civilian government on November 1, but failed to gain popular support and resigned on November 16.

25 UN Secretary General Kurt Waldheim calls for an "urgent meeting" of the Security Council to deal with the Iranian-U. S. crisis.

26 The International Olympic Committee approves a resolution that assures the People's Republic of China's participation in Olympic competition.

28 Pope John Paul II arrives in Turkey for a three-day visit with leaders of the Eastern Orthodox churches.

UPI

In November, (Joseph) Lane Kirkland, 57, was elected to succeed George Meany as president of the AFL-CIO.

ALAIN MINGAM, GAMMA/LIAISON

On November 4, Iranian students, demanding the return of the Shah to Iran, seized the U. S. Embassy in Tehran and took Americans as hostages. The students issued a statement from the Ayatollah Khomeini stating that Iran "must clean up its situation vis-à-vis the United States."

DECEMBER

3 Puerto Rican nationalists kill two U. S. sailors and injure 10 others as they ambush a busload of Navy personnel outside San Juan. A note said that the action was in retaliation for the killing of three Puerto Rican nationalists.

6 South Korea's acting president, Choi Kyu Hah, is proclaimed president by the National Conference for Unification.

7 As Japan's Prime Minister Masayoshi Ohira concludes a three-day visit to Peking, a series of new Sino-Japanese economic, technical, and cultural agreements is announced.

11 Charles Haughey, who was elected leader of Ireland's Fianna Fail Party on December 7, is formally chosen as prime minister of Ireland. Prime Minister John Lynch had resigned.

U. S. District Judge Joyce Hens Green orders an immediate halt to special immigration checks on Iranian students in the United States, declaring the checks unconstitutional.

12 Zimbabwe Rhodesia returns to legality as a colony of Britain, as Lord Soames, newly-appointed governor, arrives in Salisbury to work toward the establishment of black majority rule.

The North Atlantic Treaty Organization agrees to the installation of U. S. medium-range nuclear missiles in Europe.

13 The Canadian Supreme Court declares unconstitutional sections of Quebec's Bill 101, establishing French as Quebec's sole official language.

15 The deposed Shah of Iran takes up residence in Panama.

The International Court of Justice rules that Iran must release immediately the American hostages held in Tehran. On December 4, the UN Security Council had adopted a resolution demanding the release of the hostages.

17 Britain's Margaret Thatcher arrives in Washington for her first official visit to the United States as prime minister.

18 Canada's former prime minister Pierre Elliott Trudeau accepts a draft to remain leader of the Liberal Party through the general election scheduled for Feb. 18, 1980. The government of Joseph Clark had suffered a motion of no confidence on December 18.

19 Members of the U. S. Senate approve a $1.5 billion loan guarantee to the Chrysler Corporation; the bill was approved by the House of Representatives on December 18.

21 In London, the conflicting parties in Rhodesia's seven-year civil war sign a peace agreement, promising a cease-fire, a new constitution, and elections leading to independence.

26 For the first time ever, New York's gold price soars past $500 per ounce.

27 Afghanistan's President Hafizullah Amin is ousted from power and executed in a coup apparently planned and carried out by the USSR; Babrak Karmal is the new president.

Portugal's interim Prime Minister Maria de Lurdes Pintassilgo resigns, making way for Dr. Francisco Sá Carneiro, the leader of the rightist Democratic Alliance, elected on December 2, to select a cabinet.

29 "Substantial numbers" of Soviet troops are reported to be crossing into Afghanistan.

RAGHU RAI, MAGNUM

In the words of the Nobel Peace Prize Committee, 1979 was the year the world "turned its attention to the plight of children and refugees, and these are precisely the categories for whom Mother Teresa (a 69-year-old Albanian nun who works in Calcutta, India) has for many years worked so selflessly."

REVIEW OF THE YEAR

ACCIDENTS AND DISASTERS

AVIATION

March 14—In Peking, a Trident jet crashes into a factory; 44 persons are killed.

March 14—A Jordanian airliner crashes while trying to land in Doha, Qatar, killing 45 persons.

March 17—A Soviet Aeroflot TU-104 crashes shortly after takeoff from Moscow, killing 90 persons.

May 25—An American Airlines DC-10 jetliner loses an engine and crashes shortly after takeoff from Chicago's O'Hare Airport, killing all 273 persons on board.

July 11—An Indonesian domestic airliner crashes into a mountain in North Sumatra, killing all 61 persons aboard.

August 11—Two Soviet Aeroflot jetliners collide in air over the Ukraine, killing 173 persons.

Oct. 31—A Western Airlines DC-10 crashes on landing at the Mexico City airport, killing at least 74 persons.

Nov. 26—A Pakistan International Airlines jetliner crashes shortly after takeoff from Jidda airport in Saudi Arabia, killing all 156 persons on board.

Nov. 28—An Air New Zealand DC-10 crashes into the side of a volcano on Ross Island off the Antarctic coast, killing 257 persons.

EARTHQUAKES

Jan. 16—An earthquake strikes northeastern Iran, killing at least 199 persons and destroying approximately 1,000 homes and other buildings.

April 15—An earthquake hits the southern Adriatic coast of Yugoslavia, killing at least 101 persons; 35 more persons are killed and 350 others injured in Albania, to the south of Yugoslavia.

Nov. 14—An earthquake destroys at least 14 villages in northeastern Iran, killing 242 persons and injuring 72 others.

Nov. 24—An earthquake hits Colombia, South America, killing 44 persons and injuring 600 more.

FIRES AND EXPLOSIONS

Feb. 21—At least 175 persons are killed as a volcano on central Java (Indonesia) erupts.

April 2—Twenty-five persons die in a boardinghouse fire in Farmington, MO.

April 14—Twenty-six coal miners are killed and 40 others injured when explosive charges ignite in a mine shaft in Chungsun, South Korea.

April 19—A fire in a dormitory at George Washington University, Washington, DC, injures 35 students.

July 12—Fire rushes through a luxury hotel in Saragossa, Spain, killing 80 persons.

July 29—A fire starts in a movie theater in Tuticorin, southern India, killing at least 92 persons and injuring 80 others.

Sept. 28—A pre-dawn fire sweeps through a Vienna hotel, killing 25 persons.

Oct. 27—A fire breaks out in the Unsong Mine in Munkyong, 80 mi (129 km) south of Seoul, South Korea, killing 30 miners.

LAND AND SEA TRANSPORTATION

Jan. 4—Two express trains traveling on the same track between Ankara and Istanbul, Turkey, collide; an estimated 56 persons are believed dead.

Jan. 8—During the unloading of crude oil in Ireland, the French tanker *Betelgeuse* explodes, killing 50 persons.

Jan. 16—A bus collides with a truck west of Caracas, Venezuela, killing 32 people.

March 14—A Greek bus collides with a Yugoslav gasoline tanker truck on the Greek side of the border, killing 30 people.

April 17—A bus falls into the Paraiba do Sul River in eastern Rio de Janeiro state, killing an estimated 25 to 30 persons.

April 22—Two trains collide 50 mi (80 km) northeast of Karachi, Pakistan, killing 44 persons and injuring 37 more.

June 2—In Thailand's Phang Nga province, a gasoline truck collides with a bus, causing an explosion which kills 52 persons.

July 14—A bus falls into Lake Victoria in Africa, killing 60 persons.

July 19—In heavy rain east of the island of Tobago, two supertankers collide; 26 crewmen are missing and large amounts of crude oil are spilled into the Atlantic.

August 18—A vehicle pile-up of a bus and several trucks in the Great Rift Valley of Kenya results in the deaths of at least 44 persons.

Sept. 13—The collision of a freight train with an express train near Stalac, Yugoslavia, kills at least 60 persons.

Oct. 12—About 30 mi (48 km) south of Chicago, an Amtrak passenger train slams the rear of a parked Illinois Central Gulf Railroad freight train, causing the deaths of two crewmen, the injuries of 43 others, and the death by heart attack of a fireman helping in the rescue efforts.

Oct. 16—A crash involving three commuter trains in Philadelphia injures more than 400 persons.

Oct. 20—Near Lourdes, in France, a bus carrying a group of Spaniards who had visited the shrine is struck by a train after becoming stuck on a railroad crossing; 21 persons are killed and 32 injured.

Oct. 30—A Djibouti-Addis Ababa train derails and crashes just north of the Ethiopian border post of Ali Sabieh, killing 50 persons and injuring 30 more.

Nov. 10—A Canadian Pacific train derails and burns, spreading deadly gas fumes over the area around Mississauga, Ontario, and causing the evacuation of nearly 250,000 residents.

Nov. 22—Thirty-five Vietnamese refugees die when their boat breaks up in rough waters in the South China Sea near Kuala Trengganu, a Malaysian port.

Dec. 21—A bus transporting Filipinos home for Christmas falls into a river, killing at least 43 persons.

STORMS AND FLOODS

Jan. 12–15—A blizzard hits much of the Midwest, most particularly Chicago, leaving an accumulation of 33 in (76 cm) of snow, closing O'Hare International Airport, and causing the deaths of at least 100 persons.

Feb. 7—A month of flooding in east central Brazil causes the deaths of 204 persons and leaves 200,000 homeless.

April 10—Tornados strike Wichita Falls, TX, and sweep the Texas-Oklahoma border, killing at least 60 persons and causing extensive property damage.

May 12–13—Six hundred persons are killed by hurricanes (with winds of up to 100 mph) and floods on the southeast Indian coast, in Andhra Pradesh state.

June 24—It is reported that at least 32 persons are drowned and 25 others are missing as a result of flooding in Montego Bay, Jamaica.

July 2—A flash flood hits Valdepenas, Spain, killing 24 persons and injuring more than 50 others.

July 22—It is reported that the tidal wave that struck Lomblem Island, Indonesia, in mid-July resulted in the deaths of 700 persons.

August 11—Hundreds of persons are killed as a dam collapses, sending the Machu River into the city of Morvi, India.

August 14—Due to storms at sea, at least 18 persons are drowned in the yachting race *Fastnet*, which takes place in the English Channel and the Irish Sea.

August 25–26—Torrential downpours caused by Typhoon Judy produce flooding in southern South Korea; at least 43 deaths are confirmed and about 60 persons are feared dead.

August 29–Sept. 5—Hurricane David, with winds of up to 150 mph, sweeps through Dominica, Puerto Rico, the Dominican Republic, Haiti, and the east coast of the United States, killing about 1,000 persons and destroying thousands of homes.

Sept. 12—Hurricane Frederic hits the central Gulf coast along a 100-mi (161-km) front in Florida, Alabama, and Mississippi; the death toll is low, but property damage is reported in the hundreds of millions of dollars.

Sept. 13—It is reported that 100 persons are dead as a result of a tidal wave which struck the east coast of Yapen, Indonesia.

Oct. 19—A storm causing winds and flooding moves through eastern, central, and then northern Japan; 400 persons are injured and 25 are dead as a result.

MISCELLANEOUS

March 28—An accident at the three-month-old nuclear power plant at Three Mile Island, PA, causes the release of above-normal levels of radiation.

August 11–12—Fifty-four persons are drowned off crowded Japanese beaches during this weekend period.

ADVERTISING

The stock market, U. S. dollar, and consumer faced difficult times in 1979, yet the advertising industry managed to have a very good year. While the gross national product registered its smallest increase since the 1974–75 recession (6.7% in the second quarter), the amount of money spent on advertising increased by 8.4%.

Recession-like conditions were evidenced by a decline in the number of new products introduced, the bread and butter of the agency business. In the first seven months of 1979, 674 new products made their national debuts, compared with 719 for the same period the year before. The success of the advertising industry was therefore difficult to explain. Some observers felt it was because advertisers had to compete harder for fewer and smaller client investments.

Law and Regulations. Perhaps the most significant action for the advertising industry since 1975, when Congress gave rule-making power to the Federal Trade Commission (FTC), came late in 1979 when the House Appropriations Committee effectively muzzled that agency until Congress and the president could redefine its authority. Pending FTC proposals would have required foods claiming to be "natural," "nutritious," "pure," and the like to disclose additional information in advertising materials; restricted or banned television advertising for children; and required the use of government-approved descriptions and warnings on drug labels.

The U. S. Justice Department filed a civil antitrust suit challenging television regulations limiting the amount of advertising aired on any given show. The standard 9½-minute limit per prime-time hour restricts competition and drives up costs, said the government. Ironically, the broadcasters themselves, roundly criticized for cluttering programs with as much as 9½ minutes of advertising, were attempting to reduce the time of commercials shown in order to avoid government (FTC) intervention.

Media. Advertisers and viewers who balked at the television networks' unsettling habit of changing, shifting, or preempting regularly scheduled shows were given cause for optimism in 1979. All three major networks promised to be more stalwart when it comes to programming.

Independent television production companies grew significantly in 1979. Together they supplied more hours of programming for the new fall network schedule than all the major studios combined. Even corporations got into the act: for the first time in a decade, one advertiser, Procter & Gamble, sponsored a one-hour weekly series. Despite these developments, television program costs continued to soar, particularly for local stations. Reruns of successful off-network properties brought prices in excess of $500,000 per episode in the commercial syndication market.

While 1979 was a good year financially for the magazine industry, some dark clouds began to form. A paper shortage forced several slick publications to downgrade the quality of their stock. Circulation began to soften at several major publications, and some were forced to rebate advertising money for failing to reach readership quotas. The self-designated authorities on magazine readership—Simmons Market Research Bureau and the Magazine Research Institute—not only often disagreed with each other but usually contradicted the publishers as well. Magazine research continued to baffle industry experts and confound advertisers still looking for a fail-safe method of measuring readership.

Meanwhile, the new mass communications media—cable television, satellite transmission, over-the-air pay television, and video cassette and video disc systems—were hungry for programming.

Volume. Media advertising expenditures reached $47.4 billion in 1979, an 8.4% increase over 1978. However, the tentativeness of the industry was reflected by the fact that a 14.7% increase was recorded in 1978. The largest single outlays were for newspapers—$13.4 billion (up 7.9%) and television—$9.9 billion (up 11.4%). Television network spending was the only category to outstrip the previous year's pace—$4.5 billion, or a 15% increase (compared with a 12% jump in 1978). Local television purchases equaled $2.6 billion (up 9%); spot, $2.8 billion (up 8%). A total of $2.9 billion was spent on magazine advertising, a 12% gain. All other increases were below 10%: radio, up 9.4% to $3.2 billion; outdoor, up 8.8% to $506 million; direct mail, up 8% to $6.5 billion; business publications, up 2% to $1.4 billion; and miscellaneous, up 5.9% to $9.1 billion.

Canada. The growth of advertising in Canada dropped from 11.6% in 1978 to 7.9% in '79. This was attributed to a generally sluggish national economy. Media costs increased at a staggering rate, creating problems for small-budget advertisers.

The industry continued to move toward self-regulation, as advertising guidelines were drawn up for cosmetics, toiletries, feminine hygiene, and over-the-counter drugs. Following the example of Quebec, which in 1978 levied a 2% tax on commercials, Newfoundland proposed a 4% tax on all advertising in the province.

Canadian advertisers spent a total of $2.5 billion in 1979, nearly half of which went to newspapers ($1 billion, up 10%). Next came television ($495 million, up 15%); radio ($364 million, up 20%); outdoor ($202 million, up 9%); directories ($190 million, up 4%); magazines ($102 million, up 36%), business publications ($65 million, up 10%); weekend supplements ($40 million, up 67%); and farm publications ($15 million, up 20%).

EDWARD H. MEYER
Grey Advertising Inc.

AFGHANISTAN

It was a turbulent year in Afghanistan. Government takeovers, rebel violence, political arrests, army mutinies, and 12 months of general upheaval culminated in late December with a massive invasion by Soviet troops and the installation of a puppet president.

Politics. As the year began, the pro-Communist government of President Nur Mohammed Taraki was losing support and facing severe and growing Islamic tribal insurgency. To defuse the Islamic revolt the government claimed to respect Islam and ordered public meetings to start with prayers from the Koran. However, dissident religious leaders were imprisoned or exiled. The government also instituted widespread purges of civilian and military officials. Having first purged the rival leftist Parcham party, Khalq (Masses) leaders turned on their own members. "Unreliables" were expelled or imprisoned. The military leaders who led the original coup in April 1978 that put the Khalq into power were imprisoned. Political prisoners at the Pul-i-Charkhi jails numbered thousands according to reliable reports. There were numerous attempted coups and revolts both in Kabul and other cities. In March, Afghanistan's third largest city, Herat, was captured by a popular uprising and held for several days. In August a major revolt occurred in Kabul in which mutinous Afghan army units participated. Both revolts were put down ruthlessly with hundreds of casualties reported.

Reflecting the unrest, Foreign Minister Hafizullah Amin was named premier on March 27. Taraki retained his posts as president and defense minister, but the Revolutionary Council empowered Amin to revamp the government. On September 16 he staged a coup in which Taraki reportedly was killed. Amin emerged as the new president and leader of the Khalq party.

But not for long. Dismayed by the overthrow of its friend Taraki and dissatisfied with the rule of Amin, the Soviet Union launched some 30,000 troops into Afghanistan during the last week in December. Amin was ousted from power and executed, and former Deputy Prime Minister Babrak Karmal was returned from exile to assume nominal leadership of the country. But it was the Kremlin that was calling the shots. The early weeks of 1980 saw an increase of Soviet troops to put down continuing tribal rebellion and heard protests from around the world against the brazen Soviet maneuver.

Rebellion. The growing insurgency, led by refugee religious leaders operating from Peshawar, Pakistan, at first involved only the war-like Pushtun tribes of the Eastern frontier but soon spread to the North and to the Central Plateau of the Hazara Jat. The rebels were fragmented into seven groups unable to form a united front. In April, a prominent religious leader, Soghatullah Moajadidi, announced an *Afghan National Liberation Front,* but other important rebel groups refused to join. Disunity was the rebels' chief handicap throughout the year.

Foreign Relations. The Soviets had first responded to the rebel threat by increasing economic, political, and military support. In March, Afghanistan's Council of Ministers ratified a 20-year treaty of "friendship, good neighborliness, and cooperation" with the USSR. An official Soviet declaration stated that "the Afghan revolution is a socialist revolution which it is our duty to defend."

Afghanistan's relations with the United States deteriorated rapidly following the assassination in February of the U. S. ambassador, Adolph Dubs, in Kabul. The United States blamed Afghan heedlessness and Soviet involvement for the clumsy attempt to rescue Dubs from a terrorist kidnapping. In July the United States evacuated American dependents and drastically reduced its embassy staff. Economic aid programs were allowed to lapse and no new ones were authorized. The Peace Corps withdrew and Fulbright exchange programs were halted. The United States was strongly critical of the Soviet incursion and the installation of Karmal. It declared a grain embargo against the USSR, threatened a boycott of the 1980 Olympics in Moscow, and called for other international sanctions.

As the Soviet Union became more deeply involved in Afghanistan, Afghan relations with its neighbors, Pakistan and Iran, worsened and its friendly ties with most other Islamic countries were loosened. During 1979 Afghanistan definitely became a member of the extreme radical group of Third World countries.

Economics. Afghanistan became increasingly dependent on the USSR for economic survival. It was estimated that the Soviet Union has contributed a total of $1.3 billion in economic aid and $600 million in military assistance to Afghanistan since 1954. Afghan exports to the West declined in 1979. A principal export, karakul (Persian lamb), which comes from northern areas controlled by guerrillas, completely stopped. Because of the insurgency many farmers did not plant, and there was a threat of serious famine in 1980.

LEON B. POULLADA
Northern Arizona University

―――― AFGHANISTAN • Information Highlights ――――

Official Name: Democratic Republic of Afghanistan.
Location: Central Asia.
Area: 250,000 square miles (647 497 km²).
Population (1979 est.): 18,300,000.
Chief Cities (1975 est.): Kabul, the capital, 749,000 (met. area); Kandahar, 209,000; Herat, 157,000.
Government: *Head of state and government,* Babrak Karmal, president and premier (took power Dec. 1979). *Policymaking body*—35-member Revolutionary Council.
Monetary Unit: Afghani (43.50 afghanis equal U. S.$1, July 1979).
Manufactures (major products): Textiles, cement, carpets, furniture, soap, shoes, fertilizer.
Agriculture (major products): Wheat, cotton, fruit and nuts, karakul pelts, wool, mutton.

AFRICA

For Africa, 1979 was to a large extent a year to regain control over its own destiny. Politics and economics were disorderly—as had been customary for a decade—but the removal of the most despotic dictators ended several major sources of instability. The great powers undertook major efforts to lower the visibility of their intrusions into African affairs, and while the Soviet Union, France, and the United States remained active in particular areas, they appeared willing to focus less competition in the African arena. One indirect casualty of this lowered interest in Africa was the departure from his post of U. S. Ambassador to the UN Andrew Young.

WEST AFRICA

Despite the anarchy that ruled in Chad, West Africa was a region of stability in 1979, as three governments made the planned return from military to civilian and democratic rule.

Nigeria, the most populous state on the continent, concluded a successful transition to multiparty democracy at the beginning of October. More than 13 years of military rule ended when Alhaji Shehu Shagari assumed the presidency. The new constitution bore a striking resemblance to the American system, with a separation of powers between the legislative, judiciary, and executive branches. To hinder tribalism and to ensure the federal character of the new government, a successful candidate for the presidency has to obtain at least one quarter of all votes cast in two thirds of the 19 states. Also, the presidential and vice-presidential candidates of each party have to be from different ethnic groups. In elections for the bicameral legislature held during July, Shehu Shagari's National Party of Nigeria (NPN) did not command an overall majority but the NPN did receive more votes than any of the other four registered parties.

Oil-production revenues in Nigeria climbed to a record high of $15 billion. As the second largest supplier of crude oil to the United States, Nigeria considered its oil embargo weapon as a form of pressure against American recognition of Zimbabwe Rhodesia. In late July, all British Petroleum oil interests in Nigeria were nationalized as a retaliatory measure against British exports of oil to South Africa and as a move calculated to deter the British government from lifting economic sanctions on Zimbabwe Rhodesia.

Ghana also returned to multiparty democratic rule in September, but the change did not proceed according to the original plan. A coup by junior officers in June overthrew the military government of Gen. Fred Akuffo, following an attempt that failed only a month before. The coup leaders expressed dissatisfaction with the widespread corruption in the Akuffo government, the dire state of Ghana's economy, and the dominance of foreign interests in the country. The junta, headed by Air Force Lt. Jerry Rawlings, did not interfere with the presidential and parliamentary elections preliminary to the return of civilian rule.

As the Ghanaian people voted in mid-June, choosing from among six registered presidential candidates and seven parliamentary parties, Rawlings' Armed Forces Revolutionary Committee purged a number of army officers, executing three former Ghanaian heads of state and several other top-level officials. All of those executed were convicted of embezzlement of public funds or similar charges.

An international outcry against the executions was heard from numerous African states,

ETIENNE MONTES, GAMMA/LIAISON

Residents of the town of Bata, Equatorial Guinea, cut up for the cameras following the overthrow of President Francisco Macias Nguema in August. Two other African dictators—Amin in Uganda and Bokassa in the Central African Empire—were also overthrown in 1979.

as well as from overseas. The most damaging protest move was Nigeria's cutoff of oil shipments to Ghana in late June, depriving Ghana of 80% of its oil supply. Also, the Ivory Coast and Upper Volta reportedly halted deliveries of meat, and Benin, of corn and oil. Rawlings, bowing to such pressures, subsequently announced there would be no more executions and pledged that Ghana would respect human rights.

In a second, runoff election in mid-July, Hilla Limann was elected president of the future civilian government, while his People's National Party gained 68 of the 140 parliamentary seats. Limann vowed to continue Rawlings' house cleaning process, peacefully, and added that Ghana's economic crisis would receive his "serious attention."

To turn Mali over to "constitutional rule," presidential and legislative elections were held in June. The military had controlled Mali for ten years. Mali's president, Gen. Moussa Traoré, the only candidate, was returned to power. Delegates to the national assembly were also voted in; all were members of the country's sole political party, the Democratic Union for Malian People. The new regime was predominantly civilian, but the military retained a strong role.

French and OAU attempts to mediate peace between ethnic and religious groups in war torn Chad failed repeatedly in 1979. Provisional coalition governments, hoping to strike a balance between Muslims from the north and southern Christians, rose and fell after little more than a month's existence. In March, France announced the intended withdrawal of its 2,500-man peacekeeping force, stationed in Chad since April 1978. The action followed the signing of a peace pact in Kano, Nigeria, between rival factions. Nigeria agreed to dispatch its own peacekeeping brigade to monitor the cease-fire.

A second provisional government was announced in late April, but the exclusion of representation from the Libyan-backed southern secessionist force led to the outbreak of fighting in mid-May. Yet another conference on Chad was held in Lagos, Nigeria, in late May, with representatives from Cameroon, the Central African Empire, Libya, Niger, Nigeria, and Sudan attending. The newest provisional administration was not represented and the conference ended with a condemnation of the Chadian government, which was described as "contrary to the provisions of the Kano accord," and with an appeal to the government to dissolve itself so as to bring other groups into the government. The Chadian coalition responded by expelling the 850-strong Nigerian peacekeeping force.

Yet a third provisional government was formed in late August by nine warring groups who met in Lagos, Nigeria. Late in the year, it was reported that some rival groups still refused to disband their private armies, leading observers to conclude that the latest transitional government was as precarious as the previous one.

EAST AFRICA

Border fighting at the beginning of 1979 between Tanzania and Uganda turned into a full-scale invasion by Tanzanian-backed forces determined to overthrow Ugandan President Idi Amin. The invasion coincided with a series of bombings by anti-Amin sabotage groups in the Ugandan capital city of Kampala and an appeal to the Ugandan people by Milton Obote, in exile in Tanzania since Major General Amin overthrew him in January 1971, to rise up against the Amin regime.

The Ugandan dictator's army was bolstered by the airlift of Libyan troops and materiel during March, but the invaders, composed of Ugandan exiles and Tanzanian soldiers, marched slowly through southern Uganda, finally entering Kampala in April. The Uganda National Liberation Front, a broad-based coalition of anti-Amin exiles formed in northern Tanzania, established a caretaker government and appointed Dr. Yusufu Lule to lead the country until elections could be held. By early June, the remnants of Amin's army, including tens of thousands of pro-Amin refugees, had fled into neighboring Sudan. Amin was given asylum in Libya.

In late June, President Lule was forced out and replaced by Godfrey Binaisa, who had served as attorney general under former President Obote. Lule was accused of ignoring the council on important national decisions. Lule subsequently spent several weeks in Dar es-Salaam, Tanzania, under house arrest—an effort to exact his support for his replacement. He was permitted to fly to London in July.

After Lule's dismissal, more than 20,000 Tanzanian troops remained in Uganda to aid the Binaisa government's efforts to halt the lawlessness that plagued the country into September. Binaisa estimated national reconstruction costs at $2 billion, but promised relief, from a number of international sources, amounted to little more than $100 million.

The possibility of resumed cooperation in east Africa was raised in August when Julius Nyerere proposed a summit meeting of the former partners in the defunct East African Community. Kenyan President Daniel arap Moi and President Binaisa responded favorably to the idea, but Moi questioned the possibility of such cooperation when the Kenyan-Tanzanian border remained closed. Negotiations between Moi and Nyerere during May reestablished air links between their two countries, but the heads of state did not agree immediately to open the common border closed by Tanzania in early 1977.

HORN OF AFRICA

Tensions that dominated the Horn during 1978 continued to rule events in 1979. The Ethiopian civil war dragged on inconclusively as Chairman Mengistu Haile Mariam's government

After the signing of an August peace agreement between the Polisario and Mauritania, fighting between Morocco and the Polisario continued.

troops and peasant militia were unable to end armed secessionist movements in Eritrea, the Tigre, and the Ogaden regions. Soviet support for the Mengistu regime expanded in 1979, changing from its primarily military orientation to a greater commitment to the faltering Ethiopian economy. Although Cuba's military force was downgraded and restricted to a training role, its mere presence buttressed Mengistu.

An OAU-mediated effort to normalize relations between Ethiopia and neighboring Sudan failed in February. The summit meeting between Mengistu and President Jaafar al-Nemery ended only in mutual recriminations. Nemery accused Mengistu of backing attempts to overthrow him and Mengistu asserted that the Sudan was fomenting rebellion in Eritrea. Somalia's President Siad Barre's pan-Somali aspirations kept the Ethiopian-Somali conflict at the brink of outright war. Somali irredentism also induced Kenyan President arap Moi to sign an unlikely treaty of friendship and cooperation with Ethiopia as a proclamation of the two countries' opposition to "expansionist policies" in the Horn.

Barre sought to find a rapprochement with President Moi, but it miscarried in September. It was a serious setback for Barre, since his chances for receiving more economic or rudimentary military aid from the West were in large part dependent upon his ability to convince potential benefactors that a strengthened Somalia would not be seen as a threat by Kenya. Somalia then turned to the People's Republic of China for military support and to anti-Soviet Arab states. Trying to obtain Arab economic aid, while at the same time pursuing close cooperation with Egypt, was a delicate balancing act for Barre.

WESTERN SAHARA

The conclusion of a Mauritanian-Polisario peace treaty in early August did not mitigate the steady escalation of fighting in the Western Saharan war. The four-year-long conflict, which until mid-1979 was confined to sporadic outbreaks of guerrilla warfare, enlarged into a series of major battles between Moroccan and Polisario forces. Sweeping changes at the top level in both the Algerian and Mauritanian governments further contributed to regional uncertainty.

The discreet meetings between Algerian President Houari Boumedienne and King Hassan II of Morocco had extended hope for a negotiated solution to the Saharan conflict. Boumedienne's death in late 1978, however, left no clear successors and Algeria focused inward on the bidding for new leadership. Boumedienne's political vehicle, the National Liberation Front (FLN), nominated Benjedid Chadli as the sole candidate for president. Pro-Polisario elements again predominated in the new government, but with the change in leadership, Algeria's advocacy of Sahrawi self-determination was not accompanied by the previous willingness to further peace negotiations. This new intransigence was reinforced by Polisario military and political gains during 1979.

A year-long cease-fire between Mauritania and the Polisario ended in July when the Polisario raided the town of Tichla, which is located in the southern Mauritanian-controlled sector of the Western Sahara. Mauritania had at the time barely recovered from the death of its prime minister in a plane crash in late May, and the resignation of its president for "personal reasons" in June, but observers believed that resumption of attacks was the catalyst for Mauritania's decision to hold discussions with the Polisario in late July. Further negotiations in early August at Algiers led to the final peace treaty, in which Mauritania ceded its southern third of the Western Sahara to the Sahrawi Arab

Democratic Republic, the Polisario's Algerian-based government-in-exile, and renounced its collaboration agreements with Morocco. Morocco denounced the agreement and swiftly annexed the Western Saharan territory that had been held by Mauritania. Moroccan soldiers left Mauritanian soil and relations between Rabat and Nouakchott deteriorated, resulting in accusations of subversive activity against Morocco by Mauritania. In September, the new Mauritanian prime minister, Mohamed Khouna Ould Haydalla, traveled to Paris where he reportedly drew French President Giscard d'Estaing's attention to the "maneuvers" of several countries —particularly Morocco and Senegal—that threatened Mauritanian territorial integrity. Haydalla returned home armed with a promise for French air support in the event of attack, military equipment, and assistance in armed forces training.

After mid-1979, the Polisario staged full-scale attacks on Moroccan towns and military garrisons, both in southern Morocco and in its annexed Saharan provinces. Increasingly, the Polisario forces behaved like a disciplined regular army, due to a growing arsenal of sophisticated Soviet-built armament, as well as to the tactical consultation of Soviet-bloc military advisers, particularly Cubans. Polisario forces posted important victories during August and September but on October 5, at Smara, Western Sahara's holy city, the Moroccan army and air force routed a 5,000-man Polisario assault, the largest clash in the war's history.

During July the Organization of African Unity (OAU) passed a resolution calling for a cease-fire in the conflict and for the organization of a referendum to consult the population of the Western Sahara as to who should be its legitimate governor. Morocco flatly refused to accept any internationally supervised referendum, citing its historical right to the territory.

Aid to King Hassan came in September when Egyptian President Anwar el-Sadat pledged his full support of Morocco and sent arms, despite Hassan's public break with Egypt over the peace treaty with Israel. Also, in October, U. S. President Carter sought congressional approval for the sale of armed reconnaissance planes and helicopter gunships to Morocco. The move was welcomed by Sadat, and Saudi Arabia reportedly offered to finance the sales. Carter's decision was coupled with a call for peace negotiations.

SOUTHERN AFRICA

Southern Africa underwent dramatic changes during the year. International attention centered upon efforts to mediate peace in the Zimbabwe Rhodesian and South West Africa/Namibian conflicts.

Prime Minister Ian Smith's internal settlement with moderate black leaders won the constitutional approval of Rhodesia's white minority early in 1979 and led to the first universal suffrage elections in the history of the breakaway British colony. Bishop Abel Muzorewa emerged in April as the first black prime minister of Rhodesia, then renamed Zimbabwe Rhodesia.

One of his administration's foremost tasks was to attract diplomatic recognition, and thereby bring an end to economic sanctions. Muzorewa was not only unable to obtain international diplomatic recognition for his government, but was also unable to bring an end to civil war, since both wings of the Patriotic Front condemned the April elections and vowed to intensify the guerrilla war against Salisbury. Zimbabwe Rhodesian air and ground forces, beefed up by an extension of draft registration to include all blacks and whites between the ages of 16 and 60, also expanded the war, carrying out retaliatory attacks and preventive raids against Patriotic Front bases in Botswana, Mozambique, Zambia and, for the first time, Angola. Zimbabwe Rhodesian forces began to confront regular government troops as the raids penetrated deeper into neighboring states, sometimes lasting several days. Estimates of the daily toll in lives reached into the hundreds.

Western pessimism in the early part of the year over the possibility of assembling an all-parties conference turned about in the summer, when the Patriotic Front and representatives of the Muzorewa government agreed to meet in London under British mediation to forge an internationally acceptable constitution and a political settlement in Zimbabwe Rhodesia. A set of proposals that outlined the basis for a new constitution and called for holding elections under British supervision had been endorsed by the Commonwealth heads of state after an August conference in Lusaka, Zambia. Joshua Nkomo and Robert Mugabe, the joint leaders of the Patriotic Front, formulated a unified approach to the upcoming Lancaster House talks. They ruled out a preconference cease-fire, which had been urged.

Negotiations proceeded haltingly, but after hard-fought concessions from both sides the conference completed the first of its two principal tasks in mid-October, with agreement on the parameters of a new constitution. The five African front line states (Angola, Botswana, Mozambique, Tanzania, and Zambia) were able to bring their influence with the Patriotic Front to bear, pressuring Mugabe and Nkomo to stay at the conference table. The draft constitution still reserved parliamentary seats for the white minority although without legislative blocking power. In addition, it prohibited property seizures without financial compensation. A major problem for the British was finding a way to reduce the entrenched power of the Rhodesian white minority without causing a further exodus of whites. More than 14,000 whites fled Rhodesia in 1978 and official statistics put the number over 5,000 for the first half of 1979. The second phase of the negotiations, agreement on

David Dacko (*left*), the Central African Empire's new leader, marches with Bokassa during pre-coup days.

implementing the constitution, proved to be more difficult. As the talks carried into November, Bishop Muzorewa's delegation gave its conditional acceptance of British proposals for the transition period prior to new elections, but the Patriotic Front still demanded a number of alterations in "the modalities" of the transition period. Finally, in a ceremony in Lancaster House on December 21, the parties to the Rhodesian civil war signed a peace agreement. The pact called for a cease-fire, a new constitution, and elections leading to independence for Zimbabwe Rhodesia. Lord Carrington, Britain's foreign secretary, noted that the signing "heralds the end of a war which has caused immense hardship and suffering. The people of Rhodesia will now be able to settle their future by peaceful means." Lord Soames, former British ambassador to France, was named to oversee the cease-fire and the elections. On the same day as the signing, the United Nations Security Council removed its economic sanctions against Zimbabwe Rhodesia.

Hopes for a peaceful transition to independence in Namibia were running high at the beginning of 1979 following the South African government's December 1978 acceptance of a UN plan for a cease-fire and supervised elections. However, in March South Africa rejected the implementation of that plan by the UN secretary-general, objecting to inadequate controls on guerrilla activity by South West Africa People's Organization (SWAPO) within Namibia. South Africa also feared that SWAPO guerrillas, seeking to influence the elections or to take over a new government by force, would infiltrate Namibia from neighboring countries.

South Africa wanted SWAPO forces to be confined to bases inside neighboring Angola and Zambia and to be monitored by the UN. SWAPO, as well as Angola and Zambia, opposed such monitoring. South African retaliatory strikes against SWAPO bases in Angola and Zambia became more intense as the year wore on.

The five Western nations (the United States, Britain, France, West Germany, and Canada), which originally drafted the UN plan pursued diplomatic contacts with Pretoria, and in October submitted a substantially revised plan. Initially suggested by the late President Agostinho Neto of Angola, the new plan proposed the creation of a demilitarized zone along both sides of the Angolan-Namibian border, in which South African and SWAPO military enclaves would be patrolled by a UN peace-keeping force. A conference on Namibia was proposed for mid-November, with the participation of South Africa, SWAPO, the Front Line States, and the five Western powers. But Pretoria insisted in early November that representatives of the Democratic Tunhalle Alliance, the major indigenous Namibian party, be invited to the Geneva negotiations.

In South Africa, Prime Minister Botha's first year in office registered a healthy economic upswing, despite the cutoff of Iranian oil supplies. The skyrocketing price of gold in the world market made an important contribution, and the finance ministry was able to announce in July that South African exports, excluding gold, were greater in value than imports for the first time.

Venda, South Africa's third black homeland, proclaimed its independence in September. The

OAU chairman William Tolbert of Liberia presides at the organization's 16th annual summit.

president, Chief Patrick Mphephu, called for more land from the South African government and recognition of its independent status from foreign countries.

CENTRAL AFRICA

The countries of central Africa were clearly in transition as three heads of state were deposed in bloodless coups.

The overthrow of Macías Nguema in Equatorial Guinea and Emperor Jean-Bedel Bokassa in the Central African Empire relieved the region of two dictators. Nguema was overthrown in a military coup in August and was succeeded by a military junta, the Revolutionary Military Council. Former Defense Minister Teodoro Obiang Nguema, the president's cousin, emerged as the new leader. Nguema and six associates were executed in September. Amnesty International charged that Nguema's personal reign of terror was responsible for the deaths of thousands of his people. Over one quarter of the Equatorial Guinean population fled the country during Nguema's rule. Spain, which had cut off diplomatic relations with Equatorial Guinea because of its human rights violations, announced a hasty recognition of the new government and the airlift of massive economic assistance.

Emperor Bokassa's corrupt rule increased in international condemnation after Amnesty International and a Committee of African jurists accused Bokassa of participating in the April massacre of several hundred schoolchildren. The French government, whose aid reportedly made up 50% of the CAE's budget, cut off all its financial assistance in August, precipitating Bokassa's overthrow. David Dacko, the emperor's cousin and first president of the Central African

Republic, dethroned Bokassa in September with the help of 300 French troops.

The first president of Angola, Agostinho Neto, died in a hospital in Moscow after surgery for cancer. His government faced deepening resistance from guerrillas in the countryside despite the continued presence of some 19,000 troops from Cuba and military advisers from Soviet-bloc nations.

The inter-African defense force, composed of units from Gabon, Ivory Coast, Morocco, Senegal, and Togo, stationed in Zaire's Shaba province since the 1978 rebel invasion, withdrew by the end of the summer. The defense force was to be replaced with a 9,000-man brigade of the Zairian army, trained by Belgium, China, and France.

ORGANIZATION OF AFRICAN UNITY

At the 16th annual summit of the Organization of African Unity (OAU) in Monrovia, Liberia, in July, the conflict-ridden continent was not able to keep its regional and ideological disputes behind the scenes as acrimonious debates arose over the Egyptian-Israeli peace treaty, the Western Saharan dispute, and the Tanzanian-Ugandan war. Resolutions issued at the end of the summit condemned Israel but not Egyptian peace efforts and called for a UN-supervised referendum in the Western Sahara. Other resolutions warned the outside world not to recognize Zimbabwe Rhodesia and approved the creation of a pan-African news agency. Liberian President William Tolbert, the current chairman of the OAU, tried to win approval for the creation of a pan-African defense force, but his resolution was rejected.

RICHARD E. BISSELL
Managing Editor, "Orbis"

AGRICULTURE

World grain production for 1979–80 was nearly 1.6 billion tons (1.5 billion metric tons), 4% less than 1978–79 but the second largest crop on record. Wheat production was down about 7%, with sharp reductions in major producing regions, including Australia, Canada, and Europe. The U. S. crop was 17% greater than in 1978. India harvested its fourth successive record crop. World rice production nearly matched the record level of the previous year. China had a large increase in rice production, but crops were smaller elsewhere in Southeast Asia. While coarse grain production was down in Western Europe and the USSR, the U. S. crop was a record. World soybean production also was at a record level. The existence of large grain stocks and the record harvest in the United States helped fill out the world's supply of grain. The United States produced 7.6 billion bushels (267.5 million m³) of corn and 2.2 billion bushels (77.5 million m³) of soybeans. Both developed and developing countries had enough grain available to help increase somewhat average food per person. However, it was estimated that nearly 500 million poor families in the less developed countries had insufficient food and suffered malnutrition.

Shortfalls in 1978 seedings, above-average winterkill, and poor growing weather sharply reduced the Soviet 1979 harvest of grains. More feed was also needed for growing livestock herds. Cattle, hog, sheep, poultry, and goat numbers reached record levels. However, even with greater animal numbers, meat production in the socialized sector was less than expected due to cold weather and reduced production efficiency. Harsh winter conditions also lowered grain production elsewhere in East Europe. Frost in late April reduced fruit and vegetable yields in Hungary and Yugoslavia. Growing conditions were good in China. Rains in the late fall of 1978, a mild winter, and ample spring rains contributed to a favorable crop. However, grain imports increased to new levels because of growth in population and incomes.

Coffee production continued to increase, following severe freezes which killed trees in Latin American countries several years ago. However, the 1979–80 world coffee crop was only slightly larger than 1978–79 because Ecuador's production declined by about 10% and Brazil's crop was less than its potential before the 1978 freeze. A freeze in May and June 1979 reduced Brazil's potential coffee crop for 1980–81 by about 25%. This outlook caused Brazil and Colombia temporarily to halt export registration until the situation could be evaluated. Nevertheless, world exportable supplies for 1979–80 were up about 4% over the previous year. Coffee prices rose during the year due to increased disorders in Africa and higher minimum price guarantees in Brazil and Colombia. World cocoa production was down slightly due to unfavorable weather in Ghana and Nigeria. World cotton production increased by about 6% over the previous year. Australia, Brazil, China, Ivory Coast, Mexico, Pakistan, Sudan, and the USSR had improved yields of cotton. Greece, Iran, and Turkey had smaller crops than in the previous year.

U. S. Production, Prices, and Income. While U. S. stocks of grain were large and production reached record levels at the beginning of the year, grain prices improved substantially during the year. Improved prices resulted from greater export demand, particularly by the Soviet Union, and from somewhat unfavorable crop conditions in Australia and Canada. In July 1979, average national grain prices were: wheat, $3.95, as compared with $2.81 in 1978; corn, $2.73, as compared with $2.16; and soybeans, $7.38, as compared with $6.40. Cotton was 59.8 cents per bale in 1979, compared with 56.5 in 1978. Grain prices declined in the fall as a result of the large crop and of inadequate transportation early in the season. Also, a strike by workers of the Rock Island Railroad complicated the situation.

U. S. beef production was down considerably

UPI

U. S. Secretary of Agriculture Bob Bergland (*right*) and Rep. Thomas Harkin (D-IA) inspect the Iowa corn crop. American farmers produced 7.6 billion bushels (267.5 million m³) of corn during 1979.

in 1979, after high production in recent years. Beef slaughtered in the first half of the year was down 34% from 1978. Ranchers, seeking to rebuild their herds and produce more beef, were holding 8% more beef females than in the previous year. Pork production ran about 16% above 1978 and broilers and turkeys were about 9% greater. Egg and milk production increased slightly over the previous year. These supply changes had noticeable impact on prices for livestock and meat. Beef prices rose rather sharply in the first part of the year then declined slightly but averaged above 1978 levels. In contrast, hog prices were down more than 20%. Broiler and turkey prices also declined in 1979. Egg and milk prices were up slightly.

Due to improved prices from greater exports and record crops, net farm income in the United States improved markedly during the year. U. S. net farm income was at about the same level as in 1973, the previous record year, when mammoth exports went to the Soviet Union.

With such large exports and improved farm income, U. S. Secretary of Agriculture Bob Bergland decided not to have a crop set-aside program in 1980. Under the program, farmers were paid to keep land idle as a means of reducing crop supplies to increase prices to farmers. The set-aside program had been in effect since 1977 and had been used previously during the period 1961–73.

World Trade. World trade in grains was up in 1979, due especially to the larger exports of U. S. grains to the Soviet Union. The United States increased the amount of grains that could be exported to the USSR. Limits had been in effect since 1975 when the large Soviet purchase pushed grain prices very high for U. S. consumers. The USSR was allowed to buy 17.1 million tons (15.7 million metric tons) of grain from the United States in 1978–79 but there was agreement between the two countries that Soviet purchases could approach 27.3 million tons (25.0 million metric tons) in 1979–80. At midyear, U. S. exports to the Soviet Union were running 29% ahead of 1978. U. S. exports to Africa, Asia—including China and Japan—and the European Community (EC) increased substantially.

The sharp increase in exports to China during 1979 resulted from improved U. S.-Chinese relations and especially from the substantial increase in total Chinese farm imports. Grain production in China has been running below the record levels of the 1950's. While food output has increased slowly, population has increased recently at a rate of about 1.5% per year and per capita income has risen to meet food demand. China had record imports, especially wheat, from all countries during the year. Most deals were on a cash basis. China eased its foreign trade policies and allowed imports to fill important domestic gaps. It made import agreements with Argentina, Australia, and Canada to purchase 6 to 7 million tons (5.5–6.4 million metric tons) of grain, mainly wheat, through 1981. A traditional exporter of soybeans, China again imported that commodity in 1979. While China's grain imports have increased markedly, the nation showed signs of a more cautious approach to future trade pacts and international debts.

In contrast to the food shortages India experienced in the 1960's, the nation exported more than 764,000 tons (700 000 metric tons) of wheat and 546,000 tons (500 000 metric tons) of rice mainly to Bangladesh, Mauritius, USSR, and Vietnam. South Africa's drought allowed only a million tons of corn to be exported. Thailand resumed exports to Taiwan, the country's second largest market after Japan. Transportation bottlenecks restricted Canada's ability to export. While annual export capacity is 24 million tons (22 million metric tons) of grains and oilseeds, rail car shortages, bad weather, and labor problems reduced the effective capacity to 21.8 million tons (20 million metric tons) during the year.

The members of the Organization of Petroleum Exporting Countries (OPEC) increased agricultural imports to more than $14 billion in 1979, representing 8% of total trade in farm commodities. The U. S. share of OPEC imports was 19%. Competition to supply OPEC's imports is keen among Australia, EC nations, and Turkey. Australia shipped 2 million tons (1.83 million metric tons) of wheat to OPEC countries and large amounts to Indonesia and Iraq. Tur-

Farmer Jon Vessey examines lettuce, rotting as a result of a strike by United Farm Workers.

UPI

key made large deliveries to Algeria, Iran, Iraq, and Libya.

Western Europe continued to export wheat and import soybeans. It increased coarse grain imports in line with increased livestock production and a reduced grain crop.

With the 1979–80 world rice crop about equal to the 1978–79 record, world trade in rice continued to grow, especially in Africa and the Middle East. A production shortfall in Korea caused imports of more than 546,000 tons (500 000 metric tons) in 1979. At the same time that it increased grain production, Indonesia increased imports to keep up with a growing population and a small increase in per capita income.

Representatives from 41 nations initialed agreements in Geneva concluding the Tokyo Round of trade talks. The agreements were to take effect in January 1980. The keystone of the Tokyo Round is new nontariff measures (NTM) Codes of Conduct. Accordingly, there will be international discipline over agricultural subsidies which distort world trade patterns. The code bans the use of agricultural export subsidies to displace or undercut other exporters in third-country markets. A general agreement on agriculture should enable countries to anticipate better and to prevent disputes. Increased U. S. exports to Canada, Europe, Japan, and some developing countries are allowed as a result of the Tokyo Round agreements.

Agricultural Policies. The United States went into 1979 with a set-aside program in effect for wheat, feed grains, and cotton to curtail supplies and increase prices. Farmers were also granted loans for their crops. If the price proved to be lower than the loan rate, they could keep the loan proceeds and let the government take over the crop. Also, target prices were used. If the market price was below the target price, the government would pay the difference to the farmer as a deficiency payment. However, grain prices increased in 1979 and the loan and target price programs were somewhat ineffective.

The EC agricultural ministers increased 1979–80 farm commodity prices by 1.5%, as compared with an average 6.0% increase in recent years. An increase was not allowed for milk because it was in surplus. Measures taken would increase farm level prices in France, Italy, and the United Kingdom. Hence, the EC would move closer to achieving common prices for agricultural commodities in member countries. The higher farm level prices would stimulate production of grain and livestock and alter EC production and trade patterns.

Plans for agricultural growth in East European nations ranged from a 2% growth in East Germany to a 7% increase in Bulgaria. All plans called for a reduction in agricultural imports. The area devoted to feed grains and oilseed would be increased to allow greater livestock production. The Hungarian government raised food prices to consumers by 50% in midsummer. China increased state assistance to agriculture in 1979, particularly in key regions and projects. New policies emphasized a greater use of prices to guide production.

Issues discussed at conferences of both the Food and Agricultural Organization (FAO) and the Organization for Economic Cooperation and Development (OECD) indicated a need to improve world buffer stock systems so that grain supplies would vary less due to weather. The Association of Southeast Asian Nations (ASEAN—Indonesia, Malaysia, the Philippines, Singapore, and Thailand) completed an agreement, effective in 1979, by which each member contributes a stated physical amount to storage inventories. Then, a member nation that has been affected by drought would be allowed to draw on these buffer stocks to prevent high food prices or famine. Although the buffer stock includes only 54,600 tons (50 000 metric tons) of rice, the ASEAN agreement sets a precedent.

Concerned over the future state of agriculture and world food supplies, the FAO conducted a study and held a conference in November under the theme "Agriculture: Towards 2000." Conclusions reached at the conference indicated that if food production grows only at trend rates until the year 2000, food supplies in the less developed countries would tighten and prices would be high. Also, with growth at only trend rates, about 2.5% annually, improvements in diets cannot be attained for the 500 million persons who suffer malnutrition. The study indicates, however, that resources are available for food production in those countries to grow by as much as 4.0% per annum until the year 2000. Under these conditions, the world food situation could be considerably improved. However, to attain these rates of growth, some intensive agricultural policies would have to be implemented. To encourage farmers to increase their investments in agriculture, prices for farm inputs and commodities produced would need to be put at favorable levels. A study completed by the World Bank in 1979 indicated that the price policies used by 90% of the less developed countries served as a disincentive for agricultural production. The tendency in the less developed countries is to keep food prices low for urban consumers. But the low prices discourage innovation and the use of new technologies by farmers.

The OECD also held a meeting to analyze the future structure of agriculture and indicated that world food production could be increased at a rate exceeding population growth for the remainder of the century. However, much larger investments in agricultural research must be made in the less developed countries. More manpower must be trained to conduct research and provide extension education. The main source of increase must be from higher yields.

EARL O. HEADY, *Iowa State University*

ALABAMA

In Alabama, the most notable events of 1979 involved the legislature, the federal judiciary, gasoline supplies, race relations, and the weather.

Legislative Actions. The legislature convened in organizational session on January 9. Ordinarily, the regular session would have been held in February. Convinced that a new administration required additional time to develop its own budgetary policies, Gov. Forrest (Fob) H. James, Jr., called a special session that met on January 18 and shifted the meeting date of the first regular session in a new term to April.

During the regular session, the legislature mainly was concerned with three major administration proposals: a revised state constitution, an extensive highway maintenance program to be financed with an additional tax on gasoline, and a "war on illiteracy" to improve instruction in basic educational skills. Only the latter passed.

Judicial Actions. During the year, the U. S. Supreme Court made three notable decisions involving the state. In March, the court invalidated the state's law preventing former husbands from receiving alimony in divorce cases. Shortly thereafter, in a dramatic action taken at the last moment, the court stayed the execution of John Louis Evans, 3rd, who had received the death penalty following conviction for murder. The execution had been set for April 6. In December the court stayed the execution of Eugene Ritter, a convicted murderer, so that it could consider a review of the case

In late October a federal grand jury indicted seven persons, including an Alabama legislator and three coal-mining company officials, on charges of racketeering, mail fraud, and extortion.

Gasoline Shortage. The spring fuel shortage was heightened by the independent truckers' strike and was accompanied by violence. State military personnel were used to assist law enforcement officers in escorting tanker trucks and, in some instances, in delivering gasoline. By midsummer, the truckers' strike had ended and gasoline supplies were more plentiful.

Race Relations. Racial disturbances continued during 1979. In June, demonstrations were precipitated in Birmingham by a shooting incident in which a black woman was killed by a policeman. On October 9, in an election undoubtedly influenced by developments associated with the incident, Dr. Richard Arrington, a black candidate who had served on the city council, received a substantial plurality of the votes cast for the office of Birmingham's mayor. Having narrowly failed to achieve a majority, Dr. Arrington was forced into an October 30 run-off with Frank Parsons. By winning the run-off, Arrington became the city's first black mayor.

Renewed Ku Klux Klan activity, which had arisen in 1978 in connection with the trial of Tommy Lee Hines, was centered mainly in north Alabama. In August a Klan demonstration described as a "reverse Selma-to-Montgomery march for white civil rights" culminated in the arrest and conviction in Montgomery of many of the marchers on charges of parading without license.

September Hurricane. On the night of September 12–13, Hurricane Frederic swept savagely ashore in the area of Mobile, severely damaging the state's coastal region. Other areas were affected by the storm as it traveled northward over the state. Property damage was estimated at more than $1 billion.

JAMES D. THOMAS
The University of Alabama

City Councilman Richard Arrington became the first black to be elected mayor of Birmingham, AL.

UPI

ALASKA

The main concern of Alaskans during 1979 was the federal reservation of over 100 million acres (40 million ha) for wilderness areas, wildlife reserves, and parks. The land issue has sparked controversy in the state, and efforts by the U. S. Congress to deal with it have not been successful. In late 1978, just before Congress adjourned, Sen. Mike Gravel (D) had stunned his Republican colleague, Ted Stevens, by effectively killing a lands bill, which had been passed by the House of Representatives. The House passed a similar bill, which was favored by conservationists, in 1979.

After nearly a year's discussions the state and the U. S. Department of Interior reached agreement on conditions for the sale of prospecting leases in the Beaufort Sea. Both environmental and energy groups were involved.

Legislature. The 11th state legislature convened with Senate President Clem Tillion (R-Halibut Cove) committed to keeping the session close to 90 days. The legislature adjourned after about 120 days, but only at the cost of a number of key issues. Topics not dealt with included state participation in gas-line construction and the funding of salary increases negotiated by state employees. The latter issue forced the calling of a special session of the legislature during the summer.

Economy. The chief economic topic was the fate of the line to take natural gas from Prudhoe Bay to the "lower 48." The major obstacle to its construction is the role of the state in financing the private builder. Some Alaskans feel that only private sources of funding should be used, but the state government seemed to be searching for a method of providing some public support. The president of Northwest Pipeline Company requested federal assistance in obtaining state funding. This profoundly irritated many Alaskans. Another question related to the gas line is the location of a processing plant, which many hoped to establish in or near Fairbanks. After hearings in Alaska, Matthew Holden of the federal Energy Regulatory Commission affirmed a pressure limit on the gas line which requires that the plant be located near Prudhoe Bay.

A number of minor problems arose along the oil pipeline. Two leaks were discovered where the pipe had "wrinkled" due to settling of the underlying permafrost. The spill of oil was not detected by the automatic warning system but by flyovers or passersby. Also, the line was in the news for several weeks when a "pig," a monitoring device designed to crawl through the line and check for defects, got stuck in a by-pass valve near Anaktuvik Pass. Over 8 million barrels of oil were going through the line daily by October 1.

The salmon catch was higher, especially in areas like Bristol Bay where conservation efforts

ALYESKA PIPELINE SERVICE CO.

A measuring device, lodged in the Alaskan pipeline, was removed by a special technique, "stoppeling."

several years ago caused controversy. There was some indication that the commercial harvest would cause a glut.

In July 1979 the state's unemployment rate was 7.6% compared with a 10% rate in July 1978. However, employment prospects pertaining to the gas line were not good. Only 8,000 temporary jobs would result.

University of Alaska. Jay Barton II, provost for academic affairs at the University of West Virginia, succeeded Foster Diebold, former executive secretary to the Board of Regents, as president of the University of Alaska.

ANDREA R. C. HELMS
University of Alaska

——— ALASKA • Information Highlights ———

Area: 586,412 square miles (1 518 807 km²).
Population (Jan. 1979 est.): 404,000.
Chief Cities (1970 census): Juneau, the capital, 6,050; Anchorage, 48,081; Fairbanks, 14,771.
Government (1979): *Chief Officers*—governor, Jay S. Hammond (R); lt. gov., Terry Miller (R). *Legislature* —Senate, 20 members; House of Representatives, 40 members.
Education (1978–79): *Enrollment*—public elementary schools, 49,895 pupils; public secondary, 40,833; colleges and universities, 26,351. *Public school expenditures* (1977–78), $338,525,000 ($3,123 per pupil).
State Finances (fiscal year 1978): *Revenues,* $1,317,-902,000; *expenditures,* $1,289,246,000.
Personal Income (1978): $4,415,000,000; per capita, $10,963.
Labor Force (July 1979): *Nonagricultural wage and salary earners,* 171,400; *unemployed,* 14,900 (7.6% of total force).

ALBANIA

The year 1979 marked the 35th anniversary of the liberation of Albania from Nazi occupation and the establishment of the Communist regime.

Government. On Dec. 26, 1978, Maj. Gen. Mehmet Shehu was reelected prime minister by the People's Assembly. There were no changes in his cabinet, suggesting that the political purges which had brought 21 cabinet changes between 1972 and 1977 were over. Hysni Kapo, the third-ranking member of the Albanian ruling elite, died on Sept. 23, 1979, in Paris, where he was being treated for cancer. Kapo had been responsible for the day-to-day administration of the ruling Albanian Party of Labor.

The regime acknowledged that there was still some resistance to its hard-line policies, especially among younger Albanians. The latter were strongly criticized for their unwillingness to accept work assignments in those sectors of the economy and those regions of the country in which they were needed most.

Foreign Relations. Although Albania and China resumed diplomatic ties on the ambassadorial level, relations between the two countries remained cool. The publication of First Secretary Enver Hoxha's two-volume commentary on Sino-Albanian relations between 1962 and 1977 represented a further polemical escalation. Hoping to replace China as Albania's leading foreign aid donor, the Soviet Union offered to reestablish commercial ties with Tiranë. The overture was rejected. Albania also reiterated its opposition to any relationship with the United States, Israel, or what it termed "other Fascist states." It did, however, actively seek increased economic and cultural ties with its neighbors—Yugoslavia and Greece—as well as with France, Italy, Austria, the Scandinavian countries, and the Benelux states. The Albanians indicated a willingness to establish diplomatic relations with West Germany, provided that Bonn offer indemnities for the destruction of Albania under Nazi occupation. Albania stood alone among the European nations in its opposition to the SALT II treaty and its support of the seizure of the U. S. embassy in Tehran.

Natural Disasters. On April 15, northern Albania was hit by what was described as the country's most destructive earthquake in the 20th century. The quake caused 35 deaths and 382 injuries, destroyed some 2,500 buildings, and left 100,000 persons homeless. In early October, the government announced that all repairs had been made without external assistance. This was hailed as a "great victory" for the regime's policy of "self-reliance." In mid-November the western coastal region was buffeted by strong winds and torrential rains, causing heavy crop losses and extensive property damage.

NICHOLAS C. PANO
Western Illinois University

ALBERTA

In 1979 Alberta's population neared two million, and unemployment remained under 4.5%, substantially below the national figure. Inflation continued serious, but the abundance of low-cost fossil fuel, the absence of gasoline and sales taxes, and the lowest income tax in Canada mitigated its impact. Labor unrest was markedly under 1978 levels.

Government. Conservatives emerged triumphant in both federal and provincial elections. Under Peter Lougheed's leadership, they captured 74 of 79 seats in the provincial legislature and all 21 Alberta seats in parliament. Among Alberta winners in the latter contest was Canada's new prime minister, Joe Clark. The expiration of the term of Ralph Steinhauer, Canada's first Indian lieutenant-governor, was followed by the appointment of Frank Lynch-Staunton, an Alberta rancher.

During its spring session, Alberta's legislature gave approval to some 30 laws, including legislation to grant $1.045 billion to the province's municipalities for debt reduction; benefits to low income taxpayers; and an estimated $40-million tax cut to more than 17,000 small businesses.

The change of government in Ottawa did little to alleviate federal-provincial confrontation on pricing of Alberta-produced oil and gas. At year's end, the Local Authorities Board and the government were considering Edmonton's application for a vast expansion of its municipal boundaries. In another area, the growing practice of extra billing by the medical profession led to increased tension with the provincial government over its health insurance plan.

Agriculture. Harvesting weather was excellent in 1979, and grain crops were satisfactory, if not outstanding. However, serious problems remained in grain movement to foreign markets, and beef prices remained high.

Business and Industry. Urban construction continued at high levels, except for some decline in residential building due to higher mortgage rates. Exploration and development increased in the oil sands and heavy oil deposits, but the coal industry was threatened with declining export markets.

Environment. In 1979, Albertans protested a number of proposed projects, including dams on the Red Deer and Milk rivers, limited exploitation of wilderness reserves, mineral exploration in foothills' forested areas, and the location of a dangerous wastes disposal plant near industrial Fort Saskatchewan.

Other News. In the sports world, Edmonton's Commonwealth Stadium became home field for the Drillers soccer club. The Edmonton Oilers moved from the collapsing World Hockey Association to the National Hockey League.

The Department of Education's Heritage Learning Resources Project reached fruition.

JOHN W. CHALMERS, *Concordia College*

ALGERIA

Col. Benjedid Chadli succeeded the late Houari Boumedienne, Algeria's president for 13 years, as head of state in 1979. The 49-year-old former defense minister continued most of his predecessor's policies, particularly his support for the Polisario Front in the Western Sahara war. New economic directions, with a focus on agricultural development to be financed by exports of oil and natural gas, were charted.

Politics. Chadli, formerly Oran's military commander, was elected president of Algeria in February. He was chosen as sole candidate by the ruling National Liberation Front (FLN) after Boumedienne's December 1978 death, as a compromise between the party's left wing, headed by its Executive Secretary Mohammed Salah Yahiaoui, and the right, led by the former Foreign Minister Abdelaziz Bouteflika.

Chadli, who also took over as secretary general of the Liberation Front, formed a new government in March. He replaced Bouteflika, who became a presidential adviser, with former Finance Minister Sedik Ben Yahia. The president waived a constitutional option of assuming the duties of prime minister himself by appointing Interior Minister Mohammed Ben Ahmed Abdelghani to serve also as head of government.

Although there were no significant departures from the previous regime's policies, a more relaxed and confident mood prevailed under Chadli. The April release of several political prisoners, the freeing from three-year house arrest of two former presidents of the Provisional Algerian government (Youssef Benkhedda and Ferhat Abbas), and the July

---

ALGERIA • Information Highlights

Official Name: Democratic and Popular Republic of Algeria.
Location: North Africa.
Area: 919,595 square miles (2 381 751 km²).
Population (1979 est.): 19,100,000.
Chief Cities (1974): Algiers, the capital, 1,000,000; Oran, 330,000; Constantine, 254,000.
Government: *Head of state*, Benjedid Chadli, president (took office Feb. 1979). *Head of government*, Mohammed Ben Ahmed Abdelghani, prime minister (took office March 1979).
Monetary Unit: Dinar (3.84 dinars equal U. S.$1, Aug. 1979).
Manufactures (major products): Petroleum, gas, petrochemicals, fertilizer, iron and steel, textiles, transportation equipment.
Agriculture (major products): Wheat, barley, oats, wine, fruits, olives, vegetables, livestock.

Algeria marks the 25th anniversary of the beginning of its war for independence. Floats depict each year of the struggle.

WIDE WORLD

release of former President Ahmed Ben Bella from 14 years of house arrest added to the new atmosphere.

Economy. Chadli's plans were to place a higher priority on infrastructural development and the raising of production levels in agriculture. In contrast, Boumedienne had concentrated on heavy industrialization. Relying on revenues generated from increased oil prices and liquefied natural gas sales, estimated at $8 to $10 billion for 1979, a 75% increase from 1978's totals, the government injected more funds into housing, water and food distribution, transport, agriculture, and fishing.

Self-sufficiency in food is a goal of the new regime as Algeria spends more than 20% of its oil and gas earnings on food purchases. A contract for the third gas liquefaction plant, LNG-3, was signed with a group of French banks and it was projected to be the largest of its kind.

Foreign Relations. France extended its hand to the new government in hopes of improving relations between the two nations. In June, France sent Foreign Minister Jean François-Poncet to Algiers to meet with members of Chadli's regime. The meeting paved the way for further talks between the two nations. Foreign Minister Ben Yahia was expected to go to Paris before the end of the year. France refused, however, to yield in its support of Morocco in the Western Sahara war against the Algerian-backed Polisario Front.

Chadli's government continued Algeria's strong backing of the Polisario despite Morocco's increased intransigence and its threats of launching retaliatory attacks into Algerian territory. A high security council composed of leading members of the government was formed in June to deal with the possibility of the attacks and a Moroccan offer for discussion was refused.

MARGARET NOVICKI, *"African Update"*
African-American Institute

ANGOLA

Signs of economic revival and improving foreign relations in 1979 were marred by the death of President Agostinho Neto and persistent warfare in the south of the country. At year's end, questions abounded concerning the future of Angola's domestic and foreign policy.

Domestic Affairs. After cancer surgery in Moscow, Neto died on September 10. A poet and medical doctor, he had been the key figure in the *Movimento Popular de Libertação de Angola* (MPLA) since its formation in 1956. In spite of massive Soviet aid during the civil war, Neto was on occasion at odds with Moscow. He denied it naval bases, sacked pro-Soviet officials, and looked to the West for development assistance. José Eduardo dos Santos, the minister of planning who was trained in Russia, succeeded Neto as president. Dos Santos, a former deputy

premier, is a member of the political bureau of the ruling party.

The ruling Marxist MPLA still had to wage antiguerrilla warfare in the southern region as one of the aftereffects of the civil war. Despite thousands of Cuban troops and Soviet bloc weapons, the MPLA could not root out the *União Nacional para Independência Total* (UNITA). Supported by South African military assistance and conservative Arab funds, UNITA continued to mine the Benguela railway. Although it operates locally, the line's disruption is a setback to economic recovery. South African and Rhodesian air raids also did much harm to refugee-guerrilla camps of their respective opponents from Namibia and Zimbabwe (Rhodesia) who enjoy sanctuary in southern Angola.

Foreign Affairs. Relations improved with Portugal, France, West Germany, and, significantly, China. Peking gave discreet aid to the MPLA's opponents in the civil war. However, the United States, also a backer of the MPLA's enemies, has refused diplomatic recognition until the 25,000 Cuban troops are withdrawn. State department officials and Sen. George McGovern (D-SD) visited Luanda, whose help is needed in settling the Namibian conflict. Recognition from Western countries caused no slackening of ties with the Soviet bloc.

Economy. Angola broadened its policy of economic nonalignment to secure Western investment and technology to help develop its considerable resources. Drilling rights agreements were signed with Western firms; funds from the European Community were accepted; and French experts arrived to build naval yards and telecommunications. Yet East Europeans and Cubans continued their prominent role in construction and agriculture.

Peace with Zaire allowed agriculture to begin again in the north. Cotton and coffee yields were higher but did not reach pre-independence levels. Diamond mining revived and phosphate mining for local fertilizer began.

Neto defended his tolerance of small private enterprise on the grounds that it "did not necessarily clash with the revolutionary principles of the MPLA." But the official Marxist policy remained hostile to the black market system.

THOMAS H. HENRIKSEN, *Hoover Institution on War, Revolution and Peace*

─── **ANGOLA • Information Highlights** ───

Official Name: People's Republic of Angola.
Location: Southwestern Africa.
Area: 481,351 square miles (1 246 700 km²).
Population (1979 est.): 6,900,000.
Chief Cities (1973): Luanda, the capital, 540,000; Huambo, 89,000; Lobito, 74,000.
Government: Head of state, José Eduardo dos Santos, president (took office Sept. 1979).
Monetary Unit: Kwanza (49.29 kwanzas equal U.S.$1, Aug. 1979).
Manufactures (major products): Cement, textiles, fuel oil.
Agriculture (major products): Manioc, coffee, cotton, sisal, tobacco.

ANTHROPOLOGY

In 1979, the field of anthropology was highlighted by a debate over the classification of fossils found in Africa between 1973 and 1977.

New Fossil Named. At a press conference Jan. 18, 1979, Dr. Donald C. Johanson, curator of physical anthropology at the Cleveland Museum of Natural History, and Dr. Tim White, an anthropologist at the University of California at Berkeley, announced that some 350 fragments discovered in Afar, Ethiopia, and Laetolil, Tanzania, from 1973 to 1977 are evidence of a human ancestor 3 to 4 million years old.

According to the two scientists, the new fossil species, which they named *Australopithecus afarensis,* or Afar ape-man, was the common ancestor of two divergent evolutionary strains—the genus Homo, which culminated in man, and the *Australopithecus* lineage, which became extinct about one million years ago. This new hominid species was small-brained, with an ape-like head and jaws and a fully erect body. Johanson and White contended that the fossils found by Dr. Mary Leakey at Laetolil in 1978 belong to the same species.

Debate Intensifies. A month later, Kenyan anthropologist Richard E. Leakey reported that he had discovered new Homo habilis fossils that challenged Johanson's and White's conclusions. According to Leakey, these new fossils, the ones found by Mary Leakey in Tanzania, and the remains discovered by Johanson and White all dated from about 3.5 million years ago. Afar ape-man, Leakey concluded, could not have been ancestral to the human lineage because an early form of homo had already been in existence by that time.

Theory of Bipedalism. The discovery of *Australopithecus afarensis* suggested that human ancestors walked erect but still had small, ape-like brains. Dr. Owen Lovejoy, an anthropologist at Kent State University (OH), developed a theory of bipedalism that does not include substantial brain enlargement and thereby lends credibility to the contention of Johanson and White. Bipedalism, Lovejoy maintains, is linked to the development of a social system, which enabled increased amounts of food to be carried back to females tending more than one infant. The theory implies that bipedalism is tied to the sexual division of labor, the development of a strong family bond, the abandonment of primate patterns of sexual promiscuity, the development of male-female pair-bonding, and extensive food sharing.

Chinese Fossils. Chinese anthropologists reported the discovery of an ape skull, at least 8 million years old, in a coal mine in Yunnan Province. It is believed to be the first such ape fossil to be recovered from the late Miocene–early Pliocene periods.

China also announced that it was engaged in extensive excavations at Zhou Kodian (Chou KouTien), the site where Peking Man fossils had been found. Many fossils were expected to be found at the original entrance of the main cave, yet to be uncovered.

Early Human Diets. Dr. Alan Walker, a Johns Hopkins University (MD) anthropologist, made the startling suggestion that early hominid forms ate fruit rather than meat, seeds, shoots, leaves, and/or grass. Studies of fossil hominid teeth which predate *Homo erectus* show microscopic wear patterns characteristic of fruit eaters. Walker also invented a method of detecting scratches and pits with an electron microscope.

Ancient Voyaging. Among the major ethnological studies reported in 1979 was an analysis of the techniques used by Polynesian peoples who made long, open-sea voyages without charts or instruments.

Books. Important anthropology books published in 1979 included George N. Appell's *Ethical Dilemmas in Anthropological Inquiry* (Crossroads Press); Marvin Harris' controversial *Cultural Materialism* (Random House); William Arens' *Man-Eating Myth* (Oxford), a response to Michael Harner's theories (1977) about Aztec cannibalism; and Claude Levi-Strauss' *The Origins of Table Manners* (Harper and Row), the third volume in his noted Science of Mythology series.

HERMAN J. JAFFE
Department of Anthropology
Brooklyn College, City University of New York

The skull of "Afar ape-man," center, more resembles that of a chimpanzee, top, than that of modern man, bottom.

UPI

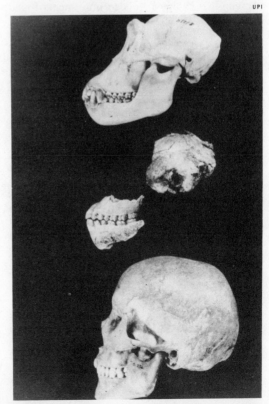

ARCHAEOLOGY

In 1979, laboratory development was as important as field work for the advancement of archaeology in the Eastern Hemisphere. In the Americas the most notable discoveries came from excavations in either very early or historic era sites.

EASTERN HEMISPHERE

Physicists and archaeologists at the University of Missouri developed a new technique for dating burnt flints—the analysis of Electron Spin Resonance. The new technique is more precise than thermoluminescent dating and extends well beyond the 50,000-year range of radiocarbon dating.

A University of Tubingen (West Germany) team developed chemical techniques for tracing organic materials on prehistoric tools, pottery, and even the ground of archaeological sites. A fat content of 2 grams (.07 oz) per kilo (2.2 lbs) of soil from a late Mousterian site in Württemberg was identified as lanolin residue from bear and mammoth hides used as covers and blankets.

Far Eastern Stone Age Hunters and Farmers. Australian National University archaeologists digging in a peat bog at Wyrie Swamp, South Australia, found stone and wooden tools of hunter-gatherers who exploited the marsh resources. Along with scrapers made on flake cores were three complete boomerangs. Radiocarbon tests placed their origin in the period of 7,000 to 8,000 B.C.; they are the oldest evidences of returning boomerangs yet discovered. Among the 25 other wooden implements found were digging sticks and two kinds of spears.

Indian archaeologists tested the hypothesis of B. K. Sinha that northeastern India was one of the earliest sites of agricultural development. Test excavations in Assam produced rice and other plant remains with cord-marked pottery and Hoabhinian-like stone tools dated by radiocarbon analysis to about 5,500 B.C.

Iron Age Royalty. After ten years of excavation on Mount Moriah (Israel), site of the Temple of Jerusalem, archaeologists discovered traces of the royal portico—four rows of 162 monolithic pillars 9 m (29′ 6½″) high and 1.5 m (4′ 11″) in diameter. A secret tunnel was found under the storehouse for valuables, which was used during the Crusades as a stable. An inscription on one of the large blocks, which weighs more than 50 tons (45 359kg), is a quotation from Isiah 66:14. The royal tombs of King Uzziah and other monarchs of Israel were excavated and reburied on the Mount of Olives.

An Egyptian mummy, preserved at Wesleyan University (CT) and unwrapped in honor of the visit of Egyptian President Anwar el-Sadat, proved to be a man of the 26th dynasty, dating to the 7th century B.C. Inside the wrappings were pitch-soaked scrolls; in the body itself, near the vertebrae, lay two tubes, one apparently gold.

Celtic graves in west-central Europe dating from the Hallstatt and La Tene periods (750 B.C. to A.D. 15) had in recent years produced many nobles but very few chiefs. In 1979, however, at Hochdorf, West Germany, the Baden-Württemberg Antiquities service uncovered a grave that was indisputably that of a king. Under the stone-covered burial mound, 60 m (196′ 10″) in diameter, lay a man wearing a golden torc and golden serpentine fibulae, with gold shoe-fittings. His sword had a gold-covered anthropoid handle and a golden sheath. A bronze cauldron, more than 1 m (3′ 3″) in diameter, still contained a golden goblet. An iron drinking horn and iron and bronze arrowheads were also found, along with a four-wheel wagon, bridles of leather, bronze chains, and a yoke made of wood and bronze. Most remarkable of all was the king's engraved bronze couch supported by eight bronze figurines.

An archaeological dig at Mézières (Ardennes), France, produced the remains of several Frankish nobles from the sixth century. Recovered with the bodies were swords with knotted pommels (symbolic of the tie of the warrior to his chief), *angon* spears, razors, and lead beads. A gold coin of the Byzantine Emperor Anastasius helped date the find.

Heathens and Saints. Excavations by the Schleswig Prehistoric Museum yielded from a fjord near the Danish Viking Age border town

Researchers at Wesleyan University (CT) examine a mummy, proved to date to the 7th century B. C.

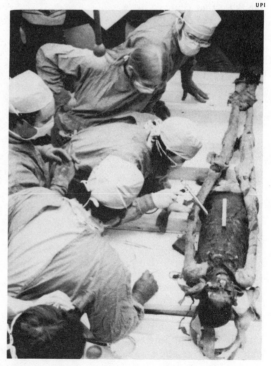

UPI

A coin, discovered by an amateur archaeologist, was identified as an 11th century Norse penny.

of Hedeby the remnants of a burned and sunken long ship, perhaps part of the attack fleet used by Norwegian King Harold Harderade in 1050. A fabulous bronze bell belonging to the church of Saint-Ansgar, the missionary who built the first church in Vikingland in 848, was also recovered during the year.

At Nietlica, Poland, a joint team of U. S. and Polish archaeologists explored the ruins of an early Slavic fortress from a late Bronze Lusatian culture. The remains include a two-room pit house with clay uprights forming a double rectangle. Ziz-zag and linear decorated pots found inside are 50–60 cm (19.7–23.6 inches) tall. The complex was thought to be a rare Slavic temple dating from the 7–8th centuries.

WESTERN HEMISPHERE

Palaeo-Indians. Fossilized bones of bison, musk oxen, horses, and woolly mammoths found in the Yukon Tanana uplands and dated by radiocarbon to c. 28,000 B. C. had chop marks, burnt areas, and spiral fractures implying that they were slaughtered by human beings. However, no stone tools were found among the bones.

At the famous Kimmswick site south of St. Louis, MO, scientists of the Illinois State Museum found an 11,000-year-old fluted stone point with what were identified as mastodon bones. It marked the first time that a projectile from the Palaeo-Indian Clovis culture could be associated with the killing of a mastodon.

Stone tools were found with a mastodon tooth and horse bones at Loltun Cave, in Mexico. The remains lay under a stratum of pottery from the early Olmec Civilization of the San Lorenzo Horizon. The pottery, from approximately 1800 B. C., is the oldest ever found on the Yucatán Peninsula.

Little Salt Spring in southwest Florida fills a 50-m (164-ft) deep biconical sinkhole which collected and preserved organic artifacts and other evidence of Palaeo-Indian and Archaic Indian civilizations between 12,000 and 5,200 years ago. One of the oldest remnants is a socketed projectile point with part of the dart shaft and the base of a carved oak mortar intact. Also found was a nonreturning boomerang, virtually identical in shape and lenticular cross-section to the ethnographic "swan-necked" type of northern Queensland, Australia.

Indian High Culture. Carved stone artwork of the Hopewell Culture (c. A. D. 1 to 500) is normally found in rich burials inhumed in mounds. However, a team of archaeologists from the University of Missouri and Joseph Smith Historic Center digging 19th century Mormon ruins at Nauvoo, IL, chanced upon several Hopewell flat burials. Two contained pipes, one of them a cardinal effigy sculpted in mottled red catlinite pipestone. In a nearby mound lay 7–8 skeletons *without* grave relics.

The ruined city of El Mirador in the steamy lowland jungles of Guatemala was investigated by a team of archaeologists from three U. S. universities. Twin altars were discovered at one end of a vast public plaza. Sculpted artifacts bear the horizon style of the second century, while potsherds date back to 600 B. C. El Mirador must have been one of the earliest and largest of Mayan cities but also one of the first to be abandoned, having been deserted about A. D. 500.

New World Settlers. A silver and copper coin found in 1961 by an amateur archaeologist near Bar Harbor, ME, was identified by archaeologists in early 1979 as a Norse penny made between 1065 and 1080. It was the oldest datable Viking artifact found in North America, but questions about how it got there left the significance of the discovery in doubt.

The remains of a 17th century Puritan hamlet were discovered by construction crews working on an extension of the Boston subway system. Archaeologists were called in after builders found the remains of a sheep buried 150 to 250 years ago near the Wadsworth Gate on the edge of the grounds of Harvard University. Also found were two British farthings from 1613, a variety of jugs, tobacco pipes, and pins, and a pewter spoon.

On Wolstenholme Street in old Martin's Hundred near Williamsburg, VA, two plate armor helmets left by early 17th century English settlers were unearthed. Excavations at the scene of an Indian massacre uncovered the body of a dutiful English swordsman, probably Richard Kean. The settlers had invited the Indians for breakfast, only to be attacked. Kean stood by the door trying to protect his escaping comrades and was struck down.

RALPH M. ROWLETT
University of Missouri-Columbia

ARCHITECTURE

It was a great year for architects, but not for architecture. Most architects had lots of work; unemployment in the profession was low; interesting new architectural trends developed. But significant new buildings were few.

Building in general was relatively scarce, with experts estimating housing starts down about 15% from 1978 and public construction down 10% to 15%. Construction of private, non-residential buildings increased about 10%, thanks mostly to new office and industrial space. Inflationary conditions drove construction costs steadily upward throughout the year to a figure approximately 13% above 1978. It was one of the biggest increases in the past quarter century. Although interest rates hit new highs, money generally was available, particularly during the first three quarters of the year, for those willing and able to pay.

Attention to History. An architectural trend became a mode, as the work of more and more architects reflected the history of their profession. Insistence on totally modern design gave way to respect for the efficiency and beauty of architecture through history, and a willingness to incorporate the best of yesteryear in today's buildings.

So architectural shapes, precedents, and materials of the past received new attention. Arcades appeared with increased frequency; structures lined streets rather than being set back from them; big buildings included retail outlets at street level and with street access; brick and granite walls rose where steel and glass would have been a year or two earlier. As a result of this attention to history, buildings became more hospitable to pedestrians, both aesthetically and practically. Urban street environments improved and showed every sign of continuing to do so in the future.

Fascination with architectural history extended to one of the profession's most important segments: schools of architecture. There, interest developed in the work of men who practiced in the late 19th and early 20th centuries, including English architect Sir Edwin Lutyens and the American Richard Morris Hunt.

Schools also placed new emphasis on the symbolic meaning of architectural shapes, as the slick, glass-skinned buildings championed by Ludwig Mies van der Rohe fell further into disfavor and forms such as pediments, arches, columns, and colonnades attracted new attention.

Solar Heating. More attention was certainly paid to the solar heating and cooling of buildings, particularly homes. Architects increasingly used the orientation, landscaping, and design of homes to take full advantage of the sun. Emphasis was on incorporation of passive solar systems, non-mechanical means of using the sun, such as situating massive concrete walls or water-filled containers so as to absorb the sun's heat during the day and radiate the stored calories into living spaces at night. In commercial buildings, there was new emphasis on utilizing daylight for illumination, particularly in low rise structures where skylights, courtyards, and atria could be employed to particular advantage.

While the use of passive solar systems increased, there was considerable research in sophisticated, active systems involving electronics and complicated hardware, especially in the area of photovoltaic devices that transform the sun's energy into usable electricity.

Preservation Movement. The architectural preservation movement continued to gain momentum, spurred by the general focus on architectural history. Buildings were restored for the love of fine architecture as well as for the purpose of saving a dollar. As preservationists redoubled their efforts, so did their opposition.

Works honored by the American Institute of Architects in 1979 included: Mechanics Hall, which "has been reborn as a social and community center" for Worcester, MA . . .

SERT, JACKSON AND ASSOCIATES

... the Joan Miró Foundation Center for Studies of Contemporary Art in Barcelona, Spain ...

Leaders in the movement to save worthwhile architecture said they faced more and heavier pressures from developers than they had in previous years.

The U. S. House Appropriations Subcommittee on the Interior implemented a victory for antipreservation forces by declaring that permission must be granted by owners before their industrial properties can be declared national historic landmarks by the U. S. Department of the Interior. Preservationists worried that expected Congressional support of the committee decision on industrial structures would start a trend so that owner permission would be required before other kinds of buildings (churches, schools, homes) could be designated as historic landmarks. Such a trend would make it more difficult to get buildings declared landmarks, due to owner opposition on grounds that restrictions on razing and remodeling landmark buildings decrease the flexibility of property and lower its value.

Preservationists got something to cheer about in the form of a study indicating that old buildings can save energy. The document was released by the Advisory Council on Historic Preservation, a federally funded group charged with advising the president and Congress on energy matters.

The Prizewinners. The American Institute of Architects gave 15 honor awards for projects completed in the past seven years. Six awards were for contributions to "extended use" of older buildings; in other words, for preservation and renovation.

"Extended use" awards went to a renovated concert hall in Worcester, MA (Anderson, Notter, Feingold, architects); a natural history and science museum in Louisville, KY (Louis and Henry, architects); a 70-year-old art museum in St. Louis (Hardy Holzman Pfeiffer, architects); a public library and cultural center in Chicago (Holabird & Root, architects); partially underground galleries and a lecture hall that preserved an existing environment at Yale University in New Haven, CT (Herbert S. Newman Associates, architects); and an office building in Princeton, NJ (Michael Graves, architect).

... the Louisville (KY) Museum of Natural History and Science, which was designed by Louis and Henry ...

COURTESY, AIA

COURTESY, AIA

... Harvard University's Undergraduate Science Center, a work "handled skillfully."

Winners in the "new buildings" category were the Undergraduate Science Center at Harvard University in Cambridge, MA, and the Joan Miró Foundation Center for Studies of Contemporary Art in Barcelona, Spain (architects for both projects were Sert, Jackson and Associates); Citicorp Center in New York City (Hugh Stubbins and Associates, architects); the Johns-Manville Corp. headquarters in Jefferson County, CO (The Architects Collaborative, architects); the 22-block Transit Mall in Portland, OR (Skidmore, Owings & Merrill and CHNMB Associates, architects); a wooden cabin on the Washington coast (Arne Bystrom, architect); a home in Bainbridge Island, WA (Morgan and Lindstrom, architects); Pembroke Dormitories at Brown University in Providence, RI (MLTW/Moore, Lyndon, Turnbull, and Lyndon Associates, architects); and the Angela Athletic Facility at St. Mary's College, Notre Dame, IN (C. F. Murphy Associates, architects).

Two of America's leading architects won the nation's two leading architectural awards. I. M. Pei received the American Institute of Architects' Gold Medal, the institute's highest honor, for "most distinguished service to the architectural profession." Philip Johnson won the $100,000 Pritzker Architectural Prize, named for its donor, Jay A. Pritzker, chairman of Hyatt Hotels. Johnson's prize was for "doing more than anyone in the world to keep modern architecture lively and unpredictable."

Developers, Exhibitions, Books. An incipient trend gained strength as major developers hired excellent architects to design projects that cost more than normal but result in significant structures that create a higher than average profit for their owners. A lender of that trend was Gerald D. Hines, head of Gerald D. Hines Interests in Houston, TX. Since 1971, the firm has commissioned buildings by such noted architects as Philip Johnson and John H. Burgee, I. M. Pei, Gyo Obata of Hellmuth, Obata & Kassabaum, and Bruce Graham and Chuck Bassett, both of Skidmore, Owings & Merrill.

One of the most successful architectural exhibitions of the year was a retrospective of the work of Finnish architect Alvar Aalto at the Cooper-Hewitt Museum in New York City. Perhaps the nation's least successful major architectural exhibit was "Transformations in Modern Architecture" at the Museum of Modern Art in New York. Critics attacked the show as a grab bag that lacked continuity and focus.

How-to-do-it books, with an emphasis on energy conservation, were popular. One of the year's outstanding books was *Cities of the American West,* a Princeton University Press volume in which John W. Reps outlined the calculated way in which many western towns were planned. *The City Observed* by Paul Goldberger was an interesting Random House publication offering an architectural tour of New York. The publisher was planning companion volumes on Los Angeles by Charles Moore, on Boston by Donlyn Lyndon, and on Chicago by Stuart Cohen.

Obituary. World famous architect Pier Luigi Nervi died at his home in Rome on January 9 at the age of 87. The honored Italian created reinforced concrete buildings noted for their structural lightness and their ability to enclose huge open spaces. Nervi's buildings included numerous European structures, among them the Vatican Audience Hall in Vatican City. He also designed St. Mary's Cathedral in San Francisco and a cultural center in Norfolk, VA.

JOHN DREYFUSS, *"Los Angeles Times"*

Journalist-businessman Jacobo Timerman (*right*), who was released in September following 2½ years as a political prisoner in Argentina, receives an Anti-Defamation League award from the association's vice president, Benjamin Epstein.

ARGENTINA

During 1979 Argentina experienced a brief rebellion against the government, an illegal general strike, an improved economy, and the dedication of a major hydroelectric complex on the Uruguay River.

Politics and Government. The regime of President Jorge Videla was abruptly shaken in September by a short-lived rebellion, led by rightist Gen. Luciano B. Menéndez, commander of the III Corps in Córdoba. Menéndez called for Roberto Viola, a moderate, representing the army on the ruling junta, to step aside, after he had joined navy and air force members of the junta in accepting a judicial decision releasing Jacobo Timerman from custody. A journalist-businessman, Timerman had been the best-known political prisoner in Argentina. Menéndez' action, along with bombings of homes belonging to ranking members of Videla's economic-planning team, reflected deep dissatisfaction on the right and perhaps the left, with official policies.

An announcement in August by Gen. Carlos Suárez Mason, chairman of the joint chiefs of staff, that the next two presidents would be military men dashed all hopes of an early return to civilian and democratic rule. Interior Minister Albano Harguindeguy added that it was premature to talk of the military sharing political power with civilians, but, when initiated, the process would begin at the municipal level and move to state and federal governments. The church joined political parties and trade unions in opposing the military hardliners' delay in political normalization.

President Videla received the Inter-American Human Rights Commission on September 20, following its three-week investigation into the human rights situation in Argentina. The commission left a list of recommendations for early action with the chief executive, who was said to have promised the release of Timerman and an improvement in respect for human rights. Just prior to the commission's visit, the junta passed a law dealing with the "disappeared" persons who number into the thousands. Under the new law, a person need be missing only a few months, before being declared legally dead by the government.

An illegal general strike, called for April 27 to protest official economic policy, was ably handled by the Videla government. Of the two labor organizations, representing 3.5 million largely Peronista workers, only the smaller and more militant "Group of 25" participated in the strike. Prior to the strike date, the government decreed a 15% wage increase and arrested 32 union leaders. With militant union leaders in jail and only a 30% participation in the stoppage, the government went ahead and finalized its "Professional Associations Law," which was forwarded to a legislative commission in July. The law was drafted to curtail the influence of unions.

Economy. The Argentine economy revived somewhat in 1979. During the first quarter of the year the gross domestic product rose by 12%. Economic growth fueled inflation, which was projected to 170% for 1979. The recovery was

───── **ARGENTINA • Information Highlights** ─────

Official Name: Republic of Argentina.
Location: Southern South America.
Area: 1,072,158 square miles (2 776 889 km²).
Population (1979 est.): 26,700,000.
Chief Cities (1970 census): Buenos Aires, the capital, 2,972,453; Córdoba, 781,565; Rosario, 750,455.
Government: *Head of state and government,* Jorge Videla, president (assumed office March 1976). *Legislature*—Congress (dissolved March 24, 1976); Legislative Advisory Commission established.
Monetary Unit: New Peso (1,549 new pesos equal U. S.$1, Nov. 1979).
Manufactures (major products): Processed foods, motor vehicles, textiles, chemicals, metal and metal products, electrical appliances.
Agriculture (major products): Grains, oilseeds, livestock products.

attributed, in part, to reduced government monetary controls and a tightening of state and federal spending. More money was available for loans, as banks dropped reserve requirements from 45 to 27%. Automotive output in the first four months of 1979 was more than 62,000 units, an increase of 80% over that period in 1978. Unemployment stood at only 1.8%. Central bank reserves reached an unprecedented $8 billion in June.

Responding to government incentives, agricultural exports led the economic recovery. Argentina exported a record 3.7 million metric tons (4 tons) of soybeans in 1979. The 1978–79 wheat crop yielded 8 million metric tons (8.7 tons), a 53% increase over the previous season. According to estimates late in the year the maize harvest was expected to increase by 13.4% over 1978.

Foreign investment in Argentina increased. Renault, Ford Motor Co., and Mercedes Benz Argentina were increasing their operations.

Energy Development. With the dedication in June of the first of 16 turbines in the $900 million Salto Grande binational hydroelectric complex on the Uruguay River, Argentina moved ahead with a $58 billion energy development plan that would triple energy output by the year 2000. Accordingly, Videla and Paraguayan President Alfredo Stroessner met on the northeastern border in November to sign documents permitting the joint construction of a $4.5 billion hydroelectric project on the Paraná River. Upon completion, the Yacyretá dam would be the seventh largest in the world, supplying 65% of Argentina's present energy needs. Financing of $410 million for the Yacyretá project was arranged through the World and the Inter-American Development banks.

In accordance with an agreement signed by the foreign ministers of Argentina, Brazil, and Paraguay in October, the Itaipú, the world's largest hydroelectric project being built on the Paraná River by Brazil and Paraguay, would have 18 turbines operating at one time, with the capacity for 20. In addition, the height of the Corpus dam would be 105 meters (344 ft).

Foreign Relations. Papal efforts to mediate the Beagle Channel dispute between Argentina and Chile resumed in September in the Vatican, after a recess of one month. Pope John Paul II was represented in the mediation by Antonio Cardinal Samoré of Italy. Maritime jurisdictions in the disputed South Atlantic area and also the ownership of three tiny islands in the channel were considered.

While denying the formation of an anti-Chile alliance, Argentine officials did receive President Francisco Morales Bermúdez of Peru and Bolivia's Foreign Minister Raúl Botelho Gonsalvez, whose respective countries have century-old border disputes with Chile. During his state visit to Buenos Aires in June, the Peruvian chief executive stated to the press that he would be discussing the coordination of foreign policy actions with his Argentine counterpart. Botelho reiterated in Buenos Aires that Bolivia would not reestablish diplomatic relations with Chile until his landlocked country had regained an outlet to the Pacific Ocean, taken by Chile in 1879.

Regarding an Argentine claim to the British-held Falkland (Malvinas) Islands, bilateral discussions were held in March and September. No progress was made toward a settlement of the Argentine claim, but the two countries agreed to restore full diplomatic relations.

LARRY L. PIPPIN, *Elbert Covell College*
University of the Pacific

ARIZONA

During 1979, public attention in Arizona focused on issues related to water use, a white-collar criminal network, population growth, and a balanced state budget.

The Economy. Arizona's population growth rate was estimated at 3.3% at midyear. Employment was up almost 8%, bringing the number employed in the state to a record high.

The state's major industries continued to grow. The copper industry showed sales up 83% over 1978 and employment up 7%. It was a bumper year for the state's large cotton crop, and the construction industry showed similar patterns of expansion. Tourism suffered a decline, due to the nationwide gasoline shortage in the spring and early summer months.

The Legislature. A record one billion dollar budget was passed in the state legislature. The biggest budget outlay, $700 million, went for the operation of the state's educational system. Arizona had a record budget surplus in excess of $100 million. In response to 1978's citizen tax revolt, a $95 million property-tax rebate was effected.

Environmental Issues. The controversial Central Arizona Project (CAP), now under construction, was brought to public attention when Secretary of the Interior Cecil Andrus announced that its completion was dependent on state water law reform. Andrus declared that federal fund-

---
ARIZONA • Information Highlights

Area: 113,909 square miles (295 024 km²).

Population (Jan. 1979 est.): 2,378,000.

Chief Cities (1976 est.): Phoenix, the capital, 679,512; Tucson, 302,359; (1970 census): Scottsdale, 67,823.

Government (1979): Chief Officers—governor, Bruce Babbitt (D); secy. of state, Rose Mofford (D). *Legislature*—Senate, 30 members; House of Representatives, 60 members.

Education (1978–79): *Enrollment*—public elementary schools, 349,695 pupils; public secondary, 160,135; colleges and universities, 176,612 students. *Public school expenditures,* $953,733,000 ($1,504 per pupil).

State Finances (fiscal year 1978): *Revenues,* $2,423,-112,000; *expenditures,* $2,067,347,000.

Personal Income (1978): $17,352,000,000; per capita, $7,372.

Labor Force (July 1979): *Nonagricultural wage and salary earners,* 932,100; *unemployed,* 55,300 (5.4% of total force).

ing of CAP hinged on groundwater law reform and the resolution of litigation involving Native American tribal water rights.

Arizona's Governor Bruce Babbitt was appointed in April to President Carter's Commission to investigate the Three-Mile Island nuclear accident. The issue of radiation hazards and public safety was brought to public notice in Arizona with the discovery in May of contaminated food in Tucson. The contamination was traced to a privately owned manufacturing firm, American Atomics. In June, the Arizona Atomic Energy Commission shut down the residentially-located plant, and in September the governor used his emergency powers to confiscate the remaining radioactive material. The incident focused public attention and concern on the construction of Arizona's first nuclear power facility, the Palo Verde plant.

White Collar Crime. In a broad investigation prompted by the 1976 murder of Phoenix reporter Don Bolles, federal, state, and local investigators continued to uncover a vast array of sophisticated fraud, much of it seemingly tied to Eastern-based organized crime. The schemes, operating out of locations in Phoenix and suburban Scottsdale, are estimated by the investigators to have extracted over $100 million from the American public yearly. The investigation has resulted in indictments of 165 individuals and 16 corporations, many of which have Mafia connections.

Former U. S. Attorney General Richard Kleindienst, now an Arizona resident, agreed to pay $150,000, along with two other defendants, to settle a civil suit which accused them of involvement in a large insurance fraud scheme.

JEANNE NIENABER
The University of Arizona

ARKANSAS

Events during 1979 demonstrated that resolution of state problems would be neither easy nor rapid, despite exemplary intentions and ambitious undertakings. A state supreme court order for a ten-year statewide property reappraisal program to end extreme property-tax inequities generated a multitude of court suits, legislative actions, and constitutional amendments to neutralize the adverse impact of higher tax bills on numerous property owners. Gov. Bill Clinton discovered that more than his pleas were needed to achieve energy conservation after a follow-up study on his executive order reducing the state auto fleet by 15% revealed an increase in vehicles. A vestige of past racial discrimination was removed when Governor Clinton signed at Washington, AR, site of the state Civil War capitol, a bill repealing state segregation laws.

State Government. Youthful, first-term Democrat Bill Clinton skillfully assumed his role as state executive leader. He sought a more responsive state bureaucracy by expanding executive authority over the budgetary process and by replacing most top executives appointed by former Democratic governors Dale Bumpers and David Pryor. In an 87-day regular biennial session the legislature adopted most of his programs for moving Arkansas into an "Era of Excellence," including a one-cent raise in the gasoline tax to finance increased spending for state highways; measures such as mandatory achievement tests for public school students, standardized competency tests for new teachers, a fair dismissal law for teachers, and a $1,200 per year teacher salary increase to improve the quality of public education; a state energy department; and an ambitious capital construction program. However, inflation and meager revenue collections cast doubt on the ability to finance all the programs.

Constitutional Convention. A 100-delegate constitutional convention, with Dr. Robert A. Leflar, professor emeritus of law at the University of Arkansas, as presiding officer, proposed a new constitution to replace the existing constitution of 1874. After the convention, delegates began sponsoring community forums to persuade the public to accept and to vote for the new document in November 1980. Among the proposed changes were an increase from two to four years in the length of term for elected state and county executives, a combining of the offices of state auditor and treasurer, replacement of the justices of peace and city courts with county trial courts staffed by judges trained in law, selection of judges in nonpartisan elections, home rule to cities and counties, and creation of a new right-to-privacy and of a right-to-own-guns-for-hunting.

Controversies. State banks and savings and loan associations attempted to get state courts to nullify the constitutional limit of 10% on interest rates. Federal courts ordered consolidation of four school districts to eliminate black public schools in Conway County. Racial tensions increased when the Ku Klux Klan held rallies in state-owned buildings.

WILLIAM C. NOLAN
Southern Arkansas University

―――― **ARKANSAS · Information Highlights** ――――

Area: 53,104 square miles (137 539 km²).
Population (Jan. 1979 est.): 2,206,000.
Chief Cities (1976 est.): Little Rock, the capital, 151,-649; (1970 census): Fort Smith, 62,802.
Government (1979): *Chief Officers*—governor, Bill Clinton (D); lt. gov., Joe Purcell (D). *General Assembly* —Senate, 35 members; House of Representatives, 100 members.
Education (1978–79): *Enrollment*—public elementary schools, 241,178 pupils; public secondary, 215,520; colleges and universities, 72,318 students. *Public school expenditures,* $618,246,000 ($1,158 per pupil).
State Finances (fiscal year 1978): *Revenues,* $1,839,-706,000; *expenditures,* $1,684,539,000.
Personal Income (1978): $13,047,000,000; per capita, $5,969.
Labor Force (July 1979): *Nonagricultural wage and salary earners,* 745,000; *unemployed,* 57,400 (5.7% of total force).

ART

In 1979 the art world saw the continued escalation of art auctioning and dealing, major exhibitions of the art of Russia, a rediscovery of Victorian art, a controversy over the Gilbert Stuart portraits of George and Martha Washington, and terrorist activity aimed at Rome's Palace of the Senators, designed by Michelangelo.

Art Dealing and Auctioning. In Paris, a former department store across the street from the Louvre Museum was converted into the largest antiques center in Europe. Some 240 dealers permanently exhibit there. The building is owned by the British Post Office's retirement fund, and this venture is typical of the investment policies of such funds, which turned to the selling of art works and antiques in an attempt to beat inflation. Collectors, large and small, are following this trend, and smaller auction halls are doing a large-scale business among less wealthy and experienced buyers.

Glamorous auctions also continued to make headlines. The record-breaking event of the year took place at Sotheby's in Monaco before a fashionable audience of rich and famous people, many of whom found themselves in the unfamiliar position of having difficulties paying the inflated prices. The occasion was the auction of the collection acquired by Akram Ojieh, a Saudi Arabian, from Daniel Wildenstein, only two years before. It consisted mainly of 18th century French furniture destined for an abortive reconversion of the liner *France*. Many of the best pieces had come from the palace of the Vienna Rothschilds. At the auction, the top price ($1.7 million) ever paid for a single piece of furniture was given for a Louis XV encoignure, a corner cabinet with ormolu decoration and surmounted by a clock. It was bought by a London dealer for the J. Paul Getty Museum in Malibu, CA. The total realized at this auction was $12.7 million, outstripping 1978's furniture auction at Mentmore, which brought $10.3 million. In 1979 it was clear that furniture was being bought as an investment.

In New York, the collection of Benjamin Sonnenberg—the entire contents of his large house in Gramercy Park—was sold by Sotheby Parke Bernet. It, too, was a social event, attended by many of the deceased collector's friends and acquaintances who had enjoyed his hospitality and had admired the treasures with which he had surrounded himself during a lifetime of collecting. These included portraits by and of famous people, rugs, bronzes, porcelains, and furniture. The collection attracted more buyers and spectators than any other auction in Sotheby's history; in nine sessions the total sales reached $4.7 million. The highest price paid was for a Sargent portrait of the Duchess of Sutherland.

Specialty Sales. New specialties were added to already established popular categories of art and antiques at auctions. Beside such items as dolls and photographs, there were coins and clothes, the latter including not only rare and precious 17th and 18th century costumes but also Victorian lingerie and day and evening dresses of the 1920's and 1930's. These sold very well, some possibly to be worn again. An entire auction at Phillips, Son, and Neale was devoted to the Art Deco glass of René Lalique. At Sotheby's the Christner silver collection was sold, and sale prices far exceeded the estimates, totaling a record $766,730. The most expensive item, a Paul de Lamerie cake basket (1740), went for $49,000, but it was the 19th-century silver that provided the greatest excitement. Several works by Paul Storr sold for considerably more than the expected prices. At Christie's a Storr service attained $533,598. Other specialized sales were of tin soldiers, writing instruments, and old stoves. An entire stamp collection, amassed by financier Marc Haas, was sold to a British buyer for over $10 million.

Museum and Gallery Exhibitions. At the Brooklyn Museum a show, "Victorian High Renaissance," and another entitled "The Second Empire: Art in France under Napoleon III," organized by the Philadelphia Museum with the cooperation of the Musées de France, and shown also at the Detroit Institute of Arts, brought back to public attention the once-admired academic painters who were scorned by artists and critics of the last few generations. Society painters such as Franz Winterhalter, allegorical and sentimental artists such as Frederick Leighton and William-Adolphe Bouguereau, and the court painter of Napoleon, Jean-Léon Gérome, were represented. In Germany, too, there were exhibitions drawing on the 19th century, among them one at the Kunstmuseum in Düsseldorf. The respectability again accorded this style of art paralleled an interest in representational and objective art seen in contemporary sculpture and painting. Another aspect of 19th-century taste was explored in the exhibition "Designs for the Dream King" at the Cooper-Hewitt Museum in New York. The king, Ludwig II of Bavaria, built several lavish palaces and castles in a historicizing mode, providing them with furniture and accessories both anachronistic and theatrical. This art was formerly looked down upon as eclectic, tasteless, and good only for the ignorant delight of untutored but revenue-producing hordes of tourists who visited the original sites. More recently, however, it was the subject of exhibitions and critical writings and was admired for its high level of craftsmanship and imagination.

A dissimilar rediscovery—of a fundamental period of art history—was the theme of the exhibition "Berenson and the Connoisseurship of Italian Painting" shown at the National Gallery in Washington, DC. Bernard Berenson

GIFT OF KATE L. BREWSTER

THE ART INSTITUTE OF CHICAGO

An exhibition of 109 paintings by Henri de Toulouse-Lautrec, including "Miss May Milton, 1895" (above), was a 1979 highlight at the Art Institute of Chicago.

LENT BY THE STATE MUSEUMS OF THE MOSCOW KREMLIN

THE METROPOLITAN MUSEUM OF ART

A 1904 Fabergé model of the Kremlin was displayed at New York City's Metropolitan Museum of Art during the popular "Treasures from the Kremlin" exhibition.

The "Victorian High Renaissance" show at the Brooklyn (NY) Museum helped to renew an interest in Victorian art, which recently had been scorned by the critics.

THE BROOKLYN MUSEUM

(1865–1959), who advised such major American collectors as Isabella Stewart Gardner, Joseph Widener, and Samuel H. Kress, laid the groundwork for the study of the history of Italian painting. His searching and cataloging, by artist and style, uncovered paintings in museums, collections, and churches that had previously been either unknown or improperly attributed. If subsequent scholarship frequently disagreed with Berenson's opinions in individual cases, it did not alter the validity of his method and the main outlines of his work. He, more than anyone else, was responsible for the rediscovery of early Italian painting.

Another "tastemaker" who ran a gallery in Paris from 1924 to 1964, the dealer Pierre Loeb, was honored with an exhibition at the Museum of Modern Art in Paris. The exhibit featured works by Kandinsky, Picasso, Zao-Wuoki, and Giacometti, as well as Coptic and New Guinean art.

At the Whitney Museum in New York, founder Gertrude Vanderbilt Whitney, the most active patron of American art of her time and a distinguished sculptor, was remembered with an exhibition "Tradition and Modernism in American Art, 1900–30." The show included documentary material on the 1913 Armory show, John Sloan's first exhibition at the Whitney Studio Club in 1916, and the museum's collection of paintings, drawings, watercolors, prints, and sculptures.

The same time span was covered by the "Paris-Moscow" exhibition at the Pompidou Center in Paris. The exhibition featured works of the Russian "avant garde," which formerly were in the "reserve" section of Russian museums and considered the antithesis of official and approved Russian art. Inspired by early modern Western European painting in the post-Impressionist and Cubist mode, Russian artists of the early 20th century developed a unique modernist art that is close to recent trends in abstract and minimal art in the West. Some of these artists became known when they left Russia to work for the Diaghilev Ballet, but most were only recently discovered. The more than 2,500 items included painting and sculpture, theater documents, film, literature, photographs, posters, architectural designs, furniture, and textiles. More than two thirds of the items came from the Soviet Union. Some Russian collections, influential to this period, of Western artists such as Picasso, Matisse, Braque, Derain, and Bonnard, were seen outside Russia for the first time since the early years of this century.

Henri Matisse was the subject of a major show at the Guggenheim Museum in New York. Most of the pieces came from the Baltimore Museum of Art. It was not only an impressive retrospective of Matisse but also a reminder of the collecting activities of Baltimore's Cone sisters, who originally owned most of the loan paintings, drawings, and sculptures. These two ladies, friends of Gertrude Stein's brother, became acquainted through him with contemporary artists working in Paris and started collections of the artists' works before they became acknowledged masterworks.

Another rediscovered modern master was the Norwegian Edvard Munch. Most of his paintings are in public and private collections in Norway, and it was a great occasion when more than 200 were permitted to go to the National Gallery in Washington. Of these, 23 were later shown at the Museum of Modern Art in New York. In the development of themes of psychological relationships and alienation, Munch, a most individualistic artist, was closer to the expressionist playwrights August Strindberg and Henrik Ibsen than to contemporary artists.

On the occasion of its 100th anniversary, the Art Institute of Chicago in October 1979 mounted two excellent exhibitions—a large retrospective of the work of Henri de Toulouse-Lautrec and an exhibit of 16th-century Roman drawings from the collection of the Louvre in Paris. The Toulouse-Lautrec exhibit provided 109 paintings and a group of drawings and prints. The Roman drawings showed examples of the work of Michelangelo, Raphael, and others of the High Renaissance and Mannerist styles.

At New York's Museum of Modern Art, only a small print show commemorated the centenary of the birth of Paul Klee. As *New York Times* critic Hilton Kramer observed, Klee is now "unfashionable." A more representative show was mounted by the Saidenberg Gallery in New York.

In contrast to the modest Klee celebration, the Museum of Modern Art participated in plans to bring together a mammoth retrospective of Pablo Picasso. More than 700 of his paintings, sculptures, ceramics, drawings, and prints were seen in late 1979 in Paris, and are to be seen in May 1980 at the Museum of Modern Art in New York. The Paris showing marked the settlement of the painter's estate, which left the French government with about 30% to 40% of his works in lieu of taxes. In addition to the works from his estate, the exhibition presented objects from Barcelona, London, Leningrad, Moscow, Prague, Paris, and New York. At the 1980 showing in New York, the entire floor space of the Museum of Modern Art is to be dedicated to this one exhibition. It very well may be the last time that the famous painting "Guernica" is seen in New York. Following this exhibition the Museum of Modern Art is scheduled to close for alterations. The sale of the air rights to a developer for $17 million will provide a welcome increase in the museum's funds. In addition, the museum extension will double the present gallery space and provide related support facilities, such as storage space. A luxury 44-story apartment tower is to be built on top of a portion of the extended museum and is to be

Many Americans rebelled against the proposed sale of Gilbert Stuart's portraits of George and Martha Washington to the National Portrait Gallery of the Smithsonian Institution. It was the general feeling that the famous paintings should remain in Boston.

completely separate from it. However, the two buildings will be compatible in design.

Probably the only museum in the world which did not suffer from lack of funds was the Getty Museum in Malibu, which is endowed with Getty Oil Company stock.

Loan Exhibitions. In addition to the Paris-Moscow show, there were several other loan exhibitions from Russia. "Treasures from the Kremlin" brought thousands of objects to the Metropolitan Museum. Ranging over eight centuries, coronation regalia, icons, and liturgical objects of Russian origin vied with European armor and silver and goldsmith work presented by western monarchs to the Czars. Spiritual and political significance, splendid decoration and pathetic memories of the dying Russian Empire were evoked and seemingly much appreciated by the visitors. Eleven paintings from the Hermitage Museum in Leningrad, "From Leonardo to Titian," visited the National Gallery, the Los Angeles County Museum, the Detroit Institute of Arts, and the Knoedler Gallery in New York. In Paris, 30 of Wassily Kandinsky's paintings—most never before seen outside Russia—were visible at the Pompidou Center. Not all the Russian loans were concluded smoothly. A yearlong United States tour entitled "The Art of Russia 1800–1850," ran into trouble at the University of Michigan and in Washington at the Renwick Gallery.

Other countries also provided great exhibitions for the United States. Under its French-born director the Metropolitan Museum developed cooperation with France that resulted in two shows. One presented some of the fragments from Notre Dame in Paris, found in 1976 after having been removed, mutilated, and buried during the French Revolution. The second exhibition, "Greek Art of the Aegean Islands," brought together treasures from the Metropolitan, the Louvre, and Greek museums. Of the latter many were objects recently excavated and not before seen abroad.

The Gilbert Stuart Portraits Controversy. The familiar Gilbert Stuart portrait of George Washington suddenly became a cause célèbre when

it was learned that the Boston Athenaeum was contemplating its sale, together with the companion portrait of Martha Washington, to the Smithsonian Institute's National Portrait Gallery. The two paintings, acquired by the Athenaeum from the artist's widow and on loan to the Boston Museum of Fine Arts for over a century, are well known to all Americans, but the extent of the controversy stirred by the reports of a sale took everyone by surprise. The Athenaeum, a private library with a limited endowment, had sold some of its paintings, in recent years, without attracting any publicity. The Boston Museum had received the first offer to acquire these two pictures, and only after their refusal was the National Portrait Gallery approached, as it seemed the most suitable repository. Suddenly, not only Bostonians, but also Philadelphians and New Yorkers, claimed the paintings, citing historical or sentimental associations superior to Washington's. By year's end a final solution was not announced. Meanwhile, five Stuart portraits of American presidents, known as the Gibbs-Coolidge set and in the possession of a prominent Bostonian family since the 19th century, were acquired by the National Gallery without causing any comments or protests.

Art and Terrorism in Rome. Italy has been plagued by bomb and terrorist attacks for several years, but an April 20 attack on the Palace of the Senators on the Capitoline Hill marked the first time that one of its monuments was damaged. In the attack part of the façade of the palace was blown away, and cracks appeared in both flanking buildings. Large patches of frescoed ceiling fell, and many parts were loosened. The Capitol, which has been the center of civic life in Rome since antiquity, was redesigned by Michelangelo. Three palaces (housing municipal offices, halls for council meetings and ceremonial events, as well as the art collections of the Capitoline Museums); a piazza, with the antique bronze equestrian statue of the Roman Emperor Marcus Aurelius; and a monumental staircase leading up to it were built by the great Renaissance artist.

ISA RAGUSA, *Princeton University*

The Museum of Modern Art

The Museum of Modern Art (MoMA) celebrated its 50th anniversary in 1979. The Museum, 40,000 members strong, has an annual attendance of 1,200,000. In the past 50 years, 29,500,000 people have visited this collection of modern art's major accomplishments.

Continuing its recognition of the interrelationship of the visual arts, the Museum scheduled such special anniversary exhibits as *Transformations in Modern Architecture, Contemporary Sculpture: Selections from the Collection of The Museum of Modern Art, Ansel Adams and the West, Art of the Twenties, Printed Art Since 1965,* and *Pablo Picasso: A Retrospective.*

History. The Museum was founded in New York City in 1929 by seven patrons of the arts, of whom three, Lillie P. Bliss, Mrs. Cornelius J. Sullivan, and Abby Aldrich Rockefeller, were particularly influential. Its purpose was "to help people enjoy, understand, and use the visual arts of our time." Alfred H. Barr, Jr., who later published his famous monographs *Matisse: His Art and His Public* and *Picasso: Fifty Years of His Art,* was appointed the Museum's first director. Works of Cézanne, Gauguin, Seurat, and van Gogh made up the opening exhibition. Public acceptance was immediate, with attendance during the first month reaching 47,000. During the next decade the Museum expanded so rapidly that it relocated twice before completion of a new building at the present site on West 53d Street in May 1939. At the time of its dedication, President Franklin Roosevelt referred to the Museum as "a citadel of civilization."

In addition to collecting paintings and sculptures, drawings and prints, the Museum was a pioneer in recognizing photography, film, architecture, and design as important art forms of our time. This broad and innovative concept of the proper scope of a modern museum set examples followed by other institutions around the world.

In 1930, the first photograph (*Lehmbruck: Head of Man* by Walker Evans) was acquired for the collection, and the first photography exhibition was held in 1932. In 1940, the Department of Photography was established, the first such department in any museum. The Film Library (now the Department of Film) was founded in 1935. As the first international film archive, its work in preserving significant motion pictures and in fostering study and appreciation of film as a uniquely modern art has been enormously influential. The Department of Architecture and Design was also the first of its kind, and its programs have affected our landscape.

During its 50-year history, MoMA has collected and exhibited the works of such diverse artists as Ansel Adams, Luis Buñuel, Alexander Calder, Anthony Caro, Paul Cézanne, Marcel Duchamp, Buckminster Fuller, D. W. Griffith, Edward Hopper, Ellsworth Kelly, Sol LeWitt, Henri Matisse, Joan Miró, Piet Mondrian, Barnett Newman, Georgia O'Keeffe, Claes Oldenburg, Pablo Picasso, Jackson Pollock, Robert Rauschenberg, Edward Steichen, Frank Stella, Vincent van Gogh, Jacqueline Winsor, and Frank Lloyd Wright. Special shows have also had a wide-ranging scope: modern architecture, machine art, African Negro art, cubism and abstract art, contemporary film and photography, posters, furniture and textiles, and the auto.

The Museum has undergone considerable physical expansion during its 50 years. Important additions have been the Abby Aldrich Rockefeller Sculpture Garden, the Philip L. Goodwin Galleries for Architecture and Design, the Edward Steichen Photography Galleries, and the Paul J. Sachs Galleries for Drawings and Prints. In 1963, the Museum acquired the adjacent former Whitney Museum building.

Present Scope. The Museum's collections of painting, sculpture, drawings, prints, photography, film, architecture, and industrial and graphic design now number more than 100,000 items. Included are such master paintings as van Gogh's *The Starry Night,* Picasso's *Demoiselles d'Avignon,* and Jackson Pollock's *One* (*Number 31, 1950*).

The Department of Film, its archive housing some 8,000 films, programs cycles that range from retrospectives of distinguished directors to national and historical film surveys. The Department also circulates films from its collection to colleges and film societies throughout the United States. CINEPROBE, established in 1969, gives visitors the opportunity to investigate recent films by independent filmmakers who are present at the screenings to discuss their work. In recognition of the Museum's ongoing program of film preservation and its continuing support of the motion picture as an art form, the Academy of Motion Picture Arts and Sciences in 1979 presented an honorary Academy Award to its Department of Film.

The Museum maintains a 70,000 volume library. The Publications Department has issued more than 500 authoritative books and catalogs. The Education Department serves a diverse audience of students, scholars, and community groups.

Although the 50th anniversary presented a happy occasion on which to review the Museum's achievements, it was also recognized as a time of planning for the future, of meeting challenges and opportunities in some ways as great as those that confronted its founders in 1929. For, as President Roosevelt noted, The Museum of Modern Art is "a living museum."

RICHARD E. OLDENBURG

50 Years

Works of art that have special meaning for New York City's Museum of Modern Art (1929–79) include:

Pablo Picasso's *Les Demoiselles d'Avignon* **(1907)**

The sculpture of the Abby Aldrich Rockefeller Sculpture Garden

The Museum of Modern Art

50th Anniversary

Vincent Van Gogh's *The Starry Night* (1889)

Jackson Pollock's *Number One* (1948)

Marc Chagall's *I and the Village* (1911)

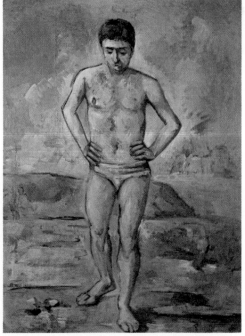

Paul Cézanne's *The Bather* (c. 1885)

Henri Matisse's *The Dance* (1909)

Vietnamese troops patrol near Pho Lu during Vietnam's 17-day war with China.

ASIA

War and peace curiously coexisted in the transition year of 1979 in Asia. On the whole, great power relations improved, but military quarrels among smaller states threatened to involve larger patron nations.

Mixed Beginning. The year began auspiciously for the United States, a major loser in the Vietnam War that ended with a Communist victory in 1975. Agreement was announced January 1 on the terms of continued U. S. use of the important Clark air and Subic Bay naval bases in the Philippines. The terms, including a pledge of $500 million in U. S. military and economic aid over five years, were reached late New Year's Eve.

January 1 also witnessed the establishment of normal diplomatic relations between China and the United States. Within the month, Chinese Deputy Premier Deng Xiaoping (Teng Hsiao-ping) visited the United States.

But war also greeted the advent of a new year. Seven days earlier, on December 25, Vietnam had invaded Cambodia. And by February 17, China and Vietnam, former allies, were fighting one another on Vietnamese soil. The new "Vietnam wars"—pitting Hanoi against China and those Cambodians unwilling to be subservient to the Vietnamese—underscored the importance of Sino-American rapprochement and the revalidated U. S. presence in the Philippines.

Cambodian Crisis. Vietnamese troops in a blitzkrieg-like invasion of Cambodia reached and captured the capital city of Phnom Penh by January 7. Although the Vietnamese have historically harbored designs on Cambodian territory, the 1978–79 attack was partly provoked by persistent Cambodian-initiated incidents along the two states' common border. The Chinese, allies of Cambodia, may have encouraged such activity in view of Vietnam's increasingly close ties with China's chief rival, the USSR. After the Chinese-leaning Pol Pot government was driven from office in January, the Vietnamese immediately substituted the puppet regime of Heng Samrin in its place. When the anti-Vietnamese Pol Pot Communists came to power in 1975, there were an estimated 8 million Cambodians. By the time Hanoi placed Heng Samrin in office, there were only 4.5 million. And, by the end of 1979, the possibility of the death of another two million—from famine, disease, or war—was real.

Approximately 100,000 Vietnamese troops took part in the Cambodian invasion, and these subsequently were joined by an additional 100,-000 in the face of continued resistance in the western extremities of the country. Vietnam and its protégé, Heng Samrin, initially opposed international relief assistance—apparently because of the fear that it would largely benefit resistance forces. The United States pledged $69 million in help and 34 other UN members promised another $130 million.

Sino-Vietnamese War. Vietnam's other war—with China—was a direct outcome of its invasion of Cambodia. Hanoi was a Soviet ally, and China supported, albeit reluctantly, the brutal Pol Pot Cambodian regime in an effort to contain the influence of the Soviet Union in Southeast Asia. Vietnam's conquest of Cambodia and the establishment of the Heng Samrin government were in Peking's eyes a major threat to China's national security.

The 17-day Sino-Vietnamese war began on February 17 as tens of thousands of Chinese troops crossed the border into Vietnam. An estimated 50,000 Vietnamese casualties were inflicted by the Chinese before they withdrew in March. But, while they probably taught the Vietnamese "a lesson," the announced intention of their attack, the Chinese did not force Hanoi to quit Cambodian soil.

Unquestionably China also made the point that Hanoi's ally, the USSR, was not able to prevent the death of a very substantial number of Vietnamese. Vietnam's attack against Cambodia was, more than anything else, a revival of historically rooted local imperialism. But China's response to the action reflected 20th century big power rivalries. Indochina had by no means settled down to a new status quo in 1979, and the Chinese invasion of Vietnam was viewed in many capitals as the first step in a new great-power struggle.

The Bloody Struggle. The struggle for power was also a bloody one in Afghanistan, Korea, and Pakistan.

President Carter's decision to suspend the withdrawal of U. S. ground troops from South Korea, announced in July, reflected the political-military instability in Southeast Asia. The South Korean government itself announced an increase of $500 million in military spending for 1980 (to $3.5 billion). The Korean situation, however, became suddenly uncertain in late October when President Park Chung Hee, Seoul's strong-armed ruler for 18 years, was assassinated by his own intelligence chief.

Violent death also figured in the brutal politics of Pakistan, where former Prime Minister Zulfikar Ali Bhutto died on the gallows in April for a political murder for which he may not have been responsible. His de facto hangman, President Zia-ul Haq, later in the year postponed general elections scheduled for November—reflecting his fear of lacking popular acceptance of his regime.

Not only did Muslim dissidents wage an escalating jihad (holy war) against a pro-Soviet government in Afghanistan, but death also played a prominent part in the jockeying for power among the country's Communist rulers. Communist President Nur Mohammed Taraki, who unseated non-Communist Mohammed Daud in 1978, died following a coup in Kabul that elevated rival Hafizullah Amin to the presidency. Hafizullah Amin was ousted and killed in late December. The Soviet-inspired coup and the large number of Soviet troops in Afghanistan were causing major concern as 1980 began.

Peaceful Politics. Jockeying for ascendency also was notable in Asia's three most important countries—China, India, and Japan.

Japan's Diet (lower house) reelected Masayoshi Ohira by a narrow 138–121 margin—raising questions about the durability of the Liberal-Democratic coalition that largely has governed the country since the end of the American occupation. In India, the badly splintered Janata Party, in power since 1977, came to an end, and Indira Gandhi campaigned to return to office in elections planned for January 1980.

China's internal politics were also outwardly peaceful, but force was clearly implied in the continuing campaign against "Maoist" influences. Deputy Premier Deng Xiaoping gained near-complete control of the top levels of the Chinese government as a result of the National People's Congress in June–July. Student, peasant, and anti-military demonstrations, however, suggested that the Deng-Premier Hua Guofeng (Hua Kuofeng) duumvirate presided over a far from fully stabilized Chinese polity.

U. S.-USSR. The Soviet Union seemed to lose more than it gained in Asia in 1979. China announced that it would not renew its friendship treaty with the USSR when it expired in 1980, and Japan took serious exception to Moscow's efforts to expand its military presence in the northern islands taken from the Japanese in the late days of World War II. The Soviets and the Chinese failed to agree on an agenda for Moscow talks aimed at improving relations between the two countries. Afghanistan, moreover, gave evidence of becoming the Soviet Union's "Vietnam," as Moscow increased its support of the Communist Kabul government fighting Muslim insurrectionists. And, while its ally Vietnam seemed to be successful in its invasion of Cambodia, the USSR was not able to deter China from attacking the Vietnamese.

The United States, for its part, consolidated its relationship with China, Japan, the Philippines, South Korea, and Thailand. In particular, it dramatically expanded its aid to Thailand in the wake of a growing Vietnamese presence in neighboring Cambodia. The United States failed, however, to stimulate American-South Korean-North Korean diplomatic talks. And Washington's ties with Pakistan visibly weakened following the Bhutto execution, the discontinuance of United States developmental aid due to the Pakistani government's construction of a nuclear plant capable of producing weapons, and the late November attack on the U. S. embassy in Islamabad (in which two Americans died).

RICHARD BUTWELL, *Murray State University*

UPI

A Hong Kong police launch guides the freighter, *Skyluck*, jammed with Vietnamese refugees, to a dock.

ASIA—SPECIAL REPORT:

The Indochinese Refugees

In 1979 the plight of the Indochinese refugees became a source of major world concern, first with the dramatic increase in "boat people" fleeing persecution in Vietnam, and later with the influx into Thailand of Cambodians fleeing war and famine in Cambodia (Kampuchea).

The prospect of continuing waves of refugees led some of the governments in the surrounding region to take the desperate measure of refusing to grant even temporary asylum to the Indochinese. The result was mounting loss of life, chaotic camp conditions, and threats to the stability of the region.

The international community took steps to increase assistance to the political refugees and famine victims, ease the burden of the Southeast Asian countries of first asylum, and discourage the regimes of Indochina from pursuing the policies that contributed to the refugee outflow. Nonetheless, by the end of 1979, food and medical relief were reaching only a fraction of the needy Cambodians, and about 310,000 other Indochinese were still in UN-sponsored refugee camps awaiting offers of permanent resettlement.

Background. The largest previous exodus of Indochinese refugees was in 1975, following the fall of the governments of South Vietnam, Laos, and Cambodia. At that time, about 135,000 Indochinese, mostly Vietnamese, were admitted to the United States, and thousands more were accepted by other countries such as France, Canada, and Australia. After the first wave of refugees, a steady but small number of Indochinese continued to flee the new communist regimes and to find temporary asylum in Southeast Asia. However, none of the first-asylum countries would resettle the Indochinese permanently. They insisted that the rest of the world must assume the burden of refugee resettlement.

In response, the United Nations High Commissioner for Refugees (UNHCR) established programs to care for the Indochinese where they sought refuge (principally Thailand, Malaysia, Indonesia, Hong Kong, and the Philippines) and to provide legal protection for them until they could be resettled elsewhere. Although other Western countries also responded to appeals for assistance, the United States accepted

After landing in Manila, the Philippines, boat people acquire temporary living quarters along Manila Bay.

almost twice as many Indochinese as the rest of the world combined.

In the autumn of 1978, a deterioration of political and economic conditions in the countries of Indochina led to an upsurge in the refugee flow, particularly among the ethnic Chinese. For generations, ethnic Chinese had lived in urban areas of Indochina as merchants and professionals. They were traditionally mistrusted because of their adherence to their own culture and language, and they were among the first victims of efforts by Communist authorities to eliminate urban commercial and professional classes. As tensions rose between Vietnam and China in 1978, the Vietnamese also came to see the ethnic Chinese as a security threat. Because of systematic discrimination, almost 200,000 ethnic Chinese fled to China before Chinese authorities closed the border. The Vietnamese then gave the remaining ethnic Chinese the choice of banishment to bleak and undeveloped "new economic zones" or "assisted departures" from Vietnam by boat, for which they would have to pay in gold. The Vietnamese also increased discrimination against ethnic Chinese in the areas of Laos and Cambodia.

Increasingly, the Chinese chose to flee these intolerable conditions. Joining this exodus of "boat people" were also many ethnic Vietnamese who had to escape secretly or pretend they were of Chinese origin. Coincidentally, a steady stream of refugees entered Thailand overland from Laos and Cambodia, fleeing persecution and expanding Vietnamese control.

The exodus by boat and land reached crisis proportions during the spring of 1979. In the month of May alone, 65,000 Indochinese arrived in first-asylum countries. In the face of these numbers, Malaysia, Indonesia, and Thailand hardened their policies of granting asylum and threatened to expel new arrivals and even some refugees already in camps.

Geneva Conference. In response to mounting international concern and the requests of first-asylum countries for help, UN Secretary General Kurt Waldheim convened an international meeting in Geneva in July to focus on the Indochinese refugee crisis. Some 60 governments attended the conference and pledged almost $200 million to the efforts of the UNHCR. They also provided offers of permanent resettlement for about 260,000 Indochinese over

PHOTOS UPI

Refugees of varying ages endure a difficult journey aboard an overcrowded boat. Their immediate goal is a refugee center, such as the one in the Philippines (left).

UPI

Flimsy shelters, offering little protection from the weather, are common at a first-asylum center in Malaysia.

the following 18 months (as compared with 120,000 resettlement opportunities available only three months before). Vice President Walter Mondale repeated President Carter's earlier commitment that the United States would double its resettlement rate from 7,000 to 14,000 Indochinese refugees a month, for a total of 168,000 in the following fiscal year. The Vietnamese, bowing to international pressure, informed Secretary General Waldheim that they would try to stem the refugee flow from Vietnam for an indefinite period of time and would cooperate with the UNHCR to establish a means of "orderly departure" of people from Vietnam.

The Vietnamese moratorium on departures of ethnic Chinese resulted in an immediate decline in arrivals of "boat people" in first-asylum countries (down to 2,500 in November 1979). Land escapes from Laos also declined. The simultaneous increase in departures for resettlement countries reduced camp populations and eased political tension in Southeast Asia.

Cambodian Refugees. At the same time, however, the deteriorating situation within Cambodia contributed to a new outpouring of Cambodian refugees into Thailand and again brought international attention to the suffering of the Indochinese. This new dimension of the refugee problem stemmed primarily from the Vietnamese invasion and occupation of Cambodia

that began in December 1978. The invasion followed almost four years of brutal rule by the Pol Pot regime, during which perhaps two million of the 1975 population of seven to eight million were executed or died of starvation or disease. Although the Vietnamese who overthrew Pol Pot were originally greeted as liberators, their harsh policies and military operations resulted in further population dislocation and hindered the rice harvest and distribution.

By July there was evidence of widespread food shortages, and international relief organizations began negotiations for the delivery of badly needed food and medical supplies with the two groups contesting control over Cambodia. By the time the first supplies arrived in Cambodia in October, thousands of additional Cambodians had crossed into Thailand in search of food and medical care, and additional hundreds of thousands were massing in abject condition on the Thai-Cambodian border. International organizations such as UNICEF and the International Committee of the Red Cross began massive deliveries to Cambodia. But much of the supplies remained in warehouses because the authorities were preoccupied with the continuing civil war, and services essential to a distribution system—roads, railroads, and communications—remained in poor condition.

VICTOR PALMIERI
U. S. Coordinator for Refugee Affairs

ASTRONOMY

Although the most spectacular developments related to astronomy in 1979 may have been the close inspection of the planet Jupiter by the spacecrafts Voyager I and II, other astronomical news may be of even more lasting importance.

Instruments. On board the second High Energy Astronomical Observatory, which was launched in late 1978 and named the Einstein Observatory, is an X-ray telescope (the Einstein telescope) which is a thousand times more effective than previous X-ray instruments. It forms images by the use of grazing incidence optics that consist of four concentric sets of parabolic and hyberbolic cylinders. The total effective aperture is 58 cm; it achieves a 3″ resolution with a 1° field of view. The system functions best in the soft X-ray region (0.25–4 keV, i.e. 50A–3A).

The Multiple Mirror Telescope (MMT), a joint project of the Smithsonian Astrophysical Observatory and the University of Arizona, was put into operation at the Mt. Hopkins Observatory in Arizona. The Canadian-French-Hawaiian 1.85 meter telescope, atop Mauna Kea, Hawaii (20° N latitude), was completed. The new Russian RATAN-600 radio telescope consists of a circular array (diameter equals 576 m) of 895 panels (each 2 m x 7.4 m) with various detectors to cover a wavelength range of 8 mm to 20 cm.

Eclipses. A total solar eclipse was seen in northwestern United States on February 26. It was the last one that will be seen in the United States during the twentieth century. The track passed from north Oregon to Manitoba, Canada. Successful observations were obtained in several sites. An annular solar eclipse was seen as a partial eclipse in South America on August 22, and the associated lunar eclipse was seen in western North America on September 6.

Venus. Pioneer Venus I, which began orbiting the planet on Dec. 4, 1978, included an orbiter and five separate probes that entered the atmosphere at different places. Also in December 1978, two Russian probes descended to the surface of the planet, obtaining evidence of lightning discharges en route. Although the size and mass of Venus are similar to earth's, Venus shows little other resemblance. It rotates from east to west instead of west to east as do earth and most other planets; with a period of about 243 days, its solar day is about 117 earth days. Its dense atmosphere is composed almost entirely of carbon dioxide which exerts a surface pressure of 91 earth atmospheres. There are two principal cloud decks which totally obscure the surface, where the level of illumination is akin to that of an overcast day on earth. The upper cloud deck, cresting at 63 km, consists mostly of small liquid droplets with a diameter of about 1 micron. It reflects back about half the impinging sunlight. The haze thins out slightly from 58 km to 52 km; there is a dense

cloud layer extending down to 48 km. Then the atmosphere is relatively clear to the surface. The clouds consist mostly of sulfuric acid droplets, but intricate reactions occur among carbon oxide (CO), water (H_2O), oxygen (O), and free sulfur. The surface of Venus is not smooth.

Saturn. In early September, the Pioneer II probe reached Saturn. It detected a faint outer ring, corroborated the existence of an eleventh satellite, and found the temperature of the cloud tops of Titan to be about −200° C (−392° F). The magnetic field of Saturn is about half that of the earth and appears to be aligned well with the axis of rotation.

Stars. Ultraviolet and X-ray observations showed that highly ionized and excited structures, akin to the outer solar envelopes, i.e. the chromosphere and corona, also exist in cool stars, hot luminous stars, and some dwarf stars. In the sun, strong winds blow from coronal holes along magnetic lines of force. Similar winds may occur in other stars. Although accretion binaries are the strongest sources of energy, the X-ray emission from hot O-stars may rival the entire energy output of the sun.

Startling X-ray Observations. By opening a new window in the domain of high energy astrophysics, X rays have revealed startling insights. For example, it has been found that the η Carinae nebula is filled with an X-ray glow from hot interstellar gas, presumably of supernova origin. The shells (but not any remnant neutron stars) of Cass A and Tycho's supernova appear. In the Cass A shell, X-ray lines of magnesium (Mg), silicon (Si), sulfur (S), calcium (CA), and argon (AR) show an enhanced abundance due to element building in supernovae. Observations of nearby galaxies reveal discrete X-ray sources, e.g. the nucleus and four globular clusters. X-ray activity ranges from a very low level in "normal" galaxies to high levels in quasars. In clusters, such as Virgo, X-ray emission tends to be concentrated around individual galaxies. The chemical composition of the heated gas resembles that of the sun. The material is not primordial but has been processed through stars. X-ray luminosities as high as 10^{10}–10^{13} that of the sun have been observed. Sometimes, the emissions are variable, e.g. OX 169 varied by a factor of 2 in 3 hours, which implies that an associated black hole must have a mass exceeding 2 million suns. Earlier measurements revealed a general X-ray sky background. With deep exposures the Einstein satellite revealed point sources emerging from the background. Perhaps all of this general radiation comes from discrete sources (mostly quasars). The cosmological implication is that there is not enough matter to "close" the universe. The bizarre object SS 433 was catalogued by Nicolas Sanduleak and Charles Stephenson as #433 on their list. It is a faint (14th^{mag}) "star" variable optically, in radio range, and in X rays. From interstellar extinction, its distance was estimated as 11,000 light years. Spectroscopic observations by B. Margon and associates at UCLA and Lick Observatory showed that although one set of lines remained stationary, two other sets showed rapid shifts in opposite directions, fitting sinusoidal curves with a period of 164 days. What is striking is the size of the shifts, exceeding those of any other galactic object. The data are fitted by a model of a spinning, precessing object that emits 2 well-collimated beams of hot material with a velocity of 81,000 km/sec. The energy carried by each particle is about 30 MeV. A Russian astrophysicist, Skhlovsky, interpreted the object as a pulsar spinning with a period of .001 seconds.

Gravity Waves? During 1979, the centennial of Albert Einstein's birth, further evidence emerged in support of his predictions. P. McCulloch (University of Tasmania) and Joseph Taylor and L. Fowler of the University of Massachusetts clocked a remarkable binary pulsar, PSR 1913 + 16, which emits a sharp pulse every 0.059[s]. This pulsar (fast spinning neutron star) moves in an 8-hour orbit about its companion with a velocity of 300 km/sec. General relativity predicts that the system should lose energy by radiation of gravity waves. The observers succeeded in measuring a tiny slowdown, evidence in favor of gravity waves!

LAWRENCE H. ALLER, *University of California*

AUSTRALIA

Australia experienced a year of sharpened political contention as well as of mixed economic fortunes, including unrelieved price advances, 6% unemployment, a hesitant though improved economic growth rate, and greater business confidence. Wages rose slightly less than prices, and a favorable balance-of-payments current account and a buoyant capital inflow helped encourage stock market gains.

Economic Policy. In fiscal 1979 a ballooning federal deficit and excessive growth in the money supply impaired Prime Minister Malcolm Fraser's drive to curb inflation, but the gains elsewhere were promising: gross domestic product up 4.7% (with gross farm product up 36% and nonfarm product up 2.8%). Capital expenditures rose slightly, with house-building up from earlier depressed levels, but growth in retail sales was sluggish. A high savings rate was maintained. There was a noticeable increase in unemployment among young people, especially those seeking their first jobs, and among women.

Measures adopted in May dampened growth and expectations by introducing a stiff tax on local crude oil (to skim off company gains as local prices moved closer to world parity) and by extending the operation of personal income tax surcharges through November. The August budget further lessened inflation pressures and provided supports for the balance-of-payments position. Strengthened efforts to restrain growth in the volume of money and to curb pressures on

―――― **AUSTRALIA · Information Highlights** ――――
Official Name: Commonwealth of Australia.
Location: Southwestern Pacific Ocean.
Area: 2,967,900 square miles (7 686 861 km[2]).
Population (1979 est.): 14,400,000.
Chief Cities (1977 est.): Canberra, the capital, 228,040; Sydney, 3,121,800; Melbourne, 2,694,100.
Government: *Head of state,* Elizabeth II, queen; represented by Sir Zelman Cowen, governor general (took office December 1977). *Head of government,* Malcolm Fraser, prime minister (took office December 1975). *Legislature*—Parliament: Senate and House of Representatives.
Monetary Unit: Australian dollar (0.90 A. dollar equals U.S.$1, Oct. 1979).
Manufactures (major products): Motor vehicles, iron and steel, textiles, chemicals.
Agriculture (major products): Cereals, sugarcane, fruits, wine grapes, sheep, cattle, dairy products.

interest rates were major elements of the budget's deflationary thrust; revenue was set to rise 15% and outlays 9.4%. The stock market applauded the budget with a strong advance, especially in the mining sector.

As well as pursuing its policy of reducing inflation, the government continued to move toward a more traditional balance of income share between wages and profits. Wage-earners (who did well in the mid-1970's) slipped, while business profits (which had suffered a decline for years) showed clear gains.

Political Developments. Within Labor, differences polarized members around Australian Labor Party parliamentary leader Bill Hayden and the president of the Australian Council of Trade Unions, Robert J. Hawke. At the ALP triennial conference in July Hayden sided with the left on some key issues, while Hawke had less success in defending his pragmatic views on these and other policy matters. At a follow-up ACTU congress, Hawke lost ground when a more militant group gained congressional endorsement for its uncompromising policies on uranium (a ban on all mining as well as on nuclear power use), wages (pressure for maximum increase), and technology (a demand for compensation for "lost" jobs that would, if applied, effectively block the introduction of labor-saving equipment). Hawke's subsequent emergence as a candidate for parliament came after opinion polls showed that he could expect strong popular support in any challenge for ALP parliamentary leadership.

In the non-Labor parties, policy differences surfaced between Liberals and members of the National Party, especially in the key states of Queensland and Victoria. In part the discord stemmed from growing differences in economic thrust and in part from city/rural tensions.

A leading National Party member, Ian Sinclair, resigned his portfolio of primary industry after a damaging report by an investigator appointed by the New South Wales Labor administration which dealt with irregularities concerning a family company run by Sinclair's father (who died in 1976). The inquiry was not a public one but the report was made public in the New South Wales parliament, and the prime minister and others immediately accused Labor of base political motives in the matter. Subsequently, court proceedings were initiated against Sinclair.

State elections showed mixed trends: in Tasmania Labor's position strengthened, in Victoria the Liberals won a narrow victory, and in South Australia Labor suffered a sharp defeat.

Trade and Foreign Affairs. A government-sponsored report on the nation's manufacturing industries explored existing trade barriers as well as opportunities for Australia's participation in the rapid growth occurring in some Asian economies.

In foreign affairs, discussion centered on a government-appointed committee's paper, *Australia and the Third World*, which recommended that Australia's public stance on many issues should be less oriented to supporting the viewpoint of its Western allies and should move closer to the nations of the region.

The Mining Industry. Most mining companies reported improved prospects arising from metal price increases, and shares in gold-mining enterprises were keenly sought. Important new coal and uranium mining activities were initiated in spite of demonstrations by antinuclear power activists. A feature of the financial scene was the spate of mergers and takeovers, including many that involved mining companies.

Considerable media attention was given to a conference organized by the Australian Mining Industry Council to air problems. Industry leaders urged more responsible labor attitudes in order to put an end to strike-engendered delays in ore output and delivery, and they also criticized government intervention in the affairs of ore traders. A general complaint was that average profit margins of mining enterprises were too low, and the government was urged to offer incentives that would stimulate the search for oil and other energy sources.

A National Milestone. Although expenditure on public works was generally out of favor, the government decided to go ahead with construction of a $170 million Parliament House in Canberra.

R. M. YOUNGER, *Author,*
Australia and The Australians

AUSTRIA

In 1979 attention in Austria focused on national and local elections and on important international conferences held in Vienna. The economy showed strong signs of improvement.

Politics. On Jan. 11, 1979, the government announced that national elections would be held May 6. Provincial elections in Lower Austria and Salzburg on March 25 brought the Socialist Party significant gains. Chancellor Bruno Kreisky conducted a vigorous national campaign and was elected to an unprecedented fourth term by a surprising margin. His Socialist Party won 95

seats in parliament, increasing by two its representation in the 183-member body. The conservative opposition People's Party won 77 seats, a loss of two, and the right-wing Freedom Party took 11 seats. After the formal resignation of the cabinet on May 9, Kreisky was asked to form a new administration. On June 5 the same cabinet was sworn in again. In the aftermath of the election, Joseph Taus resigned as head of the People's Party and was replaced by Alois Mock, the party's parliamentary leader.

Economic Developments. The Austrian economy was one of the most stable in Europe during 1979. A midyear inflation rate of only 3.3% and an unemployment figure of only 2.2% were a boon to the reelection campaign of Chancellor Kreisky. Exports continued to increase during 1979, but a steady rise in imports caused the national trade deficit, which had been reduced in 1978, to expand. Still, economic growth was estimated at 3.5% for 1979, compared with 1.5% the year before.

Foreign Affairs. Austrian President Rudolf Kirchschläger acted as host to U. S. President Jimmy Carter and Soviet President Leonid Brezhnev during their meeting in Vienna, June 15–18, for the signing of the SALT II agreement. Chancellor Kreisky and former West German Chancellor Willy Brandt, acting as vice president and president respectively of the Socialist International (the organization of Western socialist parties) conferred in Vienna with Yasir Arafat, leader of the Palestine Liberation Organization (PLO), July 6–8. The three men issued a communiqué expressing "extreme concern" over Israeli settlements on the West Bank and over the fighting in Lebanon. Israel issued a sharp protest to the Austrian government, but it was rejected as "an interference in Austrian internal affairs."

On August 23, the United Nations formally took over the $55-million office and conference complex known as the Vienna International Center. The complex, which already housed the International Atomic Energy Agency and the UN Industrial Development Organization, was built by the Austrian government and is rented to the UN for one schilling (7.5 cents, U. S.) per year.

ERNST C. HELMREICH
Bowdoin College

——————AUSTRIA • Information Highlights ——————
Official Name: Republic of Austria.
Location: Central Europe.
Area: 32,376 square miles (83 853 km²).
Population (1979 est.): 7,500,000.
Chief Cities (1975 est.): Vienna, the capital, 1,650,000; Graz, 253,000; Linz, 207,000; Salzburg, 132,000.
Government: *Head of state,* Rudolf Kirchschläger, president (took office July 1974). *Head of government,* Bruno Kreisky, chancellor (took office April 1970). *Legislature*—Federal Assembly: Federal Council and National Council.
Monetary Unit: Schilling (12.99 schillings equal U. S.$1, Oct. 1979).
Manufactures (major products): Iron and steel, chemicals, capital equipment, consumer goods.
Agriculture (major products): Livestock, dairy products, grains, barley, oats, corn, sugar beets, potatoes.

Lee Iacocca (*left*) and John Riccardo, president and chairman of the board of Chrysler Corp., respectively, meet with the press after requesting federal assistance to help overcome Chrysler's financial losses.

UPI

AUTOMOBILES

Fuel shortages increased sales of smaller "fuel-efficient" vehicles and reduced demand for full-size and intermediate cars, as well as light trucks and utility vehicles. Primarily affected by the sudden shift in market preferences were the Big Three—General Motors, Ford Motor Co., and Chrysler Corp.—and the situation became so critical for Chrysler that it sought federal loan guarantees or tax credits from the federal government to help overcome severe financial losses.

Actually, a political revolution in Iran and subsequent gasoline-supply shortfalls in the United States accelerated the trend toward lighter and more economical vehicles. Weight reductions of up to 1,000 pounds (454 kg) in the largest American-made cars had begun in the fall of 1976—a full year before every auto manufacturer or importer was required to meet a Federal Corporate Average Fuel Economy (CAFE) standard of 18 miles (29 km) per gallon. The CAFE advanced to 19 miles (30.5 km) per gallon on 1979 models and to 20 miles (32 km) per gallon on 1980 models, accompanying massive "downsizing" and weight shrinkage programs and facilitating the growth in use of four-cylinder engines and manual transmissions.

Setting the industry's pace in development of small cars was GM, which began production of new front-wheel-drive compacts (called the GM X cars after their code name) in April 1979. GM "downsized" its largest cars 2½ years earlier and its intermediates 1½ years earlier, not only leading its competition in each case but raising its share of production and sales to close to 60% in the 1979 model year.

The 1979-model run totaled 9,613,727 cars, a 6.9% rise from the previous model production of 8,995,418. GM assembled 5,530,943 cars in the '79-model run, up 5.5%; Ford Motor, 2,-752,978, a gain of 11%; Chrysler Corp., 1,027,-

545, off 9.4%; and American Motors, 169,439, up 23.4%. Volkswagen's new assembly plant in Pennsylvania built 132,822 Rabbit subcompacts.

Truck demand was less affected by the gasoline shortage. A total of 2,757,000 trucks were built in the first nine months of 1979, compared with 2,490,000 for the same period of 1978. Truck output in the '78-model run had set a record of 4 million units.

The full-sized Chevrolet dropped 19% in sales from the 1978-model year, but once again was easily the top-selling U. S. model.

Five of the top ten sellers were Chevrolet models, two were Oldsmobiles, and three were Fords. Only one, the Chevrolet Chevette, was a subcompact and three, including the new front-wheel-drive Chevrolet Citation, were compacts.

Chevrolet widened its margin over Ford as the number 1 seller despite Ford's introduction

WORLD MOTOR VEHICLE DATA 1978

Country	Passenger Car Production	Truck and Bus Production	Motor Vehicle Registration
Argentina	134,118	45,757	3,900,000
Australia	355,683	29,322	6,900,000
Austria	...	2,541	2,320,000
Belgium	28,000	23,754	3,431,725
Brazil	535,442	526,755	8,700,000
Canada	1,139,263	667,839	12,800,000
Czechoslovakia	162,820	46,169	2,180,986
France	3,111,380	396,550	21,330,000
East Germany	170,000	41,000	3,000,000
West Germany	3,890,176*	296,188	23,196,156
Hungary	...	15,973	1,026,100
India	33,886	64,538	1,889,245
Italy	1,508,669	147,502	19,313,999
Japan	5,975,968	3,293,185	34,120,734
Mexico	242,519	141,608	4,212,000
Netherlands	51,617	8,714	4,197,000
Poland	328,000	80,000	2,200,000
Portugal	...	592	1,102,500
Rumania	72,000	40,000	500,000
Spain	986,116	157,715	7,826,652
Sweden	254,256	51,278	3,041,638
Switzerland	...	1,050	2,218,442
United Kingdom	1,282,987	384,518	15,941,000
United States	9,176,635	3,722,567	146,775,000**
USSR	1,312,000	839,000	12,800,000
Yugoslavia	252,075	27,684	2,358,966
World total	31,255,610	11,051,799	367,450,000

* Includes 264,675 micro-buses. ** U.S. total includes 116,395,000 cars and 30,380,000 trucks and buses. Source: Motor Vehicle Manufacturers Association of the United States, Inc.

in the fall of 1978 of restyled full-size LTD and Mustang subcompact series. Another GM division, Oldsmobile, topped 1 million sales for the second year in a row.

Ford division's top-selling makes were the compact Fairmont and subcompact Mustang. Similarly, Chrysler Corp.'s most popular nameplates were its compacts, the Dodge Aspen and Plymouth Volare, and its subcompacts, the Dodge Omni and Plymouth Horizon. AMC's only gainer in '79 sales was a subcompact, the Spirit. Luxury makes—Cadillac, Lincoln, and Chrysler—fell in sales as a result of the swing to more economical vehicles. A boon for Cadillac and Oldsmobile was the availability of a fuel-saving diesel engine.

The 1980 Models. The season began early when GM staged a spring introduction of its '80 front-wheel-drive compacts—the Chevrolet Citation, Pontiac Phoenix, Oldsmobile Omega, and Buick Skylark. The only other major 1980 styling change by GM came in the Cadillac Seville, which was equipped with front-wheel drive for the first time and was assigned a diesel engine as standard equipment. With only its full-size cars reduced in weight, GM turned to economy-engine moves in 1980 as its main efforts to meet the 20-mile (32 km)-per-gallon corporate average. Diesel engines were offered on large GM models.

Midsize cars were restyled and reduced in poundage by Ford and Chrysler Corp. Ford chopped 800 pounds (363 kg) from the '80 Lincoln. The midsize Dodge Mirada replaced the Magnum and a full-size Gran Fury was restored to the Plymouth lineup. AMC introduced the domestic industry's first four-wheel-drive car—the Eagle, a derivative of its compact Concord. An automatic transmission with overdrive was pioneered by Ford—another fuel economy move.

Imported Cars. After a slow start because of steep price increases ascribed to foreign-currency revaluations, imports surged to new record levels. Japanese makes were the primary beneficiaries of the boom.

For the first nine months of 1979, import sales reached 1,817,000 cars and 300,000 mini-pickup trucks. During the months between May and September foreign-built cars accounted for about 22% of the U. S. new-car market. Toyota maintained its leading sales position, up 8% to 388,000 cars for the January–September period; Datsun was next, up 31%; Honda, third, up 24%; Mazda, fourth, up 111%.

Nine European makes, stressing front-wheel drive and diesel or four-cylinder engines, also showed higher sales in 1979. GM discontinued import of its Japanese-built Opel and AMC took over marketing of the French-made Renault. Toyota introduced its first front-drive model, the subcompact Tercel. Datsun restyled its 200ZX sports coupe, and VW offered an imported Rabbit convertible.

MAYNARD M. GORDON, *"Motor News Analysis"*

BANGLADESH

Although many of the usual problems remained unsolved, 1979 was a relatively quiet and uneventful year for Bangladesh.

Internal Politics. Those who monitor "human rights" agreed that Bangladesh had improved its position. To some degree, this was the result of the success of the parliamentary elections held in February. That President Ziaur Rahman's Bangladesh Nationalist Party won two thirds of the seats was less surprising than that there was an election at all—one, moreover, that permitted opposition parties to run. The Awami League won 40 seats. This was in contrast to Pakistan (of which Bangladesh was once a part) where its strong man, a general named Zia, canceled not only elections scheduled for year's end, but "western-style democracy" as well.

General Ziaur of Bangladesh remained popular. He claimed to have released the bulk of the political prisoners. And in April he announced the end of martial law, which had been in effect since 1975. Undoubtedly the Bangladesh economy had improved, although jute still claimed 50% of export revenues. Increased food production has been a victory for the government. Although there has been little success in controlling the increase in a population of 87 million people, reliance on food imports declined by some 50%. Some exotic foods—for example, frogs legs—have been exported.

Large numbers of skilled Bangladesh workers were lured to the Persian Gulf for work in one of the oil-rich states. Although the government, eager for the foreign exchange remittances sent home to families in Bangladesh, did not discourage the exit, the departure of so many (perhaps 100,000) skilled workers put a severe strain on domestic industry. The exit also made it even more difficult to absorb efficiently foreign aid (estimated at $1.2 billion in 1979).

Foreign Affairs. The issue of the Burmese Muslim refugees in Bangladesh seemed to have run its course, with most refugees repatriated to Burma. Bangladesh and India announced a series of agreements regarding allocation of irrigation waters, boundary adjustments, demarcation of offshore oil exploration, and trade.

CARL LEIDEN, *The University of Texas*

—— **BANGLADESH • Information Highlights** ——

Official Name: People's Republic of Bangladesh.
Location: South Asia.
Area: 55,126 square miles (142 776 km²).
Population (1979 est.): 87,100,000.
Chief Cities (1974 census): Dacca, the capital, 1,310,-972; Khulna, 436,000; Chittagong, 416,733.
Government: *Head of state,* Ziaur Rahman, president (took office April 1977). *Head of government,* Shah Azizur Rahman, prime minister (took office April 1979). *Legislature*—Parliament.
Monetary Unit: Taka (15.12 takas equal U. S.$1, June 1979).
Manufactures (major products): Jute products, cotton textiles, processed foods, wood products.
Agriculture (major products): Rice, sugarcane, tea, oilseeds, pulses.

BANKING

The year 1979 saw continued flux in the operations of American banks and in the role the banks play in regulating economic activity.

Basically the trend toward broader powers for all financial institutions continued unabated. Banks pushed for new ways to serve their customers through the introduction of automatic transfer service, which allows money to move automatically from checking to savings accounts and in effect gives the saver interest on checking.

Saving banks and savings and loans associations pushed for growth of their Remote Service Units. Such service gives customers the interest return that thrift accounts offer plus the convenience of being able to move money in and out of the accounts at such accessible locations as supermarkets. And credit unions developed further their share drafts, which actually do offer interest on checking accounts.

Finally, however, the U. S. Court of Appeals stated that Congress must specifically authorize the above mentioned services, which had only been approved by regulators, or the financial institutions would have to stop offering them at the end of the year.

Thus the likelihood was that all financial institutions would be given broader powers by Congress to offer interest on checking in the same manner that banks and thrifts in the six New England states and New York are authorized to offer their NOW (negotiable order of withdrawal) accounts.

But while the public was likely to gain this added bank service, all financial institutions were becoming more selective in their pricing of services. They were not so anxious to be all things to all people, and they were more willing to sacrifice their image of friendliness to gain higher service charges, higher minimum balances, and more profits from their accounts.

The profits squeeze that made the sharper pricing necessary was also leading to greater acceptance of automated banking, through electronic tellers, use of point of sale terminals, and telephonic transfer of funds, as banks tried to reduce the ever soaring cost of personnel. This too was making both banks and thrift institutions less friendly in image but more efficient in operation.

Behind the profits squeeze was the rapid rise in interest rates. For with banks limited to paying 5.25% on passbook savings and thrift institutions limited to 5.5%, while open market interest rates have soared above 10%, banks and thrift institutions had to rely more on high cost money market certificates. On top of this, some $35 billion left the banks and was invested in money market mutual funds.

And while most financial people agreed that high cost deposits were better than no deposits, they also recognized that they must improve the efficiency of their operations to be able to pay the costs of competing for money at rates of 10% or higher.

To add to this pressure, at the end of the year, the Federal Reserve announced that it would place its anti-inflationary emphasis on controlling the money supply no matter how high interest rates rose. The Fed not only sharply increased its discount rate (i.e. the interest it charges to banks), but it also took steps to prevent banks from increasing borrowing. These steps created an even greater squeeze on bank profits. They meant that deposit funds bought from the public at going rates would cost even more, while much of bank and savings institution portfolios were locked into mortgages and consumer loans whose yields do not rise as rapidly as costs of bank funds do.

Thus bankers and thrift executives were becoming much more selective in offering loans and in soliciting high cost deposits. They were striving to match asset maturities and liability maturities better, even if it meant less aggressiveness in serving the public.

While the Federal Reserve's restraint measures were costly to banking, most bankers applauded them. For they recognized that continuation of a rate of inflation approaching 15% could lead to even sharper declines in savings.

And financial people recognized that if the public is so worried about inflation that most people spend their money rather than save, then the banking system and the economy are both likely to experience drastic and unpleasant changes.

Thus 1979 was a year of less friendly bankers, bankers more anxious to pull in their horns, and bankers and thrift executives worried about what inflation was doing to their profits and to the health of the economy.

Bankers also believed that they were the chosen instrument of the Federal Reserve as it tried to slow inflation and that they would feel the restraint more than any other group in the economy. But as 1979 ended bankers hoped that the Federal Reserve's actions would lead to less inflation, better real rewards for savers, and a dollar whose value could be depended upon again both at home and abroad.

Canada. Due to "a rapidly increasing demand for money and credit in Canada," the Bank of Canada raised its bank rate (the interest rate the central bank charges on loans to chartered banks) nine times during the first nine months of the year, in an anti-inflationary move similar to that in the United States.

Legislation to approve long delayed revisions of the Bank Act, allowing foreign-owned banks to operate more freely in Canada, establishing branches, and providing banking services now restricted to Canadian banks, neared enactment.

See also feature article (pages 25–28); CANADA: Economy; UNITED STATES: Economy.

PAUL S. NADLER
Rutgers—The State University of New Jersey

BELGIUM

Nearly six months of political disarray came to an end April 2, 1979, when Belgian King Baudouin announced the formation of a new government coalition. Since October 1978, when former Prime Minister Leo Tindemans submitted the resignation of his ministry, the country had been run by the caretaker government of Paul Vanden Boeynants.

The new five-party coalition was headed by 42-year-old Wilfried Martens, president of the Flemish branch of the Social Christian party. Martens was sworn in as prime minister April 3. The other four parties in the coalition are the French-speaking Social Christians, the Flemish Socialists, the French-speaking Socialists, and the French-speaking Democratic Front. Boeynants remained in the government as deputy premier.

A plan to create separate assemblies and executive agencies for Dutch-speaking Flanders, French-speaking Wallonia, and bilingual Brussels continued to be a sensitive political issue in 1979. A new language legislation package, called the Egmont Pact, was the most comprehensive proposal for regional autonomy since the formation of modern Belgium in 1830. Although Martens put together his cabinet with that issue in mind, economic policy still gained the most attention in domestic affairs.

Economy. Inflation, the status of the franc, and the prospect of a shorter work week were the central economic concerns during the year. Although the per capita gross national product of Belgium was sixth in the world in 1978, inflation continued to hurt consumer spending power in 1979 and government policies were largely ineffectual. By midyear, the annual rate of inflation was approximately 8%. A proposal to reduce the work week to 36 hours not only created new friction between labor and management but also raised questions about its effect on and implications for European Community (EC) policy. The new European Monetary System (*see* EUROPE) was expected to help stabilize the currency, but apprehensions persisted.

Nuclear Energy. A growing environmental movement and the accident at the Three Mile Island (PA) nuclear power plant in late March gave rise to heated public debate in Belgium and the nation's first major antinuclear demonstrations. On April 7, Socialist mayor Fernand Hubin ordered the immediate shutdown of a nuclear power station in the town of Huy, contending that the plant's safety procedures were inadequate. At an emergency session the next day, the Belgian cabinet reversed the mayor's order. Because Belgium has insufficient domestic energy resources and is completely dependent on imported oil, an accelerated nuclear power program seemed vital. Belgian officials therefore expected nuclear energy to be a potentially volatile issue in the future.

BELGIUM CONSULATE GENERAL

Wilfried Martens, a member of the Belgian parliament since 1974, became prime minister in April 1979.

Terrorism. At the Brussels airport on April 16, Belgian police and Israeli security men thwarted an attempt by Palestine Liberation Organization (PLO) terrorists to take over an Israeli El-Al passenger plane. The guerrillas dropped a bomb in a crowded arrival lounge, injuring five Belgians, and wounded seven others in a shootout at a nearby restaurant. Two of the terrorists were apprehended.

Cardinal Resigns. Leo Josef Cardinal Suenens, a powerful mediating force in the Flemish-Walloon conflict, was forced to resign because of a ruling by Pope Paul VI specifying 75 as the maximum age of service. Suenens had been acknowledged for nearly 20 years as a leader of the more progressive wing of the Roman Catholic Church and was reportedly a prime candidate for the papacy in the two 1978 elections.

PIERRE-HENRI LAURENT, *Tufts University*

───── **BELGIUM · Information Highlights** ─────

Official Name: Kingdom of Belgium.
Location: Northwestern Europe.
Area: 11,781 square miles (30 513 km²).
Population (1979 est.): 9,800,000.
Chief Cities (1976 est.): Brussels, the capital, 1,042,-052; Antwerp, 206,786; Liège, 135,347.
Government: *Head of state,* Baudouin I, king (acceded 1951). *Head of government,* Wilfried Martens, prime minister (took office April 1979). *Legislature—*Parliament: Senate and Chamber of Representatives.
Monetary Unit: Franc (28.88 francs equal U. S.$1, Nov. 1979).
Manufactures (major products): Fabricated metal, iron and steel, coal, textiles, chemicals.
Agriculture (major products): Sugarbeets, potatoes, grain, tobacco, vegetables, fruits, livestock, poultry.

BIOCHEMISTRY

Research in the areas of growth hormone, genetic manipulation, and the genetic code were of particular interest to biochemists in 1979.

Growth Hormone. During 1979, bacteria were engineered to produce human growth hormone, a substance of medical importance. Limited amounts of the hormone had been available from cadavers for treatment of a rare hereditary disorder, pituitary dwarfism. Although preliminary experiments suggested that the hormone might be valuable in treating burns and gastrointestinal bleeding, insufficient material had been available for pursuing other medical applications. In July two research teams announced that they had bacteria producing human growth hormone by somewhat different methods. A group at San Francisco Medical Center had spliced the gene for human growth hormone onto a gene for a bacterial product, so that the genetically engineered bacteria made a hybrid product.

In contrast, scientists at Genentech, Inc. engineered bacteria to make human growth hormone not linked to any bacterial product. The scientists chemically synthesized the "start" signal for bacterial protein production, as well as the first part of the human growth hormone gene, and linked that genetic material to a copy of the remainder of the human gene. Both teams contracted with drug companies to pursue large-scale bacterial production of the hormone.

Genetic Manipulation. Experiments in 1979 reassured many scientists of the safety of research involving the deoxyribonucleic acid (DNA) of a wide variety of organisms spliced into DNA of bacteria and inserted into bacterial cells. The greatest worry had been that cancer-causing genes accidentally transferred into bacteria might cause a cancer epidemic among people. A set of experiments to assess the likelihood of such an event was performed at the high-containment research facility at Fort Detrick, MD, by Malcolm Martin and Wallace Rowe of the National Institutes of Health. The scientists transferred into bacteria the genes from a virus that causes tumors in some animals. The bacteria were of a widely used strain that is enfeebled to limit survival outside laboratory conditions. The scientists fed or injected into mice the bacteria containing viral genes, and then tested for any viral infection. They found no evidence that the viral genes were able to survive and function in the mice. From those experiments Martin and Rowe concluded that there is little risk in most experiments using recombinant DNA in the enfeebled bacteria.

Genetic Code. The power plants of cells, the mitochondria, provided the first exception to the genetic code, which scientists had thought to be universal. Those subcellular structures are comprised in part of protein imported from the surrounding cell. But they also contain the genetic material and protein-synthesizing machinery necessary to make some mitochondrial components independently. Methods for identifying the nucleotide subunits that make up genetic material allowed scientists to compare the sequence of nucleotides in the DNA with the sequence of amino acid subunits in the protein for which it codes.

In all bacteria of plants and animals that had been studied previously a given sequence of three nucleotides corresponded to the same amino acid in the protein or to a "stop" signal. However, researchers at the Medical Research Council in Cambridge, England, and another group at Columbia University discovered two unusual codes in mitochondrial DNA. In one case a three-nucleotide sequence that in cells serves as a stop signal, causes insertion of a specific amino acid in mitochondria. In the other instance, a nucleotide sequence in the mitochondria directs insertion of a different amino acid than in the surrounding cell. Alexander Tzagoloff of Columbia University speculated that the mitochondrial genetic code is either a more advanced, simplified form, or else a primitive version of the more common genetic code.

Scent Chemistry. A single chemical compound was shown to trigger in male dogs behavior normally aroused only by a female dog in heat. Purdue University scientists Michael R. Goodwin and Fred E. Regnier identified the chemical in volatile material from dog vaginal smears. The compound, methyl para-hydroxybenzoate, was present only in samples taken on the days the females showed maximal sexual receptivity. If the chemical was rubbed on female dogs not in heat, however, male dogs exhibited the full range of sexual behavior to unreceptive, barking, snapping females. That finding indicated that although scent glands of vertebrates generate a mix of compounds, a single chemical can trigger complex behavior.

Developmental Signal. Collisions between immature abalone and red algae were shown to provide a crucial signal in the mollusk's development. This unusual coming-of-age was discovered by Daniel Morse at the University of California at Santa Barbara. The chemical signal sensed by the abalone larvae is a simple amino acid, gamma-aminobutyric acid (GABA), which is a potent neurotransmitter in the human brain and other animal tissues. When the free-swimming, immature abalone contacts GABA or an algal red pigment with GABA-like regions, it settles to the ocean bottom, loses its swimming appendages, and grows the rayed shell of an adult. Two applications of this observation were suggested. The metamorphosis signal should aid commercial cultivation of abalone and related mollusks, which are important foods in many areas of the world. In addition, environmental stress, including sublethal doses of pesticides, prevent the settling, so that behavior may be a sensitive test for pollutants.

JULIE ANN MILLER, *"Science News"*

BIOGRAPHY

A selection of profiles of persons prominent in the news during 1979 appears on pages 129–140. The affiliation of the contributor is listed on pages 589–592. Included are sketches of:

BAKER, Russell

Once described as "a quiet subversive among the hortatory voices of the *Times* editorial page," columnist Russell Baker was awarded the Pulitzer Prize for commentary on April 16, 1979, the first humorist to be so honored since that category was established in 1970. Baker, whose 750-word "Observer" column appears three times weekly in *The New York Times* and is syndicated to 475 newspapers, received the award for his writings during 1978. A social critic in the tradition of Benjamin Franklin, Mark Twain, and Finley Peter Dunne, Baker expresses his wide-ranging New Deal humanitarianism through various stances as a humorist, satirist, stylist, or essayist. According to critic R. Z. Sheppard, Baker is "a man of range, sensitive intellect, and fertile imagination," who writes each column "to preserve his sanity for at least one more day."

Background. Russell Wayne Baker, the son of a stonemason, was born in Loudoun County, VA, on Aug. 14, 1925. When he was five his father died, and the family struggled amid poverty through the Depression. From an early age, Baker was "fascinated by the ironies of life," and in high school he won some recognition as a humorist with a senior-year essay, "The Art of Eating Spaghetti." He won a scholarship to Johns Hopkins University in 1942 and, after time out for service in the U. S. Navy, was graduated with a B. A. in 1947. He worked for the Baltimore *Sun* (1947–54) and then was invited by James Reston, at that time Washington bureau chief of *The New York Times,* to join his staff as a reporter in 1954. Baker soon gained a reputation as a brilliant stylist. In 1962 he began writing the "Observer" column for the *Times.*

Collections of Baker's newspaper articles include *An American in Washington* (1961), *No Cause for Panic* (1964), *Baker's Dozen* (1964), *All Things Considered* (1965), and *Poor Russell's Almanac* (1972). He has also written a fictional account of the 1968 elections, a children's book, an unsuccessful musical comedy, and many magazine articles.

Baker and his wife, Miriam ("Mimi"), have two sons and a daughter. They reside in a brownstone house in Manhattan and have a summer home on Nantucket Island.

HENRY S. SLOAN

RUSSELL BAKER

BILL ADLER, NEW YORK TIMES PICTURES

BYRNE, Jane Margaret

Hardly anyone believed Jane Margaret Burke Byrne in the spring of 1978 when she vowed to topple Chicago Mayor Michael A. Bilandic from office. "That's not a mayor," she said of Bilandic.

Bilandic himself expressed little worry over her challenge, saying rather contemptuously, "Mayor of what?"

Jane Byrne's lonely challenge of the powerful Democratic machine in Chicago seemed doomed until the final stretch. The Bilandic administration, she kept saying through all of 1978, was corrupt and inefficient and allowing Chicago's neighborhoods to rot. Not many listened. Two January 1979 blizzards changed all that as Chicagoans, crippled for weeks, saw that the "city that works" did not work, at least not under Bilandic. His political future melted away with the February thaw.

Background. Jane Burke was born May 24, 1934, the daughter of a steel executive and the second oldest in a family of two boys and four girls. She attended Catholic grammar and high school in Chicago and Barat College in Lake Forest, IL.

After college she married William P. Byrne, a Notre Dame graduate and Marine lieutenant. They had one daughter, Kathy, born on New Year's Eve of 1956. Bill Byrne died May 31, 1959, when his jet crashed in heavy fog just north of Chicago. Widowed and without any plans for the future, Jane Byrne became a Kennedy volunteer worker in the 1960 campaign.

JOHN CHEEVER

UPI

Chicago Mayor Richard J. Daley noticed her one day, took a liking to her, and gave her some advice: Help the Chicago Democratic machine if you're going to get anywhere politically. Mrs. Byrne took the advice. In 1968 Daley rewarded her with the post of city commissioner of sales, weights, and measures, the first woman in Daley's cabinet. In that post she championed the consumer against powerful business interests. Daley always backed her up. The mayor had her named a Democratic National Committeewoman and appointed her to the honorary post of co-chairperson of the Cook County Democratic Committee.

She lost her cabinet job in November 1977, when she charged that the new mayor, Mike Bilandic, had "greased" a cab fare increase.

Jane Byrne remarried on March 17, 1978, to Chicago newsman Jay McMullen. She and Jay then gambled most of their savings on the uphill fight against Mike Bilandic—a battle she won in 1979 on primary day, February 27, and on election day, April 3.

ROBERT ENSTAD

CHEEVER, John

The critical and popular success of *The Collected Short Stories of John Cheever,* which in 1979 won both the National Book Critics Circle award and the Pulitzer Prize for fiction, must have been particularly satisfying to its author. About the publication of that work, Cheever remarked: "A collection of short stories is generally thought to be a horrendous clinker, an enforced courtesy for the elderly writer who wants to display the trophies of his youth, along with his trout flies." At times evasive, coy, or simply ironic, Cheever is in fact one of the master storytellers of his time. Evoking in brilliant prose the failure of contemporary manners and morals, his twelve books have shed penetrating light into the deeper mysteries of modern American life.

Background. John Cheever was born on May 27, 1912, in Quincy, MA. He was a precocious but apparently difficult child whose formal education ended at the age of 17, when he was expelled from preparatory school, Thayer Academy in South Braintree. A talented writer even as a teenager, his stories found quick acceptance by a number of magazines, including *The New Yorker,* which over the years has been his most important outlet. After marrying Mary Winternitz in 1941 and serving in the army during World War II, he wrote television scripts—some for the popular situation comedy "Life With Father"—and more short stories.

His first collection, *The Way Some People Live* (1943), won several awards and brought Cheever wide acclaim. His novels also received high praise, but the applause was not universal. Although *The Wapshot Chronicle* (1957) won the National Book Award, and its sequel, *The Wapshot Scandal* (1964), won him the coveted Howells Medal for fiction, Cheever's novels were criticized for being episodic and superficial. Some criticized them for dealing exclusively with bourgeois malaise from the point of view of orthodox morality. Cheever confounded his detractors, however, with *Falconer* (1977), a brutal portrait of life in prison. In 1979, "Three Cheever Stories" were adapted and televised by the Public Broadcasting System (PBS).

John Cheever lives in Ossining, NY.

JEROME H. STERN

CIVILETTI, Benjamin R.

The naming of Benjamin R. Civiletti as attorney general brought a change in style to the top post at the U. S. Justice Department. But Civiletti vowed that his appointment would not lessen the department's determination, which had been fostered by his predecessor, Griffin Bell, to resist political pressure. "I have no doubts about maintaining the same type of independent Department of Justice," he said, shortly after his name was submitted to the Senate for confirmation.

Civiletti lacks Bell's flamboyance and folksy humor, as well as the close personal relationship with Carter that Bell had developed with his fellow Georgian. But the 44-year-old Civiletti had gained the respect and trust of the president during his first 30 months at justice by his handling of a number of sensitive matters, first as head of the criminal division, then as deputy attorney general. These included the probe into Korean influence peddling on Capitol Hill; the dismissal of David Marston, the Republican U. S. attorney in Philadelphia; and the investigation into the financial affairs of Bert Lance, Carter's close friend and the former head of the Office of Management and Budget. Though Civiletti's role in some of these cases was controversial, he was generally acknowledged to be efficient and firm in the face of criticism.

At his Senate confirmation hearings Civiletti was accused of being insensitive to the rights of Hispanic Americans, who charged that he was lax in prosecuting cases of police brutality. He promised to establish a special advisory panel to look into the grievances of Hispanic Americans and pledged his commitment to equal rights for all citizens. Known as an experienced trial lawyer, Civiletti was expected to become more directly involved in major department cases than his predecessor.

Background. Benjamin R. Civiletti was born on July 17, 1935, in Peekskill, NY. He was educated at Johns Hopkins University and the University of Maryland law school. Following admission to the Maryland bar in 1961, he became a law clerk to a district judge and an assistant U. S. attorney (1962–64). From 1964 until January 1977, he was a member of the Baltimore law firm of Venable, Baetjer & Howard.

He and his wife, the former Gale Lundgren, are the parents of three children.

ROBERT SHOGAN

CLARK, Charles Joseph ("Joe")

On June 4, 1979, The Right Honorable Charles Joseph Clark, leader of Canada's Progressive Conservative party, became the nation's 16th prime minister. Taking office on the eve of his 40th birthday, Clark became the youngest prime minister in Canada's history. He succeeded Pierre Elliott Trudeau, 59, who had been prime minister of Canada since April 20, 1968. It was the nation's first Conservative government in 16 years.

In the May 22 federal elections, Clark's Conservatives returned 136 seats to the Liberals' 114, the New Democratic party's 26, and the Social Credit party's 6.

Background. Charles Joseph ("Joe") Clark was born in High River, Alberta, June 5, 1939, son of newspaper publisher Charles Clark and Grace Welch. Educated in High River schools, a graduate of the University of Alberta with a B. A. in history and an M. A. in political science, Clark did not complete his legal studies. He was a lecturer in political science at the University of Alberta (1965–67) and was a journalist for a brief period.

His rapid rise to political predominance in Canada derived from his successful work as a political manager and backroom man within the Progressive Conservative party. He was secretary to the leader of the Alberta Conservatives at age 20, became national president of the Progressive Conservative Student Federation, and was active in the struggle to oust John George Diefenbaker as leader of the Progressive Conservative party (1967). Also in 1967 he served as director of organization for Tory leader Peter Lougheed in the Alberta election, but failed in his own bid to be elected to the Alberta legislature.

In 1967 Clark went to Ottawa as special assistant to Progressive Conservative cabinet minister Davie Fulton and had the good fortune to be named to the staff of Robert Stanfield, Leader of the Opposition, a position Clark held until 1970. Clark was elected Member of Parliament for Rocky Mountain in the 1972 election and was reelected in 1974. In February 1976, on a narrow fourth ballot vote, Clark was chosen to succeed Stan-

field as Leader of the Opposition. At 36, he was the youngest person to head a major political party in Canada. At that time he was still a "dark horse," a fact underlined by an Ottawa newspaper headline the day after the election: "Joe Who?" As Opposition leader, Clark sought to make his party "an open, active party, a home for all Canadians."

Clark is married to Maureen Anne McTeer, daughter of John McTeer of Cumberland, Ontario. Miss McTeer, as she prefers to be called, is an active campaigner for husband and party. They have one daughter, Cathy.

BARRY M. GOUGH

DOBRYNIN, Anatoliy F.

Anatoliy Dobrynin, Soviet ambassador to the United States since March 30, 1962, became dean of the Washington diplomatic corps in 1979. Once described by W. Averell Harriman as Washington's "favorite Bolshevik," the ambassador has easy access to all U. S. officials. He can demand to see the U. S. secretary of state without delay and "won't take a summons from anybody lower than the secretary." Throughout 1979, the ambassador, a student of Broadway musical comedies and a fast-foods enthusiast, played a major role in U. S.-Soviet SALT II negotiations.

Background. Anatoliy F. Dobrynin was born on Nov. 16, 1919, in Krasnaya Gorka, near Gorki, in the Soviet Union. He was educated at a technical college and holds a master's degree in history. During World War II he served as an engineer at an aircraft plant. In 1944 Dobrynin became a member of the Soviet diplomatic service and he served as counselor and minister-counselor at the Soviet Embassy in Washington (1952–55). From 1955 to 1957 he was assistant deputy minister of foreign affairs and from 1957 to 1960 he was UN undersecretary without portfolio and undersecretary general for political and Security Council affairs.

One of the world's outstanding authorities on Soviet-American affairs, Dobrynin, who speaks fluent English and French, has become accustomed to speaking to U. S. presidents and diplomats without the services of an interpreter. He and his wife, the former Irina Nikolaevna, have traveled widely in the United States.

A member of the Soviet Communist Party since 1945, Dobrynin has been a member of the party's Central Committee since 1971.

DUNCAN, Charles William

After more than two years as deputy secretary of defense, Charles William Duncan wanted a bigger challenge. He could hardly have asked for a more formidable task than the one President Carter presented him with when he nominated the wealthy Texan to be U. S. secretary of energy. The 53-year-old Duncan had little experience in the energy field, except for a brief stint as an oil company roustabout as a young man.

When Duncan took over from James Schlesinger in late August 1979, energy problems were generally cited as one of the major reasons for Carter's low standings in the opinion polls. And the Department of Energy was held in such low repute that a number of critics suggested that it should be abolished.

But Duncan's associates in business and government said he was well suited to deal with those difficulties. In his private and public career he had demonstrated considerable managerial skill, a talent badly needed at the two-year-old agency he was called upon to lead. And Duncan indicated at the start that he would concentrate his efforts on increasing the efficiency of the department and implementing Administration programs, rather than blazing new policy trails.

Background. Born in Houston, Sept. 9, 1926, the nation's second energy secretary earned a bachelor's degree in chemical engineering from Rice University and did postgraduate work in management at the University of Texas. Following service with the U. S. Air Force, Duncan became president of a food company owned by his family. When that company was merged with Coca Cola, Duncan moved up the corporate ladder to become president of the giant soft drink corporation in 1971. Operating out of Coca Cola's headquarters in Atlanta, Duncan came to know Jimmy Carter, who was then governor of Georgia. He resigned from Coca Cola in 1974 to head a Houston investment banking firm.

At the Defense Department Duncan was no stranger to controversy. He was responsible for closing down military bases no longer deemed necessary and for negotiating contract disputes between the Navy and civilian shipbuilders.

He is married to the former Thetis Anne Smith. The couple are the parents of two children.

ROBERT SHOGAN

FIGUEIREDO, João Baptista de

"I will impose democracy—whatever the cost," declared Gen. João Baptista de Figueiredo during his campaign for the presidency of Brazil in 1978. Few observers doubted that Figueiredo, the chosen successor of the incumbent president, Ernesto Geisel, would win the election, but many were skeptical about his commitment to political freedom. A shadowy figure who habitually wore dark glasses and avoided reporters and photographers, the four-star general was chief of the National Intelligence Service before becoming the presidential candidate of the ruling National Renovation Alliance (ARENA).

During the campaign, however, Figueiredo gave up his secretive ways, made constant appearances in the Brazilian news media, and promised an administration of "openness"—abertura. In October 1978 the electoral college gave him the presidency by a vote of 355 to 226. Following his inauguration in March 1979, Figueiredo began cultivating a folksy image—asking to be called "President João"—and pushed ahead with his liberalization program. Among his first decisions as president were to grant amnesty to most political prisoners and to permit the organization of new political parties. The 61-year-old president attributed his appreciation of democratic principles to his father, also an army general, who took part in the 1932 Constitutional Revolt against the dictatorship of President Getúlio Vargas.

Background. Born in Rio de Janeiro on Jan. 15, 1918, João Baptista de Figueiredo spent most of his boyhood in the town of Alegrete, on the pampas of Brazil's gaucho state, Rio Grande do Sul, where he developed a passion for horseback riding. He attended the military preparatory school in Porto Alegre and went on to the national military academy at Realengo, where he was graduated in 1937 as a cavalry officer. After fifteen years in the cavalry, Figueiredo switched to the intelligence branch of the army. He took part in the military coup of 1964 and in subsequent years rose from colonel to four-star general.

His brother Euclides de Oliveira Figueiredo is a high-ranking army general, while another brother, Guilherme de Figueiredo, is a noted playwright and essayist.

NEILL MACAULAY

GOLDSCHMIDT, Neil Edward

When 39-year-old Neil Edward Goldschmidt became the youngest member of President Carter's cabinet upon his swearing in as secretary of transportation, it was a familiar distinction for him. In 1973 Goldschmidt had become the youngest big city mayor in the nation, when he took office as chief executive of Portland, OR.

In subsequent years, through his activities in city hall and in national forums, Goldschmidt established himself as a young politician of considerable ambition and ability. Richard Carver, mayor of Peoria, IL, head of the U. S. Conference of Mayors, called Goldschmidt one of the best of the "new breed" of mayors, a type of urban leader who is prepared to tackle the manifold problems of the cities with verve and imagination.

Goldschmidt made his mark especially in mass tran-

sit, and the expertise he developed in this area made him a logical choice to head the Transportation Department. In Portland he worked to defeat a proposal for a federally funded highway project. Then he helped get federal funds to support a transit mall, an area reserved for buses and pedestrians, which was credited with revitalizing downtown Portland. He also served as chairman of the transportation committee of the U. S. Conference of Mayors. And after his smashing reelection victory in 1976, Goldschmidt played a major role in gaining state and local approval for Portland's first light rail public transit system.

Apart from his transit experience, Goldschmidt's background made him a politically appealing choice for the president. His western origins matched those of his predecessor, Brock Adams of Washington. And as an active member of the Jewish faith, Goldschmidt is in a position to help improve Carter's strained relations with that Democratic constituency.

Background. Born in Eugene, OR, on June 16, 1940, Goldschmidt was graduated from the University of Oregon and from the University of California at Berkeley Law School. A civil rights worker in the South in the 1960's, Goldschmidt worked for the Portland Legal Aid Service before entering politics. From 1971 to 1972, he was city commissioner of Portland.

He and his wife, Margaret, have two children.

ROBERT SHOGAN

HUFSTEDLER, Shirley M.

On Oct. 30, 1979, President Carter named Judge Shirley M. Hufstedler the secretary of the Department of Education, a recently created cabinet-level post. The appointment came as a surprise to many, as it was long speculated that Judge Hufstedler, a liberal activist, would at some time become the first woman appointee to the U. S. Supreme Court. President Carter reportedly informed Judge Hufstedler that her position in the Department of Education need not rule out a future appointment to the Supreme Court. Her activities in the field of education had been limited—private pursuits and service as a trustee of the California In-

SHIRLEY M. HUFSTEDLER

UPI

stitute of Technology, Occidental College, and the Aspen Institute for Humanistic Studies.

Background. Shirley Mount Hufstedler was born in Denver, CO, on Aug. 24, 1925. She was educated at the University of New Mexico (B. A. 1945; LL. D. 1972) and at Stanford University (LL. B. 1949). Following graduation from the Stanford Law School she and her husband moved to Los Angeles where she practiced law until her appointment as judge of the Los Angeles Superior Court (1961). In 1966 she was appointed to the California Supreme Court of Appeals, and in 1969, President Johnson nominated her as circuit judge of the U. S. Court of Appeals for the Ninth Circuit. Judge Hufstedler was the second woman to be appointed to a federal appeals court post.

Since August 1949, Judge Hufstedler has been married to Seth Martin Hufstedler, also a prominent lawyer. They have one son, Steven Mark. She is an avid hiker; in 1977 she climbed Annapurna in the Himalayas to a level of 17,000 feet (5 181 m).

SAUNDRA FRANCE

JOEL, Billy

Billy Joel, a "street-wise" singer, songwriter, and musician from New York, whose "Just the Way You Are" on Feb. 16, 1979 won Grammy awards as best record and best song of 1978 from the National Academy of Recording Arts and Sciences, has a style which ranges from the contemporary rock idiom to that of bygone "Tin Pan Alley" romantic ballads. He has made several best-selling albums, including *Piano Man* (1973), *The Stranger* (1977), and *52nd Street* (1978).

In March 1979, Joel appeared in Cuba at "Havana Jam 1979," the first cultural exchange effort between Cuba and the United States in 20 years.

Background. A native of the Bronx, NY, William Martin Joel was born on May 9, 1949, the son of an engineer of Alsatian Jewish background. When he was seven, his parents separated, and Billy and his sister were reared in Hicksville, NY, on their mother's modest earnings from secretarial work. An important early influence was his maternal grandfather, who stimulated his interests in literature and music. At his mother's urging, Joel took classical piano lessons for 12 years, but he also found time to run with a street gang and take part in sports.

In the early 1960's, Joel became interested in popular music and at 14 organized a combo. Later he joined an ensemble called the Hassles and eventually dropped out of high school. In 1972 after recovering from emotional depression that had put him briefly in a hospital psychiatric ward, Joel recorded his first solo album of original songs, *Cold Spring Harbor.* Then, as a result of a legal conflict with his managers, he went to Los Angeles, where he played piano under the name of Bill Martin, recorded his first hit single, "Piano Man," and the album of the same title. The singer also won plaudits for his third album, *Streetlife Serenade* (1974), earning *Cashbox* magazine's designation as best new male vocalist of 1974.

In 1975, Joel took up residence in New York City, where he produced *Turnstiles* (1976). After taking on Phil Ramone as his producer in 1977, he reached the top of the record charts with his fifth and sixth albums.

Billy Joel and his manager-wife, Elizabeth, live on a Long Island estate and keep a Manhattan apartment.

HENRY S. SLOAN

KHOMEINI, Ayatollah Ruhollah

After a February 1979 meeting with the new leader of Iran, the then U.S. Ambassador to the United Nations, Andrew Young, described the 78-year-old Ayatollah Khomeini as "something of a saint." During the course of the year, however, others were given to less favorable assessments. Whatever the reaction, two things were hardly open to dispute. The ayatollah is a man of blazing religious conviction and dominating personality, unshakeably convinced that he is the messenger of Allah. Secondly, he spearheaded a revolution which had untold consequences in Middle East and world affairs.

The ayatollah, a holy man of the Shi'ite Muslim sect, had lived in exile in Iraq from 1964 to 1978. On Oct. 6, 1978, he was expelled from that country and moved to France. From a château outside Paris, Khomeini engineered a revolution by Muslims and political dissidents in Iran. Both his calls for a one-day general strike in October and an oil strike in November were heeded. Civilian violence spread throughout the country, and by year's end the government was in disarray. Shah Mohammed Reza Pahlavi left with his family in early January 1979, and Khomeini returned on February 1 to assume control of the new Islamic state. Anti-American, anti-Israeli, anti-feminist, and anti-modernist, Khomeini seemed to enunciate his hostilities more clearly than his positive precepts and policies. In November 1979, apparently with Khomeini's backing, Iranian students seized the U.S. embassy in Tehran, took hostage some 60 U.S. citizens, and demanded the return of the shah.

Background. Although the early stages of Khomeini's life remain obscure, his family probably came from Khorasan in northeast Iran and adhered to the Sufi version of Shi'ite Islam. The family name was Hendi. Ruhollah Hendi was probably born on May 17, 1900, in the town of Khumain (from which he later derived his surname). Ruhollah was still young, perhaps even an infant, when his father was murdered. Young Ruhollah gradually became known as a distinguished Islamic scholar. His patron was the eminent Abdul Karim Haeri, who in 1920 opened the Madresseh Faizieh, a center of Islamic studies in Qum. Ruhollah studied and taught there for more than 40 years. In the 1950's he became an *ayatollah* by popular acclaim, and by the 1960's he had become an uncompromising critic of the shah. His opposition to the reduction of church-owned landed estates and the emancipation of women led to his imprisonment in 1963 and exile in 1964.

Khomeini has been married either once or twice and has six children.

ARTHUR CAMPBELL TURNER

BILLY JOEL

UPI

KLUTZNICK, Philip M.

In mid-November U.S. President Jimmy Carter named Philip M. Klutznick secretary of commerce. Klutznick, a 72-year-old Chicago banker and real-estate developer and a prominent Jewish leader, succeeded Juanita M. Kreps, who had resigned for personal reasons.

In announcing the appointment, the White House pointed out that Klutznick is "a very active 72" and stressed that he was vice-chairman of the Committee for Economic Development, a group of American industrial leaders. Following hearings by the Senate Commerce Committee and confirmation by the full Senate, Klutznick was sworn in as commerce secretary as the year ended. A White House ceremony followed later.

Background. Born in Kansas City, MO, July 9, 1907, Philip M. Klutznick was educated at the universities of Kansas and Nebraska. After earning a law degree from Creighton University in 1929, he was admitted to the bar in 1930. From 1944 to 1946, he served as U.S. commissioner of the Federal Public Housing Authority. Klutznick later founded and headed the Urban Investment and Development Company, now a wholly-owned subsidiary of Aetna Life. He also has worked for the Salomon Brothers.

Klutznick has been a member of several U.S. delegations to the United Nations, a member of the national council of the Boy Scouts of America, a trustee of the Eleanor Roosevelt Institute, and a member of the President's Advisory Committee on Indo-Chinese Refugees and of several other prestigious councils and committees. An active member of the American Jewish community, he was elected president of the World Jewish Congress in 1977 and has held high positions with B'nai B'rith, the National Jewish Welfare Board, and the Institute for Jewish Policy Planning. A strong supporter of President Carter and a personal friend of Vice-President Walter Mondale, the investment banker has been a major fund-raiser for the Democratic Party. He could be expected to play an important role in President Carter's bid for a second term.

He married the former Ethel Reikes in June 1930. They are the parents of one daughter and five sons.

LANDRIEU, Moon

When Moon Landrieu left New Orleans' City Hall in 1978 after eight stormy years as mayor, he claimed that he was relieved to be free of the pressures and frictions of public life. But Landrieu is a man who thrives on attention and argument. And after a brief period as head of a real estate development company, he could not resist the opportunity to return to the public arena as secretary of the Department of Housing and Urban Development (HUD), replacing Patricia Roberts Harris. There was some controversy during the Senate confirmation hearings regarding a real estate deal that then Mayor Landrieu had with a real estate developer who also did business with the city of New Orleans. Following discussion of the issue, the Senate confirmed his nomination without a dissenting vote.

If his past record is any guide, the 49-year-old Landrieu's tenure at HUD is likely to be a contentious one. As mayor of New Orleans he was involved in one struggle after another. He brought blacks into key posts in city government over the opposition of segregationists. And despite the resistance of traditionalists, he changed the appearance of the historic city—renovating the French Market, building a new promenade along the Mississippi, and, most notably, pushing through construction of the $163 million Superdome. The disputes surrounding the creation of this huge sports arena were so intense and bitter that in the midst of one debate Landrieu was publicly moved to tears.

Background. Born in New Orleans on July 23, 1930, Landrieu was graduated in 1954 from the Loyola University law school. He began his political career as a state legislator in 1960 and plunged immediately into the furor over school segregation. He was one of the few lawmakers who challenged the efforts of Louisiana Gov. Jimmie Davis to forestall desegregation, and his efforts helped win him support from New Orleans' black majority in his campaigns for mayor.

Landrieu became head of the U.S. Conference of Mayors in 1975 and used that post to argue vigorously for federal aid to cities, particularly financially beleaguered New York City which was then on the verge of bankruptcy.

Landrieu legally changed his name from Maurice to Moon, a boyhood nickname, before he ran for mayor. He and his wife, Verna, have nine children, each of whose names begins with "M".

ROBERT SHOGAN

LEWIS, Sir [William] Arthur

Sir Arthur Lewis, 64-year-old native of the Caribbean island of St. Lucia, was named co-winner with Theodore W. Schultz of the University of Chicago of the 1979 Nobel Prize in Economics. Sir Arthur, an expert on the Third World and the first black to win the award in a category other than peace, was honored for his concern about "need and poverty in the world" and for looking for "ways out of underdevelopment." His most famous book, *The Theory of Economic Growth,* was published in 1955. He is most noted for his theoretical models explaining the problems of underdevelopment. He sees an industrial revolution as impossible unless preceded by an agrarian revolution.

Background. Born on the island of St. Lucia in the British West Indies on Jan. 23, 1915, he moved at the age of three with his family to London. He returned to St. Lucia as a student at St. Mary's College (1924–29) and, going back to England, continued his education at the London School of Economics, where he received his Ph.D. in 1940. Of his appointment as lecturer at the London School of Economics in 1938, the future Nobelist said: "I'm the kind of person you guys like the least; I'm an educated native."

He was a professor at the University of Manchester (1948–59), and principal and vice chancellor of the University of the West Indies (1959–63). For his services as vice chancellor he was knighted by Queen Elizabeth in 1963. Since 1963 he has been professor of economics and international affairs at Princeton University, and since 1968, he also has been the James Madison Professor of Political Economy there. In addition to writing many books and official papers, he has served as economic adviser to numerous governments of Third World nations, particularly in Africa. He was the first president of the Caribbean Development Bank (1970–73).

Sir Arthur is married and has two daughters.

SAUNDRA FRANCE

McHENRY, Donald F.

On August 31, 1979, President Jimmy Carter nominated Donald F. McHenry, a 42-year-old black career diplomat, as U.S. ambassador to the United Nations, succeeding Andrew Young, whose unauthorized contacts with the Palestine Liberation Organization had resulted in his resignation on August 15. In announcing his choice, the president praised McHenry as a "highly qualified professional." McHenry assumed his post at the opening of the 34th session of the UN General Assembly on September 18 and was formally sworn in on September 23 at a White House ceremony.

Shortly before his nomination, McHenry had headed the U.S. negotiating team engaged in three days of talks with Soviet representatives at New York's Kennedy Airport, where a Soviet jetliner had been detained on State Department orders to ensure that the ballerina Lyudmila Vlasova—whose husband, Bolshoi ballet star Alexander Godunov, had been granted U.S. asylum—was returning to Moscow of her own free will.

As U.S. deputy representative to the UN since 1977, McHenry, whose emphasis on "quiet diplomacy" contrasted with Young's more flamboyant style, played a key role in formulating the Carter administration's policies on southern Africa.

Background. Donald McHenry was born in St. Louis, MO, on Oct. 13, 1936. He was graduated from Illinois State University (B.S., 1957), from Southern Illinois University (M.S., 1959), and did additional graduate work in international relations at Georgetown University. After teaching English at Howard University (1959–62), he joined the State Department (1963). He resigned ten years later and joined the Carnegie Endowment for International Peace.

When Carter was elected president in 1976, McHenry became a member of the transition team, and in 1977 he was appointed Andrew Young's deputy at the UN. Through painstaking negotiations in 1977–78, McHenry played a major role in the conclusion of a complex agreement that was to transform the South African-ruled territory of South-West Africa into the independent nation of Namibia, under UN auspices. Although South Africa later reneged on the agreement, it was considered a major diplomatic achievement for the Carter administration. McHenry also helped to improve U.S.-Angolan relations.

Donald F. McHenry is divorced and has two teenage daughters and a son, a student at Oxford.

HENRY S. SLOAN

MARTIN, Steve

A zany, uninhibited clown, Steve Martin won his second consecutive Grammy award for best comedy recording from the National Academy of Recording Arts and Sciences in February 1979 for his album *Wild and Crazy Guy*. In 1978 he had received the same award for the album *Let's Get Small*. That year, he also received an Oscar nomination for his short film *The Absent-minded Waiter*.

Since attaining instant popularity in the mid-1970's as a standup comic, Martin has become a familiar figure on the nightclub circuit and on such television programs as the *Tonight Show* and *Saturday Night Live*. Usually dressed in an immaculate white suit and aided by such props as bunny ears or an arrow through the head, Martin presents an act that includes bizarre tales, humorous songs and poems, one-liners, non-sequiturs, slapstick routines, and parodies of show business, punctuated by such widely-mimicked expressions as, "Well, excuuuuse me!"

He writes nearly all of his material, and he is under contract to write and star in several films. His book *Cruel Shoes,* a collection of his sketches, poems, and jokes, was on the best-seller list in mid-1979.

Background. Born about 1945, Steve Martin moved with his family at the age of five from Waco, TX, to California. At the age of 10 he sold guidebooks at Disneyland and at 16 was featured in a vaudeville show there. Two years later he appeared at nearby Knott's Berry Farm. An honor student of philosophy at Long Beach State College, he dropped out without graduating after deciding that show business "was the only thing that had real meaning because it had no meaning."

After taking a writing course at UCLA, Martin was hired as a writer for the *Smothers Brothers Comedy Hour* and in 1968 shared an Emmy award for a script on which he had worked. Later he wrote routines for other notable performers. Working as a performer himself, Martin appeared with little success in second-rate California clubs and on the Las Vegas circuit, until in 1975 he changed his routine to the bizarre and outrageous type of humor that became his trademark.

A bachelor, and something of a recluse, Steve Martin makes his home in Aspen, CO.

HENRY S. SLOAN

MEHTA, Zubin

One of the brilliant musical conductors of our time, Zubin Mehta has had a meteoric career, and at age 43, 21 years after his debut in Vienna, he is the New York Philharmonic's music director. He began in that post in 1978, with a concert in Central Park for 140,000 people, and a tour of Argentina and the Dominican Republic. During the orchestra's 137th season (1978–79), he performed three major television concerts, made an east coast tour, and recorded four albums. In June 1979, the orchestra and Mehta received the American Society of Composers, Authors and Publishers (ASCAP) award for contemporary music programming. In September 1979, before the start of his second season in New York, he toured with the Israel Philharmonic with which he has been associated since 1961.

Background. Zubin Mehta was born a Parsi (a member of the Persian religion Zoroastrianism and a descendant of Persian refugees) in Bombay, India, on April 29, 1936. He is the son of the Bombay Symphony's founder, Mehli Mehta. At age 16, he gave up medical studies to attend the Vienna Academy of Music where he quickly turned from lessons in string bass and other subjects to conducting. In rapid succession, his natural gifts brought him the first prize in the Liverpool International Conducting Competition (1958), the music directorship of the Montreal Sym-

GORDON CLARKE

ZUBIN MEHTA

phony (1961), and the directorship of the Los Angeles Philharmonic (1962). For 16 years, Mehta conducted the Los Angeles Philharmonic, in over 1,000 concerts, 11 tours, and numerous recording sessions.

Even by Los Angeles standards, Mehta was a star of highly publicized but nonetheless real personal glamor and appeal. In 1969, he was married for the second time to Nancy Kovack, a former actress. He has two children by his first wife.

Mehta has a flamboyant style and temperament but also a strong, clear technique. He is noted for romantic symphonic repertory as well as opera, which he conducts for the Metropolitan and Vienna State Opera companies.

ROBERT COMMANDAY

MUZOREWA, Abel T.

On May 29, 1979, Bishop Abel Muzorewa (54) was sworn in as the first black prime minister of Zimbabwe Rhodesia, thus ending 89 years of white rule. The following day the bishop named a 17-member cabinet of 12 blacks and 5 whites. It included both the outgoing prime minister, Ian Smith, and the former foreign minister, Pieter K. Van der Byl. These events followed Bishop Muzorewa's triumph in the country's first majority-rule elections held in April 1979, but they were the outcome of an agreement Mr. Smith had reached with the internal black leaders in March 1978. World opinion was almost wholly opposed to that agreement, as well as to the subsequent constitutional arrangements which culminated in the exclusion of the external black leaders—the Patriotic Front. By year's end, the burden of Mr. Smith's white supremacy legacy proved too great, and Bishop Muzorewa agreed to restore the break-away

colony to British rule and, under British supervision, to contest new elections with the Patriotic Front leaders.

Background. Abel Tendekayi Muzorewa, the eldest of eight children, was born to parents of the Shona language tribal group on April 14, 1925, near Umtali. Educated at the Old Umtali Secondary School, in 1958 he went to the United States to study at Central Methodist College in Fayette, MO (M. A. 1962) and Scarritt College in Nashville, TN (M. A. 1963). He returned to the Old Umtali Mission as pastor in 1963, and was consecrated in 1968. He emerged as a political figure in 1971 when, as chairman of the new, temporary, and only unbanned black political organization—the African National Council (ANC)—he successfully organized opposition to the Sir Alec Douglas-Home–Ian Smith independence proposals. Regarded by the veteran nationalist leaders—who were in prison or exile—as only a caretaker, the bishop steadily built up a large following. By 1976, he had become a serious rival, having formed a new organization, the United African National Council (UANC). Never supported by the "front-line" black states, the Organization of African Unity (OAU), or the United Nations, and fiercely opposed by the external guerrilla leaders, Bishop Muzorewa nonetheless became Rhodesia's leading internal black politician.

Bishop Muzorewa and his wife, the former Maggie Rutendo Chigodora, have five children. His advocation is raising chickens and pigs on his farm in Dowa.

R. B. BALLINGER

NAVRATILOVA, Martina

Martina Navratilova began 1979 ranked as the number one women's tennis player in the world. She held on shakily to that position despite being replaced briefly by Chris Evert Lloyd in midsummer. The computer accurately reflected the state of women's tennis for 1979—Navratilova started and finished the year as number one, but with some doubting moments in between.

Although she has won the official women's tour twice—in 1978 (Virginia Slims) and 1979 (Avon)—and successfully defended her Wimbledon championship in 1979, Martina has not yet established herself as the clear-cut number one in the same fashion as her rival Chris Evert did from 1974 through 1978.

Since 1978, Navratilova's awesome start has been overshadowed by her late season letdown at the U. S. Open where she has been upset in the semifinals (1978 by Pam Shriver, 1979 by Tracy Austin). Some have attributed her inexplicable defeats to nervousness and being extraordinarily high-strung. A more accurate reason is that she is constantly being compared to Evert Lloyd and Austin, whose firm resolve and concentration under pressure do not permit the luxury of an artist's temperament.

Background. Martina Navratilova was born in Prague, Czechoslovakia, Oct. 10, 1956. Both her mother and stepfather were tennis administrators for the Czech government and her grandmother had been a nationally ranked tennis star. Martina was the national champion of her native Czechoslovakia from 1972–75 before she defected to the United States in 1975 to accelerate her professional career.

Now living in Dallas, she is considered by her peer pros to have more ability physically (5′ 7″ and 145 lbs, or 1.7 m and 65.8 kg) than anyone else on the circuit. Navratilova's serve is a savage left-handed sweeper that draws rivals clear off the court. Her volley is a veritable rapier and her shoulder strength makes her groundstrokes potent yet effortless.

Off the court, she demonstrates a lively extrovert personality, often joining the disco scene and enjoying her stylish vacation condominium in Palm Springs—both facilitated by her $500,000-plus earnings during 1979. It is expected that she will be granted U. S. citizenship within a year, when she can become a member of the U. S. Federation and Wightman Cup teams.

EUGENE L. SCOTT

MARTINA NAVRATILOVA

UPI

OHIRA, Masayoshi

On Dec. 7, 1978, 68-year-old Masayoshi Ohira was inaugurated as the new prime minister of Japan. His installation culminated a surprising series of events of the previous month. As the election campaign began on November 1, incumbent Prime Minister Takeo Fukuda was the choice of the Liberal-Democratic party (LDP), which held a slim coalition majority in the Japanese Diet (legislature). But in the November 27 party primary, Ohira defeated Fukuda 748 points to 638 (one point equals 1,000 votes). A run-off ballot was scheduled for December 1, but Fukuda withdrew and Ohira became president of the party. His election as prime minister by the full Diet was then routine.

In June 1979, Prime Minister Ohira welcomed to Tokyo the leaders of the six major Western powers for a summit conference on energy and world economy. On September 7, hoping to solidify his political standing, Ohira called for new national elections for the House of Representatives. Although the LDP actually lost ground in the October 7 balloting, the support of independents maintained for it a paper-thin majority and Ohira was returned as prime minister.

Background. Born on March 12, 1910, in remote Kagawa prefecture on Shikoku island, Ohira was the second son in a poor farm family. Studying secretly, he prepared for and passed stiff entrance exams for Tokyo University of Commerce (now Hitotsubashi University), from which he was graduated in 1936. As a student, Ohira joined a Christian sect whose doctrines resemble those of the Quakers.

After graduation, Ohira entered the ministry of finance and served there until the early 1950's. He was first elected to the House of Representatives in 1952 and won ten consecutive terms. In July 1960, he became chief cabinet secretary under Premier Hayato Ikeda and in July 1962 was appointed foreign minister. He later served as minister of international trade and industry (1968–70), foreign minister again (1972–74), finance minister (1974–76), and secretary general of the LDP. In the 1960's Ohira helped prepare the successful national income-doubling plan, and in 1972, as foreign minister, played a key role in normalizing relations with Peking.

ARDATH W. BURKS

SCHREYER, Edward Richard

At age 43 Edward Richard Schreyer became the 22nd governor-general of Canada, the youngest person, the first western Canadian, and the first non-French or non-English Canadian ever to hold the position.

Installed on Jan. 22, 1979, he succeeded Jules Léger, former diplomat, who retired after five years in the post. The installation involved signing oaths of office pledging allegiance to Elizabeth II as Queen of Canada and service to Canadians. In his address following the swearing-in, Schreyer said, "The freedoms we now share and cherish are equal to the best of the countries on this planet; . . . to accept the shattering of the Canadian mosaic is to break faith with all who endured so much to build so well what we have today." His reference was aimed chiefly at Quebec separatists. During the address, Schreyer spoke in English, French, German, Ukrainian, and Polish.

As governor-general his duties include serving as Canada's host to visiting heads of state, presiding over the opening of Parliament, and signing parliamentary bills into law. His office is also the ultimate safeguard of the Canadian constitution.

Background. Edward Schreyer was born in Beausejour, Manitoba, on Dec. 21, 1935, to parents of Austro-German descent. A former school teacher and lecturer at the University of Manitoba, he was first elected to the Manitoba legislature in 1958, the youngest member of the house.

Elected twice (1965 and 1968) to the Canadian House of Commons, he became leader of the Manitoba New Democratic party in 1969. In June 1969 he became premier of Manitoba, a position he held until his party's defeat by the Progressive Conservative party on Oct. 11, 1977. With the approval of Queen Elizabeth, Prime Minister Pierre Elliott Trudeau selected Schreyer to be governor-general of Canada in December 1978.

His Excellency lives at the official residence of the governor-general, Rideau Hall in Ottawa, with his wife Lilly and children Lisa, Karmel, Jason, and Toban.

BARRY M. GOUGH

STARGELL, Willie

In a baseball season highlighted by the outstanding accomplishments of such veteran stars as Lou Brock, Carl Yastrzemski, Gaylord Perry, Pete Rose, and other players approaching or passing their 40th birthdays, the performance of 38-year-old slugger Willie Stargell was perhaps the most wondrous and most heartily congratulated by teammates and opposing players alike.

The affable first baseman, known to his Pittsburgh Pirate teammates as "Pops," led the tightly-knit Bucs to a World Series victory over the Baltimore Orioles. A total of 12 hits, three home runs, seven RBIs, and a .400 batting average in the Series—including four hits, two RBIs, and a dramatic game-winning homer in the decisive seventh game—made him the oldest Most Valuable Player (MVP) in the 25-year history of that World Series award. His leadership both on and off the field won him the MVP in the National League playoffs and a share of the league MVP award (with Keith Hernandez of the St. Louis Cardinals) for the regular season. Although he batted .281, with 32 homers and 82 RBIs, it was his enthusiasm and inspiration to younger players that was most valuable to

WILLIE STARGELL

UPI

his Pirate "family." His devotion to the city and his work on the Sickle Cell Anemia Association have made him a loved and respected figure in Pittsburgh.

Background. Wilver Dornel Stargell was born on March 6, 1941, in Earlsboro, OK. His love for baseball began as early as age 7 and hasn't diminished since. His enthusiasm and light-hearted approach to the game make him in many ways still a kid. Stargell broke into the major leagues with the Pittsburgh Pirates in 1962 and has been with that team ever since. Perhaps his best year was 1973, when he led the league in home runs (43), RBIs (119), and doubles (43); the MVP, however, went that year to Pete Rose. Willie's only World Series appearance prior to 1979 came in 1971, when the Pirates defeated the Baltimore Orioles, 4 games to 3. Following relatively poor seasons in 1976 and 1977, Stargell appeared ready for retirement. In 1978, however, he was the National League Comeback Player of the Year and his performance in 1979 showed that he was anything but washed up.

JEFF HACKER

THATCHER, Margaret

On May 4, 1979, Margaret Thatcher was called to Buckingham Palace and asked by Queen Elizabeth II to form a new British government. She thus became the first female to head a government in Western Europe. For a woman only 53 years old, a member of Britain's oldest and most traditional political party, it was a formidable achievement and a tribute to her own remarkable determination.

Mrs. Thatcher, a hard-liner on most issues, is opposed to the power of the British labor unions, high taxation, and government intervention of most kinds. In terms of foreign affairs, she is suspicious of the policy of détente with the USSR. As prime minister, she hopes to encourage the skills and efforts of the British people.

Background. Margaret Hilda Roberts Thatcher was born on October 13, 1925, in Grantham, a small town in Eastern England. Her family was religious and fairly strict, and her father, a local storekeeper, instilled in his two daughters the virtues of hard work and self-

MARGARET THATCHER

UPI

reliance. She was a successful student at the local grammar (public) school and won a place in Oxford University, where she studied chemistry. For four years (1947–51) she was a research chemist, before suddenly switching to the study of law. She was called to the bar in 1953.

Her political ambitions meant that she tried several times to win a seat in Parliament, succeeding in the Oct. 3, 1959, general election when she was elected for Finchley, a north London suburb. Her quick analytical mind and capacity for hard work were soon noticed, and only two years later Prime Minister Harold Macmillan appointed her a junior pensions minister. She retained the post until Labour's victory in 1964. She later served in Edward Heath's Opposition (shadow) cabinet.

After the Conservative election victory of 1970 she emerged as an important figure on the right wing of the party. Prime Minister Heath appointed her Secretary of State for Education and Science. Although she antagonized much of Britain's traditionally liberal educational establishment, she was highly respected for her competence and clarity.

When Heath was forced to stand for reelection as party leader in 1975, Thatcher was the only candidate of weight prepared to challenge him directly. "The best man we have" became a common description of her in Tory circles. She was elected by a large majority, even receiving votes from Conservative members of Parliament of more liberal persuasion.

In 1951 the future leader of Britain married Denis Thatcher, a businessman. They are the parents of twins, Mark and Carol, born in 1953.

SIMON HOGGART

MOTHER TERESA

Mother Teresa of Calcutta, a Roman Catholic nun who has cared for the poor and sick in India for more than three decades, was named the recipient of the Nobel Peace Prize on Oct. 17, 1979. Upon hearing that she had been chosen for the award, the 69-year-old nun told a reporter: "Thank God for his gift for the poor. God's blessing will be with the people who have given the prize. I hope it will be a real means of giving peace and happiness in the world today." She added that the prize money, equal to about $190,000 (U. S.), would be used to build homes for the destitute, "especially for the lepers."

Background. Agnes Gonxha Bojaxhiu was born to an Albanian grocer and his wife on Aug. 27, 1910, in Skopje (now in Yugoslavia). Attending a non-Catholic school but inspired by village priests, she knew at age 12 that her calling was to become a nun. Stirred by the accounts of missionaries working in India, she set sail at age 17. She took her first vows on May 24, 1928. She joined a community of Irish nuns, the Sisters of Loreto, and became a teacher—and later principal—at a Loreto school for the daughters of prosperous families in Calcutta. Although she worked in the school's sheltered environment for 20 years, she was deeply aware of the hunger, poverty, and sickness in the surrounding slums. In 1948, Mother Teresa received permission to leave the convent and devote her life to the poor and destitute. She founded a new religious order, the Society of the Missionaries of Charities. The society received canonical sanction on Oct. 7, 1950, and Mother Teresa took Indian citizenship. As the new order grew, Mother Teresa's work carried beyond the slums of Calcutta to the other cities in India. By 1979, the Missionaries of Charities had grown to 158 branches, 1,800 nuns, and 12,000 co-workers; it operates children's homes, medical stations, havens for the dying, and leper colonies throughout the world.

In her coarse white sari bordered by three blue stripes, Mother Teresa became one of the most loved figures in the Catholic Church. In addition to the Nobel Prize, she has won several other awards.

JEFF HACKER

TUCHMAN, Barbara

In February 1979, historian Barbara Tuchman, a two-time Pulitzer Prize-winner, was elected president of the 250-member American Academy and Institute of Arts and Letters, becoming the first woman to head that 80-year-old prestigious organization.

Mrs. Tuchman, who combines readability with meticulous scholarship, received her first Pulitzer Prize, for general nonfiction, in 1963 for her best-selling *The Guns of August* (1962). Her book *Stilwell and the American Experience in China, 1911–45* (1971), brought her another Pulitzer Prize in the same category in 1972.

An adherent of the "How" school, rather than the "Why," and "a seeker of the small facts, not the big Explanation," Mrs. Tuchman has tried to follow the dictum of the 19th-century German historian Leopold von Ranke, that the historian must make every effort to reconstruct history as it actually happened. Her book, *A Distant Mirror; The Calamitous 14th Century* (1978), the product of several years of intensive research, remained on the best seller lists in 1979.

Background. Barbara Wertheim Tuchman, a daughter of the financier Maurice Wertheim, and a granddaughter of the noted diplomat Henry Morgenthau, Sr., was born in New York City on Jan. 30, 1912. A voracious reader, she became fascinated with history and world affairs in early childhood. After attending New York City private schools she studied history and literature at Radcliffe College, where she earned her B. A. in 1933. She worked as a research assistant for the Institute of Pacific Relations (1934–35), and she was successively editorial assistant, correspondent in Spain, and free-lance writer for the *Nation* (1935–38). In 1939 she was American correspondent for the British *New Statesman and Nation,* and during part of World War II she worked at the Far Eastern news desk of the Office of War Information.

Others of her books are *The Lost British Policy; Britain and Spain since 1700* (1938); *Bible and Sword; England and Palestine from the Bronze Age to Balfour* (1956); *The Zimmerman Telegram* (1958); *The Proud Tower: A Portrait of the World Before the War, 1890–1914* (1966); and *Notes from China* (1972).

Married in 1940 to Dr. Lester R. Tuchman, a physician, Barbara Tuchman has three daughters. She divides her time between her homes in New York and Connecticut.

HENRY S. SLOAN

VEIL, Simone

The election of French Minister of Health Simone Veil as president of the first popularly-elected Parliament of the European Community (EC), coming in the same year as the installation of Margaret Thatcher as prime minister of Great Britain and Maria de Lurdes Pintassilgo as premier of Portugal, led many to call 1979 Europe's Year of Women.

Since 1974, when she joined the cabinet of President Valéry Giscard d'Estaing, Veil has been regarded as one of France's most popular and capable politicians. Quiet, elegant, and forceful, she worked to reduce medical costs, improve prison and hospital facilities, and combat smoking and alcoholism. Despite harsh opposition, she also pushed through liberal abortion and contraception laws.

At Giscard's urging, Veil agreed to head the party ticket of his own Union pour la Démocratie Française in the EC presidential election. Her candidacy won the support of most Christian Democrats, Liberals, British Conservatives, and ultimately, French Gaullists. On June 10, Veil received 192 of 377 votes on the second ballot to become the first president of a popularly elected European Parliament. Italian Socialist Mario Zagari won 138 votes, and Italian Communist Giorgio Amendola 47. As president, Veil promised to work for aid to underdeveloped nations, improvement in the status of women, and the strengthening of the new European Parliament.

© 1978 MIRIAM CARAVELLA

BARBARA TUCHMAN

Background. Simone Veil, née Jacob, was born in Nice, France, on July 13, 1927. A Jew, she was deported with her father, brother, and sister to Auschwitz in 1944 and later to Bergen-Belsen. She alone survived. After the war, she entered the prestigious Institut d'Etudes Politiques and later took a law degree. She became a magistrate in 1956 and worked in the ministry of justice from 1957 to 1965. In 1969 she joined the staff of Minister of Justice René Pleven and in 1970 became general secretary of the High Council of the Magistrature. Over the years, Veil became known as an expert on juvenile delinquency and the problems of the mentally ill.

In a magazine interview after leaving Giscard's cabinet, she commented: "I am an alibi-woman. Men put us there to give themselves a good conscience."

F. ROY WILLIS

VOIGHT, Jon

A conscientious actor, more concerned with craftsmanship than with glamour or material gain, Jon Voight received the best actor award of the Academy of Motion Picture Arts and Sciences on April 9, 1979, for his distinguished portrayal of a paraplegic Vietnam war veteran in *Coming Home* (1978). The performance brought him, in addition, the New York and Los Angeles Film Critics' awards, the National Board of Review prize, the Cannes Festival prize, and the Golden Globe. In 1979 Voight also received plaudits for his portrayal of a down-and-out boxer in *The Champ,* a remake of the 1931 Wallace Beery-Jackie Cooper film.

Ten years earlier, Voight had appeared in his first starring film role in John Schlesinger's *Midnight Cowboy* (1969). That performance had brought him an Oscar nomination and awards from the New York Film Critics and the National Society of Film Critics.

In 1979 Voight was at work on a film script, *The Shore,* in collaboration with Dory Previn.

Background. Jon Voight, the son of a golf professional of Czech ancestry, was born on Dec. 29, 1938, in Yonkers, NY. He attended parochial schools there and in White Plains. At an early age he demonstrated

On Oct. 6, Volcker, saying he saw "no reasonable alternative," took strong steps to curb that demand even at the risk of pushing the country into a deep recession. For the time being, Volcker had, with only mild grumbling, the public support of members of the Carter administration, Congress, and the banking and business communities.

Background. Volcker was born in Cape May, NJ, Sept. 5, 1927, and reared in Teaneck, NJ, where his father served as city manager. He was graduated summa cum laude from Princeton (1949), earned a master of arts from Harvard University Graduate School of Public Administration (1951), and spent a year as Rotary Foundation Fellow at the London School of Economics (1951–52).

The towering Volcker (he stands 6' 7" or 2 m) has spent much of his career in the fiscal and monetary arena. As head of the New York Fed, which acts for the Federal Reserve System and the Department of the Treasury in foreign exchange matters, the cigar-smoking monetarist established a reputation among international central bankers. During his earlier years as undersecretary of the treasury (1969–74), the dollar was unpegged from gold and he played a key role in the transition from fixed to floating exchange rates. After a year at Princeton as senior fellow at the Woodrow Wilson School of Public and International Affairs, Volcker returned to the New York Fed in 1975 (he had been a research assistant, 1952–57) to complete the unexpired term of Alfred Hayes. In 1976 he was appointed to a five-year term.

Volcker worked as an economist for Chase Manhattan Bank (1957–61) and as the bank's vice president and director of planning (1965–69). He was also with the U. S. Department of the Treasury (1961–65).

MARY TOBIN

UPI

JON VOIGHT

a talent for mimicry and comedy, and in high school he performed in school plays. After graduation from Catholic University in 1960, he studied acting for four years at Stanford Meisner's Neighborhood Playhouse in New York City. In the early 1960's he made his Broadway debut in *The Sound of Music,* singing "I am Sixteen Going on Seventeen . . ." to actress Lauri Peters. (The couple were later married for five years.) In 1965 Voight appeared off Broadway in *A View from the Bridge.* In 1967 he starred in the short-lived Broadway production of *That Summer—That Fall,* earning a Theater World award. During those years he also worked in summer stock and television.

Other Voight films include *Catch-22* (1970), *The Revolutionary* (1970), *Deliverance* (1972), *All-American Boy* (1973), *Conrack* (1974), and *The Odessa File* (1974).

Jon Voight married a second time and is the father of two children. A pacifist, he has been active in Jane Fonda's Entertainment People for Peace and Freedom. He continues to hone his skills as an actor by attending classes at a Hollywood drama school.

HENRY S. SLOAN

VOLCKER, Paul A.

The appointment of Paul A. Volcker as chairman of the Federal Reserve Board on Aug. 6, 1979, was acclaimed by domestic and international financial leaders. The conservative president of the Federal Reserve Bank of New York inherited the post with inflation soaring, the money supply expanding, and business borrowing at a hectic pace. In contrast to the "slow and easy" approach of his predecessor G. William Miller, Volcker responded aggressively, pushing interest rates to record levels within the first month of his chairmanship. Because of continued demand for credit, the money supply surged despite these actions.

WATSON, Thomas J., Jr.

When President Jimmy Carter met with Soviet President Leonid Brezhnev at the Vienna summit conference in June 1979 he introduced Thomas J. Watson, Jr., the retired board chairman of International Business Machines Corp. (IBM), as the new U. S. ambassador to the USSR. Watson, who attended the summit in his capacity as head of the General Advisory Committee of the Arms Control and Disarmament Agency, was the first noncareer diplomat in many years to be named to the Moscow post. Soviet officials, who had come to look on Ambassador Malcolm Toon with disfavor, welcomed the appointment of Watson. President Carter formally nominated Watson on July 20, 1979, and Ambassador Watson presented his credentials in a Kremlin ceremony on October 29.

Background. Thomas John Watson, Jr., was born in Dayton, OH, on Jan. 8, 1914, the eldest son of Thomas J. Watson, Sr., founder of IBM. After graduation from Brown University (B. A., 1937), he joined IBM as a junior salesman. As an Army Air Force pilot in World War II, he spent six months in Russia under the lend-lease airlift program. Discharged in 1946 with the rank of lieutenant colonel and awarded an Air Medal, he returned to IBM and rose rapidly through the corporate ranks, succeeding his father as president in 1952. He served as IBM chairman (1961–74) and then as chairman of IBM's executive committee. He was also a member of the boards of directors of several other large companies.

Watson, who believes that the enlightened use of technology may be the answer to the problems of hunger, disease, and drudgery, served in 1977 on the American Committee on U. S.-Soviet Relations, which recommended greater cooperation between the two powers. His many honors include the Presidential Medal of Freedom.

Watson enjoys yachting and skiing and flies his own plane. He and his wife have a son and five daughters.

HENRY S. SLOAN

BOLIVIA

Deadlocked elections, military coups, general strikes and protests, and the implementation of censorship and martial law made 1979 a year of unremitting political turmoil in Bolivia. By year's end there had been four different heads of government, and the crisis situation still had not been fully resolved.

Government and Politics. In a move to smooth the way for a return from military to democratic rule, 15 cabinet ministers under President David Padella Arancibia resigned on January 15. Presidential elections, scheduled for July 1, had been promised by Arancibia when he took power in November 1978. The months prior to the election saw jockeying for position among numerous candidates. Former President Hugo Banzer Suárez, who was overthrown in 1978, returned from exile in Argentina. Banzer promised to lead "nationalist forces" in the election. The seven other candidates were headed by leftist Hernan Siles Zuazo, who was apparently robbed of a clear victory in 1978, and Victor Paz Estenssoro, the leader of a centrist alliance. Labor leader Juan Lechin Oquendo, another favorite of the left, chose not to run.

Evidence that a military coup had been averted surfaced two days before the election, when the defense minister, Gen. Hugo Cespedes suddenly resigned. Candidate Siles took an early lead in the voting, but the final outcome was a stalemate with Paz; Banzer finished third. With none of the candidates able to gain a stable legislative majority, Congress met to resolve the dilemma. After seven inconclusive votes, the Congress finally compromised August 6 by electing Walter Guevara Arce as provisional president of the republic until new elections in May 1980. Civilian government had been restored—temporarily.

On October 11 an army commander in the northeast, Col. Walter Salame, announced that he had led a "peaceful" rebellion against the government. On November 1, army troops led by Col. Alberto Natusch Busch surrounded the presidential palace; Natusch announced the formation of a new military government, and proclaimed himself president. Bolivian labor unions immediately called a general strike to protest the coup, and crowds of demonstrators expressed their opposition. Natusch dissolved parliament November 2 and declared martial law the following day. Strict censorship was also imposed, and planes and tanks were used to quell public disorder. Within one week, 60 persons had been killed and 100 wounded.

Faced with unrelenting opposition, Natusch finally agreed to step down, providing that Guevara would not be reinstated as acting president. On November 16, Congress selected Senate President Lydia Gueiler Tejada as the new interim

Interim President Walter Guevara Arce (*with medallion*) leaves the legislature in the company of his predecessor, David Padilla Arancibia (*in uniform*), and eventual successor, Senate President Lydia Gueiler Tejada.

UPI

After a November military coup, Col. Alberto Natusch Busch posted troops in La Paz to quell protestors.

president. Gueiler, a close political ally of labor leader Lechin, would remain in office until the installation of a freely elected president in August 1980. Democratic rule had again been restored, but again it was shaky.

President Gueiler ordered the resignation November 23 of Bolivia's army commander, Gen. Luis García Meza. The latter refused to step down, however, and threatened revolt. Gueiler named a replacement the following day, and Garcia Meza made clear that the rebellion was not against the new government but against the military officials appointed by it. As the year came to an end Gueiler's government faced continued resistance from the military and protests from Bolivian peasants against tough new economic policies. The path to stable democratic government still appeared to be long and rocky.

——————— **BOLIVIA • Information Highlights** ———————

Official Name: Republic of Bolivia.
Location: West-central South America.
Area: 424,164 square miles (1 098 581 km²).
Population (1979 est.): 5,200,000.
Chief Cities (1976 census): Sucre, the legal capital, 63,259; La Paz, the actual capital, 654,713; Santa Cruz de la Sierra, 255,568; Cochabamba, 204,414.
Government: *Head of state and government,* Lydia Gueiler Tejada, interim president (took office Nov. 1979). *Legislature*—Congress: Senate and Chamber of Deputies.
Monetary Unit: Peso (25 pesos equal U. S.$1, Dec. 1979).
Manufactures (major products): Textiles, cottage industry goods, processed goods, vegetables.
Agriculture (major products): Potatoes, corn, sugarcane, cassava, cotton, barley, rice, wheat, coffee, bananas.
Major Export Commodities: Tin, petroleum.

Economy and Foreign Affairs. The continuing political crisis further delayed vital decisions in all areas of the nation's economy. Banzer's ambitious investment program, heavily dependent on oil production, failed miserably. According to that plan, oil production was to increase to 280,000 barrels per day by 1980; actual production decreased to less than 32,000 barrels per day, 30% less than the 1973 peak and barely enough to support rising domestic demand. Despite buoyant tin prices, the balance of payments deficit became even more acute than it already was, partly because of increased foreign debt.

In late October, Bolivia set aside its political woes to host the ninth General Assembly of the Organization of American States (OAS). Ministers from the 26 OAS member nations, including U. S. Secretary of State Cyrus Vance, attended the meetings in La Paz, October 22–31. In his opening address, then interim President Guevara brought up two issues of concern to Bolivia. He demanded that Chile return territory ceded 100 years before that would provide Bolivia with a corridor to the Pacific Ocean; and he protested U. S. plans to sell stockpiled tin as a "grave threat to the economy of a friendly country." On October 26 the body voted, 25–0, in support of a sovereign access to the Pacific. Vance praised Bolivia for its return to democratic rule.

PAUL CAMMACK
University of Glasgow (Scotland)

BOTANY

Bamboo, allelopathy, and phylogenetics were topics of special interest to botanists during 1979.

Umbrella Bamboo. A beautiful species of bamboo, called "umbrella," whose genus had been incorrectly identified until June, began to blossom for the first time in 100 years in northern Europe and was expected to bloom shortly in the United States and the rest of the world. Flowers sent from Germany to the Smithsonian Institution in Washington, DC, enabled Dr. Thomas Soderstrom, a curator of botany at the museum, to identify the plant correctly. The bamboo was renamed Thamnocalamus spathaceus (Franchet) Soderstrom after the men (Adrien Franchet and Dr. Soderstrom) who identified the species and genus, respectively. Because most bamboo species have a genetic "clock" that determines their longevity, botanists expected the world's umbrella bamboo to die after the current resurgence.

Allelopathy. Allelopathy, a condition in which one kind of plant produces a chemical substance poisonous to another plant or plants, is a word that botanists have been using increasingly in recent years. The classic example of an allelopathic plant is the walnut tree; the fruit and leaves of the walnut tree inhibit the growth of any plants around it. Scientists have attempted to solve the replanting problems that may occur with fruit trees as a result of the allelopathic influence of trees previously planted in the immediate area.

Although wide use of the term is a fairly recent development, awareness of the phenomenon certainly is not. Farmers have recognized the principle and put it to good use for centuries. For example, barley is used as a "smother crop" to limit the growth of weeds.

Phylogenetic Systems. Taxonomic systems that reflect the evolution of flora and fauna are called phylogenetic. Since the identification of any plant or animal implies knowledge of its biological affinities and evolutionary relationships, one of the advantages of phylogenetic systems is that they are rich in informational content. The classification of the plant kingdom continues to be modified, therefore, as new information becomes available. In 1979, the classification of flowering plants again benefited from research in paleobotany and biochemical systematics and the use of scanning and transmission electron microscopes. Data obtained from these sources, used in conjunction with more traditionally derived information, helped to refine further botanical classification systems. Indeed it was the complicated procedures of plant taxonomy that allowed Dr. Soderstrom to identify correctly the umbrella bamboo.

DONALD W. NEWSOM
Department of Horticulture
Louisiana State University

BRAZIL

Gen. João Baptista Figueiredo was sworn in as the new president of Brazil on March 15, 1979, reaffirming his dedication to the full restoration of democracy and freedom of expression. To the surprise of many, he steadfastly pursued this policy of political liberalization. The choice of outgoing President Ernesto Geisel in the October 1978 election, President Figueiredo adopted populist style and refused to be provoked into repressive actions by widespread strikes and general labor unrest. Left-wing political exiles were allowed to return to the country under a new amnesty program, and the Figueiredo administration's foreign policy moved Brazil closer to the "nonaligned" nations.

Political "Opening." Institutional Act Number Five, the legal cornerstone of the repressive regime fashioned in the late 1960's, expired at the beginning of 1979. The abrogation of this act, which had empowered the president to dismiss Congress and suspend the civil rights of any citizen, was the culmination of President Geisel's program of *distensão*—"decompression." The liberalization continued under Figueiredo's policy of *abertura*—"opening"—which called for amnesty for most political prisoners, the return of political exiles, the lifting of restrictions on the formation of new political parties, and an eventual return to direct elections for the nation's president, senators, and state governors.

In June, Figueiredo's amnesty bill was introduced in Congress, where some legislators denounced it for not going far enough: prisoners convicted of "terrorism" or "armed resistance" were not covered, and former government employees were not guaranteed job reinstatement. Opposition to the proposal was dramatized by a mass rally in Rio de Janeiro and by a hunger strike in the same city by 31 excluded prisoners. In August, however, the bill was enacted without any major amendments. The new law restored civil rights to some 6,000 Brazilians, opened the door for the return of exiled politicians, and lifted the ban on the formation of new political parties.

Among the first prominent exiles to return was Leonel Brizola, the governor of Rio Grande do Sul prior to the 1964 military coup and a powerful force in the Brazilian Labor Party (PTB), which was dissolved by the government in 1966. The disappointingly small crowd—fewer than 3,000—that greeted Brizola upon his return in September boded ill for his plans to revive the PTB.

Much more impressive was Pernambuco's reception later in the month for its pre-1964 governor, Miguel Arraes. Some 60,000 citizens turned out in Recife, the state capital, for the welcome. On hand to greet Arraes was the rising star of the Brazilian labor movement, Luís Inácio da Silva, popularly known as "Lula."

In Brasília, March 15, Luis Viana Filho, president of the Senate, presides as Gen. João Baptista Figueiredo takes the presidential oath of office.

Da Silva traveled from his home in São Paulo to welcome Arraes in Pernambuco.

In October the most celebrated of all the exiles, the legendary Luís Carlos Prestes, secretary general of the Brazilian Communist Party, returned to a warm reception in Rio.

Labor Unrest. Shortly after President Figueiredo's inauguration in March, 180,000 metalworkers walked off their jobs in São Paulo. Complaining that their wage increases had fallen far behind rises in the cost of living, the workers demanded an immediate 77% wage hike. Their employers, supported by Planning Minister Mário Henrique Simonsen, refused the demand. The resulting strike was officially declared illegal, but the government moved cautiously. It occupied union headquarters and arrested strike leaders, but soon released them. Although some union officials urged acceptance of a 63% pay raise offered by the employers, most of the metalworkers followed the leadership of the charismatic young Lula and held out for a greater increase. The strike finally ended after 13 days, when Lula and the government came to a bargaining agreement. The final settlement was reached in May, and although it held the workers to a 63% wage increase, it protected them from employer and government reprisals, recognized their elected leaders, and

elevated Lula to national prominence. He became a featured speaker at labor rallies around the country.

The defiance of the government by the striking metalworkers encouraged walkouts in countless other industries. Even the public sector, in which strikes were expressly forbidden, was crippled by work stoppages. As the cost of living rose to an annual rate of nearly 80% in March and April, the highest since 1964, hospital workers, bus drivers, schoolteachers, journalists, construction workers, and other public and private employees throughout Brazil went on strike. The strikes continued through most of the year, with an estimated 100,000 or more workers on strike on any given workday. Faced with these massive walkouts, President Figueiredo still eschewed repressive action, preached conciliation, and approved wage hikes of as much as 100%.

Such large wage increases were resisted by Planning Minister Simonsen—Brazil's economic "czar"—whose anti-inflationary program called for holding wages at or below the rise in the cost of living. In May, Simonsen's wishes were granted, as the government limited the annual readjustment of the minimum wage to 45.4%. However, this served only to fuel labor unrest and Simonsen resigned three months later. He was replaced by Antônio Delfim Neto, who had been finance minister during 1967–1974 and was regarded as the author of Brazil's economic "miracle" of that period. (The nation's economy grew at an annual rate of more than 10% during those years.) Hardly considered a friend of labor in the past, Delfim cultivated a populist image in his new post and advocated such measures as a semiannual minimum wage adjustment to keep workers' incomes abreast of the cost of living.

Foreign Affairs. Dependent on foreign suppliers for 80% of its petroleum, Brazil pushed ahead in its search for domestic oil and alternative sources of energy. A promising technology was the substitution of alcohol, derived from the country's abundant sugarcane crops, for gasoline. (*See also* CHEMISTRY.)

At the same time, however, the government took care to maintain good relations with the

─────── **BRAZIL · Information Highlights** ───────

Official Name: Federative Republic of Brazil.
Location: Eastern South America.
Area: 3,286,478 square miles (8 511 965 km²).
Population (1979 est.): 118,700,000.
Chief Cities (1975 est.): Brasília, the capital, 241,543; São Paulo, 7,200,000; Rio de Janeiro, 4,860,000; Belo Horizonte, 1,560,000.
Government: *Head of state and government,* João Baptista Figueiredo, president (took office March 1979). *Legislature*—National Congress: Federal Senate and Chamber of Deputies.
Monetary Unit: New Cruzeiro (31.01 n. cruzeiros equal U. S.$1, Nov. 1979).
Manufactures (major products): Steel, chemicals, petrochemicals, machinery, consumer goods.
Agriculture (major products): Coffee, rice, beef, corn, milk, sugarcane, soybeans, cacao.

oil-producing nations of the Middle East and Africa. In May, during a visit by the vice president of Iraq, Brazil recognized the Palestine Liberation Organization (PLO) as the sole representative of the Palestinian people.

Energy was the prime topic of discussion during the April visit of West German Chancellor Helmut Schmidt. Figueiredo assured his guest that Brazil would honor its agreement to buy eight nuclear power plants from West Germany, despite increasing popular concern about the program's exceedingly high cost and possible safety problems.

In South America, Brazil shifted its attention from its conservative southern neighbors— Argentina, Uruguay, and Paraguay—to the more Third World–oriented nations of the north, its partners in the Amazon Pact. In the Nicaraguan crisis, Brazil followed the lead of Venezuela and the other Andean countries by breaking diplomatic relations with the Somoza dictatorship in June.

Trade and Monetary Policy. In his inaugural speech, President Figueiredo specified reversing the nation's balance-of-payments deficit as a primary goal of his administration. The government subsequently announced an immediate 90–100% reduction in the 360-day prior deposit levied on imports; a 10% cut in tax exemptions for exports of manufactured goods; and a 2.5% devaluation of the cruzeiro. By the end of May, after seven more devaluations, the cruzeiro had decreased in value by 22% as against the U. S. dollar.

NEILL MACAULAY
Department of History
University of Florida

BRITISH COLUMBIA

A controversial budget, provincial elections, and a major private investment initiative held the attention of British Columbians in 1979.

Budget. On April 2, Finance Minister Evan Wolfe presented to the legislature a $4.57 billion balanced budget for fiscal 1979–80. The provincial budget called for a reduction in the sales tax from 5 to 4%, a lower personal income tax, an increase of $100 in grants to homeowners, and other tax cuts to encourage private investment.

Elections. Immediately following the introduction of the budget, Premier William R. Bennett called for provincial general elections to gain public endorsement of his policies. He appealed to the electorate to choose private enterprise with individual ownership over what he termed "national socialism." The opposition stressed integrity in government. In the May 10 elections, Premier Bennett's Social Credit party was returned to power, but with a reduced majority in the Legislative Assembly. The legislature was expanded from 55 to 57 seats, with the Socreds winning 31 (a loss of 4) and the

New Democrats 26 (an increase of 8). The Liberals and Conservatives together captured only 5% of the popular vote and failed to win a single seat. The Social Credit party took 49% of the popular vote and the New Democrats 46%.

Legislature. The throne speech opening the new parliament on June 6 included government promises of a dental care program and human rights legislation. Two days later, the budget was reintroduced. The session was also marked by passage of 35 bills, including a provision for nondiscriminatory automobile insurance rates, pay increases for members of the legislature, and a controversial measure for the development of the Whistler resort. In August, the legislature was hastily recalled to repeal the Obsolete Statutes Repeal Act passed earlier in the regular session. Hearings continued on uranium mining in the province.

Ownership Initiative. As part of his overall policy to provide greater ownership and investment opportunities to British Columbians, Premier Bennett announced January 11 that his government would distribute to eligible persons in the province five free shares in the crown-owned British Columbia Resources Investment Corporation. Canadian citizens would be allowed to purchase an additional 5,000 shares in the $151.5-million company. The corporation holds oil and gas rights, pulp mills, sawmills, a plywood plant, and pipelines. Bennett's plan resulted in the distribution of 86 million shares.

Other. Political controversy erupted in the fall with revelations of activities by Social Credit workers in the so-called "lettergate" affair and the release of land from the agricultural land reserve.

The province's compulsory heroin treatment program was ruled unconstitutional by the British Columbia Supreme Court. Nathaniel Nemetz was appointed Chief Justice of the Court of Appeal after the resignation of John Ferris.

The province mourned the passing of W. A. C. Bennett, its premier from 1952 to 1972. Bennett died on February 23 at the age of 78.

NORMAN J. RUFF
University of Victoria

— BRITISH COLUMBIA · Information Highlights —

Area: 366,255 square miles (948 600 km²).
Population (1979 est.): 2,562,600.
Chief Cities (1976 census): Victoria, the capital, 62,551; Vancouver, 410,188.
Government (1979): *Chief Officers*—lt. gov., Henry Bell-Irving; premier, William R. Bennett (Social Credit party); chief justice, Court of Appeal, Nathaniel T. Nemetz; Supreme Court, Allan McEachern. *Legislature*—Legislative Assembly, 57 members.
Education (1979–80 est.): *Enrollment*—public elementary and secondary schools, 513,870 pupils; private schools, 23,950; Indian (federal) schools, 2,715; post-secondary, 47,960 students.
Public Finance (1977–78): *Revenues,* $4,196,600,000; *expenditures,* $4,266,300,000.
Personal Income (average weekly salary, May 1979): $323.26.
Unemployment Rate (July 1979, seasonally adjusted): 7.3%.
(All monetary figures are in Canadian dollars.)

BULGARIA

In 1979, the government of Todor Zhivkov, first secretary of the Communist party and president of the State Council, faced the two main problems confronting the rest of the world—energy shortages and economic instability.

Domestic Affairs. On May 21, three days before Soviet Premier Aleksei N. Kosygin called for the Communist-bloc nations to adopt "stringent" energy conservation measures, the Bulgarian government instituted an "odd-even" plan which banned the driving of private automobiles on certain days. It also raised by about 50% the price of gasoline for private motorists.

According to official sources, national income and industrial production in 1978 increased by 7%; agricultural production and labor productivity increased by 5 and 6%, respectively. Still, the gross national product per capita did not exceed $2,000 (U. S.), falling short of the projected 7%, and the standard of living in Bulgaria continued to be the lowest in Europe. A nationwide campaign for "quality and efficiency" included a new pay-incentive program; a reduction in imports of consumer goods; and an increase in the private ownership of land from 12 to 30%.

Municipal elections were held on March 12, and 99.95% of the nation's 6,446,443 eligible voters took part. Candidates sponsored by the Fatherland Front received 99.88% of the vote.

Foreign Affairs and Trade. Pledging "eternal and fraternal friendship," Bulgaria continued to follow Soviet leadership in international affairs. Maj. Georgi Ivanov became the first Bulgarian to go into space, as he joined Nikolai Rukavishnikov of the Soviet Union on the Soviet Soyuz 33 spacecraft, launched April 10. (*See also* SPACE EXPLORATION.)

Bulgarian leaders made state visits to Turkey, Greece, Cuba, Mexico, and Hungary in 1979. Officials from the Soviet Union, West Germany, Portugal, Poland, Hungary, Rumania, and South Yemen were welcomed in Sofia. Several economic and cultural exchange agreements were reached during the visits.

Foreign trade exceeded 13.346 million leva in 1978, an increase of 10% over the year before.

JAN KARSKI
Georgetown University

——— **BULGARIA · Information Highlights** ———

Official Name: People's Republic of Bulgaria.
Location: Southeastern Europe.
Area: 42,758 square miles (110 743 km²).
Population (1979 est.): 8,900,000.
Government: *Head of state,* Todor Zhivkov, president of the State Council and first secretary of the Communist party (took office July 1971). *Head of government,* Stanko Todorov, chairman of the Council of Ministers (took office July 1971).
Monetary Unit: Lev (0.88 lev equals U. S.$1, 1979).
Manufactures (major products): Processed agricultural products, machinery.
Agriculture (major products): Grain, tobacco, fruits, vegetables.

BURMA

Burma moved in new directions in 1979, recognizing its need for external assistance while attacking the partisanship of "nonaligned" summitry.

Politics. There were no new political challenges to the authoritarian rule of President Ne Win, who observed his 17th year in power. The only expressed opposition was that of various insurgent groups which have been battling the government since the return of independence in 1948. An estimated 15,000 Communist rebels continued to fight government forces in northeast Burma near China. The level of conflict declined from the year before, however, and government casualties were reduced by more than half. Karen, Shan, and Kachin ethnic minority insurrections also persisted but did not seriously threaten the government.

Economy. Rice production in the 1978–79 growing year was 10.4 million tons, compared with 9.37 million the previous year. The gain reflected good weather conditions, use of higher yield seeds and more fertilizer, better government pricing, and improved political and security conditions. The increase in rice output was the main reason for a 5% increase in the country's previously stagnant gross national product. Petroleum output also increased, and a major gasoline sale was made to Japan.

But the main economic development was the government's request in April for $400 million in aid from a three-year-old foreign assistance group (including the United States). The government also expressed a new willingness to receive private foreign investments.

Foreign Relations. One of the first "neutralist" countries in the early 1950's, Burma announced in September that it was quitting the "nonaligned" group of nations and would not attend the Third World summit conference in Havana. But the Burmese were not abandoning their neutralism. Indeed the reason they left the bloc was that they no longer perceived it as neutral.

For the first time in 17 years, the Ne Win government asked the United States for direct assistance and signed an aid pact with China.

RICHARD BUTWELL, *Murray State University*

——— **BURMA · Information Highlights** ———

Official Name: Socialist Republic of the Union of Burma.
Location: Southeast Asia.
Area: 261,218 square miles (676 555 km²).
Population (1979 est.): 32,900,000.
Chief Cities (1975 est.): Rangoon, the capital, 2,100,-000; Mandalay, 417,000; Moulmein, 202,000.
Government: *Head of state,* U Ne Win, president (took office March 1974). *Head of government,* U Maung Maung Kha, prime minister (took office March 1977). *Legislature* (unicameral)—People's Assembly.
Monetary Unit: Kyat (6.150 kyats equal U. S.$1, June 1979).
Manufactures (major products): Agricultural products, textiles, wood and its products, refined petroleum.
Agriculture (major products): Rice, jute, sesame, ground nuts, tobacco, cotton, pulses, sugarcane, corn.

BUSINESS AND CORPORATE AFFAIRS

Despite a difficult economic environment, marked by high inflation and soaring interest rates, U. S. business had a good year in 1979.

Corporate Profits. Predictions of a general economic recession did not keep corporate profits from showing consistent growth. In the first quarter, profits after taxes increased by 33% over the same period in 1978. Corporate profits climbed by 13.8% in the second quarter and by 18.7% in the third, compared with the same periods the year before. Expectations for the fourth quarter were somewhat lower, but most companies reported that order books were still strong going into the Christmas season.

The Strong and the Weak. The nation's most successful companies were concentrated in the oil, mining, paper, farm equipment, and machine tool industries. Automobile companies, steel producers, airlines, tire and rubber manufacturers, and department stores made weak showings.

The oil companies were able to capitalize on a tight supply, caused in large part by the cutback in Iranian exports. In foreign countries with no gasoline price controls, U. S. oil companies were able to expand their profit margins considerably. Inventory profits abroad, a rebound in the sale of chemicals, and lowered taxes in Great Britain further fattened the bottom line. The sharp rise in profits prompted some critics, including President Jimmy Carter, to favor a windfall profits tax; others favored outright nationalization.

The oil companies were hard pressed to find ways to reinvest their profits. New lease sales were postponed by the courts and diversification ran the danger of antitrust litigation. Nevertheless, in June, Exxon Corporation decided to buy the Reliance Electric Company for a reported $1.2 billion. A subsidiary of Exxon had invented a device which the company claimed could save electricity. Exxon maintained that it needed to buy Reliance in order to manufacture the product in the shortest possible time. The government challenged the takeover.

The airline industry attracted passengers by offering more reduced fares, but rising costs ate into profit margins. Deregulation of the industry also increased competition. National Airlines became the object of a takeover fight among Pan American World Airways, Eastern Airlines, and Texas International Airlines—eventually won by Pan Am. Airplane manufacturers had near record book orders, as low capital investment in the early 1970's caught up with the airlines industry. Boeing introduced a new line, but McDonnell Douglas had a tough time after the May crash of a DC-10 in Chicago.

The computer industry also had a good year, although its growth rate began to slow. International Business Machines (IBM) reported some disappointing earnings, as many of its customers began to lease computers rather than buy them. In order to finance its changing business mix and meet the demand for a new computer series, IBM arranged to borrow $1.5 billion from a group of banks and floated a $1 billion bond issue.

While such companies were reporting earnings, the nation's steel and automobile industries went into a slump. Steel manufacturers keenly felt the impact of imports on their own production. U. S. producers complained that foreign steel was still being sold at unfairly low prices, despite restrictions imposed by the treasury department. The Big Three auto manufacturers—General Motors, Ford Motor Company, and Chrysler Corporation—reported serious declines in production and sales. Meanwhile, the sale of fuel-efficient cars enabled foreign manufacturers to increase their share of the U. S. market to 22%.

Chrysler. Hardest hit among the car companies was Chrysler Corporation, the nation's third largest auto manufacturer and tenth largest company overall. Chrysler's major problem was its inability to manufacture enough small cars to meet the changing U. S. market. The company also faced substantial capital investments in order to meet federal fuel efficiency standards and stricter environmental safeguards.

Anticipating a loss of more than $1 billion for the year—the largest annual deficit ever recorded by a U. S. corporation—Chrysler on September 15 submitted to the Carter Administration a request for $1.2 billion in federal loan guarantees. Secretary of the Treasury G. William Miller immediately turned down the request. Chrysler Chairman John J. Riccardo announced his retirement two days later and was replaced by President Lee A. Iacocca. On November 1, the Carter Administration proposed a $1.5 billion loan guarantee program, which was passed with minor changes by the House and Senate in late December. The legislation, which requires Chrysler to raise an additional $2 million in new capital, was the largest aid package ever given a U. S. corporation.

Other Mergers and Acquisitions. Many cash-rich companies decided that the best way to put their money to work was through acquisitions or mergers. Among the year's major transactions were International Paper's purchase of Bodcaw Companies for $805 million; RCA's acquisition of CIT Financial, worth $1.4 billion; Raytheon's buyout of Beech Aircraft for $580 million; and Penn Central's acquisition of Marathon Manufacturing for $340 million.

Not all companies, however, were interested in being acquired. F. W. Woolworth resisted a takeover by Brascan, and McGraw-Hill fought off the advances of American Express.

Personnel Change. An era came to an end at Ford Motor Co. as Henry Ford II retired as chairman and Philip Caldwell took over.

RON SCHERER
"The Christian Science Monitor"

CALIFORNIA

In 1979, Californians formed the nation's first lines for gasoline, withstood two major earthquakes, welcomed large numbers of Southeast Asian refugees, saw a loss in the prestige of their Supreme Court, watched bemusedly the antics of a politically ambitious governor, and witnessed complex jousting over the state's financing system.

Petroleum. Although there were ample supplies in the state's gasoline storage tanks, and although refineries in both the San Francisco and Los Angeles areas were working at capacity, shortages were reported and long lines began to form at service stations throughout urban California in May. The panic was controlled by the imposition of "odd-even" rationing, and the alleged shortage ended almost as quickly as it began. In December, after President Jimmy Carter announced the embargo on Iranian oil, Gov. Jerry Brown reinstated the odd-even system.

On June 29, various petroleum producing firms bid almost $1 billion for federal offshore drilling rights for gas and oil.

Earthquakes. The state experienced two moderately strong earthquakes during the year. On August 6 the strongest tremor in more than 50 years, measuring 5.9 on the Richter scale, struck the San Francisco area. Its epicenter was on the Calaveras fault near Hollister, about 100 miles (161 km) south of the city. There was little damage. On October 17 a quake along the Imperial fault in the rich agricultural region along the Mexican border caused at least $25 million in property damage and injured about 100 persons. The quake, which registered Richter 6.4, brought considerable damage to the important All-American canal.

Refugees. California received far more Southeast Asian refugees than did any other state in 1979. About 2,500 arrived each month in San Francisco alone, causing a strain on public health facilities. The refugees were found to have high disease rates, especially of tuberculosis and parasites, but were not a general health threat to the population.

Supreme Court. Until 1979, the California Supreme Court was widely considered the best state court in the nation. In late 1978, however, the court was accused of deliberately delaying a controversial decision in order to assist the reelection campaign of Chief Justice Rose Bird. On June 14, the Commission on Judicial Performance opened hearings to determine the facts. The hearings were conducted in a generally open and polite manner until July 17, when a court ruled that the hearings had to be held in closed session. Charges then were made that various justices and staff members were politically motivated liars and backbiters. The justices finally were cleared, but the final report was kept secret. While the hearings were going on, two justices dubiously refused to disqualify themselves from cases. The state comptroller found that the court was taking too long on some cases and temporarily withheld their salaries. The overall result was a considerable loss of prestige for the court.

Governor. Gov. Edmund G. (Jerry) Brown, Jr., launched his campaign for the 1980 Democratic presidential nomination and was out of the state for much of the year; at one point he had not been in Sacramento for three months. During the year Brown also lost a highly publicized battle with the state Senate over the appointment of the politically controversial actress Jane Fonda to the state Arts Commission; angered Orange County Democrats with another appointment; and lost struggles with the Regents of the University and the proponents of the $1.4-billion Diablo Canyon nuclear power plant.

State Budget and Finance. The year began with the governor promising a $1.2 billion tax cut, but the legislature used up much of the state surplus on salary increases for state employees. To replace revenue lost through Proposition 13, it also set aside $4.85 billion in "bail out" funds for local governments.

Legislation. Major legislative action in 1979 had the state taking over 80% of the cost of running public schools (up from 34% in fiscal 1978). Other bills provided money to plan new prison facilities, tax credits for employers who hire welfare recipients, and $1 billion for public transit development. But no action was taken on two politically important items on the agenda: the containment of hospital costs and the reform of a wasteful and costly medical care program for the poor.

CHARLES R. ADRIAN
University of California, Riverside

─────── CALIFORNIA • Information Highlights ───────

Area: 158,693 square miles (411 015 km²).
Population (Jan. 1979 est.): 22,505,000.
Chief Cities (1976 est.): Sacramento, the capital, 262,-305; Los Angeles, 2,743,994; San Francisco, 663,478.
Government (1979): *Chief Officers*—governor, Edmund G. Brown, Jr. (D); lt. gov., Mike Curb (R). *Legislature*—Senate, 40 members; Assembly, 80 members.
Education (1978–79): *Enrollment*—public elementary schools, 2,728,637 pupils; public secondary, 1,459,-330; colleges and universities, 1,650,155 students. *Public school expenditures,* $9,102,883,000.
State Finances (fiscal year 1978): *Revenues,* $29,486,-935,000; *expenditures,* $24,628,536,000.
Personal Income (1978): $199,010,000,000; per capita, $8,927.
Labor Force (July 1979): *Nonagricultural wage and salary earners,* 9,631,400; *unemployed,* 690,700 (6.2% of total force).

CAMBODIA

Cambodia, historically called "the land of fruit," became known as "the land of walking skeletons" in 1979. When the government of the Communist Pol Pot came to power in April 1975, there were an estimated 8 million people living in Cambodia. By the time a Vietnamese invasion had replaced this ruthless ruler with the puppet Heng Samrin in early January 1979, the country's population reportedly had declined to approximately 4.5 million. And, as the year advanced, fear was expressed by many governments that another 2 million Cambodians might die if a major emergency food relief program were not mounted.

The January overthrow of the tyrannical Pol Pot was more than just the replacement of one government by another. Vietnam's invasion that caused the change—followed by civil war and widespread starvation and disease—seemed veritably to threaten the existence of the Khmer (Cambodian) people and their ancient and once great civilization.

Warfare. Vietnam's invasion, which began in late December 1978, overthrew the harsh Chinese-supported Pol Pot regime in two weeks. An estimated 100,000 Vietnamese soldiers, using tanks and backed by air and artillery strikes, took part in the lightning-like assault. The eastern part of the country was quickly overrun, but fighting against remnant Pol Pot forces in the extreme west of the land continued throughout the year.

Before the year ended, an estimated 200,000 Vietnamese troops had entered the country and carried the main burden of the fighting against the remaining Pol Pot "Khmer Rouge" forces. The successor Heng Samrin regime claimed total victory on July 22, stating that 42,000 "enemy troops" had been killed, wounded, or captured during the previous six months.

Khmer Rouge elements continued their resistance in the west and southwest. However, 10,000 of a reported 30,000 Khmer Rouge slipped into neighboring Thailand in April to travel a neutral route to their destination in the Cardamon mountains in the Cambodian southwest. The end of the monsoon rains in October, aiding the westward advance of Vietnamese troops, threatened the survival of the last remaining substantial Khmer Rouge troops.

Politics. The new Cambodian leader, 45-year-old Heng Samrin, had defected earlier from the Khmer Rouge, and his political movement, the Kampuchean National United Front for National Salvation, was clearly Hanoi-inspired. The main institution in the government he established was an eight-member Revolutionary Council.

The ousted Khmer Rouge leadership offered to form a political alliance with former non-Communist Chief of State (Prince) Norodom Sihanouk, once their prisoner but now an exile in Peking. The longtime neutralist refused, however, and proposed a new coalition of Cambodians under his leadership.

Economy. Cambodia's all but destroyed economy was a direct result of the harsh and bizarre policies pursued by Pol Pot during his rule and of the savage warfare that engulfed the land in 1979. The main rice crop, normally sown in May and harvested in December–January, had not been planted by November. Opposed Khmer Rouge and Vietnamese armies seized or burned limited rice reserves and drove away peasants in the western part of the country at planting time. Earlier drought had reduced the off-season winter crop.

Famine. By November there were widespread predictions that 2 million (or more) Cambodians would die if $100 million in food relief did not reach the country soon. Malaria and bleeding dysentery added to the problems of malnutrition—and survival—posed by exhausted food supplies. Snakes and tree-bark were eaten in the absence of alternatives, and rats and other vermin reportedly increased dramatically. The very survival of the race seemed to be threatened by the loss of the lives of children. There were reportedly few children in the land under five years of age and another 10,000 were orphans.

International Relief. President Jimmy Carter pledged $70 million in relief aid in late October. The U.S. effort generally was regarded as somewhat belated. However, the chief reason for the delay was the opposition of the Heng Samrin government, which feared that such assistance literally would give new life to foes of the regime. The earliest and most effective relief efforts were mounted by the Red Cross and UNICEF. A total of 51 nations, attending a UN conference on November 5, pledged more than $200 million for food and relief supplies to Cambodians over the next 12 months.

Foreign Relations. The Heng Samrin regime signed a Treaty of Peace and Friendship with Vietnam in February. The new government had difficulty, however, in gaining international recognition. Indonesia, Malaysia, and Singapore, for example, favored seating the Pol Pot representative at a Third World conference in Sri Lanka in June.

China, opposed to domination of Cambodia by Vietnam, a close Soviet ally, initially provided substantial material aid to the Pol Pot forces but, as they were driven back, shifted its support to the political efforts of neutralist non-Communist Norodom Sihanouk. Thailand, which received an estimated 80,000 Cambodian refugees in the first half of the year, followed a generally tolerant, if not partial, policy toward the Pol Pot forces—regarding them as a buffer against the aggressive Vietnamese. Accordingly, Thailand viewed the late 1979 Vietnamese offensive with considerable alarm.

RICHARD BUTWELL
Murray State University

--- **CAMBODIA · Information Highlights** ---

Official Name: Democratic Kampuchea.
Location: Southeast Asia.
Area: 69,898 square miles (181 035 km²).
Population (1979 est.): 8,900,000.
Chief City (1976 est.): Phnom Penh, the capital, 100,000.
Government: *Head of state and government,* Heng Samrin, president of People's Revolutionary Council (took office Jan. 1979).
Monetary Unit: Riel (1,111.11 riels equal U.S.$1, Dec. 1976).
Manufactures (major products): Textiles, cement, paper products.
Agriculture (major products): Rice, rubber, sugarcane.

CANADA

During the year 1979, Canadians faced three major national issues—the election of a new parliament (*see* special report pages 153–55), the supply of energy, and the threat of Quebec separatism. In addition, Canadians continued to experience uncertain economic performance, particularly higher interest rates, and the decentralization of power from the national to the provincial governments. Joe Clark took the oath of office as prime minister, Edward Schreyer was installed as governor-general, and the nation lost one of its favorite sons, John George Diefenbaker. The Clark government suffered a sudden vote of no-confidence in December and an election was scheduled for February 1980.

DOMESTIC AND INTERNATIONAL AFFAIRS

Politics. On May 22, the 16-year-old Liberal government under Pierre Elliott Trudeau, prime minister for 11 years, ended with the election of the Progressive Conservatives under Joe Clark, 39-year-old Albertan who had been leader of the Opposition since February 1976. To the parliament the Progressive Conservatives elected 136, the Liberals 114, the New Democratic Party 26, and Social Credit 6. After May 22 one Social Credit member joined the Progressive Conservatives, still leaving them without a clear majority in the House of Commons. Later Opposition victories in by-elections made the new government even more dependent on the Social Credit Party for support.

In keeping with certain election promises, Finance Minister John Crosbie on September 17 announced measures for phasing in mortgage payments and homeowner taxes as income tax credits. In the face of the threat of Arab economic retaliation and of the demonstrated loss of contracts in Saudi Arabia and elsewhere, the Clark government permanently delayed implementing its promise to move the Canadian embassy in Israel from Tel Aviv to Jerusalem. This was done after Robert Stanfield, former Conservative Party leader, made a Middle East tour to investigate the political consequences of such a diplomatic move.

During the first six months of the new government, 5,000 civil service jobs were eliminated. This was part of the Conservatives' planned reduction of federal public employees by 65,000 over a three-year period. Several new deputy ministers were hired and others transferred. Bryce Mackasey, chairman of Air Canada and a former Liberal cabinet minister, was fired on obvious partisan grounds. The government announced plans to sell eight government corporations to the private sector and, after much confusion, decided to introduce legislation to divide state-run Petro-Canada into private and public wings. New Democrat Party leader Ed Broadbent condemned the plan to return government-owned business to the public sector as "doctrinaire stupidity at its worst." The government also announced intentions of giving British Columbia, Newfoundland, and Nova Scotia power over offshore oil and mineral resources and rights, hitherto a federal jurisdiction.

In the Speech from the Throne on October 9, outlining legislative proposals of the new government during its first parliamentary session, the Clark administration noted that it would place more reliance on the private sector for economic stimulus and for the reduction of unemployment. The speech called for Canadian energy self-sufficiency by 1990 and for a freedom of information act, giving the public access to government documents and controlling the amount of classified material.

CP PHOTO

Justice Ronald Martland administers the oath of allegiance as Edward Schreyer becomes Canada's 22nd governor-general. Lily Schreyer, wife of the former Manitoba premier, watches attentively.

Stronger parliamentary committees and greater provincial power in the area of lotteries were also sought. James Jerome, Liberal M. P., was installed as speaker, a position he held during the previous government.

On December 13, while the House of Commons was considering an 18-cent a gallon increase in gasoline taxes, a part of Clark's first budget package, the New Democratic Party presented a no-confidence motion against the Clark government. The prime minister's budget had included a corporate-profits surtax and an increase in taxes on liquor and tobacco. The no-confidence motion, which succeeded by a 139–133 vote, charged the government with "an outright betrayal of its election promises to lower interest rates, cut taxes, and stimulate the growth of the Canadian economy." Early the next day, a February election was planned. Trudeau, who had said that he was stepping down as Liberal Party leader, was persuaded to lead the opposition in the election.

Energy. While the Clark government announced its aim of energy self-sufficiency by 1990, the major question Canadians faced in 1979 was how to achieve that goal. In March the House of Commons gave final approval to legislation allowing the government rationing powers in petroleum and coal in the event of an energy emergency. During the election campaign the Liberals, backed by the New Democrats, favored the retention and expansion of the government-backed Petro-Canada. By contrast, the Conservatives proposed selling it to the private sector. Continued uncertainty over overseas supplies led to the sending of a special delegation to Mexico. In May, Mexico agreed to sell Canada 100,000 barrels of crude a day for at least ten years. Earlier a new deal was reached with Venezuela.

In November, provincial premiers joined Prime Minister Clark at the first Ministers' Conference on Energy. Alberta, under Premier Peter Lougheed, argued for raising the prices of crude oil to "world prices." Saskatchewan Premier Allan Blakeney, whose province produces less oil than Alberta, proposed a pricing structure of benefit to all Canadians. Ontario Premier William Davis strongly advocated raising the prices but only in relationship to Canada's needs. Clark threatened to use federal powers to force an agreement. The price of oil was raised by $1.00 a barrel, effective Jan. 1, 1980, and by an additional $3.00, effective July 1, 1980.

Quebec Separatism. In January the Task Force on Canadian Unity, chaired by Jean-Luc Pepin and John Robarts, reported that Canadians should accept Quebec's right to self-assertiveness in cultural and linguistic matters. Noting that "Canadians are in the midst of a crisis," the report proposed reorganization of the House of Commons and Senate to give better representation for minorities and minority parties, changes in the Supreme Court, and provincial legislation to ensure linguistic rights. The task force championed the cause of a united Canada but stated Quebec's right to leave the federation if its residents voted for separation, a policy adopted in 1978 by the Parti Québécois, the ruling party in Quebec.

In November the Quebec government under René Lévesque published a white paper, "Quebec-Canada, a New Deal," urging "sovereignty association" with Canada. Citing historical grievances over economics, politics, and language rights, the Parti Québécois' stated position is that Québécois have the right to determine their own destiny not totally outside of Canada but in a working relationship with the dominion. Critics of the separatist position, including Trudeau, Broadbent, and Davis, have argued that separatism is unacceptable to Canadians.

Quebec Liberal leader Claude Ryan, whose strength in the Quebec National assembly increased through by-election victories over rival Parti Québécois candidates, led the fight for a Quebec within Canada. Trudeau led the federal Liberal forces against separatism. Lévesque set the date for the Quebec referendum for the spring of 1980. Separatism, an emotional issue which threatens the dismemberment of the nation, continued to be a major preoccupation of Canadians.

Provincial Developments. The year 1979 also saw changes in government in various provinces. In Alberta in March, Peter Lougheed's Progres-

THE CANADIAN MINISTRY
(According to precedence, December 1979)

Joe Clark, prime minister

Sen. Jacques Flynn, Justice minister and leader of the government in the Senate

John Crosbie, finance minister

Flora MacDonald, minister of external affairs

Sinclair Stevens, president of the treasury board

Allan McKinnon, defence minister

Ray Hnatyshyn, minister for energy, mines and resources

David Crombie, health and welfare minister

Robert de Cotret, trade and commerce minister

Walter Baker, president of the Privy Council and revenue minister

John Wise, agriculture minister

Don Mazankowski, transport minister and minister responsible for the wheat board

Lincoln Alexander, minister of labour

James McGrath, minister of fisheries

David MacDonald, state secretary and minister of communications

Roch LaSalle, minister of supply and services

Ron Atkey, minister of employment and immigration

John Fraser, postmaster general and minister of environment

Allan Lawrence, solicitor general and consumer affairs minister

Erik Nielsen, minister of public works

Elmer MacKay, minister of regional expansion

Jake Epp, minister of Indian affairs and northern development

Sen. Martial Asselin, minister of state for the Canadian International Development Agency

Bill Jarvis, minister of state for federal-provincial relations

Howard Grafftey, minister of state for social programs

Perrin Beatty, minister of state for the treasury board

Robert Howie, minister of state for transport

Steve Paproski, minister of state for fitness and amateur sport and multiculturalism

Ron Huntington, minister of state for small business and industry

Michael Wilson, minister of state for international trade

CP PHOTO

Flora I. MacDonald, 53-year-old high-school dropout, became the highest ranking woman ever in the Canadian
government when she became minister for external
affairs in the Clark cabinet. Miss MacDonald has been
a Conservative member of parliament since 1972.

sive Conservatives were returned with a landslide victory.

During the campaign, Lougheed emphasized
the importance of protecting the province's
oil revenues. In British Columbia in June, William Bennett's Social Credit Party won but with
a reduced majority. The New Democrats, under
David Barrett, made gains, capturing 46% of
the popular vote, as opposed to Social Credit's
49%. In April the Conservatives won a majority in Prince Edward Island and in June the
Conservatives did the same in Newfoundland.
With the federal Liberal defeat May 22 not one

──────── CANADA · Information Highlights ────────

Official Name: Canada.
Location: Northern North America.
Area: 3,851,809 square miles (9 976 185 km²).
Population (1979 est.): 23,700,000.
Chief Cities (1977 met. est.): Ottawa, the capital, 702,-
200; Montreal, 2,809,900; Toronto, 2,849,000.
Government: *Head of state,* Elizabeth II, queen; repre-
sented by Edward Schreyer, governor-general (took
office Jan. 22, 1979). *Head of government,* (Charles)
Joseph Clark, prime minister (took office June
1979). *Legislature*—Parliament: Senate and House
of Commons.
Monetary Unit: Canadian dollar (1.1714 dollars equal
U. S.$1, Nov. 29, 1979).
Manufactures (major products): Motor vehicles and
parts, fish and forest products, petroleum and
natural gas, processed and unprocessed minerals.
Agriculture (major products): Wheat, livestock and
meat, feedgrains, oilseeds, dairy products, tobacco,
fruits and vegetables.

Liberal administration existed in national or
provincial legislatures. The New Democrats
hold power in Saskatchewan.

Within the provinces, important developments included reports that acid rain (sulfur
and nitrogen oxides) dissolving in snow and
rain contaminating Ontario lakes, rivers, and
forests was a major health danger and would
have to be countered through a treaty with the
United States. Workers at International Nickel
Company in Sudbury signed a new contract in
June, bringing an eight-month strike, perhaps
the longest in Canadian history, to an end. In
November, 250,000 persons were evacuated
from Mississauga, Ont., when derailed tank
cars carrying lethal chlorine threatened to leak.
It was the largest evacuation in North American
history. In October, the world's largest hydroelectric facility at James Bay, Quebec, began
hydro production for markets in Canada and the
United States.

In 1979 Canada lost one of its great public
servants, John George Diefenbaker, age 83. A
distinguished defense counsel and member of
Parliament from 1940, he served thirteen successive terms for a Saskatchewan riding and
was reelected in 1979. He was prime minister
from 1958 to 1963. Humorous, articulate, and
vain, he died while doing parliamentary work
in Ottawa on August 16 and was accorded a
state funeral planned by himself. On August
22 he was buried in Saskatoon, Sask.

International Affairs. In June, Prime Minister
Clark joined the leaders of the six other Western
powers (Britain, France, Germany, Italy, Japan,
and the United States) in Tokyo for the fifth
annual economic summit. To counter the Organization of Petroleum Exporting Countries
(OPEC), the leaders signed an agreement to
set oil import limits through 1985. Because Canada's domestic oil production is expected to
decline, its quotas were actually raised, in sharp
contrast to the other signatories'.

Other international activities included the
signing of four agreements with the United
States regarding fishing rights and maritime
boundaries. Under one of the agreements Canadian fishermen received the bulk of scallops
while American fishermen would get increased
access to other fish in eastern waters. In February Canada signed a three-year contract with
China to sell 10.5 million metric tons (11.5
million tons) of wheat.

In May, a Yugoslav diplomat based in Toronto was deported for harassing Yugoslav-Cana-
dians. In November, U. S. President Jimmy
Carter canceled his scheduled visit to Ottawa
after Iranian students seized the U. S. embassy
in Tehran.

See also separate articles on each of the
provinces and territories.

BARRY GOUGH
Department of History
Wilfrid Laurier University

The Year of the Tories and Young Joe Clark

Eleven years of Trudeau government ended in 1979. Following the defeat of Pierre Elliott Trudeau's Liberal Party in the May 22 federal elections, a new minority Progressive Conservative Cabinet, with former journalist and university lecturer (Charles) Joseph Clark as prime minister, took the oath of office on June 4. It was the first Canadian swearing-in ceremony to be televised. The new government was Canada's first Progressive Conservative administration since 1963, the year the Liberals, led by Lester B. Pearson, defeated John George Diefenbaker's Conservatives. Since the formation of the Dominion of Canada in 1867, the Liberals have won 18 of the nation's 31 elections and the Conservatives 12; one had installed Sir Robert Borden's Unionist government (1917–21).

The Election Call. Following months of speculation, Allan MacEachen, the deputy prime minister and government leader in the House of Commons, announced on March 26, 1979, that Parliament was dissolved and that Canadians would go to the polls on May 22. Cheers went up from all sides. The various political parties—Liberals, Progressive Conservatives, New Democrats (NDP), and Social Credit (Creditistes)—had been waiting to do battle. When MacEachen made his announcement, Prime Minister Trudeau was asking Governor-General Edward Schreyer to dissolve the 30th Parliament. Also, at that moment, the leader of the Opposition, Joe Clark, was attending a Progressive Conservative Party dinner in Regina, Sask. Clark, who was surprised by the announcement, promised to fight a relentless campaign and to win.

At dissolution, the Liberals held 133 House seats, the Progressive Conservatives 98, the New Democrats 17, the Creditistes 9, and independents 5. Two seats were vacant. The Liberals had gained a majority on July 8, 1974.

The 1979 election call came when Trudeau, at age 59, was approaching his eleventh anniversary as prime minister, having been sworn in as Lester Pearson's successor on April 20, 1968. The election was Trudeau's fourth as party leader. A three-time victor, he had won a majority in June 1968 with his concept of a "Just Society," a minority in October 1972 under the banner "The Land is Strong," and a majority in July 1974 with a plea for strong government to face Canada's economic problems.

The Campaign. In 1979 the Liberals selected strong leadership as their campaign theme. Party advertising featured Trudeau as the only person sufficiently strong and capable to lead the country. Trudeau campaigned on five planks—fighting Quebec separatism, developing the economy in the 1980's, providing job and income security, reducing government deficits, and assuring energy supplies. The goal of bringing the last vestiges of the Canadian constitution home from Britain was also a favorite topic. Party strategy involved giving Trudeau maximum exposure across the nation. Party followers attested to his popularity at large rallies in Toronto and Montreal, but there was some heckling by postal workers, political dissidents, and unemployed persons. The English-Canadian media, increasingly critical of the prime minister who often spoke of the irrationality of the press, concen-

The Canadian election campaign begins: Pierre Trudeau (left) visits Liberal party headquarters; Joe Clark (PC) greets a future voter.

trated attention on what they regarded as Trudeau's arrogance and insensitivity. Yet various polls taken during the campaign revealed that Canadians clearly favored Trudeau over Clark and Ed Broadbent, the leader of the New Democrats, as the person most capable to lead.

The Progressive Conservatives under Clark ran a low-key campaign but with very heavy advertising aimed at discrediting Trudeau and the Liberals. The Tory slogan was "Let's Get Canada Working Again." The Conservatives offered a 23-point list of election promises. The most attractive promise was offered to home owners: a federal income tax deduction for mortgage interest payments and a similar credit for municipal taxes paid on dwellings. The Conservatives also promised to grant more power to the provinces (whose fiscal powers and needs have grown substantially since 1945) in certain fields of legislation, including resource control. Clark promised to sell PetroCanada to the private sector. PetroCanada, a Crown corporation which was created in 1975 by the Liberal government to ensure a steady supply of petroleum for Canadian needs by developing new finds, had been opposed by private oil interests whose political sympathies lay behind Clark and his party. In the realm of foreign affairs, Clark promised, in a move aimed at capturing Jewish votes, to move Canada's embassy in Israel from Tel Aviv to Jerusalem, a proposition that sparked heavy resistance from Arab interests in Canada

and caution from the Department of External Affairs in Ottawa.

Clark held few mass rallies, preferring smaller meetings as a way to develop a small town image. For the first month of the campaign he shied away from debating Trudeau and his other adversary, Broadbent, on television. On May 13, however, Clark faced his two antagonists, debating various election issues in a two-hour confrontation. An estimated six million viewers watched the debate, the first since 1968. Opinion polls showed Trudeau to be clearly the viewers' choice. Various polls taken at this time showed a narrow Liberal lead over the Conservatives, with the "undecided" vote swinging to the Conservatives, especially in the "swing" areas of southern Ontario where the outcome was expected to be decided.

The NDP, under energetic Ed Broadbent, 43-year-old Member of Parliament for Oshawa, fought a hard campaign and made full use of the media. More jobs, greater resource control by Canadians, and price controls, particularly on food, were major issues for the party. The manpower and resources of the large Canadian Labour Congress were placed at the party's disposal. Many workers, however, felt alienated by union partisanship and voted independently. Social Credit (Creditistes), under new leader Fabien Roy, centered their campaign in Quebec.

The Results. On May 22 the Progressive Conservatives won 136 seats in the expanded 282-

Outgoing Prime Minister Pierre Trudeau announces that he "will be a pretty good leader of the opposition."

Joe Clark, the youngest prime minister in Canadian history, promised a new spirit and a new life for Canada.

PHOTOS MICHAEL EVANS, LIAISON

Pierre Trudeau and Joe Clark discuss pressing national and international problems prior to the swearing in of Clark's new Cabinet, Canada's first Conservative government in 16 years.

seat House of Commons. The Liberals returned 114, the New Democrats 26, and the Creditistes 6. These results left Clark six seats short of a majority. Regionally the Conservatives had been aided by the expected swing in Ontario (57 of 95 seats) and their dominance in the four western provinces of Manitoba, Saskatchewan, Alberta, and British Columbia (57 of 77 seats). The Liberals lost heavily in British Columbia, returning only one of 28 seats. Few changes occurred in the Atlantic provinces. In Quebec the Liberals swept 67 of 75 seats; the Conservatives took only two and the Creditistes only six, down three from the previously held number in the House. NDP strength lay in Ontario (6 seats) and the western provinces (17 seats), with scattered support elsewhere. Tabulation of voting showed that the Liberals amassed 40% (down 3% from 1974), the Conservatives 36% (up 1%), the New Democrats 18% (up 3%), and the Creditistes 5% (no change). Though Conservative strength increased by only 1% since the previous election, Liberal losses to the Conservatives and to the New Democrats were sufficient to topple the Trudeau government. At midnight Trudeau told supporters that it was his duty to "recommend to the governor-general that he ask Mr. Clark to form a government."

In his riding of Yellowhead, Clark told supporters that the Progressive Conservatives "represent a new team that can bring a new spirit and a new life to our country." Immediately following Trudeau's resignation on June 4, Clark took the oath of office as Canada's 16th prime minister. About to turn 40, he became the youngest prime minister in the history of the nation.

It is not insignificant that Clark is the first prime minister from western Canada and that the oath was administered by the first governor-general from western Canada, Edward Schreyer. The voting economic powers of the Canadian West had increased substantially in the 1970's. Clark's power rests on that rise and on traditional Western resentment against Ottawa, particularly the bilingual policy of Trudeau and the Liberals. Quebec, however, heavily allied with Trudeau and the Liberals, gave virtually no support to Clark's Conservatives and, in turn, received scant representation in the Clark government. Thus the Clark administration is primarily a right-of-center, English-Canadian government. The new 29-member Cabinet included 12 members from Ontario alone. Flora MacDonald, 53-year-old member of Parliament from Kingston, became the first woman to be named secretary of state for external affairs. John Crosbie of St. John's, Nfld., and Alan MacKinnon of Victoria, B. C., were appointed ministers of finance and national defense, respectively.

BARRY M. GOUGH

THE ECONOMY

For the Canadian economy, there was mixed performance for most of the year. Inflation, measured by the Consumer Price Index, stabilized within a percentage point of a 9% rate of increase. The rate of increase in the money supply (M 1) was 13.5%. The seasonally adjusted monthly rate of unemployment ranged between 7.1% and 8.1%. Industry output did not advance, and the gross national product, which advanced by 1.6% in real terms in the first quarter, fell by 0.6% in the second quarter of the year.

Bank lending consistently ran at 15% to 20% above 1978 levels. Pretax profits ran at 20% to 30% above 1978 levels. A deficit on international merchandise trade turned into a surplus by fall. Automobile and truck sales turned down in early summer, and housing starts were down 10% to 20% below 1978 levels for all of 1979. While the Toronto Stock Exchange composite index ranged between a low of 1,315 and a high of 1,804.7 during the first eleven months of the year, long term and short term (91 day) interest rates, though high at 10% and 11%, respectively, remained steady. In midsummer interest rates began to climb but it was not until the Bank of Canada raised its rate to historic highs in response to increases in the United States that the stock market fell to about 1,700 in late November.

The explanation seems fairly straightforward. The oil boom in Alberta was supplemented by a general resources and farm products boom due to the lower value of the Canadian dollar which stabilized at about (U. S.) $.84. Mining, particularly copper and zinc, picked up, and even nickel was showing signs of recovery by midyear. Good conditions for mineral and paper sales gave New Brunswick and British Columbia minor boom conditions. Newfoundland needed no such stimulus, as by summer it was anticipating economic expansion based on oil discoveries on the Grand Banks. Basic steel and machine tool manufacturers found good markets in the United States and Canada. By midsummer, however, expansion was pressing on the money supply. By September major wage settlements were rising above the rate of inflation for the first time in three years.

The advance of 1979 was largely a primary products boom, much of it generated by domestic and foreign credit which financed expansion in oil and natural gas. But other primary products and high technology manufacturing did well. Manufacturing in general did not do so well. The result was a further narrowing of the gap in average personal income between regions.

The merchandising and financial services sectors were characterized by an unusually high level of takeover and merger activity.

It was a good spring for a Conservative government to come to power with a program of "privatization." By the end of the year, however, high interest rates, Arab money muscle, and leaping oil prices were making matters difficult for the Clark administration.

R. F. NEILL
Department of Economics, Carleton University

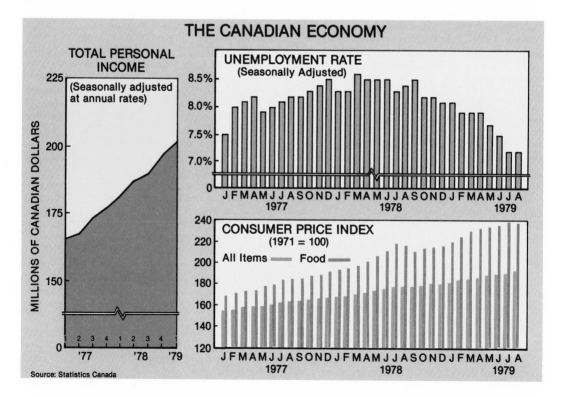

THE CANADIAN ECONOMY

TOTAL PERSONAL INCOME
(Seasonally adjusted at annual rates)

MILLIONS OF CANADIAN DOLLARS

UNEMPLOYMENT RATE (Seasonally Adjusted)

CONSUMER PRICE INDEX (1971 = 100)
All Items — Food —

Source: Statistics Canada

THE ARTS

From one point of view—that of the artists and managers—the 1979 cultural year in Canada tended to be joyless and fractious. The troubled atmosphere was a spin-off from broad national conditions. Severe economic inflation and frightening unemployment intensified bad tempers between employees and employers. Determined unionization of performers in all artistic areas encouraged a new element of confrontation and recrimination. The organizing of arts executives into strong pressure groups enlarged the area of cultural politics. All levels of government, under taxpayer pressure, stuck grimly to their provisional belt-tightening guidelines. And 1979 was a federal election year—when cultural promises were made and broken frequently, carelessly, and confusingly.

If mass media coverage may be taken as a reliable indication of public interest, two Canadian cultural events were outstanding in 1979—the National Arts Centre (NAC) summer festival and the Peter Ustinov performance of *King Lear* at Stratford.

Music. The NAC in Ottawa, generously subsidized by the federal government, maintained a low profile during its early years. A fortunate combination of shrewd business management and top-level artistic direction gradually developed the center into an important national cultural presence. To celebrate the tenth anniversary of its symphony orchestra the NAC staged Festival Ottawa 1979 (July 3–28), under the direction of resident maestro Mario Bernardi. The opera program, which included *Così fan tutte,* in Italian; *The Queen of Spades,* in English; and

Cendrillon, in French, was the highlight of the festival. Lead parts were sung by stars from several great American and European opera companies.

Theater. The Stratford Festival's presentation of *King Lear,* with Peter Ustinov as Lear, was a smash hit which attracted Shakespeare buffs from many parts of Canada and the United States. The Stratford season presented seven Shakespeare plays interspersed with half a dozen contemporary works. At Niagara-on-the-Lake, the Shaw Festival produced three Shaw plays and four Shaw-related works. The small but superb Neptune Theatre in Halifax announced that Tony Randall, who played recently in Neptune's *Seagull,* would return there for the 1979–80 season to direct *The Master Builder.* In the far west, Edmonton's Citadel Theatre was embroiled in a nasty, newsworthy donnybrook relating to the employment of the eminent English director Peter Coe. Involved in the controversy were the theater management, the assistant director, the Canada Council, Equity, the Alberta government, the federal department of immigration, the people of Edmonton, and Mr. Coe. French-language theater did exceptionally well in the 1979 season. The French section of the national theater gave 425 performances in 105 locations in eight provinces. In October, Montréal's *Théâtre d'aujourd'hui* performed in Washington, DC, during the Theater in America Festival.

Dance. Canadian interest in professional dance was late in developing, but during the 1970's it rapidly reached a position of high public favor. The most noteworthy event was the August invitational appearance of Toronto's Na-

Members of Toronto's National Ballet Company take a bow after a performance at London's Covent Garden.

NATIONAL BALLET OF CANADA

One of the Stratford Festival's 1979 offerings, *Love's Labour's Lost*, was given a special performance in September to benefit Southeast Asian refugees through an organization which the Stratford Festival employees had established.

PHOTO BY ZOE DOMINIC, COURTESY, STRATFORD FESTIVAL, CANADA

tional Ballet Company at London's Covent Garden. The performances were an artistic success, although London critics were not pleased by the company's selection of works. In April the Royal Winnipeg Ballet fled from the cold of Canadian spring to the warmth of Alabama where it performed at the Birmingham Arts Festival. The company's never-failing production of Agnes de Mille's *Rodeo* was especially pleasing. The Canada Council made grants totaling $350,000 to promote in-Canada tours by Les Grands Ballets Canadiens, the Royal Winnipeg, and Toronto's National Ballet; in addition the Council awarded $755,000 to small modern dance groups. The National Arts Centre's 1979–80 season featured visits by Ballet International de Caracas, Ballet du XXe Siècle (Brussels), the Paul Taylor Dance Company (New York), and the Pilobolus Dancers (Connecticut). In February the big non-stage event of the year was the 20th anniversary reunion of graduates of the Toronto-based National Ballet School. More than 200 alumni—professional dancers from many parts of the world—gathered to pay homage to Betty Oliphant, the school's founder and continuing principal. In June, Miss Oliphant was awarded the Canada Council's prestigious $20,000 Molson Prize.

Motion Pictures. A recent development in the Canadian entertainment world has been a phenomenal expansion of the film-making industry. In 1979 the $125-million sales of made-in-Canada films were 1,100% above the 1978 figure. The Canadian feature film *Meatballs* was shown in 1,200 movie houses in the United States and was expected to gross $100 million at the box office. Of the several reasons given for the boom, the most important is a scheme of tax incentives offered to domestic film producers by the federal government through its Canadian Film Development Corporation (CFDC). In mid-1979 Canadians were making 43 feature films, of which 32 were backed by the CFDC.

Observers on both sides of the border wondered when big American film interest groups would find it expedient to start diplomatic protests against unfair competition. Meanwhile, Canadian investors, producers, and actors enjoyed unaccustomed good fortune.

Financial Support News. The beginnings of an unpleasant battle for control of arts subsidy funds were evident in 1979, with special reference to anticipated windfall monies from excess profits, taxation revenues, and from government-sponsored lotteries. In a matter involving many millions of dollars, the chief contestants were the department of the federal secretary of state and the tough arts administrative agencies. The former, which supervised the expenditure of $734 million of arts money in 1979, was determined to hold a tight rein on all federal support of the arts. The latter demanded that a very large portion of the federal money be handled through the Canada Council. The Council, while a part of the federal government, by law has enjoyed extraordinary independence in making grants to cultural organizations and individuals. In 1979 its grants totaled about $40 million. Curiously, the arts executives have been harshly critical of the Council in recent years—largely because of natural covetousness among the various arts groups of the largest slices of the pie. One upshot of this situation was the rather urgent establishment by the Council of a small task force to study and report on the future of the agency. The task force was urged to bear in mind "the considerable financial and political pressures" under which the Council is now obliged to work. Of importance to the affairs of the Council was the appointment in 1979 of Dr. Mavor Moore as the new chairman. Dr. Moore, 60, is experienced as a playwright, producer, actor, drama critic, and professor of theater at York University.

WALTER B. HERBERT
Consultant on Canadian Cultural Affairs

CARIBBEAN

Natural disasters and a political shift to the left brought attention to the Caribbean in 1979. Volcanic eruptions on St. Vincent, hurricane destruction in Dominica and the Dominican Republic, and a leftist coup in Grenada highlighted the year. Two new nations—St. Lucia and St. Vincent and the Grenadines—were born (*see* pages 438–39).

Volcanic Eruptions. On Friday, April 13, the volcanic Mt. Soufrière on St. Vincent erupted with towering clouds of smoke and steam, scattering volcanic ash as far as the neighboring islands of Martinique, Barbados, and St. Lucia. Remembering that the last major eruption in 1902 had killed 1,565 persons, government authorities quickly evacuated some 18,000 persons from the 30 villages within a 15-mile (24-km) radius of the mountain. Although there was no loss of life among the 95,000 inhabitants of the island, the cost of emergency relief alone was far beyond the resources of this predominantly agricultural island. Canada, the United States, and Great Britain contributed emergency funds and equipment for the refugees. The volcanic ash left ugly black marks on the bananas grown on St. Vincent and the surrounding islands, making the fruit hard to sell in London and Paris. By the end of May, islanders were allowed to return to their farms and start the massive cleanup process.

Tropical Storms. The end of August and beginning of September brought two extremely destructive tropical storms into the Caribbean. The first was the powerful Hurricane David, which struck the tiny island of Dominica on the morning of August 29. With winds of about 150 miles (241 km) per hour, the storm destroyed every town and village on the island and devastated its large virgin forests. Of the 80,000 persons living on Dominica, 65,000 were left without homes and 42 were killed. The cost of reconstructing the island's communication system, roads, and economy in general was placed at approximately $1.5 billion. Hurricane David then continued its journey westward, skirting the southern coasts of St. Croix and Puerto Rico. It again touched land late in the afternoon, hitting the Dominican Republic west of the capital city of Santo Domingo. The island sustained massive property damage, and fatalities were estimated between two and three thousand. The United States and Puerto Rico rushed aid.

Less than a week after David had departed, another tropical storm, Frederic, blew into the Caribbean from the Atlantic Ocean. The first island to be hit was St. Martin, where Frederic dropped 12 inches (30.5 cm) of rain in 48 hours. As the storm moved westward, the winds dissipated, but flooding caused extensive damage in St. Thomas, the northern coast of Puerto Rico—which was declared a disaster area by U. S. President Jimmy Carter—and the northern regions of the Dominican Republic. Frederic finally moved on to Cuba, where it stalled for several hours, deluging the area around Havana with its worst flooding in more than 60 years.

Earlier in the storm season, in mid-June, Jamaica was struck by a storm that Prime Minister Michael Manley called one of the worst natural disasters in the country's history. More than 40 persons lost their lives, and heavy flooding caused property and crop damage—especially in the western sections of the island—estimated in the millions of dollars.

UPI

The crippled *Atlantic Empress* was allowed to burn after crashing with another supertanker near the coast of Tobago in mid-July. The tactic helped contain a huge oil spill that threatened nearby island beaches.

Oil Spill. Another disaster, this one man-made, was narrowly averted on July 21, when two supertankers filled with oil collided and burned at the eastern edge of the Caribbean Sea, just north of the island of Tobago. Rescue work and favorable sea currents prevented extensive damage to Caribbean beaches and averted what might have been the largest oil spill in history.

Politics. Political upheaval—some peaceful, some not—brought new left-wing governments to the islands of Grenada, Dominica, and St. Lucia.

In Grenada, the government of Prime Minister Eric Gairy was taken over at gunpoint in the early morning of March 13. The takeover was led by Maurice Bishop, the head of the leftist New Jewel Movement. Two policemen were killed in the coup, and the 300-man army was caught completely unprepared and unarmed. Gairy, who was perhaps best known for his interest in UFOs, had left the island the previous day. The new government immediately suspended the constitution but retained its ties with Great Britain and opened formal diplomatic relations with Cuba. The United States officially recognized the new government, but the neighboring islands of Barbados, Trinidad and Tobago, and St. Vincent delayed recognition for several months. The new government rejected pressure to hold early elections, and in October it closed the island's only independent newspaper.

In St. Lucia, which had gained independence from Great Britain on February 21, the government of Prime Minister John Compton was defeated in national elections by the left-wing opposition party. The St. Lucia Labour Party took 12 of the 17 seats in the legislature and elected Allan Louisy as the new prime minister.

In Dominica, Prime Minister Patrick John was voted out of office by parliament on June 21. His defeat followed a month of civil unrest, which had culminated in the shooting death of two unarmed demonstrators by the police. A former member of John's cabinet, Oliver J. Seraphine, was elected interim prime minister until new elections—planned for early 1980—were held.

The new leaders of Grenada and St. Vincent joined with Prime Minister Manley of Jamaica and Prime Minister Forbes Burnham of Guyana in issuing a declaration condemning increased U. S. military presence in the Caribbean. President Carter had ordered the step-up after disclosures of a Soviet combat brigade in Cuba.

THOMAS MATHEWS
University of Puerto Rico

CENTRAL AMERICA

The overriding political question facing Central America in 1979 was the degree to which the recent troubles in Nicaragua might spread to the neighboring states. Many of the same conditions prompting Nicaragua's civil war and the overthrow of President Anastasio Somoza could be found elsewhere in Central America, and an increase in political and social turbulence in El Salvador and Guatemala was evident.

In spite of the severe unrest and continued inflation, all of the Central American republics, except Nicaragua, showed a substantial increase in productivity. Honduras announced exceptional gains in agriculture, and if El Salvador could avoid civil war, it could look forward to unusually high food production in the 1980's. Trade within the Central American Common Market (CACM), of which Panama is only an associate, expanded slowly in spite of the continued tensions—including periodic border closings—between Honduras and El Salvador and Nicaragua and Costa Rica. Agreements were concluded on new intrazonal tax incentives for industry, and a number of badly needed highways were completed in the region. Most economic indicators appeared positive, but the influence of inflation made conclusions risky.

COSTA RICA

Costa Rica's reputation for stability was tested by the war in Nicaragua. Somoza accused Costa Rica of interference in the war, as thousands of opposition Sandinistas used Costa Rica for training sites, supplies, and occasional refuge. But Costa Rica, which had broken diplomatic relations with Nicaragua in November 1978, was a haven for Somoza followers as well, many of whom planned to return to their homeland when the economy was restored. Meanwhile Costa Rica did not suffer from the violence and terrorism found elsewhere in Central America. The major disturbance during the year was a mid-August strike centered in Limón. Seven unions, members of the Workers Federation of Limón (including dock, banana, refinery, and railroad workers), sought a number of benefits including some back pay. Perhaps 100 individuals were injured before agreements were made for future arbitration. The government attributed the ten-day strike to "political subversion" and ordered the top Soviet diplomats in Costa Rica to leave the country during the trouble.

In October the opposition National Liberation Party asked President Rodrigo Carazo to meet with four former presidents in an effort to find solutions to the nation's more pressing economic problems. Although business remained good, inflation was reported to be 9.6% by the government and 20% by the opposition.

EL SALVADOR

As an uneasy quiet descended upon Nicaragua, it became clear that the most tormented land in all of Central America was now El Salvador. Riots, kidnappings, assassinations, guerrilla action from the left and the right, tore at the tiny republic. Reasons abounded; income extremes were enormous. Perhaps the most crowded nation in America, its 4.5 million peo-

(Continued on page 163)

CENTRAL AMERICA—
SPECIAL REPORT:

Nicaragua

Nicaragua has never had an easy existence. The region was fought over by conquistadores almost from Columbus' time; it battled poverty, disease, and tropical climate, then and now; after independence in the early 19th century its two chief towns—León and Granada—battled one another for the role of capital and chief commercial center. Their rivalry made possible a struggle among Anglo-Saxon businessmen for control of a railroad route across Nicaragua, culminating in the "National War." This bitter struggle drove out most of the foreigners, but left North American interests in control of the railway and the Nicaraguan conservatives in control of the nation. The conservative dictatorship provided some stability and peace from the 1860's until its overthrow in 1893 by José Santos Zelaya, a Liberal Party tyrant. Santos Zelaya had no respect for human rights, but he encouraged business and progress. His defeat in 1909 left a political vacuum into which the United States felt it must enter to prevent complete anarchy in Nicaragua and foreign intervention throughout Central America. For almost the entire period from 1912 to 1933 U. S. marines occupied Nicaraguan territory and supervised national elections. In 1926, 2,000 marines aided the conservatives in quelling civil war, and incidentally helped create a folk hero, Augusto César Sandino, one of the few Nicaraguans who resisted the compromise imposed from Washington. But the leader of the insurgents soon made peace with the newest Nicaraguan dictatorship, which was supported by the National Guard and in turn supported by the United States.

This arrangement made possible a government by a new strong man, and there rose to the top Anastasio Somoza, one of whose first acts was to approve the murder of Sandino by the Guard. The Somoza family has dominated Nicaragua since 1933. Anastasio ruled with efficient brutality until his assassination in 1956. Acquiring more power and wealth, the Somozas and their puppets maintained the land as their own fief until 1979.

In recent years the people of Nicaragua increasingly expressed their distaste for the regime of Anastasio Somoza Debayle, a son of the first Somoza. The government had long tolerated a certain amount of criticism from the opposition, but younger generations of businessmen increasingly resented the lack of opportunities resulting from Somozan control of most of the economy.

New challenges arose to Somoza's control of the republic. In the early 1960's the Sandinist National Liberation Front, a small, tight organization modeled after Fidel Castro's July 26

UPI

In the jungles of Nicaragua, President Anastasio Somoza discusses military plans with National Guardsmen.

movement, entered the scene. It grew very slowly for many years, but it was the first movement in Nicaragua to hold appeal for the mass of peasants, 200,000 of whom were landless. A second factor was the devastating earthquake of 1972; the middle classes were appalled by the mismanagement of the reconstruction program and charged Somoza with profiteering from the tragedy. In the mid-1970's the Sandinistas began a moderately successful program of kidnappings as a means of purchasing arms. While they had little military success against the Guard, they attracted sympathizers from a broad political spectrum. The archbishop's attacks upon the government as corrupt and brutal swayed many neutrals. In January 1978, the government's best known opponent, the respected newspaper publisher, Pedro Joaquin Chamorro, was shot to death in Managua; the perpetrators were unknown, but the government was blamed. Rioting and a two-week general strike precipitated sporadic civil war.

In the summer of 1978 the Sandinistas captured several government strongholds, and there were frequent demands that Somoza resign; but the Guard regained virtually every major town in less than two weeks. Hundreds of Nicaraguans, mostly civilians, were killed in the bom-

Large crowd gathers in Managua's main square following the victory of the Sandinist National Liberation Front and the overthrow of President Somoza.

Members of the new junta hold postwar news conference to announce reconstruction plans.

PHOTOS UPI

bardments and shooting. Renewed repression by the Guard drove thousands of peasants into the countryside, where the Sandinistas were able to recruit many followers. Heavier and better weapons were obtained through Venezuela and Panama, and at the same time the United States ceased providing military aid to Somoza. Other nations broke diplomatic relations with his government, and by May 1979 the war had resumed on a fierce scale. In an address to the Organization of American States, U. S. Secretary of State Cyrus Vance called upon Somoza to resign.

As the United States increasingly put diplomatic pressures upon Somoza, his opponents became more confident. In June 1979 they created a large provisional junta composed mostly of businessmen, obviously to minimize the stigma of Marxism. The military aspect of the campaign was almost over; the Guard had not given up, but it was being defeated regularly. On July 17, Somoza announced his resignation and left for Florida, ending a 43-year dynasty.

In a peculiar move, his hand-picked successor, Francisco Urcuyo Malianos, refused to wind down affairs for Somoza and announced his intention to complete his predecessor's term. But when the Guard surrendered, Urcuyo departed. The guerrilla army occupied Managua, and the victors established a new five-member governing junta. Somoza's party moved from Miami to the Bahamas. The war was over.

The new government faced vast problems. Fifty thousand persons were dead. Property damage was estimated at $5 billion. Hundreds of thousands of people had lost their homes or places of employment. Suspicion and distrust prevailed and probably would continue for years. The currency was weak and the foreign debt was impossible. The junta begged for, and received large quantities of food, mostly from the United States. All private banks and Somoza's 51 corporations were nationalized, and the International Development Bank took steps to grant millions for reconstruction. The independent daily *La Prensa* was permitted to resume publishing and a bill of rights, including freedom of expression, was announced.

Months after the war's end the mood was still one of uncertainty. The government was too radical for some, too cautious for others. Some Nicaraguans wanted revenge on the Guard, especially when it appeared that armed attacks were recurring as the guardsmen were released from jail. Some peasants seized private lands, and businessmen invested reluctantly. Nicaraguans were now faced with the task of working together to rebuild a new Nicaragua.

THOMAS L. KARNES

ple occupy only 8,260 square miles (21 392 km²) of land. Yet 60% of the farm land is owned by a handful of families who total 2% of the population. The unemployment rate was estimated at 30%. The republic has been governed by the military since 1932. In the decades since, the army has kept tight control, regularly conducting elections but permitting only new military groups to rule, often through fraud and violence. In February 1977 Carlos Humberto Romero was elected in that fashion and during his administration, which lasted until Oct. 15, 1979, some 200 opponents were killed and 125 others disappeared. Several varieties of left-wing groups emerged, their tactics running the gamut from silent protest, special masses by the archbishop, occupation of embassies as inducement for releasing political prisoners, kidnappings of international businessmen for vast sums, to outright assassination of government figures, including the minister of education and the brother of the president. Violence broke out again in September amid reports that the United States was asking Romero to call for an early presidential election under outside supervision.

The sudden overthrow of Romero by another military junta surprised most observers, and there were hopes that conditions might be moderated after several peace-oriented announcements by the new regime. But it soon became apparent that the new "colonels' clique" could not or would not change conditions very soon. Some prisoners were released, but hundreds were still unaccounted for; demonstrators battled police as usual and a score were killed; a national guard officer was assassinated; and the U. S. embassy was bombed.

GUATEMALA

Guatemala shares many of the problems of its neighbor, El Salvador, except that the land area is some five times greater. Guatemala, too, has been under military control—for all but four of the last 25 years—and the battles between leftist guerrillas and rightist vigilantes, with an authoritarian government caught in between, are much the same as El Salvador's. The difference is merely one of degree, with the Guatemalan case somewhat less violent. But hundreds of peasants have been killed, the most popular leader of the leftists was assassinated, the deputy foreign minister was kidnapped, and the chief of staff of the Army was machine-gunned —all within four months. In one day in Octo-

ber, 15 persons were killed in political shootings, and a cousin of the president was kidnapped. Earthquakes, declining coffee prices, and the continued discussions of the Belize situation seemed almost anticlimactic.

HONDURAS

Among the Central American states ruled by a military regime, only Honduras appeared to be relatively peaceful. There were, however, occasional quarrels between university students and the military. Development of the huge pine forests proceeded slowly, and relations between the nation and the large banana producers seemed to have been normalized again. Agrarian reform made little progress; the government often arrested the leaders of peasant groups who attempted to seize lands on the north coast. Honduras had its share of Nicaraguan fugitives, including an important Somoza commander who was assassinated, apparently in Honduras. Of more concern to most Hondurans were the torrential rains late in the year which drove thousands from their homes and livelihood.

PANAMA

To the great joy of the Panamanians the Panama Canal treaties became effective on Oct. 1, 1979, and the first steps were taken toward the ultimate transfer of the Canal to Panama's control. Some last minute objections were raised in the U. S. Congress, but in the end the implementing legislation was enacted. Formal ceremonies were attended by President Aristides Royo and U. S. Vice President Walter Mondale. For the next ten years the canal will be operated by a bi-national commission of five Americans, including the chief commissioner, and four Panamanians. For a second ten-year period, the makeup of the commission will be reversed. At the conclusion of those two periods—Dec. 31, 1999—Panama will take complete control. Meanwhile the United States retains the right of defense against a threat to the operation of the canal and still occupies several military establishments in the zone.

A crucial matter was the status of Canal employees. About one fourth, or 3,200, of the workers are U. S. citizens, compared with some 9,000 non-Americans, mostly Panamanians. Training programs got under way to smooth the transition, as many of the Americans retired or transferred to jobs in the United States.

THOMAS L. KARNES, *Arizona State University*

CENTRAL AMERICA · Information Highlights

Nation	Population (in millions)	Area In sq mi (km²)	Capital	Head of State and Government
Costa Rica	2.2	19,575 (50 700)	San José	Rodrigo Carazo Odio, president
El Salvador	4.5	8,260 (21 392)	San Salvador	Junta, Ruben Zamora, minister of the presidency
Guatemala	6.8	42,042 (108 890)	Guatemala City	Romeo Lucas García, president
Honduras	3.1	43,277 (112 087)	Tegucigalpa	Policarpo Paz García, leader, ruling junta
Nicaragua	2.5	50,193 (130 000)	Managua	Five-member junta
Panama	1.9	29,209 (75 650)	Panama City	Omar Torrijos Herrera, commander, National Guard Aristides Royo, president

CHEMISTRY

For chemistry, 1979 was marked more by the continuation of trends and developments of previous years than by startling innovations.

Energy. To rid the United States of its dependence on imported petroleum, effort turned toward a massive program for development of synthetic fuels (synfuels), synthetic liquid and gas fuels derived from coal, oil shale, and tar sands. With the United States possessing more than a fourth of the world's known coal supply, phrases such as "the middle east of the world in coal" were heard. Plans were reconsidered, however, after economic and environmental concerns were factored in. Synfuels are expensive to produce, and both the recovery of coal from the ground and its conversion to a liquid pose environmental hazards. Large amounts of water are required, sulfur dioxide is produced, and heavy dependence on synfuels might speed an already worrisome buildup of carbon dioxide in the atmosphere. (*See also* ENERGY: Alternative to Petroleum, page 204.)

With the economic, environmental, and political drawbacks of fossil fuels becoming more obvious, attention has increasingly turned to renewable resources. Brazil is a leader in this area, especially in its ambitious program of producing ethanol from sugarcane. The ethanol is used as a motor fuel and in chemical products. A major program to produce methanol from eucalyptus trees was under consideration in 1979. Melvin Calvin, the 1961 Chemistry Nobel laureate from Berkeley, CA, is enthusiastic about the possibilities of using another Brazilian tree, the copaiba tree, which grows wild and can be tapped to yield an oil resembling diesel fuel. Calvin feels that such trees can be developed to yield substantial quantities of oil.

General Motors announced development of a zinc-nickel oxide battery, which is lighter and has a higher energy-storing capability than conventional lead acid batteries. A 900-pound (408-kg) pack of the new batteries can power a 3,000-pound (1 361-kg) car 100 miles (161 km) before recharging; however, the batteries must be replaced after 30,000 miles (48 280 km) and costs remain high.

Pollution. Hazardous waste disposal became a prime chemical concern of the year as unsafe chemical waste sites seemed to pop up throughout the United States. Hooker Chemical revealed that three of its dump sites in the Niagara Falls, NY, area contain 3,700 tons (3 357 metric tons) of wastes from trichlorophenol production, deposited over a 45-year period. Most alarming was the potential presence of over 100 pounds (45 kg) of chlorinated dioxin (TCDD), an extremely toxic by-product of trichlorophenol manufacture. On a wider scale, U. S. environmental experts regard many of the country's waste sites as "chemical time bombs," the result of careless and negligent disposal practices. Cost estimates for cleaning up all present hazardous waste sites run to billions of dollars.

The origin of environmental chlorinated dioxins became a controversial subject when Dow Chemical released a report claiming that these compounds are formed in small amounts in a variety of common combustion processes and are widespread in the environment. Dow scientists analyzed samples from a number of commercial and domestic sources, including incineration and power plant stacks, auto mufflers, and cigarette smoke. In each case the researchers detected chlorinated dioxins in the particulate matter. They suggested that ash from local combustion sources might be responsible for dioxins detected in fish from a river near Dow's Midland, MI, pesticide plant. However, independent investigators disputed some of the Dow findings.

Chemicals and Cancer. In reaction to the common view that "everything causes cancer," Douglas Costle of the Environmental Protection Agency noted that of 7,000 chemicals tested, only about 500 (7%) have turned out to be carcinogens. The Supreme Court heard arguments on proper exposure limits in the workplace for benzene, which has been linked to leukemia. And preliminary tests by Batelle Corporation indicated that rats exposed to formaldehyde vapor developed nasal cancer.

One group of well-known carcinogens, the nitrosamines, was found to occur in trace amounts in several brands of beer and scotch whiskey. Previous warnings concerning these compounds have centered on bacon, where nitrosamines can form during cooking from nitrites added to the bacon as preservatives. Polychlorinated biphenyls (PCBs) were also in the news. Animal feed, contaminated by PCBs leaking from an electrical transformer, was distributed in several western states, necessitating the destruction of many chickens and eggs.

Nobel Prize. The 1979 Nobel Prize in Chemistry was shared by two synthetic organic chemists, Herbert C. Brown of Purdue University and Georg Wittig of the University of Heidelberg, West Germany. Brown is known for his work on organoboron compounds, especially hydroboration and the use of sodium borohydride. Wittig, now retired, is noted for the Wittig reaction, a technique for synthesizing alkenes from carbonyls.

USSR-China. Many scientists pledged to restrict or end scientific cooperation with the USSR over the question of treatment of Soviet scientists and human rights activists. For the first time a large delegation of chemists from Communist China attended the joint American Chemical Society/Chemical Society of Japan meeting held in Honolulu. A U. S.-China agreement on scientific and technical cooperation was signed, and the United States and other western countries prepared to receive Chinese science and engineering students.

PAUL G. SEYBOLD, *Wright State University*

UPI

Chicago's Jane Byrne, her husband, Jay McMullen, and her daughter, Kathy, greet supporters on election night.

CHICAGO

A New Year's Eve blizzard ushered in a year of almost unparalleled change. A record winter snow of nearly 90 inches (229 cm), a new mayor, and a papal visit made 1979 a year Chicagoans will not soon forget.

The snow and prolonged cold crippled people in their efforts to go about their daily chores. And it dealt a fatal blow to Mayor Michael A. Bilandic, whose incompetence in handling snow removal became a joke. Minor scandal also hit his administration—all of it just before a mayoral election.

Jane Margaret Byrne (McMullen), a feisty woman and the city's consumer affairs commissioner whom Bilandic had fired, made the most of Bilandic's troubles. She edged him out in the Democratic primary and then, just a month later, swamped her Republican opponent by the biggest margin ever in a Chicago mayoralty election. (*See also* BIOGRAPHY.)

Byrne, whose personal dislike of Bilandic was well known, moved fast in her new job. She promptly fired Bilandic's key aides, exposed waste in the Bilandic administration, and went about establishing her own political machine. President Jimmy Carter openly courted her support, coming to her high-rise apartment for a political fund raiser. But in October, Byrne endorsed Sen. Edward M. Kennedy for president, damaging relations with the White House.

Byrne also became known for her daily "bombshells." She openly attacked the old alliance between City Hall and organized labor, proposed a city-run casino and a new monorail transit line, and fired hundreds of city employees in an economy move.

But as her first year in office began to wear on, some of her key aides left in disillusionment. And many Chicagoans began to ask whether the Byrne administration was stronger in rhetoric than in substance.

The new State Street mall neared completion at year's end. Retail merchants were hoping the downtown mall would revitalize department store sales, but few were expecting overnight wonders for a street now known for its honkytonk shops, cheap-food emporiums, and pornographic salons.

In May, Chicago's O'Hare International Airport, the world's busiest, experienced the worst single air disaster in U. S. history. An American Airlines DC-10 jumbo jet lost an engine on take-off, killing 273 persons as the plane plunged to the ground in a ball of fire. The disaster led to the grounding of all domestic DC-10s for six weeks.

The year ended on a sour note as strikes by city transit workers and by truck drivers who deliver gasoline crippled the city. The school system, cited in April for violating federal civil rights laws, neared bankruptcy in December.

ROBERT ENSTAD, *Chicago Tribune*

CHILE

In 1979, Chile's political atmosphere was clouded by opposition unrest and deteriorating diplomatic relations with the United States. In the economic sphere, however, large U. S. corporations made substantial investments.

Pinochet Bars Civilian Rule. In a state of the nation address on September 11, marking the sixth anniversary of the military overthrow of the late Salvador Allende Gossens, President Augusto Pinochet Ugarte rejected opposition demands for a timetable for the restoration of representative government. Pinochet said: "The political process remains in total force, particularly in the face of those who want to drag us toward Marxist totalitarianism." President Pinochet also accused the United States of allowing "Soviet imperialism" to spread in Latin America because of "a vacuum created by the country that should be the leader of the free world."

Opposition Unrest. More than 400 persons were arrested by *carabineros* (special police) during May Day demonstrations banned by the police. One week earlier, growing student militancy was shown in elections at the University of Chile when government supporters received only 28.6% of the vote, compared with 59.2% for the opposition and 12.2% for independents. Following the May Day arrests, there were almost daily demonstrations of up to 500 persons outside military tribunals where some of the detainees were being tried. Other protest meetings and hunger strikes at universities and churches continued through September.

In July a special civil judge charged an army captain and seven men under his command with killing 15 persons whose remains were found in an abandoned lime kiln in Lonquen, 25 miles (40 km) southwest of Santiago; their subsequent release under a decree of amnesty further angered many Chileans at home and abroad.

The government forbade the media to disclose the contents of an August 24 speech by former President Eduardo Frei calling for a return to democracy. Between May and September, several bombs exploded at the Santiago homes of high government officials and university professors, and at a government building.

Letelier Case. George W. Landau, the U. S. ambassador to Chile, was recalled for discussions after a decision by Chile's Supreme Court rejecting a U. S. appeal for the extradition of three former army officers indicted for the 1976 murders in Washington, DC, of Orlando Letelier, a former Chilean Foreign Minister under President Allende. The three were Gen. Manuel Contreras Sepúlveda, former head of the Secret Service, and two aides—Lt. Col. Pedro Espinoza Bravo and Capt. Armando Fernández Larios. Michael Vernon Townley, an American using a special Chilean passport, and three Cuban exiles were convicted and sentenced to prison for their roles in the murder of Letelier and an American assistant. Although the United States restricted economic and military aid to Chile, Landau resumed his post in December.

U. S. Investments and the Economy. Anaconda, now an Atlantic-Richfield subsidiary, bought several mines near Salamanca in Coquimbo Province for $20 million and began exploratory work to determine the extent of future operations that could lead to annual production of 150,000 tons of copper. Exxon, another international oil giant, invested $110 million in a mining operation at La Disputada, while the St. Joe Minerals Corporation began developing gold and copper resources at another site. Dow Chemical resumed operation of polyethylene and sodium chloride plants taken over by workers during the Allende regime.

Copper prices, which had fallen to 51 cents a pound in August 1977, stayed at 90 cents a pound in October 1979, after having risen to a record $1.02 in April. Although affected by declining U. S. automobile production and building construction, production problems in Zaire and Zambia, and short strikes in Peru and Canada, prices remained high.

Continued high mineral prices would help improve export earnings necessary to repay Chile's growing foreign debt of $6.5 billion, up from $3.5 billion in 1973. High mineral prices might also ease unemployment which was between 15–20%.

Government planners were hoping that inflation would rise no higher than 35% in 1979, compared with 30.3% in 1978, 63.5% in 1977, and 174.3% in 1976. An annual growth rate of 7% for the 1980's was predicted. Since the mid-1970's, Chile's annual growth rate has averaged about 6%.

Anti-Labor Laws Decreed. In early July, Minister of Labor José Pinera Echenique issued decrees which prevented unions from collecting dues from paychecks, allowed employer lockouts, and limited collective bargaining. The decrees were a surprise reversal of January offers by Pinera to permit more freedom by the unions in a successful effort to persuade foreign labor unions to lift planned boycotts of Chilean goods.

NEALE J. PEARSON, *Texas Tech University*

CHILE • Information Highlights

Official Name: Republic of Chile.
Location: Southwestern coast of South America.
Area: 292,257 square miles (756 945 km²).
Population (1979 est.): 11,000,000.
Chief Cities (1978 met. est.): Santiago, the capital, 3,448,700; Valparaíso, 248,200; Viña del Mar, 362,100.
Government: *Head of state and government,* Gen. Augusto Pinochet Ugarte, president (took power Sept. 1973). *Legislature*—Congress (dissolved Sept. 1973).
Monetary Unit: Peso (39.00 pesos equal U. S.$1, Nov. 1979).
Manufactures (major products): Small manufactures, refinery products.
Agriculture (major products): Wheat, rice, oats, barley, fruits, vegetables, corn, sugar beets, beans, wine, livestock.

Movie posters replace revolutionary slogan signs as China becomes more Westernized.

CHINA, PEOPLE'S REPUBLIC OF

The establishment of diplomatic relations with the United States in January 1979 brought an end to China's long isolation from the West. The Chinese government made extensive efforts to import science and technology from capitalist countries and to learn Western ways in industry and agriculture. Antagonism between China and the Soviet Union grew even more heated, with Peking calling for resistance to Soviet "expansionism" on all fronts. China's full-scale conflict with Vietnam amounted to a proxy war with the Soviet Union.

Determined to make China a strong and prosperous nation before the year 2000, Peking shifted from political revolution to economic development. But shortages of capital and technical manpower required the government to scale down its ambitious plans of industrial growth. The Chinese leadership supported limited democracy and the rule of law but dealt firmly with what it called "anarchy and factionalism."

DOMESTIC AFFAIRS

Party Leadership. Although Hua Guofeng (Hua Kuo-feng) remained chairman of the Chinese Communist Party and premier of the government, senior Deputy Premier Deng Xiaoping (Teng Hsiao-ping) clearly was the dominant power and final decision-maker.

In the interest of domestic stability and of his modernization plans, Deng chose not to purge high-ranking adversaries within the party. He thus allowed Hua to retain the highest position in the party hierarchy and expressed his intention "to add but not subtract" from the nation's leadership. The addition of 12 new members to the Central Committee—all victims of the 1966–69 Cultural Revolution—and the naming of two new Politburo members—including Peng Zhen, a mayor of Peking purged during the Cultural Revolution—strengthened Deng's power.

The National People's Congress ended its two-week session July 1 by appointing three economic experts as deputy premiers. Among them was Chen Yun, who became head of the new State Economic and Finance Commission.

While Deng seemed to be succeeding in his efforts to preserve party unity, factionalism was not entirely eliminated. Several old-time Maoists, including Wang Dongxing, a former bodyguard of Mao Zedong (Mao Tse-tung), and Chen Xilin, the commander of the Peking military region, aligned with Hua and were a force for Deng to reckon with. And Chen Yun, whom Deng had helped restore to government power, was said to be critical of the deputy premier's economic plan and of his war on Vietnam. Despite a general stability within the party, such

167

divisions did force Deng to compromise on important decisions.

Ideological Issues. The memory of Mao Zedong continued to be a delicate and far-reaching issue. An intensive campaign was launched in late 1978 to downgrade Mao and discredit his Cultural Revolution. The former chairman was harshly attacked in wall posters appearing throughout the country and accused of directly supporting the "Gang of Four," the radical leaders of the Cultural Revolution. A violent reaction by the Maoists, however, forced Deng Xiaoping to adopt a milder attitude. He stated that Mao's contributions to Chinese society were "beyond the description of words," but at the same time reaffirmed his utilitarian notion that "*practice* is the sole criterion of truth" (emphasis added). The efforts to demythologize Mao's precepts continued. In a speech on September 29, Ye Jianying, senior deputy chairman of the Communist Party, repeated the generally held view that Mao was "a great man, not a god," and added that the Cultural Revolution was "an appalling catastrophe suffered by all our people."

Democracy. After the downfall of the "Gang of Four" in 1976, the Chinese people began demonstrating for democratic principles and the rule of law. Rallies for freedom of speech and human rights grew in size and passion, and wall posters violently criticizing government leaders became common. Whether the masses have a right to attack the party leadership was a question debated at the plenary session of the Central Committee in December 1978. At that meeting it was resolved that while "bourgeois factionalism and anarchism" must be firmly opposed, it was desirable to promote democracy and eliminate suppressive persecution. The implementation of that resolution, however, was not simple. In April 1979, four members of an active group named the Human Rights Alliance were arrested for putting up a wall poster denouncing China's "bureaucratic system and its masters." Peking ordered the removal of all posters considered antigovernment or anti-Communist. Government leaders like Deng Xiaoping, who had first favored freedom of expression, were apparently taken aback by the vociferous attacks on the party leadership. On March 16, Deng reportedly delivered a strong warning against pushing too strongly for domestic reforms. The government made clear that it would not deal gently with human rights activists.

UPI

Classical Chinese opera, marked by beautiful, elaborate costumes and precise movement, has returned to Peking.

UPI

A hydroelectric power station in Guangxi (Kwangsi) province is the largest of its kind in China. A more moderate approach toward modernization had to be adopted during 1979.

Of great embarrassment to the government were groups of petitioners—totaling more than 10,000—who traveled to Peking from various provinces seeking redress of a variety of grievances. They complained of unemployment, shortages of housing and food, and injustices dating back to the Cultural Revolution. The government appointed 1,000 officials to investigate their complaints, accompany them back to their home districts, and help resolve their problems.

New Laws. In July the People's Congress, China's nominal legislature, adopted a new criminal code and a law of criminal procedure barring arbitrary prosecutions. The new code restricts political prosecution by defining a counterrevolutionary offense as an act committed, not just thoughts harbored, against the dictatorship of the proletariat and the socialist system. It also declared that everyone, regardless of rank, is equal before the law. The new criminal procedure law provides that the family of a detained person must be notified of the arrest within 24 hours and that the courts must try the case within six months. Defendants have the right to a lawyer, and the courts must rely on hard evidence, not just confessions, in reaching a verdict. The new laws were intended to quell fears of prosecution so that intellectuals and professionals could more freely devote themselves to building the country.

Business Class and Ex-landowners. As an attempt to enlist the talents and experience of former industrialists in the nation's modernization plans, the government announced in late January that the rights of the business class would be fully restored. Assets and bank accounts confiscated during the Cultural Revolution were to be returned, with interest. Businessmen could return to their requisitioned homes, and their children would not be discriminated against in schools or jobs. Their professional titles would be restored, and those with special talents would be given political advancements.

The rights policy was then extended to former landowners and "counterrevolutionaries" whose holdings had been seized during the Cultural Revolution and who had been subjected to continued discrimination. According to Peking, these groups had been reformed and should no longer be treated as a subclass.

Modernization. As part of the effort to make China a powerful and prosperous nation by the end of the 20th century, the government in 1978 launched the Four Modernizations program for industry, agriculture, defense, and science and technology. At first, rapid economic growth was projected, but during 1979 a more moderate approach was adopted. The war against Vietnam required increases in the military budget, making difficult the vast purchase of imported technologies. There also proved to be an insufficient number of technicians and skilled workers to handle the sophisticated foreign equipment. In May, Chen Yun began to readjust the nation's economic plans, looking toward a more gradual and balanced growth. Before the National People's Congress on June 18, Hua Guofeng admitted that "some of the measures we adopted were not prudent enough."

Economic Development. The original development program called for the construction of 120 new facilities, including 10 steel plants, 9 nonferrous metal complexes, 10 oil and gas fields, 30 power stations, 8 coal mines, 6 new railways, and 5 harbors—all to be completed by 1985 at a cost of $75 billion a year. It soon became apparent, however, that the plan was simply too ambitious for a poor country, despite its abundant natural resources. By mid-1979, Peking was moving to slow development and to concentrate on only the most needed projects. The construction of steel mills and the development of other heavy industries were reduced substantially. The projected industrial growth for 1979 was revised down from 10% to 8%. The nation's overall budget for 1979 projected total revenues of $70.7 billion, with approximately equal expenditures. However, a deficit was expected.

With 75% of the Chinese population living on farms, the role of agriculture in economic growth was increasingly recognized. To spur agricultural output, Peking adopted the following measures: it raised the prices of grains to give peasants 20% more money for their produce; it reduced the tax on harvests, as well as the prices of chemical fertilizer and farm equipment; and it encouraged peasants to seek profits from produce grown on their private land, as well as from such sideline activities as fishing and raising poultry. The government projected a 4% growth in agricultural output for 1979.

Population Problems. With the population of China reaching 950 million and increasing at a rate of 1.5% a year, Peking discouraged further growth through taxation and other economic sanctions against couples with more than two children. The government seeks to reduce population growth to 5 births per 1,000 people by 1985.

─ **COMMUNIST CHINA • Information Highlights** ─

Official Name: People's Republic of China.
Location: Central part of eastern Asia.
Area: 3,705,396 square miles (9 596 976 km²).
Population (1979 est.): 950,000,000.
Chief Cities (1974 est.): Peking, the capital, 7,600,000; Shanghai, 10,800,000; Tientsin, 4,000,000.
Government: *Chairman of the Chinese Communist Party:* Hua Guofeng (took office Oct. 1976). *Head of government,* Hua Guofeng, premier (took office April 1976); Deng Xiaoping, senior deputy premier. *Legislature* (unicameral)—National People's Congress.
Monetary Unit: Yüan (1.55 yüan equal U.S.$1, 1979—noncommercial rate).
Manufactures (major products): Iron and steel, coal, machinery, cotton textiles, light industrial products.
Agriculture (major products): Rice, wheat, corn, millet, cotton, sweet potatoes.

Meanwhile, the rapid growth of the population had serious economic repercussions. According to an official estimate, about 10% of China's population did not have enough food in 1979, and about 20 million workers were unemployed. Despite its primary commitment to industrial growth, the government found it necessary to increase state investments in agriculture and light industries to help improve the standard of living.

Trade. To attract foreign investment, Peking guaranteed profits to foreign participants in joint-venture enterprises in China. Foreign companies were allowed to repatriate part of their profits and to employ outside managers, engineers, and accountants.

China's exports for the first seven months of 1979 rose to $4.64 billion, a 40% increase over the same period in 1978. Imports increased by 70% to $5.6 billion, leaving a trade deficit of nearly $1 billion.

INTERNATIONAL AFFAIRS

United States. After 30 years of what Deng called the "abnormal state of Sino-U. S. relations," China and the United States established formal diplomatic ties on Jan. 1, 1979. At the same time, the United States severed diplomatic relations with Taiwan and terminated its mutual defense treaty with the Chinese Nationalist government.

U. S. President Jimmy Carter acknowledged that Taiwan was part of China but made it clear that normalization with Peking would not jeopardize the well-being of Taiwan. The United States would maintain commercial, cultural, and other relations with Taiwan through nongovernmental means.

China's decision to speed up normalization with the West was influenced by two considerations: the fear of encirclement by the new Soviet-Vietnamese alliance and the desire to achieve economic modernization by expanded trade with the United States. Peking softened its opposition with respect to U. S. arms supplies to Taiwan and, although refusing to rule out the use of force in recovering the island, made a number of conciliatory gestures in the interest of peaceful unification. It was this subtle change in policy which at last brought about the normalization sought by President Richard M. Nixon during his visit to China in 1972.

On January 28, senior Deputy Premier Deng Xiaoping arrived in the United States for a nine-day visit to discuss global problems and cooperation between the two countries. Deng was given a full-dress welcome on the White House lawn, honored at a formal state dinner, and made the guest of honor at a gala performance at Washington's Kennedy Center. In statements to the media, Deng criticized any U. S.-Soviet strategic arms agreement and called for curbs on Soviet expansionism. He was perhaps more moderate in private conferences with President Carter but made clear that China differed considerably with the United States in its perception of Soviet designs. On the whole, Deng's talks with President Carter were fruitful, and his genial response and pleasant manner generated much enthusiasm among the American public. In a joint communiqué issued February 1, the two governments stated their opposition to efforts by any country to establish "hegemony or domination" over others. Hegemony is the term commonly used by the Chinese to refer to Soviet expansionism.

On January 31, Carter and Deng signed a series of agreements on scientific and cultural exchanges. These included an overall pact on cooperation in science and technology; a separate accord on cooperation in the field of high energy physics; an agreement on space technology that would enable China to enlist the aid of the U. S. National Aeronautics and Space Administration (NASA) in launching a civilian communications satellite; an agreement aimed at increasing cultural contacts in a variety of fields; a scientific agreement calling for student exchange programs; and an interim agreement providing for the establishment of American consulates in Shanghai and Canton and for Chinese consulates in Houston and San Francisco.

Deng left Washington on February 1 for visits to Atlanta, Houston, and Seattle. Leaving Seattle for China on February 5, he issued a statement of warm thanks to the American people, saying that he looked forward to "everlasting friendship and cooperation" between the two countries.

In early May, U. S. Secretary of Commerce Juanita M. Kreps arrived in Peking to help restore full trade relations between China and the United States. On May 11 negotiators overcame a major obstacle by agreeing on settlements of mutual, pre-existing financial claims in both the public and private sectors. On May 14, the two nations reached a trade agreement that would be the foundation of full economic cooperation. China would be granted most-favored-nation trading status; tariff restrictions on Chinese exports to the United States would be significantly lowered. The amount of Chinese textiles exported to the United States was still to be worked out, however, and the accord required final approval by the U. S. Congress.

To reassure China of continued American friendship and support, U. S. Vice President Walter Mondale visited Peking on August 25. There the vice president told the Chinese that "a strong and secure and modernizing China" was in the American interest and that the United States was committed to joining China in advancing their "many parallel strategic and bilateral interests." Mondale and Chinese leaders signed a cultural exchange pact and an agreement for the United States to help China develop hydroelectric power.

In Peking on August 28, China's Deputy Premier Deng Xiaoping and Walter Mondale enjoy a laugh during an official toast. The U. S. vice president and Chinese officials signed a cultural exchange pact and a hydroelectric-power development agreement.

UPI

Western Europe. On October 15, Hua Guofeng arrived in Paris, France, to begin a 23-day, four-country tour of Western Europe. It was the first visit to Western Europe ever made by a Chinese head of government. At welcoming ceremonies in Paris, Hua noted Europe's "pivotal role in international affairs" and urged that France and China strengthen their cooperation in opposing foreign (Soviet) aggression. Hua's next stop was Bonn, West Germany, where government officials, anxious to improve relations with Moscow, had hoped that Hua would not carry his anti-Soviet rhetoric. In Munich, however, Hua called on Western Europe to bolster its military strength against hegemony, or Soviet domination. But it was in Great Britain that Hua delivered his strongest attack on the Soviets. At a dinner with Prime Minister Margaret Thatcher on October 28, Hua implicitly compared the USSR to the Nazis and identified it as the major threat to world peace. Arriving in Rome on November 3 for the last leg of his tour, Hua conferred with Prime Minister Francesco Cossiga and then traveled to Venice to visit the house of Marco Polo. Back in Rome he met informally with Enrico Berlinguer, head of the Italian Communist party. Hua returned to China November 6.

Soviet Union. The normalization of relations between the United States and China was a source of deep concern to the Soviet Union. It was especially displeased with the joint Sino-American communiqué condemning "hegemony." The Soviet Union loomed large in the background of China's military action against Vietnam. Peking considered the Soviet-Vietnamese alliance a threat to China's security. When Chinese forces attacked Vietnam in February, Moscow warned Peking to stop "before it is too late." Although Soviet planes and ships were rushing military supplies to Vietnam, no Soviet military activity was reported along the Chinese border.

On April 3, China announced that it would not renew its 1950 friendship treaty with the Soviet Union when it expires on April 11, 1980. Said Peking, the treaty "has long ceased to exist except in name."

Vietnam War. Relations between China and Vietnam had been deteriorating since 1978, when Hanoi's harsh treatment of its ethnic-Chinese minority was followed by its invasion of Cambodia, an ally of China. Increasingly frequent border incidents heightened the tension and finally convinced Peking that Hanoi "must be taught a lesson." On Feb. 17, 1979, China launched a major attack along its 500-mile (805-km) border with Vietnam. Supported by artillery and tanks, Chinese forces invaded four Vietnamese provinces.

After a pause for new supplies, the Chinese on February 21 renewed their advance in the direction of Lang Son in northwest Vietnam. By March 2, the Chinese had taken Lang Son, Cao Band, and Lao Cai, penetrating some 25 miles (40 km) into Vietnamese territory. Having reached its goal, Peking announced that its forces were withdrawing to Chinese territory. The withdrawal was completed by March 16, when Vietnam offered to hold talks to ensure peace along the border and ultimately to normalize relations. The first two sessions, held in Hanoi April 18 and 26, were immediately deadlocked. Subsequent meetings during the year also served merely as an opportunity to exchange accusations. The chief difficulty in the negotiations was Hanoi's refusal to consider the Chinese demand that Vietnamese forces be withdrawn completely from Cambodia.

See also TAIWAN (Republic of China).

CHESTER C. TAN
New York University

Pinyin

Unlike English or European scripts, which employ the Roman alphabet, Chinese writing is ideographic. Written characters express the meaning of words graphically but do not indicate pronunciation. Hence it usually takes years of study to acquire a functional reading knowledge of Chinese. And although the written language is uniform throughout the country, spoken Chinese varies from region to region. About 70% of the population speak one of several Mandarin dialects, about 29% of Chinese speak some other mutually intelligible dialect, and 1% speaks non-Chinese minority languages.

Soon after the establishment of the People's Republic of China in 1949, the problems of adopting a new script to increase literacy and of unifying the spoken language were intensively studied and discussed. Early in 1956, three forceful measures of langauge reform were announced: the simplification of written characters; the popularization of a national language called *putonghua*, which is based on Mandarin; and the creation of a new phonetic alphabet. The "First Draft of the Scheme of Phonetic Spellings" was issued on Feb. 12, 1956, and adopted with major revisions as the "Scheme of Phonetic Spellings" by the First National Congress of People's Representatives on Feb. 11, 1958. These decrees established *pinyin*—literally, "it spells the sounds"—as the official romanization system of the People's Republic of China.

A number of phonetic alphabets have been used in the West for the transliteration of Chinese characters. The most commonly employed has been the 19th century English Wade-Giles system. In China, *pinyin* was intended to replace ideographic characters, but the changeover has been gradual. At present the system is used primarily to teach Chinese characters, although books, newspapers, wall posters, and official publications employ both methods. Foreign publications have increasingly appeared in *pinyin*, and in August 1977, the Third United Nations Conference on Standardization of Geographical Names accepted China's request to adopt *pinyin* as the international method for romanization of place names. On Jan. 23, 1979, the U. S. Board on Geographical Names announced its approval of *pinyin* as the official government system for the spelling of geographic names in China. This decision prompted the nation's major news agencies, newspapers, and magazines to change over also.

Pinyin offers many practical advantages. As an aid to pronunciation, it has helped popularize the common language of *putonghua* and facilitate the learning of written language; it has enabled previously unwritten minority languages to be put down on paper; and it has been a valuable tool for teaching Chinese to foreigners. In addition, it serves as a convenient means for alphabetical indexing and for arranging dictionaries. Other possible uses include telegraph communication; flag signalling; braille for the blind; and an iconic sign language for the deaf and mute.

The problems posed by *pinyin* are by comparison minor and pertain to the system *per se*. Such questions include: how to represent tonal variation, an integral part of the Chinese language; how to distinguish homophones; whether to combine familiar terms into one word or to separate them by hyphens; and whether foreign names should be transliterated or retained in their original spellings. In the case of tone representation, there is no uniform practice; in some publications tones are indicated by diacritics, but in other reading materials, such as newspapers, tones generally are not indicated. The problem of homophones, which is acute only when the two words appear in the same context, is perhaps best resolved by choosing a synonym for one of the terms. The question of word division is as yet unsettled. And with respect to foreign names, the transliterated form seems to be preferred.

DIANA L. KAO

The Pinyin Alphabet

The *pinyin* system consists of the 26 letters in the Roman alphabet, arranged into 26 initials and 35 finals. (A final consists of a vocalic $+/-$ ending.) The following list indicates the pronunciation of all 26 letters and 2 unique combinations. Corresponding letters used in the Wade-Giles system are given in parentheses.

a (a)	as in *far*	**p** (p)	as in *par*
b (p)	as in *be*	**q** (ch)	as in *cheer*
c (ts)	as in *its*	**r** (r)	as in *right* or
ch (ch)	as in *church*		as z in *azure*
d (t)	as in *do*	**s** (s, ss, sz)	as in *sister*
e (e)	as in *her*	**t** (t)	as in *top*
f (f)	as in *foot*	**u** (u)	as in *too*
g (k)	as in *go*	**v** (v)	used only for for-
h (h)	as in *her*		eign words, minor-
i (i)	as in *eat* or *sir*		ity words, or local
j (ch)	as in *jeep*		dialects
k (k)	as in *kind*	**w** (w)	as in *want*
l (l)	as in *land*	**x** (hs)	as in *she*
m (m)	as in *me*	**y**	as in *yet*
n (n)	as in *no*	**z** (ts, tz)	as in *adze*
o (o)	as in *law*	**zh** (ch)	as dr in *dry*

Examples of Familiar Names and Words Rendered into *Pinyin*
(from the Wade-Giles or Postal system)

Zhōngguó (China)	tóngzhì (comrade)
Máo Zédōng (Mao Tse-tung)	zhǔxí (chairman)
Dèng Xiǎopíng	Běijīng (Peking)
(Teng Hsiao-p'ing)	Guǎngzhōu (Canton)
Huá Guófēng (Hua Kuo-feng)	Sìchuān (Szech'wan)
Tiānjīn (Tientsin)	Nánjīng (Nanking)
Húnán (Hunan)	

CITIES AND URBAN AFFAIRS

The U. S. urban crisis, a term coined in the 1960's to describe a host of municipal and social ills, was itself a matter of debate in 1979. Several nationally reported studies concluded that the urban crisis was over, but this view was by no means universal. While it was true that some cities attracted new business and industry, strengthened tax bases, and took new steps to manage growth and stem decline, the larger problems—loss of population, fiscal distress, aging facilities, clogged transportation arteries, crime, and poverty—remained. Indeed, several new factors—the prospect of continued energy scarcity, changing population and employment patterns, and the "tax revolt" spurred by California's Proposition 13—posed new challenges to city governments.

Fiscal Worries. The fiscal situation continued to be the number one problem for U. S. cities in 1979. The confluence of double-digit inflation, imminent recession, and state tax reductions resulted in fiscal belt-tightening in urban areas across the country. Cuts in city services, disrepair of municipal buildings and transportation facilities, and substantial reductions in government personnel were not uncommon.

These conditions were most prominent in Cleveland, OH, which in late 1978 became the first major U. S. city since the Depression to default. (*See* Special Report, page 174). But while Cleveland was the year's urban horror story, several other American cities continued to suffer deteriorating infrastructures, outflow of business and industry, loss of residents and jobs, and inability to secure a broader tax base.

Economic conditions did improve slightly in New York City and Newark, NJ, both in severe fiscal stress during recent years. But the population of New York City hit its lowest level since the Depression, and inroads into the city's long-term financial problems were modest. (*See* New York City, page 370). By the same token, Newark remained synonymous with urban crisis, consuming large amounts of federal aid—about $500 million in eight years.

Population Trends. The so-called "back-to-the-city" movement attracted considerable attention in 1979 as a possible signal of the end of urban decline. Inner city rejuvenation projects, such as Quincy Market in Boston, Capital Hill in Washington, DC, and Society Hill in Philadelphia suggested that young, middle-class professionals were moving from the suburbs back to the central cities. Commercial centers emerged in several downtown areas once abandoned by business.

Although these highly visible areas were encouraging success stories, they were isolated occurrences. The truth is that the population of central cities continued to decrease. In fact, twice as many people were moving away from the central cities during 1979 than were moving in. And contrary to popular perceptions, the new home buyers in many cities were not newcomers moving in from the suburbs but people who already lived in the city.

The U. S. Census Bureau reported in 1979 that the black urban population showed no growth for the first time since World War II. Meanwhile, black migration to the suburbs increased by 34% between 1970 and 1977.

Also reversing a post-World War II trend, poor people began moving south. The continued growth and economic health of the Sunbelt states attracted low-income families despite the area's comparatively low welfare benefits.

Many cities continued to show rapid growth during the year, presenting new management problems for mayors and city managers. According to the Census Bureau, Houston (*see* page 246) had the biggest increase. Other significant population gainers were also located in the Sunbelt region: San Diego, Dallas–Fort Worth, Atlanta, and Miami–Dade County.

Policies and Politics. In 1979 the country still did not have what could be termed a comprehensive urban policy. None of the major components of President Carter's urban program, presented in March 1978, was passed by Congress. However, the linchpin of his urban policy —a partnership of the public and private sectors —was evident in a number of programs. Inner city revitalization projects were variously managed or financed by the Department of Housing and Urban Development, the Department of Commerce, the Small Business Administration, and the Farmers Home Administration.

Carter's proposal for a federally funded "urban development bank" stalled again in Congress, but some of the more modest financial arrangements survived in the authorization of the Economic Development Administration.

A fundamental principle of President Carter's urban policy is that public dollars should be used to supplement and encourage private investment, not replace it. Accordingly, Congress in 1979 passed a 10% investment tax credit for rehabilitation and expansion of existing industrial plants, as well as for new construction. In addition, the Urban Development Action Grant Program (UDAG), which provides federal money for urban projects with private support, was slated for increased funding.

Meanwhile, some of the older urban programs—such as federal revenue-sharing and counter-cyclical aid—came under sharp attack in Congress. General revenue sharing, by which federal funds are pumped into state and local government, survived the year despite criticisms that it contributes heavily to the federal deficit. The economic developments of 1979, coupled with political pressure to balance the budget, made unsure the continuation of the program beyond its Sept. 30, 1980, expiration date.

WILLIAM GORHAM
President, The Urban Institute

Default in Cleveland

Ohio's largest city failed to pay six banks a total of $14 million owed on Dec. 15, 1978, and continued to be in default through 1979. Its 33-year-old mayor, Dennis J. Kucinich, a Democrat at odds with the party organization, had become embroiled with the city council's leadership and all efforts to draw up programs to end the default situation failed. How did Cleveland move to the brink of bankruptcy?

Kucinich's two predecessors, Carl B. Stokes, a Democrat and the first black mayor of a major U. S. city, and Republican Ralph J. Perk, had skirted financial pitfalls. Stokes in 1970 sought an increase in the municipal income tax rate in exchange for giving up an expiring real estate tax levy. Voters rejected the proposal and revenue which renewal of the levy would have given was lost. When Stokes left office in 1971, after voter rejection of another income tax increase issue, he estimated Cleveland's operating deficit at $2 million for the year. An accounting firm said the figure was nearer $27 million.

Perk managed to keep the city afloat financially by appealing, frequently and successfully, to the national Republican administrations (Nixon-Ford) for large special grants.

Kucinich, as a maverick Democrat, had no special entrée at the White House. Wage in-

creases for city workers, inflated costs, and demolition of many inner city homes, with loss of real estate taxes, tightened the fiscal bind. By late 1978, Cleveland's operating budget was seriously out of balance, and cooperation was lacking among City Hall, political factions, and banks. Ohio's largest bank, Cleveland Trust Co. (later AmeriTrust), declined in mid-December to extend its $5 million loan. Complicating the fiscal trouble was a deficit, building over several years, of about $50 million in bond fund accounts—the money had gone for operations. The city defaulted.

In January 1979, Gov. James A. Rhodes of Ohio considered forming a financial management assistance team, like New York's Emergency Financial Control Board, but Kucinich called it a "takeover" bid and nothing followed.

Two steps were proposed, requiring an election Feb. 27, 1979. Voters approved an increase from 1% to 1.5% in the municipal income tax. The move was designed to collect about $2.5 million more a month. The tax also applies to suburbanites working inside Cleveland's borders. Mayor Kucinich, though he had promised no new taxation, backed the issue. The vote was 74,402 to 34,586.

Also on the ballot was a proposal that the city sell its Municipal Electric Light System (Muny Light). The Cleveland Electrical Illuminating Co., a private utility which had sought to eliminate Muny competition, was the presumed buyer. Kucinich fought the sale of Muny Light, which has been losing money. That issue lost, 38,817 to 69,957. Meanwhile, the city kept alive a $330 million antitrust suit against CEI.

In June, Council President George L. Forbes and a member of the Kucinich cabinet announced a plan to refinance the $14 million debt and pay off $1.25 million a month. But disagreement arose over the true state of the city's financial condition. The city then did pay about $3.75 million to the banks, plus interest. The banks took no step to foreclose to get all their money.

From the time default loomed, Mayor Kucinich assailed Cleveland Trust Co. and other banks as attempting to dominate City Hall policy and to force the Muny Light sale.

Any serious attempts at resolution of a debt-payment schedule were delayed as the November 6 municipal election approached. George V. Voinovich, a Republican who had been Ohio's lieutenant governor since January, defeated Kucinich and began immediate steps to cleanse Cleveland of default, possibly with state help. Bank and business leaders repeated offers to help dig into the city's bookkeeping mess.

JOHN F. HUTH, JR.

Cleveland Mayor Dennis Kucinich votes in a special February election. Later, he lost his reelection bid.

UPI

CIVIL LIBERTIES AND CIVIL RIGHTS

The year 1979 was not a particularly outstanding one for individual and group rights in the United States. The record of the courts was mildly progressive, but there were several decisions that staunch defenders of civil liberties, such as Supreme Court Justice Thurgood Marshall, regarded as "temporary setbacks."

Job Bias. In a case likely to have even greater repercussions than the celebrated *Bakke* case of 1978, the Supreme Court upheld, by a vote of 5–2, the voluntary affirmative action employment program of Kaiser Aluminum Co. A white worker, Brian Weber, had challenged the plan on a "reverse discrimination" theory. However, the majority of the court found that the racial quota was consistent with the 1964 Civil Rights Act, as it was intended to correct a racial imbalance in the work force (*Kaiser Aluminum Company v. Weber*).

Another employer, Sears Roebuck, was unsuccessful in its challenge of federal equal employment programs. Sears had sued 10 federal agencies, charging that conflicting equal employment policies placed the company in an untenable position and that the government's own policies were responsible for creating a work force dominated by white males. Sears had asked the court to prohibit federal agencies from seeking penalties against private employers until the government could more effectively enforce equal opportunity laws in housing, education, and employment. A district court judge dismissed the case as unsuitable for judicial resolution.

School Bias. Twenty-five years after its landmark decision in *Brown v. Board of Education*, the Supreme Court heard its first school desegregation appeal in six years brought by minority plaintiffs seeking to integrate public schools. In *Dayton Board of Education v. Brinkman* and *Columbus Board of Education v. Penick* the court ruled that the two school systems had helped bring about segregation and that systemwide solutions such as busing were therefore necessary.

These decisions were handed down shortly after the publication of a provocative study by the Institute for Southern Studies. The paper concluded that public school segregation was least common in the 11 states of the old Confederacy and that the greatest failure of school integration occurred in northern cities.

The Internal Revenue Service (IRS) in 1979 challenged the tax-exempt status of private schools having discriminatory admissions policies, but supporters of church-sponsored schools and opponents of government regulation banded together and protested vigorously. One result was a Congressional amendment to the Treasury Appropriations bill forbidding the IRS from implementing review procedures for evaluating the tax-exempt status of private schools.

In another noteworthy case, a federal judge in Michigan sided with 11 black children who charged that their school had failed to provide them with an equal learning opportunity by not recognizing their language barrier. The school board was ordered to submit a plan for training a group of teachers to identify children who speak "Black English."

Sex Bias. The Supreme Court upheld claims of sex discrimination in six of eight cases. The court rejected, however, the claim of feminists that laws giving government job preference to military veterans discriminated unfairly against women.

In another case, the nation's highest court declared unconstitutional a Massachusetts law requiring an unmarried minor who wants an abortion to first obtain the approval of her parents or a judge. Although freedom-of-choicers were gratified by the Supreme Court ruling, they were disturbed that the majority opinion suggested a formula by which a state could require a judge to consider whether the teenager was "mature" enough to make such a decision on her own.

In other actions, the Supreme Court expanded the right of female employees to bring antidiscrimination suits against universities and members of Congress.

On the other side of the coin, however, the high court struck down a New York law awarding alimony to women but not to men. It struck down another New York law permitting the mother of an illegitimate child, but not the reputed father, to veto adoption of the child. And in the same spirit, it ruled that unemployed mothers have the same right to welfare benefits as out-of-work fathers if they have been the family's principal wage earners.

Defendant's Rights. Despite the Burger Court's image as a champion of law and order, the Supreme Court in 1979 decided against the police in six out of ten cases involving searches, including those of unlocked suitcases and randomly stopped automobiles.

In other actions, though, the court came down on the side of criminal justice officialdom. It held that the police do not have to obtain a written waiver of an individual's right to silence before interrogation, and it refused to apply due process standards to state parole systems.

Elsewhere, however, there were efforts to constrain police abuses. A federal judge issued an injunction prohibiting strip searches of traffic offenders without probable cause, and the Justice Department filed an unprecedented civil suit against the city of Philadelphia for systematic and widespread police brutality.

See also ETHNIC GROUPS; LAW—U. S. Supreme Court.

MARTIN GRUBERG
Professor of Political Science
University of Wisconsin, Oshkosh

THE SUSAN B. ANTHONY DOLLAR

The Susan B. Anthony dollar, honoring the famed suffragette, is the first American coin that portrays an American woman. The first Anthony dollars were minted in Denver, with subsequent issues produced in Philadelphia and San Francisco. The coin is slightly larger than a quarter, is made of nickel-covered copper, and contains no silver.

UPI

COINS AND COIN COLLECTING

Stealing the numismatic show in 1979 was the Susan B. Anthony dollar. Chief engraver of the coin was Frank Gasparro. Heralded as a boon to the public, the coin was less than successful following an enthusiastic introduction. Millions of Anthony dollars were on hand for the July 2 introduction, but the public at large rejected them, stating various reasons, including the ease of mistaking them for quarters.

The General Service Administration announced that in 1980 it would sell remaining Carson City silver dollars dated 1880, 1881, and 1885.

Inflation and the energy crisis focused attention on gold and silver metals, which resulted in the record $400-per-ounce gold prices in evidence during the autumn of 1979. This development, plus knowledge of the past investment performance of rare coins—which has sharply outpaced returns from traditional investment media—produced a strong market.

The American Numismatic Association (ANA), the leading organization of collectors, met in St. Louis for its annual convention. Auction sales held by five firms the weeks before and during the convention grossed approximately $13 million, an all-time selling record.

Walter Perschke of Chicago paid $430,000 for a 1787 Brasher doubloon, the highest recorded price for a coin ever sold at auction. A 1907 extremely high relief MCMVII Saint-Gaudens double eagle, one of 18 known, sold for $225,000 at a sale held by Stack's.

Bowers & Ruddy Galleries of Los Angeles was selected by The Johns Hopkins University to sell at public auction the Garrett Collection of coins. The Garrett Collection, formed by members of the family who controlled the B&O Railroad, was built from 1865 to 1940 and represented the most valuable collection ever to be offered publicly. Included were two examples of the famous 1787 Brasher doubloon, the 1804 silver dollar, unique 1783 Nova Constellatio silver patterns, and territorial gold issues. In November, four segments of the collection realized a record price of more than $7 million.

The Bureau of Engraving and Printing returned to the production of $2 notes after a lapse of 2½ years. The U. S. government discontinued sale of earlier-dated 1776–1976 bicentennial silver coins when the price of silver bullion rose to the point that the intrinsic value of the sets was greater than the previous offering price.

Sales of South African krugerrands containing an ounce of gold continued brisk. The Royal Canadian Mint announced the production of the United Nations International Year of the Child $100 gold coin. Canada later issued the Maple Leaf, which was minted of .999 fine gold.

Q. DAVID BOWERS
Bowers & Ruddy Galleries, Inc.

COLOMBIA

The first full year in office for Liberal President Gabriel Turbay Ayala was marked by increasing violence both in rural and urban areas. Several new guerrilla groups emerged, and government troops apparently were given a freer hand in dealing with them. Meanwhile, it was politics as usual in Bogotá, as the Liberal Party was torn by internal dissension, and the opposition Conservatives, led by the redoubtable Belisario Betancour, tried to take advantage.

The economy performed fairly well, with most economic indicators up sharply from 1978. The Turbay administration made some efforts to control the still burgeoning marijuana trade.

Politics. To many outside observers, the Colombian political system seemed to be in serious trouble by the end of 1979. A continuing state of siege and the suspension of *habeas corpus*

--- **COLOMBIA · Information Highlights** ---

Official Name: Republic of Colombia.
Location: Northwest South America.
Area: 439,737 square miles (1 138 914 km²).
Population (1979 est.): 26,100,000.
Chief Cities (1978 est.): Bogotá, the capital, 3,831,099; Medellin, 1,442,244; Cali, 1,255,198.
Government: *Head of state and government,* Gabriel Turbay Ayala, president (took office Aug. 1978). *Legislature*—Congress: Senate and Chamber of Representatives.
Monetary Unit: Peso (43.00 pesos equal U. S.$1, Nov. 1979).
Manufactures (major products): Textiles, beverages, processed food, clothing and footwear, chemicals, metal products, cement.
Agriculture (major products): Coffee, bananas, rice, cotton, sugarcane, tobacco, corn, plantains, flowers.

rights in January did not prevent guerrilla movements from increasing in number and strength. Foremost among the new groups was the 19th of April Movement (M-19), headed by Pablo Garcia. The M-19 and its leader claimed to be followers of the National Popular Alliance (ANAPO), a populist movement launched in the early 1970's by former Colombian dictator Gustavo Rojas Pinilla and his daughter, Maria Eugenia Rojas. The M-19 remained unique among the nation's underground groups for its attempts to gain mass populist support. Despite President Turbay's denials, his increasing reliance on the army to combat the M-19 and other armed opposition groups led to a deterioration in the position of the civilian government as against the military. Although few expected a military coup in the near future, the armed forces, long quiescent in Colombian politics, appeared to be playing a much larger role.

Economy. Although the annual inflation rate was estimated at 21.8%, the Colombian economy continued to perform well during 1979. Foreign investments increased by 252% for the first six months, while agricultural production and imports rose by 8.6% and 46.8%, respectively, during the same period. Coffee exports increased 64.7%, but earnings were flat as a result of lower world prices. The proposed budget for 1980 was a record 169 billion pesos.

Foreign Affairs. Domestic problems did not deter Turbay from taking a more active role in foreign affairs. His summer trips to Mexico and Europe as representative of the Andean Pact countries, and his appearance at the Panama Canal Zone ceremonies in October indicated a new leadership role in the hemisphere.

ERNEST A. DUFF
National Autonomous University of Mexico

COLORADO

Natural resources continued to provide the backdrop for many economic and political developments—good and bad—in Colorado.

Denver's Building Boom. A strong building boom in downtown Denver, paced by energy companies that used the city's central location to oversee operations in western states, continued to add tax base and jobs in the city. But the influx of new payrolls and workers, coupled with growing concern about the price and availability of gasoline and heating oil, fanned a trend to "gentrification" in formerly low to moderate income residential neighborhoods in downtown Denver. The term refers to an influx of mostly young professionals into neighborhoods where they displace less affluent residents. A spate of conversions of apartment buildings into condominiums—often selling at prices beyond the reach of the former tenants—set some to worrying about a growing shortage of low to moderate income housing.

Figures indicated that in the 12 months ending Sept. 30, 1979, housing prices in the Denver area had leaped 28.2% over the previous year. That helped fuel an overall inflation rate of 16.3% for the period, the nation's second highest. (San Diego's 16.4% is first.)

Energy. President Carter's proposal for a massive program to stimulate synthetic fuel production met widespread opposition in Colorado. Residents feared that parts of the state might become, in the words of Gov. Richard Lamm, a "national sacrifice area" or "energy colony" as the drive unfolded. Less melodramatic, but more practical, were fears that a full-scale drive to develop synthetic fuel from Colorado's vast "oil shale" deposits might overtax the state's scant water resources and dry up its flourishing agriculture. Such concerns were lessened by Congressional compromises, which prompted some Western lawmakers to give their support to the revised proposals.

Legislature. The Colorado legislature began the 1979 session agreeing that the air pollution in the Denver metropolitan region was its top priority. It adjourned without passing antipollution legislation, agreeing to study two conflicting approaches until 1980. The lawmakers passed a $118 tax relief bill, which exempted groceries from the state's 3% sales tax and trimmed other levies. The state's sagging highway system received an extra $30 million, and $8 million was sent into a fund for state financing of water projects.

People. Gaetano Delogu became the new conductor of the Denver Symphony Orchestra in September and a $13 million theater complex was set to open December 31 in the new Denver Center for the Performing Arts. Denver Mayor William McNichols easily won reelection to a third four-year term in May voting.

The University of Colorado received attention—and criticism—by hiring New England Patriots coach Chuck Fairbanks as its new football coach. The negotiations surfaced as the Patriots were entering the 1978–79 NFL play-offs. Eventually, booster groups paid the Patriots' management a reported $200,000 as part of a settlement.

BOB EWEGEN, *"The Denver Post"*

COLORADO • Information Highlights

Area: 104,247 square miles (270 000 km²).

Population (Jan. 1979 est.): 2,695,000.

Chief Cities (1976 est.): Denver, the capital, 479,513; Colorado Springs, 180,821; Pueblo, 103,918.

Government (1979): *Chief Officers*—governor, Richard D. Lamm (D); lt. gov., Nancy Dick (D). *General Assembly*—Senate, 35 members; House of Representatives, 65 members.

Education (1978–79): *Enrollment*—public elementary schools, 307,001 pupils; public secondary, 251,284; colleges and universities, 152,359 students. *Public school expenditures,* $1,268,283,000 ($2,044 per pupil).

State Finances (fiscal year 1978): *Revenues,* $2,675,-106,000; *expenditures,* $2,279,059,000.

Personal Income (1978): $21,645,000,000; per capita, $8,105.

Labor Force (July 1979): *Nonagricultural wage and salary earners,* 1,185,500; *unemployed,* 66,300 (4.8% of total force).

Windsor and Windsor Locks, CT, were declared disaster areas after a tornado caused heavy damage October 3.

CONNECTICUT

National, state, and local politics, public-school funding, gasoline, heating oil, gambling, and racial discrimination preoccupied Connecticut citizens in 1979.

Government. Under orders from the state Supreme Court to find a more equitable way of funding public schools, the Connecticut legislature responded with a new formula and approval for an additional $190 million in school funding for the next five years. No new taxes were imposed, and an austere $2.4 billion budget for fiscal 1980 was approved. Following the regular six-month session of the General Assembly, Gov. Ella Grasso called the legislature back into session on October 29 to formulate programs to help ease the looming heating oil crisis.

In politics, Abraham A. Ribicoff, Connecticut's former governor and its U. S. senator since 1963, announced his plans to retire in 1980. Connecticut's Republican Sen. Lowell P. Weicker, Jr., made a brief run in the spring for the Republican presidential nomination, but pulled out after poor showings in the polls.

In November mayoral elections, Democrats captured an additional 20 towns and kept control of the state's four largest cities. Mayor George A. Athanson (D) won a fifth term as mayor of Hartford, and former police chief Biagio "Ben" DiLieto was elected the Democratic mayor of New Haven.

The Economy. Connecticut's economy held strong even in the face of dark forecasts for the national economy. According to September figures, total employment rose 2.7% over 1978, and unemployment remained steady at 4.8%. Heavily dependent on defense contracts for submarines, aircraft engines, and helicopters, Connecticut experienced a 10.8% rise in employment related to transportation equipment. Construction contracts were also up 32% over 1978.

Energy. During the summer a gasoline shortage led to an odd-even gasoline rationing plan.

The price of heating oil nearly doubled 1978's price and was a source of great concern in Connecticut, where 72% of the households are heated with oil.

Gambling. The state agency regulating the multimillion dollar gambling industry, which includes jai alai, dog racing, off-track betting, and lotteries, was completely overhauled at the governor's request and with the legislature's concurrence. For the first time in jai alai's 45-year history in the United States, more than a dozen players, betters, and cashiers were arrested by federal and state authorities on various charges of fraud and game rigging. Using cable television, the nation's first "Teletrack," a kind of simulated horse track, with betting and live broadcasts of races, opened in New Haven.

Racial Discrimination. Racial tensions flared in the autumn with several cross burnings around the state and reports of increased activity by the Ku Klux Klan. Housing discrimination in the suburbs continued to be a major source of friction between the cities and suburbs, with several suits filed. The U. S. Justice Department joined in a suit charging the town of Manchester with racial discrimination in housing.

DIANE HENRY
"The New York Times"

------ **CONNECTICUT · Information Highlights** ------

Area: 5,009 square miles (12 973 km²).
Population (Jan. 1979 est.): 3,095,000.
Chief Cities (1976 est.): Hartford, the capital, 134,957; Bridgeport, 139,552; New Haven, 124,583.
Government (1979): *Chief Officers*—governor, Ella T. Grasso (D); lt. gov., William A. O'Neill (D). *General Assembly*—Senate, 36 members; House of Representatives, 151 members.
Education (1978–79): *Enrollment*—public elementary schools, 396,975 pupils; public secondary, 196,782; colleges and universities, 152,431 students. *Public school expenditures*, $1,290,200,000 ($1,967 per pupil).
State Finances (fiscal year 1978): *Revenues*, $2,908,-740,000; *expenditures*, $2,789,507,000
Personal Income (1978): $27,612,000,000; per capita, $8,911.
Labor Force (July 1979): *Nonagricultural wage and salary earners*, 1,397,600.

CONSUMER AFFAIRS

Inflation, the major problem confronting consumers in 1978, continued to be the number one problem in 1979. In fact, the inflation rate approached 14%. Inflation hurt even more because personal income increased at a slower rate and consumers' purchasing power fell behind.

Inflation. Most consumers felt inflation's greatest impact in the almost 50% increase in prices paid for gasoline and heating oil. The increases in the price of gasoline brought about a very significant change in the automobile buying habits of the public. While some car manufacturers offered rebates of $400 to $1,000 to help sell big cars, car dealers asked and got more than the sticker price on some small, fuel-efficient cars. Prices for small, used cars actually went up while the prices of used "gas guzzlers" dropped sharply.

Federal Policy. It was a holding year for the consumer movement in terms of federal legislation. No legislation of major significance was enacted. A potentially significant move to benefit consumers was the signing of Executive Order 12160 by President Carter on Sept. 26, 1979. The order established the Consumer Affairs Council with responsibility to "provide leadership and coordination to ensure that agency consumer programs are implemented effectively." The council, which will consist of senior-level officials from each cabinet department, will also strive "to maximize effort . . . to eliminate duplication and inconsistency among agency consumer programs."

Federal Trade Commission (FTC). The FTC, the focal point of consumer activity during 1979, pressed for additional regulations to give consumers more protection, while feeling the animosity of the business community for "going too far." FTC "truth in insulation" rules to reduce deception in the sale of insulation for the home were finalized. The commission also ruled that the three-day "cooling off" provision that applies to door-to-door sales also applies to sales made at motels and to all sales of consumer products of more than $25 not made in stores. It also ruled that eye doctors must give patients their prescriptions immediately after an eye exam. Activity by the commission in defense of consumers led to a possible backlash in Congress. Under pressure from the business community, legislation was introduced to give Congress veto power over FTC rules and to block funding for certain FTC activities, including its attempts to curb television advertising directed at children.

Food and Drug Administration (FDA). Of every dollar spent in the United States by consumers, 25¢ goes for products regulated by the FDA, including all foods, except red meat and poultry which are regulated by the Department of Agriculture; all medicines, cosmetics, medical devices, and vaccines; and such radiation-emitting products as microwave ovens and television sets. The FDA ruled in 1979 that labels on most common pharmaceuticals, both those sold over the counter and by prescription, must display expiration dates. In addition the FDA was developing regulations that would require more informative labeling, particularly nutritional information, on food products. Many in the business community strongly resist such rules.

Canada. The metric system was more extensively used in Canada. By late 1979 the weights of all ice cream, pet foods, sugar, and snack foods were in metric; all weather temperatures were given only in centigrade; and almost all highway mileage and speed signs were metric. In addition all post offices were using metric measurements.

The Canadian Supreme Court ruled that the Civil Code of Quebec prevents auto manufacturers from limiting liability for defective cars in the province. Ontario's new stringent consumer protection codes received judicial support. The Ontario Supreme Court ruled that manufacturers are liable for claims made in brochures.

STEWART M. LEE, *Geneva College*

CONSUMER AFFAIRS—SPECIAL REPORT:

The Credit Card and Personal Credit

The average American, seemingly defying talk about a possible recession, splurged on credit purchases in 1979 but at a rate lower than in 1978. Credit buying was easy. Inflation increased consumer income though it reduced discretionary income. But concern over future higher prices kept the consumer buying.

Credit-card sponsors freely bestowed cards upon customers. Retail stores eagerly welcomed credit cards. And banks invited consumers to buy not only on one but two multipurpose credit cards and to take advantage of automatic overdraft checking privileges. Only the reality of recession curtailed charge and installment purchases.

After a sharp 19% increase in consumer debt in 1978, the year 1979 got off to a slow start. Consumer credit increased by $3.1 billion in January 1979 after a $4.4 billion rise in December. Nonetheless, the January increase boosted total consumer debt outstanding to $275.6 billion, $120 billion above the level at the end of the previous recession in early 1975. Credit continued to rise during the next three months of 1979 but during the month of May it dropped again.

ANDREW PARTOS

The big jump in outstanding debt, fostered in great part by use of bank credit cards, raised fears that an increasing number of Americans had financially overextended themselves. The Consumer Credit Counseling Service of Greater New York estimated that, because of a combination of high demand and inflation, consumers had reached a state in which they were paying a record 18% of their take-home pay to cover installment debt, not including home-mortgage payments. Thus, the Counsel added, the average consumer was burdened with about $4,400 in outstanding debt.

In an unusual move, John G. Heimann, the U. S. Comptroller of the Currency, warned banks against overextending consumer credit through the excessive use of credit cards. He said that he was concerned about the use of so-called revolving credit lines and extension of multiple lines of credit to individual borrowers through credit cards. He cited reports from banks that open lines of bank credit were being used to support consumer life-styles. But the implication was that consumer-credit losses might rise substantially unless banks tightened their lending policies.

Some banks had anticipated the problem. According to a spokesman, the First National Bank of Chicago had adopted "a more aggressive stance on collections. At the first sign of a problem, we go in with counseling. We are not waiting until people get in over their heads." The bank also exerted a more rigorous scrutiny of credit applications.

Ironically, perhaps, it was the consumer's unabated appetite for buying now and paying later that, at least in the early months of 1979, seemed to defy economists' assertions that a recession had arrived.

More than 600 million credit cards were in use in 1979. Many users were convinced that physical assets would intrinsically be worth more than dollars. And credit, after all, was still easy to get. So Americans continued to be conspicuous credit consumers. Yet many were nervous about such buying. Others began to hold back during the early months of the year. But the later trend did not change much. Consumers, it seemed, were more worried about the shortage and rising price of gasoline than about their debts.

Rising prices of autos and the gasoline squeeze curtailed buying of new cars during the year. And the sharp price curve in housing, as well as the tight mortgage market, concerned potential home purchasers although sales continued high. It was clear that housing and new cars were the two major purchases about which consumers were most concerned. But the desire to beat higher prices, even if it meant buying on credit, persisted on other items.

Mortgage interest rates, however, continued to rise and overall retail sales drifted downward, not only in automobiles but in general merchandise. When the Carter administration reluctantly admitted that the United States was indeed in a recession—two consecutive fiscal quarters in which the gross national product declines—Americans began to get the message. Despite double-digit inflation, U. S. retail sales in real dollars fell off from 1978 levels.

As a result, the annual rate of installment debt in 1979 declined by an estimated 10%. And yet, some economists did not consider the estimated $375 billion in total consumer debt a worrisome load. The reason, they said, was the consumers' higher net worth, which had severely eroded in previous recessions, relative to their debt. This was due, they explained, to the rapid rise in the price of housing and the inflated value of consumer's other assets.

ISADORE BARMASH

CRIME

The close relationship between economic conditions and criminal activity was particularly notable in 1979. Inflation, energy shortages, unemployment, high interest rates, and other indexes of uneasy times all were reflected in different forms of law violation.

Take, for instance, the energy crunch. Escalating prices for gasoline created a heavy demand for smaller, fuel-efficient cars. This demand was being met in part by altered patterns of auto theft in the United States. A growing number of law-breakers also conspired with owners of big, gas-guzzling cars to "steal" or destroy such vehicles and allow the owners to file insurance claims to gain reimbursement. The National Automobile Theft Bureau predicted that a record high of 1.1 million cars would be stolen in 1979, a 15% increase from 1978. Thefts of subcompact cars nearly doubled during the year, while those of compacts almost tripled. "Anything with a four-cylinder engine is being snapped up by crooks," the head of one of the nation's largest insurance companies noted. In the past, two thirds of all cars had been stolen by joy riders who abandoned them after a brief spin. Now about 70% of the stolen cars never come back to their owners, with most of them presumably being sold on the black market.

Assaults on Teachers. The uncertain nature of the times was mirrored throughout the nation's classrooms, where pupils are more likely than in earlier times to challenge the authority of teachers. This fact was reflected in a report by the National Education Association that 5% of U. S. school teachers were physically attacked during the 1978–79 school year. This puts the total at about 110,000 teacher assaults throughout the country. Of the teachers physically assaulted, 10% required medical attention for their injuries. Another 8% suffered emotional trauma sufficiently serious to involve medical care.

Bank Robberies. Cities such as Atlanta, Washington, and San Francisco registered rates of bank robberies that were roughly twice as high as those of the previous twelve months. In addition, New York City witnessed a record number of bank holdups. Boris Melnikoff, security director of the First National Bank of Atlanta, which was robbed at least 11 times during the year, offered an explanation: "We blame it on the economy. We have a product that is very marketable. The professional bandit needs more money to survive."

The rate of capture of bank robbers has been declining, in part because of increasing attention to white-collar crime by the Federal Bureau of Investigation. Banks have taken to installing security devices such as floor-to-ceiling Plexiglas "bandit barricades" between tellers and customers. Some banks began using scented capsules which are wrapped inside rolls of bills. If squeezed, these release a strong odor of rotten eggs. The rolls are handed to robbers by the tellers at the time of holdups.

Unemployment and Crime. The continuing high levels of unemployment in the United States are reflected in particularly high rates of crime among inner city youths, who more than any other group remain unable to locate work. Such youths primarily engage in property offenses—robbery, burglary, larceny, and auto theft—but they also are 10 to 12 times more likely than other young persons to be arrested for crimes of violence. Sustained unemployment is said to breed frustration, anger, and despair, with such states of mind being expressed in criminal behavior.

A major problem is that a youngster charged with committing a crime is further stigmatized and removed from the labor market, since he or she will find it even more difficult than before to obtain a job. The situation is particularly critical for inner city black persons, who now have an unemployment rate about twice that of whites. Particularly bad is the condition for black youths. In 1979 the unemployment rate for blacks in the 16- to 18-year age bracket was about 40%, compared with 15% for whites in the same age category.

Tax Crimes. U. S. authorities persistently have put forth the view that the country's system of voluntary compliance with tax requirements

Policemen leave a New York City bank after a robbery attempt. City bank robberies increased in 1979.

UPI

works exceedingly well. In 1979 that belief was exploded by a comprehensive study. The Internal Revenue Service estimated that it failed to collect $19 to $26 billion in legitimate taxes during the year studied. This represents approximately 10% of the total $230 billion that is collected. Deductions from workers' paychecks in the form of withholding account for most of this revenue.

The stunningly high level of tax evasion, a problem common throughout the world, was believed in part to represent a response to economically uncertain times. There has been a large growth in the so-called underground economy. This economy is represented by transactions that cannot be traced by taxing authorities. It includes bartering, and other forms of business dealing, particularly the use of cash to pay for services, that leave no records in their wake. Doctors, dentists, and home-repair workers were said sometimes to be offering lower prices if they are paid in cash rather than by check. They then do not include the cash received on their income tax returns.

The Internal Revenue Service's study also reported some striking figures for the earnings of persons engaged in "victimless crime" activities. These included income of about $20 billion from illegal drug sales, about $4.5 billion from bookmaking, $2.5 billion from numbers gambling, and $1.8 billion from other forms of gambling. Persons engaged in prostitution were said to earn about $1.3 billion a year. Very little of this income is reported for tax purposes, resulting in a loss of more than $6 billion in federal revenue.

Terrorism. Political unrest in various parts of the world accounts for the growth of terrorism,

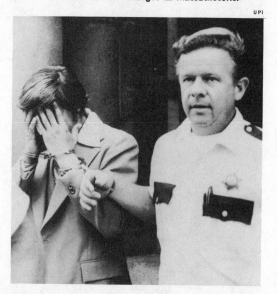

In an unusual case, James Chretien (*left*) was found guilty of raping his estranged wife. He was the first man to be tried on such charges in Massachusetts.

UPI

which often takes the form of grim, theatrical criminal acts. The International Society of Political Psychology devoted several sessions of its annual meeting to terrorism. In one, Wilfried Rasch, a German forensic psychiatrist who had examined members of the Baader-Meinhof gang before they committed suicide or were killed in prison, said that governments have a vested interest in portraying terrorists as mentally disturbed so that their claims of political grievance can readily be discredited. Rasch maintained that his interviews clearly refuted the theory that the terrorists were mentally warped.

Another research worker, after studying Basque and Latin American terrorists, concluded paradoxically that terrorist behavior such as theirs is apt to increase as governments become less dictatorial. "The more freedom, the greater violence," he maintained. It was also reported that constant terrorism can exert a deadening impact on the ambition of young persons who might become its target. Turkish youngsters, according to Ayse Kudat, are likely to become "de-motivated" because of fear of terrorist activity. Some middle-class children, Kudat said, desire only to become waiters or janitors, explaining: "I want to live. Let the university students die."

Public Attitudes. During the year, the *Sourcebook of Criminal Justice Statistics,* issued by the Law Enforcement Assistance Administration of the Department of Justice, brought together a number of surveys of public attitudes regarding aspects of the crime problem. Taken together, the surveys form a portrait of a diminishing general apprehension about crime, largely because citizens have become increasingly alarmed about other aspects of contemporary life, particularly economic conditions (including inflation) and environmental damage.

Respondents to one poll blamed the high U. S. rate of crime largely on "the leniency of the law" and "social conditions such as poverty and unemployment." Slightly fewer persons thought that the "way judges apply the law" and "the breakdown of religion and morality in families" were responsible for high crime rates. The fewest number chose the fifth alternative: "the way the police enforce the law."

The polls also pinpointed a decline during 1975–79 from 74% to 67% of teenagers who said that if they saw a stranger slashing the tires of a car they would report the incident and describe the person to the police.

A national survey also found opinion in the country evenly divided on the issue of legalization of homosexual relations between consenting adults, with 43% of the population approving, 43% disapproving, and 14% stating no opinion on the matter. The largest group in opposition to legalization (57%) was made up of unemployed persons and those with only a grade-school education. The largest group favoring

UPI

Joan Dedrick, 46-year-old wife of a New York bank executive (*right*), was released unharmed after being held by kidnappers for about 42 hours. A $300,000 ransom was paid; much of it was recovered.

legalization (58%) was constituted of persons in the 18 to 24 age group.

The Death Penalty. On May 23, John Spenkelink, 30, became the first person to be executed in the United States since 1977, when Gary Gilmore was put to death by a firing squad in Utah. Spenkelink met his death in Florida's electric chair after being sentenced for the murder of a fellow drifter. In Nevada, six months later, Jesse Bishop became the second felon executed in 1979.

Surveys reported increasing American support of capital punishment. A poll by the National Opinion Research Center found that 67% endorse the death penalty, with only 26% opposing it, and 6% offering no opinion. The increase in support rose by almost 15% during 1974–79.

At year's end, nearly 600 inmates were housed on the nation's death rows, awaiting legal determination of the status of their sentences. Southern states accounted for about four fifths of the total, with Florida alone having more than 130 persons under sentence of death.

China. For the first time since the revolution in 1949, public officials paid open attention to the issue of crime in the People's Republic of China. Newspapers devoted numerous columns to reports of criminal episodes, though they focused only on those in which the accused had been found guilty. They noted, for example, that in August a 43-year-old Peking truck driver had been convicted of raping and murdering a farm woman and had been executed for the act by a firing squad. Courts were also opened to the public for the first time, and on Jan. 1, 1980, a new Criminal Code and Law of Criminal Procedure was put into effect. People now would be able to know formally what kinds of acts are punishable and how they may defend themselves against charges.

The main purpose of criminal law enforcement in China continues to be public education. Selected trials are used as lessons on how people ought to behave and what happens to those who violate expected norms. The exact rate of criminal activity in China remains impossible to determine. But it is known that relatively few persons are imprisoned. Shanghai, with a population of almost 11 million, has only 2,600 inmates in its jails, an incarceration rate about one sixth that of the United States. The United States, for its part, has the second highest imprisonment rate per capita in the western world. South Africa is first, and the lowest rates are found in The Netherlands and Norway.

GILBERT GEIS, *University of California, Irvine*

CUBA

The revolutionary government of Cuba, appearing to be less attentive to the country's intractable economic and social problems, increased its already considerable interest in world affairs. President Fidel Castro, in control as firmly as ever after 20 years in power, indicated that Cubans would have to be prepared for at least another decade of hard work and economic hardships, but that the country would continue to honor its "international duties."

Foreign Policy. For the Havana government, the most important event of 1979 was the sixth summit conference of the organization of nonaligned nations that took place in the Cuban capital early in September. Fidel Castro, as the conference's host, became president of the 95-member organization, which has no formal structure. Consequently, he became the official spokesman of the Third World grouping. He is to hold the post until 1982 when he relinquishes it to the head of state of Iraq, where the next nonaligned nations conference is scheduled to be held.

A mural of the Che Guevara is dominant as Cuba stages a parade for the 20th anniversary of the Castro regime.

UPI

Before the week-long Havana gathering, many members of the nonaligned organization voiced concern that the Cuban leader would try to use his new position to convert the group into a tool of Soviet international policy, a charge that he denied. At the conference, the Cuban president also defended Cuba's international policy, regarded by some Third World countries as aggressive and dictated by Moscow's expansionist designs. He asserted that Cuba was sending to and maintaining military forces in Africa and elsewhere because Cuban soldiers were fighting for "just causes." He added: "We don't try to impose our radicalism on anyone, much less on the nonaligned movement."

In October, President Castro, in his first visit to the United States in 18 years, addressed the General Assembly of the United Nations as president of the Third World organization. His speech underlined Cuba's interest in foreign affairs and, contrary to some expectations, did not signal any diminution of its overseas military involvement.

An issue that in a way affected Cuba's standing among nonaligned nations was the presence of Soviet troops in Cuba. It emerged, Havana said not coincidentally, at the time when the conference was in session. The Carter administration announced that it had discovered that a part of the Soviet military personnel on the island had become a "combat brigade" of between 2,500 and 3,000 men, comprising three infantry batallions and one tank batallion. On September 5, Secretary of State Cyrus R. Vance declared that the "presence of a Soviet combat unit in Cuba is a matter of serious concern." Two days later, President Carter escalated the issue by stating that the unit's presence could affect U. S.-Soviet relations and that "the status quo is not acceptable." Both Cuba and the Soviet Union denied the existence of the combat brigade in Cuba. They stated that since the end of the October 1962 missile crisis there has been no change either in the overall number of Soviet troops in Cuba, estimated by Washington at between 10,000 and 13,500, or their function, which both Havana and Moscow said was that of training Cuban soldiers.

On October 1, after a series of discussions between Secretary Vance and Soviet Ambassador Anatoliy F. Dobrynin and an exchange of mes-

--- **CUBA · Information Highlights** ---

Official Name: Republic of Cuba.
Location: Caribbean Sea.
Area: 42,823 square miles (110 912 km²).
Population (1979 est.): 9,900,000.
Chief Cities (1977 est.): Havana, the capital, 1,981,258; Santiago de Cuba, 330,997; Camaguey, 236,116.
Government: *Head of state and government,* Fidel Castro Ruz, president (took office under a new constitution, Dec. 1976). *Legislature* (unicameral)—National Assembly of People's Power.
Monetary Unit: Peso (0.72 peso equals U. S.$1, 1979—noncommercial rate).
Manufactures (major products): Refined sugar, metals.
Agriculture (major products): Sugar, tobacco, rice, coffee, beans, meat, vegetables, tropical fruits.

U. S. marines stage a show of force at Guantanamo Bay, Cuba, following the disclosure that a Soviet "combat brigade" is stationed on the island.

UPI

sages between the White House and the Kremlin, President Carter defused the issue. But he announced a number of counter-measures to the Soviet presence in Cuba. Among the more specific were: intensifying intelligence surveillance of the island; resuming SR-71 spy planes' regular overflights of the island; establishing a Caribbean Joint Task Force headquarters in Key West, FL; holding military maneuvers in the region; and increasing economic assistance to Caribbean countries.

The Cuban military involvement in Africa and Asia appeared to have acquired a permanent character. According to U. S. government analysts, Cuba maintained approximately 50,000 troops in some 20 nations, including about 20,000 in Angola and 15,000 in Ethiopia. Cuban soldiers continued to be logistically dependent on Russian supplies, which were flown directly from the Soviet Union. In 1979, the Cubans were not involved in any major fighting in the countries in which they were stationed. But appearing to be prepared for a long stay, they reportedly have developed a "base mentality," seldom venturing from their urban bases into a countryside that is often controlled, especially in Angola, by antigovernment rebels.

Domestic Affairs. Cuba's dependence on Soviet economic aid increased in 1979 to an estimated total of $3 billion a year (or about $8 million a day), almost one quarter of the country's gross national product. According to President Castro, Cuba produced a record harvest of 7 992 000 metric tons (8.9 million tons) of sugar in 1979. But he complained that because of the low world market sugar prices the value of this entire production, which represents 80% of all Cuban exports, was not enough to pay for the petroleum the country consumes annually.

GEORGE VOLSKY
University of Miami

CYPRUS

In 1979 Cyprus remained in the quagmire into which it fell after the Turkish invasion of the summer of 1974. Turkish forces retained control of the northern part of the island, and no visible progress, was made toward resolving the conflict between the majority Greek Cypriots and the minority Turkish Cypriots.

Attitude of Kyprianou. President Spyros Kyprianou and his Democratic Party government continued to refuse to recognize the Turkish Federated State of Cyprus in the north and its president, Rauf Denktaş. The state had been proclaimed in areas occupied by Turkish Cypriots and immigrating mainland Turks after 200,-000 Greek Cypriots had been forced to flee southward in the wake of the Turkish invasion.

Settlement Initiatives. Largely because of efforts by UN Secretary General Kurt Waldheim, Kyprianou and Denktaş met in Nicosia, May 18–19, and agreed on a ten-point program for the resumption of intercommunal talks on the unification of the island. Previous negotiations had broken down more than two years before. Both sides were optimistic and negotiators were chosen for the opening of the talks on June 15. But on June 22, after only four sessions, the negotiations broke down amid serious recrimi-

─────── **CYPRUS • Information Highlights** ───────

Official Name: Republic of Cyprus.
Location: Eastern Mediterranean.
Area: 3,572 square miles (9 251 km²).
Population (1979 est.): 600,000.
Chief Cities (1974 est.): Nicosia, the capital, 117,100; Limassol, 80,600.
Government: *Head of state and government,* Spyros Kyprianou, president (took office Aug. 1977). *Legislature*—House of Representatives.
Monetary Unit: Pound (0.34941 pound equals U. S.$1, Aug. 1979).
Manufactures (major products): Processed foods, asbestos, cement.
Agriculture (major products): Potatoes, grapes, citrus fruits, wheat, barley, carobs, livestock.

nations from both sides. Kyprianou's government accused the Turkish Cypriots of not really wanting unification and of bargaining for a division of the island into two separate states. The Turkish Cypriots claimed that they had been a persecuted minority before the Turkish invasion and that they would do nothing to risk a return to that condition.

To promote Turkish Cypriot demands, Denktaş sought the support of Islamic nations in the Middle East. His efforts were backed by Turkish Prime Minister Bülent Ecevit. Süleyman Demirel, who succeeded Ecevit in November, was equally adamant in safeguarding Turkish interests on the island.

Meanwhile, President Kyprianou's strategy was to mobilize general world opinion against the Turkish occupation. He embarked on a number of initiatives toward that end, all the while keeping in close touch with Greek Premier Constantine Caramanlis. Kyprianou traveled to Rumania in June to consult with President Nicolae Ceauşescu, and at the summer gathering of Commonwealth leaders in Lusaka, Zambia, conferred with British Prime Minister Margaret Thatcher and Queen Elizabeth II. In late September and early October Kyprianou attended the conference of nonaligned states in Havana, Cuba, and saw the passing of a resolution calling for the resumption of intercommunal talks, an end to foreign intervention on the island, and the return of refugees to their homes.

On November 20 the general assembly overwhelmingly adopted a resolution calling for the establishment of a special UN committee to work with Waldheim if there was no progress in the negotiations between Greek and Turkish Cypriots by March 1980. Denktaş, however, had already dismissed in advance any UN resolution concerning the island.

GEORGE J. MARCOPOULOS, *Tufts University*

CZECHOSLOVAKIA

The year was one of deepening economic malaise for Czechoslovakia. The regime of President Gustav Husák registered little success in its stepped-up efforts to silence the nation's political dissidents.

Economy. In 1979, Czechoslovakia's economy experienced a major slowdown and failed to meet established targets in the major sectors. By midyear, modest increases over the corresponding period in 1978 were reported in industrial production (2.6%), labor productivity in industry (1.9%), construction (2.9%), foreign trade (7.3%), retail trade (0.1%), and cash income of the population (2.8%). All of these increases, however, were well below those of preceding years. As a result, industrial production lagged 1.6% behind the planned target, construction by 2.6%, and labor productivity in industry by 1.9%. Only 80% of the apartments planned for the first half of 1979 saw

completion, and as many as 46% of the nation's construction enterprises and 38% of its industrial enterprises failed to reach their goals.

Prospects in the crucial field of fuel and energy were dimmed by political developments in Iran. For all practical purposes, the 1975 agreement by which Czechoslovakia would receive from Iran 4,700 million cubic yards (3 600 million m³) annually of natural gas in the years 1981–2003, was nullified. The results in agriculture were even worse. Instead of the hoped-for 12.3 million tons (11.2 million metric tons) of cereal grains, only about 9.9 million tons (9 million metric tons) were harvested.

Price Increases. Besides growing shortages in many essential goods, consumers were hit hard by steep price increases. On July 20 and 23, the government raised the price of gasoline (by 50% to about $2.65 a gallon), electricity, fuel oil, and telephone and postal rates.

Dissidents. Despite police harassment, Czechoslovak dissidents persevered in issuing and publicizing via the Western media statements criticizing the regime's violations of human rights, attacking its economic policies, and charging widespread corruption. Frustrated by its inability to silence the dissenters by any means short of criminal prosecution, the government in May ordered the arrest of eleven leading members of the Charter 77 human rights movement and charged them with "subversion of the state." Six of them, all associated with the self-styled Committee for the Defense of the Unjustly Persecuted, were sentenced in October to prison terms ranging from 2 to 5 years. Among them was the noted playwright Vaclav Havel. The arrest and trial triggered worldwide protests and prompted the European Parliament to adopt a resolution accusing the Czechoslovak government of violating its obligations under the Final Act of Helsinki.

Communist Party. The Communist Party of Czechoslovakia (KSC) required the exchange of all membership cards and canceled the affiliation of those persons considered unworthy of the "honor."

EDWARD TABORSKY
University of Texas at Austin

DANCE

A series of startling events rocked the world of dance in 1979. The most sensational was the defection of three principal dancers from Moscow's Bolshoi Ballet—Aleksandr Godunov and Leonid and Valentina Kozlov.

A former Russian defector who continued to be in the news was the superstar Mikhail Baryshnikov. Barely a year after he had stunned his public by leaving American Ballet Theatre to join the New York City Ballet, it was announced that he would return to Ballet Theatre as its artistic director on Sept. 1, 1980. He insisted that in the interim he would continue to dance with the City Ballet. But in October 1979, at the start of his second year with the company, Baryshnikov suddenly resigned.

Ballet Company Problems. The future of the three major American ballet companies seemed momentarily clouded in 1979. Prior to Baryshnikov's appointment, the news that Lucia Chase, Ballet Theatre's founding patron, would relinquish her post as artistic director in September 1980, came as a surprise. Oliver Smith, her co-director, announced that he would resign as well. In October 1979, due to a labor contract dispute, the company's management locked out its dancers and cancelled Ballet Theatre's season at the Kennedy Center in Washington, DC.

The New York City Ballet was troubled by the illness of its chief choreographer and artistic director, George Balanchine. For the first time in 20 years, there was no Balanchine premiere in the season. But following his successful heart surgery in June, Balanchine planned new works for 1980.

Meanwhile, the Joffrey Ballet suspended activity for six months because of financial difficulties. In place of its regular repertory seasons, New York appearances were limited to a program that repeated the same four ballets nightly, with Rudolf Nureyev as guest artist.

The Ballet Season. Artistically, it was a season more noted for fine performances by individuals and by special events, such as new competitions, than by the production of great new works. Among the foreign companies that visited the United States, the Netherlands Dance Theater, with ballets by its new artistic director, the Czechoslovak-born Jiri Kylian, became an immediate hit.

High on the list of personalities who made a strong impact in 1979 was Anthony Dowell, the star of Britain's Royal Ballet, who appeared as a guest artist with Ballet Theatre. Known for his purity and elegance, Dowell danced with new assertive freedom, notably in Ballet Theatre's premiere of "Contredances," created by Glen Tetley for Dowell and Natalia Makarova.

The other Ballet Theatre premiere was Antony Tudor's "The Tiller in the Fields," in which Gelsey Kirkland startled both the public and her peasant lover in the ballet by showing off a rounded belly. This controversial naturalistic ending left critics and audiences wondering if Tudor was ·joking. Eventually, Tudor admitted that he had hoped to give the public a jolt, and that while he used music by Antonín Dvořák, he had followed a scenario in a composition by another Czech composer, Leoš Janacek.

Ballet Theatre also presented the company premieres of John Cranko's "Pas de Deux Holberg" and Ben Stevenson's "Three Preludes," in which Kirkland, partnered by John Meehan, had a tremendous personal success.

Mikhail Baryshnikov danced at the White House, but he was less visible in the City Ballet which, unlike Ballet Theatre, firmly pursues a no-star policy. After 15 months with the company, Baryshnikov left because of tendinitis and other injuries that required him to stop dancing for several months. In his tenure with the City Ballet, he danced 22 roles, many involving an adjustment to a new style. The consensus was that he made steady progress. He was considered outstanding in "Harlequinade" and in an abbreviated version of Balanchine's "Apollo."

Jerome Robbins cast Baryshnikov in two new ballets—"The Four Seasons," set to Verdi, and the Prokofiev "Opus 19." The third premiere for the City Ballet was by Peter Martins. His plotless "Sonate di Scarlatti" confirmed his promise as an inventive new choreographer.

Rudolf Nureyev danced with three companies, including Ballet Theatre and the National Ballet of Canada. The Joffrey Ballet's appearances on Broadway were built around his presence and the theme, "Homage to Diaghilev."

Boris Akimov is Mercutio in "Romeo and Juliet," presented by the Bolshoi Ballet during its U.S. tour.

© JACK VARTOOGIAN

Members of the Netherlands Dance Theater created great excitement in the New York premiere of "Sinfonietta."

Nureyev danced in three ballets originally created for Serge Diaghilev's Ballets Russes. If he was less successful in "Petrouchka" and "Le Spectre de la Rose," he was praised in the title role of a beautiful and striking revival of Vaslav Nijinsky's rarely-seen "L'Après-midi d'un Faune." The program, which included "Parade," was later repeated at Lincoln Center.

Nureyev also danced in a New York City Opera production of "Le Bourgeois Gentilhomme." The comic ballet set to Richard Strauss' music was commissioned from Balanchine who, because of his illness, shared the choreography with Robbins. Patricia McBride and Jean-Pierre Bonnefous were the other leads in this slight work.

An accent on Balanchine ballets marked the opening of the Dance Theatre of Harlem in its first full New York season in two years. It offered three premieres: "Adagietto No. 5" by Royston Maldoom, "Sensemaya" by Carmen de Lavallade, and "Mirage" by Billy Wilson.

Foreign dance companies which visited the United States during 1979 included the Irish Ballet, the International Ballet of Caracas, the Bat-Dor Dance Company from Israel, Maurice Béjart's Ballet of the 20th Century from Belgium, the Stuttgart Ballet, the National Ballet of Cuba, and a group of soloists from the Royal Danish Ballet.

The most attention went to the Netherlands Dance Theater and the Bolshoi Ballet. Jiri Kylian's exultant style was seen in the Netherlands group with such works as "Sinfonietta," "Symphony of Psalms," and "Glagolitic Mass."

The Dutch group included many American dancers. A further taste of Kylian's daring, flungout choreography was given by the Stuttgart Ballet, which performed his "Return to the Strange Land."

The Bolshoi's soldout seasons were marked by brilliant performances by Nadezhda Pavlova, Vyacheslav Gordeyev, Natalia Bessmertnova, Ludmilla Semenyaka, and Aleksandr Godunov, who defected at the end of the New York run. The ballets of Yuri Grigorovich, such as "Romeo and Juliet," "Legend of Love," and "The Stone Flower," drew mixed reactions.

Modern Dance. On the modern dance scene, Twyla Tharp presented among other premieres "Baker's Dozen." Paul Taylor's new works were "Diggity," "Profiles," and "Nightshade," a Gothic and mysterious piece inspired by Max Ernst. In "Plains Daybreak," Erick Hawkins offered a sensitive transposition to his own idiom of an American Indian ceremony.

Murray Louis, Alvin Ailey, Louis Falco, and Jennifer Muller also presented seasons. At the American Dance Festival in Durham, NC, Laura Dean presented the premiere of "Music," and Merce Cunningham created "Roadrunners."

Among 1979's special events was a Katherine Dunham gala, with revivals by the famed pioneer of black theatrical dance. The Boston Ballet's First International Choreographers Competition was won by Constantin Patsalas of the National Ballet of Canada. The first U. S. A. International Ballet Competition (IBC) was held in Jackson, MS.

ANNA KISSELGOFF, *"The New York Times"*

DELAWARE

Delaware was confronted with problems involving inflation, unemployment, and public education. Inflation was the basis for threatened strikes by construction and automotive assembly plant workers and professors at the University of Delaware. In each instance solutions were reached, averting work stoppages.

Economy. Delaware experienced a rise in unemployment to 8% at year's end. A decrease in the number of public school teachers accounted for some of the loss in employment, and layoffs also occurred in automobile plants and in the construction industry. Contracts for nonresidential building construction fell 80%, from $8.6 million to $1.7 million in 1979. Housing starts showed an increase of 3% in the same period.

The state ended fiscal 1979 with a surplus of $34.5 million. The budget for fiscal 1980 was $557 million. Although demands for an additional tax cut were voiced, state financial officials felt that the surplus should be saved in order to overcome expected shortages in gasoline and auto transfer revenues. Delaware's credit rating improved perceptibly in 1979. Profits realized from soybeans and corn were above average, but lima beans' profits dropped slightly after extremely wet weather at harvest. The total net tonnage handled by the Wilmington marine terminal increased from 2.6 million tons to 10.7 million tons. There was a drop of 3% in revenue from the Delaware Memorial Bridge and Lewes–Cape May Ferry due to the prolonged gasoline shortage.

Schools. The second year of court-ordered desegregation in northern New Castle County began without incident although there was evidence of minor clashes involving racial groups in the schools. Complaints continued from many suburban white parents whose younger children were bused to predominantly black schools in Wilmington. Enrollment in public schools in New Castle County has slumped by 8% since desegregation was decreed. The birthrate drop accounted for but 3%; the remainder was attributed to "white flight." There was an increase in the number attending parochial schools. Nonsectarian private-school enrollment rose 7%.

Legislation. The General Assembly passed the first leg of a constitutional amendment permitting initiative and referendum. To become law, approval by the legislature elected in 1980 is required. The legislature agreed to continuance of the Wilmington wage tax. Municipalities were granted additional money for repair of streets damaged by winter weather. The state supreme court refused to issue an advisory opinion limiting the governor's right to make administrative appointments during recess of the legislature. Refunding of Delaware Turnpike bonds was approved. The Turnpike Authority let contracts for the widening of the Kennedy Memorial Turnpike, a vital link in the Northeast highway corridor. Consideration of building an additional bridge over the Delaware River was postponed indefinitely. Insistent demand for revision of the law regulating pricing of alcoholic beverages met with little response from the legislature.

PAUL DOLAN, *University of Delaware*

DENMARK

The deteriorating Danish economy and an intracabinet dispute between Social Democrats and Liberals over the 1980 budget led to the resignation of Prime Minister Anker Jørgensen and his entire coalition cabinet on September 28 after 13 months in power. A new election for the Folketing (Parliament) was set for October 23, with Jørgensen's cabinet carrying on in a caretaking capacity.

Politics. The parliamentary election, which was the fourth one in six years, served to strengthen the political center, including the Social Democrats. The Social Democrats increased their representation by four for a total of 69 seats, 21 short of a majority. With 22 seats the Liberals tied for second place with the Conservative Party, which gained seven seats, while the Progressive Party's representation was reduced from 26 to 20. The Communists lost all of their 7 seats.

With 12 parties vying for votes and political power, the task of forming Danish coalition cabinets is a delicate one. This time, Jørgensen did not embark on that course, but instead

---

DELAWARE • Information Highlights

Area: 2,057 square miles (5 328 km²).
Population (Jan. 1979 est.): 582,000.
Chief Cities (1970 census): Dover, the capital, 17,488; Wilmington, 80,386; Newark, 21,078.
Government (1979): *Chief Officers*—governor, Pierre S. duPont IV (R). *General Assembly*—Senate, 21 members; House of Representatives, 41 members.
Education (1978–79): *Enrollment*—public elementary schools, 53,041; public secondary, 57,993; colleges and universities, 30,918 students. *Public school expenditures,* $233,847,000 ($1,925 per pupil).
State Finances (fiscal year 1978): *Revenues,* $800,842,000; *expenditures,* $725,031,000.
Personal Income (1978): $4,972,000,000; per capita, $8,534.
Labor Force (July 1979): *Nonagricultural wage and salary earners,* 250,500; *unemployed,* 21,900 (7.9% of total force).

DENMARK • Information Highlights

Official Name: Kingdom of Denmark.
Location: Northwest Europe.
Area: 16,631 square miles (43 074 km²).
Population (1979 est.): 5,100,000.
Chief Cities (Jan. 1, 1977): Copenhagen, the capital, 1,251,226; Aarhus, 245,866; Odense, 167,616.
Government: *Head of state,* Margrethe II, queen (acceded Jan. 1972). *Head of government,* Anker Jørgensen, prime minister (took office Feb. 1975). *Legislature* (unicameral)—Folketing.
Monetary Unit: Krone (5.2930 kroner equal U. S.$1, Nov. 1979).
Manufactures (major products): Industrial and construction equipment, furniture, textiles, electronic equipment.
Agriculture (major products): Dairy products, meat, fish, fur.

Following October elections in Denmark, Prime Minister Anker Jørgensen (*center*) formed a new minority Social Democratic government.

formed a minority Social Democratic government. Headed by Jørgensen as prime minister, the list of Social Democratic cabinet members includes Kjeld Olesen as foreign minister and Ritt Bjerregaard as minister of social affairs. In December 1978 Bjerregaard had lost her post in the cabinet because of charging exorbitant travel expenses to the government. The new cabinet faced a number of towering problems, including rampant inflation, widespread unemployment, a huge balance-of-payments deficit, and a steep rise in oil prices.

European Parliament. The first Danish elections to the European Parliament took place on June 7 with less than 48% of the eligible voters casting their ballots. Of Denmark's 16 seats in the European Parliament, the Social Democrats won 3, the Conservatives 2, the Socialist People's Party 1, the Center Democrats 1, the People's Movement against the Common Market 4, the Liberals 3, and the Progressive Party 1, to whom was added one representative for Greenland.

Anniversaries. The centennial of the birth of the great explorer Knud Rasmussen was celebrated on June 7. Rasmussen, who was born in Greenland, headed a great number of expeditions that mapped and explored wide areas of Greenland. In 1910 he founded the trading post known as Thule in an area which at that time was considered no man's land.

In June the University of Copenhagen celebrated its 500th anniversary. The anniversary was marked by the publication of a 14-volume set, depicting the history of the university.

ERIK J. FRIIS
Editor, "The Scandinavian-American Bulletin"

DIVORCE

U. S. Trends. A United States Census Bureau study, published in 1979, projected that nearly four out of every ten recent U. S. marriages might end in divorce if the current levels of divorce persist. The study provided evidence of the extent to which divorce had become a common practice.

The United States has the highest divorce rate of any nation in the world. By 1978, it reached a high of 5.1 divorces per 1,000 total population. In 1975, the number of divorces had exceeded one million for the first time. Although the rate has leveled off since then, there have been more than one million divorces (involving more than one million children) in each subsequent year. This number is more than twice that of just ten years ago. In recent years the number of children involved in divorce has tripled. In addition, even though the divorce rate has leveled off of late, the number of divorcing couples has continued to increase as a result of the large population of young adults who have married in recent years.

The 1979 Census Bureau study also indicated that as of 1975 one fourth of divorced, separated, or never-married mothers received child support. The average yearly amount of support was $2,430. This amount did not substantially increase for additional children within the family. Only 4% of separated or divorced women in 1975 received alimony. Other data disclosed that one-parent families maintained by women had increased 131% between 1960 and 1978, and that in 1978, 19% of all American children lived with just one parent.

Paths. The high divorce rates in 1979 were characteristic of all races and socioeconomic levels, but continued to be higher among blacks and among those with lesser education and income. Recent research indicated that divorce historically was more likely to occur among high school dropouts, among women who have babies prior to marriage, and among men and women with a low level of family income. Divorce was more than twice as likely to occur among persons who marry in their teenage years than among persons who marry in their 20's.

Although precise reasons for the greatly increased divorce rate are not known, it is probable that part of the increase is due to the greater willingness of unhappy couples to go through with divorce. Less social stigma is associated with divorce, and it may be easier for a divorced individual to re-enter the community as a single person. There are social clubs and organizations for divorced persons (for example, Parents Without Partners), and the increased independence of women makes it easier for them as divorcees to be treated with respect, to make new friends, obtain work, and socialize in the community. Never-married men and women are more willing to date and to consider marriage to a divorced person.

Other factors which may contribute to the advanced divorce rate are exceedingly high expectations of marriage, the lessening of commitment within the marriage, greater emphasis on individual emotional well-being, and the greater tolerance toward divorce by religious groups.

Despite divorce statistics, there were ample data to suggest that marriage is still a highly sought-after and respected institution. More than nine of every ten Americans marry, and more than 75% of divorced persons remarry.

Laws. In 1979 all but three states allowed some form of "no-fault" divorce, which replaced or supplemented traditional divorce statutes that assumed one guilty party and one innocent party in a divorce. No-fault laws assume that in a failed marriage it is possible for both spouses to have a contributing role.

While the law varies from state to state, there are in general two forms of no-fault divorce. The first form allows one or both of the spouses to testify that there are irreconcilable differences or that the spouses are incompatible to a degree that warrants dissolving the marriage. The other form of no-fault divorce allows for a mandatory period of separation.

While the issue of "fault" or "no-fault" divorce continues to be debated by some state legislatures, it is generally agreed that a no-fault system provides for a more honest and conciliatory approach to marital instability. Experts also believe that "no-fault" divorce has not increased the divorce rate but has simply made the procedure less painful.

GRAHAM B. SPANIER
The Pennsylvania State University

ECUADOR

After nine years of military dictatorship, Ecuador returned to a democratically elected civilian government in 1979. However, the establishment of a constitutional regime did not completely end the nation's political instability.

Elections. The government changed the election law three times before the elections were finally held. On January 19 it made illegal the spoiling of ballots and banned as candidates all government employees, including teachers and professors. A month later the ban on government employee candidacies was lifted. A final change forbade candidates of parties which had not received official recognition to be included on the candidate lists of the other parties.

The presidential and congressional elections finally took place on April 29, three weeks later than originally scheduled. Jaime Roldós Aguilera, the 38-year-old candidate of the leftist Concentration of Popular Forces (CPF), gained a decisive margin over Sixto Durán Ballén Cordovez of the Christian Social Party and other right-wing groups. Roldós also helped the CPF-led coalition win 45 of 69 seats in the national assembly; 57 seats in the congress were elected by district, 12 at large.

Policies and Politics. In his inaugural speech August 10, Roldós promised to fight corruption, improve health care and redistribute rural land holdings to improve the lives of the poor (most of them Indians), expand exploration for oil, and institute a sweeping program of economic development.

Roldós' reform program faced a major political obstacle, however, in the form of Assad Bucaram, the effective leader of the CPF. Bucaram, who in 1978 was barred from running for the presidency because his parents were born in Lebanon, was replaced on the ticket by Roldós. But Bucaram was allowed to run for Congress and was even elected president of that body. Personal and ideological differences soon developed between Roldós and his former patron, and with Bucaram in control of Congress, a conflict developed between that body and the president. In August and September, the president vetoed three bills passed on Bucaram's initiative. Although the dispute between the two branches of government stymied public policy-making, it did not lead to an immediate constitutional crisis.

Economy. The Ecuadorean economy was relatively prosperous during the year. According to the Inter-American Development Bank, the gross national product increased by 6.8% in 1978, and its growth seemed to continue in 1979. The nation also continued to receive international funding for research and development, but it still faced a foreign debt of $4 billion, an annual inflation rate of nearly 15%, and the possible cessation of revenues from oil exploration.

ROBERT J. ALEXANDER, *Rutgers University*

————— **ECUADOR • Information Highlights** —————

Official Name: Republic of Ecuador.
Location: Northwest South America.
Area: 104,506 square miles (270 669 km²).
Population (1979 est.): 8,000,000.
Chief Cities (1974): Quito, the capital, 557,113; Guayaquil, 814,064.
Government: *Head of state and government,* Jaime Roldós Aguilera, president (took office Aug. 1979). *Legislature* (unicameral)—Congress.
Monetary Unit: Sucre (28.10 sucres equal U. S.$1, Nov. 1979).
Manufactures (major products): Food products, textiles, light consumer goods, light industrial goods.
Agriculture (major products): Bananas, coffee, cacao, rice, corn, sugar, livestock.

EDUCATION

A new, separate cabinet-level U. S. Department of Education came into being in 1979. National testing, particularly for college entrance, and state-required competency tests for high-school graduation came under attack. Declining school enrollment, closed schools, and higher costs were national trends. Educational progress in the USSR was examined in a U. S. Central Intelligence Agency report, and Canada's McGill University faced major problems.

THE UNITED STATES

Department of Education. On September 24 the U. S. Senate by a vote of 69–22 approved the conference report on a bill establishing a separate cabinet-level Department of Education. Three days later the House of Representatives approved the report, 215–201. Following the signing of the bill by President Jimmy Carter on October 17, the thirteenth cabinet-level agency was inaugurated. The new department was expected to employ 17,400 persons and to have an initial budget of $14.1 billion. The final bill came from a Senate-House conference committee merging a Senate version passed April 30, 72–21, and a House version passed July 11, 210–206. The compromise bill eliminated the House's anti-busing, anti-abortion, and pro-prayer amendments, believed by some to have been tacked on to kill the bill.

For President Carter it was a major victory in his government reorganization plan and fulfilled his promise to the 1.8 million-member National Education Association (NEA). The smaller American Federation of Teachers (AFT) feared that its rival NEA would dominate an independent education department and opposed the action. The new department consolidated some 170 education programs from various federal agencies, including the Office of Education from Health, Education, and Welfare (HEW), the Defense Department's overseas dependents' schools, the Agriculture Department's graduate school, the Labor Department's migrant education program, some National Science Foundation programs, and Housing and Urban Development's college and student housing loans. The Interior Department would continue to oversee Indian education programs and preschool Head Start remained under HEW (renamed Department of Health and Human Services) auspices.

At a White House ceremony early in December, Shirler Hufstedler, former judge of the U. S. Court of Appeals, was sworn in by Chief Justice Warren Burger as the first secretary of education. (*See also* BIOGRAPHY.)

Teachers' Strikes. On September 19 the NEA reported 134 teachers' strikes in 18 states. Issues for which the approximately 45,000 teachers struck, affecting nearly 1 million students, included salary increases, cost of living contract

President Carter signs into law the bill establishing the U. S. Department of Education as the 13th cabinet level agency.

clauses, lesson-preparation time, class size, and extra duty pay. Michigan led in number of teachers' strikes, followed by Pennsylvania, Illinois, Ohio, New Jersey, Indiana, and Rhode Island. The 1979 teachers' strike total was below the 176 strikes of 1978 and much below the 1975–76 high of 203. Most teachers dislike having to strike. They consider it unprofessional and know that parents and the public fault them for caring more for salary than for educating children. But strikes seem to be a necessary tool for teachers, who are paid less than other professionals and also suffer from double digit inflation. On the other side of the coin, school systems are hardpressed by taxpayers' revolts and rising costs.

New York State. On June 14, the New York State legislature passed a "truth in testing" bill. The legislation, effective Jan. 1, 1980, requires testing companies to release scores, answers, and studies on the tests' intent, interpretation, reliability, and validity. Proponents of such legislation, including the NEA, and consumer advocate Ralph Nader, urged the introduction of a similar bill in the U. S. House of Representatives. Anti-testers want to make college entrance tests, such as the Scholastic Aptitude Test, less biased against minorities. Others want to undermine college entrance tests altogether. The testing industry and higher education officials who opposed the bill say that compliance will increase test costs three- to fourfold, aid private tutoring services and those who pay for coaching, start law suits challenging the rationale behind such tests, and still not affect college admissions. The dispute could force U. S. colleges and universities to change their admissions procedure. In mid-July U. S. medical and dental school representatives said that, rather than invalidate tests, they might no longer give tests in New York State. Earlier California passed a weaker version of the New York bill. Ohio considered similar legislation.

On July 27, the New York State Board of Regents voted to put any of the state's 1,100 high schools and 400 junior high schools on probation if 15% of a school's seniors fail competency exams in reading, math, and writing; if the dropout rate exceeds 5% a year; or if truancy rates surpass 10%.

On March 1, the Regents defeated a proposal to award certificates instead of diplomas to high school seniors failing minimum competency tests. Regent Kenneth B. Clark decried such "Jim Crowism," with mostly whites getting diplomas and mainly blacks and other minorities certificates. It was anticipated that during 1979–80, 7,000 of 60,000 seniors in New York City, 1,400 seniors in other cities of the state and 2,400 seniors in New York rural and suburban schools would fail the competency test. In progress is a shift of state funds from richer to poorer school districts, to redress the balance and to end using property tax for financing

schools (declared unconstitutional in June 1978).

New York City. New York City's public schools, the largest system in the United States, opened September 10 to a host of problems: lowest enrollment in 22 years (947,000 pupils, 48,000 fewer than 1978), requiring teacher layoffs and closing of some of the 1,000 schools; poor competency test results in writing (80% failed or barely passed) and in reading (50% passed); high absenteeism and dropouts, particularly among the 71% majority black-Hispanic-Asian ethnics; school violence—teachers were victims of 3,550 crimes in 1978 (5% more than in 1977) and 12% of New York City schools accounted for 58% of the crimes committed against teachers; and reduction of the school security force.

Declining New York City Catholic school enrollment leveled off to 211,000 students. Private school enrollment was expected to top 1978's total of 21,931 students, as more middle class families, disenchanted with suburban commuting and schools, moved back to New York City and chose private over public schools for their children.

U. S. Private Schools. While public school enrollments declined, private grade school enrollment rose to 5 million. Costs at such schools average $4,000 annually per pupil or $6,500 at boarding schools. Attendance at private schools (about 10% of the total U. S. school population) reflected disenchantment with public education, which often seems unable to provide the academic and individual discipline available in private institutions. Greatest growth is among the 825 private secular schools in the National Association of Independent Schools and among the so-called "segregated academies," many of which are church-run and circumvent court-ordered public school desegregation. Enrollment at Catholic schools, comprising 70% of the U. S. private school total, has in fact declined from 87% of the private school enrollment in 1965. Internal Revenue Service guidelines, which were revised under pressure from pro-integration forces to eliminate the tax-exempt status of segregated private academies, were postponed for a year by a 47-to-43 Senate vote. Reason given for this Senate and earlier House action was Congress's hesitation to infringe on constitutional rights of church-run schools.

Competency Tests. State-required courses to prepare high school seniors for minimum competency tests (MCT) provoked controversy in many states which have adopted such procedures to meet public concern over college freshman English and math deficiencies. In the first MCT case, a Florida federal judge said that the literacy tests required for graduation discriminated against blacks, most of whom had attended segregated schools as recently as 1971.

SAT Scores. The College Board reported September 8 that Scholastic Aptitude Test average scores of high-school seniors dropped again, to 427 verbal and 467 math (1969: 463 verbal, 493 math). An earlier study had cited the following reasons for the ten-year decline: excessive television watching, family changes, relaxed school standards, Vietnam and Watergate turbulence, and more low income–minority youths taking the test. There is dispute over whether coaching and cramming raise SAT scores.

Math Scores. The National Assessment of Educational Progress in mid-September reported a decline in math scores since 1974: 4% among 17-year-olds, 2% among 13-year-olds, and 1% among 9-year-olds. Observers blamed the deficiency in math reasoning on a shift from new math (problem-solving emphasis) to back-to-basics (memorization emphasis). The findings echoed a June New York City math test which two thirds of 9th and 10th graders failed.

Gallup Poll. A May 3–7 sampling of public opinion showed that 34% of those polled gave public schools an A or B grade (36% in 1978). Major problems seen confronting public schools were discipline, drugs, lack of financial support, poor curriculum and standards, difficulty in getting good teachers, and integration/busing. More than 50% of those polled favored "mainstreaming," i.e. mixing physically handicapped with nonhandicapped students, but 77% opposed mainstreaming mentally retarded children; 85% wanted teachers to pass state competency tests before being hired.

N. Y. C. Correction Department vans were used to transport children during a school-bus drivers' strike.

UPI

Enrollments Down, Costs Up. School statistics for 1979–80 (1978–79 in parentheses) were: Enrollments, kindergarten through grade 8: 31,700,000, −2% (32,200,000); high school: 15,300,000, −2% (15,600,000); higher: 11,400,000, +1% (11,300,000); total: 58,400,000, −1.2% (59,100,000). The total was 5% below 1975's record high of 61,300,000.

Percentage of age group enrolled: 92% of 5-year-olds (kindergarten); 99% of 6–13-year-olds (grades 1–8); 94% of 14–17-year-olds (grades 9–12); and 26% of 18–24-year-olds (college). Pupil-teacher ratio in public elementary and secondary schools was 19.4 pupils per teacher.

Teachers, elementary and secondary, 2,400,000 (same), plus 300,000 administrators; higher, 830,000 (same); total of 3,530,000.

Graduates, high school, 3,150,000 (same); bachelor's degrees, 950,000 (1,000,000); first professional degrees, 68,000 (67,000); master's, 330,000 (347,000); doctorates, 33,000 (37,000).

Education directly involved 62,000,000 (63,400,000), or nearly 30% of the total population. Expenditures were: public elementary and secondary schools, $92.1 billion; nonpublic elementary and secondary, $10.6 billion; public higher education, $39.3 billion; nonpublic higher, $18.7 billion; a total of $160.7 billion ($155 billion). The estimated $11 billion increase was caused by inflation.

INTERNATIONAL

USSR. A Central Intelligence Agency (CIA) report, "U. S. S. R.: Trends and Prospects in Educational Attainment, 1959–85," showed Soviet secondary education to be available nationwide. A labor shortage in the 1980's is expected to pressure students to leave school early for jobs. Median schooling completed by the labor force rose from 6.3 years in 1959 to 9.5 years in 1917. Nevertheless 22% of the labor force has under eight years of schooling and less than 10% has completed college. During 1950–59, Soviet secondary school enrollment quadrupled, from 340,000 to 1,400,000, but higher education could absorb only 17% of those graduates (compared with nearly 50% in the United States), and the academic high school left the rest unprepared for most jobs. This fact led to a hastily introduced emphasis on vocational education in 1958.

In 1977 45% of the 5,000,000 Soviet students in higher education were in part-time programs, which were criticized as inferior when compared with full-time studies. The dropout rate in such part-time programs was high. Soviet professional specialization has also been criticized as too narrow to cope with technical change. There has since been an increase in the number of full-time higher education students, with engineering students still accounting for 50% of total enrollments. There has been a shift in emphasis from defense and space-related specialties to computers, construction, transportation, and consumer goods technology. An emphasis shift from applied science to basic science, particularly math and physics, and to broader social science for technical specialists has also been seen.

Educational quality needs to be improved in rural schools, which enroll nearly half of the nation's elementary and secondary school students, particularly in the Central Asian republics where Muslim traditions are handicaps, especially to women's education. Women in vocational-technical schools increased from 18% to 30% of total enrollment between 1966 and 1977.

The CIA report concluded that Soviet education is still trying to compete with U. S. education, that the Soviets excel in math and science, that their narrow concentration on job-oriented early specialization (which many U. S. educators also advocate) more often limits than aids individual and national economic progress, and that the Soviets' considerable education gains would have been even greater if not compelled to follow the turns of five-year plans.

Canada. In 1979, McGill University, located in Montreal, Quebec, and under the leadership of new president David L. Johnston, faced not only dwindling enrollment and severe financial difficulties, common to higher education elsewhere in North America, but also severe cuts from the government of the French-oriented province. The provincial government provides McGill with 85% of its $112,000,000 annual budget and there was concern that the university would become a French-speaking institution. Of McGill's 19,500 students (a decline to 14,000 is expected in ten years), 18% are French-speaking, about the same proportion as elsewhere in Canada. The student daily is published in French one day a week, there is an intensive French course for faculty, and there are programs with Quebec's French-speaking universities. But Quebec's language law restricts English schooling to children of parents educated in Quebec's English schools. This fact, combined with the declining birthrate and the leaving of English-speaking companies and families, is decimating Quebec's English community, which has provided McGill University with 60% of its enrollment.

There were complaints about Quebec's unwillingness to expand inadequate library facilities at nearby English-speaking Concordia University (40% of its books are in a warehouse), forcing its students to use McGill's heavily used scattered libraries. In January, for alleged cost-cutting reasons, Quebec ordered McGill to reduce the number of out-of-province medical interns and residents from 200 to 130 and to eliminate non-Quebecers by 1983. No quotas were imposed on Quebec's French-speaking medical units, prompting McGill, which built its reputation partly on its fine medical school, to charge discrimination. But under pressure from physi-

UPI

Cleveland youngsters begin the school year by marching in support of a court-ordered busing plan.

cians, Quebec soon withdrew the cutback order. A government spokesman justified the original action by saying that Quebec was not going to subsidize outside medical students who did not intend to practice in Quebec.

Canadian higher education enrollment was expected to decline 1.1% in 1979–80 to a total of 610,000 (362,000 university, 248,000 college), the third consecutive year of decline. A further drop was expected in 1980–81 higher education enrollment, 598,000 (354,000 university, 244,000 college). Total expenditure on all Canadian education will increase to $19.7 billion in 1979–80 ($18.5 billion, 1978–79), or 8% of annual spending on all goods and services, of which higher education will cost $5.4 billion.

China. As part of China's modernization campaign, a vast program to educate adults got under way in China. In the past, many Chinese adults did not have a chance to complete their secondary education. Even in the late 1970's, only one tenth of 1% of the Chinese population was full-time college and university students. According to a report, some 69 million Chinese adults were participating in some type of organized learning in 1979. The courses were generally practical but at the same time technological. Although television courses were offered to a limited number of adults in some cities, radio and mimeographed pamphlets were major sources of educational instruction.

FRANKLIN PARKER, *West Virginia University*

EGYPT

It was a good and productive year for Egypt. At last a peace treaty was signed with Israel. President Anwar el-Sadat's popularity continued high and his country, although still hampered by economic problems, was in better condition than it had been for 15 years.

Peace with Israel. In late 1977 President Sadat journeyed to Jerusalem to seek peace with Israel. Following hard bargaining, Sadat and Israeli Prime Minister Menahem Begin came to a preliminary agreement at the famous Camp David (MD) meetings, an effort that was to reward them both with the Nobel Peace Prize. 1979 was the year in which Sadat and Begin actually signed the treaty in Washington at the White House on March 26. President Carter signed as a witness. Carter was praised by both Middle Eastern leaders, but particularly by President Sadat, who said that without the American president's efforts, there would have been no treaty.

The treaty was accepted rather quickly in both Israel and Egypt but equally quickly the problems of interpreting and implementing its provisions began. Essentially the treaty called for the following provisions: 1. The Israelis would withdraw from Sinai, about two thirds of its area by year's end and the remainder within three years; 2. UN personnel as well as Egyptians and Israelis would be used in establishing "security" zones along the Egyptian-Israeli border; 3. relations between Israel and Egypt would be "normalized," including recognition and an exchange of ambassadors, the reestablishment of travel and other communications, the lifting of boycotts and similar economic sanctions: in short, each side pledged not merely to end the state of war which has characterized Egyptian-Israeli relations for 31 years but to build "friendly" relations in their place; 4. Israeli cargoes and ships would have access to the Suez Canal and to the Gulf of Aqaba (through the Strait of Tiran); 5. Egypt would sell, under normal price arrange-

ments, oil to Israel from the Sinai fields; 6. the treaty would take precedence over other international obligations of Egypt, except those under the UN Charter which permit aid to countries engaged in self-defense; 7. Egypt would not use the military bases in Sinai vacated by Israel for military purposes; 8. the Israelis and Egyptians would attempt "in good faith" to work out some acceptable version of Palestinian self-rule within a year.

With respect to these provisions by year's end, the Israelis were somewhat ahead of schedule in leaving Sinai. In fact Sadat was able to pray at Mount Sinai on the second anniversary of his Jerusalem trip. The last of the oil fields in Sinai (or adjacent waters) were turned over to the Egyptians in late November. There was a flurry of arguments in late summer about "supervision" of areas within Sinai with respect to military preparedness, but according to a tentative agreement reached in September, increased U. S. surveillance would supplement Egyptian and Israeli patrols.

Generally there seemed little doubt that normalization proceeded according to the March treaty. Israelis and Egyptians in limited numbers traveled back and forth. Air arrangements and telecommunications, at least in a limited sense, were established. A variety of binational committees were created to deal with specific problems. Egyptians and Israelis seemed genuinely glad to end a military hostility that had resulted in four wars since 1948. Cargoes under Israeli flags were now traversing the Suez Canal and the Strait of Tiran without hindrance. Sadat repledged in late November his government's intention to continue selling a portion of Sinai oil to the Israelis. Economic barriers seemed to be coming down. The most troublesome problem was the negotiation of "self-rule" for the Palestinians. It must be remembered that Egyptians and Israelis were negotiating something for a group of people not represented at the bargaining tables. The Israelis refused to accept the credentials of the Palestine Liberation Organization

An Egyptian-Israeli peace treaty has been signed and Israeli warships pass through the Suez Canal for the first time, May 29.

(PLO) as the representative of the Palestinians. Outside powers—the United States and the USSR—influenced the situation but domestic politics were heavily involved. The foreign minister of Israel, Moshe Dayan, resigned in late October, partly as a result of Israeli policies on settlements in the West Bank. Begin himself was ill, and Israeli politicians—for example, Agriculture Minister Ariel Sharon—had begun politicking to succeed Begin. High among the issues were these settlements. The last week in November witnessed continued Israeli attempts—later to be abandoned—to "deport" the Palestinian Mayor of Nablus for expressing sympathy with the PLO. Antigovernment demonstrations occurred in Tel Aviv and Jerusalem over inflated budgetary allocations, reported to be $5 billion, for West Bank settlements. At the time, Israel's domestic inflation rate was 100%–150%. In the meantime the PLO picked up support, including recognition by Turkey and Portugal. Small wonder, then, that despite periodic optimistic reports of "progress," Egyptian-Israeli attempts to define "self-rule" or "autonomy" resulted in little concrete agreement.

Other Foreign Relations. Generally the Arab world reacted bitterly and uncooperatively to the Egyptian-Israeli treaty. Only Sudan, among the major Arab states, offered support. The Arab League moved its headquarters from Cairo to Tunis, and, in turn, Sadat froze the league's foreign assets. Egypt's bankers, Kuwait and Saudi Arabia, gradually withdrew their support for a variety of projects in Egypt. Trade between Egypt and other Arab countries, never very great at best, materially fell off. Nevertheless, by December 1979 it was apparent that the Arab countries had failed in their attempts to influence Egyptian policy regarding peace with Israel.

For Egypt one of the benefits of the treaty was a warmer relation with the United States. To a degree at least, the United States bought the peace treaty by promising both Israel and Egypt enormous aid packages. By September U. S. aid totalled $4.3 billion. Military aid was included, and the Egyptians were beginning to replace their old Russian weapons system with an American one. A 20-man Pentagon team went to Egypt in August. In a lavish military parade in Cairo in October, Egypt displayed its first American F-4 fighters, several dozen M-113 personnel carriers, and other equipment. Sadat, cashing in on his new friendship with the United States, submitted several military shopping lists that called for expenditures of many billions of dollars. Sadat also expressed the hope that Egypt could be the military stabilizing force in the Middle East following Iran's relinquishment of the role.

President Carter visited Egypt in March and received a tumultuous welcome. Sadat, in his own view a special friend of the United States, published his memoirs there in the spring of

UPI

As of July 21, 1979, residents of Cairo can buy Coca-Cola again. The soft drink company was expelled from Egypt in 1967 for doing business with Israel.

1978. As a result of his visits, and the popularity he had generated among Americans, the memoirs continued to sell well. When the U. S. embassy was seized in Tehran in November, Sadat condemned the Ayatollah Ruhollah Khomeini in unmeasured terms. He also offered the deposed shah asylum in Egypt. Relations with Europe, except for the Warsaw Pact countries, generally were good.

Domestic Affairs. The Egyptian economy prospered in spite of Arab efforts to damage it. Although not all Egyptians have benefited from the prosperity, enough of them have to give Sadat a larger popular base than any Egyptian leader has had, including Nasser. Sadat gambled on an Israeli peace and an American connection; as 1979 ended, the gamble was paying off.

See also ISRAEL; MIDDLE EAST.

CARL LEIDEN
University of Texas at Austin

——— **EGYPT · Information Highlights** ———

Official Name: Arab Republic of Egypt.
Location: Northeastern Africa.
Area: 386,660 square miles (1 001 449 km²).
Population (1979 est.): 40,600,000.
Chief Cities (1975 est.): Cairo, the capital, 8,400,000; Alexandria, 2,500,000.
Government: *Head of state,* Anwar el-Sadat, president (reelected for second six-year term, Sept. 1976). *Head of government,* Moustafa Khalil, prime minister (took office June 1979). *Legislature* (unicameral)—People's Assembly.
Monetary Unit: Pound (0.67 pound equals U. S.$1, Dec. 1979).
Manufactures (major products): Textiles, processed foods, tobacco manufactures, chemicals, fertilizer, petroleum and petroleum products.
Agriculture (major products): Cotton, rice, wheat, corn.

ELECTRICITY— SPECIAL REPORT:

CENTENNIAL OF LIGHT

1879 1979

In a year in which Americans were becoming increasingly concerned about energy-efficient technologies, it seemed fitting to celebrate perhaps the most seminal energy-using invention in American history—the electric light. The 100th anniversary of Thomas Edison's invention of the incandescent bulb was an occasion for newspaper features, televsion and radio stories, museum exhibits, contests, and scholarly meetings.

The highpoint of the year's observances was October 21, the date traditionally given for Edison's first successful light. At the reconstruction of Edison's Menlo Park laboratory, built by his friend Henry Ford in Dearborn, MI, ceremonies were held reenacting the historic events of 1879 and commemorating the 50th anniversary of the Henry Ford Museum, itself built to celebrate "Light's Golden Jubilee" in 1929. In New Jersey, where Edison spent most of his life, first at Menlo Park (now Edison, NJ), then in West Orange, year-long observances culminated in speeches, parades, and exhibits. Earlier in October, the Smithsonian Institution in Washington unveiled a large exhibit, "Edison: Lighting a Revolution," which drew attention not only to the light bulb, but also to the dramatic spread of electric power that followed its introduction.

Amidst all the celebrations, a lively historical debate took place over the events of Oct. 21, 1879. According to tradition, it was on that date that Edison and his associates, after a year of trial and error, put a piece of carbonized cotton thread into an evacuated glass bulb, turned on the current, and watched in jubilant amazement as the thread glowed bright and steady for 40 hours. Early in 1979, however, author Robert Conot claimed in his Edison biography, *A Streak of Luck,* that not only had no such forty-hour bulb existed, but that Edison had taken some of his key ideas from reports of the work of English inventor Joseph Swan. And, indeed, many British observers of the Centennial of Light were busy celebrating *Swan's* invention of the light bulb. Most American scholars dismissed the claims for Swan's priority as ill-founded, and errors in Conot's analysis were pointed out. Enough doubts existed, however, to spur interest

in new Edison research, highlighted by a multi-million dollar project at Rutgers University to gather and make available Edison's papers.

There were no doubts about the importance of the electric light or of the work Edison did to make it practical. Edison accompanied his success in finding a workable filament with the introduction of a new, highly-efficient electric generator. He devised such basic electrical equipment as fuses, switches, meters, sockets, regulators, and conduits. Above all, Edison envisioned his electric light as part of a *system* that would supply light and power from central stations for use in homes, offices, factories, and city streets. Edison's triumph in creating that system was marked by the success of the Pearl Street generating station that began operation in lower Manhattan in September 1882. The significance of the electric light lay not only in its liberation of mankind from the tyranny of darkness and of flickering lamps, but also in its ushering in the electrical age and a whole new way of distributing and using energy.

No one was more aware of this fact than Thomas Alva Edison himself. In a career that spanned the age of American invention, Edison emerged as the most prolific, most visionary, and most famous inventor of all. A total of 1,093 patents was issued to Edison in the years from 1869, when the twenty-one-year-old telegrapher quit his job to devote himself entirely to inventing, to 1931, when he died the most honored American of his time. Among his credits were counted important telegraph and telephone components, the phonograph, the motion-picture camera, the alkaline storage battery, and a host of lesser chemical, mechanical, and electrical discoveries. No invention was more intimately associated with Edison, however, than his light bulb.

And it is the modern light bulb—and the system that makes it work—that remains Edison's greatest achievement. It has changed in a century from a delicate glass globe enclosing an even more delicate piece of baked thread in a near-perfect vacuum. The thread was replaced quickly by Edison, first with cardboard and then with bamboo. Early in the twentieth century, the carbon filament gave way to the much more efficient tungsten. Soon thereafter, the vacuum was replaced by an atmosphere of inert gas. Then competing forms of electric lighting began to emerge—fluorescent and vapor lamps finding their niches.

Despite these changes, our bulbs are perhaps most remarkable for their similarity to the original. The modest glass bulb, with the screw base Edison devised, does not really *look* that different from the product of Menlo Park, and it still does yeoman service in just those uses for which Edison intended it. And the electrical system behind it—while a gigantic and complex network spanning continents rather than city blocks —is still, essentially, the Edison system.

ROBERT FRIEDEL

ENERGY

The intensifying problems of the U. S. energy system continued to mount during 1979. The world oil glut that existed during the summer of 1978 became a very tangible shortage by the summer of 1979. Long lines at gasoline stations became the norm in some parts of the country during the spring and early summer. These shortages were triggered by revolutionary developments in Iran which led to a period of total cessation of Iranian oil exports. Driven in part by the lack of Iranian oil, world oil prices increased by nearly 50% during the year. The total cost of U. S. oil imports jumped from $40 billion in 1978 to an estimated $60 billion in 1979.

Within the United States, energy consumption remained relatively stable during the year. Industrial users of energy continued their pattern of improving energy efficiency. Consumption of electricity grew at about half the rate projected only a few years ago. Gasoline consumption declined slightly in the face of a more fuel-efficient fleet of cars and higher prices. In sum, the most optimistic factor in the 1979 energy picture was the nation's ability to restrain continued growth in energy consumption.

Domestic energy production provided a more mixed picture. In the critical area of domestic crude oil production, the pattern of decline continued even in the face of the highest exploratory drilling program in industry history. By the end of 1979, the United States had estimated domestic reserves of approximately 25 billion barrels, down from slightly more than 27 billion barrels at the end of 1978. During the year, the nation consumed approximately 6.5 billion barrels of oil, half of which came from imports. The United States produced over 3 billion barrels during the year and discovered about 1 billion barrels of new oil. Should the nation continue to produce and discover oil at the same rates for the next decade, it would be out of crude oil by 1990.

World Oil Production. Worldwide oil production was at the highest level in history. Soviet production led all other countries at a rate of nearly 11.5 million barrels per day. Saudi Arabia increased its production by 1 million barrels per day to 9.5 million barrels to help overcome the world oil shortage. Following the overthrow of the shah, Iranian exports returned as a major factor in the world oil picture, but they were at a level of nearly 2 million barrels a day or 40% below their prerevolutionary peak.

Estimates of world oil shortages in future remained the norm. Even with continued levels of production by the Organization of Petroleum Exporting Countries (OPEC), the U. S. Central Intelligence Agency projected new oil shortages by 1981 or 1982 at the latest. Those shortages will result from continued increases in consumption plus declining production in both the United States and the Soviet Union. U. S. production has been declining since 1970. Soviet production is expected to begin declining after 1980. That will doubtless require the Communist countries presently supplied by Soviet oil to procure portions of their oil after 1980 from non-Communist countries. These new demands on the West's traditional import sources are certain to exacerbate shortages.

Late in the year, two other developments added to uncertainty surrounding future world oil supplies. Continued Iranian oil exports were made speculative by a student occupation of the U. S. embassy in Tehran. An immediate result of the occupation was a decision by President Carter to stop buying Iranian oil. The effects to the United States of the denial of the 700,000 barrels a day of Iranian oil were unclear.

The second unpredictable factor affecting future world oil supplies was the announcement by several OPEC nations that they planned to reduce production in 1980. These decisions reflect an effort by producing nations to maintain a tight supply-demand situation to keep upward pressure on oil prices. President Carter's decision to freeze Iranian assets held in American banks, triggered by the occupation of the American embassy, appeared to reinforce the intent of those producing nations to cut back production. Simply stated, some countries appear to believe that it is safer to hold their wealth as oil in the ground than as freezable assets in Western lands.

By the end of the year, the rapidly moving world energy situation had changed the key role of Saudi Arabia. The Saudis clearly had lost

their capacity to control world oil prices. Although the Saudis increased production and priced their oil $4 to $5 a barrel below other exporting nations, the other nations found ready markets for their higher priced oil. One ready indication of the loss of control over prices was the increasing world importance of the spot oil market in Rotterdam. Throughout 1979, OPEC nations sent increasing amounts of their production to the spot market, where some of it was selling at $40 a barrel by the end of the year. The $40 price was nearly double the OPEC-established price for oil sold under long-term contracts. The spot market has created powerful pressure for even larger increases in long-term contract prices.

At a December meeting in Venezuela, OPEC ministers failed to agree on a uniform oil price structure. The organization did agree to permit its members to charge their own prices. A meeting to restore price unity was expected within three months.

The unvarnished message of 1979 was that the world simply did not have the capacity to replace a 3–5 million barrel a day loss such as that associated with an Iranian shutdown. Events in Iran were said to be generating a broad policy debate in Saudi Arabia. Even with their ambitious development program, the Saudis did not use the more than $60 billion in oil revenues they received during 1979. Foreign banks were estimated to hold a long-term accumulation of over $60 billion in Saudi revenues. Some Saudis question the wisdom of massive dollar holdings when inflation is eroding those dollars at a rate of 13% a year.

Domestic Sources. Large-scale liquid and gaseous fuel production from coal, oil shale, and organic materials is at least a decade away. If the United States is to increase domestic control of its energy sources during the 1980's, it will have to rely on five major options. They are: (1) newly discovered oil and gas, (2) coal, (3) nuclear power, (4) solar energy, and (5) conservation. (*See* special report, page 204.)

In 1979 roughly 75% of the nation's energy came from oil and gas. The easiest short-term answer to U. S. energy needs would be new oil discoveries. Both industry and government experts place their hopes for major domestic discoveries in three areas: the outer continental shelf (OCS), Alaska, and the overthrust belt.

In an effort to speed the search for new oil finds, the government added new areas to its proposed five-year schedule for leasing on the OCS. Most new leasing was in frontier areas, where no previous leasing had taken place but where the greatest potential for large discoveries exists. These areas are in the northern and western Alaska OCS, offshore New England, and in deep waters. Two lease sales in frontier areas—the Beaufort Sea off northern Alaska and the Georges Bank off New England—were held in December 1979. Each of these sales represented a microcosm of the controversy between environmental concerns and energy needs that pervaded domestic energy policymaking in 1979.

Oil and gas development onshore in Alaska was equally laden with controversy. Pitted against each other were interests seeking to preserve large portions of Alaska from mineral development and those arguing that the state should be opened to rapid development. Only in the overthrust belt, running along western Wyoming and eastern Utah, did oil exploration proceed rapidly during 1979.

Coal represented the only energy source where domestic supply significantly outran demand during the year. Although coal consumption increased during 1979, its rate of growth was less than most observers hoped for. One result was the existence of substantial unemployment among miners in certain areas of the Appalachian coal region. Environmental impacts continued to play a role in limiting the use of coal. Perhaps the most optimistic coal development was the establishment of a new leasing program for coal on federal lands. This new coal leasing program ended an eight-year moratorium on the leasing of federally-owned coal.

In general, the federally-owned coal is west of the Mississippi in the states running from Montana to New Mexico. Coal development in this region has all of the complexities of offshore development plus intense state-federal controversy. Many westerners fear that their area will become an energy colony for the rest of the nation. Some areas in the West fear the boomtown effects of rapid coal development, while others welcome it. In regions such as southern Utah, local residents appear to welcome coal development, but air quality regulations are a barrier to building coal-fired electric power plants. Finally, questions of land reclamation and water availability slowed coal development throughout the arid and semiarid West.

Nuclear power will add little or nothing to the nation's energy supply during 1980 as a result of the nuclear power plant accident at Three Mile Island. The accident raised serious questions about the long-term role of nuclear power. A special commission, appointed by President Carter to study the Three Mile Island accident, found grave deficiencies in the nation's nuclear safety program. The commission found major problems with the training and procedures used by power plant personnel. Following the special commission's report, the Nuclear Regulatory Commission (NRC), the responsible government regulatory agency, established a moratorium on licensing new plants until its regulatory program could be fully reviewed. The NRC estimated that it would take from 6 months to 2 years before the review would be completed and new nuclear power plants could be brought into production.

Even with a new safety program, the future of nuclear power is clouded. No real progress

GOLDBERG, SYGMA

OPEC oil ministers, meeting in Geneva in March, agreed to raise the base price of oil by 9%.

was made during 1979 on how radioactive wastes from nuclear power plants should be handled. Increasingly, states which contain temporary storage sites began to block movement of wastes from other states into those sites. In the highly charged rhetoric of debate, no state wants to be "the nation's nuclear dumping ground." At one point during the year, every storage site in the nation was shut down, creating a real fear that disposal even of the nuclear wastes created in the process of medical treatment would become a problem. Advocates of nuclear power clearly saw 1979 as a disastrous year.

Support for solar energy continued to increase rapidly. Federal expenditures for solar research and development rose to more than $800 million from a level of about $1 million a decade earlier. Congress seemed certain to enact legislation establishing a loan support program of $100 million, called a Solar Bank. The goal of the Solar Bank, plus a program of tax credits, was to speed the use of direct solar energy for home and water heating.

Electricity on a large scale from solar sources remained a distant prospect. Solar electric technologies are economically unable to compete with other sources. Something of the enthusiasm for solar energy, however, can be seen by the sympathetic hearing Congress gave to a proposal for early study of solar space stations. The proposal sketched a 30-year program of 60 space stations, each the size of Manhattan island, which would send energy back to earth in microwave form.

Emphasis on the importance of energy conservation increased during the year, and the nation's ability to restrain energy consumption showed real progress. Energy conservation was pursued on two tracks. First, more efficient energy use, for example, better home insulation and more use of diesel cars. Second, changed life styles, requiring lower thermostats in the winter and higher ones in the summer and less car driving.

Policy. Rising energy prices and shortages triggered political controversy in the United States and caused energy to be the dominant issue in Congress. Major increases in oil industry profits in the third quarter of the year led to accusations of excess profits and demands for more government regulation. Others argued that if the government would quit regulating, industry would solve the energy problem. Clearly the nation was not able to develop a consensus on how to deal with the energy crisis. The Carter administration sought to follow an energy strategy that had four major elements. First, it would set a limit on oil imports. Second, it would move toward decontrol of oil prices. Third, it would place an excess profits tax on the increased oil industry profits resulting from decontrolled prices. Fourth, it would use the revenues generated by the excess profits tax in part to subsidize the increased costs of energy for low income families, and in part to subsidize the development of synthetic fuel substitutes from oil.

During the Tokyo economic summit conference in June, President Carter committed the United States to an import limit of 8.2 million barrels per day for 1979 and to an average of no more than 8.5 million barrels a day indefinitely thereafter. This commitment was in response to the views of U. S. allies that excessive U. S. imports are a major cause of both world energy and economic problems. It should be noted that substantial Congressional opposition to this quota was expressed. Many Congressmen feared that it would damage the U.S. economy.

Early in the year, following Congressional refusal to enact a standby rationing program and other administration proposals, the president, operating under existing authority, implemented a scheduled and incremental decontrol program for oil prices. The goal was twofold. First, higher prices were expected to lead Americans to greater oil conservation. Second, higher prices were expected to increase industry incentives to find and produce more oil. Price decontrol generated great political opposition and proposals were before Congress to withdraw the president's authority to decontrol prices.

Parallel with the decontrol program, the president proposed establishing an excess profits tax on oil which would raise an estimated $200 billion during the 1980's. Oil industry representatives and others argued that such a tax would undermine the goal of increased exploration. President Carter argued that profits remaining after the tax would provide adequate incentive for industry.

In June, the House of Representatives passed a "windfall profits" tax bill, which would tax oil company profits at a rate of 60%. The bill would raise an additional $276 billion by the year 1990. A Senate version, passed on December 17, would tax profits at a 38% rate and would increase government revenue by $178 billion by 1990. A compromise of the two, to be worked out by a Congressional conference committee, was expected early in 1980.

One of the central elements in the debate over the excess profits tax was how the new revenues would be used. The already high en-

ergy prices had created demands for assistance to low-income families. Conservative Congressmen opposed energy subsidies for low-income families. They expressed the view that it was the beginning of a massive new welfare program. The need was thought to be so compelling, however, that Congress passed an energy subsidy for low-income families in advance of passing the excess profits tax.

The major portion of the revenues from the excess profits tax was slated for support of a synthetic fuels industry based on coal and oil shale. The administration initially proposed a ten-year, $88 billion program. After Congressional debate, it appeared likely that the initial authorization would be for a three-year, approximately $20 billion program. The purpose of the three-year program was to test out alternative technologies in commercial size plants.

Congress approved the administration's proposal for an Energy Mobilization Board. This new board was to have the power to cut red tape and speed large energy construction projects, such as synthetic fuels plants. Wide support for the board was the result of a belief that the multiple federal and state agency approvals required for new construction have become major barriers to the nation's ability to respond to the energy crisis.

As 1979 ended, it appeared likely that the Congress would pass some form of standby gasoline rationing program. The change in the Congressional view of the need for a standby rationing program as well as the other energy initiatives reflected a recognition, shared by a large number of Americans, that there is a real energy crisis.

See also INTERNATIONAL TRADE AND FINANCE.

DON E. KASH, *University of Oklahoma*

Long gas lines were a common sight throughout the United States during the spring and summer.

UPI

At a solar station in Albuquerque, NM, steam is produced by reflecting the sun's rays onto a huge boiler.

Many urban commuters took to mopeds to conserve gas; one San Franciscan (*below*) used his for making deliveries. The city of Portland, OR, promoted public transit by designating special bus lanes in the downtown area.

Alternatives to Petroleum

The search for alternatives to petroleum took on added urgency during 1979 as the world experienced both oil shortages and rapid price increases. The near total dependence on petroleum of the U. S. transportation system, as well as one quarter of its home heating systems, requires development of liquid fuel alternatives.

Liquid fuel substitutes for petroleum are potentially available from four sources: coal, oil shale, tar sands, and biomass (organic materials). Producing liquids from any of the four sources requires major processing.

Coal. The U. S. government's response to the need for alternatives to petroleum has been to propose the rapid development of several commercial-scale demonstrations of coal and oil shale synthetic fuels plants. Coal has been chosen as one of the major development focuses because the nation has huge coal resources and the essentials of the conversion process are understood. South Africa presently has a commercial plant in operation. The twin goals of the proposed U. S. program will be to reduce both the economic and environmental costs of coal liquifaction technology.

Although several coal liquifaction technologies are available, they involve changing the carbon-to-hydrogen ratio in the fuel. For example, soft (bituminous) coal has 16 carbon atoms for every hydrogen atom, while fuel oil has a six-to-one ratio. If the process sounds simple, the cost and technologies for creating coal liquids are another matter. For example, a plant capable of producing 50,000 barrels a day, about one three hundred and sixtieth of daily consumption, would cost $2 billion. The mine needed to supply a single 50,000-barrel-a-day plant would be among the largest in the United States. Significant production of liquids from coal is more than a decade away.

Oil Shale. While not so large as coal, oil shale resources are substantial. Estimates are that 400 billion barrels of oil are available from high grade oil shale deposits containing 25 to 40 barrels per ton. By comparison, U. S. petroleum reserves are less than 30 billion barrels. The high quality oil shale deposits are located in a single geological formation in northwestern Colorado, northeastern Utah, and southwestern Wyoming —known as the Green River Formation.

Limited commercial production of oil from shale appears likely by the mid to late 1980's. Two major demonstration facilities are presently under construction in western Colorado. Both of the facilities under development use what is called a modified "in situ" process. In this process the shale is fractured and heated in underground cavities and the raw oil is pumped to the surface. Alternatively, oil shale may be mined, crushed, and heated at a surface plant in a reactor called a retort. Whether "in situ" or surface processing technology is utilized will depend on costs.

Estimates are that a 50,000-barrel-a-day oil shale plant will cost more than $1 billion. As with coal, the size and cost figures are impressive. A mine to support a surface facility producing 50,000 barrels a day would be 3 to 4 times larger than the large mine needed to support a similar-size coal liquids plant.

Tar Sands. Although large scale production of oil from tar sands exists at the Athabasca Tar Sands in Canada, there is presently little interest in tar sands in the United States. Tar sands are deposits of porous rock that contain oils too heavy to be extracted by normal petroleum recovery methods. Recovery requires either application of heat or use of a solvent to separate the oil from the sand.

Tar sands are receiving less attention than coal or oil shale for several reasons. Like the other alternatives to petroleum, tar sands do not appear to be economically competitive with petroleum imports. In addition, the resource base is only 5% that of oil shale, and many of the sands are deep in the ground and costly to mine. Finally, many of the potentially attractive tar sands are federally owned, and there are legal problems.

Biomass. Although liquids from biomass are presently in commercial production and come from a renewable resource, their long term potential is very much in question. Organic materials as a source of fuel have received a great amount of popular attention with the marketing of gasohol—the 10% alcohol/90% gasoline fuel. Alcohol from grains as an alternative to gasoline has been promoted. The agricultural sector argues that grain alcohol offers both a renewable energy source and a use for agricultural surpluses.

Whether liquids from biomass will be competitive with those from coal and oil shale will depend on costs and energy efficiencies. The present fermentation processes used to produce alcohol are expensive. Further, production of fuel from grains that have been grown using modern energy-intensive farming techniques may require using nearly as much energy as there is in the alcohol.

Summary. At present, no alternative to petroleum can compete economically with imported oil. Only a developmental stage that improves the technological development of the alternatives, or the continued escalation of oil prices, or both seem likely to make some of the alternatives commercially available in the 1980's.

DON E. KASH

A leak of radioactive steam from the power station at Three Mile Island on the Susquehanna River near Harrisburg, PA, in March cast doubt on the safety of nuclear energy power plants.

SPECIAL REPORT:

Three Mile Island and the Issue of Nuclear Energy

At 4:00 A. M. on Wednesday, March 23, 1979, operators of a nuclear reactor near Harrisburg, PA, noticed something was amiss. By noon, the Three Mile Island story was making headlines throughout the world. The events of that morning were the beginning of the first major commercial nuclear reactor accident in the United States, an event which immediately had a profound impact on the future of nuclear power in the United States and throughout the world. The key issue is the safety of nuclear reactors and their ability to provide reliable and economic electricity without exposing the public to unacceptable levels of radiation.

Commercial nuclear power dates from 1957, when the first commercial power reactor was opened at Shippingport, PA. By the end of 1979 there were 72 commercial nuclear generating plants in the United States, providing 12.5% of all the electricity generated. In the Chicago area, nuclear power provides as much as 55% of all electricity used.

From its inception, nuclear power has been controversial. In the early 1950's, debate centered on the effects of waste heat from nuclear plants. More recently, key issues have been the reliability of safety systems; the means of storing radioactive waste products; and the possibility of nuclear material being stolen to make weapons. Throughout the years, the nuclear industry and the federal government have maintained that nuclear power is safe and that no one has ever been killed in an accident involving a commercial reactor. The importance of nuclear energy was recognized by the U. S. Congress in 1957, when it enacted the Price-Anderson Act, by which the federal government became the co-insurer of all nuclear systems and guaranteed a minimum coverage of $560 million.

After the accident at Three Mile Island, the safety of nuclear energy became a major national concern. The antinuclear movement gained a wider following and a new urgency.

Indeed, the accident was different from anything anticipated by the industry or by most nuclear experts. It was a complicated series of events which led to severe damage to the nuclear core of the reactor and to the release of radioactive gases into the atmosphere. Whether the incident was due to errors in the design of the reactor or to operator error could not be known for sure. There was no doubt that the accident would be very expensive for both the company that owns the reactor and for the public. Even more importantly, it raised serious questions about future energy sources and potential threats to human health and safety.

The power center of a nuclear reactor is the fuel core, which includes rodlike cylinders containing pellets of fissionable uranium 235. Also in the core are many similar sized control rods made of silver-indium and cadmium, which absorb scattering neutrons and thereby prevent the fission reaction. The reactor is started by raising the control rods to a specified level within the core, allowing the fission reaction to begin and extreme heat to be produced. Water passing through the core is heated to about 600° F (316° C) and pumped under high pressure through pipes to a steam generator. The heat is transferred to uncontaminated water in a self-contained second pipe loop. This clean water (which is at a lower pressure) is quickly boiled and turned into steam, which powers a turbine-driven electrical generator.

The water passing through the reactor core plays the crucial role of cooling the operating fuel. The greatest danger of a nuclear power plant is the loss of this cooling fluid. Should the flow of cooling water be interrupted, however briefly, the reactor core will begin to heat up. Unless backup cooling is provided, the core could get so hot that it would melt, thereby releasing radioactive vapors.

Many safeguards are designed into the reactor to prevent this chain of events. The first line of defense is to stop the reaction by reinserting the control rods; the reactor's control system does this automatically. Secondly, in the event of a Loss of Cooling Accident (LOCA), the Emergency Core Cooling System (ECCS) will pump thousands of gallons of water into the core, which prevents overheating. The final line of defense is the "containment vessel." All reactors in the United States are constructed in a massive steel and/or reinforced concrete structure designed to withstand the most severe impact. The Three Mile Island reactor, for example, is designed to absorb the crash of a large passenger plane.

A number of factors—human and technological—contributed to the accident at Three Mile Island. That the accident occurred at all dramatically demonstrated that as yet no system is foolproof.

Early on March 28, 1979, Unit 2 at Three Mile Island was operating at 98% of full power when the main feedwater system (which circulates condensed steam after it has passed through the turbine and returns it to the steam generator) shut down. The resulting reduction in heat removal from the reactor system caused the reactor water pressure to increase to the point where the first line of defense was set in motion. The control rods were automatically inserted and the process of nuclear fission stopped. An electrically-operated pressure relief valve was opened and the excess reactor pressure relieved. At this point, the backup feedwater system was called into action to provide the necessary heat removal after shutdown. While the backup feedwater pumps operated, the valves supplying the water to the steam generators remained closed, a condition that continued for approximately eight minutes. During these minutes the only cooling taking place was that effected by steam passing through the open reactor relief valve. After eight minutes, the operator opened the backup feedwater valves, and that system began its heat removal and shutdown cooling task.

Damage to the fuel did not result from the closed valves or from the delay in providing backup feedwater. The ultimate damage was caused by the continued loss of reactor coolant through the reactor relief valve (which had stuck open) and by an operator's decision to override the automatic actions of the ECCS. Mistaking the instruments of an auxiliary tank for those showing the water level in the reactor system itself, and concerned not to overfill and thereby overpressure the system, the operator reduced the flow of replacement water into the reactor. The main coolant pumps continued to circulate the steam/water mixture past the fuel, but the continuing loss of coolant led to steam formation and severe pump vibration. Because of the vibration, the circulating pumps were shut off at 100 minutes. The water in the mixture then settled around the fuel rods but was insufficient to cover them completely. Those portions of the rods which were exposed to steam heated up to the point that the zirconium cladding ruptured from internal fission gas pressure. This released the contained radioactive fission gases and allowed them to pass into the reactor piping. From there, they passed through the open reactor relief valve and discharged into the reactor containment building. It was at this time (6:15 A.M.) that radiation detection equipment in the reactor building first detected high levels. Within a few minutes an emergency was declared.

After almost 15 hours, operators finally managed to repressurize the reactor and restart a main cooling pump. Adequate core cooling was established and the emergency brought to an end. The extreme heating of the fuel cladding, however, created another problem. Zirconium reacts chemically with steam, producing zirconium oxide and hydrogen gas. This is exactly what happened in the Unit 2 reactor at Three Mile Island. About 40% of the 25 tons of zirconium cladding reacted with the enveloping steam, leading to a hydrogen bubble inside the

DRAWING BY FRANK SENYK

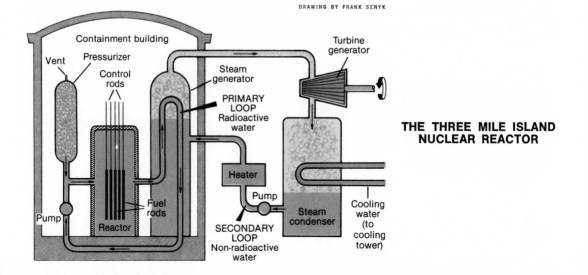

THE THREE MILE ISLAND
NUCLEAR REACTOR

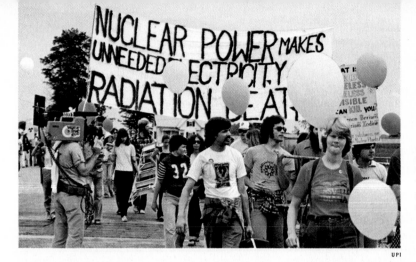

In Marble Hill, IN, demonstrators march to protest the use of nuclear power. Following the accident at Three Mile Island, antinuclear rallies were held across the country.

UPI

reactor. This gas collected at the top of the reactor and required about two days to dissolve into the cooling water. The bubble could not explode in the reactor system itself because there was too little oxygen. However, some hydrogen was released through the open relief valve into the reactor containment building. This raised the hydrogen concentration to the point where a spark caused a substantial explosion. The containment vessel proved its worth by withstanding the explosion and by containing the massive quantities of radioactive gases—primarily xenon, krypton, and volatile iodine—until they decayed sufficiently to allow cleanup to begin and families to return to town.

While the consequences of the accident at Three Mile Island will not be known for quite some time, there is no doubt that it was a great financial loss and opened serious questions about the health hazards of current nuclear technology. The mere cost of repairing the plant was estimated at more than $400 million, making Three Mile Island the most expensive industrial accident ever. Other financial losses included the interest on money borrowed to pay for the plant ($8 million per month); the cost of replacing lost electricity ($24 million per month); the loss of revenue incurred by local businesses during and after the accident; and a possible decline in area property taxes.

But the most important consequences of the accident were its effects on the health of area residents and plant personnel and on the environment.

During the accident large quantities of highly contaminated water were taken from the reactor system into the filtering and purification system located in the adjacent auxiliary building. This building was not designed to process so large a quantity of radioactive water, however, and when small amounts leaked, gas by-products of the nuclear reaction were discharged through the building's exhaust system. The majority of radioactive particles and radioiodine was removed by filter, but inert xenon and krypton gases were found in samples taken outside the plant.

Although the released radioactive materials increase slightly the incidences of cancer and genetic abnormality, the increase due to the reactor accident at Three Mile Island was so small that it could be calculated but not accurately measured. The 30,000 people within five miles (8 km) of the plant were exposed to about 17 millirem of radiation (compared with the average annual exposure of 100 millirem). The Three Mile Island exposure increased the probability of death in this population by between 0.2 and 0.3 deaths. In short, the effects were far less serious than they might have been. Although no evacuation was ever ordered, Pennsylvania Gov. Richard Thornburgh did suggest that children and pregnant women leave the area. Many families did leave, and schools and businesses were closed for days.

The environmental damage caused by the 400,000 gallons of low-level water dumped into the Susquehanna River will take years to determine. Within weeks, however, a groundswell of antinuclear sentiment spread across the country. In May, 65,000 demonstrators gathered in Washington, DC, to protest the use of nuclear energy. In September, nearly 200,000 protesters gathered in New York City to stage the largest antinuclear demonstration ever.

The events at Three Mile Island led to several investigations of the accident itself and the future of nuclear energy production in the United States. The Nuclear Regulatory Commission (NRC) conducted extensive inquiries, which led to a series of immediate recommendations, and promised that it would demand further changes in nuclear plant design and operation. Reviews by the electric utility industry and a specially-appointed presidential inquiry panel, headed by John Kemeny of Dartmouth College, and in-depth Congressional studies were expected to result in new laws governing many aspects of nuclear energy production.

The accident at Three Mile Island could damage the nuclear power industry beyond recovery. Ultimately, it could also lead to a safer and stronger industry.

PAUL P. CRAIG and DANIEL D. WHITNEY

ENGINEERING, CIVIL

Despite adverse economic conditions in much of the world, many countries continued to construct impressive new bridges, canals, dams, and tunnels.

BRIDGES

United States. The year 1979 saw completion of the Parrott's Ferry Bridge over the New Melones Dam Reservoir near Sonora, CA. The segmental, lightweight concrete box girder structure has a 640-foot (195-m) main span—the longest of its type in the country—flanked by 325-foot (99-m) side spans. The 1,290-foot (393-m) bridge carries a two-lane highway. Its two piers are 225 feet (69 m) high. The 16½-foot (5-m) long girder segments were cast in place by a balanced cantilever operation, then post-tensioned. Built in two years, the bridge cost $10 million.

Work on a new high-level crossing of the Mississippi River at New Orleans, LA, was scheduled to start in 1980. The six-lane span, downstream from the existing four-lane Greater New Orleans Bridge, will have a 1,575-foot (480-m) steel cantilever main truss span. The bridge will be 133 feet (41 m) above the river and was scheduled for completion in 1986.

Canada. Work was completed in Nova Scotia on the longest segmental concrete box girder span in North America. The two-lane highway bridge crosses the Shubenacadie River near Truro, about five miles (8 km) above the head of the Bay of Fundy. The 1,444-foot (440-m), three-span structure consists of the record 700-foot (213-m) main span, flanked by 372-foot (113-m) side spans. The superstructure was built in 15-foot (4.6-m) long segments, then post-tensioned together. The cost of the entire project was about $9 million.

Yugoslavia. Also bridged in 1979 was the Adriatic Sea between the island of Krk and the Croatian mainland. The 4,296-foot (1 310-m) prestressed concrete, high-level crossing includes two arches—a 1,280-foot (390-m) main arch 220 feet (67 m) above the sea, and an 800-foot (244-m) second arch 179 feet (55 m) above the water. The longer span is the world's longest concrete arch. St. Mark island, a small rocky outcrop, serves as an anchor for one end of each arch. The $20-million structure carries oil pipelines and a roadway 34 feet (10.3 m) wide.

West Germany. Flehe Bridge, the fifth crossing of the Rhine River at Düsseldorf, was completed during the year at a cost of $57 million. The 3,763-foot (1 147 m) structure has six traffic lanes. It includes a 1,207-foot (368-m) main steel span, one of the longest of its type, supported by cables from a single pylon. The 7,000 ton (6 410 metric ton) steel span is supported 476 feet (145 m) above the ground by seven cables fanning out asymmetrically from the east pylon. The rest of the bridge is a 2,556-foot (770-m) multi-span, prestressed concrete viaduct.

CANALS

Venezuela. The State Power Authority of Venezuela continued construction of a thermoelectric generating plant on the Caribbean coast 140 miles (225 km) west of Caracas. An important addition in 1979 was a canal for the cooling water intake.

The canal's channel is 2,297 feet (700 m) long, 131 feet (40 m) wide, and 23 feet (7 m) deep. Sheet piling was driven to form permanent bulkheads along the canal, and 235,431 cubic yards (180 000 m³) of material were dredged. Some drilling and blasting were required to cut through coral.

The Ruck-a-Chuck Bridge is scheduled to rise across a planned reservoir northeast of Sacramento, CA. High-strength cables are to be attached to the steep hillsides on both banks. The design won a major architectural award.

USSR. One of the major long-term construction projects in the Soviet Union is a 900-mile (1 448-km) irrigation canal in the Kara Kum desert. Begun in 1954, the canal reached more than 600 miles (966 km) in 1979 but was expected to take another 20 years to complete. The channel, being dug westward toward the Caspian Sea, carries water from the Amu Darya River to the dry soil of Soviet Turkmenistan. The original excavation is being enlarged to a width of 550 feet (168 m) and a depth of 21 feet (6.4 m); some time in the future it will be further enlarged to 998 feet (304 m) wide and 26 feet (7.9 m) deep. Excavation of sand and clay will total about 1.15 billion cubic yards (880 million m³). The projected cost is $1.5 billion.

DAMS

United States. Residents of Washington, DC, will be assured of a constant supply of fresh water upon completion in 1981 of the Bloomington Lake Dam, 180 miles (290 km) from the nation's capital. Started in 1971, the $158-million U. S. Corps of Engineers project will also help prevent flooding. The rock and earth dam will be located in the Shenandoah Mountains on the northern branch of the Potomac River at the Maryland–West Virginia border. The dam will be 2,310 feet (704 m) long, 296 feet (90 m) high, and 1,640 feet (500 m) wide at the base. The embankment will contain 10.2 million cubic yards (7.8 million m³) of fill and will create a reservoir containing 94,700 acre-feet of water.

In 1979, work was started on a U. S. Bureau of Reclamations dam to irrigate an arid tract of land in Utah. The Vat Diversion Dam will impound water from the Westfork River with an earth embankment 470 feet (143 m) long, 130 feet (40 m) wide at the base, and 20 feet (6 m) high. Included in the $11.8-million project is a concrete water pipeline 78 inches (198 cm) in diameter and 4.2 miles (6.8 km) long, laid 23 feet (7 m) under ground. The project is scheduled for completion in 1981.

Australia. Chaffey Dam, under construction on the Peel River near Tamworth, New South Wales, will supply domestic water to Tamworth and irrigation water to valley lands below the dam. It will consist of an earth and rockfill embankment 177 feet (54 m) high, 1,378 feet (420 m) long, and 656 feet (200 m) wide at the base. The structure will contain 1.7 million cubic yards (1.3 million m³) of material and its estimated cost is $14 million.

Nigeria. An earth and concrete dam under way on the Oyun River north of Lagos will provide water for the Nigerian capital by 1982. The 219,000 acre-feet of water impounded by the dam will also be used for irrigation in the southwest part of the country. The dam will cost $80 million to build and will be 4,593 feet (1 400 m) long and 108 feet (33 m) high.

TUNNELS

United States. A concrete gravity sewer to carry water from suburban Hales Corner, WI, to Milwaukee's South Shore treatment plant was being bored in 1979. Scheduled for completion in 1981, the $4.8 million sewer will be 6,415 feet (1 955 m) long, 60 inches (152 cm) in diameter, and 100 feet (30 m) under ground.

The U. S. Air Force has built a prototype concrete tunnel in the Arizona desert to test the feasibility of its mobile missile launching system. The tunnel is 15.7 feet (4.8 m) in diameter and 3.7 miles (6 km) long, and lies in a trench 20 feet (6.1 m) deep. The tunnel permits the movement of missiles under ground, thereby hiding their exact location. A canister carrying the missile and launcher can break through hatches in the tunnel roof and fire from any point along the tunnel. Custom-built trenchers were used for excavation, and the continuous pipe was cast in place by slip-forming equipment.

Malaysia. The first highway tunnel through a mountain in Malaysia is being bored on the East Coast Road that links Kuala Lumpur, the capital, with Karak. Located 21 miles (34 km) from the capital, the 2,851-foot (869-m) horseshoe-shaped tunnel is 30 feet (9.14 m) wide and 25.5 feet (7.77 m) high.

WILLIAM H. QUIRK
"Construction Industry International" Magazine

ENVIRONMENT

If present trends continue, what will the quality of the world's environment be at the end of this century, only 20 years away? This was the question that occupied many environmental leaders during the year 1979. Their projections underscored the magnitude of the problems that lie ahead. Forecasts released by the U. S. government, the United Nations Environmental Program (UNEP), Worldwatch Institute, and others painted a scene of continued environmental decay and, ultimately, an overall decline in the quality of human life—even among industrialized nations. However, the consensus was that there is still time to institute effective environmental reforms. In the United States, the year brought mounting concern about the safety of nuclear power plants, the environmental effects of energy development, and the adequacy of laws protecting endangered species.

WORLD DEVELOPMENTS

Despite worsening economic conditions, energy shortages, and civic turmoil, a number of nations made new commitments to safeguard the environment through self-regulation and international agreements. The International Union for Conservation of Nature and Natural Resources and the UNEP pledged to implement a new International Conservation and Development Strategy. UNEP's executive director,

Mustafa K. Tolba, said that one of the most immediate concerns is poverty and its environmental impact.

Forests. The depletion of the world's forests continued at a rapid rate, and some projections released during the year predicted that losses of woodlands could total 400 million hectares (988 million acres) by the year 2000. However, during 1979, there was some progress in attempts to stem forest losses. In Sri Lanka and the Philippines, test programs were begun to introduce such alternate sources of energy as wind power, solar energy, and biogas (derived from organic wastes). Significant advances in forest conservation were also reported in the People's Republic of China and in South Korea. In China, according to one estimate, from 30 to 60 million hectares (74 to 148 million acres) of new forests have been planted to meet village and industrial wood needs. In South Korea, nearly 645 000 hectares (1,593,150 acres) of "Village Forestry Association" woodlots have been planted since the early 1970's. These are expected to ease the country's rural fuel problems during the 1980's.

Mexican Blowout. On June 3, a Mexican oil well named Ixtoc I began spewing oil in the Gulf of Campeche. By the middle of August, millions of gallons of crude stretched nearly 1,000 miles (1 600 km) toward Texas and Louisiana, threatening a number of fragile wildlife habitats and a popular resort area on Padre Island. Attempts to contain the slick with booms continued into the fall, while crews worked to cap the well. Although relatively little of the oil reached the United States, more than 5 miles (8 km) of beaches were contaminated, and some of the spill remained adrift. It was the biggest oil spill in history, more than 100 million gallons (378.5 million liters). The full environmental consequences could not be immediately assessed.

Wildlife. A number of significant international agreements concerning wildlife were made during 1979. Twenty-two nations, most of them African and European, signed the Convention on the Conservation of Migratory Species of Wild Animals. The treaty was expected to benefit migratory birds and herds of grazing animals. The United States declined to sign the treaty on the grounds that it would conflict with existing agreements on bird migration between the United States and Canada, Mexico, the Soviet Union, and Japan. The United States and Canada did finalize plans for an agreement to manage and protect the Porcupine herd, about 100,000 caribou which migrate between the Yukon and Alaska. The International Whaling Commission banned all whaling in the Indian Ocean and issued a temporary ban on the killing by factory ships of all whale species except the abundant minke. The move was expected to save about 7,000 sperm whales, a rapidly disappearing species.

Uganda announced a five-year moratorium on hunting in an effort to rebuild wildlife populations depleted by poachers during and shortly after the reign of deposed dictator Idi Amin. Egypt announced plans to establish its first two wildlife reserves in parts of the Sinai Peninsula. Liberia, in a dramatic policy turnaround, instituted sweeping reforms; plans for three national parks and for protection of imperiled wildlife species were enacted.

U. S. DEVELOPMENTS

The year's environmental highlights included reaction to President Jimmy Carter's July message on energy, the aftermath of a nuclear power plant breakdown, and a Congressional decision to override the nation's endangered species law in order to allow construction of a controversial dam.

Energy and Environment. After the Carter administration declared energy production one of its top priorities, the prospect of some difficult trade-offs became more real: increased mining for coal and oil-bearing shale; relaxed air-quality standards to allow the burning of more coal; and the possible suspension of several environmental laws to allow power plants and other energy-related projects to go forward. In September, one such trade-off was made—a decision to allow drilling for oil and gas on the Georges Bank off Cape Cod, MA, an area that

As the International Whaling Conference opens in London, protestors demand that the whale be saved. The conference banned all whaling in the Indian Ocean and issued a temporary ban on the killing by factory ships of all whale species, except the abundant minke.

was to have been a marine sanctuary. A number of citizen-action groups called the administration's decision a "backlash" against the environmental movement.

Nuclear Reactionaries. On March 28, the Three Mile Island nuclear power plant on the Susquehanna River near Harrisburg, PA, broke down, dumping 400,000 gallons (1 514 000 liters) of low-level radioactive wastewater into the river. Although the environmental damage will take years to determine, reaction by the public and the media was immediate. Within weeks, a groundswell of antinuclear sentiment spread around the world. (*See* ENERGY—SPECIAL REPORT.)

Land Use. In response to worldwide economic and energy problems, land-use patterns in the United States continued to change in 1979. Americans increasingly turned to their public lands for much-needed renewable and nonrenewable natural resources. This, in turn, led to some new environmental concerns. In June, the Carter administration ordered the departments of agriculture and the interior to increase the timber harvest on national forests and other public lands by 1 to 3 billion board feet (2.36 to 7.08 million m^3) per year—a 10% increase. Earlier in the year, Nevada began what has been called the "sagebrush war"—an effort to claim state sovereignty over more than 50 million acres (123.5 million ha) of public land within its borders. Frank Gregg, director of the U. S. Bureau of Land Management, attributed the attempt to fears that environmental extremism would lock up such economic resources as timber, minerals, and grazing rights. (*See* feature article, page 51.)

Toxic Substances. Although concentrations of the pesticide DDT continued to disappear from the environment at faster rates than had been expected, new sources of pollution were identified in 1979. Contaminants called polychlorinated dibenzofurans (PCDFs) were detected in fish for the first time. PCDFs are chemical by-products of polychlorinated biphenyls (PCBs), which are industrial residues that have become ubiquitous in the nation's environment. The PCDFs were found in carp, catfish, lake trout, and coho salmon collected in the northern United States. The extent of the pollution is not known, but the substances are considered dangerous to human health. The discovery was announced a month after the government Toxic Substances Strategy Committee had recommended better interagency coordination in identifying and regulating toxic chemicals in the workplace and natural environment.

Acid Rain. Atmospheric fallout from industrial effluent, the so-called "acid rain" that plagued upstate New York in 1978, became a political issue in 1979. Environmentalists argued vehemently against relaxed air quality standards. Sulfur dioxide and other chemicals present in the fallout have been known to kill entire popu-

UPI

Workers lower a giant cone into the Gulf of Mexico in an effort to control the worst oil spill ever.

lations of fish in some lakes. In 1979 there was some cause for alarm as the rain began to show up in lakes in northern Wisconsin. Acid rain also appeared in Canada during 1978–79, and an international advisory group was organized to identify the extent of the problem.

Wildlife. The Endangered Species Act, which was amended by Congress in 1978, proved insufficient to stop construction of the Tellico Dam on the Little Tennessee River. The on-again, off-again project of the Tennessee Valley Authority, which had been delayed on the grounds that it threatened to destroy an endangered fish called the snail darter, will be completed by Congressional decree. President Jimmy Carter signed the authorization on September 25, with "great reluctance." The measure had been attached to a crucial bill on energy and water development. Earlier in 1979, the dam project had been quashed by a cabinet-level Endangered Species Committee—not because of the danger to the snail darter, but for economic reasons.

Two other endangered species, the American alligator and the peregrine falcon, were in the news in 1979. The alligator population has increased dramatically in parts of Louisiana and other Southern states, and the U. S. government finalized plans for resuming world trade limitations on alligator hides. Four peregrines were placed in a nest on the Interior Building in Washington, DC, to test their ability to adapt to urban environments.

BILL VOGT, *"National Wildlife"*
and "International Wildlife" Magazines

ETHIOPIA

In 1979, Ethiopia gained the upper hand in its battle against Eritrean insurgents, developed its political ties to the Soviet Union, and survived an attack of locusts that swept through the Horn of Africa.

Civil War. Throughout the year Ethiopia put heavy military pressure on the Eritrean insurgents. Major offensives, using some 90,000 Ethiopian troops and 600 Soviet advisers, were launched. So successful were the attacks that in August Cuba withdrew some 3,000 of its 18,000 soldiers stationed in Ethiopia. On August 23 the Ethiopian leader, Lt. Col. Mengistu Haile Mariam, paid public tribute to the Cubans, Russians, and South Yemenites who had lost their lives in the battle against the Eritreans and in the 1977–78 war with Somalia. The remarks were the first official admission by Ethiopia that foreign troops had been directly engaged in the various wars. Mengistu indicated that these soldiers were killed "defending the revolution."

Diplomatic Activity. In January, a Treaty of Friendship and Cooperation was signed with Kenya in order to limit the influence of Somalia, which claims territory in both states.

Ethiopia closed the Addis Ababa office of the New China News Agency in March, accusing it of leveling propaganda that was aimed at disrupting the Soviet/Ethiopian Treaty of Friendship.

Also in March, Morocco severed diplomatic relations with Ethiopia after the latter recognized the Saharan Arab Democratic Republic proclaimed by the Polisario Front in the disputed Western Sahara territory.

Ethiopia and the Horn of Africa. Djibouti had by 1979 absorbed some 35,000 refugees, most of whom had fled from the wars in Eritrea and the Ogaden (which Somalia invaded in 1977). This population influx posed a serious problem for Djibouti since the United Nations has given only limited assistance.

The Soviet Union increased its air and naval activity in the Indian Ocean during the first quarter of the year. TU-16 Soviet bombers began flying surveillance missions out of Aden, while the aircraft carrier *Minsk* and its escorts engaged in maneuvers in the western Indian Ocean.

In response the United States increased its

─────── **ETHIOPIA · Information Highlights** ───────

Official Name: Ethiopia.
Location: Eastern Africa.
Area: 471,778 square miles (1 221 905 km²).
Population (1979 est.): 31,800,000.
Chief Cities (1976 est.): Addis Ababa, the capital, 1,-242,555; Asmara, 340,206.
Government: *Head of state and government,* Mengistu Haile Mariam, chairman of the Provisional Military Administrative Committee (took office Feb. 1977).
Monetary Unit: Birr (2.07 birrs equal U.S.$1, June 1979).
Manufactures (major products): Processed foods, textiles, cement, building materials, hydroelectric power.
Agriculture (major products): Cereals, coffee, pulses, oilseeds, hides, skins, meat.

Indian Ocean naval forces. Fourteen naval vessels, including the carrier *Midway,* patrolled the area.

Natural Disasters. Famine in Wollo province continued into 1979, and in June the government began to resettle more than 250,000 people from Wollo to less populated areas.

In February a plague of locusts attacked the country and its Horn of Africa neighbors. The crisis abated by month's end, but the infestation was called by one spokesman "the worst in at least ten years."

Human Rights. The U. S. State Department's third annual report on human rights released in February indicated that the Ethiopian military government backed a campaign of violence and terror between December 1977 and April 1978 which resulted in 3,000 deaths and some 20,000 arrests. According to the report, the campaign was primarily directed at urban dwellers.

PETER SCHWAB
State University of New York at Purchase

ETHNIC GROUPS

On May 17, 1954, the U. S. Supreme Court ruled in the case of *Brown v. the Board of Education of Topeka, Kansas,* that segregated public schools were unconstitutional—and laid the foundation for perhaps the greatest social revolution in U. S. history. A quarter of a century after that landmark decision, events showed that some of the battles that were begun in 1954 continued to defy resolution. But it was also clear that America's minorities had made considerable progress.

Education. Despite continuing controversy over the quality of public education for all races, the supposed "cultural bias" in standardized tests, and the feasibility of busing to achieve racial balance, still it was obvious that black children were closing the education gap with their white counterparts. In 1960, for example, only 42% of black youngsters finished high school, as opposed to 66% of whites. By 1978, 73% of blacks were finishing, in comparison with 85% of white children. Also, 20% of black youths aged 18 to 24 were enrolled in college (as against 26% of whites), a number that nearly equaled the black percentage of the population as a whole.

There was also less encouraging news. The U. S. Civil Rights Commission invoked the Brown anniversary to chastise Congress for passing legislation that weakened school desegregation efforts and to criticize the executive branch of government for failing to enforce desegregation efforts more strongly. The commission noted that, 25 years after the nation's schools were ordered to desegregate "with all deliberate speed," nearly half the country's minority-group children remained in schools that were in some way segregated. Most of those schools, ironically, were in the North, where more than 150 school districts were under court or federal government order to desegregate.

One case in point was Chicago, which has the nation's third largest school system with 475,000 students—only about 20% of whom are white. After a lengthy investigation, the Department of Health, Education, and Welfare (HEW) accused the city of fostering segregation over a 40-year period through the location of new schools, the alteration of attendance boundaries, and discriminatory transfer policies. When Chicago's Board of Education failed to meet government requirements for correcting the situation, HEW Secretary Patricia Roberts Harris asked the Justice Department to file suit.

Employment. The Supreme Court's 1978 ruling in the Bakke case upheld the principle of affirmative action—racial preference—in college admissions, although it ruled out the use of quotas to achieve racial balance. In 1979, the court gave an even stronger endorsement to affirmative action, this time in employment. Brian Weber, a white Louisiana factory worker, sued his company, Kaiser Aluminum, and his union, the United Steelworkers of America, after he was denied admission to a skilled-crafts training program. The program had been set up by the company and union, under federal government pressure, with half the slots reserved for women and minorities. Two black workers with less seniority than Weber were admitted and he charged reverse discrimination, arguing that the Civil Rights Act prohibited any discrimination based on race.

By a 5 to 2 vote, the Supreme Court ruled against Weber. Justice William Brennan, who wrote the majority opinion, noted that the Civil Rights Act was specifically intended to improve the lot of minorities and that it allowed for voluntary preferential treatment—including quotas—by private employers to compensate for past injustices.

That may have helped pave the way for the federal government's lawsuits filed against Sears, Roebuck & Co., the world's largest retailer, for discriminating against blacks and Hispanics in hiring. Earlier in the year, Sears had challenged the government with a suit of its own, charging that conflicting federal policies had created an imbalance in the work force in favor of white males. That suit was dismissed. In its suits, the government asked for both affirmative action programs to alleviate Sears' alleged bias and back pay for affected workers.

Foreign Policy. Andrew Young, U. S. ambassador to the United Nations, resigned amid a storm of controversy after it was revealed that he had met secretly with a representative of the Palestine Liberation Organization (PLO), the Arab group seeking recognition of Palestinian rights in the Middle East. Since Young was the first black American to hold such a visible and influential position in the realm of foreign policy, his departure angered many black leaders, some of whom felt he had been dismissed unfairly.

The incident also caused a strain in relations between black and Jewish groups, traditional allies in the civil rights movement, because some blacks felt that Jewish groups had pressed for Young's ouster. At a meeting in New York, 200 black leaders issued a statement criticizing some Jewish organizations for becoming "apologists for the racial status quo" and defending the right of blacks to participate in international affairs. Some black groups, including the National Association for the Advancement of Colored People, urged the government to negotiate with the PLO to help effect peace in the Middle East. Others, like the Rev. Jesse Jackson, head of Operation PUSH, traveled to the Middle East to meet with PLO chief Yasir Arafat.

Such moves in turn angered Jewish leaders who view the PLO as a terrorist group committed to the destruction of Israel. There was dissent from other black leaders as well. Vernon Jordan of the National Urban League declared that "the black civil rights movement has nothing in common with groups whose claim to legitimacy is compromised by cold-blooded murder." By all indications, the Middle East remained a low-level priority with most black Americans. But the dispute did promise a new-found concern, at least among some black leaders, with U. S. foreign policy.

Indo-Chinese Refugees. The plight of Indo-Chinese "boat people"—refugees from Vietnam, Laos, and Cambodia by the thousands fleeing war, hunger, and brutal oppression in rickety boats—came to worldwide attention. And many of those refugees reached the United States, to become the country's newest major immigrant group. Spurred by guilt over the Vietnam war and memories of ignored Jewish refugees from Nazi Germany, the U. S. government redoubled its commitment to aid the Indo-Chinese. Since the fall of Saigon in 1975, the United States had absorbed 220,000 Indo-Chinese refugees at a cost of $1 billion. By late summer, another 14,000 refugees were entering the United States every month.

Though the resettlement was accomplished largely through the massive efforts of charitable organizations and individual sponsors, there was some backlash against the latest wave of immigrants. The most dramatic example was in tiny Seadrift, TX, on the Gulf Coast, where about 100 Vietnamese refugees had settled. Angry disputes over crab fishing led to the killing of one local man and the arrest of two Vietnamese for the crime. In apparent retaliation, Vietnamese boats were burned and most of the refugees fled town temporarily. Still, there were many more cases of refugees who were able to reunite their families, find work, and invest heavily in the American dream.

DENNIS A. WILLIAMS, *"Newsweek"*

EUROPE

The dismal pattern established during the Arab oil embargo of 1973–74—inflation and economic disruption, brought on by high fuel prices and magnified by the weakness of the American economy—continued in Europe during 1979. Election results showed an ongoing disillusionment with established political parties on both the right and left, and terrorism again challenged the will of democratic governments. But amid the gloom, there were a few bright spots. The election of John Paul II in 1978 brought a refreshing new humanity to the Catholic Church; the first popular election of the European Parliament invigorated the process of European unification; and women were finally chosen for several of the highest political offices in Europe.

Continuing Economic Problems. The economies of Europe recovered far more slowly than that of the United States after the recession of 1973–74. In the early months of 1979, however, most European countries experienced a surge of confidence. A brief revival of the U. S. dollar and a decision by the West German government to stimulate its economy were cause for optimism. But by midyear, an atmosphere of despair and at times mutual distrust pervaded the economic discussions of the industrialized powers.

After five and one-half years of talks, the "Tokyo Round" multilateral trade negotiations culminated in Geneva with the April 1979 signing of a comprehensive agreement to reduce tariffs and overcome other obstacles to world trade. In June, the leaders of Britain, Canada, France, Germany, Italy, Japan, and the United States held an economic summit in Tokyo to set country-by-country limits on oil imports. The Organization of Petroleum Exporting Countries (OPEC) had boosted oil prices by 50% since January, and individual member nations were restricting production to boost prices even higher. The immediate effects in Europe were increased rates of inflation and unemployment. In West Germany inflation rose to more than 7%, in Britain to 13%, and in Italy to 17%. In West Germany, which was attempting to reduce unemployment by restricting contracts to immigrant workers, there was 4% unemployment.

Long-term economic problems also worsened. The governments of Europe remained deeply troubled by the instability of the world monetary system. The problem of recycling OPEC monetary surpluses—more than $700 billion by 1979 —was only partially resolved by the purchase of industrial shares, capital equipment, and real estate in Europe and North America by various OPEC nations. The holders of petrodollars and 600 billion Eurodollars lent abroad by the United States were tempted by the midyear decline of the U. S. dollar to shift to such stronger European currencies as the German mark and the Swiss franc. This caused great fluctuations in European currency values. The European gold market also became volatile, as investors sought a hedge against currency weakness. In this condition of "stagflation," European governments found it difficult to reduce unemployment in such money-losing industries as textiles, shipbuilding, and steel.

A promising step toward monetary improvement was the introduction of the European Monetary System in January 1979. According to the new system, the currencies of participating nations—all members of the European Community (EC) except Great Britain—are to fluctuate no more than 2.25% above or below an assigned value. If a country needs to sell or buy its own currency to stabilize the market value, it can borrow from a $65 billion reserve fund. Each participating nation contributes 20% of its gold and dollar reserves to this fund. A new currency, the European Currency Unit (ECU) was introduced as a reserve asset to help the overstretched dollar and to eliminate the problems of fluctuating member currencies. One ECU is defined as a basket of all EC currencies.

Political Instability. As a result of these economic problems, the major political parties in Europe fared poorly in 1979. Italy was governed for more than six months by a minority cabinet under Christian Democrat Giulio Andreotti. In national elections held in June (two years ahead of schedule), both the Christian Democrats and Communists received fewer votes than in the previous national election. It seemed unlikely that a new minority government under Francesco Cossiga could restore confidence in the Christian Democrats, and after the election a challenge was mounted inside the Italian Communist party to the leadership of Enrico Berlinguer and to the concept of Eurocommunism. Although Spanish Communist Party leader Santiago Carrillo remained committed to national communism by democratic means, the French Communist Party seemed determined to return to its traditional pro-Soviet position.

Popular dissatisfaction with labor demands led to the ouster of the British Labour government, while the high cost of social programs caused voters in Sweden to reject an attempted return to power by the Social Democratic Labor Party. British labor unions, which for three years had respected a wage restraint pact with the Labour government of former Prime Minister James Callaghan, went on strike for pay increases of up to 20%. For weeks, the public had to cope with interruptions in food supplies, ambulance service, garbage collection, school administration, and even grave digging. Many of the demands were met, but an outraged public swept the Labour Party out of office in May elections. Voters gave Margaret Thatcher's Conservative Party an absolute majority, thereby endorsing her platform of reduced state intervention, lower taxation, stimulus to free enterprise, and discipline of labor. A similar solution to

With French President Valéry Giscard d'Estaing, Mme. Simone Veil, who in July became president of the new European Parliament, attends a meeting of European social welfare ministers. The scene is the Palais d'Europe in Strasbourg.

economic difficulties had been attempted in France after the appointment of Raymond Barre as premier in 1976. Although the national trade deficit was eliminated, government attempts to restructure the steel and textile industries contributed to growing unemployment, a high rate of inflation, and the disaffection of labor groups and the general public. But public reactions to economic difficulties were perhaps most acute in Turkey. Prime Minister Bülent Ecevit was compelled to declare martial law in one third of the country after clashes between rival Moslem communities and between political extremists on the left and right led to more than 1,500 deaths in 1978–79. A slight improvement in Turkey's economic situation was promised in June 1979, when 24 western European governments jointly provided $1.5 billion in emergency aid.

Rampant Terrorism. West Germany was the only European country that could claim any progress in the area of terrorism control during 1979. Italy remained prey to kidnapping, murder for profit, and political violence. The Red Brigade and Marxist student Autonomists planted bombs, "kneecapped" trial lawyers and political opponents, and were responsible for at least 15 deaths in the first half of the year alone. Basque separatists and the radical October 1 Anti-Fascist Resistance Group (GRAPO) continued their campaign of political assassinations in Spain. The military governor of Madrid, a Supreme Court justice, and numerous other officials all were murdered during the year. The most brazen terrorist act of 1979, however, was the August 27 murder of the British diplomat and war hero, Lord Mountbatten, by the Provisional Wing of the Irish Republican Army (IRA). Mountbatten and members of his family were sailing near the Irish coast when a bomb exploded on their boat. At the same time, another terrorist bomb killed 18 British soldiers in Ulster. The increasingly bold and sophisticated acts of terrorism by the IRA, possibly the result of links with other European activists, appeared only to strengthen the resolve of the British government to resist extremist demands.

Signs of Hope. Despite otherwise trying circumstances, Europe's oldest and newest institutions were invigorated by new leadership in 1979. Pope John Paul II made highly successful trips to Central America, Poland, Ireland, and the United States. The nine countries of the European Community held their first popular elections for the European Parliament. Many believed that the parliament gained more leverage in its attempt to speed up the integration of Europe. The new parliament included 44 Communists, 112 Socialists, 107 Christian-Democrats, 64 Conservatives, 21 Progressive Democrats, 40 Liberals, and 23 others. Former French Health Minister Simone Veil was elected president of the body.

The installations of Simone Veil, Margaret Thatcher, Maria de Lurdes Pintassilgo as interim premier of Portugal, and Nilde Jotti as president of the Italian Chamber of Deputies, led some to predict the end of discrimination against women in European politics.

See also individual country articles; Biography; Obituaries.

F. Roy Willis
University of California, Davis

FASHION

The major influence in 1979 on fashion was the state of world economics. Fear of a recession, the energy crisis, continuing inflation, skyrocketing gold prices, and the decline of the dollar all affected fashion design and marketing decisions. Since the higher cost of apparel made every purchase an investment, there was an emphasis on quality, a return to generally conservative styling with less radical silhouette changes, and a renewed importance placed on accessories or "items" such as camisoles, blouses, sweaters, or jackets that would update or expand an existing wardrobe.

Economics and Fashion. The devaluation of the dollar made American designer and ready-to-wear fashions attractively priced for overseas markets, and famed designers, including Geoffrey Beene, Calvin Klein, Bill Blass, and Oscar de la Renta, showed and sold their collections in international fashion centers such as Milan, Paris, London, and Tokyo.

With rising oil prices, petrochemical synthetics were more expensive and their production unreliable. Rayon, a cellulosic synthetic, enjoyed a resurgence as a replacement for nylons and polyesters. Natural fibers such as cotton, wool, linen, and mohair were the basis of every designers' line. Silk, heavily promoted by the Chinese and Koreans, was another widely-used fiber and was found at every price level.

Gold chains, bangles, earrings, and other jewelry items were popular both as accessories and as investments. Glitter hosiery, gold leather bags and shoes, as well as belts, lit up evenings; and even daytime fashions found lurex stripings on sweaters or threaded through plaids or prints. Lamé, gold lace, gilt studs, beads, and sequins appeared everywhere as evidence of a preoccupation with gold and its economic effect.

The Silhouette. In American collections there was no radical silhouette change, just a slight broadening of the shoulders, a closer body fit, a natural hip curve tapering to a narrow, slightly shorter skirt. The effect was feminine and seductive, controlled but not confining.

The Europeans exaggerated this shape with massive padding, shoulder gathers, pleats or

COURTESY, SAKS FIFTH AVENUE

Two popular fashion attractions (*shown left*) in 1979 were the slim slit skirt and the belted sweater. The suit (*below*) is right on the 1979 fall fashion mark, with its fitted jacket, narrow belt, and slim skirt; important accessories complete the look.

COURTESY, SAKS FIFTH AVENUE

epaulets, pinching waists via hard and wide belts, and adding hip curves with peplums or full gathers at the top of peg-bottomed skirts and pants. There were even some very short skirts that harked back to the days of the mini.

Emphasized Apparel. 1979 was the year of the suit. Some were variations of the easy blazer and skirt combinations of past seasons. Newer were the dressmaker suits, softened with details such as contrast piping, braid trims, tucks or darts for closer fit, and pleats or gathers at shoulder yokes. Jacket and skirt might match, but more often than not they contrasted in color, fabric, and texture. Mohair, bouclé, and poodle-cloth in stained-glass colors were used for jackets that were wrapped, boxed, cropped as boleros, or fitted and flared as blazers. They all topped the narrow slit skirt, most often black.

Camisoles and blouses in bold colors such as jade, cobalt, marigold, and fuchsia were the softening influence on the suit. Bowed or ruffled, with jabots, tuxedo-tucked fronts, or lace collars, they feminized and brightened the suit.

The shirtdress, in the same strong colors, was the single most promoted item of 1979. Touted for every occasion, day through evening, it was invariably classic in design with a softly bloused bodice, lightly sashed waist, slim, slit skirt, and full shirtsleeves. Other versions featured a lean and body-skimming chemise shape that could be worn belted or not.

Sweaters, present in every collection, were classic versions of Shetlands, in Fair Isle or argyle patterns, or cashmere crew necks accessorized by lace collars or a single strand of pearls for a demure, prim look. However, more interesting were those which were uniquely artistic handmade creations, with unusual stitches, patterns, yarn, or color combinations. While some sweater looks stopped at the waist, others were extended into tunics or lengthened into dresses. These sweater dresses were most successful when done in bright two- or three-color combinations, dividing the dress into bands, blocks, or abstract blobs of color.

Coats were shaped and fitted as reefers or princess styles, replacing the belted trench or boy-coat silhouettes of other years. Here, too, details such as piping, braid trims, velvet collars and cuffs, tucks and darts gave an air of graceful and ladylike precision. Newer lengths—from ¾ to ⅞'s—were shown over the narrow

Disco clothes (*below*) continued big in 1979, with body suits, tight jeans, and wrap skirts stealing the fashion scene. The taffeta blouse, with ruffled sleeves and neckline and worn over a bouffant silk skirt, lent romantic appeal to evening wear.

The quilted coat, in bright colors and unusual fabrics, was a popular item on college campuses in 1979.

skirt. Quilted coats, an offshoot of the down jacket, were omnipresent for day and evening in brilliant colors and unusual fabrics such as iridescent cotton, satin, taffeta, or silk jacquard—even leather or suede. The quilting was swirled, scalloped, or scrolled, as well as traditionally diamond-shaped or tunnelled.

Evening clothes were romantically Edwardian, with well-defined silhouettes. Tightly fitted bodices in the form of bustiers or corselets narrowed to nipped-in waists over bouffant skirts. Bright colors with black were a common combination, and popular fabrics were faille, velvet, and lace. Beading, sequins, and touches of gold added glamour.

Pants, while still popular, were not an important fashion. The only news was in "designer" jeans which bore identifying tags for almost every design name and provided instant status. Another new trouser making its appearance in Europe was "the baggie," which featured fullish pleating below a wide waistband tapering to a narrow pegged leg.

Fashion Accessories. Accessories were very important in 1979. In bold colors, they were the accent that completed the smartly polished look for which designers strove. They were also big business since they were an obvious and inexpensive means to update fashions.

Belts were the number one item. Narrow or wide, they instantly produced 1979's fitted look. They came in highly polished leathers or brightly colored suedes, neatly buckled or clasped, and were often embroidered, studded, quilted, perforated, and shaped or contoured to the waist.

Accessories needed to enhance the suit were handbag, hat, gloves, and shoes. An appropriate handbag was a clutch or shoulder bag—in calf, suede, or snakeskin, and in square or oblong shapes. A good choice for a hat was a small one with a narrow brim and shallow crown, often feather-trimmed or with a small veil. To complete the look, good choices were kid gloves in high colors and pumps, the shoe of the year.

The most important shoe shape, the pump came in every color and every style—D'Orsay, sling, opera, spectator—all with a higher, narrower heel, often cone-shaped, and with a softer, slightly pointed toe. Here too, details were important; bows, piping, scallop edging or shirring gave the pump new dimension and softness. Lightly textured hosiery tinted berry, navy, grey, plum, or coffee enhanced the shoe.

The boot in 1979 was short. Ankle boots—tied, buckled, or cuffed—came in highly polished leathers or softly colored suedes and had many of the dressmaker details of the pump, with the same heel and toe treatment.

Other accessory items were antique jewelry in the shape of lapel pins, bar pins, or cameos, and hair ornaments for the more controlled hairdos.

Men's Fashion. In menswear, fit was also important. The trend was toward polished, cosmopolitan dressing and body-conscious silhouettes. Wider shoulders, narrower waists, and slim-hipped fashions were the vogue both in America and Europe. Suits featured square, padded shoulders, a tighter fit through the chest, waist, and hips, with narrow, straight-cuffed trousers.

Fabrics were conservative worsteds, flannels, or tweeds in shades of brown, navy, or neutrals such as mushroom or taupe. The few plaids or patterns shown were equally subdued in color. Cotton and silk broadcloth shirts had body fit and provided a bit of color. Lavender, rust, olive, or brights such as pink or orange gave a lift to suitings' moody hues.

Even in sportswear or casual dress there was a neat and polished look. Suede replaced hard leathers for elegant bomber jackets; soft Shetland or cashmere sweaterings in shawl-collared cardigan styles topped oxford cloth or iridescent-hued, button-down shirts. Flannel trousers, properly creased, replaced jeans for casual wear.

In accessories, the clean look prevailed. Smooth leather loafers, oxfords, or ankle boots, all in rich shades of mahogany or chocolate, and ribbed hosiery, often clocked, were shown. Efficient, organized briefcases replaced the soft bag. Chains, pendants, I.D. bracelets, and other obvious jewelry were passé.

For many, fashion provided the order, quality, and control that appeared to be missing in an uncertain world.

ANN M. ELKINS
"Good Housekeeping Magazine"

FINLAND

The Finns went to the polls on March 18–19, 1979, to elect a new parliament for a four-year term. The results were to some degree rather surprising, with the Social Democrats, the biggest party in the country, ending up with 24% of the vote, a loss of two seats, and a representation in parliament limited to 52. The biggest surprise was the advance made by the Conservatives, who gained 21.7% of the votes cast. The second-largest party, the Finnish People's Democratic League (including the Communists), captured 35 seats, and the Center Party won 36 seats. The non-socialist parties controlled 113 seats, compared with 106 in 1975. The number of women in the new parliament was increased from 46 to 52, and represented the highest ratio of women in any European parliament. Compared with the 1975 elections, the votes for leftist parties declined by 2.1%, giving them 42% of the votes cast. The elections signified a setback for the parties that made up the government coalition, but the government still commanded a majority in the new parliament.

Nevertheless, the cabinet headed by Kalevi Sorsa handed in its resignation on April 4. Mauno Koivisto of the Social Democratic Party, director of the Bank of Finland and a former premier, accepted the task of heading Finland's 61st cabinet since independence, and on May 26 submitted the names of his ministers. The cabinet is a coalition of left-center parties.

The Economy. Economic developments in 1979 were generally favorable. Production figures rose markedly, with an increase in both exports and domestic demand. Employment was up more than expected, and the domestic inflation rate remained fairly modest. An action by the Council of State on September 21 changed the rate of fluctuation of the Finnish currency index, pegging it between 121.0 and 114.0.

An energy program for the 1980's was formulated by the Energy Policy Council. Among the stated aims of the program were the full utilization of labor and other production inputs, more effective exploitation of domestic natural resources, and reduced dependence on imports.

Obituaries. Mika Waltari, world-renowned author, died on August 28 at age 70. His best known novel, *The Egyptian,* an international best-seller, was published in Finland in 1945.

Armi Ratia, who helped make Finnish design world famous, died on October 3 at age 67.

ERIK J. FRIIS
Editor, "The Scandinavian-American Bulletin"

FLORIDA

Florida's dynamic new governor, Robert Graham, kept state politics in the news, but had to share the headlines with capital punishment, hurricanes, and presidential politics.

Tax Reform. Governor Graham fulfilled a promise by creating a Tax Reform Commission which was to recommend basic tax reforms. In the meantime, the legislature supported the governor by imposing a one-year freeze on *ad valorem* taxes and initiated its own tax reform by placing on the March 1980 ballot a proposed constitutional amendment that would increase the homestead tax exemption from $5,000 to $25,000.

Governor Graham called the legislature into special session in November after receiving the recommendations of the tax commission. The governor's prestige was dealt a blow when lawmakers rejected his proposals which would have resulted in increases in sales and gasoline taxes.

Education. The state shifted more financial responsibility for education from local government to the state. The state would pay 66% of the cost of education in 1980–81 compared with 59% previously. A Post-Secondary Education Act created a new funding formula and administrative reforms for the state university system as well. The law also provides tuition grants to Florida students who attend Florida's private colleges.

Budget. A record $15.78 billion two-year budget was approved, granting big increases for education and welfare services. The budget led to a constitutional controversy when Governor Graham vetoed a proviso appropriating $18 million for school books and buses, but left the

---

FINLAND • Information Highlights

Official Name: Republic of Finland.
Location: Northern Europe.
Area: 130,129 square miles (337 032 km²).
Population (1979 est.): 4,800,000.
Chief Cities (Dec. 1977): Helsinki, the capital, 487,519; Tampere, 166,118; Turku, 165,215.
Government: *Head of state,* Urho Kaleva Kekkonen, president (elected Feb. 1978 for 5th term). *Head of government,* Mauno Koivisto, prime minister (took office May 1979). *Legislature* (unicameral)—Eduskunta.
Monetary Unit: Markka, or Finnish mark (3.75 markkaa equal U.S.$1, Nov. 1979).
Manufactures (major products): Timber and forest products, machinery, ships, clothing, transportation equipment, appliances.
Agriculture (major products): Dairy products, wheat and other grains, livestock, furs.

FLORIDA • Information Highlights

Area: 58,560 square miles (151 670 km²).
Population (Jan. 1979 est.): 8,653,000.
Chief Cities (1970 census): Tallahassee, the capital, 72,586; (1976 est.): Jacksonville, 532,346; Miami, 354,993.
Government (1979): *Chief Officers*—governor, Robert Graham (D); lt. gov., Wayne Mixson (D). *Legislature* —Senate, 40 members; House of Representatives, 120 members.
Education (1978–79): *Enrollment*—public elementary schools, 776,607 pupils; public secondary, 737,212; colleges and universities, 377,100 students. *Public school expenditures,* $3,005,703,000.
State Finances (fiscal year 1978): *Revenues,* $6,442,069,000; *expenditures,* $5,712,824,000.
Personal Income (1978): $65,084,000,000; per capita, $7,573.
Labor Force (July 1979): *Nonagricultural wage and salary earners,* 3,255,200; *unemployed,* 256,100 (6.6%).

funds in the budget to be spent at his discretion. Legislative leaders were preparing to take the issue to the state Supreme Court.

Presidental Politics. As the Democratic Party made plans for caucuses to elect delegates to the 1979 state convention, supporters of Sen. Edward Kennedy began organizing in Florida to embarrass President Carter. The caucuses thus became a media event between Carter and Kennedy. President Carter, members of his family, and staff members repeatedly visited the state. Carter won an overwhelming majority, but the outcome has no effect on the selection of delegates to the 1980 national convention.

Hurricanes. Hurricane David inflicted property damages in the state estimated at $94 million. Less than two weeks later, Hurricane Frederic slammed into the Gulf coast near Pensacola, FL, and Mobile, AL, causing comparable damage. State and local officials evacuated over 300,000 people from the coastal regions. Although Florida's west coast escaped both David and Frederic, heavy rains spawned by the storms caused extensive flooding and property damage, especially in the heavily populated Tampa-St. Petersburg region.

Capital Punishment. Convicted murderer John Spenkelink was executed on May 25. At the time 133 persons were on death row in the state.

Four other death warrants were signed by the governor but the cases were being reviewed by federal courts.

J. LARRY DURRENCE
Florida Southern College

FOOD

Although issues involving energy received far more publicity in 1979, the world food supply was undergoing changes that affected much of the world's population. The changes within the developed nations were less noticed than the conflicts over food in the less developed, highly populated areas of the world. The attention of the world was focused on the problems of Southeast Asia, especially refugees and famine in Cambodia, yet weather vagaries and crop failures resulted in the purchase of near-record amounts of grain by the Soviet Union.

WORLD SUPPLY

While some nations may experience lowered crop yields due to droughts and floods, the world supply of food tends to be measured by the grain harvests in the United States and in the Soviet Union. Forecasts indicated that the Soviet grain harvest would be the lowest since 1975, when 153 million tons (140 million metric tons) were harvested. Late 1979 predictions were for a 20% drop from 1978 amounts to an estimated 202 million tons (185 million metric tons). In contrast, the U. S. Department of Agriculture predicted that the U. S. corn crop was estimated at 7.4 billion bushels. Persistent

drought in some areas and the coldest winter in 100 years in other areas caused the lowered Soviet harvest. As a result, the United States agreed to allow the Soviet Union to purchase 27 million tons (25 million metric tons) of corn and wheat in 1979–80, or an amount roughly equal to their buying in 1972. In perspective, 10 million pounds (4.5 million kg) of wheat will provide every Soviet man, woman, and child with nearly 100 one-pound (.45 kg) loaves of bread.

Other areas of the world generally maintained previous production rates of crops, except for those areas in Southeast Asia torn by conflict. A massive influx of food was needed in the Cambodian area.

The U. S. General Accounting Agency stated that U. S. food assistance is not reaching the people who need it most, especially those in remote, rural areas of low-income nations. In 1978–79, spending on U. S. food donations overseas totaled $573 million, with the 1979–80 program projected at $679 million.

In another area, the director general of the UN Food and Agriculture Organization (FAO) reported that the Third World is moving toward a massive food shortage that will increase America's role as the world's breadbasket, but possibly result in economic disaster within the next 20 years. The report stated that about 400 million people suffer from serious malnutrition, and even if drastic increases in food production are made, some 250 million will be starving in the year 2000.

U. S. FOOD SUPPLY

Availability of food in the United States was not a major problem. Price inflation was. Near-record harvests of corn and wheat combined with Soviet buying could result in higher prices for U. S. consumers in 1980. The U. S. Department of Agriculture predicted that retail food prices will rise between 9% and 11% in 1980. Hog and poultry cutbacks and higher costs of processing, transporting, and marketing were cited as factors causing the rise. Based on these predictions, a family paying $234 a month for food in 1979, could expect to pay between $250–$260 a month for food in 1980.

With the cost of energy rising at a rapid and generally unpredictable rate, the food industry, along with many federal and state agencies, sought ways to minimize the effect of energy costs on food. While many companies were routinely reducing energy costs through generally known methods, others were taking novel approaches. Tri-Valley Growers of California researched and developed an industrial boiler that derives 80% of its fuel requirements from crushed peach pits, a waste by-product of peach canning. In the future the company was expected to use olive and cherry pits, wood chips from orchard prunings, and walnut and almond shells as fuel sources. Other segments

Beverly Ribaudo, a St. Clair Shores, MI, housewife and consumer affairs activist, organized boycotts against high food prices, including meat, sugar, and coffee.

of the food industry were applying technology and equipment modification to saving energy in all areas of food processing. In a limited survey of processed-food companies, three out of four companies stated that they had energy conservation programs, with one third of the industry reporting less energy being used per unit of output. Such programs least affect the area of distribution. A USDA study concluded that attempts to increase energy savings by varying daytime and nighttime storage temperatures could result in quality loss in frozen foods.

In the consumer area, inflation, energy costs, and higher food prices initiated shifts in the market place. More interest was shown in food cooperatives, high volume warehouse-style stores, and the use of coupons. With inflation reaching 13–14% for 1979, consumers increasingly were concerned with the rapid rise of food prices. A 1979 poll indicated that consumers were concerned about rising prices, were purchasing fewer higher priced items and more specials, were adhering to fixed food budgets, and were interested more in generic food brands. Further, more consumers were interested in buying techniques, and eating more nutritiously. The USDA's Extension Service completed a pilot supermarket nutrition education project in the Washington, DC, area. Trained volunteers offered nutrition demonstrations and shopping information to shoppers in selected supermarkets. The project's success stimulated similar efforts throughout the United States.

In California, one of the most productive growing and processing areas, a new approach to food utilization sprang up. Groups of people (mostly senior citizens) joined forces to salvage produce that did not meet market requirements, at no cost other than labor. The harvest was then used by the workers or distributed through networks to other needy groups.

Nutrition. The U. S. Congress annually appropriates more than $9 billion for a number of food aid programs. In 1967, widespread hunger was reported in America. In 1979, the results of a new survey by the same Field Foundation were released covering the 1967–77 period. The report indicated that there were fewer grossly malnourished people in the United States than 10 years earlier. The report credited the Food Stamp Program, the nutritional component of Head Start, School Lunch and Breakfast programs, and the Women-Infant-Child (WIC) feeding programs with the improvement. In another area, the preliminary results of the USDA's Food Consumption Survey were released. The figures compare the spring of 1965 with the spring of 1977. Tentative interpretations indicated a lowering of calorie consumption, an increase in incidence of obesity in certain groups, a suspected lessening of physical activity, and an apparent increase in total consumption of sweeteners.

Quality. An area of continuing concern to both food processors and consumers, nitrate-free meats, was resolved. Effective Sept. 20, 1979, USDA's Food Safety and Quality Service established an amendment to the federal meat inspection regulations that permits meat-food products preserved with nitrates/nitrites to be prepared without these preservatives and sold under the same name as nitrite-preserved meats. The word "uncured" must precede the meat product name with the statements "no nitrate or nitrite added" and "not preserved—keep refrigerated below 40° F at all times." The ruling means that a consumer desiring to purchase "uncured pork strips" will now buy "uncured bacon." Further, the order prohibits the use of nitrates or nitrites in baby, junior, or toddler meat food products.

Many consumers, either for health or diet reasons, have been well aware of the non-nutritive sweetener controversy. Although without the effect of law, the House of Representatives extended the moratorium on banning saccharin until June 30, 1981. In related action, the U. S. Food and Drug Administration (FDA) reopened hearings on the safety of cyclamate, a previously withdrawn non-nutritive sweetener, and was to convene a scientific board of inquiry to recommend whether the agency should approve aspartame, an artificial sweetener. In Canada, the Canadian Health Protection Branch plans to recommend approval of aspartame as a table sweetener and for use in foods.

KIRBY M. HAYES
University of Massachusetts

France's governing coalition, *l'Union pour la Démocratie Française*, held its first Congress in February 1979.

FRANCE

"France is in a bad way," said President Valéry Giscard d'Estaing on Sept. 14, 1979. Although France's problems were perhaps not so severe as those of some other major powers, the nation did suffer a general economic slowdown, 10% inflation, an unemployment figure of 1.4 million, a seemingly endless series of labor walkouts, and a round of political scandals that touched the highest offices in the land. A bizarre mixture of high-mindedness, sleazy financial and judicial procedures, and disdain for others characterized the public life of this still prosperous country and the administrative elite that runs it.

DOMESTIC AFFAIRS

Giscard's *Union pour la Démocratie Française* (UDF)—a loosely constructed centrist alliance—remained in charge. An emergency session of the National Assembly demanded jointly by the Gaullists, Communists, and Socialists to debate economic policy March 14–16 failed to bring down the government. Prime Minister Raymond Barre, whose austerity program had little positive effect, survived censure motions in the assembly, which then subsided for the year.

With half the nation's cantonal seats up for election March 18–25, the Socialists polled

26.9% of the vote, the Communists 22.4%, and the UDF 21.2%. The Socialists and Communists gained 153 and 32 seats, respectively, and together they controlled 47 of the 96 department councils. Socialist leader François Mitterrand appealed for leftist unity at his party's congress, April 8–10. His principal rival, Michel Rocard, argued against closer ties with the Communists and a rigidly planned economy. Mitterrand drew more support (47%) than Rocard (21%) but failed to obtain a majority endorsement for the first time since he became president of the new Socialist party.

Communist Party Secretary General Georges Marchais rejected proposals for accord with the Socialist executive, suggesting instead a grassroots cooperation. On August 20, Mitterrand offered to renew the Union of the Left, but Marchais replied with charges of Socialist electioneering for the 1981 presidential contest, statements that Mitterrand sought only the ouster of Barre, and an accusation (false) that the Socialists had destroyed the Union.

This disarray was only one aspect of the republic's continued failure to achieve a genuine democratic system. Another was the Socialists' decision to circumvent the government's broadcasting monopoly by resorting to "pirate" broadcasts during the summer. On August 24, police broke into party headquarters, manhandled several deputies, injured one television worker, and charged Mitterrand with violation of the law. The Socialists called the police actions a "scandalous attack on freedom."

Thunder continued to be heard from the right. Early in the year, Jacques Chirac, leader of the Gaullist Rassemblement pour la République (RPR) and mayor of Paris, accused Giscard of selling out sovereignty to the idea of a united Europe. In June 10 elections for the new Parliament of the European Community (EC), Chirac's RPR was rebuffed, bringing up the rear with 15 seats. The UDF won 26, the Socialists 22, and the Communists 19. After the election, a stormy meeting of RPR notables reaffirmed Chirac's place of leadership, but the party remained divided. Yves Guéna, a disabused former associate, said the RPR could survive only if it could find an issue other than Chirac's ambition to displace Giscard in 1981. Essential to the government coalition, the RPR nonetheless appeared to be its prisoner.

An interesting political phenomenon was the emergence of small but well-placed ultraconservative (racist and antisemitic) groups made up of politicians and bureaucrats from the elite schools and backed by the newspaper *Le Figaro*. Attacking Soviet and American materialism, they argued for the right of a western elite to rule for the general good.

Scandals. Sharply contrasting with Giscard's austere manner was his tax return. A facsimile published in June by *Le Canard Enchaîné,* a popular leftist newspaper, disclosed stock market speculations that were questionable for a head of state. Infuriated by the leak, Giscard on October 12 had an employee in the ministry of finance arrested. Two days earlier *Le Canard* published a document, signed in 1973 by mass murderer Emperor Bokassa I of the Central African Empire (now Republic), ordering diamonds valued in excess of $250,000 to be given the then French minister of finance (Giscard). Charges of gifts being made to Giscard's family and associates then followed. Only evasions, expressions of indignation, and then silence came from the Elysée Palace. *Le Monde* castigated that reaction as unbefitting the leadership of a great nation. The political opposition demanded a full inquiry, the prospects for which were nil.

Prime Minister Barre was accused of making, with the help of Riviera officials, astonishingly profitable real-estate investments. His denial and Giscard's testimony to his honesty left the matter unresolved. Also accused of real estate profiteering was the influential labor minister, Robert Boulin. That charge and family problems made Boulin depressed, and he took his life on October 30.

At a less rarefied level, the scandal of late-night rapes and assaults by Paris and Lyon police reached the courts. The police association attributed the behavior to poor working conditions, low prestige, and some nearly illiterate recruits. In fact, it was a by-product of

officially sanctioned brutality that has a long history in France.

Strikes and Protest. Steel strikes began in January and ran on for much of the year. A giant demonstration in Paris, March 23, ended in arson and looting by "autonomous" brigades unconnected with the steel workers. Strikes also affected the nation's railways, docks, and airlines. The unrest included a brief occupation of the Eiffel Tower, sniper fire and arson in the northern city of Denain, and the closing of the Paris Bourse (stock exchange) for two weeks in March. Promising new jobs, retraining, and retirement at age 55, the government was confronted by union demands for a 35-hour week, a $638 minimum monthly wage, price freezes, increased child payments, company surtaxes, and a levy on great fortunes. "This is no longer austerity," said Georges Seguy, the head of the powerful Confédération Générale du Travail on August 7, "it's pillage."

Regional autonomy movements continued to be active during the year. The Corsican National Liberation Front repeatedly set off bombs on that island and in Paris from April through October. Separatists in Breton also resorted to bombings. Spanish Basque separatists in France responded to a government crackdown by attempting to kidnap National Assembly President Jacques Chaban-Delmas. The killing

French police call public attention to what they called the "deplorable conditions" under which they work.

JEAN LUCE HURE, NYT PICTURES

The Forum des Halles, a new multilevel shopping complex in Paris, was opened in early September.

of two Basques by unidentified gunmen in Paris at the end of June led to a bomb attack on a French bank in Madrid, July 5. Three days earlier, gunmen had fired on the Paris-Madrid express train. Symptomatic of the economic malaise and rise of right-wing extremism in France were verbal attacks alleging Jewish control of the media and actual destruction of Jewish property. A nuclear reactor being built for Iraq was destroyed near Toulon, April 6, ostensibly by ecologists, possibly by Israelis, and conceivably by order of French officials embarrassed by the contract.

Economy. "Discontent, doubt, and worry" characterized the spirit of the French people, reported Giscard in late September. Three years of "austerity" had made the rich richer but had failed to improve the economy. The balance of payments was under control but the growth rate of the GNP (gross national product) was only 2.5%. The eighth National Plan (for 1981–86), announced April 5, called for a "pause" in public spending and spoke of more equitable income distribution, but was vague about specific economic targets. The National Assembly passed legislation on May 30 to expel unemployed foreigners. Massively dependent on oil imports, France had a bill that surpassed by some $3.5 billion the projected $13.4 billion and was expected to continue its rapid rise in 1980. The output of nuclear energy was stepped up, and nine new plants were scheduled for completion within the next five years; they would provide 55% of France's electricity. One healthy sign was an intended increase in the ex-

penditure for research and development (R&D), from $9.2 to $11.1 billion. The latter figure comprised about 2.2% of the GNP, a percentage comparable to the R&D expenditures of the United States, Japan, and West Germany. The 1980 budget, approved by the cabinet September 5, provided for a 14.3% increase in spending, a $7.3 billion deficit, and heavier taxes on yachts, country homes, alcohol, tobacco, and automobiles. The wealthy groaned, the unions protested, and on September 14, Giscard proclaimed the demise of the "consumer society." The French "were not happy with this society," he said. But even if that was true, they were no more enchanted with its successor.

Defense. A 13.5% increase in French military spending was planned for 1980. The formation of a new emergency combat force was announced in September. Immensely doubtful of U. S. power and prestige in the world, France

---

FRANCE · Information Highlights

Official Name: French Republic.
Location: Western Europe.
Area: 211,207 square miles (547 026 km²).
Population (1979 est.): 53,400,000.
Chief Cities (1975 census): Paris, the capital, 2,299,830; Marseille, 908,600; Lyon, 456,716; Toulouse, 373,796.
Government: *Head of state,* Valéry Giscard d'Estaing, president (took office May 1974). *Chief minister,* Raymond Barre, prime minister (took office Aug. 1976). *Legislature*—Parliament: Senate and National Assembly.
Monetary Unit: Franc (4.02 francs equal U. S.$1, Dec. 1979).
Manufactures (major products): Chemicals, automobiles, processed foods, iron and steel, aircraft, textiles, clothing.
Agriculture (major products): Cereals, feed grains, livestock and dairy products, wine, fruits, vegetables.

declared that its own nuclear technology was on the same level as that of the great powers, continued as a major arms supplier to the third world, and stood outside nuclear arms limitations discussions.

FOREIGN POLICY

On July 17, with Giscard's backing, former French Minister of Health Simone Veil was elected assembly president of the EC parliament. France rejected every supranational pretension in that organization. At a February 15 press conference, Giscard proclaimed that a confederated Europe is the ultimate goal but that he did not wish Europe in the next century "to look like the Balkans before the First World War." In a year that saw the passing of Jean Monnet, the prophet of a united Europe, Veil pronounced dead "the federalist theories of 20 years ago."

The British and French railways planned a single-track tunnel under the English Channel, to be completed by 1990. The costly Concorde venture ended on September 21, with a decision for Britain and France to share their unsold aircraft. In two visits to France, Prime Minister Margaret Thatcher could not persuade her neighbor to accept any reduction in British payments to the EC.

During a state visit to Moscow, April 26–28, Giscard agreed to annual summit meetings, consultations in the event of any international crisis, and the participation of a French astronaut in a Soviet space mission. He refused to join the Strategic Arms Limitation Talks (SALT) and failed to persuade President Leonid I. Brezhnev to accept a general conference on conventional arms reduction.

Having harbored the Ayatollah Khomeini until his return to Iran in February, the French government (which had only once cautioned him against preaching violence from French soil), kept a low profile during subsequent developments, although it did disapprove the seizure of U. S. embassy staff in Tehran.

After helping arrange a cease-fire in the Chad civil war in February, the French government announced on March 20 that it would withdraw its 3,000 troops from that country. It continued to provide aid for the Mauritanian and Moroccan struggle against Polisario rebels.

Following reports by Amnesty International and a commission of African jurists on the massacre of schoolchildren by Emperor Bokassa, France cut off aid to the Central African Empire on August 17. It helped to carry out a coup against Bokassa September 20 and to install in office his cousin, former President David Dacko. French paratroopers carried off the imperial archives. (Giscard had known of Bokassa's sadism for years, but had cultivated him, vacationed in his country, and accepted gifts from him.) Bokassa's downfall and flight was an embarrassment to the French. On September 21 he flew to France and was confined

Chinese Premier Hua Guofeng, in an historic trip to the West, is welcomed by President Valéry Giscard d'Estaing.

in his plane on the Evreux airfield for several days. A French citizen by virtue of having served in the army as a young man, Bokassa nevertheless was denied entry and departed for the Ivory Coast, where he was given refuge, on September 24. France's refusal to grant him entrance was widely criticized.

On a state visit to Mexico, February 28– March 3, Giscard promised President José López-Portillo financial support for uranium exploration, nuclear reactor development, and bond flotation. But he could not get the Mexicans to promise more than the 100,000 barrels per day of oil provided for in their five-year agreement of December 1978.

Relations with the United States remained unenthusiastic. Giscard was almost openly critical of President Jimmy Carter and his policies at home and abroad. The French were most disturbed by what appeared to be American helplessness in the growing world disorder.

France appeared to be more circumspect in its relations with Canada. During a February visit, Prime Minister Barre refused to pronounce for an independent Quebec. As Premier René Lévesque's prospects of taking the province out of Canada began to dim, France looked less partisan than it had in years.

JOHN C. CAIRNS, *University of Toronto*

GARDENING AND HORTICULTURE

Eons ago, a simple five-petaled flower fell onto the soft earth of a primeval swamp. From the fossilized imprint of its leaf, archaeologists learned that beneath the awesome feet of dinosaurs there grew a small but tenacious flower—the rose.

The rose apparently originated in central Asia and spread from there over the northern hemisphere. Inexplicably, it never crossed the equator, for no wild species has ever been found in the southern hemisphere. Historical records indicate that wild roses were brought under cultivation in China at least 5,000 years ago. They were also grown in Egypt and Italy long before the Christian era. Centuries of cross-breeding have transformed the roses of antiquity into the vast assembly of roses that exists today. At present there are more than 13,000 identifiable varieties.

All-America Selections. The 1980 All-America Rose Selections (AARS) awards were evenly divided among the three major classifications—hybrid tea, grandiflora, and floribunda. For the first time in the 40-year history of AARS, all three winners were produced by one rose breeder, William Warriner of Tustin, CA. The

Love, a beautifully-shaped grandiflora with brilliant red blooms, was chosen as an All America Selection.

ALL AMERICA ROSE SELECTION

names of the three winners are Love, Honor, and Cherish.

Love, the award-winning grandiflora, is a rose that should please just about everyone. It flowers continuously throughout the entire growing season, furnishing long-stemmed blooms in a color combination that is strikingly beautiful. It has a delicate, spicy perfume, enough to enjoy but not overpowering. Its small, but beautifully-shaped, blooms are brilliant red with sharply contrasting silver-white reverses. The plants are heavily clothed in medium dark green foliage and thickly set with double, high-centered, recurved blooms. Not only did this grandiflora impress the AARS judges throughout the two-year trials, but it also pleased the judges at rose trials in Monza (Italy), Rome, Madrid, and Tokyo.

Honor, according to breeder Bill Warriner, is "tall, stately, and formal." This glistening white hybrid tea rose amassed six major awards from all over the world, including the AARS prize and Jackson & Perkins' 1980 "Rose of the Year." Its long, pointed 1½-inch (3.8-cm) buds are held on straight, stiff stems and open beautifully in all weather conditions to satiny 4 to 5-inch (10.2 to 12.7-cm) blooms of pure white. Most are borne singly, but even in clusters their stems are of good cutting length, with few thorns. The buds open well throughout all seasons—double enough to hold up well in the summer, but not too double to open satisfactorily in the spring. The bush is vigorous, mildew-resistant, with an upright habit and large, olive green, leathery leaves. New canes "break" abundantly from the base to produce a full, well-branched plant. Fine white hybrid tea roses are a rarity, but the clean blooms and long, strong stems of Honor make it one of the leaders.

Cherish is a floribunda as close to being trouble-free as a rose can be. It has form, color, and fragrance—all in abundance. Cherish claims the unique distinction of being able to produce hybrid tea blossoms on a floribunda bush. It blooms early and continues to flower magnificently all season long. Its high-pointed, shapely buds are carried in profusion on a broad, thickly-leaved plant. The softly-colored, shell-pink flowers are much larger—about 4 inches (10.2 cm) across—than those generally found on floribundas and are well set off by an abundance of dark green, glossy foliage. There is little change in color from bud to open flower or from season to season. Cut for arangement, the blooms last very well and their attractiveness is enhanced by a light, but pleasing fragrance. All in all, Cherish is a free-blooming rose with a compact growth habit and excellent garden value. In addition to the AARS floribunda prize for 1980, Cherish was awarded the Silver Medal at the Bagatelle Rose trials in France.

DONALD W. NEWSOM
Department of Horticulture
Louisiana State University

GARDENING AND HORTICULTURE—SPECIAL REPORT:

Home and Community Gardening

According to a Gallup poll taken in 1975, a record 35 million U. S. families—about 49% of the nation's households—cultivated home gardens. Although the number of home gardeners is reported to have decreased slightly since that time, the difference has been more than made up by a dramatic increase in the number of Americans working in shared, community plots. All in all, the number of private gardeners has been increasing astronomically. Backyards, vacant city lots, patios, and penthouse terraces all across the country are abloom in fruits and vegetables.

One of the major reasons for the boom has been the steady rise in the supermarket price of fresh fruits and vegetables—8% in 1978 and as much as 10–12% in 1979. The National Association for Gardening calculated that the average family gardener can save up to $350 per year in vegetable costs. Another reason is the fact that more and more Americans object to chemically-treated crops. A home or community garden yields fresh, tasty, and healthful produce. But perhaps the best explanation for the new popularity of gardening is the sheer pleasure of it. Nurturing one's own plants, watching them grow, and harvesting their fruits is a form of recreation that amateur gardeners find satisfying.

Recognizing the practical benefits of home and community gardening, the U. S. federal government has taken steps to further the trend throughout the country. In 1978, Congress passed a resolution introduced by the late Sen. James B. Allen (D-AL) affirming the value of vegetable gardens in fighting inflation, improving nutrition, getting exercise, and having fun. Congress later amended the Food Stamp Act so as to enable welfare recipients to purchase vegetable seeds and plants with food stamps.

The federal government has funded other initiatives to increase the number of people involved in home and community gardens. The Urban Gardening Program, a pilot program funded by Washington but administered through state Cooperative Extension Services, was begun in Newark, NJ, and five other cities. Newark was an especially good choice because it is one of the poorest cities in the country. "Community garden plots" grew out of this program, and by mid-1979 there were between 700 and 1,000 such gardens in Newark alone.

The number of cities taking part in this federally-funded program has grown to 16, and many other metropolises and towns have developed their own community garden programs. Sizeable areas of land have been set aside by enterprising farmers who realize more profit from renting the land to gardeners than they would from growing wheat, corn, or some other crop. Even the Bronx, NY, has gotten into the act. The Bronx Frontier's Community Garden Program helps support more than 60 community gardens, with 8 to 15 plots per garden.

The increased interest in gardening in the United States has been so dramatic and the market for seed, plants, fertilizer, and other supplies so great that the demand can scarcely be met. The gardening boom has also led to a series of horticultural breakthroughs. A tomato cultivar called Patio has been developed for growth in small garden plots or on patios. Watermelons that require an area of only about 9 sq ft (.84 m²) to produce also have been developed. Dwarf varieties of vegetables and small cherry, apple, pear, and peach trees are now available for small spaces. Miniature roses and many other dwarfed ornamentals are suitable for potting in sunny windows or on terraces. Probably the most popular new vegetable is a pea called the Sugar Snap. At full maturity, both pea and pod are edible—indeed sweet and crisp. During its first season on the market, more than 550,000 lbs (249 480 kg) of Sugar Snap seeds were sold in the United States.

DONALD W. NEWSOM

The home vegetable garden offers fresh, tasty produce, recreational pleasure, and a lever against rising food costs.

GENETICS

Genetic research in 1979 reflected an increasing interrelationship with studies of cell biology, embryological development, and cancer.

The power of genetic analysis was well illustrated by the work on familial hypercholesterolemia (FH) by Joseph Goldstein and Michael Brown of the University of Texas at Dallas. One person in 500 has a particular genetic predisposition to hypercholesterolemia and high risk of heart attacks. This predisposition is inherited as an autosomal dominant trait (FH heterozygote), affecting either women or men, and is manifest if just one of the pair of genes (from the two parents) is the abnormal gene for FH. One person in a million receives a "double dose" of the FH gene; these individuals (FH homozygotes) develop atherosclerosis and have heart attacks by the age of 10 years. The circulating cholesterol, which would not be soluble in plasma, is attached to proteins, especially low-density lipoproteins (LDL). Analyses of the cellular uptake of cholesterol and the regulation of cholesterol synthesis in these mutants have provided an exquisite delineation of the cellular processes and the role of cell receptors. Receptors can be expressed on fibroplasts cultured from a skin biopsy and on lymphocytes cultured from blood samples. The wisdom of the Goldstein-Brown approach lay in the study of FH homozygotes, rather than the much more common heterozygotes in whom the unknown effects of the gene would not have been discernible.

In order for LDL to deliver cholesterol to human cells, it must first bind with a high-affinity receptor on the cell surface. These receptors are located in circumscribed indented segments of the plasma membrane, called coated pits. The coated pit is internalized into the cell as an endocytic vesicle and then fuses with an intracellular lysosome, which hydrolyzes the protein and the cholesteryl ester components of the LDL. The resulting free cholesterol becomes available for synthesis of cell membranes and regulates three metabolic events: it suppresses endogenous cholesterol synthesis, activates an enzyme which re-esterifies incoming cholesterol, and suppresses synthesis of the LDL receptor. These effects adjust for variations in ingested and circulating cholesterol.

Patients with FH have mutations which affect the LDL receptor and account for their medical problems. Three types of mutations have been described: R^{bo} is a mutant allele (form of the gene) which specifies a receptor protein that cannot bind LDL. FH homozygotes (R^{bo}/R^{bo}) bind no LDL and so cannot internalize or degrade it; they have plasma LDL levels 6 times normal. The heterozygote ($+/R^{bo}$) binds, internalizes, and degrades LDL at half the normal rate and has plasma LDL concentrations 2–3 times normal. The R^{b-} mutant allele leads to markedly reduced, but detectable, LDL binding. Finally, $R^{b+,io}$ produces a clinical picture identical to R^{bo} because internalization of receptor-bound LDL is defective. Detailed family analyses revealed one patient to be a genetic compound; he had received R^{bo} from his mother and $R^{b+,io}$ from his father. Such heterogeneity is common in genetic variation and genetic disorders in all species. Experiments showed that the binding and internalization defects do not complement each other. The defects are allelic and the LDL receptor must contain two functional sites—one for binding LDL and one to mediate internalization. There can be little doubt that this process has close analogues in toxins, transport proteins, and polypeptide hormones.

Still lacking in 1979 was an animal model for FH. However, Goldstein and Brown joined forces with Beatrice Mintz of the Fox Chase Cancer Center in Philadelphia, and some progress was made. Mintz had pioneered the use of allophenic mice (formed by aggregating cells from two 8-cell embryos from two different pregnant mice of different genetic strains) for studying the genetic control of embryological development. More recently, she constructed allophenic mice using teratocarcinoma (TC) cells in place of one pair of parents. The stem cells of malignant mouse TC's can be channeled into stable differentiation if placed in the company of normal early embryo cells by microinjection into blastocysts. This phenomenon has tremendous implications for cancer biology. If the regulation of gene expression in this dramatic change from malignant cells to normal cells could be fully understood, clinically useful approaches to the containment or reversal of malignant tumors might be devised.

The first step in constructing a mouse model for familial hypercholesterolemia was to determine whether the TC cells in laboratory cultures express the LDL receptors—which they do. The affinity and specificity of binding and the intracellular effects are the same as those in normal cells. The second step was to devise a procedure to identify receptor-deficient mutants in mutagenized cell cultures. Cells with receptors capable of binding LDL were readily visualized in the fluorescence microscope after administering a fluorescent derivative of LDL. Cells treated chemically to interfere with binding showed little fluorescence and were separated from the normal cells with a fluorescence-activated cell sorter.

These results open the way for the production of LDL-receptor mutants in teratocarcinoma cells, their passage into blastocysts for full somatic tissue differentiation, and the development of mice with the same genetic disorder as persons with familial hypercholesterolemia. Such animal models are needed for relating the primary lesions in DNA and protein products to clinical pathogenesis.

GILBERT S. OMENN, *University of Washington*

GEOLOGY

Geological science advanced on all fronts during 1979. The state of the science was illustrated by the number of subfields (31) receiving separate mention in *Geotimes*, the profession's annual newsmagazine.

Planetology. The most significant discoveries were made, not on earth, but in space as Voyager 1 and Voyager 2 passed near Jupiter in March and July, respectively, and Pioneer 11 visited Saturn in September. The four large inner satellites of Jupiter came under close observation and many excellent photographs were sent back to reveal surface features of what have been called the "oldest, youngest, darkest, lightest, most active, least active, and flattest" worlds of the solar system. Io, large innermost satellite, has a density of 3.52 (water equals 1), indicating a rocky composition not unlike earth's moon. The surface shows brilliant color variations, due probably to sulfur compounds. Although there are many impact craters, they seem to be relatively young and it is believed that the planet is being "resurfaced" to erase older features at a relatively rapid rate. The present surface may be no older than 10 million years.

Europa (density 3.2, diameter 3 050 km or 1,895 mi), next in order outward, has been referred to as bland because of the flatness and uniformity of its surface. It is criss-crossed by a disorganized network of linear features hundreds to thousands of kilometers long and 50 to 100 km (31 mi to 62 mi) wide. They are flush with the surface and are thought to be planed off intrusions of lightweight material in an icy crust. The cracks could have formed by tidal action or by internal convection.

Ganymede, next in order (density 2.0, diameter 5 300 km or 3,293 mi) is larger than the planet Mercury and displays a rare combination of impact and tectonic features. Groups of parallel faults up to 100 km wide and 500 km (62 mi to 311 mi) long are the most characteristic features. Other features include examples showing linear, lateral, and rotational motions duplicating fault effects on earth. The faulted stripes divide the cratered terrane into large polygonal regions several hundred to a thousand kilometers across. The cratered regions show about the same density of impacts as do Mercury and the moon and it has been concluded that these regions are billions of years old.

In spite of having a high water content, Callisto (density 1.7, diameter 500 km or 311 mi) is the most heavily cratered of the satellites. Even very small craters are preserved and the largest ones must date back to the heavy bombardment of 4.0 billion years ago. One particularly huge multi-ringed feature, 1 500 km or 930 mi across, is thought to be due to impact but there is no central crater and no sign of ejected material. It may be that the impact was absorbed by the viscous subsurface. There are no linear grooved or faulted features.

Varied Activities. Geologists were finding themselves involved in many problems of economic, political, and social import. Investigations were made of possible disposal sites for radioactive waste, for which repositories must be secure for a minimum of 25,000 years. Geologic factors to be considered included distance from faults, earthquake history and susceptibility, possibility of solution by groundwater, depth to favorable host rock, and proximity to human populations.

The potentially political issue of earthquake prediction and precautions continued to receive scientific attention. The Palmdale Bulge, located in southern California, northeast of the intersection of the San Andreas and Garlock faults, continued to be a topic of interest and concern. An area of 32,400 square miles (83 916 km²) has undergone episodes of "quiet" uplift and collapse. An intensive leveling program conducted in 1978 by 36 teams from national, state, and local agencies revealed that the total structure has tilted northward. The question as to whether the bulge may be the precursor to a large earthquake remains to be answered. An earthquake of magnitude 5.9 shook northcentral California on August 6. This was called a geologists' earthquake because it afforded scientists an opportunity to check on data provided by many monitoring devices.

Cooperative Projects. The 18-year cooperative mapping project carried on by the U. S. Geological Survey (U. S. G. S.) and Kentucky was completed in December 1978 when the last of 707 geological maps of the state was issued. Each map covers an area of 50 to 60 square miles (130 km² to 155 km²). The project, undertaken to help revitalize the depressed coal-mining economy, cost $21 million.

International cooperation in geology is being centralized under the International Union of Geological Sciences in cooperation with UNESCO. More than 100 countries are associated, 67 being full participants. Sixty-two cooperative projects, each concerned with specific problems—such as major geologic events, distribution of mineral deposits, and data processing—were under way in 1979. Students from Columbia University's Lamont-Doherty Geological Observatory and from China were investigating the South China Sea.

U. S. G. S. Centennial. The centennial of the establishment of the U. S. G. S. was celebrated. Its 1979 budget exceeded $640 million and its permanent staff numbers about 13,000.

Dinosaur Extinction. Two additions were made to the lengthy list of dinosaur extinction theories. The first theory visualizes a cosmic event, possibly a supernova, showering the earth with death-dealing cosmic rays. The rays are known to destroy ozone and a thousandfold increase could reduce the total ozone by 89%, nitrogen oxide would increase greatly, and 10 times more ultraviolet radiation would reach the land surface This is not an entirely new concept but the investigators discovered a high concentration of the element iridium, usually rare in the earth's crust but more common in cosmic rays, in deposits dated at 65 million years old—the time of dinosaur extinction. The second theory has an earth-related mechanism. There is evidence that the Arctic Ocean became essentially landlocked during the age of dinosaurs. Consequently it is supposed that the surface waters became almost fresh by inflow from numerous north flowing rivers. At the end of the Cretaceous, so the theory goes, the fresh water "cap" was released to flood the oceans and upset climates and life everywhere.

WILLIAM LEE STOKES, *University of Utah*

GEORGIA

Business activity and crime made headline news in Georgia in 1979.

Atlanta Development. The recognized growth of the Sun Belt and the anticipated opening of the expanded airport facility stimulated business activity in Atlanta. Georgia Pacific, which announced plans in 1978 to move its corporate headquarters to Atlanta, expanded the scope of the facility to include hotel, apartments, and rental space. The new structure will become the tallest building in the southeast. Marathon Realty Company of Toronto announced plans for an office building project in downtown Atlanta. The $41.7 million Apparel Mart containing permanent display space for manufacturers and a fashion theater opened in Atlanta with the aim of dominating the southeastern apparel market. Commerzbank of West Germany, Banco do Brasil, and Lloyds Bank of London opened offices in Atlanta to meet the banking needs of international manufacturing investors.

The new midfield terminal at Hartsfield Airport will feature an international concourse allowing a 300% increase in the number of international flights out of Atlanta. The first six mile (9.6 km) link of the city's metropolitan rapid rail transit system opened in July.

Legislation. A $2.7 billion budget provided pay increases for state school teachers, university system personnel, and state employees. It also provided modest increases in benefits for welfare recipients and funds to complete the statewide kindergarten program.

Popular initiative, which would allow citizens to petition for referenda similar to California's Proposition 13, was buried in a House committee after passing the Senate. A uniform recall bill, setting up a system for recall elections for local and state officials—including members of the General Assembly—was approved.

Gov. George Busbee's proposal for permanent property tax relief for homeowners and farmers, which would require a 1980 constitutional amendment, passed the Senate but remained in a House committee. The state's usury laws were rewritten to raise the legal limit on interest rates that lending institutions may charge for loans, including home mortgages. A move to make the birthday of Martin Luther King, Jr., a state holiday was voted down by the House, and the ERA remained in committee.

Crime. Atlanta made national headlines late in the year when the homicide count soared to 183, a 63% increase over 1978. The murder rate, along with a sharp rise in other major crimes, led Governor Busbee to assign state patrol troopers to assist city police.

Other Events. Georgia Sen. Herman Talmadge was denounced by the U. S. Senate for mishandling of funds. Ted Turner, owner of Turner Communications, Inc., scheduled a 24-hour national television news program to begin in mid-1980. The program will utilize studios in Washington and New York. It will be beamed to a telecommunications satellite, which will distribute it to cable television systems.

KAY BECK, *Georgia State University*

Herman Talmadge, U. S. senator (D-GA) since 1957, was denounced by the Senate for mishandling funds.

UPI

─────── **GEORGIA • Information Highlights** ───────

Area: 58,876 square miles (152 489 km²).
Population (Jan. 1979 est.): 5,109,000.
Chief Cities (1976 est.): Atlanta, the capital, 425,666; Columbus, 162,599; Macon, 121,898.
Government (1979): *Chief Officers*—governor, George D. Busbee (D); lt. gov., Zell Miller (D). *General Assembly*—Senate, 56 members; House of Representatives, 180 members.
Education (1977–78): *Enrollment*—public elementary schools, 663,110 pupils; public secondary, 426,515; colleges and universities (1978–79), 174,867 students. *Public school expenditures* $1,336,190,000 ($1,111 per pupil).
State Finances (fiscal year 1978): *Revenues,* $4,137,-333,000; *expenditures,* $3,892,982,000.
Personal Income (1978): $34,087,000,000; per capita, $6,705.
Labor Force (July 1979): *Nonagricultural wage and salary earners,* 2,013,000; *unemployed,* 132,300 (5.6% of total force).

GERMANY

Relations between the Federal Republic of Germany (West Germany) and the German Democratic Republic (East Germany or DDR) remained fairly stable throughout 1979. New restrictions on foreign newsmen in East Germany brought protests from the Bonn government, and West German Chancellor Helmut Schmidt, who visited all the other Soviet-bloc countries during the year, made it a point to bypass the DDR. East Berlin pointed out that Schmidt could not very well have gone to the DDR since he was not invited. At the same time, both sides let it be known that they were still interested in increased economic cooperation.

Despite efforts by the West German government and various public and private agencies to keep alive a sense of community with the East German people, West German interest in the affairs of the DDR continued to decline. A public opinion poll disclosed that only 38% of the West German public followed closely the developments in the DDR; 51% were "less interested"; and 10% had no interest at all. Those who showed little interest were found primarily in the age group of 14 to 29 years—the generation which will soon determine West German politics. Of all interviewees, 70% had never been in East Germany.

Meanwhile, East German officials made it clear that they were opposed to expanding diplomatic contacts with West Germany so long as the Federal Republic adhered to its claim of an overall German nation. A change would be considered only if West Germany acknowledged the existence of a separate DDR citizenship. Without such an acknowledgement, it was averred, East German citizens would have no legal security in the Federal Republic.

Trade between East and West Germany remained at approximately the 1978 level, but for the first time East German exports to the Federal Republic exceeded slightly the latter's exports to the DDR. Tourism between the two countries also remained steady, as 8 million West Germans visited the DDR and 1.4 million East Germans visited the Federal Republic.

FEDERAL REPUBLIC OF GERMANY
(West Germany)

In May 1979, the Federal Republic celebrated the 30th anniversary of its founding. Once again, pride in what had been achieved was tempered by sadness over the existence of a separate East German state. Nor could the country's affluence conceal a growing uneasiness about the persistence of several problems. Many worried about the erosion of civil liberties resulting from antiterrorist laws enacted in recent years. Others were concerned about the deterioration of the environment, the health hazards caused by pollution and nuclear energy, and the continuing arms race between East and West.

The Chancellorship. Chancellor Helmut Schmidt, of the Social Democratic Party (SPD), continued to lead his coalition government of Social Democrats and right-of-center Free Democrats (FDP) with a steady hand. Schmidt's prestige continued to grow, but more so abroad than at home. With parliamentary elections due in 1980, the opposition parties—the conservative Christian Democratic Union (CDU) and its Bavarian offshoot, the Christian Social Union (CSU)—decided to replace the colorless Helmut Kohl with the fiery, highly articulate Franz Josef Strauss as their candidate for the chancellorship. Though ultraconservative, Strauss, the minister-president of Bavaria and a former defense and finance minister in the federal government, seemed the only one with a chance to defeat the redoubtable Schmidt.

Nazism and Neo-Nazism. One topic that preoccupied West Germans in one form or another during much of the year was Nazism. World War II Nazi war crimes became a legislative issue in 1979 when the statute of limitations was to have expired and new prosecutions barred. After a prolonged and bitter debate, the *Bundestag*, by a vote of 255 to 222, abolished the statute of limitations for murder. Many felt that the vote might have gone the other way had not the U. S. television series *Holocaust* been aired in West Germany while the issue was under consideration. *Holocaust* deeply impressed many West Germans and led them to support the abolition of the statute. Still, its removal was expected to have more symbolic than real significance since prosecution of war criminals has become extremely difficult. After more than 30 years, witnesses are hard to find and their testimony often uncertain. In 1979, a number of indictments were dismissed for lack of evidence.

Meanwhile, neo-Nazi groups grew bolder and more visible. While the number of neo-Nazis appeared to remain small, their illegal activities increased, according to the federal ministry of the interior. These right-wing extremists operate in small conspiratorial units, modeled after leftist terrorist groups. They obtain

---

—— WEST GERMANY · Information Highlights ——

Official Name: Federal Republic of Germany.
Location: North-central Europe.
Area: 97,883 square miles (253 517 km²). West Berlin, 186 square miles (481 km²).
Population (1979 est.): 61,200,000.
Chief Cities (Dec. 1977): Bonn, the capital, 284,000; Hamburg, 1,680,300; Munich, 1,313,900.
Government: *Head of state,* Karl Carstens, president (took office July 1979). *Head of government,* Helmut Schmidt, federal chancellor (took office May 1974). *Legislature*—Parliament: Bundesrat and Bundestag.
Monetary Unit: Deutsche mark (1.7860 d. marks equal U. S.$1, Nov. 1979).
Manufactures (major products): Iron, steel, coal, cement, chemicals, machinery, ships, vehicles.
Agriculture (major products): Grains, potatoes, sugar beets.

UPI

Outgoing President Walter Scheel congratulates his successor, Karl Carstens, 64-year-old president of the Bundestag.

money and arms from robberies and break-ins, harass Jews and political opponents, and are known to have planned raids on the Berlin Wall and North Atlantic Treaty Organization (NATO) installations. One such group received jail sentences of 4 to 11 years.

Presidential Elections. The Nazi issue also played a role in the May 23 presidential election. In late 1978, it was disclosed that the CDU/CSU candidate, Karl Carstens, had been a member of the Nazi party. Carstens said that he had joined the party for the sake of his education and career. In 1948, a West German tribunal ruled that his affiliation was only nominal, and it cleared him of any misdeeds. Still, his nomination for the presidency led to demonstrations in several West German cities in the early part of 1979. The issue was somewhat defused when the popular incumbent president, Walter Scheel (FDP), disclosed that he, too, had been a Nazi party member. Carstens, the speaker of the *Bundestag* and a former professor of international law, received 528 of 1,036 electoral votes to defeat Annemarie Renger (SPD), his predecessor in the *Bundestag* post, for the presidency.

Economy. On the whole, the West German economy performed remarkably well in 1979. Even a series of paralyzing snowstorms early in the year had no prolonged effects on production. In later months, however, there were signs of a possible change in the economic climate. The annual rate of inflation rose to 5.3% in September (compared with 2.2% in 1978), and car production was 9.4% lower in July 1979 than it had been in July 1978. To assure the

country's continued economic growth, the 1980 budget provided for an 11% increase in expenditures on research and development.

The Federal Republic took advantage of its still strong economic position to help bolster the U. S. dollar and other ailing currencies. Several steps were taken toward that end, including the upward revaluation of the deutsche mark by 2.5%. Allocations for international economic cooperation were increased by 12.5% in the 1980 budget. Despite these efforts, there were repeated complaints from foreign governments that Bonn did not contribute as much to the stabilization of the world economy as it could have.

Social Conditions. West Germany's birth rate, already one of the lowest in the world, continued to fall in 1979. The decline was attributed in part to the fact that increasing numbers of women no longer wished to stay home and raise children, and in part to the financial burdens that children impose on a family. The federal government provided only half as much financial aid to families with children as the Italian government and only one third of that provided by the French government. A federal commission therefore began drafting a program for the support of such families.

Continuing a trend that began in the mid-1960's, the number of marriages also declined. In 1978 there were 8.5% fewer marriages than in the previous year.

Energy and the environment were again major concerns of the government and people. The mid-year oil crisis caused Chancellor Helmut Schmidt to propose a sweeping energy conservation program. In a July 4 speech to the *Bundestag,* Schmidt called for the increased use of domestic coal reserves to meet the nation's future energy needs. The use of nuclear power would ultimately be required for continued economic growth, he said, but controversies surrounding that industry made coal the fuel of choice in the short term. Because the construction of new nuclear power plants has been banned until the problem of waste disposal is resolved, the use of nuclear power in West Germany has been increasing more slowly than in other Western European countries.

A major political scandal erupted when it was revealed that a chemical plant in Hamburg had for years been polluting the air with lethal gases. In state elections held in neighboring Bremen in October 1978, four deputies were elected from a new environmentalist coalition (*Die Grünen*).

Foreign Affairs. In January 1979, Schmidt joined the leaders of France, Great Britain, and the United States for two days of talks on the island of Guadaloupe. Topics of discussion were the SALT II negotiations; Western relations with China and the Soviet Union; and the events in Iran, Turkey, the Middle East, Vietnam and Cambodia, and Africa. As a leading economic power, Germany was asked to develop a foreign aid plan for the rehabilitation of Turkey. Chancellor Schmidt was careful to play down West Germany's rise in world status, however, so as not to arouse domestic fears about its new role. He also stressed the fact that West Germany was not and did not wish to be a nuclear power.

In keeping with this policy of restraint, Bonn was also determined to avoid any confrontation with the Soviet Union. It would not allow the

United States to install additional nuclear launchers on West German soil to counter the new and more powerful Soviet SS-20 missiles, unless other Western European states also agreed. In the same vein, Bonn worked hard for an overall improvement of Western-Soviet relations. On visits to the United States, Schmidt and Foreign Minister Hans-Dietrich Genscher urged ratification of the SALT II pact. Both men also reacted more positively than U. S. leaders to proposals by Soviet President Leonid Brezhnev for the reduction of nuclear missiles in Europe.

In the June elections for the first parliament of the European Community, nearly 66% of the West German electorate cast their ballots. The CDU/CSU won 42 seats, the SPD 35, and the FDP 4.

GERMAN DEMOCRATIC REPUBLIC
(East Germany)

The German Democratic Republic celebrated its 30th anniversary on October 7. There were extensive ceremonies and parades, with Leonid Brezhnev and other Soviet-bloc dignitaries in attendance. The East German government proclaimed a sweeping amnesty, affecting as many as 20,000 prisoners. Among the first to be released was Rudolf Bahro, the author of an incisive critique of the East German regime, *Die Alternative,* published in West Germany in 1977. The government also announced an increase in old-age pensions and other subsidies. Brezhnev used the occasion to announce the withdrawal of 20,000 Soviet troops (5% of the total) and 1,000 tanks (14%) from East Germany. At the same time, he proposed to the United States a mutual reduction of missiles stationed in Europe.

Despite all the self-congratulatory speeches at the anniversary celebrations, East Germany continued to suffer a deep malaise. The affluence of West Germany, ever visible on television and reported by West German visitors, had a demoralizing effect. The government tried to counter this by making Western goods more readily available and by limiting contacts between East Germans and Westerners. Informing foreigners about economic difficulties or po-

A shopping arcade connects an office building with apartment houses in a rebuilt section of Stuttgart.

UPI

— **EAST GERMANY** · **Information Highlights** —

Official Name: German Democratic Republic.
Location: North-central Europe.
Area: 41,768 square miles (108 179 km²).
Population (1979 est.): 16,700,000.
Chief Cities (Dec. 1977): East Berlin, the capital, 1,-118,142; Leipzig, 564,306; Dresden, 512,490.
Government: *Head of state,* Erich Honecker, chairman of the Council of State. *Head of government,* Willi Stoph, chairman of the Council of Ministers Presidium. *First secretary of the Socialist Unity (Communist) party,* Erich Honecker (took office 1971). *Legislature* (unicameral)—Volkskammer (People's Chamber).
Monetary Unit: DDR mark (2.05 DDR marks equal U. S.$1, 1978).
Manufactures (major products): Electrical and precision engineering products, fishing vessels, steel, machinery, chemicals.
Agriculture (major products): Potatoes, grains, sugar beets, meat and dairy products.

litical repression in the DDR was made a criminal offense. Western newsmen, accused of emphasizing weaknesses and ignoring positive achievements in East Germany, were subjected to new restrictions. Dissident writers were barred from publishing their works abroad, and many dissidents were expelled from the country or indicted for criminal offenses.

Economy. Agricultural and industrial production failed to meet the goals specified in the Economic Plan for 1979. This was due partly to the very severe winter of 1978–79, which interfered seriously with work and transportation. Productivity grew by only 4%, compared with 5.2% in 1978. At the same time, private consumption increased by 5.4%. Exports, upon which the DDR is especially dependent because of its lack of raw materials, increased by only 7%, as against 10% in 1978. Rising oil prices and labor shortages also weighed heavily on the economy. Despite these difficulties, government subsidies helped keep down basic food prices, utility rates, and rents.

The government planned to meet future energy needs by increasing the output of nuclear power. Existing reactors provided 5% of the nation's electricity, and eight new facilities were under construction. With the help of the Soviet Union, East Germany eventually hopes to produce half of its electricity by nuclear power.

Social Conditions. An official government survey reported in 1979 that 88% of all East German women over the age of 16 held a job, and that one third of all polytechnic and university graduates in the country were women. In addition, one fourth of all mayors and school principals, one fifth of all county medical officers, and one sixth of all agricultural and industrial managers were women. Nevertheless, there remained a serious shortage of skilled labor. To relieve the problem, efforts were made to channel high school students into engineering and technical careers.

West German telecasts of *Holocaust* were also widely viewed in the DDR. Although Nazi war crimes had been discussed for some time in East German schools and mass media, the plight of the Jews had been dealt with only peripherally. It was treated as merely one aspect of the persecution of all "antifascists." East German viewers therefore had much to learn from the *Holocaust* series. East Germany has no statute of limitations for war crimes, nor has it ever granted an amnesty for such an offense.

Foreign Affairs. Erich Honecker, the chairman of the state council and secretary general of the Socialist Unity Party, reaffirmed his opposition to the white minority governments in southern Africa. He met with the leaders of the Rhodesian and South African liberation movements and made substantial financial donations as an expression of solidarity. Early in the year, Honecker visited Angola, Zambia, and Mozambique to conclude a series of agreements on economic and cultural collaboration.

In the Far East, East Germany followed the leadership of the Soviet Union in supporting Vietnam against both China and the Pol Pot regime in Cambodia.

WEST BERLIN

West Berlin, a Western international enclave in East Germany, had another rather uneventful year in 1979. Elections in March left its parliament virtually unchanged, with an SPD/FDP coalition remaining in control. Indicative of the city's shrinking population, the electorate had decreased by 5% since the previous elections in 1975.

With foreign residents constituting more than 10% of the city's population, Mayor Dietrich Stobbe proposed measures to expedite full integration. Citizenship qualifications would be relaxed, and foreigners would be made eligible for jobs previously reserved for Germans. In order to establish better communications with the large Turkish community in West Berlin, Stobbe also suggested the appointment of Turks as policemen. The hope was that such measures would help reduce the rising crime rate among foreign youths, most of whom remained social outcasts.

To strengthen further its economic and cultural ties with West Berlin, the Bonn government agreed to reduce airplane fares to and from the city. Subsidies for individual tickets were increased by 20% and for group flights by 40%.

ANDREAS DORPALEN
The Ohio State University

Ursel Lorenzen, a West German secretary at NATO headquarters, defected to East Germany March 5.

UPI

Ghanaians stage a rally in support of the presidential bid of Hilla Limann of the People's National Party. Dr. Limann was elected in a runoff and Ghana returned to democratic rule.

GHANA

Preparations for a return to civilian rule were overshadowed by the violent overthrow of the year-old regime of Gen. F. W. K. Akuffo.

Economy. By January 1979 the estimated inflation rate exceeded 200%, the black market cedi exchange rate was c10 to the dollar (official rate c2.75 = $1), such primary goods as steel, cement, and gasoline were scarce, and even basic consumer goods could not be found. Direct government aid and commercial loans from Britain and the United States had little effect. By January more than 70,000 workers were out on strike. The cocoa crop was smaller than in previous years and the world price for the product fell. These factors provided the military the excuse for the June coup.

Politics. General Akuffo had promised a return to civilian government by July 1, 1979. A Constitutional Assembly submitted a draft report in November 1978. The military recognized the legality of political parties and ten new ones were formed. In May a Constitution was approved that created an executive president and a directly elected 140-person assembly. Akuffo's government granted amnesties for previous political offenses and boards were established to certify all candidates. Subsequently more than 100 civilians were banned from holding office. Ghana's economy continued to falter amid rumors of widespread corruption involving senior military officers. A clause in the Constitution exempting members of the military government from financial investigations started the chain of events which brought down Akuffo's government.

In May Flight-Lt. Jerry Rawlings, leader of junior officers and enlisted men, failed in an attempt to overthrow the government and was jailed. His actions had made him a hero to the common people and a further revolt was planned. On June 4 the army rank and file rebelled, released Rawlings, and after heavy fighting succeeded in seizing power on June 5. Rawlings announced the takeover as temporary and that the elections would go on as scheduled.

A newly created 14-man Armed Forces Revolutionary Council (AFRC) announced its intention to punish corrupt officers of previous regimes and to redistribute the wealth to the common people. Gen. I. K. Acheampong, former head of state, and a high ranking associate were tried and executed. Another group of 50 former government officials was accused of anti-state activities. Six were condemned to die, including General Akuffo and Gen. Akwasi A. Afrifa, a chief of state in the late 1960's. They were shot at an Accra firing range before 5,000 cheering witnesses. Pleas to stop such summary executions poured in from all parts of the world. Nigeria shut down petroleum shipments; Upper Volta reduced its export of meat; and other states refused to extend credit. Under such pressure, the AFRC limited subsequent sentences to long prison terms.

Elections for the assembly and the executive took place during the turmoil. The People's National Party, headed by Hilla Limann, won 68 assembly seats to 41 for its closest rival, the Popular Front Party of Victor Owusu. A runoff between these two leaders was necessary to determine the president, and Dr. Limann won by over 300,000 votes. The AFRC handed over power to the Third Republic of Ghana on September 24. The new president promised a concerted attack on the economic problems.

HARRY A. GAILEY
San Jose State University

GHANA • Information Highlights

Official Name: Republic of Ghana.
Location: West Africa.
Area: 92,100 square miles (238 538 km²).
Population (1979 est.): 11,300,000.
Chief Cities (1973 est.): Accra, the capital, 848,800; Kumasi, 249,000.
Government: *Head of state and government,* Hilla Limann, president (took office Sept. 1979). *Legislature*—National Assembly (dissolved Jan. 1972).
Monetary Unit: New cedi (2.75 new cedis equal U. S. $1, Aug. 1979).
Manufactures (major products): Minerals, lumber, cement, aluminum.
Agriculture (major products): Corn, manioc, coconuts, cocoa beans, sugarcane.

PHOTOS UPI

New residents at 10 Downing: Mrs. Thatcher moved in after Mr. Callaghan was forced to vacate.

GREAT BRITAIN

The most momentous event of the year in Great Britain was the general election of May 3 (*see* Special Report, page 237).

But the arrival of Margaret Thatcher (*see also* BIOGRAPHY) at 10 Downing Street had no immediate or dramatic effect on Britain's severe economic problems, which continued to worsen. The new administration argued that this deterioration was only temporary, and that its cure, though unpleasant, was a necessary precondition for the country's economic recovery. Inflation, which had been brought down to less than 10% by the outgoing Labour government, moved up toward 20% as a result of increased indirect taxes, the rise in interest rates, international price hikes, the removal of government controls over pricing, and large wage settlements. Unemployment, at 1.35 millions, showed little sign of abating, and as the year ended the lending rate stood at a record 17%. This not only discouraged industrial investment, already sluggish because of a slump in consumer demand, but hit hardest at people, especially the middle classes, buying their own homes. They found they had to pay 15% interest on capital sums which were, by British standards, already high. The massive interest rates paid in London, combined with North Sea oil which makes Britain almost self-sufficient in energy, meant that the value

of the pound sterling was high in the months following the Conservative victory. It varied between U. S. $2.10 and $2.20. In turn this made British exports, already over-priced, more expensive to buyers abroad and at home exacerbated the problems of high imports, increasing unemployment, and falling production.

Labor Movement. The year began inauspiciously. Heavy snow, much worse than is usual in Britain, cut off parts of the country and produced severe communication difficulties. These were compounded by a series of damaging strikes—in the health service, among workers for local government, including garbage collectors, and on the railroads, which are a vital part of British communications. Worst of all, truckers went on strike in support of a pay claim, which meant that goods, food, and sometimes vital supplies were not moved. A number of the striking drivers picketed factories where goods were being transported, and the violent scenes as strikers fought with working drivers were witnessed on nationwide television. This led to demands for an end to so-called "secondary picketing." Prime Minister James Callaghan, who had been attending the Guadeloupe summit of Western leaders, made a serious error on returning home when he attempted to play down the situation, asking "Crisis, what crisis?" and saying that he did not see the mounting chaos. The public, confused, worried, *(Continued on page 238)*

(Continued on page 238)

Margaret Thatcher Becomes Prime Minister

Britain's first general election since October 1974 was held on May 3, 1979, and resulted in a substantial victory for the Conservative Party, led by Margaret Thatcher. She became the nation's first female prime minister.

The election was made inevitable by the defeat of the sitting Labour government in a House of Commons vote at the end of March. Under the British parliamentary system the government of the day must command the "confidence" of the House; in effect, it must be able to put through its legislation by having the support of a majority of members of Parliament. The Labour government, headed by James Callaghan, had long been in a minority, but had managed to stay in office by a series of deals and bargains with the many smaller parties in the House. By the beginning of 1979, however, it became clear that these minor parties were beginning to fear the electoral unpopularity of supporting the government for much longer.

The end came on March 28 when the government faced a vote of "no confidence" tabled by the Conservative opposition. In spite of a host of last minute deals, the Labour side lost by a vote of 311 to 310, and Callaghan immediately announced the general election.

The voters were offered a straight choice between the two main parties. The Labourites campaigned on their record. They had brought the country through its worst economic period since the 1940's; inflation, which had been running at more than 25%, was now below 10%. The labor unions, in spite of serious difficulties at the beginning of the year, were reasonably inclined to cooperate with a Labour government and might instead oppose a Conservative administration. Callaghan argued, too, that Conservative fiscal plans would sharply increase the cost of living for ordinary families.

Mrs. Thatcher's Conservatives, by contrast, offered an entirely new start. Britain, they said, had been held back by socialist dogma which had stressed the redistribution of wealth rather than its creation. They promised a new atmosphere in which the enterprising and hardworking would be offered incentives and opportunities to get the economy working again. To this end, the Conservatives promised cuts in income tax, a relaxation of controls on businesses, and massive cuts in public expenditure which would bring a rapid fall in the rate of inflation.

The Liberals were another party hoping to do well; they had held 13 seats in the old Parliament. They claimed to offer an alternative to what they termed the "two-party dogfight." They had the most encouraging start to the campaign when their candidate in a by-election in Edge Hill, Liverpool, won a huge and unexpected victory. This result was more a tribute to the popularity and hard work of the candidate than a valid augury for the Liberals' overall performance, though their leader, David Steel, emerged as one of the most trusted and well-liked politicians in the country.

On March 30, just two days after the general election had been announced, an Irish terrorist bomb killed Airey Neave, Conservative spokesman on Northern Ireland and one of Mrs. Thatcher's closest lieutenants. One result was that all political meetings had to be conducted with strict security. Some meetings were not announced publicly and were attended only by people who had been informed privately.

From the start, the opinion polls indicated a clear Conservative victory. A single poll taken a few days before the election found a small Labour lead, but this proved false. The Conservatives decided on a low-key campaign on the grounds that only a foolish mistake on their side could deprive them of their inevitable victory. For this reason, Mrs. Thatcher declined to debate Callaghan on television.

Labour hoped to capitalize on the unpopularity of the Common Market, and the allegedly high price Britain has to pay for membership. This proved to be less than a gripping issue, and the party campaign came to stress more and more the threat to jobs and prices if the Conservatives were returned. There is some evidence that economic issues reduced the Tory lead. The Conservatives announced plans for the sale of homes built and rented by local government. This appears to have increased the Tory vote in working class areas.

Meanwhile, Labour candidates predicted that their party had an excellent chance of victory and that its total vote would be even higher than it had been in the previous election, which it had won. This proved to be true, but Labour was swamped by an even greater increase in the Conservative vote. The final result gave the Tories 339 seats in Parliament and 43.9% of the popular vote; Labour took 268 seats from 36.9% of the vote, and the Liberals managed only 11 seats from 13.8% of the vote. The splinter Scottish National Party was almost wiped out, losing 9 of its 11 seats, and the Northern Ireland Protestants captured 10 seats. The biggest swing toward the Conservatives was in southern England, while Scotland actually moved toward the outgoing Labour side. The extreme racist National Front took barely 0.5%.

Mrs. Thatcher's victory was clear only a few hours after the polls had closed. Queen Elizabeth II outlined the program of Mrs. Thatcher's new government on May 15.

Simon Hoggart

Queen Elizabeth, Mrs. Thatcher, and other leaders attend a reception during the Commonwealth Conference.

and sometimes frightened, resented this attitude from the leader of a party that had been elected largely because of its claim to have good relations with the labor unions.

The government refused to declare a state of emergency on the grounds that this would increase resentment and make the situation worse. This decision proved correct, and week by week the strikes did peter out. But the government's reaction had clearly been inadequate; the government had relaxed the (voluntary) limits on the pay of poorer workers; and later it tried to reach what it called a "concordat" with the unions about future pay scales and union bargaining. This was a vague and largely meaningless document which did not succeed in its

─── GREAT BRITAIN • Information Highlights ───

Official Name: United Kingdom of Great Britain and Northern Ireland.
Location: Island, western Europe.
Area: 94,250 square miles (244 108 km²).
Population (1979 est.): 55,800,000.
Chief Cities (1976 est.): London, the capital, 7,028,-200; Birmingham, 1,058,800; Glasgow, 856,012; Liverpool, 539,700.
Government: *Head of state,* Elizabeth II, queen (acceded Feb. 1952). *Head of government,* Margaret Thatcher, prime minister (took office May 1979). *Legislature*—Parliament: House of Lords and House of Commons.
Monetary Unit: Pound (0.4611 pound equals U. S.$1, Dec. 1979).
Manufactures (major products): Metal products, motor vehicles, aircraft, textiles, chemicals.
Agriculture (major products): Wheat, barley, oats, potatoes, livestock, livestock products.

main function, which was to persuade the public that the government still was able to cope with the unions. Callaghan's own Labour Party lost no time in telling him that his principal mistake had been to attempt to hold wage rises down to 5%. Economically, this figure might have been sensible; psychologically it seemed pitifully small to workers who had suffered cuts in their standard of living for three years and who hoped to begin retrieving losses in 1979. The result was the destruction of the government's policy on pay and a serious setback in the fight against inflation.

Pre-election Days. The disasters were not over. In March, the government's plans for a limited measure of home rule for Scotland and Wales were put to referenda. Though the plans were modest enough, offering both divisions barely more powers than a U. S. state legislature has, they failed to reach the necessary voting for implementation. In Wales the plans were thrown out by a contemptuous 4–1 margin. These results, after five years of planning, not only killed devolution, as it was called, for some time, but gave the 14 members of the nationalist parties in the Westminster parliament no further reason for supporting Callaghan's minority government and so led to his downfall.

The government lost the crucial confidence vote in the House of Commons on March 28. Two days later, before the election campaign had really begun, Irish republican terrorists murdered their most prominent victim up to that time, Mr. Airey Neave, who was a personal friend of Mrs. Thatcher and her chief spokesman on the Northern Ireland problem. Neave, a war hero, had been the first Briton to escape from the notorious Colditz (Germany) prison camp. He was killed by a bomb which had been attached to the underside of his car and which exploded as he left the Commons car park.

April was devoted to the election campaign, and was interrupted by serious rioting in the London suburb of Southall. A demonstration by opponents of the extreme right-wing racist National Front, who were holding an election meeting, turned to violence as demonstrators fought against the police. One white demonstrator, a teacher named Blair Peach, was clubbed to death, almost certainly by police, though no conclusive evidence was found against any individual. By the end of the year the National Front was in disarray, with a declining membership and a humiliating electoral record; its leaders attributed the strength of the campaign against it to the Anti-Nazi League.

Election Aftermath. On their return to office, the Conservatives swiftly set about implementing their promised changes, mainly in the economic field. Income tax was cut to 30%, with the top rate reduced from 82% to 60%. However, indirect taxes on goods were almost doubled, from 8% to 15%. All restrictions on pay claims and price rises were removed, in the hopes that the bracing forces of the free market would restore strength to British industry and commerce. The government began to sell off to private buyers parts of nationalized industries such as British Airways, where it planned to sell some of the stock. Similar plans to sell publicly-held oil interests were formulated but rejected later under the premise that only a fool would sell off oil at that time. Sweeping cuts in public spending were announced, but these proved easier to plan than to implement.

Meanwhile, the defeated Labour Party began one of its periodic bitter wrangles which threatened this time to destroy the British two-party system. The split was between "activists," prominent grassroots members of the party, who blamed moderate nonsocialist measures for the party's failure in the election. They claimed some support among members of Parliament (MPs), though the majority of MPs felt that they more truly represented the moderate bulk of Labour supporters. At Labour's annual conference in October, the left-wing succeeded in changing the party's rules so as to give themselves much greater control over policy and the choice of MPs. The left was opposed by party leader Callaghan who found himself the scapegoat for the election defeat. He attempted to defuse the issue by backing a full inquiry into the party's future, though the membership of the inquiry was successfully packed by the left. At the end of the year there were growing signs that the right, or moderate wing of Labour—which had been in government for 17 of the past 34 years—might attempt to break away or else join the centrist Liberal party.

Northern Ireland. In Northern Ireland, slight progress during the year was masked by the ap-

British troops remained in Northern Ireland as the situation continued tense after Lord Mountbatten's murder.

palling murders by the Irish Republican Army of Lord Mountbatten (*see also* OBITUARIES) and his grandson and two friends, who had been boating in the west of Ireland, and, on the same day, the killing of 18 British soldiers. These events, which horrified both the British and Irish public, led to greater cooperation on security between Britain and the Republic of Ireland. However, the cooperation did not match up to Britain's expectations and offended some of the more traditional politicians in the Republic. The Bennett Report found that security forces had "ill-treated" IRA and Protestant suspects especially when held in police custody, and the "H-block" protest by prisoners in the Maze prison continued. They were demanding status as political prisoners and backed their protests by living in conditions of absolute squalor. Political progress proved minute, largely because Ulster's politicians had no forum in which to speak. In an attempt to remedy this the new Conservative government tried to set up a round-table conference. This had to be postponed because of the refusal of several important parties to join in.

The European Community and Zimbabwe. Britain began a determined effort to get what it saw as a fairer deal from the Common Market. Because most Market funds are derived from industry to support agriculture, Britain, though the third poorest of the nine members, makes a net contribution of nearly £1,000 million. Thatcher's attempts to change this met total resistance from the other eight heads of government at the November summit meeting in Ireland.

The Thatcher government played an active role in seeking a cease-fire agreement in Zimbabwe (Rhodesia). Lord Carrington, Britain's foreign secretary, and other leaders welcomed the agreement which was signed in London on December 21. Lord Soames was named to oversee implementation of the pact.

Scandals. Jeremy Thorpe, former leader of the Liberal Party, and three other men were acquitted on charges of conspiracy to murder a man who claimed to have once had a homosexual relationship with Thorpe. In spite of the acquittal, the evidence given in court was enough to doom Thorpe's political career. Winston Churchill, grandson of the famous prime minister, admitted at the end of the year that he had had an affair with the former wife of a prominent Arab arms dealer. But Churchill, though an MP, held no government post and no action was taken against him.

Other. Robert Runcie, Bishop of St. Albans, was named as the new Archbishop of Canterbury. Police failed to track down a sex-killer, named the Yorkshire Ripper after the last century's Jack the Ripper. And Trevor Francis became the first soccer player in Britain to be transferred for a fee of £1 million.

SIMON HOGGART, *"The Guardian,"* London

THE ECONOMY

The Conservative government led by Britain's first woman Prime Minister Margaret Thatcher inherited an economy in which growth remained sluggish. When the government came to office in May, unemployment was still slowly falling but inflation had begun to accelerate again.

Output was badly hurt during the first quarter by an exceptionally hard winter and a number of strikes, of which the road haulers' was the most serious. In the second quarter there was sharp recovery fueled partly by very high consumer spending prompted by budget tax changes. But during the remainder of the year the British economy, like others in the developed world, began to move toward recession as the government became determined to squeeze out inflation. Manufacturers' investment intentions became less ambitious and gross domestic product advanced by less than 1%. Low growth in productivity kept unemployment falling for most of the year from its 1978 level of 6.2% of the working population.

At the beginning of the year inflation was not far from its 1978 levels of 9%. Rising wage settlements and the increase in oil prices produced a steady increase in spite of a strengthening pound sterling as North Sea oil production gathered pace. The rise in retail prices was accelerated by the government's switch from direct to indirect taxes which added about 3.5% to the cost and by the end of the year inflation had reached 17%. Average earnings, which grew by 13% in 1978, accelerated 15–16%. But the money stock, which grew 15% in 1978, had been brought down within the government's target range of 9–11% by the end of the year.

The current account of the balance of payments, which was in surplus by £400 million in 1978, suffered from the first quarter strikes, and the high level of consumer spending in the second quarter produced a deficit of £2,300 million during the first half. In spite of the big increase in North Sea oil production, the second half saw no erosion of the first half deficit.

The Conservative government's policies were designed to restrain inflation through strict monetary control and at the same time to restore incentives by cutting direct taxation. In his first budget, presented in June, the Chancellor of the Exchequer Sir Geoffrey Howe cut the top rate of income tax from 83% to 60% and the standard rate from 33% to 30% while reducing the public sector borrowing requirement by 20%. To facilitate these changes, 5% was cut from the planned level of public spending. By these and other similar measures, the Conservatives hoped to restore business confidence, increase investment, and improve the utilization of existing investment.

RODNEY LORD
"The Daily Telegraph," London

THE ARTS

For the British arts, money was the dominating topic of 1979. With the coming to power of a Conservative government, the subject of a cultural mixed economy combining state subsidy and private patronage received a new airing. The budget of the Arts Council was cut; high inflation pushed up costs; an increased value-added tax (VAT) raised the price of all entrance tickets; tax relief to encourage private citizens and corporations to fund artistic projects was discussed but not implemented. Nevertheless, in spite of this anxious atmosphere, a prodigious amount of cultural activity continued.

Theater. Artistic standards are set by the two big national companies, the National Theatre on the south bank of the Thames and the Royal Shakespeare Company at Stratford and at the Aldwych in London. Funded by the Arts Council and local councils, and providing equal income from the box office for every pound sterling of state subsidy, neither company is ever without financial problems or worthwhile productions. At the National, 1979 began with Albert Finney still running in a powerful *Macbeth,* Dorothy Tutin exhibiting rare comic skill in William Congreve's *The Double Dealer,* and productions of Ben Travers and Bernard Shaw comedies. Later in 1979 John Wood dominated audiences with his portrayal of Richard III (the first actor since Laurence Olivier to attempt the role), while Paul Scofield mesmerized in Peter Shaffer's new play, *Amadeus,* based on the life of Mozart. Though interrupted in midyear by a lengthy stagehands' strike, the National managed to mount new plays by Harold Pinter (*Betrayal*), Edward Bond (*The Woman*), and Simon Gray (*Close of Play*), in addition to *Amadeus.* The Royal Shakespeare Company brought Peter Brook's austere *Antony and Cleopatra,* with Glenda Jackson and Alan Howard, to London, and presented Donald Sinden as Othello in Stratford. Among new plays at the Royal Shakespeare Company, Pam Gems' *Piaf* was a sellout.

Alongside the big national companies, nearly 60 commercial theaters in London and 50 building-based companies in the regions, such as the Royal Exchange in Manchester, flourished. The Royal Exchange brought to London for an outstanding season Edward Fox in T. S. Eliot's *Family Reunion* and Vanessa Redgrave in Henrik Ibsen's *Lady from the Sea.* The "alternative theater," London fringe clubs and lunchtime pub performances, opened and closed in large numbers, but some, such as the King's Head Theatre provided, for the price of a pub lunch, plays that have finished on Broadway.

Music. London's four orchestras and the numerous summer music festivals—in Edinburgh, Aldeburgh, Bath, and Cheltenham typically—usually offer a solid year-round quantity of musical performances, although there has been criticism of unadventurous orchestral repertoire and the lack of new works in performance. In 1979, four concerts promoted by the London Orchestral Concert Board broke new ground, including as they did a first performance of a symphony by Maxwell Davies and new foreign works. John Taverner's new opera *Therese* premiered at the Royal Opera House, Covent Garden, but the Royal Opera House often seemed to be overshadowed by the greater artistic cohesion of productions at the English National Opera at the Coliseum. However, both were frequently eclipsed by the artistic level of the tiny Glyndebourne Festival Opera, which puts production talent on a level with musical values. Sir Peter Hall of the National Theatre directed both *Così fan tutte* and *Fidelio* in 1979's program.

Because of the increased level of sophistication among regional opera audiences the Arts Council disbanded its 30-year-old Opera for All and organized Opera 80 instead, to tour more elaborately with full orchestra.

Dance. The dance explosion that has hit North America is only small scale in Britain. In 1979, the scene was enlivened by important visits from international dance companies and by return visits of the Royal Ballet to North America and by the London Festival Ballet to Peking. Small dance groups in the regions have begun to grow in size and stability.

Fine Arts. The Tate Gallery was at the center of a number of events and controversies. After delays of many decades, the Tate Gallery Extension was opened in May 1979, to doubtful comments about its architecture, but general relief that 50% more exhibition space should be available. Pictures and sculpture which the outgoing director, Sir Norman Reid, chose to buy during his tenure of office were under attack by artists such as David Hockney, who accused the Tate of an obsession with abstract art. The newly-appointed director, Alan Bowness, is believed to have wider tastes. From November 1979 the Royal Academy housed a major review of Post-Impressionism, and welcomed over 3,000 visitors a day to its rooms. At its concrete monolith, the Hayward Gallery, the Arts Council organized a survey of "The Thirties," covering British painting, sculpture, and interior design. The Arts Council's work is pervading in its patronage of living artists and of galleries throughout the country.

Television. In 1979, the BBC brought evolution to the small screen with *The Voyages of Charles Darwin,* and *Tinker, Tailor, Soldier, Spy* saw Sir Alec Guinness playing spy-catcher George Smiley. Many young dramatists have found television a useful alternative discipline to live theater, and the BBC continues as the biggest single employer of actors and musicians in the country and as a substitute for a film industry close to demise.

MAUREEN GREEN
Author and Free-Lance Journalist

GREECE

Formal admission into the European Community (EC), Prime Minister Constantine Caramanlis' trip to three Eastern European Communist countries, and the awarding of the Nobel Prize for Literature to a native poet were among the notable events in Greece during 1979. The ever-present Cyprus issue continued to play an important role in foreign policy.

The Common Market. On May 28, Caramanlis and representatives of the EC countries met in Athens to sign documents formally admitting Greece as the 10th member of the Common Market. The actual date of entry was set at Jan. 1, 1981, and a five-year transition period, during which customs and other barriers would be dismantled, was established. The occasion marked a personal triumph for Prime Minister Caramanlis and his New Democracy party government. The Greek parliament ratified the treaty of accession on June 28. Andreas Papandreou, leader of the opposition Panhellenic Socialist Union (PASOK), opposed Greece's entry on the grounds that it would become subordinate to the other EC members.

Foreign Policy. Although he has long been staunchly pro-Western, Caramanlis withdrew Greece from the military wing of the North Atlantic Treaty Organization (NATO) after the Turkish invasion of Cyprus in 1974. By the end of 1979, the breach had still not healed. Irritated by what many Greeks regarded as U. S. President Jimmy Carter's pro-Turkish position in the Cyprus dispute, Caramanlis—with the encouragement of the parliamentary opposition—showed new flexibility in foreign affairs. Early in the year he visited Saudi Arabia, Syria, Yugoslavia, and Rumania. In September it was announced that Soviet vessels would be accepted for repairs at a Greek shipyard on the island of Syros. But the most forceful demonstration of the new attitude came in early October, when Caramanlis visited the Soviet Union, Hungary, and Czechoslovakia. In Moscow he met with President Leonid Brezhnev and Premier Aleksei Kosygin and reached accords for increased cooperation between the two nations. Later in the month, as if to balance matters, he visited West Germany, Great Britain, France, and Italy. In November, Caramanlis went to China, India, and Iraq.

Economy. In a major policy speech opening the International Trade Fair in Salonika September 8, Caramanlis cited inflation and energy conservation as the nation's major domestic challenges. He predicted a 4% increase in the 1979 gross national product and an annual inflation rate of about 20%. Unless some sacrifices were made, he said, the country faced "painful deprivations in the future." On August 21, the government had announced a series of measures to curb inflation: prices, profits, and wages were put under strict control; government spending and bank credit were reduced; and interest rates were increased to encourage savings. Strikes by teachers, civil servants, and bankers also hampered the Greek economy during the year.

Nobel Prize. On October 18, the Swedish Academy announced that the 1979 Nobel Prize for Literature was being awarded to the 68-year-old Greek poet Odysseus Elytis. Elytis was the second Greek poet in 16 years to be cited by the academy; George Seferis won the prize in 1963.

GEORGE J. MARCOPOULOS, *Tufts University*

――――― GREECE • Information Highlights ―――――

Official Name: Hellenic Republic.
Location: Southeastern Europe.
Area: 50,961 square miles (131 990 km²).
Population (1979 est.): 9,500,000.
Chief Cities (1971 census): Athens, the capital, 867,-023; Salonika, 345,799; Piraeus, 187,458.
Government: *Head of state,* Constantine Tsatsos, president (took office June 1975). *Head of government,* Constantine Caramanlis, prime minister (took office July 1974). *Legislature*—Parliament.
Monetary Unit: Drachma (37.37 drachmas equal U. S.$1, Nov. 1979).
Manufactures (major products): Food products, textiles, metals, chemicals, electrical goods, cement, glass.
Agriculture (major products): Grains, citrus fruits, grapes, vegetables, olives and olive oil, tobacco, cotton, livestock, and dairy products.

GREENLAND

May 1, 1979 marked the establishment of home rule for Greenland, an event that followed the holding of a plebiscite in January 1979, which had resulted in a 70% vote in favor of home rule. An election to the 21-seat legislative assembly (*Landsting;* the successor to the advisory *Landsråd*) was held on April 4, 1979.

The various powers of government and administration were to be transferred gradually to Godthaab, the capital. Areas of responsibility affected included taxes, fisheries, hunting, agriculture, labor, social affairs, education, health, and domestic transportation. The Danish government will continue to subsidize Greenland.

History. The inhabitants of Greenland are predominantly Eskimos, whose forebears arrived as long ago as 4,000 years. From 986 A. D., there existed two Norse settlements on the west coast, and Greenland in 1261 submitted to the authority of the king of Norway. When Norway entered into a personal union with Denmark, Greenland was ruled by the union king. Norway was separated from Denmark in 1814, but Greenland was retained as a Danish colony. In 1953, Denmark's new constitution changed the status of Greenland from a colony to a Danish county.

In 1972 a committee composed of Greenlanders was appointed to investigate how home rule might be carried out. In 1975 a broader Commission for Home Rule in Greenland was established, and in November 1978 the Danish parliament passed a law on Home Rule for Greenland.

ERIK J. FRIIS
"The Scandinavian-American Bulletin"

GUYANA

The Republic of Guyana suffered serious political conflict and social unrest during 1979. For the first time since coming to office in 1964 the government of Prime Minister Lynden Forbes Burnham was in real danger of losing power. During the early part of the year, the country also suffered the shock and adverse foreign publicity of the mass murder-suicide at Jonestown in November 1978.

Politics. The drafting of a new constitution by the Constituent Assembly moved very slowly while national attention focused on other domestic issues—the Jonestown débacle, strikes, the gasoline shortage, and the trial of 23 officials and businessmen for foreign exchange violations. The opposition People's Progressive Party (PPP) boycotted the drafting altogether.

Early in July, the Working People's Alliance (WPA) declared itself a formal political party. It was headed by Walter Rodney, a leading intellectual, and Kusi Kwayama, formerly Sydney King of Burnham's ruling People's National Congress (PNC). Days later, the National Development Ministry and the office of Vice Premier Ptolemy Reid, also general secretary of the PNC, were bombed. The government arrested Rodney and other WPA leaders, causing violent public demonstrations.

The arrests and demonstrations brought an apparent crisis in the armed forces. Their loyalty to Burnham was questioned for the first time since he came to power. The prime minister ousted Chief of Staff Clarence Price and Commander of the Defense Force Col. Carl Morgan, replacing them with the then head of the Guyana National Service, Norman McLean, and Col. David Granger, respectively.

Economy and Labor. The country's growing political crisis developed against a background of economic stagnation. Statistics issued on March 23 indicated that there had been no growth in the Guyanan economy in 1978. The situation did not improve in 1979. Strikes in the mining and sugar industries were among the major causes of the continued stagnation.

Workers at the state-owned bauxite company went on strike for one week in January to protest the dismissal of two union members. The walkout brought into question the loyalty of a large group of black workers to the Burnham regime. Another strike by the bauxite workers from July 23 to August 28 was supported by large sectors of the public work force, including the Guyana Agricultural Workers Union, representing the nation's sugar workers, and the Clerical and Commercial Workers Union, to which most government employees belong.

ROBERT J. ALEXANDER, *Rutgers University*

HAWAII

The year 1979 marked the 20th anniversary of statehood for Hawaii. Although formal celebration was muted, the youngest of the United States did note some important changes in the previous two decades.

Population. When Hawaii became a state, its resident population was officially listed as 622,087. In 1979 the estimated population was more than 900,000, an increase of approximately 50%. About 80% of the population still lived on Oahu, but the neighboring islands, particularly Maui, showed a greater growth rate. Hawaii's new residents come principally from the mainland United States and secondarily from nations of Asia and the Pacific.

Economy. In 1959, the gross state product (amount of goods and services sold in the state) was $1.5 billion. In 1979, the figure was estimated at $9 billion. Since the advent of statehood, tourism has replaced sugar as Hawaii's leading industry. Despite a 37-day ban on flights by all U.S.-operated DC-10s and a strike against the largest air carrier to the islands, the number of visitors to Hawaii increased to 4 million.

The sugar industry continued to struggle because of low federal subsidies and a competitive foreign market. At the same time, illegal sales of Hawaiian marijuana have been estimated to exceed those of the islands' other agricultural products.

Real estate prices, always high in the islands, continued to soar well above the rate of inflation in 1979. Many of the larger purchases were made by out-of-state investors, and the exceed-

--------- GUYANA • Information Highlights ---------

Official Name: Cooperative Republic of Guyana.
Location: Northeast coast of South America.
Area: 83,000 square miles (214 970 km²).
Population (1979 est.): 800,000.
Chief City (1976 est.): Georgetown, the capital, 205,-000 (met. area).
Government: *Head of state,* Arthur Chung, president (took office March 1970). *Head of government,* Lynden Forbes Burnham, prime minister (took office Dec. 1964). *Legislature* (unicameral)—National Assembly.
Monetary Unit: Guyana dollar (2.55 G. dollars equal U.S.$1, June 1979).
Manufactures (major product): bauxite.
Agriculture (major products): Sugar, rice.

--------- HAWAII • Information Highlights ---------

Area: 6,450 square miles (16 706 km²).
Population (Jan. 1979 est.): 897,000.
Chief Cities (1970 census): Honolulu, the capital, 324,-871; Kailua, 33,783; Kaneohe, 29,903; Hilo, 26,353; Waipahu, 22,798.
Government (1979): *Chief Officers*—governor, George R. Ariyoshi (D); lt. gov., Jean Sadako King (D). *Legislature*—Senate, 25 members; House of Representatives, 51 members.
Education (1978–79): *Enrollment*—public elementary schools, 89,630 pupils; public secondary, 81,131; colleges and universities, 47,535 students. *Public school expenditures,* $258,502,000 ($1,487 per pupil).
State Finances (fiscal year 1978): *Revenues,* $1,555,-968,000; *expenditures,* $1,495,221,000.
Personal Income (1978): $7,465,000,000; per capita, $8,437.
Labor Force (July 1979): *Nonagricultural wage and salary earners,* 386,000; *unemployed,* 25,100 (6.2% of total force).

ingly high prices for homes continued to be a problem for residents.

Energy. The initial success of an experimental ocean thermal energy conversion (OTEC) project off the Kona coast was the bright spot in Hawaii's continuing search for alternative energy sources in 1979. Research continued in the area of geothermal energy systems, and experimentation with windmills was planned in the hope of harnessing Hawaii's incessant trade winds. U. S. President Jimmy Carter, during a brief stopover in the islands at midyear, applauded the state's efforts in the energy field. The U. S. Department of Energy selected Hawaii as the site for a national conference on alternative energy sources.

Government and Politics. The effects of several constitutional amendments adopted by the electorate in 1978 began to be felt in 1979. Chief among these were limits on state spending and the requirement of a tax refund if there were a surplus in the general fund of more than 5% in any two-year period. Another set of amendments created an Office of Hawaiian Affairs to be administered for and by Hawaiians.

As the Waikiki Aquarium celebrated its 75th anniversary, plans were being made for the construction of a larger facility. Hawaii's commitment to the study of its surrounding oceans was also reflected in the $8.6 million marine sciences building under construction on the University of Hawaii campus.

RICHARD H. KOSAKI, *University of Hawaii*

HONG KONG

In September 1979, Murray MacLehose was reappointed governor of the British colony for the fourth time; he was expected to stay in office until April 1980. The reappointment suggested Britain's desire to establish stronger relations among Hong Kong, China, and itself. Accepting the first official invitation ever extended by China to a Hong Kong governor, MacLehose visited the People's Republic for 12 days in March. Chinese leaders expressed a desire to see him reappointed.

Economy. Hong Kong's trade deficit exceeded $1 billion in the first half of the year, although its domestic exports increased by 34%, reexports by 55%, and imports by 36%, compared with the same period in 1978. The gross domestic product was expected to reach 12% in real terms for the year. The growth rate was higher than originally anticipated because of a sharp rise in the population and work force, as well as greater export demands.

Hong Kong was the world's seventh largest port in terms of shipping tonnage, cargo handled, and passengers. Hong Kong was also the world's largest exporter of watches, surpassing Switzerland and Japan. Optimism about the continued growth of Hong Kong's tourism was indicated by long-term investment commitments of $1.5 billion.

Links with China. Chartered passenger flights between Hong Kong and Canton, started in October 1978, were followed in 1979 by the introduction of regular air, hovercraft, and container lorry service between the two cities. Direct passenger train service between Hong Kong and China, which had ceased for 30 years, was resumed on April 4. The Sino-British air agreement, signed in July, provided for regular flights between Peking and London, and Hong Kong. The Hong Kong Aircraft Engineering Company signed a contract with China to overhaul and repair its fleet of Boeing 707 aircraft; the Hong Kong Electric Company signed a contract to buy coal from China; and the China Light & Power Co. agreed to supply electricity to Shum Chun. Sun Hung Kai Securities, Hong Kong's largest stock brokerage firm, became the first Hong Kong company since 1949 to be permitted to establish a permanent base in China.

Refugees. In the first 10 months of the year, some 70,000 refugees entered Hong Kong and were settled temporarily in 13 refugee camps. On September 19, Hong Kong expelled 733 Vietnamese because they had been given refuge in China.

Fuel Saving. Energy conservation measures, which went into effect May 13, included a ban on the use of neon lights before 8 P. M. and after 11:30 P. M., and the restoration of daylight saving time for five months.

CHUEN-YAN DAVID LAI
University of Victoria, British Columbia

UPI

Hong Kong's new mass transit system made its inaugural run September 30 and was opened to the general public October 1.

HOUSING

Record high interest rates and tight credit slowed housing production. A weak housing market and rising energy costs indicated hard times for prospective home buyers and current home owners. Internationally, the developing nations were attempting to provide the basic services needed for adequate housing.

THE UNITED STATES

Housing production for 1979 was below 1978 and was expected to decline well into 1980. Housing starts for 1978 were just over 2 million units, making 1978 the best year for housing production since 1973. For 1979, the total was approximately 1.75 million units.

Severe weather conditions during the first quarter of 1979 hampered both homebuilders and potential home buyers. Production was down to an annual rate of about 1.6 million units but the building industry expressed cautious optimism. Mortgage interest rates were high, about 10%, but high rates were not discouraging buyers. While expensive, mortgage money was readily available and this condition of easy credit was radically different from the tight credit that was associated with the high interest rates and severe housing slump of 1974–75.

As second-quarter statistics revealed, the optimists appeared to have been correct. Production in June was at an annual rate of over 1.9 million units. Builders and lenders were saying that the mortgage market had changed and could not be affected by a recession. Thrift institutions (savings and loans; mutual savings banks) are now able to compete effectively with the federal government. Savers can buy "money market certificates" and obtain a yield equal to the yield of the treasury bills issued by the federal government. Therefore, interest rates may increase but savings will not flow out of the thrift institutions as had occurred in other periods of high interest rates.

The actions of the Federal Reserve Board during September and October quickly dispelled any residue of optimism. The Federal Reserve Board is an independent federal agency with the responsibility of controlling the money supply. The "Fed" controls the money supply by setting the rate for borrowing by banks and by regulating the reserve requirements of those banks. Therefore the actions of the Fed directly affect mortgage interest rates and the availability of mortgage loans.

During the last quarter of 1979, the Fed battled inflation by raising interest rates to record levels and by reducing the supply of money. Interest rates for single family mortgage loans rose to the 12–13% range and lenders were rationing scarce funds to only the best customers. Builders began to predict the collapse of the housing industry.

The Outlook. There is always some lag between the imposition of tighter money policy and its effect on housing production. However, in spite of projects already under way, housing production was expected to drop below 1.5 million units during the first half of 1980 and possibly go as low as 1.3 million units for the year. The actions of the Fed in making credit available would determine just how bad things would be for housing in 1980. Tight credit might force mortgage rates to the previously unbelievable level of 14%.

Energy. Higher interest rates primarily affect home buyers, but higher energy costs affect everyone. Heating oil prices were close to $1.00 per gallon by the end of 1979 and it seemed that everyone was seeking some sort of relief from rising fuel bills. As the price of energy increases, it becomes more practical to invest in saving energy. Many home owners were adding insulation, caulking to close cracks, and seeking new products and new methods to save energy. Federal programs allow tax credits of 15% for the cost of storm windows, insulation, caulking, and other energy savers. Timing devices which automatically turn down thermostats and even the correct use of the common window shade can reduce heating costs.

Home owners are seeking alternative sources of heat. The sales of wood burning stoves increased from about 1 million units in 1972 to 5 million units in 1979. The construction of homes using solar heat also increased. Solar heat requires some sort of back-up system like oil or wood to be used on cloudy days. However, a properly constructed solar heating system may provide up to 40% of a home's heating needs. Solar heating systems are expensive to build but once operating almost no cost is involved.

Conservation and alternative energy sources may help alleviate the long-term energy problem but many people were faced with the short-term problem of staying warm during the winter. The poor and the elderly were especially hard hit by rising fuel costs. State and federal officials set up emergency aid funds but no one seemed to offer any long-term solutions.

High energy costs also affect the location of housing. Since World War II, the United States has changed from an urban nation to a suburban nation. Good roads and especially the Interstate Highway System made commuting to work relatively quick and easy.

A new trend may be emerging. High gasoline prices and shortages of supply are making public transportation more desirable. Large suburban homes are more expensive to heat and maintain than smaller urban dwelling units, like townhouses and condominiums. Many families, especially young couples with both spouses employed, are showing a preference for city living. The demand for urban properties is rising. During the next decade, the cities may regain much of the vitality which they lost to the suburbs.

THE WORLD SITUATION

The developed nations are searching for the appropriate level of government involvement in housing production and management. The undeveloped nations are working to develop the necessary infrastructure to facilitate adequate housing.

Canada. The Canadian economy remained sluggish and housing starts were down, close to 200,000 units. The slow economy and a general surplus in dwelling units were cited as reasons for the low production. The government promised new economic policies to encourage homeownership. In the future, the home owner would be allowed to deduct property taxes and mortgage interest from taxable income.

Great Britain. The new Conservative government reduced the federal role in housing. Over 30% of the housing in Great Britain is government-owned. The Conservative government's plan called for encouraging the occupant of the government-owned dwelling to purchase the unit. The Labour Party and some local housing councils opposed the plan.

Soviet Union. The modernization of old rural villages is a long-term problem. Soviet agriculture has become more mechanized and collectivized. A more efficient modern rural village would provide centralized housing near where the farmers work. The old villages tend to be dispersed and the villagers are fairly self-sufficient. Old ways die hard and most villagers still prefer their huts to the modern apartment.

Undeveloped Nations. The undeveloped nations continued to try to provide the basic services that make modern housing possible. Since these nations lack the institutions which finance housing, most dwellings are built by the occupant using savings and family resources.

EDGAR J. McDOUGALL, JR.
University of Connecticut

HOUSTON

Despite fears of an economic slowdown in other parts of the United States, Houston continued to grow at a spectacular rate. Construction and energy-related industries demonstrated particular vigor, and a real estate boom in private housing and commercial property helped sustain the city's prosperity.

Growing Pains. According to the U. S. Census Bureau, Houston was the fastest growing major city in the United States in 1979. Including surrounding metropolitan areas, its population rose to 2.5 million, the fifth largest in the nation. The city itself spread to more than 521 square miles (1349 km²), seven times its size after World War II.

Such rapid growth has put a strain on public services and the city government. Houston's traffic jams have become legendary, streets are poorly maintained, and new municipal areas do not receive many essential services. Heavy rains and poor drainage led to repeated flooding in some outlying areas in 1979. As a consequence, the city took a fresh, hard look at its almost unlimited ability to annex territory.

A rising crime rate and a record jump in homicides stimulated demands for increasing the size of the police force, but charges of police brutality and failure to hire an adequate number of black and Mexican officers complicated the issue.

Politics. Black and Hispanic groups in Houston have long protested that with all the city's growth they have had little voice in public policy-making. Yielding to pressure from the U. S. Justice Department, the city instituted a new voting arrangement whereby 9 of the 14 City Council members would be elected from designated geographical areas; previously all members were elected at large. The new system allowed four black or Mexican-American candidates to win seats in the November 6 elections.

Mayor James McConn, who came under attack for financial misdeeds, also was up for reelection in 1979. On Election Day, McConn was forced into a runoff with another Democrat, Councilman Louis Macey. As expected, McConn was reelected to his second two-year term.

STANLEY E. SIEGEL, *University of Houston*

Solar home heating represents a possible area of relief for the consumer battling big heating bills. Pittsburgh students designed the house below.

UPI

HUNGARY

Improved church-state relations and a policy of economic austerity highlighted Hungarian domestic affairs in 1979.

Domestic Affairs. A highly publicized "exchange of opinion" between party leader János Kádár and Laszlo Cardinal Lekai in March led to a noteworthy improvement in the status of the Catholic Church. The bench of bishops was reconstituted, the Budapest Theological Academy was expanded, and a Catholic nursing home and a spiritual retreat house were established. In April four new bishops were appointed by the pope and approved by the government.

The economy underwent sweeping changes in price and employment policy in 1979. The program began early in the year with the elimination of price controls on many raw materials, a 25% increase in the price of gasoline, and restrictions on purchases of new cars. In July, consumer prices were raised by 9%. Food, automobiles, and energy showed overall price increases of 20%, 20%, and 34%, respectively.

The government also issued decrees aimed at increasing the productivity of farms and factories. Unprofitable facilities would be closed down, and workers on overstaffed plants would be transferred. To stimulate industrial production, the government instituted a piecework quota system in many factories.

Foreign Affairs and Trade. One result of the economic austerity plan was an improvement in Hungary's traditionally negative balance of trade. The first six months of 1979 produced a deficit of 21 million forints, compared with 40 million during the same period in 1978.

An agreement with the Soviet Union in December 1978 raised by 8% the annual trade between the two nations. In March 1979, Kádár met with Soviet President Leonid Brezhnev in Moscow, and the Soviet leader returned the visit in June. Brezhnev praised Hungary's economic policies, even though they allow more free enterprise than any other Soviet-bloc country.

As a result of improving relations with the United States, Hungary sought some $300 million in loans from U. S. banks—its first venture into the U. S. capital market since World War II. Measures to increase trade between the two nations to $1 billion were agreed upon as a result of visits to Washington by Minister of Finance Lajos Faluvegi in February and Deputy Premier Istvan Huszar in July. During a September visit to Hungary by West German Chancellor Helmut Schmidt, an agreement was reached to reduce Hungary's negative balance of trade with its most important Western trade partner.

JAN KARSKI, *Georgetown University*

ICELAND

The left-of-center government of Prime Minister Ólafur Jóhannesson resigned in October 1979, after the Social Democrats withdrew their support for his three-party coalition. The Social Democrats in turn formed a caretaker government with the informal support of Iceland's largest political party, the former opposition Independence Party. In the December 4 national elections the Independents gained one seat in the 60-member Althing (parliament), giving them a total of 21. The Progressives added five seats, giving them 17, and party head Steingrimur Hermannsson was asked to form a government. But by year's end he was unable to do so, and Social Democrat Benedikt Gröndal stayed on as interim prime minister.

Economy. A prime cause of the demise of Jóhannesson's government was its failure to cope with runaway inflation. Its aim was to decrease the inflation rate to about 30% over a 12-month period ending in late 1979, but the goal was not nearly reached. Infighting among the coalition parties was a major obstacle. Except for a lengthy shipping strike, an uneasy truce prevailed on the labor front. Still, the government faced strong pressures, and a new wage-price spiral was unleashed. The estimated rate of inflation for 1979 was 53–55%, with 10% of this blamed on the soaring cost of imported oil. While there was some economic growth, the terms of trade deteriorated, and general purchasing power went down. There was more use of foreign credit than planned, and debt-service on long-term foreign loans remained an economic burden.

HUNGARY • Information Highlights

Official Name: Hungarian People's Republic.
Location: East-central Europe.
Area: 35,920 square miles (93 032 km²).
Population (1979 est.): 10,700,000.
Chief Cities (Jan. 1978): Budapest, the capital, 2,089,-533; Miskolc, 207,828; Debrecen, 195,997.
Government: *Head of state,* Pál Losonczi, chairman of the presidential council (took office April 1967). *Head of government,* György Lázár, premier (took office 1975). First secretary of the Hungarian Socialist Workers' party, János Kádár (took office 1956). *Legislature* (unicameral)—National Assembly.
Monetary Unit: Forint (20.31 forints equal U.S.$1, 1979, noncommercial rate).
Manufactures (major products): Precision and measuring equipment, pharmaceuticals, textiles, transportation equipment.
Agriculture (major products): Corn, wheat, potatoes, sugar beets, fruits.

ICELAND • Information Highlights

Official Name: Republic of Iceland.
Location: North Atlantic Ocean.
Area: 39,709 square miles (102 846 km²).
Population (1979 est.): 200,000.
Chief City (Dec. 1977 est.): Reykjavik, the capital, 83,-887.
Government: *Head of state,* Kristján Eldjárn, president (took office for 3d 4-year term Aug. 1976). *Head of government,* Benedikt Gröndal, interim prime minister (took office Dec. 1979). *Legislature*—Althing: Upper House and Lower House.
Monetary Unit: Króna (344.0 krónur equal U.S.$1, June 1979).
Manufactures (major products): Fish products, aluminum.
Agriculture (major products): Hay, cheese, fodder, livestock.

Fisheries. The Icelandic fishing industry benefited from a good catch in 1979. Despite attempted cutbacks, the cod take was heading for a level far above that recommended by marine biologists. Although export values also were satisfactory, the industry faced a cost squeeze, stemming from both domestic inflation and rising outlays for fuel. A dispute festered between Iceland and Norway over fishing rights near the Arctic island of Jan Mayen.

Energy. The skyrocketing cost of imported oil products—long supplied by the Soviet Union but in recent years priced according to Rotterdam quotations—became a grave worry. There seemed to be little chance of winning a better deal from the Soviet Union or any other country in 1979. Public and legislative debate focused on alternative, long-term energy schemes—the use of electricity to produce methanol, exporting power via cables, and further development of hydroelectric and geothermal facilities.

HAUKUR BÖDVARSSON, *"News From Iceland"*

IDAHO

Fires and drought made the headlines in Idaho in 1979. A lack of winter snow in the mountains and a dry summer combined to cause an abundance of forest fires and a shortage of crops. The 65,000 acre (26 304 ha) Mortar Creek fire was the largest. It burned in a very steep, high, roadless area at the headwaters of the Middle Fork of the Salmon River. Three thousand people fought the $4.5 million blaze. A 38,000 acre (15 378 ha) Gallagher Peak fire in the Targhee Forest in eastern Idaho resulted from a new Forest Service policy of letting certain fires burn. It consumed far more than officials expected.

Legislature. The 1979 legislature implemented the 1% tax initiative passed by the people. Appropriations were increased by 2.7% to $357.6 million. Education received 72% of the general fund budget. It gave $30.8 million in tax relief and raised the usury rate to 13% after Gov. John Evans vetoed a bill to remove the limit entirely. Local budgets were frozen at their 1978 level for 1979–80 but can be raised by a difficult to achieve two-thirds vote of the people.

The date for the primary election was changed from August to May to coincide with the state's presidential primary. The method of paying log haulers was changed from lumber volume to weight, so the logger now receives the same for hauling defective timber as sound timber. It also abolished written examinations for the renewal of drivers' licenses.

The legislature accepted a pay raise recommended by a constitutional commission and failed to provide sufficient money to fund a 7% pay raise it had mandated for public employees, thus forcing the agencies to cut staff.

Courts. The Coeur d'Alene Indian Tribe asked for the return of the 7,000 acre (2 833 ha) Heyburn Park alleging that the state violated the terms of ownership "for public use," by leasing cottage sites on the lake.

Idaho joined Arizona in a suit to determine whether Congress had the power to extend the time for ratification of the federal Equal Rights Amendment and whether a state can rescind its ratification.

Politics. Idaho's "proposition 13," which limits property taxes to 1% of value, has slowed highway construction and has cities and counties worried over how they will serve their people. But the people who have suffered the most from the cuts are the elderly, the handicapped, the mentally ill, and drug addicts seeking rehabilitation. Governor Evans favored an increase in

---

IDAHO • Information Highlights

Area: 83,557 square miles (216 413 km²).
Population (Jan. 1979 est.): 889,000.
Chief Cities (1976 est.): Boise, the capital, 102,915; (1970 census): Pocatello, 40,036; Idaho Falls, 35,776.
Government (1979): *Chief Officers*—governor, John V. Evans (D); lt. gov., Philip E. Batt (R). *Legislature*—Senate, 35 members; House of Representatives, 70 members.
Education (1978–79): *Enrollment*—public elementary schools, 108,744; public secondary, 94,278; colleges and universities, 39,255 students. *Public school expenditures,* $311,572,000 ($1,192 per pupil).
State Finances (fiscal year 1978): *Revenues,* $887,700,-000; *expenditures,* $837,069,000.
Personal Income (1978): $6,156,000,000; per capita, $7,015.
Labor Force (July 1979): *Nonagricultural wage and salary earners,* 344,200; *unemployed,* 21,500 (5.0% of total force).

In Idaho, a lack of winter snow and a dry summer led to a series of forest fires.

sales tax to help offset the effects of the 1% limitation, but passage of such a tax did not seem likely.

Increasing prices for gold started gold fever in some who wish to dredge the streams, causing pollution problems. Four of the state's six major drainages were already declared polluted by the State Department of Health and Welfare.

Electric-power shortage looms, so the Public Utilities Commission imposed a hookup fee for new housing heated with electricity. It will cost $1,500 to $2,500 per home.

CLIFFORD DOBBLER, *University of Idaho*

ILLINOIS

Illinois citizens will remember 1979 for a bad winter that paralyzed most of the state during January and February. The frigid temperatures and record deep snow were blamed for higher costs of government, poor roads, violent crime, and a sluggish economy.

Economy. Illinois, long known for its diversified industry, appeared less desirable for industry than it had. Some believed colder winters in the state were a factor; however, the problem was much deeper, as evidenced on several fronts in 1979.

Caterpillar Tractor Co., the state's largest employer, with 55,000 workers in nine Illinois cities, announced plans for the construction of a 1,000,000 sq.-ft. (92 903 sq-m) facility near Lafayette, IN. A company spokesman said high workmen's compensation costs in Illinois were partly behind the expansion out-of-state.

An economic study by Alexander Grant and Co. found that Illinois ranked 41st among the states in terms of incentives for manufacturers. The study reported that Illinois lost 140,000 jobs in manufacturing from 1968 through 1978.

Another economic warning came from Continental Illinois Bank and Trust Company of Chicago, which indicated that the state was in danger of losing its Triple-A credit rating because of sluggish economic growth. The study found that Illinois ranked last among the 18 states whose securities were given top rating by Moody's Investor Service and Standard & Poor's Corporation. Continental Bank reported that Illinois' population increased only 1.1% from 1970 to 1979, and that its personal income rose only 89.8%, against a 91.1% average for other Triple-A states.

Illinois' agricultural economy was much better. The state's farmers continued to be the nation's leading agricultural exporters and producers of corn and soybeans. In the last decade, the U. S. Department of Agriculture reported that the value of Illinois farmland soared 312% to $1,786 an acre. Nationally, farmland value increased 200%.

Employment also remained fairly good in the state. The August 1979 unemployment rate was only 4.4%, against a national average of 6%.

UPI

Adlai Stevenson, U. S. senator from Illinois since 1971, announced that he would not seek reelection.

Government. Although Gov. James R. Thompson (R) ran as an advocate of a "tax revolt" in his 1978 reelection campaign, he and Chicago Mayor Jane Byrne pushed through the legislature a bill that allowed the Regional Transportation Authority to fund mass transit in Chicago with higher sales taxes. Thompson also vetoed and defeated a bill to phase out the state's 5% sales tax on food and medicine. On the other hand, the governor proposed constitutional amendments to limit general and road fund appropriations, to give citizens the opportunity to reject tax increases which were passed by the legislature by less than a three-fifths vote, to limit local government spending, and to improve tax collection procedures.

The legislature overturned the governor's veto of a bill establishing strict abortion controls.

ROBERT ENSTAD, *Chicago Tribune*

─────── **ILLINOIS • Information Highlights** ───────

Area: 56,400 square miles (146 076 km^2).
Population (Jan. 1979 est.): 11,258,000.
Chief Cities (1970 census): Springfield, the capital, 91,753; (1976 est.): Chicago, 3,074,084; Rockford, 141,358.
Government (1979): *Chief Officers*—governor, James R. Thompson (R); lt. gov., David C. O'Neal (R). *General Assembly*—Senate, 59 members; House of Representatives, 177 members.
Education (1978–79): *Enrollment*—public elementary schools, 1,395,192 pupils; public secondary, 704,965; colleges and universities, 611,412 students.
State Finances (fiscal year 1978): *Revenues,* $10,317,-928,000; *expenditures,* $9,952,914,000.
Personal Income (1978): $100,091,000,000; per capita, $8,903.
Labor Force (July 1979): *Nonagricultural wage and salary earners,* 4,899,600; *unemployed,* 277,700 (5.1% of total force).

Charan Singh (seated, right) holds a press conference July 28 after being sworn in as India's new prime minister by President Neelam Sanjiva Reddy (left). Singh was forced to resign 24 days later but stayed on as head of a caretaker government.

BALDEV, SYGMA

INDIA

Politically, 1979 was a troubled year for India. The Janata party government, which had won an overwhelming victory over Mrs. Indira Gandhi and her wing of the Congress party—Congress (I)—in March 1977, broke up in mid-1979. It was succeeded by an even stranger coalition headed by former Deputy Prime Minister Charan Singh, which in turn was forced to resign in late August. Charan Singh continued as head of a caretaker government until the nation's seventh general elections, finally held in early January 1980. Basing her campaign on law and order and promising an all-out attack on rising prices, both direly needed, Mrs. Gandhi and her Congress (I) party were swept back into power in an unexpected landslide victory. The character and policies of her government, however, were in doubt.

Politics. The collapse of the Janata government was due mainly to dissension within the party. At odds were its three top leaders—Prime Minister Morarji Desai, Deputy Prime Minister and Minister of Defense Jagjivan Ram, and Deputy Prime Minister and Minister of Finance Charan Singh. Additional factors were rivalries among the constituent units of the Janata party and between key members of the party in several states; the failure of the government to fulfil promises of economic decentralization and reform; and its apparent inability to deal effectively with communal and other forms of violence, strikes and lockouts in the industrial sector, police strikes, and other threats to law and order.

The political crisis reached a climax at mid-year. In May, Raj Narain, the minister of health and a member of the Janata party's national executive, demanded that Prime Minister Desai either resign or seek a vote of confidence from the party. He alleged that Desai was too much under the influence of the Jana

Sangh (BJS), a right-wing Hindu nationalist faction of the Janata, and he insisted that the BJS sever all connections with its "nonpolitical" sister organization, the Rashtriya Swayamsevak Sangh (RSS). On June 12, Narain was suspended from the Janata's national executive, and on June 23 he resigned from the party altogether.

On July 10, one day after the opening of the monsoon session of the Lok Sabha (lower house of parliament), Yeshwantrao B. Chavan, the leader of the Congress (S) opposition, introduced a motion of no-confidence in the Janata government. Five days later, following the resignation of several key members of his cabinet and the defection of nearly 100 members of his party in the Lok Sabha, Desai resigned as prime minister. The following day Charan Singh resigned and was elected head of the new Janata-Secular party, composed mainly of defecting Janata members. On July 18 President Neelam Sanjiva Reddy invited opposition leader Chavan to explore the possibilities of forming a government. When Chavan failed to muster sufficient support, President Reddy then asked Charan Singh to try to form a government. On July 28 Charan Singh was sworn in as India's fifth prime minister, heading a coalition comprised of members of his Janata-Secular party, Gandhi's Congress (I) party, and the Congress (S) party. Y. B. Chavan was made deputy prime minister.

The new coalition government lasted only 24 days. When Mrs. Gandhi withdrew her party's support, it became apparent that Singh's government could not muster a sufficient following to win a vote of confidence in the Lok Sabha. On August 20, shortly before debate on the vote of confidence motion was to begin, Singh resigned and advised President Reddy to dissolve the parliament and call new general elections. After two days of agonizing appraisal, which many described as a constitutional crisis, President Reddy decided to dissolve the Lok

A six-day visit in March by Soviet Premier Aleksei N. Kosygin (*seated at table, fifth from right*) saw the signing of a long-term mutual cooperation agreement.

Sabha and call for general elections within three months. In the meantime, he asked Singh to continue as head of a caretaker government. This decision was approved by almost all of the parties represented in the Lok Sabha, except the Janata. Jagjivan Ram, who had been chosen to replace Morarji Desai as head of the Janata party, had demanded a chance to form a government. His supporters spoke of "a pre-planned conspiracy" to prevent Ram, India's leading "untouchable," from becoming prime minister.

As head of the caretaker government, Singh was in a weak position to lead the country during a period of deteriorating economic conditions, growing violence, and political instability. His position was further weakened by friction within his government, which led him in October to request the resignation of a leading member of his cabinet, H. N. Bahuguna. This brought him into open conflict with the fiery and mercurial Raj Narain, then president of the Janata-Secular party (renamed the Lok Dal in late September).

Preparations for the seventh general elections, which were postponed until early January 1980, dominated the uncertain political scene in the last weeks of the year. Six all-India parties—the Lok Dal; the Janata party; the Congress (I); the Congress (U), formerly the Congress (S); the Communist Party of India; and the Communist Party of India (Marxist)—as well as 26 state or regional parties and a large number of independents, campaigned for the 542 seats in the Lok Sabha. Concurrent elections were also scheduled for the assemblies in the states of Gujarat and Manipur and in the union territories of Goa and Pondicherry. Mrs. Gandhi's Congress (I) appeared to have the best prospects of improving its position in the Lok Sabha, but few predicted the size of its victory. It took a two-thirds majority, enough to push through constitutional amendments.

On October 4 a presidential ordinance authorized the arrest and detention without trial of hoarders and black marketeers. This revival of preventive detention was opposed by most of the opposition parties and by all the chief ministers of individual states.

In a rare act of cooperation among the political parties, Mohammed Hidayatullah, a former chief justice of India, was chosen by a unanimous vote in both houses of parliament to succeed Vice President Basappa D. Jatti upon the expiration of his five-year term on August 31.

Economy. The economic picture was unclear. In January, the National Development Council (NDC) approved an overall figure of Rs. (rupees) 69,380 crores (1 crore = 10 million) for the Sixth Five-Year Plan (1978–83). In accordance with the Janata party's policy of democratic decentralization, the NDC decided to cut back allocations for centrally-sponsored programs and to transfer about Rs. 2,000 crores for rural schemes in the individual states. But the states continued to be financial disaster areas, and the overall planning process was virtually at a standstill.

The budget for fiscal 1979 (beginning April 1) provided for an overall expenditure of $22.6 billion, with increases in development and de-

--- **INDIA · Information Highlights** ---

Official Name: Republic of India.
Location: South Asia.
Area: 1,269,346 square miles (3 287 606 km²).
Population (1979 est.): 660,900,000.
Chief Cities (1971 est.): New Delhi, the capital, 3,600,-000; Bombay, 6,000,000; Calcutta, 3,200,000.
Government: *Head of state,* Neelam Sanjiva Reddy, president (took office July 1977). *Head of government,* Indira Gandhi, prime minister (took office January 1980). *Legislature*—Parliament: Rajya Sabha (Council of States) and Lok Sabha (House of the People).
Monetary Unit: Rupee (8.0645 rupees equal U.S.$1, Dec. 6, 1979).
Manufactures (major products): Textiles, processed food, steel, machinery, transport equipment, cement.
Agriculture (major products): Rice, pulses, oilseeds, cotton, jute, tea, wheat.

fense expenditures, sharply higher taxes, and a record budget deficit of $1.65 billion (which proved to be a serious underestimate). Rather impressive performances in many sectors of the economy were overshadowed by a sharp rise in the prices of essential imports, especially petroleum; a wayward monsoon during the summer; disastrous floods in the southeastern part of the country in May and in western India in August (the latter caused by what *The New York Times* described as "the storm of the century"); one of the severest droughts in many years in other parts of the country; strikes, lock-outs, and labor unrest (resulting in the loss of 22 million man days during the first six months of the year); power shortages; and high unemployment.

The World Bank's Annual Report, released in September, praised India's economic achievements. It reported that fiscal 1979 was the fourth consecutive year of significant economic growth in that country. Overall growth was estimated at from 3 to 4% and industrial growth at between 7 and 8%. The report commended India for increasing its foodgrain production to a record 130 million tons and for the continued growth of its foreign exchange reserves (to about $7 billion). It noted India's substantial stockpile of foodgrains, estimated at 12 million tons (other estimates ran as high as 21 million tons). It praised India for the liberalization of its trade policies, which contributed to a substantial increase in exports. (The overall balance of trade worsened, however, with the value of imports exceeding that of exports by the astronomical figure of Rs. 10,729 crores.) The Bank reported that during the fiscal year ending June 30, India received record loans of $1.492 billion from the World Bank and the International Development Association (IDA), mostly in the form of loans on concessional terms from IDA.

Until 1979, India had one of the best records in the world in controlling inflation. In March, however, prices began to show alarming increases—wholesale prices by about 18% and retail prices by at least 15%. By the end of the year the inflation rate reached a staggering figure of well above 20%.

On August 15, in his Independence Day speech at the historic Red Fort in New Delhi, Prime Minister Singh expressed the government's determination to check rising prices, reduce unemployment, and narrow the gap between rich and poor. Unfortunately, economic trends during the last weeks of the year were mostly in the other direction. India's entire development effort seemed threatened.

Foreign Policy. With the nation's political leaders inescapably preoccupied with internal problems, India played a relatively modest role in world affairs. It was greatly concerned with the traumatic events in Iran, Afghanistan, and Pakistan. Relations with the Soviet Union were highlighted by the six-day visit of Soviet Premier Aleksei N. Kosygin in March, which culminated in the signing of a long-term agreement for economic, trade, scientific, and technical cooperation. Prime Minister Morarji Desai made a four-day return visit in June. After leaving Moscow, Desai proceeded to Poland, Czechoslovakia, and Yugoslavia. He also made official visits to two of India's South Asian neighbors—Sri Lanka in February and Bangladesh in April.

In February, Minister of External Affairs Atal Behari Vajpayee traveled to China for an eight-day official visit, the first by an Indian leader since the border war in late 1962. The trip by Vajpayee, which many hoped would inaugurate a new and happier era in Sino-Indian

Demonstrators in New Delhi protest the alleged "illegalities" and "mistakes" of the Janata party government.

BALDEV, SYGMA

relations, ended on a sour note. The Chinese invasion of Vietnam, of which India strongly disapproved, was begun during Vajpayee's stay in Peking. As an expression of its disapproval, the Indian government summoned home Vajpayee days earlier than planned.

On April 18, Prime Minister Desai and Bangladeshi President Ziaur Rahman announced a series of accords to eliminate several sources of friction between their countries. Allocation of irrigation water, the demarcation of offshore zones, and the illegal movement of people across the border were among the problems covered.

In a broadcast shortly after being sworn in on July 28, Prime Minister Singh declared that he would "continue to follow the policy of non-alignment which will not lean on any super-power."

India was represented by rather undistinguished delegations, headed by the new and inexperienced minister of external affairs, S. N. Mishra, at the August meeting of the Commonwealth heads of state in Lusaka, Zambia; at the nonaligned summit conference in Havana, Cuba, in late August and early September; and at the 34th Session of the UN General Assembly, which opened on September 18. In October, India's permanent UN representative, B. C. Mishra, became chairman of the "Group of Seventy," an important voice of the world's developing countries.

Other. India lost one of its best known and most beloved public figures with the death of 76-year-old "Lok Nayak" Jayaprakesh Narayan on October 8. J. P., as he was commonly known, had great moral and political influence as a result of his nearly 50 years in public service. Although he never held elective office, he served his country in many roles. A believer in non-violence, he was one of the last remaining political figures who had worked with Mahatma Gandhi to free India from British colonial rule. He organized strikes against the British and was imprisoned several times. In later years he opposed the "emergency" rule of Mrs. Gandhi and was instrumental in her March 1977 election defeat. J. P. was widely regarded as "the conscience of the nation." Upon his death, the government declared a period of national mourning.

India also proclaimed a period of national mourning after the assassination of Lord Louis Mountbatten by Irish terrorists on August 27. Mountbatten was the last viceroy of British India and the first governor general of independent India. (*See* OBITUARIES.)

On a happier note, Indians rejoiced at the awarding of the 1979 Nobel Peace Prize to Mother Teresa, a Catholic nun who had worked selflessly for more than three decades among the "poorest of poor" in Calcutta. (*See* BIOGRAPHY.)

NORMAN D. PALMER
University of Pennsylvania

INDIANA

Budget bills and tax relief measures highlighted the regular session of the 1979 Indiana General Assembly. Problems related to nuclear power plants in the state also made the headlines during the year.

Legislation. A six-part tax and utility-bill relief program proposed by Gov. Otis R. Bowen ranked as one of the major accomplishments of the legislative session. Included were bills allowing the state to pay $200 of the utility bills for the elderly and disabled with low incomes and giving Hoosiers a 15% cut in 1979 state income taxes. Legislators also passed bills denying bail to persons appealing their convictions for serious felonies such as murder, kidnapping, or rape, and tightening Indiana's open-door, or sunshine, law. An inheritance measure exempted from tax all property transfers to a surviving spouse. Other legislation reiterated a ban on use of public funds for abortions and phased out over a 15-year period a controversial state intangibles tax.

Despite massive debate and much public unhappiness, legislators did nothing concerning the regulation of utilities and their rates. Also rejected were bills replacing the direct primary with a convention for nominating U. S. senators and certain state officers and repealing Indiana's unpopular vehicle inspection law. The legislature again failed to fund a 1977 program to compensate the victims of violent crime. "Ahead of its time" legislation providing one-day legal separation for married couples who would fare worse than their unmarried counterparts on federal income taxes also did not pass.

Budget. Three state budget bills for the 1979–81 biennium totaled more than $9 billion—about $1 billion higher than for the preceding two-year period. The operating budget increased state aid to public schools by approximately $446 million, to state universities by $138.8 million, and to mental-health programs by $57 million. The highway budget was augmented by $169 million from the state general fund, $79 million of which will go to the State Highway

---

INDIANA • Information Highlights

Area: 36,291 square miles (93 994 km²).
Population (Jan. 1979 est.): 5,394,000.
Chief Cities (1976 est.): Indianapolis, the capital, 708,-867; Fort Wayne, 183,039; Gary, 163,675; Evansville, 133,609.
Government (1979): *Chief Officers*—governor, Otis R. Bowen (R); lt. gov., Robert D. Orr (R). *General Assembly*—Senate, 50 members; House of Representatives, 100 members.
Education (1978–79): *Enrollment*—public elementary schools, 720,671 pupils; public secondary, 392,660; colleges and universities, 222,791 students. *Public school expenditures*, $1,781,000,000 ($1,389 per pupil).
State Finances (fiscal year 1978): *Revenues*, $4,223,-579,000; *expenditures*, $3,729,223,000.
Personal Income (1978): $41,412,000,000; per capita, $7,706.
Labor Force (July 1979): *Nonagricultural wage and salary earners*, 2,255,100; *unemployed*, 170,900 (6.4% of total force).

Commission, and $90 million to cities, towns, and counties. Vetoed by Bowen were five bills that would have cost an additional $33.4 million and have reduced the state's emergency reserve fund far below a $50 million projected by 1981.

Nuclear Power. Environmentalists, laborers, and the general public continued to fight construction of Bailly Nuclear Power Plant on Lake Michigan and the Marble Hill plant near Madison on the Ohio River. Alleged violations in site selection and implementation of quality control and safety procedures and charges of cover-ups of building flaws led to precedent-setting litigation, countless investigations, and continuing delays in construction.

Other. Richard G. Hatcher (D) was reelected to a fourth term as mayor of Gary, and William Hudnut (D) was returned as mayor of Indianapolis. Teachers in Indianapolis walked off their jobs September 4.

Marine Pfc. Robert T. Garwood of Adams, IN, returned to the United States more than 13 years after his capture in Vietnam to face charges of desertion and collaboration with the North Vietnamese. Heavy rains throughout the spring and summer affected Indiana's agricultural production. On Sept. 14, 1979, James "Doc" Counsilman, of Indiana University, Bloomington, became at 58 the oldest person to swim the English Channel.

LORNA LUTES SYLVESTER
Indiana University

INDONESIA

On Nov. 15, 1978, Indonesia's technocratic planners administered a shock to the economy, devaluing the *rupiah* by 50% against the U. S. dollar. The government's principal stated objective was to promote structural change by encouraging exports of both raw materials and manufactured goods and by protecting domestic industry from foreign competition. Concern was also expressed over a projected long-term decline in the country's balance of payments and in the reduced purchasing power of the rupiah in Japan and Western Europe.

The full effects of the devaluation were not known. In the first half of 1979, non-oil export earnings did increase substantially, but experts claimed that the cause was not devaluation but higher world market prices for timber, rubber, and palm oil. Increases in the price of petroleum, partly inspired by OPEC (Organization of Petroleum Exporting Countries), were expected to swell government oil revenues by about 20% in 1979–80.

For the first time in several years, there was a dramatic loss of confidence by business and a serious threat of inflation. Prices of many mass consumption goods, locally-produced as well as imported, rose immediately after the devaluation announcement. The government responded with a series of administrative measures temporarily prohibiting most price increases. The feared extra-constitutional emergency military arm of the government, *Kopkamtib* (Operational Command for the Restoration of Security and Order), was deployed by President Suharto in an attempt to force manufacturers, wholesalers, and retailers to roll back the new prices. This had little effect.

Politics. In 1978 the reelection of President Suharto for a third five-year term heated political passions to the boiling point. In 1979 the temperature was much reduced, but old problems continued to simmer. Heavily censored in the press but closely followed by the public were the simultaneous trials of 31 university students for "insulting the head of state" during anti-Suharto demonstrations in early 1978. Sentences of up to six years were requested by the state prosecutors. In defense, the students provided the court with extensive evidence of government corruption and ill-chosen, poorly implemented economic development policies. Copies of their charges were widely circulated.

Steps were taken to improve the morale of the Indonesian armed forces. The new minister of defense and security, Gen. Mohammad Jusuf, conducted a series of well-publicized tours of military units, promising a better living standard for soldiers; new equipment; the upgrading of 60 army, navy, and air force battalions; and a "closer relationship between the armed forces and the people."

The release of more political prisoners in early 1979 left a midyear total of 8,303 detainees, according to the government. Most of the prisoners have been held without trial since the late 1960's. The government promised that all but 150 would be released by year's end.

Foreign Affairs. The Indonesian government was strongly critical of Vietnam's conquest of Cambodia and its expulsion of hundreds of thousands of "boat people" into Southeast Asian waters. The nonaligned nations, meeting in Havana, Cuba, in October, condemned Indonesia for its continued occupation of the "Democratic Republic of East Timor."

R. WILLIAM LIDDLE
The Ohio State University

———— **INDONESIA · Information Highlights** ————

Official Name: Republic of Indonesia.
Location: Southeast Asia.
Area: 735,432 square miles (1 904 769 km²).
Population (1979 est.): 140,900,000.
Chief Cities (1974 est.): Jakarta, the capital, 5,000,000; Surabaja, 2,000,000; Bandung, 2,000,000; Medan, 1,000,000.
Government: *Head of state and government,* Suharto, president (took office for third 5-year term March 1978). *Legislature* (unicameral)—People's Consultative Assembly.
Monetary Unit: Rupiah (625 rupiahs equal U. S.$1, Dec. 1979).
Manufactures (major products): Textiles, food and beverages, light manufactures, cement, fertilizer.
Agriculture (major products): Rice, rubber, cassava, copra, coffee, soybeans, palm oil, tea.

INDUSTRIAL REVIEW

Industrial production worldwide increased in 1979 at a considerably slower rate than in 1978. Sharply increased oil prices, saturated demand for automobiles—especially for full-size models—and low-capacity utilization in developed countries in such mature industries as steel helped to cause the slower growth rate.

U. S. Production and Trends. U. S. industrial production faltered in the second quarter of 1979, was sluggish at midyear, and declined in the fourth quarter. The Federal Reserve Board's preliminary data indicated a 3.8% gain for the year, representing a considerable slowdown from the 5.7% gain that the FRB index of industrial production registered for 1978.

The industrial production index, prepared by the Board of Governors of the Federal Reserve System, measures the physical volume of production of U. S. factories, mines, and utilities. It covers one third of the nation's economic output as measured by the gross national product.

Production slowdown was most evident in mining, where a 0.2% drop compared with a 5% gain in 1978. Responsible for the 1979 decline was a 3.3% drop in oil and gas extraction, reversing the 5.6% advance registered in 1978. Utilities increased their output 3% in 1979, the same as in the two preceding years.

Manufacturing output grew 4.1% in 1979, sharply less than the 6.1% gain in 1978. The slowdown came in durables manufacturing where the annual increase amounted to 4.4%, compared with a 7.4% in 1978. Nondurables manufacturing production grew 3.7% in 1979, compared with 4.3% in 1978. Among product groups, defense equipment led with a 7.4% increase, followed by business equipment with a 6.6% growth. Production of consumer goods increased an estimated 1% in 1979.

The production of railroad equipment advanced by 31% for the second year in a row. Aircraft and parts also enjoyed robust growth, as production soared 17% for the second consecutive year. In addition to fixed-wing aircraft, the industry experienced brisk demand for commercial helicopters as a result of the widening search for petroleum in remote areas, increased demand for executive transport, and the growing use of helicopters in a variety of tasks, ranging from lifting felled trees out of forests to delivering construction materials and machinery over difficult terrain. Other producers of transportation equipment did not fare so well. While the group as a whole showed a 1.7% increase, motor vehicles and parts production declined nearly 6%, and the output of ships and boats decreased 1%.

Electrical machinery registered an 8% gain in 1979. Within the group, electronic components advanced nearly 16% and communication equipment by 12%. Demand was very heavy for integrated circuits, the "chips" that are being used to "computerize" products ranging from children's toys to machine tools. The electrical group's overall performance was dragged down by declines of nearly 13% in the production of television and radio sets, and a 14% drop in household appliances.

Production of nonelectrical machinery increased 7% in 1979, the fourth year of substantial gain of about the same magnitude. Production of farm equipment increased nearly 12%, a sharp departure from the lackluster performance of 1978. Output of metalworking machinery increased 10% and construction equipment had an 8% production gain. Output increased in the 6–8% range in office, service, and miscellaneous equipment and in special and general industrial machinery. The production of engines increased 3.5%.

A new rotary combine has the cylinder positioned crossways, permitting straight feeding and processing of crops. The production of agricultural equipment grew by about 12% in 1979.

Output of fabricated metal products grew 5% in 1979, after an 8% growth in 1978. Production of metal cans declined 12%, but hardware, structural materials, and other products were turned out at rates 5–7% above the previous year.

Production increase for primary metals fell short of 1%, after rising 8% in 1978. Basic steel and mill products output declined 1%, and iron and steel foundries saw their production slide by 3%. Output of nonferrous metals increased 2.5%.

Output of rubber and plastics products increased 5.5% in 1979, a considerable slowdown from 1978. While rubber products other than tires saw output rise 2%, the production of tires dropped 1.7%, repeating the 1978 performance. Plastics products posted an 8% gain.

The production index for chemicals and chemical products showed an overall gain of 6.3% in 1979, a repeat of the 1978 growth, but the record varied for individual components. Output of synthetic materials led with a 10% increase, drugs and medicines followed with 7.8%, and basic chemicals registered a 5% gain. Production of soaps and toiletries and agricultural chemicals increased a little more than 4%. Paint production declined 8%.

Production declines showed up also in the indexes of petroleum products, −0.2%; leather and leather products, −4.9%; and apparel, −2.3%. Production gains hovered near 3.5% for food, paper and paper products, and printing and publishing. Production of textile mill products and ordnance increased just a shade under 3%. Lumber and wood products output eked out a fractional gain, and tobacco products fell a little short of a 1% increase.

The gasoline shortages complicated production plans for many manufacturers. Builders of motor homes tried to boost sagging sales by offering propane power systems and steep discounts. Tire manufacturers saw their production schedules trimmed as a result of the cutback in driving and the long wearing qualities of radials. Automakers saw the production of large cars plummet 14%, squeezing total industry production to 8.4 million units in 1979, down from 9.2 million in 1978. While the demand was brisk for smaller cars, manufacturers had difficulty in expanding output. The imbalance in product mix was a factor in forcing one manufacturer—Chrysler—into severe financial difficulties. Gasoline jitters boosted the demand for bicycles and enabled manufacturers to sell out the entire year's production by the middle of the year.

Ever on the outlook for best sellers, consumer electronic equipment manufacturers turned their attention to residential electronic security systems, hoping to duplicate the success enjoyed by smoke detectors. As with smoke detectors, technological advances brought steep price cuts. With some systems selling for under $100, the consumer demand for electronic security systems grew rapidly in 1979.

Memories and expectations of cold and snowy winters helped boost sales of snow throwers and led to the introduction of a power snow shovel. Wood burning stoves and electrical heaters also were in heavy demand.

Capital spending by manufacturers amounted to $78 billion in 1979, nearly 16% more than in 1978. Durables producers boosted their expenditures for new plants and equipment almost 20%, to $38 billion, while nondurables manufacturers increased spending by 12%, to $40 billion. Mining firms spent $5.5 billion, an increase of 15.5%. Public utilities hiked expenditures by 12.5%, to $33 billion.

The largest increases in capital spending were registered by aircraft producers, 41%; nonelectrical machinery firms, 29%; and electrical machinery manufacturers, 27%. Among nondurables producers, the largest boost in outlays was recorded by paper producers, 39%. Chemical industry spending increased 18.5%.

Manufacturing industries in the United States employed 19.5 million workers in 1977, according to the Census of Manufactures that was released in 1979. There were 350,000 manufacturing establishments. They shipped products worth $1,354 billion and their payrolls totaled $263 billion. Value added by manufacture—the difference between the value of shipments and the value of materials (supplies, containers, and fuel consumed in the production process)—was $580 billion in 1977. Value added by manufacture is the best measuring stick for determining an industry's relative economic importance.

The machinery group, with $67.4 billion in value added and employing 2.1 million workers, loomed largest on the industrial scene in 1977. Transportation equipment followed, with value added at $64.2 billion and employment at 1.8

Smoke detectors have recently enjoyed remarkable sales success, as technological advances have reduced prices.

million. Chemicals and allied products producers registered $56.5 billion in value added and 878,000 in employment. Respective figures for other industries were: food and kindred products—$56.2 billion and 1.5 million; electric and electronic equipment—$49.7 billion and 1.7 million; fabricated metal products—$44.9 billion and 1.5 million; primary metals—$37.3 billion and 1.1 million; printing and publishing—$31.5 billion and 1.1 million; paper and allied products—$21.7 billion and 625,000; rubber and miscellaneous plastics products—$18.8 billion and 239,000; apparel and other textile products—$19.4 billion and 1.3 million; stone-clay-glass products—$18.8 billion and 607,000; instruments and related products—$18.7 billion and 555,000; petroleum and coal products—$16.2 billion and 148,000; lumber and wood products—$16.2 billion and 690,000; textile mill products—$16.0 billion and 870,000; miscellaneous manufacturing—$10.2 billion and 436,000; furniture and fixtures—$18.8 billion and 460,000; tobacco products—$4.3 billion and 61,000; leather and leather products—$3.7 billion and 239,000.

The Developed and Developing Countries—Production and Trends. Industrial production in the developed countries lost some of its ebullience toward year-end 1979. The composite index for Canada, France, Germany, Italy, Japan, the Netherlands, and the United Kingdom registered an overall advance of 5.7% in the third quarter of 1979 over the third quarter of 1978, compared with the U.S. 2.9% gain for the comparable time span.

Japan's industrial production growth rate, 8.8%, was the highest. Growth was slow in the United Kingdom, 1.9%, and in the Netherlands, 2.1%. Solid gains were posted by Canada, 5.1%; France, 5.5%; Italy, 5.3%, and West Germany, 4.7%.

The sketchy information available for developing countries showed the following growth statistics: South Korea—15.6%; Taiwan—14.0%; Mexico—3%; India— —0.8%; and Nigeria— —9.0%.

While steel production reached a worldwide total of 820 million tons (751 million metric tons) in 1979—a 4% increase from 1978—the industry continued to suffer from obsolescence and overcapacity in the developed countries at the same time that it remained very much the focus of industrialization in the underdeveloped countries.

As the American steel industry poured 135 million tons (123 million metric tons) of raw steel in 1979—working at 88% capacity—the steelmakers in the European Community saw their operations dip to 69% of capacity, a total of 154 million tons (141 million metric tons) of the metal.

Undaunted by the industry's difficulties in the United States, where several plants were closed, reducing production capacity by more than 1 million tons (916 000 metric tons), and in Europe, where overcapacity was a serious problem, the underdeveloped countries were planning to increase their steelmaking capacity 75% between 1978 and 1985, to 112 million tons (103 million metric tons).

Steel capacity in Latin America was scheduled to grow 84% between 1978 and 1985—to 56 million tons (51 million metric tons). In Asia, the increase was scheduled at 54%—to reach 42 million tons (38.5 million metric tons). African countries were planning for 7 million tons (6.4 million metric tons), a 310% increase. Capacity in the Middle East headed for 7.2 million tons (6.6 million metric tons), a 56% increase.

Developing countries such as Brazil, Mexico, South Korea, and Taiwan, were building steel plants that will be among the most advanced in the world. For instance, Mexico was exploiting its abundant natural gas supplies to take advantage of the direct reduction technology, a way of producing steel at much lower capital costs and substantially lower fuel costs than by conventional blast furnaces. Mexico began to sell its steel technology to the rest of the world.

Petroleum production in the world edged a bit ahead of the rate of 60 million barrels a day it reached in 1978. While Iranian production dropped sharply from the 5.5 million barrel rate of 1978, other producers—notably Saudi Arabia—managed to cover the shortfall.

The United Kingdom was well on the way to becoming self-sufficient in petroleum. With production some 50% ahead of 1978 levels, the 1.7 million barrels a day rate reached by year-end was only 15% short of oil self-sufficiency.

While pumping oil at a rate of 9.5 million barrels a day, about 12% above its normal production ceiling, Saudi Arabia pushed its vast industrial development program past the halfway mark. In various stages of completion were half a dozen petrochemical plants, steel and aluminum mills, and a variety of light and medium industries. Billions of dollars were being spent on developing power-generating stations, pipelines, desalination stations, and other facilities needed to support the nation's industrial production capacity that was being developed.

The largest oil producer in the world, the Soviet Union, produced at a daily rate of 11.5 million barrels. That was a gain of 250,000 barrels from the 1978 level. It was the smallest annual gain since the mid-1950's.

Industrial output in the Soviet Union increased 3.6% in 1979, instead of 5.7% as planned. Production goals were not reached in steel, coal, and oil. Production also fell short of planned levels in fertilizers, synthetic resins, plastics, machines and equipment, paper, and consumer goods. While coal production and steel production were the major shortfalls, production of natural gas advanced briskly.

Ago Ambre, *U. S. Department of Commerce*

The photo-mural at the Daniel Freeman Memorial Hospital, Inglewood, CA, provides an illusion of inviting parkland.

INTERIOR DESIGN

The full potential of the photographic mural as a decorating tool has only just begun to be realized. It makes possible wall-sized photographic reproduction, that can be adapted to any environment, indoors or out, and that can be used on any surface material such as vinyl, fabric, Plexiglas, plastic, wood, paper, or cement. The mural functions remarkably well as an alternate art form to tapestry, decorative tiles, or other surface decoration.

In May 1979, the Light Gallery in New York invited five prominent interior design firms to use photography in a personal or corporate setting to illustrate just how photography "is a viable and decorative means of adorning" such interior spaces. One design firm, Patino/Wolf, both of whose partners have been personally collecting photographic art for some time, created a black and white dining setting against a wall of Arnold Newman's photo-mural of Igor Stravinsky. Completing the composition was a black and white table setting.

Although this gallery exercise was somewhat visionary, there are numerous interior designers using photo-murals to great advantage in permanent installation. They see the photo-mural as visually extending space, as giving prominence to an otherwise undistinguished space, as a vehicle for color, as creating a special mood, and in some cases as a sales tool.

Shops. Architect David Kenneth Specter of New York commissioned a series of beautiful buff and white photographic images of Rosenthal USA, Ltd. products. These were enlarged into murals to be hung on walls or over counters as guides for product location.

Theater. A highlight of the recently remodeled theater/lecture hall at the Parsons School of Design in New York is a wall mural produced by means of a computerized photographic scanner process in which bars of color provide an optical illusion. The mural was conceived by Ivan Chermayeff of Chermayeff and Geismar Associates, New York. The photomural is actually an interesting presentation of colored pencils, an apt symbol for a design school. One long yellow pencil runs horizontally below a random row of rounded pencil ends sandwiching a vertical row of pencils. The general effect resembles an endless pencil box surmounted by rows of undulating pencil lines.

Offices. A pacific scene of ponds, Mt. Rainier, and a sparse conifer forest is the subject of one of many wall-size photo-murals within the New York public relations office of the 3M Company. The visual distance of this colorful landscape adds enormous dimension to the one enclosing wall of a small space. The interior designer for this project was Jerry Peterson.

In Dallas, interior designer Teddy Storm of Walhide commissioned a 9′ x 24′ (2.7 m x 7.3 m) wall-mural "Chestnut Forest," a wintery night scene mounted across the length of the wall facing the entrance to the Omega Optical Company. The photographer of the woodland scene was Dr. Greg Dimijian.

The photo-mural of the Parsons School of Design theater/lecture hall is brilliant with a unique design of brightly colored pencils.

JAIME ARDILES-ARCE, COURTESY, CHERMAYEFF & GEISMAR ASSOCS.

An early example of the "Scanamural" process is this pictorial map of North American fur trading history, located at the Telemark Lodge, Cable, WI.

COURTESY, 3M COMPANY

For the Montrose Products Company, Auburn, MA, architect Richard Lamoureux worked with art photographer Stephen Knapp, a specialist in abstract photo-murals for commercial interiors, to produce a 6' x 50' (1.8 m x 15.2 m) abstract color photograph of machinery parts.

Richard Jones and Ron Oates hung a large and arresting framed photographic color portrait of an elderly lady of strong character facing the entry to the offices of Ciranow Ltd.

Hotel. The ceiling of the Los Angeles airport La Hacienda Hotel lobby is a series of overscaled murals of radiantly lighted sun-flecked autumn leaves in golds and rusts. The photographic work was done by Joey Fisher of Los Angeles. This commission was through interior designer Harry Stoff, Jr., of Harry McCague Associates.

Restaurant. Fisher also was commissioned to create for the Hungry Tiger restaurant, Westwood, CA, an exclusive photo-mural (9' x 32', or 2.7 m x 9.7 m) of the desert plants found in the San Francisco Arboretum. The interior designer for the project was Robert Ross.

Hospital. The interior views of the Daniel Freeman Center for Diagnostic and Rehabilitative Medicine, Inglewood, CA, are a forest in Vermont and a bosky grove in Yosemite Valley. These heroic photo-murals by Joey Fisher become interior architecture that envelops patients and staff in the surrounding woodsy atmosphere. Jean Crane of United Business Interiors was the interior designer.

Residential. In the main entry of a Toronto apartment in the Palace Pier condominium, large sliding closet doors are faced with enormous neutral-toned photo-murals of unfurling fern fronds. These photo-murals create the illusion of an added dimension of unspecified depth. Jack Childs of Childs/Dreyfus Inc., Chicago, was the interior designer.

JEANNE WEEKS
American Society of Interior Designers

INTERNATIONAL TRADE AND FINANCE

Inflation and recession were marring the world economic scene as 1979 ended. A 50% increase in the price of Organization of Oil Exporting Countries (OPEC) oil added a new element to an already uncertain outlook. The 1978–79 oil price increases were not expected to have the devastating impact the Arab oil embargo and the doubling of oil prices had in 1973–74, but the flareup of hostilities in key oil-producing areas could have a major effect on supply. The earlier price rises occurred when worldwide economic activity was slowing. The 1979 increases and the enormous prices paid for oil on the "spot" market occurred with the United States in an economic slowdown and with its major trading partners in an expansionary phase.

The effect of higher-priced oil on inflation, current account balances, and economic growth of the importing countries alone slowed economic growth to an average rate of 1% worldwide. The General Agreement on Tariff and Trade (GATT) noted that the world economy may well be facing a prolonged period of restricted growth. It warned that future global world trade depended mainly on success of the fight against worldwide inflation. GATT emphasized that while the sharp increase in petroleum prices contributed to inflation, it was not the major causative factor; inflation rates already were rising in the United States and Western Europe in the middle of 1978. Between July 1978–July 1979, the consumer price index in industrial countries rose by 9%. The oil-price increases adjusted for inflation came to 10%.

GATT said the ultimate impact of the oil price increase depends on the reaction of individual countries. The West German Central Bank (Bundesbank) said part of the impact should be offset because increased spending by consumers on petroleum products would necessarily lead, because of limited incomes, to reduced spending on other goods.

Trade–Economic Growth–Oil. World trade, which amounted to $1.3 trillion in 1978, expanded at a slower rate in 1979 and, because of inflation, the growth was more in dollar value than in volume. While prices of petroleum and related products accelerated sharply, export prices of other primary, nonprimary, and manufactured products continued to move upward although not uniformly.

On July 26, President Carter signed into law an international trade agreement, initialed by the United States and 99 other countries in April. The president called the law "perhaps the most important and far-reaching trade legislation in the history of the United States." The agreement was the culmination of six years of tough negotiations at the Tokyo Round of Talks in Geneva, under the auspices of GATT. It reduced tariffs by about 33% on hundreds of items over the next eight years, opened foreign government purchases to American bidders, and greatly liberalized other trade areas.

Growth in the United States was 3.5% in the third quarter, but as the threat of a U. S. recession continued the rate was expected to decelerate. U. S. inflation for the year averaged about 14% despite monetary restraint policies in the final quarter. The U. S. merchandise trade-balance was estimated at $30 billion in 1979. The current account was in surplus in the first quarter, but the oil increases caused a deficit estimated at $7 billion for the year.

Major U. S. trading partners were poised for economic growth in 1979, but oil price increases and the rise in value of the dollar used to pay for oil—both of which fueled inflation—dampened growth. The International Monetary Fund (IMF) estimated average growth in the industrial countries at less than 3%. West Germany, after a disappointing first quarter because of the unsettled oil situation and a harsh winter, had real growth of about 4%. Japan, with a total dependence on imported oil, went into deficit on its trade figures and its rapid economic expansion of the past several years slowed to about 5.8%.

Although Germany and Switzerland expanded monetary growth slightly, most major countries showed little inclination to make up for the OPEC price hike by injecting this sort of stimulus; indeed, the 1978 monetary expansion to counter extreme downward pressure on the dollar contributed to higher inflation rates in Europe.

Revenues of OPEC countries rose sharply from the depressed 1978 level, when there was a temporary supply glut, because of higher oil prices. The effect of the huge surpluses was alleviated somewhat since much of OPEC unspendable income was recycled into investments in both government securities and private banks in the United States and Europe. There was a discernible flight of capital from the Middle East at the end of November as nervousness over the spread of hostilities concerning Iran increased; much of this private and government money was going to Europe and into gold and silver.

The increase in OPEC revenues was accompanied by a corresponding addition to the import bill of consuming countries, which the IMF estimated would mean an additional $70 billion to developed nations and $5 billion to the developing countries which are not oil exporters.

Oil production in OPEC countries declined substantially in the early part of the year and by February was 14% less than in December

1978. The reduced production and the political turmoil in Iran made future supplies uncertain. There were enormous price increases in spot market prices to over $45 a barrel as countries scrambled to obtain needed oil; indeed there were predictions that OPEC would do away with contract pricing altogether and let the spot market set the price.

Much of the reduction of imports by consuming countries in 1978 had resulted from decreased production, not decreased consumption. After OPEC countries, with the exception of Saudi Arabia, the world's largest producer, imposed additional price increases on top of the 1979 average 15% increase decided at the OPEC pricing session in December 1978, the depletion in supply was somewhat alleviated. But the overall production for the year was less than in 1978. The average price of all types of crude petroleum increased an estimated 60% through July; GATT estimated that the year-over-year increase for 1979 amounted to 35%.

OPEC's pricing meeting in Caracas, Venezuela, in December was punctuated by sharp disagreement between hardline producers, who opted for a contract price of $30 a barrel or more and moderate members, led by Saudi Arabia, who wanted a smaller increase. The meeting broke up with no agreement and with members raising prices to between $21.43 a barrel and $34.72. Saudi Arabia promised to keep its production up through the first quarter of 1980, but the supply situation after that was uncertain.

The worldwide turmoil over oil accelerated in November when Iran's revolutionary government imposed a total boycott on sales to the United States and tried to demand payment for its oil in currencies other than the dollar. Although Iran accounted for less than 10% of U. S. imports, the deteriorating political situation there unsettled the outlook for the entire Middle Eastern oil producing region.

Oil consumption decreased in most European countries and Japan, and to a slightly lower extent in the United States. Yet U. S. energy use remained distressingly high. At the Tokyo economic summit conference in June, President Carter and the other six Western leaders pledged to reduce imports dramatically, but the United States failed to enact the cohesive energy program needed to fulfill that pledge. Treasury Secretary G. William Miller traveled to the Middle East in late November in an effort to persuade Saudi Arabia and other oil producing countries that the United States would indeed cut consumption.

The exports of the developing countries which are non-oil producers increased, but because the cost of their imports rose their payments deficit reached a record $40 billion, compared with $31 billion in 1978.

The Soviet Union and other Eastern bloc countries, which in 1978 registered their slowest growth rate since World War II, experienced a further erosion to an estimated 3.5% growth. The low rate was attributed to poor results in the industrial sector, combined with severe winter weather and energy shortages. Any trade benefits the Soviet Union gained by the higher oil prices and record prices for gold—the USSR has the world's largest unmined supply after South Africa—were offset by the need for increased grain purchases.

Fueled by renewed relations with China, however, trade between the United States and 10 Communist countries grew 36% in the first 9 months of 1979, relative to the same period of 1978. The United States sold China $1.08 billions' worth of manufactured and agricultural products in 1978. Russia bought $2.8 billions' worth of U. S. products in 1978.

The interest rate increases and the measures to curtail credit that industrialized countries imposed to fight inflation added to their current-account problems and those of Third World countries. Developing nations increased borrowing, both from commercial banks and from multilateral institutions, including the IMF.

Gold. Gold bullion, which averaged $193.50 an ounce for the whole of 1978, went over $500 an ounce at the end of 1979, and financial analysts were predicting $600 an ounce early in

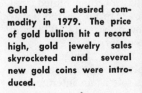
Gold was a desired commodity in 1979. The price of gold bullion hit a record high, gold jewelry sales skyrocketed and several new gold coins were introduced.

1980, primarily because much of the buying seemed to be going into "hoarding." Gold had risen to $442 an ounce on October 2, then dropped to $383.50 by October 5. It hovered around $390 an ounce through November, surged through $400 at the end of the month, and broke $500 the day after Christmas. Other precious metals also went to record prices. Silver was trading at around $30 an ounce at the end of December, compared with a price of just more than $5 an ounce as 1979 began.

But gold held center stage. The volatility—as much as $70 an ounce fluctuation in a single week during September—was unprecedented. Although much of the September surge was speculative, trading took on a different character in late November. Speculators were not in the market to any extent, as shown by the fact that the physical (cash) market led the futures, a turnaround from usual practice.

The public was not the factor in the gold market that it had been in the latter part of 1978 when the dollar was under pressure. Gold coin sales, an indicator of such participation, were lower in volume in the latter part of the year, although the dollar value rose because of the high price. Sales of the South African Krugerrand, the most widely purchased coin, declined from a high of 551,400 coins in April to 416,316 in September.

However, while not approaching the historic fascination with gold characteristic of other parts of the world, the U.S. public became more interested in the metal. Gold jewelry sales boomed and stores reported customers buying jewelry of heavier karat, such as 18-karat and 22-karat, and the public was increasingly critical of the continued sale of gold by the Department of the Treasury.

There also was a further monetization of gold in the United States. Bullion became a legitimate private portfolio investment for the first time in recent history, largely through the investment vehicle of gold certificates sold by big banks and brokerage houses. Investors in record numbers were putting varying portions of their portfolios into gold.

Yet another indication of the increasing interest in gold was new gold coins, both official and private, either minted or announced during the year. The new Canadian Maple Leaf, at one troy ounce gold weight, was aimed competitively at the Krugerrand.

Supply from production and net official sales remained about the same as the previous year. The South African Chamber of Mines estimated total free world production at 31 million ounces, and net sales from the Communist bloc at 8 million ounces. The total 39 million ounces of new supply had a worth of about $1.5 billion at current prices. The new Canadian coin will absorb most of Canada's production. South African miners, in keeping with government regulations, were forced to work the less pro-

ductive mines, which could be made to pay as a consequence of the high prices.

Unlike the reaction to sharp price increases of the past, commercial and industrial demand for gold did not fall off dramatically. Gold jewelry accounted for 28.5 million ounces, other industrial demand for 8.5 million ounces, coins for 8 million ounces, and hoarding for 15 million ounces.

A flight of money from the Middle East in December because of the increasing political unrest put additional upward pressure on gold. Because of this physical buying, speculation eased during much of the last month of the year, and many analysts were looking at the once-unheard-of $400 an ounce as a new bottom price for gold.

Currencies. The dollar was not weakened appreciably by gold's first push through $400, but the Treasury, in an attempt to "deter speculation," announced in October it would no longer hold monthly sales, which in May had been cut from 1.5 million ounces to 750,000 ounces a month. Instead, Treasury would hold auctions at unspecified times for unspecified amounts. The first such auction, for 1.25 million ounces, was held in early November. West Germany also took measures to limit the buying of gold by German banks, which had been big purchasers of official gold.

The buying by wealthy Middle Eastern interests, which began in September, was partly an alternative investment for the huge oil surpluses being accumulated, but the spread of political unrest accelerated the historic Arab buying of gold in times of danger.

If the dollar remained stronger than it had during the severely depressed 1978 level for most of the year, it was far from robust. It underwent several bouts of pressure, especially against the strong West German mark. Between the first of June and the middle of July the dollar lost about 2.5% in value against major currencies in the wake of the energy crisis and a shake-up in President Carter's cabinet. The dollar was supported heavily during this time by central banks.

The gold-market turmoil in September and October caused further selling pressure. On September 24, Treasury Undersecretary Anthony Solomon admitted that a new defense zone of 1.76 marks for the dollar had been accepted by the U.S. Federal Reserve System and the Bundesbank. U.S. and European officials attending the World Bank meeting hinted that there would be measures to prop up the dollar similar to those announced Nov. 1, 1978, and this resulted in some recovery.

Continued U.S. inflation, budget deficit, and trade deficit prevented any real strengthening of the dollar, and its role as an international reserve currency declined. But high U.S. interest rates, agreement by central banks to support the dollar at reduced levels, and the need

THE DOLLAR CLUB

LADIES WELCOME

SUSAN B. ANTHONY

"MEN—THEY FINALLY LET YOU IN WHEN IT'S NOT WORTH JOINING!"

A cartoonist makes a connection between the new Susan B. Anthony dollar and the diminishing value of the dollar.

for dollars by other countries to pay for oil provided support for most of the year.

In December, however, the dollar underwent a bout of selling that took it below the all-time low rates of Oct. 30, 1978. As with the rise in gold, this downward pressure stemmed from a movement of Arab oil money away from the dollar, primarily into the West German mark, Swiss franc, and British pound. The freeze of Iranian assets in the United States was thought to be a factor in the swing away from dollars, but the spread of anti-American demonstrations in the Near and Middle East also fueled the hedging of dollar assets by wealthy interests in that part of the world.

The dollar's value against the yen and pound fluctuated widely during 1979. Japan's worsening domestic problems and its total dependence on imported oil resulted in a sharp depreciation of the yen in November, pushing the dollar to a two-year high. Britain's pound reached a four-year high of $2.20 at midyear, fell to $2.09, then rose sharply again in the last quarter. The rise resulted because Britain's North Sea oil gave it a relatively secure position on the energy front and because the Bank of England hiked its basic interest rate to a record 17%.

The Federal Reserve's increases in the discount rate, although aimed at domestic inflation, also were taken with an eye to shoring up the dollar. West German rates in turn rose by one percentage point between August and the end of October because of Germany's announced intent to push its inflation rate of 5%

back down to the 2% to 3% range. Japan increased interest rates, as did central banks of most industrialized countries. West German officials and private bankers, in response to criticism from the United States, made it clear that they would not take the blame for any resulting turmoil in currency markets and indicated that the United States must be ready to accept a stronger medicine to fight inflation.

The Federal Reserve apparently eased its upward pressure on interest rates during November as the U. S. outlook darkened and the downward turn in short-term rates accelerated the flight from the dollar.

European Monetary System. The European Monetary System (EMS), a float agreement among European Community (EC) countries, was put into effect March 13, at a time when the dollar had strengthened and foreign exchange markets were relatively stable. The announced intention of the EMS was to foster "closer monetary stability in Europe."

Upward pressure on the West German mark, which continuously threatened to break the top of the 2.25% allowed fluctuation (6% for Italy), forced a realignment late in the year. The mark was revalued by 2% against the currencies of Belgium, France, Ireland, Italy, Luxembourg, and The Netherlands, and by 5% against the Danish kroner, the weakest currency in the float, which was again devalued at the end of November. Austria and Switzerland, although not members of the float, worked to keep their currencies within the bounds of their trading partners and to this end Switzerland in November eased restrictions on the purchase of its franc. Britain also declined to join the EMS, stating that to keep the pound within the float would put too much pressure on its reserves.

The fundamental idea of the EMS is that it would ultimately lead to a unified European currency. West Germany and France, which instigated formation of the EMS, were thought to be committed to preventing it from going the way of a former float, called the "snake," which disintegrated because of widely varying rates of inflation and economic conditions in member countries. Indeed, there seemed to be a new commitment within the European Community to foster economic cooperation.

IMF. The dollar's weakness was a primary topic of behind-the-scenes conversation at the IMF-World Bank meeting in Belgrade, Yugoslavia, where about 7,000 monetary officials and private bankers from 138 countries met October 2–5 to discuss the proposed "substitution account." The account would enable countries to exchange surplus dollar holdings for an international asset whose value would be linked to the IMF's special drawing rights. The value of the SDR, about $1.30 late in 1979, is pegged to a number of currencies and thus is more stable than the dollar. The dollars deposited in the account would be transferred into some form of U. S. government obligation. The United States, which initially was opposed to the account, indicated it would now "give it serious consideration."

MARY TOBIN
United Press International

IOWA

Major 1979 happenings in Iowa included the visits of Pope John Paul II and President Jimmy Carter, the passage of diverse legislation, a May unemployment rate of 2.9% that was approximately one half the national average, and an excellent corn crop and soybean yield.

City and County News. Oakland voters abandoned the commission form of city government after a six-year trial period. This vote left only Burlington, Ottumwa, Cedar Rapids, and Ft. Dodge with the commission system of city government.

The Iowa Supreme Court ruled that Des Moines could be sued for failure to enforce the city's building and fire codes.

Ten Iowa cities and one county applied Iowa's first-allowed local option tax on hotels and motels. Ten other cities and one county rejected by popular referendum the optional tax.

Constitutional home rule for the ninety-nine counties of Iowa went into operation following voter approval in the November 1978 elections.

Agriculture. In spite of the wettest August in Iowa history, the state's corn crop was the largest in the nation, and the soybean yield was the state's largest ever.

Marshalltown was the host to the state and national plowing matches in August.

The Legislature. The Republican-controlled General Assembly voted a $50 million rebate on income taxes paid by Iowa citizens and increased the salaries of state government officials.

Record budget appropriations for two fiscal years totaled $3.5 billion—$1.707 billion for 1979–80 and $1.768 billion for 1980–81. The appropriations provide $508 million for aid to the 447 public school districts.

Legislation was approved that limited the growth of property tax values of homes and farmland. The growth in the assessed value was limited to 6% for 1979 and 4% for 1980 and every year thereafter. The law also made permanent the "productivity" system of valuing farmland—i.e. farmland is valued on the basis of goods produced.

In other major legislation the General Assembly agreed to an income tax indexing system which would prevent a taxpayer's income tax from increasing because of inflation. However, the indexing would be ended if the balance in the state treasury dropped below $60 million at the end of a fiscal year.

The legislature joined the other states that have called upon the U. S. Congress to adopt a balanced federal budget by the 1981 fiscal year or face a possible constitutional convention. Unemployment benefits were reduced from a maximum of 39 weeks to 26 weeks. A state equal rights amendment, which parallels the proposed federal equal rights amendment (ERA), was approved. The measure will be submitted to the electorate in 1980.

Prominent Visitors. In August President Jimmy Carter, while vacationing on the stern wheeler *Delta Queen,* talked with Iowans in McGregor, Dubuque, Clinton, Davenport, Muscatine, Burlington, Ft. Madison, and Keokuk. He also held an outdoor town meeting in Burlington. Pope John Paul II visited the Iowa Living History Farms northwest of Des Moines.

RUSSELL M. ROSS, *University of Iowa*

IOWA • Information Highlights

Area: 56,290 square miles (145 791 km²).
Population (Jan. 1979 est.): 2,904,000.
Chief Cities (1976 est.): Des Moines, the capital, 195,-405; Cedar Rapids, 108,684; Davenport, 101,459.
Government (1979): *Chief Officers*—governor, Robert D. Ray (R); lt. gov., Terry E. Branstad (R). *General Assembly*—Senate, 50 members; House of Representatives, 100 members.
Education (1978–79): *Enrollment*—public elementary schools, 295,748 pupils; public secondary, 272,792; colleges and universities, 129,181 students. *Public school expenditures,* $1,218,603,000 ($2,023 per pupil).
State Finances (fiscal year 1978): *Revenues,* $2,774,-463,000; *expenditures,* $2,742,151,000.
Personal Income (1978): $23,170,000,000; per capita, $8,002.
Labor Force (July 1979): *Nonagricultural wage and salary earners,* 1,125,500; *unemployed,* 50,900 (3.5% of total force).

The once-exiled Ayatollah Ruhollah Khomeini is greeted by supporters shortly after his return to Iran to lead the revolution.

UPI

IRAN

It was for Iran a year of revolution. A theocratic autocracy of an extraordinary kind, dominated by the Ayatollah Ruhollah Khomeini, came to power, and a millenia-old monarchy and a 50-year-old dynasty were destroyed. But beyond it all lurked the question of whether the capacity of the country to function normally as a coherent entity had not also been dealt a mortal blow. Toward the end of the year, by embarking on an anti-American course of conduct wholly outside the norms of international behavior, Iran became the object of world condemnation. The economy was a shambles, the minority regions were strongly fissiparous. Nevertheless, there were no signs that internal or external pressures were soon likely to deflect or overturn the new ruler of Iran, the Ayatollah Khomeini (*see* BIOGRAPHY, page 133).

Bakhtiar Government. The widespread opposition to former Shah Mohammed Reza Pahlavi, manifested in riots and demonstrations throughout Iran in 1978, had led to concession after concession and finally to the shah's invitation on Dec. 29, 1978, to Dr. Shahpour Bakhtiar to form a new, civilian government. Bakhtiar, 63, a French-educated lawyer, had high credentials. As a young man he had fought on the Repub-

lican side in the Spanish Civil War, and in World War II as a volunteer in the French army and in the French resistance movement. He had supported Iranian Prime Minister Dr. Mohammed Mossadegh in the early 1950's, and as a member of the National Front he had been a consistent and outspoken, though not extreme, critic of the shah. His appointment at some earlier time might have defused the opposition, but the historic moment for such a gambit had passed.

Bakhtiar formed a cabinet January 1 and was formally appointed prime minister three days later. He presented his cabinet to the *Majlis* (lower house) on January 11, together with a 17-point reform program which was approved by a vote of 149 to 49. Bakhtiar also announced that Iran would no longer sell oil to Israel (which had received more than half its supplies from Iran) or to South Africa (where the figure was 90%).

Inevitably, the new government was denounced by most elements in the opposition, and Bakhtiar was expelled from the National Front. From his place of exile in France, the Ayatollah Khomeini issued a characteristic pronouncement that obedience to the new administration was tantamount to "obedience to Satan." Despite continuing violence and the decision of Gen. Feridun Djam to reject an offer to be defense minister, Bakhtiar at first received support from the middle class and some moderate members of the opposition (including three of the five eminent Muslims holding the title of Ayatollah al-Ozman or Great Ayatollah).

Initial conciliatory measures were well received, newspapers started publishing again after a break of six weeks, air traffic controllers and oil workers returned to work, and the universities reopened.

End of Shah's Rule. The opposition of the Ayatollah Khomeini, however, was adamant. On January 13, the shah appointed a regency council and three days later left for Egypt with the Empress Farah on what was nominally a vacation but was likely to be a protracted exile. On the day he left, January 16, a violent earthquake struck eastern Iran causing more than 200 deaths and destroying some 1,000 buildings. The portent proved all too real.

In his memoirs, published in Paris in the fall, the former shah criticized the United States for its lack of support during his last weeks in power. According to Pahlavi, Gen. Robert E. Huyser, deputy commander of U. S. forces in Europe, was in Iran from January 8 to February 6 with the mission of persuading leading Iranian military officers to forget their oaths of loyalty to the ruler; his departure into exile, said the shah, was strongly urged by the government of the United States.

On the same day (January 13) that the regency council was created, Khomeini, still in France, announced the formation of a provisional "revolutionary Islamic council." For more than three weeks thereafter, there were in effect two rival authorities in Iran. Riots and demonstrations—some in favor of one side and some in favor of the other—continued. The effectiveness of the Bakhtiar government steadily eroded, and its ranks were depleted by resignations of important members. Efforts to establish a modus vivendi between Bakhtiar and Khomeini failed in the face of the latter's rock-like refusal to open negotiations or even speak with representatives of what he termed an illegal regime.

Khomeini in Power. Khomeini's return to Iran, delayed for three days by the government's forced closing of the nation's airport, finally took place on February 1. He received a tumultuous welcome. The next day Bakhtiar offered to form a "government of national unity," but the pro-posal was rejected. Instead, Khomeini announced February 5 that Dr. Mehdi Bazarghan had been appointed prime minister of a provisional government and that he would shortly announce a cabinet. Bazarghan, 73, had a background similar in some ways to that of Bakhtiar. He had been partly educated in France and had served in Mossadegh's cabinet in the early 1950's. He was a devout Muslim and was regarded as a moderate among opponents of the shah. Like Bakhtiar, he had at times been a political prisoner. In the *Majlis* on February 5, Bakhtiar said that he regarded the formation of a rival government as "a joke." It was an empty bluff. After two days of street fighting in Tehran, the armed revolutionary followers of Khomeini overthrew the Bakhtiar government on February 11. Some fighting continued, however, and it was not until February 15 that a modicum of calm returned to the capital. On February 14, the U. S. embassy had been attacked by left-wing gunmen and occupied for several hours—another sketch of things to come.

Difficulties of Bazarghan. Bazarghan's tenure as prime minister lasted from early February until November 6, when he resigned in disgust over the takeover of the U. S. embassy. All along his authority was largely nominal, and he was in more or less continuous conflict with Khomeini and his followers. He complained, with justification, that they were usurping his authority, and voiced vain protests at the hundreds of summary executions. Several times previously he had submitted his resignation but then withdrawn it. On one of those occasions (August 31) he had responded to a charge of "lack of revolutionary enthusiasm" by saying "I accept the accusation," adding that he acted as he did because he respected international standards. It was clearly impossible for such a man to cooperate indefinitely with Khomeini. The Islamic leadership had been whipping up sentiment against Bazarghan because of his meeting with U. S. national security adviser Zbigniew Brzezinski in Algiers on November 1.

Bazarghan's defeated predecessor, Bakhtiar, disappeared in mid-February, and his whereabouts were unknown for almost six months. He reappeared August 1 to hold a press conference in Paris. He denounced the Islamic republic and observed with considerable accuracy that Iran was in a state of disintegration. "At present there is no government in Iran in the real sense of the word," he said. "What we have lost in a year of demonstrations and chaos exceeds all that was wasted and stolen during the reign of the shah. To get the country working again will need years and years."

Theocratic Autocracy. The Khomeini regime was consolidated by a nationwide referendum March 30–31 which gave overwhelming approval to the formation of an Islamic Republic. From that time until the end of the year there were no major changes in government. On December 2–

———— IRAN · Information Highlights ————

Official Name: Empire of Iran.
Location: Southwest Asia.
Area: 636,300 square miles (1 648 000 km²).
Population (1979 est.): 36,300,000.
Chief Cities (1976 census): Tehran, the capital, 4,496,-159 (met. area); Isfahan, 671,825; Meshed, 670,180.
Government: *Head of state and government,* Ayatollah Ruhollah Khomeini.
Monetary Unit: Rial (71.50 rials equals U. S.$1, Dec. 1979).
Manufactures (major products): Petrochemicals, textiles, cement, processed foods, steel, aluminum.
Agriculture (major products): Wheat, rice, barley.

3, however, the Islamic Republic was riveted more securely in place by a referendum (boycotted by about one third of the people), which gave approval to a draft constitution. This extraordinary document envisaged the creation of a unique religious autocracy in which the operations of an elected (but weak) president, premier, and assembly would be overseen, and if necessary overridden, by an all-powerful chief Theologian (i.e. Khomeini), assisted by mullahs (teachers of law and doctrine) throughout the country. The new constitution also established Shi'ite Islam as the official state religion and named Khomeini as Iran's political and religious leader for life.

Although Khomeini was a genius at revolution, he knew nothing of government or administration in any normal sense. He therefore found it essential to have aides with the necessary skills, but he did not find it easy to work with them. After the November 6 departure of the long-suffering Bazarghan, the office of prime minister remained vacant. It was believed, however, that the Ayatollah Mohammud Beheshti, first secretary of the Islamic Revolutionary Council—the central governing body after the revolution—was fulfilling the role. Under Bazarghan the post of foreign minister had been filled by Dr. Karim Sanjabi, a leader in the anti-Shah National Front. Sanjabi resigned on April 15, criticizing "disorders created by a government within a government." His successor, Ibrahim Yazdi, resigned with Bazarghan on November 6 and was succeeded briefly (November 11–28) by Abdul-

Hussein Bani Sadr, and he by Sadegh Ghotbzadeh. None of these figures had any genuine independent authority, and anything they said was liable to be countermanded by Khomeini or, after November 4, by the terrorists holding the U. S. embassy.

Factional Strife. The authority of the barely-functioning central government was challenged by a number of groups and factions, and violence in various forms continued. The local *komitehs* (civil organizations, usually directed by a mullah) went their own way, often in sympathy with the revolution but hardly under the control of Tehran. The long-established Tudeh (Communist) party was crippled by the minions of the Ayatollah, who destroyed many of its offices throughout the country. Other extreme groups included the People's Fedayeen—Marxist but Islamic—and the Muja Hadeen—Islamic but Marxist. A new extreme leftist underground guerrilla group, the Forghan (Koran) Fighters, came into existence in 1979 and claimed responsibility for the assassinations of General Qaraneh on April 23 and the Ayatollah Morteza Motahari on May 1. Both men were associates of Khomeini.

Domestic Policy. The domestic policy of the Khomeini regime consisted largely of an attempt to restore a somewhat mythical state of Islamic purity. Women were told to resume wearing the chador (veil) and forsake Western dress, but the adamant refusal of large numbers forced Khomeini to recant in part. Music was forbidden on the state radio, but cassette players supplied what

P. LEDRU, SYGMA

Iranian students, *left,* demanding the return of the shah, hold American hostages at the U. S. embassy. In response, Americans ask for the expulsion of all Iranians.

BART, SYGMA

radio lacked. Alcohol was officially forbidden but was obtainable on a black market.

The other principal feature of the new domestic policy was the wreaking of vengeance on all who had worked in or with the shah's regime. By the end of the year, some 800 persons had been executed after hasty, or no, trials. They included the shah's long-time prime minister, Amir Abbas Hoveida (executed April 4), senior military and police officials, members of *savak* (the shah's secret police), and civil servants. There also were rather offhand executions of prostitutes, homosexuals, and the merely rich.

The Khomeini autocracy also had no love for freedom of the press. Some 20 to 30 foreign correspondents, including representatives of *The New York Times* and the (London) *Daily Telegraph* were expelled for writing "unfriendly" reports, and the principal independent newspaper of Iran, *Ayandegan,* gave up the struggle and ceased publication May 12.

Economic Policy. Economic policy tried to undo the work of development, modernizing, and Westernization by which the shah had hoped to turn Iran into a major industrial power by the 1980's. Private ownership and economic institutions were attacked. Banks were nationalized on June 7, insurance companies on June 25, and many key industries on July 5. Most ongoing construction projects were halted early in the year and were never resumed. A variety of projects involving foreign participation were abrogated and the contracts terminated. Arms contracts with foreign governments were canceled, and on November 23 foreign debts were repudiated. The level of oil production was seriously down, and many industries were at a standstill. Although largely a matter of speculation, the gross national product for 1979 was probably about half that of 1978. The only growth industry was the cultivation of opium, which enjoyed a boom.

Regional Separatism. Iran has rightly been called an empire rather than a strictly unified and homogeneous state. Barely half the population belongs to the dominant Persian group; there are 10 million Azerbaijanis in the north and about another 8 million of smaller minorities—Kurds, Arabs, Baluchis, and Turkomans. In 1979, all these groups resisted the bonds of the central government, and (unlike the shah) the Ayatollah did not have an effective military force to control them. If the structure of Iran were to be maintained at all, moves toward regional and ethnic autonomy would have to be made. There was outright war in Kurdistan from July through early September, and although the government forces could claim victory, a long-term compromise was still pending at year's end. Azerbaijanian nationalism had its own great religious leader in the respected and moderate Ayatollah Shariat Madari, whose supporters clashed repeatedly with those of Khomeini in late 1979 and early 1980.

Foreign Policy. The main thrust of the new foreign policy was a deliberate reversal of the shah's pro-U. S. orientation. The revolution had brought an abrupt end to all military cooperation with the United States, and on February 6, Iran was withdrawn from the Central Treaty Organization (CENTO). The Khomeini regime pointedly espoused the Arab cause, drew close to the Palestine Liberation Organization (PLO), and denounced Egypt, Israel, and South Africa. There also were border disputes with Iraq.

Confrontation with the United States. Hostility toward the United States was central to Khomeini's world-view and was explicit in everything he did and said, but relations did not reach the stage of outright confrontation until the last two months of the year. This came about as a result of the movements of the exiled shah. The shah —whose assassination (along with that of his family and several past premiers) had been called for by the head of the Iranian revolutionary courts on May 13—took refuge in Egypt (January 16), Morocco (January 22), the Bahamas (March 30), and Mexico (June 10). The United States, reversing its earlier announcement, informed Pahlavi on April 19 that he would not be welcome in the United States. Former Secretary of State Henry Kissinger argued that "a man who for 37 years was a friend of the United States should not be treated like a flying Dutchman who cannot find a port of call." On October 22 the shah was permitted to enter a New York hospital for gallbladder surgery and treatment of lymphatic cancer, from which he had apparently suffered for several years. This was followed on November 4 by an action unprecedented in the annals of international relations—the seizure of the U. S. embassy in Tehran by armed, so-called students who demanded the return of the shah and who took hostage some 60 of the embassy staff. There were no disclaimers forthcoming from Khomeini, and it became clear that the takeover was welcomed, if not expressly sanctioned, by the Ayatollah. What was not known was the extent to which the terrorists would be amenable to Khomeini's commands. The embassy crisis continued into 1980 despite reconciliation efforts by the United Nations, the pleas and denunciations of the world community, threats and economic sanctions by the United States, and the December 16 departure of the shah for Panama.

Uncertainties. Although a great deal was unknown about the Iranian situation, the one clear probability was that either some serious effort had to be made to get the country going again or a downward spiral toward poverty and chaos would supervene. Oxford historian A. J. P. Taylor once wrote: "Idealists make revolutions; practical men come afterwards and clear up the mess." By early 1980 the Iranian revolution had not yet reached the second stage.

ARTHUR CAMPBELL TURNER
University of California, Riverside

Gen. Saddam Hussein, *left*, the new president of Iraq, attends the September summit of nonaligned nations in Havana. At his side is Cuba's First Vice President Raul Castro (brother of Fidel).

UPI

IRAQ

Iraq in 1979 experienced what, in the context of the nation's political history, must be reckoned an unusual event—a bloodless transfer of power from one leader to another. The changeover did not diminish, however, the political or ideological domination of the Ba'ath (Arab Socialist) Party, which since 1968 has remained resolutely in control.

Change at the Top. On July 16, President Ahmed Hassan al-Bakr, 67, citing ill health, handed over the presidency and his other offices to second-in-command Saddam Hussein Takriti, 42, vice-chairman of the Revolutionary Command Council (RCC). There was speculation that the change in leadership was the culmination of a personal rivalry between the two men. Certainly a number of older ministers whose primary loyalty was to Bakr were removed, but there was by no means a wholesale change. Of the 34 high office holders in the new and enlarged cabinet, nine were new faces; three members of the new government are close relatives of the president. Hussein's place as vice-chairman of the RCC was taken by former Interior Minister Izzat Ibrahim.

Plot Uncovered. Hardly was the new president peacefully installed when Iraqi politics resumed their normally febrile character. On July 28, five high-ranking members of the Ba'ath Party were arrested for plotting against the government with the aid of an unnamed foreign Arab power. According to some reports, more than 200 others also were arrested. Twenty-one former officials and ministers were executed by firing squad August 8. A special court had also sentenced 33 other persons to prison terms.

Internal Unrest. Whatever the reality of the alleged plot, the government in Baghdad had enough problems to justify its nervousness. About half of Iraq's Muslims are Shi'ites, and the victory of the Ayatollah Khomeini in Iran raised a specter of anti-Ba'athist cooperation between the fanatical Iranian Shia and their counterparts in Iraq. Added security precautions thwarted this threat—if it ever existed at all. The Kurdish minority, however, continued to be an all-too-real problem. A policy of gingerly treatment and increased development funds for Iraqi Kurdistan did not help.

Progress. Increasing oil revenues continued to give Iraq the means to finance its impressive development plans. The compulsive literacy law of December 1978 had a very successful first year; more than 2 million people attended the literacy centers. The national budget for 1979 provided for expenditures of $32 billion, an increase of 27% over 1978.

Foreign Affairs. The unnamed external power in the conspiracy was undoubtedly Syria. The two Ba'athist regimes had for a long time been on the worst of terms. At a January 15 meeting in Damascus, however, grandiose plans were announced not only for military cooperation but for an actual merger into a single state. Transit of Iraqi oil across Syria resumed on February 24, and a joint planning committee began meeting in Baghdad, May 3. Although relations again improved in the last five months of the year, the impetus had been lost when the plot was discovered.

Iraq took an active part in Arab discussions of sanctions against Egypt. Relations with the Soviet Union remained good, cordial cooperation with France was maintained, and mutual concessions with Great Britain warmed frosty attitudes.

ARTHUR CAMPBELL TURNER

─────── **IRAQ · Information Highlights** ───────

Official Name: Republic of Iraq.
Location: Southwest Asia.
Area: 169,284 square miles (438 446 km²).
Population (1979 est.): 12,900,000.
Chief Cities (1970 est.): Baghdad, the capital, 2,183,800 (met. area); Basra, 370,900; Mosul, 293,100.
Government: *Head of state and government,* Saddam Hussein Takriti, president (took office July 1979).
Monetary Unit: Dinar (0.2953 dinar equals U. S.$1, Aug. 1979).
Agriculture (major products): Barley, wheat, dates, vegetables, cotton.

WIDE WORLD

Charles J. Haughey, 54-year-old symbol of Irish unification, became prime minister of the Republic as 1979 ended.

IRELAND

Prime Minister Jack Lynch startled the political world by announcing his resignation December 5, several months earlier than had been predicted. Two days later, the ruling Fianna Fail party chose as his successor 54-year-old Charles J. Haughey by a vote of 44 to 38. Haughey had been ousted from the post of finance minister in 1970, when he was accused of conspiring to smuggle arms to the Irish Republican Army (IRA) in Northern Ireland. Although acquitted of those charges, Haughey continued to represent the anti-British element of his party. His election as premier caused much concern among moderates in Ireland and among Conservatives and Unionists in Britain. The Fianna Fail party lost confidence after winning only 5 of 15 seats in June 7 elections to the European Parliament. And on November 8, shortly before Lynch left for an eight-day visit to the United States, the Fine Gael opposition party captured two by-elections in his home county of Cork.

Northern Ireland and the IRA. The long struggle of the IRA to drive the British out of Northern Ireland and reunite the country reached another bloody milestone on August 27, when terrorists assassinated Earl Mountbatten of Burma, who was spending his holiday on the west coast (see OBITUARIES, page 382). The "execution" of Lord Mountbatten, along with members of his family, caused profound sorrow

and anger around the world. Shortly after the deadly bomb explosion, Irish police arrested two men on the road to Dublin and charged them with complicity in the crime.

During the year the IRA became increasingly more effective in its operations. Despite government calls for tougher measures against terrorism, a public opinion poll revealed considerable sympathy for the IRA's goals. Some 20% of those questioned supported the IRA, and another 18% remained neutral.

In what it called "the first substantive attempt to make political progress" in Northern Ireland since 1975, the British government on November 20 put forth six different plans for possible home rule in that province. British leaders also called for an all-party conference in Northern Ireland the next month, but their initiatives were widely criticized.

Pope's Visit. Pope John Paul II made a triumphal tour of Ireland from September 29 to October 1. All told, more than two million Irishmen turned out to see their spiritual leader and celebrate mass with him at Dublin's Phoenix Park, Drogheda, Galway, and the famous shrine at Knock. The first pope ever to visit Ireland, John Paul condemned violence and urged Irishmen of all parties and creeds to settle their differences by peaceful means.

Economy. Inflation and industrial strife slowed economic growth. The soaring cost of imported oil drove the price of gasoline to more than $2.00 (U. S.) a gallon in May and led experts to predict a deficit of more than £900 million for 1979. It also contributed to an inflation rate of about 9%. The government tried in vain to curb inflationary pressures by keeping wage increases below 10%. Demanding considerably more, some 13,000 postal workers and telephone operators went on strike for four and one-half months, inflicting heavy losses on the business community.

On March 30 the government severed the link between the Irish and British pounds in order to bring Ireland's currency into line with the new European Monetary System.

L. PERRY CURTIS, JR.
Brown University

———— **IRELAND · Information Highlights** ————

Official Name: Ireland.
Location: Island in the eastern North Atlantic Ocean.
Area: 27,136 square miles (70 282 km²).
Population (1979 est.): 3,300,000.
Chief Cities (1973 est.): Dublin, the capital, 680,000; Cork, 224,000; Limerick, 140,000.
Government: *Head of state,* Patrick J. Hillery, president (took office Nov. 1976). *Head of government,* Charles J. Haughey, prime minister (took office December 1979). *Legislature*—Parliament: House of Representatives (Dáil Éireann) and Senate (Seanad Éireann).
Monetary Unit: Pound (0.4735 pound equals U. S.$1, Dec. 1979).
Manufactures (major products): Processed foods, textiles, construction materials, machinery, chemicals.
Agriculture (major products): Cattle, dairy products, wheat, potatoes, barley, sugar beets, turnips, hay.

ISRAEL

The year in Israel was one of transition from a state of war to a state of peace, at least in regard to Egypt, Israel's major enemy during its three decades of existence. By far the most important event of 1979 was the signing of the Israeli-Egyptian peace treaty in March. It was, however, far from being a year of euphoria or success. The benefits of peace presumably would be very great in the long run, but the costs were immediate and very heavy. Israelis were poignantly and in some cases angrily aware that in the great peacemaking process all the tangible concessions had been extracted from Israel, while Egypt had conceded nothing but its willingness to end the state of war and accept Israel's right to normal existence.

In domestic politics the year was a difficult one for Prime Minister Menahem Begin, the head of an unstable coalition with only a narrow majority in the Knesset (parliament). Begin, however, displayed characteristic courage and persistence in the face of vote-of-confidence debates, some political defeats, appalling economic difficulties, the resignation of his most important colleague, and a serious illness.

The Peace Process. The Camp David summit meeting of September 1978 had provided a "framework for peace," but this proved hard to implement in the detailed decisions necessary for a definitive treaty. As 1979 began, negotiations were at a standstill. On January 5, Energy Minister Yitzhak Modai said that Israel would not sign a peace treaty unless assured of access to oil from the Sinai wells it had developed. Visits to Egypt and Israel by U. S. envoy Alfred Atherton, January 26–27, failed to get the talks restarted. At the end of February, Begin and

Egyptian President Anwar el-Sadat both declined to attend a renewed Camp David summit, but a meeting between Begin and U. S. President Jimmy Carter in Washington, March 2–4, was more productive. It was followed by Carter's successful Middle East mission and the signing of the Israeli-Egyptian peace treaty on March 26 (*see* MIDDLE EAST). The draft treaty and associated texts had been endorsed by the Israeli cabinet March 19, by a vote of 15 to 2. The Knesset, after a marathon 30-hour debate, approved the drafts March 22 by the surprisingly large margin of 95 to 18.

Peace brought some gains to Israel. The first Israeli cargo ship passed through the Suez Canal on April 30, followed by the first warships on May 29. The establishment of normal relations with Egypt was to be given visible form by the mutual exchange of ambassadors and the establishment of embassies on Feb. 26, 1980. In January, Begin named as Israel's first ambassador to Egypt Eliahu ben Elisar, director of the premier's office and a key figure in the negotiations.

The costs of the treaty, however, were more obvious. Compliance involved handing back to Egypt the Sinai peninsula—an area considerably larger than Israel proper—which was conquered in 1967. The transfer was carried out quite smoothly, in three steps: May 25, September 25, and November 15. A new monitoring system had to be devised when, in July, the Soviet Union vetoed extension of the United Nations Emergency Force (UNEF) and Israel and Egypt rejected UNEF's replacement by an unarmed UN truce supervisory force. The new plan called for Israeli and Egyptian patrols to monitor the truce themselves, aided by increased U. S. air and land surveillance. The third stage

Israeli Foreign Minister Moshe Dayan resigned in October, citing differences with government policy on Palestinian autonomy.

of the Israeli withdrawal, to east of the line El Arish–Ras Mohammed and leaving in Israeli hands only one third of the Sinai, was not incumbent upon Israel in terms of the treaty until Jan. 25, 1980, but as a goodwill gesture Israel advanced the date for the major part of it to November 19 and then to November 15. This enabled Sadat to attend ceremonies at the site on the second anniversary of his historic mission to Jerusalem. The November withdrawal caused particular anguish for Israel, as it involved handing back Mount Sinai, where Moses received the Ten Commandments. The remaining one third of the Sinai was not to be handed back until 1982.

The West Bank and Gaza Strip. At the same time that the Sinai transfer was being implemented, Israel and Egypt (and sometimes the United States) were holding talks on the future of the West Bank and Gaza Strip. Their aim was to implement the ambiguous treaty commitment to create an "elected self-governing authority" for those areas. The negotiations did not go well. Begin again emphasized his overriding concern for Israeli security; Sadat did not help matters by trying to drag in plans for detaching East Jerusalem (with which the treaty does not deal) from Israel. Several meetings were held in summer and autumn, but progress was essentially stalled. Nor could Sadat and Begin agree on these matters when they met for four days at Aswan, Jan. 7–10, 1980. By then, however, these matters took a back seat to concern over the Soviet invasion of Afghanistan.

Occupation Policies. Israel's policies in the occupied West Bank demonstrated that Begin contemplated nothing more than a modest degree of self-government in the area. Jewish settlements in the West Bank were still being expanded where deemed necessary for security. On October 22 a new settlement at Elon Moreh, near Nablus, was declared illegal by the Israeli Supreme Court on the grounds that it was not necessary for security. The families were given until November 30 to leave, and the government began work on a replacement site at Mt. Kabir. It twice by fiat extended the deadline for relocation, finally to February 1980. On January 2, Begin's government faced four votes of confidence on the Elon Moreh question and

won all of them by its usual narrow majority. Bassam Shaka, the Arab mayor of Nablus, was dismissed in November by the occupation authorities on grounds that he had condoned acts of terror, charges which he denied. The appeals commission overturned his deportation, December 5, and he made a triumphant return to home and office. Other West Bank mayors who had resigned in sympathy with him withdrew their resignations. This turn of events was a victory for Israeli Defense Minister Ezer Weizman and something of a defeat for Begin.

Economic Difficulties. The nation faced serious economic problems. The abolition of economic controls attempted by the Begin administration since coming to power in June 1977 simply has not worked. Largely responsible are Israel's overgrown bureaucracy (an amazing 28% of the work force, as against only 25% in industry), excessive spending on both welfare and defense, universal indexation, and an obsession with full employment. Near the end of the year inflation was running at an annual rate of more than 100%—and accelerating. Deficit on external account was more than $4 billion for the first three quarters of 1979, and the value of the pound had fallen by two thirds since the administration came to power. Yigael Horowitz, who in November replaced Simha Ehrlich as finance minister, was known to favor severe cuts in public spending. The plea of Defense Minister Weizman in Washington during the last week of the year for increased U. S. aid for fiscal 1980—from $1.785 billion to $3.45 billion—had little success.

Oil Supply. On one economic front, at least, Israel was surprisingly successful—the replacement of canceled oil shipments from Iran, which had supplied the bulk of its needs. A combination of provident alternative arrangements and active purchasing in various markets made gasoline more continuously available in Israel than in the United States. The treaty with Egypt provided that Sinai oil, which in recent years constituted one fifth of the nation's supply, was to be made available for purchase by Israel. There was also a U. S. guarantee—extended to 1990—to sell Israel as much oil as it needed if other supplies failed.

Political and Health Problems. Prime Minister Begin's complex political problems were compounded by a minor stroke suffered in July. He left the hospital on August 4, having made a virtually complete recovery. Foreign Minister Moshe Dayan also was hospitalized, on June 23, for removal of a malignant polyp. Dayan resigned his post October 21 in protest over the government's handling of the Palestinian issue. Dayan wanted more flexibility, but it did not seem that the differences between him and Begin were fundamental. Begin assumed the duties of foreign minister.

ARTHUR CAMPBELL TURNER
University of California, Riverside

——— **ISRAEL · Information Highlights** ———

Official Name: State of Israel.
Location: Southwest Asia.
Area: 7,848 square miles (20 325 km²).
Population (1979 est.): 3,800,000.
Chief Cities (1978 est.): Jerusalem, the capital, 376,000; Tel Aviv-Jaffa, 343,300; Haifa, 227,800.
Government: *Head of state,* Yitzhak Navon, president (took office May 1978). *Head of government,* Menahem Begin, premier (took office June 1977). *Legislature* (unicameral)—Knesset.
Monetary Unit: Pound (33.52 pounds equal U. S.$1, Dec. 1979).
Manufactures (major products): Processed foods, textiles, metal products.
Agriculture (major products): Wheat, hay, citrus fruits, dairy products, cotton.

SALHANI, GAMMA LIAISON

Israel Begins Withdrawal from the Sinai

The first step under the new Treaty of Peace between Israel and Egypt was taken when Israel returned the town of El-Arish, capital of the Sinai, and a 100-mile (161-km) strip of land to the west, on May 25. The occasion was marked by a ceremony attended by diplomats and military leaders from both nations.

SALHANI, GAMMA LIAISON

Mount Etna erupted in early August causing volcanic ash to fall over a large area of Sicily.

ITALY

Italy's political and economic situation continued to be unstable. The Communist Party sustained setbacks in June parliamentary elections.

POLITICS

Collapse of Christian Democratic-Communist "Partnership." As the new year began, it was clear that the precarious "partnership" between the Italian Communist Party (PCI) and Premier Giulio Andreotti's Christian Democratic (DC) government would not survive the winter. That arrangement had rested upon an understanding that the Communists would not hold cabinet posts but would be consulted by Andreotti on important issues and would vote with the government majority in parliament. Stung by setbacks in ensuing local elections, however, PCI leader Enrico Berlinguer lost interest in the accord. On January 26 he accused the Christian Democrats of ignoring the PCI and withdrew his party's support of the government. Although he disputed Berlinguer's charge, Andreotti had no choice but to submit the resignation of his government. He did so on January 31. Andreotti stayed on as caretaker, while negotiations to form a new government got under way.

President of the Republic Sandro Pertini asked Andreotti to try to form a new ministry, but that effort failed when the right wing of the DC refused to accede to Communist demands

for seats in the cabinet and when the Socialist Party (PSI) refused to back a DC government that did not have the support of the Communists.

President Pertini next invited the elderly Ugo La Malfa, the leader of the small Italian Republic Party (PRI), to try his luck. Had La Malfa succeeded, his government would have been the first since 1945 to be headed by a non-Christian Democrat. He did not.

In desperation, Pertini again turned to Andreotti. This time the veteran politician succeeded in forming a coalition with the PRI and the Social Democratic Party (PSDI). Sworn in on March 21, the new government was Andreotti's fifth and the country's 42nd since 1943. La Malfa was named to a cabinet post but died of a heart attack five days later. Because the new Cabinet did not have a parliamentary majority, it faced a tough vote of confidence in the Senate. On March 31 the confidence motion was rejected, 150–149, and the fledgling government was dissolved. Andreotti continued as caretaker pending new elections on June 3.

Political Violence. During the election campaign, political violence continued unabated throughout the country. According to PCI statistics, such acts numbered 1,599 during the first six months of 1979, compared with 1,481 for the same period in 1978. The number of groups claiming responsibility more than doubled, although police suspected that many of the same groups were simply taking on new names.

Antiterrorist forces headed by Gen. Carlo Alberto Dalla Chiesa of the Carabinieri (national police) had some success in thwarting political violence in 1979. In the course of sweeping arrests on April 7 in Padua, Milan, Rovigo, Rome, and Turin they managed to nab Antonio Negri, a Marxist professor of political science at the University of Padua and a suspected terrorist ringleader. Negri was also charged with masterminding student uprisings in 1968.

Although most terrorist acts in Italy during recent years have been committed by the radical left, it was an extreme right group that claimed responsibility for bombing Rome's city hall on April 20. That explosion caused $1.2 million damage to the Senatorial Palace that Michelangelo had designed for the Capitoline Hill.

On the morning of May 3, leftist terrorists raided the Rome headquarters of the Christian Democratic Party, wrecking two floors, killing one policeman, and seriously wounding two others. The terrorists, numbering 10 to 15 persons, escaped unharmed. Their brazen attack prompted the government to call in the regular army to help the police. Notwithstanding, the Italian Foreign Ministry was the target of the next terrorist bombing on May 24. Damage was estimated at more than half a million dollars.

On May 30, police arrested a Rome couple suspected of having participated in the 1978 murder of former Premier Aldo Moro. The downtown apartment of Valerio Morucci, age 28, and Adriana Faranda, 29, contained an arsenal of weapons, including a Czech-made machine pistol that allegedly had been used against Moro. By midsummer, some 30 suspects had been placed under arrest for Moro's abduction.

Other Political Developments. On February 9, Andreotti's caretaker government agreed to PCI demands that parliament make a full-scale investigation of the Moro kidnapping and murder. Later that month, parliament cleared the way for a trial of Giorgio Almirante, the leader of the right-wing Italian Social Movement; Almirante was charged with violating a law which prohibits the revival of the Fascist Party.

On March 1, Mario Tanassi, a Social Democratic member of parliament and former defense minister, was convicted on charges of accepting bribes from the Lockheed Aircraft Company in 1970–71; he was sentenced to 2 years and 4 months in jail. Gen. Duilio Fanali, who had been air force chief of staff in 1970, was one of five others convicted of charges stemming from the Lockheed scandal. Luigi Gui, another former minister of defense, was acquitted.

In an effort to create a fresh image under the leadership of Bettino Craxi, the Socialist Party chose a new emblem—a red carnation.

The Communist Party ended its 15th congress on April 3 with an uneasy compromise between Secretary Berlinguer's Eurocommunist majority and a pro-Soviet wing identified with

Pietro Ingrao and Armando Cossutta. The latter group had been making steady inroads among the frustrated party rank and file.

Parliamentary Elections. Italy's two leading parties—the DC and PCI—both lost ground in the parliamentary elections of June 3. Losses by the Communists—more than 1 million votes—were by far the more severe. Final returns gave the PCI 30.4% of the popular vote for the Chamber of Deputies, a decrease of 4% from the 1976 elections. In Senate elections the party received 31.5% of the vote, a drop of 2.3%. Its losses were most conspicuous in the South and among young voters.

The Christian Democrats, meanwhile, received 38.3% in the Chamber of Deputies (a drop of only 0.4%) and lost one seat. In the Senate they got 38.3%, a decline of 0.6%. The DC fell 54 seats short of a majority in the 630-seat lower house. In third place was the Socialist Party, which stayed even with 10% of the vote.

The chief benefactor of PCI and DC losses was the small Radical Party (PR), a progressive civil libertarian movement led by Marco Pannella, which tripled its share of the vote to 3.4%. The Republican Party stayed even at 3%, while the Social Democratic Party rose from 3.4% to 3.8%. The number of seats in the new parliament was divided as follows:

Party	Chamber	Senate
Christian Democrats	262	138
Communists	201	109
Socialists	62	32
Italian Social Movement	30	13
Social Democrats	20	9
Radicals	18	2
Republicans	16	6
Liberals	9	2
Proletarian Unity Party	6	—
Scattered	6	4
Total	630	315

A Communist deputy, Nilde Jotti, was elected president of the new Chamber of Deputies. She was the first woman ever to hold the post. The new president of the Senate was a Christian Democrat, Amintore Fanfani.

Election of European Parliament. None of the Italian parties was very satisfied with the results of the June 3 election. They therefore

--------- **ITALY · Information Highlights** ---------

Official Name: Italian Republic.
Location: Southern Europe.
Area: 116,318 square miles (301 264 km²).
Population (1979 est.): 56,900,000.
Chief Cities (Dec. 1977): Rome, the capital, 2,897,819; Milan, 1,706,268; Naples, 1,225,227; Turin, 1,181,569.
Government: *Head of state,* Sandro Pertini, president (took office July 1978). *Head of government,* Francesco Cossiga, prime minister (took office Aug. 1979). *Legislature*—Parliament: Senate and Chamber of Deputies.
Monetary Unit: Lira (822.60 lire equal U.S.$1, Nov. 1979).
Manufactures (major products): Automobiles, machinery, chemicals, textiles, shoes.
Agriculture (major products): Wheat, grapes, citrus fruits, rice, olives.

urged their supporters to return to the polls June 10 to try to improve their standings in the vote for Italian delegates to the new Parliament of the European Community (EC). A higher percentage of voters (85.5%) turned out in Italy than in any other EC country.

When the ballots were counted, the Christian Democrats and Communists had lost further support—2.7% and 1%, respectively—whereas the Socialists and various smaller parties improved their standings. Italy's 81-member delegation consisted of 30 Christian Democrats, 24 Communists, 9 Socialists, 4 Social Democrats, 4 Italian Social Movement members, 3 Liberals, 3 Radicals, 2 Republicans, 1 Proletarian Democrat, and 1 member of the Proletarian Union.

Cossiga Government. Attempts to form a new government began soon after the elections. Andreotti again was asked first—and failed. President Pertini then called on Bettino Craxi, the leader of the Socialist Party, to form a cabinet. He too failed. Next in line was Christian Democrat Filippo Maria Pandolfi, the treasury minister in Andreotti's caretaker government; Pandolfi soon gave up, however, because of Socialist opposition.

The seven-month political impasse was finally resolved on August 5, when a three-party coalition headed by Francesco Cossiga was sworn in. Premier Cossiga's cabinet comprised 16 ministers from his own Christian Democratic Party, 4 Social Democrats, 2 Liberals, and 2 uncommitted economic experts. Andreotti was not included in the new government. Cossiga, who had been the interior minister during the Moro kidnapping crisis, also happens to be a cousin of the Communist Berlinguer.

The new coalition then won votes of confidence in the Chamber of Deputies (287 to 242, with the Socialists and Republicans abstaining) and the Senate (153 to 118) on August 11 and 12, respectively. The Communists voted against Cossiga in both houses.

Constitutional Reform? In the autumn, Craxi's Socialist Party called for major constitutional reforms that would remove some of the checks on the executive branch of government. Surprisingly, the proposal won cautious support from the two big parties, although the smaller ones remained hostile. Talks subsequently focused on three reform possibilities: direct election of the president and assignment to him of greater powers; modification of the system of proportional representation; and abolition or reform of the Senate. At year's end, it did not seem likely that any consensus would soon be reached.

Death of Mussolini's Wife. The world was reminded of Italy's Fascist past when Rachele Guidi Mussolini, the 89-year-old widow of *Il Duce,* died on October 31.

ECONOMY

In 1979, the Italian economy showed little significant change from the year before. In October, the government conceded that the goals of its three-year (1979–81) economic plan were not being met. The plan called for a growth in the gross domestic product (GDP) of 4.5% in 1979 and 4% in each of the following two years, and a reduction of the inflation rate to 7.5% by 1981. In late 1979, Italy's inflation rate was running at 20%, unemployment at 7.6%, and the growth rate at far less than the hoped-for 4.5%. The absence of an effective government for most of the year was blamed for the country's economic troubles. On a happier note, Italy enjoyed the largest balance of payments surplus of all the EC countries—3.5 billion ECUs.

In October, Italian labor unions won a major dispute with Premier Cossiga's government over economic policy. The cabinet backed away from a series of anti-inflation measures opposed by the unions, and it dropped plans to change the system of pay hikes, which was based on the cost of living index. Instead, the government sought to trim the cost of labor to employers by picking up some of the pension outlays borne by private industry.

Italy's central bank came under attack when its head, Paolo Baffi, was accused of covering up a bank scandal. Baffi denied the charge but resigned in October. He was replaced by the bank's former director general, Carlo Azeglio Ciampi.

FOREIGN AFFAIRS

In January, Soviet Foreign Minister Andrei Gromyko visited Italy, where he met with government and Communist Party leaders, as well as Pope John Paul II. Scientific, cultural, and legal cooperation were the main topics of conversation. Gromyko also pledged nonaggression on the part of the Soviet Union.

Premier Cossiga spent two days in West Germany in October, conferring with Chancellor Schmidt on EC and security matters.

Later that month, President Pertini was invited to lunch privately with Pope John Paul II at the Vatican. It was the first time in memory that a pope had invited an Italian head of state for so informal an exchange of views.

Italy's contacts with mainland China increased during the year. In April, Italy extended to China $1.8 billion in trade credits. In midsummer, a delegation of PCI journalists visited China in what many considered a possible prelude to the establishment of relations between the Chinese and Italian Communist parties. In November, Chinese Premier Hua Guofeng paid an official visit to Italy during his tour of Western Europe. Hua conferred with government officials and also met informally with Communist leader Berlinguer.

On December 6, Italy's parliament gave its approval (328–230) to deployment by NATO of new U. S. nuclear missiles in Western Europe.

CHARLES F. DELZELL, *Vanderbilt University*

JAPAN

Although there remained little doubt as to Japan's status as an economic superpower, the nation did begin in 1979 to experience some of the problems faced by the rest of the world community. It suffered a balance of payments deficit for fiscal 1978–79 (compared with a towering surplus in 1977–78); inflation and deficit financing; the high cost of energy imports; and its highest unemployment rate in the post-World War II era.

Japanese political leaders also struggled with the impact of change. A steady increase in the number of independent and uncommitted voters translated into a decline in support for the governing Liberal-Democratic Party (LDP). The demands of coalition politics threw the factions of the LDP into disarray and led to Japan's most serious leadership crisis in years.

INTERNATIONAL AFFAIRS

Prime Minister Masayoshi Ohira hosted a two-day summit conference of the leaders of seven major Western powers in Tokyo, June 28–29. Attending the meeting were U. S. President Jimmy Carter, Canadian Prime Minister Joe Clark, British Prime Minister Margaret Thatcher, West German Chancellor Helmut Schmidt, French President Valéry Giscard d'Estaing, and Italian Premier Giulio Andreotti. What was expected to be a routine meeting took on a sense of urgency after delicate adjustments in the Tokyo-Washington relationship and the announcement of drastic price hikes by the Organization of Petroleum Exporting Countries (OPEC).

After two days of intense negotiations, the seven participating nations and the European Community (EC) issued the Tokyo Declaration, which warned against the resurgence of inflation fueled by OPEC oil price increases. Each country set oil import ceilings for the period 1980–85. They agreed to consult each other to achieve stability in the volatile foreign exchange market. Premier Ohira committed Japan to lead the wealthy, industrialized nations of the North in providing aid and technical assistance to the developing nations of the South.

Relations with the United States. Although Japan and the United States enjoyed the largest cross-ocean trade in history, the huge disparity between imports and exports caused problems for both countries. Although Japan's current account balance of payments showed a deficit of $1.7 billion for the first six months of 1979, its gold and foreign exchange reserves still totaled $31.8 billion. Meanwhile, the record U. S. deficit in merchandise exchange with Japan—$11.5 billion in 1978—constituted almost half of Japan's global surplus and more than one third of the United States' own worldwide trade deficit. U. S. Treasury Secretary Michael Blumenthal, trade representative Robert Strauss, Japanese Foreign Minister Sunao Sunoda, and trade representative Nobuhiko Ushiba shuttled back and forth between Tokyo and Washington in efforts to ease economic friction.

Another point at issue in Japanese-U. S. relations was the desire of the United States to

Prime Minister Ohira and other Japanese officials escort President Carter to a villa at Oiso.

Ikebukuro's new complex includes an office building, hotel, culture center, and the World Import Mart building.

have such giant Japanese companies as the Nippon Telephone and Telegraph Co. open its purchasing to international bidding, as AT&T does. A lack of reciprocity, it argued, was partly responsible for Japan's lopsided trade surplus. During a May visit to Washington by Prime Minister Ohira, President Carter expressed a desire for the dispute to be settled shortly, and a final settlement was signed in Tokyo on June 1. At the end of Ohira's visit, the two leaders issued a communiqué pledging "a more harmonious pattern of international trade and payments" in the next several years.

President Carter, his wife Rosalynn, and their daughter Amy were formally welcomed in Japan on June 25 in a ceremony at Tokyo's Akasaka guest house. Later, Emperor Hirohito and Empress Nagako exchanged greetings with the U. S. visitors at the Imperial Palace. President Carter then met with Premier Ohira to discuss the positions that their respective nations would take on the issue of oil import quotas at the upcoming summit conference. They also agreed to establish a high-level committee to coordinate economic policies.

Japanese leaders expressed relief when President Carter, after his visit to Tokyo in June, reassured South Korean President Park Chunghee of continued U. S. support for that country. Tokyo had strongly questioned Carter's campaign promise to reduce the number of American troops stationed in South Korea.

Relations with China. In October 1978, representatives of Japan and the People's Republic of China had exchanged ratifications of a long-delayed treaty of peace and friendship. But Japanese hopes for a sudden expansion of investment and trade gradually dimmed in 1979 as Chinese modernization plans were scaled down. On December 7, however, Chinese and Japanese leaders announced a wide range of economic, technical, and cultural accords under which Japan would treat China as a "developing nation" and thereby substantially increase trade between the two nations.

Tokyo worried about Chinese intentions in Southeast Asia. During a stopover in Tokyo after his visit to the United States early in the year, Chinese Deputy Premier Deng Xiaoping warned that China would have to take "punitive action" against Vietnam for invading Cambodia. After fighting broke out on the Vietnam border February 19, Tokyo called on Peking to withdraw its troops and urged Vietnam to withdraw from Cambodia.

Relations with the USSR. After Tokyo had normalized relations and signed a peace treaty with Peking, Japan began to feel parallel pressure from Moscow. In September, both Soviet Premier Aleksei Kosygin and Foreign Minister Andrei Gromyko warned Japan against moving toward military alliance with China and the United States. In a statement at the United Nations, Foreign Minister Sonoda replied that

Japan's new earth observation center in Hatoyama began receiving radio signals from a U. S. satellite in January.

the Japanese were concerned about the apparent Soviet military buildup in East Asia. Soviet initiatives in what the Japanese called the "northern territories" had also blocked any progress toward a Japan-USSR treaty of peace. (Tokyo and Moscow had normalized diplomatic relations, without a treaty, in 1956.) In February and again in September, Japan officially protested the increase in Soviet troops in the southern Kuril Islands, which Japan regards as its own territory. According to intelligence reports, Soviet forces in the Habomai and Shikotan group had grown to the size of a full division, despite the fact that the USSR had promised to return the islands once a peace treaty was signed.

Relations with Korea. The involvement of the Korean Central Intelligence Agency (KCIA) in the October 26 assassination of President Park in Seoul caused alarm among the leaders of Japan. In comments directed primarily at North Korea, Tokyo reasserted that the security of South Korea and the political stability of the entire peninsula were directly linked to the security of Japan itself and to the maintenance of peace in all of Northeast Asia.

DOMESTIC AFFAIRS

In primary elections held in December 1978, Masayoshi Ohira, then secretary general of the conservative LDP, successfully challenged Prime Minister Takeo Fukuda for the presidency of the party. On December 7, Ohira was installed as the new prime minister with the support of a slim majority in the legislature. In 1979, Ohira's attempts to shore up factional divisions within the LDP, strengthen the party's power base in the Diet, and gain further support for his own leadership were largely unsuccessful.

Party Politics and Elections. Encouraged by his high visibility in the Tokyo summit conference in June, and buoyed by conservative victories in quadrennial by-elections in April, Ohira set as his goals the achievement of a "stable majority" for the LDP in the Diet and a stronger position for his own faction within the party.

In local elections held April 8, LDP candidates won all 15 prefectural governorships at stake. The party's most important victory came in Tokyo, where the Socialist opposition had held that office for 12 years. With the support of the more moderate opposition, LDP candidate and former Deputy Governor Shunichi Suzuki defeated leftist Kaoru Ohta. In elections for Japan's 47 prefectural assemblies, the LDP won 1,405 of 2,645 seats. And in April 22 mayoral elections throughout the country, conservative-centrist coalitions captured a large majority of municipal offices.

Although survey research revealed some softness in the support for the Ohira cabinet, public opinion polls conducted in August showed the LDP gaining in party support. Acting under his constitutional prerogative, but against the wishes of many party elders, Ohira dissolved the House of Representatives on September 7 and scheduled a general election for October 7. By calling for the election a year ahead of time, the incumbent prime minister sought to enhance his party's narrow majority.

After the results were announced, Ohira said he was "shocked by the unexpected adverse outcome." Although the LDP retained power and increased its share of the popular vote from 41.8% in 1976 to 44.6%, the party captured only 248 seats—one less than in 1976 and eight short of a majority in the 511-seat chamber. Immediately, 10 of the 19 winning independents lent their support, and the LDP was again able to form a government. Ohira's position in the party itself had been greatly weakened, however, and a number of LDP leaders insisted that he resign.

In the month preceding the election in parliament for a new prime minister, the LDP engaged in a bitter, behind-the-scenes power struggle. Three days before the vote, former Prime Minister Fukuda decided to challenge Ohira for the office, and the LDP took the unprecedented step of placing two nominees before the Diet. For the first time in Japanese parlimentary history, a runoff between two candidates of the same party was required. Ohira was reelected by a vote of 138 to Fukuda's 121, the thinnest legislative support ever afforded a Japanese prime minister.

Prime Minister Ohira's new government also faced difficulties in Diet committees, where opposition forces, although fractured, together equalled LDP strength. Although the Japanese Socialist Party (JSP) had also lost ground (from 116 to 107 seats), the Japanese Communist Party (JCP) increased in strength (from 19 to 39 seats). Other representation in the lower house included the Clean Government Party (Komeito), 57 seats, and the Democratic Socialist Party (DSP), 35 seats. And with only a one-seat edge over the combined opposition in the House of Councillors, the LDP looked forward with some apprehension to upper house elections in 1980.

Aircraft Scandals. One reason for the poor showing by the LDP in the elections was disclosures of corruption in the procurement of foreign-built aircraft for both public and private use. In December 1978 the U. S. Securities and Exchange Commission (SEC) revealed that two American companies (McDonnell Douglas and Grumman) had paid more than $2 million in commissions for sales of aircraft to Japan. Harry F. Kern, former consultant to Grumman, named seven important Japanese politicians—including former prime ministers Fukuda and Nobusuke Kishi—involved in the purchases. By January 1979, Japan's defense agency was under investigation by the Diet in connection with its planned purchase of Grumman E-2C early warning aircraft. In February the Nissho-Iwai Co., Grumman's agent in Japan, admitted that it had once had contacts with Kern. On April 2 one of Nissho-Iwai's directors, Hachiro Kaifu, was arrested for violating foreign exchange regulations. On May 28 a former defense agency chief, Raizo Matsuno, claimed before a Diet investigation committee that payments to him had been "political donations."

In February a Tokyo court revealed testimony that had been recorded three years earlier in the United States for Japanese prosecutors.

ORION PRESS

Japanese children join youngsters from around the world in celebrating the International Year of the Child.

Former Lockheed officials admitted to having paid 500 million yen to Japanese agents for favorable consideration of the TriStar (L-1011) aircraft. It was understood that the money would be passed on to former Prime Minister Kakuei Tanaka. Tanaka, running as an independent, was reelected to the Diet in October 1979.

Economy. In August 1979, the Economic Planning Agency (EPA) released its white paper for the fiscal year April 1978–March 1979. The EPA reported that the Japanese economy was moving toward equilibrium, with domestic demand displacing aggressive promotion of exports. Since the yen had sharply appreciated (by 67.1%) over two years (1976–78), exports were inhibited and imports encouraged. A result in fiscal 1978 was a balance of payments deficit of $2.3 billion, compared with a surplus of $12.3 billion in fiscal 1977. The government continued an easy money policy in 1978, but in April 1979 the Bank of Japan raised the official discount rate for the first time in four years. Bank governor Teiichiro Morinaga explained that the action was designed to curb accelerated price increases triggered by the rising cost of OPEC oil.

At the 1978 Bonn summit conference of Western industrialized nations, Japan had promised to try to maintain a 7% annual rate of growth for 1978. Shortly after the 1979 Tokyo summit, Prime Minister Ohira stated that Japan's growth rate would fall below 7%. Despite OPEC price increases, the government was aiming at an annual inflation rate of under 5% for 1979. Meanwhile, economic planners were predicting an inflation-adjusted average annual growth rate of 5.7% through the mid-1980's.

In February, the office of the prime minister announced that the national consumer price index for 1978 had registered a 3.8% increase over 1977, to 122.6 (1975 = 100). This marked Japan's lowest inflation rate in 18 years. By September, however, wholesale prices were once again rising at a double-digit rate. The increase was reflected almost immediately in the consumer price index for the 23-ward area of Tokyo. That index, a bellwether of national trends,

─────── **JAPAN · Information Highlights** ───────

Official Name: Japan.
Location: East Asia.
Area: 147,470 square miles (381 947 km²).
Population (1979 est.): 115,900,000.
Chief Cities (Sept. 1977 est.): Tokyo, the capital, 11,-648,637; Osaka, 2,723,752; Yokohama, 2,694,569; Nagoya, 2,083,616.
Government: *Head of state,* Hirohito, emperor (acceded Dec. 1926). *Head of government,* Masayoshi Ohira, prime minister (took office Dec. 1978). *Legislature* —Diet: House of Councillors and House of Representatives.
Monetary Unit: Yen (248.75 yen equal U. S.$1, Nov. 29, 1979).
Manufactures (major products): Machinery and equipment, metals and metal products, textiles, automobiles, chemicals, electrical and electronic equipment.
Agriculture (major products): Rice, vegetables, fruits, milk, meat, natural silk.

advanced by 1.6%, the largest month-to-month gain in two years. Once again, the Bank of Japan responded by raising the discount rate by another full point, to 6.25% per annum.

Defense Debate. In the period immediately following World War II, Japan assumed a strongly pacifist and antinuclear stance. There were a variety of political, economic, and legal (Article 9 of the U. S.-influenced constitution) reasons for limiting Japan's defense expenditures. By 1979, however, several developments had caused defense policy to become a hotly debated issue: a majority of the Japanese population had been born after the war; there appeared to be a steady retreat of American influence in the Western Pacific; and there was growing instability in Southeast Asia, as well as the buildup of Russian forces in the southern Kurils.

A 1978 government poll released on March 4, 1979, indicated that some 86% of respondents had come to accept the need for the Self Defense Forces (SDF). Those opposed to the existence of the SDF dropped from 12% in 1972 to only 5%. A smaller majority (two of three respondents) continued to support the Japan-U. S. security treaty, but a significant number (12%) doubted its value.

Japan's defense agency sought expenditures of about $11.4 billion for fiscal 1980. Although the government succeeded in holding defense expenditures to below 1% of the annual GNP, the total outlay was one of the ten highest in the world. Military expenditures were intended primarily for equipment modernization and combat-readiness procedures.

"The Graying of Japan." In 1979, the Japanese media gave considerable coverage to a sociological development which they dubbed "the graying of Japan." By September 15, the number of Japanese over the age of 65 had topped the 10 million mark for the first time. That total constituted 8.9% of the national population. Expert projections indicated that the proportion of aged would increase to 18.5% by the year 2015.

The shift in population structure forced many firms to review traditional retirement policies. Japan Air Lines, for example, decided to raise the age of retirement from 55 to 60 (effective in 1980), provided that federal wage and retirement benefits for those over 58 were adjusted down. Five major steel companies— including Nippon Steel, the world's largest steel manufacturer—unanimously agreed to raise the retirement ceiling gradually, over a five-year period beginning in fiscal 1981. The 240,000-member Federation of Steelworkers' Union (*Tekkororen*) accepted the formula in principle, but wanted exact wages and benefits to be subject to negotiation.

ARDATH W. BURKS
Professor of Asian Studies
Rutgers University

A U.S. delegation, led by Zbigniew Brzezinski (*left*), tries to convince King Hussein and other Jordanian officials to support the new Egyptian-Israeli peace treaty.

UPI

JORDAN

The uncompromising resistance of Jordan's King Hussein to U.S. pressure to join Egyptian-Israeli negotiations on Palestinian autonomy sent American-Jordanian relations to an unprecedented low and helped Hussein regain much of the influence in inter-Arab politics that he had lost over the previous five years. The Jordanian monarch effectively played the role of mediator between extremist and conservative Arab powers and thereby maintained the flow of economic subsidies granted to Jordan at the 1978 Arab summit in Baghdad.

U. S.-Jordan Relations. American foreign policymakers considered Hussein a key figure in the future of the Israeli-occupied West Bank. Jordan had controlled the area prior to 1967, 50% of its population is Palestinian, and Hussein has close relations with Saudi Arabia's royal family. On March 18, 1979, U. S. National Security Adviser Zbigniew Brzezinski traveled to Amman to seek Hussein's support for the new Egyptian-Israeli peace treaty. Hussein not only refused to join in the peace efforts but complained about American "arm twisting." Other Jordanian officials accused the United States of threatening to delay promised arms shipments.

Hussein refused to accept the peace treaty on the grounds that it would provide legal sanction for an eventual Israeli annexation of the West Bank. His distrust of Israeli intentions was later amplified in his strong denunciation of a May 19 offer by Israeli Prime Minister Menahem Begin to open bilateral negotiations with Jordan.

Relations with the United States deteriorated further as President Jimmy Carter sought to compel Hussein's acquiescence by placing restrictions on or refusing to authorize arms sales to Jordan. The U. S. refusal to sell sophisticated F-16 fighter planes to Jordan prompted Hussein to purchase from France 36 F-1 Mirage fighter bombers. In mid-July the United States was informed that a Jordanian military team, led by Lt. Gen. Zaid Ibn Shaker, would be dispatched to the Soviet Union. It was the first official visit to the USSR by a Jordanian delegation in the 27-year rule of King Hussein.

In September, Hussein backed out of a proposed $300-million sale of M-60 tanks when President Carter refused to invite him to the White House after his address to the United Nations. Hussein later concluded a similar deal for British Chieftain tanks because, beyond the diplomatic snub, the United States could not promise delivery on the M-60s for at least 30 months.

Inter-Arab Affairs. By prudently avoiding extremist positions, Hussein was able to act as mediator in several Arab disputes. His most important function was to ensure that Syrian-Iraqi relations did not go beyond harsh words after the alleged Syrian involvement in a coup against Iraqi President Saddam Hussein in late July. Hussein's diplomatic efforts in inter-Arab affairs guaranteed the delivery of the $1.62 billion voted to Jordan at the Baghdad summit in November 1978.

At the Arab League summit held Nov. 20–22, 1979, in Tunis, delegates approved a modified version of a plan by Hussein to develop and promote a unified Arab peace plan. Under the resolution, Arab diplomats would travel abroad to seek support for the Palestinian cause and bring pressure on Israel to withdraw from "occupied" Arab territories.

See also MIDDLE EAST.

F. NICHOLAS WILLARD

─────── **JORDAN • Information Highlights** ───────

Official Name: Hashemite Kingdom of Jordan.
Location: Southwest Asia.
Area: 37,738 square miles (97 740 km²).
Population (1979 est.): 3,000,000.
Chief Cities (1977 est.): Amman, the capital, 732,587; Zarqa, 269,780; Irbid, 139,780.
Government: *Head of state,* Hussein ibn Talal, king (acceded Aug. 1952). *Head of government,* Sharif Abdul Hamid Sharaf, prime minister (took office December 1979). *Legislature*—National Consultative Assembly.
Monetary Unit: Dinar (0.2965 dinar equals U. S.$1, Dec. 1979).
Manufactures (major products): Cement, phosphate, petroleum products.
Agriculture (major products): Wheat, fruits, olive oil, vegetables.

KANSAS

The Kansas economy, though hampered by inflation, remained strong in 1979. While the population of the state continued to grow, Kansas maintained one of the lowest unemployment rates nationally, and the per capita income of residents increased. Manufacturing was the leading source of income, while total farm earnings continued to decline.

Agriculture. A decline in agricultural earnings occurred in spite of a record-high wheat crop. For the first time, the Kansas wheat harvest topped 400 million bushels. A record yield of 38.0 bushels per acre (93.8* bu/ha) topped the previous high of 37.0 bushels established in 1973 and surpassed the 1978 average by 8.0 bushels. Yields were higher than the year before in all parts of the state despite wet weather in late June and July that caused portions of the crop to remain unharvested.

Farmers, discontent with declining agricultural income and rising production costs, continued to support the American Agricultural Movement. Early in the year, approximately 200 farmers and their families staged a tractor rally in Topeka to bring their grievances to the attention of state legislators. Kansas farmers also participated in the national AAM rally in Washington.

Weather. Extremes were the rule in 1979, with two heavy snowstorms in January, a fall drought, and an early snowstorm in late October that left up to nine inches (23 cm) of snow in western Kansas. The early snowstorm was accompanied by heavy rains that caused flooding.

Legislation. In the 1978 elections, the Republicans regained control of the state House of Representatives and maintained a majority in the Senate. This reversed the role for Gov. John Carlin, who for two years had served as the Democratic Speaker of the House under a Republican governor. The 1979 legislature approved approximately $80 million in tax relief, including an increase in the amount allowed for personal exemptions on state income tax returns and the elimination of sales tax on residential utilities. In spite of tax relief measures, the legislature authorized a budget of $2.3 billion that would leave a balance of approximately $155 million in the state treasury in June 1980. The 1979 session dealt with several controversial issues. Governor Carlin vetoed the first death penalty bill passed by the legislature in recent years and two measures passed by the legislature on the issue of a state spending limit.

Other bills passed included the allocation of funds to upgrade the state's highway system, the liberalization of rules governing the sale of liquor in clubs, a 10% tax increase on liquor sales' gross receipts, and the reapportionment of both the House and Senate legislative districts.

Politics. The Kansas U. S. Senate delegation received increased news coverage in 1979, with Nancy Landon Kassebaum the only woman now serving in that body and with Robert Dole's May 14 announcement of his candidacy for president in the 1980 elections.

PATRICIA A. MICHAELIS
Kansas State Historical Society

KENTUCKY

Politics dominated news of Kentucky in 1979. The year began with a special session of the legislature and ended with the inauguration of a new governor.

Special Legislative Session. The special session that met in January was called by Lt. Gov. Thelma Stovall (during an absence of Gov. Julian Carroll) for the purpose of imposing limitations or reductions in a variety of state taxes and of strengthening the regulation of utility rates. The session was scheduled to meet in early December 1978; however, the state capital, Frankfort, was inundated by a major flood in December, and Governor Carroll agreed to reschedule the special session for January 1979. (The legislature meets in regular session only in even-numbered years.) Governor Carroll added a variety of other topics to the agenda.

The legislature, acting independently of the governor and the lieutenant governor, adopted a number of measures. Perhaps the most signifi-

---

KANSAS • Information Highlights

Area: 82,264 square miles (213 064 km²).
Population (Jan. 1979 est.): 2,365,000.
Chief Cities (1979 est.): Topeka, the capital, 141,236; Wichita, 261,001; Kansas City, 170,252; Overland Park, 81,271.
Government (1979): *Chief Officers*—governor, John Carlin (D); lt. gov., Paul V. Dugan (D). *Legislature*—Senate, 40 members; House of Representatives, 125 members.
Education (1978–79): *Enrollment*—public elementary schools, 227,325 pupils; public secondary, 206,222; colleges and universities, 127,323 students. *Public school expenditures,* $868,614,000 ($1,947 per pupil).
State Finances (fiscal year 1978): *Revenues,* $1,902,986,000; *expenditures,* $1,746,638,000.
Personal Income (1978): $18,505,000,000; per capita, $7,882.
Labor Force (July 1979): *Nonagricultural wage and salary earners,* 943,800; *unemployed,* 47,100 (3.9% of total force).

KENTUCKY • Information Highlights

Area: 40,395 square miles (104 623 km²).
Population (Jan. 1979 est.): 3,519,000.
Chief Cities (1970 census): Frankfort, the capital, 21,902; Covington, 52,535; (1976 est.): Louisville, 330,011; Lexington, 188,744.
Government (Jan.–Dec. 11, 1979): *Chief Officers*—governor, Julian M. Carroll (D); lt. gov., Thelma Stovall (D). *General Assembly*—Senate, 38 members; House of Representatives, 100 members.
Education (1978–79): *Enrollment*—public elementary schools, 441,712 pupils; public secondary, 251,287; colleges and universities, 132,706 students. *Public school expenditures,* $784,170,000 ($1,036 per pupil).
State Finances (fiscal year 1978): *Revenues,* $3,354,533,000; *expenditures,* $3,241,028,000.
Personal Income (1978): $23,114,000,000; per capita, $6,607.
Labor Force (July 1979): *Nonagricultural wage and salary earners,* 1,266,500; *unemployed,* 87,600 (5.6% of total force).

cant was the imposition of an annual limit of 4% on increases of local taxes on existing property, unless increases are approved by the voters of the locality. The legislature also removed the state sales tax from most home utility bills, revised the biennial budget that it had adopted in 1978, and moved to strengthen legislative control over capital construction funds.

Primary Elections. The special session had strong political overtones, not only because it was an election year, but also because Lt. Gov. Stovall was running for governor in the Democratic primary. Other Democratic contenders included former Louisville mayor Harvey Sloane, state auditor George Atkins, Congressman Carroll M. Hubbard, and the governor's choice, Terry McBrayer. A late entry in the Democratic primary was John Y. Brown, Jr., a well known business leader and son of a veteran state politician. His campaign was largely self-financed and featured skillful use of television. Brown won with only 30% of the vote. On the Republican side, former governor Louie B. Nunn (1967–71) easily won his party's nomination.

General Election. John Brown, Jr., succeeded in uniting the Democratic party, which has a large voter registration advantage in Kentucky. After a gubernatorial campaign marked by considerable bitterness, Brown defeated Nunn with a margin of nearly 60%. The margin was unusually large and included a surprisingly strong Democratic vote in the major metropolitan areas of Louisville and Lexington and represented major inroads into those rural areas that are traditionally Republican.

Constitutional Changes. Kentucky voters, who usually defeat constitutional revisions, adopted

Kentucky's Gov.-elect John Y. Brown, Jr., Lt. Gov.-elect Martha Lane Collins enjoy their election victory.

UPI

two amendments in November. One permits four rather than two amendments to be submitted to the electorate at one time. The other amendment was designed to give newly elected legislators a year to study bills before the meeting of their biennial session. This extended-time benefit was accomplished by permitting the election of legislators in even-numbered years and the election of the governor (a four-year term) in an odd-numbered year—an experiment that is unique in the United States.

MALCOLM E. JEWELL, *University of Kentucky*

KENYA

The firm establishment of the administration of President Daniel arap Moi and mixed economic changes were 1979 highlights in Kenya.

Moi. The unanimous election in late 1978 of Daniel arap Moi as president of Kenya and head of the sole party, the Kenya African National Union, came as a relief to many Kenyans who feared a bitter power struggle and possible coup upon the death in August 1978 of founding father Jomo Kenyatta.

Daniel arap ("son of") Moi was born in 1924, a member of the small Tugen tribe of the Kalenjin ethnic group. Originally named Torotich, he took the name Daniel at his baptism. He taught at a teachers' training college before entering politics as a member of the colonial Legislative Council in 1957. He founded the Kenya African Democratic Union ("KADU") in 1959, but merged his party with Kenyatta's KANU in 1964 after independence. As a result he became home minister in that year and vice president in 1967. Moi has been a highly successful businessman, holding the East African distributorship for International Harvester.

Political Affairs. President Moi moved quickly to consolidate his new powers. He chose Finance Minister Mwai Kibaki as his vice president, and began to fill many KANU and government posts that had been left vacant for years out of fear of tribal and political resentment. He also called the first all-KANU conference in many years, to revive the party's moribund organization and prepare for the regular presidential and legislative election held in November 1979. In heavy voter turnout, the electorate reconfirmed Moi as president but rejected several members of Kenyatta's cabinet. Some seats were contested by members of the KANU party and almost 50% of the incumbents were defeated.

Prior to the election, Moi kept most members of Kenyatta's family in office, and paid respect to "Mama" Ngina Kenyatta, widow of the late president. However, he dissolved the special presidential guard made up of Kiambu Kikuyu from Kenyatta's home province.

Moi's major domestic program was a severe crackdown on the corruption rampant in Kenya. His firing of many police and customs officials was widely hailed. To reassure the Kenyatta

Kenya also began to face severe land and population pressure, with a population increase of 3.5% in a country 85% rural and where only 20% of the land is arable. The redistribution of land in the fertile highlands was nearly completed and the many landless and jobless were increasing their demands on the government for a share of Kenya's relative prosperity.

Foreign Affairs. President Moi refrained from any comment on or interference in the Uganda-Tanzania war, and urged Kenyans and the many Ugandan refugees in Nairobi to do likewise.

Continuing cooperation with the United States and fear of possible military complications led Kenya to contract for $44 million in U.S. arms, including 32 helicopters and 2,000 wire-guided missiles. Fear of Uganda and Somalia were the main motives for the purchase.

Kenya established an embassy in China and opened a High Commission office in Canada.

ROBERT GARFIELD, *DePaul University*

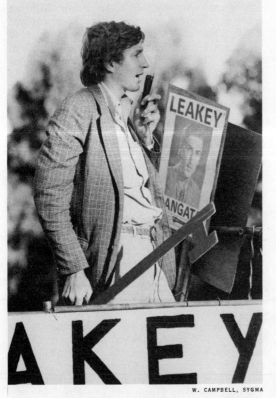

W. CAMPBELL, SYGMA

Philip Leakey, son of anthropologists Louis and Mary, is the first white to be elected to Kenya's parliament.

family, who flourished greatly in past years, Moi promised that there would be no "retroactive investigation" of past dealings. The president also freed in late 1978 all 16 political prisoners in Kenya, including radical playwright Ngugi wa Thiong'o and pro-Soviet organizer Wasonga Sijeyo.

Economy. Kenya's economy developed rapidly but unevenly in 1979. Commitment to capitalism kept foreign investment and confidence high, but a drastic fall in world coffee prices, plus bad rains and disease, hurt the crop and caused a $300 million deficit in the balance of payments. Inflation stood at 15%, while the growth in the gross national product was a bare 3.7%.

─────── **KENYA · Information Highlights** ───────

Official Name: Republic of Kenya.
Location: East coast of Africa.
Area: 224,961 square miles (582 649 km²).
Population (1979 est.): 15,400,000.
Chief Cities (1978 est.): Nairobi, the capital, 786,000; Mombasa, 374,000.
Government: *Head of state and government,* Daniel arap Moi, president (took office Oct. 1978). *Legislature* (unicameral)—National Assembly.
Monetary Unit: Kenya shilling (7.4328 shillings equal U.S.$1, Aug. 1979).
Manufactures (major products): Petroleum products, cement, beer.
Agriculture (major products): Corn, wheat, rice, sugarcane, coffee, tea, sisal, pyrethrum, meat and its products.

KIRIBATI

Kiribati (pronounced Kíri bass), formerly the Gilbert Islands, gained independence on July 12, 1979, in ceremonies on Tarawa, the principal island. In the presence of thousands of Kiribatians, who arrived at Bairiki in outrigger canoes and small boats, and representatives from 20 countries, the ceremony ended 87 years of British authority. Princess Anne represented Queen Elizabeth. Iremia Tabai, age 29, was sworn in as president.

Straddling the equator and spreading across 2 million square miles (5.8 million km²) of the southwestern Pacific, Kiribati is comprised of 33 islands and was combined administratively with the Ellice Islands (now Tuvalu) until Oct. 1, 1975. On Jan. 1, 1977, the Gilbert Islanders gained internal self-government. Independence required financial backing, and the British government provided initial funds.

Ignoring the independence festivities were the ethnically-distinct Banabans of phosphate-rich Ocean Island who during World War II were scattered to many Pacific islands. In 1945 they reassembled and settled on Rabi in the Fiji group. Recently the Banabans have pressed for separation from the Gilbertese and for greater compensation from the British Phosphate Commission.

R. M. YOUNGER, *Australian Author*

─────── **KIRIBATI · Information Highlights** ───────

Official Name: Republic of Kiribati.
Location: Western Pacific.
Area: 264 square miles (684 km²).
Population (1979 est.): 56,000.
Chief City: Bairiki, the capital.
Government: *Head of state and government:* Ieremia Tabai, president (took office July 1979). *Legislature* (unicameral)—House of Assembly.
Manufactures (major product): Phosphate.
Agriculture (major products): Copra, coconut palms, breadfruit, pandanus, bananas.

KOREA

During 1979, inter-Korean relations were tense, as knotty problems remained unresolved. The question of détente drew only peripheral interest in both Seoul and Pyongyang because the immediate concern of the rival Korean regimes was to address the respective "internal" problems on hand.

SOUTH KOREA

Politics. As in 1978, President Park Chung Hee's 1972 "Yushin" (revitalization) constitution came under attack as "illegal" and "undemocratic." Former President Yun Po Sun declared in February, "People are fed up with this dictatorial regime we have here." Dissent became more vocal after May 30 when Kim Young Sam, who pledged a campaign to restore democracy, was elected leader of the opposition New Democratic Party (NDP) at a party convention.

On September 8, a Seoul court disqualified Kim Young Sam as NDP head. On October 4, the pro-Park lawmakers expelled Kim from the legislature for having called the Park government a "minority dictatorial regime." (On October 5, Washington recalled Ambassador William H. Gleysteen, Jr., for home consultations.) On October 13, all 70 opposition lawmakers resigned to protest Kim's expulsion. Within days, student demonstrations erupted in Pusan and spread to nearby cities. Martial law was imposed in Pusan and troops were sent to the other cities.

On October 26, President Park and his chief bodyguard Cha Chi Chol were gunned down by Kim Jae Kyu, director of the Korean Central Intelligence Agency (KCIA). Prime Minister Choi Kyu Hah was named acting president and martial law was proclaimed the next day. In what was a coup that failed, Kim Jae Kyu was arrested along with several "co-conspirators." They were tried by court-martial, convicted, and all but one were condemned to death—subject to appeal. Reflecting on his motive and action, Kim Jae Kyu told the court that he had tried to remove Park from office since November 1972 and that, "I can now die in peace. I have no remorse . . . I will be judged as one who tried to restore democracy, and as a hero."

Choi Kyu Hah was formally elected president on December 6 under the 1972 constitution. The new chief executive lifted the repressive Emergency Decree No. 9 (in effect since 1975) and freed 1,646 violators. In his inaugural address on December 21, Choi pledged to have a revised constitution ready "in about a year's time" and fair elections held "as soon as possible" thereafter. The transition timetable was attacked as too indefinite.

Choi and his civilian opponents alike moved cautiously. On December 12, for reasons unclear as 1979 ended, several junior generals revolted against senior generals and removed Martial Law Commander Chung Seung Hwa and Minister of Defense Ro Jae Hyun. The junta, led by Chon Too Hwan and Lee Hui Sung, detained several generals on suspicion of complicity in Park's assassination and quickly filled key military and cabinet posts with its supporters. The cabinet, named on December 14 with Shin Hyon Hwack (a technocrat) as prime minister, bore an imprint of military influence.

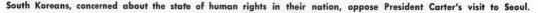

South Koreans, concerned about the state of human rights in their nation, oppose President Carter's visit to Seoul.

The politics of transition were intense but low-keyed under the watchful eyes of generals who pledged not to meddle politically. Among the leading contenders for power in the promised election was Kim Jong Pil, who had been one of Park's key supporters since 1961 and who had been elected in November to succeed Park as leader of the ruling Democratic Republican Party. Kim Jong Pil's likely rivals were Kim Dae Jung and Kim Young Sam. The political fortunes of these aspirants, not to mention the prospects for orderly and democratic changes, depended on support from students, Christian laymen, intellectuals, low-paid industrial workers, and, most importantly, military officers.

Economy. The impressive growth of recent years slowed down owing to the depressant effects of runaway inflation (26%), a tight money policy, rising global protectionism, increased raw material costs, and a slump in overseas market demand. The year-end estimate of growth of the gross national product (GNP) was 7.1% (at 1975 prices) compared with the target of 8% to 9%. GNP per capita reached $1,624 (at current prices), a 27% increase over 1978. Exports were $14.5 billion, $1 billion shy of the year's target, while imports climbed to $20 billion, $2 billion above the planned level. Rising prices for oil threatened to increase the trade gap. Indications were that the policies hitherto geared to "ambitious export targets" would be modified in favor of a strategy aimed at a "balanced" development of all economic sectors, including basic export industries.

According to a September survey in Seoul, 48% of student-youth interviewees singled out the "glaring rich-poor gap" as the foremost "social problem." Increasing layoffs and corporate bankruptcies cast dark shadows over the job market. A government survey in August showed that 51% of all 1980 school graduates may go unemployed. Living conditions improved marginally. Monthly incomes of city families ($330 to $430) fell short of the living costs ($340 to $464). Fifty-eight percent of union workers earned less than $200 a month. Meanwhile, the rural exodus to cities for jobs continued.

Foreign Policy and Defense. President Jimmy Carter visited Seoul for summit talks, June 30–July 1. In a joint communiqué, he pledged con-

K. KUEITA, GAMMA/LIAISON

In December, Choi Kyu Hah, South Korea's 60-year-old prime minister and foreign affairs specialist, succeeded as president Park Chung Hee, who was assassinated.

tinued U. S. security commitments to South Korea, and joined Park in proposing a three-way conference of North and South Korea and the United States to discuss Korean questions. Carter also urged Park to match Seoul's "dramatic economic progress" with "similar progress" in the area of "political and human rights."

South Korea welcomed the White House announcement of July 20 suspending Carter's troop withdrawal plan until 1981. After a two-day conference (October 18–19) in Seoul, the United States agreed to coassemble in South Korea F-5E and F-5F jet fighters, starting in 1982. The United States also reportedly agreed to sell 36 F-16 fighters to Seoul during 1982–86.

NORTH KOREA

Foreign Policy and Defense. North Korea continued to vilify Seoul's alleged policy of confrontation, of "two Koreas," and of war preparations. Nevertheless, it agreed to Park's proposal of January 19 to resume dialogue unconditionally. Preliminary talks were held in February and March but failed to narrow differences between Seoul's insistence that the talks be held on "an official level" and Pyongyang's demand that they be held within the framework of a "whole-nation congress" to be composed of political and social groups from both sides. Their antagonism spilled over into negotiations aimed at the formation of a single Korean team for the 35th

---

─── SOUTH KOREA • Information Highlights ───

Official Name: Republic of Korea.
Location: Northeastern Asia.
Area: 38,022 square miles (98 477 km²).
Population (October 1979): 37,355,000.
Chief Cities (October 1979): Seoul, the capital, 8,140,-021; Pusan, 3,035,000.
Government: *Head of state,* Choi Kyu Hah, president (took office Dec. 1979). *Head of government,* Shin Hyon Hwack, prime minister (took office Dec. 1979). *Legislature* (unicameral)—National Assembly.
Monetary Unit: Won (484 won equal U. S.$1, Dec. 1979).
Manufactures (major products): Textiles, clothing, electronic equipment, petrochemicals, plywood, processed foods, metal products.
Agriculture (major products): Rice, barley, wheat, soybeans, sweet potatoes, fish, livestock.

A 36-year-old Korean-American is tearfully reunited with members of his family during the table tennis championships. The interpreter had fled North Korea in 1950.

UPI

World Table Tennis Championships that Pyongyang hosted in late April. The games were held with teams from 76 nations participating—excluding South Korea. In December, North Korea proposed the formation of a single North-South team for the 1980 Summer Olympics.

In early May, UN Secretary-General Kurt Waldheim visited the two Koreas to explore the possibility of reconciliation. No new initiatives emerged but the rival governments informed Waldheim of their readiness to use his good offices for constructive purposes.

The Park-Carter proposal in July for a three-way conference drew mixed responses from Pyongyang. North Korea termed the proposal "utterly infeasible" but, nonetheless, reaffirmed its readiness to hold separate talks any time—one with Seoul on the question of reunification and the other, directly with the United States, on military questions. Although admittedly "disappointed," U. S. officials declined to consider Pyongyang's response as "final." At the same time, they stressed that none of the Korean questions could be settled without "the full participation of both North and South Korea."

North Korea earmarked $1.47 billion of its budget for defense. (South Korea's defense budget was $3.2 billion.) In midyear, Gen. O Kuk Yol (air force) became the chief of the general staff; the post had been held since 1969 by Gen. O Chin U, the current defense minister.

The size of the North Korean defense establishment was an object of much-publicized reassessments in Washington in light of "new evidence" pointing to a buildup much larger than had been reported. The new U. S. estimates placed the army as the world's fifth largest (550,000 to 600,000 men). In October, South Korea claimed that North Korea had an army of 720,000 men. Pyongyang denounced these estimates as fabrications designed to rationalize Carter's abandonment of his troop withdrawal plan.

Politics. In December, the Korean Workers Party (KWP) announced that its long-delayed Sixth Party Congress would convene in October 1980. This came against the backdrop of growing international speculations about President Kim Il Sung's successor. A sustained media campaign, focusing on the critical importance of party loyalty and discipline, was under way. An unmistakable theme was that Kim Il Sung's "glorious revolutionary tradition" must be "inherited and developed" by the new generation of party members—and that in this process everyone should unfailingly follow the guidance of "the party center" (code words for Kim Chong Il, President Kim's son).

Economy. Economic worries centered on extractive industries, foreign trade (more and better-quality export goods), and the transport sector. Some $2 billion in outstanding foreign debts remained a problem, despite the public optimism that all debts would be paid by 1984. In August, North Korea reached an accord with its Japanese creditors on a ten-year repayment schedule beginning in 1980, with an annual interest of 1.25%. In December, the ruling KWP claimed "brilliant successes in fulfilling the national economic plan for this year" but gave no details. Total trade turnover was estimated at $2 billion, and GNP (in 1975 prices), $11 billion. A South Korean study released in October predicted a $20 billion GNP for North Korea by 1984; South Korea surpassed that level in 1975.

RINN-SUP SHINN, *Foreign Area Studies*
The American University

—— **NORTH KOREA • Information Highlights** ——

Official Name: Democratic People's Republic of Korea.
Location: Northeastern Asia.
Area: 46,540 square miles (120 538 km²).
Population (July 1979 est.): 18,717,000.
Chief Cities (July 1979 est.): Pyongyang, the capital, 1,420,000; Chongjin, 353,700.
Government: *Head of state,* Kim Il Sung, president (nominally since Dec. 1972; actually in power since May 1948). *Head of government,* Li Jong-ok, premier (took office Dec. 1977). *Legislature* (unicameral)—Supreme People's Assembly. The Korean Workers (Communist) Party: General Secretary, Kim Il Sung.
Monetary Unit: Won (1.79 won equal U. S.$1, July 1979).
Manufactures (major products): Cement, coke, pig iron, ferroalloys, textiles.
Agriculture (major products): Rice, corn, potatoes, barley, millet, soybeans, livestock, fish.

LABOR

For American labor, 1979 was more than the end of a decade, it was the end of an era. On November 19, George Meany stepped down after 24 years as president of the American Federation of Labor and Congress of Industrial Organizations. (Meany died Jan. 10, 1980.)

In Canada, unemployment was relatively high, and Japanese workers, like workers everywhere, were concerned about inflation.

UNITED STATES

AFL-CIO Leadership. Although Meany's mind and memory were still sharp at 85, his body had begun to fail. The one-time Bronx plumber nominated as his successor Lane Kirkland, a former executive assistant who for ten years had served as secretary-treasurer of the AFL-CIO. Kirkland, 57, was elected by unanimous vote of the AFL-CIO's 13th biennial convention in Washington, DC.

Unlike his predecessor, who dropped out of high school in his junior year, Kirkland brought to the leadership of the nation's dominant labor organization two degrees: one from the U. S. Merchant Marine Academy, from which he was graduated in 1942, and the other a bachelor of science earned at Georgetown University's foreign service school.

Except for six years when he worked as a deck officer in the U. S. Merchant Marine and as a nautical scientist with the Navy Department during and after World War II, Kirkland has spent his career in the organized labor movement, including service as Meany's assistant.

The organization Kirkland heads is far different from the two groups from which it emerged 24 years earlier. No longer do the building and construction trade unions dominate. Manufacturing unions, too, are being overshadowed by organizations of public employees and workers in service industries. The steady migration of factories from the northeast to the sunbelt, automation, and the transfer of production to overseas plants continue to reduce factory employment.

Union Membership. In 1979, trade union membership was the highest in U. S. history— 21,734,000. However, union membership has been growing more slowly than the work force. During 1979 about one in every five American workers was a union member. In 1949, the proportion was one in three.

In late 1978 and 1979, several union mergers occurred. The most important was the merger of the Retail Clerks and the Meat Cutters and Butcher Workers to form the second largest AFL-CIO union, the Food and Commercial Workers.

National Accord. On September 29, with Kirkland as labor's chief negotiator, the AFL-CIO reached an unprecedented agreement with the Carter administration, a national accord for labor's participation in the development of the government's economic and social policies. The

George Meany, who retired as AFL-CIO president, listens as Alfred Kahn addresses an "operation price watch" rally.

UPI

CAMERA HAWAII

State and county workers in Hawaii picket during a six-week strike, which ended early in December.

document set the terms under which the AFL-CIO agreed to participate in a new wage and price restraint program. It emphasized the need for equality of sacrifice in the struggle against inflation and enumerated essential policies on employment, trade, and energy. The two unaffiliated unions, the Teamsters and the Auto Workers, concurred.

Wage restraints were to be handled by an 18-member Pay Advisory Committee, with equal representation of management, labor, and the public, serving as an advisory panel to the Council on Wage and Price Stability (COWPS). John T. Dunlop, a Harvard professor and a former secretary of labor in the Ford administration, was named Pay Advisory Committee chairman. An all-public board was to monitor prices.

The Pay Advisory Committee was expected to modify the administration's 7% wage guideline with a flexible policy tailored to individual bargaining situations. If that fails to slow price increases, which topped 13% in 1979, the AFL-

U. S. UNION MEMBERSHIP: 1979

Teamsters	1,924,000
Auto Workers	1,500,000
Steelworkers	1,286,000
Food and Commercial Workers	1,235,000
State, County, & Municipal Employees	1,020,000
Electrical Workers, Brotherhood of	1,012,000
Machinists & Aerospace Workers	920,000
Carpenters	768,000
Service Employees	625,000
Laborers	610,000
Communications Workers	508,000
Teachers	500,000

Source: U. S. Bureau of Labor Statistics

CIO was committed to support mandatory wage and price controls.

Employment. The U. S. civilian work force reached a new peak in September when 103,498,000 Americans were at work, an increase of 2.5 million in 12 months. Unemployment fluctuated between 5.6% and 6% of the civilian labor force. That meant that some 6 million workers were hunting jobs. Among blacks, unemployment was 10.6% in September, improved from 11.3% a year earlier. Unemployment among teenagers was 16.4%. Employment declined during the year in agriculture and among domestics and unskilled workers. The number employed in service industries, public services, and in technical and professional occupations increased.

Wages. Weekly earnings of nonsupervisory employees averaged $223.48 in September; in manufacturing the average was $271.88. Real earnings—purchasing power—actually declined 5.9% from September 1978.

Settlements. Collective bargaining agreements covering more than 4 million workers expired in 1979 and were renegotiated. Wage adjustments amounted to 8.2% the first year with similar increases for subsequent years of the contract. The administration's wage guideline of 7% was stretched in several settlements: in trucking the increase was 29% over three years; in the airline industry, 35–40%; in rubber, 39%; longshoremen got 32%; auto workers, 33.4%; and railroaders, 36%. Other agreements, especially those involving public service, kept within the guidelines.

The United Farm Workers Union negotiated a three-year contract with Sun Harvest Inc., the nation's largest lettuce grower, ending an eight-month strike and boycott. The pact raised maximum hourly wages for laborers from $3.70 to $5 with adjustments in 1980 to $5.40 and in 1981 to $5.71.

To deal with the double threat of inflation and low productivity, some union contracts included so-called "harmony clauses" aimed at cutting cost and raising productivity. An example is the 1979 General Motors contract. To cut costly absenteeism, particularly among younger employees, the union agreed to a lower wage rate for newly-hired employees and postponement of some benefits for one year.

Strikes. A total of 3,815 strikes occurred in the first eight months of 1979, 27% more than during the same period a year earlier. In all, 1 million workers lost 23,623,000 working days, or about 0.15% of the total estimated working time for the period. Major strikes involved Newport News Shipbuilding, Uniroyal, United Airlines, Norfolk & Western Railroad, over-the-road truckers, California lettuce growers, and New York and New Jersey dock workers.

Legislation. The major piece of labor legislation before Congress in 1979 was an employer-backed effort to repeal the Davis-Bacon Act of

1931. That act authorized the secretary of labor to set minimum wages and working conditions, based on prevailing wages in a locality, for employees working on federal construction projects, including the alteration and repair of public buildings and public works. The law was intended to guard against the undercutting of community wage standards by government contractors. The repeal effort failed to win Congressional approval.

A Federal Labor Relations Authority, created to enforce the right of federal employees to join unions and bargain collectively guaranteed by the 1978 Civil Service Reform Act, began functioning on Jan. 15, 1979.

Congress restored the prohibition against representatives of labor organizations in totalitarian countries from obtaining visitors' visas to enter the United States. The action came on a motion introduced by Sen. Jacob Javits of New York at the request of the AFL-CIO. The ban had been lifted in 1977 by the so-called McGovern amendment to a State Department appropriation bill.

Occupational Safety. The Occupational Safety and Health Administration (OSHA) penalized a chemical manufacturer $10,000 for requiring female employees to undergo sterilization if they wished to continue working in an area where they would be exposed to toxic substances.

Co-determination. Although American unions generally subscribe to the adversary relationship of collective bargaining in the United States, the Automobile Workers Union accepted an offer by Chrysler Corporation to elect the union's president to its board of directors as a trade-off for concessions granted by the union to the financially troubled auto manufacturer. Union representation on management boards is common in Europe, notably West Germany.

Racial Quotas. The U. S. Supreme Court ruled, 5–2, that unions and employers have the right to adopt quotas in hiring to overcome racial imbalance in "traditionally segregated job categories." AFL-CIO leaders welcomed the decision since it reinforces efforts to end racial injustice through collective bargaining.

Sex Discrimination. The U. S. Department of Labor blacklisted a company, disqualifying it from bidding on government contracts, until it complies with an order to end sex discrimination against women.

INTERNATIONAL

Canada. The legislative program of the new Conservative government promised improvement in industrial relations and reform of the employment program to "ensure equity and remove disincentives to work."

The National Commission on Inflation was disbanded in August 1979 in response to demands of the Canadian Labor Congress. For the first time since 1975 Canada was without a wage and price monitoring agency.

Unemployment in September was 7.1% of the work force, an improvement from the 8.4% rate for all of 1978. For men 25 to 54 the unemployment rate was 4.2%. Consumer prices, rising at an annual rate of 8.4% in the summer, were expected to reach 9% for the year.

Labor-management relations were troubled during 1979. Strikes during the first four months and workdays lost were 55% higher than for the same period of 1978.

Wages rose 7.1% in the first quarter and 8.1% in the second. Some settlements raised wages 20% over two years. An eight-month strike against Vancouver's two daily newspapers brought increases of 34.25% over 40 months, plus 3.5% for other benefits.

The new three-year agreement for West Coast longshoremen contained a reopening clause if inflation rose more than 20% during the first two years of the contract.

Canadian unions grew in pace with the work force. Union membership reached 3.3 million in 1979, representing nearly one in every three Canadian workers. Union mergers reduced the hazard of jurisdictional disputes. Relations with the government improved.

UPI

A three-month walkout by major league baseball umpires came to an end in mid-May. A new contract called for pay increases and additional summer vacations.

Japan. Inflation continued to worry Japanese workers. Consumer prices advanced at an annual rate of 6%. In July 2.2% of the Japanese work force was unemployed, unchanged from the 1978 rate. Productivity continued to increase in manufacturing and mining.

The annual spring negotiations between unions and management produced wage increases averaging 6% in private industry and 5.6% for public employees. Extension of the retirement age was the focus of intense negotiations among unions, management, and government. Traditionally, Japanese workers retire at age 55 although Japanese social security benefits do not start until a worker reaches 60. A deterrent to change is another Japanese tradition, a seniority-based wage system which provides automatic wage increases based on age and length of service, irrespective of position or performance.

The fractured Japanese labor movement sought to unite. A five-point proposal was approved in principle by the three largest federations.

Western Europe. European workers struggled to cope with the shocks of exorbitant increases in oil prices.

Great Britain. The voluntary "social contract" between British unions and the Labour government was abandoned by the Tory government as was the Price Commission. Wage settlements ranged from 12% to 14% despite anticipated 16% increases in consumer prices. By September, unemployment had dropped to 5.2% of the work force, the lowest since 1975.

Relations between the Tory government and the Trades Union Congress (TUC) were strained. The government was seeking to curb union power, discourage strikes, and increase productivity. It proposed to limit picketing, ban the closed shop, require a secret ballot for union elections, tax unemployment benefits, and withhold welfare benefits from those on strike. British unions opposed the government's plan but were divided on strategy. Proposals to resort to mass demonstrations or a one-day general strike failed by a narrow margin at the annual TUC conference.

British unions continued to grow, notably in white collar occupations, engineering and scientific personnel, and in the public service.

Federal Republic of Germany. Workers benefited from a strong economy, growing at an inflation rate of 4.6%, and little serious unemployment. More than 400,000 workers were added to payrolls in the third quarter of 1979.

Co-determination, a system of worker-representation on boards of management, was upheld by the nation's highest court and is now in force in all enterprises with more than 2,000 employees.

New labor legislation strengthened health and safety standards in industry. About 80,000 safety specialists, including physicians and safety engineers, function at the plant level. All plants employing 20 persons or more have safety stewards.

A dispute over the reduction of the work week from 40 to 35 hours, which shut down the steel industry for six weeks, ended in January. The union failed to cut the work week, settling for a precedent-setting annual paid vacation of six weeks by the end of 1982.

France. After three years of government economies, the French emphasis switched to more public spending to reduce unemployment, which totaled 1,250,000 in July. France continued to employ an estimated 3 million foreign "guest workers." The National Employment Pact continued to exempt employers from social security taxes on wages for newly employed youth and financed job training programs.

By autumn, consumer prices were running 11% ahead of 1978.

Strikes, often without authorization of the union, were a recurring problem. In April, a steel strike cut monthly industrial output 40% as workers protested mass layoffs proposed as part of a plan to modernize French steel mills. In October, workers in many cities struck to protest rising prices and unemployment.

Italy. By the fall of 1979, though the economy was advancing at a healthy real growth rate of 4%, the consumer price index was soaring at an annual rate of 16% above 1978.

Italy's new government, installed in August, attempted to replace the traditional quarterly wage escalator with a semiannual adjustment, offering employee tax reductions as a trade-off. In September, all unions joined in a series of four-hour strikes to back up their wage demands.

An estimated 5 million Italians worked full time or part time in the so-called "underground" economy at home or in unregistered enterprises at low wages and paying no taxes.

Brazil. The new Brazilian government permitted the decrees suspending constitutional freedoms to expire and relaxed restrictions on union activity. A ten-day strike of São Paulo metal workers touched off a wave of strikes protesting a 69% rate of inflation. The strikers were arrested but later freed.

In September, the government announced its intention to aid lower income groups through semiannual wage increases over and above adjustments for the cost of living. In October, sugar mill owners signed their first union contract covering 250,000 workers.

Chile. In January, the Latin American Labor Confederation and the AFL-CIO jointly declared a boycott of Chilean shipping, protesting the government's repression of Chilean workers. All forms of union security were prohibited, the antitrust laws were extended to union activity, and collective bargaining was limited to a single plant or shop. In July, the government announced decrees, limiting union activity.

GORDON H. COLE and JOSEPH MIRE

LAOS

The continued emergence of Laos as a Vietnamese-Soviet satellite was more apparent in international affairs than in economic terms. In 1979, the establishment of a fully Communist economy continued in Laos at a slow pace, but there was no doubt that Vientiane was a completely committed ally of Hanoi and Moscow against China.

Politics. Reported differences within the Communist political elite that governed Laos did not diminish the stability of the regime. President (and Prince) Souphanouvong, a long-time nationalist-Communist, and Deputy Premier Phoumi Vongvichit were opposed to becoming as outspoken opponents of neighboring China as Vietnam desired. Premier Kaysone Phomvihane followed Hanoi's lead, however. There were 50,000 Vietnamese troops in the country.

Armed dissident groups, including many pre-1975 anti-Communist soldiers, continued to fight government forces in the field. Since they were dispersed throughout the country and lacked common leadership, the rebels posed no threat to the government. Other military officers and bureaucrats of the pre-Communist Souvanna Phouma regime—numbering as many as 15,000—had been sent to re-education camps in the north in 1976.

Refugees. The Laotian refugee exodus was the largest per capita in the world in 1979. In fact, the rate of exit increased 50% over the previous year. The total who fled to adjacent Thailand exceeded 170,000 by the year's end. Two out of three remained in refugee camps near the Thai border with Laos. Many vowed to return to fight the Communist government.

Economy. Rice comprised approximately 90% of the agricultural output of the land and was much more plentiful than in 1977 or 1978. An International Monetary Fund study group noted, however, "continued depressed levels of output in all sectors." The per capita gross national product was estimated at $90.

The leadership sought to sell food, clothing, and other goods through Soviet-style government shops at subsidized prices, but the store shelves were often empty. Black marketing and smuggling prospered. Agricultural collectivization also proceeded slowly. Two thirds of all

--------- **LAOS • Information Highlights** ---------

Official Name: Lao People's Democratic Republic.
Location: Southeast Asia.
Area: 91,429 square miles (236 800 km²).
Population (1979 est.): 3,700,000.
Chief Cities (1973 census): Vientiane, the capital, 176,-637; Savannakhet, 50,690.
Government: *Head of state,* Prince Souphanouvong, president. *Head of government,* Kaysone Phomvihane, prime minister. *Legislature* (unicameral)—National Congress of People's Representatives.
Monetary Unit: Liberation kip (400 liberation kips equal U. S.$1, 1979).
Manufactures (major products): Tin, lumber.
Agriculture (major products): Rice, corn, coffee, cotton, tobacco.

farming was done on private plots. The government endeavored to encourage collective production through free or inexpensive supplies.

Foreign Relations. The presence of a token force of Laotian troops in neighboring Cambodia—fighting on the side of the Hanoi-established Heng Samrin regime—indicated that the Vientiane government had abandoned even the pretense of neutrality and had become a full ally of Vietnam and the USSR.

In March, the Soviet Union accused China of massing troops along its border with Laos. Vietnam and then the Laotian government followed in their protests. The Soviets, for their part, had earlier established a military and intelligence-seeking presence along the Chinese-Laotian frontier—long before the Vientiane government accused Peking of arming dissidents.

Vietnam pledged to withdraw its troops provided that China no longer posed a threat to Laotian independence. Hanoi's troops, however, were moved closer to the Laotian-Chinese border during the year.

Laos received foreign assistance from many countries but was unsuccessful in its efforts to obtain such aid from the United States.

See also ASIA.

RICHARD BUTWELL
Murray State University

LASERS

The number and variety of applications of lasers increased at a rapid rate in 1979. The wide range of uses stems from the nature of this remarkably pure light beam.

General Applications. Lasers have been used in the treatment of ear infections. A common procedure in the treatment of repeated ear infections has been to puncture the eardrum and insert tubes for drainage. An alternative new procedure is to drill a hole in the eardrum with a laser beam. Since the hole remains open long enough during the healing process to permit drainage, no tubes are needed.

Laser beams are also excellent for cutting hard materials, including diamonds. Since no contact is actually made, the "cutting edge" never wears out. High-power lasers are used to apply coatings both to metals and refractory materials. Typical uses produce longer-lasting, tougher coatings for equipment that operates in environmental extremes. Tests conducted in Israel in 1979 successfully utilized laser beams to extract oil and gas from shale. The shale is ignited by the laser beam, and some of the released gases are collected at the top of the well. The fraction of the gas which condenses is siphoned away by pumping.

In the military sector, laser-gyroscope navigation systems are being developed for combat aircraft. Laser guns are currently employed in war games conducted by the Department of Energy. These mock conflicts are part of a training program for personnel who protect vehicles loaded with nuclear materials. The laser guns (gallium arsenide lasers attached to M16 rifle barrels) are ideal for training purposes, since the intensity is low enough for complete safety and the power is great enough to be recorded electronically. This combination of intensity and power provides a precise but hazard-free method by which to evaluate the guards' accuracy.

Energy Applications. One approach to controlled thermonuclear fusion is to direct powerful laser beams at hydrogen and deuterium pellets, and to achieve the ultra-high temperatures necessary for fusion during the resulting implosion. Construction of the most powerful laser system in the world (Nova) has begun at Lawrence Livermore (CA) Laboratory adjacent to the present Shiva laser system. The Nova laser fusion system, which will have operating characteristics closer to those expected for an actual operating plant, will be capable of producing 300 million million watts.

Present nuclear power applications utilize the fission process, which uses as fuel the uranium enriched in isotope 235. Isotope separation by gaseous diffusion is complex, expensive, and energy-intensive. A new separation technique relies on the remarkable purity of the light emitted by the laser. The laser light can label an atom or compound of one isotope while leaving the other isotopes unaffected. The major application for laser separation would be for uranium enrichment, since laser separation of uranium could reduce the energy cost by a large factor compared with gaseous diffusion. The laser separation would also remove essentially all of the uranium 235 in the ore; one could even mine the stored wastes from gaseous diffusion plants to increase uranium reserves.

Communications. The number of telecommunications systems consisting of optical fibers and lasers is expanding rapidly. Signals are converted into light pulses by a laser, transmitted through a fiber, and then reconverted. These cables carry much more information per unit size than the traditional ones and increase the accuracy of digital signal transmission. Field trials for telephone communications are under way at a variety of locations, including Pennsylvania, Lake Placid (NY), Canada, Disney World (Orlando, FL), and Germany. Typical lengths for these experimental systems are 5–20 kilometers (3.1–12.4 mi). Other applications include linkage of computers, military fiber optic radar links, and cable television. These developments are just the beginning. Fiber optical systems are expected to advance and to become a multibillion dollar a year business by the end of the 1980's.

See also PHYSICS.

GARY MITCHELL
Department of Physics
North Carolina State University

LATIN AMERICA

The year 1979 was one of political upheaval in Latin America. The most dramatic case was the victory of Sandinista rebels over the government of Nicaraguan strong man Anastasio Somoza Debayle. Elsewhere in the hemisphere, coups d'etat overturned the governments of Grenada, El Salvador, and Bolivia, while a confused election led finally to the installation of a civilian president in Ecuador. Hurricanes lashed the Caribbean, and a political tempest raged over the alleged installation of Soviet combat troops in Cuba.

Nicaraguan Crisis. The National Guard of Nicaragua—a combined army and police force organized by U. S. Marines and commanded by a member of the Somoza family since 1933—went down in defeat at the hands of Sandinista guerrillas in July 1979. The victors took their name from Gen. Augusto C. Sandino, who led the armed resistance to U. S. occupation of Nicaragua from 1927 to 1933. An underlying anti-Yankee sentiment made the Sandinista cause a popular one among nationalistic elements throughout Latin America.

In May 1979, while rebels battled the National Guard in northern Nicaragua, Cuban President Fidel Castro, whose guerrilla experts had been training Sandinista leaders, discussed the situation with Mexican President José López Portillo in Cozumel, Mexico. Shortly after Castro's departure, Costa Rican President Rodrigo Carazo arrived in Cozumel to confer with López Portillo. Mexico and Costa Rica then broke diplomatic relations with the Nicaraguan government and urged other Latin American countries to follow suit. Many did, including Brazil and the members of the Andean Pact—Bolivia, Colombia, Ecuador, Peru, and Venezuela. Panama, long at odds with the Somoza regime, stepped up military aid to the Sandinistas.

In June, several hundred Sandinistas crossed the Costa Rican border into southern Nicaragua, while rebel leaders in the slums of Managua sparked a mass uprising in the nation's capital. With the National Guard fighting desperately to contain the nationwide insurrection, the United States called for Somoza's resignation and the dispatch of an inter-American armed force to impose peace. The foreign ministers of the Organization of American States (OAS), meeting in special session in Washington, welcomed the call for Somoza's resignation but strongly opposed OAS military intervention. The United States withdrew its proposal and supported a resolution calling for Somoza's resignation and condemning any outside military interference. Only Paraguay and Somoza's own delegate voted against the resolution.

In July, U. S. negotiators reached an agreement with both Somoza and the Sandinista National Liberation Front (FSLN) for the transfer of power to a junta named by the FSLN. So-

Soldiers stand guard in a main street in San Marcos, El Salvador, as President Carlos Humberto Romero is removed from power in an October 1979 coup.

UPI

moza resigned and turned over the presidency to Francisco Urcuyo before flying to the United States on July 17. Instead of surrendering to the FSLN, Urcuyo attempted to retain power for himself and prolonged the war for days. The result was a complete victory for the FSLN and the disbanding of the National Guard. Fearing that the United States might extradite him, Somoza moved to Paraguay in August. Members of the junta—which was composed of three moderates and two radicals—were received in the United States, Cuba, and several other countries during the year. (*See also* CENTRAL AMERICA.)

Coup in El Salvador. While the Sandinistas disavowed any intentions of exporting revolution, their success seemed to inspire revolutionaries in neighboring El Salvador. Antigovernment demonstrations and terrorist activities in that country grew rapidly over the next few months. The Salvadorean rebels, like their Nicaraguan counterparts, received considerable support from Roman Catholic clergy, although Pope John Paul II, during his January visit to Mexico, condemned "liberation theology" and any clerical involvement in left-wing movements. The major change came in October, however, as President Carlos Humberto Romero was ousted in a coup by younger army officers. The new junta promised reforms and sought an accommodation with rebel forces.

Nonaligned Nations. Nicaragua officially joiend the "nonaligned" in 1979, as did the Caribbean nation of Grenada. That island underwent a brief popular uprising in March, during which the 12-year-old regime of Prime Minister Sir Eric Gairy was replaced by a left-leaning government headed by Maurice Bishop. Other Western Hemisphere nations represented at the September summit of nonaligned countries in Havana included Argentina and Peru, which had previously shunned "third world" activism, and Panama, whose President Aristides Royo praised U. S. President Jimmy Carter's handling of the Panama Canal question. (The Canal Zone was returned to Panama in October.)

In September the United States charged that a Soviet combat brigade of 2,000–3,000 men was stationed on Cuba. Both Cuba and the Soviet Union denied the charge, insisting that Soviet personnel on the island were there only to train Cuban troops.

Tropical Storms. Cuba and most of the other Caribbean islands suffered considerable hurricane damage during 1979. Hardest hit was the Dominican Republic, which was struck in September by hurricanes David and Frederic; several thousand people were killed and many more were left homeless.

Peaceful Changes. In South America, a continent long dominated by military strong men, there were turnovers of executive power in four countries during the year. In Brazil, one military leader succeeded another, as Gen. João Baptista Figueiredo was inaugurated in March (*see* BIOGRAPHY; BRAZIL). In Venezuela, one civilian president replaced another, as Luis Herrera Campíns took office in March (*see* VENEZUELA). In Ecuador, a runoff presidential election was held in April—nine months after the original balloting—and Jaime Roldós Aguilera of the centerleft won by a landslide; his election brought to an end nine years of military rule (*see* ECUADOR). In August, Bolivia restored a constitutional government, after 11 years of military rule, with the election by the Congress of a provisional president, Walter Guevara Arce, who pledged to hold new popular elections in 1980. But on November 1, the country was set in turmoil by a military takeover. A general strike was called to protest the new regime, which responded by calling a state of siege. On November 16 the military again withdrew and allowed the installation of Lydia Gueiler, Bolivia's first woman president (*see* BOLIVIA).

NEILL MACAULAY
University of Florida

LAW

The 1978–79 term of the U. S. Supreme Court was marked by noteworthy and sometimes controversial decisions in such varied areas as reverse discrimination, the First Amendment, civil rights, and police searches. No clear ideological position emerged, as the justices tended to rule on a case-by-case basis. But probably the most widely publicized decision in the United States during 1979 was that of a California Superior Court in *Marvin v. Marvin,* a case concerning unmarried cohabitation. (The issues are detailed in a special report beginning on page 298.) In international law, the most significant developments again occurred in the areas of human rights, the law of the sea, pollution control, space, and the succession of states.

U. S. SUPREME COURT

The 10th year of the Burger Court lacked any consistent direction but had some unusual and controversial aspects. In a rare breach of security, a television news reporter correctly predicted the rulings in two cases. Evidencing mounting tension on the court, Justice Thurgood Marshall publicly criticized several decisions; Chief Justice Warren Burger, in a dissenting opinion, called one decision "intellectually dishonest"; and two justices issued a detailed list of cases that they felt raised important questions of law but that the court did not hear because its workload was too heavy.

The Burger Court, generally regarded as conservative, was unexpectedly favorable to civil rights litigation, authorizing massive system-wide

In a major case involving reverse discrimination, the U. S. Supreme Court ruled against Brian Weber.

UPI

school desegregation for two northern cities and approving affirmative action programs for the employment of racial minorities. Equal rights for women were generally favored. Limits were imposed on police searches, and several decisions favored criminal defendants. The only consistent loser was the First Amendment, the court continuing what many regarded as a vendetta against the press.

With two conservatives on the court—Chief Justice Burger and William H. Rehnquist—and two committed liberals—William J. Brennan and Thurgood Marshall—the balance of power lay with the five center justices, whose positions became increasingly unpredictable during 1979. Harry A. Blackmun (13 dissents), Byron R. White (18), and Lewis F. Powell, Jr. (18) were closest to the center, with Potter Stewart (25) and John Paul Stevens (31) more likely to vote with the liberals. Of the 130 signed opinions only 51 were unanimous. There were 5-to-4 votes in 21 of the other 79 decisions.

The First Amendment and the Press. Two decisions made it easier for persons not voluntarily involved in public controversies to win libel suits. One plaintiff had been wrongly named in a book as a Soviet spy, and the other was a university professor whose federal research grant Sen. William Proxmire (D-WI) had ridiculed with a "Golden Fleece" award. The court held that neither was a "public figure" and therefore did not have to show malice in order to prove libel (*Wolston v. Reader's Digest, Hutchinson v. Proxmire*). The Proxmire decision also limited congressional protection under the Constitution's "speech and debate" clause, holding that the clause does not cover press releases, newsletters, or telephone calls.

In another libel case, the court held that in order to prove malice the lawyers of a Vietnam veteran—a "public figure" who had appeared on CBS television's *Sixty Minutes*—must be permitted to query the broadcasters about their thoughts, motivations, and internal editorial processes in preparing the program (*Herbert v. Lando*). A further blow to the press was the court's refusal to review a lower court ruling that reporters need not be given advance notice when government agents subpoena their long distance telephone records from the telephone company (*Reporters Committee v. AT&T*). One of the few victories for the "fourth estate" was the court's ruling that a state cannot prohibit newspapers from publishing the names of juveniles charged with a crime (*Smith v. Daily Mail*).

Church-state issues continued to crop up during 1979. A New Jersey income tax deduction for parents who send their children to private schools was held to advance religion in violation of the "establishment" clause of the First Amendment (*Byrne v. Public Funds for Public Schools*). According to the decision in *NLRB v. Catholic Bishop of Chicago,* officials of parochial schools are not required to bargain with lay teachers' unions under federal labor law.

Equal Protection. In a major decision on reverse discrimination the court upheld, 5–2, an employee training program, to which equal numbers of whites and blacks were admitted, voluntarily adopted by Kaiser Aluminum Co. The court ruled that Title VII of the 1964 Civil Rights Act, while on its face forbidding racial preferences in hiring, was enacted for the purpose of increasing economic opportunities for blacks and therefore was not intended to prohibit race-conscious programs to remedy past societal discrimination (*Kaiser Aluminum Co. v. Weber*).

In cases from Columbus and Dayton, OH, the court affirmed the authority of federal judges to impose sweeping desegregation plans in cities where the public schools become nearly all-white or all-black as a result of school board policies (*Columbus Board of Education v. Penick, Dayton Board of Education v. Brinkman*). Also, a town and its residents can bring suit under the Fair Housing Act when they believe that real estate agents are illegally trying to tip the racial balance of an integrated neighborhood (*Gladstone Realtors v. Bellwood*).

The court upheld claims of sex discrimination in six of eight cases. The major failure of women's rights advocates came in their effort to have veterans-preference public employment laws declared unconstitutional because veterans are overwhelmingly male (*Personnel Administrator v. Feeney*). But they succeeded in establishing that a congressional employee can sue a congressman on grounds of sex or race discrimination (*Davis v. Passman*), and that individuals as well as the government may bring sex discrimination suits under Title IX of the 1964 Civil Rights Act (*Cannon v. University of Chicago*). The court also held that unemployed mothers are as entitled to welfare benefits for children as are unemployed fathers (*Califano v. Westcott*).

Male equality was served by a ruling that New York state laws were unconstitutional which required divorced husbands, but not divorced wives, to pay alimony (*Orr v. Orr*). A New York law allowing an unwed mother to block the proposed adoption of her illegitimate child, but denying the same right to the unmarried father, was struck down (*Caban v. Mohammed*). But the court upheld a Georgia law permitting the mother of an illegitimate child, but not the father, to sue for damages for the child's accidental death (*Parham v. Hughes*).

The court also upheld a New York law requiring public school teachers to be American citizens (*Ambach v. Norwick*) and a federal law requiring Foreign Service employees to retire at age 60 (*Vance v. Bradley*).

Criminal Prosecutions. In one of the term's most debated decisions, the court held, 5–4, that the press and public do not have a constitutional right to attend criminal trials; the decision granted judges the authority to close a courtroom upon the request of defense counsel and the consent of the prosecutors. The Sixth Amendment guarantee of a "public trial" was held to apply only to defendants (*Gannett v. DePasquale*).

Police cannot stop a person on the street and ask for identification unless they have a specific reason to suspect criminal activity (*Brown v. Texas*), nor can they detain a criminal suspect for questioning unless they have probable cause for an arrest (*Dunaway v. New York*).

Police may not stop motorists at random to check for licenses and registration unless there is some reason to believe that they are violating the law (*Delaware v. Prouse*); and police must obtain a warrant before searching a suitcase taken from an automobile (*Arkansas v. Sanders*). Mere passengers, however, cannot challenge a police search of the car in which they are riding (*Rakas v. Illinois*).

An "open-ended" search warrant allowing police to seize anything they could find in an alleged pornography shop was declared unconstitutional (*Lo-Ji Sales v. New York*). But the Fourth Amendment does not prevent federal agents from breaking and entering to install bugging equipment authorized by a judge under the Crime Control Act (*Dalia v. United States*). And according to another decision, the police do not need a search warrant before installing a "pen register" to record the numbers dialed on a telephone (*Smith v. Maryland*).

The "Miranda rule" was weakened by a 5–3 ruling that a criminal suspect does not have to sign a form specifically waiving his right to consult a lawyer in order for the police to conduct a valid interrogation (*North Carolina v. Butler*). Nor must police cease interrogation of a juvenile suspect who asks to speak to his or her probation officer (*Fare v. Michael C.*). Limiting a 1972 decision, the court held that a defendant unable to pay for a lawyer has the right to appointed counsel only if conviction leads to a jail sentence (*Scott v. Illinois*).

Grand jury testimony given by an individual under grant of immunity cannot be used later to attack his credibility as a defendant in a criminal trial (*New Jersey v. Portash*). Relaxing its recent campaign against federal habeas corpus, the court held, 5–4, that a person convicted of a crime in state court is entitled to federal court review on a claim of racial discrimination in selecting the grand jury (*Rose v. Mitchell*).

Evidence taken by the police in a "good faith" arrest can be admitted at trial even if the law under which the arrest was made is then found to be unconstitutional (*Michigan v. DeFillippo*). Evidence obtained by a federal agency in violation of its own rules can be introduced at trial (*United States v. Caceres*).

The automatic exemption of all women from jury service violates the constitutional right to trial by a cross-section of the population (*Duren v. Missouri*). Extending a previous decision affirming the constitutionality of six-member juries, the court ruled in 1979 that the verdicts of such juries must be unanimous (*Burch v. Louisiana*).

An individual cannot be committed unwillingly to a mental institution without convincing evidence of being both mentally ill and likely to be dangerous (*Addington v. Texas*). However, a minor does not have the right to a hearing to contest a parental decision to commit him (*Parham v. J. R.*).

Persons held in jail awaiting trial, usually because they cannot make bail, are presumed innocent until proved guilty. But in 1979 the court held that such individuals do not have a constitutional right to minimal restrictions. Several of them may be confined in a cell designed for one prisoner, and their bodily cavities may be checked for drugs or weapons after they receive visitors (*Bell v. Wolfish*). In *Greenholtz v. Inmates*, the Supreme Court ruled that states are free to administer their parole systems in any way they choose.

Abortion. The court struck down a Massachusetts law requiring unmarried minors to get permission from their parents or a judge before having an abortion (*Bellotti v. Baird*). It also voided as unconstitutionally vague a Pennsylvania law requiring doctors to attempt to save the life of a fetus if it "may be" viable (*Colautti v. Franklin*). But the court let stand a lower court ruling that permitted Cleveland, OH, to use its zoning powers to exclude abortion clinics from certain areas (*West Side Women's Services v. Cleveland*).

Federalism. While the Eleventh Amendment protects states from suit in their own courts, a 1979 decision allows them to be sued in the courts of another state (*Nevada v. Hall*). Also, a state cannot ordinarily block another state's request for extradition of a fugitive by conducting its own examination of the basis for the request (*Michigan v. Doran*).

The court ruled that a state may not tax electricity exported to another state more heavily than the electricity used within its own borders (*Arizona Public Service Co. v. Snead*).

The authority of the federal government to ban interstate shipment of laetrile was upheld (*United States v. Rutherford*), as was the authority of municipal government over persons residing in unincorporated areas outside city limits, even if such persons cannot vote in city elections (*Holt Civic Club v. Tuscaloosa*).

Economic Issues and Labor Law. In a suit brought by the AFL-CIO, the court declined to interfere with the use of government purchasing power by the president of the United States to enforce anti-inflation and price guidelines.

It allowed the states to pay unemployment compensation to striking workers (*N. Y. Telephone Co. v. N. Y. Dept. of Labor*) and limited the liability that a labor union can incur for failing to represent one of its members adequately in processing a grievance (*Electrical Workers v. Foust*).

C. HERMAN PRITCHETT
University of California, Santa Barbara

LAW—SPECIAL REPORT:

The Issue of Unmarried Cohabitation

April 18, 1979 was a date that ended years of waiting for actor Lee Marvin and his former mistress Michelle Triola Marvin. It was the day that California Superior Court Judge Arthur K. Marshall handed down his decision in the much-publicized case regarding the legal obligations between a man and a woman who live together out of wedlock. What did not end was speculation and conjecture on the increasingly prevalent trend of unmarried cohabitation—its legal, moral, and ethical status; its staying power; and its effect on the institution of marriage.

Judge Marshall's opinion brought to an end the breach of contract claim by Michelle Triola Marvin after three-and-a-half months at trial. The action against Lee Marvin had called for damages of $1.8 million, half of the actor's earnings during the six-year period in which the couple lived together. That trial followed a 1976 decision by the California Supreme Court in a preliminary aspect of the litigation. The high court had determined that unmarried cohabitants could regulate their property rights by contract, so long as the contract does not rest on the consideration of "meretricious" sexual services alone. A trial was ordered to determine what type of contract or other property arrangement existed between the two parties.

The stage was set. If a contract could be proven it would be enforced. Most followers of the case thought that if a contract could *not* be proven, the matter would end. But Judge Marshall saw it differently. Although no contract was proven, he interpreted some of the wording in the 1976 decision as authorizing an alternative basis for payment—rehabilitation. Accordingly, he ordered Mr. Marvin to pay his former mistress a sum of $104,000, with which to reeducate herself and to learn new, employable skills.

The *Marvin* case was not an isolated outcropping. In the last few years, more than twenty state supreme courts have catalogued

PHOTOS UPI

"Marvin v. Marvin": Michelle Triola and her lawyer; at right, actor Lee Marvin.

holdings involving unmarried cohabitation. Many more are pending. These cases all confront one common issue: should courts lend themselves to a solution of property-ownership questions of persons who voluntarily opt out of the legal and social institution of marriage?

A majority of the courts have held that the parties before them should retain access to the dispute-resolution mechanism of the judicial system, married or not. The few that disagree reiterate an old doctrine to support their position: courts should not allow the judicial system to become available to resolve disputes between parties to a meretricious relationship. The great majority of courts reason that as long as there are discernible economic elements distinct from a sexual relationship, such economic matters can be considered separately and resolved as they would be between any other litigants. In a few cases, courts have indicated that they would simply "look at the modern world" without concerning themselves with the effects of a sexual relationship.

The publicity given to *Marvin v. Marvin* was a reflection of the widespread practice of unmarried cohabitation itself. Hard statistics do not exist; no central bureau or agency records the formation or disintegration of such relations. However, estimates from various sources place the number of U. S. couples living together at three to six million. That the figure for conventionally married couples is approximately 50 million indicates the extent to which the more traditional practice is being rejected. While the 1980 U. S. census may better identify the demography of unmarried cohabitation, casual observation will convince most that living together

without ceremonial marriage is a major social trend. And it shows no sign of abating.

Regulating the property rights of unmarried "spouses" by contracts and other legal means may formalize and structure the living arrangement. Situations such as *Marvin v. Marvin,* in which no binding agreement was made, demonstrate that efforts to avoid one set of legal strictures—those of marriage and divorce—sometimes lead to even more lengthy, expensive, and complicated involvements with the law. The growth of the "cohabitation contract" will make it possible to settle disputes privately and in advance of separation. Few couples who decide to live together would dismiss such contracts, given the opportunity to read the records of cases litigated in the past. One state legislature is considering a law requiring a written contract as a prerequisite to any recognition of legal rights arising out of cohabitation.

Common-law marriage—legal matrimony without a certificate or license, based on the parties' agreement to consider themselves married—has been abolished in most American states. But as a response to the problems incident to the spread of unmarried cohabitation, legal resurrection of common-law marriage is being proposed in one U. S. state and a variant of it has been newly adopted in a Canadian province. Its continued existence in a few states, however, may serve to entrap some living-together couples into an actual marriage. That risk is but one example of the confusion that has been spawned by the experimentation with conventional forms of marriage. The final answers are certain to be many years in the making.

WILLIAM P. CANTWELL

INTERNATIONAL LAW

As bilateral treaties on diplomatic and trade relations, strategic arms, and economic aid grabbed most of the headlines during 1979, there emerged from less publicized conferences a variety of important multilateral agreements.

Law of the Seas. The United Nations Conference on the Law of the Seas (UNCLOS) held its eighth session in five years March 9–April 27, 1979, in Geneva and New York. Although no general accord was concluded, the 159-nation forum had resolved about 90% of the issues before it. A treaty of about 400 articles was hoped for in the future.

There was progress on the controversial question of deep seabed mining, and a compromise was worked out on the right of landlocked countries to fish in waters of nearby coastal nations. General agreement was also reached on the definition of the outer limit of the continental shelf, and on a draft legal code to prevent marine pollution. There was still no agreement on the sea boundaries between adjacent nations; the issue may be left to individual governments to resolve.

Previously enacted were agreements covering a 12-mile (22.2-km) zone of offshore sovereignty, a 200-mile (370-km) economic exploitation zone under the control of each coastal nation, and free passage for all ships through international straits within the 12-mile sovereignty zone.

Although UNCLOS is a testing ground for peaceful, multilateral solutions to world problems, disputes and disagreements have often arisen which threatened the successful conclusion of the conference. These occurred most frequently between nations which have the technological means to exploit the riches of the sea and developing countries which view the ocean as the common heritage of mankind.

In the absence of a formal international agreement, individual nations continued to declare 200-mile offshore fishing jurisdictions. Bilateral negotiations on reciprocal fishing rights also continued in 1979. The United States and Canada arrived at a settlement regarding fishing boundaries in the Atlantic and Pacific, but the two nations squabbled over U. S. vessels pursuing the migratory albacore tuna into Canada's 200-mile fishing control zone.

In its 31st annual meeting, the International Whaling Commission heeded the pleas of conservation groups and dismissed the objection of Japan and the Soviet Union by voting for a worldwide moratorium on whaling from factory ships. Compliance with the moratorium was expected to save 10,000 sperm whales in 1980.

A dispute between Mexico and the United States developed over the May 3 blowout of an oil well off Mexico's Yucatan Peninsula. The blowout caused a massive oil slick that began washing up on the shores of Texas by August 9 and threatened substantial environmental damage. However, the circumstances of such an accident were not anticipated in existing international accords on liability for oil spills, and Mexico disclaimed any obligation for compensation.

Space. The disintegration of man-made satellites presents another question of liability for scattered debris. Although some 75 nations, including the United States and Soviet Union, have ratified the Treaty on International Liability for Damage Caused by Space Objects, the USSR did not respond to a bill submitted by Canada for cleanup expenses after a Soviet satellite broke up over Canada in 1978.

In 1979, after seven years of work, the United Nations Committee on Outer Space approved the draft of an international treaty governing the exploitation of any riches found on the moon.

Human Rights. The European Court of Human Rights delivered a verdict in a freedom of press case brought against the British government by the *London Sunday Times*. The paper had been prohibited by the House of Lords, which serves as the nation's Supreme Court, from publishing an article on the thalidomide tragedy of the 1950's. The court concluded that the prohibition constituted prior restraint and was a breach of the Human Rights Convention guaranteeing freedom of expression.

In 1979, the 32-member UN Commission on Human Rights passed resolutions dealing with Palestinian rights, apartheid, and racism.

Succession of States. The International Law Commission published a draft of articles on succession of states in respect of state property and state debts. It also considered the topics of the responsibility of states for internationally wrongful acts; the succession of states in respect of matters other than treaties; the applicability of treaties concluded between states and international organizations or between two or more such organizations; the status of the diplomatic courier and the diplomatic bag not accompanied by diplomatic courier; the non-navigational uses of international watercourses; and the techniques and procedures for creating multilateral treaties.

At the same time, the UN Conference on the Succession of States in Respect of Treaties agreed on a convention freeing any new state from obligations deriving from its predecessor's treaties. However, the document held that the succession of states does not affect the boundaries established by a treaty.

Iran. After only days of deliberation the World Court in The Hague responded to U. S. pleadings in mid-December by issuing an unequivocal statement calling on Islamic regime in Iran to release the 50 U. S. embassy personnel held hostage in Tehran.

MARTIN GRUBERG
University of Wisconsin, Oshkosh

LEBANON

The year saw no respite from the bitter dispute among Muslim leftists, Palestinian guerrillas, and Christian rightists that has plagued Lebanon since the 1975–1976 civil war. The unsettling presence of guerrillas, the 30,000-man Arab Deterrent Force (ADF), a contingent of United Nations peacekeeping troops (UNIFIL), and an alliance between rebellious Christian troops and Israeli forces in southern Lebanon made it all but impossible for President Elias Sarkis to restore the authority of the central government or bring stability to the devastated republic.

Government Policy. Sarkis continued his attempts to form a "national reconciliation" government in which all of Lebanon's diverse factions would be represented. Such a political solution, however, would require the cessation of Palestine Liberation Organization (PLO) attacks on Israel from Lebanon, the reestablishment of the authority of the shattered Lebanese Army in Beirut and along the Lebanon-Israel border, and the eventual withdrawal of ADF and UNIFIL troops. More importantly, it would require the agreement of both Muslim and Christian factions.

While the presence of the predominantly Syrian ADF troops had forced something of a reconciliation among leftists, its effect on Christian factions was just the opposite. In mid-1978, former President Suleiman Franjieh's faction defected from the loose rightist coalition—the National Front—over the issue of Syrian troops. The murder in July 1978 of Franjieh's son by rival Pierre Geyamel's Phalange Party militia initiated a series of revenge slayings and kidnappings that have perpetuated divisions among the Christian rightists. Moreover, Camille Chamoun's National Liberal Party (NLP) joined Franjieh in accusing Geyamel of trying to dominate the right. Fighting among themselves and against Syrian forces, the Christians paralyzed reconstruction efforts through July 1979.

Christian Separatism. The destabilizing effects of the Christians' internecine strife were exacerbated by Sarkis' policy in southern Lebanon, the activities of the PLO, and an ad hoc alliance between Israel and troops commanded by former

HENRI BUREAU, SYGMA

Troops march in support of Saad Haddad, leader of a self-proclaimed "Independent Lebanon" in the south.

Lebanese Army Maj. Saad Haddad. With Israeli assistance, Haddad's men occupied and denied from PLO and UNIFIL troops the six-mile (9.7-km)-wide border strip taken over by Israel during its 1978 incursion into southern Lebanon.

On April 18, 1979, a battalion of Lebanese Army troops moved south in the first phase of Sarkis' attempt to retake control of the border region. In response, Haddad declared the creation of an "Independent Lebanon" in that area and threatened to fire on Sarkis' troops. On April 23, after Prime Minister Selim al-Hoss branded him a traitor, Haddad and Israeli forces began an offensive against PLO positions. Combining Israeli airstrikes and almost daily artillery bombardments, the campaign continued through the summer and demonstrated the impotence of the central government.

Government Resigns. The Israeli-led fighting, which brought hundreds of civilian casualties and more than 150,000 new refugees, also created a severe political crisis for Sarkis. Israel apparently sought to perpetuate the chaos in Lebanon to keep the cost of Syria's involvement as high as possible while punishing the PLO. An emergency summit meeting between Sarkis and Syrian President Hafez al-Assad momentarily boosted the government's confidence. But after Lebanese Foreign Minister Fuad Butros rejected Israeli Prime Minister Menahem Begin's May 8 offer to open peace talks, an intensification of attacks in the south forced Sarkis to accept the resignation of Hoss' cabinet on May 16.

─── **LEBANON · Information Highlights** ───

Official Name: Republic of Lebanon.
Location: Southwest Asia.
Area: 4,000 square miles (10 360 km²).
Population (1979 est.): 3,100,000.
Chief Cities (1974 est.): Beirut, the capital, 1,000,000; Tripoli, 128,000.
Government: *Head of state,* Elias Sarkis, president (took office Sept. 1976). *Head of government,* Selim al-Hoss, prime minister (took office Dec. 1976). *Legislature* (unicameral)—National Assembly.
Monetary Unit: Lebanese pound (3.4760 pounds equal U.S.$1, Dec. 1979).
Manufactures (major products): Petroleum products, lumber, cement.
Agriculture (major products): Fruits, wheat, corn, barley, potatoes, olives, onions, tobacco.

Hoss, the prime minister since December 1976, stated that he was resigning to make way for a national unity coalition of civilian political factions. Despite the almost immediate announcement of plans for a merger between Chamoun's NLP and Geyamel's Phalange, however, leftist leaders Walid Jumblatt and Rashid Karami declared on May 24 that reconciliation with the Christians was impossible so long as Christian elements were allied with the Israelis.

Lebanon's Dilemma. With the exception of Franjieh, who urged cooperation with Sarkis, most Christian factions continued to demand both the withdrawal of Syrian forces and the cessation of PLO attacks on Israel from Lebanese soil. It was the cumulative effect of Israel's retaliatory raids on PLO bases and consequent Christian anti-PLO violence that precipitated the civil war three years earlier and that continued to prolong Lebanon's search for stability.

Neither Sarkis nor Syria's Assad could persuade or compel PLO leader Yasir Arafat either to stop guerrilla activities or, at the least, to move PLO bases from civilian areas. So long as guerrilla attacks originated from Lebanon, Israel announced, it would continue preemptive strikes against the PLO and deny the border to the Lebanese Army and UNIFIL.

A June 1 ceasefire in the south and an unconvincing promise six days later by the PLO to move its bases away from civilian centers provided little more than a short lull before another devastating Israeli airstrike on June 9. A June 14 decision to extend UNIFIL's mandate for another six months also was of little significance to Sarkis, as intense fighting again erupted in Beirut on June 20. Syrian ADF forces were deployed in renewed skirmishing between the NLP and Phalangists in the southeastern suburbs of Beirut. But the ADF immediately became involved in unprecedented fighting with Lebanese Army units supported by the Christians. Another shaky ceasefire was arranged.

At the November 20–22 Arab summit, Sarkis insisted on complete withdrawal of the PLO from its bases in southern Lebanon but, unable to attract full support, was forced to accept Arafat's promise to halt attacks on Israel temporarily while retaining the bases. As compensation to Sarkis, Lebanon was granted $2 billion over five years for reconstruction.

F. NICHOLAS WILLARD

LIBRARIES

During much of 1979 intense preparations were evident in the states and at the National Commission on Libraries and Information Science for the White House Conference on Library and Information Services held November 15–19.

White House Conference. For more than two years, some 100,000 people were involved in 57 preliminary meetings held in all of the states and territories. A total of 911 delegates from the U. S. states and territories attended the five-day meeting, which was chaired by Charles Benton, who is also chairman of the National Commission on Libraries and Information Science.

The conference delegates approved 29 resolutions. These were to be presented to President Carter and Congressional committees within 120 days, and 90 days later President Carter was to make his recommendations to Congress.

Key resolutions passed by the delegates called for: 1) a library and information services office within the Department of Education; 2) a national information policy to ensure that government agencies at all levels work together to make available all new and existing library and information services to the maximum extent possible; 3) the cooperation of the local, state, and federal governments for the purpose of identifying the functionally illiterate and coordinating fund-sharing programs to train them; 4) the establishment of libraries to reach such special groups as children, youth, the aged, homebound, racial and ethnic minorities, physically handicapped, and emotionally disturbed; and 5) the establishment of a federal program to provide international training and exchange of library and information personnel and the free flow of library materials across national borders.

National Enquiry on Scholarly Communication. In May 1979, the National Enquiry on Scholarly Communication, conducted by the American Council of Learned Societies, with support from the National Endowment for the Humanities, the Ford Foundation, the Andrew W. Mellon Foundation, and the Rockefeller Foundation, released its final report, *Scholarly Communication*. The Board of Governors of the National Enquiry, which was composed of librarians, scholars, pub-

Major Library Awards of 1979

Beta Phi Mu Award for distinguished service to education for librarianship: Conrad Rawski, dean, School of Library Science, Case Western Reserve Univ.

Randolph J. Caldecott Medal for distinction in picture book illustration: Paul Goble, *The Girl Who Loved Wild Horses*

Melvil Dewey Medal for creative professional achievement of a high order: Russell E. Bidlack, dean, School of Library Science, University of Michigan

Grolier Foundation Award for unusual contribution to the stimulation and guidance of reading by children and young people: Anne Pellowski, director, Information Center on Children's Cultures, United States Committee for UNICEF

Joseph W. Lippincott Award for distinguished service to the profession of librarianship: Helen Lyman, professor emeritus, Library School, University of Wisconsin—Madison

John Newbery Medal for the most distinguished contribution to children's literature: Ellen Raskin, *The Westing Game*

Ralph R. Shaw Award for outstanding contribution to library literature: Joan K. Marshall, Associate Librarian for Technical Services, Brooklyn College of the City University of New York for her book, *On Equal Terms: A Thesaurus for Nonsexist Indexing and Cataloging*

H. W. Wilson Company Periodical Award: *Southeastern Librarian*, Leland Park, editor

President Carter is welcomed to the White House Conference on Library and Information Services, held Nov. 15–19, 1979.

lishers, and other specialists in communication, recommended the creation of a National Library Agency and an Office of Scholarly Communication in the National Endowment for the Humanities. The former would embrace a National Periodicals Center, from which scholars and librarians might obtain copies of articles from journals to which they have no access, and a bureau for the development of a national bibliographic system. A plan for the development of a National Periodicals Center was produced by the Council on Library Resources and endorsed by the American Library Association at an open forum in Arlington, VA, March 19–20, and by the National Commission on Libraries and Information Science in May. The latter would monitor and conduct studies of the system for scholarly communication in the humanities and the social sciences—areas which have been rather neglected in favor of inquiries into communication in the natural sciences. The report reviewed the respective functions of scholars, editors, journals, publishers, libraries, and librarians in an information system serving scholars and scientists.

Library Activity at the Federal Level. On May 14, Sen. Jacob Javits of New York and Sen. Edward Kennedy of Massachusetts introduced into the Senate a "study bill" designed to specify the intent of the proposed National Library Act (S-1124) and to provide a focus for debating key issues for library legislation in connection with the White House Conference. The proposed bill would replace the Library Services and Construction Act with an enlarged program of assistance to public libraries governed by a National Library Agency with a director and board of control appointed by the president. This proposed legislation would provide funds to public libraries on a matching 20% federal, 50% state, and 30% local basis. Finally, in late 1978, the Library of Congress announced a delay from January 1980, to January 1981, in the closing of its card catalog and in its adoption of the second edition of the *Anglo-American Cataloging Rules,* in order to give U. S. libraries sufficient time to prepare for these important changes.

American Library Association. The 98th annual conference of the American Library Association was held in Dallas, TX, June 23–29, 1979. Peggy Sullivan, assistant commissioner for extension services of the Chicago Public Library, was elected vice president and president-elect for 1980–1981. Presiding over the June meeting was Dean Thomas J. Galvin of the Graduate School of Library and Information Sciences, the University of Pittsburgh. In April 1979, the membership of the association set aside, by mail ballot, a January 9 action of the association's council and decided to hold the midwinter 1980 meeting in Chicago even though Illinois had not ratified the Equal Rights Amendment (ERA). During 1979 the association also considered increasing its basic dues from $35 to $50 per annum, discussed direct financial support to the forces promoting the passage of the ERA, and accredited, for the first time under its 1972 standards, the master's degree programs in librarianship at the School of Library Science, University of Oklahoma; the Graduate Library School, University of Rhode Island; and the Division of Librarianship, San Jose (California) State University. The association again sponsored National Library Week, April 1–7, the theme of which was "The Library is Filled with Success Stories."

International Library Activities. The 45th Council Meeting of the International Federation of Library Associations and Institutions convened in Copenhagen in the late summer of 1979 with conferees paying special attention to library legislation and to the management of libraries. On May 4–6, a group of seven Soviet librarians, led by V. V. Serov, head of the Directorate for Libraries in the Soviet Union's Ministry of Culture, visited Washington for the first Soviet-American Library Seminar.

DAN BERGEN, *Graduate Library School University of Rhode Island, Kingston*

LIBYA

Making liberal use of its vast oil revenues, the Libyan government helped support several radical causes in Africa and the Middle East during 1979. In an effort to continue transforming Libya in accordance with the goals of the 1969 revolution, some important changes were also made in the country's internal political structure.

Foreign Affairs. As a leader of the Arab rejectionist front, Libya vehemently attacked Egypt for negotiating and signing a separate peace treaty with Israel. On the diplomatic front, the Libyan delegation to the Conference of Islamic States led an unsuccessful attempt to have Egypt expelled from that group, although Egyptian membership was suspended. The most dynamic aspects of Libyan international activity, however, occurred in sub-Saharan Africa. Early in March, with rebels about to topple the government of Ugandan President Idi Amin, Libya sent large quantities of supplies, as well as some 2,000 troops, to the aid of the embattled dictator. In the closing days of the Amin regime, Libyan forces sustained several hundred casualties. After Kampala fell to Amin's opponents, the former dictator was granted asylum in Libya.

Elsewhere in Africa, Libyan soldiers provided backing for Muslim Chadian rebels who ousted President Felix Malloum in March. In exchange for its support, Libya reportedly was promised a strip of land in northern Chad rich in uranium and other minerals. The new Chadian government declined to cede the territory, however, and Libya launched a military offensive into Chad. On April 20 sources reported that the invasion had been repelled, but the long-standing tension over the Libya-Chad border continued throughout the year.

In the Central African Empire (now Republic), Libyan forces were also reported to have helped support Emperor Bokassa I prior to his overthrow in September.

In the wake of its African adventures, Libya came under strong criticism from the United States and other Western nations. In response,

Col. Muammar el-Qaddafi made veiled threats of terminating oil exports to the West. At the time, the United States relied on Libya for approximately 10% of its total oil imports. In mid-December, however, Qaddafi set aside the threats and stated that his government sought improved U. S.-Libyan relations. Although oil shipments did not cease, Libya late in the year did increase the price of its petroleum by more than 10%, bringing the price of its top crude to $26.27 a barrel. This was considerably above the price ceiling set by the Organization of Petroleum Exporting Countries (OPEC).

Economy and Government. With its oil revenues increasing to almost $16 billion, compared with $10 billion in 1978, Libya ranked among the world's 15 richest nations; per capita income reached $6,520. Price hikes for exported oil were required, however, by relatively sluggish production. Libya's five-year energy plan called for an oil output of 2.4 million barrels per day in 1979, but actual production fell short of this target. Experts attributed the problem to insufficient new investments in the industry. They predicted that the stagnation would last until the middle of the 1980's, although new development would prevent any actual loss. Supplies of liquid natural gas, on the other hand, reached an all-time high of 367 million cubic feet (10.3 million m³) per day in 1979 and were expected to continue to mount.

Marking the 10th anniversary of the military coup that brought him to power, Colonel Qaddafi took several steps to vest more political power in the hands of the public. "People's Committees" and "People's Congresses" were to replace the Revolutionary Command Council and work directly with government ministries. Plans were drawn up to redistribute wealth and abolish the army in favor of a people's militia. Observers speculated that the abolition of the army stemmed from government fear of opposition, evidenced by an attempted coup early in the year.

Qaddafi's populist-revolutionary ideology was further reflected in the early September anniversary celebrations, when he urged citizens living abroad to take control of Libyan embassies and open what he called "people's bureaus." Libya's foreign missions, he said, were staffed by diplomats of the former government of King Idris. Responding to his call, Libyans in Washington, London, Bonn, Rome, Athens, Madrid, and Malta took over the nation's embassies and replaced the diplomatic personnel.

With all its wealth, Libya relied increasingly on foreign technology and skilled labor, and its ultimate goal of self-sufficiency was in many ways frustrated. The private sector of the economy has been all but destroyed, and foreigners were expected to fill about 40% of the nation's jobs in 1980.

KENNETH J. PERKINS
University of South Carolina

——————— LIBYA · Information Highlights ———————

Official Name: Socialist People's Libyan Arab *Jamahiriya* ("state of the masses").
Location: North Africa.
Area: 679,360 square miles (1 759 540 km²).
Population (1979 est.): 2,800,000.
Chief Cities (1975 est.): Tripoli, the capital, 295,000; Benghazi, 190,000.
Government: *Head of state,* Muammar el-Qaddafi, secretary general of the General People's Congress (took office 1969). *Head of government,* Abdullah Obeidi, chairman of the General Popular Committee. *Legislature*—General People's Congress (met initially Nov. 1976).
Monetary Unit: Dinar (0.296 dinar equals U. S.$1, Aug. 1979).
Manufactures (major products): Crude petroleum, processed foods, textiles, paper products.
Agriculture (major products): Wheat, barley, dates, olives, peanuts, citrus fruits, livestock.

LITERATURE

The 1979 Nobel Prize for literature was awarded to Odysseus Elytis (family name Alepoudhelis), a 68-year-old Greek lyric poet whose work is noted for its mythical evocations of Greece. He is the second of a group of Greek poets, sometimes called the "Generation of the 30's," to be so honored. (George Seferis received the award in 1963.) The Swedish Academy praised him especially for his work *To Axion Esti* (1959), which has been described as "one of twentieth century literature's most concentrated and ritually faceted poems."

Elytis once said: "I consider poetry a source of innocence full of revolutionary forces. It is my mission to direct those forces against a world my conscience cannot accept." Of the Nobel award, the poet, a bachelor and something of a recluse, said: "The Swedish Academy's decision was not only an honor for me but for Greece and its history through the ages. I believe that it was a decision to bring international attention to the most ancient tradition in Europe, since from Homer's time to the present there has not been a single century during which poetry has not been written in the Greek language."

Reviews of the year's developments in the major literatures follow.

American Literature

Despite a faltering economy, the U. S. book publishing industry had a strong year in 1979 and several works of high literary achievement made their appearance.

The National Book Award Winners for 1979 were: Fiction—Tim O'Brien's *Going After Cacciato;* Poetry—James Merrill's *Mirabell: Books of Numbers;* History—Richard Beale Davis' *Intellectual Life in the Colonial South 1585–1763;* Biography—Arthur M. Schlesinger, Jr.'s *Robert Kennedy and His Times;* Contemporary Thought—Peter Matthiessen's *The Snow Leopard;* Translation—Cesar Vallejo's *The Complete Posthumous Poetry,* translated by Clayton Eshleman and José Rubia Barcia; and Children's Literature—Katherine Paterson's *The Great Gilly Hopkins.* A new format, altering the submission procedures and increasing the number of prizes to 15, was announced for 1980. Important critics and publishers denounced the changes as commercialism. (*See also* PRIZES AND AWARDS.)

Novels. Although American novelists continued to examine social, political, and religious issues, their main interest seemed to be the complex interlocking of life and art. Interestingly, the central characters in many of the year's best novels are writers.

The main characters in Philip Roth's *The Ghost Writer* are Zuckerman, an earnest young writer who has upset his father by satirizing the family, and Lonoff, an older, highly successful writer who is so devoted to his art that he has no time or passion for life itself. In an encounter between the excited Zuckerman and wry Lonoff, Roth demonstrates how the writer of fiction creates a world of beauty and fantasy out of the facts of everyday life.

William Styron's *Sophie's Choice* is an overtly autobiographical narrative of a young southerner named Stingo who goes to New York City to try to write his first novel. The naive, emotional 22-year-old is introduced to the depths of human suffering by Sophie, a Polish Catholic who survived the German concentration camp at Auschwitz. As the two become close friends, Sophie reveals the horrors of her past and the depth of her guilt. Styron's narrative is an eloquent meditation on history and evil.

The protagonist in Bernard Malamud's *Dubin's Lives* is a middle-aged free-lance biographer who is profoundly influenced by his latest subject, D. H. Lawrence, and by a young woman who draws him into a relationship which imperils his marriage. Malamud again demonstrates his sensitivity to the personal details which form the complex texture of life.

Good as Gold is Joseph Heller's story about a Jewish author and professor, Bruce Gold, who yearns for a career in Washington politics. Heller's satire on the federal bureaucracy is often brilliant, but his comic exaggeration ultimately gives way to serious polemic and more painful humor about the contemporary American experience.

Kurt Vonnegut's *Jailbird* is another novel about Washington. It is the story of a fumbling, middle-aged bureaucrat who is made President Nixon's special adviser on youth affairs, only to be jailed for an insignificant role in the Watergate conspiracy. Vonnegut's rueful comments on recent history make this one of his best works.

John Barth's fascination with the uncertain boundaries of life and literature is manifested in *Letters,* an enormous epistolary novel. The characters, some of whom appear in one of Barth's earlier novels, recognize that they are fictional creations. Their comments about life, literary creation, and Barth himself are made in a series of letters which help support a wildly complicated story line.

Gilbert Sorrentino's *Mulligan Stew* also clouds the distinction between literature and life. Judged unsellable by a number of publishers, the book includes actual rejection letters from editors. It is an ingenious and vital work.

Norman Mailer raises both moral and literary questions in *The Executioner's Song,* the story of condemned murderer Gary Gilmore. Told in flat, simple prose, it reconstructs the brutal, pathetic life of a man who, in asking to be put to death, dramatized American society's unresolved attitudes about capital punishment.

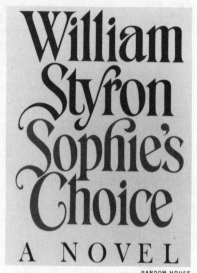

In *Sophie's Choice*, written by former Pulitzer Prize-winner William Styron, Sophie is a Polish Catholic who spent time in a concentration camp; Nathan, her lover, is a Jewish intellectual; and Stingo, a "South'n" boy, is the storyteller.

RANDOM HOUSE

By calling this enormous work a "True Life Novel," Mailer invited comparison to Truman Capote's "nonfiction novel" *In Cold Blood* (1965).

Not since Mark Twain has irreverence had as bitterly humorous a practitioner as Stanley Elkin. His newest work, *The Living End*, is a fantasy about a dead liquor store owner who is shocked by the unfairness of the afterlife and the pettiness of God.

James Baldwin's *Just Above My Head* centers on a black gospel singer and her family entanglements. In this ambitious work Baldwin renders the worlds of gospel and soul, white and black, religion and art, New York and Paris. Mary McCarthy's *Cannibals and Missionaries*, the suspenseful story of a plane hijacking, dramatizes the ironies of contemporary politics. Jerzy Kosinski pursues his interest in violence in *Passion Play*. And John Hawkes continues his inquiry into sexual obsession in *The Passion Artist*.

Ellease Sutherland's *Let the Lion Eat Straw*, Alan Saperstein's *Mom Kills Dad and Self*, and Jacob Epstein's *Wild Oats* were promising first novels published in 1979.

Short Stories. Fresh sources of material and energy were evidenced in several of the year's new short story collections. The three long stories in Jim Harrison's *Legends of the Fall* are vivid accounts of men acting with uncommon decisiveness in a threatening and violent world. John Updike's *Problems* is a collection of masterful stories from the previous seven years. In *Great Days*, Donald Barthelme includes a provocative set of pieces which deal playfully with serious matters. Guy Davenport peoples his witty stories in *Da Vinci's Bicycle* with real historical characters. Arturo Vivante's gracefully written *Run to the Waterfall* focuses on three characters in Italy; Jayne Anne Phillips demonstrates a formidable talent in *Black Tick-*

ets; Kay Boyle's long career is reflected in her *Fifty Stories;* and *Old Love* is Isaac Bashevis Singer's latest collection.

Posthumous collections included *Of This Time, Of That Place*, five stories by Lionel Trilling; *The Price was High*, billed as "The Last Uncollected Stories" of F. Scott Fitzgerald; and *Johnny Panic and the Bible of Dreams*, early stories and other prose of Sylvia Plath.

Poetry. Increasingly neglected by readers and reviewers, American poetry is kept alive—and remarkably healthy—by poets who continue to produce innovative verse and who openly promote each other's work. In 1979, small presses continued to publish the bulk of new American poetry. The Godine Poetry Chapbook Series, for example, published works ranging from Gail Mazur's warm and personal *Nightfire* to John Peck's difficult *The Broken Blockhouse Wall*.

The vitality of established American poets was demonstrated in 1979 by the appearance of several new works: Denise Levertov's *Life in the Forest;* John Hollander's *Blue Wine;* David Wagoner's *In Broken Country;* John Ashbery's *As We Know;* Irving Feldman's *New and Selected Poems;* Kenneth Koch's *The Burning Mystery of Anna in 1951;* and Lawrence Ferlinghetti's *Landscapes of Living & Dying*.

Robert Penn Warren's revised version of his *Brother to Dragons* (orig. 1953), an inquiry into human evil; the first complete edition of Louis Zukofsky's *A*, an 826-page personal epic; and *The Poems of Stanley Kunitz 1928–1978* were significant additions to American letters.

Noteworthy anthologies included *Social Poetry of the 1930's*, edited by Jack Salzman and Leo Zanderer, and *The Oxford Book of American Light Verse*, compiled by William Harmon.

Literary History and Criticism. New insights into American literary history were provided by the previously unpublished letters and memoirs of major figures. *The Habit of Being*, edited

Joan Didion's *The White Album* focuses on today's world, beginning with the late 1960's. David Halberstam's *The Powers That Be* is an historical account of four communications institutions—CBS, Time Incorporated, The Washington Post, and The Los Angeles Times.

SIMON & SCHUSTER   KNOPF

by Sally Fitzgerald, presents the sharp, wise, and courageous letters of Flannery O'Connor. Simon Karlinsky's *The Nabokov-Wilson Letters* documents the blooming and withering of the friendship between the brilliant novelist and the powerful literary critic.

End to Torment is the poet Hilda Doolittle's memoir of her long and ultimately unhappy relationship with Ezra Pound. It was Pound who gave her the pen name H. D. and who dubbed her unique style "imagisme." Pound also wrote a series of poems called "Hilda's Book," which is included in this volume.

John Steinbeck's deep dependence on and enduring friendship with his editor, Pascal Covici, is chronicled in *Steinbeck and Covici*, a letter collection edited by Thomas Fensch. Lionel Trilling's *The Last Decade* gathers his essays and reviews between 1965 and 1975.

The ongoing debate on the general health of American letters is continued by Marvin Mudrick, whose unorthodox positions are argued in *Books Are Not Life But Then What Is?* Gerald Graff's *Literature Against Itself* is a worried attack on the parochialism of contemporary literary criticism. Richard Gilman's *Decadence* discusses the history of that term, arguing that it is so misunderstood and so misused that it only confuses critics and readers.

In *Telling Lives*, Marc Pachter gathers essays by seven well-known biographers who reflect on the difficulties and rewards of their art. *Of Poetry and Poets* is Richard Eberhart's collection of essays on poetry in the United States. Adrienne Rich's literary essays and other writing between 1966 and 1978 comprise *On Lies, Secrets, and Silence*. The reflections of Louis Auchincloss are brought together in *Life, Law and Letters*.

The unique contribution of southern writers to 20th century American literature is the subject of Louis D. Rubin, Jr.'s *The Wary Fugitives*.

The book discusses the classic modernists—Robert Penn Warren, John Crowe Ransom, Allen Tate, and Donald Grady Davidson. Robert Coles' *Walker Percy* focuses on the philosophical speculations of that southern novelist.

History and Biography. As evidenced by the appearance of several new biographies, the Beat Generation has become part of the American literary heritage. Dennis McNally's life of Jack Kerouac, *Desolate Angel,* is a lively evocation of the era. More prosaic is Neeli Cherkovski's *Ferlinghetti,* a somewhat dry account of the San Francisco poet and publisher. The story of Henry Miller, an important influence on the Beat movement, is told in Jay Martin's *Always Merry and Bright.*

Milton Lomask's *Aaron Burr* and Edmund Morris' *The Rise of Theodore Roosevelt* are the beginnings of multivolume works on two fascinating political figures. Kevin Tierney's *Darrow* is an insightful look at the lawyer who has become part of history. Marshall Frady's *Billy Graham,* subtitled "A Parable of American Righteousness," is a revealing portrait of the powerful evangelist.

The profound effect of English culture on modern American literature is suggested by the number of new books on early 20th century British life and letters. Frederick Karl's massive biography, *Joseph Conrad,* is a thorough study of the seminal modern novelist. Leon Edel's *Bloomsbury* is a group portrait of the coterie whose art, criticism, and political theory are still influential. In *The London Yankees,* Stanley Weintraub tells of the American writers and artists who visited England between 1894 and 1914.

Among the best autobiographies of the year were Joseph Wechsberg's *The Vienna I Knew,* a childhood recollection; Geoffrey Wolff's *The Duke of Deception,* about life with his roguish father; and Freeman Dyson's *Disturbing the*

Universe, a reflection on the social implications of his scientific work. The first volume of Henry Kissinger's memoirs created a stir late in the year.

Leon F. Litwack's *Been in the Storm So Long* is an important and moving study of black Americans immediately after the Civil War. Anthony F. C. Wallace's *Rockdale* focuses on a single town to demonstrate the effects of the early industrial revolution on the fabric of American life. A town in France that resisted the extermination of Jews by the Nazis inspired Phillip P. Hallie's speculation on the nature of goodness, *Lest Innocent Blood Be Shed.*

The broader sweep of history was also intelligently represented. Walter Karp's *The Politics of War* examines American imperialism between 1890 and 1920. Geoffrey Perrett's *A Dream of Greatness* chronicles the American loss of direction between 1945 and 1963. The first part of an important study by Philip S. Foner, *Women and the American Labor Movement,* covers the period up to World War I. Paul Boyer's *Urban Masses and Moral Order in America, 1820–1920* argues that urban reform movements were often based on the conception of the village as the ideal community.

General. Contemporary life was the subject of inquiry for a number of trenchant writers. The surreal quality of recent political history is captured by the wild, idiosyncratic essays of Hunter Thompson in *The Great Shark Hunt.* More reflective is Joan Didion's *The White Album,* which comments perceptively on social phenomena of the last ten years. Tom Wolfe successfully controls his stylistic exuberance in *The Right Stuff,* a penetrating study of the American astronauts. In *The Culture of Narcissism* Christopher Lasch expresses a deep pessimism about our times.

Well-written books on science not only clarified technical concepts and problems but also seemed to have enduring literary value. Lewis Thomas' *The Medusa and the Snail* and Carl Sagan's *Broca's Brain* collect their lively, graceful essays. Douglas Hofstadter's *Gödel, Escher, Bach,* is an ingenious discussion of the similarities among mathematics, art, and music.

In *The Old Patagonian Express,* Paul Theroux recounts his tedious journey by train from Boston to the tip of South America. Edward Hoagland's *African Calliope,* about his travels through the desolate Sudan, is full of rich observations.

William Saroyan's *Obituaries,* a meditation on the deaths of various celebrities, is a celebration of their lives and of life itself.

Deaths. The passing of James T. Farrell, author of the classic *Studs Lonigan* trilogy (1932–35), and of Jean Stafford, the Pulitzer Prize–winning novelist and short story writer, marked the end of two notable literary careers.

JEROME H. STERN
Florida State University

Children's Literature

By the end of 1979 the outlook for children's books was not promising. Spiraling costs and a shortage of library funds had caused book prices to rise and sales to lag. As a result, a cutback in publishing programs for children seemed likely in 1980.

The individual title production for 1979 was estimated at nearly 2,000, with considerable emphasis on paperbacks. Publishing for the very young emphasized pop-up books and new editions of stories from the Brothers Grimm, Hans Christian Andersen, and Oscar Wilde. Older children saw innumerable volumes devoted to soccer, jogging, and tennis. Teen-agers and young adults could choose from among many books—fiction and nonfiction—about death, physical disabilities, alcoholism, divorce, child abuse, and runaways.

The year saw special birthday tributes to two prominent author-illustrators—Maurice Sendak, celebrating his 50th birthday, and Theodore Geisel (Dr. Seuss), his 75th. Many publishers attempted to associate new books with the International Year of the Child, but most of those volumes were of little interest.

Awards. The American Library Association's (ALA's) John Newbery Medal for the most distinguished contribution to American literature for children was awarded to Ellen Raskin for *The Westing Game,* a sophisticated mystery/puzzle about 16 zany heirs to the fortune of an eccentric millionaire. The ALA's Randolph Caldecott Medal for the most distinguished picture book of the year was awarded to Paul Goble, the illustrator and author of *The Girl Who Loved Wild Horses,* a story about the kinship of an American Indian girl with horses. The National Book Award for children's books went to a previous winner, Katherine Paterson, for *The Great Gilly Hopkins,* about the schemes of a feisty 11-year-old foster child. Doris Orgel won the Child Study Children's Book Committee Award for *The Devil in Vienna,* about the plight of two girls, one Jewish and the other Catholic, during the Nazi invasion of their country.

Perhaps the most outstanding new work of the year was Donald Hall's *Ox-Cart Man,* a picture book about the life of a farm family in 19th-century New Hampshire. The illustrations by Barbara Cooney, evocative of primitive folk art, are breathtaking in their detail of the land and people.

For Young Readers. Among other noteworthy publications for the picture book audience (ages 3 to 7) was Chris Van Allsburg's *The Garden of Abdul Gasazi.* Superbly drawn in black and white with a surreal, slightly ominous glow, it is about a boy who intrudes upon a vast estate while searching for a runaway dog. Capturing the splendid vitality and variety of Polish folk art, Janina Domanska retells an old Polish legend in *King Krakus and the Dragon.* Helme

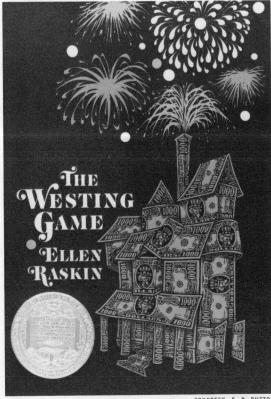

THE GIRL WHO LOVED
WILD HORSES
by PAUL GOBLE

The 1979 John Newbery Medal went to Ellen Raskin's
The Westing Game. Paul Goble's *The Girl Who Loved
Wild Horses* won the Randolph Caldecott Medal.

Heine colorfully depicts all the preparations, feasting, and frolicking of *The Pig's Wedding.* Uri Shulevitz's *The Treasure* is a fable set in an old Eastern European ghetto. Susan Jeffers provides polished, handsomely conceived illustrations for Amy Ehrlich's retelling of Hans Christian Andersen's *Thumbelina.*

For children between 6 and 10, the most outstanding new works were Arnold Lobel's *Days With Frog and Toad,* the fourth book about that companionable twosome; Piero Ventura's *Christopher Columbus,* a succinct, informative account—with brightly-colored aerial and panoramic views—of the explorer's first voyage; Guy Billout's *By Camel or By Car,* a personal view of 14 different means of transportation, depicted in bold, witty illustrations; David Lasker's *The Boy Who Loved Music,* with illustrations by Joe Lasker, telling why Joseph Haydn wrote his famous "Farewell" Symphony; and Faith McNulty's *How to Dig a Hole to the Other Side of the World,* illustrated by Marc Simont.

In the 9-to-12 category, the best new books were Richard Kennedy's scary and amusing fairy tale, *Inside My Feet,* in which two enormous empty boots carry off a boy's parents and try to get him, too; *The New York Kid's Book,* in which 167 writers and artists celebrate New York City; Betsy Byars' *Good-bye, Chicken Little,* a story about life, death, and a boy coming to grips with his fears; and Norma Farber's *How Does It Feel to Be Old?,* a sharp, lonesome,

and nostalgic poem written from the point of view of a grandmother, illustrated by Trina Schart Hyman.

Teen-Age Literature. Among the year's best novels for teen-agers and young adults was Robert Cormier's *After the First Death,* in which a busload of small children is held hostage by terrorists. *All Together Now,* by Sue Ellen Bridgers, is a warm, gentle story about the friendship between a young girl and a retarded man. Rosa Guy's *The Disappearance* is about a family that befriends a Harlem street boy who has been acquitted of murder, only to have their youngest daughter disappear. Harry Mazer's *The Last Mission* is the story of an underage Jewish boy who enlists in the Air Force during World War II. Ouida Sebestyen's *Words by Heart* is about a 12-year-old black girl trying to succeed in a small, all white, southwestern town. In Jean McCord's *Turkeylegs Thompson,* an unhappy young girl learns to live again after a summer of tragedy and humiliation. Peter Dickinson's *Tulku* recounts the adventures of a young Christian boy in turn-of-the-century Tibet.

The year also saw publication of quality biographies of Margaret Mead, Mao Tse-tung, William O. Douglas, Andrew Young, Pete Rose, Reggie Jackson, and others. Perhaps the most outstanding was *Stonewall,* Jean Fritz's study of the Confederate Civil War general, Thomas Jonathan Jackson.

GEORGE A. WOODS, *"The New York Times"*

Canadian Literature: English

For many years it seemed that Canadian authors were writing about anything but Canada. More recently, however, book after book has been devoted to some aspect of Canada's past, present, or future.

Nonfiction. The Canadian past is evoked in John and Monica Ladell's *Inheritance: Ontario Century Farms Past and Present.* Aided by the photography of Bert Hoferichter, the authors describe farms in Ontario that have been owned by the same families for at least one century.

Doris Shadbolt, former Associate Director of the Vancouver Art Gallery, has lectured brilliantly on art for many years. Her magnificent *The Art of Emily Carr* is as eloquent as her lectures, and the 200 illustrations are perfectly suited to the text.

Robert F. Legget's *The Seaway* marked the 150th anniversary of the opening of the first Welland Canal, located in the St. Lawrence Seaway. *Hurricane Hazel,* by Betty Kennedy, describes the 1954 hurricane disaster in southern Ontario. In *A Bloody War,* Hal Lawrence recalls the Canadian Navy in World War II.

William Dawson LeSueur's *William Lyon Mackenzie: A Reinterpretation* finally appeared in 1979, 70 years after it was written. This critical biography of the leader of the Upper Canada Rebellion had been barred from publication after five different court cases. The 1979 edition is an edited version with an introduction by A. B. McKillop.

In *My Working Years, 1922–1976,* Raymond Massey recalls his career as an actor. In *Exile in the Wilderness,* Jean Murray Cole tells the story of Archibald McDonald (1790–1853), former chief factor of the Hudson's Bay Company. Sonja Sinclair's *Cordial but not Cozy* is a history of the auditor general's office.

The troubled Canadian present is discussed in such books as *The Roots of Disunity—A Study of Canadian Political Culture,* by David Bell and Lorne Tepperman; and Patricia Marchak's *In Whose Interest,* about multinational corporations in Canada.

One of the most talked-about books of the year was *Beyond Reason,* the autobiography of Margaret Trudeau, estranged wife of former Prime Minister Pierre Elliott Trudeau. Although adequately written and at times painfully honest, the book actually sheds little light on the complex man who governed Canada for 11 years.

Allan Hustak's *Peter Lougheed: A Biography* describes the life of the premier of Alberta. Philip Smith's *The Treasure-Seekers* tells how Jimmy Lowery and Robert Brown built Home Oil into a powerful company.

Elliot Leyton's *The Myth of Delinquency* examines the causes of juvenile delinquency. In *My Parents are Divorced, Too* child psychiatrist Bonnie Robson describes the problems faced by children of divorced parents.

The autobiography of actor and writer Justin Thomas was published in 1979 with one of the longest titles on record: *How I Overcame My Fear of Whores, Royalty, Gays, Teachers, Hippies, Psychiatrists, Athletes, Tranvestites, Clergymen, Police, Children, Bullies, Politicians, Nuns, Grandparents, Doctors, Celebrities, Gurus, Judges, Artists, Critics, Mothers, Fathers, Publishers and Myself.*

The Canadian future is humorously portrayed in *Canada 1984: The Year in Review,* by Murray Soupcoff, with illustrations by Isaac Bickerstaff. Soupcoff predicts what several famous Canadians will be doing five years hence and makes 1984 a lot more fun than did George Orwell.

Poetry. More of the powerful poetry of Irving Layton comprises his latest volume, *Droppings from Heaven.* Lionel Kearns makes a welcome return with *Practicing Up to Be Human,* his first major collection in nine years.

Susan Musgrave's *A Man to Marry, A Man to Bury* is the newest work of one of Canada's leading poets. Michael Ondaatje's *There's A Trick with a Knife I'm Learning to Do* is a collection of the author's poems from 1963 to 1978.

Pier Giorgio Di Cicco's *The Tough Romance,* an impressive volume from one of Canada's younger poets, deals mainly with human relations. *To Say the Least,* edited by P. K. Page, is a collection of short poems by more than 100 Canadian poets.

Anniversaries is the second volume of poems by Ontario's Don Coles, and Tom Howe's *Myself in the Rain* is a promising first volume.

Fiction. Brian Moore's *The Mangan Inheritance* is one of the finest novels of a truly fine Canadian novelist. Set in New York, Montreal, and Ireland, it tells the story of Canadian Jamie Mangan, who inherits enough money from his estranged movie star wife to trace his twisted and tortured Irish roots.

Margaret Atwood has some telling things to say about life, love, and yearning in her fourth novel, *Life Before Man.* Richard Rohmer discusses the gasoline shortage in *Balls!* Jack MacLeod's epistolary novel, *Zinger and Me,* directs some sharp criticisms at academics and newspapermen.

Former federal cabinet minister Judy La Marsh's first novel, *A Very Political Lady,* is an interesting look at politics and power struggles in Ottawa.

Robert L. Pilpel's *To the Honor of the Fleet* is an intriguing novel about naval battles in World War I. Dramatist Betty Lambert's first novel, *Crossings,* is highlighted by some remarkably realistic passages.

In *Icequake,* Crawford Kilian describes the beginning of a new Ice Age; Robert Kroetsch tells an unusual and entertaining tale in *What The Crow Said;* and Ian Slater's *Sea Gold* tells of the search for riches on the ocean floor.

DAVID SAVAGE, *Simon Fraser University*

La Grosse femme d'à côté est enciente by Michel Tremblay is an account of the events in a Montreal neighborhood on a day during the year the author was born. Jacques Poulin was awarded the Governor General's award for Les Grandes marées, the tale of a translator living on an island in the St. Lawrence River.

Canadian Literature: Quebec

Activity was intense in the Quebec literary world in 1979, with significant contributions from established authors as well as from the young generation. As if to emphasize this mixing of the old and the new, the Editions de l'Hexagone celebrated its 25th anniversary.

Antonine Maillet, a 49-year-old French Canadian author and university lecturer, won the 1979 Goncourt Prize, France's most important literary award, for her novel Pelagie la Charrette. The novel is about events in her native New Brunswick in 1775.

Prose. In recent years, several Quebec novelists have been delving into the past and recreating the previously neglected Duplessis period. In 1979, Quebec's best known dramatist, Michel Tremblay, made his second foray into the world of the novel. His La Grosse femme d'à côté est enceinte chronicles the events in his Montreal neighborhood on May 2, 1942, the year he was born. La Grosse femme is the first in a series of novels still in preparation. In a different vein, Jacques Poulin's fifth novel, Les Grandes marées, appeared in 1979 and was awarded the Governor General's prize. The book tells the symbolic story of a translator living on a tiny island in the St. Lawrence River.

A number of university professors also published successful novels during the year. Among these novels are Joseph Bonenfant's Repère, Madeleine Gagnon's Lueur, François Hébert's Holyoke, and Gabrielle Poulin's Cogne la caboche.

Apart from the novel, the new prose of Quebec included Victor-Lévy Beaulieu's study of Herman Melville, Monsieur Melville. This three-volume work is not only a penetrating analysis of the author of Moby Dick but also a revealing portrait of Beaulieu himself. Louis-Philippe Hébert published a collection of highly imaginative short stories, entitled Manuscrit trouvé dans une valise, and the popular Roch Carrier brought out a volume of nouvelles called Les Enfants du bonhomme dans la lune. The Prix France-Québec was awarded to a new edition of the contes of Jean-Aubert Loranger. Finally, two well-known novelists published works about themselves: Gabrielle Roy collected her nonfiction in a volume called Fragile lumières de la terre, and Gérard Bessette offered a self-critique in Mes romans et moi.

In the realm of the essay, the most important work of the year was Pierre Vadeboncoeur's Les Deux Royaumes. This collection of literary and philosophical reflections was awarded the Prix de la Ville de Montréal.

Theater. Jean Barbeau, who had been silent for several years, staged a comeback in 1979 with two new plays. In Le Théâtre de la maintenance, maintenance workers create their own play-within-a-play. And in Une Marquise de Sade et un lézard nommé King Kong, Barbeau takes the reader into the fantasy world of the Quebec middle class. Jean-Claude Germain continued to be prolific, writing two new plays—a ritual exorcism called A Canadian Play/Une plaie canadienne and L'Ecole des rêves, an elaboration of the themes of his earlier works.

Two plays held the public's attention more for their social commentary than for their dramatic quality. The first was Denise Boucher's Les Fées ont soif, a feminist critique of political and religious myths. In attacking the Virgin Mary, Boucher touched off a heated debate in Quebec religious circles. The play continued to be presented, but the book was banned for several months. On a more positive note, David Fennario's Balconville, a play depicting life in Montreal's west end, was one of the first bilingual works ever presented. Its great popularity suggested that the "two solitudes" are not quite so isolated as they used to be.

Poetry. Several important works by well-known Quebec poets appeared during the year. Among these were Roland Giguère's Forêt vierge folle and Nicole Brossard's Le Centre blanc. Also noteworthy were works by Pierre Morency (Torrentiel) and Gilles Cyr (Sol inapparent), as well as Robert Melançon's first collection, Peinture aveugle.

JONATHAN M. WEISS
Colby College

The absence for most of 1979 (due to a labor dispute) of *The Times* of London and its ancillary publications, especially *The Sunday Times* and *The Times Literary Supplement,* was perhaps the most notable circumstance of the publishing year in Britain, for these papers are an important part of British public, intellectual, and artistic life. Fortunately, the dispute was settled, and the papers resumed publication in November.

Nonfiction. The examination of World War II continued. F. H. Hinsley and three colleagues were given access to government archives to produce the first volume of an official history, *British Intelligence in the Second World War.* This work promised to be a definitive study and to lay to rest such legends as Churchill's allowing Coventry to be sacrificed so that the Germans would not guess that their code had been broken. Another conclusive, but unofficial, history was M. R.D. Foot and J. M. Langley's *M19: Escape and Evasion 1939–1945,* an account of the intelligence agency that worked with resistance groups, prisoners of war, and escapees in enemy territory. In *Bomber Command,* Max Hastings used interviews with survivors to reconstruct life in this arm of the Royal Air Force during World War II.

In another history published during 1979, *Tales from the Dark Continent,* author Charles Allen made skillful use of oral history to describe life in colonial British Africa. Another chronicle of Britons abroad was Robert Wilkinson-Latham's *From Our Special Correspondent: Victorian War Correspondents and their Campaigns.* More recent historical accounts were given in Douglas Hurd's *An End to Promises: Sketch of a Government, 1970–74* and Harold Wilson's *Final Term: The Labour Government, 1974–76.*

Biographies of public figures included *Brendan Bracken,* by Charles Lysaght, about the minister of information in Churchill's wartime cabinet; *Clementine Churchill,* by her daughter, Mary Soames; *Sylvia Pankhurst,* by her son, Richard Pankhurst; *The Awkward Warrior,* by Geoffrey Goodman, about Frank Cousins, the trade union leader; and *Hugh Gaitskell,* by Philip M. Williams, about the man who succeeded Clement Attlee as leader of the Labour Party. In his autobiography, *Memoirs,* Jo Grimond described his experiences as leader of the Liberal Party.

More personal profiles presented were Jeanne MacKenzie's *A Victorian Courtship,* the story of the relationship between Beatrice Potter and Sidney Webb; Violet Powell's *Margaret, Countess of Jersey,* on the life of a Victorian hostess; Anne Chisholm's biography of Nancy Cunard, a 1914 debutante who became a minor poet and an active opponent of fascism and racism; and Magdalen Goffin's life of Maria Pasqua, a favorite child model of Parisian painters in the 1860's who was taken to England by an heiress so that she might be brought up as an ideal woman.

Rupert Hart-Davis' *The Arms of Time* served partly as a biography of his mother, who died when he was 19, and partly as an autobiography of his early years. Desmond Morris' *Animal Days* dealt with his life up to the publication of *The Naked Ape.* Penelope Mortimer's *About Time* described with objectivity and sympathy events of her first 21 years, including her father's attempts at incest. The playwright William Douglas Home wrote with zest about his life in *Mr. Home Pronounced Hume.*

Major biographies of men of the theater and of letters whose lives spanned the late Victorian, Edwardian, and early Georgian periods were Madeleine Bingham's *The Great Lover: The Life and Art of Herbert Beerbohm Tree,* An-

Trinidad-born V. S. Naipaul, a major force in recent English literature, in 1979 published *A Bend in the River,* a novel set in an unnamed East African country and involved with political life's more negative aspects. Naipaul's novels have been compared to those of Dostoyevsky and Conrad but are generally thought to contain less evidence of transcendental qualities.

drew Birkin's *J. M. Barrie and the Lost Boys,* Cedric Watts and Laurence Davies' *Cunninghame Graham,* Philip Graves' *A. E. Housman,* and Elizabeth Longford's *A Pilgrimage of Passion: The Life of Wilfred Scawen Blunt.*

The first volume of James T. Boulton's edition of *The Letters of D. H. Lawrence* was published.

Fiction. In novels published during 1979, three major writers—C. P. Snow, William Golding, and Muriel Spark—examined evil in man and society. Snow's *A Coat of Varnish,* ostensibly a realistic detective story, suggested that there is no more than a coat of varnish, as one character put it, "between us and the horrors beneath." Golding allowed some of the horrors to surface in *Darkness Visible.* His saintly central character, disfigured in boyhood during an air raid, later encounters conscienceless young adults and, in peacetime, another bomb. Muriel Spark portrayed evil coolly and artfully in *Territorial Rights,* a story set in Venice, where the characters, through business, crime, and terrorism, struggle for the rights referred to in the title of the book.

Two novels dealt with relationships between the artist, his art, and his audience. In Alan Sillitoe's *The Storyteller,* Ernest Cotgrave avoids trouble in Nottingham schoolyards and pubs by entertaining his companions with stories. He goes on to earn money as a storyteller on a cruise ship, using his own experiences in his tales. In Paul Breeze's *While My Guitar Gently Weeps,* Billy Dancey makes himself a successful guitarist. As his group approaches fame, thugs stamp on his fingers, which have to be partially amputated. A knife replaces his guitar, as he hunts his attackers in Stoke-on-Trent.

Industry and industrial cities and villages provided the settings for other strong novels. John Harvey's *The Plate Shop* describes vividly the shop of his title and the work and disagreements within it, until change comes from without, and most of the factory is to be closed. Stanley Middleton's *In a Strange Land* concerns life in a Midland city; Don Bannister presents a Yorkshire coal-mining village of the 1930's in *Sam Chard.* Elizabeth North's *Florence Avenue* is set in a small Yorkshire town in which postwar prosperity has produced a situation in which the characters may indulge themselves freely.

In books by Andrew Sinclair, Keith Aldritt, Mary Renault, and Rumer Godden, the novel approaches biography, but retains the license of fiction. In Sinclair's *The Facts in the Case of E. A. Poe,* E. A. Pons believes that he is Edgar Allan Poe. He writes a biography of Poe and his own diary. Aldritt's *Elgar on the Journey to Hanley* is about the composer's actual encounter with a young woman which is commemorated in one of Edward Elgar's *Enigma Variations.* In Renault's *The Praise Singer,* the ancient Greek poet Simonides tells the story of the first half of his life. Godden's *Five for*

Sorrow, Ten for Joy is about a French order of nuns who help the unfortunate and a murderess who joins them after her release from prison.

Notable collections of short stories were Penelope Lively's *Nothing Missing but the Samovar* and Pat McGrath's *People in the Crowd.*

Poetry. *The Complete Poems of Hugh MacDiarmid,* edited in two volumes by Michael Grieve and W. R. Aitken, was the most important collection of poems published in Britain in 1979. MacDiarmid, who died in 1978, was the most prolific and perhaps the greatest Scottish poet of this century. He wrote in English and in a Scots dialect. Both a lyric and a public poet, he espoused communism but showed great sympathy for the individual.

The Collected Works of Isaac Rosenberg, edited by Ian Parsons, was also published. A poet of World War I, Rosenberg was killed in 1918. In addition to the poems, his letters, prose, and reproductions of his drawings and paintings are included in this collection.

Geoffrey Hill's poems in *Tenebrae* frequently alluded to the work of other poets and of theologians. In deceptively simple blank verse, he drew on history, architecture, folklore, and ritual for his exploration of Christian beliefs.

In conversational verse that strays casually from the blank verse that is its most typical measure, D. J. Enright's *A Faust Book* examined good and evil less strenuously than did Geoffrey Hill. His Faust is a contemporary professor who would like a better post. Mephistopheles resembles a businessman who has deals to make.

Two poets of Northern Ireland, Seamus Heaney and P. J. Kavanagh, published collections. As the title of Heaney's collection, *Field Work,* may suggest, he has withdrawn from the cities of the North to the countryside of the Republic. Kavanagh found his title, *Life Before Death,* in a question written on a wall in Belfast: "Is there a life before death?" He turns it into an affirmative statement. Both poets write about the conflict in Ulster, their friends and families, and their surroundings. Heaney includes his translation of two books of Dante's *Inferno.*

Ted Hughes combined his poems with Fay Godwin's photographs in *Remains of Elmet,* a book about relics of the Celtic kingdom that once occupied Hughes' native district in northwestern England. Peter Avery and John Heath-Stubbs produced a new translation of *The Ruba'iyat of Omar Khayyam.* Kingsley Amis, the novelist, published his *Collected Poems 1944–1979.*

Other important books of poetry were Jeremy Hooker's *Solent Shore* and *Landscape of the Daylight Moon,* John Mole's *From the House Opposite,* James Berry's *Fractured Circles,* George Szirtes' *The Slant Door,* Paul Wilkins' *Pasts,* and Conn Stewart's *Under the Ice.*

J. K. JOHNSTONE
University of Saskatchewan

French Literature

The 1979 Prix Goncourt was awarded to Antonine Miller, a French Canadian (*see* Canadian Literature: Quebec).

Fiction. The best selling novels of 1979 were those with an historical background. The most successful were Jeanne Bourin's *La Chambre des Dames*, a first-rate story of men and women in Paris during the reign of Louis IX, with a preface by historian Régine Pernoud; Robert Merle's *En Nos Vertes Années*, the adventures of a young medical student in the south of France during the Renaissance; *La Motte Rouge*, by French academician Maurice Genevoix, which takes place in 1570 in the southern province of Rouergue; and *La Caverne des Pestiférés*, by Jean Carrière, a novel about the great epidemic of 1835. U. S. history was no less attractive to the French reader than to the American: Maurice Denuzière's *Fausse Rivière*, a continuation of his *Louisiane*, enjoyed immense success.

This taste for the *retro* explained the success of such "dream books" as Pierre-Jean Rémy's *Orient Express;* the appearance of several works about *la belle époque*, including the Marquis de Breteuil's *La Haute Société;* the reissue of such great 19th century novels as *La Maison Philibert* and *Les Noronsoff*, by Jean Lorraine, *La Duchesse Bleue*, by Paul Bourget, *Manette Salomon*, by Edmond and Jules de Goncourt, and *Le Vice Suprême*, by Sâr Peladan; and the comeback of Guy de Maupassant.

The feminist movement was represented mainly by the well-known Flora Groult, who published *Ni tout à fait la même ni tout à fait pareille*, and by 29-year-old newcomer Katherine Pancol, the author of *Moi d'abord*, a witty, easy book about a young woman who finds emancipation through a series of daring sexual adventures. This young writer has been compared to Colette and Françoise Sagan and may be the revelation of the year.

Among France's better known writers, Romain Gary produced another book about the stormy relations between a man and a woman, *Les Clowns Lyriques*. Marc Cholodenko's *Les Pleurs* has flashes of genius, but critics generally found it uneven and diffuse.

Stories about multimillionaires, policemen, and criminals continued to enjoy high sales. More than 100,000 copies of the following books were sold between January and August 1979: *Les Egoûts du Paradis*, by bank robber and writer Albert Spaggiari; *Le Ricain*, a police story by Roger Borniche; and *Palm Beach*, the fourth best seller in six years for Pierre Rey.

There still were, of course, novels about love and feelings. *Tendres Cousines*, by Pascal Lainé, is a very pleasant story about the sentimental awakening and romantic initiation of a handsome adolescent on the eve of World War II. *Les Années Molles*, by Jean Pierre Enard, is also a kind of contemporary *Education Sentimentale*.

Nonfiction. One of the major nonfiction works of 1979 was *Le Testament de Dieu*, by "new philosopher" Bernard-Henri Levy. In this essay, Levy "reactivates" the Bible, calling it "the only text standing up in the recent crisis of ideologies." Another notable essay by a "new philosopher" was André Glucksman's *Le Discours de la Guerre*, which several critics labeled "anti-Clausewitzian."

The year's best history books were probably Jean Baptiste Duroselle's analysis of the period 1932–70, *La Décadence*, and two biographies—*Louis XIII*, by Pierre Chevalier, and *Georges Clemenceau*, by Pierre Saulière. Also noteworthy was Armand Berard's *L'ONU, Oui ou Non*, the memoirs of France's former ambassador to the United Nations.

Memoirs by luminaries of the arts also took the fancy of French readers. The most popular and best written was actress Simone Signoret's *Le lendemain elle était souriante*.

Poetry. Lovers of poetry were offered the best recent anthology of contemporary French verse, Alain Bosquet's *La Poésie Française depuis 1950*. Bosquet also published *Poèmes I*, a collection of his own poems written between 1945 and 1967. His verse shows diversity, richness of inspiration, and a unique combination of mystery, passion, and humor.

Other notable poetry collections of the year were Luc Decaune's *Haute Provence* and *Recréations;* Claude Esteban's *Terres, Travaux du Coeur;* Pierre Torreilles' *Les Dieux Rompus;* and André Pieyre de Mandiargues' *L'Ivre Oeil*. The latter poet was awarded the French Academy's Grand Prix de Poésie for the sum of his poetical work.

PIERRE E. BRODIN
Lycée Français de New York

German Literature

Fierce competition and inflated prices characterized the German literary market in 1979. Even the critics frequently were confused.

Fiction. The end of the 1970's saw most German authors becoming less politically engaged and tending toward the private and personal. A sign of the times was the belated appreciation of the novels of Hermann Lenz. Among more established authors, Max Frisch concentrated on problems of aging in *Der Mensch erscheint im Holozän*. Günter Grass, in his new tour de force, *Das Treffen in Telgte*, withdrew into the 17th century. Even Heinrich Böll, in *Fürsorgliche Belagerung*, expressed his frustration with the contemporary scene in individual rather than social terms. Other authors distanced themselves by indulging in humor or thinly disguised autobiography.

Nonfiction. The introspective trend also was evidenced by the many reminiscences of prominent German political figures and by critical accounts of current trends and developments. Martin and Sylvia Greiffenhagen called Germany *Ein schwieriges Vaterland* (a problematic nation), and Friedrich Heer questioned the existence of a common German cultural consciousness. Sebastian Haffner's *Anmerkungen über Hitler,* a tortuous reevaluation of the past, attracted a great number of readers. Lew Kopelew's *Und schuf mir einen Götzen* faced the unpalatable truth about Nazi concentration camps. Walter Jens' *Warum ich Christ bin?* was perhaps the most impressive new work in the field of religion.

Among the year's more specialized nonfiction books the most notable were Alice Miller's study of child psychology, *Das Drama des begabten Kindes und die Suche nach dem wahren Selbst,* and Konrad Lorenz's summary of his research, *Das Wirkungsgefüge der Natur und das Schicksal des Menschen.*

Poetry. As expected, pure poetry again became a favorite vehicle of literary expression, and its formal requirements became a favorite battleground. Among young German poets whose new works attracted attention were Friederike Roth (*Tollkirschenhochzeit*), Jochen Lobe (*Augenaudienz*), and Uwe Dirk (*Ansichtskarten aus Wales*). Their names could be added to the list of more established German poets, including Ernst Jande, Paul Wühr, Hans Magnus Enzensberger, and Gabriele Wohmann. Ernst Meister died before he could receive an important literary prize.

Drama. The German stage displayed a healthy activity. One of the theatrical highlights of the 1978–79 season was Botho Strauss' *Gross und Klein,* a trenchant criticism of contemporary civilization. Thomas Bernhard's *Immanuel Kant* and his anti-Nazi tragicomedy *Vor dem Ruhestand* lampooned conventional attitudes.

East Germany. On the other side of the Berlin Wall, the East German political establishment continued its insidious campaign against dissenters. Even well-meant protests were stifled by any means available. The supporters of the regime were led by the dictatorial Hermann Kant and his unscrupulous lieutenants, Stefan Heym (*Collin*) and Rolf Schneider (*November*). Readers interested in the undisguised truth about the DDR had to turn to accounts published in West Germany, such as Margaret Bechler's *Warten auf Antwort;* Brigitte Klump's *Das rote Kloster;* and *DDR konkret,* by T. Auerbach, et al. Christa Wolf's *Kein Ort, Nirgends* is a poetic treatment of the difficulties of a writer. Erich Loest's *Pistole mit sechzehn* was a welcome addition to the anti-Nazi literature of Germany.

ERNST ROSE
Author, *"A History of German Literature"*

Italian Literature

By the government's own estimate, there were about 100,00 terrorist sympathizers in Italy during 1979; some observers placed the figure at about twice that amount. Some 500 leftists and 180 rightists were in jail as political prisoners, and a series of special laws brought the already unstable government one step closer to a police state.

Such political and social developments have cast a shadow over Italian cultural life. They have gradually disrupted the compromise within which the Italian intelligentsia had long prospered. Most Italian intellectuals are part of the establishment and their ideological comfort has been shaken; they are frightened and confused. There has been a conspicuous absence of any serious analysis of terrorism, an ever-present feature of daily life in Italy. A lack also was felt in the area of scholarly essays and critiques, as well as fictional recreations of events and public figures. In effect, literary activity in Italy has been taking place against a background of unofficial preemptive censorship.

All this seemed related to an apparent rediscovery of strictly literary values. After several years of impatience with or embarrassment by the very notion of literature, Italian writers seemed more interested in purely aesthetic concerns. This trend did bear traces of the differences in quality between prose and poetry in contemporary Italy. Whereas Italian narrative continued to be bland and derivative (as it has been since the death of Gabriele D'Annunzio), poetry was vigorous and diversified and clearly occupied a place of its own on the international scene.

In fiction, Italo Calvino's successful *Una notte d'inverno un viaggiatore* is little more than a review of different novel-writing conventions; *Amore a tre,* by Giovanni Mariotti, is an elaborate piece which echoes the style of Georges Bataille and others; and Giorgio Manganelli's *Centuria: cento piccoli romanzi fiume* captures a style somewhere between Renaissance grotesque and the humoristic vignettes of the early 1900's.

Italian poetry, on the other hand, reflected a greater liveliness and variety. Public readings at Genoa, Castel Porziano, Frascati, and elsewhere created a mass-media ambience. The actual content of the poetry also was rich and varied, but at the same time there was a scarcity of channels available to serious poets. The publication of vast anthologies was aimed at filling the void, but that medium had already become repetitive and overused. More promising was the establishment of the Societá di Poesia, a financially and culturally autonomous cooperative enterprise for the publication of contemporary Italian poets. Supported by the Guanda publishing house in Milan, the society put out seven volumes—by Cagnone, Calzavara, Conte, Greppi, Majellaro, Valesio, and Zeichen—in its first year.

PAOLO VALESIO
Yale University

Japanese Literature

The rediscovery of the past, which had made the historical novel so popular in Japan during 1978, continued unabated in 1979 and produced a literature rich in historical subject matter and theme. At the same time, the growing cosmopolitanism of Japanese culture was well reflected in all genres, with images of the West recurring even in the traditional haiku form.

Fiction. The year 1979 was a relatively quiet one for Japanese fiction. Several popular novelists published works of a different variety, including essay collections, new translations of Japanese classics (such as *The Tale of Genji*), and studies of foreign countries. No great new talent emerged, as the outstanding contributions were made by established authors. Among these were Otohiko Kaga's *Senkoku* (Condemned), a relentless novel about the life of men on death row; and Hitomi Yamaguchi's *Ketsuzoku* (Blood Relative), an autobiographical novel tracing the origins of the writer's mother. The former received a Japanese Literature Grand Prize. The Akutagawa Prizes were awarded to Yoshiko Shigekane for "Yamaai no Kemuri" (Smoke over the Valley), a short story about the operator of a crematorium, and to Sō Aono for *Gusha no Yoru* (A Fool's Night), a novelette about an unconventional Japanese-Dutch marriage.

Nonfiction. The important works of nonfiction in 1979 were biographies, critical essays, and reports on foreign countries. The most outstanding biography was Shūsaku Endō's *Jū to Jūjika* (Gun and Cross), the story of a 17th-century Christian martyr. Hiroyuki Agawa's biography of the World War II naval leader and prime minister, *Yonai Mitsumasa,* was also well received. In literary criticism, Kenkichi Yamamoto won a Japanese Literature Grand Prize for *Shi no Jikaku no Rekishi* (History of Self-Awareness in Poetry), a brilliant study of the poets included in Japan's oldest poetic anthology *Manyōshū.* Novelist Sawako Ariyoshi's report on China, *Chūkoku Ripōto,* was critically acclaimed; and Yasuko Naitō's first-hand account of massacre and starvation in Cambodia, *Kanbojia Watashi no Ai* (Cambodia My Love), was also highly regarded.

Poetry. The most significant literary event of 1979 was the publication of the 20-volume *Shōwa Manyōshū* (Ten Thousand Leaves of the Shōwa Period). Modeled after *Manyōshū,* this poetry anthology presents some 50,000 tanka by 30,000 contributors—including the emperor and empress—from all walks of Japanese life; the collection covers the years 1926–1971. Poetry continued to be as popular as ever in 1979. There were some 600 magazines devoted to haiku and an estimated 5 million poets writing in this form. In modern verse, the general trend was toward simplicity, conciseness, and lyricism. However, Gōzō Yoshimasu won critical acclaim

for his long, abstract prose poem, *Aozora* (Blue Sky). Other notable publications were the later works of Katsue Kitazono, *Blue,* and Junsaburō Nishiwaki, *Jinrui* (Human Race).

Drama. The outstanding drama of 1979 was Junji Kinoshita's *Shigosen no Matsuri* (The Meridian Festival). An innovatively staged war romance about the final defeat of the Heiki by the Genji in 1185, the play won the Yomiuri Literature Prize for drama. The most effective comedy was Hisashi Inoue's *Shimijimi Nihon; Nogi Taishō* (Ah, Japan; General Nogi), a satire based on the suicide of General Nogi, the deified World War I hero.

EMIKO SAKURAI, *University of Hawaii*

Soviet Literature

Following the course of the contemporary literary debate in the Soviet Union is no easy task for the outside observer. In 1978 it appeared that Soviet writers and critics who sought a relaxation in the dogmas of Socialist Realism were reminded that it would be a grave mistake to view the doctrine as an "open system," free to absorb ideas from other schools and ideologies. By 1979, however, there seemed to be a recognition that this verdict was too restrictive, especially because writers and artists had been so strongly encouraged to create works which would inspire a *new* sense of heroism, optimism, and faith in the ideals of Soviet society. Replacing the strict admonitions of the previous year, therefore, there were declarations that "opening the system" was unnecessary because it was already sufficiently open.

The more relaxed policy was articulated by one of the most active members of the powerful Moscow Association of Writers, Feliks Kuznetsov, during a conference of Soviet bloc writers early in the year. His declaration was published in the Literary Gazette of Jan. 10, 1979. Kuznetsov gave examples of past and contemporary works which were initially criticized for putting too much stress on the individual and not enough on the collective. Such works included stories by Valentin Rasputin (especially the controversial "Parting with Maria") and Juri Bondarev's celebrated novel, *The Shore.*

Perhaps the most sensational literary event of 1979 was the granting of the prestigious Lenin Prize, normally given to creative writers, to President and Communist Party Chief Leonid I. Brezhnev. The official announcements made specific reference to three "literary" works by President Brezhnev. The best known is a "documentary narrative," *Malaia Zemlia* (The Little Land), which recounts an episode in the author's wartime experience.

The genre of documentary narrative has always played an important role in Soviet literature, and the year 1979 saw an increasing number of volumes of this classification. The most common subject of the documentary narrative continued to be World War II. In pure fiction, too, the theme of the war was still common, although quite apparent also was the search for a "common hero." Thus, many "family chronicles," including *Dom* (The House) and other novels by the popular Fedor Abramov, met first with some criticism for their supposed "lack of social emphasis." However, Abramov's subsequent short story collection, *Dereviannye koni* (Wooden Horses), was better received after the "new" policy was declared.

The relaxation of aesthetic requirements, however limited, was perhaps best evidenced by the number of publications by authors on the fringe. Even a large edition of Mikhail Bulgakov's once infamous novel, *Master and Margarita*, was scheduled for publication. There also appeared to be an increase in the variety of themes and literary forms regarded as acceptable. This could be seen in the new short story collections of V. Shukshin and V. Soloukhin.

ZBIGNIEW FOLEJEWSKI, *University of Ottawa*

Spanish and Spanish-American Literature

The third annual Cervantes Prize, the most important Hispanic literary award, went to the poet-scholar Dámaso Alonso, member of the Generation of 1927 and renowned professor of Spanish studies.

Noteworthy were the lamented deaths in 1979 of two major literary figures: the Spanish poet Blas de Otero, perhaps the most significant voice in Spanish poetry since the Civil War, and the Uruguayan poetess Juana de Ibarbourou.

Fiction. Well-known novelists who were published during 1979 included the Argentinian Manuel Puig, whose *Pubis angelical* continued Spanish America's major contribution to the contemporary novel; the Cuban Alejo Carpentier, whose *El arpa y la sombra* capped a legendary literary career; the Iberian Juan Marsé, whose *La muchacha de las bragas de oro* received the Planeta Prize, and Juan García Hortelano, whose *Los vaqueros en el pozo* signaled a major departure from his realist norm.

Other important novels published were Luis Castillo-Puche's *El amargo sabor de la retama,* the Mexican José Agustín's *El rey se acerca a su templo,* Angel María de Lera's *El hombre que volvió del paraíso,* the Colombian Oscar Collazo's *Memoria compartida,* Jesús Fernández Santos' *Extramuros,* Antonio Ferres' *El gran gozo,* Germán Sánchez Espeso's *Narciso,* winner of the prestigious Nadal Prize, and Raúl Guerra Garrido's *Copenhague no existe.*

The number and quality of feminine novelists published were perhaps trend-setting. Most noteworthy were the two titles by Esther Tusquets: *El mismo mar todos los veranos* and *El amor es un juego solitario.* Other well-received women novelists included Rosa Montero, with *Crónica del desamor;* Montserrat Roig, with *Tiempo de cerezos;* Rosa Roma, with an unusual dialogued novel, *Lloran las cosas sobre nosotros;* and the Mexican Mercedes

Marrero, whose *Rastro de muerte* offered an unusual feminine view of Mexico's Revolution.

Interesting short-story collections published included Juan García Hortelano's *Cuentos completos,* Fernando Quiñones' *El viejo país,* the young Ecuadorian Raúl Pérez Torres' highly acclaimed *Musiquero viejo, musiquero joven,* and the Argentinian Hector Tizón's *El traidor venerado.*

Nonfiction. Significant nonfiction appearing in 1979 included Julián Marías' essay *Una jornada muy particular,* which won the León Felipe Prize; Vicente Palacio Atard's *La España del siglo XIX,* which won the Menéndez Pelayo Prize; and Dionisio Ridruejo's *Los cuadernos de Rusia,* a diary of World War II experiences on the Russian front.

Scholarly works of importance included Juan Ignacio Ferreras' *Catálogo de novelas y novelistas españoles del siglo XIX,* which won the Ribadeneyra Prize; the Peruvian Augusto Miró Quesada's *Historia y leyenda de Mariano Melgar;* Ricardo Gullón's *Psicologías del autor y lógicas del personaje;* and José María Martínez Cachero's *Historia de la novela española entre 1936 y 1975.*

Poetry. The major poetical works of 1979 were the great Cuban José Lezama Lima's posthumous *Fragmentos de su imán;* José Angel Valente's *Material memoria;* Pureza Canelo's long awaited *Habitable;* Luis Rosales' *Diario de una resurección;* and Leopoldo de Luis' *Igual que guantes grises.*

Major prizes for poetry were awarded to Felix Grande's *Los rubaiyatas de Horacio Martín* (National Prize), Joaquín Márquez' *Solo de caracol para un amor lejano* (Boscán Prize), and Arcadio López Casanova's *La oscura potestad* (Adonais Prize).

Younger and newer poets published included Francisca Aguirre (*Los trescientos escalones*); the Argentinian Horacio Salas (*Gajes del oficio*); Angel Morradán (*Cantos a la muerte*); the Chilean Carmen Orrego (*Entre nos otros*); Luis Antonio de Villena (*Hymnica*); Luis Martínez de Merlo (*Alma del tiempo*); María del Carmen Pallarés (*Del lado de la ausencia*); Alfredo Buxán (*Las ascuas de la leña combatida*); Pablo García de Baena (*Antes que el tiempo acabe*); Andrés Mirón (*El polvo del peregrino*); and Guillermo Carnero (*Ensayo de una teoría de la visión*).

Drama. The most significant event of the Spanish theatrical season was the staging of Luis Riaza's *Retrato de dama con perro.* An outstanding Spanish-American theatrical event was the presentation of the documentary play *La mudanza* by Mexico's Vicente Leñero. Also noteworthy in this category was the publication of Miguel Romeo Esteo's farces, *Pizzicato irrisoy gran pavana de lechuzas* and *Vodevil de la pálida, pálida, pálida rosa.*

ALFRED RODRIGUEZ
The University of New Mexico

LONDON

The main change in London in 1979 was the election in May of a Conservative government committed to radical fiscal policies.

Strikes. Earlier in 1979 the alliance between the unions and the Labour government collapsed. The unions rejected a 5% guideline for increases, and strikes among truck drivers, rail workers, garbage workers, ambulance men, and gravediggers helped precipitate Labour's defeat. Striking London truck drivers turned down an offer of 15% and held out for a 23% increase in pay. Erratic rail strikes in mid-January created huge traffic jams in London when commuters resorted to cars. The London Chamber of Commerce reported that 300,000 commuters decided to stay home, which further increased the economic disruptions. Garbage piled up in Leicester Square as a result of a strike.

Racism and Other Internal Conflict. In 1979 gangs of white youths tore through a Bangladeshi neighborhood in the East End of London and bombarded the houses with milk bottles, but the Asians fought back, as a new militancy among blacks and Asians became evident.

Scotland Yard came under scrutiny following the bludgeon slaying of a school teacher, allegedly by policemen. The incident was investigated by Scotland Yard's Complaints Investigation Bureau (CIB) and was one of several reports of police wrongdoing in London.

After considerable delay, a new extension (*left*) of London's famed Tate Gallery opened in May 1979.

Transport Celebration. Horse-drawn buses were employed in London during the summer as part of the celebrations of the 150th anniversary of the London Bus Service.

Lord Mountbatten's Funeral. Earl Mountbatten of Burma, Queen Elizabeth II's cousin who was killed by terrorists, was given on September 5 the most magnificent military funeral since that of the Duke of Wellington in 1852. European royalty, Commonwealth representatives, comrades of world wars I and II, and friends attended the service in Westminster Abbey.

LOS ANGELES

Although progress was made in the areas of urban renewal and subway planning, the city of Los Angeles was divided by difficult and controversial issues in 1979. Proposition 13 required cuts in both the city and school budgets, and conflict raged over school board- and court-ordered busing. Brush fires were a constant threat during the summer, and in September the city suffered its worst smog in 25 years.

Budgets. The city council approved a 1980 budget of $1.43 billion, only 2.65% larger than the previous budget and far below the rate of inflation. The council had hoped to avoid cuts by instituting a charge for garbage collection, but strong taxpayer resistance forced the plan to be abandoned. Instead, cuts were to be made in city vehicle replacement and street maintenance, and all personnel vacancies were required to be left unfilled for three months.

The Los Angeles School District adopted a $1.64 billion budget, 7% higher than the year before but still below the inflation rate. Cuts in service were made by reducing after-school playground activities, increasing class size in the first three grades, and reducing the number of school principals.

Politics and Administration. A court-ordered busing plan caused great conflict among Los Angeles residents and a split in the board of education. Attempts to have the order rescinded were unsuccessful, and pressure from minority groups to replace the at-large election system resulted in the adoption of a district plan. In the spring, School Board President Howard Miller, a strong advocate of the court's position, was recalled and replaced by an anti-busing advocate. E. Erwin Piper, the city administrator for 17 years, retired in August.

Urban Renewal and Transportation. The Community Redevelopment Agency placed on the market the last of 25 blocks in the 20-year-old Bunker Hill renewal project. The area is designated for office, commercial, residential, and recreational space, including the newly organized Los Angeles Museum of Modern Art. The local share of funding was finally arranged for the city's proposed first subway, to run from downtown along Wilshire Blvd. to North Hollywood.

CHARLES R. ADRIAN

LOUISIANA

For the first time since Reconstruction, Louisiana elected a Republican governor in 1979. In perhaps the state's most interesting gubernatorial election in years, U. S. Rep. David Treen defeated state Public Service Commissioner Louis Lambert by 10,000 votes out of 1.37 million cast in the second primary on December 8. Treen, with strong backing from the middle class and business interests, broke the Democratic Party's power base of city workers, blacks, and rural populists, which had been the key to state politics for many years. Although Treen narrowly lost New Orleans, he carried the rest of the state's cities, including Baton Rouge and Shreveport, and won overwhelmingly in his home parish (county) of Jefferson, New Orleans' principal suburban community.

In the first primary, which Treen led, Lt. Gov. James Fitzmorris, Jr., of New Orleans claimed that Lambert had stolen enough votes to edge him out of the runoff. Fitzmorris filed suit against Lambert, who is from the small town of Gonzales, but the courts ruled that Fitzmorris' claims were not proven. In the second primary, Treen received the endorsement of Fitzmorris, as well as the four other major Democratic candidates who failed to make the runoff. Gov. Edwin Edwards, who, having served two terms, could not immediately succeed himself, endorsed Lambert, but with qualifying statements.

In the race for lieutenant governor, State Rep. Bobby Freeman had the support of the black-labor coalition and defeated fellow Democrat James Donelon, who was supported by more conservative middle class interests. Other winners in top statewide elections were State Sen. James Brown as secretary of state and farmer Bob Odom, who ousted Commissioner of Agriculture Gil Dozier. The latter's first term had been tainted by claims of scandal.

Otto Passman. Former U. S. Rep. Otto Passman was cleared of charges by a federal court jury in his hometown of Monroe. The former 30-year congressman, now 79, had been charged with illegally accepting up to $213,000 from Korean rice dealer and influence peddler Tongsun Park. Passman also had been accused of failing to pay income tax on most of the money gained from Park, but the jury apparently accepted the defense's claim that Passman was an innocent dupe of evil Korean business interests.

New Orleans. It was a year of troubles and turmoil for the state's largest city, New Orleans. A bitter police strike early in the year caused cancelation of the city's famed Mardi Gras parades. State police and National Guardsmen were called in to protect the city during the 16-day walkout but, as city officials proudly pointed out after the patrolmen returned to their jobs, New Orleans suffered no crime wave or violence during the strike. However, some officers were accused of vandalism during the walkout, which some veteran cops said would split the department for years to come. The strike began over the question of the city's recognizing the Teamsters' Union as the officers' bargaining agent. When the strike finally collapsed, the officers won some $4,000 in extra pay and benefits, but the Teamsters still were not recognized.

Later in the year, statistics showed that New Orleans had the highest murder rate in the country. And at year's end, city officials were struggling with a 1980 budget with a $25 million revenue shortfall and the prospect of having to lay off several hundred city workers.

The Port of New Orleans, the city's principal industry, was way down both in volume and value of cargo handled in 1978. Port officials attributed the losses to strikes, outdated facilities, and a major grain elevator explosion.

River Basin. Of major statewide interest was a debate on the future of the Atchafalaya River basin, the last great river basin swamp in the United States. The U. S. Army Corps of Engineers held a series of hearings throughout the state. Various interests tried to reconcile the needs of flood control, the rights of private landowners, and the protection of the ecologically valuable wetlands and the state's fish and wildlife. The Corps was scheduled to present its plan, after further study, in 1981.

JOSEPH W. DARBY III
"The Times-Picayune," New Orleans

—— LOUISIANA · Information Highlights ——

Area: 48,523 square miles (125 675 km²).

Population (Jan. 1979 est.): 3,992,000.

Chief Cities (1976 est.): Baton Rouge, the capital, 302,-236; New Orleans, 580,959; Shreveport, 187,583.

Government (1979): *Chief Officers*—governor, Edwin W. Edwards (D); lt. gov., James E. Fitzmorris, Jr. (D). *Legislature*—Senate, 39 members; House of Representatives, 105 members.

Education (1978–79): *Enrollment*—public elementary schools, 565,844 pupils; public secondary, 250,825; colleges and universities, 152,207 students. *Public school expenditures*, $1,315,690,000 ($1,446 per pupil).

State Finances (fiscal year 1978): *Revenues*, $4,115,-184,000; *expenditures*, $3,918,087,000.

Personal Income (1978): $26,638,000,000; per capita, $6,716.

Labor Force (July 1979): *Nonagricultural wage and salary earners*, 1,442,200; *unemployed*, 111,800 (6.7% of total force).

LUXEMBOURG

On June 11, Prime Minister Gaston Thorn announced the resignation of his Liberal-Socialist government. The resignation came a day after the coalition had been defeated in parliamentary elections. Thorn's own Liberal Party actually increased its representation in the 59-seat Chamber of Deputies to 15, an increase of one seat, but the Socialists dropped three seats, to 14. The Christian Social Party of Pierre Werner won 42% of the popular vote and 24 legislative seats. On July 19, a new coalition government, with Werner as prime minister, was sworn in. The cabinet comprised six Chris-

—— LUXEMBOURG · Information Highlights ——
Official Name: Grand Duchy of Luxembourg.
Location: Western Europe.
Area: 999 square miles (2 586 km²).
Population (1979 est.): 400,000.
Chief Cities (1977 est.): Luxembourg, the capital, 76,-500; (1975 est.): Esch-sur-Alzette, 27,700; Differdange, 18,300.
Government: *Head of state,* Jean, grand duke (acceded 1964). *Head of government,* Pierre Werner, prime minister (took office July 1979). *Legislature* (unicameral)—Chamber of Deputies.
Monetary Unit: Franc (29.29 francs equal U. S.$1, Aug. 1979).
Manufactures (major products): Steel, rubber products, synthetic fibers.
Agriculture (major products): Livestock, dairy products.

tian Socialists and five Liberals. Thorn was made foreign minister.

No major policy shifts emerged, as Werner wrestled with a recession in the steel industry. To combat unemployment, expected to average 1% for the year, the government increased public spending. A new army regiment was created, leaving the duchy with an armed force of 660. Proposed budget deficits and tax cuts early in the year were widely opposed and may have accounted for the election results. Plans for an expensive new building for the European Parliament were set aside in favor of a more modest project.

The banking industry continued to grow. By year's end, more than 100 international banks had offices in the duchy. Tax revenue from the banking sector remained the government's largest source of income. Radio Tele Luxembourg, a private broadcast company, ranked as the second largest taxpayer, ahead of the suffering steel industry. An economic growth rate of 2.2%, a 3.5% increase in retail prices, and a positive balance of payments were expected for 1979.

JONATHAN E. HELMREICH, *Allegheny College*

MAINE

In 1979 issues of concern in Maine included possible fuel shortages and rising fuel costs; the economic impact of the Loring Air Force Base closing; numerous considerations of the state's environmentalists; and the continuing problem of the Indian Land Claim.

The Fuel Issue. Adequate gasoline for the summer tourists and adequate fuel supplies for the winter heating season were major issues. Gov. Joseph Brennan proposed a plan to assist about 49,000 low-income families in meeting the high cost of heating oil.

Economy and Environment Issues. The impending shutdown of Loring Air Force Base presented an economic threat to Aroostook County. State officials, the Maine Congressional delegation, and representatives from the county attempted to convince the federal government that the base was required for defense as well as for the economic well being of the county. It appeared as if an alternative to the base would have to be found.

The Pittston Company's renewal of application to build an oil refinery at Eastport continued to polarize advocates of economic development and environmentalists. Approval of the application by state and federal authorities appeared doubtful.

Environmentalists maintained their campaign against any damming in the Allagash, an irreplaceable wilderness area of northernmost Aroostook County that is coveted by developers and power company planners.

Aerial spraying of the spruce budworm evoked a greater-than-usual amount of opposition from those who feared human health effects, as well as from those who objected to the high costs of spraying. A mishap at Dennysville, which polluted the vegetable gardens of private citizens, heightened the opposition.

A campaign was begun to ban further construction of nuclear facilities in Maine. A few petitioners wanted to close Maine Yankee Atomic at Wiscasset, the only nuclear facility currently operating in Maine. The accident at Three Mile Island, PA, helped stir opposition.

The Drug Issue. Drug smuggling along the Maine coast has presented difficulties in recent years. The state's long, fretted coastline affords uncounted places of concealment for these illegal activities. Efforts of law enforcement authorities have met with mixed success, even though several large caches of drugs were seized.

Indian Land Claim Issue. A continuing, emotional issue is the intractable Indian Land Claim. Initially, the Penobscot and Passamaquoddy Indians claimed that 12 million acres (4 860 000 ha) of land were taken from them illegally by a breach of the Non-Intercourse Act of 1790 which required the approval of all land transfers by the federal government. In 1978, the Indians, the state, and the federal government seemingly accepted a plan originally presented by former Sen. William Hathaway. However, in 1979, the Indians asked for additional funds in order to buy back more land from private landowners. With this change, the situation appeared a stalemate. The claim, if realized, would give the Indians a large portion of the northern part of the state.

EDWARD SCHRIVER, *University of Maine, Orono*

——— MAINE · Information Highlights ———
Area: 33,215 square miles (86 027 km²).
Population (Jan. 1979 est.): 1,096,000.
Chief Cities (1970 census): Augusta, the capital, 21,945; Portland, 65,116; Lewiston, 41,779; Bangor, 33,168.
Government (1979): *Chief Officers*—governor, Joseph R. Brennan (D). *Legislature*—Senate, 33; House of Representatives, 151 members.
Education (1978–79): *Enrollment*—public elementary schools, 161,797 pupils; public secondary, 78,219; colleges and universities, 41,460 students. *Public school expenditures,* $356,800,000 ($1,386 per pupil).
State Finances (fiscal year 1978): *Revenues,* $1,161,-242,000; *expenditures,* $1,118,225,000.
Personal Income (1978): $6,867,000,000; per capita, $6,292.
Labor Force (July 1979): *Nonagricultural wage and salary earners,* 415,700; *unemployed,* 43,400 (8.6% of total force).

MALAYSIA

The tough stand taken by Malaysia against the continued influx of "boat people" from Vietnam was considered heartless by many outsiders, especially those in Western industrialized countries. But to the Malaysian government, the strong measures seemed necessary.

The flow of Vietnamese refugees, most of them ethnic Chinese, proved particularly hard for Malaysia to handle because of the delicate racial balance in the country. Malaysia's National Front government has long tried to keep smoldering racial enmity under control. At the same time, it has tried to increase the economic role of the Malay majority. This has caused resentment among the big Chinese and Indian minorities. All three groups are represented in the National Front. The arrival of thousands of ethnic Chinese from Vietnam scared many Malays and threatened to ignite the potentially explosive racial situation.

At the beginning of the year, the Malaysians, already hard-pressed to care for the refugees arriving on their shores, announced that they would not accept any more boat people. The government of Prime Minister Hussein bin Dato Onn hoped that word of its hard-line policy would reach Vietnam and encourage would-be refugees there to sail for other lands.

The Malaysians soon showed that they meant business. Starting in mid-February, thousands of newly arriving refugees were put back into boats and towed away. Many apparently died at sea. Still, the Malaysians found themselves swamped by the sheer number of arrivals. In April, more than 100 Vietnamese drowned after their boat sank. The survivors claimed that their rickety boat was recklessly towed by a Malaysian naval vessel when it foundered. The government disputed the charges, but still Malaysia's reputation was damaged.

June again brought headlines when Deputy Prime Minister Mohamad bin Mahathir said that all refugees in Malaysia would be shipped out to sea. He also said that the government would shoot on sight any refugees trying to land in Malaysia. The government quickly disowned the remarks, and there were assertions that Dr. Mahathir had been misquoted.

------- MALAYSIA • Information Highlights -------

Official Name: Malaysia.
Location: Southeast Asia.
Area: 127,315 square miles (239 744 km²).
Population (1979 est.): 13,300,000.
Chief Cities (1975 est.): Kuala Lumpur, the capital, 500,000; George Town, 280,000; Ipoh, 255,000.
Government: *Head of state,* Sultan Ahmad Shah (took office April 1979). *Head of government,* Hussein bin Dato Onn, prime minister (took office Jan. 1976). *Legislature*—Parliament: Dewan Negara (Senate) and Dewan Ra'ayat (House of Representatives).
Monetary Unit: Ringgit (Malaysian dollar) (2.16 ringgits equal U. S.$1, Aug. 1979).
Manufactures (major products): Steel, automobiles, electronic equipment.
Agriculture (major products): Rubber, palm oil, pepper.

Malaysia's anger at Vietnam for the refugee exodus was preceded by a strong denunciation of Vietnam's invasion of Cambodia. Malaysia and its partners in the Association of Southeast Asian Nations (ASEAN)—Indonesia, the Philippines, Singapore, and Thailand—were especially incensed at Hanoi because throughout 1978 Vietnam had been trumpeting its peaceful intentions toward its neighbors.

Domestically, Malaysia's economy, supported by strong prices for its top exports, did well in 1979. The inflation rate was only 5%.

On March 29, Sultan Yahya Petra, the country's 62-year-old elected king, died of a heart attack. In April, the hereditary rulers of 9 of Malaysia's 13 states elected Sultan Ahmad Shah of Pahang State to a five-year term as the figurehead king.

EDWARD EPSTEIN
"The Asian Wall Street Journal"

MALTA

The stationing of British armed forces on Malta, a practice which dated to the Napoleonic Wars, ended with the expiration of the Anglo-Maltese Defense Agreement on March 31, 1979. Malta's Labor Prime Minister Dom Mintoff hailed the withdrawal of the last British naval forces as "Freedom Day" and stressed his nation's neutrality and nonalignment. Malta, he declared, would form a "bridge of peace" between Europe and North Africa. Not all Maltese shared his optimism, however. The opposition Nationalist Party expressed fear that the British departure would leave Malta defenseless.

Several years earlier, anticipating the loss of $80 million (U. S.) in annual revenue which the British evacuation would entail, Mr. Mintoff had begun seeking outside support for the Maltese economy. He also attempted to secure international guarantees, especially from France, Italy, Algeria, and Libya, for Malta's sovereignty and neutrality. The reluctance of the Europeans to enter into such an arrangement caused Mr. Mintoff to seek closer ties with the Arabs.

Although Libyan President Muammar el-Qaddafi repeated vague assurances of economic and diplomatic support early in 1979, little concrete assistance materialized. The Maltese government had originally requested that Libya match the lost funds for a five-year period, dur-

------- MALTA • Information Highlights -------

Official Name: Republic of Malta.
Location: Mediterranean Sea.
Area: 121 square miles (313 km²).
Population (1979 est.): 300,000.
Chief Cities (1976 est.): Valletta, the capital, 14,071; Victoria, 5,027.
Government: *Head of state,* Anton Buttigieg, president (took office Dec. 1976). *Head of government,* Dominic Mintoff, prime minister (took office June 1971). *Legislature* (unicameral)—House of Representatives.
Monetary Unit: Maltese pound (.3519 M. pound equals U. S.$1, July 1979).

The Salerno Company of the British Royal Marines prepare to embark on the "Sir Lancelot," as all British troops are withdrawn from the Mediterranean island of Malta, March 1979.

DEPARTMENT OF INFORMATION, MALTA

ing which tourism and other industries could be developed. No funds of this magnitude were forthcoming, nor was Malta able to complete negotiations on such issues as the preferential purchase of Libyan oil and the establishment of tariff accords. Even more importantly, the two nations remained at odds over a disputed offshore zone earmarked for oil exploration.

Malta's relations with Britain also were strained, owing to a number of incidents prior to the withdrawal of troops. British journalists were banned from the island in the summer of 1978, ostensibly for their critical reporting of Malta's position regarding the naval bases and the growing entente with Libya. The restrictions were not lifted until February 1979. Great Britain's refusal to allow the importation of certain Maltese textile products in 1978 led Malta to curb the entry of some British goods, which worsened relations even further.

The administration insisted on minimal contact with the USSR until that country committed itself to supporting Malta's development. China, on the other hand, became involved in the construction of a major new dry dock which Maltese officials hoped would boost the economy.

KENNETH J. PERKINS
University of South Carolina

MANITOBA

"The best thing that governments do," said Premier Sterling R. Lyon of Manitoba, "is nothing." His statement reflected the philosophy by which the Progressive Conservative government continued to manage the province in 1979. Fiscal austerity, private enterprise, and provincial rights were the key terms in Manitoban affairs during the year.

Economy. On May 15, Finance Minister Donald Craik presented a budget of $1.6 billion for fiscal 1979–80. The package called for a 3% cut in the growth of government spending. The administration also announced a five-year freeze on hydroelectric rates for individuals and most industries. The freeze was expected to attract new businesses to Manitoba, but would cost $31.3 million in 1979–80 and would raise the province's annual deficit from $114 to $122.6 million. However, most of the deficit was for capital spending, not current expenses. The premier's support for private business and his view that "less government is better" were further reflected in the sale of several crown-owned corporations, including McKenzie Steele Briggs Seeds Ltd.

Politics and the Legislature. The 1979 session of the Manitoba legislature was opened with the February 15 throne speech of the Progressive Conservative government. In addition to suggesting a larger role for the private sector in automobile insurance and retail liquor sales, the administration promised to provide new

─────── **MANITOBA • Information Highlights** ───────

Area: 251,000 square miles (650 090 km²).
Population (1979 est.): 1,030,000.
Chief City (1976 census): Winnipeg, the capital, 560,874.
Government (1979): *Chief Officers*—lt. gov., Francis L. Jobin; premier, Sterling R. Lyon (Progressive Conservative party); chief justice, Court of Appeal, Samuel Freedman; Court of Queen's Bench, A. S. Dewar. *Legislature*—Legislative Assembly, 57 members.
Education (1979–80 est.): *Enrollment:* public elementary and secondary schools, 212,400; private schools, 8,230; Indian (federal) schools, 8,025; post-secondary, 21,150 students. *Total expenditures,* $758,265,-000.
Personal Income (average weekly salary, May 1979): $256.19.
Unemployment Rate (July 1979, seasonally adjusted): 5.5%.
(All monetary figures given in Canadian dollars.)

health, education, and social-service programs for the needy. The spring session ended on June 16, when the house was prorogued by the lieutenant governor. A total of 58 bills were passed, including a change in the electoral boundaries for the next provincial election. The most heated debates concerned the freeze on electricity rates and other budget proposals. At the close of the session, the 57-seat house comprised 32 Conservatives, 22 Liberals, and three vacancies. The Manitoba Liberal party lost its only seat in the chamber April 6, when Lloyd Axworthy resigned to run in the May 22 federal election. Sidney Spivak, a Progressive Conservative, also resigned to run for federal office. The third vacancy was that left by Ed Schreyer in December 1978 when he resigned to become governor-general of Canada. In the federal elections, Manitoba's 14 seats in the 282-seat House of Commons went to 7 Progressive Conservative, 5 New Democratic, and 2 Liberal candidates.

Protest. In a peaceful protest aimed at securing a long-term job program, a group of Metis demonstrators occupied a federal employment office in Winnipeg for one week in early April. The protestors left the office when Employment Minister Bud Cullen agreed to a number of proposals to alleviate high unemployment among Metis.

Flooding. The longest winter since 1936, a fast spring thaw, and heavy rains in April caused the 60-mile (96-km) stretch of the Red River valley south of Winnipeg to rise several feet above the disastrous level of the 1950 "Black Friday" flood. More than 10,000 residents fled the area, and the cost of repairs reached tens of millions of dollars.

JEFF HACKER

MARYLAND

Twenty inches (50.8 cm) of wind-driven snow buried central Maryland February 18–19. In Baltimore a 7 P. M. curfew was imposed February 19 and 20 because of looting in commercial areas. Some 500 persons were arrested.

Tropical Storm David's high winds and torrential rains ripped through Maryland on September 5. Flood damage exceeded $66 million.

Energy. The gasoline shortage struck Maryland in May, June, and July. Odd-even gas rationing, minimum purchases, and higher cargo weights for trucks were imposed, and the state filed an unsuccessful lawsuit against the U. S. Department of Energy seeking changes in the allocation system.

Experts were disappointed when a 5,567-foot (1 670 m) well on the lower Eastern Shore yielded water of 133° F (56° C), not the 159° F (71° C) needed for economical geothermal energy.

Crime. Blaming technical trial errors, a three-judge panel of the Fourth U. S. Circuit Court of Appeals on January 11 overturned the 1977 conviction of former Gov. Marvin Mandel and five associates on political corruption and mail fraud charges. Mandel resumed his old office for 36 hours until Harry R. Hughes was sworn in for the new term. The conviction was restored July 20 by a 3–3 vote of the entire circuit court. A later appeal was refused.

Mary Rose Robaczynski, a nurse, was charged with murdering four comatose hospital patients whose respirators were unplugged. She was tried on one charge but the jury could not reach a verdict. The other charges were dropped after the nurse surrendered her license.

Sports. The Baltimore Orioles, who won the American League pennant, were sold by the Hoffberger brewing family to Edward Bennett Williams, a Washington, DC, attorney and president of the Washington Redskins. Williams promised the team would remain in Baltimore for the 1980 season, but fans worried that eventually the franchise would be moved to Washington. Robert Irsay, owner of the Baltimore Colts, inspected football facilities at Memphis, TN, and Jacksonville, FL, to back up his threats to move the team unless massive improvements are made at Baltimore's Memorial Stadium.

Spectacular Bid, of Hawksworth Farm on Maryland's Eastern Shore, won the Kentucky Derby May 5, the Preakness May 19, and came in third in the Belmont Stakes on June 19.

People. The first Pulitzer Prize for feature writing in journalism was awarded to Jon B. Franklin, science writer for *The Baltimore Evening Sun,* for a two-part article on a complicated brain operation.

Mary A. Moylan, 43, one of the "Catonsville Nine" Vietnam war protesters who burned files at the suburban draft board in 1968, surrendered to federal authorities June 18. She had gone underground after appeals of her two-year prison term failed in 1970.

By surgery at the University of Maryland Hospital, Jessie Thomas, a Baltimore housewife, became the first person to get an artificial backbone section.

PEGGY CUNNINGHAM
"The News American," Baltimore

——— MARYLAND • Information Highlights ———

Area: 10,577 square miles (27 394 km²).
Population (Jan. 1979 est.): 4,148,000.
Chief Cities (1970 census): Annapolis, the capital, 30,-095; Rockville, 41,821; Hagerstown, 35,862; (1976 est.): Baltimore, 827,439.
Government (1979): *Chief Officers*—governor, Harry Hughes (D); lt. gov., Samuel W. Bogley (D). *General Assembly*—Senate, 47 members; House of Delegates, 141 members.
Education (1978–79): *Enrollment*—public elementary schools, 402,609 pupils; public secondary, 407,324; colleges and universities, 214,734 students. *Public school expenditures,* $1,628,191,000 ($1,814 per pupil).
State Finances (fiscal year 1978): *Revenues,* $4,538,-033,000; *expenditures,* $4,128,035,000.
Personal Income (1978): $34,646,000,000; per capita, $8,363.
Labor Force (July 1979): *Nonagricultural wage and salary earners,* 1,634,800; *unemployed,* 126,000 (5.9% of total force).

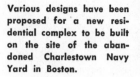

Various designs have been proposed for a new residential complex to be built on the site of the abandoned Charlestown Navy Yard in Boston.

BOSTON REDEVELOPMENT AUTHORITY

MASSACHUSETTS

The political battles of a new governor, racial conflict in Boston, the death of one national institution, and the opening of another made headlines in Massachusetts in 1979.

Politics. Democratic Governor Edward J. King had a stormy first year in office, as he confronted the state legislature on fiscal policy and faced unexpected problems within his own administration. The year began poorly for King, as three major cabinet appointees were forced to resign. The state insurance commissioner and secretary of Elderly Affairs both quit after allegations of past improprieties were lodged. King's nominee for corrections commissioner unexpectedly and abruptly took another position in neighboring Rhode Island. King's selection of Robert M. Foster as chairman of the Massachusetts Bay Transportation Authority (MBTA) sparked considerable controversy, which continued throughout the year; the MBTA, which operates an extensive transportation network in eastern Massachusetts, experienced serious problems in delivering service.

During the first months of the year, Governor King also became embroiled with the legislature over passage of a law requiring cities and towns to limit budget increases for the 1980 fiscal year. King had campaigned on a promise of no increases in local spending, but the lawmakers disagreed. After weeks of wrangling, King and legislative leaders agreed on a compromise bill calling for a maximum 4% increase in local spending.

Racial Problems. The Boston public school system, since 1974 under federal court order to desegregate, experienced a sharp increase in racial tension during 1979. The September 28 shooting of a black high school football player during a game sparked other violent incidents throughout the city school system. Opposition to school busing by various groups continued to add fuel to racial tensions.

Fiedler Dies. Only two months after celebrating his 50th year as conductor of the Boston Pops Orchestra, Arthur Fiedler died at his Brookline home on July 10 at age 85 (see Obituaries, page 381). A memorial concert reenacting Fiedler's nationally televised Bicentennial Concert of July 4, 1976, attracted more than 150,000 people to the banks of Boston's Charles River. The Boston Symphony Orchestra, parent organization of the "Pops," had not named a successor by year's end.

Kennedy Library Opens. Sixteen years after the death of John F. Kennedy, a memorial library and museum was dedicated in Boston on Oct. 20, 1979. A major reason for the long delay in construction was a change in the site of the building. President Kennedy had himself selected a site near Harvard University in Cambridge. But the prospect of thousands of visitors each month crowding an already busy neighborhood prompted the library corporation to choose a new location. The final site overlooks Boston Harbor near the new Boston campus of the University of Massachusetts. Designed by I. M. Pei, the ten-story, starkly modern structure was immediately praised as a major architectural achievement. The building houses permanent exhibits on the life and career of the former president, as well as the papers of John and Robert Kennedy.

The dedication ceremonies brought together two expected rivals for the Democratic presidential nomination in 1980, President Jimmy Carter and Sen. Edward M. Kennedy (MA). (*See* UNITED STATES: Domestic Affairs.)

HARVEY BOULAY, *Boston University*

——MASSACHUSETTS • Information Highlights——

Area: 8,257 square miles (21 386 km²).
Population (Jan. 1979 est.): 5,767,000.
Chief Cities (1976 est.): Boston, the capital, 618,250; Worcester, 168,619; Springfield, 167,577.
Government (1979): *Chief Officers*—governor, Edward J. King (D); lt. gov., Thomas P. O'Neill III (D). *General Court*—Senate, 40 members; House of Representatives, 160 members.
Education (1978–79): *Enrollment*—public elementary schools, 544,746 pupils; public secondary, 536,718; colleges and universities, 384,500 students. *Public school expenditures,* $2,692,305,000 ($2,246 per pupil).
State Finances (fiscal year 1978): *Revenues,* $6,259,-387,000; *expenditures,* $5,894,639,000.
Personal Income (1978): $45,751,000,000; per capita, $7,933.
Labor Force (July 1979): *Nonagricultural wage and salary earners,* 2,578,600; *unemployed,* 146,200 (5.0%).

MEDICINE AND HEALTH

It was a year of controversy in the field of medicine and health. The American Medical Association (AMA) slugged it out with chiropractors, competing national health insurance bills languished in the U. S. Congress, the ways and means of childbirth and infant feeding were debated, popular tranquilizers and painkillers were criticized, and the issues surrounding the detection and treatment of breast cancer remained emotional and unresolved.

On the hopeful side, a new painkiller was being tested that seemed to have the analgesic effect of morphine but not its addictive effect. The American Cancer Society sponsored trials of interferon for certain forms of malignancy and the initial results were promising. Microsurgeons were sewing on limbs seemingly as fast as people could accidentally sever them. Smallpox once and for all was declared dead. And new ways were introduced to get insulin to diabetics in the right dose at the right time.

A federal report on smoking left doubt only in the minds of the tobacco industry as to how to reduce the incidences of cancer and cardiovascular and lung diseases. The report called smoking the "largest preventable cause of death" in the United States (*see* page 329).

In the cardiovascular field there was heartening news about a stunning reduction in premature deaths from strokes and heart attacks by controlling what doctors had previously regarded as "mild" high blood pressure.

There was the continuing battle over laetrile and the pathetic death of little Chad Green, whose parents defied a Massachusetts court order and whisked him off to Mexico for treatment of leukemia with the controversial drug. The U. S. Supreme Court upheld the government's right to ban interstate commerce in a drug it considers ineffective or unsafe even for the terminally ill.

The debate over saccharin kept up, and the artificial sweetener stayed on the market despite the end of the Congressional moratorium against banning it. The search for carcinogenic substances revealed that nitrosamines, known to cause cancer in mice, were found in six of seven brands of whiskey tested.

Cancer. There was a variety of developments in the generally frustrating field of cancer research and therapy. One of the more interesting was an announcement by Dr. Arthur Upton, director of the National Cancer Institute, that there is a strong link between cancer and diet. Although the evidence was admittedly incomplete, Upton recommended eating less fat and more fiber, drinking less alcohol, and keeping weight down. The notion that vitamin C is effective against cancer, however, received a serious blow. A study at the Mayo Clinic showed that vitamin C was no more effective against advanced cancer than a placebo.

First results of a national study suggested that the risk of cancer for daughters of women who took diethylstilbestrol (DES) during pregnancy to prevent miscarriage is considerably lower than once feared. Of the 3,339 DES daughters in the study, only four had developed vaginal cancer.

At a meeting on mastectomy sponsored by the National Institutes of Health, experts designated the modified radical mastectomy as the "current treatment standard." This operation, in which the breast is removed but the pectoral muscles are preserved, replaced the full radical mastectomy as the preferred procedure. There was increasing discussion during the year about so-called prophylactic (preventive) mastectomies for women at high risk of breast cancer. In one study, 19 of 76 women whose breasts were removed on this basis were found to have cancer that had not been detected by mammography. Proponents of mammography reported that radiation doses had fallen back dra-

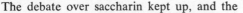

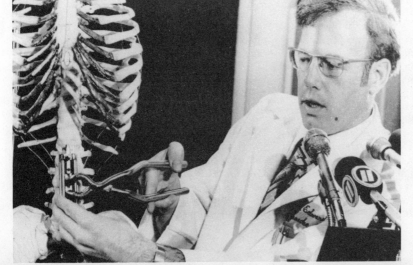

UPI

Dr. Charles Edwards of the University of Maryland Hospital in Baltimore demonstrates how he will replace the spine of a 33-year-old housewife with a 6-inch (15-cm) piece of metal. It was the first such operation ever performed.

matically since the diagnostic tool was attacked a few years earlier for causing as much cancer as it detected in routine annual use for women under age 45. It appeared that routine mammography might be making a comeback.

The cancer drug of the year was interferon. Occurring naturally in the body to attack viruses, the substance has long been regarded as potentially effective against cancer. But because interferon must be made from human blood, its cost is staggering, and large-scale studies had been prohibitively expensive. In 1979, however, the American Cancer Society ordered $2 million dollars worth of the drug for the largest study ever carried out. Initial results held promise for several different forms of cancer, and the National Cancer Institute ordered more than $6 million worth for its own trials.

In lung cancer, Canadian and U. S. researchers reported progress toward developing a vaccine based on the stimulation of the body's own immune system. In another immunological approach to the cancer puzzle, scientists reported that tumors in guinea pigs survive the normal immunological attack by growing inside protective fibrin gel cocoons. Although the cocoons have not as yet been disclosed in human cancer, potential new treatments would attack the cocoons instead of every tumor cell.

Nuclear Testing and Defoliation. The U. S. Defense Department had its hands full with allegations that its nuclear tests in the 1950's and defoliation of Vietnam's Ho Chi Minh trail in the 1960's led to the appearance of cancer today. Vietnam veterans insisted that the toxic ingredient dioxin—banned as a carcinogen by the Environmental Protection Agency (EPA) in 1978—in the defoliant known as Agent Orange had led to a variety of diseases. More than 12 million gallons (45.4 million liters) of Agent Orange were sprayed over Vietnam from 1962 to 1972. A U. S. Public Health Service study made public after 15 years revealed that persons exposed to low-level radiation during Nevada nuclear weapons tests in the 1950's had a high rate of leukemia. This report, combined with claims of high cancer rates among marines stationed in Nagasaki, Japan, after the atomic bombing of that city in 1945, led to an agreement by the Veterans Administration to reassess demands for radiation-related compensations to former servicemen.

Heart Disease. A long-overlooked phenomenon called the coronary spasm began to be looked at with sharp interest. Cardiologists reported that these sudden contractions of coronary arteries may be a significant cause of heart attacks and the pain of angina pectoris, particularly among patients whose arteries are not clogged by fatty plaque. There was excitement over several experimental drugs to inhibit the calcium buildup that may trigger these spasms.

For those whose coronary arteries are clogged, a new and straightforward approach

was devised for unclogging them, a method which one day may compete with coronary bypass surgery. In this technique, a balloon is tunneled through the clogged artery and gradually inflated, pushing the fatty deposits against the wall of the artery to form a channel for blood flow. Another encouraging development was a study showing that the drug sulfinpyrazone had reduced by half the sudden-death rate in the first seven months after a heart attack. Meanwhile, the report of a long-term study on clofibrate, which was used for years to reduce serum cholesterol and coronary artery deposits, revealed that the drug causes a significant increase in gall bladder disease and does not lower the overall cardiovascular death rate. West Germany banned the drug, and other countries, including the United States, restricted its use.

Diabetes. Among the year's wide-ranging developments in diabetes research was the introduction of an experimental portable "artificial pancreas" to provide the diabetic with the right amount of insulin at the right time. Such lightweight portable pumps, which are strapped to the diabetic's belt, were expected to become widespread within one year.

For the adult-onset diabetic, who does not need daily insulin, the use of oral drugs to lower blood sugar was reported to have declined sharply since its peak in 1973. In 1970, a government-sponsored study found that patients who use such drugs face a greater risk of dying of heart disease than those who control blood sugar with diet alone or even insulin. Now, according to the American Diabetes Association, doctors are emphasizing weight loss, and the oral drugs are generally given only if weight reduction fails.

Another important development in the fight against diabetes was the discovery of a case of juvenile-onset diabetes that was almost unquestionably caused by a virus. Although the report was called "highly important" by leading medical scientists, the possibility of a vaccine seemed remote because of countless scientific hurdles still to be cleared.

Drugs. A new six-shot rabies vaccine made from human tissue widely replaced the painful 23-injection duck-embryo vaccine that had been in use for many years. In addition to being as effective as, and less painful than, the old vaccine, it is less likely to cause side effects.

A chicken pox vaccine developed by Japanese scientists posed a dilemma for doctors. While the vaccine is effective against chicken pox, no one seemed to know whether it might cause another disease that sometimes emerges from the same virus in middle age—shingles.

From several directions came accusations that doctors were prescribing too many drugs. One report said that despite more than 10 years of warnings, office-based doctors in 1978 wrote 248,000 prescriptions for the antibiotic chloramphenicol, even though that drug should be used only in a hospital setting when less hazardous antibiotics fail. Another report suggested that doctors wasted $100 million every year by giving antibiotics to postsurgery patients far longer than necessary. Although the American College of Surgeons recommends antibiotics for only 24 hours, they sometimes are given for weeks, the report said.

There was spirited debate over the use of Darvon, the nation's second most widely prescribed painkiller. Dr. Sidney Wolfe of Ralph Nader's Health Research Group called for a government ban because of the thousands of deaths associated with its misuse. The government refused the demand, but it called on the drug's manufacturer to issue stronger warnings about the hazards associated with the drug and ordered a study to see whether it should be put in a special prescription category. Another highly criticized drug was the tranquilizer Valium, which was described at U. S. Senate hearings as causing agonizing withdrawal symptoms when efforts were made to stop taking it. The drug manufacturer insisted that the addiction potential was extremely light.

Surgery. Replantation was the talk of the year in surgery. Legs, feet, arms, hands, and fingers were stitched back in place by microsurgeons around the country. The new expertise in microsurgery came as a direct result of the normalization of relations with China. As American surgeons learned during their visits in recent years, the Chinese had moved far ahead of the rest of the world in replantation techniques.

A development which may help surgery in the absence of sufficient amounts of donated blood is a synthetic, temporary, partial blood substitute pioneered by Japanese scientists. At least one life was saved in Japan with this fluorocarbon substance. Although the first American recipient died, the transfusion was a success.

At the University of Maryland Hospital in Baltimore, doctors inserted a six-inch (15-cm) prosthetic device into a woman who had five vertebrae and a melon-size tumor removed from her back. The device provided support and protection for her spinal cord and allowed her to sit up in a wheel chair and care for her children.

Obstetrics and Child Care. Early in the year, Dr. Patrick Steptoe announced the birth of a second child as a result of his technique of fertilizing the human egg outside the body. But his clinical efforts were halted by his retirement from the British National Health Service, and his plans for a private clinic in England were delayed. In the United States, a government ethics advisory board ended its five-year ban on federal support for research in this area. In December, a clinic in Virginia was given preliminary approval to set up an *in vitro* fertilization laboratory. There was also increasing interest among medical ethicists about the propriety of amniocentesis—sampling the fluid in

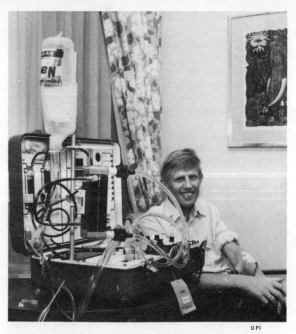

A new artificial kidney machine, which can be carried in an attaché case, makes dialysis more convenient.

which the fetus grows—if the parents plan to abort a baby of the "wrong" sex. Doctors often refuse to do such procedures simply for sex determination, but parents can easily enough claim a different reason. Meanwhile, the use of birth control pills was down sharply in the United States, but for the first time the number of abortions exceeded the total of live births.

One of the year's major battles in obstetrics involved a study indicating that anesthesia during labor or delivery sometimes leads to development and learning defects in children. The results were bitterly disputed.

The committee on nutrition of the American Academy of Pediatrics issued a statement that hailed breast feeding as highly beneficial to the newborn infant. Japanese scientists also had good news for some newborns. They have developed a new therapy for premature infants born with Hyaline-membrane disease. That disorder, which often is fatal, is caused by a deficiency in the air sacs of the immature lungs of some infants, especially those born prematurely. The Japanese technique involves injecting a mixture of synthetic and cow-lung surfactant.

The Chinese reported that they have developed a birth-control pill for men that was more than 99% successful in a study sample, did not interfere with sexual activity, and had no serious side effects. One medical journal did report, however, such side effects as transient weakness, changes in appetite, stomach discomfort, and nausea. The pill is based on a substance called gossypol, which is made from cottonseed oil.

Law and Public Policy. A major mandatory hospital cost-control bill proposed by the Carter administration was rejected by Congress, opponents saying that the voluntary effort program favored by the AMA was sufficient to hold down hospital costs. But the Federal Trade Commission (FTC) ordered the AMA to stop banning its members from advertising consultation fees, a move that it says will make medicine more competitive and less expensive. The AMA appealed. The FTC also won a consent agreement from the California Medical Association to stop issuing guides to the relative value of services by doctors, a practice which the FTC said was in restraint of trade. But the Justice Department lost a federal court battle against the American Society of Anesthesiologists for issuing similar guidelines.

Both the Carter administration and Sen. Edward M. Kennedy (D-MA) introduced bills calling for mandatory national health insurance coverage. The Kennedy bill was far more extensive—and expensive—but neither got anywhere.

American chiropractors, long deprecated by physicians, struck back in the courts with three antitrust suits, forcing the AMA to back down somewhat from its antichiropractic position. The AMA agreed to stop calling chiropractic an "unscientific cult," its theory "irrational," and its education "substandard."

(*See also* GENETICS; MICROBIOLOGY.)

MARK BLOOM
"Medical World News" Magazine

Mental Health

Recommendations made by the President's Commission on Mental Health (PCMH) exerted a strong influence on the national mental health program in 1979. The commission reported that during the course of a year, an estimated 15% of the U. S. population—about 32 million persons—had a diagnosable mental disorder and urged increased federal activity in this area. Of particular concern in federal policy development were the mental health needs of special groups—the chronically mentally ill, children, the elderly, and minorities—who frequently lack access to the most appropriate care.

Basic Research. Information of critical significance continued to emerge from the fields of neuroscience and developmental psychology. In May, the first successful graft of brain tissue in animals was reported by an international team of scientists from the U. S. National Institute of Mental Health (NIMH), the University of Colorado Medical Center, and the Karolinska Institute in Stockholm, Sweden. The host brains in the experimental animals had lesions which impaired motor activity; subsequent to the graft, motor activity improved. The research eventually may be applied to the treatment of certain human brain disorders.

The discovery in 1974 of a specific neuronal receptor to which opiates attach and act on the brain, and the subsequent discovery of two kinds of substances with morphine-like effects—endorphins and enkephalins—that occur naturally in the brain, spurred the search for other naturally-occurring substances that bind to receptors for other drugs. A team of Danish scientists reported the "highly probable" discovery of a substance, termed "gamma compound," that binds to the same receptors in the brain as do a class of anti-anxiety drugs called the benzodiazepines. The significance of this line of research lies in its potential for the synthesis of new and more effective drugs.

Clinical Research. Field testing of the revised *Diagnostic and Statistical Manual* (DSM-III), issued by the American Psychiatric Association (APA), was conducted in 1979. On the basis of research diagnostic criteria, the revised manual will afford clinicians a greater degree of precision in determining the nature of and treatment for a patient's disorder.

Studies aimed at determining what treatments are most effective assumed increasing significance as mental health benefits approached parity with health benefits under many third-party reimbursement plans. A major federal research program was launched to determine the outcome of various treatments for depression, the most widespread major mental disorder.

Mental Health Services. At the close of 1979, federal funds had been awarded to 761 community mental health centers across the country, making comprehensive services available locally to an estimated 110 million people.

The Mental Health Systems Bill, recommended by the PCMH as a response to the needs of the chronically mentally ill, was introduced into the Congress in May. The proposed legislation would strengthen federal-state relationships in the care of the mentally ill and provide support for persistently ill adults and seriously disturbed children.

Behavioral Health. In July the U. S. surgeon general released a report titled *Healthy People,* which stressed the need for individuals to incorporate more healthful patterns of behavior in their lifestyles. The report illustrated an emerging trend in mental health: to link more closely the sometimes isolated fields of physical and mental health.

Patient Advocacy. The formation of the National Alliance for the Mentally Ill—comprised of patients, former patients, and the immediate families of mental patients and complementing the efforts of such longstanding groups as the Mental Health Association—marked a major advance for mentally ill persons. Long burdened by a pervasive social stigma, the mentally ill are frequently subjected to loss of rights and opportunities. The efforts of the alliance will be bolstered by recent federal initiatives to assess and promulgate effective models of advocacy.

HERBERT PARDES
National Institute of Mental Health

MEDICINE AND HEALTH—SPECIAL REPORT:

Cigarette Smoking

The 1979 U. S. Surgeon General's Report on Smoking and Health affirmed what the experts have been saying for years—that smoking is hazardous to health. The 1,200-page tome, a summary of some 30,000 scientific studies, documented that in the United States smoking is the number one health problem and largest preventable cause of death, linking it to lung cancer; cancers of the mouth, esophagus, and bladder; and many kinds of heart disease. In addition diseases caused by smoking account for $5–8 billion of the nation's annual $205 billion health-care bill and result in $12–18 billion more in lost wages and absenteeism.

While earlier reports were uncertain about hazards for women, the new report erased any lingering doubts. The death rate from lung cancer among women smokers increased fivefold in the past 20 years and is continuing to increase at a pace that has caused experts to predict that by the early 1980's lung cancer will overtake malignancies of the breast as the leading cause of cancer among women. And, while overall death rates for women smokers are still lower than for male smokers, women who have smoking habits similar to those of men also have similar death rates.

The report contains specific warnings for younger women who smoke. When women both smoke and use oral contraceptives (containing estrogen), the risk for heart attack and sudden death increases about 10 times. Smoking is particularly dangerous during pregnancy. The offspring of women who smoke are likely to be small and their physical growth, mental development, and behavior can be affected throughout childhood. Also, smoking was found to increase the risk of spontaneous abortion, fetal death, and many complications of pregnancy.

The importance of these findings and their implicit warning was underscored by the statistics showing an eightfold increase between 1968 and 1974 in the number of 12- to 14-year-old girls who smoke, coupled with studies showing that the earlier that smoking begins and the longer it continues, the harder it is to stop.

Other significant report findings included:

—Smoking increases the risk of lung cancer to workers in such industries as asbestos, rubber, coal, textile, uranium, and chemical.

—Smoking deaths are disproportionately high in certain groups. The death rate among black men who smoke is ten times that of white men who smoke. And blue collar workers who smoke have a higher death rate than their non-blue collar counterparts.

—In any year, smokers have a 70% greater risk of dying than non-smokers, a risk that increases to 100% for two pack a day smokers.

—Mortality rates are higher for those who smoke more, inhale, start at a younger age, and use cigarettes with higher tar and nicotine content.

There was also some good news. Government figures showed that within one year the total smoking consumption in the United States had dropped by some two billion cigarettes, or 100 million packages, bringing per capita consumption to its lowest levels in 20 years. Among men, the percentage who smoke dropped from 51 in 1965 to less than 38 in 1978. The percentage of women who smoke dropped from 33 to 27 in the same period.

The report was criticized by both industry and anti-smoking groups. Calling it a "rehash" and "a selective review," industry critics claimed that if the relationship between heart disease and infant mortality and smoking is so clear, "then one has to wonder why the death rate for both is dropping."

Anti-smoking groups argued that the report did not go far enough. They said it failed to document that smoking can be as addictive as heroin or to reveal the extent of the health hazards from ambient smoke for non-smokers with allergies, heart, circulatory, and respiratory difficulties.

In addition to the decline in smoking, the number of low tar and nicotine cigarettes has proliferated in the past few years. These "safer" products now account for 35% of the market.

MARY HAGER

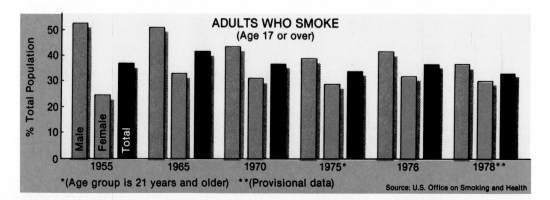

During an eight-day sweep across the Caribbean and the U. S. eastern seaboard in August, Hurricane David left more than 1,100 persons dead and billions of dollars in damage.

METEOROLOGY

The great Global Atmospheric Research Program (GARP) got fully underway in 1979. It is the largest international experiment ever undertaken, using 10 satellites, 50 research vessels, 110 airplanes, 300 high-altitude drifting balloons, and 300 drifting buoys in the southern oceans. In a concerted attack on the problems of forecasting weather, both for a given day and for two weeks in advance, 40,000 observations daily reached forecast centers in a smooth flow of data from both hemispheres. Investigations of Asian and African monsoons and polar weather analysis were also carried out. The floating weather buoys were particularly successful at southern hemisphere observational coverage.

The impact of long-neglected atmospheric events south of the equator and in the tropics in general was being investigated. The large-scale wave patterns in the northern hemisphere are notably affected by changes in the tropics, and scientists at the National Center for Atmospheric Research (Boulder, CO) have been able to produce fairly accurate five-day forecasts by using global instead of only hemispheric data.

Large mountain ranges have also been shown to affect the wave number in the wind flow around the hemisphere. These very long waves tend to move westward with periods of 5 or 15 days. In one case a 5-day wave was followed by 18 circles around the hemisphere—a period of 90 days. If such persistence could be recognized the timing of disturbed weather could also be predicted with greater precision.

Notable effects of sea ice on atmospheric circulation have been discovered. The formation of the ice in the fall affects temperatures up to several months later.

For the public, especially farmers, a new television-type weather information scheme was being tested in two Kentucky counties. It linked television sets, a data processor, and telephone lines to forecast centers. The rapid transmission of information on current and expected weather should help farmers plan their operations better. Another video relay of satellite data was underway at Colorado State University. Dubbed ADVISAR (All Digital Video Imaging System for Atmospheric Research), it permits enhanced imaging of cloud conditions in various hues. This detailed visual representation is especially designed as guidance for cloud seeding activities to increase rainfall.

A new satellite in the Tyros-N series, NOAA-6, was launched on June 27, 1979, to improve surveillance of the ocean-atmosphere system. NOAA-6 monitors the intensity of incoming solar radiation and in addition to providing the usual weather data, will collect and relay data on sea surface temperatures, water vapor concentration, and wave heights from the buoys and balloons. In the meantime Nimbus 6 continued to gather data on the earth radiation budget in an 18-month interval. Since its launching in 1975 it has fixed the average heat loss of planet Earth at 234 watts per square meter and the reflectivity for incoming solar radiation at 31%. The scanning microwave spectrometer on Nimbus 6 has also provided useful information on typhoon winds that are comparable to those obtained by reconnaissance aircraft. High frequency radio and optical receivers on satellites also have given superior data on global lighting frequency.

The difficult job of issuing tornado warnings and improving understanding of severe local storms has been aided by Doppler radar. This device can measure wind speeds at many points inside the storm systems. The equipment measures hundreds of thousands of frequency changes per minute caused by motion of cloud particles. Through new computers and electronic displays it has become possible to probe the interior of storms. Tornado warnings can be issued 20 to 30 minutes earlier than heretofore in areas guarded by Doppler radar. These de-

Wichita Falls, TX, is a disaster area after a tornado took 44 lives and destroyed 2,000 homes.

Malibu, CA, August 1979. High winds and a long drought intensified forest fires in 8 Western states.

vices can also be used in cloud-free areas to estimate low-level wind conditions by watching the motion of dust particles. This permits discovery of violent downward motions of air and intense wind shear near the surface. To warn landing aircraft of sudden intense shifts in wind speed and direction, the Federal Aviation Administration plans installation of experimental alerting systems for such events at several airports. Such shifts in the past have caused serious accidents.

Doppler radar can also spot lightning at distances as far away as 180 km (110 mi). Traffic controllers can thus reroute airplanes.

No major weather modification projects were reported but new substances affecting cloud, rain, and ice crystal formation were evaluated. Among these was aluminum sulfide, which acts as a freezing nucleus at $-3.5°$ C ($26°$ F) and appears to be a highly efficient substance for initiating precipitation in sub-cooled clouds. Other research on rain formation disclosed important effects of turbulence within clouds. Turbulent collisions enhance the growth process of cloud droplets.

Man-made pollution also interferes with precipitation processes. Experiments in the Los Angeles area have shown that traffic smog pollution tends to inhibit precipitation, but nuclei coming from oil refineries tend to create larger droplets in clouds and thus promote rainfall from clouds under the influence of their plumes. In the Soviet Union, large black experimental balloons, intensely heated by solar radiation, have been suspended over polluted areas of the city of Alma Ata and have created vertical air currents which carry the pollutants aloft.

Some of the predicted effects of pollutants on the stratospheric ozone layers appeared to be less than anticipated. The oxides of nitrogen appeared to have no negative effect in the lower stratosphere. Chlorine monoxide, a decay product of fluorocarbons, formerly used in spray cans, has also caused less ozone destruction than present knowledge of atmospheric chemistry suggests it will.

The impact of rising climatic fluctuations has prompted a number of actions. The National Climate Program Act of 1978 (Public Law 95-367) has resulted in preparation of a five-year plan for accelerated research and improved services by the U. S. government. The energy crisis has prompted meteorologists to initiate a major study of the potential effects of increased carbon dioxide (CO_2) concentration in the atmosphere. Continued and increasing use of fossil fuels is expected to lead to a doubling of pre-industrial CO_2 in the next five decades. Mathematical models indicate that this will lead to a global warming of 2 to $3°$ C ($4–5°$ F), with the major effect felt in polar regions where a temperature rise of $6–10°$ C ($11–18°$F) will melt large ice masses. Some scientists predict drastic global changes in climate.

The Eighth World Meteorological Congress, which met in Geneva in May 1979, also approved a world-wide program of research and applications of climatology. The Congress elected Dr. R. L. Kintanar of the Philippines and Dr. A. Wijn-Nielsen of Denmark as its president and secretary-general, respectively.

H. E. Landsberg
Professor Emeritus, University of Maryland

The Weather Year

The weather year was marked by major tropical storms and the failure of the East Asian monsoon.

December 1978–February 1979. For many sections of the United States, the winter of 1978–1979 was one of the coldest and snowiest on record. Satellite measurements revealed that more of North America was covered by snow in the last month of 1978 than in 13 previous Decembers. Exceptional cold was recorded from the Rocky Mountain States, across the Great Plains, to the Midwestern States. Minimum temperature records, some of which had been set only the previous winter, were broken in many areas. In Montana, Wyoming, Colorado, Nebraska, and South Dakota, it was not uncommon for average temperatures to reach 12° F (6.7° C) below average.

Frequent storms crossed the midsection of the country, bringing high winds and heavy snows to the Ohio Valley Region. By the end of February, Chicago had received an incredible 87.4 inches (222 cm) of snow. In mid-February, a large snowstorm traveled up the Eastern seaboard, closing airports, canceling schools, and stranding travelers from Georgia to New England. Washington, DC, received 19.7 inches (50 cm) from the storm, its worst since 1922.

Record cold also affected Europe, Scandinavia, and the western USSR. Moscow recorded its coldest temperatures, −40° F (−40° C), in nearly a hundred years. Snowfalls were frequent and heavy in the British Isles and on the western European continent. Snow fell on the French Riviera and in Sicily for the first time in a quarter century. Dry weather plagued Zambia, Australia, and Brazil. Crop losses were estimated at $1 billion (U. S.) in Rio Grande do Sul, a major grain-producing province in southern Brazil.

March–May. Spring was generally mild and wet from the Ohio Valley eastward to the Atlantic coast and from the Rocky Mountains westward to the Pacific shore. Only the Great Plains experienced relatively cool weather; North Dakota averaged 4° F (2.2° C) below normal. During March, precipitation was as high as 300% of average in New England, the Great Plains, the Middle Atlantic region, the northern Great Lakes, and parts of the South. In April, there was extensive flooding of the Mississippi Valley. The Pearl River crested at 43 ft (13 m) in Jackson, MI, with statewide damage estimated at $700 million. In Canada, North Dakota, and Minnesota, the Red River crested at 21 ft (6.4 m) above flood stage.

Overall, tornado activity was low. However, on April 10, a devastating tornado hit northern Texas, killing 60 people (45 of them in the small town of Witchita Falls) and injuring 1,000 others.

In Europe, spring was cool and wet, with temperatures averaging 5° F (2.7° C) below normal and precipitation averaging one inch (2.5 cm) per week. Widespread flooding in eastern and central Poland inundated 2 million acres (810 000 ha) of farmland in late March. In the third week of May, temperatures 6° F (3.3° C) below average were recorded in the British Isles. Parts of southern England and northwestern France were entering their fifth consecutive month of below-normal temperatures and fourth straight month of above-normal precipitation.

June–August. The first two months of summer brought cool temperatures to the eastern United States, with slightly warmer readings along the West Coast and in the Intermountain Region. August temperatures were above average along the Atlantic seaboard and the upper Pacific Northwest. Precipitation was heavy throughout the lower Mississippi Valley. Texas and Louisiana were hit by heavy rains from tropical storm Claudette in the third week of July, with flash floods resulting in many areas. Drier than average conditions were prevalent west of the Rockies during the first half of the season, becoming wetter than average during August. Elsewhere, precipitation was generally above average.

In India, the summer monsoon season began two to three weeks late. Rainfall was as much as 50% below average in northern portions of the country. A heat wave in the same region produced temperatures of up to 118° F (48° C). In mid-July, a tropical depression brought 20.6 inches (52 cm) of rain in 24 hours to the town of Morvi. Western Pacific typhoons produced torrential rains in the Philippines, coastal China, Hong Kong, South Korea, and Japan. By the end of July, areas in the southern Japanese island of Kyushu had received almost 50 inches (127 cm) of rain.

Summer temperatures in Europe were near average, with precipitation heavy over Scandinavia and northern portions of the USSR. Parts of Spain, Portugal, and France experienced continuing dry weather. Hot, dry conditions in the Soviet provinces of the Ukraine and Kazakhstan played havoc with the wheat crop.

Hurricane David brought death and destruction to the Lesser and Greater Antilles during the last days of August. Maximum winds of 150 miles (241 km) per hour and a central pressure of 27.29 inches (924 mb) caused this storm to be labeled one of the "most ferocious of this century."

September–November. The western half of the United States was warmer than average during the first two months of autumn, becoming cooler than average in November. Temperatures in the East were below average during the first third of the season, but November was a record warm month for much of the region. Precipitation was heavy over the eastern third of the country and in the coastal regions of Oregon and northern California. Heavy rains associated with Hurricane Frederic drenched many parts of the lower Mississippi Valley.

A powerful snowstorm swept through Wyoming and Colorado during the third week of November. Cheyenne, WY, received a record 20 inches (51 cm) of snow on November 20; drifts up to 8 ft (2.4 m) high were common.

A stationary high pressure ridge in the Los Angeles basin brought record high temperatures and heavy smog in mid-September.

Hurricane Frederic, one of the Gulf of Mexico's most intense storms in the last 100 years, slammed into the Gulf Coast near Mobile, AL, on September 12. Winds of 130 miles (209 km) per hour, heavy rains, and tornadoes spawned by the storm combined to produce damages estimated at $2 billion. There were few fatalities, primarily due to advance warning and prompt evacuation. October was an active tornado month, with 40 twisters, twice the climatological average. Seven people were killed by these storms.

Autumn temperatures throughout central Europe and Scandinavia were slightly below average. Northwestern Europe was drier than average, but the Iberian Peninsula, Germany, Czechoslovakia, Turkey, and Yugoslavia received heavy rains. Flooding problems were reported in the latter two nations.

Northwestern and north central India and Pakistan faced serious drought as the monsoon retreated approximately three weeks earlier than average.

The Philippines, Southeast Asia, and Japan continued to feel the effects of typhoons and tropical storms. The Royal Observatory at Hong Kong reported 42 inches (107 cm) of rain during the seven-week period from August to September 10. Japan was particularly hard hit by Typhoon Tip, October 17–19.

IDA HAKKARINEN

More than 17,000 persons were left homeless in Jackson, MS, when the Pearl River crested at record levels in April.

Strong winds and unusually high seas halted the 605 mile (970 km) yacht race from the Isle of Wight to Fastnet Rock off the Irish coast. At least 18 participants drowned and some 40 yachts were lost. Helicopters transported rescued yachtsmen to the Royal Navy's Air Station at Culdrose (left).

Life in Chicago came to a virtual halt as a record snow of nearly 90 inches (229 cm) fell on the city as the year opened.

MEXICO

Increased oil and gas revenues, skillful government planning and economic stimulation, and President José López Portillo's restoration of business confidence produced an economic boom in 1979. Domestic tranquility and energy resources were the foundations of a new assertiveness in foreign policy, as visiting U. S. President Jimmy Carter discovered in February.

Mexico played a key role in the late-year Iranian crisis, when it refused to allow deposed Shah Mohammed Reza Pahlevi to regain asylum after undergoing cancer treatment in New York City. Since mid-June, the former shah had been living in Cuernevaca under a tourist visa granted by the Mexican government (*see* IRAN).

Politics. In congressional elections held July 1, the ruling Institutional Revolutionary Party (PRI) won 296 of the first 300 seats in the Chamber of Deputies, the lower house of the National Congress. The centrist opposition National Action Party (PAN) won only 4 seats, a loss of 16 from the previous chamber. However, election reforms adopted in 1978 called for the expansion of the chamber to 400 seats. The 100 additional seats were to be apportioned to the minority fringe parties. On the basis of the vote in three regional districts, the PAN won 39 of the new seats, the Mexican Communist Party (PCM) took 18, the Popular Socialist Party (PPM) 12, the Authentic Party of the Mexican Revolution (PARM) 11, the Socialist Workers' Party (PST) 10, and the Mexican Democratic Party (PDM) 10.

The new election laws also stipulated that opposition parties had to win 1.5% of the popular vote in order to gain permanent recognition and be able to enter a candidate in the 1982 presidential election. The Communist party, which was allowed to run congressional candidates for the first time in decades, captured 5% of the vote and emerged as the country's third largest political party. Also winning permanent registration were the PST and PDM.

Although voting is compulsory in Mexico, between 40 and 50% of eligible voters did not take part in the election. The showing was disappointing for the government, which hoped for a large turnout in support of its policies.

In other political developments, López Portillo pursued his efforts to make the government more efficient and responsive to the needs of the people. In May, he reshuffled the cabinet to create a team more supportive of his own domestic planning and foreign policy initiatives. Efforts continued to decentralize the national government by moving key offices out of Mexico City, opening branches in other principal cities, and giving more authority to state governments. In May, the López Portillo administration stepped up its campaign against government corruption. A new law defined more precisely the responsibilities of federal employees and made it easier for them to be dismissed. Government workers earning 15,000 pesos a month or less were granted a 13.5% salary increase, while those earning more received a smaller percentage. These pay hikes also served as a wage guideline for Mexican labor unions. Similar increases were awarded to retired government workers, and new legislation doubled the value of social security pensions. López Portillo announced that since 1978 a total of 1,539 prisoners, many of them incarcerated for political reasons, had been pardoned.

Economic Policy. In 1979 the rate of inflation in Mexico was less than 20%, only about half the rate of 1978. Still, the government sought to counter inflationary pressures and further industrialize the economy by redoubling its efforts to increase production. There was continued emphasis on the Alliance for Production, calling for cooperation among business, industry,

A booming oil industry helped boost other sectors of the Mexican economy and brought new confidence to the nation's foreign policy.

Cuban President Fidel Castro, *left*, meets with Mexican President José López Portillo on the island of Cozumel in May. Castro's two-day visit was his first to Mexico in 23 years.

UPI

labor, agriculture, and government. This was augmented by the $15-billion (U. S.) National Industrial Development Plan (1979–1990), the first such program to extend beyond a single presidential term.

Mexican economic policy again sought to curb runaway inflation and avoid the economic distortions threatened by vast new revenues from petroleum sales. Oil revenues were invested in other areas of the economy to increase and diversify production. López Portillo funded increases to the fishing industry to boost exports and increase domestic consumption. In agriculture, the government announced plans to guarantee the production of basic subsistence commodities and to increase the supply of raw materials for foreign trade and domestic use. Long-term policies called for a decrease in consumer subsidies, concentration on high-yield crops, and increased imports of more basic foodstuffs. To promote tourism, the government passed a new law providing for the improvement and creation of tourist facilities and sites. A new vacation policy for federal employees was expected to enhance the domestic tourist industry.

Budget. The 1979 budget of $54.7 billion (U. S.) was structured primarily to foster the economic growth rate (about 7.5% during the year). Some 24% of the expenditures was to be spent on expanding industrial production; 23.4% on debt service; 10.7% on health care and social security; 8.9% on education, culture, science, and technology; 6.4% on agriculture and forestry; and the rest on a variety of other programs and institutions. Significantly, expenditures for fisheries and human resettlement were increased by 54.5%, while industrial expenditures, already large, were increased by 31%. Investments accounted for more than 21% of the total expenditure. The tax on mercantile income was replaced by a value added tax of 10%;

along the U. S.-Mexican border, however, the rate was set at 6% to stimulate manufacturing.

Social Policy. To relieve overcrowding on Mexico's central plateau, the government encouraged families to resettle in the humid tropics. A new antimonopoly law, prescribing criminal penalties for truth in packaging violations and failure to use maximum price labels, was enacted to protect consumers. As part of a national effort to increase the number and effectiveness of teachers, the new Pedagogical University was opened in the spring. Rural medical clinics, which numbered 2,000 by the end of the year, brought health protection to 10 million Mexicans who had no such care in the past. In 1979, more than half the national population was covered by social security.

Energy Policy. In September 1979, President López Portillo called on the United Nations to develop an international energy policy to protect the rights of individual producing nations and to end world overdependence on oil and gas. Mexico has proven crude oil reserves of 45.8 billion barrels, enough to meet domestic needs for an estimated 60 years. The government admitted having potential reserves of more than 200 billion barrels, equal to those of Saudi Arabia, but some geologists estimated Mexico's potential at 700 billion barrels, equal to that of the entire Middle East. Regardless, López Portillo restated his government's determination to follow a balanced energy policy. Mexican gas and oil resources would be exploited at a rate sufficient only to meet domestic needs and to close the nation's trade gap. Gas and oil exports would be priced at prevailing world market values.

Foreign Affairs. Pope John Paul II was enthusiastically received by the Mexican people when he arrived January 26 to open the third (continued on page 338)

During a diplomatically difficult visit to Mexico in February 1979, President and Mrs. Carter visited a local farm.

The flow of Mexicans into the United States, many of whom can find work only as farmhands, is a volatile issue between Mexico and the United States. Mexico has long been a favorite spot for the American traveler.

U.S.-Mexican Relations

The cool but correct reception given U. S. President Jimmy Carter on his state visit to Mexico Feb. 14–16, 1979, served notice that the United States could no longer treat Mexico as a client state. During that visit, Mexican President López Portillo emphasized that agreements had to be reached on numerous issues, not just the sale of oil and natural gas. López Portillo demanded "definitive agreements, not circumstantial concessions" and warned against "surprise moves and sudden deceit or abuse." Carter emphasized that the United States, too, was interested in settling differences and would no longer treat Mexico as a junior partner. Surprised at the forcefulness of Portillo's remarks at a luncheon, Carter tried but failed to ease the tension with an unfortunate pun about "Montezuma's Revenge." The two presidents agreed to meet again later in the year, after diplomatic aides had completed negotiations on natural gas pricing.

Although Mexican suspicion of the United States is long-standing, the events of the last ten years have brought it to a head. In 1969, former U. S. President Richard Nixon ordered a car-by-car drug search at the Mexican border, which disrupted traffic and cost businesses on both sides millions of tourist dollars. The same year, Nixon waited eight months before appointing a replacement for the departing U. S. ambassador. In 1971 he imposed an import surcharge without warning the Mexican government. After taking office in 1977, President Carter tried to ease strained relations by making López Portillo his first invitee for a state visit to Washington. In August, however, Carter sent to Congress a proposal on illegal aliens without consulting Mexico, as he had promised. In December, then Secretary of Energy James Schlesinger canceled a contract for the sale of natural gas to U. S. companies, despite the fact that Mexico had begun construction of a pipeline to the United States. More recently, Washington refused to return uranium sent by Mexico to the United States to be enriched for use in a nuclear power plant, claiming that the southern nation had inadequate security arrangements.

Dividing the two nations are a number of issues: trade policy, energy prices, smuggling, and the influx of illegal aliens into the United States. Because of high unemployment and comparatively low wages in their own country, millions of Mexicans have illegally crossed the border and obtained work in the United States. Washington has long attempted to stop the flow of illegal aliens and to encourage those present to leave. Mexico contends that it cannot reabsorb these people without economic chaos. It argues also that the problem must be solved by easing trade restrictions against Mexican products, thereby allowing industry and agriculture to expand and create new jobs at home. Washington wants Mexico to lower its tariffs, but Mexico hesitates for fear that increased imports would undermine its producers. In exchange for further Mexican aid in halting the flow of marijuana and narcotics into the United States, López Portillo wants the U. S. government to take steps to stop the smuggling of American merchandise across the border.

Mexico's vast oil supply—reserves of up to 200 million barrels, one of the highest in the world—and its natural gas resources stir the most attention in the energy-hungry United States. Mexico charges the world market (OPEC) price for oil, but its proximity means lower transportation costs for the United States. Suddenly courted by the world's industrialized nations, Mexico patiently bargains for deals which will help solve its economic problems.

Despite international bargaining power, the Mexican economy remains heavily dependent on the United States and has much to gain from increased trade with its northern neighbor. The United States, recognizing Mexican skittishness, has done little to dispel the impression of its economic leverage. This disposition has been the cause of some tension. President Carter initiated new negotiations for the purchase of natural gas, even though an angry López Portillo vowed after the 1977 cancellation that Mexico would use the gas domestically. Negotiations stalled in August 1979, when Mexico tried to tie its prices to that of No. 2 fuel oil in New York to guarantee profits against future inflation. However, on September 21, the two nations reached agreement on the sale of some 300 million cubic feet per day of Mexican natural gas to U. S. companies.

Beyond oil and gas, the United States has much to gain from Mexico, and its large stake in that nation demands that cordial relations be maintained. Mexico is the fifth largest trading partner of the United States, with more than $9 billion in goods being exchanged. In addition, the United States has more than $4.5 billion invested in Mexico; private and government-sponsored loans total more than $15 billion.

Future relations between the two nations depend upon the willingness of both to bargain realistically and openly. A new attitude was suggested by U. S. patience when the blowout of a Mexican oil well fouled the Texas shoreline in the summer of 1979. The agreement on natural gas in September and a state visit to Washington by López Portillo later that month boded well for the future of Mexican-U. S. relations.

DONALD J. MABRY

─────── MEXICO · Information Highlights ───────
Official Name: The United Mexican States.
Location: Southern North America.
Area: 761,602 square miles (1 972 549 km²).
Population (1979 est.): 67,700,000.
Chief Cities (1977 est.): Mexico City, the capital, 8,-785,236; Guadalajara, 1,724,656; Monterrey, 1,041,-565.
Government: *Head of state and government,* José López Portillo, president (took office Dec. 1976). *Legislature*—Congress: Senate and Chamber of Deputies.
Monetary Unit: Peso (22.86 pesos equal U. S.$1, Oct. 1979).
Manufactures (major products): Processed foods, chemicals, basic metals and metal products, petroleum products.
Agriculture (major products): Corn, cotton, sugarcane, wheat, coffee.

meeting of the Latin American Episcopal Conference (CELAM) in Puebla. Huge throngs, estimated in the millions, cheered the pontiff as he traveled throughout the nation for six days. Although 90% of the population is Roman Catholic, there is a strong tradition of anticlericalism in Mexican government and the country has no formal diplomatic relations with the Vatican. Consequently, President López Portillo could not greet the pope in an official capacity.

U. S.-Mexican relations showed improvement by year's end (*see* Special Report, page 336).

Leaders of other nations also visited Mexico during the year, most of them seeking access to Mexican hydrocarbons. French President Valéry Giscard D'Estaing promised increased trade and continued technological assistance in the construction of nuclear power plants, while carefully avoiding pressing Mexico for more oil. López Portillo and Cuba's Fidel Castro agreed to exchange technical experts, but Mexico refused to endorse the resolutions adopted by the Conference of Nonaligned Nations held in Havana later in the year.

DONALD J. MABRY
Mississippi State University

MICHIGAN

Economic problems, affecting both the private and public sectors, claimed major attention in Michigan during 1979.

Economy. Wayne County, which includes the city of Detroit, failed to issue paychecks for 3,000 of its 5,300 employees on October 19, but made the payments late. Other payrolls also were late as the county fought a continuing cash crisis. The crisis had been predicted for months, after the state Municipal Finance Commission denied the county permission to borrow against 1979–80 revenues to cover its deficit. Many, including Gov. William G. Milliken, saw the crisis as the result of the county's diffuse governmental structure and chaotic bureaucracy. The governor appointed a special task force to assess the problem and recommend solutions. The commission suggested that there be an elected, mayor-like executive to centralize authority and responsibility.

In an effort to balance the Detroit budget, which faced a deficit of $68 million, Mayor Coleman Young ordered the layoffs of 1,238 city workers, including 400 policemen. The layoffs, coupled with a freeze on hiring, reduced the number of city employees from 26,000 to 22,900.

Michigan's largest city was given a boost, however, by the August 20 opening of the Philip A. Hart Plaza, whose centerpiece is the Dodge Fountain. The nearby Joe Louis Sports Arena also was completed in 1979 and helped attract the 1980 Republican National Convention to Detroit.

The state's automotive industry also faced major crises in 1979. Chrysler Corporation projected a loss of $1 billion in 1979 and asked the federal government for loan guarantees to help the company avoid bankruptcy (*see* BUSINESS AND CORPORATE AFFAIRS). Chrysler announced several cost-cutting moves, including the shutdown of its Hamtramck·assembly plant, and rebates of up to $400 on the purchase of large cars and trucks. The United Auto Workers (UAW) made concessions in labor contract negotiations. Meanwhile, the Ford Motor Company and General Motors Corporation reached contract agreements with the UAW shortly before strike deadlines.

Miscellaneous. The effects of the chemical PBB (polybrominated biphenyl) on the health of Michigan residents was reported in 1979. PBB has been a controversial issue since 1973, when the chemical was accidentally mixed with animal feed which contaminated much of the state's livestock. The new study reported no short-term effects, but stated that the long-term effects could not yet be determined. According to the study, 90% of Michigan residents retained some PBB in their bodies but none of the chemical remained in the food.

In September, teacher strikes delayed the opening of public schools for an estimated 240,000 students. The longest strike, in Detroit, lasted 17 days.

Governor Milliken twice vetoed legislative attempts to cut off welfare payments for abortions. The state Court of Appeals upheld the governor in a September 5 decision.

CHARLES THEISEN, *The Detroit News*

─────── MICHIGAN · Information Highlights ───────
Area: 58,216 square miles (150 779 km²).
Population (Jan. 1979 est.): 9,211,000.
Chief Cities (1976 est.): Lansing, the capital, 126,071; Detroit, 1,314,206; Grand Rapids, 185,558.
Government (1979): *Chief Officers*—governor, William G. Milliken (R). *Legislature*—Senate, 38 members; House of Representatives, 110 members.
Education (1978–79): *Enrollment*—public elementary schools, 961,821 pupils; public secondary, 949,524; colleges and universities, 485,292 students. *Public school expenditures,* $3,959,295,000.
State Finances (fiscal year 1978): *Revenues,* $10,505,-213,000; *expenditures,* $9,490,177,000.
Personal Income (1978): $77,943,000,000; per capita, $8,483.
Labor Force (June 1979): *Nonagricultural wage and salary earners,* 3,638,400; *unemployed,* 316,900 (7.2% of total force).

MICROBIOLOGY

In 1979, microbiologists made significant progress toward solving a variety of problems affecting the quality of everyday life. Noteworthy developments were reported in research on tumor formation, the production of human growth hormone, alternate fuel supplies, disease control, the breakdown of PCB, and the behavior of bacteria.

Tumor-inducing Viruses. For the first time scientists identified a specific biochemical change as a key process in the formation of tumors. Raymond L. Erickson of the University of Colorado Medical School determined the mechanism by which the sarcoma virus causes tumors in several different animals. A similar mechanism was detected by David Baltimore of the Massachusetts Institute of Technology (MIT) for a leukemia virus in mice. In the infected cells, each virus produces, according to directions encoded in its own genetic material, an enzyme that catalyzes the transfer of phosphate groups to protein. The enzymes produced by the viruses are very similar to enzymes found in normal cells. However, in a cell made cancerous by these viruses, the virus-encoded enzyme is present in far greater amounts than the normal cellular enzyme. Erickson speculated that the malignant change is the result of an extra dose of enzyme overriding the cell's normal growth controls.

Growth Hormone and Recombinant DNA Research. Human growth hormone was produced by genetically engineered bacteria in two laboratories. A bacterial source for that material is of great medical importance because there is currently no adequate substitute. The hormone currently is obtained from cadavers. It is essential in the treatment of children with pituitary dwarfism, a rare genetic condition, and has also shown potential for controlling gastrointestinal bleeding and healing burns. The two laboratories—one at Genentech, a small company in San Francisco, and the other at the University of California at San Francisco—made arrangements with drug companies for the further development of related recombinant DNA techniques.

Recombinant DNA research passed risk-assessment experiments both at the U. S. National Institutes of Health (NIH) and in Great Britain. Scientists discovered that genes from a cancer-causing virus in mice did not infect animals fed or injected with bacteria containing the viral genes in recombinant DNA molecules. This result reassured scientists of the safety of experiments using recombinant DNA in the bacterium *Escherichia coli* K 12. The NIH advisory committee on recombinant DNA research proposed a relaxation of its guidelines.

Alcohol Production. The 1979 petroleum shortage focused attention on the need for economical alternative fuels. At the annual meeting of the American Society for Microbiology, scientists suggested new approaches to bacterial ethanol production. Such ethanol would be useful for making industrial raw materials and for combining with gasoline to make "gasohol." Jurgen Wiegel and Lars G. Ljungdahl of the University of Georgia reported the isolation of two promising new strains of bacteria from hot springs at Yellowstone National Park (WY). The bacteria live without oxygen at temperatures of up to 200° F (93° C). A wide range of sugars and even cellulose can be used by these bacteria as the raw material for producing ethanol. The high temperature would be an advantage in industrial production of alcohol because it would discourage contamination by other microorganisms and allow distillation of ethanol during fermentation. Other scientists at the meeting described a technique for obtaining alcohols from microorganisms trapped in polymer lattices. Ethanol was produced continuously for several months from immobilized yeast and amino acid from immobilized bacteria.

PCB Breakdown. Natural bacteria were found to be capable of decomposing polychlorinated biphenyls (PCBs), extremely stable compounds harmful to human health. Chemical procedures have failed to degrade these dangerous compounds, which have found their way into water supplies and fish sold at market. However, in 1979, scientists at the University of Georgia examined 13 species of *Bacillus* bacteria isolated from a local sewer system and found two species capable of breaking down most of the PCBs in a commercial mixture.

Diseases. Among the important medical advances of 1979 was the success of a new drug, 2-deoxy-D-glucose, in the treatment of genital herpes. This disease, for which there had been no satisfactory therapy, can cause the death of fetuses and may be linked with cervical cancer. Another significant development was a report from the U. S. Center for Disease Control (CDC) of a rapid technique for diagnosing Legionnaires' Disease from simple sputum samples. CDC scientists also developed an experimental vaccine using material from bacterial strains less virulent than those that cause the human disease.

Bacteria with Compasses. Bacteria found in such diverse places as the Baltic Sea, San Francisco Bay, and a Cape Cod swamp may share the tendency to swim in a northerly direction. Richard B. Frankel of MIT and collaborators reported how these microorganisms chart their course. Each bacterium picks up from its surroundings a chain of cubic crystals made of magnetite, the iron oxide used to make early compasses. When magnetotactic bacteria were grown for several generations in an iron-deficient medium, they could no longer orient in a magnetic field. When scientists changed the polarity of the internal magnets, the bacteria swam south instead of north. Frankel suggested that the bacteria use their magnets not to navigate the globe, but for vertical orientation.

Julie Ann Miller, *"Science News"*

MIDDLE EAST

In December 1978, when the Saudi Arabian ambassador hosted a dinner in honor of the departing Pakistani ambassador, he expressed the view that the outlook in the Middle East was extremely ominous. "Our friends do not seem to realize," he said, "that a crisis of historic magnitude is close at hand for the Western world and for those who share its values in our entire area." The guest of honor endorsed his view: "I fear that historians will look back at 1978 as a watershed year when the balance of power shifted against the Western world."

Nothing in the succeeding twelve months suggested that these apprehensions were in any way exaggerated. On the contrary, events in the Middle East in 1979 reinforced the view that, in the words of Winston Churchill, "the sky was dark with chickens coming home to roost." Western interests in the Middle East were manifestly in the gravest peril. This area, which is the main source of oil for Japan and Western Europe and an important source for the United States, was beset by threats—and in some instances more than threats—of internal instability and revolutionary changes prejudicial to every government of a friendly or even moderate character. There was hardly a single country or a single part of the region that could be viewed with complacency.

Undoubtedly, there had been too much complacency in the past. The ominous situation had been created by a lack of willingness to look at long-term problems and by a frivolous disregard of the underlying realities of geopolitics and power. The situation was not altogether beyond remedy, but any improvement would call for a will and a consistency of purpose on the part of the democratic West, especially the United States, that might or might not be present.

Main Foci of Events. The one reasonably encouraging development in this gloomy scene was provided in 1979 by the conclusion of the Egyptian-Israeli peace treaty. The series of events leading to and resulting from its signing on March 26 was the focus of attention in the first half of the year. Later, other matters thrust themselves forward with such urgent importunity that the Arab-Israeli conflict went somewhat into eclipse. Three other questions of peculiarly comfortless kind came to the fore. These were the developments in Iran, in Saudi Arabia, and in Afghanistan. Iran, of course, had been an area of instability and rapid change from the beginning of the year, but it was only toward the end of 1979 that events there rose to crisis level. Saudi Arabia's monarchical structure, although unchanged at the end of the year, experienced a terrorist attack that was violently traumatic and raised questions about the future of the country. Finally, in the last week of the year, the explosion of Soviet power in Afghanistan caused a shock wave that rippled around the world and led to some basic reassessments.

Peace between Egypt and Israel. The conclusion of a peace treaty between Egypt and Israel was above all the achievement of three men —Egyptian President Anwar el-Sadat, Israeli Prime Minister Menahem Begin, and U. S. President Jimmy Carter. Without a great deal of courage and determination on the part of all three it simply would not have been accomplished. The signing of the treaty in Washington was certainly a unique historical landmark—the first peace treaty ever signed by the state of Israel and an Arab country. It ended the state of war that had existed between the two countries for more than 30 years. There was no reason to suppose, either in the preliminary negotiations, or in the aftermath, that henceforth all would be friendship and good will, and the reaction of the rest of the Arab world was almost unanimously hostile. Nevertheless, it was a remarkable achievement.

Preceding Negotiations. The basis for the final treaty had, of course, been laid in the Camp

PHOTOS UPI

The Egyptian cabinet, chaired by Prime Minister Mustafa Khalil (*left*), announced its approval of the peace treaty with Israel March 15. The Israeli cabinet, *below*, followed suit four days later.

David framework agreements signed in Washington in September 1978. The major compromises, concessions, silences, and omissions of the Camp David accords formed the basis of the treaty, with some passages reproduced verbatim. Aside from substantive issues resolved through negotiation, the Camp David accords and peace treaty were made possible by certain facts of political life. Sadat and Begin both recognized that peace between their countries would be a prize worth buying, even at a high price. For Sadat a large part of the price would be the hostility of the Arab world for what it viewed as his "betrayal." For Begin, similar accusations of betrayal would come from the more intransigent members of his own right wing Likud party. To achieve peace, Sadat was prepared to limit his support to the Palestinian cause, while Begin was constrained, however reluctantly, to accept a somewhat vague formula for the future "autonomy" of the West Bank and Gaza and (the greatest concession of all) to withdraw from the Sinai peninsula acquired in 1967.

The Golan Heights were not mentioned, and on the future of Jerusalem the two parties simply recorded their strong differences.

After the Camp David accords, the peace treaty negotiations had to be prolonged several times and were frequently on the verge of breaking down altogether. In retrospect, this was somewhat surprising. The remaining points at issue were not truly of major importance, but they did prove effective stumbling-blocks. The target date that had been set at Camp David for the conclusion of a peace treaty—December 17—was not met. Alfred Atherton, the U. S. assistant secretary of state, conducted "shuttle diplomacy" in the Middle East from January 16 to 28, but without concrete results. It took the personal initiative of President Carter—as it had the previous autumn—to move things off dead center. His mission to Egypt and Israel, March 5–13, succeeded in resolving the major issues still outstanding and prepared the way for the ceremonial signing in Washington on March 26.

The most significant points settled during this last period of negotiation are mostly reflected in the annexed "understandings" that accompany the treaty. These issues concerned: first, the extent of "linkage" between the treaty and actual progress toward self-government for the Palestinians. This was really a post–Camp David afterthought that Sadat had brought forward in the last months of 1978. Israel, backed on this point by the United States, was dead against making normal peaceful relations and the exchange of ambassadors dependent on the progress of negotiations regarding West Bank and Gaza. The issue was settled in favor of Israel. Second, there was the question of the future availability of oil from the Alma field in the Sinai. Developed by Israel, the Alma field had been supplying about one fifth of the nation's petroleum needs. Israel wanted the guaranteed

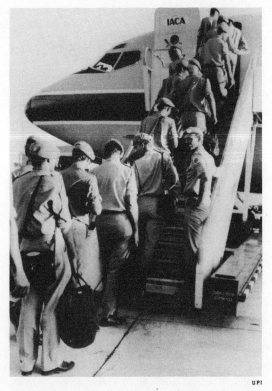

Swedish troops of the UN Emergency Force were the first to leave the Sinai after the lapse of the UNEF mandate.

right to purchase its oil on a preferential basis. All it got was access on a nondiscriminatory basis at world prices. Third, there was the question of whether the treaty should take precedence over treaties with other countries. What this referred to was the possibility that Egypt might feel obliged to help some other Arab country in a war against Israel. This question was left largely unresolved. The language of Article VI, Paragraph 5 and the agreed "minute" on the subject was thought to mean that neither commitment took precedence over the other. A last-minute hitch came up March 24–25 on the question of when the Sinai oilfields should be handed over to Egypt: should it be nine months after ratification of the treaty, as Israel wished, or six, as the Egyptian demanded? The parties compromised on seven.

Protocols of Peace. The protocols of peace constitute a voluminous series of documents running into many thousands of words. There is, first, the "Treaty of Peace between the Arab Republic of Egypt and the State of Israel," supplemented by four annexes, one with maps. Certain articles are supplemented by agreed-upon minutes. Last, there is a set of letters exchanged among the three leaders. To summarize briefly, the key provisions are as follows:

• The state of war between the parties ends with ratification of the treaty. Israel agrees to withdraw its armed forces and settlements from the Sinai and return to Egyptian sovereignty the area up to the boundary of mandated Palestine.

- When the first stage of withdrawal, up to the line El Arish–Ras Mohammed, is completed, normal and friendly relations will be established. This first stage of the Israeli withdrawal returns to Egypt about two thirds of the Sinai.
- UN forces will monitor the agreement in some areas and receive assistance from U. S. surveillance.
- Egypt will end its economic boycott of Israel and would permit free passage of Israeli ships and cargoes through the Suez Canal. Israel may purchase oil from Sinai wells at normal commercial prices.
- Israel and Egypt will start negotiations on autonomy for the Palestinians of Gaza and the West Bank one month after ratification of the treaty.

The supplementary letters ("Memorandums of Understanding") given by the United States to Israel on March 28 provided reassurances to Israel of American support (but no direct promise of military aid) in the event that Egypt should attack Israel and guaranteed that until 1990 the United States would provide Israel needed oil which it could not obtain from other sources. The first of the memorandums evoked from Egypt an angry denunciation of what it regarded as an offensive implication and a one-sided commitment. By the end of the year, however, in the context of the Soviet incursion into Afghanistan, such concerns seemed of little real consequence.

Arab Reaction. Although the rest of the Arab world was not expected to welcome the March 26 peace, the virulence and near-unanimity of its reaction were somewhat unexpected. Especially surprising was the extent to which the reaction was orchestrated by King Hussein of Jordan, conventionally regarded as one of the Arab moderates. Hussein met with the leaders of Iraq, Syria, and the Palestine Liberation Organization (PLO), and on the basis of his contacts a meeting of Arab League ministers was convened in Baghdad, March 27. The conference was attended by 18 member states and the PLO. Although sharp differences developed between moderates and hard-liners, unanimous approval finally was given to resolutions condemning Egypt and projecting a wide-ranging political and economic boycott. Only Sudan and Oman did not oppose the treaty. Even Morocco, which had not objected to the Camp David accords, now joined the anti-Egyptian majority. In the aftermath of these meetings, the Arab countries withdrew their ambassadors from Egypt and the Arab League headquarters were moved from Cairo to Tunis.

On the whole, however, the breach was not so complete nor the damage to Egypt so great as at first appeared possible. Egypt is, after all, by far the most populous and powerful of all the Arab countries. Moreover, Sadat's domestic situation was strengthened by his political adroitness. On April 25 the treaty documents were approved by overwhelming majorities both in the People's Assembly (parliament) and in a national referendum. The return of each slice of territory, especially the Mt. Sinai in November, became a gala event. Economic reports from Egypt in the summer and autumn indicated that the country was in better shape than at any time in the previous decade. It enjoyed a healthy annual growth in productivity of 8 to 9%. Foreign earnings continued to grow and provided a healthy balance of payments surplus. The cutting-off of various forms of continuous assistance from other Arab countries proved to be technically difficult and did not come to pass in some cases.

In 1979, at least, the peace appeared to damage Israel more than Egypt. By the end of the year inflation was running at more than 100%, and the nation's balance of payments deficit was higher than ever. Nor was Prime Minister Begin's political position nearly so secure as that of President Sadat.

In the months following the treaty signing, the various provisions began to be carried out smoothly. The schedule for the Israeli withdrawal was met—at times even accelerated—and two thirds of the Sinai had been returned by year's end. Negotiations began on the central and basically unsolved question of autonomy for Palestinians, but in the face of Israeli concerns over security, the ambiguity of the treaty, and the continuation of Israel's policy of creating new West Bank settlements, they could hardly be said to be going well.

In view of the events in Iran and Afghanistan, Egypt and Israel seemed to draw closer on questions of Mideast security at the very end of the year. Both expressed willingness, even enthusiasm, for having U. S. troops and military bases on their soil. Indeed, it was revealed that U. S. and Egyptian planes had conducted joint exercises in late December.

Impact of Events in Iran. The Iranian revolution, consummated in February by the return from exile of the Ayatollah Ruhollah Khomeini, sent a shock through the whole Middle East. The triumph of Islamic fundamentalism and anti-Western, anti-American policies in so large and important a country as Iran raised the question of whether some kind of political infection might spread such change to other states. On the whole this did not happen in 1979, but the possibility certainly remained. The same kind of strains and tensions that existed in Iran—the conflict between Islamic traditional values and a developing, money-based urban economy—certainly existed elsewhere in all the oil-rich Gulf states. The rulers of these states, too, for the most part enjoy all-too-conspicuous wealth and are largely out of touch with their subjects.

U. S. civil rights spokesman Rev. Jesse Jackson, *left*, one of several black leaders who expressed an interest in increased dialogue between members of the black and Palestinian communities, confers in Beirut with Palestine Liberation Organization leader Yasir Arafat.

UPI

In terms of military security, the end of Iran's role as the bulwark of defense was a disquieting turn of events to the West. The Central Treaty Organization (CENTO) was destroyed, and no obstacle to Communist expansion in the region seemed to exist. Some commentators, however, and perhaps some policy-makers in the United States, saw Egypt as the "new Iran."

Saudi Arabia. Saudi Arabia, the greatest oil supplier of the region and, like Iran, formerly a linchpin of stability in a volatile area, suddenly began to look vulnerable. In a bizarre and unforeseeable episode, the Grand Mosque at Mecca, the holiest shrine in Islam, was seized on November 20 by several hundred militants. Their leader, killed in the ensuing struggle, regarded himself as a mahdi, or messiah, but there were elements in the episode that remained obscure and disquieting. In the protracted two-week battle that followed, 244 militants and security force members were killed. On Jan. 9, 1980, 63 surviving militants were executed by beheading in various cities in Saudi Arabia. They included 41 Saudis, ten Egyptians, six South Yemenis, and three Kuwaitis.

Further disquiet was caused by the December 5 riots in Saudi Arabia's oil-rich eastern provinces. At least five people were killed. Saudi Arabia's vast oil revenues are distributed very unequally among its people, and the country's many immigrant workers are another element of instability. On the other hand, the country does not face the situation which proved disastrous in Iran—a large urban concentration of uprooted peasants.

Year-end Crises. As the year drew to an end, the atmosphere of tension, confusion, and instability in the Middle East became ever more intense. The fighting in the Grand Mosque occurred after the militants in Tehran had seized the American embassy (November 4) and made hostages of its staff. The embassy takeover was only the latest and worst of the breaches of diplomatic immunity that occurred in the region during the year—the killing of the U. S. ambassador to Afghanistan, attacks on the U. S. embassies in Pakistan and Libya, as well as incidents affecting the embassies of other states. These events all testified to a prevailing readiness on the part of some extreme political groups to ignore all rules, however long-established and however well they had hitherto been observed. The seizure of the U. S. embassy in Tehran, endorsed as it was by the Ayatollah Khomeini, introduced the appalling novelty of a state itself assuming the role of terrorist.

By contrast, the Soviet takeover in Afghanistan, even if highly threatening, had a somewhat traditional quality about it—imperialist aggression by a great power intent on furthering its interests. Strange as it seems, the takeover of countries is more common than the takeover of embassies. Still, world reaction to the Soviet operation was one of well-justified alarm. It resulted in a sudden warming in the U. S. attitude toward Pakistan and an apparent realization by the Carter administration that, in international politics, power is the name of the game. There was a sudden flurry of discussions about the possibility of establishing U. S. military bases in the area, whether in Oman, Saudi Arabia, Somalia, or some other country. This was the second time in 1979 that U. S. policy in the Middle East was reoriented toward realism and the role of power. The first came in the spring, when the Carter administration began sending aid to North Yemen in its war against South Yemen. Because the threats are so much greater and more palpable, no doubt the second conversion will be more lasting.

(*See* article on individual countries.)

ARTHUR CAMPBELL TURNER
Professor of Political Science
University of California, Riverside

MILITARY AFFAIRS

Although the SALT II negotiations dominated the news headlines during 1979 (*see* feature article, pp. 6–14), a number of other military events worthy of note occurred. The two superpowers, the Soviet Union and the United States, considered new strategic weapons which could be deployed under the SALT II provisions; both nations sought to strengthen their respective military alliances—the North Atlantic Treaty Organization (NATO) and the Warsaw Pact—in Europe; both powers continued to provide substantial quantities of arms to other nations; and both nations jockeyed for military advantage in far-away locations where previously their presence was less visible.

Strategic Nuclear Weapons. According to the provisions of the SALT II treaty each signatory may deploy one new ICBM. While it was not entirely clear which system the Soviets would construct next, the United States made known its intentions in September. President Jimmy Carter stated that the United States would build 200 MX ICBMs, with initial testing of the missile to begin by 1983. The missiles would be housed in 4,600 underground blast-resistant shelters. The cost was estimated at $33 billion. The deployment of the MXs would be in a race-track-like pattern proposed for Nevada and Utah. The missiles would be moved about among the shelters in a manner intended to preclude Soviet planners from knowing where the missiles are at any given time. It was hoped that the MX deployment would thus prevent a surprise Soviet first strike, a matter which has become a problem in regard to the 1,000 Minutemen ICBMs, which are at fixed sites known to the Soviet Union.

NATO–Warsaw Pact Competition. It was the year when many American military planners and their NATO counterparts argued successfully

that the United States and its allies had no choice but to initiate a rearming program designed to narrow the gap that has developed between Western and Communist strength in Europe. In October President Carter reflected such a perspective when he stated, "The decision ought to be made to modernize the Western allies' military strength . . . so that we can regain equivalence of military strength, equity of military strength." Earlier the president had announced that his administration would seek to increase the U. S. military budget by 3% in real growth, i.e., beyond whatever the inflation rate is. Washington secured a commitment from the NATO allies that they too would increase their military budgets by 3% real growth.

In the United States, part of the debate on whether and how the NATO forces should be strengthened centered on the politically sensitive question of whether the military draft, which was suspended in 1973, should be resumed. Those Pentagon planners who supported reinstatement of some kind of draft based their case on the contention that the NATO allies did not have the manpower to resist a Soviet attack for more than 30 days without resorting to either tactical nuclear or strategic nuclear war. Given the destructive characteristics of such weapons, using them in the highly populated areas of Western Europe is neither attractive nor particularly credible. Proponents of the draft argued that by increasing the U. S. military manpower pool, reinforcements could be rushed to a European battlefront in time to stem the tide of a Soviet offensive. Thus it would be Moscow, not Washington, that would be forced into the difficult position of having to decide whether to initiate nuclear war.

The various draft proposals were unpopular in the nation's colleges and universities. But plans by those opposing the draft to hold demonstrations in the fall were not implemented be-

UPI

Gen. Bernard W. Rogers (*left*) succeeds Gen. Alexander Haig as supreme commander of the North Atlantic Treaty Organization. Rogers was the chief of staff of the U. S. Army.

cause politicians preparing for 1980 elections chose not to push draft legislation in 1979.

Another controversial facet of the U. S. efforts to strengthen its NATO capabilities involved the possible deployment of 572 extended-range Pershing II missiles, which carry a nuclear warhead, to Western Europe. This missile has a range of approximately 1,000 miles (1 600 km) which would place targets in the Western Soviet Union within striking distance.

Discussions of the deployment were held up until late fall because the West German government set as a condition of accepting the missiles that other NATO nations also accept them. West Germany, which does not possess its own nuclear weapons, apparently did not wish to appear to Moscow as entering into a bilateral nuclear weapons agreement with the United States. At a November NATO Ministerial meeting, it was announced that Great Britain, Italy, and Belgium had also agreed to accept some of the American missiles.

Although the United States could deploy its recently developed enhanced radiation weapon (the neutron bomb) to Western Europe, the president did not order the deployment in 1979.

Much of NATO's concern regarding the military balance in Europe stemmed from the growth in the strength of the Soviet nuclear forces targeted on Western Europe. Many believed that means to counter the Russian Backfire jet bomber and the SS-20 IRBM should be explored.

While the continental members of NATO examined alternative new arms postures, the British under their new prime minister, Margaret Thatcher, moved directly to bolster the British contribution to the common defense of Europe. Major points in Mrs. Thatcher's Ministry of Defense program included the replacement of the aging SLBM force and deployment of cruise missiles and possibly Pershing II IRBMs. Regarding the SLBM, the British plan to replace four British-built submarines which carry U. S. Polaris SLBMs with five new submarines. Each of the submarines will carry 16 American Trident SLBMs equipped with British-manufactured MIRVs. The Trident's range of 5,000 miles (8 000 km) is nearly double that of the Polaris. The American-built land-based cruise missile and Pershing are to be placed in the Midlands and East Anglia. While the British were showing considerable initiative regarding rearming, time required for new weapons production and incomplete negotiations with the United States meant that some years would pass before the new forces could be operationally deployed.

In something of a contrast to Great Britain, the new Canadian government announced that it would not permit nuclear weapons to be stationed in Canada. This meant that the Voodoo anti-aircraft missile would be phased out. While continuing to meet their NATO troop commitments, the Canadians reaffirmed their policy of not equipping their troops, stationed in Europe, with nuclear weapons. The National Defense Minister, Allan McKinnon, explained the Canadian position by saying, "We continue to feel that the fewer countries which have nuclear weapons, the better for the world."

The NATO rearming movement elicited a verbal response from the Soviet Union on October 6. Speaking in East Berlin, Soviet President Leonid Brezhnev announced his intention of withdrawing up to 20,000 Soviet troops and 1,000 Soviet tanks from East Germany over a 12-month period. The Soviet president also offered to reduce the number of Soviet medium range missiles based in the Western regions of the USSR provided that NATO does not deploy its own medium range missiles.

The official U. S. response to the Soviet proposal was cool. It was pointed out that a reduction of 20,000 troops from a total of 500,000 and 1,000 tanks, presumably the older ones, from a force of 10,000 tanks, might not amount to much in the way of arms concessions.

The Conventional Arms Traffic. U. S. concern about maintaining friendly and stable nations in the troubled Islamic world was the basis for important arms negotiations between Washington and the nations of Saudi Arabia, Morocco, and Egypt. Following the fall of the Shah of Iran, Saudi Arabia became the single largest purchaser of American arms in the world. Major components of the U. S.-Saudi arms program included the sale of 60 F-15s, the most advanced U. S. Air Force jet fighter, and new base complexes built to service the aircraft. U. S. military equipment of a less sophisticated character was also being purchased by the Saudi government in order to modernize its Army and Navy as well.

In the wake of the Egyptian-Israeli peace treaty, Cairo became a new and major recipient of U. S. military hardware. Included in a $1.5 billion deal were 35 F-4 Phantom jet fighter-bombers, armored personnel carriers, and air-to-air and surface-to-air anti-aircraft missiles. This military equipment was to be added to aging Soviet material which dates from the days of friendly Egyptian-Soviet relations, and equipment later acquired from Great Britain, China, and France.

In October, President Carter announced plans to sell such military items as the OV-10 armed reconnaissance strike plane and the Cobra attack helicopter to King Hassan of Morocco. The purpose of the sales was both military and political. The equipment was to be used in the anti-guerrilla campaign Morocco was waging against Algerian-backed guerrillas in the Western Sahara. From a political perspective, the United States wanted to reward King Hassan who had played a useful role in initiating the Egyptian-Israeli peace talks and who had taken pro-Western stances regarding other matters.

The United States did not push ahead with arms sales to China. Although Defense Secre-

The new McDonnell Douglas F-18A Hornet undergoes a test flight at the Naval Air Test Center, MD.

tary Harold Brown visited Peking, and thereby sparked rumors of possible arms sales, the United States stuck with its policy of "no American military sales, but no objections from Washington to arms purchases by the Chinese from U. S. allies, such as Great Britain and France." However, in certain gray areas, such as civilian jet transport planes which could be converted for military transport use, the United States continued sales to the Chinese. Specifically, an order was taken for three Boeing 747 jet transports, to be added to the 10 Boeing 707s previously purchased. At year's end the question of when Washington would play its "China card" —i.e., confront the Soviet Union by granting direct military assistance to China—remained unanswered.

The Superpowers and Worldwide Military Presence. Late in the summer the U. S. government confirmed that a Soviet combat brigade was stationed in Cuba. There was some dispute about how long the brigade had been in Cuba and what its purpose was. Nevertheless, President Carter, worried that a lack of response would be interpreted as weakness, at a time when he was being criticized as being a weak leader, addressed the nation on the Cuban situation in somber terms. Among the military responses announced by the president were the resumption of intelligence-gathering flights over Cuba by SR-71 aircraft, more closely to monitor Soviet activity; expansion of U. S. military maneuvers in the Caribbean and at the Guantanamo Bay naval base on the island of Cuba; and the establishment of a special military headquarters at Key West, FL, to provide greater military capability in the area. Following the U. S. deployments, Secretary of Defense Brown stated that the U. S. had neutralized the Soviet military threat in Cuba.

By the year's end, the Soviets were deeply involved militarily in a civil war in Afghanistan. To support the pro-Soviet government in its war with Muslim guerrillas, the USSR flew in large quantities of arms and other military equipment to the Bagram airfield, near the capital of Kabul. Some observers started to refer to the conflict as Russia's "Vietnam." There was also the belief that the Soviets sought to use Afghanistan as a primary military base for all of its operations in Southwest Asia.

Purported Soviet military expansionism in another part of the world also caused concern in 1979. According to the Japanese government there was a Soviet troop build-up on the islands of Etorofu and Kunashiri, at the southern end of the Kurile chain. Both Japan and the USSR claim the islands.

During 1979 there was growing acceptance of the proposition that national security policy must be broadened to include the security of energy supplies to the United States and its allies. Responding to this view—following the loss of its ally, the Shah of Iran, and in light of the possibility of additional turmoil in the Persian Gulf area—the United States moved to protect the oil shipping lane leading out from the Persian Gulf, through the Strait of Hormuz, into the open ocean. In addition to increasing the Navy squadron in the Persian Gulf from three to five ships, the United States began to consider substantial increases of military assistance to Oman, a nation which borders the Hormuz Strait. The United States also promised South Korea and Japan that American naval strength would be used to protect the very long oil supply route from the Persian Gulf to the Pacific.

Another facet of U. S. preparation to use military force if necessary to maintain the flow of oil to itself and its allies was the formation in early summer of a 110,000-man "quick strike" force. The purpose of the unit was to be able to project U. S. troops quickly into a deteriorating situation in the Persian Gulf area or other trouble spots by using airlift and sealift. Possible situations in which such a force might be used include protection of the Saudi Arabian oil fields; protection of the government of Oman from Palestinian guerrillas; and support for moderate Islamic regimes against what is considered the fanatical religious politics of such leaders as Iran's Ayatollah Khomeini.

In support of the heightened American military interest in the security of the Persian Gulf region, Washington's military presence has increased in the Indian Ocean. For example, in the fall a "show the flag" operation was conducted which involved the 64,000-ton (58 048-metric ton) aircraft carrier *Midway* and six other ships, which steamed into the Indian Ocean from the South China Sea. While the *Midway* battle group was not permanently assigned to the area, the move demonstrated the U. S. ability rapidly to place substantial air and naval force alongside the oil supply lines branching out from the Persian Gulf.

ROBERT M. LAWRENCE
Colorado State University

MINING

The world's mining and mineral processing industry in 1979 generally registered upturns in activity relative to 1978 levels, but these upturns were not distributed uniformly throughout the world. Expansions in metallic ore and metal production were most pronounced among Communist nations; growth in nonmetallics was not generally so concentrated, with the developed nations of the non-Communist world sharing in expansion. Inflation, partly related to soaring fuel prices, and unemployment apparently were principal factors in slowing metals industry growth in the non-Communist world. As demand for major consumer goods fell, requirements for their raw materials dropped.

As U. S.-China relations improved, actual reports on output levels of some of China's major mineral commodities came to the surface. Figures were reported for coal, crude oil, pig iron, crude steel, cement, and salt.

Value of World Output. Value of world crude mineral output in 1979 was an estimated (U. S.) $220 billion (constant 1973 dollars), compared with $216.9 billion for 1978; $211.7 billion for 1977; $201.8 billion for 1976; $191.9 billion for 1975; $195 billion for 1973. (Most figures have been revised from those published previously.) Exact details on geographic distribution of these totals are not available, but as in recent years, the United States and the USSR were in contention for first rank, with each accounting for nearly 20% of the total, far ahead of China, Canada, Iran, and Venezuela (each with 5 to 6%).

The Carter administration continued efforts to deal with the energy shortage. However, there seemed to be no significant concern regarding other mineral commodities that must be imported to meet U. S. demand. Proposals to establish a department of natural resources were withdrawn when congressional opposition became apparent.

Ferrous Ores and Metals. Preliminary information suggests that 1979 world iron ore output only slightly exceeded the 1978 level of 845 million metric tons, remaining substantially below the historic high of 913 million tons set in 1974. Manganese ore output again was of the order of 21 million tons, and world chromite output apparently remained near the 1978 level of 9.6 million tons, which, in turn, was slightly below the record 1977 high.

It is noteworthy that recent growth in world production of the major ferrous metal ores has been chiefly the result of higher output levels by the Communist countries of Europe and China; some non-Communist developing nations have shown output increases, but, by and large, expansion of non-Communist world output during 1975–79 was much slower than that in the Communist nations.

World steel output in 1979 was estimated at about 735 million tons, about 4% higher than in 1978, with the USSR, United States, Japan, West Germany, and China remaining the dominant producers and together accounting for nearly two thirds of the world total.

Nonferrous Ores and Metals. Partial data indicated that 1979 world production of aluminum, bauxite, copper, lead, magnesium, and zinc would slightly exceed 1978 levels; that world antimony, nickel, and tin outputs would closely approximate those of 1978; that cobalt would recover to pre-1978 levels; and that mercury output at best would be on a par with that of 1978 and may have declined again.

Precious Metals. The continuing irrational growth in world gold prices was one of the most newsworthy mineral industry events of 1979. Despite prices topping $400 per ounce, world production did not advance nearly so sharply as might have been expected. Incomplete returns indicated that a level of no more than 40 million ounces was anticipated, far below the 1969 record high of 50.6 million ounces.

World silver output in 1979 was expected to total about 340 million ounces. World platinum output—speculative at best because neither of the leading producers (South Africa and the USSR) officially reports production—was believed to be of the order of 6 million ounces in both 1978 and 1979.

Fertilizer Materials. World 1979 production of phosphate rock, potash, and nitrogen fertilizer compounds evidently set new records, topping the previous highs of 1978. In the year ending June 30, 1978, world nitrogen fertilizer output, in terms of nitrogen content, totaled 49.4 million tons, up 6.7% over the preceding year. Leading 1977–78 producers (output in million tons) were: United States, 10.0; USSR, 9.0; China, 4.3 (estimated); India, 2.0; France, 1.6; Japan, 1.4; Netherlands, 1.4; Rumania, 1.4; West Germany, 1.3; Canada, 1.2; United Kingdom, 1.1; and Italy, 1.1. All of these nations, except China and India, produced enough for their own needs and more.

Other Trends. World 1979 asbestos production levels remained clouded; market conditions for some grades remained strong, but questions regarding the environmental hazards of this insulation raw material apparently retarded output growth. There was a slight decline in world output between 1977–78, despite growth in the USSR and favorable market conditions for some grades. World cement output in 1979 apparently totaled about 870 million tons and gypsum production approached 75 million tons. Returns on diamond production were incomplete, but a more stable situation in Zaire may have made it possible for that nation to exceed the USSR and regain first rank. World output of sulfur in all forms (including by-product) was of the order of 57 million tons, about 3% above that of 1978.

See also Production Tables, pages 578–79.

CHARLES L. KIMBELL, *U. S. Bureau of the Mines*

MINNESOTA

Tax relief, doubling of fuel costs, bumper crops, and a costly grain handlers' strike distinguished the year in Minnesota.

Legislature. An evenly divided House of Representatives and a Democratic-Farmer-Labor (DFL) Senate joined Independent-Republican (I-R) Gov. Albert H. Quie in voting a $661.5 million tax relief package for the 1979–81 biennium. The election of an I-R speaker when a DFL member was hospitalized gave the Republicans a brief 67–66 advantage in the House. Later, the DFL gained a majority when an I-R member was disqualified in an election challenge and a DFL candidate won his seat in a special election.

Politics. Still reeling from the death of former party leader Hubert Humphrey and from its 1978 loss of the governorship and two U. S. Senate seats, the DFL again showed signs of division as campaigning for the 1980 presidential election got under way. Factions supporting President Jimmy Carter and Sen. Edward Kennedy (D-MA) both were concerned about how the split would affect native son Vice President Walter Mondale. The DFL was cheered by the landslide victory of former U. S. Rep. Donald M. Fraser in his bid to become mayor of Minneapolis.

Energy. By late 1979 the price of heating oil had reached 95¢ per gallon, compared with 50¢ the year before. The elderly, minorities, and labor pressured Governor Quie to call a special legislative session to help the "energy poor." Many worried about the state's fuel supply when Canada—its main supporter—ended crude oil exports on October 1. St. Paul attracted national attention for its concentrated attack on the energy problem. A malfunction at the Prairie Island nuclear plant caused considerable public concern, but officials of the Northern States Power Company reported that backup safety features had worked properly.

Economy. The state's economy was strong. Average weekly labor force earnings were $272.05, 23.7% above the national average. Unemployment in June was 3.9%, compared with the national rate of 5.6%. The state's two leading crops had bumper yields. Soybean production was a record 173.6 million bushels, and corn production, while down from the 1978 record, was strong at 572.3 million.

Civil Strife. An 11-week strike by grain handlers at Duluth, MN, and Superior, WI, seriously curtailed the nation's grain shipments during the summer and resulted in losses estimated in the millions. An internal dispute and demonstrations against the Bureau of Indian Affairs erupted in violence May 20 at the Chippewa Indian reservation at Red Lake.

Culture. Stanislaw Skrowaczewski resigned after 19 years as music director of the Minnesota Orchestra and was succeeded by Neville Marriner. The opening of a new arts center was an important first step in the rehabilitation of Minneapolis' aging entertainment district.

ARTHUR NAFTALIN, *University of Minnesota*

MISSISSIPPI

Natural disasters, quadrennial elections, and two productive legislative sessions were events of major significance for Mississippians in 1979.

Natural Disasters. Fed by record rainfall over a widespread area, the Pearl River went on a rampage in mid-April, forcing the evacuation of thousands of persons and inflicting property damage estimated in the hundreds of millions of dollars. In Jackson, the river crested 25 feet (7.6 m) above flood stage, inundating parts of downtown and fashionable residential areas. Monticello and Columbia, small towns lying downstream, also were hard hit.

On September 13, Hurricane Frederic slammed into the coastal area of the state, knocking out electrical power, spawning numerous tornadoes, and causing property damage estimated at more than $500 million. While Pascagoula and Jackson County sustained the most damage, a total of 14 counties were declared eligible for federal disaster assistance.

Elections. Democrats not only maintained their hold on all state offices in the November 6 balloting, but also continued their traditional

---

MINNESOTA • Information Highlights

Area: 84,068 square miles (217 736 km²).
Population (Jan. 1979 est.): 4,025,000.
Chief Cities (1976 est.): St. Paul, the capital, 272,465; Minneapolis, 371,896.
Government (1979): *Chief Officers*—governor, Albert Quie (I-R); lt. gov., Lou Wangberg (I-R). *Legislature* —Senate, 67 members; House of Representatives, 134 members.
Education (1978–79): *Enrollment*—public elementary schools, 390,437 pupils; public secondary, 417,279; colleges and universities, 189,087 students. *Public school expenditures,* $1,749,717,000 ($1,821 per pupil).
State Finances (fiscal year 1978): *Revenues,* $4,799,-408,000; *expenditures,* $4,473,952,000.
Personal Income (1978): $31,703,000,000; per capita, $7,910.
Labor Force (July 1979): *Nonagricultural wage and salary earners,* 1,761,300; *unemployed,* 74,700 (3.6% of total force).

MISSISSIPPI • Information Highlights

Area: 47,716 square miles (123 584 km²).
Population (Jan. 1979 est.): 2,415,000.
Chief Cities (1976 est.): Jackson, the capital, 188,205; (1970 census): Biloxi, 48,486; Meridian, 45,083.
Government (1979): *Chief Officers*—governor, Cliff Finch (D); lt. gov., Evelyn Gandy (D). *Legislature*— Senate, 52 members; House of Representatives, 122 members.
Education (1978–79): *Enrollment*—public elementary schools, 274,173 pupils; public secondary, 219,537; colleges and universities, 97,569 students. *Public school expenditures,* $617,178,000 ($1,129 per pupil).
State Finances (fiscal year 1978): *Revenues,* $2,342,-334,000; *expenditures,* $2,059,724,000.
Personal Income (1978): $13,290,000,000; per capita, $5,529.
Labor Force (July 1979): *Nonagricultural wage and salary earners,* 829,400; *unemployed,* 58,000 (5.8% of total force).

dominance of legislative and local posts. In the governor's race, William F. Winter, a 56-year-old Jackson attorney who had lost gubernatorial primaries in 1967 and 1975, gained a landslide victory over Republican Gil Carmichael, a Meridian car dealer. Winter, a former lieutenant governor (1972–1976) and veteran state officeholder who earlier had overtaken incumbent Lt. Gov. Evelyn Gandy in the Democratic primary runoff, received 61% of the votes cast.

Under a new single-member-district plan, the product of 14 years of litigation, 17 blacks were elected to the Mississippi legislature, a net gain of 11. Republicans elected 8 members, increasing their number by 4. Numerous blacks ran for local posts. In local contests, blacks not only increased their numbers on county governing boards but also won the sheriff's position in three jurisdictions. Constitutional amendments providing for a system of disciplining judges and establishing a regular mechanism for legislative reapportionment won ratification.

The Legislature. At its regular 90-day session, the election-year legislature promptly overrode Gov. Cliff Finch's 1978 veto of sunset legislation and approved measures to reduce income and sales tax revenue by an estimated $83 million over a three-year period. Other significant actions included the creation of an ethics commission, the reorganization of the Agricultural and Industrial Board, and the requirement that state funds be deposited daily in interest-bearing accounts.

A three-day special session was convened on May 1 to approve tax-relief measures to benefit the victims of catastrophic spring flooding.

Other Events. Environmentalists continued to fail in their efforts to halt construction of the Tennessee-Tombigbee Waterway; Jackson was the scene of the nation's first international ballet competition; the economy showed signs of slowing; and the state produced some of its best crops in years. There were fewer racial boycotts and demonstrations than in 1978.

The year ended with Governor Finch joining the race for the White House.

DANA B. BRAMMER
The University of Mississippi

MISSOURI

Missouri's 1980 race for governor got under way in mid-1979. Incumbent Joseph P. Teasdale made no secret of his desire to succeed himself, while the state treasurer, James Spainhower, announced in August his intention to contest Teasdale for the Democratic nomination. In the Republican camp, former Gov. Christopher S. Bond was expected to make another bid for the office, and Lt. Gov. William Phelps looked very much like a challenger.

Legislation. After a dilatory start, the Missouri General Assembly ended a five-and-a-half-month session by passing some significant legisla-

──────── **MISSOURI · Information Highlights** ────────

Area: 69,686 square miles (180 487 km²).
Population (Jan. 1979 est.): 4,886,000.
Chief Cities (1970 census): Jefferson City, the capital, 32,407; (1976 est.): St. Louis, 519,345; Kansas City, 458,251.
Government (1979): *Chief Officers*—governor, Joseph P. Teasdale (D); lt. gov., William C. Phelps (R). *General Assembly*—Senate, 34 members; House of Representatives, 163 members.
Education (1978–79): *Enrollment*—public elementary schools, 489,283 pupils; public secondary, 410,719; colleges and universities, 221,281 students.
State Finances (fiscal year 1978): *Revenues*, $3,401,-585,000; *expenditures*, $3,009,139,000.
Personal Income (1978): $35,538,000,000; per capita, $7,313.
Labor Force (July 1979): *Nonagricultural wage and salary earners*, 1,959,000; *unemployed*, 100,300 (4.3% of total force).

tion, including a hike in the legal interest rates, more generous exemptions from creditors' claims for bankrupt persons, opportunity for voters to relax the ban on bingo if the games were operated by religious or charitable groups, and special reductions in the sales tax. The last measure was designed to please both urbanites by exempting residential utility bills and farmers by freeing agricultural equipment and diesel fuel from the sales tax. The measure was to cost the state an estimated $50 million in lost revenue. A perennial controversy involving efforts to repeal the antiquated blue law was resolved by a compromise that permits a county upon voter petition to hold an election to determine whether the ban on Sunday sales should be repealed.

A bill establishing more stringent regulations for nursing and boarding homes received wide support. It set stricter licensing and inspection standards, required doctors and nurses to report patient abuse, and ordained a patient bill of rights. The legislation was enacted following the tragic death of 25 patients in a boardinghouse fire at Farmington April 2.

The Governor. Many legislators, including members of his own party, sharply criticized the governor for failing to play a more active role in the legislative process. The governor kept a hands-off stance during Assembly debate.

Governor Teasdale found himself in a dilemma as a result of his decision to slash the budget of the welfare division and thereby eliminate some 400 caseworkers over a two-year period. Some of his aides then began to have second thoughts about the proposal as they realized that the cuts endangered another administration priority—reduction of Missouri's welfare error rate from 11% to 7.5% by 1980.

Finally, Teasdale created a tempest by moving his family to Kansas City for the summer where he leased a house at a cost to the state of $2,400 per month. Additional expenditures were incurred by transporting food that had been cooked in Jefferson City and by paying the travel allotments for the governor and his staff as they commuted between the two cities.

RUTH W. TOWNE
Northeast Missouri State University

MONTANA

Fiscal conservatism, energy, railroad service cuts, and polychlorinated biphenyl (PCB) contamination were major issues in Montana in 1979.

Legislature. The year began with the opening of a legislature that was characterized by fiscal conservatism. The Democratic House (led by a woman majority leader) vied with the Republican Senate in proposing tax and budget cuts, with the former pushing property tax relief and the latter income tax reductions. A legislative compromise provided modest reductions in both property and income taxes, while imposing a cent-per-gallon increase in motor fuels taxes. Industrial and business groups worked for modification of some environmental laws. Although the legislature simplified procedures under the Major (utility) Facility Siting Act, an effort to overturn the Board of Natural Resources and Conservation's 1978 allocation of Yellowstone River basin waters failed. A landmark piece of legislation established new water courts to speed up adjudication of water rights. The state's attempt to include adjudication of Indian water claims was upset when the United States Justice Department filed suits to prevent state adjudication. The legislature approved a new Montana Code Annotated, the first general revision of the legal code since 1947. Legislators continued to try to streamline the legislative process to deal with a steadily growing workload.

Energy. Northeastern Montana experienced an oil and gas boom which promised to expand to other areas of the state as energy companies engaged in extensive exploration. With increased federal funding, a magnetohydrodynamic (MHD) test center neared completion in Butte. MHD is a method of generating electricity that is twice as efficient as the conventional coal-fired generator; supporters believe it will have a significant bearing on future U. S. energy needs. A major step toward construction of two 800-megawatt plants at Colstrip was taken when the U. S. Environmental Protection Agency decided they would not violate air quality standards. Diesel fuel shortages threat-

ened agricultural production and disrupted truck transportation, while rumors of gasoline shortages helped to create a poor tourist season.

Railroad Problems. Despite protests and court action, Amtrak eliminated its Chicago-to-Seattle North Coast Hiawatha, which traversed Montana. In addition, the bankrupt Milwaukee railroad continued to cut services and on November 1 ended freight service from Miles City, MT, west to Tacoma, WA.

Other News. Coal companies and the state of Texas appealed a decision of a Montana district court upholding the constitutionality of the coal severance tax. A dry growing season led to more forest fires than in recent years and reduced production of some agricultural commodities. The rupture of an electric transformer at a Billings packing plant leaked polychlorinated biphenyl (PCB) into animal feed and resulted in costly contamination of eggs, poultry, and pork.

RICHARD B. ROEDER
Montana State University

MONTREAL

Life in Montreal began to reflect the influence of provincial Law 101, requiring the use of French language in public affairs, business, and education. The names of companies, stores, and buildings, as well as street and traffic signs began appearing in French only. The abolition of English or dual names was part of the government's effort to preserve the unity and ethnicity of its French-speaking majority.

The year also saw the closing down of *The Montreal Star* after more than 100 years of publication. The city was left with only one English-language daily newspaper, *The Gazette*. The September demise of *The Star* focused attention on the declining influence of the city's English-speaking population, which had traditionally dominated the economy, and on the growing economic and cultural pull of Toronto, Montreal's main competitor for new business and revenue. Concerned about its marked loss of financial and industrial dynamism, Montreal created a special commission to revitalize the city's economy. The Mirabel International Airport continued to be plagued with difficulties; several carriers announced that they would no longer use it as an international relay point.

The city's Metro, or subway system, was extended west, but another major project was stalled when the federal government stopped development of the Guy Favreau Complex. Instead of a high-rise government office building, Montreal was left with a gaping excavation in the China Town quarter. A new campus for the University of Quebec was inaugurated downtown.

The February visit of French Premier Raymond Barre took on strong political overtones, reminiscent of the controversial visit by Gen. Charles de Gaulle in 1967.

MONTANA · Information Highlights

Area: 147,138 square miles (381 087 km²).

Population (Jan. 1979 est.): 793,000.

Chief Cities (1970 census): Helena, the capital, 22,557; Billings, 61,581; Great Falls, 60,091.

Government (1979): *Chief Officers*—governor, Thomas L. Judge (D); lt. gov., Ted Schwinden (D). *Legislature* —Senate, 50 members; House of Representatives, 100 members.

Education (1978–79): *Enrollment*—public elementary schools, 109,463 pupils; public secondary, 54,863; colleges and universities, 31,103 students. *Public school expenditures*, $366,000,000 ($2,080 per pupil).

State Finances (fiscal year 1978): *Revenues*, $922,-568,000; *expenditures*, $868,334,000.

Personal Income (1978): $5,299,000,000; per capita, $6,755.

Labor Force (July 1979): *Nonagricultural wage and salary earners*, 303,700; *unemployed*, 17,200 (4.2% of total force).

Montreal remained a major center for international cultural and sporting events. It was the site of the International Arts Salon, a major international film festival, and the World Cup athletic competition. The Montreal Canadiens won their fourth straight championship.

FERNAND GRENIER
Télé-université, Université du Québec

MOROCCO

Morocco's continued and expanded involvement in the war over the phosphate-rich Western Sahara was central to the formulation of its foreign and domestic policies in 1979. Domestic discontent with the war and with King Hassan's utilization of the country's depleted economic resources for defense surfaced in a wave of strikes throughout the first half of the year. Increasingly isolated in his position after Mauritania's withdrawal from the war in August, Hassan turned to other nations for military support.

Sahara War. Mauritania's August peace treaty with the Polisario Front, by which it relinquished its claims to the southern portion of the Western Sahara, Tiris el-Gharbia, was condemned by Morocco, which withdrew its 6,000 defensive troops from the Mauritanian capital. Morocco then annexed the southern sector of the Sahara, renamed it Oued Eddahab, and called elections there to the Moroccan parliament, enforcing its claim by sending in 1,500 troops.

Fierce battles between Moroccan and Polisario forces continued throughout the year, with armed incursions by the Saharans into Hassan's territory. A late January attack on the southern Moroccan town of Tan Tan had resulted in Hassan's formation of an all-party national defense council to unite the country's disparate political groups behind future war moves. That was taken as an indication of the king's intention of intensifying the war. In June, there were more attacks on Tan Tan, and in August, a surprise raid on the Moroccan garrison at Lebuirate resulted in between 500 and 800 Moroccan casualties. The Lebuirate skirmish was followed by the first Moroccan admission of a defeat at Polisario hands. The largest battle in the four-year war occurred in October in the Sahara town of Smara, with casualties estimated at 1,000 on both sides. In May, Morocco formed a militia group, Aosario, to carry guerrilla warfare into Algeria, in retaliation for the attacks undertaken by Polisario, Algeria's ally.

Efforts at diplomatic mediation of the conflict failed, as did a Moroccan request in August for discussions to be held with the Algerian government. Morocco got military assistance from Egypt in the form of arms in September, and U. S. President Jimmy Carter indicated in October that he would sell reconnaissance planes and helicopters to Hassan if Congress approved the sale. Morocco retaliated against Spain's support for Saharan self-determination by stepping up claims to Spain's north African enclaves, Ceuta and Melilla, and by seizing Spanish fishing vessels off the Moroccan coast.

Politics and Economy. Prime Minister Ahmed Osman was replaced in March by the minister of justice, Maati Bouabid. Following that, the defense council was formed. Both moves were part of an attempt to unify the Moroccan political spectrum behind a domestically unpopular war. The deteriorating economy, already taxed by the cost of the war (estimated at $1 million a day), was further strained by massive strikes for higher wages during the first half of 1979. Students, railway and dock workers, miners, teachers, civil servants, and health workers were among those who walked off their jobs. The austerity plan introduced in 1978 met with harsh criticism from the labor unions and the main opposition party, the Socialist Union of Popular Forces (USFP).

MARGARET NOVICKI, *"African Update"*
African-American Institute

─────── **MOROCCO · Information Highlights** ───────

Official Name: Kingdom of Morocco.
Location: Northwest Africa.
Area: 180,602 square miles (467 759 km²).
Population (1979 est.): 19,400,000.
Chief Cities (1973 est.): Rabat, the capital, 385,000; Casablanca, 2,000,000; Marrakesh, 330,000; Fez, 322,000.
Government: *Head of state,* Hassan II, king (acceded 1961). *Head of government,* Maati Bouabid, prime minister (took office March 1979).
Monetary Unit: Dirham (3.87 dirhams equal U. S.$1, Aug. 1979).
Manufactures (major products): Coal, electric power, phosphates, iron ore, lead, zinc.
Agriculture (major products): Barley, wheat, citrus fruit, sugar beets, grapes.

MOSCOW

Moscow, the capital and largest city of the Soviet Union, continued to undergo a major face-lift in preparation for the 1980 Olympic Games. Eleven new sports centers and a total of 76 construction projects were under way, including a new airport terminal, an ultramodern communications center, international post office, 35-story hotel, and major roads and expressways. The Olympic Village, comprising eighteen 16-story apartment houses and other buildings, will be used for city housing after the Games. Everywhere buildings were repainted, trees planted, and pavements repaired to beautify the city. Taxi drivers, waitresses, and store clerks were learning useful phrases in English and other languages. Olympic memorial coins were being prepared, and cakes with Olympic emblems were already on sale. The government was spending a reported $350 million to put on the Games. At the same time, however, it warned Moscow residents of "ideological contamination" by Western visitors.

PHOTOS, TASS FROM SOVFOTO

Moscow's new Olympic village (*above*) will accommodate some 12,500 athletes during the 1980 Games and later be used for city housing. Olympic swimming and diving events will be held in a new aquatic center (*right*) on Mir Avenue. The indoor stadium will seat 45,000.

A dress rehearsal for the Olympics was held July 21–August 5 in the form of the Seventh Summer Tournament of Soviet Nations, or Spartakiade Games (*see also* SPORTS, page 457). Foreign athletes were invited to the periodic event for the first time. Approximately 2,300 of them challenged 8,338 top Soviet sportsmen. The foreigners performed well, winning 126 medals to the Soviets' 99.

Also for the first time, the International Political Science Association held its annual congress in the Soviet capital. Some 1,600 scholars from 58 countries, including the United States, attended the August 12–18 conference. Soviet authorities permitted free speech, and several foreign experts presented papers criticizing aspects of the Soviet political system.

In contrast, Soviet censors exercised strict controls over the Second Moscow International Book Fair, held September 4–10. Soviet cultural officials removed from U. S. displays 44 books which either criticized the USSR or gave detailed accounts of Hitler's regime.

The 1979 tour of the United States by Moscow's Bolshoi Ballet was marked by the defection of three of its principal dancers: Aleksandr Godunov on August 22 in New York City, and Leonid and Valentina Koslov on September 15 in Los Angeles. All three requested and received asylum from the U. S. government.

On September 27, the Moscow State Symphony Orchestra abruptly cancelled its planned five-week tour of the United States. The tour was scheduled to start in New York City during the first week in October. Soviet spokesmen claimed that the cancellation was due to a dispute with the American booking agency over choice of conductors.

ELLSWORTH RAYMOND
New York University

Jack Lemmon, Michael Douglas, and Jane Fonda are the stars of *The China Syndrome*, the story of a nuclear disaster.

MOTION PICTURES

Filmmaking entered a dramatic new boom period in the final year of the 1970's, and the upturn promised lively opportunities for the decade ahead. Motion picture production, which had dropped off significantly in favor of concentration on expensive "blockbuster" projects, rebounded with a new burst of enthusiasm, energy, and investment. More foreign-made films were also available. Critics spent more hours in the dark of movie theaters than they had in years, and for the public the boom meant greater film choices to compete with made-for-television movies or commercial-free subscription television fare.

The most timely film of 1979, and one whose subject became a front-page story, was *The China Syndrome,* released shortly before the Three Mile Island nuclear generator accident. As skeptics were accusing the film of exaggerating the fear of nuclear disaster, the mishap in Pennsylvania played out the film's scenario in many ways. It was a case of life imitating art. Statements by officials sometimes resembled lines in the script, and audiences laughed nervously at one line about the danger of an area the size of Pennsylvania being destroyed. In addition to being an entertainment in the mode of a thriller, *The China Syndrome* (starring Jane Fonda, Jack Lemmon, and Michael Douglas), was born of a desire to alert the United States to the dangers of the rush toward reliance upon nuclear energy without sufficient safeguards. The film became a textbook example of how political activists can use the medium to advance political concerns.

Vietnam. The other film that garnered massive attention was Francis Coppola's long-awaited and much-discussed $31-million Vietnam epic, *Apocalypse Now*. It was first unveiled in near-complete form before the international film audience at the Cannes Film Festival in May. The reaction was mixed, as it was when the film subsequently opened in the United States, but there was a general respectfulness for Coppola's ambitions and his arresting imagery. Like some legendary filmmakers of the past, he had gambled on "the big picture," risking his own fortune. Early returns promised that the film would recoup its investment and go on to be a moneymaker. Meanwhile, it was overwhelming audiences with the most critical, realistically violent portrayal of the Vietnam war that had thus far been presented on the movie screen.

The Deer Hunter had stolen some of the spotlight from *Apocalypse Now*. It was given limited release at the end of 1978 in time to qualify for awards. The New York Film Critics Circle voted it the best picture of the year, and it received more honors at the Academy Awards. The chief criticisms of *Apocalypse Now* tended to be artistic. But *The Deer Hunter* drew a barrage of attacks that claimed that it was not an accurate depiction of the Vietnam war and that it gave a racist portrayal of the Vietnamese. It was also argued that the violent, upsetting

Continued on page 356

MOTION PICTURES | 1979

In a scene from *Alien*, one of 1979's successful horror films, three apprehensive astronauts approach the entrance to a strange space ship.

AGATHA. Director, Michael Apted; screeplay by Kathleen Tynan, Arthur Hopcraft. With Dustin Hoffman, Vanessa Redgrave.

ALIEN. Director, Ridley Scott; screenplay by Dan O'Bannon. With Sigourney Weaver.

ALL THAT JAZZ. Director, Bob Fosse; screenplay by Robert A. Aurthur and Mr. Fosse. With Roy Scheider.

THE AMITYVILLE HORROR. Director, Stuart Rosenberg; screenplay by Sandor Stern, based on the book by Jay Anson. With James Brolin, Rod Steiger.

AN ALMOST PERFECT AFFAIR. Director, Michael Ritchie; screenplay by Walter Bernstein, Don Petersen. With Keith Carradine, Monica Vitti, Raf Vallone.

...AND JUSTICE FOR ALL. Director, Norman Jewison; screenplay by Valerie Curtin, Barry Levinson. With Al Pacino.

APOCALYPSE NOW. Director, Francis Coppola; screenplay by John Milius, Mr. Coppola. With Marlon Brando, Robert Duvall, Martin Sheen.

THE BELL JAR. Director, Larry Peerce; screenplay by Marjorie Kellogg, based on the novel by Sylvia Plath. With Marilyn Hassett, Julie Harris, Anne Jackson, Barbara Barrie, Robert Klein.

BOARDWALK. Director, Stephen Verona; screenplay by Mr. Verona, Leigh Chapman. With Lee Strasberg, Ruth Gordon, Janet Leigh.

BREAKING AWAY. Director, Peter Yates; screenplay by Steve Tesich. With Dennis Christopher, Paul Dooley, Barbara Barrie.

THE CHAMP. Director, Franco Zeffirelli; screenplay by Walter Newman, based on a story by Frances Marlon. With Jon Voight, Faye Dunaway.

THE CHINA SYNDROME. Director, James Bridges; screenplay by Mike Gray, T. S. Cook, Mr. Bridges. With Jane Fonda, Jack Lemmon, Michael Douglas.

DAWN OF THE DEAD. Director, George A. Romero; screenplay by Mr. Romero. With David Emge.

DON GIOVANNI. Director, Joseph Losey; screenplay by Patricia and Joseph Losey and Frantz Salieri, from the Mozart opera. With Ruggero Raimondi.

DRACULA. Director, John Badham; screenplay by W. D. Richter. With Frank Langella, Laurence Olivier, Donald Pleasence.

ESCAPE FROM ALCATRAZ. Director, Don Siegel; screenplay by Richard Tuggle, based on the book by J. Campbell Bruce. With Clint Eastwood.

THE EUROPEANS. Director, James Ivory; screenplay by Ruth Prawer Jhabvala, from the novel by Henry James. With Lee Remick, Lisa Eichhorn.

FEDORA. Director, Billy Wilder; screenplay by Mr. Wilder, I. A. L. Diamond, based on a story from *Crowned Heads* by Thomas Tryon. With William Holden, Marthe Keller, José Ferrer.

THE FRENCH DETECTIVE. Director, Pierre Granier-Deferre; screenplay by Francis Veber. With Lino Ventura, Patrick Dewaere, Victor Lanoux.

THE GREEN ROOM. Director, François Truffaut; screenplay by Mr. Truffaut, Jean Gruault, based partially on two stories by Henry James. With François Truffaut, Nathalie Baye.

HAIR. Director, Milos Forman; screenplay by Michael Weller. With John Savage.

HARDCORE. Director, Paul Schrader; screenplay by Mr. Schrader. With George C. Scott.

THE IN-LAWS. Director, Arthur Hiller; screenplay by Andrew Bergman. With Peter Falk, Alan Arkin.

THE INNOCENT. Director, Luchino Visconti; screenplay by Suso Cecchi D'Amico, Enrico Medioli, Mr. Visconti, based on the novel *L'Innocente* by Gabriele D'Annunzio. With Giancarlo Giannini, Jennifer O'Neill, Laura Antonelli.

THE JERK. Director, Carl Reiner; screenplay by Steve Martin, Michael Elias, Carl Gottlieb, Mr. Reiner. With Steve Martin, Bernadette Peters.

KRAMER VS. KRAMER. Director, Robert Benton; screenplay by Mr. Benton from the novel by Avery Corman. With Dustin Hoffman, Meryl Streep.

A LITTLE ROMANCE. Director, George Roy Hill; screenplay by Allan Burns. With Laurence Olivier, Arthur Hill, Diane Lane, Thelonious Bernard.

LOVE ON THE RUN. Director, François Truffaut; screenplay by Mr. Truffaut and others. With Jean Pierre Leaud, Marie-France Pisier, Claude Jade.

LUNA. Director, Bernardo Bertolucci; screenplay by Giuseppe Bertolucci, Clare Peploe, Bernardo Bertolucci. With Jill Clayburgh.

THE MAIN EVENT. Director, Howard Zieff; screenplay by Gail Parent, Andrew Smith. With Barbra Streisand, Ryan O'Neal.

A MAN, A WOMAN, AND A BANK. Director, Noel Black; screenplay by Raynold A. Gideon, Bruce A. Evans, Stuart Margolin. With Donald Sutherland.

Mariel Hemingway and Woody Allen play lovers in *Manhattan,* **Allen's black and white film about the difficulties of lasting relationships.**

MANHATTAN. Director, Woody Allen; screenplay by Mr. Allen, Marshall Brickman. With Woody Allen, Diane Keaton, Mariel Hemingway.

THE MARRIAGE OF MARIA BRAUN. Director, Rainer Werner Fassbinder; screenplay by Peter Marthesheimer, Pia Frohlich, with additional dialogue by Mr. Fassbinder. With Hanna Schygulla.

MEETINGS WITH REMARKABLE MEN. Director, Peter Brook; screenplay by Jeanne de Salzmann, Mr. Brook. With Dragan Maksimovic, Terence Stamp.

MONTY PYTHON'S LIFE OF BRIAN. Director, Terry Jones; screenplay by Graham Chapman, John Cleese, Terry Gilliam, Eric Idle, Terry Jones, Michael Palin. With Graham Chapman.

MOONRAKER. Director, Lewis Gilbert; screenplay by Christopher Wood. With Roger Moore, Lois Chiles.

THE MUPPET MOVIE. Director, James Frawley; screenplay by Jerry Juhl, Jack Burns. With Jim Henson and the Muppets.

NEWSFRONT. Director, Phillip Noyce; screenplay by Mr. Noyce, from an original screenplay by Bob Ellis. With Bill Hunter.

1941. Director, Steven Spielberg; screenplay by Robert Zemeckis, Bob Gale. With Dan Aykroyd, Ned Beatty, John Belushi.

NORMA RAE. Director, Martin Ritt; screenplay by Irving Ravetch, Harriet Frank, Jr. With Sally Field, Ron Leibman, Beau Bridges.

NORTH DALLAS FORTY. Director, Ted Kotcheff; screenplay by Frank Yablans, Mr. Kotcheff, Peter Gent, based on the novel by Mr. Gent. Wi'h Nick Nolte, Mac Davis, Charles Durning.

NOSFERATU, THE VAMPYRE. Written and directed by Werner Herzog. With Klaus Kinski.

THE ONION FIELD. Director, Harold Becker; screenplay by Joseph Wambaugh. With John Savage.

ON THE YARD. Director, Raphael D. Silver; screenplay by Malcolm Braly. With John Heard, Mike Kellin.

ORCHESTRA REHEARSAL. Director, Federico Fellini; screenplay by Mr. Fellini, with collaboration by Brunello Rondi. With Baldwin Baas.

PEPPERMINT SODA. Written and directed by Diane Kurys. With Eleonore Klarwein.

A PERFECT COUPLE. Director, Robert Altman. With Paul Dooley, Marta Heflin.

PICNIC AT HANGING ROCK. Director, Peter Weir; screenplay by Cliff Green. With Rachel Roberts.

PORTRAIT OF THE ARTIST AS A YOUNG MAN. Director, Joseph Strick; screenplay by Judith Rascoe. With Bosco Hogan.

POURQUOI PAS! Director, Coline Serreau; screenplay by Miss Serreau. With Sami Frey, Mario Gonzalez.

PROMISES IN THE DARK. Director, Jerome Hellman; screenplay by Loring Mandel. With Marsha Mason.

QUADROPHENIA. Director, Franc Roddam. Music by The Who. With Phil Daniels.

QUINTET. Director, Robert Altman; screenplay by Frank Barhydt, Robert Altman, Patricia Resnick. With Paul Newman, Bibi Andersson.

RAPE OF LOVE. Director, Yannick Bellon; screenplay by Miss Bellon. With Nathalie Nell.

RICH KIDS. Director, Robert M. Young; screenplay by Judith Ross. With Trini Alvarado, Jeremy Levy, Paul Dooley, Irene Worth.

ROCKY II. Written and directed by Sylvester Stallone. With Sylvester Stallone, Talia Shire.

THE ROSE. Director, Mark Rydell; screenplay by Bill Kerby, Bo Goldman. With Bette Midler.

RUNNING. Written and directed by Steven H. Stern. With Michael Douglas, Susan Anspach.

SAINT JACK. Director, Peter Bogdanovich; screenplay by Howard Sackler, Paul Theroux, Mr. Bogdanovich. With Ben Gazzara.

THE SEDUCTION OF JOE TYNAN. Director, Jerry Schatzberg; screenplay by Alan Alda. With Alan Alda, Barbara Harris, Meryl Streep, Rip Torn, Melvyn Douglas.

STARTING OVER. Director, Alan J. Pakula; screenplay by James L. Brooks. With Burt Reynolds, Jill Clayburgh, Candice Bergen.

STAR TREK—THE MOTION PICTURE. Director, Robert Wise; screenplay by Gene Roddenberry, Harold Livingston. With Leonard Nimoy, William Shatner.

10. Written and directed by Blake Edwards. With Dudley Moore, Julie Andrews, Bo Derek.

TIME AFTER TIME. Written and directed by Nicholas Meyer; story by Karl Alexander and Steve Hayes. With Malcolm McDowell, Mary Steenburgen.

YANKS. Director, John Schlesinger. With Richard Gere, Vanessa Redgrave, William Devane.

scenes of Russian roulette were fictional, and although it was obvious to some that they were used as a metaphor, many assumed that the deadly game was popular during the war. Despite the controversy, its director, Michael Cimino, emerged as a lauded new talent.

Woody Allen. After receiving wide acclaim for *Annie Hall* and considerable praise (along with pans) for *Interiors,* Woody Allen returned with *Manhattan,* which scored an instant success. The naysayers were barely heard in the din of adulation which stressed the creative importance of Allen to American filmmaking. Photographed in black and white with elaborate use of music by George Gershwin, *Manhattan* cemented Allen's reputation as a kind of poet laureate of the neurotic urban class; again his theme was the difficulty of establishing lasting relationships. Especially good in an excellent cast (including Allen) was Mariel Hemingway as a young, uncomplicated person who refuses to wait around for love forever.

Star Performances. Despite a new tendency to look upon directors as superstars, the public still often goes to the movies to see their favorite stars, much as earlier audiences did. A major star performance of the year was given by Bette Midler in *The Rose.* Already popular by reason of her nightclub, concert, and TV performances, Midler took a huge, challenging role as a rock singer struggling to hold herself together. Directed by Mark Rydell, the film attempted to convey the tensions and traumas of the 1960's, and the character in some ways suggested the tragic life of Janis Joplin. However, the depiction recalled similar pressures suffered by performers of various generations. Midler demon-

Jon Voight as the down and out boxer father of Ricky Schroder scores a success in *The Champ.*

UNITED ARTISTS

strated a formidable, hitherto unrecognized talent for acting.

Jill Clayburgh, already a sought-after actress, broadened her horizons by appearing in contrasting parts. Her charming portrayal opposite Burt Reynolds in the romantic comedy *Starting Over* was closer to the character she played in *An Unmarried Woman.* Her daring performance as a widowed opera singer with incestuous feelings toward her son in Bernardo Bertolucci's *Luna* revealed a new range to her talent. The film had a very mixed reception, but Clayburgh further enhanced her position as a major star.

Other key performers of the year were: Sally Field, the union organizer in *Norma Rae;* Nick Nolte, the rebellious football hero in *North Dallas Forty;* Peter Falk and Alan Arkin, involved in outrageous intrigue in *The In-Laws;* Dennis Christopher, the spunky cyclist, and Paul Dooley, his irascible father, in *Breaking Away;* James Woods, the cop-killer in *The Onion Field;* Lee Strasberg, the ·aging Brooklyn man whose world is crumbling in *Boardwalk;* Ben Gazzara, the wheeler-dealer in *Saint Jack;* Malcolm McDowell as H. G. Wells in *Time After Time;* Dustin Hoffman and Meryl Streep squaring off in the child custody battle of *Kramer vs. Kramer;* Nathalie Nell, the French actress who played a brutally assaulted nurse in *Rape of Love;* and Hanna Schygulla, the exciting German actress, brilliant in director Rainer Werner Fassbinder's *The Marriage of Maria Braun.*

Social Significance. In addition to these topical films, many American and foreign language films veered toward controversial or sensitive subjects. Norman Jewison's *. . . And Justice for All* lacerated our court system for its inequities. *Rich Kids* explored the effects of divorce on youngsters. Robert Altman's *Quintet,* praised by some but rejected by most, commented on humankind's struggle for survival. From Italy came *Orchestra Rehearsal,* a masterwork by Federico Fellini, which in 70 minutes showed the breakdown of discipline in an orchestra as a metaphor for society in turmoil. One of the most beautiful films was *The Tree of Wooden Clogs,* an Italian import that portrayed the plight of peasants at the turn of the century.

Even in the rush toward comedy—escapist entertainment was important in 1979—the emphasis was often on humor used to make a point. *La Cage Aux Folles,* the hit from France which deals hilariously and sympathetically with homosexual problems, was a case in point. It opened without much advance fanfare at New York's 68th Street Playhouse and word of mouth kept it so popular that it had remained ensconced there (seven months by year's end). *The Life of Brian,* a concoction of the uninhibited Monty Python troupe, broadly satirized religion. While generating laughs, it also drew irate protests—and one ill-fated attempt to ban it—from various religious leaders and groups. In *10* the midlife crisis that plagues many men was spoofed with an expertly comic performance by Dudley Moore.

Music. Three disparate films relying upon various facets of the music world stood out. Joseph Losey's three-hour production of Mozart's classic *Don Giovanni* demonstrated with new creative intensity the possibilities of marrying film to opera. Instead of the static staging so fatal to most attempts, Losey used elaborate outdoor and indoor locations in Italy, and obtained excellent dramatic performances from his cast. Ruggero Raimondi plays the title role. Youth of the 1960's was presented in indigenous musical surroundings; Milos Forman successfully filmed the rock musical *Hair,* giving it new verve despite its dated aspects. From England, a 1973 album by the musical rock group The Who served as the inspiration for *Quadrophenia,* a look back to 1964, the time of rival Mods and Rockers. The intensely realistic film, directed by Franc Roddam, had a sound track featuring The Who, also involved as producers.

Films for Children. With the widespread popularity on television of Jim Henson's Muppets, a film built around the marvelous characters seemed a natural. Perhaps it could have been more creative, but *The Muppet Movie,* featuring the lovable gang's trek to Hollywood to become stars, proved one of the better attractions among the slim pickings directed to youngsters. The most beautiful family-style drama was *The Black Stallion,* adapted from the first book in the series by Walter Farley. While the story grew contrived and predictable, the scenes of the storm at sea and the idyllic friendship developed between Alec, the boy hero, and his exquisite Arabian horse were filmed with impressive beauty by cinematographer Caleb Deschanel and director Carroll Ballard.

The Documentary. Of the many quality films that premiered at the New York and Toronto film festivals, one that evoked special enthusiasm and comment was *Best Boy,* an unusual, deeply moving documentary about Philly, a 52-year-old retarded man who takes his first steps toward contact with the world outside his home, where he has been confined almost all his life. The change was brought about through the efforts of his cousin, Ira Wohl, who made the film chronicling Philly's progress over a three-year period. The real life story packed more dramatic power than most fictional films. It was promptly bought for general distribution in 1980.

Potpourri. Three films about Dracula illustrated the continued horror craze. The highly stylized *Nosferatu, the Vampyre* by German director Werner Herzog, starred Klaus Kinski as the count, and in addition featured thousands of rats. The glossy, very showy, somewhat erotic *Dracula* starring Frank Langella was adapted from the Broadway play in which he appeared. A major box office success was *Love at First Bite,* an entirely satirical view of the count, with George Hamilton as the fang-toothed hero

UNITED ARTISTS

Talia Shire and Sylvester Stallone repeat their roles in *Rocky II,* the sequel to *Rocky* (1976).

who comes to New York to seek his long, lost love.

Alien, about a weird form of life taken aboard a spaceship, was one of the most popular films of the year at the box office. Fans of television's *Star Trek* series finally saw the movie version, *Star Trek—The Motion Picture,* which arrived in time for Christmas.

Among films of special quality was James Ivory's adaptation of Henry James' novel *The Europeans,* with excellent, convincing ambience and strong performances from a cast that included Lee Remick and Lisa Eichhorn. *Peppermint Soda,* directed by Diane Kurys, was a lovely reminiscence about two sisters growing up in France, a twist on the more common theme of boyhood memoirs. François Truffaut's *The Green Room* hauntingly depicted a man obsessed with remembering the dead who were important in his life to the point where it interferes with his ability to relate to the present. Truffaut's *Love on the Run,* which promised to be the last film about Truffaut's favorite character Antoine Doinel, here observed Doinel in adulthood and still unable to establish a permanent relationship. *The French Detective* was an amusing mystery about a hard-boiled detective (Lino Ventura) who resists pressure to pursue a politician with connections.

Deaths. Jean Renoir, a filmmaking titan of the century, Mary Pickford, the celebrated silent era star, and John Wayne, one of the most renowned actors in film history, died during the year (*see also* OBITUARIES).

WILLIAM WOLF, *Film Critic*
"Cue New York"

The Boston Symphony Orchestra, with Seiji Ozawa conducting, performs in Beijing's Capital Gymnasium.

MUSIC

Classical

The public's enthusiasm for good music appeared to operate independent of inflation or recession. Concert and opera activity, performances, and audiences thrived.

International Concerts. There was particular interest in musical events with international implications. The Boston Symphony's tour of China, March 12–19, was the first exchange after the newly signed cultural pact between the United States and the People's Republic of China. Concerts under Seiji Ozawa's direction were telecast and broadcast throughout China. There were open rehearsals, a joint concert with Beijing's (Peking's) Central Philharmonic Orchestra, and master classes led by BSO principal players. In April, soon after the signing of the peace pact between Egypt and Israel, Eugene Istomin, concert pianist, was the first American to give concerts in Egypt and then fly directly to Israel for performances there.

Among the U. S. orchestras that toured abroad were the New York Philharmonic, Leonard Bernstein conducting, which toured Japan and South Korea, and the Detroit Symphony, Antal Dorati conducting, which gave 24 concerts in 8 European cities. Orchestras which visited the United States, including the 26-city tour of the Dresden State Orchestra from East Germany, met with consistent success. One discordant note was the cancellation of the Moscow Philharmonic's tour after defections to the United States of Bolshoi Ballet stars.

The visit, October 25–November 15, of the illustrious Vienna Philharmonic and State Opera was the most ambitious gesture, even to patrons of Kennedy Center, by now well accustomed to international cultural events. The Vienna Philharmonic gave an opening concert under Karl Böhm, 85, then two more in Washington and three in New York City, under Leonard Bernstein. There were 14 performances of 4 operas: Beethoven's *Fidelio* (Bernstein conducting), Strauss's *Salome* (Zubin Mehta conducting) and *Ariadne auf Naxos*, and Mozart's *The Marriage of Figaro* (Böhm conducting).

Premieres. Of international interest, as well, was the profound impression made by the world premiere of Alban Berg's opera *Lulu*, finally in a complete form. Ever since the composer's death in 1936, and even in the truncated form in which he left it, *Lulu* has been regarded as a masterpiece. After the death of Berg's widow in 1976, his fairly complete and explicit Act III materials were made available to the Austrian composer Friedrich Cerha who finished the work convincingly.

Musicians the world over acclaimed the completed opera at its historic Paris premiere in February. The dramatic impact of its form was confirmed. The opera's structure takes the form of a fateful arc. The rise of the fortunes of Lulu, the ultimate femme fatale, is mirrored by her fall. There is a reversal of the musical and dramatic sequence at the opera's midpoint, which the new third act consummates.

While opinion was sharply divided over the conducting of Pierre Boulez, the staging by Patrice Chereau, and the grandiose sets by Richard Peduzzi in Paris, the U. S. premiere, in English, by the Santa Fe Opera in August had an eminently more sympathetic reception. Michael Tilson Thomas conducted and Colin Graham directed.

Opera. Of new operas, none composed in the 1970's met with any remarkable success or appeared to claim a lasting position in the repertory. There were numerous premieres. Dominick Argento's *Miss Havisham's Fire,* to John Olon-Scrymgeour's libretto based on a character from Charles Dickens' *Great Expectations,* had a half-hearted reception in its New York City Opera premiere in March. At its U. S. premiere at the Aspen Music Festival in August, *Houdini* by the Dutch composer Peter Schat was regarded as a theatrical success (Ian Strasfogel, director) but a musical failure because of a now dated and awkwardly carpentered avant-garde approach. However, the three-year-old *The Ice Break* by Sir Michael Tippett was hailed at its first U. S. production, by Sarah Caldwell with her Opera Company of Boston.

John Harbison won a measure of critical praise for his *A Winter's Tale,* given its premiere in August by the American Opera Project under the auspices of the San Francisco Opera. San Francisco Spring Opera Theater's production of Thea Musgrave's *Mary, Queen of Scots* had a singular popular success. Musgrave's *A Christmas Carol* had its premiere in December by the Virginia Opera Association.

The opera whose first performance was most highly publicized was also the most conventional. It was Gian-Carlo Menotti's *La Loca,* based on the life of the reputedly mad queen of Spain, Juana, daughter of Ferdinand and Isabella. It was commissioned and produced by the San Diego Opera as a vehicle for Beverly Sills, and honoring her 50th birthday and imminent retirement from the stage. On July 1, she succeeded Julius Rudel as director of the New York City Opera, and that company mounted additional performances of *La Loca* in its fall season.

The Wagnerian soprano Birgit Nilsson finally settled the issue of back taxes with the U. S. Internal Revenue Service, and returned to the United States for the first time since 1975. Her engagements began with a gala concert at the Metropolitan Opera on November 4. Concluding the longest tenure of any living opera company director, Kurt Herbert Adler announced his retirement in the beginning of 1982 from the directorship of the San Francisco Opera, a post he has held since 1956. Terry McEwen, London Records' executive vice president, will succeed Adler.

Because of the continued expansion of operatic activity worldwide, there was an increasing shortage of stars to fill the bills. In turn, this encouraged a noticeable repertory shift away from heavy reliance on the popular works. The rarer and previously neglected operas were explored. New operas were cultivated mostly by smaller companies, and over 230 productions were given of American works.

Symphony Orchestras. America's 1470 symphonies performed to some 25 million people in live concerts, and a sudden rise in orchestra broadcasting increased the audience incalculably. The American Telephone and Telegraph Company launched a Bell System American Orchestras on Tour program, providing $10 million to underwrite the touring through 1982 in over 100 cities by the Boston, Chicago, and Pittsburgh symphonies, the Los Angeles and New York philharmonics, and the Philadelphia and Cleveland orchestras. The National Endowment for the Arts raised its aid to orchestras by $1.6 million

In July 1979, Beverly Sills succeeded Julius Rudel as director of the New York City Opera. The company's fall season was marred by a musicians' strike.

HENRY GROSSMAN

PHOTO BY LOUIS HOOD, COURTESY,
PHILADELPHIA ORCHESTRA

Eugene Ormandy (above) announced his retirement as director
of the Philadelphia Orchestra. The
1979 Santa Fe Chamber Music
Festival toured New Mexico for
6 weeks and included 25 events.

SANTA FE CHAMBER MUSIC FESTIVAL

over 1978's amount, to $10.8 million distributed
in 120 grants.

Two of the longest-tenured conductors announced their retirements. Eugene Ormandy,
80, would leave the Philadelphia Orchestra at the
end of the 1979–80 season, after 44 years as its
musical director, and would be succeeded by
Riccardo Muti. After 32 years as the Utah Symphony's musical director, Maurice Abravanel
stepped down, concluding his career.

Lorin Maazel was named the new director of
the Vienna State Opera as of 1982 when he
would give up the music directorship of the
Cleveland Orchestra after ten years in that position.

Michael Gielen began his first season as the
Cincinnati Symphony's music director. The
beginning of Leonard Slatkin's first season at the
helm of the St. Louis Symphony and the celebration of that orchestra's 100th anniversary
were postponed for several weeks because of the
failure of contract negotiations and an orchestra
strike.

New Music. New music appeared to be in a
conservative phase; actually, composers were
assimilating the diverse techniques and innovations that had emerged during the previous
periods of more radical change, especially the
1960's. There were experimental music festivals, and the avant-garde movement continued
but as a much thinner, less noticeable current,
and with considerable overlap on one edge with
rock music.

A renewed admiration for musical craft and
the main tradition was reflected in the attention
shown Elliott Carter and his music. Numerous
regional premieres were given of his newest

work, *Syringa,* a chamber cantata for soprano,
bass, and instruments. Honors for the composer
and the celebration of his 70th birthday, December 1978, carried over into 1979. Also, Ernst
Krenek, 79, 30 years a southern California resident, was honored in an unprecedented eight-day
festival in April in Santa Barbara, with 11 programs containing 44 of his compositions, 10 lectures by scholars and composers, and 2 exhibits.

Among the premieres of major orchestral
works were William Schuman's *Tenth Symphony*
(Minnesota Orchestra, April), and Jacob Druck-
man's *Aureole* (Leonard Bernstein, New York
Philharmonic, June). Other new orchestral
works were Morton Subotnik's *Place* (Oregon
Symphony, March), Henry Brant's *Antiphonal
Responses* (Oakland Symphony, April), Earl
Kim's *Violin Concerto* (Itzhak Perlman and
Zubin Mehta, New York Philharmonic, Octo-
ber), Barbara Kolb's *Grisaille* (Portland Sym-
phony, February), and Ezra Laderman's *Piano
Concerto* (Walter Ponce and Jose Serebrier,
American Composers Orchestra, May). Lader-
man, whose opera *Galileo Galilei* was performed
in Binghamton, NY, in February, was appointed
the new director of the music program for the
National Endowment for the Arts.

The attitude toward new music was symbo-
lized by a slogan of the Minnesota Composers
Forum, "Help Create an Old Tradition." Indeed, new music was becoming more fully absorbed into the mainstream of American musical
life, less self-consciously presented, and more
generously accepted and welcomed by the general audience.

ROBERT COMMANDAY, *"San Francisco Chronicle"*

Spoleto Festival USA — 1979

Spoleto Festival USA, which opened in May 1979, won national critical acclaim, broke attendance records, and celebrated its third successful season at Charleston, SC, the beautifully-preserved 18th century city. The festival recreated on American soil Gian-Carlo Menotti's 22-year-old "Festival of Two Worlds" founded in the Umbrian hill town of Spoleto. Like its Italian counterpart, the Charleston-based festival has drawn on Menotti's talents as composer, director, and impresario. In 1979 it offered 17 days of opera, concerts, dance, drama, films, lectures, art exhibits, and colorful street events.

Since the 1977 inaugural season the festival has given two world premieres of plays, Tennessee Williams' *Creve Cœur* and Simon Gray's *Molly,* and important operatic revivals, Samuel Barber's *Vanessa* and Menotti's *The Consul, Martin's Lie,* and *The Egg.*

The play at the 1979 festival, which subsequently moved to Broadway, was Arthur Miller's heartily applauded *The Price.* It was directed by John Stix and starred Fritz Weaver, Mitchell Ryan, Scotty Bloch, and Joseph Buloff.

In opera the 1978 season's ambitious schedule of five works was trimmed by budget considerations to two in 1979. They were Domenico Cimarosa's charming 18th century opera buffa *The Desperate Husband,* staged in Charles Kondek's clever English translation, and a new production of Menotti's *The Medium,* which was directed by the composer. Cimarosa's opera, with its formula comic plot, was given a stylishly designed production by Ulisse Santicchi. It also benefited from Giulio Chazalettes' direction, Randal Behr's adept conducting, and an excellent cast. In *The Medium* mezzo Beverly Evans was particularly effective as the alcoholic fortune teller Madame Flora, and young Lorenzo Muti skillfully conducted the chamber-sized orchestra.

Christopher Keene, music director since the festival began, further enhanced his reputation by leading two special orchestral concerts devoted to the music of Sergei Rachmaninoff and George Gershwin, the highlight being a performance of Rachmaninoff's cantata *The Bells.*

Aside from the grand events, chamber music was the festival's musical heart, and concerts—hosted by Charles Wadsworth, directed by Paula Robison and Scott Nickrenz, and featuring more than a dozen renowned musicians—were given as often as three times a day. Also, the Westminster Choir, conducted by Joseph Flummerfelt, presented Masses composed by Francis Poulenc and (Franz) Joseph Haydn, and the Kent State Chorale, under Vance George, performed a liturgical music drama, *The Play of the Three Maries.*

Dance enthusiasts found much to admire: the Ballet Repertory Company's two world premieres of works by its director Richard Englund entitled "Timepools" and "Conversations," and programs by the Bill Evans Dance Company and Douglas Norwick and Dancers. Alvin Ailey's American Dance Theater's varied and eclectic events were especially well received.

A film series spanning Roberto Rossellini's 30-year career presented 28 of the director's films, including his 1973 trilogy *The Age of the Medici.* "Piccolo Spoleto" showcased local young talent every day, including children's theater, mimes, street corner brass fanfares, poetry reading, and parades.

PETER DVARACKAS

SPOLETO FESTIVAL USA 1979

Domenico Cimarosa's three-act opera The Desperate Husband was presented at the 1979 Spoleto Festival.

Jazz

In jazz music of 1979 a trend back to acoustic playing was evident—the electric piano, guitar, bass, etc. giving way to their acoustic counterparts. The constant search for personal identification by most jazz artists fostered the trend. Tied directly to it was the swing in 1979 away from fusion. With the fusion failures of many jazz artists fresh in mind, and with dozens of newly-published solo transcriptions and improvisation books to help them, more young players were discovering past jazz giants. At the same time, there was a noticeable lack of new and accomplished American-trained jazz soloists or of recorded solos. For the talented and potentially great jazz player there seemed to be a change in expectations. Many lucrative performance areas opened up, luring young players away from the slow road of playing only jazz with jazz players that could help mold them eventually into accomplished artists.

The International Jazz Critics Poll 1979. The 1979 winners as reported in *Down Beat Magazine* were: Hall of Fame, Lennie Tristano; Composer and Record of the year, Charles Mingus, *Cumbia and Jazz Fusion;* Reissue of the year, Charlie Parker, *The Savoy Sessions;* Record Label of the year, Inner City; Record Producer, Michael Cuscuna; Arranger and Big Band (with Lew Tabackin), Toshiko Akiyoshi; Jazz Group and Alto sax, Phil Woods; Trumpet, Dizzy Gillespie; Trombone, Roswell Rudd; Soprano sax, Wayne Shorter; Tenor sax, Dexter Gordon; Baritone sax, Pepper Adams; Clarinet, Anthony Braxton; Flute, Sam Rivers; Violin, Stephane Grappelli; Acoustic piano, Cecil Taylor; Electric piano, Chick Corea; Organ, Jimmy Smith; Synthesizer, Josef Zawinul; Acoustic bass, Ron Carter; Electric bass, Jaco Pastorius; Guitar, Jim Hall; Drums, Elvin Jones; Vibes, Milt Jackson; Percussion, Airto Moreita; Miscellaneous instrument, Toots Thielemans (Harmonica); Male singer, Mel Torme; Female singer, Sarah Vaughan; Vocal group, Jackie (Cain) & Roy (Kral); Soul/R&B Artists, Stevie Wonder.

Publications. The year's important publications included *Jazz Pedagogy, a Comprehensive Method of Jazz Education for Teacher and Student,* by David Baker (Down Beat Music Workshop Publications) and *To Be or Not ... to Bop, the Memoirs of Dizzy Gillespie,* co-author, Al Fraser (Doubleday and Co.).

The Visibility of Jazz. Because of the lack of a dynamic/dominant Pop scene or personage in 1979, jazz was more visible to the American public. This visibility, as indicated through overdue publications output, jazz curriculum additions, and a new awareness of the lasting and highly creative offerings of past jazz masters, promised an even brighter future for jazz.

DOMINIC SPERA
Indiana University

Popular

Despite attempts by armchair analysts to divide popular music into neat categories, music of 1979 once again refused to cooperate.

Signs of healthy cross-fertilization were everywhere. Rock and disco melded to form a new hybrid, disco-rock. Country artists debuted at the traditionally all-jazz Montreux Festival in Switzerland. Joni Mitchell completed her transition from folk to jazz with the release of an album dedicated to the late Charles Mingus.

The most acclaimed show on Broadway, *Sweeney Todd,* winner of eight Tony awards, was operatic, and, although *Gottu Go Disco* was an abysmal failure, it paved the way for disco on Broadway.

Aretha Franklin kept the soul in her disco, while Third World practiced what might be called disco-reggae. This activity, characteristic of music in transition, was generated in part by the changing demographics of the pop audience. It was further stimulated by a midyear economic slump in the industry and new technology that accelerated the international dissemination of pop music.

By 1979 the average age of the Woodstock generation was 32, and those over 25 formed the fastest growing age group in the United States. Rock 'n' roll was 25 years old. Despite the onslaught of disco, rock remained the dominant form of popular music. There were still vast audiences for such classic rock bands as the

UPI

Jazz pianist Eubie Blake (*left*), Lucille Armstrong, and Merver H. Bernstein, president of Brandeis, publicize a benefit concert for the college's Louis Armstrong Music Fund.

Rock fans attend an open air concert to commemorate the tenth anniversary of Woodstock in Bethel, NY.

Rolling Stones and Led Zeppelin, for the commercial rock of Foreigner and Supertramp, for the Billy Joel singer-songwriter types, for heavy metal and folk-rock, and all the other hyphenated rocks, but it was the New Wave's explosion into the mainstream that made musical headlines. Led by a new British invasion, New Wavers Joe Jackson, Talking Heads, and the Police brought welcome vigor and intelligence to a too-familiar scene.

The economic slump, brought on by what an industry spokesman called "a voluntary system of massive wastes," guaranteed the New Wavers visibility. To ensure future financial stability, the music business zeroed in on two types of money-making artists: those from the New Wave who cost little to produce and, like the Knack, the Cars, and Dire Straits, had natural mass appeal; and the established superstars—Fleetwood Mac, Bob Dylan, Barbra Streisand, and the Bee Gees—who sold millions of records and concert tickets despite 1979's inflated prices.

The Who tour (minus Keith Moon who had died in 1978), the first in four years, plus the release of their two films, *The Kids Are Alright* and *Quadrophenia,* proved the group the precursors of modern punk rock.

It was a year of many significant concerts. Although the Reunion Concert, celebrating Woodstock's tenth anniversary, was a disappointment, the MUSE (Musicians United for Safe Energy) benefit concerts—starring Jackson Browne, James Taylor, Carly Simon, Bonnie Raitt, Bruce Springsteen, and many others—were an enormous success and signaled a return to social activism in the pop world. The Bee Gees led ten acts participating in a glittering concert at the UN in support of the International Year of the Child. Also under UN auspices, negotiations were begun to reunite the Beatles for a benefit concert.

American pop stars made their first appearance in Cuba at the Havana Jam in March. Elton John became the first Western rocker to perform in the USSR.

As the 1970's ended, it was apparent that disco—after Elvis Presley, the Beatles, and Woodstock—was the fourth major peak in modern pop music. It was still enormously popular in clubs, and in 1979 became the fastest-growing radio format in the country, but it had begun to change. The Bee Gees, Donna Summer, the Village People, and Chic were still hot, but their songs were interspersed on the dance floor with those by Rod Stewart and Blondie. On the east coast, especially in New York, which had gained supremacy in the music business with the advent of disco, many clubs began featuring straight rock for dancing.

Disco roller skating became the big fad, as 5,000 rinks in the United States began hiring disco DJ's.

Traditional country music held its own, but the 1979 Country Music Association awards confirmed that the new mass appeal of country was based on its revamped sound. The big winners—Kenny Rogers and Charlie Daniels—were MOR (middle-of-the-road) and Southern rock artists respectively. It seemed that country was destined to be the MOR music of the future.

Both country and pop musicians made major inroads on film and television. The variety show format was replaced by individual specials hosted by such musicians as Barry Manilow, Johnny Cash, and John Denver. Films with music as their central theme or with emphasis on their incidental music abounded. *Hair, Americathon, The Rose,* and *Apocalypse Now* were but a few.

Small revivals in blues and folk music surfaced, and women came to the fore. B. B. King took the blues to the USSR in a concert first. The California Bread and Roses festival featured an all-acoustic line-up of such stars as Joan Baez, Arlo Guthrie, and the Roches. New female artists—Carlene Carter, Rachel Sweet, Ricki Lee Jones—filled the pop chart.

Although R&B was overshadowed by disco, record companies began to beef up their black music branches, which hinted at revival in the 1980's.

Despite the success of *They're Playing Our Song* and *Eubie,* Broadway retreated to revivals of old shows like *Whoopee.*

PAULETTE WEISS, *"Stereo Review"*

NEBRASKA

Excellent crops, a calm legislative session, controversy over taxes, and growing interest in groundwater engrossed Nebraskans in 1979.

Agriculture. Nebraska grain crops were excellent in 1979. Wheat exceeded 1978's yield, while grain sorghum production was about the same. Both corn and soybeans set new production records. Ripening of fall grain crops was delayed, but a dry autumn contributed to excellent yields. Grain market prices were above those of 1978. While yields and prices were up, so were energy, fertilizer, machinery, and other fixed farm costs. Likewise, limited storage and lack of transportation to central warehouses caused problems. Limited supplies of cattle raised prices, while ample supplies kept hog prices low. Readily available grain and construction of small packing plants helped increase cattle feeding in Nebraska by about 36% in the 1970's.

Legislation. The 86th Legislature began its 90-day session on January 3 and adjourned on May 23. It showed fiscal restraint, living within the 7% increase it had mandated for local spending during the 1978 special session. Legislative cooperation with the new governor, Charles Thone (elected in 1978), was better than that with the previous administration. Important legislation included restrictions on smoking in public places, a sex crime act, an abortion law, a certificate of need requirement for expansion of medical facilities, limitation on warrants to search newsrooms, and a requirement that Omaha elect its city council members by district. Governor Thone vetoed an act to end capital punishment.

Taxes. The state sales tax has remained at 3% since 1977, but the income tax rose from 16% to 18% of federal liability on Jan. 1, 1979. The legislature extended Omaha's special half-cent sales tax for another year. Attention centered on property taxes—both personal and real estate. Since 1973 personal property taxes on farm equipment, livestock, and business inventories have been reduced or eliminated, placing additional local revenue burdens on real estate. In both Omaha and Nebraska City school districts voters, by solid majorities, placed zero-based lids on property tax collections. Likewise, the State Board of Equalization took a major step in equalizing land values for tax purposes among Nebraska's 93 counties.

Water. Concern for underground water supply, a major natural resource, increased in 1979. In December 1978 the state's 61,826 irrigation wells were the source for 83% of the acres irrigated, and irrigation expansion has directly aided rapid increase of crop yields. Despite warnings that groundwater supply was not inexhaustible, mining (pumping more than is replenished) of this resource has increased, and evidence grows that water levels are declining. Nebraska has been called "the last frontier in developing water law," and it appeared that the legislature would soon address the problem of developing and imposing a policy for groundwater conservation.

ORVILLE H. ZABEL, *Creighton University*

NETHERLANDS

In 1979 Prime Minister Andreas van Agt's center-right coalition continued the delicate task of trying to get the Dutch economy on an even keel. At the same time, the Netherland's government was confronted with a major foreign policy controversy when the United States announced plans to install medium-range missiles in North Atlantic Treaty Organization (NATO) countries.

Economy. The coalition of Christian Democrats and rightist Liberals stuck to its austerity program, attempting to cut government expenditures, reduce inflation, and make Dutch products more competitive in world markets. All did not go smoothly. On June 19 the FNV trade union federation called a one-day strike to protest the austerity measures. In addition, wildcat strikes intermittently closed the port of Rotterdam. Nevertheless, there was a national consensus that something had to be done to solve the country's economic problems. Without this consensus, the coalition, which had a slender two-seat majority in the 150-seat parliament, could not have stayed in power.

NEBRASKA • Information Highlights

Area: 77,227 square miles (200 018 km²).
Population (Jan. 1979 est.): 1,568,000.
Chief Cities (1976 est.): Lincoln, the capital, 164,035; Omaha, 371,012; (1970 census): Grand Island, 31,269; Hastings, 23,580.
Government (1979): *Chief Officers*—governor, Charles Thone (R); lt. gov., Roland A. Luedtke (R). *Legislature* (unicameral)—49 members (nonpartisan).
Education (1978–79): *Enrollment*—public elementary schools, 156,662 pupils; public secondary, 141,134; colleges and universities, 81,691 students. *Public school expenditures,* $497,600,000 ($1,655 per pupil).
State Finances (fiscal year 1978): *Revenues,* $1,231,625,000; *expenditures,* $1,144,827,000.
Personal Income (1978): $11,868,000,000; per capita, $7,582.
Labor Force (July 1979): *Nonagricultural wage and salary earners,* 619,500; *unemployed,* 24,000 (3.0% of total force).

NETHERLANDS • Information Highlights

Official Name: Kingdom of the Netherlands.
Location: Northwestern Europe.
Area: 13,054 square miles (33 811 km²).
Population (1979 est.): 14,000,000.
Chief Cities (1978): Amsterdam, the capital, 728,746; Rotterdam, 590,312; The Hague, 464,858.
Government: *Head of state,* Juliana, queen (acceded Sept. 1948). *Head of government,* Andreas van Agt, prime minister (took office Dec. 1977). *Legislature* —States General: First Chamber and Second Chamber.
Monetary Unit: Guilder (2.03 guilders equal U. S.$1, June 1979).
Manufactures (major products): Metals, textiles, chemicals, electronic equipment.
Agriculture (major products): Sugar beets, wheat, barley, fruits, potatoes, oats, flax, bulbs, flowers, meat and dairy products.

The Dutch continued to pay for past government policies, which sparked inflation and placed restrictions on the ability of free enterprise to compete in world markets. Dutch exports were often too highly priced, and Dutch businessmen often found it more profitable to invest abroad rather than at home. Toward the end of the year, Prime Minister van Agt could point to modest success in combating inflation, which was reduced to about 5%.

Foreign Policy. The U. S. proposal to place medium-range missiles in West European NATO countries created a dangerous political problem for the coalition. The Hague was not only under pressure from Washington to accept the nuclear-armed missiles, but West Germany also urged The Netherlands to share the political and strategic onus of having American missiles on its soil. The leaders of both the Christian Democratic Party and the socialist opposition Labor Party felt that The Netherlands must recognize its responsibilities to NATO. The problem was, however, an unusually massive grass roots resistance to nuclear weapons. The pervasiveness of this sentiment had far-reaching political implications. No matter how pro-NATO the Christian Democrat van Agt and Labor leader Joop den Uyl might be, both men had to face what amounted to a mutinous situation in their respective parties.

Less of a burden for the government in 1979 was the South Moluccan community in The Netherlands. In recent years some of its members resorted to violence to promote the cause of independence for their homeland. In 1979, however, there were fewer terrorist activities by South Moluccan terrorists than in the past, although Dutch police did report that there had been a South Moluccan plot to kidnap Prime Minister van Agt.

The case of Pieter Menten, the millionaire art collector accused of Nazi war crimes, continued to make headlines. In December 1978, Menten was acquitted of charges of murdering more than 20 Jews in Poland in 1941. On May 22, 1979, however, the Dutch Supreme Court ruled that Menten would have to go on trial a second time. Then on September 24, a Dutch trial court ruled that the 80-year-old Menten was physically unfit to stand trial again. The decision created a storm of international protests.

AARON R. EINFRANK, *Free-lance writer*

NEVADA

The gasoline shortage in the spring of 1979 caused at least a temporary pause in the sensational growth of Nevada's economy.

Economy. With a number of new large hotel-casinos in operation in the Reno area and extensive expansion of existing gambling facilities in both Reno and Las Vegas, the state's tourist-based economy enjoyed a boom during the first three quarters of the 1979 fiscal year. Gambling and sales tax revenues going into the state general fund increased by 22% over the previous fiscal year despite a slump in tourism due to the gasoline shortage. The spring quarter's gaming revenues were up only 11% from the previous year; however, the economy rebounded in midsummer, and the unemployment rate, which had reached a year's high of 6% in June, was down to 5.5% in August.

Near Beatty, NV, a trailer-load of low-level radioactive waste caught fire in May. Later, the dump was closed.

UPI

The Legislative Session. The major concern of the 1979 legislature, which met for a record 134 days, was to devise a tax-reduction package that would appeal to voters and cause them to reject a proposed constitutional amendment which is identical to California's Proposition 13. The legislative package, including a provision removing the sales tax from food, will be invalidated if the amendment is approved by the electorate a second time in 1980. The legislators also passed, by large margins, resolutions requesting that the U. S. Congress call a national convention for the purpose of proposing a constitutional amendment mandating an annual balanced budget and that Congress submit to the state legislatures an amendment limiting federal spending. The legislature decisively buried the Equal Rights Amendment following its strong rejection in a 1978 non-binding referendum. In one of their final acts, the legislators claimed control over most of the federal land of the state (amounting to 86.7% of the total area) on the basis of the "unconstitutional" disclaimer to such land which was forced upon the state by the enabling act of 1864. Attorney General Richard Bryan was instructed to handle the legal negotiations with the federal government. Bryan was able to line up several Western states' support.

Gambling Regulation. The disclosure in a federal grand jury indictment that FBI wiretaps had uncovered hidden ownership by Kansas City racketeering elements in some Las Vegas casinos brought charges that the staff of the state's Gaming Control Board was undermanned, underpaid, and lacked the tools to do its job effectively. Previously, the legislature had increased the staff positions but had rejected a request by the control board for wire tap authority.

Miscellaneous. Although Gov. Robert List originally strongly supported the Air Force's plan to build MX missile sites in the central Nevada desert, he later expressed concern about the tremendous service costs for local government. List also threatened to shut down the radioactive waste disposal site at Beatty because of lax enforcement of safety standards.

DON W. DRIGGS
University of Nevada, Reno

------ **NEVADA • Information Highlights** ------

Area: 110,540 square miles (286 299 km²).
Population (Jan. 1979 est.): 673,000.
Chief Cities (1970 census): Carson City, the capital, 15,468; Reno, 72,863; (1976 est.): Las Vegas, 153,553.
Government (1979): *Chief Officers*—governor, Robert List (R); lt. gov., Myron E. Leavitt (D). *Legislature*—*Senate*, 20 members; Assembly, 40 members.
Education (1978–79): *Enrollment*—public elementary schools, 74,644 pupils; public secondary, 71,637; colleges and universities, 33,539 students. *Public school expenditures*, $264,533,000 ($1,631 per pupil).
State Finances (fiscal year 1978): *Revenues,* $911,469,-000; *expenditures,* $774,145,000.
Personal Income (1978): $6,229,000,000; per capita, $9,439.
Labor Force (July 1979): *Nonagricultural wage and salary earners,* 380,300; *unemployed,* 19,000 (5.4% of total force).

NEW BRUNSWICK

The year in New Brunswick saw a swing away from the national trend in the Canadian general election, deterrent fees introduced into the province's medicare plan, and an outburst of hooliganism in Bathurst.

Politics. The voters of New Brunswick went against the tide in the May 22 national election. The province vote resulted in the election of six Liberals and four Progressive Conservatives. The Tories did only marginally better than in 1974, when they elected three members of Parliament (MPs) against six for the Liberals and one independent.

Robert Howie (50), Conservative MP for York-Sunbury since 1972, was named minister of state for transport in the Clark government.

Provincially, Premier Richard Hatfield added strength to the Conservative government by appointing a Liberal speaker of the legislature. The appointment of Robert McCready gave the Tories a 30–27 edge in the House.

The finance minister, Fernand Dube, in March presented the legislature with a record $1.583 billion budget. However, a $1.453 billion budget was later approved. A highlight was the announcement that from May 1 limited deterrent or user fees would be imposed on services provided under the provincial medicare plan.

Energy. The Council of Maritime Premiers, meeting at Brudenell, P. E. I., in June, decided to seek federal help toward a $34 million engineering and environmental impact study into Bay of Fundy tidal power. New Brunswick and Nova Scotia primarily are affected.

Law Under Siege. For five successive nights in July, drag racing, hooliganism, vandalism, public drinking, and nudity put the northern New Brunswick city of Bathurst (pop. 16,000) in newspaper headlines across Canada. The lawlessness grew out of a policemen's strike over contract demands. Feelings of bitterness and resentment among the populace lasted for months after a settlement was reached.

JOHN BEST, *Canada World News*

------ **NEW BRUNSWICK • Information Highlights** ------

Area: 28,354 square miles (73 439 km²).
Population (1979 est.): 700,200.
Chief Cities (1976 census): Fredericton, the capital, 45,248; St. John, 85,956; Moncton, 55,934.
Government (1979): *Chief Officers*—lt. gov., Hedard Robichaud; premier, Richard B. Hatfield (Progressive Conservative); chief justice, Supreme Court, Appeal Div., Charles J. A. Hughes; Queen's Bench Div., A. J. Cormier. *Legislature*—Legislative Assembly, 58 members.
Education (1979–80 est.): *Enrollment*—public elementary and secondary schools, 157,230 pupils; private schools, 420; Indian (federal) schools, 830; postsecondary, 12,790 students. *Total expenditures,* $481,199,000.
Public Finances (1978–79): *Revenues,* $1,254,000,000; *expenditures,* $1,216,000,000.
Personal Income (average weekly salary, May 1979): $251.13.
Unemployment Rate (July 1979, seasonally adjusted): 11.2%.
(All monetary figures are in Canadian dollars.)

NEWFOUNDLAND

The governing Progressive Conservative party chose a new leader in early 1979, held a winning provincial election at midyear, and could boast an improving economy by year's end.

In January, Premier F. D. Moores announced that for personal reasons he would be resigning his post and that a party convention would be held March 17 to choose his successor. Principal contenders included four cabinet members, one of them 37-year-old former school teacher Brian Peckford. Peckford was the convention's choice.

On June 4, newly elected Canadian Prime Minister Joe Clark, a Progressive Conservative, named to his new cabinet two representatives from Newfoundland—John Crosbie as minister of finance, and James McGrath as minister of fisheries. The national elections also proved fruitful for the Progressive Conservative party in Newfoundland. Hoping to be carried by the PC bandwagon and to catch the opposition Liberal party with its leadership in dispute, Peckford called for a surprise provincial election on June 18. Although they had their own party convention scheduled for August 4, the Liberals rose to the challenge and quickly called on former Minister of External Affairs Don Jamieson as their candidate. The short, sharp campaign resulted in a victory for the PC's, who took 33 of the 52 seats in the legislature. Premier Peckford reordered his cabinet in July, appointing two women as ministers for the first time in Newfoundland's history. Later that month the government issued its budget, increasing taxes for

smokers, automobile operators, advertisers, and insurance companies, and adding $7 million to an already high fisheries expenditure.

The economy of Newfoundland had an upswing in 1979, largely the result of high fish prices and good catches. The benefits of private and federal expenditures on the search for offshore oil were felt locally. In late September, the Chevron Corporation announced the discovery of a promising supply of hydrocarbon in the shallow waters off the Grand Banks.

SUSAN McCORQUODALE
Memorial University of Newfoundland

NEW HAMPSHIRE

During 1979 New Hampshire's new governor, Hugh Gallen (D), manifested more reserve and was in less open conflict with the Executive Council and the legislature than his predecessor. Gallen followed through on his promise to work for the repeal of the Public Service Company's construction work in progress (CWIP) charges on utility rates. In May he signed a bill repealing CWIP charges, which forced the company to reconsider its methods of financing the multibillion dollar Seabrook nuclear facility.

Energy. Seabrook remained for many a vivid symbol of the dangers of nuclear power. In October an attempt to occupy the construction site was thwarted by a regional force of state police and National Guardsmen.

A gasoline shortage that resulted in a severe decline in tourism during early July was also a cause of concern. New Hampshire did not ex-

---

— **NEWFOUNDLAND • Information Highlights** —

Area: 156,185 square miles (404 520 km²).
Population (1979 est.): 572,900.
Chief Cities (1976 census): St. John's, the capital, 86,576; Corner Brook, 25,198.
Government (1979): *Chief Officers*—lt. gov., Gordon Winter; premier, Brian Peckford (Progressive Conservative); chief justice, Robert S. Furlong. *Legislature*—Legislative Assembly, 51 members.
Education (1979–80 est.): *Enrollment*—public elementary and secondary schools, 151,970; private schools, 260; post-secondary, 9,120 students. *Total expenditures*, $384,494,000.
Personal Income (average weekly salary, May 1979): $272.31.
Unemployment Rate (July 1979, seasonally adjusted): 14.4%.
(All monetary figures are in Canadian dollars.)

— **NEW HAMPSHIRE • Information Highlights** —

Area: 9,304 square miles (24 097 km²).
Population (Jan. 1979 est.): 882,000.
Chief Cities (1970 census): Concord, the capital, 30,022; Manchester, 87,754; Nashua, 55,820; Portsmouth, 25,717.
Government (1979): *Chief Officers*—governor, Hugh J. Gallen (D). *General Court*—Senate, 24 members; House of Representatives, 400 members.
Education (1978–79): *Enrollment*—public elementary schools, 117,241 pupils; public secondary, 55,148; colleges and universities, 41,549 students. *Public school expenditures*, $281,863,000 ($1,530 per pupil).
State Finances (fiscal year 1978): *Revenues*, $742,887,-000; *expenditures*, $708,329,000.
Personal Income (1978): $6,409,000,000; per capita, $7,357.
Labor Force (July 1979): *Nonagricultural wage and salary earners*, 389,500; *unemployed*, 17,300 (3.7% of total force).

UPI

In Portsmouth, NH, workers from a nearby shipyard stage a protest march against President Carter's wage-guidelines policy.

perience the near-crisis situation that affected several states, but in July Governor Gallen was forced to impose minimum purchases of gasoline. At summer's end, however, tourism was near or slightly above normal levels in most areas. Although gasoline stocks had been restored to adequate levels, dire predictions were made concerning winter heating oil supplies. By mid-autumn those fears appeared groundless, but prices for heating fuel were expected to be close to one dollar a gallon. Political leaders and social agencies were concerned about the impact high prices would have on families with fixed incomes and on those with small incomes. Because of the oil problems, a return to wood as a primary fuel appeared to be a firmly established trend.

Legislation, Growth, and the Economy. The 1979 legislature adjourned on June 28 after passing a $1.4 billion budget for the fiscal years 1980 and 1981 which included a one-cent per gallon gasoline tax increase, raised the drinking age from 18 to 20, and eliminated mandatory 65-year retirement age in the public and private sectors. In April the House of Representatives refused to ratify the federal constitutional amendment granting the District of Columbia full voting representation in Congress.

New Hampshire continues to defy growth patterns occurring in much of the Northeast. In the southern half of the state, population growth remains high and yet there are labor shortages in some areas. Estimates indicate that between 1970 and 1979 the state population increased as much as 34%. Except in the far north, the overall economic situation in the state has been good and the unemployment rate low.

Energy problems, growth, and related matters caused many citizens to raise questions relative to the use of land, the quality of life, and general life styles. It seemed certain that better planning and new attitudes toward the use of resources would be forthcoming during the 1980's.

WILLIAM L. TAYLOR
Plymouth State College

NEW JERSEY

Casino gambling and economic issues made news headlines in New Jersey in 1979. In November elections, the Republicans gained ten seats in the Democratic-controlled state Assembly, a $475 million bond issue for mass transportation was approved, and a $95 million issue for higher education was defeated.

Casino Gambling. Allegations persisted that Atlantic City operators were connected with organized crime. This was particularly true with respect to Resorts International's application for a permanent license. In January, Deputy Attorney General G. Michael Brown charged that the company, which had been granted a tempo-

UPI

Atlantic City's 53-year-old Hotel President is demolished to make room for a new hotel-casino.

rary license in 1978, was allied with crime figures in its casino in the Bahamas. Lengthy hearings were held in which the top officials of Resorts and their counsel, Raymond Brown, denied any willful involvement in illegal activities. Having been reassured, the New Jersey Casino Control Commission in late February voted unanimously to grant the permanent license.

The grant to Resorts International opened the way for expansion of casino operations. Resorts itself announced plans to spend $120 million for construction of a second, and larger, casino with a new hotel on 53 acres (21 ha) near the Steel Pier. In addition, Commission Chairman Joseph P. Lordi informed the legisla-

────── **NEW JERSEY · Information Highlights** ──────

Area: 7,836 square miles (20 295 km²).

Population (Jan. 1979 est.): 7,324,000.

Chief Cities (1970 census): Trenton, the capital, 104,638; (1976 est.): Newark, 331,495; Jersey City, 239,998.

Government (1979): *Chief Officers*—governor, Brendan T. Byrne (D). *Legislature*—Senate, 40 members; General Assembly, 80 members.

Education (1978-79): *Enrollment*—public elementary schools, 827,978 pupils; public secondary, 509,349; colleges and universities, 308,304 students. *Public school expenditures*, $3,307,800,000 ($2,334 per pupil).

State Finances (fiscal year 1978): *Revenues*, $7,437,860,000; *expenditures*, $6,936,901,000.

Personal Income (1978): $64,281,000,000; per capita, $8,773.

Labor Force (July 1979): *Nonagricultural wage and salary earners*, 3,079,900; *unemployed*, 286,900 (7.9% of total force).

ture in the spring that he expected four new casinos to be active within 15 months, a prediction borne out in part by a license granted to Caesar's World in late June.

Further evidence of the possibility of new gambling operations came when the Nevada Gambling Commission reported favorably on New Jersey's controls over potential penetration by organized crime. Since Nevada law allows casinos based in that state to move outside only if other states develop regulatory systems as effective as Nevada's, the report was greeted with enthusiasm in New Jersey.

Economic Issues. Various forms of retrenchment were seen in the New Jersey economy in 1979. Gov. Brendan Byrne's 1980 budget of $4.6 billion, while $243 million larger than its predecessor, called for no programs or taxes, implying that the size of government functions would decrease in the future.

The U. S. Defense Department's announcement that facilities at Fort Dix would be closed and moved to Fort Jackson in South Carolina caused anxiety among businessmen in the central part of the state. It was estimated that the closing would eliminate 3,200 civilian and military jobs and a combined civilian and military payroll of $117 million. Faced with these objections, DoD agreed to delay the closing in order to examine further its social and economic impact.

In the autumn the Tristate Regional Planning Commission advocated slower growth for the rapidly developing Hackensack Meadowlands area for the reason that it was having an adverse effect on population trends in nearby cities. A few days later, however, the owners of the Hambletonian Trot, a famous harness race, accepted the bid of the sports complex to have the event held there beginning in 1981.

HERMANN K. PLATT, *Saint Peter's College*

NEW MEXICO

In 1979 environmental problems associated with uranium mining and nuclear waste disposal were the chief issues of concern to New Mexicans. The gas shortage produced a significant slump in the state's vital tourist industry.

Environment. On July 16 a tailings dam at United Nuclear Corporation's Church Rock uranium mill broke, spilling 100 million gallons (378 million liters) of radioactive waste into the Rio Puerco, which drains a large area of northwestern New Mexico. Navajo Indians living along the Puerco delivered a protest against the slowness of the clean-up operation and the lack of information concerning potential hazards. Officials from the federal Center for Disease Control arrived almost a month after the accident to begin an investigation. Najavo livestock that had drunk from the river after the spill were sent to Albuquerque to be tested for radiation contamination. Five Indian children and

one adult were taken to Los Alamos Scientific Laboratory to be checked. The tests revealed only normal background radioactivity.

Meanwhile, controversy continued over the U. S. Department of Energy's plan to dispose of low-level nuclear defense wastes in underground salt beds near Carlsbad and to conduct research on high-level waste storage. In August the department held public hearings in New Mexico and Texas on a draft statement regarding the proposed Waste Isolation Pilot Plant. Gov. Bruce King announced that he intended to declare the statement inadequate if provisions concerning transportation of radioactive materials and emergency preparedness were not clarified.

Hispanic residents of Rio Arriba County held a two-day rally in September to protest issuance of mining leases for uranium exploration on neighboring public lands.

Energy. Public hearings were held in August on a proposal to build the nation's first full-scale demonstration geothermal power plant in the Jemez Mountains. Hot water will be extracted from wells exceeding 2,000 feet (610 m) in depth and converted to steam to power an electrical generator. The plant would initially provide enough power for a community of 50,000 persons. If the demonstration is successful, the plant could be expanded to 400 megawatt capacity, to provide an alternative to gas, oil, and other fuels.

Crime and Land Dispute. Sen. Harrison Schmitt (R-NM) and U. S. Attorney R. E. Thompson investigated a series of mysterious cattle mutilations that has plagued New Mexico and other western states. Schmitt noted that about 8,000 mutilation reports have been received since 1973 and losses to ranchers were estimated at $2.5 million.

Hispanic heirs to the 472,000-acre (191 000-ha) San Joaquin Spanish land grant forcibly closed logging roads in July on federal forest land they claim as part of the grant. They sought to force court action that would require the U. S. government to prove its ownership of property within the grant boundary.

MARC SIMMONS
Author, "New Mexico, A History"

---- **NEW MEXICO • Information Highlights** ----

Area: 121,666 square miles (315 115 km²).
Population (Jan. 1979 est.): 1,221,000.
Chief Cities (1970 census): Santa Fe, the capital, 41,-167; Las Cruces, 37,857; Roswell, 33,908; (1976 est.): Albuquerque, 284,617.
Government (1979): *Chief Officers*—governor, Bruce King (D); lt. gov., Roberto A. Mondragon (D). *Legislature*—Senate, 42 members; House of Representatives, 70 members.
Education (1978–79): *Enrollment*—public elementary schools, 143,927 pupils; public secondary, 135,322; colleges and universities, 55,717 students. *Public school expenditures,* $549,635,000 ($1,628 per pupil).
Personal Income (1978): $7,969,000,000; per capita, $6,574.
Labor Force (July 1979): *Nonagricultural wage and salary earners,* 468,800; *unemployed,* 33,400 (6.2% of total force).

NEW YORK

In a quiet election year, energy was the issue most on the minds of New York residents and the state government. The conversion to coal of several oil-burning power plants was begun, but the question of environmental impact was left unresolved.

Energy and the Environment. The gasoline crisis of the summer of 1979 was felt most acutely in congested downstate areas and was blamed for two New York City homicides that occurred in gasoline line altercations.

On November 1 the state legislature passed a bill awarding grants of $100 to $300 for heating oil and other energy-related costs to homeowners with incomes of less than $13,400. Governor Hugh Carey vetoed the bill, but on November 20 the legislature overrode his veto.

Consolidated Edison went forward with plans to convert six oil-burning plants to coal despite opposition by the state Environmental Protection Agency (EPA). The state EPA also charged the Hooker Chemical & Plastics Co., already under federal investigation for alleged contamination of the Niagara Love Canal, with dumping 1.6 million pounds (725 750 kg) of toxic chemicals a year in a municipal landfill near their Hicksville, Long Island, plant.

On August 7, the state outlined "an energy blueprint for the future" that ruled out the construction of new nuclear power plants, not including those already underway, and called for the increased use of coal and natural gas.

Although New York State is less dependent on nuclear energy than neighboring states, nearly every nuclear installation in the state was the scene of some protest in the aftermath of the March accident at Three Mile Island (PA). Protests against the lack of emergency contingency plans at the Indian Point facility at Peekskill were among the most severe. On October 29, antinuclear demonstrators marked the 50th anniversary of the Stock Market crash by staging sit-ins in New York City's financial district to protest investments in the nuclear industry. More than 1,000 demonstrators were arrested.

NEW YORK • Information Highlights

Area: 49,576 square miles (128 402 km²).

Population (Jan. 1979 est.): 17,653,000.

Chief Cities (1976 est.): Albany, the capital, 109,196; New York, 7,422,831; Buffalo, 400,234; Rochester, 262,766.

Government (1979): *Chief Officers*—governor, Hugh L. Carey (D); lt. gov., Mario M. Cuomo (D). *Legislature*—Senate, 60 members; Assembly, 150 members.

Education (1978–79): *Enrollment*—public elementary schools, 1,520,552 pupils; public secondary, 1,573,333; colleges and universities, 955,547 students. *Public school expenditures,* $8,273,000,000 ($2,478 per pupil).

State Finances (fiscal year 1978): *Revenues,* $23,425,988,000; *expenditures,* $21,395,740,000.

Personal Income (1978): $145,963,000,000; per capita, $8,224.

Labor Force (July 1979): *Nonagricultural wage and salary earners,* 7,141,000; *unemployed,* 610,500 (7.4% of total force).

Politics. A $500-million transportation bond to finance sweeping renovations of New York City's mass transit system was approved in a state referendum November 6. Legislative action on another politically-sensitive issue—a proposed amendment to the state charter that would legalize casino gambling—was deferred until 1981. On March 30 the state legislature appropriated $375 million, half the projected cost, for a new convention and exhibition center on Manhattan's west side.

Ironically, during the year in which New York City was chosen as the site of the 1980 Democratic Convention, the party's decade-long domination of state politics appeared to be waning. Republicans picked up 13 new mayoralties and 42 new county legislature seats. In its first full election year, the antiabortion Right to Life Party showed surprising strength by polling nearly as many votes in municipal and county elections as the well-entrenched Conservative Party.

In the first year of his second term as governor, Hugh Carey continued in his role as New York City's chief lobbyist in Washington. He feuded publicly with administration officials over how much state aid had been promised for fiscal 1980.

Commerce. Although a survey conducted by several of the state's major banks found that only 17% of people doing business in the state found a "favorable business climate," Governor Carey continued a vigorous program to attract new businesses. His efforts included the creation of a "free trade zone," which exempted large business insurance companies from state taxation and regulation.

In its 19 months of operation, the "I Love New York" advertising campaign was credited with attracting $400 million in new tourist business to the state.

Education. On July 13, the state legislature passed the Admissions Testing Law of 1979 (popularly known as the "truth in testing" law), which requires scholastic testing companies to make available to students, for a small additional fee, all test questions and answers for the purpose of verifying scores. The law was considered a test for similar bills proposed nationwide and generated fierce controversy. The Association of American Medical Colleges refused to administer the Medical College Admissions Test (MCAT) in New York and sued the state Department of Higher Education.

The U. S. Supreme Court overturned a lower court ruling that had prohibited New York State from reimbursing private and parochial schools for the cost of providing such state-regulated services as the administration of Regents Examinations and maintaining various student records. The State Comptroller mailed reimbursements totaling $20 million to more than 2,000 nonpublic schools.

DAN HULBERT, *"The New York Times"*

New York Mayor Edward I. Koch announces that the city's new deputy mayor, Haskell G. Ward (right), will specialize in the area of human services.

UPI

NEW YORK CITY

With the rehiring of the last 88 police officers laid off in 1975 and a federal court ruling that absolved former mayor Abraham Beame of criminal negligence in the near-default of that year, New York City in 1979 made a symbolic break with the era of fiscal crisis. But despite a spirit of renewal in the city's cultural and financial centers, most social problems seemed as intractable as ever, and Mayor Edward I. Koch found himself confronted by minority groups who keenly felt the pinch of fiscal belt-tightening.

Finances. On July 17, 40 foreign and domestic banks announced that they would back $600 million in short-term municipal notes, enough to cover the 1979 deficit. At the same time, the city pension funds sold their Municipal Assistance Corporation (MAC) bonds at a profit. Both of these developments were firsts since 1975. Along with the U. S. Treasury's rejection of Senate Banking Committee Chairman William Proxmire's move to cut federal loan guarantees to New York City, they led MAC finance chairman Eugene Keilen to announce a "financial Indian summer" on October 28.

Labor. While even Mayor Koch confessed that city services had continued to decline in 1979, there were no strikes in critical industries. New Yorkers had to endure work stoppages by dairymen, tugboat operators, and school bus drivers. Tariff reductions cost the city 7,300 jobs in the apparel industry, although jobs overall rose by 57,000 for the first half of the year.

Politics. In a nearly election-free year, much of the city's political activity revolved around the proposed riverside highway called Westway. On September 25, the U. S. Department of Transportation denied that Gov. Hugh Carey had ever applied for, or received assurances of, the $805 million in transit aid with which the governor had won Mayor Koch's approval of the highway a year before. In late 1979, the project still awaited approval by the federal Environmental Protection Agency.

At mid-term, Koch was both praised and criticized for his bluntness and candor. His decision to close four of the city's 17 financially ailing municipal hospitals was perceived by minority groups as insensitive to their needs. State Senator Vander L. Beatty circulated an unsuccessful petition to recall the mayor.

Crime. A midsummer bank robbery spree included the most heists ever recorded in a single day: 13 on July 27. Alleged organized crime czar Carmine Gallante was gunned down while dining in a Brooklyn restaurant. And in a long and celebrated trial, longshoreman union leader Anthony M. Scotto was convicted of charges that he received illegal payoffs.

The Arts. On August 23, Aleksandr Godunov of the Soviet Union's Bolshoi Ballet defected to the United States while his troupe was performing in New York. His wife, Lyudmila Vlasova, was detained for three days inside a jetliner at Kennedy International Airport while U. S. intelligence agents tried to determine if she was under official pressure to return to the USSR.

Broadway thrived on the box-office appeal of musical revivals, but an original and daring production, *Sweeney Todd,* with music and lyrics by Stephen Sondheim, collected eight "Tony" awards and the New York Drama Critics Circle Award as the best musical of the season.

People. Several prominent figures made highly-publicized visits to New York in 1979, and their receptions ranged from adulation to the cold shoulder. Pope John Paul II swept through the city October 3–4, conducting an evening mass at Yankee Stadium, delivering an address at the United Nations, and leaving hundreds of thousands of New Yorkers deeply moved by his concern for the city's destitute. Former President Richard M. Nixon purchased a $750,000 townhouse on East 65th Street but only after wary city residents had successfully blocked his attempts to move into two other buildings. Cuban President Fidel Castro's address at the United Nations highlighted his first visit to American soil since 1959, and deposed Iranian Shah Mohammed Reza Pahlavi was flown into New York for cancer treatment.

Another controversial figure in the city's ebb and flow was former New York Yankee manager Billy Martin, who was fired, rehired, and fired again in the space of 15 months. The Yankees finished poorly in 1979 after two consecutive world championships.

DAN HULBERT, *"The New York Times"*

PHOTO BY ANTHONY HATHAWAY, COURTESY OF THE NEW ZEALAND EMBASSY

In 1979, the New Zealand Embassy's new building opened at 37 Observatory Circle N. W. in Washington.

NEW ZEALAND

Although there was conflicting evidence as to the gravity of its condition, the economy continued to be New Zealand's most vital concern in 1979. Politically, the most notable development was the resurgence of the third party, the Social Credit League.

Economy. The rate of inflation caused mounting anxiety. For the year ending March 31, 1979, it stood at 10.4%; six months later it had climbed to 15.2%. The increase was variously attributed to massive hikes in transportation, power, and postal charges; the removal of price controls on most items of sale; and liberal wage awards. In July the government withdrew the authority of the Arbitration Court to make general wage orders. Disquiet over wage-fixing procedures led the Federation of Labour on September 20 to call for the first-ever general strike. Purchases of petroleum severely taxed overseas reserves, necessitating the closing of gas stations on weekends and the introduction in late July of one carless day per week. Savings were below expectations. Prior to the introduction of the budget, sizeable sales tax increases were imposed on tools, mobile homes and trailers, power mowers, and ice cream. The budget itself was a startling mixture of carrot and stick. It called for a 5% currency devaluation, the doubling of family benefits, lower income taxes, export incentives, and radical increases in alcohol and tobacco duties. A projected rise of 12% in government spending was to be accommodated by a deficit of $1.09 billion. A leading newspaper summarized the budget as "concessions and compensations aimed at maintaining some zing in a flagging economy."

Politics. In the aftermath of the 1978 general election, the opposition Labour Party retained one seat in a by-election and lost another seat when an electoral court dispossessed a member because of election irregularities. Public opinion polls consistently gave Labour a lead of 3–10% over the governing National Party. In September, Social Credit achieved its highest rating ever, 21.7%. Other polls identified the economy, inflation, and unemployment—later joined by the energy crisis—as the issues causing the most public concern. A poll in March revealed popular dissatisfaction, by a margin of 61 to 32, with the parliament.

Foreign Relations. Prime Minister Robert Muldoon went on three major foreign tours during the year. The first was to International Monetary Fund (IMF) talks in Washington and an Organization of Economic Cooperation and Development (OECD) meeting in Paris. The second was to the conference of Commonwealth heads of state in Zambia. The third trip included the opening of the New Zealand chancery in Washington and chairing sessions of the IMF and World Bank in Belgrade.

Other. A fractional decline in New Zealand's absolute population went unchecked. The loss of 26,900 persons was 26% more than in 1977–

─── **NEW ZEALAND • Information Highlights** ───

Official Name: New Zealand.
Location: Southwest Pacific Ocean.
Area: 103,736 square miles (268 676 km²).
Population (1979 est.): 3,200,000.
Chief Cities (March 1978): Wellington, the capital, 351,000; Auckland, 804,200; Christchurch, 327,800.
Government: *Head of state,* Elizabeth II, queen, represented by Sir Keith Holyoake, governor general (took office Oct. 1977). *Head of government,* Robert Muldoon, prime minister (took office Dec. 1975). *Legislature* (unicameral)—House of Representatives.
Monetary Unit: New Zealand dollar (1.0194 N. Z. dollars equal U. S.$1, Dec. 1979).
Manufactures (major products): Processed foods, wood products, cement, fertilizer, beverages, domestic appliances.
Agriculture (major products): Wheat, corn, barley, potatoes, dairy products, wool.

78. A collapse of the Public Service Investment Society was averted only by government intervention. The nation's two television channels were partially merged, consolidating planning, scheduling, and production. At the height of the flood of Vietnamese "boat people," it was announced that 800 Southeast Asian refugees would be granted residency in New Zealand. On November 28, an Air New Zealand DC-10 passenger plane crashed into Mt. Erebus, killing all 237 passengers and 20 crew members.

GRAHAM BUSH, *University of Auckland*

NIGERIA

The return of the government to civilians for the first time in 13 years was completed by the elections of midyear and the surrender of control by the military authorities on October 1.

Economy. The decline in agricultural exports, particularly cocoa, was hardly noticed because of Nigeria's income from petroleum. The temporary restrictions on petroleum production were lifted, and more gathering pipelines were built, allowing daily output to reach 2.5 million barrels a day. Nigeria's sulfur-free, low gravity crude was in great demand, particularly in the United States, and even with the rise in price, much more could be sold if production facilities were improved. Oil profits continued to rise, reflecting the greater production and the increase in the per barrel price determined by OPEC. The Federal Military Government (FMG) increased its share in all foreign oil companies to 60% and retaliated against British Petroleum (BP) for trading with South Africa by nationalizing all BP's assets. Nigeria also cut off oil supplies to Ghana to protest the executions conducted by its revolutionary regime.

Nigeria's rapidly increasing wealth is shown by the rise in the level of federal revenues and spending. In 1978–79 the revenue was ₦ (naira) 2,171 million and allocations to the states were ₦ 324 million. For the 1979–80 year the projected figures were ₦ 8,805 million and ₦ 2,534 million. Federal capital expenditure during the 1979 fiscal year stood at ₦ 6,610 million, with the military, police, and education getting the largest amounts.

Although fiscally sound, Nigeria does have some problems. The 1979 budget deficit was expected to be at least ₦ 3,200 million and inflation reached double-digit figures. There was an acute shortage of housing in the urban areas and electrical power from the Kainji complex fell short of demand. The FMG in its 1979 budget applied more conservative economics. Import restrictions were enacted, income tax laws tightened, and government loans made more difficult to obtain. Unemployment remained high in the cities and prosperity did not extend to many rural areas. However, Nigeria's program of agricultural self-sufficiency has been successful.

Politics. Lt. Gen. Olusegun Obasanjo had promised a return to civilian control in 1979 and had taken the first steps in 1978 to implement this policy. Local governments had been established, a Constituent Assembly elected, and a new Constitution promulgated. Culminating all this preparation were the elections held between July 7 and August 11. The Constitution called for a two-house federal legislature, 19 state assemblies, state governors, and an executive president, all elected by direct vote. The Federal Elections Committee (FEDECO) employed more than 400,000 persons to work the boards and monitor the elections. It had screened the qualifications of 8,728 candidates, banning more than 1,000. Five political parties—the Nigeria People's Party (NPP) headed by former President Nnamadi Azikiwe, the United Party of Nigeria (UNP) of Chief Obafemi Awolowo, the People's Redemption Party (PRP) of Alhaji Aminu Kano, the National Party of Nigeria (NPN) led by Alhaji Shehu Shagari, and the Great Nigeria People's Party (GNPP) of Alhaji Waziri Ibrahim—contested the elections. All the leaders ran for president, but Alhaji Kano was disqualified for tax irregularities.

A high percentage of the 47 million registered voters went to the polls and by August it was clear that the NPN had won a substantial victory at all levels. It held 168 of the 494 seats in the National Assembly, 36 of the 95 seats of the Senate, 7 state governorships, and Shehu Shagari was elected president, beating his nearest rival, Chief Awolowo, by more than 700,000 votes. Having no clear majority, the NPN depends on the goodwill of the other parties, but two are Northern and Muslim-based and the feeling for unity appeared genuine. The NPN is a national party; sectionalism, although important, was relegated to a secondary role.

At the inauguration ceremonies on October 1, General Obasanjo announced his retirement from the army but pledged its continuing support for the new government. President Shagari promised to continue the forward-looking policies of the FMG, to work for "agricultural and economic self-sufficiency" and to fight racism in southern Africa.

HARRY A. GAILEY, *San Jose State University*

NIGERIA · Information Highlights

Official Name: Federal Republic of Nigeria.
Location: West Africa.
Area: 356,669 square miles (923 772 km²).
Population (1979 est.): 74,600,000.
Chief Cities (1976 est.): Lagos, the capital, 1,100,000; Ibadan, 850,000; Ogbomosho, 435,000; Kano, 400,000.
Government: *Head of state and government,* Alhaji Shehu Shagari, president (took office Oct. 1979). *Legislature*—Senate and House of Representatives.
Monetary Unit: Naira (0.58028 naira equals U. S.$1, Aug. 1979).
Manufactures (major products): Petroleum, textiles, cement, food products, footwear, metal products, lumber.
Agriculture (major products): Cocoa, rubber, palm oil, yams, cassava, sorghum, millet, corn, rice, cotton.

NORTH CAROLINA

The General Assembly adopted a record budget and cut taxes. An economic slowdown became evident in July when general fund collections increased only 10.5% and highway fund collections dropped 6.5% below the same month in 1978. Employment reached a record 2.6 million in the summer.

Agriculture and Business. Tobacco farmers felt the pinch of the energy shortage and a slackening demand for tobacco. Controversy arose over insurance settlements for crops damaged by contaminated fertilizer inadvertently sold by the Smith-Douglass Corporation. Controversy also surrounded the Virginia Electric Power Company, which declined the invitation of Gov. James B. Hunt, Jr., to relinquish its franchise in 22 northeastern counties. Wachovia, the largest banking firm in the southeast, celebrated its 100th birthday.

Education. Low competency test scores by public school pupils led to demands for accountability of educational funds. Private schools were exempt from most state regulations. Legislation placed the community college system within a 19-member Board of Community Colleges and Technical Institutes.

A federal judge blocked efforts of the Department of Health, Education, and Welfare to cut off federal funds to the University of North Carolina, but the litigation continued over the issue of minority enrollments, despite the legislature's appropriation of increased capital funds for the traditionally black campuses. Ferebee Taylor, whose eight-year chancellorship at the Chapel Hill campus led to unprecedented library development, announced his resignation for reasons of health.

The murder of Charles Frankel, director of the National Humanities Center, cast a pall over the center's dedication ceremonies, in which the building was named for Archie K. Davis, the man largely responsible for its location in North Carolina.

Women. The proposed Equal Rights Amendment again failed to pass the General Assembly. Nevertheless, North Carolina enjoyed a distinc-

tion for several months when the two highest judicial offices were held by women—Susie M. Sharp as chief justice of the State Supreme Court and Naomi E. Morris as chief judge of the Court of Appeals. Justice Sharp retired on June 30 and was succeeded by Joseph Branch. Joan Little, serving a sentence for larceny and escape, was paroled under the surveillance of New York authorities.

Ku Klux Klan. In November, five members of the Communist Workers Party were slain at a Greensboro, NC, anti–Ku Klux Klan rally. Demonstrations in support of the five were held at the cemetery, where sympathizers from several states gathered.

H. G. JONES, *University of North Carolina*

NORTH DAKOTA

The Red River flood of 1979 had a major impact on North Dakota.

Weather. Spring flooding of the 200-mile (322-km) Red River Valley drove 7,500 North Dakotans from their homes and damaged 6,000 buildings. The flood water covered nearly 425,-000 acres (172 023 ha). Urban and agricultural losses topped $60 million, and 165 local governments sought $12.5 million in federal disaster aid for rehabilitation of public works. Gov. Arthur Link of North Dakota and Gov. Al Quie of Minnesota ordered a moratorium on dike repair and construction until uniform rules could be adopted, and a citizens group from the two states and the Canadian province of Manitoba sought creation of a Red River Valley authority to stabilize the river flow.

The flood, the second in two years to exceed the 100-year highwater level, followed the coldest winter in 43 years and record snow accumulation.

Legislature. The legislature enacted a June presidential preference primary, election law revision, and executive and legislative branch reorganization. These enactments are subject to the vote of the people in 1980.

The legislature upheld its 1975 Equal Rights Amendment (ERA) ratification and rejected the District of Columbia voting rights amendment.

— NORTH CAROLINA • Information Highlights —

Area: 52,586 square miles (136 198 km²).

Population (Jan. 1979 est.): 5,605,000.

Chief Cities (1976 est.): Raleigh, the capital, 136,883; Charlotte, 281,696; Greensboro, 157,324.

Government (1979): *Chief Officers*—governor, James B. Hunt, Jr. (D); lt. gov., James C. Green (D). *General Assembly*—Senate, 50 members; House of Representatives, 120 members.

Education (1978–79): *Enrollment*—public elementary schools, 800,807 pupils; public secondary, 362,003; colleges and universities, 262,757 students. *Public school expenditures,* $1,998,506,000 ($1,406 per pupil).

State Finances (fiscal year 1978): *Revenues,* $4,854,-529,000; *expenditures,* $4,672,085,000.

Personal Income (1978): $36,671,000,000; per capita, $6,575.

Labor Force (July 1979): *Nonagricultural wage and salary earners,* 2,304,000; *unemployed,* 155,000 (5.6% of total force).

—— NORTH DAKOTA • Information Highlights——

Area: 70,665 square miles (183 022 km²).

Population (Jan. 1979 est.): 655,000.

Chief Cities (1970 census): Bismarck, the capital, 34,-703; Fargo, 53,365; Grand Forks, 39,008.

Government (1979): *Chief Officers*—governor, Arthur A. Link (D); lt. gov., Wayne G. Sanstead (D). *Legislative Assembly*—Senate, 50 members; House of Representatives, 100 members.

Education (1978–79): *Enrollment*—public elementary schools, 57,902 pupils; public secondary, 64,119; colleges and universities, 32,325 students. *Public school expenditures,* $208,527,000 ($1,551 per pupil).

State Finances (fiscal year 1978): *Revenues,* $771,-064,000; *expenditures,* $699,144,000.

Personal Income (1978): $4,677,000,000; per capita, $7,174.

Labor Force (July 1979): *Nonagricultural wage and salary earners,* 247,000; *unemployed,* 10,100 (3.0% of total force).

It also gave physicians authority to prescribe Laetrile; approved two measures tightening abortion laws (however, a federal judge halted enactment of the new measures until tested in court); authorized purchase of 10,000 acres (4 049 ha) of ranchland as a state park; revised gambling for charity legislation; and passed a state human rights act.

Garrison. A controversy over acquisition of farmland for a wildlife habitat added to problems besetting the Garrison Diversion irrigation and water supply project. The federal Fish and Wildlife Service could acquire the required mitigating acres through eminent domain, but North Dakota policy calls for purchase only from "willing sellers." During 1979, one North Dakota county asked to withdraw from the project. Meanwhile, the National Audubon Society has reinstated its federal lawsuit.

Agriculture. The April flood and spring rains delayed field work nearly a month and brought grains and sunflowers to harvest in the midst of a lengthy strike of grain handlers at Duluth-Superior terminals. Grain and cattle prices improved, but North Dakota production, except for a good crop of sunflowers, was below average.

Politics. Republican Sen. Milton R. Young's decision to retire in 1980, after 35 years in the U. S. Senate, aroused political hopes of both Republicans and Democrats. The state Supreme Court further opened the political process by a judicial redistricting plan that provided for 24 elected judges in seven districts. Many now on the bench must run in 1980.

STAN CANN, *The Fargo Forum*

NORTHWEST TERRITORIES

The appointment of a new commissioner and the expansion and election of the legislative assembly were the significant political developments of the year in Canada's Northwest Territories (NWT). Despite encouraging signs for the future, the economy was strained.

Politics. An amendment to the federal Northwest Territories Act increased the size of the Territorial Council from 15 to 22 seats. The change permits the assembly to set the number of constituencies between a minimum of 15 and a maximum of 25. New Democrat Wally Firth, then the only member of parliament from the Northwest Territories, blocked swift passage of the bill in the House of Commons, but it eventually was carried by both federal chambers. Elections for a 22-member body were held October 1. The larger assembly allows for representation of smaller groups of communities, making it easier for members to represent all constituents spread over the 1.3 million square miles (3.4 million km²) of the territory. The executive committee or cabinet also was enlarged, from three to seven elected members.

Administration. On Jan. 25, 1979, then Prime Minister Pierre Elliott Trudeau announced that

─── **NORTHWEST TERRITORIES · Information** ───
Highlights

Area: 1,304,903 square miles (3 379 700 km²).
Population (1979 est.): 43,200.
Chief City (1976 census): Yellowknife, the capital, 8,256.
Government (1979): *Chief Officers*—commissioner, John H. Parker; chief justice, Court of Appeal, William A. McGillivray; judge of the Supreme Court, C. F. Tallis. *Legislature*—Territorial Council, 22 elected members.
Education (1979–80 est.): *Enrollment*—public elementary and secondary schools, 12,470 pupils. *Public school expenditures* (1978–79), $49,053,000.
Public Finance (fiscal year 1978–79): *Revenues,* $278,- 453,362; *expenditures,* $282,166,529.
Mining (1979 est.): Production value, $437,000,000.
(All monetary figures are in Canadian dollars.)

NWT Commissioner Stuart M. Hodgson was appointed Canadian co-chairman of the International Joint Commission. Hodgson, who had served as NWT commissioner for 12 years, was replaced in April by his deputy commissioner, John H. Parker.

Economy. Exploration for oil and gas, precious and base metals, and uranium had positive results and created optimism for future production. But the year also brought considerable economic strain, as soaring energy costs hindered economic development and the delivery of government services. The legislative assembly voted a budget of more than $294 million.

Land Claims. Although discussions continued, the election of a new federal government in May slowed the processing of land claims. The new Conservative administration took the time to review claimants' papers and evaluate all agreements with the previous government.

ROSS M. HARVEY
Government of the Northwest Territories

NORWAY

Despite the apparent success of its economic policies, Norway's governing Labor Party lost support in local elections, and Prime Minister Odvar Nordli had to reshuffle his cabinet.

Economy and Trade. World developments and the restrictive measures adopted by the government during the previous year brought an overall improvement of the economy. The steep rise in world oil and gas prices following the revolution in Iran benefited Norway in several ways. It increased the value of oil and gas already being produced off the Norwegian coast and made worthwhile the development of smaller fields previously regarded as uneconomic. In addition, it sharply improved the competitive position of the country's large metal-smelting industry, which uses low-priced hydroelectric power.

At home, a wage and price freeze adopted in September 1978 and lasting until the end of 1979 was accepted by all sectors of the society. The unions did without their usual pay increases in the spring and autumn. The rate of inflation was well below that of most of Norway's trading partners; from August 1978 to August 1979, the consumer price index rose by only 4.4%. This helped make Norwegian goods more competitive abroad. Curbs on credit and other measures to restrict demand helped slow the rise in imports. At the same time exports rose dramatically (nearly 35%), reflecting an increase in both the volume and value of oil and gas exports, as well as greater demand for the traditionally strong commodities.

Unemployment declined, as the oil and gas industry provided new jobs. On October 16, the energy ministers of Norway and Great Britain signed agreements for the joint development of oil and gas fields in Statfjord and Murchison.

The government presented its 1980 budget to the Storting (parliament), October 6–7. Projected expenditures of 76.5 billion kroner ($15.3 billion) would represent an increase of 13% over 1979; revenues of 71.9 billion kroner ($14.4 billion) would be a 17.7% increase.

Government and Politics. Following the trend observed in other Western industrialized nations, the results of September 17 municipal and local elections in Norway revealed a marked swing to the right. Labor's share of the vote fell by 2% from 1975 local elections, to 36%. The Conservatives, the largest party of the right, won 30%, a gain of 7%. The six nonsocialist parties together captured 57.4% of the vote, and the results were considered a major setback for the governing Labor Party.

Soon after the elections, on October 5, Prime Minister Nordli announced a major reshuffling of the cabinet. His appointments represented an attempt to strengthen the left-wing of the cabinet. The changes included the establishment of a ministry for long-term economic planning.

In early October, public controversy over a hydroelectric project in the northern county of Finnmark focused attention on the long-neglected issue of Lapps' rights. After the Storting had approved the project on October 8, hundreds of Lapps staged a demonstration and several went on a hunger strike. They maintained that the project would spoil reindeer grazing land. A wave of public sympathy led Prime Minister Nordli temporarily to suspend work at the site, pending an investigation of the Lapps' grievances.

THOR GJESTER
Editor, "Økonomisk Revy," Oslo

NOVA SCOTIA

Improvement in real income, a decline in unemployment, and progress in the development of mineral resources marked a positive year in Nova Scotia.

Government and the Legislature. During its first year in office, the Progressive Conservative government of Premier John Buchanan moved to build a new medical complex in Halifax, establish the Fisheries Research Institute of Technology in the capital city, and keep open the Sydney Steel Plant in Cape Breton.

Before adjourning May 15, the legislative assembly considered 99 bills, of which 74 gained royal assent. The new laws included changes in municipal elections and financing, a revision of the Liquor Control Act, a higher minimum for automobile insurance coverage, and pay raises for members of the legislature. The government also handed down a $1.49 billion budget, with a projected deficit of $17.6 million for the year. Projected expenditures represented a 4.7% increase over the previous year.

Economy. Although the federal economy showed little growth, Nova Scotia turned in strong performances by several vital sectors—fishing, mining, farming, lumbering, and manufacturing. Despite a significant decline in exports and housing starts, an upsurge in retail trade, farm cash receipts, and manufacturing shipments ensured a 3% real growth rate for the provincial economy. However, on August 13, the Conference Board in Canada predicted that the growth rate would fall off to 1.1% in 1980.

Energy. The provincial government continued to consider alternative sources of energy. Exploration to determine the extent of coal deposits on the shores of Cape Breton were expedited. The government also supported the construction of a gas pipeline from Montreal to Halifax and sought federal grants for developing coal and petroleum reserves off the provincial coast. In 1979, however, Nova Scotians continued to suffer rising power rates. Increases totaled about 13.5% for the year.

R. P. SETH
Department of Economics
Mount St. Vincent University, Halifax

─────── **NORWAY · Information Highlights** ───────

Official Name: Kingdom of Norway.
Location: Northern Europe.
Area: 125,181 square miles (324 219 km²).
Population (1979 est.): 4,100,000.
Chief Cities (Jan. 1978): Oslo, the capital, 460,377; Bergen, 211,861; Trondheim, 135,085.
Government: *Head of state,* Olav V, king (acceded Sept. 1957). *Head of government,* Odvar Nordli, prime minister (took office Jan. 1976). *Legislature*—Storting: Lagting and Odelsting.
Monetary Unit: Krone (4.9895 kroner equal U. S.$1, Dec. 1979).
Manufactures (major products): Pulp and paper, ships, oil and gas, food products, aluminum, ferroalloys.
Agriculture (major products): Potatoes, barley, wheat, apples, pears, dairy products, livestock, oats.

─────── **NOVA SCOTIA · Information Highlights** ───────

Area: 21,425 square miles (55 490 km²).
Population (1979 est.): 846,700.
Chief Cities (1976 census): Halifax, the capital, 117,882; Dartmouth, 65,341; Sydney, 30,645.
Government (1979): *Chief Officers*—lt. gov., John E. Shaffner; premier, John Buchanan (Progressive Conservative). *Legislature*—Legislative Assembly, 52 members.
Education (1979–80 est.): *Enrollment*—public elementary and secondary schools, 189,960 pupils; private schools, 1,340; Indian (federal) schools, 730; postsecondary, 21,420 students.
Public Finance (1979–80 est.): *Revenues,* $1,506,661,700; *expenditures,* $1,493,629,200.
Unemployment Rate (Sept. 1979, seasonally adjusted): 10.2%.
(All monetary figures are in Canadian dollars.)

ROCKEFELLER, Nelson Aldrich

U. S. vice president and New York governor: b. Bar Harbor, ME, July 8, 1908; d. New York City, Jan. 29, 1979.

Nelson A. Rockefeller, governor of New York State (1959–73) and 41st vice president of the United States (1974–77), died suddenly of a heart attack on Jan. 29, 1979. Although he was heir to one of America's greatest family fortunes and spent more than 25 years in government service, the one job that he really wanted, the U. S. presidency, escaped him.

After graduation from Dartmouth College in 1930, he invested in a Standard Oil subsidiary in Venezuela and developed a lifelong interest in Latin America. In 1940 President Franklin Roosevelt appointed him coordinator of inter-American affairs and assistant secretary of state for American republic affairs. He left the government that year but was called back in 1950 to be the chairman of President Truman's international development advisory board. In 1953, President Eisenhower named Rockefeller to head a presidential advisory committee on government organization. The group ultimately recommended the plans that resulted in the establishment of the Department of Health, Education, and Welfare and the U. S. Information Agency, and the reorganization of the departments of agriculture, defense, and justice.

Rockefeller was elected governor of New York in 1958 and reelected three times. He inaugurated a dramatic growth in state services in the areas of education, transportation, health and welfare, housing, and environmental protection. His administration was responsible for substantial tax increases, and for many years the state operated on a pay-as-you-go basis with a balanced budget. The governor's decisions regarding the 1971 Attica prison riot stirred major controversy.

After repeatedly denying interest in the presidency, Rockefeller made it known that he would accept a draft should the 1960 Republican convention offer him the nomination, but Richard M. Nixon was already assured of the nomination. Rockefeller emerged as the clear favorite for the 1964 presidential nomination. His divorce (1962) and remarriage (1963), however, had brought about a decline in his popularity that he was not able to overcome. Sen. Barry Goldwater, leader of the Republican conservative wing, won the nomination on the first ballot. Rockefeller's third campaign for the presidency, in 1968, was marred by early indecision.

After resigning from the governorship in December 1973, Rockefeller devoted himself to the Commission on Critical Choices for America, which he organized for the purpose of developing national policy alternatives. In August 1974, President Gerald Ford nominated him to be vice

OFFICE OF THE VICE PRESIDENT

NELSON A. ROCKEFELLER (1908–79)
Businessman, art collector, philanthropist, politician

president of the United States. After extended Congressional inquiries into his financial resources he was confirmed by a vote of 287 to 128 in the House and 90 to 7 in the Senate.

Vice President Rockefeller proved to be a loyal and faithful subordinate. President Ford named him to head the domestic council and to be chairman of the president's commission on the Central Intelligence Agency. He also was designated to serve on several other commissions. He was never fully accepted by the Republican conservative wing during his term, and in November 1975 he announced that he was removing himself from consideration as a possible running mate for President Ford in 1976. After leaving office he returned to New York and his private pursuits in business, politics, and the arts. He was working on a major art project when he died.

The former vice president is the author of several books.

Rockefeller was married to Mary Todhunter Clark in 1930, a union that produced five children. After their divorce in 1962 he married Margaretta (Happy) Murphy, with whom he had two sons.

In reporting his death, *Newsweek* magazine noted that Rockefeller "cut an extraordinary figure in American political life for a perennial also-ran; he bubbled with ideas, stirred passions, compelled thought and made a powerful and lasting mark on the party that rejected him."

ROBERT J. HUCKSHORN

[1] Arranged chronologically by death date

MONNET, Jean

French internationalist and financier: b. Cognac, France, Nov. 9, 1888; d. Houjarray, France, March 16, 1979.

In his 70-year career as a businessman, international economist, and diplomatic power-broker, Jean Monnet's greatest recognition came from his role as organizer and spiritual father of the European Community (EC), or Common Market. Although by the time of his death the EC had come under criticism for failing to achieve Monnet's ultimate goal of a United States of Europe, Monnet himself never lost faith. At the age of 90, not long before his death, he wrote: "The European idea goes on; and no one seeing it, and seeing how stable the Community institutions are, can doubt that this is a . . . powerful movement on a historic scale."

Monnet began his international business career in 1906 as a Canadian sales representative for his father's cognac concern. The aging of brandy, he would later say, taught him the lesson of patience. As coordinator of the Franco-British war supply in 1916 and as deputy secretary-general of the League of Nations, 1919–23, he learned first-hand the problems of reconciling divergent national interests in a common policy. By 1939, he had become an internationally respected economic adviser. He had helped to reestablish the currencies of Poland and Rumania and to reorganize the Chinese railroad system. In 1943 he joined Charles de Gaulle's Free French movement in Algiers, and in 1945 was named by De Gaulle to create the French Modernization and Equipment Plan.

Monnet's early efforts as an economic adviser were guided by his principle of "indicative planning"—the notion that a government can realize national economic goals without restricting the initiative of individual sectors. He soon became convinced, however, that the national framework was too restrictive. In May 1950 he persuaded French Foreign Minister Robert Schuman to sponsor a plan for the partial integration of the economies of the West European states. Pooling the coal and steel industries of Western Europe, he believed, was the basis for a supranational economic community.

At age 64, Monnet became president of the High Authority of the European Coal and Steel Community. In 1957, he resigned his presidency to devote himself to work for European unification. His vehicle was the Action Committee for the United States of Europe, a group of political and trade union leaders. The committee exerted pressure on the nations of Europe to accept such proposals as Euratom and the European Economic Community (EEC, later changed to EC). Monnet's vision seemed to have been realized with the great successes of EEC after 1958 and the entry of Great Britain in 1971.

F. ROY WILLIS

KELLY, Emmett

Circus clown: b. Sedan, KS, Dec. 9, 1898; d. Sarasota, FL, March 28, 1979.

Emmett Kelly, the American circus clown who evoked both pathos and laughter with no more than a lonesome stare, died in Sarasota, FL, home of the Circus Hall of Fame and the Ringling Museums, on March 28, 1979. It was the same day that Ringling Bros. and Barnum & Bailey Circus, in which Kelly performed for 15 years, opened in New York City.

Probably the most famous of all American clowns, Kelly was identified with his character of Weary Willie—a sad-faced, bedraggled hobo in tattered clothes and a battered hat. Frustration was the main theme in the antics of Weary Willie. One of the routines for which Kelly will be best remembered was Willie's attempt first to catch a fleeting spotlight and then sweep it up with a broom.

Emmett Kelly was named after Robert Emmett, the 18th century Irish patriot, by his nationalistic Irish immigrant father. As a youngster growing up in Missouri, Emmett had no yearnings to be a circus performer, aspiring instead to become a cartoonist. Although he had only an eighth-grade education, it was at school that he first discovered his aptitude for drawing. He was encouraged by his mother to pursue a career in art but was unable to find work and instead took various jobs as a sign painter and carnival manager. He also performed with chalk-talks, comic illustrations, caricatures, and as a white-faced clown in a trapeze act. In 1920 he found work with a film advertising company, where he created the cartoon character of Weary Willie. After one year he returned to the circus. In 1931 he joined the famous Hagenback-Wallace circus and decided to concentrate on being a clown. In 1933 he brought to life his own vision of a clown, Weary Willie.

With this new character he traveled widely in the United States and abroad. In 1940 he appeared in the Broadway musical *Keep Off the Grass* with Jimmy Durante. After joining Ringling Bros. two years later, his recognition grew.

Kelly's popularity enabled him to break into other entertainment media. There were film performances in *The Fat Man* (1951) and *The Greatest Show on Earth* (1952), numerous television appearances, night club performances with his close friend Red Skelton, and even a role in the Smetana opera *The Bartered Bride,* directed by Sarah Caldwell. His autobiography, *Clown,* written with F. Beverly Kelly, was published in 1954.

His third and last wife was Elvira Gebhardt; he had two daughters from that union and two sons from his first marriage.

SAUNDRA FRANCE

RANDOLPH, Asa Philip

American civil rights and labor leader: b. Crescent City, FL, April 15, 1889; d. New York City, May 16, 1979.

For half a century, A. Philip Randolph was one of the most eloquent and effective voices for blacks' rights in the United States, a young agitator who endured to become an elder statesman to a later generation of civil-rights activists. As a young man, Randolph arrived in New York City, where he, a minister's son, began preaching socialism on Harlem street corners. In 1917 he and his collaborator, Chandler Owen, started a controversial magazine, *The Messenger,* that advanced the radical philosophies of "New Negro" intellectuals. In its pages, Randolph urged black Americans not to participate in World War I— a stand that contradicted the far more popular advice of black leader W. E. B. DuBois.

In 1925, a group of Pullman porters approached Randolph and asked him to organize a union for them. At the time, the Pullman Company was a major employer of black men, all condescendingly called "George," who served the needs of rail passengers and received unusually low wages. After a tough twelve-year fight, Randolph won a contract between Pullman and the International Brotherhood of Sleeping Car Porters—the first labor settlement between a major American company and a black labor union.

His influence on American social policy continued. In 1941, he developed a campaign to have thousands of black Americans march on Washington, DC, to demand jobs in then-segregated defense plants. The idea caught on, and President Franklin Roosevelt, yielding to the threat of the mass demonstration, issued an executive order banning racial discrimination in the defense industry. Seven years later, Randolph led a nonviolent protest campaign that prompted President Harry Truman to issue an executive order desegregating the armed forces.

By then, Randolph was beginning to be challenged by a new group of black activists, who ironically found him too conservative. But as the civil rights movement of the 1950's and 1960's grew, Randolph remained a respected mediator among disparate black-rights groups and the unquestioned dean of black American political-action leaders. In addressing the vast crowd at the historic 1963 civil rights march in Washington, Randolph said: "Let the nation and the world know the meaning of our numbers. We are not a pressure group; we are not an organization or a group of organizations; we are not a mob. We are the advance guard of a massive moral revolution for jobs and freedom." None was more advanced than the old warrior Randolph, who continued to speak out.

In 1965 the A. Philip Randolph Institute was established for the purpose of studying poverty.

DENNIS A. WILLIAMS

PICKFORD, Mary

American film actress: b. Toronto, Ont., April 9, 1893; d. Santa Monica, CA, May 29, 1979.

The phenomenal career of Mary Pickford, born Gladys Marie Smith, added generously to Hollywood's mythology—the rise to fame, public adulation, the accumulation of wealth, the glamorous social life, a fabled marriage that failed, and finally, life as a virtual recluse harboring memories of the golden years. America's Sweetheart, as she early was known, died at 86, leaving a legacy of 194 films.

Her triumph came through her ability to play emotion-wrenching child parts in silents, but her downfall was that that was the only way in which the public wished to see her. The girl with the golden curls became a public darling, typecast into a mold that had little to do with the stage career she had gone to New York to seek following appearances from age five in stock productions in her native Toronto. Director D. W. Griffith, whose film studio was in New York, discovered her and was undoubtedly responsible for helping to develop her comparatively subtle style, far removed from the exaggerated gestures typical of the time.

Her pictures include her first great success, *Tess of the Storm Country; The Poor Little Rich Girl, Rebecca of Sunnybrook Farm, Sparrows, Pollyanna,* and *Stella Maris.* The public was so attuned to her youthful image that when she finally trimmed her curls it was a national event. She was not permitted her first screen kiss until 1927, when she was 34. Sensing that she could not change this pattern, she retired in 1933 to rest on her achievements. By then she had earned a vast amount of money, having reached the salary of $10,000 weekly before other stars of her era. In 1919 she and Douglas Fairbanks, Sr., whom she married in 1920, joined with Charlie Chaplin to form United Artists for the purpose of controlling the artistic production and the distribution of their own films. Eventually her fortune reached $50 million.

Fairbanks, famed for his swashbuckling roles, and Pickford were at the center of Hollywood's social whirl. Their lavish mansion Pickfair was the place to be seen and to meet the greats in and out of the movie business. But the much-publicized marriage did not last; they were divorced in 1936. A year later she married Charles (Buddy) Rogers, actor and bandleader, who remained with her through her final years, devotedly caring for her and jealously guarding her privacy when she was confined to bed by illness. The last occasion on which the public saw her was in 1976 when a film of her receiving a special Oscar at home was televised.

WILLIAM WOLF

SYGMA/PARIS

JOHN WAYNE (1907–1979)
"the duke"

WAYNE, John

American film actor: b. Winterset, IA, May 26, 1907; d. Los Angeles, CA, June 11, 1979.

On screen John Wayne was the epitome of the Western movie hero. In real life he also took on the image of the basic role he played throughout a 50-year career that included more than 200 films. Critics sometimes made fun of his awkward style—a slow drawl that counterpointed his fast draw—but audiences flocked to see him get the bad guys. He was both lauded and denounced for his controversial rightist politics, but even his detractors acknowledged his stature as a Hollywood legend. In 1970 he won an Academy Award for his performance in *True Grit,* and shortly before his death the U. S. Congress had a medal struck in his honor. When he finally lost his 15-year battle with cancer, notables in many walks of life paid tribute to him.

Born the son of a druggist, he was named Marion Michael Morrison. Because of his father's ill health, the family moved to California when Marion was six, first to a farm, then to Glendale, where his father opened a pharmacy in the same building that housed a movie theater. The actor-to-be saw nearly every film that played there. He also watched films being made at a nearby studio. After working at odd jobs, he attended the University of Southern California on a football scholarship, then dropped out after an ankle injury. His official link with the film industry came at Fox, where he was hired to move scenery. Director John Ford then hired him as a prop boy. One day he boldly subbed for a stunt man who had qualms about an assignment. Impressed, Ford made him part of his production team.

Ford recalled that when he set about to make *Stagecoach,* the 1939 film that propelled Wayne to fame, the producer Walter Wanger wanted Gary Cooper for the part of the Ringo Kid. But Ford said that Cooper would be too expensive. Wanger asked Ford who he had in mind. "Well," said Ford, "there's a boy I know who used to be assistant prop man and he's a bit player for me. His name was Michael Morrison, but he's making five-day Westerns and calls himself John Wayne now." Wanger asked if he were good. "Yes, I think so, and we can get him for peanuts."

Prior to *Stagecoach,* Wayne had starred for Raoul Walsh in *The Big Trail* (1930) and had made some 40 grade B or C Westerns. As Ringo, he exhibited the character that was to be his thereafter—tough, straightforward, principled, bashful with women, stalwart and fearless in the face of danger. He stood 6′ 4″ (193 cm) and was always the tallest tree in the forest. Even when he played a character in another milieu, he knew how to make his image work for him.

His best-known films include *They Were Expendable* (1945), *Fort Apache* and *Red River* (1948), *She Wore a Yellow Ribbon* (1949), *The Quiet Man* (1952), *The Searchers* (1955), *The Man Who Shot Liberty Valance* (1962), *El Dorado* (1967), and *The Shootist* (1976).

Twenty-five times Wayne was listed among the outstanding box office attractions in the annual polls taken by theater exhibitors. By the early 1960's his films had grossed more than $350 million, and his salary had climbed from "peanuts" to more than $650,000 per film. However, his often stated ideas on Americanism and patriotism led him into two fiascos. To show a new generation of Americans "what their country still stands for," Wayne invested $1.2 million to make *The Alamo* in 1960, but the project failed. An ardent supporter of the U. S. involvement in the Vietnam War, he made *The Green Berets* (1968), but it was called heavy-handed by critics.

In 1964 Wayne had his first cancer surgery. Even the ensuing road to death bore the stamp of the John Wayne mystique. He publicly boasted that he had "licked the Big C" and continued to make films. But during his protracted illness he underwent open-heart and gall bladder surgery, and his stomach was removed. When he appeared at the Academy Awards presentation in April 1979, he was gaunt. The audience, including many of his friends and colleagues, sensed that it might be his farewell public appearance and gave him an ovation to suit the occasion.

Wayne was married three times and twice divorced. He had seven children.

WILLIAM WOLF

FIEDLER, Arthur

Orchestra conductor: b. Boston, MA, Dec. 17, 1894; d. Brookline, MA, July 10, 1979.

Arthur Fiedler, who conducted the Boston Pops Orchestra for half a century, was one of the most popular and colorful musical personalities of his time. A "middlebrow" artist, Fiedler bridged the gap between classical and popular music. Along with Beethoven symphonies and Wagner overtures, he featured Sousa marches, Strauss waltzes, and Broadway show tunes, as well as symphonic arrangements of rock'n'roll songs. His Boston Pops recordings sold as many as 50 million copies, and his *Evening at Pops* broadcasts, presented in recent years on National Educational Television, received consistently high ratings. A highlight of his career was his Bicentennial concert of July 4, 1976, on the banks of the Charles River, attended by a record audience of some 400,000.

Background. Descended from generations of musicians in Central Europe, Arthur Fiedler received violin lessons as a child and attended Boston private schools. He was taken to Europe by his family in 1910, where he studied at the Royal Academy of Music in Berlin (1911–15). At age 17 he made his debut as a conductor. In 1915 he returned to Boston and became second violinist with the Boston Symphony; later he also played the viola, the piano, and other instruments with that orchestra. During the 1920's he became, in addition, director of the Cecilia Society Chorus, the MacDowell Orchestra Club, and the Boston University student orchestra, and he founded the Boston Sinfonietta. His free outdoor series of Boston Esplanade concerts, organized in 1929, became an annual summer event.

In January 1930, Fiedler became director of the then 45-year-old Boston Pops Orchestra, which was essentially the Boston Symphony without its principal players. A master showman with a straightforward, no-nonsense style of conducting, Fiedler guided the Boston Pops to unprecedented popularity. Over the years, Fiedler appeared as a guest conductor of many leading orchestras in the United States and abroad, and beginning in the 1950's, he conducted the San Francisco Symphony in an annual series of pops concerts.

After undergoing brain surgery in December 1978, Fiedler returned to the podium the following March to conduct the Boston Symphony, and on May 1, 1979, he opened his 50th season as conductor of the Boston Pops.

Among many other honors, Fiedler was the recipient of the French Legion of Honor (1954) and the Medal of Freedom (1977). An avid firechaser, he was made an honorary fire chief by some 350 communities.

HENRY S. SLOAN

DIEFENBAKER, John George

Canadian politician: b. Grey County, Ontario, Sept. 18, 1895; d. Ottawa, Aug. 16, 1979.

Prime minister of Canada from 1957 to 1963, John George Diefenbaker was easily the most controversial individual to hold that office in modern times and although he seldom stopped trying to explain himself, he remained a mysterious mixture of vanity and charm, vulnerability and brass, outrage and mischief. Perhaps his most lasting legacy was the fact that he single-handedly transformed Canadian politics into the country's leading spectator sport.

His life spanned much of the nation's history. The son of a homesteader in northern Saskatchewan, he served briefly in World War I and later became a successful defense attorney in Prince Albert, Sask. But his heart was always in politics. He was soundly beaten in five election campaigns (including an abortive attempt in 1933 to become mayor of Prince Albert), before finally squeaking into the House of Commons as a member of the Conservative opposition in 1940. In 1956 he fooled the pundits by capturing the leadership of Canada's Progressive Conservative Party and the following year managed to win a minority mandate.

Trumpeting his "vision" of Northern development, he went on a charismatic rampage in the 1958 campaign that made his audiences quiver. His party won 208 seats, wiping out the Liberals in six provinces. It was the largest mandate ever given a Canadian prime minister.

John Diefenbaker had heard his party vilified so often for being too cautious that, once in power, he indulged freely in the populist radicalism that was his natural instinct. His conviction that the economically underprivileged can help themselves only through collective political action found its expression in the notion that every Canadian has the right to expect equality of opportunity.

During his stormy stewardship, the Prince Albert politician was responsible for much enlightened legislation. But by 1963, his administration had collapsed from within, with 17 ministers leaving during its last 10 months. By the time Diefenbaker had lost his last election as party leader in 1965, his once-great Conservative party had been hived into a coalition of the discontented and the dispossessed.

It was always possible to admire John Diefenbaker's instincts without respecting his performance. His was the most primitive of partisanships, but he shattered the idea that the Conservative party was an instrument of big business and the long-accepted convention that Canada's political leaders should talk grey and act neutral.

PETER C. NEWMAN

MOUNTBATTEN, Louis

First Earl Mountbatten of Burma, Admiral of the Fleet, last viceroy of India: b. Windsor, England, June 25, 1900; d. at sea, northwest Ireland, Aug. 27, 1979.

Lord Mountbatten of Burma, second only to Winston Churchill in Britain's pantheon of recent war heroes, died in August 1979 when his fishing boat was blown up by members of the Irish Republican Army. The earl had been vacationing in western Ireland with his family.

Lord Mountbatten was a cousin of Queen Elizabeth and a much-loved intimate of the royal family all his life. Yet he had a common touch which endeared him to ordinary people.

As a youth, Mountbatten had the reputation of a playboy and appeared frequently in the gossip columns of the day. But in 1916, in the thick of World War I, he joined the Royal Navy and rose steadily in rank. It became clear that he was an inspired officer.

In 1939 he became commander of the destroyer *HMS Kelly*. When it was sunk in 1941, Mountbatten remained on the bridge to the last moment, finally swimming to safety. In 1941 Churchill called him back to London to become chief of combined operations, and soon afterward supreme commander of Southeast Asia. Here he not only commanded the reconquest of Burma but also managed to win the loyalty of Burmese nationalists.

After the war, Mountbatten was given his most difficult assignment—to supervise the independence of India. Despite the opposition of many British politicians and the mutual antagonism of Hindus and Muslims, he managed to bring independence in only five months and persuade both sides of the partitioned nation to remain in the British commonwealth.

SIMON HOGGART

PERELMAN, Sidney Joseph

U. S. humorist and author: b. Brooklyn, NY, Feb. 1, 1904; d. New York City, Oct. 17, 1979.

"Button cute, rapier keen, cucumber cool, and gall bitter" was how S. J. Perelman once described himself. A master of satire, parody, spoof, and wordplay, Perelman was the most appreciated American humorist of his time.

Perelman's zany insights found expression in a variety of forms and media. He worked on the scripts for the early Marx Brothers films, *Monkey Business* (1931) and *Horse Feathers* (1932), and in 1956 he won an Academy Award for the screenplay of Jules Verne's *Around the World in 80 Days.* His work in the theater also was widely acclaimed. He collaborated with Ogden Nash on the book for the 1943 hit musical *One Touch of Venus,* worked with his wife Laura in writing the 1933 play *All Good Americans,* and wrote the 1962 play *The Beauty Part,* which starred Bert Lahr. But his cutting humor was perhaps most finely honed in short satiric essays and light stories. His many books included *Acres and Pains* (1946), *Westward Ha!* (1948), *The Swiss Family Perelman* (1950), *The Most of S. J. Perelman* (1958), *Baby It's Cold Inside* (1970), and *Vinegar Puss* (1975).

Sidney Joseph Perelman was born in Brooklyn, NY, on Feb. 1, 1904, and grew up in Providence, RI. Young Perelman had a love for popular novels and movies, but his ambition was to be a cartoonist. He worked on the college humor magazine at Brown University and drew for the weekly *Judge,* following graduation in 1924. The cartoon captions, he later said, got longer and longer and the drawings were dropped altogether.

SHEEN, Archbishop Fulton J.

Churchman, preacher, former auxiliary bishop of New York, bishop of Rochester, NY: b. El Paso, IL, May 3, 1895; d. New York City, Dec. 9, 1979.

The foremost Catholic preacher of his time, Archbishop Fulton J. Sheen rose to national prominence in the 1950's as host of a weekly television series. By then, the author of more than 60 books and professor of philosophy at the Catholic University of America, Washington, DC, had for 25 years been a dominant force in Catholic academic and media circles.

He was for many years the most sought-after Catholic speaker and best-known prelate in the United States. His *Catholic Hour* radio broadcasts were carried by more than 100 network affiliates in 1950, and by 1955 his TV series reached 13 million persons weekly. He also wrote syndicated columns for both the Catholic and lay press.

Noted as a convert-maker of the famous, in 1950 he was named national director of the Society for the Propagation of the Faith, the church's outreach mission. In 1966 he was appointed bishop of Rochester, NY. Four years later, at age 74, he resigned that post and was given the personal title of archbishop.

Born in a small Illinois town, one of four sons of Newton and Delia (Fulton) Sheen, he grew up in Peoria and was ordained for the Peoria diocese in 1919. He was named bishop in 1951. After his retirement he continued to preach, conduct retreats, and make special appearances.

ROBERT L. JOHNSTON

RODGERS, Richard

American composer; b. New York City, June 28, 1902; d. New York City, Dec. 30, 1979.

One of Broadway's most prolific and versatile composers, Richard Rodgers played a major role in the evolution of the American musical theater from a light entertainment medium into a serious art form. During a career spanning six decades, Rodgers composed the scores for 42 Broadway musicals, including such all-time hits as *Oklahoma!* and *South Pacific.* Among his 1,500 songs are such familiar standards as "With a Song in My Heart," "Oh, What a Beautiful Mornin'," "Some Enchanted Evening," and "My Favorite Things."

Although Rodgers denied that he was able to compose instantaneously, he once said: "I don't find it work to write music, because I enjoy it."

Background. From his earliest childhood, Richard Rodgers was encouraged in his love of music by his mother, a gifted pianist, and his father, a prosperous physician. After two years at Columbia University (1919–1921), Rodgers studied under Walter Damrosch at the Institute for Musical Art (1921–1923).

Meanwhile, Rodgers had formed a partnership with lyricist Lorenz Hart, whom he met in 1918. Their first successful collaboration, *The Garrick Gaieties* (1925), was followed by dozens of Rodgers-Hart Broadway hits, including *Pal Joey* (1940)—considered a pioneering work in the development of musical comedy. Because of Hart's illness, Rodgers formed a new partnership in 1942 with Oscar Hammerstein II.

Their first collaboration, *Oklahoma!* (1943), won a special Pulitzer Prize and ran on Broadway for five years. In 1945, Rodgers and Hammerstein scored another hit with *Carousel.* Their long-running *South Pacific* (1949) was awarded a Pulitzer drama prize and brought Rodgers one of several Tony awards. Other major Rodgers-Hammerstein hits included *The King and I* (1951), *Flower Drum Song* (1958), and *The Sound of Music* (1959).

Rodgers' work in motion pictures included the Oscar-winning song "It Might as Well Be Spring" for the film *State Fair* (1945). For television he composed the scores for the documentary *Victory at Sea* (1952) and the series *Winston Churchill—The Valiant Years* (1960). After Hammerstein's death in 1960, Rodgers composed the music and lyrics for *No Strings* (1962), and worked with Stephen Sondheim on *Do I Hear a Waltz?* (1965). His last work was the musical version of *I Remember Mama.*

In 1962, Rodgers became president and producing director of the Music Theater of Lincoln Center, and over the years he served on several boards of directors, including those of the Juilliard School and the American Theatre Wing.

HENRY S. SLOAN

Acheampong, Ignatius K. (47), General and head of state of Ghana; executed following a coup: d. Accra, Ghana, June 16.

Ager, Milton (85), composer; was known for such hits as *Ain't She Sweet?* and the theme song for Democratic Party, *Happy Days Are Here Again:* d. Inglewood, CA, May 6.

Allbritton, Louise (59?), actress; appeared in such films as *The Egg and I* and *Walk a Crooked Mile;* made her Broadway debut in *Third Person:* d. Puerto Vallarta, Mexico, Feb. 16.

Alphand, Nicole (60?), wife of the former French ambassador to the United States; she became known as the most elegant hostess in Washington when she transformed the French embassy during her husband's tenure (1958–65): d. Paris, Feb. 15.

Angoff, Charles (77), writer, professor; he joined *The American Mercury* with H. L. Mencken in 1925 and remained with the magazine until 1950. He wrote some 30 books which included criticism, fiction, poetry, and plays: d. New York City, May 3.

Arzner, Dorothy (82), film director; she was the sole woman director in the 1930's and 1940's: d. La Quinta, CA, Oct. 1.

Barnett, Lincoln (70), former editor of *Life* magazine and author; probably best known for his 1949 book *The Universe and Dr. Einstein* which was translated into 28 languages: d. Plattsburgh, NY, September 8.

Barr, John Andrew (70), former chairman of Montgomery Ward and Company and former dean of the Graduate School of Management at Northwestern University. He became chairman of Montgomery Ward in 1955 and began a large business expansion of the company: d. Evanston, IL, Jan. 16.

Barth, Alan (né Alan Barth Lauchheimer) (73), former editorial writer for *The Washington Post* (1943–73); wrote *The Loyalty of Free Men, Government by Investigation,* and *The Price of Liberty:* d. Washington, DC, Nov. 20.

Bartlett, Dewey F. (59), former governor of Oklahoma (1967–71); U. S. senator (1973–79): d. Tulsa, OK, March 1.

Barzani, Mustafa al- (76), Kurdish leader from Iraq; from 1960 to 1975 General Bazarni led a guerrilla army, the Pesh Merga, in an attempt to win autonomy for the Kurds, the Muslim peoples who live in Turkey, Iran, Iraq, and the Soviet Union. In 1975 he sought asylum in the United States after his armies were overrun by Iraqi forces: d. Washington, DC, March 1.

Bayh, Marvella (46), wife of Sen. Birch Bayh of Indiana: her book, *Marvella: A Personal Journey* (1979) is an account of her battle against cancer: d. Rockville, MD, April 24.

Bernac, Pierre (né Pierre Bertin) (80), French baritone and a teacher of art-song interpretation; he came to fame initially as the performing partner for 25 years of the composer and pianist Francis Poulenc: d. Villeneuve-les-Avignon, France, Oct. 17.

Bhutto, Zulfikar Ali (51), former prime minister of Pakistan (1973–77); he was overthrown in a coup led by General Zia in July 1977. After a year in jail he was found guilty of plotting an opponent's murder, and hanged: d. Rawalpindi, Pakistan, April 4.

Bishop, Elizabeth (68), American poet; in 1946 she published her first volume, *North and South,* and then began work as a poetry consultant to the Library of Congress. In 1955 she published a second volume, *A Cold Spring* and in 1956 was awarded the Pulitzer Prize: d. Boston, Oct. 6.

Blokhintsev, Dmitri (71), Russian physicist; he directed the construction of the first atomic power plant in the Soviet Union (1954) and served as director of the Joint Nuclear Research Institute in Dubna (1956–65). He was head of the Institute's Laboratory of Theoretical Physics at the time of his death. He was instrumental in the discovery in 1964 of synthesized element No. 104, the 12th radioactive element heavier than uranium created by man since 1940: d. USSR, Jan. 27.

Blondell, Joan (70), motion picture and television actress; during a career that spanned nearly 50 years, she often portrayed the self-reliant, wisecracking blonde; she was nominated for an Academy Award as a supporting actress in *The Blue Veil:* d. Santa Monica, CA, Dec. 25.

Bolton, Guy (96), author of Broadway musicals; famed for his collaborations with P. G. Wodehouse. His work includes the books for *Oh, Kay, Anything Goes,* and *Follow the Girls.* He also wrote the drama *Anastasia* which was on Broadway during the 1954–55 season: d. London, Sept. 5.

UPI   UPI

Z. A. BHUTTO   **JOAN BLONDELL**

Boulanger, Nadia (92), French teacher of musical composition whose many famous pupils included Aaron Copland, Virgil Thomson, Roy Harris, Elliott Carter, and David Diamond. Mr. Thomson once referred to her as a "one-woman graduate school...." For three decades after her discovery by the American music world in 1921, she exerted great influence on American musical development: d. Paris, Oct. 22.

Brent, George (75), film and stage actor; appeared in more than 100 movies and 300 plays: d. Solana Beach, CA, May 26.

Brown, John Nicholas (79), former assistant secretary of the Navy and a member of one of Rhode Island's most prominent families. He was a senior fellow of Brown University and a direct descendant of its founders: d. Annapolis, MD, Oct. 9.

Buchanan, Edgar (76), motion picture and television actor; best known for his role as Uncle Joe in television's *Petticoat Junction:* d. Palm Desert, CA, April 4.

Capehart, Homer E. (82), former U.S. senator (R-IN, 1945–63); a conservative Republican, he was often considered an isolationist. He was chairman of the Banking and Currency Committee: d. Indianapolis, Sept. 3.

Capp, Al (né Alfred Gerald Caplin) (70), cartoonist; creator of *Li'l Abner.* The comic strip began in 1934 in eight newspapers and eventually appeared in more than 900 papers. Mr. Capp discontinued the strip in 1977. Mr. Capp was for years a political liberal, but grew disenchanted and embraced political conservatism. As he grew more polemical, fewer newspapers carried *Li'l Abner:* d. Cambridge, MA, Nov. 5.

Cavanagh, Jerome P. (51), former mayor of Detroit (1960–68): d. Lexington, KY, Nov. 27.

Cavanaugh, John Joseph (80), Roman Catholic priest and university president; he served as president of Notre Dame University (1946–52): d. South Bend, IN, Dec. 28.

Challe, Maurice (73), French general; after the fall of France during World War II, he set up an air intelligence network and later flew bombing missions with the French Air Force. He was named commander in chief of French forces in Algeria in 1958. In 1961 he attempted to overthrow President de Gaulle to prevent him from granting Algeria independence. The coup failed, Challe was stripped of his rank, and sentenced to 15 years in prison. After serving five and a half years he was pardoned by De Gaulle and later was granted complete amnesty: d. Paris, Jan. 18.

Chang Kuo-tao (82), last surviving founder of the Chinese Communist Party; he was one of 12 students and scholars (including Mao Zedong) who met secretly in a Shanghai tenement house and later on a boat offshore to design and found the Communist Party. He had disagreements with Mao and finally broke with the Communists in 1938: d. Toronto, Dec. 3.

Chapman, Ceil (née Cecilia Mitchell) (67), American fashion designer; was particularly influential in the 1940's and 1950's as a designer of evening gowns: d. New York City, July 10.

Chapple, Charles (75), retired pediatrician and professor; invented an incubator that greatly enhanced the care of premature infants: d. Lincoln, NE, March 23.

Conrad, Max (76), pioneer aviator of light planes; he logged more than 50,000 hours in the air and crossed the Atlantic and Pacific oceans more than 200 times: d. Summit, NJ, April 3.

Costello, Dolores (73), actress; appeared in such films as *The Sea Beast,* with John Barrymore (whom she married in 1928 and divorced in 1935), *Moby Dick,* and *The Magnificent Ambersons,* and on stage in *The Great Man:* d. Fallbrook, CA, March 1.

Coughlin, Charles E. (88), Roman Catholic priest; became known as the "radio priest" of the Depression with broadcasts from Michigan that, at their peak, reached an audience of 40 million. He spoke on such issues as the evils of Communism, capitalism, labor unions, Wall Street, and in time was accused of anti-Semitism. He also published a magazine, *Social Justice.* During World War II, he was silenced by the U.S. government and the Roman Catholic Church: d. Birmingham, MI, Oct. 27.

Cousteau, Philippe (39), award-winning cinematographer and aquanaut; he worked with his father Jacques-Yves Cousteau, the oceanographer: d. near Alverca, Portugal, June 28.

Dalgliesh, Alice (85), children's author; wrote more than 40 books for children and wrote books for adults on the subject of children's literature: d. Woodbury, CT, June 11.

Dasburg, Andrew (92), American abstract painter: d. Taos, NM, Aug. 13.

Davis, Jerome (87), educator, author, and espouser of world peace; first became interested in the world peace movement in 1917 when he visited World War I prison camps in Russia. He taught at Dartmouth College (1921–24) and at the Yale Divinity School (1924–37). His books include *Labor Problems in America, Religion in Action, Behind Soviet Power,* and *Peace, War, and You.* In 1952 he founded Promoting Enduring Peace and was active in the international organization until 1974: d. Olney, MD, Oct. 19.

Delaney, Beauford (77), black artist; did portraits of many prominent black people. His last American exhibition was mostly abstracts: d. Paris, March 26.

Deller, Alfred (67), British countertenor; credited with reviving the art of solo male alto singing: d. Bologna, Italy, July 16.

Dempsey, James Charles (70), retired rear admiral in the U.S. Navy; he was the submarine commander who sank the first Japanese destroyer in World War II. He helped evacuate the last Americans from the island of Corregidor: d. Norfolk, VA, July 9.

Devers, Jacob Loucks (92), retired U.S. Army 4-star general; he served 44 years in the Army, and as chief of Armored Forces (1941–43), he activated, equipped, and trained a dozen armored divisions and several independent tank battalions: d. Washington, DC, Oct. 15.

AL CAPP   **MAURICE CHALLE**   **G. DIAZ ORDAZ**   **ADOLPH DUBS**

UPI   UPI   UPI   U.S. STATE DEPARTMENT

CYRUS EATON

MAMIE EISENHOWER

JAMES T. FARRELL

GRACIE FIELDS

Díaz Ordaz, Gustavo (68), former president of Mexico (1964–70): d. Mexico City, July 15.

Draper, Christopher (86), World War I British flier; given the nickname "Mad Major" for flying low over German trenches and sweeping them with machine gun fire; awarded the Distinguished Service Cross and the Croix de Guerre: d. London, Jan. 16.

Dubs, Adolph (58), U. S. ambassador to Afghanistan (1978–79); killed by terrorists: d. Kabul, Afghanistan, Feb. 14.

Dupee, Frederick Wilcox (74), former professor of English at Columbia University (1948–71); he helped found the *Partisan Review* in 1937: d. Carmel, CA, Jan. 19.

Dutschke, Rudi (39), German leftist; known as the "Red Rudi" of the European student rebellion of the late 1960's: d. Aarhus, Denmark, Dec. 24.

Eaton, Cyrus (95), American industrialist; he was a personal friend of many top Soviet political leaders and became known for his views on the need for cooperation between the West and the Communist states. He studied for the Baptist ministry, but a meeting with John D. Rockefeller, Sr., eventually persuaded him to take up business. He got his start in 1907, taking on a venture for Mr. Rockefeller. In the stock market crash of 1929 he lost $100 million and was nearly penniless in 1933. By 1942 he had recouped his losses and by the end of his life his industrial empire was said to be worth $2 billion. He controlled two railroads—the Chesapeake and Ohio and the Baltimore and Ohio—six major steel companies, including Republic Steel, and utilities, coal, iron, and other metal companies: d. Acacia Farm, near Cleveland, May 9.

Eisenhower, Marie Geneva (Mamie) (82), widow of Dwight D. Eisenhower, 34th president of the United States; she married in 1916 over the objections of her father after knowing Second Lieutenant Eisenhower only nine months. Because of her husband's military career, she once moved seven times in one year. As first lady of the United States she remained in the background politically. She suffered a massive stroke on September 25: d. Washington, DC, Nov. 1.

Farrell, James T. (75), novelist; most famous as the author of the Studs Lonigan trilogy—*Young Lonigan* (1932), *The Young Manhood of Studs Lonigan* (1934), and *Judgement Day* (1935): d. New York City, August 22.

Fields, Gracie (81), British music hall, stage, and film entertainer, loved by the British public. She entertained troops in every theater of operations during World War II, raised millions of pounds for charity, and gave 10 command performances for British royalty: d. Capri, Sept. 27.

Flatt, Lester (64), singer and guitarist; he performed for 35 years with the Grand Ole Opry in Nashville and was best known for the bluegrass music he performed with Earl Scruggs: d. Nashville, TN, May 11.

Forssmann, Werner (73), German doctor and 1956 Nobel Prize winner in medicine; on himself he demonstrated that a catheter inserted into the vein at the elbow could safely extend all the way to the heart: d. Schopfheim, West Germany, June 1.

Gabor, Dennis (78), physicist; was the winner of the 1971 Nobel Prize in physics for his invention of holography: d. London, Feb. 8.

Gagnon, René (55), one of six U. S. marines in the famous Joe Rosenthal AP photograph of the U. S. flag raising on Iwo Jima during World War II: d. Hooksett, NH, Oct. 12.

Galento, Tony (69), former heavyweight boxer (1929–44); he fought and lost a 1939 championship match with Joe Louis. He had a total of 114 career fights, with 82 wins, 26 losses, and 6 draws: d. Livingston, NJ, July 22.

Giles, Warren (82), former general manager (1936–48) and president (1948–51) of the Cincinnati Reds baseball team and president of the National League (1951–69): d. Cincinnati, Feb. 7.

Granahan, Kathryn O'Hay (83), former U. S. Treasurer (1962–66). She had served as Democratic Congresswoman from Pennsylvania (1957–62): d. Norristown, PA, July 10.

Grosvenor, Robert George (fifth Duke of Westminster) (68), head of one of the richest families in Great Britain; he sat in the House of Commons (1955–64) and in the Northern Ireland Parliament as a senator (1964–67): d. Enniskillen, Northern Ireland, Feb. 19.

Guggenheim, Peggy (81), collector of modern art; living a Bohemian life-style in Europe, she adopted the motto "buy a picture a day" and amassed an art collection worth at least $30 million: d. Venice, Italy, Dec. 23.

Haley, Jack, Sr. (79), actor; best known for his role of the Tin Woodsman in the film classic *The Wizard of Oz*: d. Los Angeles, June 6.

Hall, Leonard (78), U. S. politician; former congressman (R-NY, 1939–53), chairman, Republican National Committee (1953–57): d. Glen Cove, NY, June 2.

Halsman, Philippe (73), photographer; famed for his portraits of such persons as Albert Einstein, Winston Churchill, and John F. Kennedy. *Life* magazine used his photos for 101 of its covers: d. New York City, June 25.

Hartnell, Sir Norman (78), British dressmaker to Queen Elizabeth II; he designed her wedding dress and coronation gown. He was awarded the French Legion of Honor in 1939, and in 1977 was knighted: d. Windsor, England, June 8.

Hathaway, Donny (33), composer-singer of pop and blues songs with black gospel undertones; with Roberta Flack he made the Grammy award-winning album *Roberta Flack and Donny Hathaway*: d. New York City, Jan. 13.

Haworth, Leland J. (74), physicist; director of the Brookhaven National Laboratory (1948–61), of the National Science Foundation (1963–69): d. Port Jefferson, NY, March 5.

Hayward, Max (54), British translator of Russian literature: d. Oxford, England, March 18.

Hébert, F. Edward (78), former U. S. representative (D-LA, 1941–77); a Southern conservative and an opponent of the "no win" policy in Korea and Vietnam, he became chairman of the House Armed Services Committee in 1971. He was removed from the post by young House liberals in 1975: d. New Orleans, Dec. 29.

Heinl, Robert, Jr. (62), retired Marine Corps colonel, columnist, and author; he was chief of the U. S. naval mission to Haiti (1959–63). In 1963 he wrote *Soldiers of the Sea*, considered a definitive work on the Marine Corps: d. Saint Barthélemy, May 5.

JACK HALEY, SR.

CONRAD HILTON

Hilton, Conrad (91), hotel owner. From a first hotel in Cisco, TX, he expanded to form (1946) the Hilton Hotel Corporation, acquire (1949) the Waldorf-Astoria, and take over (1954) the Statler hotel chain. At the time of his death he owned 185 hotels and inns in the United States and 75 more in foreign countries. He was also responsible for the establishment of the credit card company Carte Blanche: d. Santa Monica, CA, Jan. 3.

Hodge, Al (66), actor; famous as Captain Video on the TV series of the same name; he earlier appeared on the *Green Hornet* radio program: d. New York City, March 19.

Hutton, Barbara (66), much-married heiress of the Woolworth fortune; died of an apparent heart attack. During the last several years of her life she became something of a recluse: d. Los Angeles, May 11.

Hutton, Jim (45), actor; best known for his television role of detective Ellery Queen in the series of the same name: d. Los Angeles, June 3.

Jefferson, Eddie (60), jazz lyricist; best known for fitting lyrics to instrumental jazz solos: d. Detroit, MI, May 9.

Johnson, Ivan Willard (Ching) (81), hockey player; played defense for the New York Rangers hockey team for 11 years. He helped lead the team to its first Stanley Cup championship in 1927–28 and its second in 1932–33. He was selected to the league's All-Star team four times and was enshrined in 1958: d. Silver Spring, MD, June 16.

Kadar, Jan (61), Hungarian-born film director; his most acclaimed film, *The Shop on Main Street*, won the 1965 Academy Award for best foreign film and the New York Film Critics Award: d. Los Angeles, June 1.

Kaldis, Aristodimos (79), artist; was known for his paintings of Greek landscapes and New England scenes: d. New York City, May 2.

Kardelj, Edvard (69), top member of the Collective Presidency of Yugoslavia and a close comrade of Tito for 40 years; he created the worker self-management and foreign nonalignment policies of Yugoslavia: d. Belgrade, Yugoslavia, Feb. 10.

Kasznar, Kurt (65), stage, film, and television actor; best known for his Broadway roles in *Barefoot in the Park*, *The Sound of Music*, and *Waiting for Godot*: d. Santa Monica, CA, Aug. 6.

Kenton, Stan (67), jazz band leader; the last major band leader of the big band era, he was a pianist who sometimes soloed with his band. His interest later shifted to writing and arranging, then to music education and jazz clinics: d. Hollywood, CA, Aug. 25.

Kleberg, Richard M., Jr. (62), board chairman of King Ranch Inc.; he headed the Texas ranching concern that owned 860,000 acres (348 000 ha) of cattle and oil lands and millions of acres in other states and abroad. His ranch is famous for the development of the Santa Gertrudis cattle breed, the first officially recognized native breed in the Western Hemisphere: d. Corpus Christi, TX, May 8.

Knowles, John H. (52), president of the Rockefeller Foundation and a leading medical figure; Dr. Knowles earlier had served as director of the Massachusetts General Hospital (1962–71): d. Boston, March 6.

Korda, Vincent (81), painter and art director for motion pictures; received an Academy Award in 1941 for art direction on the film *Thief of Bagdad*: d. London, Jan. 4.

Kuznetsov, Anatoly (49), USSR writer who defected to Britain in 1969, after which he called himself A. Anatol. His most famous book was *Babi Yar* (1966): d. London, June 13.

La Malfa, Ugo (75), Italian economist and deputy prime minister; as a financial expert he served eight governments in 33 years: d. Rome, March 26.

Lauri-Volpi, Giacomo (86), operatic tenor; he made his debut in 1920 in Rome in *Manon* and in 1923 appeared at the Metropolitan in New York in *Rigoletto*. He sang with the Met for 10 years: d. Valencia, Spain, March 17.

Lavelle, John (62), United States Air Force general; he was relieved of his command in Vietnam and demoted from 4-star to 2-star general after ordering unauthorized air attacks against North Vietnam in 1971 and 1972: d. Fairfax, VA, July 10.

Lawrence, Marjorie (71), Australian-born operatic soprano; was best known for her Wagnerian roles. She made her debut in Monte Carlo in *Tannhäuser* and was a member of the Paris Opéra (1933–38). She made her Metropolitan Opera (New York) debut in 1935 in *Die Walküre*. In 1941 she was stricken with infantile paralysis; in the years following she devoted herself primarily to teaching: d. Hot Springs, AR, Jan. 13.

Lazzari, Pietro (80), painter and sculptor who was part of the 1920's Futurist movement in art; he became known for his bronze busts: d. Bethesda, MD, May 1.

Leemans, Alphonse (Tuffy) (66), New York Giants football star (1936–43). As a rookie in 1936 he won the National

BARBARA HUTTON   LOU LITTLE

UPI   WIDE WORLD

Football League rushing title with 830 yards. He was recently named to the Pro Football Hall of Fame: d. Hillsboro Beach, FL, Jan. 19.

Leonetti, Tommy (50), singer; most famous for his appearances as a member of the 1957–58 cast of the television series *Your Hit Parade:* d. Houston, TX, Sept. 15.

Little, Lou (85), former football coach for Columbia University (1930–56); in 1934 he took the Columbia team to victory at the Rose Bowl when his team upset Stanford. He was a member of the College Football Hall of Fame and served as president of the American Football Coaches Association: d. Delray Beach, FL, May 28.

Lucas, Bill (43), vice president of the Atlanta Braves baseball club and de facto general manager: d. Atlanta, GA, May 5.

Lyon, Ben (78), silent pictures movie actor, later talent director of 20th Century Fox; he is credited with discovering Jean Harlow and Marilyn Monroe: d. aboard a Pacific cruise ship, March 22.

McIntyre, James Francis Cardinal (93), cardinal of the Roman Catholic church (1953–79); he was a rising figure in the Wall Street securities business in New York City prior to entering the priesthood. Following seminary studies he served the church for 25 years as a cleric-administrator in New York. He was archbishop of Los Angeles (1948–70): d. Los Angeles, July 16.

Marcuse, Herbert (81), philosopher and professor; he gained prominence for his radical neo-Marxist philosophy. His most influential book was *One Dimensional Man* (1964): d. Starnberg, West Germany, July 29.

Marx, Zeppo (78), the sole surviving member of the Marx Brothers comedy team; appeared in the group's first five films—*The Coconuts* (1929), *Animal Crackers* (1930), *Monkey Business* (1931), *Horse Feathers* (1932), and *Duck Soup* (1933): d. Palm Springs, CA, Nov. 30.

Massine, Léonide (83), ballet dancer and choreographer; he was greatly influenced by Diaghilev's Ballets Russes and in 1917 scored his first success with that company in *Parade* in collaboration with Erik Satie, Picasso, and Jean Cocteau. By 1920 the Ballets Russes had turned to modernism through Massine's influence; ballets created by him that year were *La Boutique Fantasque, Le Tricorne*, and *Pulcinella*. He left the Ballets Russes and opened a studio in London, but in 1925 returned to that company until he went to the United States in 1928. He later worked for the Ballets Russes de Monte Carlo. He then formed his own company. He did some choreography for the American Ballet Theater in the 1940's, and continued for the remainder of his career to stage his ballets and to create dances for operatic companies: d. Cologne, West Germany, March 16.

Maudling, Reginald (61), member of the House of Commons in Great Britain; he first entered Parliament in 1950, elected on the Conservative Party ticket; he served as junior minister and economic secretary to the Treasury, and in 1959 became president of the Board of Trade. He served as colonial secretary (1961–62), became chancellor of the exchequer (1962–64), and in 1965 was elected deputy leader. Under Prime Minister Heath, in 1970, he was appointed Home secretary, but because of certain connections with businessmen who were indicted for crimes, he was forced to retire from that post in 1972: d. London, Feb. 14.

Maze, Paul (92), French-born artist; was a painting companion of Sir Winston Churchill. He first exhibited in Paris in 1914, and his first New York show was in 1939: d. near Mishurst, Sussex, England, Sept. 17.

Merritt, H. Houston (78), neurologist, co-developer of the anti-epilepsy drug Dilantin, and former dean of Columbia University's College of Physicians and Surgeons; he also contributed to the understanding of the effects of syphilis upon the brain: d. New York City, Jan. 9.

Meurisse, Paul (66), French stage and film actor, best known for his role as the husband in the 1955 film *Diabolique.* He spent two years with the Comédie Française and appeared in cabarets and music halls: d. Paris, Jan. 19.

Miller, Don C. (77), retired U.S. Bankruptcy Court judge and famed football star of Notre Dame (1922–24); he was a right halfback for Notre Dame who gained fame as one of the Four Horsemen of the Apocalypse: d. Cleveland, July 28.

Mingus, Charles (56), jazz composer and bass player; started in the 1940's in California; moved to New York in 1951; started composing in the mid-1950's, and during the 1960's appeared regularly in New York clubs and at important jazz festivals. He also made many recordings. He was a strong spokesman for black rights: d. Cuernavaca, Mexico, Jan. 5.

Monsarrat, Nicholas (69), British novelist who drew on his experiences in the British Navy (1940–46) to write his best-selling and most famous novel *The Cruel Sea* (1951). He wrote 25 books: d. London, August 7.

Morton, Rogers C. B. (64), former U.S. representative (R-MD, 1963–71) and former cabinet member; he served as secretary of the Interior (1971–75) and as secretary of Commerce (1975–76): d. Easton, MD, April 19.

Muir, Malcolm (93), former president, editor in chief, publisher, and chairman of *Newsweek* magazine (1937–61); also served as president of McGraw-Hill (1928–37) and was the founder of *Business Week* magazine (1929): d. New York, Jan. 30.

Munson, Thurman (32), New York Yankee baseball catcher; he was the American League rookie of the year in 1970 and in 1976 the American League's most valuable player. In 1976 he was named Yankee team captain. He was killed in the crash of the plane he was flying: d. Akron, OH, August 2.

Murchison, Loren (80), Olympic track star; he was a gold-medal winner for the U.S. in the 1920 and 1924 Olympic Games. In 1927 he was stricken with cerebrospinal meningitis and spent the rest of his life in a wheelchair: d. Point Pleasant, NJ, June 11.

Murdock, Abe (86), former U.S. congressman (1933–41) and senator (1941–46) from Utah. In 1947 he was appointed to the National Labor Relations Board. He retired from that service in 1957: d. Bethesda, MD, Sept. 15.

Murphy, Fred P. (90), honorary chairman of Grolier, Incorporated; he first worked as a book salesman in 1908. He took control of the company in 1936, and by 1968 was credited with pushing Grolier to sales of more than $181 million a year: d. Stamford, NY, Oct. 27.

Murphy, Gardner (83), psychologist and professor, a pioneer in the field of parapsychology: d. Washington, DC, March 19.

Mussolini, Rachele Guidi (89), widow of Benito Mussolini; she was a nonpolitical person who remained in the background during Mussolini's reign in Italy. Following Mussolini's death, she returned to her native northeastern Italy and opened a restaurant: d. near Forli, Italy, Oct. 30.

Nagy, Ferenc (75), former prime minister of Hungary (1946–47); in 1947 while vacationing in Switzerland he was ousted by the Communists: d. Washington, DC, June 12.

Narayan, Jayaprakash (76), Indian political leader who united opposition forces to defeat Indira Gandhi in 1977; he was a disciple of Mohandas K. Gandhi, but he sometimes veered from Gandhi's teachings to organize strikes, train wrecks, and riots. When Mrs. Gandhi declared a national emergency she had Narayan jailed; his health

WIDE WORLD

PIER LUIGI NERVI

WIDE WORLD

SAMUEL I. NEWHOUSE

was seriously impaired during his jail term: d. Patna, India, Oct. 8.

Neave, Airey M. S. (63), leader in the British House of Commons; he was killed by a bomb, allegedly set in his car by the Irish Republican Army terrorists: d. London, March 30.

Nervi, Pier Luigi (87), Italian engineer-architect whose innovative designs earned him the AIA's Gold Medal Award in 1964. Buildings he designed include the Turin Exhibition Hall, the Palace of Labor in Turin, a series of buildings for the 1960 Olympics in Rome, the UNESCO auditorium in Paris, the Pirelli Rubber Company in Milan, and the George Washington Bridge Bus Station in New York. His favorite material was concrete, and he introduced a new material—ferro-cement—which combined concrete and steel mesh: d. Rome, Jan. 9.

Neto, Agostinho (56), president of Angola; he took office in 1975 with the help of Cuban troops, while civil war was still going on between his forces and those of two other guerrilla movements. Neto was also a Marxist poet and a physician and had been in and out of prison for political agitation and nationalistic poems prior to becoming president: d. Moscow, Sept. 10.

Newhouse, Samuel I. (84), publisher; he built one of the largest communications empires in the United States, owning 31 newspapers in 22 cities; magazines in America, Britain, France, and Italy; five radio stations; and cable-television systems in many areas: d. New York City, August 29.

Novaes, Guiomar (83?), Brazilian pianist. She was noted as a colorist and an intuitive pianist: d. São Paulo, Brazil, March 7.

Oberon, Merle (née Estelle Merle O'Brien Thompson) (68), motion picture actress; best known for the role of Cathy in *Wuthering Heights* (1939): d. Malibu, CA, Nov. 23.

O'Brien-Moore, Erin (77), actress of stage, films, and television: d. Los Angeles, May 3.

Ohlin, Bertil (80), professor and Nobel Prize winner in economic science (1977); he attended Oxford University and Harvard in the 1920's and in 1933 published *Interregional and International Trade.* In 1931 he returned to his native Sweden to become professor of economics at the University of Stockholm. He led the Swedish Liberal Party in 1944 and was a major political figure for 23 years: d. northern Sweden, August 3.

O'Malley, Walter F. (75), chairman of the board of the Los Angeles Dodgers baseball team, famous as the man who moved the Dodgers from Brooklyn to Los Angeles. The move was finally lucrative, and O'Malley gained a reputation as a financial wizard: d. Rochester, MN, August 9.

Paray, Paul (93), French orchestra conductor; he was music director of the Detroit Symphony (1952–63), with which he made many recordings. In 1977, he led a concert in Nice as part of a 90th birthday celebration for his friend, painter Marc Chagall: d. Monte Carlo, Oct. 10.

Park, Chung Hee (62), president of South Korea (1961–79); he was assassinated by the chief of the Korean Central Intelligence Agency. President Park was trained as a teacher and an officer at a college in Manchuria run by the Japanese Imperial Army. He was a major general in the South Korean military when he came to power following a coup against Syngman Rhee on May 16, 1961. He was elected president in 1963. Under his rule, South Korea's constitution was twice changed to give him nearly unlimited authority. He created a large body of secret police who sometimes jailed or purged his opponents. He also reduced the legislative assembly to a

CHARLES MINGUS   **THURMAN MUNSON**

UPI   UPI

"rubber stamp" organization, with one third of the members appointed by him, and he censored the press. While suppressing human rights, he advanced economic growth. The economy expanded at a real growth rate of more than 10% a year—the highest rate of any developing nation of its size: d. Seoul, South Korea, Oct. 26.

Parodi, Alexandre (77), leader of the French resistance movement during World War II; he set up a Free French administration capable of taking over the operation of the government with the liberation of France. In 1944 when De Gaulle took over the government, Parodi became the labor minister. He was later a representative at the UN Security Council. In 1949 he became secretary general in the Foreign Ministry, and in 1956 was made representative to the North Atlantic Treaty Organization. From 1964 to 1971 he served with the World Court at The Hague: d. Paris, March 15.

Parsons, Talcott (76), former Harvard sociologist and author: d. Munich, West Germany, May 8.

Partridge, Eric (85), lexicographer and writer; his books include *A Dictionary of Clichés, A Dictionary of Slang and Unconventional English, Name This Child, Origins: A Short Etymological Dictionary of Modern English, You Have a Point There, English Gone Wrong,* and *English for Human Beings:* d. southwest England, June 1.

Pérez Alfonso, Juan Pablo (75), former oil minister of Venezuela; he served in that capacity during the late 1950's and was instrumental in establishing the Organization of Petroleum Exporting Countries (OPEC). He retired from office in 1963: d. Washington, DC, September 3.

Piasecki, Boleslaw (64), chairman of the Polish pro-Communist Catholic association, Pax; at the age of 20 he formed the right-wing National Falangist Party. During World War II he worked against both the Germans and the Soviet Union. It is believed that he escaped Communist execution by establishing Pax, which became a business enterprise, controlling many facets of Polish life. His writings were banned early by the Catholic Church, but in later years the church attitude softened: d. Warsaw, Jan. 1.

Pious, Minerva (75), actress; most famous for her role as Mrs. Nussbaum on the Fred Allen radio show of the 1930's and 1940's: d. New York City, March 16.

Pospelov, Pyotr N. (80), former editor of *Pravda,* the Communist party newspaper of Russia: death announced in Moscow, April 24.

Price, Garrett (82), artist and cartoonist for *The New Yorker* and other magazines over a 50-year period: d. Norwalk, CT, April 8.

Rand, Sally (née Helen Gould Beck) (75), fan dancer; she was a sensation at the 1933 Chicago World's Fair: d. Glendora, CA, August 31.

Ray, Nicholas (67), American film director; his more important films were *Johnny Guitar, Rebel Without a Cause, 55 Days at Peking,* and *They Live by Night:* d. New York City, June 16.

Renoir, Jean (84), international film director; born in Paris, the son of Pierre-Auguste Renoir. As a child he was the model in four Renoir paintings. He started filmmaking in 1924 and established his reputation with his 1937 antiwar film, *The Grand Illusion.* Many critics rate *The Rules of the Game* (1939) as his finest: d. Los Angeles, Feb. 12.

Rhys, Jean (84), British novelist; her work, praised by writers and critics, included *Wide Sargasso Sea* (1966) and *Sleep It Off Lady* (1976): d. Devonshire, England, May 14.

Richards, (I)vor (A)rmstrong (86), teacher, writer, and literary critic; a brilliant lecturer at Cambridge University in the 1920's and in the 1930's, he became a proponent of Basic English as the best means for teaching English to foreigners. In the 1930's he worked on linguistics and primary education and taught at Qinghua University in Pe-

king. He taught English at Harvard University (1944–63). Some of his influential writings include *Principles of Literary Criticism,* and *The Meaning of Meaning,* a collaboration with Charles Ogden. He also wrote plays and poetry: d. Cambridge, England, Sept. 7.

Richards, James P. (84), former U.S. congressman (D-SC, 1933–57); he served as chairman of the House Foreign Affairs Committee (1955–57). Following retirement from the House, he became a special ambassador to the Middle East in President Eisenhower's administration: d. Lancaster, SC, Feb. 21.

Robb, Inez (78), nationally syndicated columnist who retired in 1969; Mrs. Robb worked for the International News Service and later for the Scripps-Howard Newspapers and the United Feature Syndicate. In addition to newspaper and magazine work, she wrote *Don't Just Stand There* (1962): d. Tucson, AZ, April 4.

Roosevelt, Archibald Bulloch (85), soldier, Wall Street figure, conservationist, and last surviving son of President Theodore Roosevelt; he served in both World War I and World War II, receiving the Croix de Guerre and the Silver Star. After World War II he joined the firm of Roosevelt and Weigold. A hunter and outdoorsman, he was president of the Boone and Crockett Club that his father had founded in 1887: d. Hobe Sound, FL, Oct. 13.

Rovere, Richard H. (64), political columnist (1948–79) for *The New Yorker* magazine; he joined the staff of the magazine in 1944 following stints with *The New Masses* (1937–39), *The Nation* (1940–43), and *Common Sense* (1943–44). His books include *Affairs of State: The Eisenhower Years* (1956) and *Senator Joe McCarthy* (1959): d. Poughkeepsie, NY, Nov. 23.

Rudolph, Mendy (53), U.S. professional basketball referee: d. New York City, July 4.

Ryan, Elizabeth (87), U.S. tennis star, won 19 Wimbledon titles: d. Wimbledon, England, July 6.

Saltonstall, Leverett (86), former Massachusetts governor (1939–44), U.S. senator (R-MA, 1945–66); at retirement from the Senate, he was the ranking Republican on the Appropriations and Armed Services committees: d. Dover, MA, June 17.

Schenken, Howard (75), bridge player and author; he was regarded as a leading authority on contract bridge and won most of the bridge honors possible: d. Palm Springs, CA, Feb. 20.

Seaton, George (68), film director, screenwriter; he twice won the Academy Award—in 1947 for the screenplay of *Miracle on 34th Street* and in 1952 for his adaptation of Odet's play *The Country Girl,* which he also directed: d. Beverly Hills, CA, July 28.

Short, Dewey (82), former Republican congressman from Missouri (1929–31, 1935–57); he became Assistant Secretary of the Army under President Eisenhower (1957–61): d. Washington, DC, Nov. 19.

Shumlin, Herman (80), producer/director of numerous hit plays; he produced such works as *The Children's Hour; The Little Foxes; The Corn Is Green; The Male Animal; Inherit the Wind; Grand Hotel;* and *The Deputy:* d. New York City, June 14.

Simonov, Konstantin (63), Soviet writer; author of *The Living and the Dead* (1959), a novel about the Red Army's retreat from the Nazis in 1941. He was an honored member of the literary establishment and was secretary of the Union of Writers (1967–79). He held three Orders of Lenin: d. USSR, August 28.

Skinner, Cornelia Otis (78), actress and writer; she was the daughter of Otis Skinner, the actor, and in 1921 appeared with him in *Blood and Sand.* During the 1930's she became well known for monodramas which she created, produced, and performed. In addition to her acting she

L. SALTONSTALL

UPI

C. O. SKINNER

UPI

CHARLIE SMITH

BOB ENGINTON, LIAISON

ALLEN TATE

WIDE WORLD

| REXFORD G. TUGWELL | VIVIAN VANCE | JEAN CARDINAL VILLOT | ROBERT WOODWARD |

UPI · VIACOM · UPI · HARVARD UNIVERSITY

was also a playwright, memoirist, and biographer: d. New York City, July 9.

Slade, Paul Stewart (47), photojournalist; he became a staff member of *Paris Match* in 1953 and later worked for *Look:* d. New York City, June 7.

Smith, Charlie (137?), claimed to be the oldest person in the United States, although the editor of the *Guiness Book of World Records* disputes this claim. Mr. Smith asserted that he was sold into slavery in 1854 after being taken to the United States from West Africa. His name prior to leaving Africa was said to be Mitchell Watkins, and Mr. Smith had said that he rode with the Jesse James gang and had once gone with Billy the Kid to "get the man who killed President Garfield": d. Bartow, FL, Oct. 5.

Soderberg, C. Richard (83), professor and pioneer developer of the turbine engine: d. Cambridge, MA, Oct. 17.

Soo, Jack (né Goro Suzuki) (63), actor; best known for his role as Sgt. Yemana in the television series *Barney Miller:* d. Los Angeles, Jan. 11.

Stafford, Jean (63), short-story writer and novelist; she published her first book, *Boston Adventure*, in 1944. Her *Collected Stories* won a Pulitzer Prize in 1970: d. White Plains, NY, March 26.

Stewart, William "Bill" (37), television correspondent for ABC News; he was shot to death by a Nicaraguan soldier while covering the Nicaraguan civil war: d. Managua, Nicaragua, June 20.

Sugiura, Kanematsu (89), research scientist and pioneer in the development of chemotherapy for treating cancer; he began work on chemotherapeutic techniques in 1912. Born in Japan, he went to the United States at age 15. During World War II his research work was nearly cut off because of his nationality. Following World War II he joined the newly-formed Memorial Sloan-Kettering Institute for Cancer Research in New York City. He became a member of that institute in 1959: d. White Plains, NY, Oct. 21.

Svoboda, Ludvik (83), former president of Czechoslovakia (1968–75): d. Czechoslovakia, Sept. 20.

Tate, Allen (79), biographer, novelist, editor, teacher, critic, and poet. His poetry was formal and classical, and his criticism became part of the New Criticism: d. Nashville, TN, Feb. 9.

Todman, William S. (63), radio and television producer; with Mark Goodson, he produced such long-running television shows as *What's My Line?*, *The Price is Right*, *I've Got a Secret*, *To Tell the Truth*, and *Password:* d. New York City, July 29.

Tolstoy, Alexandra (95), author, founder of the Tolstoy Foundation, and daughter of Leo Tolstoy. During World War I she was a nurse on the Western front. After the war she helped prepare a complete edition of her father's writings. She was later arrested by the Communist government and accused of allowing White Russians to meet secretly in her home. She was sentenced to a year in jail. In 1939 she set up the Tolstoy Foundation to aid refugees. She became a United States citizen in 1941. She wrote *The Tragedy of Tolstoy* (1933) and *A Life of My Father* (1953): d. Valley Cottage, NY, Sept. 26.

Tomonaga Shinichiro (73), Japanese physicist; in 1965 he received the Nobel Prize for Physics for his research in quantum electrodynamics that contributed to the understanding of elementary particles in high-energy physics: d. Tokyo, July 8.

Tugwell, Rexford Guy (88), economist, educator, and political theorist; he was an economics professor at Columbia University when he was recruited into Franklin Roosevelt's inner circle of advisors known as the "brains trust." He served four years with the Roosevelt adminis-

tration in the Department of Agriculture, but he advised Roosevelt on numerous policies for recovery from the Depression of the 1930's. In 1938 he became the chairman of the New York City Planning Commission. In 1941, President Roosevelt sent him to Puerto Rico as chancellor of the University of Puerto Rico; later that year he was appointed governor of Puerto Rico. After leaving San Juan in 1946, he served four years as director of the University of Chicago's Institute of Planning. Following retirement in 1957, he was a visiting professor in the United States and abroad, and in 1970 he was a senior staff member of the Center for the Study of Democratic Institutions. His books include *The Brains Trust* (1968), which won the Bancroft Prize, and *In Search of Roosevelt* (1972): d. Santa Barbara, CA, July 21.

Vance, Vivian (66), actress; she was best known as the sidekick of Lucille Ball in the *I Love Lucy* television series (1951–59) and *The Lucy Show* (1962–65): d. Belvedere, CA, August 17.

Velasco Ibarra, Jose Maria (86), former president of Ecuador; he was five times president but was able to complete only one full term as he frequently ran afoul of military factions in the country. He was first elected in 1934 and last served in 1972: d. Quito, Ecuador, March 30.

Viansson-Ponte, Pierre (58), French editor and author; he became in 1958 chief editor of the domestic political sections of the newspaper *Le Monde*. He also wrote several books on Gaullism and the Gaullists. His last book, written with a French cancer specialist, was *How to Change Dying:* d. Paris, May 7.

Jean Cardinal Villot (73), Vatican Secretary of State (1969–1979): d. Rome, March 9.

Weber, Ben (62), composer; his best known works include *Symphony on Poems of William Blake, Violin Concerto, Piano Concerto, Concert Aria After Solomon, Consort of Winds*, and *String Quartet No. 2:* d. New York City, May 9.

White, Charles W. (61), artist; a leading black artist who portrayed only blacks: d. Los Angeles, Oct. 3.

Wilding, Michael (66), British film and stage actor; he appeared in Hitchcock's *Stage Fright* (1950) and on stage in the Noël Coward play *Nude With Violin* (1957): d. Chichester, England, July 8.

Williams, T. Harry (70), professor and writer; one of the foremost scholars on Civil War political and military history, he early gained attention with his book *Lincoln and the Radicals* (1941). In 1970 he won the Pulitzer Prize for his biography *Huey P. Long:* d. Baton Rouge, LA, July 6.

Woodward, Robert (62), Harvard professor of chemistry and 1965 Nobel Prize winner for chemistry; he was described as "the greatest synthetic organic chemist of modern times." In 1944 he first synthesized quinine, and in 1972 he was instrumental in the synthesizing of vitamin B-12. He also synthesized chlorophyll, strychnine, cholesterol, lysergic acid, and reserpine: d. Cambridge, MA, July 8.

John Cardinal Wright (70), since 1969 the Vatican's chief administrator for the world's 500,000 priests; he became a professor of philosophy at St. John's Seminary and was secretary to the Archbishop of Boston (1939), monsignor in 1944, Auxiliary Bishop of Boston in 1947, Bishop of Worcester (1950), and Bishop of Pittsburgh (1958). In 1969 he was named a cardinal. He was the highest-ranking American in the Vatican: d. Cambridge, MA, August 10.

Zanuck, Darryl F. (77), award-winning motion-picture producer; a flamboyant, self-made man, his motion pictures include the first talkie, *The Jazz Singer, The Sun Also Rises, The Longest Day*, and the 1961 version of *Cleopatra:* d. Palm Springs, CA, Dec. 22.

OCEANOGRAPHY

Launched with much fanfare in June 1978, the Seasat-A satellite for continuous monitoring of the ocean had a short life of only 105 days. A short circuit drained the craft's batteries faster than its banks of solar energy collectors could recharge them. Even so, in its three months of orbital operations, Seasat collected a unique set of global synoptic data on ocean winds, waves, temperature, and topography. Indications from preliminary analysis of the data were that most of the mission's objective—the demonstration of nearly all-weather microwave surveillance of the world's ocean—would be met, establishing the validity of the concept of satellite oceanography. However, no immediate replacement for Seasat was scheduled.

Other satellites supplied data. The Nimbus series of weather satellites were used to study the ocean and the Arctic environment, and also to investigate Gulf Stream eddies in the Sargasso Sea. The Geodetic Earth and Ocean Satellites (GEOS-2 and GEOS-3) were used to measure deviations in the strength of the earth's magnetic field. They provided comparisons with monthly records of cyclone eddy positions prepared by the National Weather Service. The polar-orbiting TIROS-N series satellites provided analysis of cloud cover and fog distribution, storm circulation determinations, ocean surface temperatures, tropical storm warning, hurricane tracking, and polar ice observations and snowmelt determinations. A geostationary operational environment satellite (GOES) can map in two days all the currents of the Gulf Stream from the Yucatán Strait off Mexico and Cuba to the Grand Banks near Labrador.

Eddies. Much use of satellites has been made by the joint U. S.-Soviet program for mid-ocean dynamic experiments (POLYMODE), which has sought to probe the circulation in areas of the North Atlantic. Field observations ended in the fall of 1979, after five years of activity in areas near Bermuda, east of Martinique, and on both sides of the mid-Atlantic ridge near 28° N. The studies showed that eddies both large and small have significant effects on the circulation, rather like undersea storms. Generally, the eddies are strongest near the Gulf Stream and decrease in energy with distance from that current. In most cases, eddies are weaker near the ocean bottom than they are near the surface. From POLYMODE and related studies of the Atlantic circulation conducted by French, British, German, and Canadian marine scientists, eddies are now recognized as playing an important role in ocean flow.

OTEC. The world's first ocean thermal energy conversion (OTEC) plant began testing off Hawaii in the summer of 1979. The power plant runs off a temperature difference of about 19° C (66° F) between surface water and cold deep water pumped up a 660-meter (2,165-ft) vertical pipe. These heat sources vaporize and condense ammonia in a closed power system which runs a turbine generator and produces 50 kw. This OTEC project is being conducted by the United States; similar projects got underway in Japan and in Europe.

Weather. From December 1978 to December 1979, the weather in every part of the world was monitored by a vast array of observing systems in the Global Weather Experiment (GWE). The World Meteorological Organization (WMO), representing more than 140 countries,

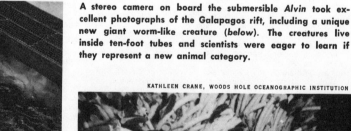

A stereo camera on board the submersible *Alvin* took excellent photographs of the Galapagos rift, including a unique new giant worm-like creature (*below*). The creatures live inside ten-foot tubes and scientists were eager to learn if they represent a new animal category.

originally named the effort the First GARP (Global Atmospheric Research Program) Global Experiment or FGGE. The program was as big as its name—10 space satellites, more than 50 oceanographic research vessels, 110 aircraft (including 10 research planes), 300 high altitude balloons, and 300 instrumented drifting buoys were involved. Four area centers in the United States, Japan, the United Kingdom, and the USSR collected, processed and controlled the quality of data observations. Each center was responsible for a section of the world.

During GWE special emphasis was placed on the Monsoon Experiment (MONEX) in the Indian Ocean. The Asian monsoon, which has great social and economic effect in the eastern hemisphere, was studied. A West African Monsoon Experiment (WAMEX) in the equatorial Atlantic involved ships from West Germany, France, Spain, the USSR, Brazil, East Germany, and Senegal. Drifting data buoys were deployed extensively in the southern hemisphere near Antarctica for observations there. A global data inventory of oceanic climate data was developed from the information obtained. Forecasting results in Australia were significantly improved and some aircraft were able to save fuel and avoid storms because of the information gathered in the experiment.

As in past years, activity of the Deep Sea Drilling Project (DSDP) added much to an understanding of the ocean floor. The puzzling Ninetyeast Ridge in the Indian Ocean, which is 50 kilometers (31 mi) to more than 100 kilometers (62 mi) wide and stretches for 4500 kilometers (2,796 mi) along the 90° east meridian of longitude, rises 2 kilometers (1.2 mi) on the average above the sea floor. Data now available indicate the ridge was formed progressively from north to south, but at a point near 50° S, much farther south than its present position. This position corresponds to a known hot spot, or site of volcanic magma, in the earth's mantle. It is now believed that the Ninetyeast Ridge is derived from a magmatic source providing substance by eruption onto the overriding crustal plate as it moved past. DSDP drilling showed that a similar origin accounts for the Hawaiian Islands and the Emperor seamount chain in the Pacific Ocean. In the latter case, the hot spot currently lies under the active volcanoes of the Hawaiian Islands.

In 1979 surveys, the DSDP research ship *Glomar Challenger* examined the Middle America Trench, the boundary along which the crust of the Pacific Ocean slowly plunges below Central America. This process, called subduction, involves the Cocos Plate (a small portion of the floor of the Pacific) and the overriding Caribbean plate which includes the land mass of Central America. Before the onset of subduction a broad, open passage was thought to exist between the two oceans. The sequence of sediments recovered indicates that a trench was in the area for at least the last 7 million years. Correlated observations on land suggest that the ancient seaway was possibly much narrower than previously believed.

At a site between Ecuador and the Galapagos Islands extensive experiments were carried out for the first time within the actual drilling hole, to examine the alteration of the crustal rocks after formation. The interior of the drilled hole was scanned by television with an ultrasonic beam. A magnetometer surveyed the entire length of the hole for the magnetic characteristics of the rock, from which some dating of the rock formation is possible. Other measurements included density, porosity, temperature, and pore water chemistry. U. S., Soviet, French, and West German scientists participated in these DSDP activities; the downhole studies were coordinated by JOIDES (Joint Oceanographic Institutions Deep Earth Sampling).

Working near the East Pacific Rise off the west coast of Mexico, an expedition from the United States, France, and Mexico found superheated water at temperatures above 300° C (570° F) spewing violently out of vents in the sea floor, forming chimney-like deposits as the metals in solution precipitated. French scientists reported that samples of deposits collected in 1978 around nearby defunct chimneys were rich in copper, iron, zinc, and sulfur, with lesser quantities of cobalt, lead, silver, and cadmium. It is believed that a large percentage of the world's ore deposits originates from such hydrothermal activity, where seawater percolates deep into hot rock erupted from within the earth, extracts metals from the rock, and then percolates upward again to erupt in geysers that lay deposits on the sea floor. Scientists in the submersible *Alvin* were the first people to see the process in action.

A total of more than 40 vents occurring on the rift at about 1500 meters (8,000 feet) has been photographed with a camera sled towed by a surface ship or explored and photographed from *Alvin*. Excellent still photographs were taken with a new stereo camera of special design that allowed close-ups of animals in their natural habitat. Water samples and filters for bacteria and particulate organic matter were collected. Samples were found of a unique new giant worm-like animal that lives inside ten-foot tubes of its own making. These creatures are so novel that they may represent an entirely new major animal category. It is believed that the food chain is based on sulfur compounds that erupt from the sea floor geysers and support a population of bacteria that in turn provides food to the worms and to the giant clams observed on the previous expedition to the Galapagos rift in 1977.

See also METEOROLOGY.

DAVID A. McGILL
Professor of Ocean Science
U. S. Coast Guard Academy

OHIO

Public school problems involving finances, teacher strikes, and adjustment to busing of students to achieve racial balance created frequent page-one news in Ohio in 1979.

In numerous communities, voters rejected money requests by school boards trying to meet increased costs. The legislature appropriated more funds, but not so much as the school leaders had hoped.

Late in the year, Cincinnati's schools, with a deficit of $7.7 million, closed for three weeks. Cleveland, forced by a federal court decision to start busing of students in September, in mid-October was distressed by its second strike in two years as teachers and others demanded more pay from budgets already stretched thin by busing costs. On Jan. 3, 1980, the teachers accepted an immediate 10% pay raise and 14% more in the 1980–81 school year. The busing program had begun without incident, but several thousand fewer students enrolled than had been expected.

Columbus started its desegregation busing without incident in September. In Dayton, where busing began its third year, black enrollment increased to 55% from 48% in 1977.

Finances. Inflation, higher interest rates, and fear of a recession complicated the state's budgeting, and that of many communities. The legislature hurriedly eased its usury statute October 31 so that the interest ceiling on municipal bonds and notes could be increased from 8% to 10.5%, as many cities feared that they would be unable to borrow needed funds.

Earlier, Ohio Auditor Thomas E. Ferguson issued a report stating that 844 local governments and school districts in 1977 had deficits in one or more of their funds, up from 577 in 1976. But many community finance directors said that the deficits were temporary or minor.

Building. A proposal by Gov. James A. Rhodes, that the state undertake $775 million in construction of new college buildings, hospitals, parks, recreational facilities, and other improvements, faced slashing. All but about $100 million was expected to be financed by bonds.

Elections. Ohio voters rejected an initiative petition to require refundable deposits on all beverage containers sold in the state. In mayoralty races, Cleveland's Dennis J. Kuchinich (D) lost out to George V. Voinovich; Columbus' Tom Moody (R) was given a third term; Roy L. Ray (R) was elected in Akron; and Canton's Stanley A. Cmich (R) and Toledo's Doug De-Good (D) were returned.

Trials. Three members of the Cleveland Council, tried for alleged theft in connection with street carnival "kickbacks" in their wards, were acquitted in July, September, and October.

Other. Cincinnati's first black city manager, Sylvester Murray, 36, took office in September.

Fourteen persons were killed in a fire at a boarding house in the village of Pioneer in November.

JOHN F. HUTH, JR.
Reporter, "The Plain Dealer," Cleveland

OKLAHOMA

The state legislature met from January 2 to June 1. It reconvened July 2 to approve a $30-million capital improvements appropriation, the first phase of a $120-million state capital expenditures "pay-as-you-go" program. The legislature appropriated a general fund budget of $928 million, $73 million more than in 1978. Major increases went to elementary schools, higher education, highways, and state correctional institutions, the latter expenditure to comply with a federal court order to reach minimum standards or be closed.

Gov. George Nigh praised the $15 million tax-cut package reached by compromise with legislative leaders as a means of controlling the growth of state government. The tax relief plan allows individual taxpayers to deduct all federal income taxes paid and it limits state income tax rates to 6%. The result was an estimated $35-million tax reduction, partly offset by an additional cigarette tax of 5¢ per package.

Inquiries by a special legislative committee into the operation of the department of corrections led to the firing of Director Ned Benton,

---

who had been actively opposed by House Speaker Dan Draper and other legislators.

Salary increases of approximately 6%, with a minimum annual increase of $600, were authorized for state employees. Increases also were made in assistance to the needy, aged, blind, and totally disabled ($20 per month) and to dependent children ($10 per month).

Business. In April, General Motors opened an auto assembly plant in Oklahoma City that employed 5,500 production and skilled workers, with an annual payroll of $120 million. Employees voted to make the United Auto Workers (UAW) their collective bargaining agent.

Att. Gen. Jan Eric Cartwright ruled that the Oklahoma constitution forbids ownership of land by foreigners unless they are actual residents of the state. Cartwright also ruled that corporations operating on land owned by city-county industrial trusts must pay full property taxes.

Education. School teachers in Oklahoma City went on strike for higher salaries when their bargaining agent, the American Federation of Teachers (AFT), failed to reach agreement with the municipal school board. Almost half of the 2,300 public school teachers joined the strike on August 23. Salary demands were not met and a district court panel ruled that the teachers must resume their classroom duties. The school board was prohibited from recognizing the AFT as the bargaining agent pending a new election.

The University of Oklahoma received a special $200,000 legislative appropriation to establish the Carl Albert Congressional Research and Studies Center.

Other. On November 4, Oklahoma honored another native son, humorist Will Rogers, on the 100th anniversary of his birth.

U. S. Sen. Henry Bellmon (R) announced in January that he would not seek reelection.

JOHN W. WOOD
Department of Political Science
The University of Oklahoma

OLDER POPULATION

Older Americans, 65 years and over and numbering upward of 24 million, continue to be the fastest growing segment of the American population. The increase in longevity was due largely to the improvement of health and living conditions in the United States. Since 1900, more than 25 years has been added to the average American life. A major concern for the legislators and planners in 1979 was to make the added years of life expectancy a benefit for older persons. The rising cost of home heating oil for the elderly also was a major issue and led to federal legislation.

The Public Interest. The Comprehensive Amendments to the Older Americans Act, which were signed by President Carter in October 1978, gave great impetus to the development of coordinated and comprehensive programs, and to setting priorities of service for the neediest and the frail. The spending level for programs and services for the elderly was projected at $652.22 million for fiscals 1979 and 1980. The Administration on Aging (AoA), which oversees the allocation of funds and the development of services for older Americans, sought primarily to make primary care services more accessible to the older population.

The funds also will be used to support senior citizen programs, nutrition programs, case work, mental health, and other programs. Monies will also support career preparation and in-service training of the many service workers involved with the elderly.

Housing. The Department of Housing and Urban Development (HUD) committed $20 million over a two-year span (fiscal years 1979 and 1980) for congregate services in public housing in addition to the construction of new housing units for the elderly poor.

The housing needs of elderly persons living in rural areas received more attention. The Department of Agriculture's Farmers Home Administration provided a minimum of $6 million to construct housing for the rural elderly. The AoA provided $1.5 million to hire full-time directors who would coordinate and provide support services for elderly residents at six designated rural areas. Services were to include meals, housekeeping for those unable to perform their own, personal care for those who need daily assistance, transportation, and social and recreational activities. These services reflect the broad goals of AoA in providing comprehensive and coordinated service systems that foster independence and reduce the need for institutionalization.

Older American Advocacy Assistance Program. State agencies on aging are now required to establish long-term care ombudsman programs to investigate complaints from residents of long-term care facilities. Moreover, area agencies on aging will be required to enter into contracts with legal service providers in furthering legal service activities on behalf of older persons.

Senate Committee on Aging. On Jan. 23, 1979, Sen. Lawton Chiles (D-FL) was named chairman of the Senate Committee on Aging. The Senate had increased the membership of this important committee to ten. In March 1979, it was increased again to 12. This committee plays an important role in safeguarding the rights and entitlements of older Americans, as well as initiating legislation on their behalf.

Elderhostels. For the elderly who are physically well and busy enjoying their retired years, Elderhostels have proven to be worthwhile and popular. The program, which started in 1975 as an experimental project, offers summer study programs for older Americans. Originally, five campuses in New Hampshire were utilized to offer educational programs and dormitory facilities to 300 hostelers. By the summer of 1979, Elderhostels grew into a national organization, publishing a national catalog containing information regarding courses and facilities throughout the United States. In 1979, the program operated on 235 college campuses in 38 states. It served 15,000 elderly hostelers. The number of hostelers served was expected to increase to 60,000 during the next few years.

Bonuses. For income tax purposes, personal exemptions for older Americans were raised from $750 to $1,000. Persons over 55 who sell their homes now have a one-time capital gains tax break.

In July social security benefits were raised 9.9%.

See also SOCIAL WELFARE.

CELIA B. WEISMAN
Director, Gerontological Institute
Yeshiva University

ONTARIO

Energy was perhaps the primary concern of Ontario, Canada's most industrialized and populous province, in 1979. Premier William Davis was strongly opposed to attempts by the federal government to raise the price of Canadian oil nearer to world levels. At the premiers' conference in August, Davis objected to any major price increase and to any further swelling of Alberta's bulging treasury. The discovery in September of a major oil supply at Sarnia was heartening, although its future benefits remained unclear.

While oil presented one problem, an excess of electrical generating capacity presented another. Ontario Hydro came under attack, especially by opposition members of the legislature, for overestimating future demands and embarking on a construction program of unnecessary generating stations. Hydro already had excess capacity, estimated by some to be as high as 47%. Many claimed that the company was raising its rates unnecessarily to service the capital debt. Hydro replied that the power may be needed in the future and will provide a valuable export commodity. Minor structural failures and water leaks in some of its nuclear stations also were an embarrassment to Hydro, although there was no evidence of any health hazard or environmental damage.

Economy. In an attempt to increase revenue and reduce the provincial deficit from $1.5 billion to $1.15 billion, Treasurer Frank Miller introduced a budget on April 10 that called for increased taxes on diesel fuel and gasoline (0.4¢ per liter) and on wine, beer, spirits, and tobacco. Provincial health insurance premiums were increased by 5.3%, and the 7% sales tax was extended to all telecommunications services, including cable television, telex, and teletype systems. To stimulate employment, the government allowed tax write-offs for investments in small businesses, set up an employment development fund of $200 million to attract major companies to the province, and abolished several duties. The ailing tourist industry also received tax concessions.

There was good news for the economy in October when General Motors announced its intention to spend $2 billion to convert and expand its plants in Windsor and St. Catherine's; 3,300 new jobs were expected to be created.

Environment. Acid rain, which is causing considerable damage to Ontario's lakes and forests, emerged as a major issue. Early in the year, the government blamed much of it on pollution from the United States, but in September a new study indicated that at least 50% of it originated in Ontario. Nevertheless, Environment Minister Harry Parrott refused to stiffen antipollution regulations until an agreement was made with the United States, perhaps fearing the effects of such a move on the provincial mining industry.

To extend further the rights of French-speaking Ontarians, the attorney general announced that plans were being made to conduct criminal trials in either English or French. The good effect of this gesture was partly offset, however, by the refusal of Education Minister Bette Stephenson to provide financial support for a private French high school in Penatanguishene. The school was set up by parents who believe that it is impossible for French-speaking students to preserve and develop their identity and culture in a mixed environment.

A contract dispute in Peel County led to a strike in October by elementary school teachers, the first in the history of the province. Liberal Party leader Dr. Stuart Smith, sensing a potentially popular issue, called for the removel of the teachers' right to strike; that right had been granted by the province's Progressive Conservative government.

Religion in public schools also emerged as a lively issue, as many protested the required daily recitation of the Lord's Prayer.

PETER J. KING
Carleton University

ONTARIO • Information Highlights

Area: 412,582 square miles (1 068 587 km²).
Population (1979 est.): 8,493,300.
Chief Cities (1976 census): Toronto, the provincial capital, 633,318; Ottawa, the federal capital, 304,462.
Government (1979): *Chief Officers*—lt. gov., Pauline McGibbon; premier, William G. Davis (Progressive Conservative); chief justice, Supreme Court, High Court of Justice, Gregory T. Evans. *Legislature*—Legislative Assembly, 125 members.
Education (1979–80 est.): *Enrollment*—public elementary and secondary schools, 1,885,250 pupils; private schools, 63,700; Indian (federal) schools, 7,530; postsecondary, 226,280 students. *Total expenditures,* $7,154,457,000.
Public Finance (1979–80 est.): *Revenues,* $14,405,000,000; *expenditures,* $15,558,000,000.
Personal Income (average weekly salary, May 1979): $282.75.
Unemployment Rate (July 1979, seasonally adjusted): 6.5%.
(All monetary figures are in Canadian dollars.)

OREGON

Environmental issues greatly concerned Oregonians in 1979.

Environment. The public debate over nuclear power generation was accelerated. A sit-in protest at the Trojan nuclear generating plant near Rainier, OR, resulted in a number of criminal trespass convictions. In October, hearings were proposed to determine whether the Trojan plant was in compliance with the terms of its license, particularly in the matter of spent fuel storage.

Another issue was the alleged effect of the herbicide 2,4-D on human health. The Forest Service traditionally sprays newly seeded cutover areas as a brush control measure. In western Oregon a group of pediatricians reported an unusually high incidence of an otherwise rather rare type of birth defect, apparently among populations living near sprayed areas.

The discovery of corroded and leaking nerve gas cannisters at the Umatilla Army Depot in eastern Oregon aroused both anger and anxiety. And, once again, the field burning in the Willamette Valley was contested.

Drought. A drought over the Pacific Northwest region began to affect power supplies in October. The pools behind the Columbia River dams fell so low that power distributors were predicting brown-outs if the drought continued. The growing anti-nuclear sentiment in the state added to the power producers' gloom. After a temporary license was issued, the Portland General Electric Company again began operation of its Bethel generating plant near Salem to supplement its power supply. The Bethel plant, an oil-fueled facility, had been idle for years because of emission standards.

Extraordinarily high grasshopper hatches, another effect of the drought, caused serious damage to crops and rangeland forage in central and eastern Oregon. Insecticide spraying in the affected areas touched off environmental debates. Forest fires caused losses substantially higher than normal.

Economy. The combination of high interest rates, Oregon's usury laws, and a resultant short-age of mortgage capital threatened the state's economy, which depends heavily on the timber industry. Although demand for single family houses remained high, unsold house inventories were abnormally high—reaching 200%.

The Wacker Chemical Company of West Germany began work on a plant in Portland. The Portland facility will produce silicon crystals and wafers used in solar generators.

During the summer, natural gas in commercial quantities was discovered near Mist. A system of pipelines is under construction for the purpose of marketing the gas within Oregon.

Other. The Department of Transportation discontinued one of Oregon's two Amtrak lines that connected Portland with several eastern Oregon communities and points east.

Connie McCready succeeded Neil Goldschmidt, who became U. S. secretary of transportation in September, as mayor of Portland.

L. CARL BRANDHORST
Oregon College of Education

OREGON • Information Highlights

Area: 96,981 square miles (251 181 km²).
Population (Jan. 1979 est.): 2,477,000.
Chief Cities (1970 census): Salem, the capital, 68,856; Eugene, 78,389; (1976 est.): Portland, 379,826.
Government (1979): *Chief Officers*—governor, Victor Atiyeh (R); secy. of state, Norma Paulus (R). *Legislative Assembly*—Senate, 30 members; House of Representatives, 60 members.
Education (1978–79): *Enrollment*—public elementary schools, 276,905 pupils; public secondary, 194,469; colleges and universities, 146,349 students. *Public school expenditures*, $962,500,000 ($1,856 per pupil).
State Finances (fiscal year 1978): *Revenues*, $3,052,-187,000; *expenditures*, $2,593,369,000.
Personal Income (1978): $19,775,000,000; per capita, $8,092.
Labor Force (June 1979): *Nonagricultural wage and salary earners*, 1,066,500; *unemployed*, 78,100 (6.4% of total force).

OTTAWA

As the capital of Canada and with the federal government as its largest employer, Ottawa viewed with concern the elections that installed the Progressive Conservative federal government in May 1979. Indeed two of the city's prominent members of Parliament, Robert De Cotret and Jean Piggot, both Conservatives and both considered potential cabinet ministers, lost their seats. Fears of losing government offices to other cities or provinces were partially allayed when the decentralization plans of the former Liberal government were shelved. In any case, two surveys published in the fall indicated that previous departmental relocations outside the city did not so greatly affect Ottawa's economic life as had been expected.

In July, Mayor Marion Dewar attracted national attention by launching "Project 4000," a campaign to have Ottawa citizens take in 4,000 Vietnamese "boat people." The first refugees began to arrive in late summer.

A decision by the city council to revise market value assessments of taxable property did not increase total tax revenues but was expected to affect a number of individual tax bills. Taxes in the previously undervalued inner city were expected to rise, while those in the suburbs were expected to fall.

The concept of regional government again came under attack. Rural municipalities, which felt they were paying for services they neither wanted nor received, expressed a desire to secede. Meanwhile, Nepean, the second largest component of the Ottawa-Carleton Municipality, officially gained the status of a city in 1979.

In a bid to gain more readers, the *Ottawa Journal* switched from afternoon to morning publication.

PETER J. KING, *Carleton University*

WIDE WORLD

Zia ul-Haq emphasized Pakistan's role as an Islamic state but was unable to form a permanent government.

PAKISTAN

It was another year of turmoil and uncertainty in Pakistan, with the execution of former Prime Minister Zulfikar Ali Bhutto, the confused attempts of the strongman, Gen. Zia ul-Haq, to form a permanent government, and the continued impact of religious extremism.

Domestic Affairs. General Zia had ousted popular Prime Minister Bhutto in 1977. Finding it impossible to schedule elections or form a reasonably democratic government as long as Bhutto was free, Zia had Bhutto arrested and ultimately tried for the murder of political opponents. Bhutto was found guilty in March 1978 and sentenced to death. About a year of appeals and political jockeying ensued. Apparently Zia was willing to let Bhutto go into exile, but political events in neighboring Iran and Afghanistan were influential in changing his mind. In Iran the shah was under increasing pressure from the Islamic clerics, and in Afghanistan there were the beginnings of what became by late 1979 a civil war. Zia was supposed to have remarked, "If Ayatollah Khomeini could, while living in Paris, bring down the powerful shah, what could we expect of a Bhutto in exile?"

The only solution was to permit the execution of Bhutto, and this Zia did, ignoring in do-

ing so not only the integrity of the Pakistan judiciary but countless appeals for mercy from all over the world. Bhutto was hanged on April 4.

Although there were some riots and demonstrations, the army was able to keep control. Bhutto's wife and daughter were held under tight security. Still, all evidence pointed to the unpalatable fact that an election held in Pakistan would bring back a strong phalanx of Bhutto followers. During the late spring and summer, Zia attempted to find a way to hold elections in November without losing them to Bhutto's widow who heads her husband's party, the Pakistan People's Party. In September he moved against Bhutto's daughter, accusing her of "bringing the country's armed forces into disrepute, creating alarm and despondency, and holding an unauthorized political meeting."

On October 16, Zia did as expected and canceled the elections indefinitely, banned all sorts of political activity, and once again moved against the nation's press. Three newspapers were closed. More than 100 opposition leaders were arrested. He reiterated the need to maintain martial law and forbade the appeal to civil courts of military tribunal decisions.

Besides strengthening the military control of the country, Zia fell back on his oft-repeated attachment to "Islamic governments." It must be remembered that some form of Muslim religious reaction has manifested itself in Pakistan, Afghanistan, Iran, and Turkey; the episodes in Iran were merely the most dramatic. On February 12, Pakistan was the first nation to extend diplomatic recognition to the new Islamic republic.

By late 1979 Zia completely abandoned any formal attachment to western democratic models. He vowed in late October to establish "a genuine Islamic" country; there "is no provision," he said, "for western-type elections in Islam." Earlier he had been quoted as saying that, in accordance with Islam, "if the majority is misguided, its verdict should be ignored." In ignoring the popular feeling in Pakistan, he has given his country the most repressive government in its history (i.e. since 1947). And almost certainly he has sowed the seeds for further rebellion and bloodshed. It is an understatement to say that, faced with these

——— PAKISTAN · Information Highlights ———

Official Name: Islamic Republic of Pakistan.
Location: South Asia.
Area: 310,403 square miles (803 943 km²).
Population (1979 est.): 79,900,000.
Chief Cities (1974): Islamabad, the capital, 250,000; Karachi, 3,500,000; Lahore, 2,100,000.
Government: *Head of state and government,* Mohammed Zia ul-Haq, president (took power Sept. 1978). *Legislature*—Parliament: Senate and National Assembly (dissolved July 1977).
Monetary Unit: Rupee (9.931 rupees equal U. S.$1, Aug. 1979).
Manufactures (major products): Cotton, textiles, processed foods, tobacco, chemicals, natural gas.
Agriculture (major products): Wheat, cotton, rice.

monumental issues, the Zia government was able to do little about Pakistan's perennial problems—poverty, overpopulation, and linguistic separatism.

Foreign Affairs. Relations with the pro-Soviet government in Afghanistan were not good, and as an indigenous revolutionary movement, flying the Islamic banner, began to develop against Afghanistan's government it was apparent that it was centered in northwest Pakistan and aided and abetted by the Zia government.

Relations with India, Pakistan's traditional enemy, were strained as usual. Zia is viewed with deep suspicion in India, which follows his "ambitions" with deep and constant interest. Prime among those ambitions apparently has been the construction of nuclear weapons. For several years Pakistan has attempted to obtain nuclear technology from regular European (mainly French) sources. Now apparently depending more upon clandestine acquisition of technology and fuel, Pakistan has been reported building at Kahuta, near Islamabad, a plant capable of producing simple nuclear weapons. Emphasizing the potential skills of its scientists, a Pakistani shared in a 1979 Nobel prize.

Although Zia has denied that such a plant is being built and has stated that any nuclear effort is for peaceful purposes, the United States took the threat seriously enough to cut off all aid (except food) to Pakistan in the spring.

In late November religious fanatics seized the great mosque in Mecca (Saudi Arabia); subsequently, incendiary broadcasts accusing the United States and Israel of complicity in this affair were beamed from Iran eastward to Pakistan. As a consequence a mob of about 20,000 stormed and burned the U. S. embassy complex in Islamabad, killing two marines in the process. The American staff retreating to the embassy "vault" were rescued by Pakistani army units after some six hours' delay. The United States recalled all nonessential American personnel and dependents from Pakistan. General Zia publicly apologized to the United States.

The Soviet invasion of Afghanistan as the year ended caused a complete reassessment of U. S.–Pakistan relations early in 1980.

CARL LEIDEN, *University of Texas, Austin*

PARAGUAY

After 25 continuous years of "peace and progress" under President Alfredo Stroessner, curtailment of political and individual freedoms persisted. The Revolutionary Febrerista Party claimed that 5,000 people have been jailed for political reasons since 1970. The Inter-American Association for Democracy and Freedom asserted that the government remains in power by unusual forms of torture. Freedom House, on the other hand, classified Paraguay as a country "partly free" rather than "not free."

The Inter-American Press Association noted that the Paraguayan press exercises self-censorship, with the president, his family, and all high military officials off limits to critics.

Stroessner's present term ends in 1983, but a 1977 constitutional amendment allows him to run for office as many times as he wishes. In spite of the restrictive political climate, four opposition parties—the Revolutionary Febrerista, the Authentic Liberal, the Popular Colorado Movement, and the Christian Democratic—agreed to cooperate for common goals, including the removal of the armed forces from politics. After eight years, the government still refuses to confer official recognition on the Christian Democrats. In 1979 the government stripped Paraguayan citizenship from the Nazi war criminal Josef Mengele, accused of responsibility for the murder of 400,000 Jews at Auschwitz. Mengele's whereabouts are unknown.

Economic Developments. Despite the fact that Paraguay has no oil production, little manufacturing, and no capital equipment, the economy has grown of late at an average rate of 10%. Notwithstanding efforts to improve the all-important agriculture base, agricultural production as a whole declined between 3% and 7% from 1978 levels. Although the soybean harvest was 15% larger than in 1978, the cotton crop was reduced. Heavy rains and severe flooding followed the 1977–78 drought and caused problems.

Some 5,000 small farmers were expected to benefit from a World Bank loan of $25 million for various agricultural projects, including the construction of a wholesale market in Asunción.

The economy continued to benefit from the ongoing construction of the giant hydroelectrical complex on the Parana river. It employs 15,000 persons and generates $200 million in foreign exchange a year. The Inter-American Development Bank (IDB) was planning to lend $210 million to a joint venture by Argentina and Paraguay to build another complex on their portion of the Parana river. A side benefit would be the addition of 360,000 new irrigated acres (145 750 ha) to production.

Paraguay granted sanctuary to Nicaragua's former President Anastasio Somoza Debayle.

LEO B. LOTT, *University of Montana*

PENNSYLVANIA

It will be remembered with a shudder as the year in which the state was confronted by a major nuclear accident, a polio epidemic, and a persistent gasoline shortage. But 1979 also will be treasured by Pennsylvanians as the year in which Pope John Paul II came to visit, the Pittsburgh Pirates won the World Series, and the city's Steelers won the Super Bowl.

Three Mile Island. Although central Pennsylvania escaped a catastrophe when safety procedures and back-up systems failed at the nuclear generating plant near Harrisburg on March 28 (*see* ENERGY), the problems encountered tormented state and local officials throughout the remainder of the year. Left hanging in doubt was the future of nuclear energy in Pennsylvania, especially the reactivation of the heavily damaged Unit No. 2 at Three Mile Island and its sister reactor, which had been shut down for refueling prior to the accident.

Civil Defense. In the six days immediately following the accident, officials grappled with the logistics of evacuating some 500,000 people living within a 20-mile (32-km) radius of the plant. Although the move was never instituted, the situation underlined the inadequacy of the existing Emergency Management (civil defense) system. In addition to developing plans for mass evacuations, preparedness personnel spent much of the year establishing procedures for dealing with accidents arising from the transportation of hazardous materials. There were several such incidents in the state in 1979, but no injuries.

Energy Options. Gov. Richard Thornburgh, citing the state's extensive coal reserves as an alternate source of energy, broke ground in August for a coal-gasification plant designed to supply the energy needs of an entire industrial park at Hazleton. Arrangements also were under way to construct a large coal-fired generating facility to be situated directly at a mine site in the long-depressed anthracite fields northeast of Harrisburg. Pressure was exerted on the Environmental Protection Agency to revise emission control rules to spur the use of coal, particularly the cleaner-burning anthracite.

State Politics. In the first year of his administration, Thornburgh, a Republican, encountered trouble from the Democratic-controlled Senate. In late October, the Democrats blocked nominations to fill three vacancies on the five-man Public Utilities Commission, which was wrestling with the aftereffects of Three Mile Island. Also at issue were several hundred other posts on regulatory boards and commissions. The governor juggled his cabinet to improve the momentum of his administration and fired Commonwealth Secretary Ethel Allen for spending too much time away from the post. In November elections, former Rep. William J. Green (D) defeated former U. S. District Attorney David J. Marston (R) in Philadelphia's mayoralty race. Frank Rizzo was barred by statute from seeking another term.

Transportation. The gasoline and diesel fuel shortage struck with virtually no warning in early spring and lingered into fall. State officials channeled emergency supplies into the Harrisburg area to permit the voluntary exodus of an estimated 150,000 residents during the nuclear crisis. An odd-even rationing plan was in operation from June 28 into September.

Health. A spring outbreak of polio among the state's 18,000 Amish resulted in eight cases of the Type I variety, the most frequent cause of paralysis. Although many members of the sect at first declined to be vaccinated, the state Department of Health estimated that 88% of the Amish subsequently were vaccinated and the epidemic subsided. In September, two additional cases were reported, but they were attributed to the vaccine; both victims were infants.

Crime. W. A. "Tony" Boyle, 78, former chief of the United Mine Workers, was sentenced a second time to three life terms for setting up the 1969 murders of union rival Joseph Yablonski, his wife, and daughter. Boyle's first conviction was set aside by the state Supreme Court in 1977, and he was found guilty again in 1978.

Civil Rights. In an unprecedented move, the U. S. Justice Department in August filed suit against the Philadelphia Police Department, Mayor Frank Rizzo, and 18 other city officials, charging them with systematic police abuse of minorities. The suit was dismissed by a federal judge who criticized the Justice Department for filing the suit during the final days of the Rizzo administration, thus denying the defendants their day in court.

Economy. Unemployment dipped slightly through most of the year, but rose to slightly more than 8% for October. Steel and several other industries attributed sales declines to growing competition from imports. Agriculture had a good year. The tourist industry was dealt a blow by the notoriety of Three Mile Island, the polio epidemic, and the gas shortage.

RICHARD ELGIN
State Desk, "The Patriot-News," Harrisburg

—— PENNSYLVANIA · Information Highlights ——

Area: 45,333 square miles (177 412 km²).

Population (Jan. 1979 est.): 11,737,000.

Chief Cities (1970 census): Harrisburg, the capital, 63,061; (1976 est.): Philadelphia, 1,797,403; Pittsburgh, 449,092.

Government (1979): *Chief Officers*—governor, Richard L. Thornburgh (R); lt. gov., William W. Scranton, III (R). *General Assembly*—Senate, 50 members; House of Representatives, 203 members.

Education (1978–79): *Enrollment*—public elementary schools, 1,008,664; public secondary, 1,038,082; colleges and universities, 472,577 students. *Public school expenditures*, $5,017,900,000; $2,135 per pupil.

State Finances (fiscal year 1978): *Revenues*, $12,106,-282,000; *expenditures*, $11,723,405,000.

Personal Income (1978): $90,939,000,000; per capita, $7,740.

Labor Force (July 1979): *Nonagricultural wage and salary earners*, 4,695,700; *unemployed*, 340,300 (6.3% of total force).

PERU

Major 1979 events in Peru were the promulgation of a new Constitution providing for the transfer of political power from military rulers to an elected civilian government in 1980 and the death of 84-year-old Víctor Raúl Haya de la Torre, founder in 1924 and leader of the center-left American Popular Revolutionary Alliance (APRA).

New Constitution. A new constitution, promulgated on July 12, 1979, and signed by Assembly president Víctor Raúl Haya de la Torre on his sick bed, was rejected by 30-odd left-wing representatives and was sent back to the assembly by the cabinet. Provisions concerning additional protection to individuals, abolishing the death penalty except for treason during wartime, allowing state employees to form unions, and cancelling debts owed by recipients of land under agrarian reform were especially disputed. In response, the assembly unanimously rejected the cabinet's objections and adjourned.

Nevertheless plans went forward for elections. The Constitution provides that if no one wins more than 36% of the vote in May 1980 elections, Congress will select a president from the two front-runners. In future elections, a runoff is to be held if no one wins 50% of the first vote. As 1979 ended, it was expected that the three principal candidates for the 1980 presidential election, the first since 1963, would be Armando Villanueva del Campo of the Apristas; former president (1963–68) Fernando Belaúnde Terry of Popular Action; and Genaro Ledesma of the extreme left Workers, Peasants, and Students Front (FOCEP). The new Constitution establishes a bicameral Congress consisting of a 68-member Senate and a 180-member Chamber of Deputies, both elected for five-year terms. Presidential budgetary power and the power to make executive agreements with other nations are increased. Illiterates are given the right to vote for the first time in Peruvian history.

New Cabinet. Maj.-Gen. Pedro Richter Prada, a conservative, was sworn in as prime minister, war minister, and commander of the Army in February, replacing Gen. Oscar Molina Pallochia, who retired. After criticism over his conciliatory attitude toward Chile—despite the arrest of four Chileans for spying in December 1978—Foreign Minister José de la Puente Radbill was replaced by Carlos Garcia Bedoya, the ambassador to the United States.

Economy. The Peruvian sol continued to decline in value as inflation reached a 60% annual rate in September after having been 73.8% in 1978 and 32% in 1977. A 40% decline in real wages in 1978, plus reductions in government food and fuel subsidies, contributed to short-lived strikes broken up by the government.

Mining Output Improved. Discovery in January by Occidental Petroleum of a new oil field in an Amazon region abandoned by another U. S. firm was expected to increase oil exports by 20,000 barrels daily. The discovery was expected to lead to the renegotiation of an agreement with Japan over oil prices. Oil-sale income is to pay for construction of the North Andean Pipeline. PETROPERU, the government oil corporation, however, was in considerable trouble with the Central Bank and foreign banks over its financial management.

Continued high world demand and the impact of strikes not only in Peru but also in Canada and Zambia were expected to increase revenues from Peru's copper exports.

NEALE J. PEARSON, *Texas Tech University*

PHILIPPINES

Ferdinand E. Marcos, simultaneously president and prime minister of the Philippines, began in September 1979 his eighth year of rule by martial law in the face of growing opposition to his "constitutional authoritarianism."

Politics. Jaime Cardinal Sin, the Philippines' ranking Catholic clergyman, publicly called, for the first time, for an end to martial law. President Marcos, he said, should hold elections or step down as the nation's leader. The cardinal's action was in response to increasing support of the country's Communist rebels by some priests and nuns as well as to the 62-year-old Marcos' cancellation in January of plans for local elections of 1,575 governors and mayors. Such voting was last held in 1971.

By October, as signs of growing discontent with his authoritarian regime increased, President Marcos announced that he would consider

---

PERU • Information Highlights

Official Name: Republic of Peru.
Location: West coast of South America.
Area: 496,223 square miles (1 285 216 km²).
Population (1979 est.): 17,300,000.
Chief City (1972 census): Lima, the capital, 3,350,000 (met. area).
Government: *Head of state,* Gen. Francisco Morales Bermúdez, president (took office Aug. 1975). *Head of government,* Maj.-Gen. Pedro Richter Prada, prime minister (took office Feb. 1979). *Legislature*—Congress: Senate and Chamber of Deputies.
Monetary Unit: Sol (239.72 soles equal U. S.$1, Nov. 1979).
Manufactures (major products): Mineral and petroleum products, fish meal, textiles.
Agriculture (major products): Cotton, sugar, coffee.

PHILIPPINES • Information Highlights

Official Name: Republic of the Philippines.
Location: Southeast Asia.
Area: 115,830 square miles (300 000 km²).
Population (1979 est.): 46,200,000.
Chief Cities (May 1975): Manila, the capital, 1,479,116; Quezon City, 956,864; Cebu, 413,025.
Government: *Head of state and government,* Ferdinand E. Marcos, president and prime minister. *Legislature* (unicameral)—National Assembly.
Monetary Unit: Peso (7.35 pesos equal U. S.$1, Nov. 1979).
Manufactures (major products): Processed foods, tobacco, beverages, rubber products, cement, glass, textiles.
Agriculture (major products): Rice, corn, sugar, copra, coconut oil.

holding governors' and mayors' elections within 18 months and a new national assembly vote by 1984. There was widespread skepticism that such balloting would occur or be free if it did.

Political opposition to the Marcos regime focused on continuing human rights violations, widespread corruption involving the president's relatives and friends, and markedly increased abuse of power by the military—especially in the countryside. The size of the armed forces was variously estimated to have increased by 60% to 80% since Marcos terminated constitutional government in 1972.

Former President Diosdado Macapagal was charged with incitement to sedition as a result of a book, first published in 1976, calling on the army to rise up against Marcos.

Economy. Economic conditions worsened in the Philippines in 1979. Inflation increased at an annual rate of nearly 30%—with many Filipino families spending as much as 70% of their income for food. An estimated one third of all children suffered from major nutritional deficiencies (with the number higher in poorer rural regions).

The Philippines' foreign debt rose to almost $9 billion and the oil import bill to $1.4 billion a year. The pace of new investment from abroad slackened, and there were reports of foreign capital leaving the country by various clandestine means.

Rebellions. Two significant insurgencies continued to rage in the country. The largest of these—on behalf of autonomy for two million Muslims in the southern Philippines—involved an estimated 10,000 partisans. The war against the Moro Liberation Front, in its fifth year, shifted from large set battles to smaller but no less costly or intense hit-and-run raids.

The second insurrection—by the Communist New People's Army—comprised no more than 3,000 rebels, but their number was growing. Communist military activity was mainly concentrated on central Luzon and in the middle islands of the archipelago.

Foreign Affairs. The Sino-Vietnamese war that broke out early in the year, coupled with strong Soviet support of the Vietnamese, clearly frightened the Filipino leader, who subsequently reiterated his country's military dependence on the United States.

Taking advantage of Vietnam's preoccupation with continued resistance to its handpicked satellite regime in neighboring Cambodia, the Philippines formally annexed much of the contested Spratly Island group in the South China Sea. Claimed by Vietnam, China, and Taiwan, the Kalayaans, as the Filipinos call them, are a potentially oil-rich group of islands. Several of the islands had been fortified by the Philippines as early as 1971.

Mrs. Imelda Marcos, wife of the president and herself governor of metropolitan Manila, visited Peking in July to sign an aviation pact with China and to discuss unstable conditions in the Asian rimland with the Chinese.

U. S. Relations. Agreement was announced January 1 on the terms of continued American access to the large Clark Air Force base and to the no less important Subic Bay naval facility. The United States recognized Philippine sovereignty over the bases which it has used since granting the country its independence in 1946. In return, Washington promised the Marcos government $500 million in economic and military aid over the next five years, although it was by no means certain that the U. S. Congress would provide the necessary funding. The Filipino tricolor was raised over the bases, for the first time ever, on February 17.

Anti-Americanism in the country visibly grew—part of the popular reaction against an autocratic government with which the United States was closely allied. Former President Macapagal criticized the Carter administration for coddling an "overstaying and corrupt dictatorship."

RICHARD BUTWELL
Professor of Political Science
Murray State University

UPI

Long lines for gasoline are also common in Manila, the Philippines. In addition, inflation runs at annual rate of 30% and as much as 70% of the family income is spent on the purchase of food.

PHOTOGRAPHY

Nikon's EM

COURTESY, NIKON

A last hurrah in a decade-long photographic boom called "nothing less than spectacular" by New York gallery owner Lee Witkin characterized the year 1979. Automation and ever-shrinking hardware, faster color films and optics, multiplying galleries and museum departments, more exposure in books and in the media generally, additional university and art school courses, and the acceptance of the medium as a fine art as well as everyman's expressive form marked photography's fabulous seventies. The decade ended, however, with a harvest of technological refinements and a retrospective air in exhibitions and publications.

New Equipment. The annual Photo Marketing Association (PMA) trade show in Chicago was the launching pad for an all-out campaign by single-lens reflex (SLR) 35mm camera manufacturers to broaden the market. Economy and simplicity characterized the avalanche of compact, light-weight, automatic-exposure, "entry-level" cameras designed for the 110 or instant photography snapshooter moving to a 35mm SLR for the first time. Canon's AV-1, Nikon's EM (its first entry in the amateur market), and the Olympus OM-10 had in common a considerable use of plastic, simplified operation with no external shutter speed dial, and a matching flash unit and auto-winder. Pentax's MV, the smallest and lightest 35mm SLR to date, even went so far as to replace the traditional aperture and shutter-speed viewfinder symbols with red, green, and yellow lights to tell the user when to stop, shoot, or proceed with caution, i.e., flash. And manufacturers promoted these cameras as easy to use in $70 million advertising campaigns.

New non-interchangeable lens 35s appeared with built-in pop-up flash and auto (automatic) focusing. The Fuji Flash Focus added a method of projecting a sensor beam on the subject to assure enough light for the auto-focus mechanism to operate. And the Olympus XA with rangefinder focusing was so compact that its 4 x 2½ x 1½ in. (10 x 6 x 4 cm) dimensions and 8 ounce (.2 kg) weight made it about the size of a package of cigarettes.

The traditional 110-format pocket cameras continued to gain in sophistication. Agfa-Gevaert brought out its Agfamatic 910E motor, the first non-SLR 110 with a motorized film advance, while Kodak introduced three new Ektras, two with built-in electronic flash and tele (telephoto) lens.

For the first time, instant-camera giants Kodak and Polaroid began to appeal to different audiences: Kodak to the average consumer with three new models, including the Colorburst 50 and the Colorburst 250; Polaroid to the professional with the 3¼ x 4¼ in. (8 x 11 cm) format 600SE. For its instant Polavision movie system, Polaroid announced the development of sound via phototapes.

The size of lenses continued to shrink, matching the compactness of new camera bodies; the zoom lens boom went on, especially among wide angles; and *Popular Photography* magazine popularized a new method for maximizing lens performance—ISFO, i.e. image surface-to-film optimization—by ensuring that the film is kept as flat as possible in the camera.

"Dedicated" electronic flash units—in which a current is triggered in the camera to set the body's shutter speed at the correct synch (synchroflash) speed—continued to be produced. For example, Nikon marketed the SB-E for its EM. Flash units for instant cameras proliferated —for example, Kodak's Model C for the new Colorburst 50—as did flashes with extremely rapid cycling for use with motor drives. "Double-header" flashes were also popular as a means to provide bounce and direct lighting from one unit.

Most film manufacturers opted to refine existing products rather than introduce new ones. Kodak brought out a new version of PR10 (Kodak Instant Color Print film) with full development in four minutes, sharper images, and improved color rendition; Polaroid demonstrated its SX-70 film that develops fully in one minute.

Sharpness, color rendition, and shadow detail also improved in Kodacolor 110 ASA 400 film. Kodak introduced 12-exposure 35mm cartridges, shortened the film leader on Ektachrome 200 for easier loading, started to sell its film in China, and announced the adoption of International Standards Organization (ISO) emulsion-speed designations which are to appear on its packages.

For the darkroom, improvements in color paper occurred and new "silver-rich" black-and-white exhibition-quality fiber-based paper—Ilford's Ilfobrom "Gallerie"—became available. The development of a laser color printer represented a technological breakthrough because it allowed for faithful reproduction from a transparency and unlimited artistic and corrective variations, while bucking the complex problems and cost of producing dye transfer prints.

Court Cases. In the civil antitrust suit brought by Berkey Photo Inc. against Eastman Kodak, a federal court of appeals reduced the $87 million originally awarded Berkey to less than $1 million. Berkey appealed the decision to the U. S. Supreme Court. But Kodak was found to have conspired illegally in its development of magicube flash with Sylvania and of flipflash with GE, and a new trial was to determine the damages to Berkey. Most importantly, the appeals court also set aside the trial court's decision that Kodak must give advance notice to competitors of its plans to introduce new products. In the meantime, Argus Inc. brought a suit against Kodak charging that it has used its hold on the amateur film market in the United States to stifle camera sales by competitors; Argus is trying to divest Kodak of its camera business or force it to create film formats in any form required by a competing manufacturer.

Exhibitions. "Distinctly retrospective" sums up the 1979 trend of major photographic shows.

Classical American photography shows abounded in New York. At the Museum of Modern Art (MoMA), "Ansel Adams and the West," 153 black-and-white prints of Yosemite Valley and the Sierra Nevada, celebrated the landscapist's 50 years in the medium. The Metropolitan Museum of Art showed 50 color prints by Eliot Porter in honor of his 40 years as a naturalistic photographer. At the Whitney Museum of American Art, a survey of American photography between 1900 and 1930 traced soft-focus pictorialism to hard-edged modern. And the photographs by women born or working around the turn of the century came under scrutiny—Gertrude Käsebier at the Brooklyn Museum and two surveys at the International Center of Photography.

French photography of all periods came in for much attention. Prince Gustav Le Gray's 19th-century French landscapes were shown in New York as well as Brassai's photographs of artists and studios in Paris. Henri Cartier-Bresson celebrated his 50-year retrospective, and Eugène Atget's photographs of gardens around Paris were shown. A survey show, "France Between the Wars," covered the years 1925–40.

At the Witkin Gallery, one of the nerve centers of fine art photography in the United States, "A Ten Year Salute" included 150 images by 54 photographers who had shown there since it opened in 1969.

Major museums outside of New York that have established a collection or acquisition policy during the 1970's showed some of their fruits—examples of American pictorialism at the Brooklyn Museum, the traveling Target Collection of up-to-the-minute work acquired by the Museum of Fine Arts in Houston, and Paul Strand's photographs in the Stieglitz Gallery at the Museum of Art in Philadelphia. During a three-month period, Venice was the site of 35 shows and 46 workshops celebrating "Trends and Masters of the 20th Century."

Ansel Adams' 50 years in photography were marked by an exhibit, at MoMA in New York City, which included his rock landscape.

DAVID HUME KENNERLY, CONTACT

FROM THE COLLECTION OF ANSEL ADAMS, COURTESY, MUSEUM OF MODERN ART, NEW YORK

Eliot Porter's photo (*above*) was shown at the "Intimate Landscapes" exhibition which the Metropolitan Museum of Art mounted to celebrate his 40 years as a naturalist photographer. The collage by Linda Connor is from the "One of a Kind," Polaroid survey show.

At the Witkin Gallery (NY), "A Ten Year Salute" exhibit celebrated the gallery's first ten years.

Storm, Provincetown, by Joel Meyerowitz, is from the "Cape Light" show of views of Cape Cod, which toured the United States during 1979.

Galleries were ablaze with color. Joel Meyerowitz's "Cape Light" show of views of Cape Cod, MA, toured the United States, as did the Polaroid survey "One of a Kind." Well-known photojournalist Gordon Parks took a different tack in his "Eye Music" exhibition of large-scale abstractions in brilliant colors.

Personal journalism also continued to be recognized. Robert Frank's photographs from *The Americans* coincided with the 20th anniversary of the publication of his famous book, which was reissued in 1979 by Aperture; Larry Fink's photography was shown at MoMA, while the work from *Jean Pigozzi's Journal of the Seventies* appeared in conjunction with book publication.

Books and Periodicals. Another plethora of books of and about photography appeared, more than ever from the large publishing houses. From American Heritage came Oliver Jensen's *America's Yesterday, Images of Our Lost Past Discovered in the Photographic Archives of the Library of Congress,* with 325 pictures from the 1800's through 1945. *The History of Fashion Photography* (Chanticleer Press) counteracted the theory that commercial photography is not art, and the New York Graphic Society produced a book of *Marie Cosindas Color Photographs* (Polaroid). Harper and Row published *Walker Evans First and Last,* and *The Book of Color Photography* came from Knopf. The introspective trend of the 1970's and the growing popularity of self-portraiture led to a how-to book called *Self-Exposure: A Workbook in Photographic Self-Portraiture.* The increased interest in self-publishing was fed by photojournalist Bill Owens' *Publish Your Photo Book.*

The exploding interest in photography resulted in increased coverage in newspapers and magazines. Critic A. D. Coleman came out with a collection of his *Light Readings: A Photogra-*

phy Critic's Writings 1968–78, while David Godine was preparing a collection of Janet Malcolm's writing on photography. And interviews of photographers and historians that originally appeared in (Swiss) *Camera* magazine were gathered together in *Dialogue with Photography.*

General periodicals used photographs more than ever before, and the big picture magazines returned—*Life* as a monthly, *Look* as a biweekly (though it folded before the end of 1979). There was also an influx of European magazines, including *Geo.*

In the photographic press, *Darkroom* magazine was established, while *American Photographer* completed its second year. With the exception of the *Photography Annual,* which in 1979 ran more color pages (32) than ever before, special editions of *Popular Photography* ceased publication.

BARBARA LOBRON, *Writer and Photographer*

PHYSICS

During 1979, the centennial anniversary of the birth of Albert Einstein, exciting results were obtained in particle physics and major developments were reported in the fields of nuclear physics and controlled thermonuclear fusion.

Particle Physics. The class of elementary particles called hadrons (protons, neutrons, pi mesons) is thought to consist of subparticles called quarks. The discovery of the J/psi particle in 1974 required the introduction of a fourth (charmed) quark. In 1978 a new, more massive particle, the upsilon, was found at Fermilab (Batavia, IL) and later confirmed by a series of experiments at DESY (Hamburg, West Germany). This fifth quark is called the bottom (or beauty) quark. Most physicists agree that there should be a sixth quark (the top quark) and a more massive corresponding particle.

The new particle will likely be found through the use of one of two new machines: PETRA (Hamburg, West Germany) and PEP (Stanford, CA). These machines utilize colliding beams. When one fast particle strikes a stationary target, much energy goes into moving the target, but when two particles crash head-on none of their energy is wasted. Storage rings are used to increase the number of particles. Electrons and positrons (antielectrons) seem ideally suited for such experiments, since they annihilate each other. A machine employing this principle was used to discover the J/psi particle. A new intermediate energy machine at Cornell (Ithaca, NY) may be best suited for the study of upsilon particles.

An important experiment at SLAC (Stanford Linear Accelerator) provided strong evidence for parity nonconservation in neutral currents. Some processes conserve parity (show no preference for left or right handedness), while others do not. The electromagnetic interaction conserves parity, while the weak interaction does not. If two particles interact and exchange a unit of electric charge, the process is called a charged-current interaction; if no charge is exchanged, it is called a neutral-current interaction. Parity was known to be violated for charged-current processes, and predicted to be violated for neutral-current processes. Previous experiments yielded negative results. In the recent experiment at SLAC polarized electrons were scattered from a deuterium target, and an asymmetry in the number of scattered electrons was measured to be about one part in ten thousand, in excellent agreement with theoretical predictions.

Nuclear Physics. The recent direction of nuclear physics has been toward larger facilities and heavy ions. In the United States, a major heavy ion facility is to be built at Michigan State University. The beam from a superconducting cyclotron under construction in 1979 will be injected into a second, larger superconducting cyclotron. Uranium ions can be accelerated to over 40 GeV (about 18 MeV/nucleon), while mass 40 ions would have nearly 200 MeV/nucleon. The construction at Oak Ridge (TN) National Laboratory of the 25 MV tandem electrostatic accelerator neared completion in 1979. The accelerator was to be combined with a cyclotron for heavy ion research.

The most interesting recent development in heavy ion research has been deep inelastic scattering, in which a massive transfer of energy takes place between heavy projectiles and targets. The search for superheavy elements (elements far beyond those presently found in nature) had proven fruitless by late 1979. Such attempts have emphasized the fusion of heavy projectile and target. The production of superheavies via deep inelastic scattering is now being tried in a variety of reactions. However, there is growing pessimism about the likelihood of producing superheavy elements via conventional heavy ion reactions.

Gravity Waves. As electromagnetic waves are produced by accelerated charges, gravity waves should be produced by accelerated masses. The usual methods to detect gravity waves involve a large cylinder whose ends should be set into very small oscillations by the waves. Piezoelectric crystals would be squeezed to produce a voltage. Many groups have obtained negative results with such apparatus. Laser interferometers are under construction which will search for a shift in interference fringes between light traveling in horizontal and vertical directions. Although astronomers from the University of Massachusetts have presented a detailed analysis of radiation from a pulsar and have suggested that gravity waves are being emitted in the amount predicted by general relativity, experimental observation of gravity waves will probably not be achieved for many years.

Controlled Thermonuclear Fusion. Since the "fuel" used in nuclear fusion is essentially unlimited, controlled fusion remains an appealing long-term solution to the energy problem. The fundamental difficulty with this method is the high temperature required to initiate fusion (10 to 100 million degrees Kelvin). Since no ordinary matter can exist at these temperatures, containment is exceptionally difficult.

Most containment methods utilize magnetic fields. The most popular configuration has been a doughnut shape, usually labelled tokamak (a Russian acronym). In 1979 the fusion test reactor at Princeton (NJ) achieved a temperature of 60 million degrees. In addition to temperature, density and containment time are also crucial. Although the 60 million degree temperature achieved at Princeton was the highest ever recorded, other important variables were well below record values. An old magnetic field approach using magnetic mirrors has been revitalized at Lawrence Livermore (CA) Laboratory. A fusion reactor with a straight tube and magnetic mirrors at each end would have enormous practical advantages. The device could be scaled up to suit power requirements and could be built in modular units. Unfortunately, particles tend to leak out the ends. This problem was solved by bending the tube into a doughnut. However, new designs for magnetic mirrors to plug the leaky ends of the tube may make it possible to return to linear geometries. A mirror fusion test facility with superconducting magnets was under construction at Livermore. However, the basic problem—that more energy is absorbed than produced in these test fusion reactors—remains, and the fundamental choice between alternate approaches has not been made.

See also feature article on Albert Einstein, pages 29–34.

GARY MITCHELL, *North Carolina State University*

John Paul II Goes Home

Pope John Paul II's return to his native Poland—seven and a half months after his election to the papacy—was by all accounts the most significant religious event of 1979. It was also a "political triumph" in terms of asserting the importance of religion in Poland and in Eastern Europe's other Communist-ruled nations.

The pope was prevented by the Polish government from making the trip in May for the normal celebration of the ninth centenary of the death of St. Stanislaus, the symbol of Polish unity and religious nationalism. But the pontiff simply extended the celebration to include the time of his trip and culminated his visit with a special Mass in honor of the saint celebrated before one million people in Cracow.

The nine-day trip, June 2–10, described by the Vatican as a "religious pilgrimage," was fraught with political implications as the pope made specific pleas for religious freedom and human rights.

The itinerary was staggering, beginning with a one-day stop in Warsaw, the nation's capital and base of Poland's most powerful religious leader, Stefan Cardinal Wyszynski. The initial stop included a meeting with top government leaders and an outdoor Mass in the city's center.

The pilgrimage encompassed Gniezno, an early center of Polish Catholicism; the historic monastery of Jasna Gora; the famous Shrine of Our Lady of Czestochowa; side trips to rural villages and mountain areas; a memorial Mass at the former Nazi concentration camp in Brzezinka, near Auschwitz; a visit to the pope's native town, Wadowice; and the final stop in Cracow, his former archbishopric.

A highly emotional experience for Pope John Paul, who often wept, sang, shouted, and ad libbed during his sermons and exchanges with the crowds, the pilgrimage drew millions of fervent Polish Catholics, thousands of visitors, and more than 1,000 journalists from the West.

In Warsaw's Victory Square, on that first day of his visit, Pope John Paul hurled a basic challenge to the Polish government's efforts to create an atheistic state. He said: "It is impossible without Christ to understand the history of the Polish nation."

During two subsequent days in Gniezno, his homilies contained strong pleas for religious freedom and recognition of God-given human dignity. He stated that he wished to play a major role in the unification of Christians in both Eastern and Western Europe.

In Czestochowa, the pope set the tone of his entire trip by pleading for Church freedom, declaring himself an "apostle to the Slavs" (which includes peoples of other Eastern European nations) and by consecrating the Church in Poland and the world to Mary, Christ's mother.

Although the pope's remarks were expressed in religious terms, significant political implications were present in almost every major talk. At one point he interpreted his own election as pope as a call to Poland to become a "particularly responsible witness" to the Church in Eastern Europe.

Ironically, when the pope was greeted, quite warmly, by Communist leaders in Warsaw, he was treated as a visiting head of state. Henryk Jablonski, chairman of the Polish Council of State who received the pope in the name of the government, noted the increasing commitment of the papacy to efforts "most significant for the whole of mankind—peace, friendly coexistence, and social justice."

In his first utterance on Polish soil as pope, the former Karol Cardinal Wojtyla of Cracow

UPI

At the Warsaw airport, Stefan Cardinal Wyszynski, primate of Poland, welcomes John Paul to the pope's homeland.

UPI

At an outdoor, televised Mass in Warsaw's Victory Square, Pope John Paul declared that "Christ cannot be kept out of the history of man in any part of the globe."

stressed that his visit was "dictated by strictly religious motives" but added that he hoped it would serve the "great cause of rapprochement and of collaboration among nations" and that "it might be useful . . . for reconciliation and for peace" in today's world.

John Paul II expressed the hope that his visit, the first by a pontiff to a communist-governed state, would aid the "development of relations between the state and Church" in Poland.

Edward Gierek, first secretary of the Polish Communist Party, later praised the pope's efforts "to promote dialogue and peace." He vowed that Poland's government would "encourage further development" of relations between Poland and the Vatican "for the sake of . . . supporting the supreme cause of peace."

Pope John Paul, in response, recalled Poland's many struggles to attain nationhood. He said peace depends on respect for the rights of the nation and declared that the Church seeks to serve both state and society, asking only for what is essential to accomplish her mission.

During an outdoor Mass in Warsaw, the pope made an impassioned plea for Poland to remain faithful to its religious heritage, and placed a heavy emphasis on the nation's Christian roots.

Wherever the Polish-born pontiff went throughout the country, thousands gathered along streets and rural lanes. Some wore gaily colored costumes and waved papal and Polish flags. Crowds swelled into the hundreds of thousands for outdoor Masses in Gniezno, Czestochowa, and Cracow. Millions more, normally deprived of religious radio and television programming by the government, saw live coverage of the pope's Mass in Warsaw.

During his visit to Jasna Gora and Czestochowa, the 59-year-old pontiff addressed the opening of the 169th assembly of Polish bishops in the monastery of Jasna Gora.

Citing the life of St. Stanislaus, who was slain for opposing policies of an unjust king, he said the martyrdom shows "how deeply the moral order penetrates the structures and levels" of the nation and its political life.

At Brzezinka, the site of Nazi atrocities, Pope John Paul again focused on human rights, calling the concentration camps a "testimony to war" and "to hatred, destruction, and cruelty."

In Cracow, where he had served as archbishop for 20 years, the pope recalled his early life and declared that for him Cracow was a "synthesis" of all that it means to be Polish and Catholic. In effect, during his nine-day visit to the land of 35 million (90 percent of whom are Catholic), the pope stressed that Poland's culture, history, tradition, and nationhood are "fundamentally Christian" and that any effort by the state to hinder Church activity affronts the nation.

ROBERT L. JOHNSTON

Pope John Paul II kneels and prays at the former Nazi concentration camp in Brzezinka, near Auschwitz. Some 6 million Poles, including 3 million Jews, were killed during World War II.

UPI

At a meeting with the pope, Edward Gierek, the first secretary of the Polish Communist Party, observed that "cooperation between the church and state should embrace everything that serves the development of Poland."

GAMMA, LIAISON

UPI

Dressed in native costume and displaying copies of the portrait of the "Black Madonna," Polish women prepare to greet the pontiff at the historic monastery of Jasna Gora.

POLAND

The outstanding issue in Poland during 1979 was the relationship between church and state, brought to the fore by the June visit of Pope John Paul II (*see* Special Report, page 406).

In other domestic developments, the PZPR (Polish United Workers' Party) on July 22 celebrated the 35th anniversary of the founding of Communist rule in Poland. Among the more significant political changes during the year were the February demotions of Jozef Kepa and Jozef Tejchma from their posts as vice premiers. The two Politburo members were blamed for failures in transportation and agricultural development, respectively.

Opposition. Activities by the political opposition were widespread for most of the year. Some of the dissension was in behalf of Kazimierz Switon, a member of the movement for the Defense of Human and Civil Rights who was arrested and jailed in late 1978. In January 1979, Polish intellectuals made widely publicized appeals to Chairman Henryk Jabłonski on behalf of Switon. On the night of April 17–18, the statue of Lenin at Nowa Huta was damaged by a bomb. This led to even more intense police action against protesters. On April 18, Jacek Kuron and Adam Michnik, two prominent dissidents, were arrested in a new government campaign against underground or "flying" universities. The two scholars, who had been giving lectures not included in official university curricula, were released on May 25.

In mid-June several dissident groups announced that they would join forces, and on September 1 an oppositional organization, called the Confederation of Independent Poland (KPN), was formed.

Economy. Although official estimates were lacking, independent observers estimated that the rate of inflation in 1979 was between 6 and 8%. Even according to official statistics, real income was stagnant. Production lagged in agriculture; housing construction, energy resources, and transport failed to expand. Despite heavy indebtedness, Poland succeeded in securing some new foreign loans, including $550 million from a group of U.S. and West German banks, and $100 million from Japan.

On June 18 officials of Pol-Mat, the foreign trade organization of the Polish automotive industry, and Fiat, the Italian car manufacturer, signed an agreement to cooperate in the production of two new vehicles. The agreement, valued at $700 million a year, also requires Poland to supply a specified number of cars to Fiat dealers abroad and permits Fiat to export to Poland car models not produced there.

To improve the quality and availability of goods and services to consumers, the government on July 1 introduced on a trial basis a measure decentralizing retail store management in 13 cities and towns.

--- POLAND · Information Highlights ---

Official Name: Polish People's Republic.
Location: Eastern Europe.
Area: 120,727 square miles (312 683 km²).
Population (1979 est.): 35,400,000.
Chief Cities (Dec. 1977): Warsaw, the capital, 1,532,-100; Łodz, 818,400; Cracow, 712,600.
Government: *Head of state,* Henryk Jabłonski, president of the Council of State (took office 1972). *Head of government,* Piotr Jaroszewicz, chairman of the Council of Ministers (1970). *First secretary of the United Polish Workers' Party,* Edward Gierek (1970). *Legislature* (unicameral)—Sejm.
Monetary Unit: Złoty (33.20 złotys equal U.S.$1, 1979).
Manufactures (major products): Iron and steel, chemicals, textiles, processed foods, ships, transport equipment.
Agriculture (major products): Grains, sugar beets, potatoes, hogs, livestock.

Church-State Relations. Boleslaw Piasecki, the long-time leader of a pro-regime Catholic lay association (PAX), died on Jan. 1, 1979. The passing of Piasecki was expected to weaken further the government's attempts to penetrate and direct Catholic opinion in Poland. Piasecki was succeeded by Ryszard Reiff.

On January 24, Stefan Cardinal Wyszynski and Party leader Edward Gierek met for the first time since 1977. They discussed church-state relations and reportedly agreed on the terms of the pope's visit.

In September, Poland's bishops issued a series of pronouncements challenging the regime on a number of issues: birth control, censorship of the press, and indoctrination in government schools. During the summer, some 300 Catholic intellectuals in Poland addressed a letter to Cardinal Tomasek of Prague on behalf of Czech dissidents. Dissidents in the two countries had maintained contact for more than a year.

Foreign Affairs. The year 1979 was a busy one in Polish diplomacy. In February, Czech Party leader Gustav Husák visited his counterpart in Poland, Edward Gierek. The two leaders expressed their support for pro-Soviet Vietnam and attacked the "anti-Socialist and chauvinist" policies of China. In March, Gierek traveled to Moscow to discuss various bilateral and world problems. The same month, Premier Piotr Jaroszewicz visited Cuba to hold talks on trade relations and aid for developing Cuban industry. In July, Gierek met again with Soviet President Leonid Brezhnev, this time to endorse the SALT II treaty and détente and to reaffirm "the brotherly friendship of the Polish and Soviet nations."

Also in July, French Foreign Minister Jean François-Poncet visited Warsaw to discuss increased economic cooperation and cultural relations, and two months later Gierek met in Paris with French President Valéry Giscard d'Estaing. Trade, détente, and the repatriation of ethnic Germans in Poland were the topics of discussion when Gierek met with West German Chancellor Helmut Schmidt in August.

ALEXANDER J. GROTH
Department of Political Science
University of California, Davis

POLAR RESEARCH

Antarctic. More than 300 U. S. scientists traveled to Antarctica to conduct 85 science projects during the 1978–79 austral field season.

Investigators melted three new holes through the 412-m (1,350-ft)-thick Ross Ice Shelf with a new hot-water drill. Cameras lowered through the holes allowed scientists to study changes in the ice fabric at increasing depths.

Scientists also took 35 sphincter sediment cores—the longest being 25 cm (9.8 inches)—and 40 gravity cores—the longest, 125 cm (49.2 inches)—from the sea bottom beneath the drill site. Some of the sediment contained dead gastropods and foraminifera. Several copepods and about 4,000 living amphipods of five different species were collected through the access hole.

Instruments designed to measure the mass balance and heat flow of seawater, rates of freezing and melting, and currents beneath the shelf were lowered and locked in place as the water in the holes froze.

A team of Soviet researchers used a thermal alcohol drill to obtain 381 m (1,250 ft) of ice core through the Ross Ice Shelf near the drill site. The core included 6 m (19.7 ft) of briny ice from the very bottom of the shelf; the lower end of the core confirmed that sea water is freezing onto the bottom of the Ross Ice Shelf.

Elsewhere in Antarctica, researchers found 309 meteorites, including a metallic fragment weighing 136 kg (300 lbs) and two carbonaceous chondrites. Chemical analyses of carbonaceous chondrites found in 1977–78 revealed 18 amino acids evenly divided between right-handed and left-handed molecules. Because almost all amino acid molecules on earth are left-handed, the meteorite amino acids probably are extraterrestrial in origin.

Scientists examining ecological adaptation to polar environments discovered algal mats living beneath the ice cover in dry valley lakes in less than one tenth the amount of light necessary for algae to photosynthesize in temperate regions. An aeromagnetic survey of the Dufek Massif indicated that this basic layered intrusion is much larger than geologists previously had supposed. Scientists visited the Darwin and Byrd glacier regions to study the local geology and the dynamic interaction of the Byrd Glacier, which drains about 6% of the East Antarctic Ice Sheet, with the Ross Ice Shelf.

Arctic. Investigators analyzing a graphite-bearing ironstone from Isua, Greenland, found evidence of primitive organic compounds that may shed light on the chemistry and time of the emergence of life on earth. The hydrocarbons identified may represent original compounds that survived the intense metamorphism that these rocks—the oldest known on earth—have undergone since their deposition some 3.8 billion years ago.

U. S. airplanes equipped with special radio echo sounding antennas completed their coverage of the Greenland Ice Sheet in May 1979. Scientists will use the sounding data to complete an ice thickness map of the Greenland Ice Sheet. A new deep drill was tested in Greenland during the summer. The drill may enable engineers to extract an ice core completely through the ice sheet and obtain a great deal of information about the earth's past climates.

Research into the optical and chemical properties of Arctic atmospheric haze confirmed that the haze often extends thousands of miles, that it has a strong seasonal variation, and that it contains a considerable amount of sulfate, generally in the form of dilute sulfuric acid. Scientists could not yet determine the source of the haze, but there was evidence that it comes from the industrialized areas of the northern hemisphere. Researchers continued to examine the effects of the haze on the radiation balance of arctic and global climates and the effects of sulfuric acid fallout on the fragile tundra. Research in the Bering Sea concentrated on the influence of oceanic fronts on the distribution of dissolved nutrients and living organisms. Large schools of Alaskan pollack make the Bering Sea the world's second largest single-species fishery. The southeastern Bering Sea apparently has a complex system of three oceanic zones separated by two interfront zones. Winds and tides, not cyclonic eddies, provide the energy that transports nutrients from one region to another.

RICHARD P. MULDOON
Polar Programs
National Science Foundation

PORTUGAL

Disenchantment with political haggling and the absence of a concerted attack on severe economic problems led Portuguese voters to give strong support to a center-right political grouping, reviving hope that the country's short-lived experiment in democracy might succeed.

Government and Politics. Francisco Sá Carneiro became prime minister following the victory in the December 2 parliamentary elections of the "Democratic Alliance," composed of Social Democrats, Center Democrats, and the tiny monarchist party. In capturing 44.6% of the ballots cast, this coalition secured the first majority in the 250-seat parliament since a coup in 1974 ended 46 years of authoritarian, corporate state rule by Antonio Salazar and Marcello Caetano. The once-dominant Socialist Party declined in strength from 34.8% to 27.4% of the popular vote, while the pro-Soviet Communists rose from 14.3% to 19%.

The 45-year-old Sá Carneiro, a lawyer from the staunchly Catholic North, promised to form a government "not based on collectivism [but] stability and authority of the state. . . ." He pledged to cut taxes, lessen price controls, and reduce regulation of banking and industry. He took over from Maria de Lurdes Pintassilgo, who had become Iberia's first woman premier on August 1.

The year's political developments were characterized by discord and uncertainty over the attempted reversal of radical leftist policies instituted after the fall of elitist, authoritarian rule in 1974. Moderates and conservatives, supportive of President Antonio Ramalho Eanes, continued to dismantle such post-1974 reforms as nationalization of key industries, worker administration of factories, and the seizure of land by inefficient cooperatives. But partisan disagreements slowed efforts to restore the national economy and left the political situation still uncertain.

Economy. Since coming to power in mid-1976, General Eanes has followed an austerity program (approved by the International Monetary Fund) to undo the excesses of the radicals by restricting credit, boosting taxes, promoting exports, and encouraging private investment. However, parliamentary squabbling, attended by frequent cabinet changes, gradually slowed efforts to put the country's economy on a sound footing. The dizzying rise in oil prices also proved a stunning blow to this import-dependent nation, although revenues from tourism and emigrant remittances rose.

Despite the return of farmland to many dispossessed owners and a notable reduction in the number of worker-run companies, economic conditions remained grim. In 1979, the gross domestic product grew by only 2%, a rate equal to that of the previous year. The account deficit hovered around $776 million, the same figure as in 1978. Meanwhile, unemployment—swollen by one million refugees from former Portuguese colonies in Africa—beset approximately one quarter of the labor force, and prices shot up by 23%. Inflation combined with government belt-tightening measures drove real wages below the level of 1974, when they were the lowest in Western Europe.

Contributing to the dismal picture was a decline in grain production caused by inclement weather in January and February, when four major rivers overflowed their banks. The pro-

SAMUEL IAVELBERG, GAMMA/LIAISON

Maria de Lurdes Pintassilgo, the head of a caretaker government, became Iberia's first woman premier.

PORTUGAL • Information Highlights

Official Name: Republic of Portugal.
Location: Southwestern Europe.
Area: 35,553 square miles (92 082 km²).
Population (1979 est.): 10,000,000.
Chief Cities (1979 est.): Lisbon, the capital, 1,100,000; Oporto, 350,000.
Government: *Head of state,* António Ramalho Eanes, president (took office July 1976). *Head of government,* Francisco Sá Carneiro, prime minister (took office Dec. 1979). *Legislature* (unicameral)—Assembly of the Republic.
Monetary Unit: Escudo (50 escudos equal U. S.$1, Dec. 1979).
Manufactures (major products): Textiles, clothing, cork products, chemicals, transport equipment.
Agriculture (major products): Wine, grapes, tomatoes, wheat, olives, fruit, rice, cereals.

duction of wine, a key commodity, was expected to rise by almost 50% over the low 1978 level.

Persistent problems required this predominantly agricultural country to seek assistance from its European neighbors. Perhaps fearing Portugal's further economic distress and the consequent emergence of another right-wing dictatorship, they largely complied. The European Investment Bank extended credits for the modernization and development of small and medium-sized industry. West Germany, The Netherlands, and the World Bank also made sizable loans.

Portugal's application to join the European Community (EC) was accepted in principle in May 1978, with the accession period to begin in 1983. Formal entry must await the outcome of negotiations on such sensitive matters as taxation, capital movements, and projected EC tariff reductions.

The integration of Portugal into the mainstream of European affairs seemed to offer the best prospect of nurturing a fragile democracy afflicted by domestic discord and the threat of world recession.

GEORGE W. GRAYSON
College of William and Mary

POSTAL SERVICE

The most welcome news concerning the U. S. Postal Service (USPS) during its fiscal year (FY) ending Sept. 30, 1979, was that revenues exceeded expenditures by $469 million. The office of Postmaster General William F. Bolger released the figures. The previous year in which the USPS (then the nonindependent U. S. Post Office) ran in the black was 1945 when the surplus reached $169.1 million.

The 1979 revenue figure did not represent a profit, for it included an annual subsidy of nearly $1 billion which also contributed to an income of nearly $18 billion in fiscal 1979. Moreover, the trend was expected to be temporary; because of the impact of inflation on its fixed-rate structure, the USPS was anticipating a deficit of at least $475 million during FY 1980 and was predicting a rates increase request by 1981.

Underlying the 1979 excellent performance were two developments—continued mechanization and a new marketing strategy.

Mechanization. Large capital expenditures were allotted during the 1960's and 1970's for new, fast sorting and handling equipment. Use of the well-known five-digit ZIP code, dating from 1963, has sped procedures, and a new nine-digit code will be introduced in 1980 to simplify bulk mailings. The standardization of letter and package sizes has continued and new size limits for all classes of mail—especially first and third—went into effect on July 15, 1979. The full mechanization effort is expected to be completed by the mid-1980's.

This program has permitted a large rise in productivity plus a decline in postal employment of more than 50,000 since 1970. The annual number of pieces of mail handled per postal worker now totals nearly 150,000, by far the world's highest.

Marketing. The USPS's marketing strategy of 1978–79 helped push mail volume to a record of nearly 99 billion pieces during FY 1979. Discounts are offered to high-volume customers who agree to save the USPS much expensive labor by presorting their bulk letter or advertising circular mail. In return such mailers have received a 13-cent letter rate instead of the usual 15 cents, and advertisers gained a savings of 1.5 cents per piece. However, efforts to apply the same policy to such bulk parcel mailers as Sears Roebuck have been held up by a court injunction obtained by the United Parcel Service, charging below-cost pricing.

Electronic Communications. Of greater significance has been a major controversy which stirred during 1979 over the entry of the USPS into the electronic sector of the communications market. In 1979, only 20% of all transmitted messages were by post.

During the winter of 1977–78 the USPS proposed to enter what was termed "Generations I and II" of the electronic communications era on an experimental basis. By Generation I is meant an input by hard copy (such as a letter), electronic transmittal, and output in the form of a hard copy delivered by the USPS. Generation II refers to an input of messages by electronic means (from computers or other devices) with a hard copy output delivered by the USPS. Generation III, some time away, contemplates both inputs and outputs as electronic.

Responding in part to private interests, which have thus far had the electronics field to themselves, President Carter appointed a special commission to advise the administration about further USPS penetration into electronics. As a result, the president announced on July 19, 1979, that he would support Generations I and II efforts by the USPS provided its electronic operations were not subsidized by tax money or by revenues from other USPS services.

However, by August the Federal Communications Commission (FCC), disputing jurisdiction over electronic proposals with the Postal Rate Commission, had stalled experimental contracts involving joint efforts with Western Union and other companies. By the middle of October, USPS had gone to court seeking to overturn the FCC's claim of complete jurisdiction over all aspects of electronic mail. Congress, too, was seriously considering modifications not only of the Postal Reform Act of 1970 and other basic communications control laws, but also of the Private Express Statutes giving USPS a monopoly of letter mail, with few proposals favoring any larger role for the USPS.

Although it was clear that USPS could operate efficiently, its future was uncertain.

Other Activities. During 1979 the USPS also undertook to simplify its regulations. Metropolitan express service was expanded, as were efforts to control mail order fraud. And a Postal Career Executive Service was created to parallel a similar managerial corps provided for the rest of the federal government in 1978.

Worldwide Postal Notes. For the second consecutive year the British postal service, which also controls the telephone and telegraph, ran in the black. Statutes and practices similar to those behind the USPS, plus lower personnel costs, appeared responsible.

The Canada Post Office, covering great distances and servicing many small volume units, has modernized and maintained schedules well, but at the cost of large deficits. During its FY ending March 31, 1979, expenditures of $1.6 billion exceeded revenues by $485 million. In April 1979 the first class letter rate was raised to 17 cents (Canadian). Partly as a result of U. S. and British experience, the new Conservative government was expected to propose in 1980 that the Canada Post Office be put more on its own as a largely self-financed public corporation.

PAUL P. VAN RIPER
Texas A&M University

PRINCE EDWARD ISLAND

Prince Edward Island Progressive Conservatives have cause to remember 1979. It was the year that Tories swept into office provincially and also carried the province in a federal vote. One of the first actions of the new provincial government was to turn thumbs-down on nuclear energy.

Politics. The only remaining Liberal provincial government in Canada was thrown out of office with the election of a new Conservative administration in P. E. I. on April 23. The Tories, under J. Angus MacLean, a 64-year-old blueberry farmer and former federal MP, took 21 of the 32 legislature seats, against 11 for the Liberals. The Liberals, under Premier Bennett Campbell, had been seeking their fifth consecutive mandate.

MacLean and a nine-member cabinet were sworn in on May 3. The legislature opened June 29, and in the speech from the throne MacLean's government pledged to back away from any involvement in nuclear power. The new government announced that "It is intended to take whatever action is necessary to assure that Prince Edward Island will not be involved in support of nuclear energy production." Instead, development of renewable, alternative energy sources would be encouraged.

For P. E. I. Conservatives the provincial triumph was repeated a month later when Tories took all of the Island's four federal seats in the federal general election. Previously, the Tories held two seats and the Liberals two. Among the defeated candidates was Liberal Veterans Affairs Minister Dan MacDonald in Cardigan riding. David MacDonald, a 42-year-old United Church minister and an MP since 1968, was named state secretary and minister of communications in the new Conservative administration in Ottawa. He represents Egmont riding.

Transportation. A meeting between federal and provincial transportation officials in Charlottetown in September cleared the way for a major study of rail transportation in P. E. I. The study was conducted by federal and provincial representatives, the Canadian National Railways, and the P. E. I. Potato Marketing Board.

The panel was to examine the movement of freight and farm produce, particularly potatoes, within the province. The ultimate objective, said Agriculture and Forestry Minister Prowse Chappell, is development of the "optimum transportation system." The federal government is paying the cost of the study—about $65,000.

Judicial. A ruling by Justice C. R. McQuaid at a hearing in Summerside on September 19 upheld the right of access to court cases by the press and public as an important part of the island's juridical system. McQuaid quashed an application by Summerside lawyer Bloyce McLellan to bar press and public from an indecent assault case heard in Supreme Court. McLellan's client, Joseph Bernard, 20, pleaded guilty to a charge involving a 17-year-old girl and subsequently received a suspended sentence. McLellan argued that publication of details of the case would offend public morals. But Justice McQuaid said the public had a common-law right to view criminal matters in open court.

JOHN BEST, *Chief, Canadian World News*

PRISONS

While public attention generally remained focused on such dramatic events as capital punishment and prison escapes, the conditions inside U. S. prisons continued to deteriorate in 1979. Overcrowding, often in antiquated and unsafe facilities, contributed to growing tensions. The year was marked by a number of violent outbursts, lawsuits by inmates alleging cruel and inadequate care, and job actions by prison guards. As the number of male, female, and juvenile prisoners rose to record levels for the fifth year in a row, prison officials talked much less about rehabilitation and corrections and more about security and control under stress. Escapes, although much rarer than assaults and murders within prisons, generated far more activity and concern on the part of prison authorities—and headline writers.

Conditions. In June 1979, the Law Enforcement Assistance Administration announced that the inmate population of federal and state facilities had reached a new high of 307,384. Including local jails and juvenile detention centers, the number of U. S. prisoners was estimated to be well over the 600,000 mark. The rate of incarceration in the United States was exceeded only by South Africa and the Soviet Union. Texas, with the largest state prison system, reported a 10% increase in the number of prisoners. Houston was the scene of a year-long class action suit brought by inmates alleging overcrowding, brutality, poor food, and inadequate medical care. Testimony from more than 300 witnesses on both sides concluded in September, but a decision was not expected for several months. State

Special rehabilitation in a Bermuda prison: Henry Edwards teaches inmates the art of gourmet cooking.

UPI

attorneys did concede that at times up to 1,000 prisoners in the Texas system had to sleep on floors because of a lack of space, but denied the brutality charges. Regardless of the final decision, both sides expected the case to wind up in the U. S. Supreme Court. The Texas Corrections System is noted for its low escape rate as well as its low per diem cost per prisoner—$7.31, compared with the national average of $27.

Violence. The federal penitentiary in Atlanta, GA, built in 1902, houses approximately 1,500 prisoners, most of whom are serving long-term sentences for serious crimes. In the 32-month period from November 1976 to July 1979 twelve prisoners were murdered, apparently by other prisoners. In almost all cases, the victims were stabbed to death. Motives for these attacks ranged from jealousy arising out of homosexual triangles, to drug disputes and rumors that the victims might be cooperating with law enforcement officials. There were no indictments.

In another federal penitentiary, Stateville Prison in Joliet, IL, it had become increasingly apparent in recent years that control and authority were shifting from prison officials to the inmates themselves. Although the problem was most severe at Stateville, it remained typical of prisons throughout the country. As lockup facilities become more overcrowded, stricter and longer sentences are reserved for the toughest and least controllable offenders. Over the past years, prison authorities from guards to wardens have found themselves increasingly faced with younger and more violent inmates. Many observers report that homosexual rape and strongarm intimidation among prisoners, although seldom officially reported, have been increasing dramatically. At Stateville, full-scale gang wars, the killing of several guards, and mounting evidence of contraband smuggling, led to a major crackdown. On February 24, some 200 riot-equipped state guards and 60 state troopers with dogs entered the prison, put all 2,013 inmates in 24-hour lockup, suspended all showers, visits,

and recreational activities, and began a systematic search and cleanup operation that lasted weeks. Before the search was half over, the guards had uncovered two guns, more than 400 knives, saw blades, bomb components, and a variety of narcotics. Officials were disappointed with the small amount of contraband recovered and surmised that large supplies of drugs and small weapons were flushed down toilets, thrown out windows, or given to sympathetic guards for disposal.

Racial tensions are not unusual in many of the nation's prisons. On June 4, in an exercise yard in Attica, NY, an inmate was stabbed to death in a brawl involving some 60 black and white prisoners. According to prison officials, the fight started as a result of an earlier stabbing. Tensions built up so quickly that for some time prison officers were unable to move the prisoners back into their cells.

Job Action. A 16-day strike by New York State corrections officers was settled early in May. National Guardsmen and state troopers were temporarily moved in to take charge of the 21,000 inmates housed in the 33 state prisons. Conflicts between the striking officers and state militia erupted at several facilities. On Staten Island, 25 striking guards with drawn guns surrounded a group of National Guardsmen, but police officers were able to separate the two groups. At the height of the strike, union leader Hollis Chase was sent to jail for ignoring a court back-to-work order. Although negotiations to settle the bitter strike seemed to focus mainly on such financial issues as cost of living increases and fringe benefits, some observers argued that the emotional pitch among the strikers could only be explained by a deeper examination of the strains and conflicts under which the officers are routinely required to work.

See also CRIME; LAW.

DONALD GOODMAN
John Jay College of Criminal Justice
City University of New York

PRIZES AND AWARDS

NOBEL PRIZES ($190,000 each)

Chemistry: Herbert C. Brown, professor of chemistry, Purdue University, and Georg Wittig, professor emeritus, Heidelberg University, for helping to develop a group of substances capable of facilitating otherwise very difficult chemical reactions. Their research work makes possible the production of hundreds of important pharmaceutical and industrial chemicals that otherwise would be prohibitively expensive.

Economics: Sir Arthur Lewis, professor of economics, Princeton University, and Theodore Schultz, professor emeritus of economics, University of Chicago; cited because they are "deeply concerned about the need and poverty in the world and are engaged in finding ways out of underdevelopment."

Literature: Odysseus Elytis, Greek poet, cited "for his poetry, which, against the background of Greek tradition, depicts with sensuous strength and intellectual clearsightedness modern man's struggle for freedom and creativeness."

Medicine or Physiology: Allan MacLeod Cormack, physicist, Tufts University, and Godfrey Newbold Hounsfield, electronics engineer, EMI, Ltd., Great Britain, for the development of a revolutionary X-ray technique, computed axial tomography (CAT) scan. The Nobel Committee said in its citation: "It is no exaggeration to state that no other method within X-ray diagnostics within such a short period of time has led to such remarkable advances in research and in a multitude of applications."

Peace Prize: Mother Teresa of Calcutta, Roman Catholic nun, cited because "this year, the world has turned its attention to the plight of children and refugees, and these are precisely the categories for whom Mother Teresa has for many years worked so selflessly."

Physics: Steven Weinberg and Sheldon L. Glashow, physicists at Harvard University, and Abdus Salam, physicist, University of London, and director of the International Center for Theoretical Physics, Trieste, Italy, cited for their complementary research on the Weinberg-Salam Theory of Weak Interactions.

ART

American Academy and Institute of Arts and Letters Awards
Academy-Institute Awards ($4,000 ea.): art—Fletcher Benton, Anne Healy, Randall Deihl, Wolf Kahn, Arthur Levine; music—Paul Chihara, Vivian Fine, Robert Starer, Morton Subotnick
Arnold W. Brunner Prize in Architecture ($1,000): Charles W. Moore
Distinguished Service to the Arts: Lloyd Goodrich
Gold Medal for Architecture: I. M. Pei
Charles Ives Scholarships in Music ($4,000 ea.): Robert Beaser, Susan Blaustein, Marilyn S. Bliss, Carl Brenner, David B. Goodman, Tobias Picker
Charles Ives Award for the preparation of new and critical editions of the works of Charles Ives ($23,000): Charles Ives Society
Goddard Lieberson Fellowships ($10,000 ea.): Gerald Levinson, Bruce MacCombie
Richard and Hinda Rosenthal Foundation Award ($3,000): Nicholas Isaak (in art)

American Institute of Architects Awards
Gold Medal Award: I. M. Pei
25-Year Award: Louis I. Kahn

Avery Fisher Prize ($5,000): Emanuel Ax

Capezio Award: Alvin Ailey, American Dance Theater

Dancemagazine Awards: Erick Hawkins, Aaron Copland, Jorge Donn

John F. Kennedy Center for the Performing Arts Awards for lifetime achievement in the performing arts: Aaron Copland, Ella Fitzgerald, Henry Fonda, Martha Graham, and Tennessee Williams

Leopold Stokowski Award: Calvin Simmons

National Academy of Recording Arts and Sciences Grammy Awards for excellence in phonograph records
Album of the year: *Saturday Night Fever,* The Bee Gees, and others
Classical album of the year: *Brahms: Concerto for Violin in D Major,* Itzhak Perlman, with Carlo Maria Giulini

UPI

The Bee Gees copped a Grammy for *Saturday Night Fever,* the largest selling soundtrack in album history.

Country music song: *The Gambler,* Don Schlitz, writer
Jazz vocal performance: *All Fly Home,* Al Jarreau
New artist: A Taste of Honey
Record of the year: *Just the Way You Are,* Billy Joel
Song of the year: *Just the Way You Are,* Billy Joel

Pritzker Architecture Prize ($100,000): Philip Johnson

Pulitzer Prize for Music: Joseph Schwantner, *Aftertones of Infinity*

Richard Tucker Foundation Award ($5,000): Diana Soviera, lyric soprano with the New York City Opera (the award also subsidizes productions in which she sings)

JOURNALISM

George Polk Memorial Awards
Commentary: Russell Baker, *The New York Times*
Education reporting: *Chronicle of Higher Education*
Film documentary: Golden West Television Productions, *Scared Straight*
Foreign reporting: John F. Burns, John Darnton, Michael T. Kaufman, *The New York Times*
Local reporting: *The Dallas Times-Herald*
News photography award: Eddie Adams, The Associated Press
National reporting: Ronald Kessler, *The Washington Post*
Public service reporting: Jane Shoemaker, Thomas Ferrick, Jr., William Ecenbarger, *The Philadelphia Inquirer*
Regional reporting: *Southern Exposure*
Television reporting: Don Harris and Bob Brown (posthumously), NBC News, for coverage of the Jonestown, Guyana tragedy
Special award for lifetime achievement in gathering news: Richard S. Salant, CBS News

Maria Moors Cabot Prizes ($1,000 ea.): Juan Zuleta Ferrer, Jeremiah O'Leary, Jr.

National Magazine Awards
Essays and criticism: *Life*
Fiction: *The Atlantic Monthly*
Public service: *New West* magazine
Reporting excellence: *The Texas Monthly*
Service to the individual: *The American Journal of Nursing*
Single topic issue: *Progressive Architecture*
Specialized journalism: *The National Journal*
Visual excellence: *Audubon*

Overseas Press Club Awards
Book on foreign affairs: Tad Szulc, *The Illusion of Peace: Foreign Policy in the Nixon Years*
Business news reporting from abroad: Andrew Nagorski, *Newsweek International*

Cartoon on foreign affairs: Jim Morin, *Miami Herald*
Daily newspaper or wire service reporting from abroad: Charles Krause, *The Washington Post*
Magazine interpretation of foreign affairs: Donald R. Katz, *Rolling Stone*
Magazine reporting from abroad: Peter A. Iseman, *Harper's Magazine*
Photographic reporting from abroad: Frank B. Johnston, *Newsweek*
Radio interpretation of foreign news: Josh Darsa, National Public Radio, "Dialogues on a Tightrope: An Italian Mosaic"
Radio spot news from abroad: Tom Fenton, Lew Wheaton, Hal Moore, Associated Press Radio Network, "Four Weeks in September"
Television interpretation of foreign affairs: ABC News Close-Up, "Terror in the Promised Land"
Television spot reporting from abroad: Don Harris, Bob Brown, NBC (posthumously)
Bob Considine Memorial Award: Flora Lewis, *The New York Times*
Robert Capa Gold Medal: Susan Meiselas, *Time*
Madeline Dane Ross Award: Alvaro Joe Brenes de Peralta and Jeannine Yeomans, KRON-TV

Pulitzer Prizes
Commentary: Russell Baker, *The New York Times*
Criticism: Paul Gapp, *The Chicago Tribune*
Editorial cartooning: Herbert L. Block, *The Washington Post*
Editorial writing: Edwin M. Yoder, Jr., *The Washington Star*
Feature photography: *The Boston Herald American*'s entire photography staff (for pictures of the February 1978 New England snowstorm)
Feature writing: Jon D. Franklin, *The Baltimore Evening Sun*
General local reporting: *The San Diego* (CA) *Evening Tribune*'s entire staff (for reportage on the midair airplane collision over San Diego, Sept. 25, 1978)
International reporting: Richard Ben Cramer, *The Philadelphia Inquirer*

For her work in *Coming Home*, Jane Fonda captured her second Oscar for best actress in a leading role.

UPI

National reporting: James Risser, *The Des Moines Register*
Public service: David and Catherine Mitchell, *The Point Reyes* (CA) *Light*
Special local reporting: Gilbert M. Gaul and Elliot G. Jaspin, *The Pottsville* (PA) *Republican*
Spot news photography: Thomas J. Kelley III, *The Pottstown* (PA) *Mercury*

LITERATURE

Academy of American Poets Fellowship Award ($10,-000): May Swenson
Academy of American Poets Walt Whitman Award ($1,000 and publication of the book by William Morrow and Company): David Bottoms for *Shooting Rats at the Bibb County Dump*
American Academy and Institute of Arts and Letters Awards
American Academy in Rome Fellowship in Creative Writing: Joseph Caldwell
Academy-Institute Awards ($4,000 ea.): Arlene Croce, Barry Hannah, James McConkey, John N. Morris, Robert M. Pirsig, Richard Poirier, Philip Schultz, Dave Smith
E. M. Forster Award ($5,000): Bruce Chatwin
Gold Medal for Poetry: Archibald MacLeish
Award of Merit Medal ($1,000): William H. Gass
Richard and Hinda Rosenthal Foundation Award ($3,000): Diane Johnson (in writing)
Harold D. Vursell Memorial Award ($5,000): Wallace Fowlie
Marjorie Peabody Waite Award ($1,500): James Still
Morton Dauwen Zabel Award ($2,500): Richard Gilman
Bancroft Prizes for best books in American history or diplomacy ($4,000 ea.): Christopher Thorne, *Allies of a Kind: The United States, Britain and the War Against Japan, 1941–45;* Anthony F.C. Wallace, *Rockdale: The Growth of an American Village in the Early Industrial Revolution*
Bollingen Prize in Poetry ($5,000): W. S. Merwin
Canada's Governor General's Literary Awards
English fiction: Alice Munro, *Who Do You Think You Are?*
French fiction: Jacques Poulin, *Les grandes marées*
English nonfiction: Roger Caron, *Go Boy*
French nonfiction: François-Marc Gagnon, *Paul-Emile Borduas*
English poetry and drama: Patrick Lane, *Poems New and Selected*
French poetry and drama: Gilbert Langevin, *Mon refuge est un volcan*
International Book Committee Award: Léopold S. Senghor, president of Senegal
National Arts Club's Medal of Honor for Literature: Allen Ginsberg
National Book Awards ($1,000)
Biography: Arthur M. Schlesinger, Jr., *Robert Kennedy and His Times*
Children's literature: Katherine Paterson, *The Great Gilly Hopkins*
Contemporary thought: Peter Matthiessen, *The Snow Leopard*
Fiction: Tim O'Brien, *Going After Cacciato*
History: Richard Beale Davis, *Intellectual Life in the Colonial South, 1585–1763*
Poetry: James Merrill, *Mirabell: Books of Numbers*
Translation: Clayton Eshleman and José Rubia Barcia, César Vallejo's *The Complete Posthumous Poetry*
National Book Critics Circle
Fiction: John Cheever, *The Stories of John Cheever*
Poetry: *Hello, Darkness: The Collected Poems of L. E. Sissman*, edited by Peter Davison
Criticism: Meyer Schapiro, *Modern Art: 19th and 20th Centuries, Selected Papers*
General nonfiction: Maureen Howard, *Facts of Life;* Garry Wills, *Inventing America: Jefferson's Declaration of Independence*
Pulitzer Prizes
Biography: Leonard Baker, *Days of Sorrow and Pain: Leo Baeck and the Berlin Jews*
Fiction: John Cheever, *The Stories of John Cheever*
General nonfiction: Edward O. Wilson, *On Human Nature*
History: Don E. Fehrenbacher, *The Dred Scott Case*
Poetry: Robert Penn Warren, *Now and Then*
Ralph Waldo Emerson Prize ($2,500): Bruce Kuklick, *The Rise of American Philosophy*

Television talk-show host Phil Donahue, here with actress Marlo Thomas, holds an Emmy he received as outstanding host on a daytime television talk show. His show, *Donahue,* also received an Emmy as outstanding talk show.

UPI

MOTION PICTURES

Academy of Motion Picture Arts and Sciences ("Oscar") Awards
Actor: Jon Voight, *Coming Home*
Actress: Jane Fonda, *Coming Home*
Cinematography: Nestor Almendros, *Days of Heaven*
Costume design: Anthony Powell, *Death on the Nile*
Director: Michael Cimino, *The Deer Hunter*
Documentary feature: *Scared Straight*
Film: *The Deer Hunter*
Foreign language film: *Get Out Your Handkerchiefs*
Original score: Giorgio Moroder, *Midnight Express*
Original screenplay: Nancy Dowd, Robert C. Jones, Waldo Salt, *Coming Home*
Original song score and adaptation: Joe Renzetti, *The Buddy Holly Story*
Screenplay based on material from another medium: Oliver Stone, *Midnight Express*
Song: Paul Jabara, *Last Dance,* from *Thank God It's Friday*
Supporting actor: Christopher Walken, *The Deer Hunter*
Supporting actress: Maggie Smith, *California Suite*
Jean Hersholt Humanitarian Award: Leo Jaffe
Honorary Awards: Laurence Olivier, King Vidor, Walter Lantz, and the Museum of Modern Art
Special Achievement Award: *Superman,* for visual effects
American Film Institute's Lifetime Achievement Award: Alfred Hitchcock
Cannes Film Festival Awards
Best actor: Jack Lemmon, *The China Syndrome*
Best actress: Sally Field, *Norma Rae*
Best director: Terrence Malick, *Days of Heaven*
Best film (shared): *Apocalypse Now* (United States); *The Tin Drum* (West Germany)
New York Film Critics Circle Awards
Actor: Dustin Hoffman, *Kramer vs. Kramer*
Actress: Sally Field, *Norma Rae*
Director: Woody Allen, *Manhattan*
Picture: *Kramer vs. Kramer*
Supporting actor: Melvyn Douglas, *Being There*
Supporting actress: Meryl Streep, *Kramer vs. Kramer* and *The Seduction of Joe Tynan*

PUBLIC SERVICE

The University of Chicago Albert Pick, Jr., Award for "outstanding contributions to international understanding" ($25,000): Robert S. McNamara
International Institute for Human Rights Gold Medal: President Jimmy Carter
Rockefeller Public Service Awards ($10,000 each):
Conservation: George R. Palmiter, Norfolk and Western Railway
Health (shared): Dr. Abraham B. Bergman, Seattle Children's Orthopedic Hospital; Dr. Emery A. Johnson, Indian Health Service, U. S. Public Health Service

Justice: Richard E. Gerstein, Miami attorney and former Dade County state attorney
Public service: Raul Yzaguirre, National Council of La Raza
Revitalizing communities (shared): Gale Cincotta, president and founder, National People's Actions; Macler C. Shepard, president, Jeff-Vander-Lou, Inc.
U. S. Presidential Medal of Freedom (presented by U. S. ambassador to the UN, Andrew Young, on behalf of President Jimmy Carter, Jan. 20, 1979): Dr. Margaret Mead (posthumously)

SCIENCE

Albert Lasker Awards ($15,000)
Basic medical research (shared): Dr. Walter Gilbert, Harvard University; Dr. Frederick Sanger, Britain's Medical Research Council
Clinical medical research: Dr. Roger W. Sperry, California Institute of Technology
Special award for contributions to a worldwide campaign against blindness: Sir John Wilson, International Agency for the Prevention of Blindness
Bristol-Myers Award ($25,000): Dr. Werner Henle and his wife, Gertrude Henle
Columbia University's Louisa Gross Horwitz Prize for research in biology and biochemistry ($22,000): Walter Gilbert, Harvard University; Frederick Sanger, England's Medical Research Council Laboratory of Molecular Biology
General Motors Cancer Research Foundation Awards ($100,000)
Charles F. Kettering Prize: Dr. Henry S. Kaplan, Stanford University
Charles S. Mott Award: Sir Richard Doll, Oxford University
Alfred P. Sloan, Jr., Prize: Dr. George Klein, Karolinska Institute Medical School in Stockholm
Inventor of the Year for 1978: Barbara S. Askins, chemist, Marshall Space Flight Center
Lita Annenberg Hazen Award for clinical research ($100,000): Dr. Jesse Roth
U. S. National Medals of Science: Robert H. Burris, University of Wisconsin; Elizabeth Brosby, University of Michigan, Ann Arbor; Joseph L. Doob, University of Illinois, Urbana; Richard P. Feynman, California Institute of Technology; Donald E. Knuth, Stanford University; Arthur Kornberg, Stanford University; Emmett Leith, University of Michigan; Herman F. Mark, Polytechnic Institute of New York; Raymond D. Mindlin, Columbia University; Robert N. Noyce, Intel Corporation; Severo Ochoa, Roche Institute of Molecular Biology; Earl R. Parker, University of California, Berkeley; Edward M. Purcell, Harvard University; Simon Ramo, TRW Inc.; John H. Sinfelt, Exxon Corporate Research Laboratories; Lyman Spitzer, Jr., Princeton University; Earl R. Stadtman, National Institutes of Health; George L. Stebbins, University of California, Davis; Paul A. Weiss, Rocke-

Winners of the 1979 Tony awards (*left to right*)—Angela Lansbury, Len Cariou, Tom Conti, and Carole Shelley—get together following the presentations. Miss Lansbury and Mr. Cariou were named best actress and actor in a musical; Mr. Conti and Miss Shelley were given awards as best actor and actress in a play.

UPI

feller University; Victor F. Weisskopf, Massachusetts Institute of Technology

TELEVISION AND RADIO

Academy of Television Arts and Sciences ("Emmy") Awards

Actor—comedy series: Carroll O'Connor, *All in the Family* (CBS)

Actor—drama series: Ron Leibman, *Kaz* (CBS)

Actor—limited series or special: Peter Strauss, *The Jericho Mile* (ABC)

Actress—comedy series: Ruth Gordon, "Sugar Mama," *Taxi* (ABC)

Actress—drama series: Mariette Hartley, "Married," *The Incredible Hulk* (CBS)

Actress—limited series or special: Bette Davis, *Strangers: The Story of a Mother and Daughter* (CBS)

Children's special: *Christmas Eve on Sesame Street* (PBS)

Classical program in the performing arts: "Balanchine IV—Dance in America," *Great Performances* (PBS)

Comedy series: *Taxi* (ABC)

Drama series: *Lou Grant* (CBS)

Individual achievement—special events: Mikhail Baryshnikov, *Baryshnikov at the White House* (PBS)

Informational program: *Scared Straight* (SYN)

Limited series: *Roots: The Next Generations* (ABC)

Program achievement: *The Tonight Show Starring Johnny Carson* (NBC); *Lifeline* (NBC)

Special—drama or comedy: *Friendly Fire* (ABC)

Supporting actor—comedy series: Robert Guillaume, *Soap* (ABC)

Supporting actor—drama series: Stuart Margolin, *The Rockford Files* (NBC)

Supporting actress—comedy series: Sally Struthers, "California, Here We Are," *All in the Family* (CBS)

Supporting actress—drama series: Kristy McNichol, *Family* (ABC)

Second Annual Governors' Award: Walter Cronkite

Friars Club of New York Entertainer of the Year Award: Johnny Carson

George Foster Peabody Awards

Radio: CBS News, *World News Roundup;* National Radio Theater, Chicago, for imaginative radio drama; WMUK, Kalamazoo, MI, for live radio dramas presented as part of the city's Super Summer Arts Festival; WABE-FM, Atlanta, *The Eyewitness Who Wasn't;* National Public Radio, Washington, *Dialogues on a Tightrope: An Italian Mosaic;* NBC radio, *Second Sunday;* WOCB, West Yarmouth, MA, *The Last Voyage of the Cap'n Bill;* Jewish Theological Seminary of America, *The Eternal Light*

Television: ABC and Four D Productions-Trisene Corp., *Barney Miller;* CBS and MTM Productions, *Lou Grant;* Jim Henson, *The Muppets;* Baptist Radio and TV Commission, Fort Worth, *A River to the Sea;* WDVM-TV, Washington, *Your Health and Your Wallet;* WENH-TV, Durham, NH, *Arts in New Hampshire;* CBS News, anchored by Bill Moyers, *The Battle for South Africa;* CBS, Tomorrow Entertainment-Medcome Co., *The Body Human: The Vital Connection;* NBC, Survival Anglia Ltd.-World Wildlife Fund, *Mysterious Castles of Clay;* KGO-TV, San Francisco, *Old Age: Do Not Go Gentle;* WEVM-TV, Washington, *Race War in Rhodesia;* KQED, San Francisco, *Over Easy;* Newsweek Broadcasting, *Cartoon-A-Torial;* KHET, Honolulu, *Damien;* CBS, *30 Minutes;* WAVE-TV, Louisville, KY, *Whose Child Is This?;* WQED, Pittsburgh, *Once Upon a Classic,* "A Connecticut Yankee in King Arthur's Court"; NBC, Titus Productions Inc., *Holocaust*

Individual Awards: Bob Keeshan (Captain Kangaroo); Richard S. Salant, CBS News

THEATER

Antoinette Perry ("Tony") Awards

Actor (drama): Tom Conti, *Whose Life Is It Anyway?*

Actor (musical): Len Cariou, *Sweeney Todd*

Actress (drama): Constance Cumming, *Wings;* Carole Shelley, *The Elephant Man* (tie)

Actress (musical): Angela Lansbury, *Sweeney Todd*

Choreography: Michael Bennett, Bob Avian, *Ballroom*

Costume design: Franne Lee, *Sweeney Todd*

Director (drama): Jack Hofsiss, *The Elephant Man*

Director (musical): Harold Prince, *Sweeney Todd*

Featured actor (drama): Michael Gough, *Bedroom Farce*

Featured actor (musical): Henderson Forsythe, *The Best Little Whorehouse in Texas*

Featured actress (drama): Joan Hickson, *Bedroom Farce*

Featured actress (musical): Carlin Glynn, *The Best Little Whorehouse in Texas*

Musical: *Sweeney Todd*

Play: *The Elephant Man*

Score: Stephen Sondheim, *Sweeney Todd*

Special awards: Henry Fonda; Walter F. Diehl; Eugene O'Neill Theater Center, Waterford, CT; American Conservatory Theater, San Francisco

Lawrence Langer Award for distinguished lifetime achievement in the theater: Richard Rodgers

Drama League Award, the Delia Austrian Medal: Frances Sternhagen, *On Golden Pond*

New York Drama Critics' Circle Theater Awards

American play: *The Elephant Man*

Musical: *Sweeney Todd*

Foreign play: no award

Pulitzer Prize for Drama: Sam Shepard, *Buried Child*

PUBLISHING

Economic issues were of prime concern to publishers of books, magazines, and newspapers. Postage rates continued upward; newsprint reached $375 a ton, while paper generally was in short supply. Other costs were expected to increase media expenses some 10% in 1980.

The unsettled economic situation threatened newsstand and bookstore sales and advertising growth. Nevertheless, records were made in 1979 and more were expected in 1980 as inflation was the prevailing economic trend.

Court Suit. In March 1979, a federal judge in Milwaukee, WI, issued an injunction preventing the *Progressive* magazine from publishing an article describing the workings of the hydrogen bomb. It was the first time in U. S. history that a publication was prohibited from running an article for reasons of national security. Opponents of the decision contended that the injunction was "prior restraint" and a violation of the First Amendment. The *Progressive* appealed the decision and the case seemed headed for the Supreme Court. In late September, however, a small newspaper in the state capital, the *Madison Press Connection*, printed an 18-page letter from a computer programmer in California explaining how the hydrogen bomb works. Included was a cross-section diagram of the bomb. The authors and editors of both publications insisted that all their information had been culled from sources available to the public. With the information now published in the *Connection*, the U. S. Justice Department withdrew its suit against the *Progressive*.

BOOKS

Overall View. In the intensely competitive book publishing industry a spirit of cautious optimism prevailed. For 1979, the Department of Commerce estimated publishers' receipts at $5.2 billion, up 9% over 1978. Gains were expected to be lower in 1980. Publishers wondered if inflation and gasoline shortages would affect book sales. Despite fewer shoppers, sales of paperbacks were expected to top 400 million copies in 1979. Concern about the economy led to the popularity of such books as Jane Bryant Quinn's *Everyone's Money Book* and Sylvia Porter's *New Money Guide for the 80's.*

Publishers Weekly, the authority for the book industry, noted a slight decline in number of titles, with 41,216 in 1978 compared with 42,780 in 1977. The decline came in first printings. Average prices inched upward, with mass hardcover books at $19.30, paperbacks at $1.90.

Pocket Books, which pioneered the paperback business, celebrated its 40th birthday. Starting with James Hilton's *Lost Horizon* in 1939, the firm now has 2,200 titles in print. Bantam Books set an all-time-high advance of $3.2 million for Judith Krantz's *Princess Daisy,* set for 1981 paperback.

Piracy of American books continued in some foreign countries. However, U. S. publishers visited China to discuss copyright and other book-related subjects. *Publishers Weekly* reported book exports for 1978 were up 18% to more than $380 million. About 150 American publishers attended the Moscow Book Fair, where some American books were removed from the displays by the Soviet government.

The "swelling tide" of information sources concerned publishers. Bowker's *International Periodicals Directory* listed 92,000 periodicals.

Computers gained wider acceptance in preparing copy, distribution, and record keeping. More in-house type composition was performed, according to *Publishers Weekly.* More printing companies shifted from sheet to web operations.

The *New King James Bible,* representing the work of 119 scholars, arrived in updated language for today's readers.

Best-Sellers. Early in the year, *Publishers Weekly*'s best-seller lists included Herman Wouk's *War and Remembrance,* James Michener's *Chesapeake,* John Updike's *The Coup,* and

UPI

In March a federal court judge issued a temporary injunction preventing the magazine *Progressive* from publishing an article on the hydrogen bomb. Free-lancer Howard Morland (*left*) wrote the article; Edwin Knoll (*right*) is editor of the magazine.

Jann Wenner, publisher of *Rolling Stone*, and *Look* owner Daniel Filipacchi (left) discuss the acquisition of *Look* by *Rolling Stone*. *Look*'s revival was a short one.

Mario Puzo's *Fools Die*. Arthur Hailey's *Overload* next appeared and for three months Robert Ludlum's *The Matarese Circle* was first. Kurt Vonnegut's *Jailbird* led in the fall.

Biographies and books about diet and energy use led the nonfiction lists. Christina Crawford's *Mommie Dearest* created a stir. Lauren Bacall's *By Myself* was Knopf's biggest seller, with 126,000 copies sold in four weeks. Theodore H. White's *In Search of History: A Personal Adventure* and William Manchester's *American Caesar: Douglas MacArthur, 1880–1964* added heavier subject matter to the list. *The Complete Scarsdale Medical Diet* was also a winner.

Among paperbacks the leaders were Jay Anson's *The Amityville Horror: A True Story*, Colleen McCullough's *The Thorn Birds*, James A. Michener's *Centennial* and *Chesapeake*, John Irving's *The World According to Garp*, Erma Bombeck's *If Life Is a Bowl of Cherries—What Am I Doing in the Pits?*, Nancy Friday's *My Mother/My Self: The Daughter's Search for Identity*, Belva Plain's *Evergreen*, Sidney Sheldon's *Bloodline*, and others.

Alex Comfort's *The Joy of Sex*, Mary Ellen Pinkham's *Best of Helpful Hints*, White's *In Search of History*, Richard Bolles' *What Color is Your Parachute?*, and Jim Evenroad's *How to Flatten Your Stomach* led the trade list.

MAGAZINES

Although new magazines arrived and others recorded circulation and advertising gains, the industry viewed the future with concern.

Folio magazine reported a "cover-price sensitive" market. Barbara Love wrote that "the magazine business will be tough, unyielding, and unforgiving for those who make mistakes, and richly rewarding for those who have mastered their craft." The industry continued to spend some $100 million annually to survey readers.

The Leaders. At mid-1979, *TV Guide* continued its circulation and advertising leadership, with weekly sales of 19.5 million and six-month ad revenues of $108 million. *Time,* which nosed out *TV Guide* for top ad income in 1978, was close with $106 million for mid-1979. *Reader's Digest,* still selling more than 18 million copies monthly, accepted liquor ads. For the first time, *Changing Times, The Kiplinger Magazine* and a group of four publications oriented for the senior citizens market announced that they would carry advertisements.

National Geographic joined the exclusive more-than-10-million-circulation club. Others in the top ten were *Better Homes & Gardens,* 8 million; *Family Circle,* 7.6; *Woman's Day,* 6.5; *McCall's,* 6.5; *Ladies' Home Journal,* 5.6; *Playboy,* 5.5; and *Good Housekeeping,* 5.1. *Playboy*'s December 1979 issue had nearly 500 pages. *Family Circle* and *Woman's Day* reported sizable declines in newsstand sales.

Panorama was scheduled to be introduced in early 1980. Merrill Panitt, Triangle Publications' editorial director, said "*Panorama* will concern itself more with the impact of television, with unusual people and programs, and with the new program sources."

Business Week continued its domination as ad page leader, followed by *TV Guide, New Yorker, People, Newsweek, Time, Sports Illustrated, Forbes, Yachting,* and *Cosmopolitan.*

Following *TV Guide* and *Time* in ad revenue for mid-1979 were *Newsweek, Business Week, Sports Illustrated, Reader's Digest, Better Homes & Gardens, Family Circle, Woman's Day,* and *People,* all with $40 million or more for the half-year.

Milestones. The Jehovah's Witnesses' *Watchtower* observed its 100th birthday, *Sunset* became 50, *TV Guide* 25, and *People* 5. Media Records celebrated 50 years of measuring ad contents. *Scientific American, Time,* and *Reader's Digest* were among early publications working closer with the Chinese.

Meanwhile, older citizens, women, and the sports-minded gained more specialized publications directed toward their interests. City and regional publications increased. An association was formed to promote these publications.

Magazines continued to die, with *New Times, Vital,* and *Human Nature* among the departed. *Life* continued upward, with 1.2 million circulation, but *Look* made a brief return, encountered personnel and marketing problems, and disappeared quickly.

Kent Rhodes, formerly with *Reader's Digest,* became president of the Magazine Publications Association.

NEWSPAPERS

Publishers and the courts continued at odds over interpretations of the First Amendment. Some $322 million were earmarked for plant expansion by U. S. publishers and nearly $50 million by Canadian publishers in 1979.

Acquisitions. Newspaper groups expanded. The year's major transaction involved the acquisition of the Hartford (CT) *Courant* by Los Angeles Times–Mirror Inc. for $105 million. In Nashville, TN, Gannett Co., Inc. acquired the *Tennessean* and sold its *Banner* to a local group.

Thirteen groups had total daily circulations in excess of one million, led by Knight-Ridder with 3.7 million daily and 4.3 million Sundays in 25 markets. Gannett, with 80 newspapers, had 3.3 million daily/Sunday in 68 markets.

The Newspaper Guild and the International Typographical Union came nearer to a merger, although "serious and complicated" differences remained to be ironed out. The Guild urged the government to limit the size and influence of groups.

Prices continued upward. The trend was for more dailies to cost 20–25 cents and for Sunday editions to be priced at least 35 cents.

Technology. The Atlanta *Journal* and *Constitution* used recycled newsprint plus pine wood chips; other mills experimented with Kenaf as a substitute pulp for newsprint. Papers used nearly 11 million tons of newsprint in 1979.

Nearly 1,300 dailies have converted to offset; many have expanded their computer operations. Dr. Wayne Danielson of the University of Texas predicted that computer systems would be "designed to check spelling, style, grammar, and readability and to point out missing facts or give leaders to related stories." Others viewed growing opportunities in the "technologies of lasers, fiber optics, satellite communications," according to *Editor & Publisher.* The Associated Press planned earth stations in 37 cities for delivery of radio network and some services for newspapers.

Robert Marbut, of Harte-Hankes Communications, visualized a satellite network for the 1980's, with "devices such as magnetic bubble memories, which can store 1,000 newspaper pages of text in one square inch; electronic photography to eliminate need for film; and eventually, plateless printing with electronically controlled printing at full press speeds."

Circulation and Milestones. *Editor & Publisher 1979 Year Book* reported 1,756 dailies with a morning circulation of 27,656,739, and evening circulation of 34,333,258 for a total of 61,989,997, up slightly over the previous year. Sunday papers increased to 696, with a circulation of 53,990,033. For smalltown and suburban weeklies, the National Newspaper Association reported circulation totals of 40,243,795, nearly double the 1960 figure. This represented 7,673 weeklies, an increase of 206 during the year.

"Gasoline Alley" celebrated its 60th year on the comic page. The Overseas Press Club observed its 40th birthday.

Researchers Yankelovich, Skelly and White said readers wanted more local news but warned papers not to imitate "what everyone else seems to be doing" and called for each to look "at its own market and judge accordingly."

Chicago *Daily Defender* publisher John H. Sengstacke urged his colleagues to continue to fight discrimination. According to Sengstacke, "the black press believes that America can best lead the world away from racial and national antagonisms when it accords to every person, regardless of race, color, or creed, full human and legal rights."

Canada. The 110-year-old *Montreal Star,* one of Canada's major afternoon newspapers, suddenly ceased publication in September. Although the afternoon daily has long been a dominant force in Canadian journalism, the end of the *Star* was a clear indication that Canada, like the United States before it, was moving away from the afternoon/evening newspaper.

Late in the year, Canada's two weekend magazines, *Weekend* and *The Canadian,* merged into a single publication, *Canadian Weekend.* The new publication is distributed to the largest single subscribing paper in each Canadian city. Its circulation is 2.9 million.

WILLIAM H. TAFT, *University of Missouri*

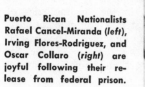
Puerto Rican Nationalists Rafael Cancel-Miranda (*left*), Irving Flores-Rodriguez, and Oscar Collaro (*right*) are joyful following their release from federal prison.

UPI

PUERTO RICO

A struggling economy, political violence, and three major storms made 1979 a difficult year in Puerto Rico.

Economy. The island's economy could best be described as sluggish. The improvements recorded in 1978 continued, albeit at a slower pace, during the first months of 1979. Economic performance reached a high in April but then declined steadily as a result of the economic slowdown on the mainland United States. Both the manufacturing and construction sectors performed poorly. In manufacturing, some 5,000 jobs were lost in the first six months of the year. Although a slight improvement (1,000 more jobs) was noted in the construction industry, a six-week strike by truck drivers virtually halted all construction in the last months of the year. The official unemployment rate rose to 17% of the labor force at midyear and approached 18% during the last six months. With a registered work force of 1 million, this translated into about 170,000 eligible persons out of work; the unofficial estimate, however, was more than twice that amount. Of the unemployed, 70% were under 35 years old and 28% were women. In contrast to the sluggish economy the rate of inflation moved into high gear, reaching double digits for the year. All goods and services increased in cost; transportation, reflecting the $1.10 average price of a gallon of gasoline, showed the most marked increase, closely followed by food and housing.

A number of factors contributed to the negative economic picture. In October several federal employment programs, including the Comprehensive Employment and Training Administration, substantially reduced their payrolls; the reductions followed an economic study ordered by the White House which indicated that such short-term programs had little effect in reducing unemployment. In agriculture, the insular government continued to cut back sugar production. Its own Sugar Corporation, which has taken over the industry, has registered steady and substantial losses in recent years ($61.9 million in 1977, $57.7 million in 1978); in 1979 it had a total indebtedness of about $400 million. Although above-average rainfall had increased the output of some agricultural products in previous years, the yield from sugarcane steadily decreased. At 1979 prices, the Sugar Corporation suffered a loss of $20 on every hundredweight produced.

Independence Movement. In September, U. S. President Jimmy Carter freed from federal prison four Puerto Rican Nationalists. One had been imprisoned since 1950 for an attempt on the life of President Harry Truman. The other three, including Lolita Lobron, a folk heroine of the Puerto Rican independence movement, were jailed for an attack on the floor of the U. S. House of Representatives in 1954. About 5,000 sympathizers received the freed prisoners upon their arrival in San Juan, September 12.

The Fuerzas Armadas de Liberacion Nacional (FALN), a terrorist independence group, claimed responsibility for the bombing of office and government buildings in Chicago and Puerto Rico, October 18. On December 3, three radical nationalist groups attacked a U. S. Navy bus outside San Juan, killing two sailors and injuring ten others; the attack was said to be in retaliation for the deaths of two advocates of Puerto Rican independence.

Storms. Three major tropical storms brushed by Puerto Rico within a period of six weeks—Claudette on July 18, David on August 30, and

--- **PUERTO RICO · Information Highlights** ---

Area: 3,421 square miles (8 860 km²).
Population (1979 est.): 3,500,000.
Chief Cities (1978 est.): San Juan, the capital, 544,596; Bayamon, 231,456; Ponce, 206,282.
Government (1979): *Chief Officers*—governor, Carlos Romero Barceló (New Progressive Party); secretary of state, Pedro R. Vázquez. *Legislature*—Senate, 27 members; House of Representatives, 51 members.
Manufactures (major products): Rum, distilled spirits, beer, cement, electricity.
Agriculture (major products): Sugarcane, coffee, tobacco, pineapple, molasses.

Frederic on September 4. All three brought heavy rains and extensive flood damage. As a result of flood damage caused by David and Frederic, estimated at close to $20 million, President Carter declared the island a disaster area.

Sports. San Juan was the site of the VIII Pan American Games, July 1–15 (*see* page 461).

THOMAS MATHEWS
University of Puerto Rico

QUEBEC

Political activity in Quebec focused increasingly on preparations for the 1980 referendum to determine the political status of the province. The election to the National Assembly in April of Claude Ryan, leader of the Quebec Liberal party, gave new direction to the "federalist forces" opposing Premier René Lévesque's Parti Québécois. Under Ryan's direction, the Liberals won all six by-elections called during the year to fill vacancies in the Assembly, although the Parti Québécois retained a clear majority (68 of the 110 seats). In November, the Parti Québécois administration published a detailed explanation of its sovereignty-association proposal. That document, titled "A New Deal" in its English-language version, proposes that Quebec negotiate a system of political and economic association with the rest of Canada, thus realizing sovereignty. A council of ministers would be appointed by the province and federal government to implement a treaty of association. The essential principle would be equal partnership, but the Canadian dollar would remain the common currency and Quebec would be represented on a joint economic council proportional to the relative weight of its economy. Premier Lévesque estimated that negotiations for such an arrangement would take two years if Quebec citizens voted in the referendum to give the government a mandate to negotiate. There were, however, strongly negative reactions to the New Deal proposal from elsewhere in Canada, notably from the province of Ontario.

In other political developments, Fabien Roy quit the Quebec National Assembly to run for and be elected as the leader of the Social Credit party in the Canadian Parliament. The Quebec government passed legislation strictly controlling the use of agricultural land for nonagricultural purposes and prohibiting the sale of agricultural land to nonresidents of Quebec.

Economy. Relations between the Quebec government and the Conseil du patronat, representing most of the province's employers, were marked by accusations of bad faith from both sides. Although the administration conceded that there were some problems in Montreal, it maintained that the overall economy of the province was growing more rapidly than ever. Legislation allowing Quebeckers to deduct from their taxable incomes money invested in new shares of companies operating extensively in Quebec was judged a success in terms of building up risk capital for the economy. Legislation reforming municipal financing took direct taxing powers away from local school commissions but promised to reduce the level of taxation for homeowners. The Quebec government permanently eliminated the 8% consumer sales tax on footwear and clothing in an attempt to help Quebec manufacturers, who were flagging under import pressure. Two banks whose principal interests are in Quebec—the Banque Canadienne Nationale (Canada's 6th largest, assets $9 billion) and the Provincial Bank (7th largest, assets $6 billion)—merged to form the National Bank. At year's end, the Quebec government had not taken definite action under legislation it had passed to expropriate the Quebec assets of Asbestos Corp., whose owner, General Dynamics Corp. of St. Louis, MO, continued to reject Quebec's offers to purchase controlling interest in the mining operation. The first phase of the $15.1 billion James Bay hydroelectric development, already the largest in North America, was opened officially.

Social Climate. For the first time in the 1970's, the Quebec government negotiated labor contracts with most of the 300,000 public and parapublic workers without plunging the province into a general strike. There were scattered strikes in hospitals, despite legislation making them temporarily illegal. Legal strikes closed the government's liquor outlets, paralyzed public transportation in Montreal and Quebec City, and disrupted service to some Hydro-Quebec clients. A government inquiry commission recommended legislation to establish a framework for relations between the Quebec government and the province's universities, but at year's end debate on the recommendation and its implications for university autonomy had not begun. The government's UHF (ultrahigh frequency) television network, Radio-Québec, made important improvements in its programming under a new president, Gérard Barbin.

See also MONTREAL.

FERNAND GRENIER
*Télé-Université, Université
du Québec*

——— **QUEBEC • Information Highlights** ———

Area: 594,860 square miles (1 540 687 km²).
Population (1979 est.): 6,298,100.
Chief Cities (1976 census): Quebec, the capital, 177,082; Montreal, 1,080,546; Laval, 246,243.
Government (1979): *Chief Officers*—lt. gov., Jean-Pierre Coté; premier, René Lévesque (Parti Québécois). *Legislature*—Legislative Assembly, 110 members.
Education (1979–80 est.): *Enrollment*—public elementary and secondary schools, 1,108,150 pupils; private schools, 72,120; Indian (federal) schools, 4,820; post-secondary, 204,160 students. *Total expenditures,* $5,670,467,000.
Public Finance (1979–80 est.): *Revenues,* $13,510,000,-000; *expenditures,* $14,960,000,000.
Personal Income (average weekly salary, May 1979): $281.63.
Unemployment Rate (July 1979, seasonally adjusted): 8.8%.
(All monetary figures are in Canadian dollars.)

ANDREW PARTOS

RECORDINGS

The U. S. recording industry closed out the 1970's with a healthy burst of activity despite an unexpected economic slump in the decade's last year. By 1979 the industry had grown 500% since the Beatles arrived in the United States in 1964.

Classical. Classical recording featured a little of everything and a lot of a few things. Digital recording proved that standard repertoire could achieve hit status all over again. Many digital discs came from small companies such as Telarc and Denon who distributed them through audio stores. Their success encouraged major labels to essay the new technique.

Opera also was a major factor in the year's classical releases. Such works as Hindemith's *Mathis der Maler* and Massenet's *Cendrillon* were completely recorded for the first time. New releases and reissues emerged from the record companies in a never-ending stream.

Luciano Pavarotti and Beverly Sills were 1979's most visible opera stars, while Frederica Von Stade established herself as a major name in the vocal field. The pianists Youri Egorov and Bella Davidovich aroused considerable interest, and flutist James Galway began to reach the almost-pop star status he had in Britain.

Pop. Rock was 25 years old and still king. Albums by Led Zeppelin, Supertramp, and the Eagles dominated the charts.

Although disco recordings had threatened to overtake rock, by the end of 1979 disco sold less vinyl than its great popularity in clubs and on radio had indicated. The Bee Gees were still ruling artists in the disco realm. With their fifth album, *Spirits Having Flown,* they were approaching the Beatles' top standing of six number-one albums in a row. But disco diva Donna Summer's number-one album, *Bad Girls,* pointed the way to the future with its blending of rock and disco. Disco-rock gained ground as rock

stars like Rod Stewart had disco hits, and major labels renamed their disco branches "dance music" departments.

The divisions between categories of recordings blurred in all areas. The jazz charts contained disco and easy-listening discs. Middle-of-the-road recordings dominated the country charts. Philip Glass' *Einstein on the Beach* floated between classical and jazz. Pop superstar Barbra Streisand recorded a disco duet with Donna Summer, and Ethel Merman discoized Gershwin and Porter.

Discs by New Wave artists as diverse as Joe Jackson and Talking Heads entered the mainstream in droves. Small New Wave labels like Stiff and Virgin increased their U. S. distribution by uniting with the majors. This went hand in hand with a new British invasion reminiscent of the early 1970's.

A totally unknown group, the Knack, went gold in 13 days without the benefit of heavy promotion. This repeated the recent pattern of the Cars and Dire Straits, and convinced major labels to change their policies and support more such acts in the future. The industry's midyear economic crisis, which found the music business touched by recession for the first time, made these unknowns particularly attractive; their discs cost little to produce and required minimal promotion.

A second result of the crisis was a flood of sure-selling superstar products. In the fall, the market was jammed with new discs by Fleetwood Mac, Elton John, Bob Dylan, and scores of others at increased prices, while new budget labels were introduced to stimulate sagging sales. Other results of the slump were the fading of commercial picture discs and 12-inch singles, new Recording Industry of America Association (RIAA) requirements for gold and platinum awards, a marked increase in blank tape sales, and exploration of new markets like China and Africa.

RECORDINGS OF 1979

CLASSICAL

BARRIOS: *Guitar Music;* John Williams (Columbia).

BARTÓK: *Concerto for Orchestra;* Ormandy, Philadelphia Orchestra (RCA).

BEETHOVEN: *Fidelio;* Janowitz, Kollo, Bernstein, et al., Vienna Philharmonic (Deutsche Grammophon).

BEETHOVEN: *String Quartets, Op. 59, 74, 95;* Cleveland Quartet (RCA).

BERNSTEIN: *Songfest;* Dale, Elias, Bernstein, et al., National Symphony Orchestra (Deutsche Grammophon).

BIZET: *Carmen;* Berganza, Domingo, Abbado, et al., London Symphony Orchestra (Deutsche Grammophon).

BRITTEN: *Peter Grimes;* Harper, Vickers, Davis, Royal Opera Company (Philips).

CHOPIN: *Piano Concerto No. 1;* Zimerman, Giulini, Los Angeles Philharmonic (Deutsche Grammophon).

CHOPIN: *Piano Concerto No. 2;* Ax, Ormandy, Philadelphia Orchestra (RCA).

MASSENET: *Cendrillon;* Von Stade, Gedda, Rudel, Philharmonic Orchestra (Columbia).

MILHAUD: *Protée (Suite symphonique No. 2);* Abravanel, Utah Symphony (Angel).

MOZART: *Marriage of Figaro;* Vienna Philharmonic (London).

MUSSORGSKY: *Pictures at an Exhibition;* Maazel, Philharmonic Orchestra (Telarc).

SCHUBERT: *Alfonso und Estrella;* Mathis, Schreier, Suitner, et al., Berlin State Opera (Angel).

SCHUMANN: *Piano Concerto;* **FRANCK:** *Symphonic Variations;* Moravec, Neumann, Czech Philharmonic (Supraphon).

SHOSTAKOVICH: *Lady Macbeth of Mtsensk;* Vishnevskaya, Rostropovich, London Philharmonic (Angel).

R. STRAUSS: *Die Schweigsame Frau;* Scovotti, Adam, Janowski, Dresden State Opera (Angel).

STRAVINSKY: *Firebird Suite;* **BORODIN:** *Polovtsian Dances;* Shaw, Atlanta Symphony Orchestra (Telarc).

VIVALDI: *Sacred Choral Music, Vols. 1 and 2;* Negri, Alldis Choir, English Chamber Orchestra (Philips).

COMEDY

STEVE MARTIN: *Comedy Is Not Pretty* (Warner Bros.).

ROBIN WILLIAMS: *Reality . . . What a Concept* (Casablanca).

JAZZ

GEORGE BENSON: *Livin' Inside Your Love* (Warner Bros.).

ANGELA BOFILL: *Angel of the Night* (Arista).

GARY BURTON & CHICK COREA: *Duet* (ECM).

CRUSADERS: *Street Life* (MCA).

EGBERTO GISMONTI: *Sol do meo Dia* (ECM).

JOHNNY GRIFFIN: *Live in Tokyo* (Inner City).

EARL HINES: *Fatha Plays Hits He Missed* (M & K Real Time).

MILESTONE JAZZSTARS: *In Concert* (Milestone).

JONI MITCHELL: *Mingus* (Asylum).

SONNY ROLLINS: *Don't Ask* (Milestone).

SPYRO GYRA: *Morning Dance* (Infinity).

WEATHER REPORT: *8:30* (Columbia).

MUSICALS, MOVIES

HAIR: soundtrack (RCA).

JOHNNY THROUGH THE SECRET LIFE OF PLANTS: Stevie Wonder, soundtrack (Tamla).

THE KIDS ARE ALRIGHT: The Who, soundtrack (MCA).

THE MAIN EVENT: soundtrack (CBS).

QUADROPHENIA: soundtrack (Polydor).

SWEENEY TODD: original cast (RCA).

THEY'RE PLAYING OUR SONG: original cast (Casablanca).

POPULAR

ALLMAN BROTHERS BAND: *Enlightened Rogues* (Capricorn).

HERB ALPERT: *Rise* (A & M).

ATLANTA RHYTHM SECTION: *Underdog* (Polydor).

BAD COMPANY: *Desolation Angels* (Swan Song).

BEE GEES: *Spirits Having Flown* (RSO).

BLONDIE: *Eat to the Beat* (Chrysalis).

PEABO BRYSON: *Crosswinds* (Capitol).

JIMMY BUFFETT: *Volcano* (MCA).

THE CARS: *Candy-o* (Elektra).

CHEAP TRICK: *Live at Budokan* and *Dream Police* (Epic).

CHER: *Take Me Home* and *Prisoner* (Casablanca).

CHIC: *Risqué* (Atlantic).

NATALIE COLE: *I Love You So* (Capitol).

ELVIS COSTELLO: *Armed Forces* (Columbia).

CHARLIE DANIELS: *Million Mile Reflections* (Epic).

JOHN DENVER: *John Denver* (RCA).

NEIL DIAMOND: *September Morn* (Columbia).

DIRE STRAITS: *Communiqué* (Warner Bros.).

DR. HOOK: *Pleasure and Pain* (Capitol).

BOB DYLAN: *Slow Train Coming* (Columbia).

EAGLES: *The Long Run* (Asylum).

EARTH, WIND, & FIRE: *I Am* (ARC).

ELECTRIC LIGHT ORCHESTRA: *Discovery* (Jet).

EMERSON, LAKE & PALMER: *Love Beach* and *Live* (Atlantic).

FLEETWOOD MAC: *Tusk* (Warner Bros.).

STEVE FORBERT: *Jackrabbit Slim* (Newperor).

FOREIGNER: *Head Games* (Atlantic).

PETER FRAMPTON: *Where I Should Be* (A & M).

G. Q.: *Disco Nights* (Arista).

GLORIA GAYNOR: *Love Tracks* (Polydor).

J. GEILS BAND: *Sanctuary* (EMI/America).

GEORGE HARRISON: *George Harrison* (Dark Horse).

MOLLY HATCHET: *Flirtin' with Disaster* (Epic).

HEATWAVE: *Hot Property* (Epic).

ISLEY BROTHERS: *Winner Takes All* (T-Neck).

JOE JACKSON: *Look Sharp* and *I'm the Man* (A & M).

MICHAEL JACKSON: *Off the Wall* (Epic).

MILLIE JACKSON & ISAAC HAYES: *Royal Rappin's* (Polydor).

THE JACKSONS: *Destiny* (Epic).

RICK JAMES: *Fire It Up* (Gordy).

JEFFERSON STARSHIP: *Freedom at Point Zero* (RCA).

WAYLON JENNINGS: *Greatest Hits* (RCA).

JETHRO TULL: *Stormwatch* (Chrysalis).

ELTON JOHN: *Victim of Love* (MCA).

RICKIE LEE JONES: *Rickie Lee Jones* (Warner Bros.).

JOURNEY: *Evolution* (Columbia).

KANSAS: *Monolith* (Kirshner).

EVELYN CHAMPAGNE KING: *Music Box* (RCA).

THE KINKS: *Superman* (Arista).

KISS: *Dynasty* (Casablanca).

THE KNACK: *Get the Knack* (Capitol).

LED ZEPPELIN: *In Through the Out Door* (Swan Song).

BARRY MANILOW: *One Voice* (Arista).

BETTE MIDLER: *Thighs and Whispers* (Atlantic).

STEPHANIE MILLS: *Whatcha Gonna Do With My Lovin'* (20th Century).

WILLIE NELSON: *Willie Nelson Sings Kris Kristofferson* (Columbia).

WILLIE NELSON AND LEON RUSSELL: *One for the Road* (Columbia).

TED NUGENT: *State of Shock* (Epic).

THE O'JAYS: *Identify Yourself* (P. I. R.).

THE OUTLAWS: *In the Eye of the Storm* (Arista).

PEACHES AND HERB: *Twice the Fire* (Polydor).

TEDDY PENDERGRASS: *Teddy* (Philadelphia International).

TOM PETTY AND THE HEARTBREAKERS: *Damn the Torpedoes* (Backstreet).

PINK FLOYD: *The Wall* (Columbia).

POLICE: *Reggatta De Blanc* (A & M).

QUEEN: *Live Killers* (Elektra).

GERRY RAFFERTY: *Night Owl* (United Artists).

BONNIE RAITT: *The Glow* (Warner Bros.).

RAYDIO: *Rock On* (Arista).

SMOKEY ROBINSON: *Where There's Smoke* (Tamla).

KENNY ROGERS: *Kenny* (United Artists).

KENNY ROGERS & DOTTY WEST: *Classics* (United Artists).

DIANA ROSS: *The Boss* (Motown).

SISTER SLEDGE: *We Are Family* (Cotillion).

REX SMITH: *Sooner or Later* (Columbia).

AMII STEWART: *Knock on Wood* (Ariola/America).

BARBRA STREISAND: *Wet* (Columbia).

DONNA SUMMER: *Bad Girls* (Casablanca).

SUPERTRAMP: *Breakfast in America* (A & M).

TALKING HEADS: *Fear of Music* (Sire).

JAMES TAYLOR: *Flag* (Columbia).

TANYA TUCKER: *Tear Me Apart* (MCA).

EDWARD VAN HALEN: *Van Halen II* (Warner Bros.).

VARIOUS ARTISTS: *No Nukes/The Muse Concerts* (Asylum).

VILLAGE PEOPLE: *Go West* and *Live & Sleazy* (Casablanca).

WAR: *The Music Band* (MCA).

DIONNE WARWICK: *Dionne* (Arista).

WINGS: *Back to the Egg* (Columbia).

NEIL YOUNG: *Rust Never Sleeps* (Reprise).

CASABLANCA

UPI

Donna Summer's *Bad Girls* was one of the year's big albums. Barry Manilow took a Grammy for pop vocal performance.

Get the Knack by the unknown group The Knack became a gold record in 13 weeks.

CAPITOL RECORDS

Jazz. Jazz, which early in 1979 had seen vigorous activity on both traditional and fusion labels, was cut back as the year closed, although it still sold in greater volume than ever before. Like classical music, jazz was particularly suited to the new sound-enhancing recording techniques. Quantities of direct-to-disc and the newer digital discs were released by small labels, followed by the tag-along majors.

Equipment. Ry Cooder's *Bop Till You Drop* was the first major label rock digital recording, and Giorgio Moroder's $E=MC^2$ was the first for disco. The first commercial videodisc machine was marketed by MCA/Philips/Magnavox in late 1978. By November 1979, the first International Video Music Conference had been held.

Country, R&B, and Blues. Discs by traditional country artists continued to be popular, but "country" albums by middle-of-the-roader Kenny Rogers and southern rocker Charlie Daniels had nationwide appeal. R&B artists suffered in disco's shadow, but Stevie Wonder, Earth Wind & Fire, and Ashford & Simpson retained their large audiences.

The success of *The Blues Brothers* LP stimulated a minor blues revival. Folk music on disc also picked up, activated by newcomers Steve Forbert and the Roches.

Comedy and Show Music. Comedy recordings had not been so popular since the 1960's; Steve Martin and Robin Williams were among the top sellers. The innovative original cast recording of *Sweeney Todd* was Broadway's hottest album, actually appearing on pop charts in the Top 100. However, after many new shows had failed, the general trend was to reissue old show discs and record Broadway revivals.

As more rock, pop, and country music artists became involved in films, the popularity of film soundtracks grew. Three very successful LP's were *Every Which Way but Loose*, which featured many country music figures, and two from the Who—*The Kids Are Alright* and *Quadrophenia*.

It was truly a year of transition, filled with musical and technical recording innovations and new trends certain to blossom in the 1980's.

PAULETTE WEISS, *"Stereo Review"*

RELIGION

Survey

The extraordinary first year in the papacy of John Paul II, the rise of an Islamic republic in Iran, and the aftermath of a ritual massacre in Jonestown, Guyana, were among the most prominent news items to emerge in the world of religion in 1979. In addition, developments in the Middle East, especially regarding the Palestine Liberation Organization (PLO), were of particular interest to the world's Jewish community.

Having served the Catholic Church in a Marxist state, John Paul II had learned that Catholicism must be sure of itself in a hostile world. In less than a year, he carried his message of love and forgiveness to the peoples of Mexico, his native Poland, Ireland and the United States, and Turkey. The papal journeys represented an extraordinary pastoral achievement. In each of these nations the pope pledged to preserve the Gospel and to prevent it from being identified with other doctrines and ideologies. A moral and theological conservative, he demonstrated an amazing ability to bring hope and unity to our chaotic times.

The return of the Ayatollah Ruhollah Khomeini to Iran after 15 years of exile was symbolic of the gathering force of the Islamic religion. Khomeini, a Shi'ite Muslim who successfully ousted the shah from power, dedicated himself to the establishment of a republic based on the laws of Islam. He shied away from use of the word "democratic" because it is a Western term, an indication of his antipathy to foreign influence.

To many observers, the religious revolution in Iran was evidence of what seems to be a worldwide Islamic revival. However, much of the Islamic world expressed disapproval of Iran's holding Americans as hostages late in the year.

In Jonestown, Guyana, late in 1978, the Rev. Jim Jones, an ordained Protestant minister with strong convictions about social justice, led a group of his followers in a ritual of collective murder and suicide. Throughout 1979, numerous investigations, analyses, and soul-searchings endeavored to determine the exact reasons for the Jonestown tragedy.

RICHARD E. WENTZ
Arizona State University

U. S. CHURCH AND RELIGIOUS ASSOCIATION MEMBERSHIP

Religious Body	Members	Religious Body	Members
African Methodist Episcopal Church	1,950,000	General Baptists (General Association of)	72,030
African Methodist Episcopal Zion Church	1,083,391	Greek Orthodox Archdiocese of North	
American Baptist Association	1,350,000	and South America	1,950,000
American Baptist Churches in the U. S. A.	1,304,088	Independent Fundamental Churches of America	87,582[1]
The American Lutheran Church	2,390,076	International Church of the Foursquare	
The Antiochian Orthodox Christian		Gospel	89,215[7]
Archdiocese of North America	152,000	Jehovah's Witnesses	554,018
Apostolic Overcoming Holy Church of God	75,000[10]	Jewish Congregations	5,775,935
Armenian Apostolic Church of America	125,000[2]	Lutheran Church in America	2,967,168
Armenian Church of America, Diocese of the		The Lutheran Church-Missouri Synod	2,673,321
(including Diocese of California)	326,500	Mennonite Church	96,609
Assemblies of God	1,283,892	National Baptist Convention of America	2,668,799[10]
Associate Reformed Presbyterian Church		National Baptist Convention, U. S. A., Inc.	5,500,000[9]
(General Synod)	31,867	National Primitive Baptist Convention, Inc.	250,000[1]
Baptist General Conference	120,222	North American Baptist Conference	42,724
Baptist Missionary Association of America	218,361	North American Old Roman Catholic Church	60,214
Buddhist Churches of America	60,000[1]	Orthodox Church in America	1,000,000
Bulgarian Eastern Orthodox Church (Diocese		Pentecostal Church of God of America, Inc.	110,670
of N. & S. America and Australia)	86,000[3]	Pentecostal Holiness Church	86,103
Christian and Missionary Alliance	152,841	Plymouth Brethren	74,000
Christian Church (Disciples of Christ)	1,256,849	Polish National Catholic Church of America	282,411[8]
Christian Churches and Churches of Christ	1,044,842	Presbyterian Church in America	73,899
The Christian Congregation, Inc.	80,411	Presbyterian Church in the United States	869,693
Christian Methodist Episcopal Church	466,718[6]	Progressive National Baptist Convention, Inc.	521,692[4]
Christian Reformed Church in North America	210,088	Reformed Church in America	351,438
The Church of God	75,890	Reorganized Church of Jesus Christ of	
Church of God (Anderson, IN)	171,947	Latter-Day Saints	186,414
Church of God (Cleveland, TN)	377,765	The Roman Catholic Church	49,836,176
The Church of God in Christ	425,000[6]	The Romanian Orthodox Episcopate of America	40,000
The Church of Christ, International	501,000[3]	Russian Orthodox Church in the U. S. A.,	
The Church of God of Prophecy	65,801[1]	Patriarchal Parishes of the	51,500[1]
The Church of Jesus Christ of Latter-Day Saints	2,486,261	The Salvation Army	396,238
Church of the Brethren	177,534	Serbian Eastern Orthodox Church for the U. S. A.	
Church of the Nazarene	455,648	and Canada	65,000[4]
Churches of Christ	2,500,000	Seventh-Day Adventists	522,317
Community Churches, National Council of	125,000	Southern Baptist Convention	13,078,239
Congregational Christian Churches, Nat. Assoc.	95,000	Triumph the Church and Kingdom of	
Conservative Baptist Association of America	300,000	God in Christ (International)	54,307[2]
Cumberland Presbyterian Church	93,200	Ukrainian Orthodox Church in the U. S. A.	87,745[5]
The Episcopal Church	2,818,830	Unitarian Universalist Association	180,240
Evangelical Covenant Church of America	74,060	United Church of Christ	1,785,652
Evangelical Free Church in America	100,000	United Free Will Baptist Church	100,000[11]
Evangelical Lutheran Churches,		The United Methodist Church	9,785,534
The Association of	106,684	United Pentecostal Church, International	420,000
Free Methodist Church of North America	69,134	The United Presbyterian Church in the	
Free Will Baptists	216,831	United States of America	2,561,234
Friends United Meeting	65,348	The Wesleyan Church	97,859
General Association of Regular Baptist Churches	235,918	Wisconsin Evangelical Lutheran Synod	401,489

Figures are mainly for the years 1977 and 1978. [1]1975. [2]1972. [3]1971. [4]1967. [5]1966. [6]1965. [7]1963. [8]1960. [9]1958. [10]1956. [11]1952. (Source: National Council of the Churches of Christ in the U. S. A., *Yearbook of American and Canadian Churches 1979*).

Views on the issue of women priests are clearly visible as a large Washington crowd awaits the arrival of Pope John Paul II. The Dalai Lama (*above*) toured the United States for 49 days.

PHOTOS UPI

Far Eastern

The Dalai Lama, spiritual head of Tibetan Buddhism, visited the United States for 49 days during 1979. He has been exiled from his native land since the People's Republic of China took over Tibet. Regarded by his people as the incarnate Lord of Compassion, he is thought to be a reincarnation of his predecessors. He was discovered at the age of two by Buddhist leaders assigned to find a successor to the Tibetan throne and verify his reincarnation. Since 1959 he has lived in Dharmsala, India. The Dalai Lama regards himself as a simple monk and, during a visit to St. Patrick's Roman Catholic Cathedral in New York City, referred to all religions as "basically the same." The Dalai Lama hopes for a change in Chinese policy that will permit his return to Tibet to serve the needs of his people. The religious leader told *Newsweek* magazine: "The problem is not religion, ideology or racism by the Chinese, but the fact that they treat us (the Buddhists) as inferiors."

Among the continuing incidents of religio-political strife were clashes between Hindus and Muslims in India. Rioting, looting, and arson occurred in such cities as Jamshedpur. It was estimated that hundreds were injured and more than a hundred killed in this communal violence. The fatal stabbing of a Hindu by a Muslim set off one incident.

The USSR renewed its efforts to suppress Buddhism among the Mongol-derived tribes of eastern Siberia. The official home of these Buddhists is Ivolginsk, a barren region of Siberia with one monastery and 28 monks. Aga in the Chita region has 12 monks. In addition there are some 300 district monks. These figures contrast with the year 1916 when there were 16,000 monks at 36 monasteries, along with 600,00 district monks.

Attempts by Chinese leaders to improve living standards and bring on more rapid modernization have produced a new skepticism among the people. Officials have had to step up their campaign against such surrogates for religion as witchcraft and fortune-telling. There has also been increased interest in visitations to the mausoleum of Maó Zédōng (Mao Tse-tung) and in the call for class struggle. Such matters were considered by some to be indicative of a spiritual hunger within the People's Republic.

RICHARD E. WENTZ

Islam

An upsurge of religious activism linked with political objectives characterized the Middle Eastern heartlands of the Islamic faith during 1979. Iran, where religious leaders spearheaded a revolution that overthrew Shah Mohammed Reza Pahlavi and then began to mold a theocratic state, provided the most striking example of this trend. On November 20, some 200 armed fundamentalist Muslims seized the Grand Mosque in Mecca and battled with Saudi militia for several days before giving up the shrine.

In Turkey, sporadic violence flared between

Muslim sects, endangering the country's precarious political balance. Parallel outbursts in Syria resulted in numerous casualties, while Lebanon, still in tatters from a devastating civil war, also experienced sectarian unrest. Muslim tribesmen in Afghanistan took up arms against a central government that they regarded as too willing to subvert traditional practices. A more peaceful example of the growing appeal of Islam was Pakistan's decision to introduce the Islamic legal code as the law of the land.

The Muslim reawakening seemed evident in all parts of the world. By the end of the year there were approximately 750 million Muslims in the world, compared with 985 million Christians. Participation in the annual pilgrimage to Mecca has grown markedly since 1974. In the United States, many former Black Muslims have rejoined the Islamic mainstream.

Iran. Exiled Shi'ite Muslim leader Ayatollah Ruhollah Khomeini provided much of the impetus for the Iranian revolution. When prolonged disturbances drove the shah from Tehran in January 1979, Khomeini called for the creation of an Islamic government to correct the abuses of the old regime. The ayatollah subsequently returned to Iran and created an Islamic Revolutionary Council, which took charge of the country in February. A referendum the next month gave an overwhelming endorsement to the establishment of an Islamic republic. Later, Khomeini made public a draft constitution which clarified the Muslim nature of the new regime. It demanded that political, economic, and social affairs conform to Islamic ethics; advocated the organization of a watchdog committee to nullify un-Islamic laws proposed by the legislature; and declared Islam the state religion.

Turkey. Religious difficulties in Turkey revolved around its nearly eight million Shi'ite Muslims, called Alevis. Fighting between this group and the Sunni majority claimed hundreds of lives in 1978 and continued into the new year. The crux of their differences was political—the Alevis tending to be less conservative than the Sunnis—but splits also occurred along religious lines. The government imposed martial law in many provinces with large Alevi populations, but intermittent violence continued.

Syria. The Alawites, a Shi'ite minority which nevertheless has great influence in Syrian politics, also suffered assaults by Sunni Muslims. In June, some 60 Alawite military cadets were murdered in Aleppo by the right-wing Muslim Brotherhood. Again, political disagreements precipitated the disorders. Members of the Brotherhood were punished for the crime, but renewed attacks against Alawites brought on more riots in Latakia in September.

Lebanon. The Shi'a are also a minority in Lebanon. In 1978, their religious leader, the Imam Sadr, disappeared during a visit to Libya. During 1979, his followers resorted to plane hijackings and other violent acts to protest what they assumed was his murder or exile. Their actions led to outbreaks of sectarian strife and the loss of many lives.

Afghanistan. The government of Afghanistan was bogged down for much of the year in a guerrilla war with rebellious tribesmen. Afghan leaders were accused of modernizing the country too quickly and becoming too closely allied with the Soviet Union. The government was unable to control the rebels, who solicited external support for their bid to preserve Islamic values. Soviet forces, which crossed into Afghanistan late in the year, stepped up the campaign.

Pakistan. In Pakistan, the implementation of Muslim law, including punishments prescribed by the Koran, was seen by many as an effort to win conservative religious support for the troubled government of Gen. Zia ul-Haq.

KENNETH J. PERKINS
University of South Carolina

UPI

Early in the year, supporters of the Ayatollah Khomeini demonstrate in favor of the establishment of an Islamic government in Iran. Such a state was formed and gave evidence of a growing Islamic revival.

Rabbis Arthur J. Lelyveld and Bernard Mandelbaum (*center*) present Jimmy Carter with a shofar, the traditional ram's-horn trumpet, symbol of the Jewish High Holy days. The president had just received the Synagogue Council of America's International Human Rights Award.

UPI

Judaism

The year 1979 was one of great hope and grave concern for world Jewry. The peace negotiations between Israel and Egypt opened vistas of cooperation and encouraged hope for harmony with other Arab neighbors. The Islamic revolution in Iran, however, stepped up anti-Jewish ferment among Muslims and inspired an increase of Arab terrorism in Israel. Commemorations of the holocaust in many countries suggested a growing awareness of the plight of Jews in World War II. At the same time, however, there was an increasing number of anti-Semitic acts in many parts of the world. Emigration restrictions in the Soviet Union were relaxed and leading "prisoners of Zion" were released from that country, but the Soviet propaganda campaign against Jews seemed to intensify. In the United States, a rift developed between blacks and Jews over calls for formal negotiations with the Palestine Liberation Organization (PLO) by former U. N. Representative Andrew Young, the Rev. Jesse Jackson, and other black leaders.

Israel and World Jewry. The issues of territorial concessions and Jewish settlements in Judea and Samaria were sources of nationalistic-religious controversy throughout the year. Territorial concession became a reality when parts of the Sinai were handed over to Egypt in compliance with the new peace treaty. Rabbinic authorities issued "halachic" (Jewish legal) statements and lay groups demonstrated both for and against the giving up of land. The issue of Jewish settlements on the West Bank stirred even more controversy. A small group of settlers called "Elon Moreh" became a symbol for proponents of settlement when the Israeli Supreme Court ordered its removal from sites near the town of Nablus. The clash of views between traditionalists, who viewed these areas as a sacred trust to the people of Israel, and the secularists, who felt that the settlements jeopardized the peace process, threatened to topple the government of Prime Minister Menahem Begin.

Arab terrorism, incited by the Islamic revolution in Iran and by fierce opposition to the Israeli-Egyptian peace accord, claimed many lives in Israel during the year.

Jewish scholarship was given a boost when a group of rabbis and academics was granted permission to examine medieval Jewish texts at the old Cairo synagogue and when a valuable Torah scroll was presented by Alexandrian Jews to Begin. The autumn ushered in a year of *shmitta,* during which, according to a biblical injunction, the land must lie fallow. A special enactment by the Chief Rabbinate enabled Israeli produce to be harvested and marketed.

Soviet Jews and Anti-Semitism. A rise in the number of emigration visas granted to Jews in the Soviet Union was coupled with the unprecedented release of numerous Jewish dissidents and activists. As if to balance these positive gestures, however, the Soviet government stepped up its anti-Semitic propaganda in literature and the public media. Soviet missions abroad were used for the dissemination of anti-Semitic material throughout the world.

Desecration or destruction of synagogues, Jewish cemeteries, and private homes occurred in such diverse places as England, Argentina, Mexico, Syria, Denmark, and United States, and West Germany. Jewish antidefamation groups attempted to halt the spread of anti-Semitic literature, which they regarded as responsible for these acts.

United States. The Presidential Commission on the Holocaust, headed by author Elie Wiesel, visited sites of Nazi brutality and made recommendations for a permanent memorial to Jewish victims. The activities of that commission and reactions to the television series *Holocaust,* broadcast for the first time in Germany and rebroadcast in the United States in 1979, resulted in various commemorative projects in Europe and North America.

American Jewish leaders were deeply concerned over the open support of Arab terrorist organizations by black leaders and religious groups. The traditional solidarity and cooperation between the Jewish and black communities seemed irreparably damaged.

LIVIA E. BITTON JACKSON
Herbert H. Lehman College, CUNY

Orthodox Eastern Church

The autocephalous (self-governing) Orthodox Church in America, led by Metropolitan Theodosius of New York, elected two new American-born bishops—Boris Geeza in Chicago and Mark Forsberg in Boston. It also received the communities of the Monastery of the New Skete in Cambridge, NY, from the Roman Catholic Church on February 23. The New Skete, which has both monks and nuns, is headed by Abbot Laurence Mancuso. The OCA was also in dialogue with the newly formed Evangelical Orthodox Church, a Protestant group centered in Santa Barbara, CA.

The Greek Orthodox Archdiocese in America, headed by Archbishop Iakovos, who celebrated his 20th anniversary as its leader, received a new charter from its patriarchate in Constantinople. The charter gives greater freedom and authority to diocesan bishops. Texas-born Christopher Kovacevich became bishop of the eastern diocese of the Serbian Orthodox Church in America.

The Ecumenical Patriarch of Constantinople, Dimitrios, accused the government of Turkey of illegal activities in regard to Orthodox institutions. The patriarch was supported by other Orthodox leaders who fear for Christian rights in predominately Muslim lands. The number of Orthodox in Turkey continued to diminish, and the position of the patriarchate was more precarious than ever.

Pope John Paul II visited Turkey in November to discuss the reunification of the Catholic and Eastern Orthodox Churches. The Pope attended Orthodox services with Patriarch Dimitrios and urged ties of friendship with Islam.

Metropolitan Ignatios Hazim of Latakia in Syria was elected the Orthodox Patriarch of Antioch on July 2. He succeeded Elias IV who died on June 21.

The Greek Orthodox Patriarchate of Alexandria continued to be troubled by accusations of neglect and racism in its dioceses in East Africa, especially in Kenya and Uganda. New dioceses were being formed in West Africa. In Ghana a local church, which has considered itself as Orthodox since its formation in the 1930's, sought official inclusion in the patriarchate.

In the USSR the Moscow patriarchate appeared to be enjoying mild government support for certain of its official activities and institutions. The number of students in the church's theological seminaries has greatly increased (totaling about 1,500), with certain institutions allowed to improve their material conditions and to build new facilities. However, dissenters in the church, especially those without international reputation, continued to suffer fierce suppression. Igor Ogourtsov in Leningrad and Alexander Ogorodnik in Moscow were exiled to Siberia for leading discussion groups about Orthodoxy.

Visitors to the USSR also reported increased governmental inspection and harassment in regard to religious matters.

The Church of Greece opposed vehemently new laws about divorce and abortion. Certain voices, including that of the bishop of Pireus, called for the official separation of church and state in the country. The monastic revival on Mount Athos continued to flourish.

The Serbian Orthodox Church in Yugoslavia lost a great theologian when Father Justin Popovich died on April 7. Under house arrest in a monastery in Celije for 25 years, Father Popovich wrote many books and articles on theological, spiritual, and philosophical subjects.

REV. THOMAS HOPKO
St. Vladimir's Orthodox Theological Seminary

Protestantism

In advertising parlance, 1979 was not a good "image" year for the Protestant churches of the United States. The eight-year-old son of a Pennsylvania Presbyterian minister told his father that he wanted to become a Roman Catholic because his own Presbyterian church did not have a "pope like John Paul II."

Pope John Paul II. With a remarkable sense of projecting a pastoral, warm image, the pope left American Protestants with mixed feelings during his triumphant tour in October. His presence highlighted interest in religion, but his expression of conservative views did not encourage

Bishop Robert Runcie and Mrs. Lindi Runcie. In September, the 57-year-old theological scholar was designated the 102d Archbishop of Canterbury.

Protestants to feel that the pope would be working to ease differences with "separated brethren" in the United States.

Speaking to Protestant and Eastern Orthodox leaders in a Washington service, the pope appeared to reintroduce the concept of the "one true church" which was essentially down-played after the strong ecumenical emphasis of the Second Vatican Council. And by stressing the importance of traditional Catholic belief regarding moral issues, including remarriage of divorced persons, celibate clergy, abortion, and birth control, the pope made it more difficult for Protestants to move toward unity with the Catholic Church since all of those issues are viewed with a greater sense of tolerance by Protestants.

Still, in spite of the nagging belief that ecumenism might suffer under Pope John Paul II, the fact that so many Americans responded so warmly to the presence of a major religious leader indicated to Protestant leaders that there is a genuine longing for a spiritual dimension.

Television Services. Another indication that religious interest outside of mainline Protestant churches was heightened among the populace was the increasing support American viewers were giving to the so-called "electronic church," television programs produced by independent ministers. During the telecasts, many of these ministers have abandoned the traditional worship service format and have adapted a talk show structure. Pat Robertson, for example, host of the *700 Club* has a large listening audience that responds to his low-keyed appeals for salvation, financial contributions, and prayer. Clearly, programs such as the *700 Club* or the *PTL* (*Praise the Lord or People that Love*) *Club*

Adrian Rogers, a pastor in Memphis, TN, was elected president of the Southern Baptist Convention.

SOUTHERN BAPTIST PRESS ASSOCIATION

are attracting a wide audience of persons who find that they meet a need in their lives. Mainline church leaders are concerned, however, that the "electronic church" drains resources from organized religion without providing the sense of personal contact or community found in local congregations.

Jonestown. The darkest hour for American churches, however, was an event that shocked the world and cost the lives of more than 900 religious cult members in Jonestown, Guyana. News of the tragic event broke in November 1978, but the impact continued well into 1979 as religious leaders struggled to assess the meaning of the mass murders and suicides. In addition to the fact that more than 900 people died, the ongoing issues raised by the deaths involved separation of church and state and the fear that public horror over the deaths could lead to religious repression.

Before he organized Peoples Temple in San Francisco, CA, the Rev. Jim Jones had served briefly in a United Methodist Church in Indiana and had been ordained by the Christian Church (Disciples of Christ). When Jones took his congregation to Guyana and formed his own private Jonestown community, he was still technically under the jurisdiction of the Christian Church, but since that denomination emphasizes the importance of local authority, there was no way that ecclesiastical authorities could anticipate or prevent the deaths. But since Jones used Christian belief as the organizing force behind his cult, a few officials suggested that the separation of church and state should not be allowed to protect ministers from exploiting believers. Cults as such became a negative term in American thought, even though most current Protestant bodies began as small groups protesting the lack of commitment and faith, or adherence to particular doctrine within established churches. A year after the November 18–19 tragedy at Jonestown, there was no indication that religious repression might move against persons seeking to express their faith in ways different from the conventional. But the question—How does the secular state protect citizens from bodily harm or exploitation by religious groups without violating First Amendment rights protecting freedom of religion?—had been raised and not answered.

Southern Baptist. If the Roman Catholic pope's homilies in the United States indicated a move toward conservatism in his church, the election of a new Southern Baptist president represented a victory for conservative forces in that largest of Protestant denominations. Adrian Rogers, pastor of Bellevue Baptist Church, Memphis, TN, succeeded Jimmy Allen, considered a moderate, following an election held in Houston, TX, in July. Rogers is a believer in the inerrancy (absolute, literal truth) of the Bible. Some more liberal members of that church feared a setback for seminary education, but the same "messengers" (delegates) who elected Rogers also applauded six seminary presidents—"liberal" by Baptist measure—during the convention.

Ordination of Homosexuals. On the conservative-liberal continuum, the Episcopal Church in the United States came down on the conservative side of the on-going debate on the issue of ordaining persons of a homosexual orientation. Meeting in Denver in early fall, the Episcopal church reaffirmed the "traditional teaching of the church on marriage, marital fidelity, and sexual chastity as the standard of Christian sexual morality." Since candidates for ordination are expected to conform to this standard, the church's General Convention asserted that "it is not appropriate for the church to ordain a practicing homosexual, or any person who is engaged in heterosexual relations outside of marriage." A minority of 23 bishops issued a "statement of conscience" objecting to the official judgment of the denomination.

Earlier, the United Methodist Church had dismissed a female staff member for her public assertion that she was a lesbian. The Methodists will confront the issue of homosexuality at the church's 1980 General Conference in Indianapolis. Efforts will be made at that time to have the denomination change its present policy of not ordaining homosexuals.

JAMES M. WALL
Editor, "The Christian Century"

Roman Catholicism

Pope John Paul II, Catholicism's first Polish pope, dominated the Catholic scene in 1979 with an unprecedented show of energy, decisiveness, and pastoral sweep that took him literally around the world on trips to the Dominican Republic and Mexico; Poland, Ireland and the United States; and Turkey.

He issued a major encyclical, *Redemptor Hominis* (Redeemer of Man), a "state of the church" document outlining the church's role in world affairs, ranging from the arms race to threats to religious freedom and human dignity, and providing a "Christocentric" approach to church life.

Besides visiting different parishes in his Rome diocese each Sunday and personalizing his many audiences, the pope authorized publication of documents on such topics as priestly life, seminary education, life after death, and sexual morality; he called on the 1980 Synod of Bishops to study marriage and family life; and summoned the world's cardinals to a rare conclave to treat a variety of issues, including Vatican finances, and to analyze his pontificate thus far.

In solidifying his position as a world spokesman, the pope went to Mexico early in the year to speak on behalf of the poor and oppressed, later returned to his homeland, Poland, to plead for human rights and religious freedom (*see also* pages 406–08), journeyed to Ireland to de-

UPI
Before the UN, Pope John Paul II pleads for peace linked with human rights and social justice.

nounce civil strife, and made a week-long pastoral visit to the United States—which included an address at the United Nations in behalf of world peace and justice.

The journey to Ireland and the United States, which involved some 70 speeches by the pope, began with a papal call for peace in Northern Ireland and ended with a plea for increased attention to the "sacredness" of human life.

The papal "pilgrimage," which included Dublin and the Marian shrine at Knock in Ireland, touched Boston, New York, Philadelphia, Des Moines (IA), Chicago, and the U. S. capital. The papal Masses in Philadelphia and Chicago drew more than one million. Television coverage was unprecedented, as was the pope's White House meeting with President Carter.

Not a year into his job, Pope John Paul II took steps to mediate a serious territorial dispute between Chile and Argentina; sought to "normalize" relations with a changing Communist regime in China; named 14 new cardinals; sought unsuccessfully to reconcile the suspended traditionalist Archbishop Marcel Lefebvre; and moved to encourage new initiatives for evangelization and the strengthening of family life.

In December the Vatican censured the Rev. Hans Küng, a liberal Swiss theologian, and barred him from "functioning in a teaching role."

Church Dilemmas. While the church challenged the world community on such issues as aid for Southeast Asian refugees, world hunger, and disarmament, it continued to face continuing internal dissent, especially on the role of women in the ministry.

In the United States, efforts against abortion were stepped up in the courts and legislatures.

Concluding his U. S. trip, Pope John Paul II celebrates mass on the Washington Mall.

Catholic officials fought moves by government to change the tax status of church-related schools. For the first time, the U. S. bishops filed a law suit against the federal government, challenging a regulation forcing employers to pay for employee abortions. The National Catechetical Directory, guidelines developed over a period of five years for religious education, was issued.

Charismatics and Ecumenism. The first special collection for the Catholic communications media was authorized by the U. S. bishops for use in evangelization efforts. On June 2, 17 "Jesus rallies," sponsored by Catholic charismatics, were held across the country. And in August, a lay celebration took place in Washington to coordinate and spur evangelization efforts throughout the country.

On the ecumenical front, major Catholic-Protestant dialogues continued, as did those between Catholics and Orthodox Christians. In Venice, Anglicans and Catholics reported a "real convergence" on the questions of papal authority and infallibility.

Shroud of Turin. Scientists who examined the Shroud of Turin, venerated as the burial cloth of Jesus, said after extensive testing that the impressions on the cloth could not have been forged. But, scientifically, they could not prove its authenticity.

Central America. Not long after the pope's visit to Mexico, the government of Anastasio Somoza in Nicaragua was overthrown by largely Church-supported guerrilla forces. Among the leading members of the anti-Somoza forces were two priests, a Maryknoller and a Jesuit.

Archbishop Oscar Romero of San Salvador, El Salvador, defied the remainder of his country's bishops, and denounced the government and rich landholders as oppressors of the poor.

Transition. Among those who died were John Cardinal Wright, U. S.-born head of the Vatican Congregation for the Clergy; Jean Cardinal Villot, French-born Vatican secretary of state; James Cardinal McIntyre, retired archbishop of Los Angeles; Alfredo Cardinal Ottaviani, former prefect of the Vatican doctrinal congregation; Father Charles Coughlin; and Archbishop Fulton J. Sheen.

Those who resigned in 1979 include Leo Joseph Cardinal Suenens, primate of Belgium, and John Cardinal Carberry of St. Louis.

ROBERT L. JOHNSTON, *"The Catholic Review"*

RETAILING

In 1979, retailers in the United States ran into their severest pressures since the late 1974–early 1975 recession. High costs, stiff competition, a nervous consumer squeezed by inflation, and a gasoline shortage and resultant price increases led to a yearlong fight by retailers for their share of the consumer dollar.

Before the year ended, sales had undergone months of erosion, running virtually flat after inflation in some of the nation's best-known chains. Profits were hurt. Expense-cutting programs and careful inventory controls were not enough to offset slower consumer buying. The hardest hit were the middle-price stores. Market-dominant stores, specialty retailers catering to affluents, and discount or promotional stores which aim their goods at low-income shoppers did relatively well.

Because of the weakened dollar and high financing costs, foreign companies with ready cash and an interest in an American foothold bought a major stake in American retailing—or tried to. The most ambitious effort was the $1.1 billion attempted takeover of the F. W. Woolworth Company, the fifth largest American retail chain, by Brascan Ltd., a Canadian conglomerate. After weeks of verbal fireworks and complex litigation, Brascan withdrew but only because another Canadian holding company, Edper Equities Ltd., made its own successful effort to acquire a major interest in Brascan and insisted that the Woolworth offensive be dropped.

Other foreigners were more successful. The Tengelmann Group, West Germany's largest supermarket chain, took a major interest, with later option for control, in the Great Atlantic & Pacific Tea Company (A&P). The Dutch Brenninckmeyer interests, which already own Ohrbach's, added Maurice's, a Midwest apparel chain. Agache-Willot, a French textile and merchandising company, acquired the Korvette department-store chain based in New York. And the Imperial Group Ltd., Britain's sixth-largest company and the world's biggest tobacco company, made a $630 million offer for the Howard Johnson Company and obtained preliminary approval from the hotel-restaurant-food concern.

There were also acquisitions of American retailers by American companies, fostered on the buyer's part to diversify or improve market share and on the seller's part to obtain a capital influx or gear better for the future. Allied Stores Corporation, a large department-store chain, bought the Bonwit Teller stores and decided to revive that chain's flagship store in Manhattan after it had been closed. Alexander's, Inc., the New York chain, purchased Margo La Modes, a Texas retailer, and Hess's Inc., a Pennsylvania department-store group, welcomed a takeover offer from Crown-American Corporation, a shopping-center developer.

W. R. Grace & Company, the chemicals and natural-resources company, bought Daylin, Inc., a California retailer, adding that firm's Diana Apparel Shops and home-improvement stores to Grace's growing retailing group. Grace also bought Berman Buckskin, a Midwest leather-goods retailer. And Loews Corporation, the hotel, movie-theater, and insurance company, increased its small investment in F. W. Woolworth.

A business drama unfolded at Sears, Roebuck & Company, the Chicago department-store and catalog seller which is the world's biggest retailer. The firm's size—$18 billion in annual sales—and market clout—several thousand producers depend upon their Sears business for survival—made a daring shift in policy by Sears in 1978 a matter of national concern. But by late 1979, that change from an aggressive program of price reductions to one of fewer sales promotions intended to improve profits had apparently produced benefits.

In October, Sears happily reported a 2.4% sales increase over the same month of 1978, the company's first monthly sales rise in a year. By spurning considerable volume on low-profit items, Sears willingly risked a sharp slump in business in 1978 and most of 1979 but its goal of emphasizing higher-markup goods returned the giant retailer to better earnings. But whether the company can sustain its improved performance must await an answer in the years ahead. In the meantime, the concurrent programs of sharp expense cuts and of tight buying controls adversely affected several thousand Sears employees and more than a few suppliers.

As in 1978, specialty-store chains achieved above-average gains. This was due to customers turning more discriminating because of the inflation squeeze and to the specialty stores' keener skills in controlling their needs. Shortly before the takeover bid for it failed, Woolworth announced a plan to establish a nationally branded apparel chain at discount prices which would eventually have 100 stores. The name chosen was "J. Brannam" (an acronym for "Just Brand Names"). A related action was taken by the B. W. I Retail group, a subsidiary of Brown & Williamson Industries which in 1974 acquired through its British parent, BAT Industries, the Gimbel Brothers and Saks Fifth Avenue chains. B. W. I. said it planned to open a national chain of regular-priced apparel.

In other developments, suburban shopping centers were hurt by the gasoline shortage while downtown stores reaped the benefit. Retailers began paying more attention to either dressing up their downtown stores or opening in-city sites which they had previously overlooked. A fallout in the specialty-store field was the Franklin Simon chain which was closed when its parent, City Stores Company, New York, filed for court protection under the federal bankruptcy laws.

ISADORE BARMASH
"The New York Times"

MOUNTAIN VALLEY WATER

KRISTIA ASSOCIATES   UPI

Retailers constantly introduce new products. For one reason or another, some enjoy instant success in terms of sales. In 1979, the energy crisis and the high cost of home heating oil led to the popularity of the wood-burning stove; bottled water was "in"; and for the kids, shoe skates and an accompanying specially-tailored outfit were the rage.

National Guardsmen prepare to leave the Institute of Mental Health complex in Cranston, RI, following the settlement of an eight-day strike by nurses. A lower staff-patient ratio, not wages, was the issue.

RHODE ISLAND

Energy, especially a midyear gasoline shortage, was the critical issue in Rhode Island in 1979.

Energy. Gas lines lengthened in late spring and early summer, and the important tourist industry feared a disastrous season. Rhode Island joined neighboring states in adopting an odd-even gasoline rationing system, and the numbers of people taking public transportation soared. By midsummer, gas lines were gone and supplies were adequate, though at increased prices.

The state's householders looked apprehensively toward 1979's winter. The price of the oil that heats the bulk of Rhode Island homes was 85¢ a gallon by fall, up 65% from a year ago. Middle income families faced huge bills, and the poor needed massive aid. It was hoped that a combination of federal and state programs would benefit them.

The Environment. The controversial nuclear power plant planned for surplus Navy land in Charlestown was dealt a severe blow by a General Services Administration decision not to sell the land for that purpose. The breakdown of Providence's antiquated treatment plant allowed the dumping of sewage into the Bay for months while repairs were being made.

The Economy. Despite inflation and predictions of recession, the Rhode Island economy continued to prosper. August figures showed employment topping 400,000 and unemployment falling to 5.9% from 6.6% in May. Manufacturing employment patterns were less encouraging, although factory jobs were at a 26-year high at midyear. In September it was announced that Electric Boat, builder of nuclear submarines, would add another 500 to its work force of 3,800 in the state. Despite these favorable trends, hourly earnings in Rhode Island remained well below the New England average and far below national figures.

Government. At its regular January 1979 session, the General Assembly adopted a budget within previously mandated growth ceilings, and one which called for no new taxes. By fall, above-estimate tax revenues promised a surplus. Comprehensive open-records legislation was also passed. A new Department for Children and Their Families, to consolidate services for these clients, was established. An October special session raised welfare benefits 12% to offset inflation and high heating bills. Also in October the two houses elected Superior Court Presiding Justice Florence K. Murray to the Supreme Court, the first woman to sit there.

Politics. Providence's mayor Vincent Cianci, Jr., seemed certain to run for governor in 1980. Also, in a state long a Kennedy stronghold, it was no surprise to see the formation of an organization, headed by former governor Dennis Roberts, to promote Edward Kennedy for president.

Other News. The fall brought a faculty strike at the University of Rhode Island. In October the state was saddened by the death of John Nicholas Brown, wealthy philanthropist and public benefactor. Brown University was named for an earlier Nicholas Brown.

ELMER E. CORNWELL, JR., *Brown University*

RHODE ISLAND · Information Highlights

Area: 1,214 square miles (3 144 km²).
Population (Jan. 1979 est.): 935,000.
Chief Cities (1976 est.): Providence, the capital, 164,989; (1970 census): Warwick, 83,694; Pawtucket, 76,984.
Government (1979): *Chief Officers*—governor, J. Joseph Garrahy (D); lt. gov., Thomas R. DiLuglio (D). *Assembly*—Senate, 50 members; House of Representatives, 100 members.
Education (1978–79): *Enrollment*—public elementary schools, 85,771 pupils; public secondary, 74,885; colleges and universities, 63,553 students. *Public school expenditures,* $308,853,000 ($1,890 per pupil).
State Finances (fiscal year 1978): *Revenues,* $1,086,921,-000; *expenditures,* $1,066,996,000.
Personal Income (1978): $6,984,000,000; per capita, $7,472.
Labor Force (July 1979): *Nonagricultural wage and salary earners,* 400,100; *unemployed,* 32,500 (7.1% of total force).

RUMANIA

Key changes were made in the government of President Nicolae Ceauşescu early in the year, apparently to help strengthen the Rumanian economy. In foreign affairs, Rumania opposed the Soviet Union on several issues and maintained open friendship with China.

Government and Politics. On Jan. 31, 1979, Ceauşescu reassigned several cabinet members holding vital economic posts. Emil Bobu replaced Gheorghe Pana as minister of labor; Pana was named mayor and Communist party leader of Bucharest. Former Bucharest Mayor Ion Dinca was appointed minister of industrial production and deputy premier, and Gheorghe Cioara became minister of electrical energy.

On March 31, Ceauşescu replaced Premier Manea Manescu with long-time associate Ilie Verdet. Verdet had been first deputy premier and chairman of the state planning commission, the body that devises the country's economic programs. His place on the commission was taken by Nicolae Constantin.

Economy. In 1978, for the third year in a row, Rumania's agricultural output failed to reach projected goals. Grain, meat, vegetables, fruit, and dairy products yielded a total increase of 2.4%, compared with a planned increase of 7%. The poor performance caused President Ceauşescu to issue new regulations centralizing the nation's agricultural production. Central units were set up to administer all collective farms, state farms, farm machinery distribution centers, and agricultural research facilities. Each council was issued plans for the fulfillment of production goals.

Substantial price increases were put into effect during the course of the year. Gasoline and various foods were hardest hit. On March 28, increases averaging 28% were instituted for washing machines, children's clothing, glassware, bicycles, many wood and paper products, and some medicines.

Foreign Affairs. At the November 1978 meeting of the Warsaw Pact leaders in Moscow, President Ceauşescu resisted the Soviet Union on several issues. He expressed the view that the defense pact calls for mutual aid in the event of an "imperialist aggression in Europe only," and thereby disengaged Rumania from conflicts in Asia. He opposed Soviet demands for increased military budgets; criticized Soviet policies in the Middle East; and refused to sign a declaration condemning China, the United States, and the Middle East peace accords. At the July 1979 meeting of the Soviet-bloc party leaders, the Rumanian delegation refused to sign a joint declaration, "For International Solidarity." In October, the Rumanian delegation was conspicuously absent from another meeting of Warsaw Pact leaders, this one to celebrate the 30th anniversary of the establishment of the German Democratic Republic (East Germany). And in November, Ceauşescu opened the Communist Party congress in Bucharest with a careful but firm restatement of Rumania's independence from the USSR in foreign affairs.

The Rumanian president also sought to play a "positive and active role" in establishing peace in the Middle East. He was hosted by Syrian President Hafez al-Assad and Palestine Liberation Organization (PLO) leader Yasir Arafat. In September, an emissary held secret talks with Israeli Prime Minister Menahem Begin in Jerusalem. Unlike other Warsaw Pact countries, Rumania maintained diplomatic relations with Israel and refused to recognize the Vietnam-sponsored government in Cambodia. Deputy Prime Minister Paul Niculescu further promoted relations with China during a May visit.

JAN KARSKI
Georgetown University

------- RUMANIA · Information Highlights -------

Official Name: Socialist Republic of Rumania.
Location: Southeastern Europe.
Area: 91,700 square miles (237 500 km²).
Population (1979 est.): 22,100,000.
Chief Cities (July 1978): Bucharest, the capital, 1,948,-314; Constanta, 293,713; Iaşi, 288,752.
Government: *Head of state,* Nicolae Ceauşescu, president and secretary general of the Communist Party (took office 1965). *Head of government,* Ilie Verdet, premier (took office March 1979). *Legislature* (unicameral)—Grand National Assembly.
Monetary Unit: Leu (4.47 leu equal U. S.$1, 1978).
Manufactures (major products): Power; mining, forestry, and construction materials; metal products; chemicals; machines; processed foods; textiles.
Agriculture (major products): Corn, potatoes, wheat, oil seeds.

SAINT LUCIA

Saint Lucia, island of the Windward Islands of the eastern Caribbean, attained full independence on Feb. 22, 1979 as the 40th member state of the Commonwealth. Independence came amid the disruption of a civil servants' strike, the burning of St. Lucia's prison, and the boycott of the celebrations by the St. Lucia Labour Party (SLP). Outgoing governor Sir Allen Montgomery Lewis was appointed governor-general, and John G. M. Compton, head of the United Workers' Party, retained the prime ministership. Political and social unrest following independence contributed to a rising robbery rate, vandalism, and an apparent political power struggle.

Compton was turned out of office on July 2 when the SLP, a coalition of conservatives and radicals in common opposition to the United Workers' Party, won St. Lucia's first democratic elections after independence. Allan Louisy became prime minister, although it was generally

------- ST. LUCIA · Information Highlights -------

Location: Windward Islands, eastern Caribbean.
Area: 238 sq mi (616 km²).
Population (Jan. 1979 est.): 120,000.
Chief City: Castries, the capital.
Agriculture (major products): Bananas, coconuts.

thought that George Odlum, deputy prime minister, and Peter Josie, the minister in charge of agriculture, lands, fisheries, labor, and cooperatives, were running the new government.

British power in St. Lucia dated back to 1803. In recent decades successive measures enlarged local jurisdiction. Moves for independence grew with a 1976 resolution of the House of Assembly. The SLP pressed for a pre-independence referendum on the issue, but British Foreign and Commonwealth Minister Edward Rowlands mediated local differences to the point of "near-unanimity." A Westminster-style constitution, providing for an elected House of Assembly and an Upper House of nominated senators, was adopted.

The economic prospects for St. Lucia are relatively bright. All 1979 budget expenditure and a fifth of development outlays came from local revenues. An oil refinery and transportation complex are under development.

St. Lucia joined the United Nations.

R. M. YOUNGER

SAINT VINCENT AND THE GRENADINES

In ceremonies at the capital, Kingstown, on Oct. 27, 1979, the Caribbean island state of St. Vincent (located in the Windward Islands) was granted full independence as the 42d member state of the Commonwealth.

Moves for independence followed a 1976 resolution of the St. Vincent House of Assembly seeking termination of the status of Associated State voluntarily established with Great Britain in 1969. English in speech and largely Protestant, St. Vincent chose to remain a monarchy, with Her Majesty Queen Elizabeth represented by a governor-general, J. S. Arthur. R. Milton Cato became the nation's first prime minister. In December 5 elections, Cato's Labor Party won 11 of 13 Parliamentary seats.

British power dated back to 1627. The Carib population was undisturbed when St. Vincent formally became a British colony in 1763. The French held the island for a few years; Britain regained control, and most of the Caribs were transferred to Honduras in the 1790's. Over recent decades the British government approved successive measures enlarging local jurisdiction.

Fertile valleys of the volcano of Soufrière have long supported diversified agriculture. The government still holds more than 40% of the land. The chief export crops are bananas, arrowroot, coconuts, and vegetables. Efforts are being made to establish processing industries. International tourism has grown.

R. M. YOUNGER

─── SAINT VINCENT AND THE GRENADINES ───
Information Highlights

Location: Caribbean.
Area: 150 square miles (389 km²).
Population (1979 est.): 110,000.
Chief City (1979 est.): Kingstown (capital): 25,000.

SAN FRANCISCO

On December 11, Mayor Dianne Feinstein retained her post in a runoff election against Supervisor Quentin Kopp. The final balloting removed from office the district attorney, sheriff, and four supervisors.

Crime. On May 22, former Supervisor Dan White was found guilty of voluntary manslaughter in the 1978 killings of Mayor George Moscone and Supervisor Harvey Milk, a spokesman for the city's many homosexuals. The prosecutor had asked for first-degree murder convictions, but the Superior Court jury found White guilty on only two counts of the lesser charge. The verdict carried a maximum prison sentence of less than eight years and caused a riot by 5,000 San Franciscans. The protestors stormed City Hall, breaking windows, and set fire to 12 police cars. Damage was estimated at $200,000.

In October, 18 members of the Hell's Angels motorcycle gang went on trial under a federal indictment for racketeering.

Transportation. In late August, workers of the Bay Area Rapid Transit system went on strike in a wage dispute. The strike continued into early October, but limited service was resumed with supervisory personnel.

The city's famous cable car system was closed down for a major overhaul after the tourist season. Police were assigned to the city's buses in an attempt to quell rising youth violence.

Earthquake. On August 6, the San Francisco Bay Area was shaken by its worst earthquake in more than 50 years. There were no deaths, however, and property damage was not extensive.

Refugees. By mid-July, more than 13,000 Indochinese refugees had settled in San Francisco, with another 2,500 arriving monthly. The refugees suffered high rates of tuberculosis, leprosy, and parasites, and local health services were strained "beyond capacity."

CHARLES R. ADRIAN
University of California, Riverside

Many San Franciscans felt that Dan White's sentence for the slaying of a mayor and supervisor was too lenient.

WIDE WORLD

SASKATCHEWAN

The New Democratic Party (NDP) government of Saskatchewan opened its third term Feb. 22, 1979, with a throne speech outlining programs to consolidate the province's human rights codes, monitor uranium mining, and give rebates on farm fuel costs. The farm fuel rebate, originally announced in 1977, in 1979 returned to farmers up to $300. During its first session, the 19th legislature passed a bill consolidating the province's bill of rights, Human Rights Commission Act, fair employment practices act, and fair accommodation practices act; the issue of homosexual rights was not addressed. Other bills passed by the body included a new matrimonial property act, providing an even division of property if a marriage is dissolved; workers' compensation legislation, linking compensation to lost incomes and increases in the cost of living; and a law creating a new department of intergovernmental affairs. The minimum wage was increased to $3.50 per hour.

Uranium. A decision by Premier Allan Blakeney at midyear was expected to make Saskatchewan one of the world's leading producers of uranium. Sparsely inhabited areas in the northern part of the province hold an estimated 10 to 15% of all the uranium supplies in the Western Hemisphere and about 30% of the known reserves in Canada. Foreign companies have been seeking to develop large deposits in the northwest Cluff Lake region. In early June, a special commission issued a lengthy report on all aspects of uranium mining in Saskatchewan. One week later, the Blakeney government gave its go-ahead. By 1984, Saskatchewan would provide more than half of Canada's uranium production. Tax and royalty earnings were expected to reach $2 million in 1979 and about $125 million by 1982.

Economy. Efforts to diversify the provincial economy, long dependent on agriculture alone, brought a rapid growth in mineral resource development during 1979. Increases were expected to reach 6% before the end of the year. Oil was the most valuable nonfarm commodity, with heavy deposits in Lloydminster; more than 1,400

SASKATCHEWAN • Information Highlights

Area: 251,700 square miles (651 900 km²).
Population (1979 est.): 954,900.
Chief Cities (1976 census): Regina, the capital, 149,-593; Saskatoon, 133,750; Moose Jaw, 32,581.
Government (1979): *Chief Officers*—lt. gov., C. Irwin McIntosh; premier, Allan Blakeney; chief justice, Court of Appeal, E. M. Culliton; Queen's Bench, F. W. Johnson. *Legislature*—Legislative Assembly, 61 members.
Education (1979–80 est.): *Enrollment*—public elementary and secondary schools, 207,790 pupils; private schools, 1,830; Indian (federal) schools, 7,300 students; post-secondary, 17,740 students. *Total expenditures,* $706,565,000.
Personal Income (average weekly salary, May 1979): $271.76.
Unemployment Rate (July 1979, seasonally adjusted): 3.7%.
(All monetary figures are in Canadian dollars.)

---

wells were drilled in that area in 1979. Potash sales increased by 25%, with China a major buyer. The Potash Corporation of Saskatchewan continued to expand its transportation and warehouse facilities; it constructed a unit train terminal in the midwestern United States. Late seeding and drought in some regions caused some crops to decline, but the cattle market increased by 37.4% in the first six months of the year.

Diefenbaker Dies. The people of Saskatchewan were deeply saddened by the death of The Right Honorable John Diefenbaker, Canada's 13th prime minister, on August 16. Saskatchewan was his home for 76 years (*see* Obituaries, page 381).

DOROTHY HAYDEN
Regina Public Library

SAUDI ARABIA

Saudi Arabia and the United States became even more mutually dependent in 1979, as a variety of economic problems and foreign policy dilemmas confronted both nations.

An occupation of the great mosque of Mecca by religious extremists in November was ended by Saudi troops after a week of fighting, but damage to the government's prestige was great.

Foreign Affairs. Because Saudi Arabia continued to hold vast amounts of U. S. dollars, Finance Minister Mohammad Aba al-Khail expressed concern that rising inflation would erode his nation's oil income. U. S. Secretary of the Treasury Michael Blumenthal and Secretary of Commerce Juanita Kreps visited Saudi Arabia early in the year to offer reassurances.

Border clashes between North and South Yemen in February–March also affected U. S.-Saudi relations. To aid North Yemen, Saudi Arabia purchased U. S. military supplies, placed its troops on alert, and recalled its forces from Lebanon. U. S. assistance to Yemen was regarded by some as an attempt to reassure the Saudis of its continued interest in the area.

The Saudis persisted in opposing, however, the American-backed Egyptian-Israeli peace treaty. On March 18 in Riyadh, U. S. National Security Adviser Zbigniew Brzezinski was told that the treaty remained unacceptable because it ignored the rights of the Palestinians and did not require complete Israeli withdrawal from all occupied territory. Under pressure from Iraq and Syria, the Saudis agreed on March 31 to move the Arab League headquarters from Cairo to Tunis, cut diplomatic ties with Egypt, and discontinue its $1 billion in aid.

The United States nevertheless remained committed to the defense of Saudi Arabia. Offers to send U. S. troops and to build U. S. military bases on Saudi soil were rejected, but diplomatic support during the revolution in Iran was gratefully accepted.

In June, Crown Prince Fahd, and in October, Foreign Minister Saud Al-Faisal, reiterated

UPI

Saudi Arabia's Foreign Minister, Prince Saud Al-Faisal, and Zbigniew Brzezinski, assistant to President Carter for national security affairs, review the Egyptian-Israeli peace treaty.

Saudi willingness to end hostilities with Israel and to accept its pre-1967 frontiers if there was complete Israeli withdrawal from occupied territories and if a solution to the Palestinian problem was reached. Saudi Arabia gave monetary support to the Palestine Liberation Organization (PLO) and urged the United States to negotiate with that group.

Economy and Finance. The continuing influx of money from oil sales helped Saudi Arabia become a permanent member of the board of directors of the International Monetary Fund in September 1978.

During the year, the Saudi government reluctantly agreed to several price increases by the Organization of Petroleum Exporting Countries (OPEC). To help compensate for shortages in world oil production, Saudi Arabia increased its production from 8.8 million barrels per day in the last six months of 1978 to 9.5 million barrels per day in the first quarter of 1979. However, Oil Minister Ahmed Zaki Yamani warned the consuming nations that this high level of production would continue only until the end of 1979. The immediate solution to the world energy problem, he stated repeatedly, was for the Western industrialized nations to reduce drastically their consumption of oil.

According to official government reports, the annual rate of inflation in Saudi Arabia during 1979 was estimated at 10%, a marked improvement over the previous year. The decline was largely due to improvements in the housing and shipping industries and to the success of a food subsidy program.

The 1979–80 budget showed little growth over the previous year. Total revenues and expenditures remained in balance at approximately $48 billion. A major difference, however, was an increase in security and defense spending to about $16 billion, or one third of the budgeted expenditures.

Government. King Khalid's long absences from the country due to illness left Crown Prince Fahd in charge of the government for much of the year. The cabinet, government bureaucracy, and officer corps remained practically unchanged.

───**SAUDI ARABIA · Information Highlights**───

Official Name: Kingdom of Saudi Arabia.
Location: Arabian peninsula in southwest Asia.
Area: 830,000 square miles (2 149 690 km²).
Population (1979 est.): 8,100,000.
Chief Cities (1976 est.): Riyadh, the capital, 667,000; Jidda, 561,000; Mecca, 367,000.
Government: *Head of state and government,* Khalid ibn Abd al-Aziz al-Saud, king (acceded March 1975).
Monetary Unit: Riyal (3.370 riyals equal U. S.$1, Oct. 1979).
Manufactures (major products): Petroleum products, cement, fertilizers.
Agriculture (major products): Dates, vegetables, grains.

Minister of the Interior Prince Nayef took an active role in domestic affairs, deporting thousands of illegal aliens, attacking the expanding role of women in business, and banning the wearing of all jewelry with religious inscriptions. A U. S. report on human rights issued in February concluded that torture was not being used by the Saudi government but criticized the treatment of Saudi women, the severe punishments for minor crimes, and the banning of trade unions and political parties.

Military. The United States continued to sell vast quantities of arms to Saudi Arabia. In fact, more than half of all U. S. foreign military sales went to the Saudis. The U. S. Army Corps of Engineers continued work in Saudi Arabia on construction projects costing $4 billion, and another $6 billion in construction was proposed for the future. Nevertheless, the Saudi government felt insecure because of dangers posed to its ruling family by nearby revolutionary states, by the Arab-Israeli conflict, Soviet expansionism, and the possibility of internal opposition. Despite protests from Israel, the United States sent twelve F-15 fighter planes to Saudi Arabia in January 1979, two airborne control planes in March, and a training team to assist in the deployment of Saudi troops in April.

There was still no military conscription in Saudi Arabia in 1979, but the government announced in July that it was considering the possibility of a draft.

WILLIAM OCHSENWALD
Department of History
Virginia Polytechnic Institute

SINGAPORE

Lee Kuan Yew celebrated his twentieth anniversary as Singapore's prime minister in 1979. The occasion provided an opportunity for Lee and others to reflect on how far Singapore has advanced economically and socially. The nation of 2.4 million people now has the second highest per capita gross national product in Asia, trailing only Japan.

Domestic Policies. As he marked the anniversary, Lee, a savvy politician and a skillful administrator, became concerned about the issue of who would succeed him. Still only 56 years old as the year ended, Lee realized that his country needed a whole new generation of leaders, even if he remained in power for several more years, as seemed likely. Lee had acted on his concern in early January, when six members of the government-dominated Parliament resigned. The prime minister said that three members were asked to resign while the others left voluntarily to make way for younger blood. Lee's People's Action Party, which controlled all 69 seats in Parliament, handpicked candidates for the seats in hopes of bringing some new faces into the government.

The opposition Workers Party, which claims it is intimidated by the Lee government, contested five of the seven seats filled in a February by-election. The leading opposition candidate managed to get 38% of the vote. Lee appointed some of the new legislators to his cabinet. Tony Tan, a banker before his election, became minister of state for education. Howe Yoon Chong, who had headed the civil service system, was named defense minister.

The country's GNP, aided by a manufacturing boom and by healthy prices for Malaysia's commodities which are processed and marketed in Singapore, grew by about 9.5%. Inflation remained below the 7% level. Singapore feared that its economy would be hurt by a new Australian civil aviation policy limiting the stopover rights of passengers on the "kangaroo route" from London to Australia. Singapore long has been a popular tourist stop on the run. The island nation did lose some Australian business, but this was more than offset by big gains in arrivals from other countries.

In 1979, Lee initiated a campaign to teach Singaporeans to be more courteous to each other and to tourists. Initial results were mixed.

The year also saw Lee's government intensify efforts to get Singaporeans, 76% of whom are Chinese, to drop their dozen or so Chinese dialects in favor of Mandarin, the national tongue of China. Mandarin is one of four official languages in multiracial Singapore, along with English, Malay, and Tamil (a Ceylonese dialect). This was all part of Lee's longstanding program to get his country's Chinese majority to stop thinking of themselves as overseas Chinese and start realizing that they are part of a polyglot Singapore, along with Malay and Indian minorities.

Foreign Affairs. With Indonesia, Malaysia, the Philippines, and Thailand—its four partners in the Association of Southeast Asian Nations— Singapore strongly denounced Vietnam's invasion of Cambodia early in the year. Later, Singapore joined its ASEAN allies in only mildly rebuking China when it attacked Vietnam.

Concerned about the Soviet Union's increasing military presence in Southeast Asia, Lee in October called on the United States to bolster its naval forces in the region.

EDWARD EPSTEIN
"The Asian Wall Street Journal"

--------- **SINGAPORE · Information Highlights** ---------

Official Name: Republic of Singapore.
Location: Southeast Asia.
Area: 224 square miles (580 km²).
Population (1979 est.): 2,400,000.
Chief City (1974 est.): Singapore, the capital, 1,327,500.
Government: *Head of state,* Benjamin H. Sheares, president (took office Jan. 1971). *Head of government,* Lee Kuan Yew, prime minister (took office 1959). *Legislature* (unicameral)—Parliament.
Monetary Unit: Singapore dollar (2.155 S. dollars equal U. S.$1, Oct. 1979).
Manufactures (major products): Refined petroleum, processed rubber.
Agriculture (major products): Tobacco, vegetables, fruits, rubber and coconut palms.

SOCIAL WELFARE

The United Nations proclaimed 1979 as the International Year of the Child, seeking to focus attention on needed improvements in the welfare of the young. There was, nevertheless, major deterioration in that welfare in areas where infants and children made up a disproportionate share of refugee and famine victims.

Refugees. At the beginning of the year, the "boat people" fleeing Vietnam captured much attention and threatened to overwhelm the capacities of Malaysia and other neighboring countries to receive them. The United States and some other Western nations eased their immigration restrictions to allow more refugees in and also contributed to the maintenance of the roughly 200,000 people still interned in camps in Southeast Asia. The number of new arrivals from that source dropped sharply by December. In the meantime, however, the continued military struggle between Vietnam and Cambodia destroyed much of the food supply for millions, and the plight of some 2 to 3 million people, facing starvation in Cambodia or in the refugee camps of neighboring Thailand, elicited the most publicized concern.

The United Nations High Commission for Refugees estimated that five countries of sub-Saharan Africa—Burundi, Rwanda, Tanzania, Uganda, and Zaire—had pursued policies that helped create in 1979 approximately 3 million new refugees, many of them children facing starvation. Their plight was alleviated by well-organized efforts of UN organizations and by such private groups as the 37-year-old Oxford Committee for Famine Relief (an England-based group known as Oxfam).

Other Problems Affecting Children. A study by the International Labor Organization on the global exploitation of child labor showed that the worst abuses were probably on the Indian subcontinent, where more than 10 million youngsters were subjected to appalling conditions. But millions more suffered from similar cruelties in other Third World nations.

Renewed and continuing interest in child welfare accounted for a large share of study and action in the United States, too. A 1980 White House Conference on the Family was to define and study an agenda for policymakers on related problems. An estimated 87% of welfare recipients are children and mothers, primarily under the Aid to Families with Dependent Children (AFDC) grants. New family realities, it was believed, demanded adjustments in welfare programs. For example, since the proportion of children with working mothers was expected to increase further, the care of preschool children was becoming a more pressing issue. A related concern was for the expansion of job programs for disadvantaged young people, about one third of whom were unemployed.

A report by the National Institute of Mental Health addressed itself to the problem of child abuse and neglect. As many as 1.5 million children annually are the victims of such maltreatment within their homes, a number at least matched by the number of wives who are abused. In December, the House of Representatives approved and sent to the Senate a $65 million, three-year program to provide shelters and other aid for battered wives and children.

Meanwhile, the self-abuse that children and young adults resort to in an affluent society seemed to spread further, even with some apparent tapering off in the misuse of hard drugs and with the stabilization of marijuana consumption, though the latter still was prevalent among adolescents. The most serious problem in terms of rate of increase was teenage alcoholism. During the year, several states raised or were considering raising the minimum legal drinking age. However, such changes generally are regarded as only marginally effective. A new series of educational campaigns for prevention of alcoholism, made possible by rapidly increased spending, was directed at teenagers through the National Institute of Alcohol Abuse and Alcoholism. The agency raised its annual budget for combating the problem among adolescents from a nominal sum to $3.1 million.

Equally nagging was the problem of assuring adequate foster care for children. An exhaustive study by the Childrens' Defense Fund, issued in March, and Congressional hearings in the spring, came to the same basic conclusions as the 1909 White House Conference on Dependent Children—whenever possible children should be kept in their own or in permanent homes. About $700 per child per year in federal funds, and several times that sum in state funds, went to keep nearly 500,000 children, a number that had quadrupled since 1961, in foster homes. Several bills to provide more financial aid and counseling to help keep families intact were in the congressional hopper, though prospects for passage looked slim. On the other hand, there was no suggestion that the United States should imitate Sweden's 1979 legislation that provided mechanisms by which children could "divorce" themselves from their parents.

The Supreme Court handled two major cases dealing with children's rights. In June, it concluded that parents have the right to sign their children into mental facilities without a prior judicial hearing. On July 2, it struck down a Massachusetts law requiring an unmarried woman younger than 18 years to have the consent of both parents for an abortion. During the year, about 170,000 women under 18 years obtained legal abortions, an increasingly controversial matter.

Abortion. Meanwhile, the broader controversies over abortion remained as heated as ever. The Supreme Court agreed to hear arguments in 1980 on an Illinois appeal challenging the constitutionality of the Hyde amendment, the four-year-old congressional ban on medicaid financing for most abortions. Essential appropriations again were held up in Congress over efforts, only partially successful, to allow more exceptions to the ban. Only a last-minute compromise settled the annual struggle to tighten or liberalize public financing of abortions. The struggle over the legality of abortions went deeper. Anti-abortion forces busily prepared for the 1980 elections. Right to Life parties won places on the ballot in several states. The movement had relatively limited campaign funds, but through the cooperation of the Life Amendment Political Action Committee and the National Right to Life Committee gained maximum effect in the drive to obtain a constitutional prohibition of abortion. The passions stirred were reflected in the continued, but isolated, attacks on planned parenthood or abortion clinics and the harassment of patients. On the other hand, the National Abortion Rights Action League mounted its own extended propaganda counterattack. Another American response to the prospect of unwanted births was an increase, to more than 500,000 per year, double the 1900–75 rate, in tubal sterilizations.

The abortion struggle was not limited to the United States. In France, adherents and opponents fought bitterly over the renewal of the 1974 law that had made abortions legal for five years. A narrow victory for renewal was counterbalanced to some degree by further liberalization of family subsidies.

HEW. The resignation of the colorful, outspoken Joseph Califano as secretary of Health, Education, and Welfare was accepted as part of a general cabinet shake-up in July. Califano's opposition to creating a separate cabinet-level department of education, in spite of strong political pressures for it, and his close personal ties with Sen. Edward Kennedy, were probably major reasons for his departure. Secretary of Housing and Urban Development Patricia Roberts Harris succeeded him and pledged to continue Califano's tradition of vigorous enforcement and action, but acceded to the loss of education as part of her bailiwick. Her department assumed the new title of Health and Human Resources. The differences between President Carter and Senator Kennedy, both announced 1980 presidential candidates by December, over approaches to developing a national health care program continued, but became somewhat blurred. Carter submitted a bill to provide universal catastrophic health insurance in gradual steps. Kennedy planned to present a more comprehensive health care program later.

Welfare Expenditures. The unremitting worldwide inflation spurred by rising oil prices, along with real and prospective recessions, brought further pressures to stem welfare expenditures in all industrialized nations. In the United Kingdom, the "social contract" was broken by a wave of strikes, including the first walkout ever of about 3,000 social workers, at the beginning of the year. Meanwhile, a Royal Commission on the National Health Service began receiving its first testimony in a mounting debate over whether Britons should pay higher user charges under that system. A backlash against the strikes helped topple the Labour government in the May 3 election. Conservative Margaret Thatcher, the new prime minister, showed a tough, energetic approach soon after her victory by announcing plans to encourage the sale of government-owned Council Houses to tenants. Later Prime Minister Thatcher pushed for an austerity budget that would hold or reduce other welfare costs.

A similar shift took place in Canada, where Pierre Elliott Trudeau's Liberal Party was defeated by Conservatives about the same time. Prime Minister Joe Clark also pledged to cut budgets. A somewhat different change took place in Italy, where wholesale reorganization of the nation's health care system went into effect after ten years of study, conflict, and compromise. The new service is designed to replace gradually a fragmented and uncoordinated national health scheme with a more centralized, efficient, and less wasteful arrangement. The goal in Italy was to deliver equal health care to all citizens through a system eventually financed out of general revenues, but with much local participation in its administration.

In the United States, the pressure against welfare expenditures, or at least their increases, took different forms. A nationwide movement for required limits on federal spending gained momentum. Thirty states, four short of the number needed, passed resolutions calling for an unprecedented national constitutional convention for adoption of an amendment stipulating that the budget must be in balance. With automatic increases in welfare payments in the offing, and social expenditures running at almost 50% of the total federal outlay, other solutions also were proposed. Some leaders suggested limited federal welfare expenditures to less than 25% of gross national product (GNP), though current spending was still well below that level. In California, businessman Paul Gann, cosponsor of Proposition 13 in 1977, led the drive that won approval in November by a 3 to 1 margin for Proposition 4, imposing constitutional limits on future spending by the state and local governments. In California and elsewhere, legislatures also responded to the inflationary skewing of individual tax liabilities by enacting rebates and indexing their income tax schedules to prevent cost of living increases in salaries from bumping workers into higher brackets. Neither these nor other efforts at tax reform presented a direct attack on welfare spending, but a deep cut in federal funding for CETA programs had a very pronounced effect in large

Mrs. Rosalynn Carter and Joseph Califano listen as President Carter addresses a White House briefing on mental health. The forthright Califano was forced to resign as secretary of Health, Education, and Welfare in mid-July.

UPI

cities throughout the nation, where most of those short-term job training funds had gone.

Carter Programs. On other fronts, the Carter administration again tried for most of the year to push through Congress a bill to restrain future rises in the cost of hospital care, without success. Secretary Harris did, however, provide short-term help to at least one hospital threatened with bankruptcy and closure, when she joined Gov. Hugh Carey of New York in furnishing a well-publicized joint federal-state grant of $14 million to the Jewish Hospital and Medical Center of Brooklyn for a pilot project designed to make better health care more directly available to poor residents of the adjoining neighborhoods. At all levels of government there were responses, usually under the threat of suits and with federal aid, to demands by physically handicapped citizens for the changes required by law in equipment and services that would make buildings, streets, and transport facilities more accessible to them. In October, Judge David Bazelon, head of the U. S. Court of Appeals, handed down a decision reaffirming the Federal Occupational Safety and Health Administration's standards and enforcement authority to set maximum levels of cotton dust permissible in textile mills. The restrictions were intended to reduce and prevent byssinosis, or "brown lung" disease. As the cost of fuel oil shot up during the year, state legislatures turned to various programs to help the elderly and the working poor meet the higher heating bills of the coming winter. By the end of the year, Congress also had passed supplementary legislation for the same purpose. Finally, President Carter appointed a Commission on Pension Policy to engage in a two-year study of the nation's pension systems and the future of retirement income policies, giving special attention to areas where private, state, and local sectors overlap or leave gaps.

Social Security. Disability rolls in the American and foreign systems were rising faster than expected, and more workers were choosing early retirement. Such demands had pushed social security taxes up in all advanced nations, with further rises anticipated.

In the United States, a consensus was emerging that a reduction rather than further increase in Social Security taxes was desirable; the maximum level was due to rise from $1,403 per year to $1,587 on Jan. 1, 1980, then to $1,975 the next year. In addition, the prestigious Advisory Council on Social Security, headed by former Assistant Secretary of HEW Henry Aaron, conducted hearings throughout the country early in the year as part of an 18-month study and began submitting recommendations in November for basic improvements. The panel suggested that husbands and wives pool and split their earnings credits evenly if they divorce, and that survivors should inherit a deceased spouse's Social Security earnings credits. Such changes would give women more equitable treatment under the law, but would also require an increase in the tax rate of about 5%. Meanwhile, new regulations effective November 1 made more people eligible for payments under the Supplementary Security Income (SSI) program, though excluding individuals whose total assets are worth more than $1,500 and couples with assets worth more than $2,500.

To counter pressures on costs, Congress was considering such proposals as allowing an income tax credit of 20% of a person's Social Security levy, financing medicare and related payments from general revenue sources, and eliminating survivor benefit payments, currently running at more than $2.2 million annually, to post-secondary school students. Public concern about the mounting costs and future of the system grew to the point that some agencies, public and private, whose membership in it is voluntary, were considering withdrawal. The city government of San Jose, CA, gave the most publicized case of actual withdrawal, setting up instead its own plan for employees.

MORTON ROTHSTEIN
University of Wisconsin, Madison

SOUTH AFRICA

The year witnessed a number of highly dramatic developments and the promise of significant change in racial legislation, but it brought little relief from the uncertainty, tension, and continuing international pressure which marked 1978. In both external and internal affairs, the year was dominated by the unfinished business of 1978. Since the emergence of Angola and Mozambique as independent neighbors in 1975 and the Soweto disturbances and internal unrest of 1976–77, the Nationalist government has been preoccupied with two fundamental problems—the security of its frontiers and the stability of the apartheid state. Aside from the strengthening of the armed forces, attention has focused primarily on the efforts to ensure that the succession states in Zimbabwe Rhodesia and Namibia (South West Africa) will be cooperative and stable; and then on the need for internal nonwhite allies and the concessions necessary to gain at least their limited cooperation in a new system of consultative institutions.

But at the end of 1979, despite the agreement at the London conference, the future of Zimbabwe remained unclear. Pretoria's concern with the fragility of any cease-fire arrangements after the seven years of bloodshed was evidenced in speeches by the prime minister and foreign minister during November. Both warned that South Africa would not stand by and tolerate chaos on its northern border. With regard to Namibia the future remained equally unclear. The differences between South Africa and the United Nations over the final arrangements for the transfer of power in the territory and the holding of UN-supervised elections were, apparently, as far from resolution as in 1978. Meanwhile in both areas the guerrilla war and the killing went on.

Internally the first half of the year was overshadowed by the continuing fallout from the multimillion dollar scandal involving the Information Department. The scandal threatened to paralyze if not bring down Prime Minister P. W. Botha's government. The government-appointed commission implicated the state president, John Vorster, who abruptly resigned on June 4, less than nine months after his resignation as prime minister. In the second half of the year the confusion and tensions within the National Party ranks increased considerably as Botha tightened his grip on the party, encouraged his colleagues, and repeatedly urged the need for a new approach to race relations. He challenged his party followers to "adapt or die" and provoked a considerable backlash.

Internal Affairs. The Information Department scandal continued to dominate politics as the country and press awaited the Erasmus Commission's report and reacted to the "revelations" from abroad of the central figure, Dr. Eschel Rhoodie. Botha promised to resign if members of his cabinet were implicated. In February, the opposition parties refused to join in a vote of congratulations to State President Vorster and on March 22 called on him to resign. Serious attacks also were made on Finance Minister Owen Horwood. In April, former Information Minister Connie Mulder was expelled from the National Party. On June 4 Prime Minister Botha presented the commission's report and, at the same time, announced Mr. Vorster's resigna-

South African troops patrol near the Namibia-Angola border, the scene of increased guerrilla activity.

tion. In a reversal of its first report, the commission found that Mr. Vorster had knowledge of the department's secret funding and the spending of funds for propaganda projects. It exonerated Botha, Horwood, and Dr. P. G. J. Koornhof, the minister of cooperation and development.

Mr. Vorster was succeeded as president by Marais Viljoen, the president of the Senate. In August, Dr. Rhoodie was extradited from France and on October 8 he was sentenced to six years in prison for fraud. No other former officials were charged.

Mr. Botha's reaction to these events was to seek greater curbs on the press and to use the opportunity to reshuffle his cabinet. No longer able to keep his chief rival and ideological opponent, Dr. Andries Treurnicht, out of the government, Botha named him minister of public works, statistics, and tourism. Minister of Justice James Kruger, another hardliner, became president of the Senate, while two other new faces were brought in and posts were reallocated.

The conflict between the prime minister and the right wing Afrikaners, inside and outside the party, deepened with the unfolding of the scandal, the decision not to demolish the Crossroads squatter settlement at the Cape, the maintenance of Alexandra township as a family residential township, and the acceptance in principle of two major commission reports—the so-called Wiehahn and Riekert reports. The first recommended that Africans be allowed to unionize and that job discrimination be largely eliminated. The second urged far-reaching changes in the hated influx control laws. Together they constituted a major shift in official thinking.

A confrontation seemed imminent in late June when Dr. Treurnicht repudiated statements —called deviations from basic party principles— made in the United States by Dr. Koornhof, the most active liberal in the cabinet. After the prime minister stoutly defended Dr. Koornhof, the Transvaal leader became more cautious. But conservative reaction continued to grow. Botha continued to hammer at the need for change and to question such tenets of apartheid as the mixed marriages and immorality acts.

On August 31 Prime Minister Botha made

PETER JORDAN, LIAISON

John Vorster, state president since Oct. 12, 1978, resigned as the result of a Department of Information scandal.

—— SOUTH AFRICA • Information Highlights ——

Official Name: Republic of South Africa.
Location: Southern tip of Africa.
Area: 471,445 square miles (1 221 043 km²).
Population (1979 est.): 28,200,000.
Chief Cities (1970 census): Pretoria, the administrative capital, 543,950; Cape Town, the legislative capital, 691,296; Johannesburg, 642,967; Durban, 495,458.
Government: Head of state, Marais Viljoen, president (took office June 1979). Head of government, P. W. Botha, prime minister (took office Sept. 1978). Legislature—Parliament: Senate and House of Assembly.
Monetary Unit: Rand (0.7689 rand equals U. S.$1, Dec. 1979).
Manufactures (major products): Textiles, chemicals, fertilizers, automobiles, fabricated metals, fish.
Agriculture (major products): Sugarcane, tobacco, corn, citrus fruits, wheat, dairy products, wool.

history by becoming the first prime minister to visit the black township of Soweto. But in four by-elections held on October 3 the ruling party saw its majorities reduced as voters stayed away in unprecedented numbers. Although the National Party retained the four seats, the rightwing Herstigte Nasionale Party (HNP) increased its share of the vote. Connie Mulder called the results a vote of no confidence and announced the formation of a new party. And in November 7 by-elections, Botha suffered another disappointment when his party lost its Edenvale seat to the official opposition, the Progressive Federal Party (PFP). The PFP had surmounted a crisis over image and leadership when on September 3 Dr. Fredrik van Zyl Slabbert, 39, replaced Colin Eglin as party leader.

Black reaction to Mr. Botha's extraordinary first year was mixed. While they welcomed his statements and ideas, many black leaders were quick to point out that the structure of racial discrimination remains largely intact. The fear that white backlash would, as hitherto, force a retreat, also remained. During the year the government launched the third independent "homeland," Venda, in the northeast, but like Transkei and Bophuthatswana before it, it was refused international recognition.

Namibia. Despite the 1978 UN-backed, five Western powers' plan for the independence of Namibia, Pretoria continued to reject the detailed proposals for its implementation. In February, the two-year-old-search for an alternative to UN-imposed sanctions against South Africa seemed over and a breakthrough appeared close. It proved illusory. Pretoria charged and continued to reiterate that the detailed proposals breached the original 1978 agreement. Since the plan set up a guerrilla base inside Namibia and failed adequately to monitor South West African People's Organization (SWAPO) bases in Angola and Zambia, the government clearly considered the plan pro-SWAPO. The five states and the UN submitted a revised plan, which included a proposal of the late Angolan President Agostinho Neto for a demilitarized zone on both sides of the frontiers. South Africa demurred. The government's suspicion that the UN is committed to a SWAPO victory in any UN-supervised elections was difficult to overcome. Clearly Pretoria preferred an "internal" settlement based on the result of 1978 elections. Guerrilla activity continued to escalate, as did 'hot pursuit' across the Angolan border.

The United Nations. The condemnation of South Africa, together with General Assembly resolutions calling on the Security Council for measures to ensure its compliance over Namibia and reiterating support for the armed struggle against the republic, continued throughout the year. When South Africa reoccupied its seat on May 23, for the first time since its credentials were rejected in 1974, the General Assembly once more voted to reject them (96–19–9) and expelled the delegates the following day. The Security Council condemned the republic for its "aggression against Angola" and for the proclamation of Venda independence.

Foreign Affairs. Relations with the United States continued to deteriorate. On April 12 Botha levelled charges of spying, which involved the use of the ambassador's light plant, against the U. S. embassy and expelled three military attachés. Washington denied the charges, refused to apologize, and expelled two South African military attachés. When subsequently Mr. Botha said the matter was closed and replacements would be permitted, the United States showed no haste to alter the situation. On October 25 U. S. State Department officials announced that signs of a low yield nuclear explosion in the Indian Ocean were detected on September 22. It was suggested that South Africa might secretly have joined the nuclear weapon states. Pretoria strongly denied the charge, and the interpretation of the September 22 data remained uncertain. But the exchange did little to improve U. S.–South African relations.

R. B. BALLINGER, *Rhode Island College*

SOUTH CAROLINA

In 1979, South Carolina experienced significant industrial growth, bountiful agricultural production, constant friction over the regulation of utilities and nuclear wastes, and efforts to upgrade public schools.

Government. In his first year Governor Richard W. Riley exerted strong leadership as he

Matthew J. Perry, Jr., of the Court of Military Appeals was named U. S. District Court Judge for South Carolina.

pushed for a different method of selecting public service commissioners (utility regulators), halted additional agents from using the Barnwell nuclear waste storage facility, successfully vetoed 15 capital improvement items, and created a state intergovernmental commission. The general assembly had the second longest session in history. The chief laws enacted brought about the addition of six circuit judges, establishment of a 5-member intermediate court of criminal appeals, increase of the gasoline tax by one cent, revision of standards for certifying teachers, reinstatement of merit raises for state employees, and reduction to one year of the separation time for divorce.

Economy. Industrial expansion was the largest in years. Developments in electronics and graph-

— **SOUTH CAROLINA • Information Highlights** —

Area: 31,055 square miles (80 432 km²).
Population (Jan. 1979 est.): 2,942,000.
Chief Cities (1976 est.): Columbia, the capital, 112,-779; (1970 census): Charleston, 66,945; Greenville, 61,436.
Government (1979): *Chief Officers*—governor, Richard W. Riley, (D); lt. gov., Nancy Stevenson (D). *General Assembly*—Senate, 46 members; House of Representatives, 124 members.
Education (1978–79): *Enrollment*—public elementary schools, 428,682 pupils; public secondary, 196,249; colleges and universities, 130,076 students. *Public school expenditures,* $843,839,000 ($1,229 per pupil).
State Finances (fiscal year 1978): *Revenues,* $2,768,-427,000; *expenditures,* $2,584,661,000.
Personal Income (1978): $18,346,000,000; per capita, $6,288.
Labor Force (July 1979): *Nonagricultural wage and salary earners,* 1,165,200; *unemployed,* 65,800 (4.9%).

ite added diversity. Foreign capital continued to flow into the state, and significant industrial plants were located in rural areas. Personal income increased more than the southeastern or national average. Unemployment was below the national average. Growth patterns were reflected through the addition of many new industrial plants, major expansions in existing ones, increased immigration, and increased state tax collections.

In agriculture, soybean and corn production increased significantly, and there were bountiful yields of tobacco and peaches. Soybeans replaced tobacco as the number one cash crop.

Education. New presidents were installed at Clemson and the Citadel. The higher education commission released a major long-range plan to control growth and development. The Department of Health, Education, and Welfare reviewed the institutions of higher education to determine if affirmative action was being accomplished. Teacher certification changes required that teachers pass a skills test and be evaluated regularly. First-grade students must be tested and when necessary given remedial work. Measuring the attainment of students at other levels was also required. Financial programs to achieve educational equalization improved education, especially in the low income districts.

Social and Cultural. The state enhanced its programs to prevent child abuse and adopted the interstate compact on the placement of children. It improved training for the disadvantaged and provided for the development and control of a state health plan. Under a permanent loan, 26 works by artist Andrew Wyeth were displayed as a unit in the ultramodern Greenville County Museum of Art. The Spoleto Festival had its third successful season (*see also* page 361).

ROBERT H. STOUDEMIRE
University of South Carolina

SOUTH DAKOTA

Conservatives who controlled the 1979 legislature lifted a ban on dove hunting, abolished the South Dakota (political) Ethics Commission, reinstated the death penalty, and rescinded the state's previous acceptance of the proposed Equal Rights Amendment to the U. S. Constitution. The legislators voted to restrict nonresident alien ownership of land, to rebate one third of the 9¢ state fuel tax to consumers of gasohol, to correct billboard placement policies in order to qualify for maximum federal aid in road construction, and to join the demand for a constitutional amendment that would require a balanced federal budget. They passed and Gov. William Janklow signed a bill allowing physicians to prescribe laetrile, and another to establish a pilot center for widows who need jobs.

The appropriation act for fiscal year 1980 supplied $194.5 million, most of which was allocated for social services ($30 million), public schools ($47 million), and higher education ($50.8 million.)

Economy. The gross state product increased by 8% over the previous year. Crops thrived under favorable weather conditions and livestock prices rose. Nonagricultural employment increased by approximately 2%. However, operators of tourist facilities reported losses due to the scarcity and high price of gasoline. Farmers paid large transportation fees to truckers because railroad cars were scarce. The shipment of their farm produce was hampered by the Milwaukee railroad shutdown.

American Indian Affairs. The United States Court of Claims rendered a decision favorable to the Sioux tribes. The case concerned the transfer of title to the Black Hills from the Sioux to the United States by an "agreement" written into federal law in 1877. After the Sioux massacred General Custer and his cavalry, the avenging U. S. Army forced the Sioux to surrender the Hills in return for only nominal compensation.

About fifteen years later, spokesmen for the western Sioux tribes began to prepare a claim against the government for abrogating the 1868 Fort Laramie treaty which provided that no part of the Black Hills could be surrendered without the consent of three fourths of the adult male Sioux. For more than 90 years the claim met only neglect or rejection. Then, with encouragement from a special act of Congress, the Claims Court reviewed the case in the spring of 1979 and recommended compensation for the Sioux in the amount of $17,553,484 plus 5% interest for a period of 102 years—a total award of some $105 million. Individual Indians will reap limited returns; after all fees are paid, and funds are set aside for tribal use, some 60,000 tribal members will receive little more than $1,000 each.

Other. The Interior Department proposed on September 7 to add South Dakota's Badlands to the list of primitive and historic areas to be protected from spoilage of air pollution and unfettered industrial development.

HERBERT T. HOOVER
University of South Dakota

— **SOUTH DAKOTA · Information Highlights** —

Area: 77,047 square miles (199 552 km²).
Population (Jan. 1979 est.): 690,000.
Chief Cities (1970 census): Pierre, the capital, 9,699; Sioux Falls, 74,488; Rapid City, 43,836.
Government (1979): *Chief Officers*—governor, William J. Janklow, (R); lt. gov., Lowell C. Hansen II (R). *Legislature*—Senate, 35 members; House of Representatives, 70 members.
Education (1978–79): *Enrollment*—public elementary schools, 90,437 pupils; public secondary, 47,791; colleges and universities, 30,931 students. *Public school expenditures,* $237,050,000 ($1,586 per pupil).
State Finances (fiscal year 1978): *Revenues,* $597,-683,000; *expenditures,* $581,674,000.
Personal Income (1978): $4,733,000,000; per capita, $6,864.
Labor Force (July 1979): *Nonagricultural wage and salary earners,* 239,700; *unemployed,* 10,600 (3.0% of total force).

SPACE EXPLORATION

July 20, 1979, marked the 10th anniversary of the first manned lunar landing. The success of the Apollo 11 mission has since served as a model of high technological achievement by the U. S. National Aeronautics and Space Administration (NASA) and has prompted many to ask: "If we can land men on the moon, why can't we ...?" Although the socioeconomic concerns of nations and governments make the situation considerably more complex, the manned lunar landing of 1969 continues to be an example of what can be accomplished with a national commitment. For as President Carter noted: "The touchdown of the Apollo 11 *Eagle* in the Sea of Tranquillity is an unforgettable milestone in the history of exploration. Whatever else historians say about this century, they will surely describe our nation as dynamic and resourceful. Not only did we fulfill mankind's age-old dream of human flight, but we also successfully ventured into space." Although progress in the field of space exploration during 1979 was not nearly so dramatic, there were significant developments.

A new manned orbital endurance record of 175 days was set by Soviet cosmonauts Lt. Col. Vladimir Lyakhov and Valery Ryumin in the Salyut 6 space station. In planetary exploration, the U. S. Voyager 1 and 2 spaceprobes provided a close-up view of Jupiter (*see* special report, page 354), and Pioneer 11 gathered valuable information while flying past Saturn. Closer to home, new earth-orbiting satellites were launched in support of scientific investi-gation and communications networks. After six years in low earth orbit, the Skylab space station reentered the atmosphere and broke up.

MANNED SPACE FLIGHT

The Salyut 6 space station, reactivated after a four-month shutdown, was occupied for a record-breaking 175 days by the Soviet space crew of Lt. Col. Vladimir Lyakhov and Valery Ryumin. (The previous record of 139 days was set by another Soviet space team in 1978.) They were launched February 25 in Soyuz 32, docked with Salyut 6 a day later, and returned to earth August 19 in Soyuz 34 to complete the record-breaking flight. Two hours of daily exercise, regular work and sleep schedules, and the use of a lower body-pressure suit enabled Lyakhov and Ryumin to readapt to the earth's gravity with no ill effects. Three unmanned Soviet tanker/transport satellites, Progress 5, 6, and 7, were used to resupply Salyut 6 during the lengthy mission; this was carried out March 12, June 15, and June 28. In addition to regular resupply functions, Progress 5 boosted the Salyut 6/Soyuz 32 complex into a higher orbit, while Progress 7 brought an antenna 33 feet (10 m) in diameter to support radiotelescope experiments. Soyuz 33 and 34 were also involved in the mission. Soyuz 33 was launched April 10 with Soviet citizen Nikolai Rukavishnikov and Bulgarian Maj. Georgi Ivanov aboard. Ivanov was the first Bulgarian to go into space. Because of problems with its "approach correction power unit," Soyuz 33 returned to earth April 12.

PLANETARY PROBES

A significant number of planetary probes contributed to the further understanding of the

UPI

Ten years after a man's first walk on the moon, former astronaut Neil Armstrong shows guests at a Paris luncheon the spot on the Sea of Tranquillity where *Eagle* landed.

origin and evolution of the solar system. Voyager 1 and 2 returned important and unexpected data on the planet Jupiter, while the Pioneer 11 mission to Saturn presented scientists with a wealth of new information and acted as pathfinder for Voyager 1 and 2, which were expected to arrive in 1980 and 1981.

Meanwhile, on Mars, three planetary spacecraft—Viking Orbiter 1 and Viking Lander 1 and 2—continued to supply meteorological and geological data. Cameras on Viking Lander 2 revealed a new layer of water frost on the surface of the Utopia Plains landing site. Previously it was felt that the frost collection was associated with major dust storm activity. However, since there were no major dust storms on Mars in 1979, new theories were being formulated to explain the phenomenon.

After more than three years, the Viking spacecrafts continued to operate in a survey mission stage. The Viking Landers were to continue operating in this mode until the Viking Orbiter ceases operation in 1980. Viking Lander 1 was then to operate in an automatic mode for the following ten years, transmitting data directly to earth on command.

The Pioneer Venus Orbiter also continued to return high quality data after completing its basic mission of one Venus sidereal year (242 earth days); the spacecraft was expected to remain in operation for one more year. Information about Venus' cloud characteristics and atmospheric composition was extracted from the data. Extremely high temperatures (up to 900° F, 482° C) on the surface of the planet were explained by some scientists on the basis of water vapor beneath the cloud. This water vapor is present in sufficient quantities to insulate the planet, blocking the emission of heat.

Additional atmospheric information, including cloud images and atmospheric temperature and pressure variations, provided a new understanding of planetary circulations. The radar altimeter aboard the Pioneer Venus Orbiter experienced data acquisition problems, but the malfunction was corrected and surface topographic data were forthcoming.

The Soviet Venera 11 and 12 spacecrafts, which landed on Venus in December 1978, transmitted data on the surface environment for approximately two hours. No television pictures were transmitted during this mission.

After a six-year journey of three billion miles, Pioneer 11 arrived near Saturn on September 1. Launched in April 1973, the Pioneer 11 spacecraft passed within 13,000 mi (21 400 km) of the planet, permitting photographs to be taken with five to six times more detail than the best pictures taken from earth. They were the first close-up photographs and measurements ever made of Saturn. Pioneer 11 survived several micrometeroid impacts during its close passages of the planet rings, providing additional confidence that Voyager 2 can continue on to Uranus after its Saturn encounter in 1981. Saturn is the second largest planet in the solar system, only slightly smaller than Jupiter. It is also the least dense planet, appearing to be composed principally of helium and hydrogen and tending to behave like a liquid mass. Saturn's most distinctive features are its rings, discovered by Galileo in 1610. Approximately 150 pictures were taken from the spacecraft. They required 86 minutes to reach earth, compared with the 52-minute transmission time for Voyager 2 data from Jupiter. Pioneer 11 instruments collected data for ongoing scientific investigations of Saturn's magnetic field, atmo-

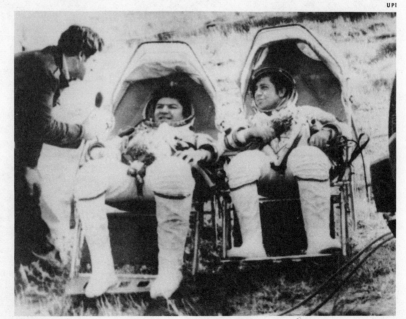

Soyuz 32 cosmonauts Col. Vladimir Lyakhov and Valery Ryumin return to earth following a record 175 days in space.

sphere, thermal radiation, and composition of rings and moons. Imaging observations revealed a previously unknown ring and moon which lie outside the rings visible from earth. Pioneer 11 then left the solar system in a manner similar to the exit of Pioneer 10 after its encounter with Jupiter in 1973. Both Pioneers carry plaques with a message from earth in the event that they are retrieved by intelligent alien species during their endless voyages among the stars.

EARTH ORBITING SATELLITES

A series of earth application and science satellites was launched during the year. These spacecraft supported earth and space science investigations and continued to provide weather monitoring and communication capabilities.

Earth Application Satellites. A Stratospheric Aerosol and Gas Experiment (SAGE) was launched with a Scout vehicle on February 18. The objective of the SAGE mission was to improve man's understanding of the stratosphere by obtaining information on aerosol and ozone content. The stratosphere begins above the cloud tops at approximately 7 miles (11.3 km) and extends to approximately 30 miles (48 km). The stratosphere contains small dustlike particles, or aerosols, which tend to reduce the solar energy input and thermal energy emitted from the earth. Changes in the aerosol concentration can affect the earth's climate. The stratosphere also contains ozone, which protects the earth by filtering ultraviolet sunlight. These changes in gas and aerosol concentration can be naturally induced—by volcanic eruptions and tropospheric generation—and man-influenced—by high flying jet aircraft and chlorofluormethane (freon) emissions, which deplete the ozone layer. The data from SAGE compliments the Stratospheric Aerosol Measurement (SAM-II) experiment launched aboard the Nimbus spacecraft in 1978.

The U. S. Magnetic Field Satellite (MAGSAT) was launched on October 30 into a 350-km (217-mi) x 550-km (342-mi) sun-synchronous polar orbit. The objectives of the mission were to obtain an accurate quantitative description of the earth's magnetic field; provide data suitable for an update of the world magnetic field model; compile magnetic anomaly maps; and interpret crustal anomaly maps in conjunction with ancillary data to improve future geologic exploration strategies. MAGSAT improves upon the measurements made by Polar Orbiting Geophysical Observatories (POGO) 2, 4, and 6, which operated from 1965 to 1971. The U. S. Geological Survey will be the principal user of the data from MAGSAT, assisted by a team of scientific investigators.

The National Oceanic and Atmospheric Administration NOAA-6 weather satellite was launched by an Atlas-F vehicle from the Vandenberg Air Force Base in California on June 27. The satellite provides information on solar

The Pioneer 11 spacecraft passed within 21 400 km (13,375 mi) of Saturn, permitting an imaging photopolarimeter to produce photos. Saturn's moon Rhea is a spot just below the planet.

UPI

radiation and collects and relays ocean-atmosphere data from buoys and balloons.

The Soviet Union launched two weather satellites in its Meteor series on January 25 and March 1.

Scientific Satellites. The British satellite UK 6 was launched into a 625-kilometer (388-mi) circular orbit, at an inclination of 55°, from Wallops Island, VA, on June 2 aboard the 100th Scout Vehicle. (The first Scout was launched in 1960.) Science experiments aboard UK 6 include a cosmic ray detector and two X-ray astronomy studies. The data from these experiments will provide a better understanding of high energy astrophysical phenomena, such as quasars, radio galaxies, supernovae, and pulsars.

The third in a series of High Energy Astronomical Observatories (HEAO-C) was launched on September 20. It was launched with an Atlas Centaur vehicle from Cape Canaveral, FL, and sent into a 499-km (310-mi) orbit with a 44° inclination. The spacecraft contains three scientific experiments, two to study cosmic rays and one to study gamma rays. Meanwhile, HEAO 2, launched in 1978, continued to return valuable data on X-ray sources. The HEAO 1 spacecraft ended 17 months of operation in January 1979 after its consumable gas supply was depleted. The *X-ray Source Catalog,* based on HEAO data and covering 30% of the sky, was published in 1979. It contains more than 1,000 X-ray sources, some three to four times as many as are contained in all earlier catalogs combined.

A total eclipse of the sun, the last one observable from the North American continent in the 20th century, took place on February 26. A joint U. S.-Canadian sounding rocket program was conducted to study its effects on the earth's atmosphere and ionosphere. Twelve U. S. satellites also provided scientific data associated with the eclipse.

Thirteen U. S. life science experiments, together with experiments from the Soviet Union and several other countries, were launched on September 29 aboard an unmanned Soviet Vostok series spacecraft. The mission was similar to previous cooperative Life Science Cosmos Flights in 1975 and 1977. Soviet scientists would be attempting to breed mammals in space for the first time, while U. S. experiments concentrated on changes in animal muscle fibers and bone formation, turnover, and strength. The U. S. experiments were aimed at gaining a better understanding of the loss of muscle strength and bone calcium during extended manned space flights.

Communication Satellites. At least eight major communications satellites, three by the United States and five by the USSR, were launched in 1979.

FLTSATCOM-B, the second of five Navy communications satellites in the FLTSATCOM series, was launched on May 3 by an Atlas Cen-

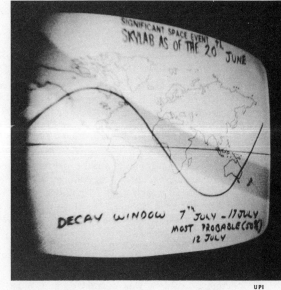

UPI

The orbital path of Skylab is tracked carefully as the station reentered the earth's atmosphere in July.

taur vehicle from the Kennedy Space Center. It was the 50th launching for Atlas Centaur, the first coming in 1962. FLTSATCOM was placed in a geostationary orbit at 23° west longitude over the Atlantic Ocean. The satellite provides a new communications capability for the U. S. Department of Defense.

Westar-C, the third in a series of Western Union communications satellites, was launched on a Delta vehicle from the Kennedy Space Center on August 9. Westar-C was placed in a geostationary orbit at 91° west longitude over the equator, due south of New Orleans, LA. The satellite will be used for television, telephone, and commercial data relay.

RCA-C, a domestic communications satellite for the Radio Corporation of America (RCA), was launched on a Delta Vehicle from the Kennedy Space Center on December 6. Unfortunately, a failure in the satellite system prevented operation of this geostationary communications satellite.

Communications satellites launched by the USSR in 1979 included two in the MOLNIYA 3 series, on January 18 and June 5; RADUGA 5, on April 25; and two in the MOLNIYA 1 series, on April 12 and July 1. The 1980 Olympics will be broadcast from Moscow via the Soviet Gorizont Series communication satellites. The Communications Technology Satellites (CTS), a joint U. S.-Canadian project, terminated television transmissions in October 1979, after more than three years of operation. CTS demonstrated that powerful satellite systems can bring low-cost transmission to remote locations anywhere on earth. More than 160 communications experiments, ranging from business teleconferencing to emergency information linkup, were conducted by the United States in 1979. Satellite communications was expected to be one of the fastest growing technologies in the coming decade.

SPACE TRANSPORTATION DEVELOPMENTS

The first orbital flight of the U. S. Space Shuttle was expected to take place in 1980; the flight test would be made by Orbiter 102-Columbia. Meanwhile, three other orbiters were named—Challenger, Discovery, and Atlantis. The development-model Enterprise, the first of the series, will probably not be orbited but has served as an excellent test vehicle. These tests included approaches and landings while mounted on top of a Boeing 747 aircraft, mated vertical ground vibration tests, and shuttle facility verification tests.

Problems encountered during the development of the orbiter included main engine malfunctions and thermal tile installation. The main engine problem was corrected, and most test firings were completed. The time required to install thermal protection tiles on the skin of the orbiter was found to be longer than expected. Both problems contributed to the delay of the initial orbital flight to 1980.

A presidential review of these shuttle development, flight schedule, and cost problems produced the following vote of confidence for NASA: "I fully support the space shuttle program because of its integral relationship to our national goals. . . . I recognize we must expect and encounter setbacks in the course of a bold development effort of this kind, but I am certain they will be successfully overcome as they occur." Progress in 1979 included the delivery and testing of the external tank development article and the successful outcome of solid rocket motor firings. In order to prepare for full operation of the Shuttle, scheduled to begin in 1981, launch service agreements were consummated with users in the private sector. The development of the European Space Agency spacelab continued in 1979; the first engineering model pallet was delivered to NASA. Delivery of experiments for Columbia's first payload was also made at the Kennedy Space Center during the year.

The cancellation of the proposed Skylab reboost/deorbit mission was a result of system deterioration, increased sunspots leading to accelerated orbital decay, and the delayed Shuttle schedule. Skylab, launched on May 14, 1973, safely reentered the earth's atmosphere on July 11 over the Indian Ocean and southwest Australia. Although visual sightings of hot debris were recorded in Australia, no bodily injury or property damage was reported.

See also METEOROLOGY; OCEANOGRAPHY.

MICHAEL A. CALABRESE

SPACE EXPLORATION—SPECIAL REPORT:

Jupiter

In 1979, the first close-up studies of the planet Jupiter were carried out by two U. S. spacecraft. After journeys of more than a year, Voyager 1 made its closest approach on March 5 and Voyager 2 on July 9. During periods of about two months each, the spacecraft sent back to earth a wealth of new and sometimes unexpected data about this, the largest planet in our solar system, and its major satellites. Among the principal discoveries made by the Voyager probes were the complex nature of the cloud structure and dynamic properties of Jupiter's atmosphere; the existence of an unexpected ring of tiny particles surrounding the planet; a new, small satellite which orbits just inside the outer edge of the ring; and widespread volcanic activity on the innermost Galilean satellite, Io.

The Great Red Spot (GRS), perhaps the best known and most enigmatic cloud formation in Jupiter's atmosphere, was found to be merely the largest member of a class of oval-shaped atmospheric vortices. These vortices are characterized by anticyclone rotation (clockwise in the northern hemisphere, counterclockwise in the southern) about their centers and gentle vertical convection. Smaller clouds circulating the perimeter of the GRS take approximately six days to complete the circuit, implying vortical wind speeds of about 360 km (225 mi) per hour. Elsewhere, the planetary wind system is dominated by easterly and westerly jet streams with speeds of up to 600 km (375 mi) per hour. Numerous small eddies appear to be the main source of energy and momentum for these high-velocity jet streams. The eddies themselves are assumed to draw their energy from Jupiter's internal heat, which is convected outward from the interior of the planet.

In one of the more surprising discoveries of the Voyager missions, spacecraft cameras recorded a thin, sparse ring of very small particles surrounding Jupiter and extending outward to a distance of 130 000 km (81,000 mi, or 1.8 Jupiter radii) from the center of the planet. Although both Saturn and Uranus have planetary rings, the ring system of Jupiter is unique in that it extends inward to the very top of the planet's atmosphere. Just within the outer edge of the ring system are two narrow, brighter rings having widths of 800 and 6 000 km (500 and 3,700 mi); the outer, narrower ring is slightly brighter. Nongravitational forces, such as pressure of light and magnetic field interaction, cause all of the small ring particles to

Bradford A. Smith announces that Viking 1 has discovered a thin, flat ring of particles around Jupiter.

spiral continuously inward and ultimately to be deposited in the planet's upper atmosphere. Scientists conclude that these lost particles must be replaced from some other source. Whether that source is a group of larger bodies orbiting just inside the outer edge of the ring system or whether the supply is located beyond the rings altogether is not known. However, Voyager did discover a new satellite orbiting at a radius of 129 000 km (80,000 mi), just inside the outermost ring material. Although the size of this body is not precisely known, it is estimated to be in the 20–40 km (12–25 mi) range. Its orbital period and speed are 7 hours, 8 minutes and 32 km (20 mi) per second, respectively, giving it the shortest period and highest orbital velocity of any known natural satellite in the solar system. The new satellite, temporarily designated as 1979 J1, brought to 14 the number of known Jovian satellites. There is little doubt that 1979 J1 is somehow associated with the ring system, but whether it represents a source for ring particles or merely establishes the approximate outer boundary of the rings is not yet known.

Jupiter's four large Galilean satellites are themselves planet-size bodies. Voyager data suggested that they fall into two general groups. The inner satellites Io and Europa are smaller—about the size of the earth's moon—are relatively dense, have high albedo (reflectivity), and have geologically young, active surfaces. The outer Ganymede and Callisto are larger—about the size of Mercury—are lower in density, and have low albedo and older surfaces. Europa, Ganymede, and Callisto all have water ice crusts. Callisto shows a surface scarred by eons of meteoric bombardment. Ganymede also has a heavily cratered surface but shows evidence of early tectonic activity which modified several large areas. These regions exhibit curvilinear ridges and grooves, suggesting the movement of large crustal ice plates similar to the drifting of the earth's continents.

Io may be the most geologically active body in the solar system. No less than nine active volcanoes were seen by the Voyager spacecraft. Their eruptions seem to involve both sulfur and sulfur compounds, as opposed to the molten silicates at work in terrestrial volcanism. The reddish color of the satellite is probably caused by deposits of elemental sulfur and sulfur dioxide which rain down from massive volcanic plumes. Volcanic eruptions on Io appear to be more violent but cooler than their terrestrial counterparts. The reason for Io's remarkable volcanic activity is not fully understood, but it is believed that the energy is derived from periodic, inelastic warping of the satellite's crust due to the enormous land tides raised by the mother planet.

See also ASTRONOMY.

BRADFORD A. SMITH
Head, Voyager Photography Team

SPAIN

Spain continued its miraculous transition from fascism to democracy throughout 1979 under the astute, forceful leadership of King Juan Carlos I, the 41-year-old handpicked successor to the late dictator Generalissimo Francisco Franco.

Politics. The most significant political event of the year was the victory of the Union of the Democratic Center (UDC)—the party of Prime Minister Adolfo Suárez González—in the March 1 parliamentary elections. The UDC won 35.2% of the popular vote to capture 168 of the 350 seats in Congress. The Spanish Socialist Workers' Party, which had been given a chance of winning by pollsters, finished second, with 29.4% of the vote and 121 congressional seats, still the largest opposition group and the major party of the Spanish left.

Meanwhile, the "Eurocommunist" Communist Party, which has effusively praised the king's leadership, increased its parliamentary strength from 20 to 23 seats as it secured 10.7% of the ballots cast. The principal loser was the Democratic Coalition, an amalgam of right-wing leaders who saw their vote drop from 8.5% (1977) to 5% and their number of seats cut from 16 to 10.

Also notable was the success of regional nationalist parties which secured 30 seats—12 in the Basque provinces, 10 in Catalonia, 5 in Andalusia, and 3 in Aragon and the Canary Islands. Later in the year, voters in Catalonia and the Basque country approved regional autonomy in their areas. In advisory referendums, moderate leaders favoring greater control over local affairs were pitted against fringe groups of the far left and right urging abstention or a "no" vote.

Despite sporadic violence before and after the campaign, the parliamentary elections—the first under Spain's new Constitution—appeared to have consolidated the country's democratic system. The one cause of concern was a relatively high level of voter abstention—35% nationwide and 49% in the northwest province of Galicia.

Economy and Energy. In mid-July the government announced its medium-term economic plan, which commits Spain to a market economy and spurns protectionism as a solution to the problems besetting the economy. Spiraling energy costs helped reduce the growth of the gross domestic product to 2.7% in 1979, compared with 4% and 5% in previous years. Oil imports also helped drive up the rate of inflation from 12% (1978) to 16%.

The parliament ratified a ten-year National Energy Plan to spur the use of coal and nuclear power, promote conservation, and reduce dependence on foreign oil which accounts for 97% of the 50 million metric tons that Spaniards annually consume.

Foreign Affairs. Spain continued to strengthen its ties to the rest of Western Europe. On June 26, the Iberian nation signed an agreement with the European Free Trade Association to reduce sharply duties on industrial imports. At the same time, negotiations began in Brussels on the country's proposed membership in the European Community.

As Spanish diplomats promoted European unity, Prime Minister Suárez continued his nation's courtship of Latin America. He visited Brazil, Ecuador, and the Dominican Republic between August 6 and 14. Spain also dispatched a representative to the nonaligned nations' conference that convened in Cuba.

GEORGE W. GRAYSON
College of William and Mary

─────── **SPAIN • Information Highlights** ───────

Official Name: Spanish State.
Location: Iberian Peninsula in southwestern Europe.
Area: 195,270 square miles (505 750 km²).
Population (1979 est.): 37,600,000.
Chief Cities (1975 est.): Madrid, the capital, 3,500,000; Barcelona, 2,000,000; Valencia, 700,000.
Government: *Head of state,* Juan Carlos I, king (took office Nov. 1975). *Head of government,* Adolfo Suárez González, prime minister (took office July 1976). *Legislature*—Cortes: Senate and Chamber of Deputies.
Monetary Unit: Peseta (66.55 pesetas equal U.S.$1, Nov. 1979).
Manufactures (major products): Textiles, footwear, petrochemicals, steel, automobiles, ships, cement.
Agriculture (major products): Cereals, vegetables, citrus fruits, feedgrains, wine, olives and olive oil, livestock.

In Ecuador for the presidential inauguration of Jaime Roldós, Spain's Prime Minister Adolfo Suárez greets Violetta Chamorro, a member of Nicaragua's new junta. Spain generally courted Latin America in 1979.

SPORTS

An Overall View

There were some unusual occurrences in sports in 1979. The New York Yankees failed to win their fourth straight pennant. Ray Kroc, the originator of McDonald's hamburgers and owner of baseball's San Diego Padres, was fined $100,000 for allegedly tampering with future free agents. Ann Meyers, a 24-year-old UCLA basketball star, became the first woman to sign a National Basketball Association (NBA) contract. Sebastian Coe of Britain ran the fastest mile in history, 3 minutes 49 seconds. And amateur athletes throughout the world were busy training for the 1980 Olympics—scheduled for Lake Placid, NY, and Moscow.

The fining of Kroc created controversy. He said publicly he wanted to improve his team by eventually signing the Yankees' Graig Nettles and Cincinnati's Joe Morgan, who would become free agents after the 1979 season. Bowie Kuhn, baseball commissioner, contended that Kroc's mention in the press of his intentions constituted tampering and fined him. Kroc threatened to sell his club and get out of baseball altogether. He withdrew the threat, however, and instead turned over the operation of the team to his son-in-law.

Ann Meyers and Title 9. Miss Meyers' signing by the Indiana Pacers to a one-year contract, worth $50,000 whether or not she won a place on the 11-player roster, seemed to bring to fruition, superficially at least, efforts by the women's movement to gain equality in sports.

In the background of Miss Meyers' signing was Title 9, the federal law passed in 1972 to guarantee women equal educational opportunities. It helped to bring the aspirations of female athletes to public attention. Miss Meyers benefited as the first woman to win a four-year athletic scholarship (nonexistent for women before Title 9) at UCLA, where she was a four-time all-American and led the team to the 1978 national title. She was a member of the women's 1976 Olympic squad that won a silver medal.

Whether the 5′9″ (17.2 m), 135-pound (61.2 kg) Miss Meyers could compete on equal footing with men in pro basketball or whether her signing served only as a publicity gimmick was decided quickly. She was dropped from the Pacers before the season began and later signed to play in the Women's Basketball League.

Title 9 has also stirred controversy. While it spawned heavy recruiting by colleges for talented female athletes and opened many doors, protesting women's groups claimed that it had not gone far enough, that funds for women's athletic programs were still not distributed on parity with men's programs, and that women were still denied basic opportunities in other fields and job categories. However women have benefited most through athletics. A 1979 study showed that in the American public high school system one third of the athletes were women, compared with 18% in 1972.

On the reverse side of the coin, a federal judge ruled that a Providence, RI, male high school senior had been barred unconstitutionally from playing on a girls' volleyball team. After a court of appeals stayed the order pending a hearing, the U. S. Supreme Court rejected without comment the plea of the 19-year-old.

Spartakiade. In Moscow, Olympic preparations advanced so dramatically that the Russians invited 2,500 athletes from 60 nations to compete in their seventh Spartakiade, a quadrennial event in all Olympic disciplines. The competition offered foreign athletes an opportunity to become accustomed to the atmosphere and to inspect the facilities.

At the opening ceremonies in Lenin Stadium, which holds more than 100,000 spectators and will be the centerpiece for the Olympic track and field competition, the Russians put on a spectacular dress rehearsal for the Games.

More than 800 journalists covered the Spartakiade. Reviews were mixed. Some voiced criticism over delays in scheduling and getting quick access to information.

The United States sent a token group of athletes to the competition. American athletes were concerned about bureaucratic rigidity, food, and training logistics. One American coach was critical of the long waits imposed on athletes during warm-ups. They were confined to special areas so they would be available promptly for starting calls.

The Olympics. Some political overtones developed. New Zealand and Israel were excluded from the invitation list to Spartakiade. For the Olympics, the first ever to be held in a Communist country, the Soviets promised entry for all nations in good standing with the International Olympic Committee (IOC).

American prospects for the Olympics were bright. For the first time, the United States was engaged in a national training program, with centers at Squaw Valley, CA, and at Colorado Springs, CO. Job opportunity programs and large-scale commitments from corporations funneled funds into the program. The U. S. women's volleyball team, for example, has worked as a unit on a full-time basis since 1977, competing against the best teams in the world. Some players left college and well-paid jobs to join the team, which had a paid, full-time coach. These developments were a departure from the U. S. concept of "amateurism for its own sake," a principle that had seemed to put Americans at a disadvantage in past international competition.

GEORGE DE GREGORIO, *"The New York Times"*

UPI

CHUCK SOLOMON

The Year In Sports

In 1979, the Soviet Union invited foreign athletes to its national Spartakiade Games for the first time. The opening ceremonies (*above*) provided a glimpse of the pageantry planned for the 1980 Moscow Olympics and enabled athletes to test the newly constructed sports facilities. Oscar Fabbiani (*left*) led the North American Soccer League in scoring, but his Tampa Bay Rowdies lost to the Vancouver Whitecaps, 2–1, in Soccer Bowl '79.

Ann Meyers (*left*) scored a victory for women's sports by signing a contract with an NBA team. Gymnast Kurt Thomas (*above*) displays his patented "Thomas Flair" on the pommel horse. In the NCAA men's basketball final, Earvin Johnson (with ball) led Michigan State to victory over Indiana State and Player of the Year Larry Bird (33).

Outstanding performers of 1979: English middle-distance runner Sebastian Coe (*left*) set three world records; Spectacular Bid (*above*) won the Kentucky Derby by three lengths; and the ever-mighty Montreal Canadiens (in white) won their fourth straight Stanley Cup.

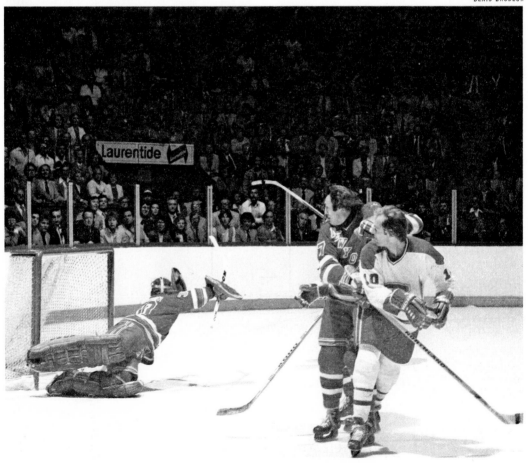

VIII Pan American Games

The Pan American Games were founded on the principle that a sports celebration for the nations of the Western Hemisphere would not only provide a showcase of athletic excellence but would help build new and closer ties among the participating nations. The Games are also regarded as a sort of Olympic preview, an important preliminary test for aspiring amateur athletes from North, South, and Central America and the Caribbean.

Between July 1 and 15, 1979, some. 4,400 athletes from 33 nations performed in the VIII Pan American Games in San Juan, PR. It was the largest, most colorful, and most successful Pan Am Games to date. Previous celebrations were held in Buenos Aires (1951), Mexico City (1955, 1975), Chicago (1959), São Paulo (1963), Winnipeg (1967), and Cali (1971).

The team representing the United States, which consisted of 550 athletes and 200 coaches, managers, and staff, was the most successful in the history of the Games. U. S. athletes won a total of 263 medals—126 gold, 92 silver, and 45 bronze. Cuba was a distant second with 146 medals, including 65 golds.

The strength and depth of the U. S. team were evidenced by the fact that its athletes failed to win a medal in only two individual events.

The United States was especially strong in track and field, capturing 25 gold medals (14 by men, 11 by women) and setting a total of 14 Pan Am Games records. U. S. athletes were no less awesome in swimming, racking up 29 gold medals. Archery, men's basketball, women's softball, and water polo were other sports in which the United States excelled.

Cuba was most impressive in the team sports, winning titles in baseball, women's basketball, and both men's and women's volleyball. Argentina took home gold medals in field hockey and roller derby, and Brazil won the hotly contested soccer tournament.

Among the outstanding individual performers in the VIII Pan American Games was 15-year-old U. S. swimmer Cynthia ("Sippy") Woodhead, who won an amazing five gold medals, including a world-record in the 200-m freestyle. Teammate Tracy Caulkins came away with 4 gold and 2 silver medals. The most surprising triumphs were scored by runners James Robinson (800 m) and Tony Darden (400 m) of the United States, both of whom upset Cuban Olympic gold medalist Alberto Juantorena. Sprinter Evelyn Ashford, also of the United States, won both the 100-m and 200-m dashes. Among Cuba's five gold medalists in boxing, the

Roberto Clemente, Jr., and Cynthia Guaialupe light the torch marking the opening of the VIII Pan American Games.

UPI

Pan Am highlights included the win of James Robinson (above) over A. Juantorena in the 800 m, the introduction of roller skating, and the overall performance of Tracy Caulkins.

FINAL MEDAL STANDINGS

COUNTRY	GOLD	SILVER	BRONZE	TOTAL
USA	126	92	45	263
Cuba	65	49	32	146
Canada	24	44	67	135
Mexico	3	6	28	37
Argentina	12	7	17	36
Brazil	9	13	14	36
Puerto Rico	2	9	11	22
Venezuela	1	4	7	12
Dominican Republic	0	5	7	12
Chile	1	4	6	11
Colombia	0	1	8	9
Panama	0	3	1	4
Jamaica	0	3	0	3
Guyana	0	2	1	3
Peru	0	1	2	3
Ecuador	0	0	2	2
Bahamas	0	1	0	1
Belize	0	0	1	1
El Salvador	0	0	1	1
Netherlands Antilles	0	0	1	1
Virgin Islands	0	0	1	1

most impressive performer was two-time Olympic heavyweight gold medal winner Teofilo Stevenson. Stevenson registered two easy knockouts to establish himself as the 1980 Olympic favorite.

Roller skating and softball were new additions to the Pan American Games in 1979. In roller skating, the United States and Argentina were dominant. Thomas Peterson, 20, of Tacoma, Wash., won four gold medals, as did Argentine speed skater Nora Vega. The U. S. women's team captured the gold in softball with a 2–0 win over Puerto Rico in the championship game. The favored U. S. men's team, however, lost a 1–0 decision to Canada in the final match.

But even the most outstanding individual and team performances in the VIII Pan American Games were brightened by a general spirit of friendly competition and camaraderie. Beyond everything else, the Pan Am Games of 1979 were simply the bringing together of thousands of young people to share in competition and culture, and in the celebration of sport. That sort of internationalism is hard to come by.

MICHAEL MORAN

AUTO RACING

In the closest finish in the history of the National Association for Stock Car Racing (NASCAR), Richard Petty nosed out Darrell Waltrip by 11 points for the grand national championship. For Petty, a Southern stock car legend, it was his seventh NASCAR title. Waltrip had the most victories for the season—seven.

Consistent driving won the Formula One World Title for South African Jody Scheckter, who scored points in 12 of 15 races. Scheckter nipped Ferrari teammate Gilles Villeneuve of Canada by four points. But the pair had to fight off a surge by Alan Jones of Australia, who won four races late in the season.

While constructors and organizers quarreled in Europe, a long-simmering feud erupted in the United States. The United States Auto Club, sole governing body of American open cockpit racing since 1956, was crippled by the formation of Championship Auto Racing Teams (CART). Most of the leading drivers and teams ran under the CART banner during the season. But the great A. J. Foyt returned to USAC after first joining CART. Hurt by the defections, USAC ran only seven races and Foyt won five of them, more than enough to gain his sixth USAC driving crown. However, by the end of the season both sanctioning bodies were having trouble filling fields.

USAC was in charge of the Pocono 500-mile race, which was won by Foyt, while CART ran the California 500, won by Bobby Unser. The rival groups competed against each other only in the Indianapolis 500-mile race. Rick Mears, in his second season of big-time racing, took the checkered flag after a late-race gear failure forced Bobby Unser to accept fifth place.

BOB COLLINS, *"The Indianapolis Star"*

AUTO RACING

World Champion: Jody Scheckter, South Africa	NASCAR: Richard Petty, U. S.
USAC: A. J. Foyt, U. S.	CART: Rick Mears, U. S.
Can-Am: Jackie Ickx, Belgium	

Major Races

Indianapolis 500: Rick Mears, U. S.	Pocono 500: A. J. Foyt, U. S.
California 500: Bobby Unser, U. S.	Daytona 500: Darrell Waltrip, U. S.

Grand Prix for Formula One Cars, 1979

Argentina: Jacques Laffite, France	Britain: Clay Regazzoni, Switzerland
Brazil: Jacques Laffite	Germany: Alan Jones, Australia
South Africa: Gilles Villeneuve, Canada	Austria: Alan Jones
Long Beach: Gilles Villeneuve	Netherlands: Alan Jones
Spain: Patrick Depailler, France	Italy: Jody Scheckter
Belgium: Jody Scheckter	Canada: Alan Jones
Monaco: Jody Scheckter	United States: Gilles Villeneuve
France: Jean-Pierre Jabouille, France	

On May 27, Rick Mears, a 27-year-old Californian, captured the Indianapolis 500.

UPI

BASEBALL

It was a year of seemingly overage players not acting their ages at all.

Heroes. Lou Brock, 40, who had been considered "washed up" after hitting .221 in 1978, bounced back to hit .304 in his final major league season. But, most importantly, the St. Louis Cardinal outfielder became the 14th player in major league history to reach the 3,000-hit plateau. Brock's milestone came on August 13, and 30 days later 40-year-old Boston Red Sox star Carl Yastrzemski became the 15th member of the 3,000-hit club. Earlier, the outfielder-first baseman had become the 18th major leaguer to hit 400 home runs.

Finally, there was 38-year-old Willie Stargell, who pulled off a unique triple by being named co-winner with St. Louis' Keith Hernandez of the Most Valuable Player (MVP) Award in the National League, MVP in the National League play-offs, and MVP in the World Series.

Stargell hit 32 homers and drove in 82 runs during the regular season as the Pirates outlasted the Montreal Expos in the tight National League East race. Then, as the Bucs swept the three-game play-offs from the Cincinnati Reds, Stargell hit .455 with two homers and six runs batted in.

In the World Series, Stargell, affectionately called "Pops" by his teammates, hit .400, blasted three home runs, and drove in seven runs as the Pirates pulled off an improbable comeback after being down three games to one to the Baltimore Orioles.

World Series. It was only the fourth time in history that a club had erased a 3–1 deficit to win a seven-game World Series and it was Stargell's two-run homer in the sixth inning of the last game that sent the Pirates ahead to stay. Two insurance runs in the ninth inning gave the Pirates a 4–1 victory in game seven and their first world title since 1971, when, also in the seventh game, they defeated the Orioles in Baltimore.

American League Cy Young Award winner Mike Flanagan, a 23-game winner in the regular season, had given the Orioles the jump in the series by pitching a 5–4 victory in the first game but 35-year-old Pirate reserve Manny Sanguillen evened the score with a ninth-inning pinch-single that won the second game, 3–2.

Another spear carrier, Baltimore's backup shortstop, Kiko Garcia, drove in three runs to spark the Orioles to an 8–4 third-game triumph and pinch-hitters John Lowenstein and Terry Crowley gave the Orioles a 9–6 win in game four.

Then, Pittsburgh began its resurgence behind 37-year-old lefthander Jim Rooker and Bert Blyleven, who combined to pitch a 7–1 victory in the fifth game. In the sixth game, John Candelaria and Kent Tekulve teamed on a 4–0 victory and in the seventh game it was Stargell,

BASEBALL

Professional—Major Leagues

AMERICAN LEAGUE
(Final Standings, 1979)

Eastern Division	W	L	Pct.	Western Division	W	L	Pct.
Baltimore	102	57	.642	California	88	74	.543
Milwaukee	95	66	.590	Kansas City	85	77	.525
Boston	91	69	.569	Texas	83	79	.512
New York	89	71	.556	Minnesota	82	80	.506
Detroit	85	76	.528	Chicago	73	87	.456
Cleveland	81	80	.503	Seattle	67	95	.414
Toronto	53	109	.327	Oakland	54	108	.333

NATIONAL LEAGUE
(Final Standings, 1979)

Eastern Division	W	L	Pct.	Western Division	W	L	Pct.
Pittsburgh	98	64	.605	Cincinnati	90	71	.559
Montreal	95	65	.594	Houston	89	73	.549
St. Louis	86	76	.531	Los Angeles	79	83	.488
Philadelphia	84	78	.519	San Francisco	71	91	.438
Chicago	80	82	.494	San Diego	68	93	.422
New York	63	99	.389	Atlanta	66	94	.413

Play-offs—American League: Baltimore defeated California, 3 games to 1; National League: Pittsburgh defeated Cincinnati, 3 games to 0.

World Series—Pittsburgh defeated Baltimore, 4 games to 3. First Game (Memorial Stadium, Baltimore, Oct. 10, attendance 53,735): Baltimore 5, Pittsburgh 4; Second Game (Memorial Stadium, Oct. 11, attendance 53,739): Pittsburgh 3, Baltimore 2; Third Game (Three Rivers Stadium, Pittsburgh, Oct. 12, attendance 50,848): Baltimore 8, Pittsburgh 4; Fourth Game (Three Rivers Stadium, Oct. 13, attendance 50,883): Baltimore 9, Pittsburgh 6; Fifth Game (Three Rivers Stadium, Oct. 14, attendance 50,920): Pittsburgh 7, Baltimore 1; Sixth Game (Memorial Stadium, Oct. 16, attendance 53,739): Pittsburgh 4, Baltimore 0; Seventh Game (Memorial Stadium, Oct. 17, attendance 53,733): Pittsburgh 4, Baltimore 1.

All-Star Game (Seattle Kingdome, July 17, attendance 58,905): National League 7, American League 6.

Most Valuable Players—American League: Don Baylor, California; National League: Keith Hernandez, St. Louis, and Willie Stargell, Pittsburgh.

Cy Young Memorial Awards (outstanding pitchers)—American League: Mike Flanagan, Baltimore; National League: Bruce Sutter, Chicago.

Managers of the Year—American League: Earl Weaver, Baltimore; National League: Bill Verdon, Houston, and Dick Williams, Montreal.

Rookies of the Year—American League: Alfredo Griffin, Toronto' and John Castino, Minnesota; National League: Rick Sutcliffe, Los Angeles.

Leading Hitters—(Percentage) American League: Fred Lynn' Boston (.333); National League: Keith Hernandez, St. Louis (.344). (Runs Batted In) American League: Don Baylor, California (139); National League: Dave Winfield, San Diego (118). (Home Runs) American League: Gorman Thomas, Milwaukee (45); National League: Dave Kingman, Chicago (48). (Runs) American League: Baylor (120); National League: Hernandez (116).

Leading Pitchers—(Earned run average) American League: Jim Kean, Texas, 1.57; National League: Joe Sambito, Houston, 1.78. (Victories) American League: Mike Flanagan, 23; National League: Joe Niekro, Phil Niekro, 21. (Strikeouts) American League: Nolan Ryan, California, 223; National League: J. R. Richard, Houston, 313.

No-Hit Games Pitched—Ken Forsch, Houston.

Professional—Minor Leagues, Class AAA

American Association (play-offs): Evansville
International League (Governor's Cup): Columbus
Pacific Coast League (play-offs): Salt Lake City

Amateur

NCAA Division I: Cal State, Fullerton; Division II: Valdosta State; Division III: Glassboro State
Little League World Series: Taiwan

Willie "Pops" Stargell (*above*) leads the Pittsburgh Pirates to World Series victory. Earl Weaver, Baltimore's manager of the year, chats with Al Bumbry.

the man who had been passing out plastic stars to his teammates all year long for jobs well done, who was the star of stars.

Play-offs and Regular Season. The Reds survived the loss of 38-year-old Pete Rose to the Phillies to win the National League Western division title after a year-long struggle with the surprising Houston Astros. In the American League, the California Angels gave their cowboy owner Gene Autry his first division title by nosing out Kansas City in the West. However, the Angels were defeated in the play-offs, 3 games to 1, by the Orioles, who led all major league teams with 102 victories. After the season, the Angels' pitching star, Nolan Ryan, signed as a free agent to play for Houston.

Baltimore was not expected to win the East but the Boston Red Sox fell short of pitching and the New York Yankees, two-time world champions, could not overcome two disastrous events. Early in the season, the Yankees lost their ace reliever, Rich Gossage, for more than two months when he suffered a fractured thumb in a shower-room scuffle with reserve catcher Cliff Johnson. Then, in August, the Yankees lost their great catcher, Thurman Munson. Munson, 32, died tragically when the private plane he was piloting crashed near his home in Canton, OH.

Owner George Steinbrenner sought to give his flagging Yankees a lift by bringing back Billy Martin as manager in June—he had previously said he would bring back Martin in 1980—but Martin had no magical powers and the Yankees finished a distant fourth in the AL East. A month after the season, Martin was no longer the Yankees manager—again. Steinbrenner dismissed Battlin' Billy after an incident in a Bloomington, MN, hotel bar in which Martin and another customer reportedly exchanged punches.

Houston's Ken Forsch pitched the only no-hitter of the season in the season's first week and joined brother Bob of St. Louis, who had a no-hitter in 1978, as the first brother combination to accomplish that feat.

Bruce Sutter of the Chicago Cubs was the National League Cy Young Award winner on the basis of his record-tying 37 saves. Houston's Joe Niekro, the Cy Young runner-up, and brother Phil Niekro of Atlanta each won 21 games, marking the second time in baseball history that brothers had won more than 20 games in the same season. Jim and Gaylord Perry had won 24 and 23 games in 1970.

The Niekros were the only 20-game winners in the National League, while Flanagan, Tommy John of the Yankees, and Jerry Koosman of the Minnesota Twins all won at least 20 games in the American League. Koosman's total represented a rise of 17 from his three-victory season with the New York Mets in 1978.

Boston's Fred Lynn (.333) and St. Louis' Keith Hernandez (.344) won the American and

High baseball drama: St. Louis Cardinal star Lou Brock becomes the 14th major leaguer to get 3,000 hits.

Carl Yastrzemski of the Red Sox waves to his Boston fans after he, too, joined the 3,000-hit club.

National League batting titles, respectively, the first championship for each. Gorman Thomas, of Milwaukee, despite hitting just .244, won the AL home-run title with 45, while Dave Kingman clobbered 48 for the Cubs to win the National League crown.

California's Don Baylor led all run producers with 139 runs-batted-in, while San Diego slugger Dave Winfield paced the National League with 118, three ahead of Kingman.

Baseball had only the fourth forfeited game in its annals when the Chicago White Sox were forced by American League president Lee Mac-Phail to forfeit a game to the Detroit Tigers. The White Sox field had become unplayable after a "Disco Demolition" promotion had turned into a mob scene between games of a doubleheader and great chunks of sod had been displaced.

People. Former New York and San Francisco Giants star and New York Mets coach Willie Mays not only made it to the Hall of Fame but was also dissociated from baseball by commissioner Bowie Kuhn for his involvement with a New Jersey gambling casino. Other new Hall of Fame members were Hack Wilson, the former Chicago Cubs slugger who holds the season record for RBIs, 190, and former National League president Warren Giles, who died in February. Death also claimed Los Angeles Dodgers owner Walter O'Malley.

BOB BROEG, *"St. Louis Post Dispatch"*

BASKETBALL

In the first rematch of play-off finalists in six years, the Seattle SuperSonics avenged their 1978 loss by defeating the Washington Bullets, four games to one, for the National Basketball Association (NBA) championship. The Sonics, coached by Lenny Wilkens, captured their first title since the club was formed in 1967. Michigan State culminated a topsy-turvy college season by winning the men's NCAA crown. Old Dominion completed a near perfect season by winning the women's title.

THE PROFESSIONAL SEASON

The NBA final paired the teams with the two best records in the regular season—Washington (54–28) and Seattle (52–30). The team-oriented SuperSonics featured none of the league's individual statistical leaders and did not

JERRY WACHTER, FOCUS ON SPORTS

Seattle guard Dennis Johnson goes up for two as the Sonics defeat the Bullets for the NBA championship.

PROFESSIONAL BASKETBALL

National Basketball Association
(Final Standings, 1978–79)

Eastern Conference

Atlantic Division	W	L	Pct.
*Washington Bullets	54	28	.659
*Philadelphia '76ers	47	35	.573
*New Jersey Nets	37	45	.451
New York Knickerbockers	31	51	.378
Boston Celtics	29	53	.354

Central Division	W	L	Pct.
*San Antonio Spurs	48	34	.585
*Houston Rockets	47	35	.573
*Atlantic Hawks	46	36	.561
Cleveland Cavaliers	30	52	.366
Detroit Pistons	30	52	.366
New Orleans Jazz	26	56	.317

Western Conference

Midwest Division	W	L	Pct.
*Kansas City Kings	48	34	.585
*Denver Nuggets	47	35	.573
Indiana Pacers	38	44	.463
Milwaukee Bucks	38	44	.463
Chicago Bulls	31	51	.378

Pacific Division	W	L	Pct.
*Seattle SuperSonics	52	30	.634
*Phoenix Suns	50	32	.610
*Los Angeles Lakers	47	35	.573
*Portland Trail Blazers	45	37	.549
San Diego Clippers	43	39	.524
Golden State Warriors	38	44	.463

*Qualified for play-offs

Play-offs
Eastern Conference

First Round	Philadelphia	2 games	New Jersey	0
	Atlanta	2 games	Houston	0
Semifinals	Washington	4 games	Atlanta	3
	San Antonio	4 games	Philadelphia	3
Finals	Washington	4 games	San Antonio	3

Western Conference

First Round	Los Angeles	2 games	Denver	1
	Phoenix	2 games	Portland	1
Semifinals	Phoenix	4 games	Kansas City	1
	Seattle	4 games	Los Angeles	1
Finals	Seattle	4 games	Phoenix	3

Championship	Seattle	4 games	Washington	1

All Star Game: West 134, East 129

Individual Honors

Most Valuable Player: Moses Malone, Houston
Most Valuable Player (play-offs): Dennis Johnson, Seattle
Rookie of the Year: Phil Ford, Kansas City
Coach of the Year: Cotton Fitzsimmons, Kansas City
Leading Scorer: George Gervin, San Antonio; 2,365 points; 29.6 per game
Leading Rebounder: Moses Malone, Houston; 17.6 per game

---

place a single player on the all-star team named at season's end. To reach the top, the Sonics relied on the league's No. 1 defense and Wilkens' "share the wealth" brand of offense.

Seattle guard Dennis Johnson, who received the most votes on the NBA all-defensive team, was named most valuable player for the final play-off series. Ironically, it was Johnson's foul at the final buzzer of Game 1 that enabled the Bullets to pull out a 99–97 victory, their only one of the series.

Game 2, also played at Landover, Md., yielded a 92–82 decision for Seattle. The SuperSonic defense, which limited the Bullets to a season-low 30 points in the second half, deserved most of the credit for the win.

The Sonics won the next two games on their home court by scores of 105–95 and 114–112. Their overtime victory in Game 4 was all but assured when the Bullets' superb front line of Wes Unseld, Elvin Hayes, and Bob Dandridge fouled out. Johnson clinched the victory by deflecting a shot by Kevin Grevey at the buzzer.

Game 5, back in Landover, brought the SuperSonics their first NBA crown and marked the end of a long season for both teams. Seattle trailed by eight points at halftime, but rallied to win, 97–93. Igniting the comeback was Gus Williams, whose 26-point average over 17 play-off games led the Sonics. Two Bullet guards, Grevey and Tom Henderson, were injured in the final game and joined ace reserve forward Mitch Kupchak, who missed the entire play-offs, on the bench.

Seattle had qualified for its second straight appearance in the finals by eliminating the Los Angeles Lakers, four games to one, and the Phoenix Suns, four games to three. The Super-Sonics narrowly escaped elimination in Game 6 of the Phoenix series. A missed shot at the buzzer by the Suns' Garfield Heard gave Seattle a dramatic 106–105 victory.

Washington earned the chance to defend its 1977–78 title by ousting the Atlanta Hawks and San Antonio Spurs, each in seven games. In the semifinal series against San Antonio, the Bullets became only the third team in the history of the league to rally from a play-off deficit of three games to one.

San Antonio's George Gervin became the sixth player in league history to win two consecutive scoring titles. He averaged 29.6 points per game during the regular season. Houston's Moses Malone, the league's most valuable player during the regular season, easily was the top rebounder, averaging 17.6 per game. Teammate Rick Barry set a single-season record by netting 94.7% of his free throws, and Detroit's Kevin Porter became the first player ever to pass for more than 1,000 assists in one campaign. Cotton Fitzsimmons of the Kansas City Kings was voted coach of the year, while his outstanding guard, Phil Ford, was rookie of the year.

Bill Walton, who won the 1977–78 MVP award while at Portland, sat out the season with a foot injury and ultimately signed a lucrative contract with the San Diego Clippers. In other post-season developments, the league's board of governors abandoned after one year its assignment of three officials to each game; in 1979–80 there would be a return to two. The governors also approved the move of the New Orleans Jazz to Salt Lake City, Utah, and decided to expand the league by two teams, making a total of 24, for the 1980–81 season.

THE COLLEGE SEASON

The Michigan State Spartans' first NCAA basketball title was almost overshadowed by the Cinderella season of the Indiana State Sycamores. Overlooked in the pre-season polls, the Sycamores won all of their first 33 games before losing to the Spartans in the title contest, 75–64, at Salt Lake City's Salt Palace. The Sycamores were led by Player of the Year Larry Bird.

Michigan State (26–6) featured balanced scoring and a defense that held Bird to 19 points, 10 below his average. Bird's principal defender, Earvin "Magic" Johnson, scored 24 points, and Greg Kelser pitched in 19. Johnson, a 6'8" (2.03 m) sophomore guard, elected to turn pro-

---

COLLEGE BASKETBALL

Conference Champions

Atlantic Coast: North Carolina
Big Eight: Oklahoma
Big Sky: Weber State
Big Ten: (tie) Michigan State; Iowa; Purdue
East Coast: Temple
Eastern Eight: Rutgers
Ivy League: Pennsylvania
Metro-7: Louisville
Mid-American: (tie) Toledo; Central Michigan
Missouri Valley: Indiana State
Ohio Valley: Eastern Kentucky
Pacific-10: UCLA
Southeastern: Tennessee
Southern: Appalachian State
Southland: Lamar
Southwest: Arkansas
Southwestern: Alcorn State
Sun Belt: Jacksonville
West Coast Athletic: San Francisco
Western Athletic: Brigham Young

Tournaments

NCAA: Michigan State
NIT: Indiana
NCAA Div. II: North Alabama
NCAA Div. III: North Park College
NAIA: Drury College
AIAW (Women): Old Dominion

---

fessional after the season and was drafted by Los Angeles as the NBA's No. 1 pick.

Michigan State, from the Big Ten, reached the final by winning a lopsided 101–67 semifinal contest over Pennsylvania. Indiana State, from the Missouri Valley Conference, earned a berth in the final by beating DePaul, 75–74.

Indiana State was not listed among the top 20 teams when the season began, and Michigan State was ranked seventh. Duke was No. 1, but the Blue Devils fell from the top spot after consecutive losses to Ohio State, 90–82, and St. John's, 69–66.

The No. 1 ranking changed hands several more times during the season. Michigan State earned the distinction in January, but a loss to Purdue left Notre Dame in the top spot. The UCLA Bruins then avenged an early season loss to Notre Dame, upsetting the Fighting Irish, 56–52, in South Bend, Ind., and replacing them as No. 1. UCLA's hopes of retaining the top ranking disappeared in mid-February, however, when the Bruins were beaten, 69–68, by the University of Washington. Still unbeaten Indiana State finally moved into the No. 1 position, where it remained entering the NCAA finals.

Indiana, another Big Ten school, toppled arch-rival Purdue, 53–52, to win the National Invitational Tournament (NIT) in New York City's Madison Square Garden.

In the women's competition, the Old Dominion Lady Monarchs completed a 35–1 season by defeating Louisiana Tech, 75–65, in the championship game of the Association of Intercollegiate Athletics for Women (AIAW). Inge Nissen's 22 points led the way for the Norfolk, Va., school, with Player of the Year Nancy Lieberman adding another 20. Tennessee finished third in the tournament by beating defending champion UCLA, 104–86.

GREG HEBERLEIN, *"Seattle Times"*

BOXING

Muhammad Ali, who had announced his retirement several times previously, made it official in July 1979. His retirement left vacant for three months the World Boxing Association (WBA) heavyweight championship and opened the door for a historic title bout in South Africa.

In his 19-year, 59-bout professional career, Ali compiled a record of 56 victories (37 by knockout), three defeats, and no draws. He was never knocked out; he earned some $50 million in purses alone.

By relinquishing the championship, the 37-year-old Ali gave the WBA an opportunity to sanction an October title fight in Pretoria, South Africa, between John Tate, a black American from Knoxville, TN, and Gerrie Coetzee, a South African white. Tate gained a unanimous 15-round decision, but his victory was hardly impressive. There was little action in the early rounds, and by the halfway mark Coetzee held a slim lead. But Tate picked up the tempo in the last seven rounds and took command of the fight. A right to the chin sent Coetzee reeling across the ring in the 14th. There were no knockdowns.

The Tate-Coetzee bout was the first heavyweight title fight ever held in South Africa. More importantly, it was the first sporting event in that country in which an integrated crowd was allowed to view the competition. The crowd of 81,000 at Loftus Versfeldt Stadium, where no blacks had ever been permitted before, paid $3,267,000 (U. S.) to see the fight. The bout aroused considerable anti-apartheid sentiment in the United States and other countries.

The World Boxing Council (WBC) heavyweight champion, Larry Holmes, defended his title three times in 1979. He knocked out Puerto Rico's Ossie Ocasio in the 11th round of a March bout in Las Vegas, NV; scored a 12th round knockout against Mike Weaver in New York City's Madison Square Garden; and in late September stopped Ernie Shavers at Caesars Palace in Las Vegas. He was most impressive in the win against Shavers. From the outset, Holmes dominated the hard-punching Ohioan with his quick left jab and all-around boxing skill. But in the seventh round he walked into one of Shavers' powerful rights and was knocked to the canvas. Holmes' ability to recover from the blow and continue pummeling the tired Shavers won him a technical knockout in the 11th round and the praise of boxing experts. A fight between Tate and Holmes for the undisputed title was expected in 1980.

In other weight divisions, Roberto Duran of Panama gave up his lightweight title to become a welterweight. Another welterweight, 1976 Olympic gold medalist Sugar Ray Leonard, scored his 25th consecutive victory without a loss by knocking out Andy Price in the first round of their October bout; the fight was on the same card as the Holmes-Shavers encounter.

M. EVANS, GAMMA LIAISON

After his retirement, "The Greatest" devoted himself to acting, public speaking, and promoting the Islamic faith.

On November 30, Leonard met WBC welterweight champion Wilfredo Benitez of Puerto Rico and took the title on a 15th-round knockout at Las Vegas. In New Orleans, Victor Galindez, the Argentine WBA light-heavyweight champion, was dethroned by Marvin Johnson of Indianapolis on an 11th-round knockout. Galindez had regained the title from Mike Rossman.

GEORGE DE GREGORIO

BOXING

World Professional Champions
(Year of achieving title in parentheses)

Junior Flyweight—Yoko Gushiken, Japan (1976), World Boxing Association (WBA); Kim Sung-Jun, South Korea (1978), World Boxing Council (WBC).

Flyweight—Betulio Gonzalez, Venezuela (1978), WBA; Park Chan-Hee, South Korea (1978), WBC.

Bantamweight—Jorge Lujan, Panama (1977), WBA; Lupe Pintor, Mexico (1979), WBC.

Junior Featherweight—Ricardo Cardona, Colombia (1978), WBA; Wilfredo Gomez, Puerto Rico (1977), WBC.

Featherweight—Eusebio Pedroza, Panama (1978), WBA; Danny Lopez, Los Angeles (1976), WBC.

Junior Lightweight—Samuel Serrano, Puerto Rico (1976), WBA; Alexis Arguello, Nicaragua (1978), WBC.

Lightweight—Ernesto Espana, Venezuela (1979), WBA; Jim Watt, Scotland (1979), WBC.

Junior Welterweight—Antonio Cervantes, Colombia (1977), WBA; Kim Sang Hyun, South Korea (1978), WBC.

Welterweight—José Cuevas, Mexico (1976), WBA; Sugar Ray Leonard, Palmer Park, MD (1979), WBC.

Junior Middleweight—Ayud Kalule, Uganda (1979), WBA; Maurice Hope, England (1979), WBC.

Middleweight—Vito Antuofermo, Brooklyn, NY (1979). Title undisputed.

Light Heavyweight—Marvin Johnson, Indianapolis, IN (1979), WBA; Matthew Saad Muhammad, Philadelphia, PA (1979), WBC.

Heavyweight—John Tate, Knoxville, TN (1979), WBA; Larry Holmes, Easton, PA (1978), WBC.

FOOTBALL

For the first time in 29 seasons, Ohio State's Buckeyes took the field in 1979 without Woody Hayes prowling the sidelines. On the pro level, the Pittsburgh Steelers took on the Los Angeles Rams in the 1980 Super Bowl.

THE COLLEGE SEASON

Woody Hayes, a veritable institution in Columbus, had been dismissed after punching a Clemson player in the last minutes of a losing Gator Bowl game. But such was Hayes' high standing among Ohio State supporters that some doubted whether Earle Bruce (or anyone else) could prove to be an adequate replacement. Not that Bruce was without credentials. He had been an Ohio State back and an aide to Hayes for six years. In 1973 he accepted the top job at Iowa State and lifted the Cyclones' sagging fortunes, compiling an overall winning record in his six-year stay.

In short order Bruce convinced the doubters. He opened up Ohio State's staid offense by installing an effective passing game, directed by sophomore quarterback Art Schlichter. Consequently, Ohio State wound up with an 11–0 won-lost record, the Big Ten title, and its first trip to the Rose Bowl since 1975.

The clincher came in the traditional climactic finale against Michigan, played at Ann Arbor before 106,255 fans, the largest crowd ever to see a regular season game. Although Ohio State won, 18–15, and Schlichter typically starred by completing 12 of 22 passes for 196 yards, the Buckeyes had to employ a rehearsed punt-block play to provide the winning points in the final period. The victory was the first over the Wolverines in four years.

The University of Southern California thought they were Rose Bowl–bound after defeating Washington for a 1½-game lead over the Huskies with one contest left. But a few days later Arizona State was required to forfeit its three conference victories (including one over Washington) when eight players were declared ineligible. So the Huskies' bowl hopes were still alive, but USC ended them by romping over the University of California, Los Angeles, 49–14.

The trojan among the Trojans was Charles White, whose four touchdowns against the Bruins put the finishing touches on a tremendous season-long performance. He paced the nation's rushers with 1,803 yards and in tribute was voted the 45th winner of the Heisman Trophy.

White was also the Rose Bowl hero in USC's 17–16 triumph. Powering a late 83-yard drive, the durable tailback ran for 72 yards, including the final yard for the deciding score with 92 seconds left to play. He set a Rose Bowl rushing record of 247 yards in 39 carries.

While Bruce was enjoying a fine rookie season at Ohio State, a veteran head coach, Paul (Bear) Bryant, who had considered retiring, was up to his custom, piloting Alabama to its fourth unbeaten season in the last nine and into the Sugar Bowl for the third straight year. What made the 66-year-old Bryant change his mind and sign a new five-year contract was the realization that he was within hailing distance of becoming the winningest college coach in history. Bryant's total of 295 victories placed him third on the career list—19 behind Amos Alonzo Stagg and 18 in back of Glenn (Pop) Warner.

Alabama continued its winning Sugar Bowl ways for coach Bryant by disposing of Arkansas, 24–9. Steadman Shealy magnificently directed the Tide's wishbone attack and never resorted to a pass. Major Ogilvie was the top runner, scoring twice.

COLLEGE FOOTBALL

Conference Champions

Atlantic Coast—North Carolina State
Big Eight—Oklahoma
Big Ten—Ohio State
Ivy League—Yale
Mid-American—Central Michigan
Missouri Valley—West Texas State
Pacific Ten—Southern California
Southeastern—Alabama
Southern—Tennessee-Chattanooga
Southwest—Arkansas, Houston (tied)
Southwestern—Alcorn State, Grambling (tied)
Western Athletic—Brigham Young
Yankee—Massachusetts

Heisman Trophy—Charles White, USC

NCAA Champions

Division I—Eastern Kentucky
Division II—Delaware
Division III—Ithaca

NAIA Champions

Division I—Texas A&I
Division II—Findlay

Major Bowl Games

Holiday Bowl (San Diego, Dec. 21)—Indiana 38, Brigham Young 37
Liberty Bowl (Memphis, Dec. 22)—Penn State 9, Tulane 6
Sun Bowl (El Paso, TX, Dec. 22)—Washington 14, Texas 7
Tangerine Bowl (Orlando, FL, Dec. 22)—Louisiana State 34, Wake Forest 10
Blue-Gray Game (Montgomery, AL, Dec. 25)—Blue 22, Gray 13
Fiesta Bowl (Tempe, AZ, Dec. 25)—Pittsburgh 16, Arizona 10
Gator Bowl (Jacksonville, FL, Dec. 28)—North Carolina 17, Michigan 15
Hall of Fame (Birmingham, AL, Dec. 29)—Missouri 24, South Carolina 14
Bluebonnet Bowl (Houston, Dec. 31)—Purdue 27, Tennessee 22
Peach Bowl (Atlanta, Dec. 31)—Baylor 24, Clemson 18
Cotton Bowl (Dallas, Jan. 1)—Houston 17, University of Nebraska 14
Orange Bowl (Miami, Jan. 1)—Oklahoma 24, Florida State 7
Rose Bowl (Pasadena, Jan. 1)—USC 17, Ohio State 16
Sugar Bowl (New Orleans, Jan. 1)—Alabama 24, Arkansas 9

Final College Rankings

	AP Writers	UPI Coaches		AP Writers	UPI Coaches
1	Alabama	Alabama	6	Florida State	Pittsburgh
2	USC	USC	7	Pittsburgh	Nebraska
3	Oklahoma	Oklahoma	8	Arkansas	Florida State
4	Ohio State	Ohio State	9	Nebraska	Arkansas
5	Houston	Houston	10	Purdue	Purdue

Pushovers during their first three years in the NFL, the Tampa Bay Buccaneers relied on a strong defense and the quarterbacking of Doug Williams (12) in reaching the National Conference championship game. A 9–0 defeat by Los Angeles ended their Super Bowl hopes.

Oklahoma qualified for the Orange Bowl after its star, Billy Sims, had his best game of the season in the Big Eight showdown against Nebraska. The 1978 Heisman winner galloped for 247 yards as the Sooners won, 20–17. That gave Barry Switzer an enviable record of having his teams win or tie for the league title all seven years he has coached at Oklahoma.

The Sooners' foe in Miami was Florida State, which parlayed the passing of Jimmy Jordan and Wally Woodham and a sturdy defense, led by nose guard Ron Simmons, into an undefeated campaign. The Seminoles, in their first major bowl appearance, were unequal to the job of stopping Oklahoma, which built a 17–7 first-half lead into a 24–7 victory. In addition to Sims, J. C. Watts proved to be a Sooner rushing threat.

In a dramatic finish, Houston won its Cotton Bowl joust with Nebraska, 17–14, on a tipped pass in the last 12 seconds.

THE PROFESSIONAL SEASON

The fact that 10 Pittsburgh Steelers were selected to play in the Pro Bowl—which pits the elite of the two National Football League (NFL) conferences—explained why that team was seeking a record fourth Super Bowl championship.

The Steelers, who were heavily favored to defeat the Los Angeles Rams in their Pasadena, CA, showdown on Jan. 20, 1980, presented a familiar cast. The Pittsburgh veterans gave an impressive demonstration of their ability to rise to the occasion when they whipped the powerful Houston Oilers, 27–13, in the American Conference (AFC) title contest. The unflappable Terry Bradshaw, after giving up a 75-yard touchdown interception to Vernon Perry in the first 2½ minutes, pitched scoring passes to John Stallworth and Bennie Cunningham in the course of a 219-yard aerial effort. On the ground, Rocky Bleier, at 34 the second oldest running back in the NFL, plunged over for the final Pittsburgh touchdown. The vaunted Steel Curtain defense, spearheaded by Mean Joe Greene, limited Earl Campbell, the league's leading rusher, to only 15 yards.

If the Steelers' drive to the Super Bowl was as predictable as a steamroller, the Rams' arrival was not. Los Angeles had to survive turmoil in the front office, a horrendous streak of injuries, and the loss of six of its first 11 games before earning its first try at a Super Bowl ring. Although the Steelers won the Super Bowl as predicted, the Rams did not go down to defeat easily. Before 103,985 persons, Bradshaw threw 2 touchdown passes and led his team to a 31–19 win.

The Tampa Bay Buccaneers were the other surprising National Conference (NFC) finalists. Picked for another last-place finish in the Central Division, the four-year-old expansion club took its first five games. At that point it

PROFESSIONAL FOOTBALL

National Football League
Final Standings

AMERICAN CONFERENCE

Eastern Division

	W	L	T	Pct.	Points For	Agst.
Miami	10	6	0	.625	341	257
New England	9	7	0	.563	411	326
Jets	8	8	0	.500	337	383
Buffalo	7	9	0	.438	268	279
Baltimore	5	11	0	.313	271	352

Central Division

	W	L	T	Pct.	For	Agst.
Pittsburgh	12	4	0	.750	416	262
Houston	11	5	0	.688	362	331
Cleveland	9	7	0	.563	359	352
Cincinnati	4	12	0	.250	337	421

Western Division

	W	L	T	Pct.	For	Agst.
San Diego	12	4	0	.750	411	246
Denver	10	6	0	.625	289	262
Oakland	9	7	0	.563	365	337
Seattle	9	7	0	.563	378	372
Kansas City	7	9	0	.438	238	262

NATIONAL CONFERENCE

Eastern Division

	W	L	T	Pct.	Points For	Agst.
Dallas	11	5	0	.688	371	313
Philadelphia	11	5	0	.688	339	282
Washington	10	6	0	.625	348	295
Giants	6	10	0	.375	237	323
St. Louis	5	11	0	.313	307	358

Central Division

	W	L	T	Pct.	For	Agst.
Tampa Bay	10	6	0	.625	273	237
Chicago	10	6	0	.625	306	249
Minnesota	7	9	0	.438	259	337
Green Bay	5	11	0	.313	246	316
Detroit	2	14	0	.125	219	365

Western Division

	W	L	T	Pct.	For	Agst.
Los Angeles	9	7	0	.563	323	309
New Orleans	8	8	0	.500	370	360
Atlanta	6	10	0	.375	300	388
San Francisco	2	14	0	.125	308	416

Play-offs
Houston 13, Denver 7
Pittsburgh 34, Miami 14
Houston 17, San Diego 14
Pittsburgh 27, Houston 13

Play-offs
Philadelphia 27, Chicago 17
Los Angeles 21, Dallas 19
Tampa Bay 24, Philadelphia 17
Los Angeles 9, Tampa Bay 0

Super Bowl: Pittsburgh 31, Los Angeles 19

was the only undefeated team in the league. A sputtering offense made the rest of the season rocky for the Bucs, who had to win on the final day to clinch the division crown. Tampa Bay owed its play-off status to a tenacious defense. Sparked by all-pro end Lee Roy Selmon, the Bucs yielded a league-low of 237 points and only 246.8 yards per game.

Although they won the Western Division for the seventh year in a row, the Rams were the perennial conference bridesmaids, having been the losers in four of the last five NFC finals. With six regulars out for the year, including first-string quarterback Pat Haden, coach Ray Malavasi faced a rebuilding task after the 5–6 beginning. Putting Vince Ferragamo at the helm, the Rams turned things around, capturing four of their last five games. An improving offensive line, a steady defense, and the emergence of second-year running back Wendell Tyler were factors in the Los Angeles comeback.

The Rams-Bucs match proved to be a defensive struggle, Los Angeles prevailing by Frank Corral's three field goals, 9–0. Doug Williams, Tampa Bay's quarterback, had an off day, connecting on only 2 of 13 passes for 12 yards until he left with a muscle injury. His successor, Mike Rae, did not fare any better. The Rams' defense, with end Jack Youngblood playing in spite of a hairline fracture in his left leg, shut down Tampa Bay's running attack, holding star Ricky Bell to 59 yards.

Upsets were the order in the conference semifinals. In perhaps the most inspired victory of the season, the Oilers jolted the San Diego Chargers, 17–14, even though quarterback Dan Pastorini, Campbell, and wide receiver Ken Burrough were unavailable because of injuries. Credit for the win belonged in large part to

Eddie Biles, Houston's defensive coordinator, who broke the hand-signal code used by the San Diego coaches to deliver the plays to quarterback Dan Fouts. Fouts had already had a banner season, erasing Joe Namath's single-season passing record with a total of 4,082 yards. But the forewarned Oilers intercepted him five times, as the Charger quarterback found himself throwing into double coverage much of the time.

A tactical gimmick developed by Bud Carson, the Rams' defensive planner, helped produce another surprise result: Los Angeles' 21–19 victory over the Dallas Cowboys. To blunt Dallas' deadly air attack, the Rams used a "7-defense" on obvious passing downs, taking out linebackers and employing seven backs.

In the third upset, Tampa Bay keyed on Philadelphia Eagle running back Wilbert Montgomery and came away with a 24–17 triumph.

Only the Steelers were immune to upset. Manhandling Miami's three-front defensive line, the Steelers rolled to an early 20–0 advantage and trounced the Dolphins, 34–14.

The 1979–80 season marked the end of two illustrious careers, as O. J. Simpson and Jim Marshall decided to hang up their cleats. After 11 seasons with the Buffalo Bills and San Francisco 49'ers, Simpson retired with a career total of 11,236 yards—including an incredible 2,003 in 1973—second only to Jim Brown's 12,312. Marshall, who starred at defensive end for the Minnesota Vikings for 20 years, extended his consecutive-game playing streak to 282 regular season contests.

In the Canadian Football League, the Edmonton Eskimos defeated the Montreal Alouettes, 17–9, for their second consecutive Grey Cup.

LUD DUROSKA, *The New York Times*

GOLF

It was the same old story, with some variations, on the United States professional golf tours in 1979. Tom Watson and Nancy Lopez again were the dominant players, but there was enough glory and plenty of money left over for a lot of others.

On the Professional Golfers Association (PGA) Tour, Watson led all categories for the third year in a row. He won five tournaments, banked a record $462,636 in winnings, won the Vardon Trophy for low stroke average with a 70.21, topped the *Golf Digest* performance averages with a .799 rating, and again was named the PGA player of the year.

But Watson came up empty in the major tournaments for the second straight year. The closest he came was in the Masters, where he tied with Fuzzy Zoeller and Ed Sneed, who bogeyed the last three holes to toss away a seemingly sure victory. Zoeller won it with a birdie on the second play-off hole.

The U. S. Open at Inverness in Toledo was, as usual, a survival test. Hale Irwin, the 1974 Open winner, survived again with even-par 284, to become only the 14th golfer to win this championship more than once.

Severiano Ballesteros, the young Spanish star, played mostly from the rough and sand traps but shot 283 for a three-stroke victory in the British Open over Americans Ben Crenshaw and Jack Nicklaus.

In the PGA, David Graham double-bogeyed the last hole, but still shot 65 and won the title on the third hole of a play-off with Crenshaw at Oakland Hill, Birmingham, MI.

Lon Hinkle deliberately skipped a shot across a pond in the third round and went on to win the World Series of Golf at Firestone C. C. in Akron, OH. Larry Nelson, who double-bogeyed the 71st hole in the World Series to lose the $100,000 first prize, won the first two tournaments of his career in 1979 and was second on the money list with $281,022. He also starred in the United States' 17–11 victory over Great Britain-Europe in the Ryder Cup matches, participating in five winning matches. All this earned Nelson *Golf Digest*'s most improved professional award.

John Fought won back-to-back tournaments late in the year and was named rookie of the year by *Golf Digest*.

Perhaps the biggest story of 1979 was the fact that Jack Nicklaus played in only 12 U. S. tournaments, won none and earned only $59,434, his worst season ever after dominating world golf since 1962. Nicklaus, who would turn 40 in January 1980, hinted that he would cut back his schedule even more in 1980.

On the Ladies Professional Golfers Association tour, Nancy Lopez won eight tournaments and a record $197,489. She won the Vare Trophy for low stroke average with 71.20, topped the *Golf Digest* performance averages with .816, and repeated as player of the year.

But Lopez also failed to win a major tournament. Donna Caponi Young out-dueled Jerilyn Britz to win the LPGA Championship at Kings Island in Ohio with a 279 total. Five weeks later, Britz won the U. S. Women's Open at Brooklawn in Fairfield, CT, with an even-par 284 total. It was the first victory of her six-year professional career and earned her the *Golf Digest* most improved professional of the year award.

LARRY DENNIS
Associate Editor, "Golf Digest"

WIDE WORLD

Jerilyn Britz (*left*) displays her cup after winning the 1979 U. S. Women's Open. Fuzzy Zoeller dons the Green Jacket, symbolic of the Masters Tournament championship.

UPI

GOLF

Winners—1979 PGA Tour

Bob Hope Desert Classic: John Mahaffey (343)
Phoenix Open: Ben Crenshaw (199)
San Diego Open: Fuzzy Zoeller (282)
Bing Crosby National Pro-Am: Lon Hinkle (284*)
Tucson Open: Bruce Lietzke (265)
Tournament Players Championship: Lanny Wadkins (283)
Masters: Fuzzy Zoeller (280*)
Tournament of Champions: Tom Watson (275)
Byron Nelson Classic: Tom Watson (275*)
Kemper Open: Jerry McGee (272)
U.S. Open: Hale Irwin (284)
Canadian Open: Lee Trevino (281)
Western Open: Larry Nelson (286*)
PGA: D. Graham (272*)
Hall of Fame Classic: Tom Watson (272*)
B. C. Open: Howard Twitty (270)
World Series: Lon Hinkle (272)
Pensacola Open: C. Strange (271)
National Team Classic: Burns/Crenshaw

Winners—LPGA Tour

Elizabeth Arden: Amy Alcott (285*)
Sunstar Classic: Nancy Lopez (280)
Sahara National: Nancy Lopez (274)
Kemper Open: JoAnne Carner (286*)
Colgate-Dinah Shore Tournament: Sandra Post (276)
Lady Citrus Classic: Jane Blalock (286*)
Women's International: Nancy Lopez (282)
Coca-Cola Classic: Nancy Lopez (216*)
Golden Lights: Nancy Lopez (280)
LPGA: Donna Young (279)
Sarah Coventry: Jane Blalock (280)
Lady Keystone Open: Nancy Lopez (212)
U.S. Open: Jerilyn Britz (284)
European Open: Nancy Lopez (282)
Team Championship: Nancy Lopez/Jo Ann Washam (198)
Dallas: Nancy Lopez (274)

Other Tournaments

British Amateur: Jay Sigel
British Open: Severiano Ballesteros, Spain
Ryder Cup: United States
U.S. Amateur: Mark O'Meara
U.S. Public Links: Dennis Walsh
U.S. Women's Amateur: Carolyn Hill
Walker Cup: United States

* denotes play-off

HOCKEY

The 1978–79 National Hockey League (NHL) season was an exquisite reflection of the year before. The Montreal Canadiens, despite finishing second behind the New York Islanders in the regular season standings, won their fourth consecutive Stanley Cup and the 22nd in their impeccable history. The Winnipeg Jets won the World Hockey Association's (WHA's) Avco Cup—and the league's last championship—for the second straight year. And the Soviet Union, which manhandled the NHL all-stars in a three-game, midseason series in New York, swept to its 14th world championship in 17 seasons.

NHL. There were several notable developments during the season, but the one which attracted the most attention took place away from the thud and thwack of the arena. On March 22, 1979, the NHL Board of Governors ratified a proposal to merge with the rival WHA for the 1979–80 season. According to the agreement, four WHA teams—Edmonton, Winnipeg, Quebec City, and New England (to become Hartford)—would enter the NHL as "expansion" clubs at a fee of $6 million each. The merger brought to an end seven years of litigation, competition for players, and other expensive infighting between the two leagues.

On the ice, cracks started to show in the ranks of the Canadiens' dynasty even though the team won its fourth straight Stanley Cup. Montreal finished one point behind the Islanders (116–115) in the regular season race, and many observers regarded their presence in the Stanley Cup final as the product of remarkably good fortune. The Canadiens had trailed with less than two minutes left in the seventh and deciding game of their semifinal series against the Boston Bruins. Guy Lafleur scored the tying goal with only 1:14 remaining, and Yvon Lambert knocked home the winning shot in overtime after the Bruins had missed several shots.

As the Canadiens were squeaking past the Bruins, the New York Rangers were eliminating the crosstown Islanders in what could be de-

UPI

Superior goaltending by the New York Rangers' John Davidson could not keep the Montreal Canadiens—or the puck—away from the net in the Stanley Cup finals.

scribed as a thunderous upset. Formidable goal-tending by John Davidson and an aroused defense stymied NHL scoring champion Bryan Trottier and goal-scoring leader Mike Bossy. The Rangers won the series 4 games to 2 and gained a berth in the finals against Montreal.

Suddenly, Stanley Cup fever was in New York. The last time the Rangers had reached the finals was 1972, and a New York team had

not won the Cup since 1940. But when the Rangers came into Montreal for the first game of the Stanley Cup final and outclassed Canadiens, 4–1, the fever reached epidemic proportions. The Cup seemed destined for New York.

Alas, it was not to be. After falling behind, 2–0, early in the second game, the Canadiens regained their poise and stormed back to win 6–2. In New York's Madison Square Garden, the defending champions won the next two games, 4–1 and 4–3, and then closed out the series with a 4–1 victory on home ice.

After the season, however, the cracks in Montreal seemed to widen even further. Coach Scott Bowman was lost to the Buffalo Sabres; goalie Ken Dryden, co-winner of the Vezina Trophy, retired to pursue his legal career; veteran center Jacques Lemaire, who led the playoffs in scoring with 11 goals and 12 assists, left to be the player-coach for a team in Switzerland; and Director of Player Personnel Al MacNeil accepted an offer to coach the Atlanta Flames, replacing Fred Creighton.

WHA. Edmonton Oilers finished first in a reduced (six-team) World Hockey Association, but then lost to Winnipeg in the play-off finals. The Jets' victory, 4 games to 2, was an upset of generous proportions because they had gone into the season without Bobby Hull, who had retired, and Swedish superstars Anders Hedberg and Ulf Nilsson, who had been snatched away by the NHL's Rangers.

World Cup. The high point of the season for the Soviet national team was their 9–2 defeat of Canada for their second consecutive amateur world championship. But the accomplishment that attracted the most attention was their resounding victory over the NHL's best in the February Challenge Cup. In the three-game series at Madison Square Garden, the NHL won the first game, 4–2, lost the second game, 5–4, and was shelled, 6–0, by the Soviets in Game 3.

RED FISHER
Sports Editor, "The Montreal Star"

HOCKEY

National Hockey League
(Final Standings, 1978–79)

Campbell Conference

Patrick Division

	W	L	T	Pts.	Goals For	Goals Against
*N.Y. Islanders	51	15	14	116	358	214
*Philadelphia	40	25	15	95	281	248
*N.Y. Rangers	40	29	11	91	316	292
*Atlanta	41	31	8	90	327	280

Smythe Division

	W	L	T	Pts.	For	Against
*Chicago	29	36	15	73	244	277
*Vancouver	25	42	13	63	217	291
St. Louis	18	50	12	48	249	348
Colorado	15	53	12	42	210	331

Wales Conference

Norris Division

	W	L	T	Pts.	For	Against
*Montreal	52	17	11	115	337	204
*Pittsburgh	36	31	13	85	281	279
*Los Angeles	34	34	12	80	292	286
Washington	24	41	15	63	273	338
Detroit	23	41	16	62	252	295

Adams Division

	W	L	T	Pts.	For	Against
*Boston	43	23	14	100	316	270
*Buffalo	36	28	16	88	280	263
*Toronto	34	33	13	81	267	252
Minnesota	28	40	12	68	257	289

*Made play-offs

Stanley Cup: Montreal Canadiens

Challenge Cup: USSR 2 games, NHL All-Stars 1

INDIVIDUAL HONORS

Hart Trophy (most valuable player): Bryan Trottier, N.Y. Islanders
Ross Trophy (leading scorer): Bryan Trottier
Norris Trophy (best defenseman): Denis Potvin, N.Y. Islanders
Lady Byng Trophy (sportsmanship): Bob MacMillan, Atlanta Flames
Vezina Trophy (top goaltender, shared): Ken Dryden and Michel Larocque, Montreal Canadiens
Calder Trophy (rookie of the year): Bobby Smith, Minnesota North Stars
Conn Smythe Trophy (most valuable in play-offs): Bob Gainey, Montreal Canadiens
Coach of the Year: Al Arbour, N.Y. Islanders

World Hockey Association
(Final Standings, 1978–79)

	W	L	T	Pts.	Goals For	Goals Against
*Edmonton	48	30	2	98	340	266
*Quebec	41	34	5	87	288	271
*Winnipeg	39	35	6	84	307	306
*New England	37	34	9	83	298	287
*Cincinnati	33	41	6	72	274	284
Birmingham	32	42	6	70	286	311
**Indianapolis	5	18	2	12	78	130

* Made play-offs
** Team disbanded in 1978

Avco Cup: Winnipeg Jets

INDIVIDUAL HONORS

Gordie Howe Trophy (most valuable player): Dave Dryden, Edmonton Oilers
Leading Scorer: Réal Cloutier, Québec Nordiques
Murphy Trophy (best defenseman): Rick Ley, New England Whalers
Deneau Trophy (sportsmanship): Kent Nilsson, Winnipeg Jets
Hatskin Trophy (top goaltender): Dave Dryden
Kaplan Award (rookie of the year): Wayne Gretzky, Edmonton Oilers
Most Valuable Player in Play-offs: Rich Preston, Winnipeg Jets
Coach of the Year: John Brophy, Birmingham Bulls

Intercollegiate Champions

NCAA: University of Minnesota

HORSE RACING

In 1979, Affirmed won the Horse of the Year award for the second year in a row and in the process became the leading money-winner in thoroughbred racing history. Owned by the Harbor View Farm of Louis Wolfson, Affirmed finished his career with earnings of $2,393,818, breaking the record of $1,977,896 set by Kelso.

Affirmed, who was bred in Florida and finally retired to stud at Spendthrift Farm in Kentucky, won 22 of 29 races in his three-year career. In 1979, he triumphed in seven of nine starts and earned $1,148,800. His 1979 victories included the Strub Stakes, Santa Anita Handicap, Californian, Hollywood Gold Cup, Woodward, and Jockey Club Gold Cup.

In the Jockey Club Gold Cup, Affirmed defeated two standout 3-year-olds—Spectacular

Bid, the winner of the Kentucky Derby and Preakness, and Coastal, who captured the Belmont Stakes.

Spectacular Bid, owned by the Hawksworth Farm, won 10 of 12 races and set a record for most money earned in a single season, $1,279,-334.

Laz Barrera, the conditioner of Affirmed, and Laffit Pincay, Jr., who rode that horse to all seven of his 1979 victories, also set records for most money earned in one year by a trainer and jockey, respectively. Barrera's horses earned $3,-563,147, and Pincay's mounts won $8,183,535. Barrera and Pincay also won Eclipse awards for best trainer and best jockey, respectively, the fourth time that each has been so honored.

Rockhill Native, trained by veteran Kentucky horseman Herb Stevens, was voted the best racehorse among 2-year-old colts and geldings. Greentree Stable's Bowl Game won acclaim as the best male grass horse.

Harness Racing. Niatross won all 13 of his starts in 1979 to become the first 2-year-old pacing colt to go undefeated since Bret Hanover in 1964. Niatross earned $604,900, a record for 2-year-old harness horses or thoroughbreds.

Quarter Horses. Pie In The Sky won the $1.2-million All American Futurity at Ruidoso Downs. He triumphed by a length-and-a-half and was timed in 21.76 seconds for the 440 yards.

Sales. At Keeneland's summer auction, Tom Gentry sold a son of Hoist the Flag for $1.6 million, a record price for a yearling sold at public auction.

JIM BOLUS
Sports Department
"The Louisville Times," Louisville, KY

UPI

Regina Sackl of Austria slaloms to victory in women's World Cup skiing competition at Les Gets, France.

SKIING

Peter Luescher of Switzerland and Annemarie Proell Moser of Austria won overall World Cup titles in 1979. Ingemar Stenmark of Sweden, 1978 overall champion, swept 10 giant slaloms in posting 13 victories and breaking the record of 12 set by Jean-Claude Killy of France. In the Nations Cup team standing, Austria was first (1,757 points), followed by Switzerland (1,224), Italy (996), and the United States (959).

Stenmark took both slalom crowns, but was fifth overall. He did not compete in the downhill. Peter Mueller of Switzerland, with 109 points, took the downhill.

Luescher won with 186 points. Leonard Stock of Austria was runner-up with 183. Phil Mahre of White Pass, WA, who missed the last six races because of a broken leg, was third with 155, and Piero Gros of Italy wound up fourth with 152. Stenmark had 150 points.

Mrs. Moser captured her sixth overall crown. Her second place in the season's last race, the giant slalom, enabled her to overtake Hanni Wenzel of Liechtenstein, the 1978 champion. She trailed Miss Wenzel, 240–220, going into the final. She earned 23 points and won with 243. Miss Wenzel finished fifth in the event and failed to score any points. Regina Sackl of Austria took the slalom title with 105 points and Christa Kinshofer of East Germany gained giant slalom honors with 125. Mrs. Moser also won the downhill championship with a total of 125 points.

GEORGE DE GREGORIO

HORSE RACING

Major U. S. Thoroughbred Races

Alabama Stakes: It's in the Air, $108,300 (value of race)
Belmont Stakes: Coastal, $269,000
Californian: Affirmed, $272,400
Coaching Club American Oaks: Davona Dale, $132,625
Gulfstream Park Handicap: Sensitive Prince, $150,000
Hialeah Turf Cup: Bowl Game, $132,250
Hollywood Gold Cup: Affirmed, $500,000
Jockey Club Gold Cup: Affirmed, $375,000
Kentucky Derby: Spectacular Bid, $317,400
Man O' War Stakes: Bowl Game, $137,375
Marlboro Cup: Spectacular Bid, $300,000
Meadowlands Cup: Spectacular Bid, $361,000
Preakness Stakes: Spectacular Bid, $235,300
Ruffian Handicap: It's in the Air, $133,125
San Juan Capistrano Handicap: Tiller, $200,000
Santa Anita Handicap: Affirmed, $312,800
Suburban Handicap: State Dinner, $131,875
Travers: General Assembly, $134,750
Turf Classic: Bowl Game, $250,000
Washington, DC International: Bowl Game, $200,000
Woodward Stakes: Affirmed, $191,000

Major U. S. Harness Races

Cane Pace: Happy Motoring, $336,420
Hambletonian: Legend Hanover, $300,000
Kentucky Futurity: Classical Way, $100,000
Kentucky Pacing Derby: Niatross, $204,000
Little Brown Jug: Hot Hitter, $226,455
Meadowlands Pace: Sonsam, $750,000
Messenger Stake: Hot Hitter, $180,225
Roosevelt International: Doublemint, $200,000
Woodrow Wilson: Niatross, $862,750
Yonkers Trot: Chiola Hanover, $237,765

SOCCER

In 1979, U. S. soccer continued to grow, both on and off the field. The North American Soccer League (NASL) reported the highest attendance figures in its 13-year history—5,800,-459 total and an average of 14,911 per match. And even though the league remained at 24 teams, it also grew in the sense that it got rid of its one-horse image.

Ever since Pelé first stepped on the field in 1976, the NASL had been totally dominated by the New York Cosmos. The Cosmos, who won consecutive league titles in 1977 and 1978, appeared well on the way to a third championship in 1979. Their 24–6 regular season record was the best in the league.

But a funny thing happened to the Cosmos on the way to Soccer Bowl '79. They lost the National Conference finals to the Vancouver Whitecaps in a dramatic shootout on their home field. Vancouver then completed its Cinderella season by beating the Tampa Bay Rowdies, 2–1, in the September 8 title game, also held at the Cosmos' Giants Stadium. It was the second straight Soccer Bowl defeat for the Rowdies.

The Cosmos' Giorgio Chinaglia failed in his bid for a third consecutive scoring title, losing out to Tampa Bay's Oscar Fabbiani, 58–57. The NASL crowned a new most valuable player (MVP) in 1979—the legendary Dutch star Johan Cruyff. Cruyff, who scored two goals in his first seven minutes of play for the Los Angeles Aztecs, was the biggest name in a horde of internationally-known players who came into the league during the season. Others were Fabbiani, a four-time scoring champion in Chile; West German international Gerd Mueller and Peruvian World Cup star Teofilo Cubillas, both to Fort Lauderdale; English first division scoring champion Frank Worthington, to Philadelphia; Mexican internationals Leonardo Cuellar and Hugo Sanchez, to San Diego; Dutch star Johan Neeskens, to the Cosmos; English standout Alan Hudson, to Seattle; and Scottish international Willie Johnston, to Vancouver.

But the NASL also lost some big names in 1979. New England's Mike Flanagan, the 1978 MVP, did not return from England. Tampa Bay superstar Rodney Marsh announced his retirement, effective after Soccer Bowl '79. Coach Eddie Firmani of the Cosmos was fired in midseason despite a 9–2 start and two straight Soccer Bowl titles.

Firmani wound up coaching the New Jersey Americans of the American Soccer League (ASL), and his presence gave that league new credibility. The Sacramento Gold won the ASL title, beating the Columbus Magic, 1–0, in the championship match. Ian Filby of Sacramento won the league scoring title and Poli Garcia of California the MVP award.

A new soccer league began play during the winter of 1978–79 and took the game indoors. The Major Indoor Soccer League (MISL) did not compete with the NASL on or off the field, but it did borrow one full team (Houston) and a number of top-notch players. Among these was goalie Shep Messing of Rochester, who led the New York Arrows to the MISL title and won the league's MVP award.

On the international circuit, it was a year of Olympic qualifying matches. The United States lost consecutive first round matches to Mexico but protested both defeats, claiming that the Mexicans had used professional players. Mexico later withdrew because of the claim, and the U. S. team advanced to the next round against Bermuda.

JIM HENDERSON, *"Tampa Tribune"*

SOCCER

North American Soccer League
(Final Standings, 1979)

National Conference

East

	W.	L	G.F.	G.A.	Pts.
New York.	24	6	84	52	216
Washington	19	11	68	50	172
Toronto	14	16	52	65	133
Rochester	15	15	43	57	132

Central

Minnesota	21	9	67	48	184
Dallas	17	13	53	51	152
Tulsa	14	16	61	56	139
Atlanta	12	18	59	61	121

West

Vancouver	20	10	54	34	172
Los Angeles	18	12	62	47	162
Seattle	13	17	58	52	125
Portland	11	19	50	75	112

American Conference

East

Tampa Bay	19	11	67	46	169
Fort Lauderdale	17	13	75	65	165
Philadelphia	10	20	55	60	111
New England	12	18	41	56	110

Central

Houston	22	8	61	46	187
Chicago	16	14	70	62	159
Detroit	14	16	61	56	133
Memphis	6	24	38	74	73

West

San Diego	15	15	59	55	140
California	15	15	53	56	140
Edmonton	8	22	43	78	88
San Jose	8	22	41	74	86

NASL Champion: Vancouver Whitecaps
NASL MVP: John Cruyff, Los Angeles Aztecs
ASL Champion: Sacramento Gold
MISL Champion: New York Arrows
European Cup: Nottingham Forest
NCAA Champion: University of Southern Illinois, Edwardsville

SWIMMING

U. S. swimmers dominated every meet they entered in 1979. The combined men's and women's team walked off with 28 of 29 gold medals at the Pan American Games in San Juan, PR, and made a strong showing at the World Cup in Tokyo (see table below). The U. S. women's team, which failed to win a single individual event at the Montreal Olympics in 1976, established itself as a formidable threat to East German supremacy at the 1980 Games in Moscow.

Cynthia Woodhead, Tracy Caulkins, Kim Linehan, and 14-year-old butterfly specialist

Mary T. Meagher led the way. Miss Meagher, from Louisville, KY, bettered the world record in the 200-m butterfly three times in six weeks. Her time of 2 minutes 9.77 seconds in San Juan in July clipped 0.1 second from the world mark. Then at the long-course championships in Fort Lauderdale, FL, she lowered it to 2:08.41 in a preliminary heat and to 2:07.1 in the final.

Miss Woodhead, 15, from Riverside, CA, won five gold medals at the Pan Am Games, captured three events at the AAU long-course meet and lowered her world record in the 200-m freestyle to 1:58.23 in the World Cup. Miss Caulkins, 16, from Nashville, TN, set five U. S. records in the AAU short-course championships and won the two individual medleys and one breaststroke title in the long-course meet. Miss Linehan, 16, of Sarasota, FL, set a world mark of 16:04.49 in the 1,500-m freestyle at Fort Lauderdale.

In the men's AAU long-course championships, freestylist Ambrose Gaines won four gold medals, Brian Goodell posted two victories in long-distance freestyle events, and Jesse Vassallo won both individual medleys, with a world mark of 2:03.29 in the 200 m.

GEORGE DE GREGORIO

TENNIS

If 1979 was what the United Nations decreed as the International Year of the Child, tennis fit the pattern perfectly. Kids took over the professional game. John McEnroe, 20, the brash basher from Douglaston, NY, won the U. S. Open at Flushing Meadow, 10 minutes from where he grew up—though some cynics insist he has not. The fiery McEnroe soared from 255 to 3 in the world rankings in 18 months. He is clearly the most gifted all-around athlete in tennis today, and if he continues to develop as comprehensively as he did in 1979, tennis historians will start to look for him among the "all-time greats." McEnroe's serve is devastating, his ability to change direction uncanny, and his flair for the volley magical. As a tribute to his versatility, he is the only superstar who excels in doubles as well as singles—ranking number one in the world with Peter Fleming in the tandem game.

Tracy Austin, 17, started to do what Chris Evert (now Mrs. John Lloyd) did in 1974—except that she is doing it at a younger age. Austin at 16 became the youngest player ever to win the U. S. Open, destroying Martina Navratilova and Evert without losing a set. As 1979 ended, Austin ranked number three among all professionals, and, on a slow surface, no one is better. It is hard to imagine, but Austin's strokes are more compact than Evert's, which means Tracy hits the ball harder with less effort and greater consistency than the Cinderella who gave new dimension to the trait "steady" during her five years as undisputed queen of tennis.

The youth parade did not stop with Austin. Czech Hana Mandlikova (17), and the Americans Bettina Bunge (17) and Pam Shriver (17), all slotted for sure future stardom, were being chased themselves by Americans Andrea Jaeger (15) and Kathleen Horvath (14). And in terms of total racquet handling ability, the brigade of boys and girls in the 12 and 14 age divisions was astounding.

Two personal achievements bear particular mention. Martina Navratilova, the Czech defector, won Wimbledon for the second straight year (see BIOGRAPHY). More notable, however, was the performance of Björn Borg who set a modern record by winning Wimbledon for the fourth year in succession. Borg also won the French Championship, and, with two legs of the Grand Slam in hand going into the U. S. Open, he was the clear favorite for the title. But he was ambushed at Flushing by the rifle serve of Roscoe Tanner who had already nearly defeated the great Swede in a five-set Wimbledon final.

Since 1978, there has been only a reshuffling of the superstar deck with the major change being Guillermo Vilas sinking from three to six and Borg clearly topping Jimmy Connors for the first time in five years. The year's final order was: 1. Borg, 2. Connors, 3. McEnroe, 4. Vitas Gerulaitis, 5. Tanner, 6. Vilas. The major change among the women was the disappearance of Billie Jean King from the ranks of the top ten, though the inimitable leader of the women's movement in sports and elsewhere began her fourth comeback and finally fetched that record 20th title at Wimbledon. She and Navratilova took the doubles.

The United States dominated the men's and women's team competitions, winning the Federation, Wightman, and Davis cups.

TENNIS

Major Team Competitions

Davis Cup: United States.
Federation Cup: United States.
Wightman: United States.

Major Tournaments

U.S. Open—Men's Singles: John McEnroe; women's singles: Tracy Austin; men's doubles: Peter Fleming and John McEnroe; women's doubles: Betty Stove and Wendy Turnbull; men's 35 singles: Marty Riessen; women's 35 singles: Renée Richards; junior men's singles: Scott Davis; junior women's singles: Alycia Moulton; Hall of Fame doubles: Fred Stolle and Dick Savitt.

U.S. Open Clay Court Championships—Men's Singles: Jimmy Connors; women's singles: Chris Evert Lloyd; men's doubles: John McEnroe and Gene Mayer; women's doubles: Kathy Jordan and Anne Smith.

U.S. National Indoors—Men's Singles: Jimmy Connors; men's doubles: Wojtek Fibak and Tom Okker.

National Men's 35 Clay Court Championship—Men's Singles: Butch Newman; men's doubles: Butch Newman and Jimmy Parker.

U.S.T.A. Women's Clay Court Championship—Women's Senior Singles: Nancy Richey; 35 doubles: Cathie Anderson and Nancy Richey; 45 singles: Nancy Reed; 45 doubles: Charlene Grafton and Nancy Neeld; 55 singles: Dodo Cheney; 55 doubles: Phyllis Adler and Dodo Cheney.

National Jr. Boy's 18's—Singles: Scott Davis; doubles: DePalmer and Harmon.

National Girl's 18's—Singles: Andrea Jaeger; doubles: Andrea Jaegar and Susan Jaegar.

Colgate Grand Prix Masters—Men's Singles: John McEnroe; men's doubles: Peter Fleming and John McEnroe.

Other U. S. Championships

NCAA (Division 1)—Singles: Kevin Curren (Texas); doubles: Erik Iskersky and Ben McKown.

NAIA—Singles: Garry Seymour (S. W. Texas State).

AIAW—Singles: Kathy Jordan (Stanford); doubles Kathy Jordan and Alycia Moulton; team: University of Southern California.

Professional Championships

U.S. Pro Championships—Men's Singles: José Higueras; men's doubles: Wojtek Fibak and Tom Okker.

World Championship Tennis Tour—Men's Singles: John McEnroe; men's doubles: John McEnroe and Peter Fleming.

Other Countries

Wimbledon—Men's Singles: Björn Borg; women's singles: Martina Navratilova; men's doubles: Peter Fleming and John McEnroe; women's doubles: Billy Jean King and Martina Navratilova; junior boys: Ramesh Kirshnan; junior girls: Mary Louise Piatek.

Australian Open—Men's Singles: Guillermo Vilas; men's doubles: Wojtek Fibak and Kim Warwick; women's singles: Chris O'Neil; women's doubles: Betsy Nagelsen and Renata Tomanova.

French Open—Men's Singles: Björn Borg; men's doubles: Sandy Mayer and Gene Mayer; women's singles: Chris Evert Lloyd; women's doubles: Betty Stove and Wendy Turnbull.

Italian Open—Men's Singles: Vitas Gerulaitis; men's doubles: Peter Fleming and Tomas Smid; women's singles: Tracy Austin; women's doubles: Betty Stove and Wendy Turnbull.

Canadian Open—Men's Singles: Björn Borg; men's doubles: John McEnroe and Peter Fleming; women's singles: Laura DuPont; women's doubles: Lea Antonopolis and Dianne Evers.

LEADING MONEY WINNERS IN 1979

Men's Tournament Earnings

Björn Borg	$659,345	Guillermo Vilas	$244,195
John McEnroe	600,238	Eddie Dibbs	206,793
Jimmy Connors	476,340	Roscoe Tanner	203,433
Vitas Gerulaitis	324,515	Wojtek Fibak	192,452
Peter Fleming	290,715	Harold Solomon	174,578

Men's Overall Earnings

Björn Borg	$1,019,345	Peter Fleming	$353,315
John McEnroe	1,005,238	Roscoe Tanner	263,433
Jimmy Connors	701,340	Eddie Dibbs	249,293
Vitas Gerulaitis	414,515	Wojtek Fibak	234,452
Guillermo Vilas	374,195	Harold Solomon	222,078

Women's Tournament Earnings

Martina Navratilova	$594,248	Sue Barker	$158,519
Tracy Austin	343,010	Betty Stove	155,006
Chris Evert Lloyd	329,632	Evonne Goolagong	132,573
Wendy Turnbull	255,463	Virginia Wade	127,950
Dianne Fromholtz	161,690	Billie Jean King	115,804

Women's Overall Earnings

Martina Navratilova	$747,548	Billie Jean King	$185,804
Chris Evert Lloyd	564,398	Betty Stove	182,006
Tracy Austin	541,676	Sue Barker	175,542
Wendell Turnbull	317,463	Evonne Goolagong	171,573
Dianne Fromholtz	265,990	Virginia Wade	146,283

Youth conquers at the U. S. Open: John McEnroe, 20, won the men's singles title and Tracy Austin, 16, became the youngest to capture the women's single crown.

UPI   UPI

Politically, the world of tennis was relatively quiet for the first time in ten years, though the game's gentle disturbances would be enough to traumatize other sports totally. Despite last minute gasps, World Team Tennis finally died after five seasons of near success. The world's top five players were not intimidated by coercive grand prix rules and refused to play the major men's circuit until modifications were made.

Avon replaced Virginia Slims as the biggest sponsor of women's tennis and Colgate surprised everyone by stating that 1979 would be their last year of supporting the Men's Grand Prix. Volvo was recruited to lead the men's tour.

Arthur Ashe, 36, suffered a heart attack after completing a dramatic comeback that saw him reach the finals of the Colgate Masters and U. S. Pro Indoors. Doctors disagreed with Ashe's prediction that he would be back on the tour in four months.

EUGENE L. SCOTT
Publisher, "Tennis Week"

TRACK AND FIELD

Sebastian Coe, a 22-year-old Englishman, became the toast of the track world in 1979 as he set world records in the mile, 1,500-m, and 800-m runs during July and August. No other runner had ever held simultaneously the world records for those three distances.

Coe, an honors graduate in economics and social history from Loughborough University in Leicestershire, began his assault on the record books July 5 at Bislet Stadium in Oslo, Norway. He captured the 800-m run with a clocking of 1 minute 42.4 seconds, 1.07 seconds faster than the established world record of Cuba's Alberto Juantorena.

Then on July 17, the 5′ 9½″ (1.77 m), 129 lb (58.5 kg) Coe, who is coached by his father, returned to Bislet and shattered the four-year-old world mark in the mile. His time was 3:49, 0.4 second better than the previous record of New Zealand's John Walker. Coe's startling achievement came in the fastest mile ever run; the first 10 finishers in a field of 13 were clocked under 3:55.3. Steve Scott of the United States finished second with a time of 3:51.11; another American, Craig Mosback, was third, with 3:52.02.

On August 15, before a crowd of 26,000 at Letzigrud Stadium in Zurich, Switzerland, Coe capped his remarkable season by clipping 0.1 second from the 1,500-m mark of 3:32.2 set by Tanzania's Filbert Bayi in 1974.

Track and field athletes aiming for the 1980 Olympics had several opportunities to test their skills against top international competition. The World Cup II meet in Montreal (see table), the Spartakiade Games in Moscow, and the Pan American Games in Puerto Rico were the highlights of the 1979 track and field season.

GEORGE DE GREGORIO

UPI

Defending champion Bill Rodgers wins the 83rd, and his third, Boston Marathon. He later captured New York's Marathon. Such races gained in popularity.

TRACK AND FIELD

World Cup II Championships
Men

100-m dash: James Sanford, U.S.A.
200-m dash: Silvio Leonard, Cuba
400-m dash: Kasheef Hassan, Sudan
800-m run: James Maina, Kenya
1,500-m run: Thomas Wessinghage, W. Germany
5,000-m run: Miruts Yifter, Ethiopia
10,000-m run: Miruts Yifter
3,000-m steeplechase: Kiproth Rono, Kenya
110-m hurdles: Renaldo Nehemiah, U.S.A.
400-m hurdles: Edwin Moses, U.S.A.
Pole vault: Mike Tully, U.S.A.
High jump: Franklin Jacobs, U.S.A.
Long jump: Larry Myricks, U.S.A.
Triple jump: João de Oliveira, Brazil
Hammer throw: Sergei Litvinov, U.S.S.R.
Javelin: Wolfgang Hanisch, E. Germany
Discus: Wolfgang Schmidt, E. Germany
Shot put: Udo Beyer, E. Germany
4 x 100-m relay: The Americas
4 x 400-m relay: U.S.A.

Women

100-m dash: Evelyn Ashford, U.S.A.
200-m dash: Evelyn Ashford
400-m dash: Marita Koch, E. Germany
800-m run: Nikolina Shtereva, Bulgaria
1,500-m run: Totka Petrova, Bulgaria
3,000-m run: Svetlana Ulmasova, U.S.S.R.
100-m hurdles: Grazina Rabsztyn, Poland
400-m hurdles: Barbara Klepp, E. Germany
High jump: Debbie Brill, Canada
Long jump: Anita Stukane, U.S.S.R.
Javelin throw: Ruth Fuchs, E. Germany
Discus: Evelin Jahl, E. Germany
Shot put: Ilona Slupianek, E. Germany
4 x 100-m relay: Europe

SPORTS SUMMARIES[1]

ARCHERY—World Champions: freestyle: men: Darrell Pace, Cincinnati, OH; women: Jin Ho Ki, South Korea. **National Field Archery Association:** barebow: men: Roger Arnold; women: Gloria Shelley; freestyle, open: Richard Johnson; women's open: Lonna Carter.

BADMINTON—World Champions: men: Liem Swie King, Indonesia; women: Lene Kappen, Denmark.

BIATHLON—World Champion: 20 kilometers: Klaus Seibert, East Germany; **United States:** 10 kilometers: Lyle Nelson, McCall, ID; 20 kilometers: Ken Alligood, Anchorage, AK.

BILLIARDS—World Champions: 3-cushion: Raymond Ceulemans, Belgium; pocket: Mike Segal, Towson, MD; women's pocket: Jean Balukas, Brooklyn, NY.

BOBSLEDDING—World Champions: two-man: Erich Schaerer and Josef Benz, Switzerland; four-man: West Germany.

BOWLING—American Bowling Congress: Classic Division: singles: Ed Bird, Kingston, NY (739); doubles: Nelson Burton, Jr., and Neil Burton, St. Louis (1,413); all-events: Nelson Burton, Jr. (2,079); team: Robby Automatic Positioner, Glendale, CA (3,110). Regular Division: singles: Rick Peters, Franklin, OH (761); doubles: Mike Turnbull, and Jack Wilson, Akron, OH (1,388); all-events: Bob Bessachi, Detroit (2,097); team: Hal Lieber Trophies, Gary, IN (3,262). Masters: singles: Doug Myers, El Toro, CA. **Women's International Bowling Congress:** open division: singles: Betty Morris, Stockton, CA (699); doubles: Mary Ann Deptula, Warren, MI, and Geri Beattie, Dearborn, MI; all-events: Betty Morris; team: Alpine Lanes, Euless, TX.

CANOEING—Flatwater: men's kayak: 500 and 1,000 meters: Terry White, Manchester, VT; 10,000 meters: Brent Turner, St. Charles, IL; women's kayak: 500 meters: Linda Dragan, Washington, DC; 5,000 meters: Ann Turner, St. Charles, IL; men's canoe: 500 and 1,000 meters: Roland Muhlen, Cincinnati, OH; 10,000 meters: Kurt Doberstein, Lombard, IL.

COURT TENNIS—World Champion: Howard Angus, London; **U. S. Open:** Barry Toates, Boston; **U. S. Amateur:** Ralph Howe, New York City; **U. S. Pro:** Jimmy Burke, Philadelphia.

CROSS-COUNTRY—World Champions: men: John Treacy, Ireland; women: Grete Waitz, Norway. **AAU:** men: Alberto Salazar; women: Margaret Groos.

CURLING—World Champion: Norway; **United States:** men: Bemidji, MN; women: Washington State; **Canada:** Barry Fry.

CYCLING—World Champions: track: men's sprint: Lutz Hesslich, East Germany; women's sprint: Galina Zareva, USSR; pursuit: Mikolai Makarov; time trials: Lothar Thoms, East Germany; pro sprint: Koichi Nakano, Japan; road: men: Gianni Giacomini, Italy; women: Petra de Bruin, Netherlands; pro: Jan Raas; Tour de France: Bernard Hinault. **United States Champions:** road: men: Steve Wood, Albuquerque, NM; women: Connie Carpenter, Berkeley, CA; track: men's sprint: Leigh Barczewski, West Allis, WI; women's sprint: Sue Novara, Flint, MI; men's pursuit: Dave Grylls, Grosse Point, MI; women's pursuit: Connie Carpenter; time trials: men: Andrew Weaver, Gainsville, FL; women: Beth Heiden, Madison, WI.

DOG SHOWS—Westminster (New York): Best: Ch. Oak Tree's Irishtocrat, Irish water spaniel, Anne E. Snelling owner. **International** (Chicago): Best: Ch. Lou-Gins Kiss Me Kate, standard poodle, Terri Meyers and Jack and Paulann Phelan owners.

FENCING—World Champions: men's foil: Aleksandr Romankov, USSR; men's épée: Philippe Riboud, France; men's saber: Vladimir Lazlymov, USSR; women's foil: Cornelia Hanisch, West Germany; team: men's foil, épée, and saber: USSR; women's foil: USSR. **United States Champions:** men's foil: Michael Marx, Portland, OR; men's épée: Tim Glass, San Antonio, TX; men's saber: Peter Westerbrook, New York Fencers Club; women's foil: Jana Angelakis, Peabody, MA, College. **NCAA:** foil: Andy Bonk, Notre Dame; épée: Carlo Songini, Cleveland State; saber: Yuri Rabinovich, Wayne State; team: Wayne State. **Intercollegiate Women's Fencing Association:** foil: Joy Ellingson, San Jose State; team: San Jose State.

GYMNASTICS—World Champions: men: all-round: Aleksandr Ditiatin, USSR; floor exercise: Kurt Thomas, Terre Haute, IN; rings: Aleksandr Ditiatin; vault: Aleksandr Ditiatin; horse: Zoltan Magyar, Hungary; high bar: Kurt Thomas; parallel bars: Bart Conner, Norman, OK. Women: all-round: Nelli Kim, USSR; floor exercise: Maria Filatova, USSR; balance beam: Nadia Comaneci, Rumania; bars: tie between Yanhong Ma and Maxi Gnauck; vault: tie among Dumitria Turner, Melita Ruhn, Nelli Kim, and Steffi Kraker; team: Rumania. **United States AAU:** men: all-round: Peter Kormann, New York Athletic Club; floor exercise: Steve Elliott, Nebraska; pommel horse: Dave Stoldt, Illinois; still rings: Jim Hartung, Nebraska; vault: Ron Galimore, Iowa State; parallel bars: Mike Nadour, Athletes in Action; horizontal bars: Al Kwiatkowski, unattached; team: New York A. C. Women: all-round: Jackie Cassello, Hempstead, NY; floor exercise: Kathy Johnson, Belcher, LA; balance beam: Kathy Johnson; uneven parallel bars: Shari Mann, Silver Springs, MD; vault: Jackie Cassello; team: Olympia Training Center, Belcher, LA, College. **NCAA:** all-round: Kurt Thomas; team: Nebraska. **AIAW** (women): all-round: Kolleen Casey, Southwest Missouri; team: California State-Fullerton.

HANDBALL—United States Handball Association Champions: 4-wall: singles: Naty Alvarado, Pomona, CA; doubles: Stuffy Singer and Marty Decatur, Van Nuys, CA; masters singles: Jim McKee, Memphis, TN; masters doubles: Ron Earl and Marty Goffstein, California.

HORSESHOE PITCHING—World Champions: Mark Seibold, Huntington, IN; women: Phyllis Negaard, St. Joseph, MN; senior: Stan Maker, Martinsville, OH.

HORSE SHOWS—World Cup: Hugo Simon, Austria.

ICE SKATING, FIGURE—World Champions: men: Vladimir Kovalev, USSR; women: Linda Fratianne, Northridge, CA; pairs: Tai Babalonia, Mission Hills, CA, and Randy Gardner, Los Angeles; dance: Natalie Linichuk and Gennadi Karponosov, USSR. **United States Champions:** men: Charles Tickner, Littleton, CO; women: Linda Fratianne; pairs: Tai Babalonia and Randy Gardner; dance: Stacy Smith and John Summers, Wilmington, DE.

ICE SKATING, SPEED—World Champions: men: Eric Heiden, Madison, WI; women: Beth Heiden, Madison, WI; sprint: men: Eric Heiden; women: Leah Poulos, Milwaukee. **United States Champions:** outdoors: men: Erik Henriksen, Champaign, IL; women: Gretchen Byrne, Syracuse, NY; indoors: men: Bill Lanigan, Teaneck, NJ; women: Patti Lyman, Boulder, CO.

JUDO—AAU Champions: men: 132-pound class: Keith Naksone, Honolulu; 143: James Martin, Wheeling, IL; 156: Steve Sack, Chatsworth, CA; 172: Brett Barron, San Mateo, CA; 189: Leo White, Seaside, CA; under 209: Miguel Tudela, Los Angeles; over 209: Dewey Mitchell, Tuscaloosa, AL; open: Shawn Gibbons, St. Petersburg, FL; women: 104: Mary Lewis, East Berne, NY; 113: Robin Takemori, Alexandria, VA; 123: Monica Emmerson, Daly City, CA; 134: Anne Marie Fuller, Salem, OR; 143: Dolores Brodie, Los Angeles; under 158: Christine Penick, Los Angeles; over 158: Margaret Castro, New York City; open: Barbara Fest, Boston.

KARATE—AAU Champions: men's kata, advanced: Albert Pena, Haverstraw, NY; women's kata, advanced: Vickie Johnson, Central; men's weapon kata: Glen Hart, New England; women's weapon kata: Katherine Loakopolos, Metropolitan; men's kumite: open: Tokay Hill, Chillicothe, OH; advanced heavyweight: Mike Powell, New Jersey; women's kumite, advanced: Andrea Clark, Metropolitan.

LACROSSE—NCAA: Division I: Johns Hopkins; Division II: Roanoke; women: Penn State.

LUGE—World: men: Detlef Guenther, East Germany; women: Melitta Sollmann, East Germany; doubles: Hans Brandner and Balthasar Schwarm, West Germany. **United States Champions:** men: Frank Masley, Newark, DE; women: Donna Burke, Lake Placid, NY; doubles: Gary Schmeusner, Wilmington, DE, and Ty Danco, Pepper Pike, OH.

MODERN PENTATHLON—World Champion: men: Robert Nieman, Hinsdale, IL. **United States Champion:** men: Mike Burley, Berea, OH.

PADDLE TENNIS—United States Open Doubles Champions: Sol Hauptman and Jeff Fleitner, Brooklyn, NY.

POLO—National Champions: open division: Retama, San Antonio, TX; gold cup: Retama.

PLATFORM TENNIS—United States Champions: men's doubles: Clark Graebner, Greenwich, CT, and Doug Russell, New York City; women's doubles: Yvonne Hackenberg, Kalamazoo, MI, and Linda Wolf, New Canaan, CT.

RACQUETS—United States Champions: singles: William Surtees, New York City; doubles: William Surtees and Ed Ullmann, New York City; open: William Surtees.

RACQUETBALL—United States Champions: men: Marty Hogan, St. Louis; women: Karin Walton, San Clemente.

RODEO—United States Champion: all-round: Tom Ferguson, Miami, OK.

ROLLER SKATING—World Champions: men: Michael Butske, West Germany; women: Petra Schneider, West Germany; dance: Fleurette Arseneault, Cambridge, MA, and Dan Littel. Farmingdale, NJ; pairs: Karen Mejia, Chicago, and Ray Chappatta, Palos Hills, IL. **United States Champions:** men: singles: Michael Glatz, San Diego, CA; women: singles: Moana Pitcher, San Diego; international singles: men: Lex Kane, Toledo, OH; women: Joanne Young, Virginia Beach, VA; pairs: Tina Kneisley and Paul Price, Mansfield, OH; dance: Fleurette Arseneault and Dan Littel.

ROWING—World: heavyweight: single sculls: Pertti Karppinen, Finland; double sculls: Frank and Alf Hansen, Norway; pairs without coxswain: Jorg and Bernd Landvoigt, East Germany; pairs with coxswain: Gerd Uebler, Juergen Pfeiffer, Georg Spohr (coxswain), East Germany; fours with coxswain: East Germany; fours without coxswain: East Germany; eights: East Germany; women: single sculls: Sanda Toma; double sculls: Cornelia Linse and Heidi Westphal; quadruple sculls: East Germany; pairs: East Germany; fours: East Germany; eights: East Germany. **United States Champions:** men: singles: Greg Stone, Harvard; singles (quarter-mile dash): Jim Dietz, New York Athletic Club; lightweight singles: Bill Belden, New York A. C.; doubles: Bill Belden and Jim Dietz, New York A. C.; pairs with coxswain: Tom Woodman, John Chatzky, Philip Stekl (coxswain), University of Pennsylvania; lightweight doubles: Larry Klecatsky and Bill Belden, New York A. C.; pairs with coxswain: David Fellows and Richard Cashin, Harvard; lightweight pairs:

Tai Babalonia and Randy Gardner of California give a beautiful performance to win the pairs competition at the World Figure Skating Championships in Vienna, Austria, in March.

UPI

J. Duke and H. Hodgson, Union Boat Club; fours: University of Pennsylvania; fours with coxswain: Harvard Combination; lightweight fours without coxswain: St. Catherines, Ontario; lightweight fours: U.S. Lightweight Eight Team A; eights: University of Pennsylvania Combination; lightweight eights: U.S. Lightweight Camp. **Intercollegiate Champions:** IRA: eights: Brown; junior varsity eights: Northeastern; freshman eights: Wisconsin; pairs with coxswain: Princeton; pairs without coxswain: Connecticut College; fours with coxswain: Washington State; fours without coxswain: Pennsylvania; freshman fours: Rutgers.

SKIING—United States Champions: men's alpine: slalom: Cary Adgate, Boyne City, MI; giant slalom: Phil Mahre, White Pass, WA; downhill: Sepp Ferstl, West Germany, women's alpine: slalom: Cindy Nelson, Lutsen, MN; giant slalom: Viki Fleckenstein, Syracuse, NY; downhill: Irene Epple, West Germany; nordic: class A jumping: Jeff Davis, Steamboat Springs, CO; junior jumping: John Denney, Duluth, MN; women's jumping: Theresa Altabelli, Iron Mountain, MI; veterans class jumping: Dave Engstrom, Rockford, MI; men's cross-country: 15 kilometers: Bill Koch, Guilford, VT; 30 kilometers: Tim Caldwell, Putney, VT; 50 kilometers: Stan Dunklee, Brattleboro, VT; women's cross-country: 7.5 kilometers: Alison Owen-Spencer, Anchorage, AK; 10 kilometers: Alison Owen-Spencer; 20 kilometers: Beth Paxson, Morehead, KY.

SOFTBALL—United States Amateur Softball Association: men's fast pitch: Midland, MI; men's slow pitch: Nelson Manufacturing, Oklahoma City; men's 16-inch slow pitch: Chicago Bobcats; men's industrial slow pitch: Leslie Fay, Wilkes-Barre, PA; men's Class A fast pitch: Clark and Sons, East Providence, RI; women's fast pitch: Sun City, AZ; women's slow pitch: Miami (FL) Dots.

SQUASH RACQUETS—United States Squash Racquets Association: open singles: Mario Sanchez, Mexico City; 35–40: Tom Poor, Boston; 40–45: Raul Sanchez, Mexico City; 45–50: Les Harding, Seattle, WA; 50–55: Henri Salaun, Boston; 55–60: Richard Daly, Seattle; 60–65: Taft Toribara, Rochester, NY; class B: Sewall Hodges, New York City; class C: Fred Bass, New York City; doubles: Tom Poor and Gil Mateer, Philadelphia; veterans doubles: Mel Sokolow, New York City, and Ted Simmons, St. Louis; senior doubles: Darwin Kingsley, New York City, and Alfie Hunter, Philadelphia. College: class A singles: Ned Edwards, Pennsylvania; class B: John Nimick, Princeton; class C: Peter Thompson, Princeton; team: Princeton. **World Pro Champion:** men: Sharif Khan, Toronto. **United States Women's Squash Racquets Association Champions:** open singles: Heather McKay, Australia; 35 and over: Joyce Davenport, Pittsburgh; 40 and over: Goldie Edwards, Pittsburgh; mixed doubles: Carol Thesieres, Bryn Mawr, PA, and Gil Mateer, Philadelphia.

SQUASH TENNIS—singles: Pedro Bacallao, New York City.

TABLE TENNIS—World Champions: men's singles: Seiji Ono, Japan; women's singles: Ge Xinai, China; men's doubles: Anton Stipancic and Dragutin Surbek, Hungary; women's doubles: Zhang Deying and Zhang Li, China; mixed doubles: Liang Geliang and Ge Xinai, China. Men's team (Swaythling Cup): Hungary. Women's team (Corbillon Cup): China. **United States Champions:** men's singles: Milan Orlowski, Czechoslovakia; women's singles: Ki Won Lee, South Korea; men's doubles: Josef Dvoracek and Jindrich Pansky, Czechoslovakia; women's doubles: Kayo Kawahigashi and Shoko Takahashi, Japan; mixed doubles: Jacques Secretin and Claude Bergeret, France; senior men (over 40): Vincent Purkart, France; senior women

(over 40): Yvonne Kronlage, Columbia, MD; senior men (over 50): Bernie Bukiet, Hollywood, CA.

WATER POLO—United States Champions: men's outdoor: Newport, CA; men's indoor: Pepperdine; women's outdoor: Seal Beach, CA; women's indoor: Long Beach, CA. **World Cup:** Hungary. **NCAA:** University of California, Santa Barbara.

WATER SKIING—United States: men's open overall: Ricky McCormick, Winter Haven, FL; men's seniors: Brad Conger, San Diego; men's veterans: Jud Spencer, Oswego, NY; women's open: Karin Roberge, San Diego; women's seniors: Thelma Salmas, Lantana, FL. **World:** men's overall: Joel McClintock, Canada; women's overall: Cindy Todd, United States.

WEIGHT LIFTING—AAU: 114½-pound class: Jon Chappell, Philadelphia (391 total pounds); 123: Pat Omari, Hilo, HI (446½); 132: Phil Sanderson, Billings, MT (555½); 148: Dave Jones, Eastman, GA (594); 165: Dave Reigle, York, PA (632½); 181: Tom Hirtz, San Francisco (698½); 198: Jim Curry, Jr., Berkeley, CA (715); 220: Kurt Setterberg, Masury, OH (770); 242: Mark Cameron, Hyattsville, MD (847); super heavyweight: Tom Stock, Belleville, IL (830½); team: York (PA) Barbell Club (58 points).

WRESTLING—AAU: 105½-pound class: Bob Weaver, New York Athletic Club; 114½: Tom Dursee, New York A. C.; 125½: Joe Corso, Hawkeye Wrestling Club, Iowa City; 136½: Andre Metzger, Oklahoma; 149½: Chuck Yagla, Hawkeye W. C.; 163.1: Lee Kemp, Wisconsin Wrestling Club, Madison, WI; 181.1: Dan Lewis, Fullerton, CA; 198.1: Laurent Soucie, Wisconsin W. C.; 221.1: Russ Hellickson, Wisconsin W. C.; heavyweight: Greg Wojciechowski, Ohio Wrestling Club, Toledo, OH; team: New York A. C. **Greco-Roman:** 105½: Greg Williams, San Francisco; 114½: Raymond Pavia, United States Air Force; 125½: Bruce Thompson, Rosemount, MN; 136½: Hachiro Oishi, New York A. C.; 149½: Abdul Raheem-Ali, Minnesota W. C.; 163: John Matthews, Lansing, MI; 180½: Don Chandler, Minneapolis; 198: Frank Anderson, Sweden; 220: Brad Rheingans, Minnesota W. C.; heavyweight: Greg Wojciechowski, Toledo, OH. **NCAA:** 118-pound class: Gene Mills, Syracuse; 126: Dan Lewis, Iowa; 134: Darryl Burley, Lehigh; 142: Dan Hicks, Oregon State; 150: Bruce Kinseth, Iowa; 158: Kelly Ward, Iowa State; 167: Mark Churella, Michigan; 177: Mark Lieberman, Lehigh; 190: Eric Wais, Oklahoma State; heavyweight: Fred Bohna, UCLA; team: Iowa. **NAIA:** 118: Bill DePaoli, California (PA) State; 126: Scott Whirley, Augsburg (MN); 134: David James, Central (OK) State; 142: Johnny Powell, Central (OK) State; 150: Dave LaMott, West Liberty; 158: Bob Gruner, Wisconsin-Parkside; 167: Jeff Swenson, Augsburg (MN); 177: Bruce Hinkle, Fairmont (WV); 190: Tony Huck, Valley City (ND); heavyweight: Herbert Stanley, Adams (CO) State; team: Central (OK) State.

YACHTING—United States Yacht Racing Union Champions: Mallory Cup (men): Glenn Darden, Fort Worth, TX; Adams Trophy (women): Allison Jolly, St. Petersburg, FL; Mertz Trophy (women's single-handed): Betsey Gelenitis, Bricktown, NJ; Adams Memorial (women's double-handed): Nell Taylor and Charlotte Lewis, New Haven, CT; Sears Cup (juniors): Bill Lynne, Jr., Rye, NY; Smythe Trophy (juniors single-handed): Baird Loberee, Coconut Grove, FL; Prince of Wales (club): Dr. John W. Jennings, St. Petersburg, FL; National Sea Exploring: Ron A. Baerwitz, North Hollywood, CA. **Youth Champions:** single-handed: Kevin Kempton, Ocean Gate, NJ; double-handed: Gerald Braun, Tom Tompkins, Marble, MA; Annapolis-to-Newport Race: Class I, Ted Turner, *Tenacious;* Class II: Steve Nichols, *Obsession.*

SRI LANKA

Under the strong presidential system provided for in the new (September 1978) constitution, President Junius R. Jayewardene seemed to be firmly in control of the Democratic Socialist Republic of Sri Lanka. The political and social scenes were marred, however, by widespread violence instigated by young Tamil-speaking separatists. Mainly as a result of basic changes in philosophy and policy, the nation's economy showed considerable improvement for the first time in many years.

Politics. The overwhelming majority of the United National Party (UNP) in the National State Assembly was reiterated on the local level in municipal council elections on May 19. The UNP won a majority of seats on all of the local councils, except for three in the north, where the Tamil United Liberation Front (TULF) was victorious.

Dissatisfaction among the Tamil-speaking minority rose steadily, as the TULF sought greater local autonomy and extremist groups demanded an independent Tamil state. An extremist Tamil youth group known as the "Liberation Tigers" was responsible for a wave of killings and other acts of violence. In July the UNP government proclaimed a state of emergency in the northern district of Jaffna and passed laws to curb violence by Tamil separatists. Tensions between the Sinhala majority and the Tamil minority were somewhat eased by the appointment in August of a presidential commission to devise a plan for vesting greater authority in district councils and by the agreement of the TULF to participate.

Economy. Reversing the socialist policies and economic restraints of the previous regime, the UNP regime eliminated numerous price controls, licensing and permit requirements, import duties, and taxes on profits and exports. Food subsidies on rice and flour, which had comprised more than 30% of the national budget, were eliminated for persons whose average income exceeded $18 a month and were largely replaced by a food stamp program for the 7.5 million people (half the total population) whose incomes fell below that level.

--- **SRI LANKA · Information Highlights** ---

Official Name: Democratic Socialist Republic of Sri Lanka.
Location: Island off the southeastern coast of India.
Area: 25,332 square miles (65 610 km²).
Population (1979 est.): 14,500,000.
Chief City (1977 est.): Colombo, the capital, 616,000.
Government: *Head of state,* Junius R. Jayewardene, president (took office Feb. 1978). *Head of government,* Ranasinghe Premadasa, prime minister (took office Feb. 1978). *Legislature* (unicameral)—National State Assembly.
Monetary Unit: Rupee (15.615 rupees equal U. S.$1, Aug. 1979).
Manufactures (major products): Consumer goods, textiles, chemicals and chemical products.
Agriculture (major products): Tea, rubber, coconuts, rice, spices.

The more liberal economic policies gave an unprecedented boost to the economy. The economic growth rate rose to 6%, twice that of the previous year, and external reserves increased to nearly $8 billion. Private foreign investment also showed a remarkable increase. However, the majority of people benefited little, as the rate of inflation reached more than 17%.

Foreign Policy. President Jayewardene led a delegation to the sixth nonaligned summit conference in Havana, Cuba, in late August and early September. After the conference he made official visits to Japan and Singapore. In March, Sri Lanka became the 107th nation to adhere to the nuclear nonproliferation treaty.

NORMAN D. PALMER, *University of Pennsylvania*

STAMPS AND STAMP COLLECTING

The year in philately was punctuated by the sale of rare items for sensational record prices. In a private sale, Stanley Gibbons International, a London stamp dealer, paid $10 million to New York financier Marc Haas for his collection of U. S. classic issues. The collection included stamps issued before the Civil War, as well as Pony Express and Wells Fargo covers.

At the Swiss CORINPHILA auction in May, a Baden "Stockach provisional" stamp on the original 1858 cover brought $178,000, the highest price ever fetched by a single German item.

More than 6,500 new stamps were issued around the world, many for the 1980 Olympic Games, UN-sponsored International Year of the Child, and 100th anniversary of the death of Rowland Hill, the English "inventor" of the adhesive postage stamp.

The United Nations, which prints stamps for sale to collectors but depends on U. S. and Swiss post offices to handle its mail, added an office in Vienna, Austria, for which special stamps will be produced and sold to the philatelic market.

Two scandals rocked the stamp world in 1979. On August 2, Kenny International Corp., a small New York–based stamp distributing firm, became the first company to be prosecuted under the 1977 Foreign Corrupt Practices Act. The firm pleaded guilty to having diverted $337,000 from the sale of Cook Island postage stamps to rig 1978 gubernatorial elections and thereby retain the right to distribute the territory's stamps. Kenny agreed to pay a $50,000 fine, repay the diverted revenue, and pleaded guilty on similar charges in Rarotonga.

In another unsavory affair, the former director and deputy director of the U. S. Bureau of Engraving and Printing were indicted for the improper awarding of stamp printing contracts to a private New York firm and then resigning to accept positions with that firm. In December, however, the charges were dismissed.

The "Benjamin Franklin Stamp Club" program, sponsored by the U. S. Postal Service to promote stamp collecting in 30,000 grammar schools, bogged down "for lack of funds." To revitalize the program a multimillion-dollar ad campaign was renewed on prime time television and in the printed media to boost the sale of stamps to the public.

ERNEST A. KEHR
Stamp News Bureau

PHOTOS U. S. POSTAL SERVICE

SELECTED U. S. COMMEMORATIVE STAMPS, 1979

Subject	Denomination	Date
Robert Kennedy	15¢	Jan. 12
Martin Luther King	15¢	Jan. 13
International Child Year	15¢	Feb. 15
G. R. Clark postal card	10¢	Feb. 23
John Steinbeck	15¢	Feb. 27
Albert Einstein	15¢	March 4
Chanute air-mail	2x21¢	March 29
PA Toleware	4x15¢	April 19
U. S. Architecture	4x15¢	June 4
Blinds' Guide Dogs	15¢	June 15
Special Olympics	15¢	Aug. 9
Olympics (decathlon)	10¢	Sept. 5
Olympics postal card	10¢	Sept. 17
John Paul Jones	15¢	Sept. 23
Summer Olympics	4x15¢	Sept. 28
Pulaski postal card	10¢	Oct. 11
Christmas stamps	2x15¢	Oct. 18
Olympics (high jump)	31¢	Nov. 1
Wiley Post	25¢	Nov. 20
Olympics postal card	21¢	Dec. 1
Olympics aerogramme	22¢	Dec. 1
Olympics envelopes	4x15¢	Dec. 10

STOCKS AND BONDS

The U. S. stock market overcame a formidable array of economic problems to register some healthy gains in 1979. The bad news seemed to come from every direction: a battle of wills with a new revolutionary regime in Iran, record-high interest rates, a deepening energy crisis, and double-digit domestic inflation. But except for one precipitous two-week drop in October that evoked memories of the Great Crash on Wall Street 50 years before, the market gave a good account of itself.

The Dow Jones average of 30 blue-chip industrials posted a modest advance of 4.2% to 838.74. Other indicators with a broader representation of stocks rose more sharply, however, as the smaller issues, known as "secondary stocks," outperformed the big names of American industry for the third consecutive year.

The New York Stock Exchange (NYSE) index of more than 1,500 common stocks was up 15.5% from January through December. Standard & Poor's 500-stock composite index gained 12.2%.

Most impressive of all was a 64.1% rise for the market value index at the American Stock Exchange, which benefited from a bull market in energy issues, particularly those of Canadian oil and gas producers.

Trading volume on the Big Board reached a new high of 8.16 billion shares, surpassing the previous record of 7.2 billion shares set in 1978. The exchange also had by far the busiest day in its history on October 10, when 81.6 million shares changed hands as investors scrambled to respond to a new set of credit-tightening plans by the Federal Reserve System. Under the direction of Paul Volcker, named by President Carter to the chairmanship of the central bank in July, the Fed disclosed on October 6 that it was administering some strong new medicine against the nation's most troublesome economic ill, inflation. Instead of its past practice of gradually nudging interest rates up and down, the Fed said it would shift its strategy toward direct efforts to control the supply of credit.

Interest rates, cut free from their traditional restraints, immediately soared. And while the stock market had a bad couple of weeks, with the Dow Jones industrials falling about 90 points, the damage was even worse in the bond market.

Bond prices, which move inversely with interest rates, lapsed into a free-fall decline. "October was the worst month on record for bonds and exploded the myth about bonds providing stability and low volatility," said Robert Farrell, a market analyst at Merrill, Lynch, Pierce, Fenner & Smith Inc. In the waning days of the year, Farrell calculated that stocks showed a total return—price change plus yield—of more than 15% from January 1, against a minus 5% return for bonds.

A Chicago securities processor reads of Oct. 10, 1979, New York Stock Exchange developments—volume hit a record level and the Dow Jones average dropped 8.27 points.

UPI

Collectibles. Both stocks and bonds continued to get stiff competition from other types of investments. The price of gold, the traditional haven from economic uncertainty and inflation, more than doubled in 1979, reaching all-time highs above $500 an ounce. "Gold is now so high you can't buy it with money," joked New York disk jockey Don Imus with only a touch of hyperbole. Gold was but one symbol of the inflation-induced rage for collectibles—art, stamps, rare coins, old baseball cards, any non-financial asset that could be regarded as a store of value.

A study issued by the investment banking firm of Salomon Brothers reported that, from 1968 to 1979, gold ranked first among 15 types of investments, with a compound annual rate of gain of 19.4%. Next, in order, came Chinese ceramics, up 19.1% per year; stamps, up 18.9%; rare books, up 15.7%; silver, up 13.4%; coins, up 12.7%; old masters, up 12.5%, and diamonds, up 11.8%. For investors without the means or the expertise to take part in such markets, there was another inflation hedge—houses, which rose 9.6% a year. At the bottom of Salomon Brothers' list were bonds, up 5.8%, and stocks, up 3.1%.

As popular as collectibles were, the year's biggest success story on Wall Street grew out of a much newer idea: the money-market mutual fund, investing in short-term securities such as Treasury bills, bank certificates of deposit, and commercial paper issued by corporations. After a modest start in the mid-1970's, the money funds were swamped with business in 1979 as their yields rose, along with interest rates generally, to unprecedented two-digit levels. At the end of 1978, the funds had about $8 billion in assets. By late 1979, the Investment Company Institute reported the total had surged to nearly $40 billion.

Another hot new product, aimed primarily at investing institutions and sophisticated spec-ulators, was the interest-rate futures contract, modeled after the contracts traded on farm and industrial commodities. Many Wall Street organizations, including the NYSE, with its plans to open the New York Futures Exchange, were banking on further growth in financial futures in the 1980's.

Overseas Stock Markets. Stock markets in many of the world's financial centers equaled or bettered the gains in the United States. According to analyst William Lefevre of Granger & Co., the top performer among the ten major world stock markets from November 1978 to November 1979 was that of gold-rich South Africa, up 54.6%. The Hong Kong market, known worldwide for its volatility, was second, up 52.5%. Canada, with its energy and other natural resources, ranked third with a 33.2% rise. France, Italy, Switzerland, and Japan recorded smaller gains. Only West Germany, off 10.8%, and England, off 15.8%, fell into the minus column.

Outlook. Although the picture presented by the U. S. economy at the end of 1979 was anything but rosy, Wall Streeters saw some cause for hope that the stock and bond markets could fare better in the 1980's than they did in the lackluster 1970's.

The nation was still struggling to cut its enormous outlays for imported oil from uncertain sources. But with gasoline prices exceeding $1 a gallon and heating oil not far below it, there were signs that Americans were at last getting serious about conservation.

In addition, the bank prime lending rate, after soaring from 7.75% to 15.75% in two years' time, inched downward a half point in late November and early December.

And despite the initial shock effects, most leaders of the financial community expressed their firm support of the Federal Reserve's stringent new anti-inflation tactics.

CHET CURRIER, *The Associated Press*

SUDAN

The regime of Sudan's President Jaafar al-Nemery faced its toughest test during its ninth year in power—a severe economic crisis which provoked riots, strikes, and antigovernment plots. Nemery introduced some political and economic reforms in 1979, allowing him temporarily to overcome the growing domestic dissatisfaction with his rule.

Politics. Nemery grappled with serious popular unrest motivated by the country's economic crisis. First, while attending an April London meeting with Sherif al-Hindi, an exile opposition leader who refused to accept Nemery's 1978 national reconciliation program, there were reported discoveries of up to three coup plots against the president.

In mid-August, a government-imposed 66% price increase for sugar, fuel, and other basic commodities sparked widespread rioting in the capital, Khartoum, and in Omdurman, followed by a strike of the 250,000-member Sudanese Railways Union. Nemery blamed Sudanese communists for the disturbances, but deep-seated popular discontent with the state of the economy appeared to be the real cause of the unrest.

In August, to quell the unrest, Nemery cancelled the gas price increase, introduced some price controls, and authorized a pay boost for transit workers. He also fired the nation's first vice president and secretary-general of the only political party, the Sudanese Socialist Union, Abdel Kassim Mohammed Ibrahim, and replaced him with the Defense Minister Abdel Magid Hamid Khali. The president then undertook a drastic government shake-up, sacking eight top ministers and appointing two political opponents to the government. A new finance and economy minister, Badreddin Suleiman, began his term in office with some needed economic reforms.

Economy. Still suffering from development overspending and heavy foreign borrowing without available short-term financing, the Sudanese economy worsened, with an unofficial inflation rate of 50% a year and a foreign debt estimated to exceed $1.3 billion. A poor transport system complicated the situation, with exports of such cash crops as cotton and groundnuts frequently stranded. In addition, transport workers' strikes halted the system completely.

In May, an agreement was reached allowing Sudan to borrow $260 million from the International Monetary Fund over the next three years. The pact was contingent on reductions in official spending and domestic borrowing and the adoption of a strictly export-oriented development strategy. Financial austerity plans would continue despite the high inflation rate and severe shortages of most staple goods.

In September Finance Minister Suleiman announced the lifting of many of the government-imposed controls on the flow of foreign exchange in order to ease the country's balance of payments problems. It was hoped that the measure would stimulate production, allow a freer flow of imports and exports, and stimulate a capital inflow from Sudanese working abroad. A two-tier exchange rate was introduced, legitimizing the existing black market rates in foreign currency. In October, Sudan also asked Western banks for a large refinancing loan on concessional terms to be used to pay off its overdue commercial foreign debt.

Some hopes for added income were raised with the discovery by Chevron of oil deposits in western Sudan in July. The wells were netting 500 barrels a day. However, it was too early to predict if the oil would become a marketable commodity.

MARGARET NOVICKI, *"African Update"*
African-American Institute

SWEDEN

The general election in Sweden, held September 16, was won by the non-Socialist bloc of Moderates, Center, and Liberals. The non-Socialists won by a single seat in the parliament (175 seats of 349). By a margin of 2,000, the vote favored the non-Socialists, but proportional representation awarded a contested seat to the Social-Democrats. However, when the votes were completely counted the non-Socialists had a plurality of 8,000, and the Moderates received the last seat. Election victory was thus taken from the Social-Democrats and Communists by 52,000 absentee voters, of whom 4,000 were living abroad. The Moderates

---
SUDAN • Information Highlights

Official Name: Democratic Republic of Sudan.
Location: Northeast Africa.
Area: 967,500 square miles (2 505 825 km²).
Population (1979 est.): 17,900,000.
Chief Cities (April 1973): Khartoum, the capital, 333,-906; Omdurman, 299,399.
Government: *Head of state,* Gen. Jaafar Mohammed al-Nemery, president (took office Oct. 1971). *Legislature* (unicameral)—People's Assembly.
Monetary Unit: Pound (0.4 pound equals U. S.$1, Aug. 1979).
Manufactures (major products): Cement, textiles, pharmaceuticals, shoes, processed foods.
Agriculture (major products): Cotton, sesame seeds, peanuts, gum arabic, sorghum, wheat, sugarcane.

SWEDEN • Information Highlights

Official Name: Kingdom of Sweden.
Location: Northern Europe.
Area: 173,000 square miles (448 068 km²).
Population (1979 est.): 8,300,000.
Chief Cities (1976): Stockholm, the capital, 661,258; Göteborg, 442,410; Malmö, 240,220.
Government: *Head of state,* Carl XVI Gustaf, king (acceded Sept. 1973). *Head of government,* Thorbjörn Fälldin, prime minister (took office Oct. 1979). *Legislature* (unicameral)—Riksdag.
Monetary Unit: Krona (4.24 kronor equal U. S.$1, Nov. 15, 1979).
Manufactures (major products): Machinery, instruments, metal products, automobiles, aircraft.
Agriculture (major products): Dairy, grains, sugar beets, potatoes, wood.

gained 18 seats; the Center lost 22 and the Liberals one.

The minority government headed by Ola Ullsten, Liberal, officially resigned and was asked by the speaker of parliament to continue as a caretaker government. On September 20, Ullsten resigned as prime minister to negotiate with the two other non-Socialist parties on forming a new government. Social-Democrat Ingemund Bengtsson was chosen Speaker of the Parliament on October 1. The result was generally considered a severe setback for the three non-Socialist parties. On October 9, the Center Party's Thorbjörn Fälldin, prime minister in 1976–78, again took over the post. The other two parties had opposed naming Moderate Gösta Bohman to the premiership.

Economy. A devaluation of the krona and a restrained wage agreement reestablished Swedish competitiveness in export markets. The gross national product expanded at a rate of about 5%, one of the highest in the West. Unemployment was at 2.2%, and inflation ran at about 6%. The budget deficit, ten times larger than in 1976, was close to $12 billion, and for the first time Sweden had foreign debts.

Foreign Relations. Sweden's total annual contribution to the United Nations amounted to more than $140 million, making the country the second largest contributor after the United States to the entire UN system. In March and May, strong protests against Soviet espionage in Sweden were delivered to the Soviet ambassador in Stockholm. U. S. Vice President Walter Mondale visited Sweden in April. A trade treaty was signed with China on May 15.

Royal Family. King Carl Gustaf and Queen Silvia made an official eight-day visit to West Germany in March. On May 13, the queen gave birth to a son, christened Carl Philip in the Royal Palace Chapel on September 7.

Other. Bertil Ohlin, 80-year-old winner of the Nobel Prize in Economics, died on August 3.

MAC LINDAHL, *Harvard University*

SWITZERLAND

Continued economic prosperity, the creation of a new canton, and debate over the regulation of nuclear power plants marked an eventful year in Swiss domestic affairs.

Economy. Switzerland was cited as the world's richest country in 1978, after surpassing Kuwait with a per capita gross national product of $13,853 (U. S.). The trade deficit was reduced from $512 million in 1977 to $307 million in 1978. But although exports for the first half of 1979 rose by 16% (to $12,610 million) over the same period in 1978, imports increased by 19.5% (to $13,527 million).

The stability and strength of the Swiss franc led many countries to seek loans from Swiss investors to shore up their own currencies. In January 1979, the United States sold to Swiss investors $1.7 billion in notes in order to use francs to purchase dollars on the international money market.

On April 11, the government announced plans to spend $990 million on armaments, its largest such purchase since the Korean War. Opponents of the move cited the nation's increasing balance of payments deficit.

Jura Canton. More than 10 years of separatist agitation and political maneuvering came to an end on Jan. 1, 1979, with the creation of Switzerland's 23rd canton. Jura Canton, the nation's first new canton since the establishment of the Swiss Confederation in 1848, gained final separation from the French-speaking Bern Canton. Jura's 60-seat parliament opened with six political parties represented.

Elections. Parliamentary elections in late October wrought little change in the national government. The four-party coalition that had been running Switzerland for 20 years—comprising the Socialist Party, Radical Democratic Party, Christian Democratic Party, and Swiss People's Party—was returned to power with 169 seats, the same number that it held previously.

Nuclear Regulation. On February 18, Swiss voters narrowly rejected a proposal (also opposed by the government) that would have greatly tightened licensing procedures for nuclear power plants, removed all limits on the liability of power companies in the advent of a nuclear accident, and granted to local communities control over the siting of all nuclear plants. Clearly influenced by the subsequent Three Mile Island (PA) accident, however, Swiss voters on May 20 overwhelmingly approved a stiffer set of regulations proposed by the government. The construction and operation of nuclear plants would be strictly controlled, and final licensing authority would be reserved for the national parliament.

Other Referenda. A program to increase federal aid for the protection and maintenance of footpaths was approved, but the electorate rejected proposals to create a federal police force, to ban all advertising of alcohol, to reduce the voting age from 20 to 18, and to establish an 8% value added tax.

PAUL C. HELMREICH, *Wheaton College, MA*

—— **SWITZERLAND** • **Information Highlights** ——

Official Name: Swiss Confederation.
Location: Central Europe.
Area: 15,943.4 square miles (41 923.2 km²).
Population (1979 est.): 6,300,000.
Chief Cities (1978 est.): Bern, the capital, 145,500; Zurich, 379,600; Basel, 185,300.
Government: *Head of state,* Georges-André Chevallaz, president (took office Jan. 1980). *Legislature*— Federal Assembly: Council of States and National Council.
Monetary Unit: Franc (1.66 francs equal U. S.$1, Nov. 15, 1979).
Manufactures (major products): Watches, clocks, precision instruments, machinery, chemicals, pharmaceuticals, textiles, generators, and turbines.
Agriculture (major products): High-quality cheese and other dairy products, livestock, fruits, grains, potatoes, and wine.

A new American flag is raised at the U.S. legation in Damascus; an Arab mob destroyed the former one.

SYRIA

A steady escalation of sectarian fighting posed the first serious domestic challenge to the nine-year-old regime of President Hafez al-Assad. Urban violence diverted the president's attention and caused him to falter in his attempts to establish a new Arab alignment in the wake of the March 1979 Egyptian-Israeli peace treaty. At the same time, Assad attempted to extricate his army from the unceasingly volatile situation in Lebanon.

Domestic Upheaval. The June 16 massacre of 60 Army cadets at a military academy in Aleppo was the murderous high point of a relentless program of assassination by the antigovernment Muslim Brotherhood. Fueled by sectarian jealousies, a revival of orthodox Islam, and widespread resentment of official corruption, the terrorists—part of the country's Sunni majority—singled out members of the minority Alawite sect who held key positions in the government and the military. Att. Gen. Adel Mini, an Alawite, was murdered April 11.

Assad publicly held the Muslim Brotherhood responsible for the wave of killings, and 15 members of the group were summarily executed after the June 16 slaughter. The Brotherhood, a loose-knit fanatic sect established in Egypt in 1928, has caused sporadic problems for Syria's ruling Baathist Socialist Party since 1963

by its fundamentalist rejection of secular, pan-Arab policies. As in Lebanon, however, the outbreak of sectarian violence more accurately reflected the underlying political and socio-economic dissatisfaction of the Sunni Muslim majority with the ascendancy of the traditionally lower-class Alawites. Despite comprising less than 15% of the nation's population, Alawites held the most important positions of power.

Mounting tension after June 16 required the government to deploy military troops and tanks in Damascus, while security police arrested more than 250 religious and political leaders. Security forces remained on alert status for the duration of the year. In addition to weekly hit-and-run assassinations, larger-scale sectarian fighting broke out in Latakia, an Alawite stronghold, in September and October. In the wake of more than 40 deaths, the government announced steps to quell the rising unrest. The authority of the National Progressive Front—comprising members of the ruling Baath party, the Syrian Communist Party, and two smaller left-wing parties—would be expanded; the civil service would be purged; and efforts would be made to improve the nation's economy and ensure the supply of basic commodities.

Foreign Policy. Frustration characterized Assad's attempts to achieve his major foreign policy goals in 1979. As Egypt concluded a peace treaty with Israel in March, Assad sought a new and solid ally to confront Israel with a viable political and military threat and to regain what the Syrian president called "Arab Rights." Early in 1979, Assad and Iraqi President Ahmed Hassan al-Bakr announced plans to establish "one flag and one presidency." If consummated, the unification promised a decisive change in the Middle Eastern balance of power. Negotiations proceeded until summer, when a series of domestic problems in Syria, a clash between Syrian and Israeli aircraft over Lebanon, and an unexpected change in Iraqi leadership combined to sink the talks.

In the first air combat between Syria and Israel in five years, five of Syria's Soviet-made MiG-21s were shot down by American-made F-15s over Lebanon on June 27. The Syrian aircraft had been attempting to block an Israeli

---

SYRIA • Information Highlights

Official Name: Syrian Arab Republic.
Location: Southwest Asia.
Area: 71,500 square miles (185 184 km²).
Population (1979 est.): 8,400,000.
Chief Cities (1975 est.): Damascus, the capital, 1,042,-245; Aleppo, 778,523; Homs, 267,132.
Government: Head of state, Lt. Gen. Hafez al-Assad, president (took office March 1971). Head of government, Muhammad Ali al-Halabi, prime minister (took office March 1978). Legislature (unicameral)—People's Council.
Monetary Unit: Pound (3.95 pounds equal U.S.$1, Aug. 1979).
Manufactures (major products): Petroleum, textiles, cement, glass, soap, processed foods, phosphates.
Agriculture (major products): Wheat, barley, sugar beets, tobacco, sheep, goats, grapes, tomatoes.

attack on Palestinian guerrilla positions near Sidon. The incident prompted fears of war and thereby delayed Syrian-Iraqi negotiations.

On July 16, Iraqi President Bakr abruptly resigned and was replaced by second-in-command Saddam Hussein. Subsequent accusations that Syria was involved in an attempted coup against Hussein rekindled old suspicions between the two countries. On September 7, Assad was forced to admit that the unification talks were stalled.

Lebanon. Syrian mediation efforts in Lebanon met with no better success than the attempt to unite with Iraq. Despite attempts by Assad and Foreign Minister Abdel Halim Khaddam to bring the warring Lebanese factions to an agreement, the Christians remained intransigent and fighting along the Israeli border continued. It was costing Syria approximately $1 million a day to maintain its 22,000 troops in Lebanon. (*See* LEBANON.)

Soviet Union. A visit to the USSR by President Assad, October 15–18, marked a significant improvement in Syrian-Soviet relations. Assad was promised more sophisticated weapons, and the Soviet Union reportedly canceled Syria's $500 million debt.

F. NICHOLAS WILLARD

TAIWAN (REPUBLIC OF CHINA)

After an initial outburst of anger, Taiwan quickly adjusted to the new situation created by the severance of formal diplomatic relations with the United States. The government maintained diplomatic ties with only 21 nations but had trade relations with more than 140. Its economy continued to grow, foreign trade expanded, and foreign investments in Taiwan advanced to a new high.

Despite the adverse development in its foreign affairs, Taiwan was determined to preserve its democratic form of government, firmly adhering to its staunch anti-Communist position. The Nationalists announced categorically that under no circumstances would they negotiate with the Chinese Communists.

With the United States terminating the mutual defense treaty and with Peking refusing to swear off the use of force against Taiwan, the Nationalists were anxious to strengthen the island's defense. They were particularly interested in equipping their army with modern, sophisticated weapons.

U. S. Break. On Dec. 16, 1978, U. S. Ambassador Leonard Unger informed President Chiang Ching-kuo that the United States had decided to establish diplomatic relations with Peking and to sever its ties with the Republic of China. In a bitter protest to the United States, President Chiang denounced the American action as seriously damaging the rights and interests of his nation.

Deputy Secretary of State Warren M. Christopher and other members of a U. S. delegation arrived in Taipei December 27 to discuss the shape of future relations between the two countries. The Americans were attacked by an angry mob, resulting in slight injuries to Mr. Christopher and Ambassador Unger. Taiwan promptly apologized, and after the government took measures to ensure the personal safety of the visiting delegation, negotiations were begun. A crucial topic in the talks was the security of Taiwan. The Nationalists insisted that its security must be ensured by appropriate U. S. legislation.

Influential members of Congress exerted strong pressure to restore security assurances to Taiwan, but President Jimmy Carter was afraid that such measures might offend Peking. After considerable debate and deliberation, a compromise bill was approved by both houses of Congress. On April 10, 1979, President Carter signed legislation establishing unofficial relations with Taiwan and providing some security assurances to the island. The bill declared that the United States would consider any warlike pressure on Taiwan "a threat to the peace and security" of the Western Pacific and a matter "of grave concern." It also stipulated that the United States would provide Taiwan with "arms of a defensive character."

To preserve economic and cultural relations, the United States established the American Institute on Taiwan, which was to provide much

Charles T. Cross is head of the American Institute in Taiwan, which now handles U. S.-Taiwanese relations.

AMERICAN INSTITUTE IN TAIWAN

In Houston, TX, in February, demonstrators, carrying Taiwanese flags, protest the visit of China's Vice Premier Deng Xiaoping.

UPI

the same service as the former American embassy in Taipei. On its part, Taiwan established the Coordinated Council for North American Affairs to handle nondiplomatic functions formerly the responsibility of the Chinese Embassy in Washington. The two countries kept in force all agreements except for the mutual defense treaty, which was to terminate at the end of 1979. (A U. S. District judge ruled October 17 that the president could not end the treaty without the consent of Congress. The Justice Department immediately announced its intention to appeal, and in December the Supreme Court upheld the president's authority.)

Territorial Waters. On September 6, the Nationalist government announced the extension of its territorial waters to 12 miles (22.2 km) and declared a 200-mile (370-km) economic zone to protect its coastal natural resources. It also reaffirmed its sovereignty over the continental shelf near its coast.

Anti-Communism. In response to the question of a journalist, President Chiang Ching-kuo declared in July that statements from Peking about possible nonpolitical links with Taiwan—trade, postal service, family visits, and cultural programs—were "simply deceitful." The president directed his anti-Communist rhetoric to other countries as well, especially the USSR.

– TAIWAN (REPUBLIC OF CHINA) · Information –
Highlights

Official Name: Republic of China.
Location: Island off the southeastern coast of mainland China.
Area: 13,885 square miles (35 961 km²).
Population (1979 est.): 17,300,000.
Chief Cities (Dec. 1977): Taipei, the capital, 2,127,625; Kaohsiung, 1,041,364; Taichung, 570,661.
Government: *Head of state,* Chiang Ching-kuo, president (installed May 1978). *Head of government,* Sun Yun-suan, premier (took office May 1978). *Legislature* (unicameral)—Legislative Yüan.
Monetary Unit: New Taiwan dollar (38 NT dollars equal U. S.$1, Dec. 1979).
Manufactures (major products): Textiles, electronic equipment, light manufactures, cement.
Agriculture (major products): Sugarcane, sweet potatoes, rice, vegetables.

Internal Policy. Taiwan continued to emphasize its commitment to democratic government and respect for human rights. At the same time it also sought an orderly society ruled by law. "We cannot," said Premier Sun Yun-suan, "tolerate anyone who violates law and discipline and undermines our solidarity." Efforts were made to ensure an honest and efficient government and to maintain close contact between administrative agencies and the people. Anticorruption tribunals were set up to hear cases involving improper conduct by government officials. Taiwan's social policy was aimed at narrowing the income gap between rich and poor. Attention was given to more effective use of land resources and to providing broader land benefits to the people. Provincial and municipal governments planned more public housing.

Economy. Stability continued to be the government's primary economic goal. Agricultural prices fell because of oversupply, while a severe labor drain developed in the countryside. This forced the government to reduce rice production on the one hand, and foster farm mechanization on the other. It also raised the price of its own rice purchases and suspended land taxes for the latter part of the year.

In the industrial sector, priority was given to chemical, machine, and electronics industries, where the government assisted in introducing new technologies. Among transportation projects completed in 1979 were Taichung Harbor, Chiang Kai-shek International Airport, and the southern section of the North Ling Railway.

Taiwan's gross national product was estimated to have increased by 10% in 1979, and export growth by 20–25%. In the first eight months of the year, Taiwan registered a trade surplus of $838 million. Its overall foreign trade was expected to increase by some 30% over 1978.

See also CHINA, PEOPLE'S REPUBLIC OF.
CHESTER C. TAN
New York University

The rule of Uganda's President Idi Amin ended April 11, 1979, as Tanzanian soldiers joined Ugandan rebels in taking Kampala, Uganda's capital.

FRANCOLON, GAMMA, LIAISON

TANZANIA

A major war with Uganda and continuing involvement in the Rhodesian crisis were the major events of the year for Tanzania.

Ugandan War. Tanzania fought one of modern Africa's biggest wars in 1978–79 against the Uganda of dictator Idi Amin. Bad relations had existed for years between the two countries, especially after Tanzania granted asylum to Uganda's former president, Milton Obote, who used Tanzania as a base to plan a return to power. The war began in October 1978, when Ugandan forces captured a 710 square mile (1 839 km²) area of remote northwest Tanzania. Uganda claimed that the area was rightfully Ugandan and that it had been used as a staging area for raids into Uganda by pro-Obote guerrillas. The occupation lasted a month, and the withdrawal of Ugandan forces revealed enormous death and destruction in the battle area along the Kagera River—10,000 Tanzanians murdered and 40,000 expelled by Amin's troops.

Despairing of aid or support from the Organization of African Unity (OAU), Tanzania's President Julius K. Nyerere determined to crush Amin, whom he detested. General mobilization was ordered, and new fighting began in February 1979. More than 20,000 troops, with armor, artillery, and air support, and aided by Ugandan exiles, invaded Uganda. Amin's bloody and tyrannical rule had left him little support in Uganda, and his army, after initial defeats, collapsed. Tanzanian forces and Ugandan exiles took Kampala, the Ugandan capital, on April 11, thoroughly defeating the last garrison in Kampala, a force of Libyans sent by that country to reinforce Amin. After securing the rest of the country for the new Ugandan government, the Tanzanian forces withdrew, leaving Nyerere with enormous prestige and influence. However, the war cost impoverished Tanzania over $1 million daily, draining the reserve of foreign exchange and crippling the internal economy.

Rhodesian Crisis. Tanzania continued to play a leading role in seeking a solution to the problem of Rhodesia. As the leader of the "front-line" states demanding African rule in Rhodesia, Tanzania refused to accept any settlement that excluded the Rhodesian nationalist guerrillas from a major share in power. Tanzania also denounced the continued power of the white minority. To show its displeasure, Tanzania nationalized the local holdings of the huge British Lonrho conglomerate, charging the company with secretly cooperating with the racist Ian Smith to undermine genuine black rule in Rhodesia. President Nyerere also denounced the secret meetings among Smith, Zambian President Kenneth Kaunda, and nationalist leader Joshua Nkomo, calling it a sellout of African interests. These events only underscored Nyerere's often repeated demand for an end to white rule and racism in all of southern Africa.

Peace Corps. Better relations with the United States were foreseen as a result of Tanzania's decision to reaccept Peace Corps volunteers following an absence of many years.

Economy. Even without the effects of the war, the Tanzanian economy suffered in 1979. A 30% drop in coffee exports led to a $277 million trade deficit. This was combined with 15% inflation. The country continued, however, to push for a classless socialist economy based on agricultural self-sufficiency. Despite the economic downturn, there was little hunger or major suffering in the country. Foreign investment, and even tourism, was discouraged.

ROBERT GARFIELD, *DePaul University*

―――――― **TANZANIA · Information Highlights** ――――――

Official Name: United Republic of Tanzania.
Location: East Africa.
Area: 364,900 square miles (945 087 km²).
Population (1979 est.): 17,000,000.
Chief City (1975 est.): Dar es Salaam, the capital, 517,000.
Government: *Head of state,* Julius K. Nyerere, president (took office 1964). *Head of government,* Edward Moringe Sokoine, prime minister (took office Feb. 1977). *Legislature* (unicameral)—National Assembly.
Monetary Unit: Shilling (8.268 shillings equal U. S.$1, March 1979).
Manufactures (major products): Textiles, agricultural products, light manufactures, refined oil, cement.
Agriculture (major products): Sugar, maize, rice, wheat, cotton, coffee, sisal, cashew nuts, tea, tobacco.

TAXATION

In most nations, 1979 tax policy decisions reflected concern over problems resulting from continued high inflation, slow economic growth, and threatened energy shortages. The most prevalent government tax actions were those reducing income taxes, especially for those with lower and moderate incomes, and raising the rates of taxes on consumption.

THE UNITED STATES

Congressional Action. Tax deliberations during the first session of the 96th Congress were almost exclusively concerned with the so-called "windfall profits tax," proposed by President Carter in April, when he announced his decision to phase out controls on oil prices. The proposed tax, which is an excise or severance tax on domestically produced crude oil, was designed to capture for public use a share of the large new revenues that U. S. oil producers would receive from the decontrol of domestic oil prices and from increases in the world price.

The House of Representatives and the Senate approved substantially different bills establishing such an excise tax. In late December, a House-Senate conference committee began work to reconcile the two measures, but did not complete its action. A compromise measure was expected to be approved early in 1980.

In October Al Ullman, chairman of the House Ways and Means Committee, proposed the introduction of a value-added tax, a device common in Europe but never levied at the national level in the United States. Russell B. Long, chairman of the Senate Finance Committee, also indicated support for such a levy. Generally regarded as a type of sales tax, the tax would apply to the value imparted to goods and services at each stage of the production process. Representative Ullman suggested a 10% tax, to be applied uniformly and broadly (possibly excepting food) to yield an estimated $130 billion annually. The proceeds would be used to finance cuts in individual and corporate income taxes and to cut back the sharp increases in Social Security taxes scheduled to take effect beginning in 1981. After three days of hearings before the Ways and Means Committee in November, the committee rescheduled private-sector testimony for early January.

Congress also considered a number of other tax matters—including mortgage revenue bonds, bankruptcy, technical corrections, and tax simplification. Final decisions were withheld.

Supreme Court. In a case which attracted wide attention in the business community, *Thor Power Tool Company v. Commissioner of Internal Revenue,* the court voted unanimously to affirm a lower court finding that the Internal Revenue Service (IRS) had not abused its discretion in refusing to allow Thor Power Tool Company a substantial write-down in the inventory value of replacement parts. The company manufactures handheld power tools, parts and accessories, and rubber products. Requirements for replacement parts were difficult to forecast, and to avoid future production runs Thor produced a generous supply on the original run. In 1964 new management assumed control of the company and, among other changes, wrote down what it regarded as excess inventory to the company's own estimate of net realizable value of the excess goods. The write-down resulted in a $926,952 reduction in inventory and a corresponding decrease in 1964 taxable income. Nonetheless, Thor continued to hold the goods for sale at original prices. The Internal Revenue Service held that Thor had to maintain its parts inventory at replacement cost rather than net realizable value until it actually scrapped them. The court decided that the inventory write-down was not supported by objective evidence of the inventory's reduced value, as required by Treasury regulations, and was thus properly disallowed by the IRS as not clearly reflective of income. The case may have far-reaching implications, since several hundred similar cases, involving added tax costs of at least $125 million, are pending in the U. S. Tax Court or before the Internal Revenue Service Audit Division.

In *Arizona Public Service Company v. Snead,* the court ruled that New Mexico's 2% gross receipts tax on electric energy conflicted with federal law and was therefore invalid. Imposed in 1975, the tax effectively applied only to electricity sold outside New Mexico, because instate consumers received a credit for the tax against the state's 4% gross receipts tax. In its decision the court relied on a federal law enacted in 1976 that prohibited state taxes that result in a greater tax burden on electricity consumed outside the taxing state.

The court summarily affirmed, without a written opinion, a lower court ruling that invalidated New Jersey's $1,000 state income tax deduction allowed taxpayers for each dependent child attending nonpublic schools. The lower court had ruled that the deduction aids religion in violation of the establishment clause of the Constitution.

In a decision with implications for communities in at least 35 states, the court upheld a law that permits a municipality to impose fees or taxes on nearby nonresidents who receive certain city services but are not permitted to vote in municipal elections. The case, *Holt Civic Club et al. v. City of Tuscaloosa,* came on appeal in a statewide class action by a civic association and several residents of Holt, AL, a small, unincorporated community outside the corporate limits of Tuscaloosa. The court ruled that Alabama's police jurisdiction laws do not violate the equal protection clause of the 14th amendment, that a government unit legitimately may restrict the right to vote to those who reside within its borders, and further, that it is not unreasonable to require residents in a police jurisdiction to pay license fees to support services provided them by the city.

In a decision regarded as a victory for international shipping interests, the court declared unconstitutional a property tax levied by two California cities on foreign-owned cargo containers. The case, *Japan Line v. County of Los Angeles,* was brought by six Japanese shipping companies after they had been assessed more than $500,000 in taxes on containers that had been on Los Angeles piers in 1970, 1971, and 1972. The companies paid the tax under protest and sued for refunds in the California courts. After the California Supreme Court upheld the tax, the companies appealed to the Supreme Court. The court held that the local taxes conflicted with the constitution's commerce clause because they resulted in multiple taxation of property involved in foreign commerce and interfered with Congress constitutional power to regulate foreign commerce.

State and Local Revenue. Growth in state and local government revenue in 1979 was the smallest in many years, reflecting statutory tax reductions and a slowing in the expansion of federal aid. Primarily as a result of Proposition 13, which slashed local property taxes in California by 70%, property taxes nationwide declined by 3% in 1979 from 1978, the first annual reduction since 1940. Total state and local tax collections were $203 billion, an increase of $11 billion or 6% over 1978, as compared with a gain of 10% in 1978 over the previous year. Federal grants to states and localities increased by only 5% in 1979, as compared with 14% in 1978 and 16% in 1977. The slowing in revenues was not accompanied by comparable restraint in expenditures; as a result, state and local governments, which had experienced surpluses in their general budgets in 1977 and 1978, moved into deficit operations.

Despite the decline in revenue growth, state legislatures for the second straight year approved significant reductions in taxes. Taxpayers in 24 states would benefit from tax cuts totaling more than $2.6 billion a year, largely in personal income and sales levies. Partly offsetting were tax increases totaling $610 million annually, mainly in higher motor fuel taxes enacted by 10 states.

OTHER COUNTRIES

Canada. In a move to narrow the deficit and to cut the inflation rate, the new Canadian government in December 1979 proposed sharp increases in corporate income taxes and several excise levies. Corporations would face a 5% profit surtax to run to December 1981. The federal excise tax on gasoline would rise in four steps to 40 cents a gallon by Dec. 1, 1980, boosting the price of gasoline from $1.07 before the tax increase to $1.47 a gallon by Dec. 1,

1980. Cigarette taxes would go up by 10%, and taxes on liquor, wine, and beer would increase. There would also be higher taxes on energy companies, as part of a new Canadian energy strategy. To ease the sharply higher energy prices, the government would grant an energy tax credit for low- and middle-income Canadians, with the amount reduced progressively with the taxpayer's income. Almost immediately, Parliament rejected the budget package, leading to the fall of the Clark government. New elections were to be held in February 1980.

Europe. Britain's new government introduced measures designed to strengthen incentives and encourage private industry to expand. The major effect of the changes was to shift more of the tax burden to consumption and to reduce taxes on income. Included among the changes were reductions in the lowest income tax rate for individuals from 33% to 30%, and in the highest marginal tax rate from 82% to 60%. The top tax rate on investment income was cut from 98% to 75%. In addition, personal exemptions were increased by about 18%; and the minimum level at which taxes begin was raised, exempting 1.3 million more people from paying income tax. The income tax cuts were expected to cost the Treasury $7 billion in 1979. Most of the revenue would be recouped by an increase in the value-added tax to a flat 15%. Previously the rate had been 8% for general items and 12.5% for so-called luxury goods, including autos.

West Germany raised its value-added tax rates from 6% to 6.5% for items taxed at the reduced rate and from 12% to 13% for items taxed at the standard rate.

France's 1980 budget included a new special tax on companies producing oil and natural gas; partial indexing for inflation of all but the highest income tax brackets; an increase in personal exemptions; increases in tax rates on alcohol and tobacco; and new taxes on certain "luxury" items, including large motorboats, planes, and helicopters.

Italy raised the consumption tax on beer and bananas and introduced a tax on the production of picture tubes for certain color television sets. The Italian government proposed increases in several tax credits against income tax, including the credit for children and the employment tax credit.

Japan. In September the prime minister of Japan, Masayoshi Ohira, recommended either an increase in income taxes or the introduction of a consumption tax to reduce deficit financing, which was currently estimated at about 40% of the total budget. In recent years the Japanese government has increased public spending in an effort to revive domestic economic activity, and many observers hold that the resulting deficits have encouraged inflation. The prime minister's proposal was met by strong opposition.

ELSIE M. WATTERS, *Tax Foundation*

Melissa Gilbert is Helen Keller and Patty Duke Austin is Annie Sullivan in NBC's *The Miracle Worker.*

TELEVISION AND RADIO

Talk of new technologies filled the air and the advertising pages during the 1979 broadcasting year. Home video-cassette recorders as well as video disks and playbacks were becoming increasingly familiar to the public. The probability of satellite-to-home transmission and the development of the superstation, a leap forward in pay television, were discussed. What the viewer saw on the television screen, however, was the usual potpourri. To be sure, a few network executives gave lip service to the possibility that the new technologies and ever-expanding cable services might someday transform the nature of both network and local broadcasting. Television might someday, they observed, have to serve specialized audiences, as radio does, rather than the mass audience.

Programs and Ratings. The television year began with ABC (American Broadcasting Company) still firmly leading the ratings, and NBC (National Broadcasting Company) and CBS (Columbia Broadcasting System) struggling mightily to catch up. In fact, with generous dollops of special programming, CBS managed to emerge as number one for a few weeks in the winter and spring. NBC languished. Few of the new programs offered in the "second season" captured the fancy of the audience. The sum-

mer program doldrums did nothing to alter the ratings order. However, with the advent of the "new season," spread out over much of September, there came some surprises. NBC won the first full week of the new season, with CBS a distant third. Two strong movies and special episodes of *CHiPS* and *Diff'rent Strokes* made the difference. ABC took the second week. Baseball's major league play-offs helped NBC win the third week and the World Series won the next two for ABC. The sixth week went to CBS as *Dallas* crashed into the magic Top Ten to join CBS's *60 Minutes* (number one) and four other CBS shows. The seesaw continued-- an amusing game to the interested onlooker, but a serious matter to the networks. Domination in the ratings meant increased profits and stronger affiliate loyalties.

Of the new shows, only *Archie Bunker's Place* (CBS) was strong enough to crack the Top Ten. The show had a new format.

Children's Programs. Almost from the day that Saturday morning became children's time on network television, the programming has been under attack. Action for Children's Television (ACT) made its first petition to the Federal Communications Commission (FCC) in February 1970. In 1974 the FCC issued a policy statement urging certain restraints on broadcasters, but dissatisfactions persisted. In January 1979 the FCC received industry comments on its inquiry into children's programming. At the same time the Federal Trade Commission (FTC) was conducting hearings in San Francisco on advertising on children's programs. The hearings were continued in Washington during March. In both situations, broadcasters, cereal companies, and toy manufacturers made much the same response, indicating that "further intrusion into programming and advertising" by both commissions "would have serious constitutional implications" and would be "counterproductive." Early in November the FCC issued a staff study which found that the television industry had not complied with the 1974 guidelines, and which indicated that only mandated standards, however "imperfect and temporary," would resolve the problems. The only results in 1979 were unhappy broadcasters, advertisers, commissioners, members of Congress, and parents. The issues were carried over to 1980.

News. News divisions of the three networks during 1979 provided an uncommon amount of news from within. Richard S. Salant, the successful president of CBS News for 16 years, became 65 years old, a fact that would have little significance were it not that CBS has a policy of mandatory executive retirement at age 65, the only exception to the rule being the 75-year-old chairman and founder, William S. Paley. April 30 was the day that Mr. Salant was to retire, but at the beginning of the month he announced that he would join NBC as vice chairman of the board, with responsibility for NBC News and corporate planning.

During the summer, ABC's *World News Tonight,* long a lowly third in the audience draw, began—with the help of format changes and greatly improved news-reporting and production teams—to overtake NBC's *Nightly News.* To counter, Salant hired William J. Small, the veteran CBS news executive, as president of NBC News. Shortly thereafter, the decision was made to have John Chancellor as the sole anchorman on the NBC *Nightly News,* with David Brinkley doing regular commentary.

The CBS weekly newsmagazine, *60 Minutes,* more often than not was rated among the Top Ten programs in 1979. Hoping to emulate that success, ABC designed *20/20.* After early stumbling, *20/20* during the summer established a firm place in the weekly schedule. NBC's entry, *Prime Time Sunday,* with Tom Snyder and, later, Jessica Savitch, made its debut on June 24. Like *60 Minutes* and *20/20* in their early months of airtime, *Prime Time Sunday* had difficulty finding an audience, but was expected to continue.

Sports. A typical autumn week provided the fan with 18, and sometimes 21, hours of college and professional football. When to these hours were added local radio broadcasts of school and college games and pre-season and post-season

professional games, culminating in the Super Bowl, the amount of football available to the chair-bound fan was staggering. Radio and TV rights to all these events in 1979 cost an impressive $201,216,571.

Impressive, too, was the $225 million figure with which ABC won the rights to the 1984 Olympics in Los Angeles.

Public Broadcasting. The Carnegie Commission on the Future of Public Broadcasting issued its report at the beginning of February. There were three major recommendations: 1) a dramatic increase in support for the system, reaching $1.6 billion by 1985; 2) further protection for public broadcasting from political control or interference; and 3) the creation of a Public Telecommunications Trust to replace the unwieldy Corporation for Public Broadcasting. The report suggested that much of the increased support funding should be derived from a special "spectrum space" fee levied on commercial broadcasters and based on the size of the individual markets.

Carnegie II, as the report was dubbed, did not address problems within the Public Broadcasting Service (PBS). In June, PBS itself approved a restructuring and voted to create three networks: a national service of cultural and entertainment programs for prime time, a regional service open to local station and independent production, and an instructional service for in-school and home-study purposes. Each service was to function under its own manager. A Center for Public Television, much like the National Association of Broadcasters (NAB), was suggested for the running of nonprogram functions. PBS, already with three satellite channels for program distribution, had options on a fourth.

Cable. High optimism was the mood of the National Cable Television Association as it gathered for its annual convention in late May. The keywords came from Charles Ferris, chairman of the FCC, who called 1979 the "end of the beginning" for cable "as an independent and creative industry." For cable television, Ferris promised a future free of the hampering regulations the FCC had originally adopted to protect on-air television.

The superstation, which delivers its signals via satellite, emerged late in 1978 as an important source of programming for cable companies. The first such station was Ted Turner III's independent WTCG-TV Atlanta. It was followed in early 1979 by independent WGN-TV Chicago, and then by WOR-TV New York and KTVU-TV San Francisco-Oakland. By midyear WTCG-TV Atlanta was serving by satellite 4.8 million cable subscribers, and at least 500,000 more via microwave and over-the-air transmission.

Competition for subscription cable grew when the FCC, in September, allowed greater freedom for the growth of pay television by repealing the rule that limited one pay television station to a market. There were six such stations operating in 1979. Pay cable had begun to cut into audiences for prime time network programs. A study of pay cable viewers made by the A. C. Nielsen Co. during February showed pay cable drawing 16%, on average, of the total audience, as compared with a 23% average for each of the networks. In 1979, pay cable served about five million homes.

Television and the Candidates. The first contention between the networks and a candidate in 1980's presidential campaign came when President Carter's campaign group asked to buy a prime time half hour early in December, following the president's announcement of his candidacy for a second term. NBC and ABC refused on the ground that it was too early to sell political time. CBS offered to sell a five-minute spot, pleading that a half hour "would involve massive disruptions" of its schedule. The networks had previously refused comparable time to Ronald Reagan and John Connally. The Carter-Mondale Committee filed with the FCC a complaint against the three networks. At issue was the interpretation of the "reasonable access" provision that had been written into the Communications Act in 1971. Sen. Barry Goldwater (R-AZ) made it clear that the Congress would step in if the FCC didn't act expeditiously to find "a satisfactory solution."

CBS had scheduled a *CBS Reports* on Sen. Edward Kennedy (D-MA) for November 7. When the network found out that Senator Kennedy would announce his presidential candidacy

George Cukor directed Katharine Hepburn in *The Corn is Green*, adapted from Emlyn Williams' play.

UPI

on that date, it was forced to schedule the documentary on November 4, to avoid having to give equal time to all other candidates, as provided for under the Communications Act. Thus Senator Kennedy ran head-to-head against the movie *Jaws,* in its first television showing. *Jaws* drew a smashing 57% share of the audience, putting it in the same league with *Gone with the Wind* and *Bridge on the River Kwai* in their TV debuts. *CBS Reports* drew a respectable 20% share.

Congress and TV. Early in March the House of Representatives began televising its daily floor proceedings. Broadcasters—network and local—showed little or no interest (other than to use an occasional brief clip on a news broadcast) because the House insisted on controlling the cameras. The House proceedings, however, were fed to cable systems across the country by way of the Cable Satellite Public Affairs Network (C-SPAN), set up for the purpose. There was no similar action in the Senate.

Radio. The deregulation of radio was high on the FCC agenda. In September, issuing a notice of inquiry and proposed rule making, the Commission invited comments on its proposal to eliminate requirements on program and commercials logging, on commercial time, on amounts of news and public affairs programming, and on reporting by licensees of their methods of ascertaining their community's needs. Reaction came quickly, ranging from doubt on the part of some commissioners and NAB officials through praise from licensees to sharp condemnation by such citizens groups as the Office of Communication of the United Church of Christ and the National Citizens Committee for Broadcasting.

Radio Conference. In late September, the World Administrative Radio Conference (WARC) was opened in Geneva, Switzerland. Some 1,500 delegates from 140 nations attended to discuss a number of issues, including the allocation of the world's radio broadcasting frequencies. Since 1958, when the last world radio conference was held, the number of short-wave transmitters has more than doubled. The increasing number of countries broadcasting news around the globe has resulted in serious overcrowding of shortwave bands and bad reception.

When the conference ended, on December 6, six days later than planned, the U. S. delegation was able to say that it had won at least partial victories on several counts, and was "satisfied." Among its victories was agreement on the extension of the lower end of the AM band by 10 kHz, and of the upper end by 100 kHz, thus allowing room for additional AM radio stations. The U. S. delegation was especially pleased that the conference did not "degenerate into a confrontation between industrialized and developing countries." The next WARC conference, on space services, was planned for 1984.

See feature article on SITUATION COMEDY, pp. 43–50.

JOHN M. GUNN

THE 1979 TELEVISION SEASON
—Some Sample Programs

Andrés Segovia at the White House—The classical guitar master presented a program televised from the White House which included selections from Bach and Luys de Navarez. PBS, March 11.

An American Ism: Joe McCarthy—A biography of Joe McCarthy made by the use of newsreels and from interviews with those who knew him. PBS, April 24.

Backstairs at the White House—A four-part miniseries based on Lillian Parks' book, *My Thirty Years Backstairs at the White House;* the drama covers the administrations of William Taft through Dwight Eisenhower. NBC, Jan. 29.

Baryshnikov at the White House—Mikhail Baryshnikov performed in four ballet pieces at the White House. PBS, April 15.

Blind Ambition—A miniseries based on John Dean's book of the same name and on his wife Maureen's book *Mo;* with Martin Sheen. CBS, May 20.

The Boston Symphony in China—A *CBS Reports* telecast on the March 1979 concert tour of China by the Boston Symphony Orchestra. CBS, April 27.

Dorothy Hamill—A 60-minute special on Dorothy Hamill's return to Lake Placid. ABC, April 23.

Edward the King—A 13-part series on Edward VII of England; hosted by Robert MacNeil; with Annette Crosbie, Robert Hardy, Charles Sturridge, and Timothy West. Independent, Jan. 17.

Einstein's Universe—A two-hour discussion of Einstein's theories by scientists at the McDonald Observatory of the University of Texas; hosted by Peter Ustinov. PBS, March 13.

Evening at Pops—A special 50th-year celebration for Arthur Fiedler, conductor of the Boston Pops. PBS, May 1.

Examined: The American Family—An *NBC News Special* three-hour report on the changing American family; hosted by Edwin Newman and Betty Rollin. NBC, Jan. 2.

Fidelio—A *Great Performances* telecast of Beethoven's only opera; performed by the Vienna State Opera and the Vienna Philharmonic; conducted by Leonard Bernstein. PBS, Feb. 21.

Freedom Road—A two-part television movie about an emancipated slave fighting for civil rights just after the American Civil War; with Muhammad Ali and Kris Kristofferson. NBC, Oct. 29.

Friendly Fire—An *ABC Theatre* telecast adapted from the book by C. D. B. Bryan about the death of an American soldier in Vietnam by "friendly fire" and his parents' search for the truth; with Carol Burnett. ABC, April 22.

From Here to Eternity—A three-part miniseries based on James Jones' novel; with Natalie Wood, William Devane, and Steve Railsback. NBC, Feb. 14.

George Burns—A 100th birthday celebration for George Burns 17 years early; with guests Goldie Hawn, Milton Berle, Debby Boone, Johnny Carson, Bob Hope, Gregory Peck, and Jimmy Stewart. CBS, Jan. 22.

Great Jazz Pianos—First in the summer series *Summerfest '79,* a series of concerts from around the United States; with Eubie Blake, Marian McPartland, George Shearing, and Teddy Wilson. PBS, July 7.

Great Performances—Three dramatizations of John Cheever stories—*The Sorrows of Gin, O Youth and Beauty!,* and *The Five Forty-Eight.* PBS, Oct. 24, Oct. 31, Nov. 7.

Henry Kissinger Interview—The former secretary of state was interviewed by David Frost. NBC, Oct. 11.

The Jericho Mile—A 1979 made-for-television movie about a prisoner who trained himself to run in the Olympics; with Peter Strauss. ABC, March 18.

John Denver—A variety hour of music and comedy; Denver's guests included Cheryl Ladd, Tina Turner, Valerie Harper, Cheryl Tiegs, and Erma Bombeck. ABC, March 8.

The Kennedy Center Honors—An evening of tribute to five Americans. CBS, Dec. 29.

Lillie—A 13-part series based on the life of Lillie Langtry, English actress and a mistress of Edward VII. PBS, March 11.

Live from Lincoln Center—A recital by Joan Sutherland and Luciano Pavarotti; Richard Bonynge conducted. PBS, Jan. 22.

Leopard of the Wild—A documentary about an orphaned leopard and how it is trained to survive in the wild. NBC, March 1.

The Magic Sense—A documentary from *The Body Human* series exploring the human eye. CBS, Sept. 6.

Muppets Go Hollywood—A special Muppets show; with numerous celebrities, including Dick Van Dyke, Rita Moreno, and Johnny Mathis. CBS, May 16.

Music by Russian Composers—A *Live from Lincoln Center* telecast of works by Tchaikovsky, Stravinsky, and Mussorgsky; with the New York Philharmonic; conducted by Zubin Mehta; hosted by Mrs. Joan Mondale. PBS, Jan. 17.

The Music for UNICEF Concert—Charity performances taped from the UN General Assembly in New York; guests included Rod Stewart, Elton John, the Bee Gees, Henry Winkler, Henry Fonda, Rita Coolidge, Kris Kristofferson, and Olivia Newton-John. NBC, Jan. 10.

Oil and American Power—An NBC White Paper documentary on the problem of America's dependency on Middle East oil. NBC, Sept. 4.

Palestine—A British series on Palestine's history from 1914 to the present. PBS, Jan. 18.

Paul Robeson—A one-man show based on the life of the actor, singer, and social activist; with James Earl Jones. PBS, Oct. 8.

The Prime of Miss Jean Brodie—A six-part miniseries, based on the novel of the same name, about a school teacher who earmarks certain girls as "Brodie girls" and attempts to bestow upon them her expertise in all manner of subjects. PBS, May 18.

Raised in Anger—A documentary exploring the child abuse problem; hosted by Edward Asner. PBS, Jan. 11.

Roots: The Next Generations—A seven-part sequel to the original *Roots* which begins in 1882 and goes to 1976; with Marlon Brando, Olivia de Havilland, Henry Fonda, and James Earl Jones. ABC, Feb. 18.

Scared Straight—A documentary in which teenagers from correctional homes visit lifers in Rahway (NJ) State Prison under a Juvenile Awareness Program; hosted by Peter Falk. Independent, March 8.

The Scarlet Letter—A four-part dramatization of the Nathaniel Hawthorne novel; with Meg Foster, John Heard, and Kevin Conway. PBS, April 2.

Shakespeare Plays—The debut of this six-year series, in which all 37 of the plays of William Shakespeare will be presented, began with *Julius Caesar.* Other plays presented during 1979 were *As You Like It, Romeo and Juliet, Richard II, Measure for Measure, Henry VIII.* PBS, Feb. 14, 28; March 14, 28; April 11, 25.

The Shooting of "Big Man": Anatomy of a Criminal Case—An *ABC News Closeup* documentary which followed the procedures of a murder case. ABC, June 8.

Strangers: The Story of a Mother and Daughter—A 1979 made-for-television movie about a reunion between a mother and daughter after the daughter's 20-year absence; with Bette Davis and Gena Rowlands. CBS, May 13.

Studs Lonigan—A special three-part series based on the trilogy by James T. Farrell about a boy growing up in the Chicago of the 1920's; with Harry Hamlin. NBC, March 7.

Thor Heyerdahl and the Tigris—A documentary in which Heyerdahl set out to test the navigational skills of the Sumerians. PBS, April 1.

Too Far to Go—A drama adapted from John Updike's short stories which traced the failure of a 20-year marriage; with Michael Moriarty and Blythe Danner. NBC, March 12.

TV Guide—The First 25 Years—A retrospective of television news, sports broadcasts, comedies, dramas, and westerns; with host Phil Donahue. NBC, Oct. 21.

Verdi's Otello—A *Live from the Met* telecast, based on Shakespeare's *Othello;* with Placido Domingo, Gilda Cruz-Romo, and Sherrill Milnes; conducted by James Levine. PBS, Sept. 24.

TENNESSEE

A political scandal, good agricultural yields, and state college mergers dominated news in Tennessee in 1979.

Government. On January 17 Lamar Alexander became the state's fifth Republican governor in more than a hundred years. In a surprising and unprecedented move, sanctioned by Democratic leaders in both legislative houses, Alexander was sworn into office three days ahead of schedule after a federal prosecutor warned that outgoing Gov. Ray Blanton might pardon several convicts who were targets of a federal grand jury probe. Six persons, including three Blanton aides, already had been indicted, following action by the grand jury in a widely publicized clemency-for-cash allegation. A few days before Alexander's early inauguration, Blanton had pardoned 52 convicts—an action that outraged the public.

Alexander assumed office with characteristic vigor; his recommendations for conservative spending on the state level met with favor. Lawmakers passed legislation which continued the 4.5% sales tax and provided for a $3.5 billion budget.

Economy. Despite a slight increase in the state's unemployment rate in the late summer and early fall, officials pointed to a substantial increase in the total work force in describing the state's economy as "healthy and growing." Farmers, enjoying the largest income in history, benefited particularly from increased beef cattle prices and a conversion of considerable acreage of corn and cotton to soybeans. Beef cattle claimed the number one sales position, with soybeans a close second.

Education. Following a federal court ruling ordering the merger of the University of Tennessee at Nashville with Tennessee State University under the name and administration of the latter, the school year began for the predominantly black institution without incident, although enrollment was more than 10% off original projections. On nearby Vanderbilt University campus, a merger of the George Peabody College for Teachers with Vanderbilt was accomplished. With the opening of the fall semester, Peabody became the Vanderbilt University College of Education.

Dr. Homer Adams became president of Trevecca Nazarene College. King College of Bristol, which earlier had announced plans to close with the spring semester of 1979, opened again in September.

People in the News. John J. Hooker, three times a gubernatorial candidate, became publisher of the Nashville *Banner*. The Gannett Corporation, former owner of the *Banner,* purchased the Nashville *Tennessean,* published since 1938 by the Silliman Evans family.

Appointed to seats on the United States District Court were Judge John Nixon and former State Treasurer and gubernatorial candidate Tom Wiseman.

ROBERT E. CORLEW
Middle Tennessee State University

TEXAS

A sunbelt state without many of the energy problems plaguing the North and Midwest, Texas continued to undergo rapid growth in 1979.

Politics. William Clements, Jr., the first Republican since Reconstruction to be sworn in as governor of Texas, encountered strong resistance from a Democratic legislature during his first year in office. Clements had campaigned on a pledge of fiscal austerity and the return of part of the state's surplus as tax relief. In 1979 he sought to carry out those promises. Public school teachers were held to a 5.1% salary increase, and a reduction of 20,000 state civil service jobs was planned. Responding to this threat, state employees considered the possibility of unionizing. Disappointed by the token tax relief granted by the legislature, Clements called for a special session to discuss that issue and the possibility of increased compensation for state civil servants.

In a political maneuver that seemed bizarre to those unfamiliar with the workings of the Texas legislature, 12 state senators went into hiding for five days in May to kill a controversial legislative proposal. The "Killer Bees," as the 12 lawmakers became known, fled the state capital, denied the Senate a quorum, and thereby destroyed a bill to establish an early presidential primary in 1980. The bill was seen as favorable to the state's conservative Democrats and to the chances of John B. Connally winning the Republican primary.

Oil and the Economy. In late summer, the Texas shoreline was dealt a devastating blow by the largest oil spill in history. The June 3 blowout of a Mexican oil well in the Bay of Campeche washed ugly globs of oil on the beaches of southern Texas by early September. Hardest hit were the resort areas of Corpus Christi and Padre Island. The damage occurred at the height of the summer season, and the loss in tourism was very heavy. The Gulf Coast fishing industry suffered substantial losses, and the ecological damage to the area's birds and other wildlife was beyond estimation. The spill became a political issue when Texas Attorney General Mark White threatened a lawsuit against Mexico, which refused to pay cleanup costs, and Governor Clements opposed the move. Private lawsuits on behalf of Texas fishermen were filed, but no decisions had been rendered by year's end.

President Carter's energy proposals stirred considerable controversy in Texas during 1979. Oilmen insisted that excess profits be reinvested in research and exploration, while consumers demanded relief from rising gas and utility prices. With coal an abundant resource in Texas, many favored diversification and the development of alternative fuel sources.

Gas shortages occasioned the implementation of an "odd-even" rationing plan June 25. Although gas lines dwindled and the scheme was abandoned, the price of gasoline remained high.

See also HOUSTON.

STANLEY E. SIEGEL, *University of Houston*

THAILAND

The eyes of Thailand's leaders were fixed nervously on neighboring Cambodia throughout 1979. Fighting there between the forces of the Vietnamese-backed regime of Heng Samrin and Chinese-supported guerrillas led by ousted Premier Pol Pot threatened to spill over into eastern Thailand. Tens of thousands of refugees from the Cambodian fighting crossed the border into Thailand, joining masses of refugees from the Communist regimes of Laos and Vietnam. Mass famine resulted.

By late January, elements of at least ten Vietnamese divisions had largely routed Pol Pot's forces and were poised along Cambodia's border with Thailand. Their presence meant that for the first time in centuries, Thailand and Vietnam faced each other along a common frontier. The Thai government of Prime Minister Kriangsak Chamanan, a retired army general, reacted to the potential threat by stepping up military

spending and training and by seeking support from Thai allies.

In Washington in February, Prime Minister Kriangsak received pledges of more military aid. U. S. military sales thereafter increased.

But Thailand's leaders recognized that their 200,000-man armed forces would be no match for Vietnam's 600,000 battle-hardened troops. In an effort to prevent confrontation with Vietnam, the Thais repeatedly called on Vietnam to withdraw its forces from Cambodia.

In late March, Kriangsak went to Moscow for talks with Soviet officials, the main backers of Vietnam and of Cambodia's Heng Samrin government. Kriangsak tried to get Soviet President Leonid Brezhnev to restrain Vietnam.

Throughout the year, there were reports that China was sending supplies to the Pol Pot forces through Thailand. The Thais denied the reports, but not very vigorously.

In late April the Thais allowed a column of about 50,000 of Pol Pot's troops and their families to march through Thai territory and then back into Cambodia to escape encirclement by Vietnamese forces. Bangkok's decision was denounced bitterly by the Vietnamese and the Heng Samrin government in Cambodia. Then, in late September, Thailand tightened controls on Soviet cargo flights through its air space.

Domestically, Kriangsak's military government allowed a partial return to parliamentary democracy. Elections were held in April for the 301-member House of Representatives created under a new constitution whose provisions for a two-house legislature assured that Kriangsak would remain in office. Since members of the 225-member Senate were named by Kriangsak, he needed only minimal support in the House to remain in power, and he received it. The rightwing Prachakorn Thai Party and the middle-of-the-road Social Action Party, led by former Prime Minister Kurit Pramoj, did well.

Kriangsak tried to curb inflation, estimated at 12%, recognizing that rising prices could produce political and civil unrest. Otherwise, the largely agricultural economy performed fairly well, with the gross national product growing about 8% during the year.

EDWARD EPSTEIN
"The Asian Wall Street Journal"

──────── **THAILAND · Information Highlights** ────────
Official Name: Kingdom of Thailand.
Location: Southeast Asia
Area: 209,411 square miles (542 375 km²).
Population (1979 est.): 46,200,000.
Chief Cities (1975 est.): Bangkok, the capital, 4,000,000; Chiang Mai, 100,000.
Government: *Head of state,* Bhumibol Adulyadej, king (acceded June 1946). *Head of government,* Kriangsak Chamanan, prime minister; *Legislature*—National Assembly: Senate and House of Representatives.
Monetary Unit: Baht (20.42 baht equal U. S.$1, June 1979).
Manufactures (major products): Processed foods, textiles, wood, cement.
Agriculture (major products): Rice, rubber, tapioca, corn, sugar, pineapple.

THEATER

In 1979 it became increasingly clear that a distinctive new pattern was emerging from Broadway's continuing dependence upon off-Broadway, off-off-Broadway, and regional America for most of its plays. While musicals continued to be fabricated directly for Broadway, the straight plays that reached New York's largest theater public came from more modest origins and had already been tried out before American audiences and critics. Many were plays of quality touching upon issues which might have been deemed repellant or, at best, of interest only to a very few. The subjects of these plays, whose appeal could not easily be predicted, included the impact upon others of a deformed man of overpowering ugliness, the experience of a woman who suffers a stroke and starts on the road to recovery, life in Czarist Russia seen through the eyes of a horse, and the serene existence of a retired couple who are brought back to immediate reality by encounters with their daughter and their grandson. Such plays were not the sort that had dominated Broadway for years; instead, they were expert but unsensational explorations of human problems. Their success had an effect upon even those producers who followed the older pattern of importing their plays from London; if the new Broadway pattern had not emerged, it is unlikely that we would have seen a British play about a hospital patient who argues successfully that he should be the beneficiary of a mercy killing, or a play about the brutal Nazi persecution of homosexuals. The Broadway theater was, as it always had been, an unsentimental business enterprise. Only Broadway's conception of what had box-office appeal changed.

Bernard Pomerance's *The Elephant Man* had been presented in London without winning much attention, but from its first appearance at an off-off-Broadway theater this play by an expatriate American seemed assured of a Broadway transfer and extraordinary commercial success. Its central character is an historical personage of Victorian England, John Merrick, whose spectacular deformity is made to provide other characters, and notably the distinguished physician who befriends Merrick, with opportunities to ponder the normality of their own lives. In the title role, a hitherto unknown actor, Philip Anglim, brilliantly and economically gave the impression of deformity without the appearance of deformity. The high quality of his acting was matched by that of Kevin Conway as the physician and Carole Shelley as an actress. *The Elephant Man* won both the Tony and the Drama Critics Circle awards as best play of the season. The most prominent of its producers was Richmond Crinkley, the newly appointed head of the now dormant Vivian Beaumont Theater of Lincoln Center, whose roster of executives included Edward Albee, Woody Allen, and the Rumanian director Liviu Ciulei.

In Arthur Kopit's *Wings,* originally written for radio and then performed by the Yale Repertory Theater, Constance Cummings gave vivid expression to the role of a former aviatrix disabled by a stroke and amply reinforced the play's impression of scrupulous authenticity. The American theater's continuing interest in illness and old age was reflected also in Ernest Thompson's *On Golden Pond,* an amiable comic portrait of an elderly couple which began its life at an off-off-Broadway theater in the previous year and had two 1979 Broadway openings.

Strider, Mark Rozovsky's dramatization of a story by Leo Tolstoy, was seen at the Gorky

Kevin Conway, Philip Anglim, and Carole Shelley star in Bernard Pomerance's *The Elephant Man.* The Tony Award—winning drama is the story of John Merrick, the "elephant man" of Victorian London.

Theater of Leningrad by Robert Kalfin, who co-directed it at his off-off-Broadway Chelsea Theater Center. This moving account of a long-suffering gelding's tragic life, embellished by authentic music and inventive choreography and highlighted especially by Gerald Hiken's beautifully conceived performance in the leading role, moved to Broadway late in the year. The secret of its appeal was that the story was an allegory of human life.

Even the year's most acclaimed romantic play struck a distinctively contemporary note. In *Loose Ends* Michael Weller has continued to write candidly about his own generation, following his pair of young lovers from their first casual encounter into a marriage that is shattered by new ambitions and commitments. Sympathetically directed by Alan Schneider, this play was first seen at Washington's Arena Stage. Virtually the same production opened some months later at the Circle in the Square on Broadway, a theater normally committed to a policy of limited engagements; the instant popularity of *Loose Ends* caused that policy to be abandoned to permit a continuous run that lasted beyond the end of the year.

Not all of Broadway's successes reflected new tendencies. Bernard Slade's *Romantic Comedy* originated on Broadway and, indeed, this saga of two collaborating playwrights who take more than a dozen years to discover that they are made for each other could have originated nowhere else. Anthony Perkins won particular praise for the sureness of his comic style; playing the less firmly-conceived role of his partner, Mia Farrow, in her Broadway debut, at least had no difficulty transmitting her considerable personal charm.

Like Pomerance, Martin Sherman is an American whose play was first professionally staged in England, but his *Bent* might, more properly than *The Elephant Man,* be called an importation because it enjoyed a respectable London run. *Bent* is a harrowing picture of the vicious treatment of homosexuals in a Nazi concentration camp. Richard Gere, a new comet of the film world, played the lead. A more diverting importation, with an equally dismaying subject, was Brian Clark's *Whose Life Is It Anyway?* This comic defense of euthanasia owed most of its appeal to Tom Conti's bright, resourceful performance as a sculptor whom an accident has rendered permanently incapable of living a normal life. Yet one was left with the impression that diversion was not what this subject called for. The British importations were no more unanimously devoted to solemn subjects, however, than the American originals. Alan Ayckbourn's *Bedroom Farce,* brought to America by a cast from England's National Theatre but subsequently played by substitutes recruited locally, jumbled three couples together in what was ultimately a rather innocent comedy of sexual confusion.

Among the honorable failures of the Broadway season must be counted Brian Friel's *Faith Healer,* a series of striking monologues to which James Mason contributed a memorable performance, and Abe Polsky's *Devour the Snow,* a courtroom play dealing with cannibalism in the American historical incident of the Donner Party. James McLure's *Lone Star* and *Pvt. Wars,* which originated at a regional theater, was a pair of one-acters that displayed a comic talent not yet fully developed. John Guare's sardonic comedy *Bosoms and Neglect* pursued a pattern contrary to the common one, following its brief appearance on Broadway with a new production at the Yale Repertory Theater. One of the stranger events of the Broadway season was a presentation of Shakespeare's *Richard III* in which Al Pacino played the King.

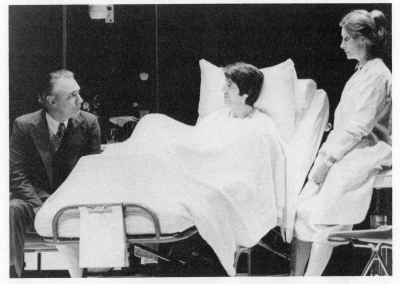

Whose Life Is It Anyway? featured Philip Bosco, Tom Conti, and Jean Marsh. The play, which won a Tony for Mr. Conti, tells of a sculptor who is badly injured in an accident and seeks mercy killing.

The best Broadway musical of the season was *Sweeney Todd* with Angela Lansbury and Len Cariou. Stephen Sondheim wrote the music and lyrics; Harold Prince directed and produced.

PHOTO BY MARTHA SWOPE, COURTESY MARY BRYANT

Musicals. Broadway's musicals tended to be more traditional, but *Sweeney Todd,* directed and produced by Harold Prince, with a musical score by Stephen Sondheim and a book by Hugh Wheeler, was as distinctive and original as all the projects which Prince sets in motion. To the old story of the mad, murderous barber of Fleet Street who delivers his victims to a neighbor to be converted into meat pies, Prince and his collaborators added new motivation and social commentary (derived from an English play by Christopher Bond): it is suggested that cannibalism is a suitable metaphor of human life in our society. To accompany this savage social criticism, Sondheim contributed disturbing tunes that reminded many of Kurt Weill. As the homicidal barber and the genial baker of meat pies, Len Cariou and Angela Lansbury gave appropriately stylized performances. General admiration for *Sweeney Todd* did not suggest to anyone that Prince and his collaborators seriously identified with its ideas. They were "trying them on" for the sake of the show.

Prince was also the director of *Evita,* a musical which he had first directed in London in the previous year, but its concept did not originate with him, and, in fact, one of the songs was popular long before *Evita* reached the stage. Again, but more emphatically than in London, the charge was made that the concept was at fault, that the show was excessively sympathetic to its title character, the wife of the Argentine dictator Peron, and that the gratuitous presence of the revolutionary Che Guevara as a critical chorus figure did not seriously answer this criticism. Nevertheless, *Evita* found its audience. However, another new play with music fell victim to what was considered to be its excessive zeal—in spite of the fact that most of its critics viewed its cause more sympathetically. *Zoot Suit,* which had been enormously successful in Los Angeles, hotly attacked the victimization of Chicanos in an unjust trial of the World War II period. The producers launched a considerable effort to overcome indifferent reviews, but their effort failed.

More conventional musicals came and went. Some of those that stayed were among those most firmly linked to the past. *They're Playing Our Song* capitalized on a perfunctory story about two songwriters, some pleasant banter, a winning title song, and a stunning performance by Lucie Arnaz (whose failure to be nominated for a Tony was one of the mysteries of the year). *Sugar Babies* was more frankly an exercise in nostalgia—a revue about burlesque, utilizing authentic burlesque routines and starring two movie stars of years ago, Mickey Rooney and Ann Miller. If the jokes were ancient, their great age contributed to their charm. *Whoopee* was even more obviously a carload of nostalgia because it was a 1920's musical, revised and directed in such a way as to make it even more antique and naive. In this context, no one could object to the tap-dancing Tapaho Indians, one of whom was a blonde. *The 1940's Radio Hour* had less impact, but as its title clearly indicates, its main ingredient was nostalgia for the golden age of radio. Two of the most eagerly received musicals of the recent past came fully equipped with their own built-in nostalgia—*Peter Pan* and *Oklahoma!*

But reminding us of the past was not enough to guarantee a musical's success. *I Remember Mama* strove mightily to awaken nostalgia for immigrant life in America or, at least, for the play, the film, and the television series that used the same Norwegian-American material—but all in vain. It had been too totally bathed in sentimentality. Richard Rodgers' pleasant score, the last which he was to compose, was not one of his best. The show's most potent ingredient, the radiant personality of its star, Liv Ullmann, was insufficient to save it. Still another revived musical, *The Most Happy Fella,* had a short life despite its proclaimed fidelity to Frank Loesser's original score and despite the operatic talents of Giorgio Tozzi in the lead. *The Grand Tour,* based on the wartime play *Jacobowsky and the Colonel* and set in the French collapse of 1940, proved not to be truly nostalgic but only remote, and the spritelike Joel Grey, as Jacobowsky, expended too much of his energy trying to beat life into this dead vehicle. The producers of one of the many doomed musicals, *Sarava,* based on a Brazilian novel, attempted to escape their fate by refusing to invite the drama critics, to no avail.

Off-Broadway. With many of its likeliest vehicles commandeered for Broadway, the off-Broadway season was not quite so bright as it has been. As usual, Joseph Papp's Public Theater led in the number of offerings, but it had no overwhelming successes to add to its popular Broadway musical, *A Chorus Line.* Among the Public's many productions were *Dispatches,* Liz Swados' vivid adaptation of Michael Herr's book about the Vietnamese war; Ntozake Shange's *Spell No. 7,* a program of songs and poems; Frederick Neumann's dramatization, for Mabou Mines, of Samuel Beckett's novel *Mercier and Camier; Tongues,* "a collaboration by Sam Shepard and Joseph Chaikin," acted by Chaikin; David Mamet's *The Woods,* a duologue which was one of Mamet's less memorable creations; and *Julius Caesar* and *Coriolanus,* the first prod-

ucts of one of Papp's new schemes—classic drama acted by black and Hispanic players. In addition to creating the black-Hispanic venture (run first by Michael Langham and later by Wilfred Leach), Papp journeyed to the Soviet Union and announced on his return that he would send *A Chorus Line* there and also export directors who would repeat their Public Theater productions with Russian casts; the Russians would send their directors to do their own plays at the Public. Subsequently the plans had to be canceled. Earlier Papp revealed that he would coproduce plays with the Kennedy Center of Washington.

Other dramatists, old and new, were staged off-Broadway. Shepard was represented by *Seduced,* about an eccentric millionaire who resembled Howard Hughes. He won the Pulitzer Prize for *Buried Child,* one more of his studies of eccentric rural families, a play seen first in San Francisco in 1978 and then in New York and New Haven. The Circle Repertory Company produced Mamet's *Reunion,* a trio of one-act plays about a father and daughter, and also Lanford Wilson's *Talley's Folly,* a love story that was part of a series about a family in Indiana. *Talley's Folly* was particularly well received, and a Broadway production was promised for 1980 with Judd Hirsch and Trish Hawkins repeating the roles they created. Marsha Norman's *Getting Out,* first seen in Louisville, was an impressive study of a woman released from prison, with different actresses playing the juvenile of-

Ann Miller and Mickey Rooney were the attractions in *Sugar Babies* at New York's Mark Hellinger.

BROADWAY OPENINGS OF 1979

MUSICALS

But Never Jam Today, book by Vinnette Carroll and Bob Larimer, music by Bert Keyes and Mr. Larimer, lyrics by Mr. Larimer; directed by Vinnette Carroll; July 31–August 5.

Carmelina, book by Alan Jay Lerner and Joseph Stein, music by Burton Lane, lyrics by Mr. Lerner; directed by José Ferrer; April 8–29.

Comin' Uptown, book by Philip Rose and Peter Udell, music by Garry Sherman, lyrics by Mr. Udell; directed by Philip Rose; with Gregory Hines; December 20–.

Evita, book by Tim Rice and Andrew Lloyd Webber, music by Mr. Webber, lyrics by Mr. Rice; directed by Harold Prince; with Patti LuPone; September 25–.

Got Tu Go Disco, book by John Zodrow, music and lyrics by Kenny Lehman and others; directed by Larry Forde; June 25–July 5.

The Grand Tour, book by Michael Stewart and Mark Bramble, music and lyrics by Jerry Herman; directed by Gerald Freedman; with Joel Grey; January 11–March 4.

I Remember Mama, book by Thomas Meehan, music by Richard Rodgers. lyrics by Martin Charnin and Raymond Jessel; directed by Cy Feuer; with Liv Ullmann; May 31–September 2.

King of Schnorrers, book, music, and lyrics by Judd Woldin; directed by Grover Dale; November 28–.

The Most Happy Fella, book, music, and lyrics by Frank Loesser; directed by Jack O'Brien; with Giorgio Tozzi; October 11–November 25.

My Old Friends, book, music, and lyrics by Mel Mandel and Norman Sachs; directed by Philip Rose; with Maxine Sullivan; April 12–May 27.

The 1940's Radio Hour, a musical written and directed by Walton Jones; October 7–.

Oklahoma!, book and lyrics by Oscar Hammerstein, music by Richard Rodgers, from a play by Lynn Riggs; directed by William Hammerstein; with Laurence Guittard and Christine Andreas; December 13–.

Peter Pan, by Sir James M. Barrie, music by Mark Charlap (additional music by Jule Styne), lyrics by Carolyn Leigh (additional lyrics by Betty Comden and Adolph Green); directed by Rob Iscove; with Sandy Duncan and George Rose; September 6–.

Sarava, book and lyrics by N. Richard Nash, music by Mitch Leigh; directed by Rick Atwell; with Tovah Feldshuh; February 9–June 17.

Snow White and the Seven Dwarfs, by Walt Disney; written for the stage by Joe Cook; directed by Frank Wagner; executive musical direction by Donald Pippin; October 18–November 18.

Sugar Babies, conceived by Ralph G. Allen and Harry Rigby, written by Mr. Allen, music by Jimmy McHugh, lyrics by Dorothy Fields, Harold Adamson, and Al Dubin, additional music and lyrics by Arthur Malvin, Jay Livingston, and Ray Evans; directed by Ernest Flatt; with Mickey Rooney and Ann Miller; October 8–.

Sweeney Todd, book by Hugh Wheeler, music and lyrics by Stephen Sondheim; directed by Harold Prince; with Angela Lansbury and Len Cariou; March 1–.

They're Playing Our Song, book by Neil Simon, music by Marvin Hamlisch, lyrics by Carole Bayer Sager; directed by Robert Moore; with Robert Klein and Lucie Arnaz; February 11–.

The Utter Glory of Morrissey Hall, book by Clark Gesner and Nagle Jackson, music and lyrics by Mr. Gesner; directed by Nagle Jackson; May 13.

Whoopee, book by William Anthony McGuire, music by Walter Donaldson, lyrics by Gus Kahn; directed by Frank Corsaro; with Charles Repole; February 14–August 14.

PLAYS

Are You Now or Have You Ever Been, by Eric Bentley; directed by John Bettenbender; January 29–February 25.

Bedroom Farce, by Alan Ayckbourn; directed by Alan Ayckbourn and Peter Hall; March 29–November 24.

Bent, by Martin Sherman; directed by Robert Allan Ackerman; with Richard Gere; December 2–.

Bosoms and Neglect, by John Guare; directed by Mel Shapiro; May 3–5.

Break a Leg, by Ira Levin; directed by Charles Nelson Reilly and Frank Dunlop; April 29.

Devour the Snow, by Abe Polsky; directed by Terry Schreiber; with Kevin O'Connor; November 7–10.

Dogg's Hamlet and Cahoot's Macbeth, by Tom Stoppard; directed by Ed Berman; October 3–28.

The Elephant Man, by Bernard Pomerance; directed by Jack Hofsiss; with Kevin Conway, Philip Anglim, and Carole Shelley; April 19–.

Every Good Boy Deserves Favour, by Tom Stoppard and André Previn; directed by Mr. Stoppard; with René Auberjonois and Eli Wallach; July 30–August 4.

Faith Healer, by Brian Friel; directed by José Quintero; with James Mason; April 5–21.

Father's Day, by Oliver Hailey; directed by Rae Allen; with Tammy Grimes; June 21–September 16.

The Goodbye People, by Herb Gardner; directed by Jeff Bleckner; with Herschel Bernardi; April 30.

G. R. Point, by David Berry; directed by William Devane; with Michael Moriarty; April 16–May 13.

Knockout, by Louis La Russo 2d; directed by Frank Corsaro; with Danny Aiello; May 6–September 16.

Last Licks, by Frank D. Gilroy; directed by Tom Conti; with Ed Flanders; November 20–December 1.

Lone Star and **Pvt. Wars,** by James McLure; *Lone Star* directed by Stuart White; *Pvt. Wars* directed by Garland Wright; with Leo Burmester and Clifford Fetters; June 7–August 5.

Loose Ends, by Michael Weller; directed by Alan Schneider; with Kevin Kline and Roxanne Hart; June 6–.

Manny, by Raymond Serra; directed by Harold J. Kennedy; with Raymond Serra; April 18–May 13.

A Meeting by the River, by Christopher Isherwood and Don Bachardy; directed by Albert Marre; with Siobhan McKenna, Sam Jaffe; March 28–April 1.

Murder at the Howard Johnson's, by Ron Clark and Sam Bobrick; directed by Marshall W. Mason; with Joyce Van Patten, Tony Roberts; May 17–19.

Night and Day, by Tom Stoppard; directed by Peter Wood; with Maggie Smith; November 27–.

Once a Catholic, by Mary O'Malley; directed by Mike Ochrent; with Rachel Roberts; October 10–13.

On Golden Pond, by Ernest Thompson; directed by Craig Anderson; with Frances Sternhagen and Tom Aldredge; February 28–June 16; September 12–.

The Price, by Arthur Miller; directed by John Stix; with Mitchell Ryan, Fritz Weaver, Joseph Buloff, and Scotty Bloch; June 19–October 21.

Richard III, by William Shakespeare; directed by David Wheeler; with Al Pacino; June 14–July 15.

Romantic Comedy, by Bernard Slade; directed by Joseph Hardy; with Anthony Perkins and Mia Farrow; November 8–.

Spokesong, by Stewart Parker; directed by Kenneth Frankel; March 15–May 20.

Strangers, by Sherman Yellen; directed by Arvin Brown; with Bruce Dern; March 4–11.

Strider, by Mark Rozovsky, adapted from a story by Leo Tolstoy, English version by Robert Kalfin and Steve Brown; directed and staged by Robert Kalfin and Lynne Gannaway; with Gerald Hiken; November 14–.

Teibele and Her Demon, by Isaac Bashevis Singer and Eve Friedman; directed by Stephen Kanee; with F. Murray Abraham and Laura Esterman; December 16–.

Whose Life Is It Anyway?, by Brian Clark; directed by Michael Lindsay-Hogg; with Tom Conti and Jean Marsh; April 17–October 27.

Wings, by Arthur Kopit; directed by John Madden; with Constance Cummings; January 28–May 5.

Zoot Suit, written and directed by Luis Valdez; choreographed by Patricia Birch; musical sequences and production by Daniel Valdez; March 25–April 29.

REVUES

Bette! Divine Madness, with Bette Midler; December 5–.

Bruce Forsyth on Broadway, one-man show; June 12–16.

Gilda Radner Live From New York, written by Gilda Radner and eight others; directed by Lorne Michaels; with Gilda Radner; August 2–September 22.

A Kurt Weill Cabaret, music by Kurt Weill; with Martha Schlamme and Alvin Epstein; December 26–.

The Madwoman of Central Park West, by Phyllis Newman and Arthur Laurents; directed by Mr. Laurents; with Phyllis Newman; June 13–August 25.

The Magnificent Christmas Spectacular, a Radio City Music Hall revue; November 22–.

Monteith and Rand, by and with John Monteith and Suzanne Rand; January 2–March 10.

A New York Summer, a Radio City Music Hall revue; June 1–September 26.

Up In One, conceived by Peter Allen and Craig Zadan; with Peter Allen; May 23–June 30.

fender and the maturer parolee. In Tennessee Williams' *A Lovely Day for Crève Cœur*, Shirley Knight played a spinster who was in danger of becoming entirely isolated from life. Ms. Knight returned in *Losing Time*, by her husband John Hopkins, a harrowing play about women's problems. In David Berry's *G. R. Point*, Michael Moriarty played an innocent recruit who is hardened by his exposure to the Vietnamese war. The leading off-Broadway musicals were *God Bless You, Mr. Rosewater*, based on the novel by Kurt Vonnegut, Jr., and *Scrambled Feet*, a satirical revue which dealt with show business.

Canada, London, Paris. The most interesting new play in Canada was probably *Jitters*, by David French, a hilarious comedy about the opening of a play; after getting its first staging at the Tarragon Theater of Toronto, it was seen at many more Canadian playhouses and at the Long Wharf Theater of New Haven. The festival of Stratford, Ontario, saw an essentially comic actor undertake one of the great tragic roles when Peter Ustinov played King Lear.

The London theater continued to be dominated by the two great subsidized companies. Among the most acclaimed plays of the National Theatre were Peter Shaffer's *Amadeus*, in which Mozart was represented as an unpleasant person and Paul Scofield played his rival Salieri; *End of Play*, a story of a family in which the ailing Michael Redgrave remained on stage throughout but spoke only eight words; *The Undiscovered Country*, by the 20th-century Viennese dramatist Arthur Schnitzler, adapted by Tom Stoppard, with Dorothy Tutin playing the long-suffering wife of John Wood; *Richard III* with a hyperactive Wood; John Dexter's production of *As You Like It;* and Arthur Miller's *Death of a Salesman*, with Warren Mitchell. The Royal Shakespeare Company offered Pamela Gems' *Piaf*, with Jane Lapotaire as the French singer; Peter Brook's production of *Antony and Cleopatra*, which moved to London from Stratford-on-Avon; Mikhail Bulgakov's *The White Guard*, a Soviet play about the Russian Revolution; and the much-appreciated Hollywood comedy by George S. Kaufman and Moss Hart, *Once in a Lifetime*. The West End had *Songbook*, a musical comedy by Monty Norman and Julian Moore about show business; *A Day in Hollywood, a Night in the Ukraine*, a musical revue employing themes from Hollywood farces; James Saunders' comedy about two married couples, *Bodies;* New Zealander Roger Hall's comedy about two married couples, *Middle Age Spread;* and some American musicals. Smaller theaters in London presented the world premiere of a striking East German play, Stefan Schutz's *Mayakovsky*, about the Soviet poet, and Tom Stoppard's playful double bill, *Dogg's Hamlet, Cahoot's Macbeth*, the first production of the British American Repertory Company and consequently seen afterward in New York.

NATIONAL THEATRE

John Wood becomes the first actor since Laurence Olivier to portray Richard III in London. The Shakespearean production was presented at the National Theatre.

Interesting plays in Paris included *The Conference of the Birds*, adapted by Jean-Claude Carrière from an old Persian poem and directed by Peter Brook for his company; *Mephisto*, based on Klaus Mann's novel about the rise of Nazism and the German theater, adapted and directed by Ariane Mnouchkine; Claude Rich's *An Outfit for Winter*, a Pinteresque representation of the strange encounter of three men, one of them played by Rich himself; Jean-Claude Grumberg's *The Workshop*, a chronicle of Jewish life in the garment industry; Fernando Arrabal's *The Tower of Babel*, a play about Spain presented by the Comédie Française, which has been trying to shake its conservative image; Eduardo Manet's *The Day Mary Shelley Met Charlotte Brontë*, in which the two novelists are confronted by their characters; *The Hunchback*, a study of some curious individuals by Slawomir Mrozek, a Polish dramatist who has become a French citizen; and *Audience* and *Private View*, a double bill about a political dissident by Vaclav Havel, a Czech dramatist who has been condemned to prison in his native land.

HENRY POPKIN
State University of New York at Buffalo

Mime

Mime, the art of silent theatrics, had a banner year in 1979. In the United States, there was mime on Broadway, off-Broadway, and in two national festivals. There were even laurels from the mayor of New York City, who proclaimed the second Tuesday in September as an official day of mime celebration. The occasion was marked by festivities honoring a mime troupe performing at the prestigious Lincoln Center in Manhattan. Abroad, mime festivals were held in London in January and in Mexico during July.

The year also marked the 81st birthday of Etienne Decroux, the French actor-teacher credited with being the "father of modern mime." Working alone, and later with his first famous student, Jean-Louis Barrault, Decroux broke ranks with the 19th century tradition of white-faced mime storytellers. The growth of interest in mime art in America is traceable directly to early motion pictures and to Etienne Decroux.

As a young acting student, Decroux had despised the costumes, mannerisms, and affectations of the actors and white-faced Pierrot storytellers who typified the 19th century mode. At the Vieux-Colombier School of Jacques Copeau in Paris, where Decroux studied, theater space

"Mummenschanz," a pantomime with three performers, enjoyed its third season on Broadway in 1979.

MUMMENSCHANZ

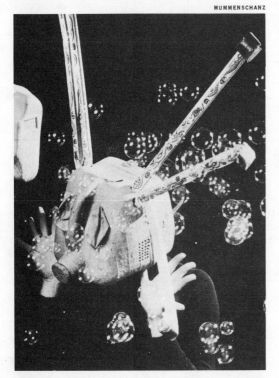

was stripped to an essential bare stage, and actors were trained to work free of manners and pretense. This enabled them to use the human body as the core element in a Theater of Ideas. Decroux seized the opportunity. He did away with costumes, plots, and texts to free the actor for studies of pure movement in space.

The isolation of body parts in rotation, inclination, and translation; changes in line, speed, and force of the body; and a focus on pure form and pure movement presented unlimited possibilities in the mind of Decroux. It was, he felt, the best way to excite the mood of an audience. One of his unique contributions to the art of mime was a "scale" of movements as basic to the mimist as a musical scale is to the musician.

In this way, Decroux aligned himself with what the French writer André Malraux described as "the distinguishing feature of modern art. Twentieth century art never tells a story." This rejection of 19th century realism and romanticism in painting, music, dance, and poetry was a revolution in form which affected all the arts and flew on the wings of 20th century science.

Still, the 19th century is referred to as the magic century of mime. Solo performers such as Sevérin, Paul Le Grand, George Wague, Felicia Mallet, Christine Kerf ("her eyes were like a voice"), and other male and female actors emerged as popular mime storytellers. Their influence was felt as late as the 1940's, when Wague, a theater critic and member of the French Académie, first brought Decroux's and Barrault's gifted student, Marcel Marceau, to public attention.

From his first public appearances more than three decades ago, Marceau has had enormous international success, becoming the most visible and well-known contemporary mime artist. His most familiar stage character is the roguish Bip, but his artistry and imagination are best reflected in his perceptive solo sketches, caricatures, illusions, and evocations of emotion.

Historians and scholars tracing the art of mime back to its ancient roots in Zuni ritual and Greek pantomime note interesting transformations. In later centuries mime was absorbed into the speaking theater, and then, in the current era, again became the silent art of signs and pure movement.

Today, mime acting is flourishing in many forms—from informal entertainment in store windows and on street corners, to rehearsed performances in elegant theater settings. It is at once a unique art form and a basic form of communication that can be understood across cultural borders.

JEWEL WALKER

THIRD WORLD

The sixth summit of nonaligned nations took 1,400 delegates from 95 nations to Havana, Cuba, Sept. 3–9, 1979. In what might be called "The Battle for the Third World," two distinct factions within the nonaligned movement engaged in often bitter debate and behind-the-scenes political maneuvering.

Cuban President Fidel Castro, the host and chairman of the summit, led the more radical, pro-Soviet wing of the alliance. In his opening speech September 3, Castro launched an aggressive attack against U. S. "imperialism" and defended his own country's "fraternal relations" with the Soviet Union. Yugoslav President Josip Broz (Tito), the last surviving founder of the organization, led the more moderate, strictly nonaligned member-nations. In his September 4 speech, Tito urged the Third World states of Africa, Asia, and Latin America to avoid close involvements with both the Western democracies *and* the Soviet bloc. Differing dramatically with Castro's address, the 87-year-old Tito warned that "all forms of political and economic hegemony" are incompatible with nonalignment and that "foreign influences" were trying to divide the movement.

In addition to the speeches and debates—sometimes taking up to 12 hours a day—there was vigorous maneuvering for committee chairmanships, priority on the speaking agenda, and wording of the final resolution. Castro was anything but an impartial chairman, using his authority to pack key committees with his radical allies and to give them prime time at the expense of the moderates. When the dust had finally settled, there were some indications of a pro-Soviet orientation. From its inception in 1961 the nonaligned movement had tended to be hostile toward the West, but its pro-Soviet tilt became more pronounced in 1979, largely because of the charisma and tactics of Castro.

One victory for the Cuban-led faction came in a dispute over whether the Cambodian seat should be occupied by representatives of the ousted Pol Pot regime or the government of Heng Samrin, installed by Vietnam in January. The "compromise" decision, by which the seat would remain empty, was a blow to the prestige of Pol Pot and considered a triumph for Castro. A move by the radicals to oust Egypt from the conference failed, but the Egyptian-Israeli peace treaty was formally condemned. Human rights violations by the Soviet Union were ignored, as were those by nonaligned dictatorial regimes. Although the final declaration was noncommital on several divisive issues and Castro closed the meeting with a vow of restraint, the Cuban president would remain the titular head of the movement until 1982 and would undoubtedly promote a pro-Soviet stance. Even less in doubt was that the nonaligned Third World states would seek to isolate the Western industrialized nations and deprive them further of valuable natural resources and markets.

Economic Plight. Invited to report on the nonaligned conference at the United Nations in October, Castro emphasized the economic disparity between the developed and nondeveloped nations of the world. The biggest threat to world peace, he said, is the concentration of wealth "in the hands of a few powers whose wasteful economies" are maintained by the exploitation of the labor and natural resources of the Third World. He repeatedly singled out the United States as the main source of the world's problems. Citing the "moral obligation" of the wealthy, Castro called on the United States and other Western "imperialists" to pay $300 billion to developing nations in the next 10 years. He did not dwell on the impact of soaring oil prices on Third World economies; the nonaligned movement includes several members of the Organization of Petroleum Exporting Countries (OPEC).

Statistics released by the United Nations and World Bank showed that the economic status of more than one and a half billion inhabitants of the Third World was not improving appreciably in 1979. In addition to rising oil prices, Third World countries continued to suffer from illiteracy, malnutrition, repressive and inefficient regimes, and high birth rates.

Communications. The dialogue between the richer countries of the northern hemisphere and the poorer nations mostly in the southern hemisphere also came to a head on issues of world communication. In late 1978 the Third World states, with the support of the Soviet Union, took an anti-Western line in talks on worldwide press information at the UN Education, Scientific, and Cultural Organization (UNESCO). The final UNESCO declaration did eliminate from an earlier document a controversial passage calling for state control of the media and endorsed the principle of freedom of the press, but it called on developed nations to help improve Third World news organizations.

In late 1979, the expected battleground was the World Administrative Radio Conference (WARC) in Geneva, Switzerland. Of the 65 new delegations since the previous conference in 1959, most were from the Third World. Almost all of the 40 issues to be decided at WARC had potential rich-versus-poor overtones. The most controversial of these was the apportionment of the world's radio frequency spectrum. Developed nations, which accounted for only 10% of the world's population, controlled 90% of the spectrum. The United States sought to maintain its monopoly and proposed to expand the AM band. When the conference ended on December 6, the U. S. delegation was able to say that it had won at least partial victory on several counts and was pleased that the conference did not "degenerate into a confrontation between industrialized and developing countries."

AARON R. EINFRANK, *Free-lance Writer*

TRANSPORTATION

The generally prosperous economic conditions of 1978 gave way to increasing uncertainty and expectations of recession in the first half of 1979. Real gross national product increased only 1.1% in the first quarter and registered a 2.4% decline in the second. Industrial production was off slightly and the continued strength of consumer demand was in doubt. Since the demand for the transportation of freight derives from the level of economic activity, the continuance of traffic growth was unlikely. Nonetheless, both rail and truck traffic showed significant increases over 1978, with the rate of increase declining as the year wore on. New records would be set for tons and ton miles.

No major legislation regarding U. S. transport policy was enacted. Regulatory relaxation both in rail and truck transportation was continued by the Interstate Commerce Commission (ICC). But bills, proposed by the Carter administration and others, seeking substantial regulatory reform for railroads and motor carriers engendered far more dispute than had airline deregulation in 1978. Rail, shipper, and labor views were at odds with one another and with the proposals of the administration. The trucking industry, while remaining sternly opposed to major regulatory reform, put forward modest proposals of its own. The right of eminent domain for slurry pipelines to transport coal was again actively pushed, but Gov. Ed Herschler of Wyoming, out of concern for the water supply, vetoed a bill that would have granted the right in that state. The proposed construction of a pipeline connection eastward from Los Angeles for the movement of Alaskan crude oil was dropped when environmental considerations and the multiplicity of required permits escalated costs. Plans moved along, however, for construction of gas pipeline connections between Alaska and the lower 48 states.

The National Transportation Policy Study Commission, a joint Congressional-executive branch group, delivered its final report after several years of searching work. Several members, in dissenting expressions, criticized the report as falling short of recommending an articulated U. S. transportation policy. The report was noteworthy, however, for calling attention to the risk generated by the absence of a national energy policy. It questioned whether the capital needs of the transport industries—forecast as $3 trillion from private and $1 trillion from government sources by the year 2000—can be met. The general tenor of the recommendations was to seek greater freedom from regulatory restraint in favor of market forces.

In ocean transport, a grand jury investigation resulted in 7 major shipping companies and 13 executives being fined a total of $6.1 million. It was said to be the largest such fine in the history of antitrust. At issue were alleged violations of the Shipping Act of 1916 through failure to file agreements and through rate fixing activities not sanctioned by approved agreements. The U. S. Department of Justice and the Federal Maritime Commission continued to pursue opposite policies regarding the desirability of open competition in the ocean-borne foreign trades. Numerous legislative proposals were addressed to the improvement of the condition of the U. S. merchant marine. Abroad, the liner code of conduct developed through the United Nations Conference on Trade and Development (UNCTAD) neared ratification, although the United States remained opposed.

Neil Goldschmidt, former mayor of Portland, OR, and a mass-transit enthusiast, succeeded Brock Adams as U. S. secretary of transportation. (*See* BIOGRAPHY.)

Fuel. Shortage and high cost of fuel were the outstanding U. S. transportation stories of 1979. The revolution in Iran, resulting in a temporary cessation of crude oil exports from that country, produced shortages of gasoline and diesel fuel resembling those at the time of the 1973–74 embargo. The United States was reminded again that all of its transportation, by whatever mode, is almost wholly dependent upon petroleum-based fuels. Despite the sharp price increases imposed by the Organization of Petroleum Exporting Countries (OPEC), U. S. demand had continued to grow and its dependence upon imported oil continued to increase in the face of gradually declining domestic crude production. Shortages at the gas pump, producing long lines, first appeared in California, but by April were spreading to the northeast and later to other parts of the country. Priority granted to farmers for spring planting generated shortages of diesel fuel at truck stops.

There are an estimated 100,000 truck owner-operators who haul agricultural commodities, including most of the nation's fresh fruits and vegetables, that are exempt from regulation. They also work for regulated trucklines on a percentage of the freight basis. Because they rely for a living on the productivity of their vehicles, the 55-mph speed limit and the lower weight limitations in some states cut their annual mileage and tonnage and squeezed their operating margins. When fuel shortages, short pumping hours and long lines at truck stops, rapidly escalating fuel prices, and the failure of large truck lines to secure rate increases and pass them through to their owner-operators all hit suddenly and severely, the owner-operators organized a strike. Highways, truck stops, and, in some cases, oil bulk stations and refineries were blockaded. Violence erupted on the highways. In several states the National Guard was called upon to protect trucks that continued to operate.

(Unlike owner-operators, large trucking companies had contracted for fuel supplies.) Negotiations with government agencies resulted in 100% fuel allocations for truckers, a required pass-through of fuel-based rate increases, emergency action to raise weight limits in a number of states, and other steps that brought an end to the disruption. Meanwhile, however, an unknown number of owner-operators had put their rigs up for sale and deserted the business while fresh produce prices increased.

Just as heavier allocations cured the gas lines in California and exported the shortage to other states, priorities for farmers and truckers reimposed shortages of diesel fuel on railroads and barge lines. Faced with reduced allocations from their regular suppliers, some diesel fuel users resorted to the spot market. Prices which had averaged 38.2 cents per gallon on January 1 had reached 62.38 cents on July 9 and fuel was being purchased in the spot market at an average cost of $1 per gallon. Stocks were run down, branch-line and switching operations were curtailed, and main-line freight services were slowed to conserve fuel. Before the embargo of 1978, fuel took 3.5% of railroad revenues; in late 1979 it was taking more than 10%. Some barge lines, resorting to the spot market, found fuel costs rising to 50% of operating expenses.

Airlines were not exempt from the problems. Some schedule cancellations occurred. Had it not been for a two-month strike of United Airlines and the grounding of DC-10 aircraft following the nation's most costly air crash, more serious disruption of service would have occurred. But fuel costs as a percent of operating costs climbed from 20% in 1978 to more than 25% by mid-1979. Airlines are the most intensive users of fuel in relation to the work they perform.

All commercial transportation has been making vigorous efforts at fuel conservation. Railroads handled 34 billion more ton miles of freight in 1978 than in 1977, but burned less fuel. New tractors for motor carrier service feature air deflectors, radial tires, improved drive trains, intermittent cooling fans, and lower engine revolutions per minute, all of which improve fuel economy. Late model jet engines for aircraft show substantial improvement over earlier models and the turbo prop is replacing jets in some short-haul services because of greater fuel efficiency. Down sizing of automobiles has increased miles per gallon despite the increasing bite of more stringent emissions standards. Yet the number of motor vehicles on the roads has for some years increased at 2.5 times the growth of the population and the reduced automobile sales of mid-1979 were generally regarded as temporary. The transportation sector consumes some 26% of the nation's energy, but 54% of its petroleum products. Thirty-nine percent of petroleum demand is for highway use and, of this, 71% goes to the automobile. (See also ENERGY.)

Air Transport. With the route and pricing freedom accorded by the airline deregulation statutes of 1978, trunk and supplemental airlines expanded service into competitive markets by acquiring dormant rights and reducing or eliminating service at smaller airports where traffic volume was unprofitably low. Commuter airlines moved into many of the abandoned markets, but complaints were heard from some points where service had diminished. Discount fares were multiplied—on one route as many as 77 separate fare packages were said to be in existence—to the confusion of passengers, travel agents, and even airline ticket agents.

Aided by a booming economy and lowered fares which induced new traffic and filled empty seats, revenue passenger miles increased 17.9% in 1978, while available seat miles grew by only 6.7%. Hence the passenger load factor climbed from 55.9% to 61.5%. The average coach fare declined from 7.91 cents per mile in 1977 to 7.80 cents in 1978 and to 7.74 cents in the first quarter of 1979. Airline profits boomed, increasing 59% from 1977 to 1978 and reaching $1,197,000,000 in that year. Profits for 1979, however, were expected to be about one half those of 1978. In the face of incipient recession, the rate of traffic increase had declined to 9.4% by July. Costs of both fuel and labor had been rapidly increasing and fares had not kept pace. The airline industry is particularly vulnerable to the economic cycle and the sharp profit contraction was cause for concern.

On May 25 a McDonnell-Douglas DC-10, American Airlines Flight 191, crashed immediately after take-off at Chicago's O'Hare International Airport. All 272 persons aboard perished. The aircraft had lost an engine, and inspection of the pylons revealed cracks which led the Federal Aviation Administration (FAA) to ground all DC-10s in the United States until inspections could be made. On restoration to service cracks continued to appear, hence the FAA grounded the aircraft from June 6 until mid-July while investigation and retrofit were accomplished. The FAA as well as the manufacturer came under heavy criticism. The schedules of those airlines with numerous DC-10s in their fleets were severely disrupted.

Mergers were in the news as Southern and North Central joined to form Republic and the Civil Aeronautics Board (CAB) disapproved a Continental-Western linkup. Texas International, Eastern, and Pan American all bid for control of National. Pan Am's application was approved. Allegheny increased its service and changed its name to US Air.

On the international front the CAB continued its attempt to export the competitive philosophy exemplified by domestic airline deregulation. Several bilateral agreements with European countries and with Israel permitted certification of additional U. S.-flag carriers to compete with those already on the routes. Other nations, including Japan, were resistant to the competitive philosophy. The CAB also called upon carrier members of the International Air Transport Association to show cause why group rate making through the IATA traffic conferences should not be disallowed. Numerous governments launched vigorous protest, but IATA itself adopted a two-tier structure which enabled carriers to participate in its service functions without joining in the traffic conferences.

A major problem for airlines is the huge prospective capital requirement for the retrofit or replacement of existing aircraft. The needs to save fuel and to meet stringent noise standards require major replacement of earlier jets. As of June 1, 1979, 452 aircraft were on order. Engine and airfoil research continues in the search for greater efficiency. The airlines forecast capital requirements of $60 billion in 1977 prices for replacements and additions to the fleet during the 1980's.

Railroads. Despite the highest freight traffic on record, earnings in 1978 were low and provided a return on investment of less than .75%. Traffic continued to show increases in 1979. But burgeoning fuel and wage costs outpaced rate increases. Rail capacity continued to be short, with car shortages exceeding 33,000 on the average day during the period of heavy agricultural movement. With a record grain crop and heavy export demand, movement was impeded by a prolonged strike by operators at the Lake Superior grain elevators. Though the order books of freight car builders stretched into 1981, no early relief from the car shortage was expected.

Conrail, the semigovernment rail corporation which operates the former Penn Central, Erie, Lehigh Valley, Reading, and Central of New Jersey and which has received $3.3 billion in government financing, logged a small profit for the first time in the second quarter of 1979.

A substantial loss, although less than the loss of 1978, was anticipated for the full year. The prospect of ultimate profitability recedes and depends upon further rail deregulation, relief from union work rules, and line abandonment. The physical condition of the properties has been greatly improved, but traffic has not attained estimated levels.

A reorganization plan for the Milwaukee Road was submitted to the court and to the Interstate Commerce Commission (ICC). It called for reducing the 9,800-mile (15 771 km) system to a 3,400-mile (5 471 km) core east of Miles City, MT. A U. S. district judge submitted the plan to the ICC. Southern Pacific's proposed acquisition of Rock Island's Santa Rosa (NM)– Kansas City line continued to face heavy opposition. The merger proceeding of Burlington Northern and St. Louis–San Francisco appeared to be approaching a favorable conclusion, while hearings moved along in the proposed Seaboard Coast Line–Chessie merger.

The Carter administration's proposed cut of 43% in the Amtrak route mileage came under sharp criticism as the fuel shortage cut back highway travel and turned passengers toward commercial carriers. Amtrak carried 2,050,000 passengers during the month of June, an increase of 24% over June 1978, and denied 1,381,685 requests for space. Plagued by equipment shortages and large numbers of aging passenger cars out of service, it was unable to expand train service to accommodate the sudden increase in load. Congress, accordingly, authorized nearly twice the subsidy which the administration proposed and set standards which would require much smaller reductions in route mileage. Railroads, however, account for only 0.7% of intercity passenger miles and expansion is dependent on the addition of new motive power and equipment for which lead times are long. Rehabilitation of the Boston-Washington corridor oper-

UPI

The first segment of MARTA, Atlanta's new rapid transit system, began operations in June 1979. When completed MARTA will consist of a 53-mile (85.3-km) subway- and elevated-train network.

ated by Amtrak continued, but the work was well behind the original schedule.

Railroads reaped some benefit from the deregulation of transportation of fresh fruits and vegetables. Especially during the strike of owner-operators on the highways, rail movement increased and high rates were obtained. But volume was held down by the limited supply of mechanically refrigerated cars and trailers. New concepts of piggyback and container flat cars were being tested, designed to reduce weight and air resistance and thus improve fuel performance. The Road Railer concept was revived and under test—a semitrailer capable of operating both over the highway and on the rails in special trains. Since the concept uses the trailer itself as the rail vehicle and eliminates the flat car, fuel savings of about 40% were anticipated.

Motor Transport. Intercity bus lines reaped additional traffic as a result of the gas shortage. But, faced with the competition of the private automobile, the airlines, and a subsidized Amtrak, their traffic trends had been down for a number of years and their business verged on the unprofitable. For this reason Holiday Inns disposed of its Trailways subsidiary. One area of improvement was the growth of express package business.

News of truck transportation was dominated by the troubles of the owner-operators, including the household goods movers, and the fight of the regulated segment of the industry (approximately 40%) against Congressional moves toward deregulation. A contract was reached with the Teamsters which was generally regarded to have broken the president's wage guidelines and which clearly affected later union negotiations in other industries. Acquisition of small truck lines by larger carriers continued.

Underlying the more noteworthy events, and little noticed by the public, were the continued growth of private carriage by industrial concerns, the spread of irregular-route truckload transportation of general and special commodities, and the continued erosion of the share of total traffic carried by railroads and by the regulated segment of the trucking industry. The service needs of shippers were not being fully met by the regulated carriers. Faced with double digit inflation, shippers sought to minimize their inventories both in transit and in warehouse. The demand for faster and more dependable movement of goods often led to new or expanded private truck operations.

Quite apart from the battles in Congress, regulatory relaxation in trucking was proceeding as the ICC further reduced its control. The ICC moves were partly designed to enhance competition in the industry and partly to improve efficiency by reducing empty backhauls and circuitous routing; both are costly in terms of fuel. The entry of new firms and the acquisition of new routes continued to be made easier. A landmark ICC decision, reversing a rule that had applied for more than 40 years, permits private carriers to seek authority to haul commercially for others in order to fill their empty backhauls. The exempt zones around airports were significantly expanded for the trucking of air freight. On the other hand, the ICC was reconsidering a controversial decision designed to limit the return on investment of regulated truckers and thus to restrain rate increases.

Urban Transit. The year was marked by the opening of the first segment of Atlanta's new rail rapid transit system (MARTA). The Washington, DC, system was further extended and hours of operation increased. Bay Area Rapid Transit (BART) similarly increased its operating hours in the San Francisco region. In August, however, BART was struck, forcing some 66,000 daily passengers back onto the highways.

Progress continued with rail system engineering in Miami, FL, and Buffalo, NY. In New York a special subway-bus service was instituted to improve access to J. F. Kennedy Airport. The New York City Transit Authority and Pullman, manufacturer of the latest large order for subway cars, entered suit and countersuit over failures of truck sideframes on delivered cars and alleged improper influence of Transit Authority personnel.

Because of the high cost of rail rapid transit and the fact that few city corridors provide the heavy volume of passenger travel necessary to use its very large capacity, increased attention was given to the potential of light rail. This is a modernized and improved version of the old street car, but intended to operate more often on separated rights of way than in city streets. In Canada, both Calgary and Edmonton were relying on light rail to accommodate urban growth, and in the United States, the Boston system was being improved with new light-rail equipment.

The fuel crisis directed new attention toward mass transit and away from private automobile use. President Carter's energy program contemplated additional federal financing for mass transit. For the most part this would involve urban bus transportation, since only a few of the largest cities have the concentrated passenger movements that can justify rail transit. Unlike the cities of Western Europe and many other parts of the world, the suburban sprawl around American cities—induced by highway construction, hitherto cheap gasoline, and other inducements—produces light housing densities and makes a return to mass transit difficult. Ironically, as interest in encouraging a trend toward mass transit grew, manufacturers were deserting both the bus and rail-car industries. The prospect emerged that only one manufacturer might remain in each of these industries and U. S. transit systems began to look to foreign sources for equipment.

ERNEST W. WILLIAMS, JR., *Columbia University*

PHOTOS UPI

Shortly after takeoff from Chicago's O'Hare International Airport on May 25, an American Airlines DC-10 dropped one of its three engines (*left*), rose to about 500 feet (150 m), rolled to the left, and plunged to earth. A total of 275 persons (272 on board and 3 on the ground) was killed in the crash and fire. The head of the Federal Aviation Administration (FAA), Langhorne Bond (*below*), ordered the grounding of all DC-10s. Before July 13, when the FAA ban against operation of all U.S.-airlines' DC-10s was finally lifted, teams of inspectors scrutinized the planes, and especially the engine mountings (*below, left*).

A report, issued by the National Transportation Safety Board as 1979 ended, blamed the crash on "improper maintenance procedures" by American Airlines. The board criticized McDonnell Douglas for designing an engine mount assembly in a manner that made it "vulnerable to damage" and recommended that the FAA improve its monitoring of aircraft production and maintenance.

TRAVEL

Domestic and international travelers in 1979 spent an estimated $504 billion, an increase of 18% over 1978. That enormous sum exceeds the annual world expenditure on health care ($464 billion) and military defense ($400 billion).

Changes in Patterns. Americans traveled as much as ever despite periodic gas shortages and panics, a shrinking dollar, double digit inflation, and travel costs that were sent skyrocketing largely by rapidly rising fuel costs. However, there were noticeable changes in the patterns of tourism—changes that caught segments of the travel industry off guard and resulted in shortages and confusion.

American travel abroad leveled off, reflecting the decreased purchasing power of the dollar overseas, while domestic travel was greatly affected by fuel availability. Some resort areas, such as the Catskills (NY), with their large and largely self-contained hotels, entertained more vacationers than usual. But areas and attractions dependent on transient automobile traffic saw business fall off sharply.

In some national parks, for instance, campground occupancy in spring and early summer was down nearly 50% from 1978. As the year went on and gas supplies increased, there was some rise in the occupancy rate.

The summer of 1979 saw the price of a gallon of regular gasoline pass the $1 mark in most of the nation, a psychological peak that made drivers more conscious of fuel costs. An appeal by President Jimmy Carter for Americans to "take no unnecessary trips" also had an inhibiting effect on pleasure travel.

Major metropolitan areas, where public transit systems make cars more a nuisance than a necessity, benefited in many cases from the scarcity of gasoline. Some were helped by promotional campaigns like "I love New York." Both Washington and New York enjoyed tourist booms that were limited only by severe hotel-room shortages.

One of the most significant developments of the year was the foreign traveler's discovery of America, a discovery stimulated by a weak dollar, which made the United States a bargain for citizens of hard currency countries, and by relatively cheap airfares. An unprecedented total of 21 million foreign visitors, including Canadians and Mexicans, arrived in the United States in 1979. Significantly, air arrivals were up about 25%. These foreign tourists spent an estimated $10 billion, an important contribution to the economy and a welcome change from the U. S. tourism deficit—about $2 billion per year—caused by U. S. travelers spending more abroad than foreign tourists do in the United States.

Air Travel. Despite some problems, air travel boomed in 1979. In the United States, the effect of federal deregulation of the airlines was dramatic, as supplemental carriers turned to scheduled routes, intrastate carriers became interstate, and domestic airlines went international. Virtually every fare change and route application was granted by the Civil Aeronautics Board (CAB), including Pan American Airways' 30-year-old request for rights to fly passengers between New York and the West Coast.

New fares and services were often launched with bargain promotional fares and these became so common that it was estimated that by summer more than half the passengers in the United States were using some sort of discounted ticket. Passenger volume increased nearly 20% in the first part of the year, leveling off to about 14% as fuel costs forced ticket prices upward and curtailed bargains.

United States domestic carriers flew a record 240 million passengers and racked up record earnings, but because of fuel costs profits totaled about $754 million—around the same as in 1977. Increased numbers of passengers created a demand for airline seats that carriers had trouble meeting, a situation worsened by a 55-day machinists' strike that idled United Airlines, the largest carrier in the western world, and forced cancellation of 1,600 flights daily. In addition, the crash of an American Airlines DC-10 in Chicago caused the grounding in early summer of 270 DC-10s belonging to 41 U. S. and foreign airlines. Thousands of passengers had to be

Construction was widespread in Washington, DC, the U. S. capital, in 1979. Generally, the shortage of gasoline forced tourists to flock to the nation's cities.

shifted to new equipment or different carriers, since many airlines lost a sizeable portion of their fleets. Laker Airways, operator of the pioneering no-frills Skytrain service from London to New York and Los Angeles, uses only DC-10s and had to shut down entirely while the aircraft were being inspected.

Cruise Revival. Cruiseship bookings were in such demand that cruise lines opened their books for 1980 reservations nine months in advance. More than a million Americans took cruises in 1979. Many lines announced plans to build new ships or renovate or enlarge—sometimes by inserting a section in the hull and "stretching"—older ones.

The old *France* was being turned, at a cost of $42 million, into the 2,000 passenger *Norway* and $30 million was being spent on the long-mothballed *United States* to enable it to cruise between Los Angeles and Hawaii.

Inter-city bus lines gained passengers as a result of gasoline shortages, although many former drivers of their own cars preferred budget flights for long distances. Bus tours grew in popularity and about half of the approximately 335 million passengers carried on inter-city lines were part of charters or tours.

Rail service in the United States continued to decline despite a gas-related increase in demand. Congress approved a reduction of about 20% in AMTRAK routes after the Department of Transportation asked for a 43% cut in passenger train mileage.

WILLIAM A. DAVIS, *Travel Editor*
"The Boston Globe"

TUNISIA

President Habib Bourguiba, ailing throughout most of 1978, reasserted his dominance of the Tunisian government in late 1979, instituting some conciliatory measures with imprisoned trade unionists and reshuffling some top leaders after the tenth congress of the ruling Socialist Destour Party (PSD). The capital, Tunis, became the new headquarters of the Arab League in June after the organization was withdrawn from Cairo, Egypt. The Tunisian Information Minister, Chedli Klibi, became secretary-general of the league.

Labor Relations. Serious conflicts between the government and the trade unionists continued in 1979, an outgrowth of the general strike of 1978 organized by Tunisia's only trade union confederation, the General Union of Tunisian Workers (UGTT). An opposition group, the Tunisian Collective of January 26, announced that in February several trade union leaders were imprisoned, adding to the more than 1,000 already jailed after the 1978 strike.

In May, Bourguiba signed a pardon for 263 people serving strike-related sentences, but investigations by Amnesty International and by a team of French jurists into the reported deplorable conditions of detention and the torture of the jailed unionists revealed that the measure was a propaganda maneuver and that no actual releases had been documented.

In August, Bourguiba pardoned Habib Achour, secretary-general of the UGTT jailed since the 1978 strike, after international concern had focused on his fate. Seriously ill with diabetes and hypertension, Achour was a victim of a poisoning attempt in June, believed to be the work of prison officials. He had been a member of the PSD political bureau until the UGTT broke into open conflict with the government's authoritarian rule and in protest of the stagnating economy.

Politics. Although Prime Minister Hedi Nouira's place as successor to President-for-Life Bourguiba, 76, seemed well-assured in 1979, intraparty jockeying to consolidate Nouira's power during the September tenth party congress resulted in a government shake-up instituted by the president. The change was a signal that Bourguiba still holds the reins of the regime in his hands. Bourguiba opened the meeting with lavish praise of Nouira, but he later fired his minister of defense and congress organizer, Abdallah Farhat, for his maneuvers to enhance the Nouira faction in the PSD against those opposed to his policies. This disrupted the delicate balance of forces which Bourguiba had long striven to achieve. Elections to the PSD's central committee demonstrated the rising strength of the anti-Nouira faction. One of the prime minister's leading critics, Mohamed Sayah, gained a seat on the decision-making body.

The defense minister, a close associate of Nouira and considered one of the government's most influential leaders, was replaced by the former minister of mines and energy, Rachid Sfar, a relative political new-comer. Farhat was not the only victim, however. The director of the Tunisian Press Agency, Mahmoud Triki, and the political affairs director on Nouira's staff, Hedi Baccouche, also were dismissed.

Succession. Hedi Nouira still appeared as the leading candidate to succeed the aging Bourguiba, who, however, seemed to have recovered from some of the ailments that kept him in the political background in 1978.

MARGARET NOVICKI, *"African Update"*
African-American Institute

TUNISIA · Information Highlights ———

Official Name: Republic of Tunisia.
Location: North Africa.
Area: 63,170 square miles (163 610 km²).
Population (1979 est.): 6,400,000.
Chief City (1975 census): Tunis, the capital, 550,404.
Government: *Head of state,* Habib Bourguiba, president-for-life (took office 1957). *Chief Minister,* Hedi Nouira, prime minister (took office Nov. 1970). *Legislature* (unicameral)—National Assembly.
Monetary Unit: Dinar (0.406 dinar equals U. S.$1, Aug. 1979).
Manufactures (major products): Crude oil, phosphates, olive oil, textiles, construction materials.
Agriculture (major products): Wheat, olives, grapes, citrus fruits.

TURKEY

Political disarray, burgeoning anarchy, and an unstable economy made 1979 a year of crisis in Turkey.

Government Falls. Parliamentary by-elections on October 14 brought down the 22-month-old government of Prime Minister Bülent Ecevit. The right-wing opposition gained enough seats in both houses to topple the coalition of Ecevit's Republican People's Party (CHP), the conservative Republic Reliance Party (CGP), and the Democratic Party (DP). Losing all five seats at stake in the National Assembly and retaining only 12 of the 50 contested seats in the Senate, Ecevit announced the resignation of his cabinet two days later. He called on the head of the opposition Justice Party (AP), former Prime Minister Süleyman Demirel, to form a new cabinet, but Demirel was reluctant to align himself with smaller right-wing groups. After nearly a month of political maneuvering and consultations with President Fahri Korutürk, Prime Minister Demirel on November 12 announced the formation of a new government. The cabinet included 28 ministers, all of them members of parliament from Demirel's Justice Party. The prime minister appealed to the public for "trust and patience," but serious ideological differences between the nation's two major parties—the AP and CHP—helped perpetuate a state of general insecurity. The new administration inherited major problems.

Unrest. Political and sectarian violence spread to all parts of Turkey during the year and continued unabated despite martial law in many provinces. Shootings and reprisals between radical fringe groups on the left and right killed more than 1,000 persons during the year. The population of Turkey has been deeply divided for years. Neighborhoods, schools, and cafés in Ankara and other major cities were considered the domain of either "antifascist" leftists or "anti-Communist" rightists. In 1979, however, violence between the two groups seemed to spread to outlying areas. Gang raids, bombings, and mass demonstrations reached epidemic proportions. Martial law, originally proclaimed in 13 provinces after sectarian violence in the southern province of Kahramanmaras left more than 100 persons dead in December 1978, was expanded to six more of Turkey's 67 provinces in 1979 and was extended for the duration of the year. A poll of terrorists conducted by the Mil Iyet daily newspaper revealed that the basic cause of the violence was economic frustration.

Economy. From mid-1978 to mid-1979, Turkey had the highest rate of inflation of any Organization for Economic Cooperation and Development (OECD) nation: 52.3%. At the beginning of 1979, Turkey's economic problems included foreign debts totaling about $12 billion, a lack of foreign exchange to pay for oil and essential machinery, and 20% unemployment.

In March, the National Assembly approved a $16-billion budget for 1979–80 proposed by the Ecevit government. Approval of the budget opened the door for new stabilization measures, with reduction of the balance-of-trade deficit a major goal. Several austerity and currency revaluation measures also were put into effect during the year.

A "comprehensive economic rescue plan" announced March 16 called for major price increases for petroleum, coal, iron, and steel products, as well as sugar and cement. On June 12 the lira was devalued by 44% against the U. S. dollar—only two months after a 5.7% devaluation—and other major price hikes were announced. Finally, the Fourth Five-Year Plan went into effect in 1979. This austerity program was intended to accelerate growth (by 2% per annum), promote industrial development, strengthen foreign payment capacity, and overcome the nation's energy problems.

Foreign Aid and Relations. As Turkish leaders planned for the future they also recognized that foreign assistance was desperately needed. Meetings in Guadaloupe and Bonn, West Germany, early in the year resulted in an aid package totaling $1.45 billion from the major Western nations. The money was intended to help Turkey finance its imports in 1979 but was made contingent on a Turkish accord with the International Monetary Fund (IMF) on its redevelopment plans. The IMF subsequently endorsed the government's programs and, on June 13 announced that it could again borrow money from the IMF. The new arrangement would grant Turkey $325.5 million in one-year standby credit and would pave the way for the release of some $1.7 billion in other loans and credits.

Western concern for Turkey's prosperity reflected the strategic importance of that nation in Europe and Asia. The political turmoil in Iran during 1979 further emphasized the need to secure the southern flank of the North Atlantic Treaty Organization (NATO).

Meanwhile, the Turkish government continued its policy of improving relations with its Balkan neighbors—especially Bulgaria, Rumania, and Yugoslavia—as well as the Soviet Union and the Arab oil-producing nations. Disagreements over offshore rights in the Aegean Sea

--------- **TURKEY · Information Highlights** ---------

Official Name: Republic of Turkey.
Location: Southeastern Europe and southwestern Asia.
Area: 306,870 square miles (794 793 km²).
Population (1979 est.): 44,300,000.
Chief Cities (1978 est.): Ankara, the capital, 2,018,000; Istanbul, 2,801,000; Izmir, 742,500.
Government: *Head of state,* Fahri Korutürk, president (took office April 1973). *Head of government,* Süleyman Demirel, prime minister (took office November 1979). *Legislature*—Grand National Assembly: Senate and National Assembly.
Monetary Unit: Lira (35.35 liras equal U. S.$1, Aug. 1979).
Manufactures (major products): Textiles, processed foods, minerals.
Agriculture (major products): Cotton, tobacco, cereals, sugar beets, fruit, nuts.

and the situation in Cyprus kept relations with Greece strained. And although serious issues remained unresolved, Turkish-U. S. relations showed improvement. In September, the United States announced that its U-2 reconnaissance planes would no longer fly over Turkish soil to gather intelligence data about the USSR; the Turkish government responded by allowing U. S. military bases to remain open for at least another three months.

HARRY N. HOWARD, *Middle East Institute*

UGANDA

A bloody war culminating in the overthrow of dictator Idi Amin, and continued economic and political chaos were the dramatic events that dominated Uganda in 1979.

War with Tanzania. Uganda began the year still under the brutal regime of Idi Amin, with an economy all but collapsed and the country in the grip of a reign of terror. Opposition to the regime's activities even surfaced in the pampered army, which was Amin's base of power. To cover a mutiny at the Mbarara barracks, Amin ordered an invasion of Tanzania in October 1978. Claiming an invasion had occurred, Amin hoped to embarrass Tanzanian President Julius Nyerere who was his mortal enemy. Ugandan forces overran 710 square miles (1 838 km²) of Tanzania, murdered almost 10,000 civilians and made 40,000 others refugees. Under pressure from the Organization of African Unity, and Tanzanian counter-

With joy, Yusufu Lule succeeded Idi Amin as Uganda's president. His term was short, however.

UPI

attacks, the Ugandans withdrew in November.

Urged by Ugandan exiles, by former President Milton Obote, and by his own feelings, Nyerere decided to carry the war into Uganda and to try to get rid of Amin once and for all. Tanzanian and exile forces numbering between 10,000 and 20,000 invaded Uganda in February 1979 and advanced quickly as Amin's army showed little willingness to fight and enjoyed absolutely no support from the brutalized civilian population. Amin received massive assistance from Muslim and Arab sources who supported his pro-Islamic policies, and above 2,000 Libyan and Palestinian troops were sent to Uganda in early March. Nothing could stop the Tanzanian advance, however, and the population welcomed the invaders as liberators. After a delay caused by political and humanitarian concerns, Kampala fell on April 12, amid scenes of wild rejoicing and massive looting. Amin fled to Jinja and thence to his home area in the northwest, where invading forces finally arrived in May. Amin then fled to Libya, and his remaining troops, now little more than an armed mob, were rounded up and disarmed. Thousands of Amin's supporters fled to Kenya and to the Sudan, creating new refugee problems and possibly a base for a comeback by Amin.

Political Reconstruction. Ugandan exiles had long dreamed of returning to the country and overthrowing Amin. With the goal finally in sight, and urged on by President Nyerere, numerous exile groups met in Moshi, Tanzania, March 23–25, 1979, to organize a provisional government. Divided into pro- and anti-Obote segments, the exiles agreed to form a united front, create a National Consultative Council (NCC) to serve as a quasi-legislature, and make Dr. Yusufu Lule, former head of Makerere University and a non-political figure, the provisional president. This organization became Uganda's new government in April. However, unity and harmony quickly faded amid charges that Lule was too aloof, too inexperienced, had made cabinet and other changes without consulting the NCC, and had favored his own Baganda tribe in official appointments. On June 20, Lule was ousted, even though he claimed that he was still the legal head of state, and thousands of Baganda rioted in the capital in protest. The largest and most progressive tribe in Uganda,

─────── **UGANDA · Information Highlights** ───────

Official Name: Republic of Uganda.
Location: East Africa.
Area: 91,134 square miles (236 037 km²).
Population (1979 est.): 13,200,000.
Chief City (1979 est.): Kampala, the capital, 350,000.
Government: *Head of state and government,* Godfrey L. Binaisa, president (took office June 1979). *Legislature*—National Consultative Council (est. May 1979).
Monetary Unit: Shilling (7.482 shillings equal U. S.$1, June 1979).
Manufactures (major products): Processed agricultural products, cement, beverages.
Agriculture (major products): Coffee, tea, cotton, tobacco. sugar.

Amin is out as president and residents of Kampala, Uganda's capital, are offered a new newspaper.

UPI

the Baganda had suffered the most under both Obote and Amin and feared that Lule's ouster was the sign of a fresh round of oppression and discrimination.

New President. The new president, replacing Lule, was Godfrey Binaisa, a lawyer. Born in Kampala May 30, 1920, he was educated at Makerere and took a law degree in London in 1955. Obote appointed him Uganda's first attorney general in 1962, but he broke with Obote in 1967 over the latter's suppression of the Baganda. Fleeing Uganda after Amin accused him of "Zionism," he lived in exile in London and New York until his return with other exiles in April 1979. A staunch Anglican, very British in speech and manner, and pro-Western, Binaisa was expected to bring political expertise to the formidable task of restoring order and creating a permanent government in a country where the rule of law and even common human decency had been all but destroyed.

Social and Economic Affairs. The brutality and chaos of the Amin years had left Uganda in a state of near-anarchy. Conservative estimates indicated that between 100,000 and 300,000 people had been killed, and 100,000 were in exile. Observers noted the destruction of the "social contract," the minimal respect for others and for laws that makes society function. As 1979 ended, Uganda was faced with the tasks of restoring social peace and order, especially trying to stop the outbreak of brutal armed robberies, and reincorporating the exiles.

The economy was also in ruins after Amin. Coffee, which represented 90% of Ugandan exports, was a victim of the war, as picking and marketing became impossible. Inflation stood at

700% for the year, and only on the black market could one buy consumer goods: gasoline at $120 a gallon and butter at $9 a pound. However, the wonderfully fertile soil of Uganda, and the fact that 80% of the population were rural and farmed their own land, prevented massive starvation. Massive aid was also promised from Western countries and in October the United States lifted the boycott on coffee imposed in 1978 to protest the Amin regime.

Other Concerns. The events of 1979 in Uganda had far-reaching effects within and outside the country. Tribalism and the possibility of Obote's return kept the country politically on edge as the unity created by opposition to Amin faded. For Africa, events of 1979 represented the first time a country on that continent had overthrown the government of another, thus calling into question the security and integrity of every one of the fragile new states there.

Arab-African hostility could also be expected to increase as a result of Amin's overthrow, since he had been violently pro-Muslim and anti-Israel. Even an Idi Amin comeback could not be ruled out.

See also AFRICA; TANZANIA.

ROBERT GARFIELD
DePaul University

Commerce begins anew in Uganda. Plantains are unloaded for sale at a market in Kampala.

UPI

Athletes march in Red Square during parade commemorating the 62nd anniversary of the Bolshevik Revolution.

USSR

The most significant development in Soviet foreign affairs during 1979 was the June signing of the Strategic Arms Limitation Talks agreement (SALT II) with the United States. If ratified, the treaty will require both superpowers to reduce their total number of nuclear missile launchers and limit their production of various other types of weapons. Elsewhere, the USSR was confronted with a Chinese invasion of its Southeast Asian ally, Vietnam; a Muslim revolution against the friendly, Marxist government of Afghanistan; and the unfriendly attitude of the new revolutionary regime in Iran. Do-

mestically, overloading and poor maintenance of the nation's railways caused a slump in industrial production, with output of several basic raw materials and some types of consumer goods falling well below 1978 levels. At the same time, bad weather throughout the year resulted in a poor grain crop—about 25% smaller than the 1978 harvest.

FOREIGN AFFAIRS

United States. Friction between the United States and the Soviet Union began early in 1979 and continued for much of the year. On March 1, more than 2,400 U. S. scientists refused to visit the USSR on a cultural exchange until the Soviet dissident scientists Yuri F. Orlov and

Anatoly B. Shcharansky were released from prison. As 1979 ended, neither dissident had been freed.

Two later incidents at the U. S. Embassy in Moscow caused concern to diplomats of both nations. On March 28, a 27-year-old Soviet merchant seaman exploded a bomb inside the embassy and killed himself after demanding U. S. assistance in obtaining an emigration visa from the USSR. Then on April 27, another young Soviet entered the embassy grounds with two sawed-off shotguns and fired two shots into the air. The man was talked into leaving by embassy personnel and arrested outside by Soviet police.

Despite a U. S.-USSR treaty supposedly forbidding maritime provocations, two naval incidents did occur during the month of August. Early in the month, Soviet warplanes conducted more than 30 mock missile attacks against two U. S. destroyers cruising in the Black Sea. On August 9, a Soviet spy ship seized a training torpedo launched by a U. S. submarine during Pacific Ocean maneuvers near the island of Guam (an American territory). At the request of the U. S. government, the Soviet Union returned the torpedo.

One of the most irritating incidents, as far as the Soviets were concerned, was the August 22 defection of Bolshoi Ballet star Aleksandr Godunov in New York City and the subsequent U. S. treatment of his wife, ballerina Lyudmila Vlasova. Vlasova, who had intended to return home on a Soviet passenger plane August 24, was detained until U. S. officials could determine whether she was leaving of her own free will. The Soviets forbade her to leave the plane. The impasse was solved on August 27, when U. S. authorities were allowed to interview her on an airport bus. Vlasova stated that she was leaving without compulsion, and the plane departed for Moscow.

U. S.-Soviet tensions reached their peak in September, when the United States strongly protested the alleged combat brigade of 3,000 Soviets on Cuban soil. The USSR replied that in fact no Soviet combat units were present in Cuba. What the U. S. intelligence reports had disclosed, said Moscow, were the same military advisers that had been openly training Cuban armed forces for 17 years. Members of the U. S. Senate and Congress were skeptical.

Despite these troublesome incidents, cooperation between the two nations continued to grow during the year. On April 27, the USSR released five Soviet dissidents to the United States in exchange for Valdik A. Enger and Rudolf P. Chernyayev, two Soviet employees of the United Nations who were convicted in 1978 of attempting to buy U. S. defense secrets. The five Soviet dissidents were Edward S. Kuznetsov and Mark Dymshits, who had planned to hijack a Soviet passenger plane to flee abroad; Georgi P. Vins, the secretary of an illegal faction of the Russian Baptist Church; Valentin Moroz, a leader of Ukrainian nationalists; and Aleksandr Ginzburg, the leader of a Moscow group which monitored human rights violations by the Soviet government.

In an encouraging effort at arms control, the USSR and United States on July 10 submitted to the Geneva Disarmament Committee of the United Nations a joint proposal for a worldwide treaty permanently banning radiological weapons. But the greatest diplomatic achievement in the area of disarmament during 1979 was the June 18 signing of the SALT II agreements by U. S. President Jimmy Carter

A Soviet jetliner, with ballerina Lyudmila Vlasova aboard, remains at JFK airport, N. Y. C., for three days.

Giscard d'Estaing and Soviet President Leonid Brezhnev inspect the troops as the French president begins an official visit to the USSR, April 26. The two leaders signed several agreements.

FRENCH EMBASSY INFORMATION

and USSR President Leonid I. Brezhnev in Vienna, Austria. SALT II required that the total number of long-range bombers, intercontinental rockets, and submarine-based missiles on each side be 2,250 from 1982 to 1985, compared with existing totals of 2,283 for the United States and 2,504 for the USSR. Of the 2,250 superweapons to be permitted, only 1,320 could be rockets with multiple warheads (MIRVs). As 1979 came to an end, the USSR was delaying its approval of SALT II until the U. S. Senate had ratified the treaty (*see* feature article, page 6).

On October 29, Thomas J. Watson, Jr., the former president and chairman of the board of the International Business Machines Corporation (IBM), replaced Malcolm Toon as U. S. ambassador to the Soviet Union. Moscow seemed to welcome the change.

Europe. Soviet relations with most of the European nations were harmonious during 1979. The USSR concluded the following treaties: a 10-year trade agreement with East Germany; a 10-year cultural exchange program with Hungary, a technical aid pact with Greece; a cultural exchange and technical aid treaty with Spain; and 10-year trade and 5-year scientific cooperation and cultural exchange agreements with France. The USSR also exchanged technical aid with all the Eastern European Communist countries except Albania, and gave support to the non-Communist nations of Cyprus, Finland, Iceland, and Portugal.

In a dramatic speech in East Berlin on October 6, Soviet President Brezhnev announced the withdrawal of 20,000 Soviet troops and 1,000 tanks from East Germany in the 12 months to come. At the time he spoke, Soviet forces in East Germany included 400,000 troops and 7,000 tanks. Moreover, if the North Atlantic Treaty Organization (NATO) were to install no new intermediate-range rockets in West-

ern Europe, the Soviet Union would reduce the number of its intermediate rockets in the western USSR.

Far East. Sino-Soviet relations remained tense throughout most of 1979. In January, Vietnamese insurgents helped overthrow the pro-Chinese Pol Pot government in Cambodia and establish a new regime. The USSR immediately recognized the new government and began sending economic and military supplies. When China retaliated by invading Vietnam in February, the USSR demanded a cessation of hostilities and increased arms shipments to its Vietnamese ally. Twelve Soviet warships were sent into the South China Sea, and Soviet troops maneuvered near the Sino-Soviet border, but the USSR refrained from any direct military attack on China. After the withdrawal of the Chinese army from Vietnam in mid-March, the Soviet Union boasted that it had remained calm despite the serious Chinese provocations.

On April 3, China announced that it would not renew the 30-year Sino-Soviet friendship treaty when it expires in April 1980. In response, the USSR on April 17 proposed a joint statement renouncing the use of force in mutual relations. China refused, and on June 4 the USSR suggested that Sino-Soviet talks be held in Moscow to discuss mutual disagreements.

On July 16 a small skirmish broke out along the border between China and Soviet Central Asia. One Chinese soldier was killed and another was captured by the Soviets. Each side claimed that the other had invaded its territory. Perhaps as a result of this incident, China agreed to negotiate with the Soviets and talks began in Moscow in late September. As 1979 ended, the negotiations were deadlocked by a variety of disputes.

In October the USSR rejected a protest by the Japanese government over the increase of

President Brezhnev welcomes Yugoslavia's President Tito to the Soviet Union, May 16. It was the first meeting between the two men since November 1976. Yugoslavia's nonalignment policy had caused a strain in relations.

Soviet troops on three south Kuril islands claimed by Japan.

Middle East and South Asia. The signing of the Israeli-Egyptian peace treaty on March 26 brought continual criticisms from the Soviet government. The treaty was regarded as a betrayal of the Arab struggle against Israel.

The Soviet Union provided technical aid to 14 Middle Eastern and South Asian nations. In March it signed new trade, technical aid, and cultural exchange agreements with India. On October 25 a technical aid pact and a 20-year friendship treaty were concluded with South Yemen.

After Afghan revolutionary terrorists assassinated U. S. Ambassador Adolph Dubs on February 14, the USSR denied charges that its advisors had precipitated the murder by urging Afghan police to storm the building where the U. S. envoy was held prisoner. By the spring, the 118 Soviet aid projects in Afghanistan had been badly disrupted by the Muslim revolt against the Soviet-supported Marxist government. When high Soviet officials hosted Afghan President Nur Mohammed Taraki in Moscow on September 10, they apparently were unaware that he would be overthrown in Kabul six days later. The USSR immediately supported Afghanistan's new Marxist president, Hafizullah Amin.

In a coup supported by airlifted Soviet troops, however, President Amin was ousted from power and executed December 27. Former Deputy Prime Minister Babrak Karmal, a friend of the Kremlin who had been living in exile in Eastern Europe, was installed as the new president and secretary general of the governing People's Democratic Party. During the last week of the year, an estimated 30,000 Soviet troops crossed the border into Afghanistan to help overthrow Amin, bring back Kar-

mal, and quell rebel violence. The United States, Great Britain, China, and other major powers vigorously protested the invasion.

In Iran, the Islamic uprising early in the year stopped the flow of natural gas to the Soviet Union, causing severe winter fuel shortages in the cities of the Soviet Caucasus. When Shah Mohammed Reza Pahlavi was finally overthrown and the Ayatollah Ruhollah Khomeini returned from exile in early February, the Soviet Union became the second nation in the world to extend recognition to the new Islamic state. (Pakistan was first.) By summer, the new Iranian regime had resumed gas shipments to the USSR but had sharply reduced the 116 industrial projects which Soviet specialists had been building in Iran. In the autumn, Soviet-Iranian relations improved; an agreement was reached for the USSR to construct an electric power station.

Africa. In 1979 the Soviet Union rendered technical aid to 38 African countries, of which about half were receiving Soviet munitions. In addition, Moscow openly admitted that it was arming rebel guerrillas in Rhodesia and South Africa, as well as the Polisario Front fighting Morocco for control of Saharan territory. The USSR also concluded a new technical aid pact with Ethiopia, and consular, cultural exchange, and technical aid agreements with Angola.

Latin America. In an effort to woo governments more within the U. S. sphere of influence, the USSR provided technical aid to 11 Latin American nations. The chief recipient continued to be Cuba, where the USSR was building or rebuilding 200 economic enterprises. Soviet-Jamaican trade and cultural exchange agreements were concluded in April.

The Soviet Union offered to reestablish diplomatic relations with Nicaragua on July 20, after Sandinista rebel forces had overthrown president Anastasio Somoza Debayle and established a new cabinet.

Canada. Despite good trade relations, friction also developed between the Soviet Union and Canada. In January, the Canadian government asked the Russians to pay $6 million toward the cost of collecting the radioactive debris which was scattered over northwest Canada upon the disintegration of the Cosmos 954 satellite in 1978. The Soviet government at first refused, claiming that the satellite had caused no damage. In autumn 1979 the USSR agreed to discuss the dispute, but by year's end negotiations had not commenced.

DOMESTIC AFFAIRS

Government and Politics. On March 4 elections were held for a new Supreme Soviet (parliament). More than 99% of the voting population elected 1,500 deputies, of whom 72% were members of the Communist Party. The election also marked the end of the political career of former Soviet President Nikolai Podgorny, who was not among the deputies returned to his seat in the nominal legislature. The newly elected legislature held its first meeting on April 18, reelecting Leonid I. Brezhnev president and Aleksei N. Kosygin premier.

Though obviously in poor health, the 73-year-old Brezhnev remained at the top of the Soviet power structure. He held simultaneously the positions of president, secretary-general of the Soviet Communist Party, and chairman of the State Defense Council. At a late November meeting of the Communist Party's Central Committee, Nikolai A. Tikhonov, Kosygin's 74-year-old first deputy prime minister, was promoted to full voting membership in the ruling Politburo. Tikhonov is considered a close political ally of President Brezhnev. In another shift, Mikhail S. Gorbachev, a national party secretary, was made a nonvoting member of the body.

Armed Forces. In 1979 the Soviet armed forces comprised about 4,400,000 men, including 375,000 rocket troops. The USSR ranked first in the world in number of tanks, intercontinental ballistic missiles, submarine-based and medium-range missiles, medium-range and fighter bombers, and naval ships. But the Soviet arsenal lagged behind that of the United States in number of aircraft carriers, long-range bombers, tactical atomic weapons, and total nuclear warheads.

In July, Soviet land and air forces conducted joint maneuvers in Lithuania, with military observers from Finland, Sweden, and seven European NATO nations permitted to attend.

Space. A series of spectacular space flights began on Feb. 25, 1979, when Soyuz 32, with Lt. Col. Vladimir Lyakhov and Valery Ryumin on board, was lofted into space. Soyuz 32 docked with the Salyut 6 space station on February 26. On April 10 came the launching of Soyuz 33, manned by Nikolai Rukavishnikov, a Soviet, and Major Georgi Ivanov, a Bulgarian. After an equipment failure prevented the cosmonauts from docking with Salyut 6, Soyuz 33 landed safely in Central Asia on April 12. Soyuz 34, an unmanned supply rocket, was launched on June 6 and docked with Salyut 6 two days later. It took the place of Soyuz 32, which returned to earth unmanned but carrying research data from the space station. Meanwhile, during the spring and summer, three other unmanned cargo rockets refueled the space station and were released to burn up in the atmosphere. After achieving a world record of 175 days in space, Lyakhov and Ryumin returned safely to earth on August 19 aboard Soyuz 34.

Population. The first Soviet population census since 1970 was taken in early 1979. Preliminary results revealed a total population of 262,442,000, of whom 62% lived in cities. The total labor force numbered 122,700,000, including 36,000,000 industrial workers and 14,200,000 collective farmers. One third of the world's doctors and one fourth of all scientists were working in the USSR.

The total Soviet population increased by 9% from 1970 to 1979, but by only 6% in the three Slavic Soviet republics—Russia, Belorussia, and the Ukraine. By contrast, large population increases were recorded in several non-Slavic republics: Armenia, 22%; Azerbaidzhan, 18%; Kirghizia, 20%; Tadzhikistan, 31%; Turkmenistan, 28%; and Uzbekistan, 30%.

Among the largest public organizations of the USSR were the Communist Party, with 17,000,000 members; sport societies, with 70,000,000; and trade unions, with 121,000,000.

Religion. The Soviet press admitted that about one half of Soviet pensioners and housewives and one fifth of all workers believe in religion despite official atheist propaganda. On March 23, Vladimir Sholokov, an 83-year-old leader of the Russian Seventh Day Adventists, was sentenced to five years in prison camp for alleged antigovernment slander.

Emigration was officially authorized for about 50,000 Soviet Jews, the largest number in one year since the Lenin era; 180,000 others had requested to leave the country. Also seeking to escape religious persecution were some 20,000 Christians, mostly Baptists and Pentecostals.

Defectors. While touring abroad in 1979, a number of Soviet performers refused to return to the USSR. Valentin A. Markov and Natalya Koloskova, members of the Leningrad Philharmonic Symphony Orchestra, defected on June 7 while on tour in Japan. Three principal dancers of the Bolshoi Ballet, Aleksandr Godunov and Leonid and Valentina Koslov, took asylum in the United States during an August–September engagement. Olympic figure skating champions Oleg Protopopov and wife Lyudmila Belousova, refused to return from Switzerland on September 18. Chess grandmaster Viktor Korchnoi, who had been living abroad as a stateless person since defecting in 1976, was granted asylum in Switzerland on September 24. In late October the West German government reported that Vladislavas Cesiunas, a champion canoeist who had defected from the Soviet Union in August, was kidnapped back to the USSR.

Crime and Imprisonment. On September 11, Soviet newspapers announced a major drive against robbery, alcoholism, student vandalism, narcotics abuse, black market activity, and embezzlement. Alcohol abuse was singled out as the cause of most crimes in the Soviet Union. A decree by the Central Committee stated that "the means of the state . . . are not being fully used in the struggle against lawlessness."

Meanwhile, a report by Yuri Orlov smuggled out of a Soviet prison alleged that at least 5 million citizens—2% of the population—are serving time in forced labor camps. This represented about 20 times the number of inmates in U. S. prisons.

ECONOMY

Trade. The USSR continued to be the world's largest exporter of raw materials, trading with 118 nations and rendering aid to 61 Communist and non-Communist countries. Foreign trade again expanded but not so much as in any of the three previous years. Because of a shortage of foreign currency, the USSR owed to Western nations alone some $17 billion which had been borrowed to buy various products, mostly machinery.

Nuclear Power. Most of the new nuclear power stations being built in the Soviet Union were located near cities in European USSR, which faced a growing shortage of energy. According to the Soviet press, atomic accidents such as the one at the Three Mile Island (PA) power plant in late March are unlikely, because Soviet safety precautions are superior to those used in the United States.

Planning. While the 20-year economic plan for 1980–2000 was still being formulated, several specific goals were revealed. Greater mechanization is expected to double the number of farm machines and abolish hand labor in industry by 1990. Mechanization is considered essential because a declining birth rate will bring only one third the number of new workers into the industrial labor force between 1981 and 1985 as the influx during the period 1976–80.

The 20-year plan also provides for fast expansion of the steel and housing industries. Development in Siberia and the Soviet Far East will have priority, while increases in the production of petroleum and natural gas take place primarily in western Siberia.

Standard of Living. The standard of living in the Soviet Union remained mediocre in 1979. There were admitted store shortages of meat, milk, potatoes, fruit, clothing, furs, medicine, and rugs. Urban housing was cramped, with an average of five people inhabiting each apartment. One third of all urban and rural homes lacked gas for cooking. On July 1, retail prices were increased by 50% for gold and silver jewelry, furs, sheepskin coats, carpets and rugs, 30% for imported furniture, 10% for domestically manufactured furniture, 18% for automobiles, and 25–45% for evening meals in restaurants.

Transportation. In 1979 the Soviet railway system controlled 11% of all the railroad track in the world but transported 53% of world rail freight. For years, the budget had allotted insufficient funds for proper railroad maintenance and by 1979 the railways could no longer cope with their heavy burden: rail freight haulage decreased well below the 1978 level. Although freight trucking and the shipment of oil through pipelines did show increases, these gains could not offset the railway slump.

Industry. The railway slump was a major contributor to an industrial recession. Total industrial output increased by about 3.6% in 1979, compared with a projected 5.7% and a 4.8% actual increase in 1978. More serious, however, were decreases in the output of a number of key products: coal, steel, cement, timber, paper, and plastics; pesticides, chemical fertilizers, and tractors; radios, refrigerators, washing machines, and shoes. A decree by the Kremlin on July 27 based fulfillment of factory and mine quotas not on output but on the delivery of products to other industries or the retail trade network.

Agriculture. A snowy spring, summer drought, and severe autumn rains caused the grain crop to decline sharply. The yield was estimated at only 175,000,000 metric tons, compared with 226,800,000 tons projected and 237,200,000 tons reaped in 1978. By the fall, the USSR had already purchased about 18,200,000 tons of foreign grain, of which 15,000,000 tons would come from the United States. Meat, butter, and cotton showed declines.

ELLSWORTH RAYMOND
New York University

——————— **USSR · Information Highlights** ———————

Official Name: Union of Soviet Socialist Republics.
Area: 8,649,540 square miles (22 402 308 km²).
Population (1979 census): 262,442,000.
Chief Cities (Jan. 1978): Moscow, the capital, 7,911,-000; Leningrad, 4,480,000; Kiev, 2,133,000.
Government: *Head of state,* Leonid I. Brezhnev, president (took office June 1977). *Head of government,* Aleksei N. Kosygin, premier (took office Oct. 1964). *Secretary general of the Communist party,* Leonid I. Brezhnev (took office 1964). *Legislature*—Supreme Soviet: Soviet of the Union, Soviet of Nationalities.
Monetary Unit: Ruble (0.65 ruble equals U. S.$1, 1979—noncommercial rate).
Manufactures (major products): Iron and steel, steel products, building materials, electrical energy, textiles, domestic and industrial machinery.
Agriculture (major products): Wheat, rye, corn, oats, linseed, sugar beets, sunflower seeds, potatoes, cotton and flax, cattle, pigs, sheep.

Dec. 4, 1979: the UN Security Council approves unanimously a resolution urging Iran to release American hostages.

UNITED NATIONS

All the major organs of the United Nations became embroiled in the two Asian crises—in Iran and in Indochina—that preoccupied the world in 1979.

In both cases, the political and legal mechanisms of the UN—the Security Council, General Assembly, and World Court—were used to manifest a consensus of international opinion but could not alter the course of events. It was the UN Secretariat, through its humanitarian agencies and the "good offices" of Secretary General Kurt Waldheim, that played a major role in both Iran and Indochina, and gained in stature as a result.

Early in the year, the Security Council debated the Vietnamese occupation of Cambodia and the subsequent Chinese incursion into Vietnam. On both occasions, council resolutions were blocked by Soviet vetoes. In July, after the massive exodus of Vietnamese "boat people" threatened the stability of neighboring Asian nations, Waldheim convened a special conference in Geneva. The meeting succeeded on July 21 in stemming the flow of refugees, doubling the resettlement rate, and funding the Asian transit camps established by Poul Hartling, UN High Commissioner for Refugees.

On November 5, after it became clear that deliveries of 1,000 tons per day of food and medicine were needed to prevent the starvation of 2.5 million Cambodians, Waldheim convened another conference, this one in New York, that produced the necessary pledges of $210 million. It also put pressure on the Vietnamese occupiers to increase the flow of supplies to those in need.

But as the year ended, there were still reports that supplies were being withheld by Hanoi from Cambodian civilians.

One day before the refugee pledging conference, on November 4, militant Iranian students invaded the U. S. Embassy in Tehran and took hostage some 70 of its personnel. Thirteen Americans and a number of non-American embassy employees were soon released. When Iranian authorities backed the militants' demand that deposed Shah Mohammed Reza Pahlavi be returned for trial before the release of the 50 remaining hostages, Waldheim quickly became an important diplomatic channel between Washington and Tehran. Backed by two unanimous Security Council appeals (on November 9 and 27) and two council resolutions (December 4 and 31), he sought, at the minimum, to guarantee the safety of the prisoners and to win access to them by a team of international observers. Waldheim's ultimate objective was some form of "package deal," under which the hostages would be freed in return for an investigation of Iran's underlying grievances against the shah and the United States. As weeks went by without a break in the impasse, Washington turned to the International Court of Justice in The Hague. On December 15, the court handed down a preliminary ruling ordering the immediate release of the hostages. The second council resolution—passed by a vote of 11–0, with four abstentions—decided in principle that economic sanctions would be imposed on Iran if the hostages were not freed by Jan. 7, 1980. Waldheim left for Tehran on the last day of the year in hopes of winning their release but returned without success. On January 13 the Security Council voted 10–2 in favor of economic sanctions, but one of the negative votes was a Soviet veto.

Other issues on the UN agenda—the perennial problems of the Middle East, southern Africa, and Cyprus, and the dialogue between the industrialized nations and the Third World—were overshadowed by the dramas in Iran and Indochina.

General Assembly. The highlights of the 34th annual General Assembly session were ceremonial visits by Pope John Paul II on October 2 and by Cuban President Fidel Castro, in his capacity as chairman of the nonaligned movement, ten days later.

The papal visit, just the second in UN history, centered on a speech dealing with two elements of human rights: the "frightful disparities" between rich and poor and the need for governments to respect the rights of the individual.

Castro's appearance was designed to enhance Cuba's claim to leadership in the Third World. In a speech that was moderate in both length and ideology (compared with most of his utterances), Castro called upon the richer nations to pay more than $300 billion to developing nations in the next decade.

Cuba's drive for global recognition included a contest with Colombia for a seat on the Security Council. But Castro's earlier attempt to lead the nonaligned movement toward the Soviet sphere caused a number of moderate Third World nations to join Latin American and Western countries in blocking the necessary two-thirds majority in the General Assembly. The deadlock persisted for a record 148 ballots, with neither contestant willing to compromise. Finally, on Jan. 7, 1980, Cuba and Colombia both agreed to withdraw their candidacies, and Mexico won the final vacant seat on the 15-member council with 133 General Assembly votes.

Another Soviet ally, Vietnam, suffered two setbacks. On September 21 the assembly voted 71 to 35, with 34 abstentions, to seat the delegation from the ousted Pol Pot regime of Cambodia and to reject Hanoi's bid for recognition of the Heng Samrin regime which it had installed in Phnom Penh. On November 14 the assembly adopted a resolution by an even wider margin (91–21, with 29 abstentions), calling for the withdrawal of all foreign forces from Cambodia and the free choice of government.

Consideration of Middle East issues demonstrated increased numerical support for the Palestinian cause and resulted in the adoption of several texts critical of the 1978 Camp David Accords and the March 1979 Egyptian-Israeli peace treaty. But the only positive proposal aimed at a comprehensive settlement of the Arab-Israeli dispute—a suggestion by Austrian Chancellor Bruno Kreisky that Israel and the Palestine Liberation Organization (PLO) enter into preliminary negotiations—was not put to vote because both parties opposed it.

Three treaties of some importance were approved without opposition. One is a code of conduct for law enforcement agencies which bans torture. Another is a convention banning the taking of hostages; nations in which the offenders are found would be expected either to extradite or prosecute them. The third is a treaty ensuring that the moon shall be used exclusively for peaceful purposes; it also sets out guidelines for lunar exploration, the exploitation of resources, and environmental protection of all celestial bodies.

The assembly opened on September 18 with an agenda of 125 items, elected Salim A. Salim of Tanzania as its president, and welcomed St. Lucia as its 152d member. Resolutions were adopted on disarmament, southern Africa, Cyprus, Belize, East Timor, and Western Sahara.

Security Council. The council's year started with Indochina and ended with Iran. In between, it grappled with a wide range of disputes—involving Namibia, Rhodesia, Cyprus, Lebanon, the Middle East, and Western Sahara—without appreciable effect.

Cambodian Prince Norodom Sihanouk made a dramatic appearance on January 11, asking the council not to recognize the new regime in Phnom Penh and to cut off all aid to Vietnam. Four days later, a resolution calling for a ceasefire and the withdrawal of Vietnamese troops from Cambodia won 13 votes, but was defeated by a Soviet veto.

The Chinese invasion of Vietnam on February 17 led to extensive but inconclusive debate in the Security Council. It was not until March 16, after the threat of a wider war had faded and the fighting had ebbed, that a resolution criticizing both countries for their respective incursions and calling once again for the withdrawal of all foreign troops was put to the vote. It suffered the same fate: 13 positive votes and a Soviet veto.

Throughout the year the council was used as a sounding board for Arab and Soviet antipathy to the Egypt-Israel peace treaty. On March 22, just four days before the treaty was signed, the council (with the United States abstaining) established a commission composed of Bolivia, Zambia, and Portugal to investigate Israeli settlements in the occupied Arab territories. After the commission reported back, the council on July 20 called on Israel to end its settlement policy. Again the United States abstained. Four days later, Soviet opposition to the UN's role in implementing the treaty forced the council to terminate the UN Emergency Force that had kept peace in the Sinai since 1973. The only UN personnel to help police the Israeli pullback were observers from the UN Truce Supervision Organization, who operated under the secretary general.

Another Middle East debate, this one regarding Palestinian rights, forced the resignation of Andrew Young as U.S. ambassador to the

In his last official trip as U. S. ambassador to the UN, Andrew Young went on a trade mission to seven African nations in September.

WILLIAM CAMPBELL, SYGMA

UN. As president of the Security Council for August, Young discussed the situation in a secret meeting with PLO representative Zehdi Labib Terzi despite the U. S. policy of avoiding formal contact with the PLO. He compounded the problem by misrepresenting the nature of the meeting to the U. S. State Department. Young's deputy, Donald McHenry, was named the new UN ambassador (*see* BIOGRAPHY).

Council members worked behind the scenes to promote an agreement for the independence of Namibia. South Africa raised objections in March to arrangements for policing a cease-fire between its troops and guerrilla units of SWAPO, the liberation movement based in Angola and Zambia. Angola proposed in July that a demilitarized zone be established to remove this last remaining obstacle to UN-supervised elections for Namibia. But it was not until December 5 that South Africa agreed to the concept. This enabled Waldheim to name Gen. Prem Chand of India to work out the final details and to head the UN peace force (UNTAG) that would police the cease-fire.

Britain informed the council on December 12 that lengthy negotiations had finally brought to an end the 14-year "rebellion" of Rhodesia. The economic sanctions imposed by the United Nations on Rhodesia in 1966 and 1968 were terminated by the Security Council on December 21, by a vote of 13–0, with Czechoslovakia and the Soviet Union abstaining.

Secretariat. Secretary General Waldheim demonstrated his activism and stamina by involving himself personally in a number of issues besides Iran and Southeast Asia. He traveled to both Seoul and Pyongyang to establish himself as a channel of communication between North and South Korea and to promote the resumption of talks on reunification. He made a similar effort at reviving intercommunal dialogue in Cyprus and was intensively involved in the negotiations for a Namibia settlement.

Throughout the Iran crisis, Waldheim was in direct communication with authorities in both Washington and Tehran. On November 25, after his initial attempts at negotiation bogged down, Waldheim invoked his power to convene the Security Council on a matter that poses a threat to the peace. It was the first time since the Congo crisis of 1960 that a secretary general had exercised that authority.

The UN effort in the Cambodian famine was led by Henry Labouisse, executive director of the UN Children's Fund, who traveled to Phnom Penh early in November to press for more efficient distribution of food supplies. UNICEF also led the celebration of 1979 as the "International Year of the Child."

In April, arrangements were completed for the UN Industrial Development Organization (UNIDO) to become the 16th specialized agency of the UN system.

Economic and Social Council. Although the council itself took no new initiatives, the Third World countries proposed—and industrial nations welcomed—a round of economic talks to begin in 1980 that would include a discussion of the energy crisis. After three years of negotiation, the UN Conference on Trade and Development reached agreement in principle to establish a "Common Fund" to help stabilize fluctuating commodity prices.

Trusteeship and Decolonization. After sending a commission to observe voting in Micronesia, the Trusteeship Council accepted the desire of the Marshall Islands and Palau to separate from the rest of the U. S. territory, the last under council jurisdiction.

Legal Activities. The UN Conference on the Law of the Sea, which began eight years earlier, ended its 1979 session on August 23 without an agreement on political and financial arrangements for the creation of an International Seabed Authority. The conference set as its goal the adoption of a new sea-law treaty during the ten weeks of negotiation scheduled for 1980.

MICHAEL J. BERLIN, *"New York Post"*

ORGANIZATION OF THE UNITED NATIONS

THE SECRETARIAT

Secretary-General: Kurt Waldheim (until Dec. 31, 1981)

THE GENERAL ASSEMBLY (1979)

President: Salim Ahmed Salim (Tanzania). The 152 member nations were as follows:

Afghanistan	German Democratic	Oman
Albania	Republic	Pakistan
Algeria	Germany, Federal	Panama
Angola	Republic of	Papua New Guinea
Argentina	Ghana	Paraguay
Australia	Greece	Peru
Austria	Grenada	Philippines
Bahamas	Guatemala	Poland
Bahrain	Guinea	Portugal
Bangladesh	Guinea-Bissau	Qatar
Barbados	Guyana	Rumania
Belgium	Haiti	Rwanda
Belorussian SSR	Honduras	Saint Lucia
Benin	Hungary	São Tomé and
Bhutan	Iceland	Príncipe
Bolivia	India	Saudi Arabia
Botswana	Indonesia	Senegal
Brazil	Iran	Seychelles
Bulgaria	Iraq	Sierra Leone
Burma	Ireland	Singapore
Burundi	Israel	Solomon Islands
Cambodia	Italy	Somalia
Cameroon	Ivory Coast	South Africa
Canada	Jamaica	Spain
Cape Verde	Japan	Sri Lanka
Central African	Jordan	Sudan
Republic	Kenya	Surinam
Chad	Kuwait	Swaziland
Chile	Laos	Sweden
China, People's	Lebanon	Syria
Republic of	Lesotho	Tanzania
Colombia	Liberia	Thailand
Comoros	Libya	Togo
Congo	Luxembourg	Trinidad and Tobago
Costa Rica	Madagascar	Tunisia
Cuba	Malawi	Turkey
Cyprus	Malaysia	Uganda
Czechoslovakia	Maldives	Ukrainian SSR
Denmark	Mali	USSR
Djibouti	Malta	United Arab
Dominica	Mauritania	Emirates
Dominican Republic	Mauritius	United Kingdom
Ecuador	Mexico	United States
Egypt	Mongolia	Upper Volta
El Salvador	Morocco	Uruguay
Equatorial Guinea	Mozambique	Venezuela
Ethiopia	Nepal	Vietnam
Fiji	Netherlands	Western Samoa
Finland	New Zealand	Yemen
France	Nicaragua	Yemen, Democratic
Gabon	Niger	Yugoslavia
Gambia	Nigeria	Zaire
	Norway	Zambia

COMMITTEES

General: Composed of 29 members as follows: The General Assembly president; the 21 General Assembly vice presidents (heads of delegations or their deputies of Belorussian SSR, Cameroon, China, Costa Rica, Cyprus, Ethiopia, France, Guyana, Iceland, Lesotho, Pakistan, Panama, Papua New Guinea, Singapore, Somalia, Togo, Turkey, USSR, United Kingdom, United States, Yemen); and the chairmen of the following main committees, which are composed of all 152 member countries:

First (Political and Security): Davidson L. Hepburn (Bahamas)

Special Political: Hammoud El-Choufi (Syria)

Second (Economic and Financial): Costin Murgescu (Rumania)

Third (Social, Humanitarian and Cultural): Samir I. Sobhy (Egypt)

Fourth (Decolonization): Thomas S. Boya (Benin)

Fifth (Administrative and Budgetary): André X. Pirson (Belgium)

Sixth (Legal): Pracha Guna-Kasem (Thailand)

THE SECURITY COUNCIL

Membership ends on December 31 of the year noted; asterisks indicate permanent membership.

Bangladesh (1980)	Mexico (1981)	Tunisia (1981)
China*	Niger (1981)	USSR*
France*	Norway (1980)	United Kingdom*
German Dem. Rep.	Philippines (1981)	United States*
(1981)	Portugal (1980)	Zambia (1980)
Jamaica (1980)		

Military Staff Committee: Representatives of chief of staffs of permanent members.

Disarmament Commission: Representatives of all UN members.

THE ECONOMIC AND SOCIAL COUNCIL

President: Hugo Scheltema (Netherlands). Membership ends on December 31 of the year noted.

Algeria (1981)	German Democratic	Pakistan (1981)
Argentina (1980)	Republic (1981)	Rumania (1980)
Australia (1982)	Germany, Federal	Senegal (1981)
Bahamas (1982)	Republic of (1981)	Spain (1981)
Barbados (1981)	Ghana (1981)	Sweden (1980)
Belgium (1982)	Hungary (1980)	Tanzania (1980)
Brazil (1981)	Indonesia (1981)	Thailand (1982)
Bulgaria (1982)	India (1980)	Trinidad and
Cameroon (1980)	Iraq (1982)	Tobago (1980)
Central African	Ireland (1981)	Turkey (1981)
Republic (1980)	Italy (1982)	USSR (1980)
Chile (1982)	Japan (1980)	United Arab
China (1980)	Jordan (1982)	Emirates (1980)
Cyprus (1981)	Lesotho (1980)	United Kingdom
Dominican Rep.	Libya (1982)	(1980)
(1980)	Malawi (1982)	United States
Ecuador (1981)	Malta (1980)	(1982)
Ethiopia (1982)	Mexico (1982)	Venezuela (1981)
Finland (1980)	Morocco (1981)	Yugoslavia (1982)
France (1981)	Nepal (1982)	Zaire (1982)
	Nigeria (1982)	Zambia (1981)

THE TRUSTEESHIP COUNCIL

President: Sheila Harden (United Kingdom)

China[2]	France[2]	United Kingdom[2]
	USSR[2]	United States[1]

[1] Administers Trust Territory. [2] Permanent member of Security Council not administering Trust Territory.

THE INTERNATIONAL COURT OF JUSTICE

Membership ends on February 5 of the year noted.

President: Sir Humphrey Waldock (United Kingdom, 1982)
Vice President: Nagendra Singh (India, 1982)

Isaac Forster (Senegal, 1982)	Salah El Dine Tarazi (Syria, 1985)
André Gros (France, 1982)	Shigeru Oda (Japan, 1985)
Manfred Lachs (Poland, 1985)	Roberto Ago (Italy, 1988)
Platon Dmitrievich Morozov (USSR, 1988)	Abdullah Ali El-Erian (Egypt, 1988)
José María Ruda (Argentina, 1982)	José Sette Câmara (Brazil, 1988)
Hermann Mosler (Fed. Rep. of Germany, 1985)	Richard R. Baxter (United States, 1988)
Taslim O. Elías (Nigeria, 1985)	

INTERGOVERNMENTAL AGENCIES

Food and Agricultural Organization (FAO); General Agreement on Tariffs and Trade (GATT); Intergovernmental Maritime Consultative Organization (IMCO); International Atomic Energy Agency (IAEA); International Bank for Reconstruction and Development (World Bank); International Civil Aviation Organization (ICAO); International Fund for Agricultural Development (IFAD); International Labor Organization (ILO); International Monetary Fund (IMF); International Telecommunication Union (ITU); United Nations Educational, Scientific and Cultural Organization (UNESCO); Universal Postal Union (UPU); World Health Organization (WHO); World Intellectual Property Organization (WIPO); World Meteorological Organization (WMO).

Residents of the Iowa town of Le Claire gather to welcome the *Delta Queen*, bearing the first family on an August cruise down the Mississippi.

UNITED STATES

In 1979 the United States continued to enjoy peace overseas and relative prosperity at home. Yet midway through the year, on July 15, President Jimmy Carter in a remarkable address to the nation warned Americans that they were undergoing "a moral and spiritual crisis," a loss of confidence that represented a "fundamental threat to American democracy."

DOMESTIC AFFAIRS

Everyone agreed that the national mood was deeply troubled. And it was easy to identify the major problem areas as the economy and energy. But there was intense disagreement over what the solutions might be.

The Economy. As the year began, hopes for curbing inflation rested mainly on the administration's wage-price guidelines, restraint in federal spending, and tighter credit. The administration hoped to hold down prices with the guidelines until the impact of its budgetary cutbacks and the higher interest rates could slow the economy.

On January 25, in his economic report to Congress, the president reiterated his assurance that the economy could be slowed down without triggering a severe recession. The President's Council of Economic Advisers predicted

an inflation rate of just under 7% compared with 9% for 1978, and forecast an unemployment rate of 6.25%, compared with 5.9% at the end of 1978.

But as the statistical reports issued throughout the year demonstrated, these forecasts did not take into account such factors as the cutoff of oil from Iran as a result of the civil upheaval in that country, the subsequent rise in OPEC oil prices, and the vagaries of agricultural production at home. Moreover, the guidelines, which depended mainly on moral suasion, seemed inadequate to the task of checking the inflationary psychology that prevailed in the country. Despite high interest rates and high prices, businesses continued to borrow and consumers to spend in anticipation of even higher interest rates and prices.

With prices and profits rising, labor resistance to the guidelines stiffened. A teamster contract reached April 10 with the trucking industry appeared to provide about a 10% annual increase in wages and benefits over three years, rather than the 7% called for by the guidelines.

The administration and Congress struggled to keep the deficit in the 1980 budget from exceeding $30 billion. But more and more the administration seemed to be relying mainly on the credit-tightening policies of the Federal Reserve Board. On October 6, in a dramatic Saturday night press conference, Federal Reserve

Chairman Paul A. Volcker announced a boost in the discount rate (the rate charged to commercial banks when they borrow money from their district federal banks) to 12% from 11%, along with other restrictions designed to curb the money supply and discourage borrowing. The financial community was thrown into turmoil and interest rates soared. By mid-November the prime rate was well above 15%.

As the year drew to a close, there was little sign that inflation was being brought under control. But there were a number of worrisome indications that the long-predicted recession was getting closer. High interest rates on mortgages threatened a slowdown in the housing industry, sales by the top three auto makers fell 23% in October from the previous year, and unemployment was at 6%.

Energy. In 1979 the impact of the energy crisis on the life of the average American became more severe. Prices for gasoline and heating fuel soared. Gasoline shortages led to long lines at service stations. And most disturbing of all was the specter of nuclear holocaust raised by an accident at one of the atomic-powered generators relied on to develop electricity without using fossil fuels.

The accident at the Three Mile Island reactor near Harrisburg, PA, was the most serious in the history of the nuclear-power industry. It resulted from a failure in the cooling system of the plant's reactor. Amid conflicting statements by the power company officials and various experts, technicians struggled to bring the situation under control. The Nuclear Regulatory Commission warned of the possibility of a disaster, either from a meltdown of the reactor's nuclear core or from the explosion of the hydrogen bubble that had formed in the overheated reactor.

On March 30, Pennsylvania Gov. Richard Thornburgh, concerned about the continuing danger of radiation, urged pregnant women and young children living near the plant to evacuate the area. Not until April 9 did the federal Nuclear Regulatory Commission announce that the crisis at the stricken plant was over.

The episode left the nuclear industry in a cloud of controversy and uncertainty. At the time of the accident 72 nuclear plants were operating, providing about 13% of the nation's electricity. And an additional 125 plants were either under construction or in the planning state. President Carter, who visited the Three Mile Island site shortly after the accident, promised "a full accounting" to the American people of the causes of the accident. He appointed a commission headed by Dartmouth College President John G. Kemeny to look into it.

The accident served to arouse the antinuclear movement. Protest demonstrations flared up near the sites of existing plants. And on May 6, a national demonstration in Washington was attended by more than 65,000 persons. On September 23, an even larger crowd, estimated at about 200,000, showed up for a protest demonstration in New York City.

The President's Commission on the Accident at Three Mile Island issued its report on October 30. It recommended the abolition of the Nuclear Regulatory Commission and in its place the creation of a new agency, headed by an executive with authority to monitor the nuclear industry and to act swiftly and decisively in case of emergency. The commission did not recommend a moratorium on new plant construction, although it did suggest changes in the way reactors are operated and regulated. In addition, the report contained the sobering warning that even if all the suggestions made by the commission were adopted, no one could be certain that "there will be no serious future nuclear accidents."

The president, whose administration had been trying to accelerate growth of nuclear power to help meet the energy crisis, said he would not decide on future nuclear-power policy until he had time to study the report.

The setback for nuclear power came as the administration was striving to get the nation to conserve oil and gas. On April 5 the president ordered the phased decontrol of domestic oil prices, so that they would rise to the higher levels being charged on the world market, thus discouraging consumption at home. The president called for a windfall tax on the extra profits that would be taken in by the oil companies. The extra funds were to be used to help low-income families meet the increased cost of heating fuel, to support mass transit, and to spur the development of new sources of energy.

Underlining the seriousness of the situation, gasoline shortages began developing, starting in California during the first week of May and then spreading to the East Coast. To meet the emergency, most states set up systems under which motorists whose license plates ended with even numbers could buy gas only on even numbered days of the month and those with odd numbered plates on odd numbered days. Gasoline dealers were allowed to raise the price of gasoline to about $1 a gallon. By midsummer the shortages had abated. But no one could promise that new shortages would not develop. Later, as cold weather approached, concern shifted to the possibility of shortages of heating oil and price rises that lower-income consumers could not meet.

The Presidency. The dilemmas posed by energy and inflation compounded President Carter's difficulty in establishing himself as a leader in whom the nation could have confidence to deal with the issues of the day. Carter and his supporters contended that the problems he confronted now were more complex and demanding than those of the past and required a greater measure of sacrifice and forebearance on the part of the citizenry.

When the president sent his "lean and austere" budget to Congress on January 22, projecting a deficit of $29 billion, he conceded that his proposed restraint in spending for social programs would "disappoint those who seek expanded federal efforts across the board." But he said the restraint was unavoidable "if we are to overcome the threat of accelerating inflation." And in his State of the Union address, delivered January 23, the president talked of a "new foundation" for the future, whose success depended heavily on the ability to control inflation.

But the president's approach did not go over well with groups who depend on government largesse, most of whom generally contributed to the electoral majorities of the Democratic Party.

And if he could not win the backing of the traditional political constituencies, Carter seemed unable to build a constituency of his own. Critics complained that his policies lacked cohesion and focus. Carter's style and rhetoric failed to inspire the public. The phrase "new foundation," used in his State of the Union Address in an apparent attempt to stir the enthusiasm evoked by such past presidential catchwords as the New Frontier and the New Deal, won little favorable reaction and was soon dropped. The president's standing in the polls dropped, too. His ratings got a boost with the signing on March 26 of the Israeli-Egyptian peace treaty which he had helped engineer, but this revival proved short-lived.

The president's troubles seemed to come to a head in late June while he was attending an economic summit conference in Tokyo. At home gas lines were lengthening and prices were soaring. In a memo quoted July 7 in *The Washington Post*, Carter's domestic policy adviser, Stuart Eizenstat, wrote the president that "in many respects this would appear to be the worst of times. I do not need to detail for you the political damage we are suffering." Eizenstat saw in the situation an opportunity for the president to regain lost political ground if he could redirect the resentment of the public from himself to the OPEC nations.

The president appeared determined to act. He canceled a Hawaii vacation planned for the end of his nine-day Far Eastern trip and returned to his desk on July 2 to confer with his energy advisers. He scheduled a televised address to the nation on energy on July 5 and withdrew to the presidential retreat at Camp David to work on the speech. But then suddenly and without immediate explanation, his press secretary, Jody Powell, announced on July 4 that the speech was cancelled. This abrupt shift startled and puzzled most of the president's closest advisers and added to the appearance of indecisiveness surrounding his administration.

The White House subsequently let it be known that the reason for the cancellation of the speech was that the president had decided to make a much broader address which would deal with the impact of energy on the economy and on other phases of national life. On July 6, the president began a six-day series of meetings at Camp David with more than 100 prominent politicians, economists, academicians, businessmen, labor officials, and religious leaders in what the White House called a domestic summit. And on July 12 the President and Mrs. Carter went by helicopter to Carnegie, PA, near Pittsburgh, to meet with a number of hastily assembled ordinary citizens for a discussion of the nation's problems. Because of the delay and other circumstances, the speech which Carter delivered to a national television audience on July 15 was probably the most important and dramatic of his presidency.

In describing the "crisis of confidence" and national "malaise," which became the most memorable phrases of his speech, Carter cited the assassinations of the 1960's, the Vietnam War, and the Watergate scandal. "These wounds are still very deep," he said. "They have never been healed."

The president called the energy crisis "a clear and present danger" to the nation. But he vowed, "We are the generation that will win the war on the energy problem and in that process rebuild the unity and confidence of America." He outlined a six-point program for meeting the energy crisis—holding oil imports down to 1977 levels, creating import quotas, making a "massive peacetime commitment" to develop "America's own alternative sources of fuel," requiring utility companies to cut their massive use of oil by 50%, establishing an energy mobilization board, and giving Congress authority for mandatory conservation measures and standby gasoline rationing.

Democrats hailed the speech as Carter's most effective oratorical effort. But Republicans, noting that the president had complained that "the gap between our citizens and our government has never been so wide," argued that the president himself should bear the brunt of such criticism.

As the president took to the road on July 16, to elaborate on his program in speeches in Kansas City and Detroit, he was warmly received

—— **UNITED STATES • Information Highlights** ——

Official Name: United States of America.
Location: Central North America.
Area: 3,615,123 square miles (9 363 169 km²).
Population (1979 est.): 220,300,000.
Chief Cities (1976 est.): Washington, DC, the capital, 700,130; New York, 7,422,831; Chicago, 3,074,084; Los Angeles, 2,743,994; Philadelphia, 1,797,403.
Government: *Head of state and government,* Jimmy Carter, president (took office Jan. 1977). *Legislature* —Congress: Senate and House of Representatives.
Monetary Unit: Dollar.
Manufactures (major products): Motor vehicles, aircraft, ships and railroad equipment, industrial machinery, processed foods, chemicals, electrical equipment and supplies, fabricated metals.
Agriculture (major products): Wheat, rye, corn, barley, oats, soybeans, tobacco, cotton, cattle, fruits.

A new Carter team held its first Cabinet meeting September 10 at the White House after a major shake-up.

and he seemed to be on his way to developing the popular support he sought. But then Carter cut the ground out from under himself with an unprecedented shake-up of his government. On July 17 the White House announced that at the president's request, all the members of the cabinet and of the White House senior staff had offered their resignations. Within the next four days, four members of the cabinet were dismissed, either because they were considered too controversial, or not sufficiently loyal, or both.

Those forced to leave were Treasury Secretary W. Michael Blumenthal; Health, Education, and Welfare Secretary Joseph Califano; Energy Secretary James R. Schlesinger; and Transportation Secretary Brock Adams. The long-planned resignation of Attorney General Griffin Bell, a close friend and confidant of the president, was also accepted.

The White House announced that Hamilton Jordan, who had been the most influential member of the White House staff, would now officially be designated White House chief of staff. In that capacity, Jordan's first act was to order an evaluation of all top-level political appointees in the administration. The purpose of the changes seemed to be to assure better coordination of the government by the president. But critics complained that the shake-up had increased the influence of Jordan and the so-called Georgia Mafia. At any rate, the consequent publicity created an impression of disarray in Washington and distracted public attention from the president's top priority, the energy crisis.

To fill the vacancies created by the shake-up, Carter moved Housing and Urban Development Secretary Patricia Harris to the top job at HEW and named Federal Reserve chairman G. William Miller to head Treasury. Deputy Defense Secretary Charles Duncan became energy secretary, former New Orleans Mayor Moon Landrieu took over at HUD, and Neil Goldschmidt, the mayor of Portland, OR, became secretary of transportation. Deputy Attorney General Benjamin Civiletti took command at Justice. Later in the year, the president named U. S. Court of Appeals Judge Shirley Hufstedler

to head the newly established Department of Education and Philip M. Klutznick, a Chicago real estate developer, to replace Commerce Secretary Juanita Kreps, who resigned for personal reasons. *See also* BIOGRAPHY.

Politics. President Carter's apparent weakness spurred early maneuvering by White House hopefuls in both parties. On the Republican side, Illinois Rep. Phil Crane had declared his candidacy in 1978. He was followed in 1979 by former Texas Gov. John Connally, 62, former Republican National Chairman George Bush, 55, Kansas Sen. Robert Dole, 56, Illinois Rep. John Anderson, 57, Tennessee Sen. Howard Baker, 54, and former California Gov. Ronald Reagan, 68.

The polls showed Reagan to be the front-runner, a premise that was supported by his victory November 17 in a straw vote on presidential preference taken at a Florida Republican convention. Reagan won the nonbinding competition with 36% of the vote.

Reagan, making his third try for the presidency, benefited from support built up over the years. His chief vulnerability was his age, a problem he hoped to overcome by vigorous campaigning. Connally mounted the most aggressive early challenge to Reagan, but he was handicapped by his negative image as a "wheeler-dealer." Bush and Baker competed for support of moderate Republicans. Bush had a better organization, but Baker was better known.

Among the Democrats, Gov. Edmund G. (Jerry) Brown of California signaled his interest in another bid for the presidency early in the year when he endorsed a proposed constitutional amendment to require a balanced federal budget. He pressed his efforts to win support from both liberals and conservatives. He announced his candidacy November 8 based on three principles: "Protect the earth, serve the people, and explore the universe."

But most of the speculation about Democratic challengers centered on Sen. Edward M. Kennedy of Massachusetts, whom most polls showed beating President Carter by large margins. At first Kennedy said he intended to support Carter for renomination. But in early

September, with Carter's position declining, Kennedy let it be known that he was reconsidering his position. On November 7 he formally announced his candidacy, pledging an "effective presidency in the thick of the action."

The 47-year-old Kennedy was in the unusual position of starting the race ahead of the incumbent president he was challenging. But he carried the burden of having to explain his conduct at Chappaquiddick, MA, in 1969, when a young woman passenger in his car died.

Carter, who formally announced his own candidacy on December 4, vowed a vigorous battle. Though he trailed Kennedy in the polls, he had the advantage of incumbency. And his campaign organization demonstrated its effectiveness by defeating Kennedy supporters in Florida caucuses on October 13.

In gubernatorial elections, Democrats rebuffed Republican hopes for gains in two Southern states. In Kentucky, John Y. Brown, a Democratic fund raiser whose wife, television personality Phyllis George, helped him campaign, defeated former GOP Gov. Louis Nunn. And in Mississippi, former Democratic Lt. Gov. William Winter won out over Republican Gil Carmichael. And in Louisiana, U. S. Rep. David C. Treen became the first Republican in more than a century to win the governorship.

In mayoralty races the biggest upset was in Chicago, where insurgent Jane Byrne defeated Democratic incumbent Michael Bilandic in the party primary and won the general election. In other big city contests, Cleveland's controversial mayor, Dennis Kucinich, was defeated by Republican George Voinovich, and Democratic Rep. William Green won easily over Republican David Marston to succeed Frank Rizzo as mayor of Philadelphia. In Minneapolis, former Democratic Congressman Donald Fraser won over former mayor Charles Stenvig, a conservative

independent, and in Boston, Democratic Mayor Kevin White was elected to an unprecedented fourth term. Birmingham, AL, once a center of racial strife, elected its first black mayor, Richard Arrington.

Republicans won two special elections to the U. S. House of Representatives in April. William H. Royer was elected in California to the seat held by Leo J. Ryan, who was killed in Jonestown, Guyana, in November 1978. In Wisconsin's 6th district, Thomas E. Petri was chosen to fill the seat vacated by the death of William A. Steiger.

Nationally, the drive to call a constitutional convention to draft an amendment requiring a balanced budget gained the support of nearly 30 states, but then lost momentum, and failed to get the backing of the required 34 states.

Congress. The 96th Congress got off to a slow start. President Carter had difficulty mustering support for his programs because of his political problems. And with the electorate concerned about inflation and suspicious of government in general, the lawmakers were reluctant to enact ambitious new programs.

The Senate made an important change in its own procedures when it voted on February 22 to curb filibusters. The change limited debate after cloture had been passed to 100 hours. In the past, post-cloture debate had often been dragged out by quorum calls and forcing votes on minor amendments.

Carter suffered a series of setbacks during the session. On January 23 Oregon Rep. Al Ullman announced that the Ways and Means Committee he chaired would not consider the president's proposals for cuts in Social Security benefits.

Congress pushed through, despite Carter's opposition, legislation permitting the completion of the Tellico Dam on the Little Tennessee

Candidates elected or reelected in November 1979 included:

William Green, mayor, Philadelphia	W. Winter, governor, Mississippi	Kevin White, mayor, Boston
GREEN CAMPAIGN HEADQUARTERS	UPI	MAYOR'S OFFICE, BOSTON

River in Tennessee by exempting the project from the Endangered Species Act. Conservationists had opposed the dam because they contended it would threaten the existence of the snail darter, a small fish protected under the Endangered Species Act. Carter signed the authorization bill reluctantly on September 26, to avoid a divisive veto battle. The bill also included funding for nine new water projects the Carter administration had not requested.

And on November 15 the House killed the president's proposal to establish standby federal cost controls on hospitals and adopted instead a voluntary plan which Carter supporters called meaningless.

Still, the president won some significant victories. Congress approved a new international trade act, which carried out the nontariff terms of a new international trade agreement.

Also approved was legislation establishing the Department of Education as the 13th Cabinet agency. Most of the new department's employees and initial functions were transferred from the Department of Health, Education, and Welfare, which was renamed the Department of Health and Human Services.

The critical legislative battleground was energy, where Carter had to overcome major obstacles to get action. On May 10 the House embarrassed the administration by rejecting Carter's proposal for standby gas rationing. Carter accused House members of political expediency and challenged them to develop their own rationing plan. On August 1 the House voted to give the president power to draft a standby rationing bill, thus avoiding the dilemma of resolving special interest pressures on the issue.

Meanwhile the President agreed to compromises on other energy measures. He had originally asked Congress for $88 billion over 10 years to develop synthetic fuels. Instead he accepted legislation which authorized the spending of $19 billion for that purpose and of an additional $1.35 billion in emergency aid to help low-income families pay their fuel bills.

Congress also approved Carter's proposal for an energy mobilization board designed to expedite construction of pipelines, refineries, synthetic fuel plants, and other energy facilities.

The controversial proposal for a windfall profits tax was ensnarled by various pressure groups in Congress. Carter asked for a permanent 50% tax on windfall profits. The House approved a 60% tax and the Senate agreed to a tax rate of 75%. The House measure was expected to produce $276.8 billion and revenue from the Senate version was estimated at $177.8 billion. A House-Senate conference committee gave tentative approval to a $227.3 billion bill. Final Congressional approval awaited 1980.

Investigations. Wrongdoing and allegations of wrongdoing by public officials again commanded public attention in 1979. A number of cases involved members and former members of Congress. On February 3 a mistrial was declared in the trial of Rep. Daniel J. Flood (D-PA) when jurors failed to reach a verdict.

Joshua Eilberg, a former Democratic House colleague of Flood's from Pennsylvania, pleaded guilty February 24 to charges that he had illegally taken money for helping his former law firm get a federal grant for a Philadelphia hospital. He was placed on probation for three to five years and fined $10,000 because of pleading guilty to a felony, and barred from again holding federal office.

Rep. Charles C. Diggs (D-MI) managed to retain his House seat (despite his conviction in 1978 for taking salary kickbacks from his staff) when the House rejected an attempt to expel him on March 1. But on June 29 Diggs admitted that he had misused his payroll to pay personal expenses and agreed to repay the House more than $40,000. On July 31 he was formally censured by the House, the first member to be so penalized since 1921. The Senate also moved against one of its members, Democrat Herman Talmadge of Georgia. On October 10 the Senate voted 81 to 15 to "denounce" Talmadge for "reprehensible" conduct, specifically for submitting false expense accounts and diverting campaign funds to his own use.

The White House was also involved directly and indirectly in federal law enforcement inquiries. Bert Lance, former director of the Office of Management and Budget, and a longtime Carter friend, was indicted May 23 along with three associates in Atlanta. The Justice Department charged that they had conspired to obtain about $20 million in loans for their own benefit from a number of banks over an eight-year period, including the time Lance served in the administration.

Meanwhile, an investigation into loans granted the Carter family warehouse business resulted in appointment of a special counsel, Paul Curran, a Republican and former U. S. attorney, to head the investigation. Curran, who was given powers similar to those granted the Watergate Special Prosecutor, announced on October 16 that he had found no evidence of criminal wrongdoing against either the president or his brother Billy. The inquiry covered the years 1975 and 1976 before Carter became president. One suspicion, which Curran's probe ruled out, was that money lent to the warehouse business had been channeled into Carter's campaign. Though the inquiry did find irregularities in the loan transactions between the warehouse and the National Bank of Georgia, which had been headed by Bert Lance, Curran evidently decided these infractions did not amount to crimes.

In another inquiry involving the White House, Arthur H. Christy was named as a special prosecutor to investigate charges that Hamilton Jordan had used cocaine.

ROBERT SHOGAN, *"Los Angeles Times"*

Former newsman Lloyd N. Unsell is a principal lobbyist for the nation's oil industry.

UNITED STATES—SPECIAL REPORT:

The Growth of Lobbies

When Jimmy Carter campaigned for the presidency in 1976, it was as an "outsider," who carefully dissociated himself from the Washington political establishment and the special interest lobbyists he perceived to be exerting undue influence on the federal government.

President Carter returned to that theme in the summer of 1979 when gasoline lines and steadily escalating prices sent his popularity plummeting to an all-time low. Attacking a "Congress twisted and pulled in every direction by hundreds of well-financed and powerful special interests," Carter sought to divert responsibility from the White House for public frustrations with energy and inflation problems.

Neither candidate Carter nor President Carter was very specific about who the special interests were. He did not have to be. The public might not have accepted Carter's suggestion that the president had little to do with the nation's problems. But Carter had no trouble convincing many citizens that powerful interest groups exerted influence on government decision-making far out of proportion to the number of people those groups represented.

Definition. In recent years, organized pressure groups representing thousands of businesses and trade associations have set up shop in Washington or hired influential Washington law firms to present their cases on Capitol Hill, before federal agencies, and at the White House. Washington special interest lobbies are commonly viewed as those organizations that seek to influence the Congress or the executive branch on behalf of the financial interests of a particular business, trade association, or union.

Some observers also include under the general special interest rubric such visible movements as the anti-abortion lobby, the gun lobby, environmental groups, Ralph Nader's organizations, and Common Cause (the so-called citizens lobby). But the term has more frequently been applied to organizations motivated by their members' financial interests rather than by broad philosophical concerns or political goals devoid of any obvious pecuniary rewards. It is the influence of such moneyed interests that Carter and other politicians have attacked. And it is largely these groups that have accounted for a dramatic growth in Washington lobbies in the 1970's.

Special Interests of 1979. Which groups the public perceives to be special interests varies from year to year. In 1979, the oil industry was singled out by the news media most frequently. And with an annual budget of more than $30 million, it is hard to deny that the American Petroleum Institute, the industry's principal lobby operation, has enormous clout on Capitol Hill. Yet, the Washington lobbying phenomenon includes a far broader range of interests.

Examples of special interest lobbying in 1979 include:

• A successful effort by defense contractors to kill the Renegotiation Board, a federal agency set up to guard against excess government contract costs, and one of the few federal agencies with a proven record of saving taxpayers' money.

- A successful effort by an association of private airline pilots to kill new air safety rules favored by professional pilots. The rules would have required installation in private planes of radar equipment designed to help avoid midair collisions.

- A successful effort by a hospital-doctor lobby to tie up legislation designed to limit rapidly escalating price increases in hospital care.

- A successful effort by business associations, including the national Chamber of Commerce, seriously to weaken an antitrust bill that would have made it easier for consumers to bring price-fixing suits.

- A well-orchestrated effort by bankers to reinstate a tax loophole that allowed heirs to the most valuable 10% of estates in the country to escape capital gains taxes.

While there have always been individual businessmen who have sought and obtained special treatment from the government, there have never been so many organized associations looking for special advantages as there were in 1979. A classic case of special interest lobbying was seen in 1979 during a prolonged debate over authorization and funding of the Federal Trade Commission (FTC). The FTC, a government agency charged with protecting the public from "unfair" and "deceptive" trade practices, came under assault from virtually every business and professional association it sought to regulate.

The oil industry tried to stop an FTC antitrust investigation designed to make the eight largest oil companies more competitive. A similar antitrust investigation of the automobile industry came under attack from leading auto manufacturers.

But the biggest industries were not the only ones attacking FTC's consumer protection actions. Funeral home directors banded together to stop the FTC from issuing regulations that would require the directors to give bereaved consumers precise price information. Used car dealers hired a law firm to lobby against proposed FTC rules that would have forced the dealers to tell purchasers of used autos which parts of a for sale car are working and which are not. And a coalition united to kill proposed rules that could have affected $600 million a year in advertising that involves children. The FTC rules would ban advertising on radio and television programs where young children compose a significant portion of the audience.

Growth. There are no precise figures available on the number of lobbyists working in Washington, which is largely a result of a 1946 lobby law stating that only organizations whose "principal purpose" is lobbying need file reports. The 1946 law leaves it largely up to the reporting organization to decide what constitutes a lobbying expenditure.

Consumers Union, the organization that publishes *Consumer Reports* magazine, stated in 1978 that the number of companies with Washington offices jumped from 100 to 500 during the 1970's. But far more companies have Washington representatives lobbying their causes. The office of the Clerk of the House of Representatives estimated that there were more than 4,700 "active" lobbyists registered in 1979. That was a dramatic increase from the 2,000 *Time* magazine estimated were registered a year earlier. But even the clerk's figures only begin to scratch the surface of the Washington lobbying phenomenon.

Two major news organizations estimated in 1978 that Washington lobbies employed at least 15,000 individuals at an annual cost of about $1 billion. And during 1978 hearings before a House Governmental Operations subcommittee, it was suggested that another $1 billion a year was spent on indirect or "grass roots" lobbying, such as newspaper and mass mail campaigns. The subcommittee estimated that 85% to 90% of those campaigns were paid for by corporations and trade associations.

A related aspect of the growth in Washington lobbying is evidenced in Federal Election Commission records which show that the number of political action committees (PACs), which donate millions of dollars to congressional and Senate campaigns, grew from 608 in 1974 to 1,938 as of Jan. 1, 1979. Many of the organizations lobbying in Washington represent companies or organizations that have set up PACs.

Urban lobbyist Richard Cherry discusses the issue of aid to cities with Rep. Corrine C. Boggs (D-LA).

And while it is difficult to point to instances of PAC contributions buying votes, nobody denies that PAC dollars make it a lot easier for an association representative to get into the office of a congressman or senator. Curiously, federal election laws requiring disclosure of campaign contributions have given lobby groups the names of thousands of potential grass roots lobbyists from virtually every major business interest in the country.

Shift in Power. While the exact dimensions of Washington lobbying remain somewhat obscure, the reasons that it is prospering are far from mysterious. Public concern about the role of special interest lobbies increased markedly as the events known as Watergate undermined faith in the government. Disclosures that lobbyists for ITT had offered secret bribes to stop a government antitrust suit and that dairy interests poured $500,000 into President Nixon's reelection fund after he hiked milk price subsidies were among the dozens of incidents that undermined public confidence in the government's ability to resist manipulation by organizations with less than the general public interest at heart.

As Watergate fostered changes in public attitudes about government, it also resulted in shifts in the base of power in government and changes in the way those seeking to influence government went about their business.

The Vietnam War and disclosures of abuses by U. S. intelligence agencies operating overseas led Congress to assert a larger role in foreign policy. In the debates regarding the 1978 Panama Canal treaties and the 1979 SALT II treaty, Congress held sway over the final decisions. At the same time, Congress asserted greater control over domestic policy. Public demands in the early 1970's that Congress address such long-neglected problems as occupational safety, air and water pollution, and toxic chemicals in the environment were responsible for expansion of federal agencies and regulations.

The resulting increased presence of government in the day-to-day conduct of business is viewed as a major cause of the proliferation of lobby groups. Business associations were organized so that they could continue to operate as they had in the past without government regulation, or at least control regulation and make their own decisions on what was best for public health and safety and for the nation's economy.

Ironically, while 1979 heard a great hue and cry against government regulation on behalf of the open marketplace, the trucking lobby succeeded in delaying an effort to deregulate that industry. At the same time the railroad industry began lobbying against an incipient move to lift government constraints from its operations. While airlines had similarly resisted deregulation in 1978, by 1979 they had found their new competitive environment profitable enough to change their tune.

Changes in Congress. But there are other reasons why lobbyists are flocking to Capitol Hill and they stem from changes on the Hill itself. Watergate not only resulted in the downfall of a president, but it also led to considerable change in both houses of Congress. More politically independent men and women, far less responsive to the pleas of party leaders and more responsive to the parochial pressures of their constituents, were sent to the House of Representatives and Senate.

In Congress there were no longer a House speaker or a majority leader of the Sam Rayburn or Lyndon Johnson mold who could command party loyalty and votes at the drop of a hat. And with one or two notable exceptions, the power of committee chairmen has been reduced drastically. Instead, more members share power over committees and subcommittees. As a result, representatives of special interest groups have to visit more members to make their cases. They need more manpower, better organization, and more money to do their job. Where they could once rely on one or two powerhouses to pass a tax break or scuttle a new regulatory effort, they now have to get a majority of a committee on their side. And with less powerful party leaders, lobbyists also have to scramble for a majority of votes on the House and Senate floors.

Lobby Legislation. Legislation to regulate lobbying at the federal level has been debated in the House and Senate since 1975. The 96th Congress, set to expire at the end of 1980, stands a better chance than any of its predecessors of passing such a law. Not surprisingly, lobby legislation has been actively opposed by dozens of major special interest groups.

Any law that is passed must balance the public's right to know about lobbying activities with the lobbyists' constitutionally protected rights of privacy and free speech.

Two questions have proved major stumbling blocks to enactment of lobby legislation. The questions are: first, whether the public should be able to learn the names of persons or organizations financing lobby groups through large contributions, and if so, whether this procedure would inhibit contributions to controversial groups and thereby interfere with their constitutional right to petition the government; second, whether lobby organizations should be required to report expenditures for grass roots lobbying, such as newspaper advertisements and letter-writing campaigns designed to influence legislation. Many reform advocates argue that grass roots lobbying accounts for a major portion of annual lobby expenditures and has become the most effective form of lobbying in recent years. Opponents claim that keeping records on grass roots efforts would be costly as well as unconstitutional.

ALAN BERLOW
Reporter, "Congressional Quarterly"

THE ECONOMY

It was a year like few others, one of anxieties and shocks, of a pervasive sense of helplessness about events, of a deep-down feeling that economic America must pay for its profligate ways. Throughout the year it seemed that in every house, including the White House, people worried about 13% inflation and 15% money, and believed almost totally in an "upcoming recession." Though at midyear even President Jimmy Carter was ready to concede that the recession had finally arrived, it still was not confirmed in December. There were omens; automakers and steelmakers were laying off workers, but officially, the recession was a forecast.

Fueled by rising oil prices, the consumer price index soared 1% a month from the first month through the last. It was the worst inflation in recent decades, exceeding the 1978 rate by four full percentage points.

Interest rates were the highest of the century. The prime lending rate to blue chip corporations hit a high of 15.75% in late November, having spurted after the Federal Reserve Board on October 6 announced a restrictive, anti-inflation money policy. Though rates were high prior to the Federal Reserve action, they had stopped neither business nor consumers from borrowing. In fact, many individuals had reduced their savings to near the vanishing point, and the national savings rate dropped below 5%, one of the lowest rates ever. Then

they borrowed. They borrowed and they spent with fervor through September, anticipating higher interest rates and devalued dollars.

At the same time, the dollar was under persistent attack from abroad, its value falling in relation to the currencies of other trading nations and to gold, which some countries, companies, and individuals believed was a safer repository for their reserves. Fear was engendered by several factors: the inability of the United States to develop a strategy for dealing with oil imports and high oil prices, the claim by some of ineffective leadership by Carter, and particularly the nation's failure to restrain inflation. Analysts worried about an ominous slowing in the growth of productivity, and about the efficiency with which goods are produced. In fact, gains in manufacturing productivity may have ceased altogether. Viewing such factors, investors and speculators pushed up the price of gold on October 2 in the New York market to more than $440 an ounce. The price of silver leaped also, by about 50% in September alone, to $16.89 an ounce.

Then, according to the popular version, just as the party was getting enjoyable, the Federal Reserve took away the punch bowl. In an unprecedented action, newly named chairman Paul Volcker rushed back from a monetary meeting in Belgrade, Yugoslavia, to lead the board in voting for three major steps: 1) raising the discount rate, the rate at which the central bank's reserves are lent to commercial bank members, to 12% from 11%; 2) raising some

FRANK H. SENYK

THE U.S. ECONOMY

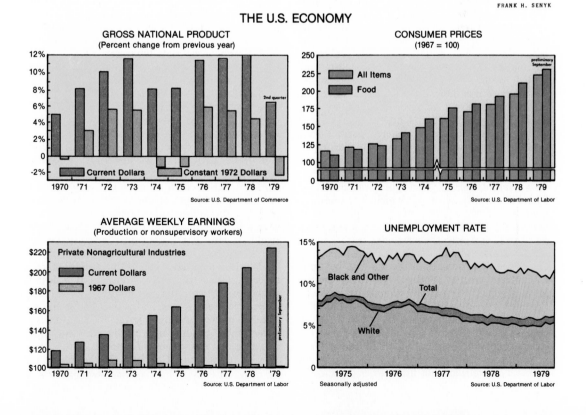

GROSS NATIONAL PRODUCT
(Percent change from previous year)
Source: U.S. Department of Commerce

CONSUMER PRICES
(1967 = 100)
Source: U.S. Department of Labor

AVERAGE WEEKLY EARNINGS
(Production or nonsupervisory workers)
Source: U.S. Department of Labor

UNEMPLOYMENT RATE
Seasonally adjusted
Source: U.S. Department of Labor

marginal reserve requirements for member banks; 3) shifting emphasis from control of the money supply toward control of bank reserves directly.

Even before the action was announced, the markets for currencies, metals, and other commodities were thrown into chaos, rising and falling and rising again as speculators sought their way out of the confusion. In the days that ensued, prices of metals, commodities, and some currencies fell lower against the dollar. Bond prices suffered but the stock market tended to gain in anticipation of lower interest rates.

Then came the Iranian crisis. As the United States sought to free diplomatic personnel held hostage at its embassy in Tehran there arose another round of fears about the dollar and, simultaneously, an excitement of those instincts that cause people to seek tangible rather than paper assets. As the year ended, the Iranian problem was compounded by the Soviet Union's involvement in Afghanistan. The dollar weakened again, and on December 31 gold soared to $533 an ounce and silver to $34.45 an ounce.

Still, the Federal Reserve's efforts were effective in some ways. Economists said the underlying strength of the dollar, apart from the Iranian impact, was improving. U. S. goods were more competitive, and the trade imbalance showed signs of shrinking. More important perhaps, the inflationary psychology was being undermined. As individuals and corporations lightened their credit demands, the prime interest rate fell sharply. Most bankers seemed to think that in a year or so, barring further shocks, it might even retreat into the single numbers again.

A decline in interest rates was unlikely to help the Chrysler Corporation. Facing a $1 billion loss for the year, the nation's third-largest automaker and tenth largest manufacturer appealed to the White House and Congress for aid. The White House offered $1.5 billion in loan guarantees, but Congress resisted, insisting among other things that Chrysler workers and executives adopt more austere policies that would preclude wage increases. Chrysler's plea set off heated debates. Just before Christmas, Congressional conferees accepted a $1.5 billion loan guarantee plan. The figure was part of a $3.5 billion package under which those with an interest in Chrysler must make $2 billion available to the company in the form of loans, stock purchases, and wage concessions.

As worries about inflation abated somewhat, even though popular indexes did not yet indicate improvement, concern about a recession grew stronger. Well-known economists said any recession would be milder than that of 1974–75, but others maintained that the "delay" in its coming would make it longer and deeper. The stricter monetary policy added to those fears.

The president repeatedly said that his policy was one of restraint, but fiscal 1979 produced a deficit of $27.28 billion, and the administration projected a deficit of $33.28 billion for fiscal 1980, which began Oct. 1, 1979. While Congress at one time sought a $30 billion limitation, private forecasters were assuming that a stimulative tax cut would be enacted in the political year of 1980, and that the deficit could exceed $50 billion. That assumption was based, of course, on the continued belief the "lost recession" would soon be found. Talked about all year long, the delay in its onset was documented statistically. Following a weak first half, the economy strengthened in late summer and early fall. Gross national product, a measure of goods and services produced, grew from an annual rate of $2.29 trillion in the first quarter to $2.33 in the second, $2.4 in the third, and $2.44 trillion in the final three months of the year, producing a rate for the year of nearly $2.37 trillion, or a gain of more than 11%.

With inflation wrung out of the numbers by using comparable (1972) dollars, the gain was less impressive, from $1.4 trillion in 1978 to $1.43 trillion in 1979, or just a bit more than 2%. The small gain documented the inroads of inflation; in the prior year the gain had been 4.4%. Carter often blamed the deterioration on higher costs for imported oil, but economists said that if oil prices had not risen the price index would still have been close to double digits.

Nevertheless, at least one big increase—a jump of 1.5% for housing in November, the highest rate for that category in three decades—was in part caused by big fuel bills. Other factors also contributed, such as mortgages, which rose to more than 13%, highest in memory. The median price of existing single-family dwellings, as measured by the National Association of Realtors, was $57,300 in September, 14.1% above the $50,200 price tag of 1978. Those who already owned houses were often ecstatic, because they believed inflation had made them wealthy. It was different for first-time buyers. Government showed the price of the typical new home had soared to about $70,000. In many states mortgage availability ceased.

Two measurements illustrated the Jekyll and Hyde personality of the 1979 economy. Americans were happy to find a big demand for workers; the civilian labor force grew by 1.9 million in a 12-month period through November, and the jobless rate ranged between 5.7% and 6%. But offsetting that were prices. The relentless rise of the consumer price index left workers with less take-home pay.

While individuals found the condition outrageous, some economists found in it a degree of hope. When inflation hinders rather than helps, economists reasoned, people then understand that they and their government and institutions must produce more efficiently and must conserve, save, and build for the future.

JOHN CUNNIFF, *Business Analyst*
The Associated Press

The John Fitzgerald Kennedy Library

The president's desk and rocking chair.

The John Fitzgerald Kennedy Library, overlooking Boston's Dochester Bay and the city's skyline, was officially dedicated Oct. 20, 1979. President Carter, the late president's family, and members of the Kennedy administration were among the 7,000 persons who attended the ceremony. Designed by I. M. Pei, the $12 million, nine-story building houses President Kennedy's papers, films, video-tapes, and other memorabilia.

The Year
in the
United States

Rosalynn Carter became an increasingly active first lady in 1979. She served as one of her husband's principal advisers, campaigned hard for the Carter administration, traveled to foreign lands, and championed her favorite cause—mental health.

GIANFRANCO GORGONI, CONTACT

DALE WITTNER

Following a tragic air accident at Chicago's O'Hare International Airport in May, the Federal Aviation Agency kept the nation's 138 DC-10s on the ground for a 37-day period.

ROGER SANDLER

Ronald Reagan, a favorite among the Republican rank and file for most of the year, made it official in November and announced that he would seek the GOP presidential nomination in Detroit in 1980.

In response to rising diesel fuel prices and general fuel shortages, independent truckers went on strike in June. Strikers blocked truck stops, particularly in the Midwest and West. The protest lasted for approximately one month.

Edward M. Kennedy enjoys a summer break. Later, Massachusetts' senior senator followed in his brothers' footsteps and announced his candidacy for the U.S. presidency.

The House of Representatives remained under the leadership of Reps. John J. Rhodes (R-AZ, right) and Thomas P. O'Neill (D-MA). The first session of the 96th Congress was a long one.

FOREIGN AFFAIRS

In terms of U. S. foreign affairs, the signing of the SALT II, Egyptian-Israeli, and Geneva trade liberalization agreements; the enactment of Panama Canal treaty legislation; the launching of normal diplomatic relations with Communist China; the stiffening of policy toward Cuba; a crisis with the new Iranian government; and moderate reaction to political changes in Nicaragua and Southeast Asia rank as major developments.

Objectives and Expectations. The United States reiterated its fundamental national goals— peace, security, and promotion of human welfare, including individual rights. President Jimmy Carter espoused U. S. leadership in moving the world closer to these objectives by marshaling American strength, supporting allies and friends, preserving the integrity of other nations, and working to resolve international conflicts.

On human rights, the United States reemphasized the rights of individuals to personal integrity, to enjoy civil and political liberties, and to fulfill such vital needs as food, shelter, health care, and education. Under legislative mandate, the Department of State monitored and reported on conditions in some 115 countries that received U. S. economic or security assistance.

President Carter warned Americans to resist "the temptation to see all change as inevitably against the interests of the United States." Secretary of State Cyrus Vance stressed the need to reorient foreign policy in response to the shift from American strategic supremacy to stable equivalency, the increasing dangers of escalating regional conflicts, the intensification of nationalism among Third World powers, growing pluralism in the global community, economic interdependence, and the demands of developing nations for a greater voice in international decision-making.

Conduct of Foreign Affairs. President Carter received some 25 foreign leaders, including Pope John Paul II. He made several trips abroad: to Guadeloupe (4-power Western summit, January), Mexico (February), Cairo and Jerusalem (March), Vienna (SALT II, June), Tokyo (Western economic summit, June), and Korea (June 29–July 1). Vice President Walter Mondale went abroad four times, and Secretary Vance went on six ministerial negotiation ventures.

During the year St. Lucia and St. Vincent and the Grenadines in the Caribbean and Kiribati (Gilbert Islands) in the Pacific became independent, increasing the community of nations to 163 members. The Department of State maintained 141 embassies and 19 other diplomatic missions, including a non-official agency in Taiwan, as well as 123 consular offices. During 1979, the United States participated in more than 1,000 international conferences and forums, including multilateral conclaves on the law of the sea, radio frequency allocation, and trade liberalization. As of January 1, 1979, the United States was a party to 966 treaties and 5,946 agreements. Approximately 400 additional accords, including SALT II and several basic multipartite trade agreements, were signed during the year.

In April the president appointed Robert S. Strauss ambassador at large and his personal envoy to the Mideast. Seven months later, Sol M. Linowitz was named to succeed Strauss. When 34 Cabinet and White House officers tendered their resignations in July, the president retained all of his principal foreign relations advisers. A month later, however, Andrew Young, ambassador to the UN, resigned and was replaced by his deputy, Donald F. McHenry. Dr. Sevilla-Sacasa, Nicaragua's ambassador to the United States since July 30, 1943, resigned following a revolt in his country. Soviet Ambassador Anatoliy Dobrynin then succeeded him as dean of the diplomatic corps.

Western Hemisphere. In March the United States and Canada signed a package of maritime agreements to end their protracted "fishing war." Despite an exchange of presidential visits, some U. S.-Mexican issues remained unsettled.

During the revolt of the Sandinistas in Nicaragua, the United States called for the replacement of the Somoza regime, which call was endorsed by the Organization of American States. Somoza fled to Miami in July and although a

UPI

In Peking, March 1, Leonard Woodcock officially becomes the first U. S. ambassador to the People's Republic of China.

President and Mrs. Carter and Egypt's President and Mrs. Sadat visit the pyramids at Giza. The American president was in Egypt to encourage support for an Egyptian-Israeli peace treaty.

revolutionary coalition junta, backed by Cuba, took over, Washington decided to continue normal relations and to provide humanitarian aid.

President Carter submitted proposals to Congress in January to implement the new Panama Canal treaty, but it was not until September, following a divisive debate, that a compromise bill was passed. On October 1 the Canal Zone was taken over by Panama and the canal came under a nine-member joint U. S.-Panamanian commission. Congressional restraints were enacted to prohibit the president from ceding the canal to Panama before the end of the century, to forbid retroactive Panamanian taxes on Americans, and to require treaty implementing costs to be paid from canal tolls before any U. S. payments are made to Panama.

Normalization of diplomatic relations with Cuba was hampered by Prime Minister Fidel Castro's attacks on the United States at the Havana Third World summit conclave in September and the mini-crisis over some 2,000–3,000 Soviet "combat troops" in Cuba. In a telecast to the nation on October 1, President Carter reported that the Soviet government denied the combat nature of the troops and refused to withdraw them. He also outlined the U. S. response: increase intelligence surveillance of the Soviet troops, provide assurance that no Soviet military unit in Cuba would be used to threaten the security of nations in this hemisphere, establish a permanent Caribbean Joint Task Force headquarters in Key West, FL, step up U. S. military

maneuvers in the area, and increase economic assistance to Caribbean countries to resist social turmoil and possible communist domination.

Mideast. When Iran erupted into mass antigovernment rebellion and the Shah fled the country in January, events were set in motion that changed the geopolitics of the Persian Gulf area. Competing factions vied for political control. The American embassy was attacked by leftist guerrillas on February 14, two marine guards were wounded, and embassy personnel was evacuated. Despite the interregnum, characterized by widespread rioting, summary executions, and repression, Washington maintained formal diplomatic relations with Tehran. The situation became even more serious in November when Iranian students seized 62 Americans at the U. S. Embassy compound in Tehran. The students, with the backing of the government of Ayatollah Khomeini, were demanding the return to Iran of the deposed Shah, who was in New York City for medical treatment. After nearly three weeks passed without the release of all the hostages, the Carter administration threatened military action. Although the Shah had left the United States, some 50 Americans remained as hostages in Iran as 1979 ended. The United States was seeking the aid of the World Court, the UN, and other channels to free the hostages.

Following six months of negotiations, a peace treaty between Egypt and Israel was signed at a televised White House ceremony on March 26. Signing as a "witness," the president declared:

President Carter and Soviet President Leonid Brezhnev extend congratulations to each other following the signing of the Strategic Arms Limitation Treaty in Vienna in June.

"We have won, at last, the first step of peace." Ratification instruments were exchanged in the Sinai on April 25 and the Israeli-Egyptian border was opened on May 27. U. S. supporting agreements provided for nearly $5 billion in security and economic assistance to Israel and Egypt over several years.

Conflict in Lebanon, epitomized by Palestinian bombings and Israeli preemptive shelling and aerial strikes, was deplored as "intolerable" by the Carter administration and condemned in the UN. The United States reconfirmed its policy: cooperating with the UN peace mission (UNIFIL), ending terrorist slaughter, and concluding a cease-fire and permanent settlement.

Asia. On January 1 the United States launched full diplomatic relations with the People's Republic of China. Two months later an agreement was initialed whereby China undertook to compensate Americans for $196,600,000 worth of property seized after the Communist takeover in 1949, and the United States agreed to free Chinese national assets frozen during the Korean War. China and the United States also signed a three-year trade pact in July, granting Peking most-favored-nation status.

Regular diplomatic relations with the Republic of China (Taiwan) were severed on January 1 and the mutual defense treaty (1954) was terminated as of the end of 1979. But all other agreements with Taiwan remained in force, and commercial and other relations, including arms sales, were continued. Washington maintained "non-official" representation in Taipei through an American Institute. Congress challenged the constitutionality of unilateral presidential treaty termination, and 24 members brought legal suit on the grounds that such action required legislative approval. In October the District Court of Washington ruled against the executive. Later the Court of Appeals reversed the decision.

American policy to normalize relations in Indochina was aborted when Vietnamese forces invaded Cambodia and created a puppet regime.

China intervened in February "to teach Vietnam a good lesson," but withdrew its forces the following month. Conflict over the status of Cambodian political authority crystallized in the matter of representation in the UN General Assembly in September. The United States joined the majority in voting to seat the Pol Pot regime. The United States led other nations in providing both sanctuary for the continuing flood of Vietnamese refugees and humanitarian relief for some 2.5 million starving Cambodians.

In January the United States signed an agreement with the Philippine Republic, providing for unhindered use of American air and naval installations in the islands. During the revolt of Muslim guerrillas against the Soviet-backed government of Afghanistan, U. S. Ambassador Adolph Dubs was murdered on February 14, and the Department of State evacuated its embassy staff. The two Koreas resumed peace negotiations in February, but North Korea rejected a proposal to include the United States. Following President Carter's visit to Seoul, the White House suspended—at least until 1981—plans for the withdrawal of American combat troops from South Korea.

Arms and Their Limitation. The Department of State reiterated U. S. policy on conventional arms transfers—to continue transfers that serve the defense needs of allies while seeking not to exacerbate local conflicts, and to induce arms suppliers to exercise restraints.

Consummating seven years of negotiations, President Carter and President Leonid Brezhnev signed the Strategic Arms Limitation Treaty—SALT II. However, early in 1980, after the USSR installed a new puppet government in Afghanistan and sent a large force of combat troops into the country during the final days of 1979, President Carter asked the Senate to postpone further consideration of SALT II. (*See also* feature article, pages 6–14.)

ELMER PLISCHKE
Professor Emeritus, University of Maryland

URUGUAY

Although headed by civilian President Aparicio Méndez, and with civilians constituting most of the cabinet, the Uruguayan government continued to be controlled by the nation's armed forces. Consequently, the most significant political developments were those involving the military.

Government and Politics. At a lengthy meeting in April, the powerful junta of generals named Lt. Gen. Luis Vicente Quevedo as head of the military command. Three colonels were promoted to the rank of general, including Julio Vonelli, who became chief of the combined general staff.

Despite its dominating role, the military leadership restated its dedication to the return of a civilian constitutional government. A presidential election, with one candidate agreed upon by existing political parties, would be held in 1981; and a general election, with competing candidates, was expected by 1986. The Consejo de Estado, the military regime's substitute for a legislature, endorsed a new Statute of Political Parties. The law established a procedure by which political parties could gain official recognition and altered the electoral process itself by limiting each party to one nominee. Another development fundamental to the reconstitutionalization process was the adoption of a far-reaching new labor law. Aimed at "social integration" and "true and real justice," the law required unions to obtain legal recognition and to function under government supervision, provided for collective bargaining, forbade closed shops, and barred unions from engaging in political or business activities.

Although Uruguay was still a police state, the regime announced efforts to locate political opponents who had "disappeared" following arrest. According to official figures, the number of political prisoners decreased to 1,600 from a high of 6,000 in 1974. Nevertheless, some dissidents continued to "disappear."

Economy. Economic policymakers sought to dismantle the extensive governmental controls which had built up over the previous 50 years. Toward that end, Minister of Economy Valentin Arizmendi began drastically reducing tariff barriers. Other policy changes were intended to boost agriculture and grazing. Increased productivity of farmland and herds was rewarded, and taxes on imported fertilizer, machinery, and other items were eliminated.

As even Arizmendi admitted, such laissez-faire policies had the effect of lowering the standard of living among workers and of increasing unemployment. Wage levels could not keep up with continued rampant inflation.

Foreign Affairs. The year saw two important developments in Uruguay's foreign affairs. The first was a January meeting in Montevideo, at which representatives of Argentina and Chile agreed to ask the Vatican to mediate their boundary dispute in the Beagle Channel. The second was an October meeting in La Paz, Bolivia, of the Assembly of the Organization of American States (OAS). The assembly accepted a report by the Inter-American Human Rights Commission which condemned Uruguay (and others) for violating the rights of political opponents and for refusing to allow the commission to send a team of investigators.

ROBERT J. ALEXANDER, *Rutgers University*

UTAH

In 1979, taxes and a change in the form of Salt Lake City's municipal government were the major issues before the citizens of Utah.

Legislature. Utah legislators, responding to the impact of California's "Proposition 13," passed tax relief legislation. Provisions were for some $74.5 million of tax relief, which included: 1) property tax rebates for homeowners and renters ($52.1 million); 2) "circuit breaker" relief of $2.6 million for senior citizens and for widows and widowers; and 3) a four-mill reduction in local school property-tax levies that would result in a $20-million reduction in school taxes. As enacted, homeowners were assured of a minimum $100 refund or 27% of the property-tax bill, up to a maximum of $400. Renters were also assured of a minimum $100 refund or 2.7% of the rent paid in the previous 12-month period. The sales tax on farm machinery was to be phased out over a four-year period.

URURUAY • Information Highlights

Official Name: Eastern Republic of Uruguay.
Location: Southeastern coast of South America.
Area: 68,536 square miles (177 508 km²).
Population (1979 est.): 2,900,000.
Chief City (1975 census): Montevideo, the capital, 1,-229,748.
Government: *Head of state,* Aparicio Méndez, president (took office Sept. 1976). *Head of government:* Lt. Gen. Luis Vicente Quevedo, head of the military junta. *Legislature*—General Assembly (suspended June 1973).
Monetary Unit: Peso (8.35 pesos equal U. S.$1, Dec. 1979).
Manufactures (major products): Processed meat, textiles, wools and hides, shoes, handbags and leather wearing apparel, cement, fish, refined petroleum.
Agriculture (major products): Livestock, grains.

UTAH • Information Highlights

Area: 84,916 square miles (219 932 km²).
Population (Jan. 1979 est.): 1,328,000.
Chief Cities (1976 est.): Salt Lake City, the capital, 168,667; (1970 census): Ogden, 69,478; Provo, 53,131.
Government (1979): *Chief Officers*—governor, Scott M. Matheson (D). *Legislature*—Senate, 29 members; House of Representatives, 75 members.
Education (1978–79): *Enrollment*—public elementary schools, 182,924 pupils; public secondary, 142,102; colleges and universities, 88,989 students. *Public school expenditures,* $572,995,000 ($1,407 per pupil).
State Finances (fiscal year 1978): *Revenues,* $1,432,-247,000; *expenditures,* $1,299,885,000.
Personal Income (1978): $8,585,000,000; per capita, $6,566.
Labor Force (July 1979): *Nonagricultural wage and salary earners,* 550,600; *unemployed,* 22,100 (3.8% of total force).

Salt Lake City's $10 million Symphony Hall, the new home of the Utah Symphony, opened in September.

Salt Lake City Government. On May 15, 1979, Salt Lake City voters adopted the optional form of municipal government known as the council-mayor form to replace the commission form of local government.

Under the council-mayor form, Salt Lake City was to be divided into seven council districts substantially equal in population, with the election of non-partisan candidates from each council district. The seven-member council was to exercise the legislative authority of the city. A mayor, elected by the voters, was to exercise executive powers for the government, including appointment of department heads, with council approval.

Other News. On May 30, 20-month-old Siamese twins Lisa and Elisa Hansen, whose heads were joined at birth, were separated in a 16½-hour operation in a Salt Lake City hospital. On July 17, they were released from the hospital.

Abe Murdock (86), former U. S. representative (1933–41) and senator (1941–47) from Utah, died September 15.

On Jan. 18, 1979, Mormon polygamist John Singer (47) was killed by a Summit County (Utah) lawman when he apparently resisted arrest. Conflicts between Singer and the courts had occurred since 1973 because of Singer's refusal to send his seven children by his first wife and, in late 1978, the three children of his second "wife" to public schools.

Although Singer had other conflicts with the Mormon church (from which he had been excommunicated in 1973), his neighbors, school officials, and the law, the primary issue in 1978–79 was his refusal to send his children to public schools. He cited as his reasons exposure to drugs, sex, homosexuality, and the school's failure to teach religion. The local school district originally exempted the children from the public school system, providing it was demonstrated that they made progress and that appropriate records of achievement were maintained. When Singer failed to comply with school district requirements, he was charged with child neglect. Several hearings and trials resulted in a warrant for his arrest.

LORENZO K. KIMBALL, *The University of Utah*

VANCOUVER

In 1979, the Vancouver City Council was again controlled by the Non-Partisan Association (NPA), whose members held 5 of 10 aldermanic seats. NPA-endorsed Mayor Jack Volrich easily won reelection against the candidate of The Electors Action Movement (TEAM), May Brown. Despite a 52% plebiscite vote in favor of a ward system for the election of aldermen, the council established a review commission to consider the proposal further. The new council approved a $25 million trade and convention center at Pier B-C, but controversy still surrounded the proposed $150–175 million Multiplex sports stadium project. Following its rejection of the Pacific National Exhibition site, the provincial government initiated a study of all possible locations. Other decisions included the abolition of the city's Equal Opportunities office and the dismantling of the Jericho Beach hangers.

Former Mayor Art Phillips was narrowly elected in the May 22 federal general election, to become the only Liberal Party member of parliament west of Manitoba. The Progressive Conservatives and New Democrats each obtained two of Vancouver's five federal seats.

A nearly eight-month strike against the city's two major newspapers—the *Vancouver Sun* and *Province*—came to an end June 25, when pressmen and drivers accepted a contract offer previously approved by four other striking unions.

In sports, the Vancouver White Caps defeated the New York Cosmos in the North American Soccer League (NASL) play-off semifinals and went on to defeat the Tampa Bay Rowdies, in Soccer Bowl '79. On the arts scene, the musical *Billy Bishop Goes to War,* on the life of the first World War Canadian flying ace, enjoyed a resounding success.

NORMAN J. RUFF, *University of Victoria*

VENEZUELA

With the inauguration of Christian Democrat (COPEI) Luís Herrera Campíns as president on March 12, 1979, Venezuela entered its 21st year of democracy and saw the third peaceful transfer of political power since 1958.

Inauguration. In his inaugural address, the new president stressed the need for austerity in both the public and private sectors, more regard for the value of work, and greater integration of all sections of society into the economic and political life of the nation. The minister of the interior further spelled out the priorities of the new administration—education, housing, agriculture, development projects, public service, and personal security.

President Herrera angered some in his party when he appointed non-party members to his cabinet. Six of the 26 portfolios were new.

Politics. President Herrera aroused the wrath of the outgoing *Accion Democratica* (AD) Party when he charged it with leaving him with a "mortgaged Venezuela" afflicted with inflation and eroded purchasing power. He also hinted at substantial corruption in the AD government. Bad blood continued between the two major parties for the rest of the year. The 109 AD members of Congress boycotted the August and September meetings of Congress because they alleged that the COPEI administration had followed irregular legislative procedures in extending the life of the Congress and had failed to supply adequate information on pending fiscal legislation. The president announced a controversial amnesty policy for political dissenters at home and abroad.

In June, AD and COPEI vigorously contested local elections, the first ever held separately from the general elections. For AD it was a chance to recoup some of its 1978 electoral losses. It was COPEI, however, which emerged the victor with 50.2% of the 2.4 million votes cast in 191 municipal districts. The party also gained control of the powerful Caracas municipal government. The AD defeat triggered an internal acrimonious debate and continuing power struggle between reformers and standpatters. Former President Carlos Andres Pérez had campaigned hard for AD and its defeat was a blow to his political fortunes.

Late in the year, Eduardo Fernández narrowly defeated Pedro Pablo Aguilar for the post of secretary-general of COPEI. Although President Herrera said that the defeat of his supporter would not affect his program, the development was expected to cause strife within the party.

The mysterious release of U. S. industrialist William Niehous after more than three years in the hands of guerrillas, and his equally mysterious departure for the United States within 12 hours of his release, caused a good deal of criticism. Skeptics rejected the "humanitarian reasons" given by the government for letting Niehous leave before he could testify before a Venezuelan court. The government denied that it had negotiated with the kidnappers.

The Economy. The government estimated that public expenditures would reach $25 billion in 1979. Early in 1979 the foreign debt was $7.4 billion, up 50% from the previous year. Since oil continued to be the key to Venezuela's future, COPEI expressed its concern over the lack of an oil conservation policy. No new fields have been discovered since 1958 and light crude reserves are expected to run out in seven years. Overall reserves now stand at about 20 billion barrels. Wells are now operating at 94% of capacity. The government-owned oil industry is said to be plagued with inefficient management, corruption, and cost overruns.

In June, the government signed a protocol with Inter-American Development Bank (IDB) placing a $500 million trust fund under IDB

Luís Herrera Campíns, a longtime Venezuelan politician, took the presidential oath of office, March 12.

WIDE WORLD

—— VENEZUELA · Information Highlights ——

Official Name: Republic of Venezuela.
Location: Northern coast of South America.
Area: 352,143 square miles (912 050 km²).
Population (1979 est.): 13,500,000.
Chief Cities (1974): Caracas, the capital, 2,400,000; Maracaibo, 900,000; Barquisimeto, 350,000.
Government: *Head of state and government,* Luís Herrera Campíns, president (took office March 1979). *Legislature*—Congress: Senate and Chamber of Deputies.
Monetary Unit: Bolivar (4.29 bolivares equal U. S.$1, Dec. 1979).
Manufactures (major products): Refined petroleum products, iron and steel, paper products, textiles, transport equipment, consumer goods.
Agriculture (major products): Coffee, bananas, sugar, rice, corn, livestock, dairy products.

administration. The money is to be used to help finance social development and to improve balance of payments for IDB members.

An agrarian reform program projected the granting of 80,000 land titles by 1984. Foreign-owned commercial enterprises had until the end of 1979 to transfer 80% of their stock to Venezuelan investors. Imports were expected to reach $13.5 billion, about one third of which would come from the United States.

Foreign Relations. On March 6, an international conference, "Democracy in Latin America: Frustrations and Expectations," met in Caracas. Eleven of the 38 constitutionally elected former presidents of Latin America attended.

Venezuela's sympathies were with the Sandinista rebels in the Nicaraguan civil war. Although Venezuela recognized Nicaragua's new regime, it had hoped for the inclusion of more moderates in the junta. The Venezuelan foreign minister visited El Salvador, Guatemala, and Honduras.

U. S. Vice President Walter Mondale conferred with President Herrera in March and got a promise from him that Venezuela would continue to supply some U. S. oil needs.

Early in 1979 tensions increased between Colombia and Venezuela with charges by Colombia that Venezuelans had murdered 400 illegal Colombian immigrants in the border provinces. The Colombians asked the Organization of American States (OAS) to investigate the situation. The presidents of the two countries agreed in May to try to find ways to end their long-standing and conflicting claims to oil-rich areas in the Gulf of Venezuela. The administration told Congress that it would give high priority to the territorial dispute with Guyana, frozen by the Port of Spain agreement in 1979.

LEO B. LOTT, *University of Montana*

VERMONT

The first action of the 1979 House session, despite its comfortable Republican majority, was to reelect a Democratic speaker. Notwithstanding an initial House resolution pledging level funding, the legislature approved an 8%, one-year reduction of the state income tax, a pay raise for state employees (including a 25% pay hike for lawmakers), and a record $215.8 million budget (6% above that of the previous year). The lawmakers raised interest ceilings but passed no significant consumer or environmental legislation. A bill transferring control of the deer herd from the legislature to the Fish and Game Department and allowing limited hunting of young and female deer was enacted after a fierce, three-month battle. Gov. Richard A. Snelling, who described the focus of the session as "narrower than I can recall it being in 23 years," nevertheless praised the legislators for their "moderation" in rejecting a zero-growth budget. Meanwhile, inflation-fed revenues left the state with a surplus of $18 million at the end of the fiscal year 1978–79; the funds were deposited in the state's Property Tax Relief Fund.

The governor's office was plagued by continuing uncertainty over a state-sponsored whey processing plant that was closed because of financial and environmental difficulties and a state lottery that failed to produce anticipated revenues. Much controversy was aroused when the governor dismissed his commissioner of public safety without a hearing. The action was sustained by the courts, but revelations that the removal had been precipitated by the commissioner's reluctance to investigate charges of police corruption re-ignited public debate.

Law enforcement became a matter of judicial concern when a nonlawyer state's attorney was barred from filing indictments, while a legally trained state's attorney fought efforts to overrule his decision not to prosecute a judge. Both cases were appealed on constitutional issues regarding the authority of elected prosecutors.

Despite the summer gasoline shortage, the nation's general economic downturn was little felt in Vermont. Per capita income rose faster than the national rate, although Vermont achieved a rank of only 43rd among all the states. While the use of wood for heating expanded rapidly, there was serious concern over the supply of fuel oil, the availability of energy grants, and credits for low-income households.

The inability of the legislature to agree on a new aid formula for Vermont schools compounded educational woes. In the wake of the state's first teachers strike, Burlington, the largest city, dismissed its school superintendent. Rutland, the second largest city, began the 1979 school year with its teachers on strike, but a court injunction compelled them to return to work without a contract. Rising costs and declining enrollments caused serious fiscal problems for the state's numerous small private colleges.

ROBERT V. DANIELS and SAMUEL B. HAND
University of Vermont

─────── **VERMONT • Information Highlights** ───────

Area: 9,609 square miles (24 887 km²).

Population (Jan. 1979 est.): 489,000.

Chief Cities (1970 census): Montpelier, the capital, 8,609; Burlington, 36,633; Rutland, 19,293; Bennington, 14,586.

Government (1979): *Chief Officers*—governor, Richard A. Snelling (R); lt. gov., Madeleine M. Kunin (D). *General Assembly*—Senate, 30 members; House of Representatives, 150 members.

Education (1978–79): *Enrollment*—public elementary schools, 57,625 pupils; public secondary, 43,667; colleges and universities, 29,577 students. *Public school expenditures,* $178,574,000 ($1,585 per pupil).

State Finances (fiscal year 1978): *Revenues,* $603,546,000; *expenditures,* $570,955,000.

Personal Income (1978): $3,197,000,000; per capita, $6,566.

Labor Force (July 1979): *Nonagricultural wage and salary earners,* 195,900; *unemployed,* 11,200 (4.6% of total force).

Vietnamese soldiers gather near the Chinese border during the Sino-Vietnamese conflict in February.

UPI

VIETNAM

Vietnam, at war for most of the nearly 30 years between 1946 and 1975, fought a two-front military struggle during the first months of 1979—against giant neighboring China and the Chinese-supported Pol Pot government in adjacent and much smaller Cambodia. The brief war with China ended in March, but the fight against remnants of the deposed Cambodian regime continued throughout the year.

The cost of invading and pacifying Cambodia, mounting a defense against attacking Chinese (and subsequently guarding a tense frontier with China), and protecting the border of neighboring and satellite Laos against the Chinese was high. Vietnam proved unable to meet the joint demands of its war and civilian sectors. A widespread food shortage and mounting malnutrition were the result.

Invasion of Cambodia. The Vietnamese invasion of Cambodia began on Christmas Day 1978, and, although 18,000 anti–Pol Pot Cambodian Communists took part, the main burden of the fighting was carried by 12 divisions of battle-hardened Vietnamese (aided by tanks, artillery, and jet aircraft). The blitzkrieg attack resulted in the fall of Phnom Penh in two weeks —and the creation of the satellite Heng Samrin regime—and the establishment of a Vietnamese military presence in Cambodia within a month.

Hanoi's assault against Cambodia clearly was designed to unseat Pol Pot and establish a puppet regime that would follow its command— creating a de facto Indochina-wide bloc of countries (Laos as well as Cambodia) led by Vietnam. However, the invasion was not wholly unprovoked. The Pol Pot Cambodian government, supported by China, had been making military raids against Vietnamese territory, the purpose of which was difficult to discern in view of the large differences in population and military strength between the two countries.

Pol Pot's supporters proved more difficult to eliminate than Hanoi apparently had calculated,

and fighting between the Vietnamese and their foes continued in the western portion of Cambodia throughout the year.

Sino-Vietnamese War. Sino-Vietnamese hostility, which has a history going back many centuries, has been stimulated in recent years by Vietnamese nationalism and Hanoi's increasingly close ties with the USSR, Peking's chief rival. China supported Pol Pot in neighboring Cambodia more to contain Soviet than Vietnamese influence, and, when it learned in 1978 of Hanoi's plot to invade Cambodia, Peking abruptly terminated its aid program in Vietnam (which totaled $10 billion through the years).

Hanoi's requirement that Chinese living in Vietnam become citizens of the country boosted tensions and resulted in large numbers of ethnic Chinese trying to leave the land—which the Vietnamese partly blocked (further worsening relations with Peking). By 1979's end, more than 250,000 displaced ethnic Chinese had fled to China.

The Vietnamese invasion of Cambodia directly led to China's attack on Vietnam. The 17-day war began on February 17 when tens of thousands of Chinese soldiers poured across the frontier with Vietnam at 26 points—in a "counterattack" against Hanoi's border "provocations." The object of the assault was to "punish" Vietnam—to "teach it a lesson." The United States and other governments urged the Vietnamese to quit Cambodia—and the Chinese to depart from Vietnam. While the Chinese withdrew from Vietnam in March, the Vietnamese clearly had no intention of getting out of Cambodia and did not do so.

China did not gain the fast and decisive victory it probably sought. But it did inflict considerable damage on Vietnam—including the destruction of 80% of the buildings in the northern Vietnamese towns of Lao Cai, Lang Son, and Cao Bang and an estimated 50,000 casualties. And it may also have undermined the credibility of the Soviet Union as an ally of Vietnam in time of obvious danger.

UPI

A wounded Vietnamese soldier is carried from battle at Lao Cai, site of heavy damage by the Chinese.

The increasing political role of the army and the priority of military goals over civilian ones was a trend. Gen. Vo Nguyen Giap, hero of the decisive battle of Dienbienphu (1954) in the Vietnamese anticolonial war against France and chief strategist and military commander in the second Vietnam War (1960–75), may have been the country's most important political leader, in fact if not in form, in 1979.

A second trend took its character from the age of the political leadership. President Ton Duc Thang, 91, Ho Chi Minh's nominal successor, was only a figurehead. Since Ho Chi Minh's death, the real leader—but only first among relative equals—has been Prime Minister Pham Van Dong. But the premier was 73 in 1979. Party Secretary Le Duan was 71 and General Giap turned 67. The average age of members of the National Assembly was 72. The

fact of the advanced age of the still stable and unified leadership was important politically in light of what appeared to be a diminishing ability to adjust and a preference for old, if successful, policies over new ideas.

Economy. Nature—and war—took a heavy toll on Vietnam economically. In 1978 the country experienced one of the best rice harvests ever, but the rice ration was still reduced in 1979 and there were severe food shortages. Although rice planting was completed in north and central Vietnam by September, more than half of 5 million acres (2 million ha) of agricultural land in the 12 southernmost provinces had not been planted. And in October the worst floods in 30 years struck parts of central Vietnam, destroying many rice fields.

The use of rice to feed an expanded army in Cambodia, Laos, and along the Chinese border and the diversion of manpower, funds, and transportation to military purposes took their toll on the civilian population.

Foreign Relations. The USSR doubled its supply of arms and other military equipment to Vietnam. Moscow also threatened in February to "honor its obligations" under the 1978 Soviet-Vietnamese friendship treaty if Chinese troops did not quit the country. Soviet aid to Vietnam was estimated at $2 million a day.

U. S.-Vietnamese talks resumed in June on American initiative, but the United States declared that normalization of relations—sought by Hanoi—was not possible at the present time because of the invasion of Cambodia and the refugee and Cambodian relief aid problems. The number of refugees fleeing the country to other Southeast Asian lands dropped sharply after June.

RICHARD BUTWELL, *Murray State University*

VIRGINIA

Major issues occupying Virginia citizens in 1979 included state elections, taxes, and energy.

Elections. In the 1979 General Assembly races, all 140 legislators were up for reelection. Republicans failed to expand significantly their small minority representation and were outnumbered approximately four to one in each chamber. A freshman Republican became the first woman elected to the state Senate. During the campaign, Gov. John Dalton, an activist Republican leader, had urged voters to give him a "veto-proof" Assembly, warning that otherwise Democrats would gerrymander legislative districts after the 1980 census.

Legislature. A long-standing urban-suburban impasse over annexation matters was partially resolved when the General Assembly approved legislation granting counties in large metropolitan areas immunity from city annexation. In return, cities were promised increased aid.

"Proposition 13" fever infected Virginia in 1979, but the Assembly defeated or tabled all

---

VIETNAM • Information Highlights

Official Name: Socialist Republic of Vietnam.
Location: Southeast Asia.
Area: 127,246 square miles (329 566 km²).
Population (1979 est.): 50,100,000.
Chief Cities (1976 est.): Hanoi, the capital, 1,443,500; Ho Chi Minh City, 3,460,500; Haiphong, 1,191,000; Da Nang, 500,000.
Government: *Head of state,* Ton Duc Thang, president (took office 1969). *Head of government,* Pham Van Dong, premier (took office 1954). *First secretary of Communist Party,* Le Duan. *Legislature* (unicameral)—National Assembly.
Monetary Unit: Dong (2.50 dongs equal U. S.$1, May 1978).
Manufactures (major products): Phosphate fertilizer, cement, electric energy, processed foods.
Agriculture (major products): Rice, sugarcane, tea, sweet potatoes, cassava, rubber, corn, fruits.

proposals establishing fixed limitations on taxes and expenditures. Larger-than-expected state revenues permitted the legislature to expend over $100 million for various capital outlays, contributions to the state's retirement system, and highway construction. Later in the year, Governor Dalton claimed that his administration had saved the commonwealth additional millions, which allowed property taxes to be cut.

In matters of education, the state added the requirement that persons seeking teaching certification after mid-1980 would have to pass a professional exam as prescribed by the Board of Education. Laws were passed guaranteeing all teachers a "duty-free" lunch period, as well as five planning hours each week. New teacher grievance procedures were also established.

A new parole law, as interpreted by the attorney general, resulted in the early release of many tenants of the state's overcrowded prisons. Ratification of the federal Equal Rights Amendment (ERA) was again defeated.

Government Mismanagement. Audits showed the state's retirement fund to have been mismanaged in recent years. Other investigations revealed a pattern of kickbacks and payoffs in the state's purchasing division.

Energy. Gas lines in northern Virginia resulted in the governor ordering an odd-even day purchasing system from June 21 through September. In the spring, two employees of Virginia Electric and Power Company's (VEPCO's) nuclear plant in Surry County poured caustic soda on fuel rods, causing damages of more than a million dollars. They defended their action as the only means to call attention to the illegal and unsafe practices which they claimed existed at the plant. The federal moratorium on licensing of new nuclear plants prevented VEPCO from opening a new facility.

Judicial. In an unprecedented move, a three-man federal court held the Virginia Supreme Court guilty of obstructing federal court rulings regarding the legalization of advertising by lawyers, and financially liable for court costs. The Virginia court appealed the ruling.

WILLIAM LARSEN, *Radford University*

--------- **VIRGINIA · Information Highlights** ---------

Area: 40,817 square miles (105 716 km²).
Population (Jan. 1979 est.): 5,160,000.
Chief Cities (1976 est.): Richmond, the capital, 226,-639; Norfolk, 284,033; Virginia Beach, 224,595.
Government (1979): *Chief Officers*—governor, John Dalton (R); lt. gov., Charles Robb (D). *General Assembly*—Senate, 40 members; House of Delegates, 100 members.
Education (1978–79): *Enrollment*—public elementary schools, 642,592 pupils; public secondary, 412,648; colleges and universities, 258,368 students. *Public school expenditures,* $1,950,691,000 ($1,664 per pupil).
State Finances (fiscal year 1978): *Revenues,* $4,706,-668,000; *expenditures,* $4,321,663,000.
Personal Income (1978): $39,492,000,000; per capita, $7,671.
Labor Force (July 1979): *Nonagricultural wage and salary earners,* 2,119,300; *unemployed,* 119,300 (4.7% of total force).

VIRGIN ISLANDS, U. S.

On March 6, 1979, voters in the Virgin Islands were presented with a proposed new constitution that would substantially increase self-government in that U. S. territory. An apathetic turnout of only 39% of eligible voters rejected the proposal by a vote of 5,986 to 4,696. In the words of one political leader it was "a national embarrassment." Behind the apathy and negativism was a concern that the constitution would establish a very expensive bureaucracy which the economy of the islands could hardly sustain. A new effort to replace the Congressional Organic Act of 1954, under which the islands are governed, was not expected for some time.

Ship Sinks. Tourism, the islands' economic mainstay, received some adverse publicity when the Italian cruise liner *Angelo Lauro* sank alongside a pier at St. Thomas, April 1, after burning out of control for six hours. Despite inadequate facilities, local fire fighters, with the help of the U. S. Coast Guard, were able to prevent an explosion and maintain the ship in an upright position. No lives were lost, and the burned-out hulk eventually was towed away for scrap. Each year some 600 cruise ships bring more than half a million tourists to St. Thomas alone.

Storms. Two major tropical storms, both within a week's time, skirted the Virgin Islands and caused considerable damage. Hurricane David brushed by the southern coast of St. Croix on August 30, and tropical storm Frederic passed over the island of St. Thomas on September 3. Winds of more than 60 miles (96 km) per hour and high seas destroyed the tourist pier at Frederiksted, St. Croix, and torrential rains brought heavy flooding and property damage to St. Thomas. With damage estimated at $25 million, the islands were declared a federal disaster area.

Economy. Although the islands' economy seemed to be sound—the rate of unemployment was only 3.3% and decreasing in all sectors except agriculture—the government did experience serious fiscal problems. Required by the U. S. Congress to end the year with a balanced budget, the islands could not cover operating costs with federal appropriations and local revenue. Regardless, local politicians in the legislative and executive branches voted themselves salary increases substantially above federal inflation guidelines. Apparently in response, Congress refused to cover the territory's debt or to appropriate funds for the refurbishing or replacement of two dilapidated hospitals. The hospitals, one in St. Croix and the other in St. Thomas, were expected to lose their accreditations and thereby become ineligible for any federal funding of medical services. The overall fiscal impasse threatened to paralyze government services in the territory.

THOMAS MATHEWS
University of Puerto Rico

© DAVID ALLEN HARVEY, WOODFIN CAMP

The U. S. Supreme Court upheld federal treaties entitling Indian fishermen to catch up to 50% of the salmon that passes through their tribal lands.

WASHINGTON

An unexpected storm, actions on a busing initiative, an Indian fishing rights dispute, and a divided House of Representatives that ultimately required joint speakers helped make up news of Washington in 1979.

Weather. An unexpected storm packing winds of more than 100 miles (161 km) per hour slammed into western Washington on Feb-

—— **WASHINGTON • Information Highlights** ——

Area: 68,192 square miles (176 617 km²).
Population (Jan. 1979 est.): 3,820,000.
Chief Cities (1970 census): Olympia, the capital, 23,111; (1976 est.): Seattle, 490,586; Spokane, 175,751; Tacoma, 153,621.
Government (1979): *Chief Officers*—governor, Dixy Lee Ray (D); lt. gov., John A. Cherberg (D). *Legislature*—Senate, 49 members; House of Representatives, 98 members.
Education (1978–79): *Enrollment*—public elementary schools, 395,560 pupils; public secondary, 373,686; colleges and universities, 275,299 students. *Public school expenditures,* $1,904,030,000 ($1,934 per pupil).
State Finances (fiscal year 1978): *Revenues,* $4,965,-154,000; *expenditures,* $4,250,017,000.
Personal Income (1978): $32,058,000,000; per capita, $8,495.
Labor Force (June 1979): *Nonagricultural wage and salary earners,* 1,634,200; *unemployed,* 125,900 (6.7% of total force).

ruary 13, dismembering and sinking 13 concrete pontoons of the 1.3-mile (2.09-km) Hood Canal Floating Bridge. The $25 million bridge, which opened in 1961 over the deep and strong Hood Canal tidal waters, connects the upper Olympic Peninsula with the rest of the Puget Sound region. Engineering studies found no major fault with the design of the bridge, and by the end of 1979 work was under way to replace the demolished pontoons.

Law Suits. The November 1978 voter initiative prohibiting the transportation of school students to other than their nearest or next nearest schools for the purpose of racially balancing the schools was declared unconstitutional on June 15. U. S. District Judge Donald S. Voorhees said in his ruling that the initiative was unconstitutional because it forbade mandatory assignment of students for racial purposes but permitted assignment for other reasons. According to the judge, the initiative was racially discriminatory in its purpose, and was overly inclusive in that it permitted only court-ordered busing for racial reasons even though a school board might be under constitutional duty to permit such busing without a court order. Judge Voorhees' decision was appealed.

On July 2, the U. S. Supreme Court upheld U. S. District Judge George H. Boldt's 1974 decision which upheld the treaty rights of Indians to catch half the harvest of all salmon returning to traditional, off-reservation waters. The 1974 decision had dealt a blow to the commercial fishing industry of the Pacific Northwest and occasioned violence between commercial fishermen and law enforcement officers. The state's congressional delegation announced plans to attempt to amend Indian treaties.

Legislature. One of the results of the 1978 elections was an even political division in the state's House of Representatives. All pre-legislative conferences failed to resolve the question of who would be speaker; therefore the House, for the first time in its history, operated with co-speakers. This circumstance contributed to the failure of the legislature to complete its work in the 60-day regular session, necessitating a special session. Partly because recent biennial sessions have run far past the constitutionally allotted 60 days, the legislature responded to pressure from Gov. Dixy Lee Ray to submit a proposal to the voters at the 1980 general election to establish annual legislative sessions of 105 days in odd-numbered years and 60 days in even-numbered years.

The 1977 legislature had taken action to provide full funding of basic education in public schools and had established a timetable to complete this task. Although the timetable did not call for the full-funding achievement during the 1979 legislative session, an improved state economy permitted its provision.

WARREN W. ETCHESON
University of Washington

WASHINGTON, DC

Government and Legislation. On May 1, 1979, special municipal elections were held in the U. S. capital to fill three posts vacated in November 1978. John Ray, a 35-year-old lawyer, defeated 10 other candidates to become an at-large representative on the City Council. Charlene Drew Jarvis, a 37-year-old neuropsychologist, outpolled 15 other candidates to win a ward council seat; her success gave the council a 7-to-6 female majority, making it unique among state and big city legislatures. Eugene Kinlow, a 38-year-old federal government administrator, won an at-large seat on the 11-member, nonpartisan school board.

A referendum proposal for the legalization of gambling was rejected by the Board of Elections and Ethics after it found that there were not enough verified signatures on the petitions. The City Council earlier had refused to call an advisory referendum on the gambling issue. The Board also ruled that the City Charter did not permit referenda on projects funded by the city, and it again rejected a petition opposing the construction of a downtown convention center.

The proposed amendment to the U. S. Constitution granting the District of Columbia voting representation in Congress was ratified by an additional four states in 1979—Michigan, Minnesota, Massachusetts, and Connecticut. New Jersey and Ohio voted for ratification in 1978.

Teachers' Strike. Members of the Washington Teachers Union went on strike for 23 days beginning March 6, after the school board refused

Marion Barry, 42-year-old former civil-rights activist, was sworn in as mayor of Washington, DC, in January.

to extend their contract and stopped automatic payroll deductions for union dues. The board sought more control of curriculum and grading, and wanted to extend the school year by 14 days and the teachers' work day to 7 hours. The city's 184 public schools remained open during the strike, but less than half the system's students attended. The walkout ended when a Superior Court judge reinstated the contract until a new one could be negotiated.

Papal Visit. Pope John Paul II arrived October 6 for the last two days of his U. S. visit. He met with President Jimmy Carter, received a gold key to the city from Mayor Marion Barry, and attracted 175,000 people to an outdoor Mass on the Washington Mall.

Blizzard. The city's largest 24-hour snowfall in 57 years, 18.7 inches (47.5 cm) on February 18–19, paralyzed the city for days.

MORRIS J. LEVITT, *Howard University*

WEST VIRGINIA

Although West Virginia's coal production did not rise so sharply as had been projected following a 110-day bituminous strike that ended in March 1978, a slow but steady gain in tonnage toward the end of 1979 led state officials to pronounce the state's economy basically strong. The analysis was seen as a positive step in the state's long battle to move its economy away from its dependence on one industry.

In 1979 the federal government designated West Virginia as a site for a major coal gasification (synthetic fuel) project, and West Virginia University was one of six major research institutes awaiting Congressional confirmation as an energy research center. As such, the institute would be eligible for federal support.

Economy. Late-in-the-year unemployment figures were roughly the same as they had been a year earlier. Although tax income was up more than 17% over 1978 and most economic indicators trended upward during the fall, the growth rate slowed considerably after a two-year spurt. The first step in the repeal of the 3% sales tax on groceries contributed to the slowdown. As a result of 1979 legislation, the food

—— **WEST VIRGINIA · Information Highlights** ——

Area: 24,181 square miles (62 629 km²).
Population (Jan. 1979 est.): 1,870,000.
Chief Cities (1970 census): Charleston, the capital, 71,505; Huntington, 74,315; Wheeling, 48,188.
Government (1979): *Chief Officers*—governor, John D. Rockefeller IV (D); secy. of state, A. James Manchin (D). *Legislature*—Senate, 34 members; House of Delegates, 100 members.
Education (1978–79): *Enrollment*—public elementary schools, 269,979 pupils; public secondary, 125,743; colleges and universities, 79,007 students. *Public school expenditures,* $625,375,000.
State Finances (fiscal year 1978): *Revenues* $2,080,-435,000; *expenditures,* $2,054,400,000.
Personal Income (1978): $12,318,000,000; per capita, $6,624.
Labor Force (July 1979): *Nonagricultural wage and salary earners,* 627,100; *unemployed,* 47,200 (6.4% of total force).

sales tax was to be eliminated in three annual steps. Gov. John D. (Jay) Rockefeller IV had asked for a one-time cut of the entire 3%.

Legislation. Overall, a major portion of the governor's legislative program was approved. A $1 billion budget for fiscal 1980 was enacted during a two-day special session.

In other actions, the delegates appropriated an additional $78 million to support continuing highway improvements and provided underwriting for the university's energy research program. In response to "get tough" warnings from witnesses at pre-legislative hearings, the lawmakers set a three-year minimum sentence without parole for anyone convicted of an armed crime, but turned down proposals for a return to capital punishment. Alarmed by rising hospital costs—in some local instances even above national norms—the legislature required public financial reports from all hospitals and nursing homes housing more than 15 patients. Demands for wider public knowledge of school board affairs led the legislature to order that each county board must conduct at least one public hearing on a proposed budget before voting on it. The salaries of certain state workers, including legislators and teachers, were increased. A 15-member legislative-citizens committee will review the existence of 40 state agencies.

The legislature also passed bills permitting the issue of Sunday horse racing to be decided by local referenda and allowing small companies to increase maximum levels on loans and to charge higher rates of interest.

St. Mary's. "Improperly aged concrete" was the verdict of both federal and state investigations aimed at fixing the blame for the 1978 accident that claimed 51 lives in the collapse of scaffolding inside a power company's cooling tower near St. Mary's.

DONOVAN H. BOND, *West Virginia University*

WISCONSIN

A divided leadership in Madison and racial problems in Milwaukee were focal points of the 1979 year in Wisconsin.

Government. For the first time since 1969, Wisconsin had a political split in its leadership positions, with a Republican governor and a Democratic-controlled legislature. Wearing his trademark red vest, Lee S. Dreyfus went to the executive office after 11 years as chancellor of the University of Wisconsin (Stevens Point) and with no political experience. Clearly, the Democratic legislative leadership had a "show me" attitude. Although relations between the executive and legislative branches were sometimes strained, there were no long-term battles. Democrats complained that the governor did not provide enough legislative initiative.

Enjoying the political fruits of an unexpected state budget surplus, Governor Dreyfus and the legislature agreed on two bills to benefit taxpayers. One reduced income tax rates permanently and declared an eight-week moratorium on the collection of state withholding taxes; the other granted property tax relief of up to $100 per homeowner. Few other major pieces of legislation were enacted. Among bills left waiting were several dealing with energy matters, including a plan to create a state energy department.

Open Primary. Since the La Follette era of the early 1900's, Wisconsin has been proud of its open primary system, which allows voters to select candidates, regardless of party. The Democratic National Committee, however, found it repugnant that Republicans could vote in the Democratic primary and told Wisconsin Democrats to come up with a new plan. The state party constituency continued to balk, and a court battle loomed when Attorney General Bronson La Follette, the grandson of the founder of the open primary, filed suit to preserve the system.

Milwaukee Race Relations. The state's largest city has prided itself on the relatively peaceful integration of its schools, begun under a federal court order. In the fall of 1979, with the desegregation program in its fourth year, the school system could report that integration was ahead of the court's timetable, with 80% of the students attending schools that had black enrollments of 20% to 60%. Unsettlingly, in some schools racial tensions increased.

In a case that might have far-reaching implications, a former Milwaukee police officer confessed that in 1958 he had shot a young black youth to death and that it had not been a case of self-defense, as claimed at the time. The disclosure caused blacks in the community to question police reports of other shootings, and the police department's general treatment of blacks. Mayor Henry Maier agreed to a U. S. Justice Department investigation of all police shootings since 1966.

Economy. Both manufacturing and agriculture registered important gains, with the state reaching eighth position nationally in agricultural receipts. Unemployment continued at a rate well below the national average.

PAUL SALSINI, *"The Milwaukee Journal"*

——— WISCONSIN • Information Highlights ———

Area: 56,154 square miles (145 439 km²).
Population (Jan. 1979 est.): 4,697,000.
Chief Cities (1976 est.): Madison, the capital, 170,493; Milwaukee, 661,082; (1970 census): Racine, 95,162.
Government (1979): *Chief Officers*—governor, Lee S. Dreyfus (R); lt. gov., Russell A. Olson (R). *Legislature*—Senate, 33 members; Assembly, 99 members.
Education (1978–79): *Enrollment*—public elementary schools, 486,599 pupils; public secondary, 399,820; colleges and universities, 241,384 students. *Public school expenditures* (1977–78), $1,601,287,000 ($1,-635 per pupil).
State Finances (fiscal year 1978): *Revenues,* $5,524,-752,000; *expenditures,* $4,755,651,000.
Personal Income (1978): $35,241,000,000; per capita, $7,532.
Labor Force (July 1979): *Nonagricultural wage and salary earners,* 1,971,500; *unemployed,* 116,700 (4.8% of total force).

WOMEN

Asked to state what progress women had made toward equality in 1979, feminists might be at a loss for an answer. It was a year of little apparent movement on the larger issues. But not all gains are obvious.

ERA. The Equal Rights Amendment (ERA) was a case in point. Despite the reprieve it won in October 1978, when Congress voted to extend the deadline for its ratification to June 30, 1982, it appeared moribund. As the original seven-year limit passed, on March 22, a drive by supporters to have it adopted in four key states—Florida, Illinois, North Carolina, and Oklahoma—had failed in three of them, as it did in the fourth shortly afterward. Foes of the amendment gathered on the anniversary in Washington, DC, to hear Phyllis Schlafly, an Illinois housewife and national chairman of the "Stop-ERA" movement, declare, "The ERA dies tonight, morally and constitutionally." Not so, said the supporters of the amendment. Their plan is to concentrate on electing pro-ERA candidates to the state legislatures. In fact, Eleanor Cutri Sneal, president of the National Organization for Women (NOW), termed 1980 the "turning point for women's rights." And the election of women delegates to the 1980 Democratic and Republican national convention was the major subject of discussion as the National Women's Political Caucus held its biennial convention in Cincinnati in July. More than 1,000 women from both parties elected Iris Mitgang, a California lawyer, as the new president of NWPC.

Dead or alive, however, ERA has had more impact than most people realize. For example, numerous states have, during the 1970's, amended their constitutions with provisions requiring equal rights for both sexes. Ironically enough, Illinois, Ms. Schlafly's home state, was among the first to do so, although rejection of ERA has since become an annual nonevent of its legislature.

Silent Changes ... Thus, an apparent standstill may be deceptive. One tangible result of the feminist movement is that all kinds of barriers that used to keep women back and prevent them from realizing their potential are falling. Sometimes this happens with a good deal of drama. Such was the case in Chicago, when Jane M. Byrne, a Democratic maverick, upset Mayor Michael Bilandic in his bid for a full term as head of the nation's second-largest city (*see* CHICAGO).

Such spectacular changes, however, do not take place without the previous, though less visible, removal of mental barriers. Had the electorate not been ready to entrust their city to a woman, no political machine is likely to have pulled off such a coup. But the public is ready; without much fanfare, women now also run two out of the three largest cities of California—San Francisco and San Diego. Partially at least, this change may be ascribed to the efforts of the women's movement. Despite all its peripheral trivia, it has not only bolstered female self-assurance, hence assertiveness, but also—and this may be even more important—managed to alert the general public, male and female, to the subtleties of the discrimination women have suffered for so long.

... and a Noisy One. At the beginning of the year President Jimmy Carter summarily dismissed former Rep. Bella Abzug (D-NY) from her unpaid post as co-chairman of the National Advisory Committee for Women; not only had the committee issued a press release critical of his policies, but Ms. Abzug's abrasive behavior in a face-to-face meeting had also, allegedly, offended him. More than 20 other women of the 40-member committee immediately resigned in protest of the president's action. The event created some ill feeling between the administration and women's organizations, at least temporarily, but President Carter was still reported to be committed to feminist goals. In May the committee was reconstituted as the President's Advisory Committee for Women, with Lynda Johnson Robb, the elder daughter of former President Lyndon B. Johnson, in the chair.

Overseas Events. Internationally, some women made big political news during the year, and none bigger than Britain's Margaret Thatcher, who in May became the first female prime min-

THE PRESIDENT'S ADVISORY COMMITTEE FOR WOMEN

In May 1979, President Carter named Lynda Bird Johnson Robb, 35, as head of the revamped President's Advisory Committee for Women. The appointment emphasized the importance the president places on women who combine "work in the home with work outside the home." Mrs. Robb, the wife of the lieutenant governor of Virginia and the mother of three daughters, is a contributing editor of *Ladies Home Journal* and vice president of the L. B. J. Co. and Northern Virginia Broadcasting.

ister of the United Kingdom. Having led her Conservative Party to victory in parliamentary elections, she immediately went on to win the respect of other world statesmen in a series of international conferences.

Portugal, likewise, entrusted its leadership in a governmental crisis to a woman, Maria de Lurdes Pintassilgo, who on July 19 was appointed prime minister until elections could be held in December. In a part of the world where male chauvinism has long been predominant, this was a sign of change as remarkable as any that occurred during the year. Yet something similar might be said of revolutionary Nicaragua, where Violeta Barrios de Chamorro was named to the five-member governing junta after dictator Anastasio Somoza was toppled in July. And late in 1979, Lydia Gueiler became president of Bolivia.

In Iran, a spontaneous women's protest movement held the world's attention for a while in March. At issue was a declaration by the Ayatollah Ruhollah Khomeini, the country's revolutionary leader, that the proper dress for women in an Islamic society was the *chador*, the traditional head-to-toe covering worn by female Muslims. Coming as it did on the eve of International Women's Day, the Ayatollah's statement provoked a fury of resentment and mass demonstrations by Tehran's women, who have been unveiled for three generations. So confronted, the holy man beat a hasty retreat, although it remained to be seen whether the withdrawal was permanent.

In other international developments, Flora MacDonald of Kingston, Ont., was named minister for external affairs in Canada's new Conservative government; and Simone Veil (see BIOGRAPHY) of France was elected president of the European Parliament.

MAY NEWMAN HALLMUNDSSON
Baruch College, City University of New York

WYOMING

Concentration on energy exploration and a busy legislative session were headline stories in Wyoming in 1979.

Energy and Environment. The search for alternate sources of energy, challenging existing environmental quality, continued in Wyoming and other resource-rich western states. Western governors pushed on several fronts, including phased development of synthetic fuels, expanded use of conservation measures, federal assistance to energy boom towns, and state/federal consultation on energy policy.

Considerable energy exploration, logging, and other production became possible when recommendations concerning millions of acres of state land were made. The land had been considered for inclusion in the wilderness system since 1964. As a result of the 1979 action, some exploration may be allowed in the Overthrust Belt, a geological formation in Wyoming thought to contain energy resources. Environmentalists were not happy with the decision, despite the fact that 15.4 million acres (6 237 000 ha) were designated wilderness.

Although the state legislature had earlier approved a new coal slurry pipeline, Gov. Ed Herschler vetoed the proposal. The pipeline had been strongly opposed by railroads, unions, Montana officials, the Crow Indian Nation in Montana, as well as some environmental groups. In other coal slurry action a U. S. Court of Appeals upheld three lower court decisions in favor of the pipeline company's plan to pass beneath the Union Pacific railroad.

Legislative Session. Of the 700 bills introduced in the 1979 legislative session, 163 became law. Passed measures included: use of mineral royalty funds for backing state bonds; sunset legislation terminating 11 state agencies by July 1981 unless continued or reestablished by the legislature for a period not to exceed six years; reduction of gasohol tax; a $30 million tax-financed building program; increased tax relief for low income elderly and disabled; revisions to state liquor laws; increased aid for schools; water development policies; reorganization of the Department of Health and Social Services; repeal of the sales tax on trade-ins; and a call for a constitutional convention to require a balanced federal budget.

Governor Herschler's campaign proposal for a 5% increase in mineral severance taxes, coupled with a one third drop in all property taxes, was defeated. The Republican-dominated legislature substituted its own property tax relief bill. By a 16–13 vote, the Senate upheld its 1973 approval of the federal Equal Rights Amendment.

Other Events. A new state university president was appointed. Tourism declined considerably because of the threatened gas shortage. An unusual tornado struck Cheyenne in mid-July, killing one infant and injuring 57. After being convicted of murder and bombing charges, Mark Hopkinson became the first death-row prisoner in years.

JOHN B. RICHARD, *University of Wyoming*

─────── **WYOMING · Information Highlights** ───────

Area: 97,914 square miles (253 597 km²).
Population (Jan. 1979 est.): 434,000.
Chief Cities (1970 census): Cheyenne, the capital, 40,-914; Casper, 39,361; Laramie, 23,143; Rock Springs, 11,657.
Government (1979): *Chief Officers*—governor, Ed Herschler (D); secy. of state, Thyra Thomson (R). *Legislature*—Senate, 30 members; House of Representatives, 62 members.
Education (1978–79): *Enrollment*—public elementary schools, 51,300; public secondary, 43,028; colleges and universities, 19,933 students. *Public school expenditures*, $261,911,000 ($1,989 per pupil).
State Finances (fiscal year 1978): *Revenues*, $670,888,-000; *expenditures*, $507,006,000.
Personal Income (1978): $3,658,000,000; per capita, $8,636.
Labor Force (July 1979): *Nonagricultural wage and salary earners*, 216,300; *unemployed*, 5,700 (2.4% of total force).

South Yemen soldiers take a break during border fighting with North Yemeni troops early in the year.

YEMENS, THE

The two small neighboring countries that share the name of Yemen became the focus of the world's attention in early 1979. The two states are the Yemen Arab Republic—also known as North Yemen or Yemen (San'a), after its capital—and the People's Democratic Republic of Yemen—also known as South Yemen or Yemen (Aden).

The politics of the Yemens are bizarre, even by the standards of the Middle East. North Yemen is generally pro-Western (although it has flirted with the Soviet Union) and has a free-enterprise economy. South Yemen has a tight, radical, Soviet-backed regime and a rigidly-controlled economy. Both states, however, are faction-ridden, and the presidents of both met violent ends in 1978. In their mutual relations the two Yemens seem capable of anything but the expected. In 1979, just as seven years before, open hostility between the two neighbors turned into a proposal for unification.

Intermittent violence by various groups in the two countries passed into something more serious on February 24, when fighting broke out along the border between North and South Yemen. Each side accused the other of initiating the fighting, but it was fairly clear that South Yemen had launched the first attack. Its forces penetrated beyond the border about 30 mi (48 km). Other Arab League countries called for an immediate truce, and at a March 6 emergency Arab League meeting in Kuwait a cease-fire was arranged. Under the supervision of an Arab League border patrol, the cease-fire went into effect March 17.

With the possibility of a Marxist takeover of North Yemen, the United States dispatched a naval force to the area, accelerated arms supplies to the North (with Saudi cooperation), and began sending military advisers. The latter program continued throughout the year.

The cease-fire had been in effect only 12 days when, in a most surprising development, North and South Yemen signed an agreement to unite under one government. The fusion project was proposed by South Yemen President Abdel Fattah Ismail to his North Yemen counterpart, Ali Abdullah Saleh, at a reconciliation session held in Kuwait. The united country would be called the People's Republic of Yemen, with San'a serving as the capital. A constitutional committee was to draft more specific details

---
NORTH YEMEN • Information Highlights ---
Official Name: Yemen Arab Republic.
Location: Arabian peninsula in southwest Asia.
Area: 75,000 sq mi (195 000 km²).
Population (1979 est.): 5,800,000.
Chief City (1975 census): San'a, the capital, 134,588.
Government: *Head of state,* Ali Abdullah Saleh, president. *Head of government, Abdel Aziz Abdel Ghani,* prime minister. *Legislature* (unicameral)—Constituent People's Assembly.
Monetary unit: Rial (4.56 rials eqaul U. S.$1, Aug. 1979).

within six months. Talks on economic cooperation began May 10 in San'a, and a number of joint meetings were held through the summer. But by the time a second agreement was signed October 4, sights had been lowered significantly. The second pact was aimed primarily at economic cooperation and, eventually, at some loose integration. During the course of the year, the common border was in fact reopened to travel, air flights, and trade.

North Yemen. In 1979 North Yemen saw a continuation and intensification of the economic trends of the previous five years. The central feature of its economy since 1974 has been the large number of emigrant Yemenis who work for high wages in Saudi Arabia (and other Gulf states) and send home substantial remittances. By 1979 about one million Yemenis were working abroad and sending home an estimated $1.5 billion a year. Consumer goods—motorcycles, cassettes, timber, clothes, and food—funnel through the port of Hodeida into Yemen. The standard of living has been raised substantially; the per capita income in 1970 was estimated at $80; in 1979 it was more than $400.

The development of the economy has freakish aspects which the government was only beginning to face in 1979. With about one third of its labor force outside the country, North Yemen has an acute manpower shortage. A national service act to keep in the country all men between the ages of 18 and 35 was passed in September, but its enforceability was in doubt. The country has no national administration worthy of the name; there is no national system of taxation; and despite prosperity, the government operates in a chronic deficit situation, bailed out by the doles of foreign governments. The national budget for 1979–80 projected a deficit of about $300 million. The chief aid donor is Saudi Arabia, which in 1979 gave Yemen about $100 million in budget assistance and an additional $300 million for arms. Apart from expatriate remittances, the government relied on agricultural export revenues, but this was in a serious decline.

Like other conservative Arab states that increasingly see U. S. support as an unreliable reed on which to lean, North Yemen in 1979 began to mend its relations with the radical Arab states. The rapprochement with South Yemen reflected the same concern, as did the August visits of Deputy Premier Hasan Makki to Syria, Libya, and Iraq. A $15 million loan

from Iraq to finance the building of an airport at Hodeida was announced in January. In June Iraq pledged another $15 million, as well as a $300 million loan from the Iraqi Development Fund to finance roads, hospital, and wells.

South Yemen. The involvement of South Yemen with the Communist bloc deepened during 1979. The number of Eastern bloc advisers in South Yemen, rising steadily in recent years, reached about 10,000; included were some 4,000 Russians, as well as East Germans and Cubans. Soviet naval activity in the area also continued to increase; a USSR missile submarine visited Aden in August. According to some sources, the USSR completed construction of a naval base on Socotra Island and a military base in the Hadhramaut. During a visit to Moscow in October, President Ismail signed a 20-year treaty of friendship which envisaged military cooperation. A broad treaty of cooperation was signed with East Germany on November 18. The compatibility of these ties with the projected fusion of the two Yemens was less than obvious.

South Yemen has long had a stagnant economy. The port of Aden handles about one third of the tonnage it did when the area was controlled by the British. The former British Petroleum refinery at Aden operates at only about 25% of capacity. However, a considerable flow of expatriate remittances has begun to raise the standard of living and stimulate the economy. A report by the World Bank issued in March viewed South Yemen's economic future with cautious optimism.

ARTHUR CAMPBELL TURNER
University of California, Riverside

YUGOSLAVIA

Yugoslav Marxism remains one of the major irritants to the Soviet Communist party. Worker self-management, diplomatic nonalignment, and efforts to gain equal standing for the League of Communists of Yugoslavia (LCY) are major Yugoslav policies that the USSR would like to change. President (Josip Broz) Tito's proposal for the first change of the 1974 constitution, which would provide for collective leadership and rotation in office, was expected to be fully implemented by the spring of 1981.

The Communist Party. According to the constitution, the LCY is Yugoslavia's only legal political party and the sole source of all ideas and policies pertaining to the fate of the country. The LCY had about 1.8 million members in 1979, or about 8% of the total population and one fourth of the working force. The Yugoslav variant of the Marxist-Leninist party model remained midway between an elitist and a mass party system. Since 1971 the emphasis had been upon reintroduction of greater centralization and party discipline. But this trend has been somewhat neutralized by the gradual re-

—— **SOUTH YEMEN · Information Highlights** ——

Official Name: People's Democratic Republic of Yemen.
Location: Arabian peninsula in southwest Asia.
Area: 112,000 square miles (290 078 km²).
Population (1979 est.): 1,900,000.
Chief City (1977 est.): Aden, the capital, 271,590.
Government: *Head of state,* Abdel Fattah Ismail, president. *Head of government,* Ali Nasser Mohammed, prime minister. Legislature (unicameral)—People's Supreme Assembly.
Monetary Unit: (.3454 dinar equals U. S.$1, July 1979).

organization of the party and the tendencey to relocate more power within basic party organizations of associated labor (BOALS). By 1979 such organizations numbered more than 50,000, and the LCY was firmly entrenched within the BOALS.

In the 24-member Presidency of the Central Committee of the LCY, which was formed to ease the transition of power after the passing of Tito, now 87, the vice presidency is rotated each year among the various Yugoslav nationalities and republics. On October 29, Stevan Doronjski (from the province of Vojvodina) became the new vice president. Also in 1979, Stane Dolanc, a long-time secretary of the party, was replaced by Branko Mikulić. The death of Edvard Kardelj, one of Tito's closest associates, removed from office one of the last members of the old guard.

Politics. While a strict rotation is practiced in the highest party body, continuity in office is maintained in the executive branch. At Tito's suggestion, Prime Minister Veselin Djuranović was reelected, as were the secretaries of foreign affairs, defense, and internal affairs.

The eight-man Presidency of the Socialist Federal Republic of Yugoslavia (SFRY), also created in anticipation of the demise of Tito, was elected May 15. The eight members, each representing one of Yugoslavia's six republics and two autonomous provinces, were elected to a five-year term by the respective assemblies. Lazar Koliševski (of Macedonia) was elected to a one-year term as vice president of that body.

Economy. Inflation (about 25%), slow economic growth, a mounting foreign trade deficit, energy shortages, unemployment (perhaps as high as 20%), and the strongest earthquake in the nation's history were on the negative side of Yugoslavia's economic balance sheet. On the positive side were the expansion of joint projects (mostly with the West), tourism, and flow of remittances in hard currency from Yugoslav workers abroad, and a relatively good agricultural crop. According to the 1979 budget, government spending would increase by 9% to 99.4 billion dinars ($5.2 billion); defense expenditures were to comprise 53% of the outlay.

Foreign Affairs. Yugoslav foreign policy con-

ALAIN NOOLEG, SYGMA

Cuba's President Fidel Castro welcomes Yugoslavia's President Tito to the Havana nonaligned nations conference.

tinued to pursue the goal of nonalignment and to condemn any interference in the internal affairs of any state. Tito's talks in Moscow with Soviet President Leonid Brezhnev in May and the friendly visit of an LCY party delegation to the United States represented the attempt by Yugoslavia to balance relations with the two superpowers. Tito's efforts at the sixth conference of nonaligned nations in Havana, Cuba, countered in part the attempts by Cuban President Fidel Castro to sway the movement closer to the Soviet fold (see THIRD WORLD). Friendly relations with China continued to flourish. Tito also visited Algeria, Libya, Syria, Iraq, Jordan, Kuwait, and Malta in 1979.

Relations with the neighboring states of Rumania, Greece, and Italy remained friendly and peaceful. A November meeting between Tito and Rumanian President Nicolae Ceauşescu reaffirmed the close technical ties between the two countries (including the Djerdap hydroelectric project) and their mutual determination to remain independent from Moscow. Relations with Bulgaria remained icy because of statements from that country implying that Macedonians are Bulgarians; Yugoslavia continued to denounce Bulgaria's denial of the rights of the Macedonian national minority. There was a gradual thaw in Yugoslavia's relations with Albania.

MICHAEL M. MILENKOVITCH
Herbert H. Lehman College, CUNY

——— **YUGOSLAVIA** • Information Highlights ———

Official Name: Socialist Federal Republic of Yugoslavia.
Location: Southwestern Europe.
Area: 98,650 square miles (255 504 km²).
Population (1979 est.): 22,200,000.
Chief Cities (1974 est.): Belgrade, the capital, 845,000; Zagreb, 602,000; Skopje, 389,000.
Government: *Head of state,* Tito (Josip Broz), president (took office 1953). *Head of government,* Veselin Djuranović, prime minister (took office March 1977). *Legislature*—Federal Assembly: Federal Chamber and Chamber of Republics and Provinces.
Monetary Unit: Dinar (21.54 dinars equal U.S.$1, Aug. 1979).
Manufactures (major products): Processed food, machinery, textiles, nonferrous metals, wood.
Agriculture (major products): Corn, wheat, sugar beets, tobacco.

559

YUKON

Moves toward self-government, the installation and resignation of a commissioner, renewed interest in exploration for gold and other minerals, and the opening of two major highways were events of note in the Yukon Territory.

Government and Politics. On Jan. 20, 1979, former Whitehorse Mayor Ione J. Christensen became the first woman and first native Yukoner to become commissioner of the territory. She replaced Arthur M. Pearson, who resigned from the position in October 1978. In the aftermath of federal and territorial elections, however, the powers of the commissioner's office were greatly reduced.

The executive committee was increased from four to six elected members; the new committee included its first native Indian. Two ministers resigned during their first year in office—Tourism and Economic Development Minister Howard Tracey stepped down over a conflict of interest, and Health Minister Grafton Njootli resigned following a police investigation into his personal activities.

Recommendations to the newly elected federal government for further modifications of the constitution resulted in major political changes for the Yukon. The first-ever "executive council" would replace the executive committee and function as a provincial cabinet. In October, after receiving instructions from the federal government that her position would not be included in the new executive council and that her powers and responsibilities would be greatly limited, Commissioner Christensen resigned.

Economy. The rising world market prices of gold and other minerals sparked renewed interest in mining. Employment in the mineral exploration industry increased by 24%, while expenditures increased by 12% to $20 million. Still, the cost of living in the Yukon continued to rank among the highest of all Canadian provinces and territories.

Transportation. The opening of two new highways added important links to the territory's transportation network. An extension of the Klondike Highway connected Whitehorse and the tidewater town of Skagway, AK. The new Dempster Highway links Dawson City and the northern reaches of the Northwest Territories.

ANDREW HUME
Free-lance writer
Whitehorse, Yukon

─────── YUKON · Information Highlights ───────

Area: 207,076 square miles (536 327 km²).
Population (1979 est.): 21,600.
Chief City (1976 census): Whitehorse, the capital, 13,311.
Government (1979): *Chief Officers*—commissioner, vacant; chief justice, Court of Appeal, and judge of the Supreme Court, H. C. B. Maddison. *Legislature*—Territorial Council, 16 members.
Education (1979–80 est.): *Enrollment*—public elementary and secondary schools, 5,350 pupils.

ZAIRE

Zaire's place in world attention slipped in 1979 from the one it had occupied in the previous two years when its Shaba province had been twice invaded by rebels. But the disarray in Zaire's internal economic management and the continued instability of the regime of President Mobuto Sese Seko remained topics of concern.

Aftermath of Invasions. The political and economic repercussions of the invasions in 1977 and 1978 from Angola by the *Front National pour la Libération du Congo* (FNLC), descendants of the old Katanga (now called Shaba) gendarmes, lingered throughout the year. To save the Mobutu regime from collapse during the second invasion, France dispatched a regiment of its Foreign Legion to the mining town of Kolwezi. Soon after, Belgian troops and a pan-African peacekeeping force, comprised chiefly of Moroccans and Senegalese, arrived.

After restoring peace the expeditionary forces turned in 1979 to training the shaky Zairian army and to ensuring the security of the tiny European community whose well-being is necessary for the operation of the copper mines. Withdrawal of the pan-African force caused misgivings in Kolwezi among local and foreign residents who fear bandits and the unruly Zairian armed forces.

When not on his frequent trips abroad the president spent much of his time in Shaba, reassuring employees of Gecamines, the national copper mining company and, in his words, "breathing new life into the army so that it becomes an instrument in the service of the people."

Economy and Mining. Although the economy stayed as precarious as in the preceding year, its apparent bankruptcy appeared less immediate in the light of a $150 million standby credit from the International Monetary Fund (IMF). The financial shot in the arm for the ailing economy carried with it stringent conditions by the IMF as part of the "stabilization plan." Dr. Erwin Blumenthal of the IMF team became principal director of the central bank where he has banned credit to scores of companies, many owned by Mobutu's closest friends and political allies.

These measures attacked the link between political influence and personal economic gain, so long a feature of Mobutu's rule. Thus the president's procrastination in signing the letter of intent for the credit is understandable, for the "Zairian sickness" (or corruption) undergirds the regime itself.

At year's end Mobutu looked mainly to rising prices in copper and cobalt to solve the financial crises. The price for copper rose in early 1979 but flattened out by midyear. Other resources —cobalt, diamonds, and zinc—were given increased production targets, but scepticism greeted the optimistic projections.

Europeans, who had withdrawn from Kolwezi following a 1978 massacre, returned to the mining center in 1979.

The Benguela railway across Angola, the shortest route for Zaire's export to the sea, was still closed as a result of sabotage by guerrillas fighting against the Luanda government. A 50% devaluation of the zaire in January reflected the poor state of the economy and the IMF requirements.

Domestic Affairs. The Executive Council (government) was reorganized in March. The most dramatic move took the form of the reinstatement of Nguza Karl-I-Bond to the cabinet as foreign minister. In the wake of the first Shaba conflict, he had been charged with high treason and sentenced to death. The removal of Mpinga Kasenda as prime minister on charges of corruption and his replacement by Boboliko Lokonga, along with other ministerial reshuffl-

ing, seemed to represent pressure from the IMF to stamp out favoritism. But the changes could conceal Mobutu's elimination of potential threats to his rule in the way his frequent moving of military commanders had in the past.

Drought caused severe food shortages, and scarcity of fuel was noted in many areas outside the capital which received more than its share. The budgetary deficit of the armed forces, urban banditry in Kinshasa, and the inadequate use of Lomé Convention credits drew criticism in the parliament but food shortages and inflation preoccupied its sessions.

Foreign Affairs. Zaire mended fences with Cuba and the Soviet Union, which it had accused of being behind the Shaba invasions. Mobutu's aim is to lessen the probability of a repetition. In another rapprochement, Kinshasa also exchanged ambassadors with East Germany. These moves toward the Soviet bloc caused no discernible shift from the friendship with China which in the past supplied military assistance.

Abruptly and with a loss of $40 million, Mobutu cancelled the contract with Otrag, the West German firm which had leased 39,000 square miles (101 000 km²) in Shaba for rocket testing. This improved his standing with Tanzania, a longtime critic of the German operation. Mobutu also improved relations with Angola and the People's Republic of the Congo.

THOMAS H. HENRIKSEN, *National Fellow*
Hoover Institution on
War, Revolution, and Peace

ZAIRE · Information Highlights

Official Name: Republic of Zaire.
Location: Central equatorial Africa.
Area: 905,365 square miles (2 344 895 km²).
Population (1979 est.): 28,000,000.
Chief Cities (1976 est.): Kinshasa, the capital, 2,443,-876; Kananga, 704,211.
Government: *Head of state,* Mobutu Sese Seko, president (took office Nov. 1965). *Head of government,* Boboliko Lokonga, prime minister (took office March 1979). *Legislature* (unicameral)—National Legislative Council.
Monetary Unit: Zaire (1.53 zaires equal U. S.$1, July 1979).
Manufactures (major products): Processed and unprocessed minerals, consumer products, metal and chemical products, construction materials, steel.
Agriculture (major products): Palm oil, coffee, rubber, tea, cotton, cocoa beans, manioc, plantains, corn, rice, vegetables, fruits, sugarcane.

ZIMBABWE (Rhodesia)

For the former British colony known at the beginning of the year as Rhodesia, at the middle as Zimbabwe Rhodesia, and by the end as Zimbabwe, 1979 brought close the end of a momentous chapter in its history.

The long expected crisis in the regime took place. Despite Prime Minister Ian Smith's success in persuading the ruling white minority to accept and implement a settlement with the internal black leaders for limited black majority rule, the settlement lasted barely six months. The new government of Prime Minister Abel Muzorewa, which came into office on June 1, found the burdens it inherited too great to overcome. The international support and recognition its creators—both black and white—had hoped for and counted on was not forthcoming. By the end of the year it had bowed to pressures even greater then those which had forced Mr. Smith's government in March 1978 to concede the principle of "one-man one-vote" and to turn to the internal black nationalist leaders. The Muzorewa government agreed to restore the breakaway colony to British rule, to step down, and to contest new elections, under British supervision, with the hitherto excluded leaders of the external Patriotic Front alliance.

Thus ended Mr. Smith's 14-year-old rebellion against Britain and his ruling party's efforts to achieve independence on its own terms. Once more the political future of Rhodesia was in doubt. These events took place in a country wracked by guerrilla war and violence on a scale that exceeded anything in the previous six years of hostilities. The new elections, which would take place on the basis of a revised constitution, a cease-fire, and the return of the Patriotic Front leaders and their guerrilla forces, were scheduled to be held early in 1980.

Internal Affairs. The first half of the year was dominated by the transitional government's preparations to hold a general election on the principle of 18-year-old universal suffrage and then to hand over the reins of government, within the limitations imposed by the internal settlement, to the victors. Originally intended to take place before Dec. 31, 1978, the elections were set forward to April. They were conditional upon the acceptance by the existing electorate—overwhelmingly white and numbering about 94,000—of the new constitution. On January 30 these voters, but not the black population, were asked to vote in a referendum to accept or reject the constitution. "If you believe you can get away without this (black rule) and the removal of racial discrimination, you are living in a fool's paradise," Smith warned his white audiences. And repeatedly he reminded them of the special privileges the constitution provided whites, and the entrenched clauses which protected them. Some 85% of the voters accepted the document. The new constitution did seriously limit black majority rule. Of 170 clauses, 123 were entrenched. In the 100-member House of Assembly 28 seats were reserved for whites for ten years, while only 23 votes were necessary to defeat a proposed constitutional change. A Senate of 30 seats would include 10 for whites. In the cabinet 28% of the seats were reserved for whites, while special

A white Rhodesian soldier stands guard as blacks prepare to vote in April elections.

Prime Minister Abel Muzorewa (*left*), Deputy Prime Minister Silas Mundawarana, and Ian Smith participate in the London Conference, which returned Rhodesia to temporary British rule and paved the way for a new constitution and new elections in 1980.

UPI

commissions were set up to control the civil service, the armed forces, the police, and the judiciary. These arrangements gave considerable ammunition to the opponents of the internal settlement who saw in it only Prime Minister Smith's latest attempt to avoid genuine majority rule.

The government turned its attention to the April elections—the first in which all Africans over the age of 18 were entitled to vote. They were to be held in three stages. The first dealt with 20 white seats, the second with the 72 common roll but essentially black seats, and the third with the selection of the remaining 8 white members by the 92 elected members from a list submitted by, as it transpired, Smith's party, the Rhodesian Front. The latter swept all 20 elected reserved seats. The government announced that it had dropped its plans to register black voters. The war, together with manpower problems, had made this impossible earlier and made it impossible now. The same was the case for the delimitation of constituencies. The government instead adopted a party list system along with proportional representation for any party gaining at least 5% of the vote. To deal with the problem of illiteracy, the black parties adopted symbols. For example, Bishop Muzorewa's United African National Council (UNAC) employed a tribal shield with a spear and a hoe; the Rev. Ndabanigni Sithole's Zimbabwe African National Union (ZANU) a flaming torch. Three other parties—Chief Jeremiah Chirau's Zimbabwe United People's Organization, Chief Kayisa Ndiweni's United National Federal Party, and Henry Chihota's National Democratic Union—contested the 72 seats. The common roll elections took place April 17–21 at some 2,000 polling points, many in areas heavily infiltrated by Patriotic Front guerrillas. Most of the country was under martial law and most of the able-bodied whites mobilized.

Those who voted, estimated at 1.8 million of the 2.8 million eligible (64%), gave Bishop Muzorewa's party 51 of the 72 seats, the Reverend Sithole's party 12, and Chief Ndiweni's 9. On May 7 the remaining 8 white seats were filled, thus giving Mr. Smith all 28. Bitterly disappointed at the results, Sithole charged "gross irregularities," called the whole process into question, and decided to boycott the new Parliament and cabinet. There were undoubtedly irregularities, and not by any one group alone, especially in the existence of "auxiliaries" or private armies recruited in 1978. But neither a team from the British Conservative Party nor a delegation from the New York–based Freedom House organization, which observed the elections, discredited the final returns. But many continued to express the opinion that the exclusion of the Patriotic Front prevented any meaningful results.

Bishop Muzorewa's victory had been widely expected. On June 1 he took office as the first black prime minister. His cabinet of 12 blacks and 5 whites included Mr. Smith as minister without portfolio and the right-wing former foreign minister, South African–born P. K. Van der Byl; the two successful rival black parties were given 2 posts each; the remainder went to the bishop's UNAC. On January 12, campaigning for the new constitution, Mr. Smith had said that although the government could fight on for years, "If we don't get support from the free world there really is not much hope."

—ZIMBABWE (Rhodesia) • Information Highlights—

Official Name: British Colony of Southern Rhodesia.
Area: 150,673 square miles (390 245 km²).
Population (1979 est.): 7,200,000.
Chief Cities (1978 est.): Salisbury, the capital, 610,000; Bulawayo, 358,000.
Government: Lord Soames, Great Britain's interim governor (see text).
Manufactures (major products): Textiles, machinery, fertilizers.
Agriculture (major products): Tobacco, sugar, tea, groundnuts, cotton, corn, millet, sorghum, wheat.

This statement essentially summed up the problems facing Bishop Muzorewa's government. International opinion, despite the hopes of Smith and the bishop, was almost wholly opposed to the internal settlement. Neither the United Nations, nor the Organization of African Unity (OAU), nor the so-called "front-line" black states could accept the exclusion of the guerrilla leaders, Joshua Nkomo and Robert Mugabe, and their Patriotic Front. Neither the United States nor, as it later proved, the new Conservative government in Britain believed that peace was possible unless a settlement included them. And no one, not even the Muzorewa government, believed that the war could be won outright without the lifting of the UN sanctions, and international recognition.

The bishop pinned his hopes on the U. S. Senate and the Case-Javits amendment of 1978 obliging the U. S. president to lift sanctions if free elections led to majority rule and the government had demonstrated willingness to negotiate with the Patriotic Front. As early as May, the Senate had called on President Carter to lift the sanctions 14 days after the new government was installed. Muzorewa looked also to Mrs. Thatcher's preelection pledge to recognize the new regime. He continued to insist that thousands of guerrillas would soon defect on the ground that the nationalists' primary objective now had been achieved with majority rule. Such hopes proved illusory.

On June 7 President Carter refused to lift the sanctions and when, on June 12, the Senate in a 52 to 41 vote called for their repeal, his administration spoke of a veto. He was spared the necessity, however, when the House of Representatives voted 350 to 37 in favor of a compromise which permitted Carter to retain sanctions if he considered it in the national interest to do so. Prime Minister Muzorewa visited both the United States and Britain in July and was received by both heads of government. Mr. Carter said he would work closely with Britain but would not lift sanctions. Prime Minister

Thatcher indicated that sanctions would probably not be renewed after November but recognition must wait. Reportedly she pressed for the removal of Smith and modifications in the constitution. The Commonwealth Conference was due to meet in Lusaka in early August and Thatcher advisers increasingly warned that not a single African state would support the bishop. Both Britain and the United States had been advised strongly against recognition by the North Atlantic Treaty Organization (NATO), the OAU, Tanzania, and Nigeria. There was strong talk in Nigeria of retaliatory measures such as the nationalization of British and U. S. companies, as well as an oil embargo. The 16th OAU meeting of heads of state in Monrovia, Liberia, condemned the April elections as a sham. Nothing would be decided before the Commonwealth Conference at Lusaka, Zambia. The British government was being pushed to a fresh diplomatic initiative despite the desire by some Tories to support the bishop.

Meanwhile, at home Prime Minister Muzorewa was having domestic difficulties. James Chikerema, his first vice president, and seven others broke away from his party to form the Zimbabwe Democratic Party. The bishop's attempt to force their resignation through the courts was not upheld. And on July 20 his security forces were involved in clashes with numbers of "auxiliaries" said to be terrorizing the tribal areas. It was reported that more than 180 auxiliaries were killed. The situation in the towns and cities continued to deteriorate as refugees from the exposed rural areas flowed into them for protection. Unemployment, inflation, and shortages continued to add to the strains of war. The budget's allocation for defense was increased by 24.3% and the cost of fighting the war was estimated at some 35% of the whole, or more than $1.7 million a day.

The Commonwealth Conference. The heads of state and delegations of 39 states opened the conference on August 1. Although it was concerned with a broad range of problems, that of

PETER JORDAN, LIAISON

Police carefully monitor roadblocks as martial law is enforced in Salisbury.

Zimbabwe Rhodesia was central. It was soon clear that opposition to the recognition of the internal settlement was near-unanimous. The Nigerian commissioner for external affairs said his government's takeover of British Petroleum interests the day before was intended as a warning against recognition or the lifting of sanctions. Zambia's President Kenneth Kaunda insisted that the country was still a British colony in rebellion; Australia's Prime Minister Malcolm Fraser said that the elections settled nothing. Prime Minister Thatcher stated that what Britain sought was true majority government based on free elections, and to bring the country to legal independence on a basis acceptable to the international community. Mrs. Thatcher spent many hours in informal talks with various African leaders, including presidents Kaunda and Julius Nyerere of Tanzania, and a compromise was hammered out. In speeches, August 3, both Mrs. Thatcher and President Nyerere criticized the terms of the constitution and both agreed a case could be made for whites holding a disproportionate number of parliamentary seats. On August 6 the 39 heads of delegations approved a proposal calling for a cease-fire, a new constitution, and new elections supervised by the British government. It also called for a constitutional conference of the Muzorewa government, the Patriotic Front, and the British government to draw up the new constitution. It was understood that presidents Kaunda and Nyerere would use their influence with Nkomo and Mugabe, and Mrs. Thatcher would be responsible for Bishop Muzorewa. President Carter pledged his support.

On August 10 President Nyerere announced that the Patriotic Front would accept the proposal and the same day the British cabinet approved a plan for a conference in London in September. Bishop Muzorewa, still protesting that new elections were unnecessary, followed suit. On August 14 Britain formally invited the representatives of the Salisbury government and the Patriotic Front to a conference beginning September 10 in London under the chairmanship of the British Foreign Secretary, Lord Carrington. Each delegation was to number 12. Bishop Muzorewa accepted the next day and the Patriotic Front on August 20. Nkomo and Mugabe made it quite clear, however, that there would be no cease-fire until agreement on all other matters had been reached.

The London Conference. The conference opened on September 10. On December 21, after fourteen weeks of hard bargaining, stalemates, threats, brinkmanship, breakthroughs, and ultimatums, the leaders of the Patriotic Front, Bishop Muzorewa, and Lord Carrington (representing the British government) signed a cease-fire agreement and the conference final report. The same day, Lord Soames, the new British Governor of Southern Rhodesia (Zimbabwe's official legal name for the present) who

took up residence on December 12, lifted the ban on proscribed political parties, and proclaimed an amnesty for all in rebellion against the Crown, and all who were in rebellion against the Salisbury government. At the UN, the Security Council voted 13–0–2 to lift the 13-year-old economic embargo.

The London agreement came in three stages. The first dealt with the draft constitution. It won acceptance from both sides on October 18. It guaranteed whites 20% of the parliamentary seats but removed from them the effective control of the government. Britain agreed that the protection of white land rights would not be a charge against future governments of the independent state. With the constitution behind them the conference turned to consider the question of the transition from guerrilla war to a general election. Agreement was reached on November 15. Lord Carrington agreed to satisfy the Patriotic Front's insistence that their forces have equal status with those of the Salisbury regime, while the Front in turn dropped demands for a share of political power during the transition and for the integration of the forces.

The third and final phase was concerned with the arrangements for the cease-fire. In terms of the accord, this would be supervised by a Commonwealth force of about 1,200 troops under British command; the elections would be held some two months after the cease-fire had gone into effect. A concern of Nkomo and Mugabe was to prevent their men from becoming easy targets in a number of vulnerable assembly points should the hostilities resume.

The War. The Patriotic Front had pledged itself to disrupt the April elections and prevent the population from voting. It succeeded in neither. But throughout the year, all three forces engaged in the struggle stepped up the war and put as many men as possible in the field. War casualties were more numerous than in any other year and the Red Cross condemned both sides for a callous disregard of basic standards and respect for human life. During the election month, April, according to Salisbury estimates, 850 persons were killed, bringing the total from January to more than 2,500. In the months of negotiations, September to November, 1,250 persons were killed. On the government side, few incidents caused as much public anger and anguish as the shooting down of another Viscount passenger plane with the loss of all 59 aboard. Nkomo forces claimed responsibility for the disaster. On the Patriotic Front side few activities produced as much devastation as the raids on bases in the neighboring countries, Zambia and Mozambique. By the end of August, Bishop Muzorewa's government had brought the total of such raids outside Zimbabwe Rhodesia to 34. Meanwhile white Rhodesians continued to emigrate.

R. B. BALLINGER, *Rhode Island College*

ZOOLOGY

In 1979 several thousand new papers and books about animals were published. Many were so technical as to be of interest only to the specialists. Almost all were ignored by the popular press. Even reports concerning the status of rare and endangered species, which once received extensive coverage, were not common nor prominently featured. The energy crunch caused many to question whether modern man can afford the environmental protection efforts necessary to guard rare or endangered species. Zoologists, however, continued to recognize that although esthetic considerations are of little importance to starving or energy-hungry people, an ecological balance is of prime importance to the long-term survival of mankind.

Animal Liberation. In the area of "animal rights," Scientists' Center for Animal Welfare focused its attention on the areas of wildlife management, factory farming, and the use of animals in research (*Science,* Oct. 6, 1978).

The American Grasshopper Crisis. The devastating effects of the locust (a grasshopper) have been recorded in North Africa since biblical times. In recent years, British, French, and UN scientists have devoted extensive efforts to control the African migratory locust. In the United States, ranchers and farmers of the high plains states will long remember 1978 and 1979 as the "years of the grasshoppers." The combination of two years of favorable conditions for grasshopper reproduction and survival, as well as a government ban against the use of effective anti-grasshopper insecticides, resulted in extensive pasture land and crop destruction.

Animal Repellers. An electromagnet insect and rodent repeller, with the purpose of destroying such harmful animals and insects as roaches and rodents, appeared on the market with a price tag of up to $1,195.00. Reportedly, the units were so effective that one would cover an area of 30 acres (12.1 ha) with protective "controclusive magnetism (CCM)," a term coined by one of the manufacturers of these devices. The U. S. Environmental Protection Agency found all such devices tested to be useless, ordered several models removed from the market, and concluded that the concept of repellency at low levels by electromagnetism is false. (*Science,* May 4, 1979).

Endangered Primates. *Primate Conservation,* a new book edited by Monaco's Prince Rainier and G. H. Bourne and published by Academic Press, New York, summarized the status of many primates. In general, the work concluded that increased competition between animal and man has resulted in the extinction of some primates and is rapidly reducing a number of others.

The popular but extremely rare giant panda remained in the news in 1979. Plans were advanced at the Washington National Zoo to try to mate its two giant pandas, Ling-Ling and Hsing-Hsing, which have been residents of the zoo since President Nixon's 1972 trip to China, through artificial insemination. Since giant pandas are difficult to breed, Washington zoo officials sought to imitate the Chinese. A female panda cub was born at the Beijing (Peking) zoo in 1978 following the artificial insemination of an eight-year-old female.

The nation of Japan mourned the death of Lan Lan, a ten-year-old giant panda. Officials at Tokyo's Ueno Zoo declared that if its prime attraction had lived one more month it might have given birth. For Lan Lan was pregnant at the time of death.

Evolution. New means of measuring evolutionary time spans and the discoveries of new fossils and "missing links" were reported. R. W. Taylor, research scientist at the Australian National Insect Collection, reported the rediscovery of a living-fossil ant. This Australian species is considered to be the most primitive living ant. Relatives with similar structures are known only from a few fossils thought to be over 60 million years old. Studies of the structure, genetics, behavior, and ecology of this ant have led to a proposed reclassification of ants.

The role of ants and termites in modern ecosystems received additional definition in a new book, *Production Ecology of Ants and Termites,* edited by M. V. Brian (Cambridge University Press, New York). The work reports that, in most parts of the world, there are between 500,000 and 50,000,000 ants and termites per acre. By weight, they make up from 1% to 20% of all animal life in an area. Many termite species have colonies made up of individuals hatched from the eggs laid by the one queen in that colony. One of these queens deposits more than 85,000 eggs each day. Such production probably continues daily for as long as 80 years.

Yuanjing, a female panda, was born at the Beijing (Peking) zoo in April 1978 following the artificial insemination of Juanjuan, an eight-year-old female.

In *Modes of Specification,* published by W. H. Freeman of San Francisco, Michael J. D. White, an Australian geneticist, provides new insights into the mechanisms of evolution. Although quite technical, the book should be required reading for any serious zoologist. *Caste and Ecology in Social Insects* by G. F. Oster and E. O. Wilson (Princeton University Press) explores the question of optimality (desirability) in evolution; G. J. Vermeij's *Biogeography and Adaptations of Marine Life* (Harvard University Press) explores evolutionary gradients.

Physiology. Emily R. Morey of NASA Ames Research Center and David J. Baylink of the University of Washington reported in *Science* (Sept. 22, 1978) that young laboratory rats decrease and may cease all bone formation during space flight. They suggested that prolonged weightlessness might well result in bone decomposition.

Magic stones that removed poison from a medieval monarch's drinks have long been recognized. These bezoar stones are calcareous concretions that develop in the digestive tracts of Persian mountain goats. Similar stones have been found in other goats, antelopes, and ruminant animals. Scientists at the Scripps Institution of Oceanography in San Diego have recently explained the development. These bezoars include partially digested animal hair. This particular protein has the ability to absorb arsenic and related arsenical chemicals that were the most common poisons of the Middle Ages. As reported in *Science* (Feb. 16, 1979), attempts have been made to develop marine algae with similar arsenic absorbing traits to help remove marine pollutants from industrial sources.

E. Satinoff of the University of Illinois suggested (*Science,* July 7, 1978) that the body-temperature regulating mechanism developed in mammals is not, as generally accepted, a single thermostat response system. Professor Satinoff proposes that the nervous system evolved as many thermostats as there are thermoregulatory responses. In other words, the ability of the mammalian to maintain a relatively uniform temperature under a range of surrounding conditions is the result of a large series of interacting neural control mechanisms.

Joseph Siebenaller and George N. Somero of Scripps Institution of Oceanography demonstrated that a physiological trait (differences in sensitivity to pressures in certain enzymes important in muscle contraction) actually determines why certain kinds of fish dwell at given depths while related species occur only at higher or lower depths. Earlier, workers had attempted to find behavioral traits, differences in temperatures, competition, and other factors as the cause (*Science,* July 21, 1978).

Behavior. P. D. Boersma of the University of Washington reported that the breeding patterns of the Galapagos penguins are an excellent indicator of oceanographic conditions. As has been

UPI

Researchers at the University of Oklahoma hope that Washoe, the first chimpanzee to learn American sign language, will teach the system to her offspring.

known for many years, multiannual variations in oceanic conditions off the west coast of South America cause large variations in the number and variety of fish available to sea birds. In extremely poor years few birds nest and many die. This report demonstrates that the condition is much more widespread than previously known—extending westward at least to the Galapagos Islands.

G. C. Ray of Johns Hopkins University and four associates from various institutions reported tracking a fin whale tagged with a radio. The whale was followed for almost 28 hours for a distance of more than 90 miles (145 km). During one period of two hours and ten minutes the whale took 58 breaths (about 2.2 minutes between breaths).

Monarch butterflies have long been cited as an example of an insect that has an odor that is distasteful to birds. Therefore, this brightly colored butterfly escaped predation. In fact, other species lacking bad taste have mimicked the color patterns of the monarch simply to avoid being fed upon. W. H. Calvert and associates of Amherst College have found that individual birds of several different species have learned to avoid the monarch butterfly's chemical defense and at some over-wintering sites in Mexico have become major predators (*Science,* May 25, 1979).

E. LENDELL COCKRUM
University of Arizona

STATISTICAL AND TABULAR DATA

TABLE OF CONTENTS

NATIONS OF THE WORLD

A PROFILE AND SYNOPSIS OF MAJOR 1979 DEVELOPMENTS*

Nation, Region	Population in millions[1]	Capital	Area Sq mi (km²)	Head of Government[2]
Bahamas, Caribbean	0.2	Nassau	5,380 (13 935)	Lynden O. Pindling, prime minister

The deposed Shah of Iran stayed in the Bahamas from March 30 to June 10. Later in the summer another deposed head of state, Anastasio Somoza Debayle of Nicaragua, was expelled, his request for a three-month visa rejected. Land sales to foreigners were restricted.

Nation, Region	Population in millions[1]	Capital	Area Sq mi (km²)	Head of Government[2]
Bahrain, W. Asia	0.3	Manama	258 (668)	Isa ibn Salman, emir Khalifa ibn Salman, prime minister

Egyptian ships were barred from Bahrain in April—an act of retaliation for Egypt's peace treaty with Israel. Shortly before, Egypt recalled its ambassador from Bahrain.

Nation, Region	Population in millions[1]	Capital	Area Sq mi (km²)	Head of Government[2]
Barbados, Caribbean	0.3	Bridgetown	166 (430)	John M. G. Adams, prime minister

Barbados was showered with volcanic ash in April, when Mount Soufrière on St. Vincent, about 100 miles (160 km) away, suddenly erupted.

Nation, Region	Population in millions[1]	Capital	Area Sq mi (km²)	Head of Government[2]
Benin, W. Africa	3.5	Porto-Novo	43,483 (112 621)	Mathieu Kérékou, president

Nearly 100 people, most of them absent, were sentenced to death in May for complicity in the mercenary raid on Cotonou on Jan. 16, 1977. Among the condemned was former President Émile Zinsou.

Nation, Region	Population in millions[1]	Capital	Area Sq mi (km²)	Head of Government[2]
Bhutan, S. Asia	1.3	Punakha	18,147 (47 000)	Jigme Singhye Wangchuk, king

Bhutanese border guards confronted their Chinese counterparts in August, after Chinese herders encroached upon Bhutanese pasture lands and were challenged. No bloodshed was reported.

Nation, Region	Population in millions[1]	Capital	Area Sq mi (km²)	Head of Government[2]
Botswana, S. Africa	0.7	Gaborone	231,804 (600 372)	Sir Seretse Khama, president

Botswana suffered several armed incursions by Zimbabwe-Rhodesian forces during the year ; the country maintained refugee transit camps for people fleeing the fighting across the border. Despite such pressures, Botswana has retained its democratic principles, with no suspension of civil liberties. General elections in October resulted in no governmental changes.

Nation, Region	Population in millions[1]	Capital	Area Sq mi (km²)	Head of Government[2]
Burundi, E. Africa	4.4	Bujumbura	10,747 (27 835)	Jean-Baptiste Bagaza, president

The European Community airlifted food and other essential supplies to Burundi in March, after rail and road links to the East African coast were severed by Ugandan-Tanzanian hostilities.

Nation, Region	Population in millions[1]	Capital	Area Sq mi (km²)	Head of Government[2]
Cameroon, Cen. Africa	8.3	Yaoundé	183,568 (475 442)	Ahmadou Ahidjo, president

A new succession law was adopted by the National Assembly in June. It provides for the prime minister to assume presidential powers in case of the president's death or resignation. Good quality light crude oil was discovered 50 miles (80 km) offshore in August ; several weeks later a find of natural gas was also reported 75 miles (120 km) offshore.

Nation, Region	Population in millions[1]	Capital	Area Sq mi (km²)	Head of Government[2]
Cape Verde, W. Africa	0.3	Praia	1,557 (4 033)	Aristides Pereira, president

Because of insufficient rain in 1978 and a resulting poor harvest of corn, the country experienced severe food shortages in the early part of the year. Unrest within President Pereira's ruling party caused the resignations of three cabinet members in March and April.

* Independent nations not covered separately or under Central America (pages 82–567).   [1] 1979 estimates.   [2] As of Dec. 31, 1979.

Nation, Region	Population in millions[1]	Capital	Area Sq mi (km²)	Head of Government[2]
Cen. Afr. Republic, Cen. Africa	2.4	Bangui	240,534 (622 984)	David Dacko, president

Emperor Bokassa was overthrown and the country reverted to republican government on September 20. The coup, ending 14 years of Bokassa's rule, was engineered by the country's previous president, David Dacko, apparently with French aid. A storm had been brewing against the emperor since January, when school children protested a law requiring them to wear expensive uniforms to classes. In mid-April, following further protests, government forces rounded up some 150 children, aged 6–20, and took them to the Ngaragba jail where more than 100 were killed. A five-member African committee of jurists concluded in August that the emperor personally was involved in the killings, and survivors later described his murderous acts in gory detail. After the coup, Bokassa flew to France, claiming citizenship and a right to residence as a former member of the French armed forces. Denied entry by an embarrassed French government, he found political asylum in the Ivory Coast.

Nation, Region	Population in millions[1]	Capital	Area Sq mi (km²)	Head of Government[2]
Chad, Cen. Africa	4.4	N'Djamena	495,752 (1 284 000)	Goukouni Oueddei, president

President Félix Malloum resigned on March 23 to facilitate an end to the civil war between his followers and those of Prime Minister Hissène Habré. A succeeding interim regime was also bedeviled by repeated clashes between warring groups, and further complications arose from Libyan incursions in the north. Libya allegedly has designs on a mineral-rich strip of land along the Libya-Chad border. In August, nine rival groups finally agreed on a government of national unity under the presidency of Goukouni Oueddei, a northern Muslim tribal chief.

Nation, Region	Population in millions[1]	Capital	Area Sq mi (km²)	Head of Government[2]
Comoros, E. Africa	0.4	Moroni	838 (2 171)	Ahmed Abdallah, president
Congo, Cen. Africa	1.5	Brazzaville	132,046 (342 000)	Denis Sassou-Nguessou, president

A palace coup on February 8 ousted President Joachim Yombi Opango. Charged with embezzlement of public funds and other crimes, Opango was to be put on trial. A new constitution was adopted in a referendum in July. It was reported in October that hundreds of Congolese children had been forcibly sent to Cuba for military training.

Nation, Region	Population in millions[1]	Capital	Area Sq mi (km²)	Head of Government[2]
Djibouti, E. Africa	0.1	Djibouti	8,494 (22 000)	Hassan Gouled, president B. G. Hamadou, prime minister

An Afar guerrilla group on June 27 attacked a government army base, killing at least four soldiers. Some 50 Afars, including two members of parliament, had been arrested shortly before, following an assassination attempt on the head of the regime's security forces.

Nation, Region	Population in millions[1]	Capital	Area Sq mi (km²)	Head of Government[2]
Dominica, Caribbean	0.1	Roseau	289 (749)	Oliver J. Seraphim, acting prime minister

Scandals and allegations of corruption forced Prime Minister Patrick John out of office on June 21. Shortly before, President Fred DeGazon had fled the country and his successor, Sir Louis Cools-Lartigue, resigned after only a day in office. Former Minister of Agriculture Oliver J. Seraphim was appointed to head an interim government. Ten weeks later, on August 30, Hurricane David flattened the capital city of Roseau, leaving at least 22 dead and 60,000 homeless.

Nation, Region	Population in millions[1]	Capital	Area Sq mi (km²)	Head of Government[2]
Dominican Republic, Caribbean	5.3	Santo Domingo	18,818 (48 739)	Antonio Guzman, president

President Guzman dismissed his finance minister and economic coordinator. According to the president, agricultural expansion should be the basis for future economic development. The island was damaged severely by Hurricane David. Pope John Paul II and the Spanish prime minister were guests. An attempted coup was thwarted in September.

Nation, Region	Population in millions[1]	Capital	Area Sq mi (km²)	Head of Government[2]
Equatorial Guinea, Cen. Africa	0.3	Malabo	10,831 (28 051)	Teodoro Obiang Nguema, president

President Macias Nguema's 11-year rule of terror came to an end with a bloodless military coup.

Nation, Region	Population in millions[1]	Capital	Area Sq mi (km²)	Head of Government[2]
Fiji, Oceania	0.6	Suva	7,055 (18 272)	Ratu Sir Kamisese Mara, prime minister

Prime Minister Mara complained in October that Fiji's large contingent of the UN peace-keeping force in Lebanon had been paid only a fraction of what the organization owed for its services, resulting in considerable financial hardship for the tiny island nation.

Nation, Region	Population in millions[1]	Capital	Area Sq mi (km²)	Head of Government[2]
Gabon, Cen. Africa	0.5	Libreville	103,346 (267 667)	Albert-Bernard Bongo, president

Several constitutional changes, among them a shortening of legislators' terms, were drawn up in January but a slated referendum for their approval was canceled for financial reasons. It was reported, however, that the country's financial status had improved considerably because of the government's stabilization program, initiated in 1978.

Nation, Region	Population in millions[1]	Capital	Area Sq mi (km²)	Head of Government[2]
Gambia, W. Africa	0.6	Banjul	4,361 (11 295)	Sir Dawda K. Jawara, president

President Jawara in May appointed Muhamadu Lamine Saho to the newly created office of attorney general and minister of justice. He also announced the formation of a special tribunal to handle charges of corruption. An agricultural development fund will be established to boost farm production.

Nation, Region	Population in millions[1]	Capital	Area Sq mi (km²)	Head of Government[2]
Grenada, Caribbean	0.1	St. George's	133 (344)	Maurice Bishop, prime minister

The 18-year-old government of Sir Eric M. Gairy was overthrown on March 13, the coup led by an opposition legislator named Maurice Bishop, whose father was killed by Sir Eric's secret police in 1974. The constitution was suspended, but the new government vowed to respect human rights. The coup appeared to have genuine popular support.

Nation, Region	Population in millions[1]	Capital	Area Sq mi (km²)	Head of Government[2]
Guinea, W. Africa	4.9	Conakry	94,925 (245 857)	Ahmed Sékou Touré, president

President Touré continued his policy, begun in 1978, of expanding Guinea's foreign relations, with an unofficial visit to the Ivory Coast in February. In August he visited the United States, trying to attract foreign investment. As a gesture of goodwill to President Tolbert of Liberia, a Christian, Muslim Touré in August released Monsignor Raymond Tchidimbo, archbishop of Conakry, who had been imprisoned since 1970 for alleged plots against the government.

Nation, Region	Population in millions[1]	Capital	Area Sq mi (km²)	Head of Government[2]
Guinea-Bissau, W. Africa	0.6	Bissau	13,948 (36 125)	Luiz de Almeida Cabral, president

President Antonio Ramalho Eanes of Portugal paid an official visit to Guinea-Bissau in March. Agreements between the two countries on judicial and consular affairs were signed.

Haiti, Caribbean	5.7	Port-au-Prince	10,714 (27 750)	Jean-Claude Duvalier, president

The poorest country in the Western Hemisphere, with a per capita income of less than $90 in 1978, Haiti has created its own version of "boat people"—economic refugees seeking entry into the United States. Six such drowned off the Florida coast in August as a result of panic when discovered by U. S. coast guards. By November, some 8,000–12,000 illegal Haitian immigrants were fighting to stay in the United States, while immigration officers rejected their claims to political asylum.

Ivory Coast, W. Africa	7.7	Abidjan	124,502 (322 462)	Félix Houphouët-Boigny, president

Visa requirements between Ghana and the Ivory Coast were mutually abolished in February, the first such accord between francophone and anglophone African states. In late September President Houphouët-Boigny granted the deposed Bokassa I of the Central African Empire political asylum as an act of "Christian charity."

Jamaica, Caribbean	2.2	Kingston	4,244 (10 991)	Michael Manley, prime minister

Six people were killed and dozens injured in January during three days of violent protests caused by increased gas prices. The austerity imposed by the perennially shaky economy drives about 1% of the population to emigrate each year, creating a drain on skilled manpower, which in turn further threatens the island's development.

Kuwait, W. Asia	1.3	Kuwait City	6,880 (17 818)	Jabir al-Ahmad al-Sabah, emir Saad al-Abdullah al-Sabah, prime minister

The revolution in neighboring Iran in 1979 stirred the Kuwaiti government to think of reviving parliamentary democracy; the National Assembly has been in abeyance since 1976, and the press is restricted. Nevertheless, Kuwaitis enjoy the best social system and the most liberal regime in the area, and the country has the highest per capita income in the world—which may be the reason why popular discontent is not too sharply focused.

Lesotho, S. Africa	1.3	Maseru	11,720 (30 355)	Moshoeshoe II, king Leabua Jonathan, prime minister

Several bombing incidents, believed to be the work of the outlawed Congress Party, took place during the year, causing considerable damage and some loss of life. Armed clashes between police and members of the opposition movement claimed additional lives. Prime Minister Jonathan announced in September that the paramilitary police mobile unit would be turned into a regular army to deal with the situation.

Liberia, W. Africa	1.8	Monrovia	43,000 (111 369)	William R. Tolbert, president

Riots caused by a proposed increase in the price of rice cost more than 40 lives in April; some 550 others were injured, and property damage was estimated at $30 million. Tanks were rolled out to face the crowds, and police shot some demonstrators. President Tolbert subsequently suspended habeas corpus for a year and closed the University of Liberia, which he described as a "breeding ground of revolutionary ideas." In late June, however, he declared a general amnesty for those arrested in connection with the riots and vowed to reopen the university.

Liechtenstein, Cen. Europe	0.024	Vaduz	62 (160)	Francis Joseph II, prince Hans Brunhart, premier
Madagascar, E. Africa	8.5	Antananarivo	226,656 (587 041)	Didier Ratsiraka, president

Former President Gabriel Ramantsoa died in Paris on May 9; he had been head of state from 1972 to 1974. A contract with the Chinese, made in July, provides for China to build a 1,200-kw hydroelectric power plant 60 miles (95 km) from the capital, Antananarivo.

Malawi, E. Africa	5.9	Lilongwe	45,747 (118 484)	Hastings K. Banda, president

President Banda in March claimed full responsibility for the sending of a letter bomb to Dr. Attati Mpakati, an exiled Malawian opposition leader residing in Mozambique. Dr. Mpakati reportedly lost several fingers in the explosion.

Maldives, S. Asia	0.1	Malé	115 (298)	Ibrahim Nasir, president

A Maldivian atoll chief, aboard an American survey ship to carry out clearance procedures, was shot and wounded by crew members in February. Three Americans were detained by authorities for a while, but the incident was played down by both sides and written off as a "genuine case of misunderstanding."

Mali, W. Africa	6.5	Bamako	478,764 (1 240 000)	Moussa Traoré, president

Presidential and parliamentary elections were held on June 19 after 10 years of military government. President Traoré, the only candidate for the presidency, received 99.89% of the vote. All 82 assembly members voted in belong to the Democratic Union of the Malian People, the only political party, which was formed at a special congress in March. The country's new constitution took effect on July 1.

Mauritania, W. Africa	1.6	Nouakchott	397,953 (1 030 700)	Mohammed Mahmud Ould Luly, president

President Mustapha Ould Salek assumed unlimited powers in late March and shortly afterward dissolved the government, installing a military council in its stead. On June 3 he resigned the presidency "for personal reasons" and was replaced by Lt. Col. Mohammed Mahmud Ould Luly. On August 5 Mauritania signed a peace agreement with the Polisario Front of the Western Sahara, labeling the four-year old war with the front "fratricidal and unjust."

Nation, Region	Population in millions[1]	Capital	Area Sq mi (km²)	Head of Government[2]
Mauritius, E. Africa	0.9	Port Louis	790 (2 045)	Sir Seewoosagur Ramgoolam, prime minister

A general strike in support of sugar workers paralyzed the economy in August; sugar accounts for 70% of the national income. Faced with a 30–35% inflation, the government was then pressed by the International Monetary Fund to devaluate the rupee by 30%. In addition, export duties on sugar were increased and new taxes imposed on the hotel and tourist industries.

Nation, Region	Population in millions[1]	Capital	Area Sq mi (km²)	Head of Government[2]
Monaco, S. Europe	0.025	Monaco-Ville	0.73 (1.89)	Rainier III, prince
Mongolia, E. Asia	1.6	Ulan Bator	604,247 (1 565 000)	Yumjaagin Tsedenbal, president Jambyn Batmönh, prime minister
Mozambique, E. Africa	10.2	Maputo	302,328 (783 029)	Samora Machel, president

The government forced the closing of 15 Catholic mission churches in January, greatly increasing the tension between the church and the regime. President Machel in a May Day speech called the church "an operational force of political and ideological subversion." More tangible subversion was provided by the Mozambique National Resistance, an opposition group based in Zimbabwe Rhodesia, which carried out several acts of sabotage during the year. In April ten people were executed by firing squad under a new law imposing the death penalty on those found guilty of sabotage, espionage, or high treason. President Machel rejected a Soviet application for naval base rights and announced that he would seek an increase in trade with the West.

Nation, Region	Population in millions[1]	Capital	Area Sq mi (km²)	Head of Government[2]
Nauru, Oceania	0.007	Nauru	8 (21)	Hammer de Roburt, president
Nepal, S. Asia	13.7	Katmandu	54,362 (140 797)	Birendra Bir Bikram, king

About 20 people were killed in repeated clashes between students and police in April and May. The unrest began when students wanted to protest the hanging of former Prime Minister Ali Bhutto of Pakistan but were forbidden to do so. Their protest then turned into demonstrations against King Birendra's regime.

Nation, Region	Population in millions[1]	Capital	Area Sq mi (km²)	Head of Government[2]
Niger, W. Africa	5.1	Niamey	489,189 (1 267 000)	Seyni Kountché, president

Rich uranium deposits were discovered near Agadez at the southern edge of the Sahara, it was reported in late August. President Kountché reorganized his cabinet in September, reshuffling several portfolios.

Nation, Region	Population in millions[1]	Capital	Area Sq mi (km²)	Head of Government[2]
Oman, W. Asia	0.9	Muscat	82,029 (212 457)	Qabus ibn Said, sultan

Sultan Qabus ibn Said, wary of the Soviet presence in neighboring Southern Yemen, appealed to the United States in May to warn the Russians against any trouble-making in the area. Aden, he said, has become a principal land, sea, and air base of the Soviets, whose long-range intention is to win control of the entire Arabian Peninsula.

Nation, Region	Population in millions[1]	Capital	Area Sq mi (km²)	Head of Government[2]
Papua New Guinea, Oceania	3.1	Port Moresby	178,259 (461 691)	Michael Somare, prime minister

Prime Minister Michael Somare declared a state of emergency on July 23 in an attempt to halt increasing tribal violence. More than 100 tribal clashes since the beginning of the year had left some 35 people dead and more than 200 wounded. At stake, too, was the coffee production of the Highlands region, which was threatened with disruption as a result of the hostilities.

Nation, Region	Population in millions[1]	Capital	Area Sq mi (km²)	Head of Government[2]
Qatar, W. Asia	0.2	Doha	4,247 (11 000)	Khalifa bin Hamad al-Thani, emir

Qatar in May followed the lead of six other OPEC nations in raising its oil prices above the official base price of the organization.

Nation, Region	Population in millions[1]	Capital	Area Sq mi (km²)	Head of Government[2]
Rwanda, E. Africa	4.9	Kigali	10,169 (26 338)	Juvénal Habyalimana, president

Twelve Belgian mercenaries, captured in February, were tried by a Rwanda court in June on charges of plotting to enter Zaire with the intent of overthrowing its government. Eleven were found guilty, but they were later allowed to return to Belgium. French President Valéry Giscard d'Estaing paid a two-day official visit in May and then stayed over an additional four days to attend the sixth Franco-African summit in Kigali.

Nation, Region	Population in millions[1]	Capital	Area Sq mi (km²)	Head of Government[2]
San Marino, S. Europe	0.02	San Marino	24.1 (61.19)	Ermemegildo Casperoni and Adriano Reffi, co-regents

Foreign Secretary Giordano Bruno Reffi officially visited the United States in May.

Nation, Region	Population in millions[1]	Capital	Area Sq mi (km²)	Head of Government[2]
São Tomé and Príncipe, W. Africa	0.1	São Tomé	372 (964)	Mañuel Pinto da Costa, president

Several political leaders were found guilty in May of conspiring to overthrow the government and assassinate the president. Afterward, the cabinet was reshuffled. In September a coup attempt by former Prime Minister Miguel Trovoada, whose office had been abolished in the reshuffle, was said to have been foiled.

Nation, Region	Population in millions[1]	Capital	Area Sq mi (km²)	Head of Government[2]
Senegal, W. Africa	5.5	Dakar	75,750 (196 192)	Léopold S. Senghor, president

The fourth political party in the country, the Senegalese Republican Movement, was legalized in February. A fifth party was formed, though not legalized, in September. A new press law that took effect in May requires all publications to be submitted to the government for approval prior to publication and empowers a magistrate to renew or revoke any journalist's press card, based on his writings.

Nation, Region	Population in millions[1]	Capital	Area Sq mi (km²)	Head of Government[2]
Seychelles, E. Africa	0.1	Victoria	108 (280)	F. Albert René, president

Elections under the country's new one-party constitution were held on June 5. President F. Albert René was elected to a five-year term with 98% of the vote. Two months earlier a Belgian mercenary had been arrested, suspected of preparing a coup on behalf of deposed former President James R. Mancham.

Nation, Region	Population in millions[1]	Capital	Area Sq mi (km²)	Head of Government[2]
Sierra Leone, W. Africa	3.7	Freetown	27,699 (71 740)	Siaka P. Stevens, president

President Siaka P. Stevens paid an official visit to France in June, discussing political and economic cooperation with his host, President Valéry Giscard d'Estaing. Earlier in the year, President Stevens had rejected recommendations by the International Monetary Fund that the leone be further devaluated. Rising
prices and lack of rice, the country's staple food, are two acute problems of his government.

Nation, Region	Population in millions[1]	Capital	Area Sq mi (km²)	Head of Government[2]
Solomon Islands, Oceania	0.2	Honiara	11,500 (29 785)	Peter Kenilorea, prime minister
Somalia, E. Africa	3.5	Mogadishu	246,200 (637 657)	Mohammed Siad Barre, president

Somalia withdrew from the Ogaden war with Ethiopia in March 1978, but fighting was still carried on
by guerrillas, who claim control of the countryside while Cuban-aided Ethiopians command the cities.
About all Somalia has gained, however, is a huge refugee problem—some 350,000 people in 21 camps—
which is seriously straining the country's resources. By mid-November, the continuing flow of fleeing
people was still about 1,000 a day. Year-end elections brought a heavy turnout.

Nation, Region	Population in millions[1]	Capital	Area Sq mi (km²)	Head of Government[2]
Surinam, S. America	0.4	Paramaribo	63,037 (163 265)	Johan H. E. Ferrier, president Henck A. E. Arron, prime minister

Surinam in March signed an agreement in a fisheries dispute with neighboring Guyana. The following
month Prime Minister Arron met with Prime Minister Burnham of Guyana to try to settle some other
outstanding differences between the nations, among them a territorial dispute over the so-called New
River Triangle. Surinam officially joined the movement of the nonaligned nations at its summit meeting
in Havana, Cuba, in September.

Nation, Region	Population in millions[1]	Capital	Area Sq mi (km²)	Head of Government[2]
Swaziland, S. Africa	0.5	Mbabane	6,704 (17 363)	Sobhuza II, king

King Sobhuza II reshuffled his cabinet in February, retaining only three of his previous ministers. The
country has been deluged with tens of thousands of South African, Malawian, and Mozambican refugees,
despite the reportedly very harsh treatment they receive in the country.

Nation, Region	Population in millions[1]	Capital	Area Sq mi (km²)	Head of Government[2]
Togo, W. Africa	2.5	Lomé	21,622 (56 000)	Gnassingbe Eyadéma, president

President Eyadéma reorganized his cabinet in March for the second time in six months. In August, 15
people accused of conspiracy to overthrow the government and kill the president were put on trial. Ten
were sentenced to death and three to prison terms; two were acquitted. Among those convicted (in ab-
sentia) were two sons of former President Sylvanus Olympio, whom Eyadéma killed during the military
coup of 1963. The president was elected to another seven-year term in December.

Nation, Region	Population in millions[1]	Capital	Area Sq mi (km²)	Head of Government[2]
Tonga, Oceania	0.1	Nuku'alofa	270 (699)	Taufa'ahau Tupou IV, king Prince Tu'ipelehake, prime minister

Tonga became a member of the United Nations Conference on Trade and Development (UNCTAD) during the conference's fifth session in Manila, the Philippines, from March 7 to June 3.

Nation, Region	Population in millions[1]	Capital	Area Sq mi (km²)	Head of Government[2]
Trinidad and Tobago, Caribbean	1.1	Port-of-Spain	1,980 (5 128)	Eric E. Williams, prime minister

The Inter-American Press Association held its annual meeting in Port-of-Spain in March. Two fully
loaded supertankers collided off the coast of Tobago on July 19, but fortunately none of the spilled oil
washed up on the beaches. Trinidad and Tobago is heavily dependent on tourism. (See also Caribbean.)

Nation, Region	Population in millions[1]	Capital	Area Sq mi (km²)	Head of Government[2]
Tuvalu, Oceania	0.01	Funafuti	9.5 (24.6)	Toalipi Lauti, prime minister

A treaty of friendship between Tuvalu and the United States was signed in April. The treaty included an
important U. S. renunciation of its claim, dating from 1856, to the country's four southernmost islands.

Nation, Region	Population in millions[1]	Capital	Area Sq mi (km²)	Head of Government[2]
United Arab Emirates, W. Asia	0.9	Abu Dhabi	32,278 (83 600)	Zaid ibn Sultan al-Nuhayan, president Maktum ibn al-Maktum, prime minister

The United Arab Emirates decided in April to withdraw its contingent from the Arab League peace-keeping
force in Lebanon. The country was cautious in its oil-price policy, choosing not to add a surcharge to
the OPEC base price, though many other nations had done so.

Nation, Region	Population in millions[1]	Capital	Area Sq mi (km²)	Head of Government[2]
Upper Volta, W. Africa	6.7	Ouagadougou	105,869 (274 200)	Sangoulé Lamizana, president

A law instituting a three-party system in Upper Volta was enacted by the National Assembly in late May.
A wave of strikes paralyzed the country in the first half of the year. Some arrests were made.

Nation, Region	Population in millions[1]	Capital	Area Sq mi (km²)	Head of Government[2]
Vatican City, S. Europe	0.001	Vatican City	0.17 (0.44)	John Paul II, pope
Western Samoa, Oceania	0.2	Apia	1,097 (2 841)	Malietoa Tanumafili II, head of state Tupuola Efi, prime minister
Zambia, E. Africa	5.6	Lusaka	290,585 (752 614)	Kenneth D. Kaunda, president

President Kaunda scored a diplomatic victory at the Commonwealth meeting in Lusaka in July, when he
prevailed upon Britain's Prime Minister Margaret Thatcher to call yet another conference to try to solve
the Rhodesian problem. Later, at a critical time of the talks, Kaunda flew to London to facilitate an agreement on a sticky point. As all this was happening, however, Zimbabwe Rhodesian forces staged one
raid after another into Zambia—one of them into the middle of Lusaka—blowing up bridges and crippling
the country's essential but vulnerable transportation routes. In late November President Kaunda called
up reservists and canceled all military leaves in order to cope with what he called a "full-scale war situation."

WORLD ECONOMIC INDEXES

The potential output of an economy is the output that would be realized if the labor force were fully employed, and labor and capital used at normal intensity. Although the concept is difficult to define and even more difficult to quantify, the need for such a measure, however imprecise, is not in doubt. Estimates of potential output and the ratio of actual to potential output—the output gap—are crucial in assessing the economic situation of a country and the appropriateness of its policies. These estimates are particularly crucial at the present time when there are serious divergences of views on whether more expansionary policies are needed in a number of industrial countries.

JACQUES R. ARTUS
Research Department, The International Monetary Fund

Name & Region	Consumer Price Index—1978 1970 = 100 All items	Food	Wholesale Price Index—1978 1970 = 100	Industrial Production Index—1978 1970 = 100	Unemployment Rate %—1978	Foreign Trade 1978—Million U.S. Dollars Imports	Exports	Estimated GNP 1978—Million U.S. Dollars	GNP Per Capita—1977 U.S. Dollars
AFGHANISTAN	142.1					498[1]	314[1]	2,300[1]	190
ALBANIA								750	610
ALGERIA	156.8[1]	187.0[1]				7,125[1]	5,814[1]	15,900	1,100
ANGOLA						625[7]	1,227[7]		330
ANTIGUA	236.0[1]	277.8[1]							
ARGENTINA	49,729.0	11,860.0	47,729.0	119	3.4[1]	4,162[1]	5,650[1]	76,400[1]	1,730
AUSTRALIA	224.0	211.4		117	6.3	13,885	14,127	108,100	7,340
AUSTRIA	166.8	158.7	104.0[5]	133	2.1	16,013	12,205	58,100	6,140
BAHAMAS	150.0	158.4				3,053[1]	1,989[1]		3,450
BAHRAIN						2,046	1,893	1,700[1]	3,790
BANGLADESH	314.8	302.1				1,294	576	8,000	90
BARBADOS	292.3	326.9			15.7[1]	314	130		1,760
BELGIUM	182.6	171.7	147.9	120	10.5	48,376[8]	44,853[8]	97,600	7,580
BENIN						246[1]	31[1]		200
BHUTAN									80
BOLIVIA	318.3	348.2			4.2[2]	618[1]	649[1]		540
BOTSWANA	154.4	153.4							440
BRAZIL	494.3	522.5	747.6	189[1]		15,054	12,659		1,390
BRUNEI	162.0[1]	171.0[1]				276[1]	1,613[1]	970	6,620
BULGARIA	102.0[1]	104.0[1]		188		7,606	7,501	25,100	2,590
BURMA	257.8	269.3				309	243	3,900[1]	140
BURUNDI	163.6[2]	171.2[2]				78[1]	92		130
CAMEROON						1,057	803		340
CANADA	180.2	210.3	212.7	140	8.4	43,434	46,065	204,000	8,450
CAPE VERDE	437.0	435.8							140
CEN. AFR. REP.	210.3	215.0	192.0			57	72		250
CHAD	144.8	155.0				118[2]	59[2]		130
CHILE	232,773.0	280,924.0	687,929.0		13.7	3,110	2,408		1,170
CHINA									410
CHINA (TAIWAN)									1,180
COLOMBIA	428.5	508.0	527.1	136[2]	9.8[1]	1,563	3,018	19,300[1]	710
CONGO	156.9[2]	158.0[2]				201	123[1]		500
COSTA RICA	216.6	221.7	280.8		4.7[1]	1,026[1]	798[1]		1,240
CUBA						4,687	4,346	12,500	900
CYPRUS	107.8	105.7	181.6		2.0	753	344	1,020[1]	1,740
CZECHOSLOVAKIA	104.6	104.1		162		12,560	12,321	61,600	4,090
DENMARK	207.6	221.6	197.2		7.4	14,810	11,886	55,300	8,050
DOMINICA	254.2	239.8							370
DOM. REP.	202.5[4]	179.2[4]	185.2			860	604		840
ECUADOR	262.6	312.1				1,627	1,494	7,000	770
EGYPT	184.4	218.0	184.6	164[2]	2.5[6]	6,480	1,901	18,100[1]	310
EL SALVADOR	204.8	198.3	234.6			1 025	629		570
EQ. GUINEA									340
ETHIOPIA	203.9	218.2				514	306	3,000	110
FIJI	210.9	222.1				356	199		1,220
FINLAND	244.3	257.5	125.8	130	7.5	7,864	8,618	30,800	6,150
FRANCE	199.8	212.5		128		81,805	76,609	463,000	7,290
FRENCH GUIANA	194.3[1]	197.8				191	7		

Name & Region	Consumer Price Index—1978 1970 = 100 All items	Food	Wholesale Price Index—1978 1970 = 100	Industrial Production Index—1978 1970 = 100	Unemployment Rate %—1978	Foreign Trade 1978—Million U.S. Dollars Imports	Exports	Estimated GNP 1978—Million U.S. Dollars	GNP Per Capita—1977 U.S. Dollars
GABON	239.6	207.4[1]	219.8[1]			589	1,307		3,730
GAMBIA	236.0	260.6				100	39		200
GERMANY, E.	96.0	100.0		159		14,572	13,267	72,700	4,940
GERMANY, W.	150.1	145.2	146.3	118	4.4	120,668	142,090	634,200	8,160
GHANA	351.5[2]	414.1[2]	278.0[2]	108[7]		862[2]	962[1]	6,000[1]	380
GIBRALTAR	277.2	324.0				38[2]	3[2]		
GREECE	255.4	280.5	276.9	183		7,648	3,341	32,300	2,810
GUADELOUPE	213.1	223.3				424	112		2,380
GUATEMALA	134.5	127.3	184.7	128[6]		1,084[1]	1,089	5,500[1]	790
GUINEA								740[1]	230
GUINEA-BISSAU									160
GUYANA	196.5	244.0				279	289		560
HAITI	208.3	213.7				225[1]	149[1]		230
HONDURAS	163.8	182.1				693	596	1,690	450
HONG KONG	125.0	122.0			4.5[1]	13,452	11,499		2,590
HUNGARY	130.8	132.1	130.0[1]	158		7,902	6,345	33,500	2,570
ICELAND	759.2	876.5			0.4[1]	674	641		4,570
INDIA	178.8	173.0	184.9	148		7,954	6,614	106,400	150
INDONESIA	351.3	402.6	354.2			6,690	11,643	22,600[1]	300
IRAN	222.4[1]	204.5	213.4[1]	177[2]		15,842	22,431	75,100	2,180
IRAQ	151.9	153.4	147.5[2]			4,213	11,008	15,500	1,530
IRELAND	269.0	290.4	152.6	155	10.7	7,097	5,678	10,200	2,880
ISRAEL	785.4	833.7		162	3.6	5,582	3,716	10,500	2,920
ITALY	265.3	271.6	300.8	126	7.2	56,446	56,047	259,000	3,450
IVORY COAST	233.3	249.1				2,325	2,322	6,110[1]	710
JAMAICA	238.0[1]	252.3[1]				872	710		1,150
JAPAN	211.4	216.4	163.6	134	2.2	78,731	97,501	930,000	5,640
JORDAN	136.6	135.7	133.5			1,499	297	1,850[1]	710
KENYA	196.0	201.2				1,710	1,025	4,200[1]	270
KOREA, N.								10,500	700
KOREA, S.	295.9	356.7	324.9	512	3.2	15,074	12,713	46,000	810
KUWAIT	166.4[9]	182.6[9]	165.0[9]			4,616	10,483	11,900[1]	12,700
LAOS								260	90
LEBANON								3,400	
LESOTHO	193.5[12]	217.6[12]							230
LIBERIA	203.6	209.6				464[1]	486	910[1]	430
LIBYA					3.2[1]	3,782[1]	9,561[2]	19,000	6,680
LUXEMBOURG	171.1	170.0		104		48,376[8]	44,853[8]	3,380	7,150
MADAGASCAR	180.0	192.5				347[1]	338[1]	2,320	210
MALAWI	185.2	190.0				339	187	1,040	140
MALAYSIA	160.3	179.3		195				14,700	930
MALI						219	107	615[1]	110
MALTA	154.0	174.8		192[2]		568	355	750	1,680
MARTINIQUE	224.1	215.0				498	125		3,340
MAURITANIA	135.3	140.2				181	119		270
MAURITIUS	238.9	232.7				496	326		760
MEXICO	309.4	311.4	334.6	147[1]		7,744	5,739	83,600	1,110
MONGOLIA				173[1]					830
MOROCCO	144.6	146.3	191.5[1]	156[1]		2,970	1,511	9,500[1]	570
MOZAMBIQUE						278[1]	129[1]	16,000	150
NEPAL	171.6	180.5						1,400[1]	110
NETHERLANDS	182.7	116.3[5]	180[1]	128	5.0	53,812	50,953	130,300	7,160
NETH. ANTILLES	186.4[4]	257.3[4]				3,128[1]	2,646[1]		1,750
NEW ZEALAND	243.7	240.7	230[1]	146[1]		3,500	3,752	16,300	4,370
NICARAGUA				165[2]		755[1]	628[1]	2,090[1]	830
NIGER	241.8	273.0				127[2]	134[2]	1,610	160
NIGERIA	285.4	358.2				12,857	9,483	34,200[1]	420
NORWAY	192.5	191.0	180	153	1.3	11,420	10,011	39,400	8,540
OMAN						1,102[2]	1,512	2,550	2,520

574

Name & Region	Consumer Price Index—1978 1970 = 100 All items	Food	Wholesale Price Index—1978 1970 = 100	Industrial Production Index—1978 1970 = 100	Unemployment Rate %—1978	Foreign Trade 1978—Million U.S. Dollars Imports	Exports	Estimated GNP 1978—Million U.S. Dollars	GNP Per Capita—1977 U.S. Dollars
PAKISTAN	249.6[6]	260.4[4]	268.6[10]	117[2]		3,275	1,470	18,500	190
PANAMA	113.3	110.9	228.5	125[1]	8.7[1]	942	244		1,220
PAPUA N.G.	183.0[4]	187.1[4]				676	780		480
PARAGUAY	218.4	251.0		148[1]		319	257	2,140	760
PERU	527.0	589.5		147[1]	5.8[1]	1,614[1]	1,433[1]	12,400	830
PHILIPPINES	215.0[9]	207.9[9]	247.0[9]	152		5,143	3,425	23,200	450
POLAND				202		15,098	13,333	112,700	3,150
PORTUGAL	346.0	402.4	352.0	165	7 5[1]	4,791	2,393	15,850	1,850
PUERTO RICO	167.8	193.7	180[1]		18.1				2,460
QATAR						1,185	2,367	1,000[1]	11,670
REUNION	210.3	232.4				604	116		2,680
RUMANIA				230[1]		7,018[1]	7,021[1]	75,700	1,580
RWANDA						79	92[1]	515[2]	130
SAMOA, W.	167.3	166.7				53	11		350
SAUDI ARABIA						14,651[1]	39,210	64,200	4,980
SENEGAL	219.8	250.2		148		640[2]	476[2]	2,140	420
SEYCHELLES	359.1								650
SIERRA LEONE	211.8	226.9			7.34[12]	277	135[1]	620[1]	200
SINGAPORE			111.6[11]	208[1]		13,049	10,134	7,540	2,890
SOMALIA	204.7	236.2				106	85[2]	425[1]	110
SOUTH AFRICA	215		252.7	101[1]				43,770	1,340
SPAIN	310.0	310.1	254.7	170[1]	4.1[1]	18,708	13,115	127,500	3,190
SRI LANKA	164.8	174.0	157.4[11]			940	847	2,620	200
SUDAN	294.9	302.2				1,060[1]	661[1]	6,150[1]	300
SURINAM	194.6	195.4				292[1]	330[2]		1,500
SWAZILAND	217.8	218.5							580
SWEDEN	198.1	211.9	188[1]	107	1.6	20,123	21,560	84,900	9,250
SWITZERLAND	150.8	146.8	128.0	103		23,804	23,561	83,900	9,960
SYRIA	229	246	240.6	191[1]	5.0[1]	2,437	1,053	7,100[1]	900
TANZANIA						748[1]	457	3,370[1]	200
THAILAND	188.2	209.0	203.7			5,360	4,093	21,700	410
TOGO	217.9	231.4				284[1]	159[1]	565[1]	300
TONGA	228.7	250.1							300
TRIN. & TOB.	252.0	263.6			13.4[1]	1,963	2,039		2,380
TUNISIA	105.4	106.2	166.6	167		2,119	1 110	5,830	860
TURKEY	483.3	523.7	509.2	172[2]		4,597	2,288	45,300	1,110
UGANDA						158[2]	352	800	260
USSR			97[1]	166		50,550	52,216	780,635	3,010
UN. ARAB EM.						4,896	9,050	12,000	14,420
UN. KINGDOM	269.6	315.2	336.3	110	6.2	78,557	71,691	302,000	4,430
USA	167.9	179.5	189.7	136	6.0	182,787	141,154	2,106,600	8,640
UPPER VOLTA						209[1]	55[1]	795[1]	110
URUGUAY	4,768.8	5,045.0	5,095	119[1]	12.8[1]	757	723	3,700	1,450
VENEZUELA	163.9	201.8	193.7		4.8[1]	9,003[1]	9,126	35,800[1]	2,820
YEMEN						1,040[1]	11	1,500	390
YEMEN, S.								500	320
YUGOSLAVIA	358.5	385.7	287	181	12.0	9,987	5,659	37,800[1]	1,960
ZAIRE	1,132.4	1,423.4				588	925	4,650[1]	130
ZAMBIA	231.2	243.4	184.5[1]	110		671[1]	898[1]	2,320[1]	450

[1] 1977.   [2] 1976.   [3] 1977 = 100.   [4] 1971 = 100.   [5] 1975 = 100.   [6] 1975.   [7] 1974.   [8] Includes Belgium and Luxembourg
[9] 1972 = 100.   [10] July 1969–June 1970 = 100.   [11] 1974 = 100.   [12] 1973 = 100.

Sources of Information: "Monthly Bulletin of Statistics"; "Statistical Yearbook," United Nations.   "The Military Balance 1979–1980," The International Institute for Strategic Studies.   "1979 World Population Data Sheet," Population Reference Bureau, Inc.

(in thousand metric tons)

	Coffee	Cotton	Eggs	Maize	Milk[1]	Potatoes	Rice	Soybeans	Wheat
AFGHANISTAN	...	54	17	800	918	250	448	...	2 830
ALBANIA	...	7	5	300	301	132	17	...	370
ALGERIA	...	...	20	...	617	520	2	...	1 800
ANGOLA	54	13	3	400	144	35	20	...	10
ARGENTINA	...	228	203	9 700	5 176	1 593	310	2 500	8 100
AUSTRALIA	...	44	200	130	5 329	734	490	77	18 300
AUSTRIA	...	...	90	1 166	3 266	1 401	...	...	1 195
BANGLADESH	...	1	28	...	1 126	863	18 898	...	343
BELGIUM[2]	...	...	235	32	4 008	1 604	...	...	1 053
BOLIVIA	22	17	16	331	97	793	89	26	60
BRAZIL	1 200	460	520	13 533	12 056	2 015	7 242	9 800	2 677
BULGARIA	...	15	119	2 300	1 985	390	50	90	3 450
BURMA	...	16	24	75	277	54	10 500	16	94
CAMEROON	90	23	8	350	61	41	20	...	10
CANADA	...	...	310	4 215	7 600	2 453	...	475	21 146
CHAD	...	54	3	10	237	12	40	...	6
CHILE	...	...	59	257	938	981	105	1	893
CHINA	6	2 100	4 064	33 120	6 969	12 048	131 775	13 257	44 003
COLOMBIA	669	82	148	862	2 500	1 996	1 715	131	38
COSTA RICA	95	7	17	98	290	25	195	...	...
CUBA	27	1	85	95	1 080	155	460	...	...
CZECHOSLOVAKIA	...	...	240	628	5 927	3 837	...	...	5 600
DENMARK	...	...	68	...	5 324	1 009	...	...	653
DOM. REP.	45	3	23	42	340	23	308	...	...
ECUADOR	89	10	45	200	838	498	285	36	38
EGYPT	...	435	76	3 197	1 922	950	2 351	79	1 933
EL SALVADOR	132	74	30	540	360	16	60	...	...
ETHIOPIA	191	15	72	1 079	714	185	...	...	423
FINLAND	...	...	76	...	3 220	746	...	...	241
FRANCE	...	...	758	9 473	31 230	7 459	45	7	21 057
GERMANY, E.	...	...	292	2	8 176	10 100	...	...	3 200
GERMANY, W.	...	...	900	620	23 313	10 510	...	...	8 118
GREECE	...	138	119	537	1 695	944	92	...	2 660
GUATEMALA	139	133	38	760	314	68	26	...	55
HONDURAS	59	9	20	340	196	5	21	...	1
HUNGARY	...	...	275	6 700	2 450	1 700	51	54	5 669
INDIA	118	1 250	85	5 500	25 890	8 153	79 010	120	31 328
INDONESIA	191	5	71	2 750	61	236	25 739	530	...
IRAN	...	150	134	60	2 505	680	1 650	130	5 700
IRAQ	...	10	19	85	474	52	172	1	910
IRELAND	...	...	37	...	5 400	1 070	...	...	247
ISRAEL	...	77	96	13	751	221	...	...	175
ITALY	...	1	638	6 040	10 675	2 856	950	...	8 764
IVORY COAST	198	37	6	325	...	5	430	...	...
JAPAN	...	...	1 960	11	6 100	3 305	16 000	190	367
KENYA	80	6	19	2 350	1 020	361	42	...	144
KOREA, N.	...	3	92	1 850	31	1 450	4 500	320	350
KOREA, S.	...	2	223	138	291	360	8 058	293	36
MADAGASCAR	87	14	11	100	28	132	1 981	...	...
MALAWI	...	8	10	1 400	36	89	43	...	1
MALAYSIA	6	...	112	35	...	...	1 590	...	...
MALI	...	43	8	85	147	...	270	...	2
MEXICO	270	332	486	9 616	6 495	837	397	324	2 643
MOROCCO	...	8	61	390	540	190	27	...	1 876
MOZAMBIQUE	...	26	10	400	67	38	35	...	3
NEPAL	...	...	14	750	716	300	2 400	...	401
NETHERLANDS	...	...	346	...	11 346	6 231	...	...	792
NEW ZEALAND	...	...	59	232	6 069	245	...	...	357
NICARAGUA	59	144	28	209	297	2	82	1	...
NIGERIA	3	37	140	1 450	324	30	580	70	21
NORWAY	...	...	38	...	1 869	576	...	...	80
PAKISTAN	...	548	71	800	9 970	294	4 706	...	8 289
PANAMA	5	...	13	83	75	11	211	...	...
PARAGUAY	8	81	19	410	126	5	75	300	32
PERU	66	81	44	550	860	1 650	400	3	90
PHILIPPINES	82	1	179	3 333	33	21	6 907	8	...
POLAND	...	...	476	400	18 085	46 600	...	...	6 000
PORTUGAL	...	...	63	443	855	1 160	131	...	252
RHODESIA	...	33	11	1 400	250	26	5	...	90
RUMANIA	...	...	330	10 179	4 847	4 450	45	230	6 235
SENEGAL	...	15	6	47	114	5	127	...	...
SOUTH AFRICA	...	47	215	9 930	2 550	750	3	37	1 730
SPAIN	...	32	581	1 933	6 296	5 316	411	19	4 795
SRI LANKA	9	2	18	25	232	30	1 992	1	...
SUDAN	...	167	23	50	1 466	25	8	...	370
SWEDEN	...	...	109	...	3 255	1 420	...	...	1 306
SWITZERLAND	...	...	43	108	3 539	893	...	...	407
SYRIA	...	145	34	66	656	165	260	...	1 651
TANZANIA	42	56	21	1 000	778	88	260	1	65
THAILAND	...	27	157	3 030	...	10	17 000	125	...
TURKEY	...	515	224	1 300	5 190	2 800	280	5	16 500
UGANDA	156	20	9	660	381	330	16	5	15
USSR	...	2 640	3 539	9 000	94 500	85 900	2 100	680	120 800
UN. KINGDOM	...	...	818	...	15 836	7 072	...	...	6 450
USA	...	2 360	3 955	179 886	55 305	16 356	6 251	50 149	48 954
URUGUAY	...	21	18	172	700	102	226	35	150
VENEZUELA	72	21	112	740	1 276	204	600	...	1
VIETNAM	14	3	117	460	64	19	9 880	22	...
YEMEN	3	1	3	54	245	106	...	...	38
YUGOSLAVIA	...	1	225	7 555	4 361	2 400	30	60	5 355
ZAIRE	95	8	7	487	...	34	202	7	5

Source: UN Statistical Yearbook 1978. Note: Some of the figures are provisional or estimates.
[1] Total production from all sources, including cows, buffaloes, sheep, and goats. [2] Includes Luxembourg.

ENERGY: PRODUCTION AND CONSUMPTION

	Coal Reserves in million metric tons	Coal Production in thousand metric tons	Electricity[1] in million kilowatt hours	Natural Gas Production in tera-calories[2]	Petroleum Reserves in million metric tons	Petroleum Production in thousand metric tons	Total Energy Production*	Total Energy Consumption*
AFGHANISTAN	...	160	700	22 300	...	...	3.61	.81
ALBANIA	...	...	2 150	1 600	17	2 600	4.55	2.21
ALGERIA	9	6	4 650	81 592	1 367	53 895	91.62	12.61
ANGOLA	...	...	1 360	600	193	8 640	6.75	1.08
ARGENTINA	155	533	32 477	64 629	318	22 167	41.82	46.40
AUSTRALIA	25 540	71 000	82 522	59 880	298	21 000	119.86	90.83
AUSTRIA	1	...	37 684	23 380	18	1 787	9.96	30.15
BANGLADESH	760	...	1 930	7 949	...	...	1.14	2.63
BELGIUM	253	7 068	47 099	321	...	...	8.81	59.82
BOLIVIA	...	...	1 150	14 800	24	1 612	5.04	1.84
BOTSWANA	506	294	348	...	...	...		
BRAZIL	3 256	3 859	99 869	9 720	149	7 810	26.47	79.84
BULGARIA	29	287	29 710	87	2	129	14.08	41.26
BURMA	13	15	1 056	1 400	9	1 301	1.78	1.51
CAMBODIA	...	...	150	...	...	...	...	.13
CAMEROON	...	...	1 346	...	...	...	.16	.64
CANADA	8 463	23 042	316 549	685 899	816	62 021	258.80	230.28
CHILE	97	1 228	9 776	13 560	70	928	5.73	10.32
CHINA	300 000	490 000	...	41 000	2 464	100 000	614.78	590.06
COLOMBIA	150	3 800	15 223	20 411	120	7 106	18.73	16.66
CONGO	...	...	118	90	63	1 582	3.00	.20
COSTA RICA	...	...	1 760	...	...	...	.18	1.02
CUBA	...	...	7 700	200	...	150	.25	11.60
CZECHOSLOVAKIA	5 540	28 354	66 501	7 539	2	123	83.84	110.34
DENMARK	...	...	22 436	...	6	503	.29	26.99
DOM. REP.	...	...	2 671	...	...	...	.02	3.30
ECUADOR	...	...	2 145	387	173	9 280	14.10	3.33
EGYPT	25	...	13 000	13 664	284	20 921	27.26	18.00
EL SALVADOR	...	...	1 354	...	...	...	.09	1.07
ETHIOPIA	...	...	682	...	...	...	.04	.76
FINLAND	...	...	31 734	...	...	...	1.41	24.47
FRANCE	1 380	22 996	210 845	71 507	7	1 037	45.10	231.92
GABON	...	...	443	1 650	74	11 234	16.69	.68
GERMANY, E.	200	349	91 996	26 535	3	60	79.25	113.96
GERMANY, W.	44 001	91 310	335 320	152 419	42	5 401	165.88	364.28
GHANA	...	...	4 300	...	...	...	.51	1.62
GREECE	...	...	19 019	...	18	...	7.68	20.62
GUATEMALA	...	...	1 291	...	...	15	.05	1.61
GUINEA	...	...	500	...	...	...	.01	.42
HONDURAS	...	...	701	...	...	...	.06	.75
HUNGARY	450	2 925	23 391	52 220	26	2 191	22.21	37.66
ICELAND	...	...	2 607	...	...	...	.29	1.00
INDIA	21 365	100 110	99 096	11 494	281	10 185	121.09	132.92
INDONESIA	163	231	4 380	53 000	1 501	82 998	113.84	30.43
IRAN	385	900	18 000	202 201	6 407	282 608	467.36	49.77
IRAQ	...	...	5 000	14 726	4 831	122 390	167.70	8.36
IRELAND	22	54	9 299	...	...	...	2.41	10.02
ISRAEL	...	...	11 108	526	...	28	.13	9.01
ITALY	1	2	166 545	125 685	43	1 083	28.43	184.46
JAPAN	7 443	18 246	532 609	29 615	3	592	38.21	414.87
JORDAN	...	...	601	...	...	...	...	1.46
KUWAIT	...	...	6 018	55 556	10 277	98 744	169.10	9.47
LEBANON	...	...	1 600	...	...	...	.10	1.58
LIBERIA	...	...	887	...	...	...	.04	.72
LIBYA	60	...	1 500	56 437	3 462	99 503	145.58	4.04
MADAGASCAR	...	...	366	...	...	...	.02	.55
MALAWI	...	...	331	...	...	...	.04	.29
MALAYSIA	...	...	6 697	849	137	8 791	12.06	7.63
MEXICO	5 316	6 610	50 632	128 395	1 425	49 279	91.44	76.40
MOROCCO	15	707	3 678	646	...	22	.95	4.86
NETHERLANDS	3 705	...	58 285	732 594	9	1 382	118.06	85.70
NEW ZEALAND	297	2 089	21 265	14 220	81	686	6.00	11.35
NICARAGUA	...	...	1 180	...	...	...	.05	1.07
NIGERIA	359	565	3 450	4 660	1 673	102 970	153.58	6.09
NORWAY	2	455	72 520	2 683	753	13 551	31.41	21.19
PAKISTAN	24	1 112	11 050	39 405	38	405	8.33	13.11
PANAMA	...	...	1 640	...	...	...	.01	1.52
PARAGUAY	...	...	626	...	...	...	.08	.52
PERU	211	...	8 557	4 590	102	4 496	7.06	10.34
PHILIPPINES	...	158	15 800	...	...	...	.76	14.38
POLAND	32 425	186 112	109 364	57 874	3	364	200.35	180.51
PORTUGAL	15	195	13 324	...	...	...	.79	10.13
RUMANIA	70	7 368	59 858	320 900	149	14 652	83.90	86.56
SAUDI ARABIA	...	...	2 500	88 000	15 527	458 460	643.99	17.56
SIERRA LEONE	...	...	200	...	...	...	...	.32
SOUTH AFRICA	24 224	85 570	80 198	...	...	...	76.32	87.40
SPAIN	1 272	12 068	93 803	9	41	844	19.00	86.31
SRI LANKA	...	...	1 331	...	...	...	.14	1.45
SWEDEN	60	2	90 018	...	...	...	8.73	49.71
SYRIA	...	...	2 043	1 100	351	10 117	14.94	5.65
TANZANIA	309	1	695	...	...	...	.06	1.07
THAILAND	...	...	11 690	...	...	8	.68	13.22
TUNISIA	...	...	1 725	2 779	...	4 265	5.80	2.61
TURKEY	191	4 410	20 565	...	8	2 712	12.20	29.83
UGANDA	...	...	725	...	...	...	.11	.58
USSR	165 802	499 768	1 150 074	2 889 335	8 067	545 799	1 674.10	1 349.86
UN. KINGDOM	98 877	122 150	283 280	376 701	1 376	37 541	198.18	295.28
UNITED STATES	317 451	603 772	2 211 031	4 932 118	4 031	402 489	2 049.70	2 485.45
URUGUAY	...	...	3 040	...	...	...	.15	3.10
VENEZUELA	14	121	23 051	122 000	2 466	117 007	199.00	35.08
YUGOSLAVIA	82	511	48 580	18 777	48	3 950	29.42	43.46
ZAIRE	720	116	4 100	...	18	1 126	2.37	1.58
ZAMBIA	74	708	8 683	...	...	...	1.62	2.81

* In million metric tons of coal equivalent.
[1] Total gross generation of electricity both from enterprises generating primarily for public use and industrial establishments generating primarily for their own use.
[2] Teracalories = U.S. trillions of calories.

Source: UN Statistical Yearbook 1978.

WORLD MINERAL PRODUCTION

Aluminum, smelter (thousand metric tons)

	1977	1978
United States	4,117	4,358
USSRe	1,640	1,670
Japan	1,188	1,058
Canada	973	1,048
West Germany	742	740
Norway	623	640
France	400	391
United Kingdom	350	346
Chinae	250	300
Italy	260	271
Australia	248	263
Netherlands	241	261
Rumania	209	213
Spain	211	212
India	184	205
Yugoslavia	197	196
Other countriesa	2,856	1,881
Total	14,689	14,053

Antimony, mineb (metric tons)

	1977	1978
Bolivia	15,156	12,672
Chinae	12,000	12,000
South Africa	11,535	10,478
USSRe	7,900	7,900
Thailand	5,238	2,873
Yugoslavia	2,248	e2,760
Canada	2,698	2,457
Morocco	1,409	2,110
Australia	1,574	2,100
Italy	808	931
United States	553	907
Peru	823	895
Other countriesa	9,453	8,823
Total	71,395	66,906

Asbestosc (thousand metric tons)

	1977	1978
USSRe	2,460	2,500
Canada	1,543	1,379
South Africa	380	257
Rhodesiae	200	225
Chinae	200	220
Italy	153	135
Brazil	93	e93
United States	92	93
Other countriesa	206	229
Total	5,327	5,131

Baritec (thousand metric tons)

	1977	1978
United States	1,355	1,700
USSRe	450	475
India	331	350
Ireland	373	344
Chinae	300	300
Perue	280	280
Italy	150	237
France	220	e225
Mexico	231	214
Iran	230	200
West Germany	271	184
Moroccoe	140	120
Other countriesa	1,190	1,275
Total	5,521	5,904

Bauxited (thousand metric tons)

	1977	1978
Australia	26,071	24,300
Jamaica	11,433	11,736
Guinea	11,300	e11,000
USSRd,e	6,180	6,180
Surinam	4,924	e4,920
Guyana	2,731	3,475
Hungary	2,949	2,898
Greece	2,882	2,630
Yugoslavia	2,044	2,566
France	2,059	1,978
United States	2,013	1,669
India	1,352	e1,600
Brazil	1,352	e1,400
Chinae	1,200	1,300
Indonesia	1,301	1,008
Other countriesa	4,292	5,000
Total	84,083	83,660

Cementc (million metric tons)

	1977	1978
USSR	127.0	129.3
Japan	73.1	84.4
United States	72.6	77.5
China	55.6	65.2
Italy	38.2	38.2
West Germany	32.2	33.5
Spain	28.0	30.2
France	29.0	29.1
Poland	21.3	21.6
Brazil	18.5	20.0
India	19.1	19.6
United Kingdom	15.5	15.9
Turkey	13.8	15.7
South Korea	15.2	15.5
Rumania	13.9	14.7
Mexico	13.2	14.1
East Germany	12.1	12.5
Other countriesa	196.5	204.2
Total	794.8	841.2

Chromitec (thousand metric tons)

	1977	1978
South Africa	3,319	3,145
USSRe	2,180	2,300
Albaniae	880	980
Turkey	690	680
Rhodesia	600	600
Philippines	538	533
Finland	602	507
India	351	266
Brazile	190	190
Irane	165	165
Madagascar	180	138
Other countriesa	172	108
Total	9,867	9,612

Coal, all gradesf (million metric tons)

	1977	1978
USSR	722	724
China	550	618
United States	630	598
East Germany	254	253
Poland	227	234
West Germany	208	214
Czechoslovakia	121	123
United Kingdom	120	122
Australia	108	108
India	104	105
South Africa	85	91
North Koreae	41	45
Yugoslavia	39	40
Canada	28	29
Rumania	27	e28
Bulgaria	25	25
Hungary	25	25
Greece	24	24
France	25	22
Other countriesa	120	187
Total	3,483	3,615

Copper, mineb (thousand metric tons)

	1977	1978
United States	1,364	1,352
Chile	1,056	1,035
USSRe	850	865
Canada	759	758
Zambia	656	643
Zaire	482	423
Peru	350	366
Poland	289	318
Philippines	268	239
Australia	220	220
South Africa	208	209
Papua New Guinea	182	199
Yugoslavia	116	113
Chinae	100	100
Mexico	90	87
Japan	81	81
Indonesia	57	55
Other countriesa	605	421
Total	7,733	7,484

Diamond (thousand carats)

	1977	1978
USSRe	10,300	10,550
Zaire	11,213	9,833
South Africa	7,643	7,727
Botswana	2,691	2,785
Ghana	1,947	1,950
South West Africa (Namibia)	2,001	1,898
Venezuela	687	738
Sierra Leone	961	707
Angola	353	400
Liberia	326	308
Tanzania	408	293
Other countriesa	271	531
Total	38,801	37,720

Fluorsparg (thousand metric tons)

	1977	1978
Mexico	955	960
USSRe	500	510
South Africa	351	393
Spain	399	372
Chinae	360	360
Mongoliae	320	360
France	283	315
Thailand	248	208
United Kingdom	194	200
Italy	186	170
United States	154	117
Other countriesa	717	734
Total	4,667	4,699

Gas, natural, marketed productionh (billion cubic feet)

	1977	1978
United States	20,025	19,721
USSR	12,219	13,137
Netherlands	3,422	3,133
Canada	3,161	3,090
Chinae	1,900	2,200
United Kingdom	1,437	1,346
Rumania	1,104	1,105
West Germany	638	738
Iran	748	650
Mexico	600	650
Libya	556	580
Italy	485	494
Other countriesa	5,099	5,241
Total	51,394	52,085

Gold, mine (thousand troy ounces)

	1977	1978
South Africa	22,502	22,649
USSRe	7,850	8,000
Canada	1,734	1,700
United States	1,100	999
Papua New Guinea	740	751
Australia	623	649
Philippines	558	610
Rhodesiae	600	600
Ghana	481	402
Dominican Republic	348	336
Colombia	257	246
Mexico	213	202
North Koreae	180	180
Brazil	172	e172
Yugoslavia	164	e164
Other countriesa	1,327	1,314
Total	38,849	38,974

Graphite (thousand metric tons)

	1977	1978
USSRe	95	95
North Koreae	75	75
South Korea	65	56
Mexico	58	52
Chinae	50	50
India	41	49
Austria	35	41
Madagascar	16	e17
West Germany	13	13
Other countriesa	40	44
Total	488	492

Gypsumc (thousand metric tons)

	1977	1978
United States	12,147	13,509
Canada	7,234	7,890
Iran	7,500	7,000
Francee	5,800	5,800
USSRe	5,200	5,300
Spain	e4,300	4,500
Italy	4,180	e4,180
United Kingdom	3,273	3,217
Mexico	1,496	1,758
Polande	1,250	1,250
Australia	900	956
India	768	854
Austria	655	626
Other countriesa	12,627	13,298
Total	67,330	70,138

Iron Orec (million metric tons)

	1977	1978
USSR	239.7	240.8
Brazil	82.0	85.0
Australia	96.1	83.2
United States	56.6	82.8
Chinae	60.0	70.0
Canada	57.6	41.8
India	42.3	38.2
France	36.6	33.5
South Africa	26.5	24.2
Sweden	24.8	21.5
Liberia	18.1	e18.8
Venezuela	13.7	13.6
Chile	7.9	9.7
North Koreae	9.5	9.5
Spain	7.9	8.1
Other countriesa	69.5	64.2
Total	848.8	844.9

Iron, steel ingots (million metric tons)

	1977	1978
USSR	146.7	151.5
United States	113.7	124.3
Japan	112.9	112.5
West Germany	39.0	41.3
China	23.5	31.0
Italy	23.3	24.3
France	22.1	22.8
United Kingdom	20.4	20.4
Poland	17.8	19.4
Czechoslovakia	15.1	15.2
Canada	13.6	14.9
Belgium	11.3	12.6
Brazil	11.1	12.1
Rumania	11.5	11.7
Spain	11.2	11.3
India	9.8	9.4
South Africa	7.4	7.8
Australia	7.3	7.6
East Germany	6.8	6.9
Mexico	5.5	6.7
Netherlands	4.9	5.6
Luxembourg	4.3	4.8
Austria	4.1	4.3
Sweden	4.0	4.3
Hungary	3.7	3.8
Yugoslavia	3.2	3.5
Other countriesa	15.4	18.0
Total	669.6	708.0

Lead, primary smelter (thousand metric tons)

	1977	1978
United States	549	565
USSRe	510	520
Australiai	337	357
Canada	187	194
Japan	170	186
France	173	170
Mexico	154	156

1977 1978 / 1977 1978 / 1977 1978

Lead, primary smelter (cont'd) (thousand metric tons)

	1977	1978
Bulgaria	112	125
China[e]	110	120
Yugoslavia	130	117
West Germany	105	105
Belgium	104	99
Spain	89	91
Poland	85	87
North Korea[e]	70	75
Peru	79	74
Sweden	52	59
Other countries[a]	423	386
Total	3,439	3,486

Magnesium (thousand metric tons)

	1977	1978
United States	114.3	135.6
USSR	65.0	70.0
Norway	38.2	39.2
Japan	9.4	10.9
Italy	7.3	9.7
France	8.7	8.5
Canada	7.6	8.3
China	1.0	1.0
India	.1	.1
Total	251.6	283.3

Manganese Ore[c] (thousand metric tons)

	1977	1978
USSR	8,595	8,600
South Africa	5,048	4,317
Gabon	1,851	1,710
India	1,940	1,567
Australia	1,387	1,290
Brazil	1,516	e1,300
China[e]	1,000	1,000
Mexico	487	523
Ghana	343	321
Hungary	161	156
Other countries[a]	319	602
Total	22,647	21,386

Mercury[b] (76-pound flasks)

	1977	1978
USSR[e]	58,000	60,000
Spain	35,013	31,039
Algeria	30,023	e30,000
United States	28,244	24,189
China[e]	20,000	17,000
Czechoslovakia[a]	5,200	5,200
West Germany	2,872	2,437
Mexico	9,660	2,205
Turkey	4,509	1,711
Finland	630	1,145
Yugoslavia	3,133	...
Other countries[a]	1,031	587
Total	198,315	175,513

Molybdenum, mine[b] (metric tons)

	1977	1978
United States	55,523	59,803
Canada	16,431	14,068
Chile	10,886	11,340
USSR[e]	9,700	9,900
China	1,500	1,500
Other countries[a]	936	872
Total	94,976	97,483

Nickel, mine (thousand metric tons)

	1977	1978
USSR[e]	142.0	148.0
Canada	235.4	127.5
Australia	84.3	81.0
New Caledonia	109.1	66.1
Cuba[e]	37.0	37.0
Indonesia	33.1	31.9
Philippines	36.8	31.0
South Africa	22.0	22.5
Greece	25.6	21.1
Botswana	12.1	16.0
Dominican Republic	24.2	14.3
United States	13.0	22.3
Rhodesia[e]	16.0	11.0
Other countries[a]	33.5	34.8
Total	824.1	654.5

Petroleum, crude (million barrels)

	1977	1978
USSR	3,991	4,176
United States	3,009	3,176
Saudi Arabia	3,290	3,009
Iran	2,080	1,879
Iraq	910	857
Kuwait	651	799
Venezuela	817	788
China	684	760
Libya	753	723
Nigeria[e]	765	704
United Arab Emirates	730	674
Indonesia	615	583
Canada	482	469
Algeria	410	452
Mexico	358	448
United Kingdom	272	389

Petroleum, crude (cont'd) (million barrels)

	1977	1978
Egypt	151	199
Qatar	162	178
Argentina	157	165
Australia	157	158
Other countries	1,488	1,444
Total	21,932	22,030

Phosphate Rock (thousand metric tons)

	1977	1978
United States	47,256	50,037
USSR	24,250	24,800
Morocco	17,572	17,279
China[e]	4,100	4,400
Tunisia	3,614	3,767
Togo	2,857	2,827
South Africa	2,403	2,699
Jordan	1,782	2,223
Nauru	1,146	1,999
Senegal	1,869	1,762
Israel	1,232	1,759
Vietnam[e]	1,500	1,500
Christmas Island	1,186	1,400
Other countries[a]	5,655	6,470
Total	116,422	122,922

Potash (thousand metric tons of K_2O equivalent)

	1977	1978
USSR	8,310	8,347
Canada	4,996	6,089
East Germany	3,161	3,229
West Germany	2,036	2,341
United States	2,177	2,229
France	1,600	1,580
Other countries[a]	1,979	1,911
Total	24,259	25,726

Pyrite[c] (thousand metric tons)

	1977	1978
USSR[e]	7,000	7,000
China[e]	2,100	2,200
Spain	2,404	2,200
Rumania	915	e920
Italy	863	787
South Africa	830	765
Japan	798	696
United States	442	e660
North Korea[e]	615	620
Sweden	402	484
West Germany	531	462
Yugoslavia	394	428
Finland	295	381
Portugal	360	314
Norway	309	293
Other countries[a]	2,020	2,474
Total	20,278	20,684

Salt (million metric tons)

	1977	1978
United States	39.41	39.65
China	17.10	19.53
USSR	14.30	14.50
West Germany	12.32	13.42
United Kingdom	8.20	8.10
France[e]	6.50	6.60
Canada	6.04	6.22
Mexico	4.90	e5.00
Rumania	4.54	4.74
Australia	4.06	4.66
Poland	4.36	4.39
India	3.00	4.38
Italy	3.67	3.72
Spain[e]	3.20	3.25
Netherlands	3.11	3.22
East Germany	2.64	2.65
Other countries[a]	20.05	20.63
Total	157.40	164.66

Silver, mine[b] (million troy ounces)

	1977	1978
Mexico	47.03	50.78
USSR[e]	45.00	46.00
Canada	42.24	38.76
United States	38.17	38.57
Peru	39.73	37.04
Australia	27.53	24.86
Poland[e]	17.70	18.97
Japan	9.65	9.73
Chile	8.45	8.21
Bolivia	5.89	6.44
Sweden	5.44	5.79
Yugoslavia	4.69	5.11
Other countries[a]	45.30	46.60
Total	336.82	336.86

Sulfur, all forms[j] (thousand metric tons)

	1977	1978
United States	10,676	11,863
USSR[e]	9,540	10,800
Canada	7,346	7,380
Poland	5,090	5,605
Japan	2,825	2,728

Sulfur, all forms[j] (cont'd) (thousand metric tons)

	1977	1978
France	2,160	2,219
Mexico	1,936	1,998
West Germany	1,602	1,564
China[e]	1,140	1,400
Spain	1,243	1,290
Iraq	675	641
Italy	702	620
Iran	547	542
Finland	570	354
Other countries[a]	5,356	5,442
Total	51,408	54,446

Tin, mine[b] (thousand metric tons)

	1977	1978
Malaysia	58.7	62.6
USSR[e]	32.0	33.0
Bolivia	32.6	30.9
Thailand	24.2	30.2
Indonesia	25.9	24.1
China[e]	20.0	20.0
Australia	10.6	11.6
Brazil	6.4	8.5
Zaire	3.7	3.5
Other countries[a]	19.1	19.9
Total	233.2	244.3

Titanium, materials[c,k] (thousand metric tons)

	1977	1978
Ilmenite		
Australia	1,081	1,222
Norway	829	767
United States	579	527
USSR[e]	400	410
Malaysia	154	e160
Finland	125	125
Other countries[a]	187	190
Total ilmenite	3,355	3,401
Rutile		
Australia	324	263
Other countries[a]	34	48
Total rutile	358	311
Titaniferous slag		
Canada	711	780
Japan	1	e1
Total titaniferous slag	712	781

Tungsten, mine[b] (metric tons)

	1977	1978
China[e]	9,000	9,000
USSR[e]	8,200	8,500
Bolivia	2,981	3,171
United States	2,732	3,130
Thailand	2,035	2,942
South Korea	2,528	2,681
Australia	2,333	e2,400
North Korea[e]	2,150	2,150
Canada	1,817	e1,800
Austria	1,116	1,179
Portugal	1,010	1,098
Brazil[e]	1,000	1,000
Turkey	1,200	e1,000
Other countries[a]	4,390	4,448
Total	42,492	44,499

Uranium Oxide (U_3O_8)[b,l] (metric tons)

	1977	1978
United States	13,426	16,783
Canada	7,020	9,439
South Africa	3,962	3,760
South West Africa	3,587	4,000
France	2,473	1,914
Niger	1,887	2,000
Gabon	1,068	1,407
Other countries[j]	1,193	1,240
Total	34,616	40,543

Zinc, smelter (thousand metric tons)

	1977	1978
USSR[e]	735	770
Japan	778	768
Canada	495	495
United States	408	407
West Germany	335	289
Australia	249	250
Belgium	240	233
Poland	228	223
France[e]	181	186
Italy	169	177
Mexico	172	170
Spain	157	168
Netherlands	109	135
Finland	138	133
North Korea[e]	135	130
China[e]	110	125
Bulgaria	90	92
Yugoslavia	99	92
South Africa	76	79
Other countries[a]	586	643
Total	5,490	5,565

[a] Estimated in part. [b] Content of ore. [c] Gross weight. [d] Includes calculated bauxite equivalent of estimated output of ores other than bauxite (nepheline concentrates and alunite ores). [e] Estimate. [f] Includes anthracitic, bituminous and lignitic coal (including that coal classified in Europe as "brown coal"). [g] Marketable gross weight. [h] Marketed production (includes gas sold or used by producers; excludes gas reinjected to reservoirs for pressure maintenance and that flared or vented to atmosphere which has no economic value and which does not represent a part of world energy consumption. [i] Includes lead bullion refined elsewhere. [j] Includes (1) Frasch process sulfur, (2) elemental sulfur mined by conventional methods, (3) by-product recovered elemental sulfur, and (4) recovered sulfur content of pyrite and other sulfide ores. [k] Excludes output (if any) by China. [l] Excludes output (if any) by Albania, Bulgaria, China, Czechoslovakia, East Germany, Hungary, North Korea, Mongolia, Poland, Rumania, the USSR, and Vietnam. Compiled by Charles L. Kimbell, U.S. Bureau of Mines.

INDUSTRIAL PRODUCTION: SELECTED COUNTRIES (1977)

	Beer	Cotton yarn	Crude steel	Cement	Gasoline	Motor vehicles	News-print	Nitrogen fertilizer[6]	Sugar
	in thousand hecto-liters	in thousand metric tons	in thousand metric tons	in thousand metric tons	in thousand metric tons	in thousands	in thousand metric tons	in thousand metric tons	in thousand metric tons
AFGHANISTAN	...	1[1]	...	136	...	...	...	38	10
ALBANIA	...	...	...	800	175	...	...	50	25
ALGERIA	616	9[2]	213	1 777	787	3[4]	...	42	25
ANGOLA	650[1]	...	...	650	61	...	...	...	65
ARGENTINA	2 710	95	2 676	6 030	4 337	219[3]	11	30	1 666
AUSTRALIA	19 391	20	7 473	5 039	10 221	379	207	215	3 452
AUSTRIA	7 778	20	4 092	5 993	1 494	2	171	265	506
BANGLADESH	...	37	108	313	51	...	...	106	115
BELGIUM	13 819	41	11 256	7 764	5 077	1 080[4]	83[5]	651[5]	757
BOLIVIA	654[2]	0.3[2]	...	265	502	...	...	...	281
BRAZIL	13 980[1]	70[1]	11 165	20 528	10 077	907[3]	107	232	8 759
BULGARIA	4 927	86	2 589	4 665	1 690	22[3]	...	705	240
BURMA	33	14	...	269	218	...	...	55	85
CANADA	20 812	63[1]	13 581	9 933	26 733	1 777	8 169	1 342	155
CHILE	1 361	...	506	1 140	937	12[4]	132	96	120
CHINA	1 750[1]	...	27 000	40 000	...	...	1 100	4 600	3 800
COLOMBIA	...	...	210	3 300	2 469	36[1,4]	...	72	853
COSTA RICA	270[2]	...	...	398	63	...	...	32	200
CUBA	2 200[1]	24	341	2 656	950	...	...	47	6 953
CZECHOSLOVAKIA	22 442	126	15 064	9 779	1 643	200	80	605	924
DENMARK	8 450	2	685	2 309	1 405	1[4]	...	117	472
DOM. REP.	556	0.4[1]	...	582[1]	322	...	...	...	1 258
ECUADOR	1 060[2]	1[2]	...	626	587	...	...	2	260
EGYPT	388	210	263	3 169	1 530	16[4]	...	195	657
EL SALVADOR	578	6	...	334	142	...	...	12	364
ETHIOPIA	376[1]	10[1]	...	100[1]	75	...	...	...	137
FINLAND	2 541	18[1]	2 196	1 712	1 839	27[1,3]	979	184	75
FRANCE	23 540	238	22 094	28 956	17 805	4 009	255	1 470	3 908
GERMANY, E.	21 705	135	6 850	12 102	3 083	207	104	838	700
GERMANY, W.	90 017	178	38 985	32 163	18 837	4 111	544	1 305	2 844[1]
GHANA	500[2]	...	...	700[1]	225	...	...	...	25
GREECE	1 440[1]	87[1]	450	10 560	995	9[1,4]	...	280	294
GUATEMALA	572[1]	...	...	474	131	...	...	6	487
HONDURAS	309	...	...	247	104	...	...	...	100
HUNGARY	6 998	60	3 723	4 620	1 144	13	...	572	476
ICELAND	32	...	...	139	...	...	...	10	...
INDIA	1 063	1 034	9 836	19 173	1 370	89	56	2 000	5 019
INDONESIA	513	...	...	2 879	2 453	89[4]	...	458	1 100
IRAN	560[1]	65[1]	...	6 000[1]	4 706	168[4]	...	178	752
IRAQ	193[2]	1[2]	...	2 500	670	...	...	125	25
IRELAND	4 400	4	48	1 600	482	52[4]	...	120	...
ISRAEL	353	22	100	1 964	950	7[4]	...	51	35
ITALY	7 402	149	23 334	38 204	15 944	1 584	234	1 029	1 758[1]
IVORY COAST	972	6[2]	...	918	254	7[4]	...	5	37
JAMAICA	558	...	...	205	221	...	...	...	297
JAPAN	42 972	409	102 405	73 138	23 072	8 522	2 370	1 446	566
KENYA	1 952	3[2]	...	1 144	366	...	...	...	185
KOREA, S.	2 430	189	2 737	14 198	812	86[4]	198	669	...
LEBANON	30[1]	...	...	1 360	330	...	...	1	10
LUXEMBOURG	703	...	4 329	291	...	...	...	...	...
MADAGASCAR	274	...	...	52	97	...	...	...	110
MALAYSIA	...	18	...	1 777	60	64[4]	...	38	60
MEXICO	21 642	158[2]	5 529	13 328	9 610	276[3]	56	611	2 790
MOROCCO	316[1]	...	1[2]	2 614	380	31[1,4]	...	15	260
MOZAMBIQUE	655[1]	3[1]	...	220	65	...	...	5	320
NETHERLANDS	13 993	28	4 927	3 896	6 530	86[3]	123	1 310	947[1]
NEW ZEALAND	4 180	...	...	910	1 276	76[4]	276	...	...
NIGERIA	3 150	5[2]	...	1 260	726	7[4]	...	...	40
NORWAY	1 875[1]	1	734	2 333	1 180	...	435	336	...
PAKISTAN	25	283	...	3 071	472	...	...	307	764
PANAMA	355	...	...	331	289	...	...	...	181
PARAGUAY	...	73	...	200	65	...	...	...	55
PERU	5 041[1]	...	379	1 970	1 430	...	...	71	900
PHILIPPINES	6 000[1]	31	...	4 112	1 768	59[4]	...	38	2 624
POLAND	12 069	219	17 262	21 301	3 355	374	84	1 529	1 810
PORTUGAL	2 809	85	354	4 258	763	70[4]	1[1]	180	10
RHODESIA	900[1]	...	300	486	...	...	...	45	200
RUMANIA	7 918	171	11 457	13 122	4 215	116	44	1 381	590
SAUDI ARABIA	...	...	...	1 104[1]	1 451	...	...	93	...
SENEGAL	248	0.2[2]	...	329	135	...	...	10	40
SOUTH AFRICA	5 608	38	7 178	6 573	3 539	190[4]	254	414	2 369
SPAIN	17 260	45	10 935	27 996	4 879	1 162	134	904	1 262
SRI LANKA	30[1]	5	...	361	103	...	...	...	23
SUDAN	88	...	...	178	130	...	...	...	151
SWEDEN	4 793[1]	7[1]	3 953	2 528	2 480	236	1 111	174	339
TANZANIA	695[1]	...	...	247	105	...	...	5	108
THAILAND	1 030	73[1]	300	5 063	1 350	...	...	9	2 361
TRIN. & TOB.	304	...	...	218	2 112	14[4]	...	43	178
TUNISIA	302	7[1]	156	629	141	5[4]	...	5	10
TURKEY	2 035	167[1]	1 488	13 390	2 421	99[4]	88	187	1 158
UGANDA	221	...	15	80	...	...	...	...	20
USSR	61 861	1 597	146 678	127 056	...	2 091	1 388	9 025	8 885
UN. KINGDOM	65 239	98	20 410	15 457	14 846	1 714	326	1 199	978
USA	167 789	1 145	113 701	72 627	303 575	15 168	3 188	9 939[7]	5 523
VENEZUELA	...	...	809	3 292	5 642	163[1,4]	...	104	445
YUGOSLAVIA	9 588	121	2 377	8 233	2 231	280[3]	96	384	647
ZAIRE	4 548[1]	...	...	489	32	...	...	...	65
ZAMBIA	...	...	...	332	190	...	...	8	71

[1] 1976. [2] 1975. [3] Production and assembly. [4] Assembly only. [5] Includes Luxembourg. [6] 1977–78. [7] Excludes sodium nitrate; includes data for Puerto Rico.

Source: UN Statistical Yearbook 1978.

THE UNITED STATES GOVERNMENT

EXECUTIVE BRANCH
(selected listing, as of Dec. 31, 1979)

President: Jimmy Carter   Vice President: Walter F. Mondale

Executive Office of the President
The White House

Assistant to the President for National Security Affairs: Zbigniew Brzezinski

Chief of Staff: Hamilton Jordan

Assistant to the President for Domestic Affairs and Policy: Stuart E. Eizenstat

Advisor to the President on Inflation: Alfred E. Kahn

Counsel to the President: Lloyd N. Cutler

Assistant to the President for Congressional Liaison: Frank B. Moore

Assistant to the President for Intergovernmental Affairs: Jack H. Watson, Jr.

Assistant to the President: Anne Wexler

Assistant to the President: Sarah C. Weddington

Senior Adviser to the President: Hedley W. Donovan

Press Secretary to the President: Joseph L. Powell

Office of Management and Budget, Director: James T. McIntyre, Jr.

Council of Economic Advisers, Chairman: Charles L. Schultze

Central Intelligence Agency, Director: Adm. Stansfield Turner

Special Representative for Trade Negotiations: Reubin O'D. Askew

Council on Environmental Quality, Chairman: J. Gustave Speth

Office of Science and Technology Policy, Director: Frank Press

Office of Administration, Director: Richard Harden

The Cabinet

Secretary of Agriculture: Bob Bergland

Secretary of Commerce: Philip M. Klutznick

Secretary of Defense: Harold Brown
  Joint Chief of Staff, Chairman: Gen. David C. Jones, USAF
  Secretary of the Air Force: Hans M. Mark
  Secretary of the Army: Clifford L. Alexander, Jr.
  Secretary of the Navy: Edward Hidalgo

Department of Education, Secretary: Shirley Hufstedler

Department of Energy, Secretary: Charles W. Duncan, Jr.

Department of Health and Human Services, Secretary: Patricia Roberts Harris
  Office for Civil Rights, Director: David Tatel
  Surgeon General: Julius B. Richmond
  Commissioner of Food and Drugs: Jere E. Goyan
  Commissioner of Social Security: Stanford G. Ross

Department of Housing and Urban Development, Secretary: Moon Landrieu

Department of the Interior, Secretary: Cecil D. Andrus

Department of Justice, Attorney General: Benjamin R. Civiletti
  Federal Bureau of Investigation, Director: William H. Webster

Department of Labor, Secretary: Ray Marshall
  Women's Bureau, Director: Alexis Herman
  Commissioner of Labor Statistics: Janet L. Norwood

Department of State, Secretary: Cyrus R. Vance
  Deputy Secretary: Warren M. Christopher

Department of Transportation, Secretary: Neil Goldschmidt

Department of the Treasury, Secretary: G. William Miller
  Internal Revenue Service, Commissioner: Jerome Kurtz

Independent Agencies

ACTION, Director: Sam Brown
  Peace Corps, Director: Richard F. Celeste

Appalachian Regional Commission, Federal cochairman: Albert P. Smith

Civil Aeronautics Board, Chairman: Marvin S. Cohen

Commission on Civil Rights, Chairman: Arthur S. Flemming

Commission of Fine Arts, Chairman: J. Carter Brown

Consumer Product Safety Commission, Chairman: Susan B. King

Environmental Protection Agency, Administrator: Douglas M. Costle

Equal Employment Opportunity Commission, Commissioner: Eleanor Holmes Norton

Export-Import Bank, President and Chairman: John L. Moore, Jr.

Farm Credit Board, Chairman: Dennis S. Lundsgaard

Federal Communications Commission, Chairman: Charles D. Ferris

Federal Deposit Insurance Corporation, Chairman, Board of Directors: Irvine H. Sprague

Federal Election Commission, Chairman: Robert O. Tiernan

Federal Home Loan Bank Board, Chairman: Jay Janis

Federal Maritime Commission, Chairman: Richard J. Daschbach

Federal Mediation and Conciliation Service, Director: Wayne L. Horvitz

Federal Reserve System, Chairman: Paul Volcker

Federal Trade Commission, Chairman: Michael Pertschuk

Foreign Claims Settlement Commission, Chairman: Richard W. Yarborough

General Services Administration, Administrator: Rowland G. Freeman III

International Communications Agency, Director: John E. Reinhardt

Interstate Commerce Commission, Chairman: Darius W. Gaskins, Jr.

National Aeronautics and Space Administration, Administrator: Robert Alan Frosch

National Foundation on the Arts and Humanities
  National Endowment for the Arts, Chairman: Livingston Biddle, Jr.
  National Endowment for the Humanities, Chairman: Joseph Duffey

National Labor Relations Board, Chairman: John H. Fanning

National Science Foundation, Chairman: Norman Hackerman

Nuclear Regulatory Commission, Chairman: John F. Ahearne

Postal Rate Commission, Chairman: A. Lee Fritschler

Securities and Exchange Commission, Chairman: Harold M. Williams

Selective Service System, Director: Bernard Daniel Rostker

Small Business Administration, Administrator: A. Vernon Weaver, Jr.

Tennessee Valley Authority, Chairman: S. David Freeman

U. S. Arms Control and Disarmament Agency, Director: George M. Seignious II

U. S. Postal Service, Postmaster General: Benjamin F. Bailar

Veterans Administration, Administrator: Max Cleland

THE SUPREME COURT

Warren E. Burger, chief justice
William J. Brennan, Jr.
Potter Stewart

Byron R. White
Thurgood Marshall
Harry A. Blackmun

Lewis F. Powell, Jr.
William H. Rehnquist
John Paul Stevens

UNITED STATES: 96TH CONGRESS

SENATE MEMBERSHIP

(As of January 1980: 59 Democrats, 41 Republicans)

Letters after senators' names refer to party affiliation—D for Democrat, R for Republican. Single asterisk (*) denotes term expiring in January 1981; double asterisk (**), term expiring in January 1983; triple asterisk (***), term expiring in January 1985; (1) ran as independent.

ALABAMA
***H. Heflin, D
*D. Stewart, D

ALASKA
***T. Stevens, R
*M. Gravel, D

ARIZONA
*B. Goldwater, R
**D. DeConcini, D

ARKANSAS
*D. Bumpers, D
***D. Pryor, D

CALIFORNIA
*A. Cranston, D
**S. I. Hayakawa, R

COLORADO
***W. Armstrong, R
*G. Hart, D

CONNECTICUT
*A. A. Ribicoff, D
**L. P. Weicker, Jr., R

DELAWARE
**W. V. Roth, Jr., R
***J. R. Biden, Jr., D

FLORIDA
**L. M. Chiles, Jr., D
*R. B. Stone, D

GEORGIA
*H. E. Talmadge, D
***S. Nunn, D

HAWAII
*D. K. Inouye, D
**S. M. Matsunaga, D

IDAHO
*F. Church, D
***J. A. McClure, R

ILLINOIS
***C. H. Percy, R
*A. E. Stevenson, D

INDIANA
*B. Bayh, D
**R. G. Lugar, R

IOWA
***R. Jepsen, R
*J. C. Culver, D

KANSAS
***N. Kassebaum, R
*R. J. Dole, R

KENTUCKY
***W. Huddleston, D
*W. H. Ford, D

LOUISIANA
*R. B. Long, D
***J. B. Johnston, D

MAINE
**E. S. Muskie, D
***W. Cohen, R

MARYLAND
*C. M. Mathias, Jr., R
**P. S. Sarbanes, D

MASSACHUSETTS
**E. M. Kennedy, D
***P. Tsongas, D

MICHIGAN
***C. Levin, D
**D. W. Riegle, Jr., D

MINNESOTA
**D. Durenberger, R
***R. Boschwitz, R

MISSISSIPPI
***T. Cochran, R
**J. C. Stennis, D

MISSOURI
*T. F. Eagleton, D
**J. C. Danforth, R

MONTANA
***M. Baucus, D
**J. Melcher, D

NEBRASKA
***J. Exon, D
**E. Zorinsky, D

NEVADA
**H. W. Cannon, D
*P. Laxalt, R

NEW HAMPSHIRE
***G. Humphrey, R
*J. A. Durkin, D

NEW JERSEY
***W. Bradley, D
**H. A. Williams, Jr., D

NEW MEXICO
***P. V. Domenici, R
**H. Schmitt, R

NEW YORK
*J. K. Javits, R
**D. P. Moynihan, D

NORTH CAROLINA
***J. Helms, R
*R. B. Morgan, D

NORTH DAKOTA
*M. R. Young, R
**Q. N. Burdick, D

OHIO
*J. H. Glenn, Jr., D
**H. M. Metzenbaum, D

OKLAHOMA
*H. L. Bellmon, R
***D. Boren, D

OREGON
***M. O. Hatfield, R
*B. Packwood, R

PENNSYLVANIA
*R. S. Schweiker, R
**H. J. Heinz, III, R

RHODE ISLAND
***C. Pell, D
*J. H. Chafee, R

SOUTH CAROLINA
***S. Thurmond, R
*E. F. Hollings, D

SOUTH DAKOTA
*G. S. McGovern, D
***L. Pressler, R

TENNESSEE
***H. H. Baker, Jr., R
**J. Sasser, D

TEXAS
***J. G. Tower, R
**L. M. Bentsen, D

UTAH
*J. Garn, R
**O. Hatch, R

VERMONT
**R. T. Stafford, R
*P. J. Leahy, D

VIRGINIA
**H. F. Byrd, Jr., D (1)
***J. Warner, R

WASHINGTON
*W. G. Magnuson, D
**H. M. Jackson, D

WEST VIRGINIA
***J. Randolph, D
**R. C. Byrd, D

WISCONSIN
**W. Proxmire, D
*G. Nelson, D

WYOMING
***A. Simpson, R
**M. Wallop, R

HOUSE MEMBERSHIP

(As of January 1980: 275 Democrats, 159 Republicans, 1 vacant)

"At-L." In place of Congressional district number means "representative at large." * Indicates elected Nov. 7, 1978; **elected in special 1979 election; all others were reelected in 1978.

ALABAMA
1. J. Edwards, R
2. W. L. Dickinson, R
3. W. Nichols, D
4. T. Bevill, D
5. R. Flippo, D
6. J. H. Buchanan, Jr., R
7. *R. Shelby, D

ALASKA
At-L. D. Young, R

ARIZONA
1. J. J. Rhodes, R
2. M. K. Udall, D
3. B. Stump, D
4. E. Rudd, R

ARKANSAS
1. W. V. Alexander, Jr., D
2. *E. Bethune, Jr., R
3. J. P. Hammerschmidt, R
4. *B. Anthony, Jr., D

CALIFORNIA
1. H. T. Johnson, D
2. D. H. Clausen, R
3. *R. Matsui, D
4. *V. Fazio, D
5. J. L. Burton, D
6. P. Burton, D

7. G. Miller, D
8. R. V. Dellums, D
9. F. H. Stark, Jr., D
10. D. Edwards, D
11. **W. H. Royer, R
12. P. N. McCloskey, Jr., R
13. N. Y. Mineta, D
14. *N. Shumway, R
15. *T. Coelho, D
16. L. E. Panetta, D
17. *C. Pashayan, R
18. *W. Thomas, R
19. R. J. Lagomarsino, R
20. B. M. Goldwater, Jr., R
21. J. C. Corman, D
22. C. J. Moorhead, R
23. A. C. Beilenson, D
24. H. A. Waxman, D
25. E. R. Roybal, D
26. J. H. Rousselot, R
27. R. K. Dornan, R
28. *J. Dixon, D
29. A. F. Hawkins, D
30. G. E. Danielson, D
31. C. H. Wilson, D
32. G. M. Anderson, D
33. *W. Grisham, R
34. *D. Lungren, R
35. J. Lloyd, D
36. G. E. Brown, Jr., D
37. *J. Lewis, R

38. J. M. Patterson, D
39. *W. Dannemeyer, R
40. R. E. Badham, R
41. B. Wilson, R
42. L. Van Deerlin, D
43. C. W. Burgener, R

COLORADO
1. P. Schroeder, D
2. T. E. Wirth, D
3. *R. Kogovsek, D
4. J. P. Johnson, R
5. *K. Kramer, R

CONNECTICUT
1. W. R. Cotter, D
2. C. J. Dodd, D
3. R. N. Giaimo, D
4. S. B. McKinney, R
5. *W. Ratchford, D
6. T. Moffett, D

DELAWARE
At-L. T. B. Evans, Jr., R

FLORIDA
1. *E. Hutto, D
2. D. Fuqua, D
3. C. E. Bennett, D
4. W. V. Chappell, Jr., D
5. R. Kelly, R

6. C. W. Young, R
7. S. M. Gibbons, D
8. A. P. Ireland, D
9. *B. Nelson, D
10. L. A. Bafalis, R
11. *D. Mica, D
12. *E. Stack, D
13. W. Lehman, D
14. C. D. Pepper, D
15. D. B. Fascell, D

GEORGIA
1. R. B. Ginn, D
2. M. D. Mathis, D
3. J. Brinkley, D
4. E. H. Levitas, D
5. W. F. Fowler, Jr., D
6. *N. Gingrich, R
7. L. P. McDonald, D
8. B. L. Evans, D
9. E. L. Jenkins, D
10. D. D. Barnard, Jr., D

HAWAII
1. C. Heftel, D
2. D. K. Akaka, D

IDAHO
1. S. D. Symms, R
2. G. V. Hansen, R

ILLINOIS
1. *B. Stewart, D
2. M. F. Murphy, D
3. M. A. Russo, D
4. E. J. Derwinski, R
5. J. G. Fary, D
6. H. J. Hyde, R
7. C. Collins, D
8. D. Rostenkowski, D
9. S. R. Yates, D
10. vacant
11. F. Annunzio, D
12. P. M. Crane, R
13. R. McClory, R
14. J. N. Erlenborn, R
15. T. J. Corcoran, R
16. J. B. Anderson, R
17. G. M. O'Brien, R
18. R. H. Michel, R
19. T. Railsback, R
20. P. Findley, R
21. E. R. Madigan, R
22. *D. Crane, R
23. C. M. Price, D
24. P. Simon, D

INDIANA
1. A. Benjamin, Jr., D
2. F. J. Fithian, D
3. J. Brademas, D
4. D. Quayle, R
5. E. H. Hillis, R
6. D. W. Evans, D
7. J. T. Myers, R
8. *H. Deckard, R
9. L. H. Hamilton, D
10. P. R. Sharp, D
11. A. Jacobs, Jr., D

IOWA
1. J. A. S. Leach, R
2. *T. Tauke, R
3. C. E. Grassley, R
4. N. Smith, D
5. T. R. Harkin, D
6. B. W. Bedell, D

KANSAS
1. K. G. Sebelius, R
2. *J. Jeffries, R
3. L. Winn, Jr., R
4. D. Glickman, D
5. *R. Whittaker, R

KENTUCKY
1. C. Hubbard, Jr., D
2. W. H. Natcher, D
3. R. L. Mazzoli, D
4. G. Snyder, R
5. T. L. Carter, R
6. *L. Hopkins, R
7. C. D. Perkins, D

LOUISIANA
1. R. L. Livingston, Jr., R
2. C. C. Boggs, D
3. D. C. Treen, R[1]
4. *C. Leach, D
5. J. Huckaby, D
6. W. H. Moore, R
7. J. B. Breaux, D
8. G. W. Long, D

MAINE
1. D. F. Emery, R
2. *O. Snowe, R

MARYLAND
1. R. E. Bauman, R
2. C. D. Long, D
3. B. A. Mikulski, D
4. M. S. Holt, R
5. G. N. Spellman, D
6. *Beverly Byron, D
7. P. J. Mitchell, D
8. *M. Barnes, D

MASSACHUSETTS
1. S. O. Conte, R
2. E. P. Boland, D
3. J. D. Early, D
4. R. F. Drinan, D
5. *J. Shannon, D
6. *N. Mavroules, D
7. E. J. Markey, D
8. T. P. O'Neill, Jr., D
9. J. J. Moakley, D
10. M. M. Heckler, R
11. *B. Donnelly, D
12. G. E. Studds, D

MICHIGAN
1. J. Conyers, Jr., D
2. C. D. Pursell, R
3. *H. Wolpe, D
4. D. A. Stockman, R
5. H. S. Sawyer, R
6. M. R. Carr, D
7. D. E. Kildee, D
8. B. Traxler, D
9. G. A. Vander Jagt, R
10. *D. Albosta, D
11. *R. Davis, R.
12. D. E. Bonior, D
13. C. C. Diggs, Jr., D
14. L. N. Nedzi, D
15. W. D. Ford, D
16. J. D. Dingell, D
17. W. M. Brodhead, D
18. J. J. Blanchard, D
19. W. S. Broomfield, R

MINNESOTA
1. *A. Erdahl, R
2. T. M. Hagedorn, R
3. B. Frenzel, R
4. B. F. Vento, D
5. *M. Sabo, D
6. R. M. Nolan, D
7. A. Stangeland, R
8. J. L. Oberstar, D

MISSISSIPPI
1. J. L. Whitten, D
2. D. R. Bowen, D
3. G. V. Montgomery, D
4. *J. Hinson, R
5. T. Lott, R.

MISSOURI
1. W. L. Clay, D
2. R. A. Young, D
3. R. A. Gephardt, D
4. I Skelton, D
5. R. Bolling, D
6. E. T. Coleman, R
7. G. Taylor, R
8. R. H. Ichord, D
9. H. L. Volkmer, D
10. B. D. Burlison, D

MONTANA
1. *P. Williams, D
2. R. Marlenee, R

NEBRASKA
1. *D. Bereuter, R
2. J. J. Cavanaugh, D
3. V. Smith, R

NEVADA
At-L. J. D. Santini, D

NEW HAMPSHIRE
1. N. E. D'Amours, D
2. J. C. Cleveland, R

NEW JERSEY
1. J. J. Florio, D
2. W. J. Hughes, D
3. J. J. Howard, D
4. F. Thompson, Jr., D
5. M. Fenwick, R
6. E. B. Forsythe, R
7. A. Maguire, D
8. R. A. Roe, D
9. H. C. Hollenbeck, R
10. P. W. Rodino, Jr., D
11. J. G. Minish, D
12. M. J. Rinaldo, R
13. *J. Courter, R
14. *F. Guarini, D
15. E. J. Patten, D

NEW MEXICO
1. M. Lujan, Jr., R
2. H. Runnels, D

NEW YORK
1. *W. Carney, R
2. T. J. Downey, D
3. J. A. Ambro, D
4. N. F. Lent, R
5. J. W. Wydler, R
6. L. L. Wolff, D
7. J. P. Addabbo, D
8. B. S. Rosenthal, D
9. *G. Ferraro, D
10. M. Biaggi, D
11. J. H. Scheuer, D
12. S. A. Chisholm, D
13. S. J. Solarz, D
14. F. W. Richmond, D
15. L. C. Zeferetti, D
16. E. Holtzman, D
17. J. M. Murphy, D
18. S. W. Green, R
19. C. B. Rangel, D
20. T. Weiss, D
21. *R. Garcia, D

NORTH CAROLINA
1. W. B. Jones, D
2. L. H. Fountain, D
3. C. O. Whitley, Sr., D
4. I. F. Andrews, D
5. S. L. Neal, D
6. L. R. Preyer, D
7. C. Rose, D
8. W. G. Hefner, D
9. J. G. Martin, R
10. J. T. Broyhill, R
11. L. Gudger, D

NORTH DAKOTA
At-L. M. Andrews, R

OHIO
1. W. D. Gradison, Jr., R
2. T. A. Luken, D
3. *T. Hall, D
4. T. Guyer, R
5. D. L. Latta, R
6. W. H. Harsha, R
7. C. J. Brown, R
8. T. N. Kindness, R
9. T. L. Ashley, D
10. C. E. Miller, R
11. J. W. Stanton, R
12. S. L. Devine, R
13. D. J. Pease, D
14. J. F. Seiberling, D
15. C. P. Wylie, R
16. R. Regula, R
17. J. M. Ashbrook, R
18. D. Applegate, D
19. L. Williams, R
20. M. R. Oakar, D
21. L. Stokes, D
22. C. A. Vanik, D
23. R. M. Mottl, D

OKLAHOMA
1. J. R. Jones, D
2. *M. Synar, D
3. W. W. Watkins, D
4. T. Steed, D
5. M. Edwards, R
6. G. English, D

OREGON
1. L. AuCoin, D
2. A. Ullman, D
3. R. B. Duncan, D
4. J. Weaver, D

PENNSYLVANIA
1. M. Myers, D
2. *W. Gray, D
3. R. F. Lederer, D
4. *C. Dougherty, R
5. R. T. Schulze, R
6. G. Yatron, D
7. R. W. Edgar, D
8. P. H. Kostmayer, D
9. B. Shuster, R
10. J. M. McDade, R
11. D. J. Flood, D
12. J. P. Murtha, D
13. L. Coughlin, R
14. W. S. Moorhead, D
15. *D. Ritter, R
16. R. S. Walker, R
17. A. E. Ertel, D
18. D. Walgren, D
19. W. F. Goodling, R
20. J. M. Gaydos, D
21. *D. Bailey, D
22. A. J. Murphy, D
23. *W. Clinger, Jr., R
24. M. L. Marks, R
25. *E. Atkinson, D

RHODE ISLAND
1. F. J. St Germain, D
2. E. P. Beard, D

SOUTH CAROLINA
1. M. J. Davis, D
2. F. D. Spence, R
3. B. C. Derrick, Jr., D
4. *C. Campbell, Jr., R
5. K. Holland, D
6. J. W. Jenrette, Jr., D

SOUTH DAKOTA
1. Tom Daschle, D
2. J. Abdnor, R

TENNESSEE
1. J. H. Quillen, R
2. J. J. Duncan, R
3. M. L. Bouquard, D
4. A. Gore, Jr., D
5. *W. H. Boner, D
6. R. L. Beard, Jr., R
7. E. Jones, D
8. H. Ford, D

TEXAS
1. S. B. Hall, Jr., D
2. C. Wilson, D
3. J. M. Collins, R
4. R. Roberts, D
5. J. A. Mattox, D
6. *P. Gramm, D
7. B. Archer, R
8. B. Eckhardt, D
9. J. Brooks, D
10. J. J. Pickle, D
11. *J. M. Leath, D
12. J. C. Wright, Jr., D
13. J. E. Hightower, D
14. *Joe Wyatt, D
15. E. de la Garza, D
16. R. C. White, D
17. *C. Stenholm, D
18. *M. Leland, D
19. *K. Hance, D
20. H. B. Gonzalez, D
21. *T. Loeffler, R
22. *R. Paul, R
23. A. Kazen, Jr., D
24. *M. Frost, D

UTAH
1. G. McKay, D
2. D. D. Marriott, R

VERMONT
At-L. J. M. Jeffords, R

VIRGINIA
1. P. S. Trible, Jr., R
2. G. W. Whitehurst, R
3. D. E. Satterfield, III, D
4. R. W. Daniel, Jr., R
5. D. Daniel, D
6. M. C. Butler, R
7. J. K. Robinson, R
8. H. E. Harris, II, D
9. W. C. Wampler, R
10. J. L. Fisher, D

WASHINGTON
1. J. M. Pritchard, R
2. *A. Swift, D
3. D. L. Bonker, D
4. M. McCormack, D
5. T. S. Foley, D
6. N. D. Dicks, D
7. *M. Lowry, D

WEST VIRGINIA
1. R. H. Mollohan, D
2. H. O. Staggers, D
3. J. Slack, D
4. N. J. Rahall, D

WISCONSIN
1. L. Aspin, D
2. R. W. Kastenmeier, D
3. A. J. Baldus, D
4. C. J. Zablocki, D
5. H. S. Reuss, D
6. **T. E. Petri, R
7. D. R. Obey, D
8. *T. Roth, R
9. *F. J. Sensenbrenner, Jr., R

WYOMING
At-L. *R. Cheney, R

PUERTO RICO
Resident Commissioner
B. Corrada

DISTRICT OF COLUMBIA
Delegate, W. E. Fauntroy, D

[1] To be inaugurated as governor

583

UNITED STATES

Major Legislation Enacted During First Session of 96th Congress

SUBJECT	PURPOSE
Taiwan	Allows commercial, cultural, and other ties with Taiwan without official government representation or formal diplomatic relations. Signed April 10. Public Law 96-8.
John Wayne	Authorized the presentation of a specially-struck medal in honor of John Wayne for his "integrity, courage, patriotism, and strength. . . ." Signed May 26. Public Law 96-15.
Hubert Humphrey	Authorized that a special gold medal be struck in tribute to the "distinguished career" of Hubert Humphrey. Signed June 13. Public Law 96-21.
Veterans' Health Care	Provides readjustment counseling, treatment of alcohol and drug dependence, and other programs for Vietnam-era veterans and their families. Signed June 14. Public Law 96-22.
Government Ethics	Strengthens safeguards against abuse of influence, acquired in high-level federal service, in subsequent employment in the private sector. Signed June 22. Public Law 96-28.
Trade	Liberalizes the rules of and removes barriers to international fair trade to aid the dollar and promote U. S. exports. Signed July 26. Public Law 96-39.
Food Stamps	Appropriates sufficient funds to continue the food stamp program, provides added benefits for the elderly and disabled, and introduces measures to avoid error and fraud. Signed August 15. Public Law 96-58.
Fishery Conservation	Establishes procedures to protect whales, provides for reductions in fishing allocations in 200-mile fishing zones, manages certification of foreign nations. Signed August 15. Public Law 96-61.
Energy and Water Development	Appropriates funds for the completion of the Tellico Dam Project on the Little Tennessee River and exempts it from the Endangered Species Act. Also provides funding for nine new water projects and annual funding for water projects. Signed September 25. Public Law 96-69.
Panama Canal	Implements the Panama Canal Treaty of 1978. Signed September 27. Public Law 96-70.
Health Care	Extends the federal health planning program; provides federal assistance to permit closure of hospital beds or their conversion to more needed uses. Signed October 4. Public Law 96-79.
Magistrates	Expands the jurisdiction of U. S. magistrates in civil and criminal cases, and ensures that they are appointed on merit. Signed October 10. Public Law 96-82.
Department of Education	Creates and provides funds for a new cabinet agency, the Department of Education. Signed October 17. Public Law 96-88. See EDUCATION.
Emergency Energy Conservation	Gives president authority to devise standby gasoline rationing plan and to put it into effect during a shortage. Also creates conservation plan giving the states primary responsibility for saving energy. Signed November 5. Public Law 96-102.
Refugees	Authorizes additional funds for migrants and refugees and assistance for victims of the famine in Cambodia. Signed November 13. Public Law 96-110.
Departments of Interior and Energy	Appropriates funds for the Interior and Energy departments for fiscal 1980, including commitment to long-range evolution of synthetic fuels and help to the poor in paying their heating bills. Signed November 27. Public Law 96-126.
Milk Prices	Supports milk prices at between 80 and 90% of parity for two years. Signed November 28. Public Law 96-127.
Naval Oil	Authorizes appropriations for conservation, exploration, development, and use of naval petroleum reserves and naval oil shale reserves. Signed December 12. Public Law 96-137.
Endangered Species	Reauthorizes the Endangered Species Act for three years; includes plant species in emergency listing and international cooperation provisions; provides funds to Department of Agriculture to enforce provisions related to plants. Signed December 28. Public Law 96-159.
Financial Institutions Deregulation	Institutes stopgap financial reforms to alleviate problems of obtaining residential mortgage loans. Signed December 28. Public Law 96-161.
Meat Imports	Changes procedures used to regulate imports of beef and veal. Signed December 31. Public Law 96-177.
Chrysler Corporation	Grants $1.5 billion in loan guarantees and other financial assistance to the financially threatened Chrysler Corporation. Signed January 7. Public Law 96-185.
Election Campaigning	Encourages more local, grass roots activity in behalf of presidential and congressional candidates; prohibits Senate and House candidates from keeping surplus campaign contributions after an election. Signed January 8. Public Law 96–187.

From U.S.	Countries	To U.S.	From U.S.	Countries	To U.S.
(Vacant)	AFGHANISTAN	Abdul G. Farahi[2]	Robert P. Smith	LIBERIA	Francis A. W. Dennis
Ulric S. Haynes, Jr.	ALGERIA	Redha Malek	(Vacant)	LIBYA	Ahmed D. A. Madfai[2]
Raul H. Castro	ARGENTINA	Jorge A. A. Espil	(Vacant)	LITHUANIA	Stasys A. Backis[2]
Philip H. Alston, Jr.	AUSTRALIA	Nicholas F. Parkinson	James G. Lowenstein	LUXEMBOURG	Adrien F. J. Meisch
Milton A. Wolf	AUSTRIA	Karl Herbert Schober	(Vacant)	MADAGASCAR	Norbert Rakotomalala[2]
William B. Schwartz, Jr.	BAHAMAS	Patricia E. J. Rodgers[2]	Harold E. Horlan	MALAWI	Jacob T. X. Muwamba
Robert H. Pelletreau, Jr.	BAHRAIN	Abdulaziz A. Buali	Robert H. Miller	MALAYSIA	Zain Azraai
David T. Schneider	BANGLADESH	Tabarak Husain	Donald R. Toussaint[3]	MALDIVE IS.	(Vacant)
Sally A. Shelton	BARBADOS	Oliver H. Jackman	Anne F. Holloway	MALI	Maki K. A. Tall
Anne C. Chambers	BELGIUM	Raoul Schoumaker	Joan M. Clark	MALTA	Leslie N. Agius[2]
(Vacant)	BENIN	Thomas Setondji Boya	E. Gregory Kryza	MAURITANIA	Sidi Bouna Ould Sidi
Paul H. Boeker	BOLIVIA	Roberto Arce Alvarez	Samuel R. Gammon	MAURITIUS	Pierre G. G. Balancy
Horace G. Dawson, Jr.	BOTSWANA	Bias Mookodi	Patrick J. Lucey	MEXICO	Hugo B. Margain
Robert M. Sayre	BRAZIL	Antonio Francisco da Silveira	Angier Biddle Duke[3]	MOROCCO	Ali Bengelloun
			Willard A. De Pree	MOZAMBIQUE	(Vacant)
			Philip H. Alston, Jr.	NAURU	(Vacant)
Jack R. Perry	BULGARIA	Konstantin N. Grigorov	L. Douglas Heck	NEPAL	Padma Bahadur Khatri
Patricia M. Byrne[3]	BURMA	U Hla Shwe	Geri M. Joseph	NETHERLANDS	Age R. Tammenoms Bakker
Thomas J. Corcoran	BURUNDI	Clement Sambira[2]			
Mabel M. Smythe	CAMEROON	Benoit Bindzi	Anne C. Martindell	NEW ZEALAND	Merwyn Norrish
Kenneth M. Curtis	CANADA	Peter M. Towe	Lawrence A. Pezzullo	NICARAGUA	Rafael Solis Cerda
Edward Marks	CAPE VERDE	Viriato de Barros[2]	James K. Bishop	NIGER	André Wright
Goodwin Cooke	CENTRAL AFR. REP.	Amédée Fanga-Mbourounda[2]	Stephen Low	NIGERIA	Olujimi Jolaoso
			Sidney A. Rand[3]	NORWAY	Knut Hedemann
			Marshall W. Wiley	OMAN	Sadek Jawad Sulaiman
Donald R. Norland	CHAD	Ali Adoum[2]	Arthur W. Hummel, Jr.	PAKISTAN	Sultan Muhammad Khan
George W. Landau	CHILE	José M. Barros	Ambler H. Moss, Jr.	PANAMA	Carlos A. Lopez-Guevara
Leonard Woodcock	CHINA (People's Rep. of)	Chai Zemin	Harvey J. Feldman	PAPUA NEW GUINEA	Paulias Nguna Matane
Diego C. Asencio	COLOMBIA	Virgilio Barco	Robert E. White	PARAGUAY	Mario L. Escobar
William L. Swing	CONGO	Nicolas Mondjo	Harry W. Shlaudeman	PERU	Alfonso Arias-Schreiber
Marvin Weissman	COSTA RICA	José R. Echeverria	Richard W. Murphy	PHILIPPINES	Eduardo Z. Romualdez
Galen L. Stone	CYPRUS	Andreas J. Jacovides	William E. Schaufele, Jr.	POLAND	Romuald Spasowski
Francis J. Meehan	CZECHOSLOVAKIA	Jaromir Johanes	Richard J. Bloomfield	PORTUGAL	João Hall Themido
Warren D. Manshel	DENMARK	Otto R. Borch	Andrew I. Killgore	QATAR	Abdullah Saleh Al-Mana
Sally A. Shelton	DOMINICA	(Vacant)	O. Rudolph Aggrey	RUMANIA	Nicolae Ionescu
Robert L. Yost	DOMINICAN REP.	Enriquillo del Rosario Ceballos	Harry R. Melone	RWANDA	Bonaventure Ubalijoro
Raymond E. Gonzalez	ECUADOR	Ricardo Zaldumbide	Sally A. Shelton	ST. LUCIA	(Vacant)
Alfred L. Atherton, Jr.	EGYPT	Ashraf A. Ghorbal	Arthur T. Tienken	SÃO TOMÉ AND PRÍNCIPE	(Vacant)
Frank J. Devine	EL SALVADOR	Roberto Quinonez Meza			
(Vacant)	ESTONIA	Ernst Jaakson[2]	John C. West	SAUDI ARABIA	Sheikh Faisal Alhegelan
Frederick L. Chapin	ETHIOPIA	Tibabu Bekele[2]	Herman J. Cohen	SENEGAL	André Coulbary
John P. Condon	FIJI	Berenado Vunibobo	Wilbert J. Le Melle	SEYCHELLES	Bernard Loustau-Lalanne
Rozanne L. Ridgway	FINLAND	Jaakko O. Iloniemi			
Arthur A. Hartman	FRANCE	François de Laboulaye	John A. Linehan	SIERRA LEONE	Mohamed Morlai Turay
Arthur T. Tienken	GABON	José-Joseph Amiar	Richard F. Kneip	SINGAPORE	Punch Coomaraswamy
Herman J. Cohen	GAMBIA	Ousman A. Sallah	Mary O. Olmstead	SOLOMON ISLANDS	Francis Bugotu
David B. Bolen	GERMANY (E)	Horst Grunert	Donald K. Petterson	SOMALIA	Abdullahi Ahmed Addou
Walter J. Stoessel, Jr.	GERMANY (W)	Peter Hermes	William B. Edmondson	SOUTH AFRICA	Donald Bell Sole
Thomas W. M. Smith	GHANA	Alex Quaison-Sackey	Terence A. Todman	SPAIN	José Llado
Kingman Brewster, Jr.	GREAT BRITAIN	Nicholas Henderson	Donald R. Toussaint[3]	SRI LANKA	W. S. Karunaratne
Robert J. McCloskey	GREECE	John Tzounis	Donald C. Bergus	SUDAN	Omer Salih Eissa
Sally A. Shelton	GRENADA	Bernard K. Radix	Nancy Ostrander	SURINAM	Roel F. Karamat
Frank V. Ortiz, Jr.	GUATEMALA	Felipe D. Monterroso	Richard C. Matheron	SWAZILAND	Simon Musa Kunene
Oliver S. Crosby	GUINEA	Mamady Lamine Conde	R. O. Kennedy-Minott	SWEDEN	Count Wilhelm Wachtmeister
Edward Marks	GUINEA-BISSAU	Gil Vicente Vaz Fernandes			
George B. Roberts, Jr.	GUYANA	Laurence E. Mann	Richard D. Vine	SWITZERLAND	Raymond Probst
William B. Jones	HAITI	Georges Salomon	Talcott W. Seelye	SYRIA	Sabah Kabbani
Mari-Luci Jaramillo	HONDURAS	Ricardo Midence Soto	Richard N. Viets	TANZANIA	Paul L. Bomani
Philip M. Kaiser	HUNGARY	Ferenc Esztergalyos	Morton I. Abramowitz	THAILAND	Klos Visessurakarn
Richard A. Ericson, Jr.	ICELAND	Hans G. Andersen	Marilyn P. Johnson	TOGO	Yao Grunitzky
Robert F. Goheen	INDIA	Ashok B. Ghokale[2]	John P. Condon	TONGA	'Inoke Faletau
Edward E. Masters	INDONESIA	D. Ashari	Irving G. Cheslaw	TRINIDAD AND TOBAGO	Victor McIntyre
Walter L. Cutler	IRAN	Ali Asghar Agah[2]			
William V. Shannon	IRELAND	Sean Donlon	Stephen W. Bosworth	TUNISIA	Ali Hedda
Samuel W. Lewis	ISRAEL	Ephraim Evron	James W. Spain[3]	TURKEY	Sukru Elekdag
Richard N. Gardner	ITALY	Paolo Pansa Cedronio	(Vacant)	TUVALU	Ionatana Ionatana
Nancy V. Rawls	IVORY COAST	Timothée N'Guetta Ahoua	(Vacant)	UGANDA	Joshua L. Zake
			Thomas J. Watson, Jr.	USSR	A. F. Dobrynin
Loren E. Lawrence	JAMAICA	Alfred A. Rattray	William D. Wolle	UNITED ARAB EMIRATES	Hamad A. R. Al Madfa
Michael J. Mansfield	JAPAN	Fumihiko Togo			
Nicholas A. Veliotes	JORDAN	Abdullah Salah	Thomas D. Boyatt	UPPER VOLTA	Télésphore Yaguibou
Wilbert J. LeMelle	KENYA	John P. Mbogua	Lyle F. Lane	URUGUAY	José Perez Caldas
William H. Gleysteen, Jr.	KOREA (S)	Yong Shik Kim	William H. Luers	VENEZUELA	Marcial Perez Chiriboga
François M. Dickman	KUWAIT	Khalid M. Jaffar	Anne C. Martindell	WESTERN SAMOA	Maiava I. Toma
(Vacant)	LAOS	Khamtan Ratanavong[2]	George M. Lane	YEMEN	Yahya M. Al-Mutawakel
(Vacant)	LATVIA	Anatol Dinbergs[2]	Lawrence S. Eagleburger	YUGOSLAVIA	Budimir Loncar
John G. Dean	LEBANON	Khalil Itani	Robert B. Oakley	ZAIRE	Kasongo Mutuale
John R. Clingerman	LESOTHO	Timothy T. Thahane	Frank G. Wisner II	ZAMBIA	Putteho M. Ngonda

[1] As of December 14, 1979; [2] Chargé d'affaires; [3] Nominated but not confirmed by Congress.

This article lists some of the most noteworthy associations, societies, foundations, and trusts of the United States and Canada. The information has been verified by the organization concerned.

Academy of Motion Picture Arts & Sciences. Membership: 4,100. Executive director, James M. Roberts. Headquarters: 8949 Wilshire Blvd., Beverly Hills, CA 90211.

Alcoholics Anonymous (The General Service Board of A. A., Inc.). Membership: over 1,000,000 in more than 30,000 affiliated groups. Chairman, Milton Maxwell, Ph. D. Headquarters: 468 Park Ave. S., New York, NY. Mailing address: Box 459, Grand Central Station, New York, NY 10017.

American Academy and Institute of Arts and Letters. Membership: 250. Executive director, Margaret M. Mills. Headquarters: 633 W. 155th St., New York, NY 10032.

American Academy of Political and Social Science. Membership: 12,500, including 6,000 libraries. No annual meeting in 1980. President, Marvin E. Wolfgang. Headquarters: 3937 Chestnut St., Philadelphia, PA 19104.

American Anthropological Association. Membership: 10,268. Executive director, Edward J. Lehman. Headquarters: 1703 New Hampshire Ave. NW, Washington, DC 20009.

American Association for the Advancement of Science. Membership: 130,000 and 287 affiliated groups. Meeting: San Francisco, Jan. 3–8, 1980. President, Kenneth E. Boulding; executive officer, William D. Carey. Headquarters: 1515 Massachusetts Ave. NW, Washington, DC 20005.

American Association of Museums. Membership: 6,500. Annual meeting: Boston, June 1980. Director, Lawrence L. Reger. Headquarters: 1055 Thomas Jefferson St., Suite 428, Washington, DC 20007.

American Association of University Professors. Membership: 77,000. President, Martha Friedman. Headquarters: One Dupont Circle NW, Washington, DC 20036.

American Association of University Women. Membership: 190,000. President, Mary Grefe. Headquarters: 2401 Virginia Ave. NW, Washington, DC 20037.

American Astronomical Society. Membership: 3,700. Meetings, 1980: San Francisco, Jan. 13–17; College Park, MD, June 14–18. President, Dr. Ivan R. King. Address: Suite 603, 1717 Massachusetts Ave. NW, Washington, DC 20036.

American Automobile Association. Membership: 21,000,000 in 210 affiliated clubs. President, James B. Creal. Headquarters: 8111 Gatehouse Rd., Falls Church, VA 22047.

American Bankers Association. Membership: 13,537. President, C. C. Hope, Jr. Headquarters: 1120 Connecticut Ave. NW, Washington, DC 20036.

American Bar Association. Membership: 247,431. President, Leonard Janofsky; executive director, Bert H. Early. Headquarters: 1155 E. 60th Street, Chicago, IL 60637.

American Bible Society. 1978 United States distribution: 127,414,817 copies. Annual meeting: New York City, May 8, 1980. President, Edmund F. Wagner. Headquarters: 1865 Broadway, New York, NY 10023.

American Booksellers Association, Inc. Membership: 5,500. Convention: Chicago, June 7–10, 1980. President, Charles S. Haslam. Headquarters: 122 E. 42nd St., New York, NY 10017.

American Cancer Society, Inc. Membership: 194 voting members; 58 chartered divisions. Executive vice president, Lane W. Adams. Headquarters: 777 Third Ave., New York, NY 10017.

American Chemical Society. Membership: 116,000. National meetings, 1980: Houston, March 23–28; San Francisco, August 24–29. President, Dr. James D. D'Ianni. Headquarters: 1155 16th St. NW, Washington, DC 20036.

American Civil Liberties Union. Membership: 200,000. Board chairman, Norman Dorsen. Headquarters: 22 E. 40th St., New York, NY 10016.

American Council of Learned Societies. Membership: 43 professional societies concerned with the humanities and the humanistic aspects of the social sciences. President, R. M. Lumiansky; vice president, Gordon B. Turner. Headquarters: 800 Third Ave., New York, NY 10022.

American Council on Education. Membership: 1,348 colleges and universities, 116 associated organizations, 60 affiliates, 64 constituent organizations, and 10 international affiliates. Annual meeting: San Francisco, Oct. 8–10, 1980. President, Jack W. Peltason. Headquarters: One Dupont Circle NW, Washington, DC 20036.

American Dental Association. Membership: 131,000. President, Joseph P. Cappuccio, D. D. S.; president-elect, I. Laurence Kerr, D. D. S.; acting executive director, John M. Coady, D. D. S. Headquarters: 211 E. Chicago Ave., Chicago, IL 60611.

American Economic Association. Membership: 18,600 and 5,900 subscribers. Annual meeting: Denver, Sept. 5–7, 1980. President, Robert M. Solow. Headquarters: 1313 21st Ave. S., Nashville, TN 37212.

American Electroplaters' Society, Inc. Membership, 7,500, with 75 branches in the United States, Canada, Australia, and South America. Annual meeting: Milwaukee, June 22–26, 1980. President, Simon P. Gary. Headquarters: 1201 Louisiana Ave., Winter Park, FL 32789.

American Farm Bureau Federation. Membership: 3,076,867 families. President, Allan Grant. Headquarters: 225 Touhy, Ave., Park Ridge, IL 60068.

American Geographical Society. Fellows and subscribers: 7,700. President, Richard Nolte; director, Sarah Myers. Headquarters: Broadway at 156th St., New York, NY 10032.

American Geophysical Union. Membership: 12,000 individuals; 32 organizations. Meetings, 1980: Toronto, May 22–27 and San Francisco, Dec. 8–12. President, Allan V. Cox. Headquarters: 2000 Florida Ave. NW, Washington, DC 20009.

American Heart Association. Membership: 140,000 in 55 affiliates, 125 chapters, and about 1,000 local subdivisions. President, Thomas N. James, M. D. Headquarters: 7320 Greenville Ave., Dallas, TX 75231.

American Historical Association. Membership: 15,000. President, David Pinkney; executive director, Mack Thompson. Headquarters: 400 A St. SE, Washington, DC 20003.

American Horticultural Society. Membership: 28,000 individuals, 400 organizations, institutions and commercial establishments. National congress: St. Louis, September 1980. President, Dr. Gilbert S. Daniels. Headquarters: Mt. Vernon, VA 22121.

American Hospital Association. Membership: 29,600 persons; 6,175 institutions. Annual meeting: Washington, DC, Feb. 3–6, 1980; convention: Montreal, July 28–31, 1980. Chairman of the board, W. Daniel Barker. Headquarters: 840 North Lake Shore Dr., Chicago, IL 60611.

American Hotel & Motel Association. Membership: 7,500. Annual convention: Washington, DC, Dec. 1–4, 1980. Executive vice president, Robert L. Richards. Headquarters: 888 Seventh Ave., New York, NY 10019.

American Institute of Aeronautics and Astronautics. Membership: 24,600, plus 4,000 student members. Executive secretary, James J. Harford. Headquarters: 1290 Avenue of the Americas, New York, NY 10019.

American Institute of Architects. Membership: 32,000. President, Charles E. Schwing, FAIA. Headquarters: 1735 New York Ave. NW, Washington, DC 20006.

American Institute of Biological Sciences. Membership: 8,000 with 45 member societies and 12 affiliate organizations. Annual meeting: Tucson, August 3–8, 1980. President, Dr. Beatrice M. Sweeney. Headquarters: 1401 Wilson Boulevard, Arlington, VA 22209.

American Institute of Certified Public Accountants. Membership: 150,000. Annual meeting: Boston, Oct. 5–7, 1980. Chairman of the Board, Joseph P. Cummings. Headquarters: 1211 Avenue of the Americas, New York, NY 10036.

American Institute of Chemical Engineers. Membership: 43,216. President, J. G. Knudsen. Headquarters: 345 E. 47th St., New York, NY 10017.

American Institute of Graphic Arts. Membership: 2,000. President, J. K. Fogleman; executive director, Caroline Hightower. Headquarters: 1059 Third Ave., New York, NY 10021.

American Institute of Mining, Metallurgical and Petroleum Engineers, Inc. Membership: 64,810. Annual meeting: Las Vegas, Feb. 24–28, 1980. President, William H. Wise. Headquarters: 345 E. 47th St., New York, NY 10017.

American Legion, The. Membership: 2,700,000. Headquarters: 700 N. Pennsylvania St., Indianapolis, IN 46206.

American Library Association. Membership: 34,706. Meetings, 1980: Midwinter, Chicago, Jan. 20–25; annual conference, New York, June 26–July 5. Executive director, Robert Wedgeworth. Headquarters: 50 E. Huron, Chicago, IL 60611.

American Lung Association. Membership: 175 affiliated groups. Annual meeting: Washington, DC, May 1980. President, G. Gordon Beck. Headquarters: 1740 Broadway, New York, NY 10019.

American Management Associations. Membership: 72,000. Chairman of the board, Lee S. Bickmore; president and chief executive officer, James L. Hayes. Headquarters: 135 W. 50th St., New York, NY 10020.

American Mathematical Society. Membership: 17,438. President, Peter D. Lax; secretary, Everett Pitcher. Headquarters: P. O. Box 6248, Providence, RI 02940.

American Medical Association. Membership: 211,000. President, Hoyt D. Gardner, M. D. Headquarters: 535 N. Dearborn St., Chicago, IL 60610.

American Meteorological Society. Membership: 9,000 including 128 corporate members. President, Dr. Chester W. Newton. Headquarters: 45 Beacon St., Boston, MA 02108.

American Newspaper Publishers Association. Membership: 1,344. Annual convention: Honolulu, April 21–23, 1980. Chairman and president, Allen H. Neuharth. Headquarters: 11600 Sunrise Valley Drive, Reston, VA 22091. Mailing address: The Newspaper Center, Box 17407, Dulles International Airport, Washington, DC 20041.

American Nurses' Association. Membership: 200,000 in 53 state and territorial associations. National convention: Houston, June 8–13, 1980. President, Barbara Nichols. Headquarters: 2420 Pershing Road, Kansas City, MO 64108.

American Physical Society. Membership: 30,446 American and foreign. Annual meeting: Chicago, Jan. 21–24, 1980. President, Herman Feshbach; executive secretary, W. W. Havens, Jr. Headquarters: 335 E. 45th, New York, NY 10017.

American Psychiatric Association. Membership: 24,879; 75 district branches. Annual meeting: San Francisco, May 3–9, 1980. President, Alan Stone, M. D. Headquarters: 1700 18th St. NW, Washington, DC 20009.

American Psychological Association. Membership: 49,047. Annual meeting: Montreal, Canada, Sept. 1–5, 1980. President, Florence Denmark. Headquarters: 1200 17th Street NW, Washington, DC 20036.

American Red Cross. Divisions: 60; Chapters: 3,124. National convention: Los Angeles, May 11–14, 1980. Chairman, Jerome H. Holland; president, George M. Elsey. Headquarters: 17th and D Sts. NW, Washington, DC 20006.

American Society of Civil Engineers. Membership: 75,062. President, Joseph Ward. Headquarters: 345 E. 47th St., New York, NY 10017.

American Society of Composers, Authors, and Publishers. Membership: 18,963 composers and authors; 6,495 publishers. President, Stanley Adams; secretary, Morton Gould. Headquarters: One Lincoln Plaza, New York, NY 10023.

American Society of Mechanical Engineers. Membership: 93,000. President, Donald N. Zwiep. Headquarters: 345 E. 47th St., New York, NY 10017.

American Society of Newspaper Editors. Membership: 800. National convention: Washington, DC, April 1980. President, William H. Hornby. Headquarters: Box 551, 1350 Sullivan Trail, Easton, PA 18042.

American Sociological Association. Membership: 14,000. Annual meeting: New York, August 27–31, 1980. President, Peter H. Rossi. Headquarters: 1722 N St. NW, Washington, DC 20036.

American Statistical Association. Membership: 13,000. President, Margaret E. Martin; secretary, Fred C. Leone. Headquarters: 806 15th St. NW, Washington, DC 20005.

American Youth Hostels, Inc. Membership: 100,000; 27 councils in the United States. Executive director, Thomas L. Newman. Headquarters: National Campus, Delaplane, VA 22025.

Archaeological Institute of America. Membership: 7,900; subscribers, 30,000. President, Robert H. Dyson, Jr. Headquarters: 53 Park Place, New York, NY 10017.

Arthritis Foundation. Membership: 73 chapters. Annual meeting: Atlanta, May 28–31, 1980. Chairman, W. W. Satterfield; president, Clifford M. Clarke. Headquarters: 3400 Peachtree Rd. NE, Atlanta, GA 30326.

Association of American Publishers. Membership: approx. 340. Annual meeting: May 1980. Chairman of the board, Alexander Hoffman; president, Townsend W. Hoopes; vice president, Thomas McKee. Addresses: One Park Ave., New York, NY 10016 and 1707 L St. NW, Washington, DC 20036.

Association of Junior Leagues, Inc. Membership: 238 member Leagues in U. S., Canada, and Mexico. Annual conference: Toronto, May 4–8, 1980. President, Alice H. Weber. Headquarters: 825 Third Ave., New York, NY 10022.

Association of Operating Room Nurses, Inc. Membership: 28,500 with 250 local chapters. Convention: March 9–14, 1980. President, Barbara Stanewick; executive director, Jerry G. Peers. Headquarters: 10170 E. Mississippi Ave., Denver, CO 80231.

Benevolent and Protective Order of Elks. Membership: 1,644,496 in 2,241 Lodges. Grand exalted ruler, Robert Grafton; grand secretary, S. F. Kocur. Headquarters: 2750 Lake View Ave., Chicago, IL 60614.

Big Brothers/Big Sisters of America. Membership: 380+ local affiliated agencies. Annual convention: Louisville, KY, June 16–21, 1980. Executive vice president, L. P. Reade. Headquarters: 117 South 17th Street, Suite 1200, Philadelphia, PA 19103.

B'nai B'rith. Membership: 500,000 in about 3,000 men's, women's, and youth units. President, Jack Spitzer; executive vice president, Daniel Thursz. Headquarters: 1640 Rhode Island Ave. NW, Washington, DC 20036.

Boys' Clubs of America. Youth served: 1,000,000 in 1,100 affiliated clubs. National conference: Miami Beach, May 25–29, 1980. President, John L. Burns; national director, William R. Bricker. Headquarters: 771 First Avenue, New York, NY 10017.

Boy Scouts of America. Membership: total youth members and leaders—4,493,491 in 417 Scouting councils. Biennial meeting: New Orleans, May 21–23, 1980. President, Downing B. Jenks; chief scout executive, J. L. Tarr. National office: 1325 Walnut Hill Lane, Irving, TX; P. O. Box 61030, Dallas/Fort Worth Airport, TX 75261.

Camp Fire Girls, Inc. Membership: 500,000 boys and girls in over 35,000 communities. President, Dr. Faith LaVelle. Headquarters: 4601 Madison Ave., Kansas City, MO 64112.

Canadian Library Association. Membership: 3,774 personal, 1,014 institutional, 4,788 total. Annual conference: 1980: Vancouver. Executive director, Paul Kitchen. Headquarters: 151 Sparks St., Ottawa, Ont. K1P 5E3.

Canadian Medical Association. Membership: 32,000. Annual meeting: Vancouver, Sept. 14–19, 1980. President, D. L. Wilson, M. D. Headquarters: 1867 Alta Vista Dr., Ottawa, Ont. K1G 0G8.

Chamber of Commerce of the United States of America. Membership about 4,000 trade associations and local and state chambers, more than 81,500 business members. President, Richard Lesher; chairman of the board, Jay Vanandel. Headquarters: 1615 H St. NW, Washington, DC 20062.

Common Cause. Membership: 220,000. Chairwoman: Nan Waterman. Headquarters: 2030 M St. NW, Washington, DC 20036.

Consumers Union of United States, Inc. Executive director: Rhoda H. Karpatkin. Headquarters: 256 Washington St., Mount Vernon, NY 10550.

Council of Better Business Bureaus. Membership: 1,000. Headquarters: 1150 17th St. NW, Washington, DC 20036.

Council on Foreign Relations, Inc. Membership: 1,800. Annual meeting: New York City, fall 1980. President, Winston Lord. Headquarters: 58 E. 68th St., New York, NY 10021.

Daughters of the American Revolution (National Society). Membership: 207,573 in 3,094 chapters. Continental congress: Washington, DC, April 17–21, 1980. President general, Mrs. George Upham Baylies. Headquarters: 1776 D St. NW, Washington, DC 20006.

Esperanto League for North America. Membership: 600. Congress: July 1980. President, William R. Harmon. Headquarters: P. O. Box 1129, El Cerrito, CA 94530.

Foreign Policy Association. Chairman, Carter L. Burgess. Headquarters: 205 Lexington Ave., New York, NY 10016.

Freemasonry, Ancient Accepted Scottish Rite of (Northern Masonic Jurisdiction): Supreme Council, 33°. Membership: 511,687 in 112 valleys. Sovereign grand commander, Stanley F. Maxwell. Headquarters: 33 Marrett Rd., Lexington, MA 02173.

Freemasonry, Ancient and Accepted Scottish Rite of (Southern Jurisdiction): Supreme Council, 33°. Membership: 658,000 in 218 affiliated groups. Sovereign grand commander, Henry C. Clausen. Headquarters: 1733 16th St. NW, Washington, DC 20009.

Future Farmers of America. Membership: 494,394 in 50 state associations. Executive secretary, Coleman Harris. Headquarters: Box 15160, Alexandria, VA 22309.

Gamblers Anonymous. Membership: 6,500. National executive secretary, James J. Zeysing. Headquarters: 2705A W. Eighth St., Los Angeles, CA 90005.

Garden Club of America, The. Membership: 13,500 in 183 member clubs. Annual meeting: Norfolk, VA, April 27–30, 1980. President, Mrs. R. Henry Norweb, Jr. Headquarters: 598 Madison Avenue, New York, NY 10022.

General Federation of Women's Clubs. Membership: 10,000,000 in 14,000 U. S. organizations and 36 abroad. National convention: St. Louis, June 6, 1980. President, Mrs. A. M. Quint. Headquarters: 1734 N Street NW, Washington, DC 20036.

Geological Society of America. Membership: 12,500. Annual meeting: Atlanta, Nov. 17–20, 1980. President:

Laurence L. Sloss; executive director, John C. Frye. Headquarters: 3300 Penrose Place, Boulder, CO 80301.

Girl Scouts of the U.S.A. Membership: 3,084,000. National president, Mrs. Orville L. Freeman; national executive director, Frances R. Hesselbein. Headquarters: 830 Third Ave., New York, NY 10022.

Humane Society of the United States. Membership: 115,000. Annual convention: San Francisco, October 1980. President, John A. Hoyt. Headquarters: 2100 L St. NW, Washington, DC 20037.

Institute of Electrical and Electronics Engineers, Inc. Membership: 200,000. President, Jerome J. Suran. Headquarters: 345 E. 47th St., New York, NY 10017.

Jewish War Veterans of the U.S.A. Membership: 100,000 in 750 units. National commander, Harris Stone; national executive director, Jerome Levinrad. Headquarters: 1712 New Hampshire Ave. NW, Washington, DC 20009.

Kiwanis International. Membership: 300,000 in 7,500 clubs in U.S. and abroad. President, Mark A. Smith, Jr. Headquarters: 101 E. Erie St., Chicago, IL 60611.

Knights of Columbus. Membership: 1,308,643. Supreme knight, Virgil C. Dechant. Headquarters: Columbus Plaza, New Haven, CT 06507.

Knights of Pythias, Supreme Lodge. Membership: 132,640 in 1,394 subordinate lodges. Supreme chancellor, Victor Vickness. Office: 47 N. Grant St., Stockton, CA 95202.

League of Women Voters of the U.S. Membership: 122,000. President, Ruth J. Hinerfeld. Headquarters: 1730 M St. NW, Washington, DC 20036.

Lions International. Membership: 1,265,672 in 33,071 clubs in 150 countries and areas. Annual convention: Chicago, July 2–5, 1980. President, Lloyd Morgan. Headquarters: 300 22nd St., Oak Brook, IL 60570.

Mental Health Association. Membership: 800 state and local organizations. Executive director, Jack McAllister. Headquarters: 1800 N. Kent St., Arlington, VA 22209.

Modern Language Association of America. Membership: 30,000. President, Helen Vendler. Headquarters: 62 Fifth Ave., New York, NY 10011.

National Academy of Sciences. Membership: approx. 1,250. Annual meeting: Washington, DC, April 1980. President, Philip Handler. Headquarters: 2101 Constitution Ave. NW, Washington, DC 20418.

National Association for the Advancement of Colored People. Membership: 450,000 in 1,700 units. National convention: Miami Beach, June 30–July 4, 1980. President, W. Montague Cobb, M.D.; board chairman, Margaret Bush Wilson; executive director, Benjamin L. Hooks. Headquarters: 1790 Broadway, New York, NY 10019.

National Association of Manufacturers. Membership: 13,000. President, Heath Larry. Headquarters: 1776 F St. NW, Washington, DC 20006.

National Audubon Society. Membership: 400,000. President, R. W. Peterson; senior vice president, P. M. Howard, Jr. Headquarters: 950 Third Ave., New York, NY 10022.

National Conference of Christians and Jews, Inc. Membership: 70 regional offices. President, David Hyatt. Headquarters: 43 W. 57th St., New York, NY 10019.

National Council of the Churches of Christ in the U.S.A. Membership: 32 Protestant, Anglican, and Orthodox denominations. President, Rev. M. William Howard; general secretary, Dr. Claire Randall. Headquarters: 475 Riverside Dr., New York, NY 10027.

National Council on the Aging. Membership: 3,600. Executive director, Jack Ossofsky. Headquarters: 1828 L St. NW, Washington, DC 20036.

National Easter Seal Society for Crippled Children and Adults. Membership: 50 state and territorial societies. President, Mrs. Edward Plaut. Headquarters: 2023 W. Ogden Ave., Chicago, IL 60612.

National Education Association of the U.S. Membership: 1,800,000 with units in every state, and 12,000 local affiliates. Annual meeting: Los Angeles, July 1980. President, Willard H. McGuire. Headquarters: 1201 16th St. NW, Washington, DC 20036.

National Federation of Business and Professional Women's Clubs, Inc. Membership: 162,999 in 3,678 clubs. President, Julia K. Arri. Headquarters: 2012 Massachusetts Ave. NW, Washington, DC 20036.

National Federation of Independent Business, Inc. Membership: 582,000. President, Wilson S. Johnson. Headquarters: 150 W. 20th Ave., San Mateo, CA 94403.

National Federation of Music Clubs. Membership: 500,000 in 4,300 clubs and 12 national affiliates. Annual fall session:

Sun Valley, ID, August 1980. President, Mrs. Jack C. Ward. Headquarters: 310 S. Michigan Ave., Chicago, IL 60604.

National Foundation—March of Dimes, The. Membership: 959 chapters. President, Charles L. Massey. Headquarters: 1275 Mamaroneck Ave., White Plains, NY 10605.

National Organization for Women (NOW). Membership: 100,000 members, 800 local groups. President, Eleanor Smeal. Headquarters: 425 13th St., Suite 1001, Washington, DC 20004.

National PTA (National Parent-Teacher Association). Membership: 6,170,141 in 28,963 local units. National convention: Honolulu, June 15–18, 1980. President, Mrs. Virginia V. Sparling. Headquarters: 700 N. Rush St., Chicago, IL 60611.

National Safety Council. Membership: 15,000. National Safety Congress and Exposition: Chicago, Oct. 20–23, 1980. President, Vincent L. Tofany. Headquarters: 444 N. Michigan Ave., Chicago, IL 60611.

National Urban League, Inc. President, Vernon E. Jordan, Jr. Headquarters: 500 E. 62nd St., New York, NY 10021.

National Woman's Christian Temperance Union. Membership: about 250,000 in 6,000 local unions. National convention: Wichita, KS, August 26–Sept. 1, 1980. President, Mrs. Herman Stanley. Headquarters: 1730 Chicago Ave., Evanston, IL 60201.

Parents Without Partners. Membership: 180,000. International convention: Dallas, July 9–13, 1980. Executive director, Virginia L. Martin. International office: 7910 Woodmont Ave., No. 1000, Washington, DC 20014.

Phi Beta Kappa. Membership: 355,000. Secretary, Kenneth M. Greene. Headquarters: 1811 Q St. NW, Washington, DC 20009.

Photographic Society of America. Membership: 18,700. Executive director, Harold J. Vermes. Headquarters: 2005 Walnut St., Philadelphia, PA 19103.

Planned Parenthood Federation of America, Inc. (Planned Parenthood—World Population). Membership: 188 U.S. affiliates. President, Faye Wattleton; chairperson of the Federation, Fred Smith. Headquarters: 810 Seventh Ave., New York, NY 10019.

Rotary International. Membership: 851,500 in 18,274 clubs functioning in 153 countries. International convention: Chicago, June 1–5, 1980. General secretary, Herbert A. Pigman. Headquarters: 1600 Ridge Ave., Evanston, IL 60201.

Salvation Army, The. Membership: 396,238. National commander: Ernest W. Holz. Headquarters: 120 W. 14th St., New York, NY 10011.

Special Libraries Association. Membership: 11,500. Annual conference: Washington, DC, June 1980. President, Joseph M. Dagnese. Headquarters: 235 Park Ave. S., New York, NY 10003.

United Dairy Industry Association (including American Dairy Association, Dairy Research Inc., National Dairy Council). Annual convention: New Orleans, March 19–22, 1980. Executive vice president, John W. Sliter. Headquarters: 6300 N. River Rd., Rosemont, IL 60018.

United States Jaycees, The. Membership: 380,000 in 9,200 affiliated groups. Annual meeting: Cleveland, June 1980. President, Terryl Bechtol. Headquarters: P.O. Box 7, Tulsa, OK 74121.

United Way of America. Service organization for over 2,200 autonomous local United Way organizations. Chairman of the board of governors, Clifton C. Garvin, Jr. Headquarters: 801 N. Fairfax St., Alexandria, VA 22314.

Veterans of Foreign Wars of the United States. Membership: V.F.W. and Auxiliary: 2,499,000. Commander-in-chief: Howard VanderClute. Headquarters: V.F.W. Building, Broadway at 34th St., Kansas City, MO 64111.

World Council of Churches (U.S. Conference). Membership: 28 churches or denominations in U.S. Moderator, Robert J. Marshall. Headquarters: 475 Riverside Dr., New York, NY 10027.

Young Men's Christian Associations (National Council). Membership: 9,801,296 in 1,821 associations. National board chairman, Elija M. Hicks, Jr. Headquarters: 291 Broadway, New York, NY 10007.

Young Women's Christian Association of the U.S.A. Members and participants: approx. 2,400,000. President, Jewel Freeman Graham. Headquarters: 600 Lexington Ave., New York, NY 10022.

Zionist Organization of America. Membership: 130,000 in 600 districts. President, Ivan J. Novick; national executive director, Paul Flacks. Headquarters: ZOA House, 4 E. 34th St., New York, NY 10016.

CONTRIBUTORS

ADRIAN, CHARLES R., Professor of Political Science, University of California, Riverside; Coauthor, *Governing Urban America:* CALIFORNIA; LOS ANGELES; SAN FRANCISCO

ALEXANDER, ROBERT J., Professor of Economics and Political Science, Rutgers University: ECUADOR; GUYANA; URUGUAY

ALLER, LAWRENCE H., Professor of Astronomy, University of California; Author, *Atoms, Stars, and Nebulae* and *Astrophysics, I and II:* ASTRONOMY

AMBRE, AGO, Economist, Bureau of Economic Analysis, U. S. Department of Commerce: INDUSTRIAL REVIEW

BALLINGER, RONALD B., Professor and Chairman, Department of History, Rhode Island College: BIOGRAPHY— *Bishop Muzorewa;* SOUTH AFRICA; ZIMBABWE RHODESIA

BARMASH, ISADORE, Financial writer, *The New York Times;* Author, *The Chief Executives:* CONSUMER AFFAIRS —*The Credit Card and Personal Credit;* RETAILING

BECK, KAY, School of Urban Life, Georgia State University: GEORGIA

BERGEN, DAN, Professor, Graduate Library School, University of Rhode Island: LIBRARIES

BERLIN, MICHAEL, Diplomatic Correspondent, *New York Post:* UNITED NATIONS

BERLOW, ALAN, Reporter for *Congressional Quarterly:* UNITED STATES—*The Growth of Lobbies*

BEST, JOHN, Chief, *Canada World News,* Ottawa: NEW BRUNSWICK; PRINCE EDWARD ISLAND

BISSELL, RICHARD E., Research Associate, Foreign Policy Research Institute; Author, *Apartheid and International Organizations;* Managing Editor, *Orbis:* AFRICA

BLOOM, MARK, Senior Writer, *Medical World News:* MEDICINE AND HEALTH

BÖDVARSSON, HAUKUR, Coeditor, *News From Iceland:* ICELAND

BOLUS, JIM, Sportswriter, *The Louisville Times;* Author, *Run for the Roses:* SPORTS—*Horse Racing*

BOND, DONOVAN H., Professor of Journalism, West Virginia University: WEST VIRGINIA

BOULAY, HARVEY, Associate Professor of Political Science, Boston University: MASSACHUSETTS

BOWERS, Q. DAVID, President, Bowers & Ruddy Galleries Inc.; member, board of governors, American Numismatic Association: COINS AND COIN COLLECTING

BRAMMER, DANA B., Associate Director, Bureau of Governmental Research, University of Mississippi: MISSISSIPPI

BRANDHORST, L. CARL, Associate Professor of Geography, Oregon College of Education: OREGON

BRODIN, PIERRE E., Director of Studies, Lycée Français de New York: LITERATURE—*French*

BROEG, ROBERT W., Sports Editor, *St. Louis Post-Dispatch:* SPORTS—*Baseball*

BURKS, ARDATH W., Professor of Asian Studies, Rutgers University; Author, *Japan, Profile of a Postindustrial Power:* BIOGRAPHY—*Masayoshi Ohira;* JAPAN

BUSH, G. W. A., Senior Lecturer in Political Studies, University of Auckland, New Zealand: NEW ZEALAND

BUTWELL, RICHARD, Vice President for Academic Programs and Professor of Political Science, Murray State University, Murray, KY; Author, *Southeast Asia Today and Tomorrow:* ASIA; BURMA; CAMBODIA; LAOS; PHILIPPINES; VIETNAM

CAIRNS, JOHN C., Professor of History, University of Toronto: FRANCE

CALABRESE, MICHAEL, Program Manager, National Aeronautics and Space Administration: SPACE EXPLORATION (article written independent of NASA)

CAMMACK, PAUL, Glasgow University, Scotland: BOLIVIA

CANN, STAN, Consultant, *The Forum,* Fargo: NORTH DAKOTA

CANTWELL, WILLIAM P., Attorney at Law, Denver, CO: LAW—*The Issue of Unmarried Cohabitation*

CHALMERS, JOHN W., Concordia College, Edmonton, Alberta: ALBERTA

COCKRUM, E. LENDELL, Professor and Head, Department of Ecology and Evolutionary Biology, University of Arizona: ZOOLOGY

COLE, GORDON H., Senior Staff Associate, George Meany Center for Labor Studies: LABOR

COLLINS, BOB, Sports Editor, *The Indianapolis Star:* SPORTS—*Auto Racing*

COMMANDAY, ROBERT, Music Critic, *San Francisco Chronicle:* BIOGRAPHY—*Zubin Mehta;* MUSIC—*Classical*

CORLEW, ROBERT E., Dean, School of Liberal Arts, Middle Tennessee State University: TENNESSEE

CORNWELL, ELMER E., JR., Professor of Political Science, Brown University: RHODE ISLAND

CRAIG, PAUL P., Professor, Department of Applied Science, University of California at Davis: ENERGY—*Three Mile Island and Nuclear Energy*

CUNNIFF, JOHN, Business Analyst, The Associated Press: UNITED STATES—*Economy*

CUNNINGHAM, PEGGY, Staff Reporter, *Baltimore News American:* MARYLAND

CURRIER, CHET, Writer on Investing and Personal Finance, The Associated Press: STOCKS AND BONDS

CURTIS, L. PERRY, JR., Professor of History, Brown University: IRELAND

DANIELS, ROBERT V., Professor of History, University of Vermont: VERMONT

DARBY, JOSEPH W., III, Reporter, *The Times-Picayune,* New Orleans: LOUISIANA

DAVIS, WILLIAM A., Travel Editor, *The Boston Globe:* TRAVEL

DeGREGORIO, GEORGE, Sports Department, *The New York Times:* SPORTS—*Introduction, Boxing, Skiing, Swimming, Track, Miscellaneous Summary*

DELZELL, CHARLES F., Professor of History, Vanderbilt University; Editor, *The Future of History:* ITALY

DENNIS, LARRY, Associate Editor, *Golf Digest;* Coauthor, *How to Become a Complete Golfer:* SPORTS—*Golf*

DOBLER, CLIFFORD I., Professor Emeritus of Business Law, University of Idaho: IDAHO

DOLAN, PAUL, Professor of Political Science, University of Delaware; Coauthor, *Government of Delaware:* DELAWARE

DORPALEN, ANDREAS, Professor Emeritus of History, The Ohio State University; 1978 recipient of the Distinguished Service Award of the Ohio Academy of History: GERMANY

DREYFUSS, JOHN, Architecture and Design Critic, *Los Angeles Times:* ARCHITECTURE

DRIGGS, DON W., Chairman, Department of Political Science, University of Nevada: NEVADA

DUFF, ERNEST A., Professor of Political Science, National Autonomous University of Mexico; Author, *Agrarian Reform in Colombia:* COLOMBIA

DUROSKA, LUD, Sports Department, *The New York Times;* Author, *Great Pro Quarterbacks:* SPORTS—*Football*

DURRENCE, J. LARRY, Department of History, Florida Southern College: FLORIDA

DVARACKAS, PETER, Editor of *DIVA,* the weekly opera newsletter: MUSIC—*The Spoleto Festival*

EDELMAN, MARIAN W., Director, Children's Defense Fund: INTERNATIONAL YEAR OF THE CHILD

EINFRANK, AARON R., Free-lance writer: THE NETHERLANDS; THE THIRD WORLD

ELGIN, RICHARD, State Desk, *The Patriot-News,* Harrisburg: PENNSYLVANIA

ELKINS, ANN M., Fashion Director, *Good Housekeeping Magazine:* FASHION

ENSTAD, ROBERT H., Reporter, *Chicago Tribune:* BIOGRAPHY—*Jane Byrne;* CHICAGO; ILLINOIS

EPSTEIN, EDWARD, Copy Editor, *The Asian Wall Street Journal:* MALAYSIA; SINGAPORE; THAILAND

ETCHESON, WARREN W., Graduate School of Business Administration, University of Washington: WASHINGTON

EWEGEN, BOB, Editorial Writer, *The Denver Post:* COLORADO

FISHER, RED, Sports Editor, *The Montreal Star:* SPORTS—*Hockey*

FOLEJEWSKI, ZBIGNIEW, Professor and Chairman, Department of Slavic Studies and Modern Languages, University of Ottawa: LITERATURE—*Soviet*

FRIEDEL, ROBERT, Clarkson College of Technology, Potsdam, NY: ELECTRICITY—*100th Anniversary of the Light Bulb*

FRIIS, ERIK J., Editor-Publisher, *The Scandinavian-American Bulletin;* Author, *The American-Scandinavian Foundation, 1910–1960: A Brief History:* DENMARK; FINLAND; GREENLAND

GAILEY, HARRY A., Professor of History and Coordinator of African Studies, San Jose State University, California: GHANA; NIGERIA

GARFIELD, ROBERT, Associate Professor of History, Co-Director, Afro-American Studies Program, DePaul University, Chicago: KENYA; TANZANIA; UGANDA

GEIS, GILBERT, Professor, Program in Social Ecology, University of California, Irvine; Author, *Man, Crime, and Society:* CRIME

GJESTER, THOR, Editor, *Økonomisk Revy,* Oslo: NORWAY

GOODMAN, DONALD, Associate Professor of Sociology, John Jay College of Criminal Justice: PRISONS

GORDON, MAYNARD M., Editor, *Motor News Analysis* and *The Imported Car Reports:* AUTOMOBILES

GORHAM, WILLIAM, President, The Urban Institute; Co-author, *The Urban Predicament:* CITIES AND URBAN AFFAIRS

GOUGH, BARRY M., Associate Professor of History, Wilfrid Laurier University; Author, *Canada:* BIOGRAPHY—*Charles Joseph Clark, Edward Schreyer;* CANADA—*Review, The Year of the Tories*

GRAYSON, GEORGE W., Professor of Government, College of William and Mary; Author, *El Partido Demócrata Cristiano Chileno:* PORTUGAL; SPAIN

GREEN, MAUREEN, Free-lance British Journalist: GREAT BRITAIN—*The Arts*

GRENIER, FERNAND, Director General, Télé-université, Université du Québéc: MONTREAL; QUEBEC

GROTH, ALEXANDER J., Professor of Political Science, University of California, Davis; Author, *People's Poland:* POLAND

GRUBERG, MARTIN, Professor of Political Science, University of Wisconsin, Oshkosh: CIVIL LIBERTIES AND CIVIL RIGHTS; LAW—*International*

GUNN, JOHN M., Former Professor of Radio-TV-Film, State University of New York, Albany: TELEVISION AND RADIO

HAGER, MARY, Correspondent, *Newsweek* Magazine: MEDICINE AND HEALTH—*Smoking*

HAKKARINEN, IDA-MARIE, Graduate Assistant, Department of Meteorology, University of Maryland: METEOROLOGY—*The Weather Year*

HALLMUNDSSON, HALLBERG, Author and editor: STATISTICAL AND TABULAR DATA—*Nations of the World*

HALLMUNDSSON, MAY NEWMAN, Adjunct Associate Professor of English, Baruch College of the City University of New York: WOMEN

HAND, SAMUEL B., Professor of History, University of Vermont: VERMONT

HARVEY, ROSS M., Assistant Director of Information, Government of the Northwest Territories: NORTHWEST TERRITORIES

HAYDEN, DOROTHY, Director, Prairie History Room, Regina Public Library: SASKATCHEWAN

HAYES, KIRBY M., Professor of Food Science and Nutrition, University of Massachusetts: FOOD

HEADY, EARL O., Distinguished Professor of Agricultural Economics, Iowa State University; Author, *Economics of Agricultural Production and Resource, Agricultural Policies Under Economic Development, Farm Records and Accounts:* AGRICULTURE

HEBERLEIN, GREG, Sports Department, *Seattle Times,* Seattle, WA: SPORTS—*Basketball*

HELMREICH, E. C., Thomas B. Reed Professor of History and Political Science, Bowdoin College, Bowdoin, ME; Author, *The German Churches Under Hitler: Background, Struggle, and Epilogue:* AUSTRIA

HELMREICH, JONATHAN E., Professor of History and Dean of Instruction, Allegheny College, Meadville, PA; Author, *Belgium and Europe: A Study in Small Power Diplomacy:* LUXEMBOURG

HELMREICH, PAUL C., Professor of History, Wheaton College: SWITZERLAND

HELMS, ANDREA R. C., Associate Professor of Political Science, University of Alaska: ALASKA

HENDERSON, JIM, Sportswriter, *The Tampa Tribune, The Sporting News;* Author, *Annual Soccer Guide:* SPORTS—*Soccer*

HENRIKSEN, THOMAS H., National Fellow, Hoover Institution, Stanford University, CA; Author, *Mozambique: A History:* ANGOLA; ZAIRE

HENRY, DIANE, Stamford (CT) Bureau, *The New York Times:* CONNECTICUT

HERBERT, WALTER B., Consultant on Canadian Cultural Matters; Fellow of the Royal Society of Arts: CANADA—*Cultural Affairs*

HOGGART, SIMON, Political Correspondent, *The Guardian,* London; Author, *The Pact:* BIOGRAPHY—*Margaret Thatcher;* GREAT BRITAIN—*Review, The Election;* OBITUARIES—*Lord Mountbatten*

HOOVER, HERBERT T., Professor of History, University of South Dakota: SOUTH DAKOTA

HOPKO, THOMAS, REV., Assistant Professor, St. Vladimir's Orthodox Theological Seminary: RELIGION—*Orthodox Eastern*

HOWARD, HARRY N., Board of Governors, Middle East Institute, Washington, DC; Author, *Turkey, the Straits and U. S. Policy:* TURKEY

HUCKSHORN, ROBERT J., Professor of Social Science, Florida Atlantic University: OBITUARIES—*Nelson A. Rockefeller*

HULBERT, DAN, *The New York Times:* NEW YORK; NEW YORK CITY

HUME, ANDREW, Free-lance writer/photographer, former reporter, *The Whitehorse* (Yukon) *Star:* YUKON TERRITORY

HUTH, JOHN F., JR., Reporter-columnist, *The Plain Dealer,* Cleveland: CITIES—*Cleveland;* OHIO

JACKSON, LIVIA E. BITTON, Professor of Judaic Studies, Herbert H. Lehman College, City University of New York: RELIGION—*Judaism*

JAFFE, HERMAN J., Department of Anthropology, Brooklyn College, City University of New York: ANTHROPOLOGY

JEWELL, MALCOLM E., Professor of Political Science, University of Kentucky; Coauthor, *Kentucky Politics:* KENTUCKY

JOHNSTON, ROBERT L., Editor, *The Catholic Review,* newsweekly of the Baltimore Archdiocese: OBITUARIES—*Archbishop Fulton Sheen;* POLAND—*The Pope's Trip;* RELIGION—*Roman Catholicism*

JOHNSTONE, J. K., Professor of English, University of Saskatchewan; Fellow of the Royal Society of Literature; Author, *The Bloomsbury Group: A Study of E. M. Forster, Lytton Strachey, Virginia Woolf, and Their Circle:* LITERATURE—*English*

JONES, H. G., Curator, North Carolina Collection, University of North Carolina Library: NORTH CAROLINA

KAO, DIANA L., Associate Professor, Asian Studies Department, The City College, City University of New York; Chairman, Chinese Language Teachers Association; Author, *Structure of the Syllable in Cantonese:* CHINA—*Pinyin*

KARNES, THOMAS L., Professor and Chairman, Department of History, Arizona State University; Author, *Latin American Policy of the United States* and *Failure of Union: Central America 1824–1960:* CENTRAL AMERICA; CENTRAL AMERICA—*Nicaragua*

KARSKI, JAN, Professor of Government, Georgetown University; Author, *Story of a Secret State:* BULGARIA; HUNGARY; RUMANIA

KASH, DON E., Professor, University of Oklahoma; Author, *Our Energy Future: The Role of Research, Development, and Demonstration in Reaching a National Consensus on Energy Supply:* ENERGY; ENERGY—*Alternatives to Petroleum*

KEHR, ERNEST A., Stamp News Bureau; Author, *The Romance of Stamp Collecting:* STAMPS AND STAMP COLLECTING

KIMBALL, LORENZO K., Professor of Political Science, University of Utah: UTAH

KIMBELL, CHARLES L., Supervisory Physical Scientist, United States Bureau of Mines: MINING; STATISTICAL AND TABULAR DATA—*World Mineral Production*

KING, PETER J., Associate Professor of History, Carleton University: ONTARIO; OTTAWA

KISSELGOFF, ANNA, Chief Dance Critic, *The New York Times:* DANCE

KOSAKI, RICHARD H., Professor of Political Science, University of Hawaii: HAWAII

LAI, CHUEN-YAN DAVID, Associate Professor of Geography, University of Victoria, B. C.: HONG KONG

LANDSBERG, H. E., Professor Emeritus, University of Maryland: METEOROLOGY

LARSEN, WILLIAM, Professor of History, Radford University; Author, *Montague of Virginia, The Making of a Southern Progressive:* VIRGINIA

LAURENT, PIERRE-HENRI, Professor of History, Tufts University; Adjunct Professor of Diplomatic History, Fletcher School of Law and Diplomacy: BELGIUM

LAWRENCE, ROBERT M., Professor, Department of Political Science, Colorado State University; Author, *Arms Control and Disarmament: Practice and Promise* and *Nuclear Proliferation: Phase II:* MILITARY AFFAIRS

LEE, STEWART M., Professor and Chairman, Department of Economics and Business Administration, Geneva College, Beaver Falls, PA; Coauthor, *Economics for Consumers;* Editor, Newsletter, American Council on Consumer Interests: CONSUMERISM

LEIDEN, CARL, Professor of History, University of Texas, Austin; Coauthor, *Politics/Middle East:* BANGLADESH; EGYPT; PAKISTAN

LEVITT, MORRIS J., Professor, Graduate Department of Political Science, Howard University; Coauthor, *State and Local Government and Politics:* WASHINGTON, DC

LIDDLE, R. WILLIAM, Professor of Political Science, Ohio State University; Author, *Political Participation in Modern Indonesia:* INDONESIA

LINDAHL, MAC, Harvard University: SWEDEN

LOBRON, BARBARA, Writer, Editor, Photographer; Founding Member and Contributing Editor, *Photograph* magazine: PHOTOGRAPHY

LORD, RODNEY, Economic Correspondent, *The Daily Telegraph,* London: GREAT BRITAIN—*The Economy*

LOTT, LEO B., Professor of Political Science, University of Montana; Author, *Venezuela and Paraguay: Political Modernity and Tradition in Conflict:* PARAGUAY; VENEZUELA

MABRY, DONALD J., Associate Professor of History, Mississippi State University; Author, *Mexico's Acción Nacional: A Catholic Alternative to Revolution:* MEXICO; MEXICO—*U. S.-Mexican Relations*

MACAULAY, NEILL, Professor of History, University of Florida; Author, *The Prestes Column; The Sandino Affair; A Rebel in Cuba:* BIOGRAPHY—*João Baptista Figueiredo;* BRAZIL; LATIN AMERICA

McCORQUODALE, SUSAN, Associate Professor, Department of Political Science, Memorial University of Newfoundland: NEWFOUNDLAND

McDOUGALL, EDGAR J., JR., Assistant Professor in Finance, Member of the Center for Real Estate and Urban Economic Studies, University of Connecticut: HOUSING

McGILL, DAVID A., Professor of Ocean Science, U. S. Coast Guard Academy: OCEANOGRAPHY

MARCOPOULOS, GEORGE J., Associate Professor of History, Tufts University, Medford, MA: CYPRUS; GREECE

MATHEWS, THOMAS G., Research Professor, Institute of Caribbean Studies, University of Puerto Rico; Author, *Politics and Economics in the Caribbean* and *Puerto Rican Politics and the New Deal:* CARIBBEAN; PUERTO RICO; VIRGIN ISLANDS

MEYER, EDWARD H., President and Chairman of the Board, Grey Advertising Inc.: ADVERTISING

MEYER, PETER, Free-lance journalist, New York City; Author, *James Earl Carter: The Man and the Myth:* LAND: *The Vast Estate—The American Dream*

MICHAELIS, PATRICIA A., Kansas State Historical Society, Topeka, KA: KANSAS

MILENKOVITCH, MICHAEL, Department of Political Science, Lehman College of City University of New York: YUGOSLAVIA

MILLER, JULIE ANN, Life Sciences Editor, *Science News,* Washington, DC: BIOCHEMISTRY; MICROBIOLOGY

MIRE, JOSEPH, Former Executive Director, National Institute for Labor Education: LABOR

MITCHELL, GARY, Professor of Physics, North Carolina State University, Raleigh: LASERS; PHYSICS

MORAN, MICHAEL, Administrative Assistant, United States Olympic Committee: SPORTS—*Pan Am Games*

MULDOON, RICHARD P., Division of Polar Programs, National Science Foundation: POLAR RESEARCH

NADLER, PAUL, Professor of Finance, Rutgers University; Author, *Commercial Banking in the Economy* and *Paul Nadler Writes About Banking:* BANKING

NAFTALIN, ARTHUR, Professor of Public Affairs, Hubert H. Humphrey Institute of Public Affairs, University of Minnesota: MINNESOTA

NEILL, R. F., Associate Professor of Economics, Carleton University, Ont.: CANADA—*The Economy*

NEWMAN, PETER C., Editor, *Maclean's Magazine;* Author, *Renegade in Power: The Diefenbaker Years:* OBITUARIES —*John Diefenbaker*

NEWSOM, DONALD W., Professor and Head, Department of Horticulture, Louisiana State University: BOTANY; GARDENING AND HORTICULTURE; GARDENING AND HORTICULTURE—*Home Gardening*

NIENABER, JEANNE, Assistant Professor, Department of Political Science, University of Arizona; Coauthor, *The Budgeting and Evaluation of Federal Recreation Programs:* ARIZONA

NOLAN, WILLIAM C., Associate Professor of Political Science, Southern Arkansas University: ARKANSAS

NOVICKI, MARGARET A., Associate Editor, *African Update,* The African-American Institute: ALGERIA; MOROCCO; SUDAN; TUNISIA

OCHSENWALD, WILLIAM L., Associate Professor of History, Virginia Polytechnic Institute; Editor, *Nationalism in a Non-National State;* Author, *The Hijaz Railroad:* SAUDI ARABIA

OLDENBURG, RICHARD E., Director, The Museum of Modern Art: ART—*The Museum of Modern Art*

OMENN, GILBERT S., Associate Professor of Medicine, Division of Medical Genetics, University of Washington, Assistant Director for Human Resources and Social and Economic Services, Office of Science and Technology Policy, Executive Office of the President, Washington, DC; Coeditor, *Genetics, Environment and Behavior: Implications for Educational Policy:* GENETICS

PALMER, NORMAN D., Professor of Political Science and South Asian Studies, University of Pennsylvania; Author, *Elections and Political Development: The South Asian Experience:* INDIA; SRI LANKA

PALMIERI, VICTOR H., Coordinator for Refugee Affairs, U. S. Department of State: ASIA—*The Refugees*

PANO, NICOLAS C., Associate Professor of History, Western Illinois University; Author, *The People's Republic of Albania:* ALBANIA

PARDES, HERBERT, Director, National Institute of Mental Health: MEDICINE AND HEALTH—*Mental Health*

PARKER, FRANKLIN, Benedum Professor of Education, West Virginia University; Author, *Battle of the Books: Kanawha County; What Can We Learn from the Schools of China?; British Schools and Ours:* EDUCATION

PEARSON, NEALE J., Associate Professor of Political Science, Texas Tech University: CHILE; PERU

PERKINS, KENNETH J., Assistant Professor of History, University of South Carolina: LIBYA; MALTA; RELIGION— *Islam*

PIPPIN, LARRY L., Professor of Political Science, Elbert Covell College, University of the Pacific; Author, *The Remón Era:* ARGENTINA

PLATT, HERMANN K., Professor of History, St. Peter's College, Jersey City: NEW JERSEY

PLISCHKE, ELMER, Professor Emeritus, University of Maryland; Adjunct Professor, Gettysburg College; Author, *Conduct of American Diplomacy* and *Microstates in World Affairs: Policy Problems and Options; Modern Diplomacy: The Art and the Artisans:* UNITED STATES— *Foreign Affairs*

POPKIN, HENRY, Professor of English, State University of New York, Buffalo; Visiting Professor, The Sorbonne, Paris: THEATER

POULLADA, LEON B., Professor of Political Science, Northern Arizona University; Author, *Reform and Rebellion in Afghanistan:* AFGHANISTAN

PRITCHETT, C. HERMAN, Professor of Political Science, University of California, Santa Barbara; Author, *The Roosevelt Court* and *The American Constitution:* LAW— *The Supreme Court*

QUIRK, WILLIAM H., North American Editor, *Construction Industry International* magazine: ENGINEERING, CIVIL

RAGUSA, ISA, Research Art Historian, Department of Art and Archaeology, Princeton University: ART

RAYMOND, ELLSWORTH L., Professor of Politics, New York University; Author, *Soviet Economic Progress* and *The Soviet State:* MOSCOW; UNION OF SOVIET SOCIALIST REPUBLICS

RICHARD, JOHN B., Department of Political Science, University of Wyoming; Author, *Government and Politics of Wyoming:* WYOMING

RODRIGUEZ, ALFRED, Professor, Department of Modern and Classical Languages, University of New Mexico: LITERATURE—*Spanish and Spanish-American*

ROEDER, RICHARD B., Professor of History, Montana State University: MONTANA

ROSE, ERNST, Professor Emeritus, New York University; Author, *A History of German Literature:* LITERATURE— *German*

ROSS, RUSSELL M., Professor of Political Science, University of Iowa; Author, *Iowa Government & Administration* and *State and Local Government & Administration:* IOWA

ROTHSTEIN, MORTON, Professor of History, University of Wisconsin, Madison: SOCIAL WELFARE

ROWLETT, RALPH M., Professor of Anthropology, University of Missouri; Coauthor, *Neolithic Levels on the Titelberg:* ARCHAEOLOGY

RUFF, NORMAN J., Assistant Professor, University of Victoria, B. C.: BRITISH COLUMBIA; VANCOUVER

SAFER, MORLEY, Correspondent, *Sixty Minutes,* CBS: MORLEY SAFER REVIEWS THE 1970's

SAKURAI, EMIKO, Professor, Department of East Asian Languages, University of Hawaii: LITERATURE—*Japanese*

SALSINI, PAUL, State Editor, *The Milwaukee Journal:* WISCONSIN

SAMUELSON, PAUL A., Institute Professor, Massachusetts Institute of Technology; Recipient, Nobel Prize: RECESSION—*Causes and Consequences*

SAMUELSON, WILLIAM F., Assistant Professor, Boston University: RECESSION—*Causes and Consequences*

SAVAGE, DAVID, Lecturer, Department of English, Simon Fraser University: LITERATURE—*Canadian: English*

SCHERER, RON, Business and Financial Correspondent, *The Christian Science Monitor:* BUSINESS AND CORPORATE AFFAIRS

SCHRIVER, EDWARD, University of Maine, Orono; Author, *Go Free: Antislavery, Maine 1833–1855:* MAINE

SCHWAB, PETER, Associate Professor of Political Science, State University of New York at Purchase; Author, *Decision-Making in Ethiopia:* ETHIOPIA

SCOTT, EUGENE L., Publisher and Founder, *Tennis Week;* Author, *Tennis: Game of Motion* and *Racquetball: A Cult:* BIOGRAPHY—*Martina Navratilova;* SPORTS—*Tennis*

SETH, R. P., Professor of Economics, Mount Saint Vincent University, Halifax: NOVA SCOTIA

SEYBOLD, PAUL G., Associate Professor of Chemistry, Wright State University, Dayton, OH: CHEMISTRY

SHINN, RINN-SUP, Senior Research Scientist, Foreign Area Studies, The American University, Washington, DC; Coauthor, *Area Handbook for North Korea; Area Handbook for South Korea:* KOREA

SHOGAN, ROBERT, National Political Correspondent, Washington Bureau, *Los Angeles Times;* Author, *A Question of Judgement* and *Promises to Keep:* BIOGRAPHY—*Benjamin R. Civiletti, Charles W. Duncan, Jr., Neil E. Goldschmidt, Moon Landrieu;* UNITED STATES—*Domestic Affairs*

SIEGEL, STANLEY E., Professor of History, University of Houston; Author, *A Political History of the Texas Republic, 1836–1845:* HOUSTON; TEXAS

SIMMONS, MARC, Author, *New Mexico, A Bicentennial History:* NEW MEXICO

SLOAN, HENRY S., Associate Editor, *Current Biography:* BIOGRAPHY—*Russell Baker, Billy Joel, Donald F. McHenry, Steve Martin, Barbara Tuchman, Jon Voight, Thomas J. Watson, Jr.;* OBITUARIES—*Arthur Fiedler, Richard Rodgers*

SMITH, BRADFORD A., Department of Planetary Sciences, University of Arizona: SPACE EXPLORATION—*Jupiter*

SPERA, DOMINIC, Associate Professor of Music, Indiana University; Author, *The Prestige Series—16 Original Compositions for Jazz Band; Jazz Improvisation Series— Book I "Blues and the Basics," Book II "Making the Changes":* MUSIC—*Jazz*

STENCEL, SANDRA L., Associate Editor, *Editorial Research Reports:* THE CHARITY BUSINESS

STERN, JEROME H., Associate Professor of English, Florida State University: BIOGRAPHY—*John Cheever;* LITERATURE —*American*

STOKES, WILLIAM LEE, Professor, Department of Geology and Geophysics, University of Utah; Author, *Essentials of Earth History* and *Introduction to Geology:* GEOLOGY

STOUDEMIRE, ROBERT H., Professor of Political Science, University of South Carolina: SOUTH CAROLINA

SYLVESTER, LORNA LUTES, Associate Editor, *Indiana Magazine of History,* Indiana University: INDIANA

TABORSKY, EDWARD, Professor of Government, University of Texas, Austin; Author, *Communism in Czechoslovakia, 1948–1960;* and *Communist Penetration of the Third World:* CZECHOSLOVAKIA

TAFT, WILLIAM H., Professor of Journalism and Director of Graduate Studies, University of Missouri; Author, *American Journalism History:* PUBLISHING

TALBOTT, STROBE, Diplomatic Correspondent, *Time Magazine;* Author, *Endgame: The Inside Story of SALT II:* SALT II—*The Embattled Treaty*

TAN, CHESTER C., Professor of History, New York University; Author, *The Boxer Catastrophe* and *Chinese Political Thought in the 20th Century:* CHINA; TAIWAN

TAYLOR, WILLIAM L., Professor of History, Plymouth State College; Author, *A Productive Monopoly: The Effect of Railroad Control of the New England Coastal Steamship Lines:* NEW HAMPSHIRE

THEISEN, CHARLES W., Staff Writer, *The Detroit News:* MICHIGAN

THOMAS, JAMES D., Professor, Department of Political Science and Bureau of Public Administration, The University of Alabama: ALABAMA

TOBIN, MARY, Business Writer, United Press International: BIOGRAPHY—*Paul Volcker;* INTERNATIONAL TRADE AND FINANCE

TOWNE, RUTH W., Professor of History, Northeast Missouri State University; Author, *Senator William J. Stone and the Politics of Compromise:* MISSOURI

TURNER, ARTHUR CAMPBELL, Professor of Political Science, University of California, Riverside: BIOGRAPHY—*Ayatollah Khomeini;* IRAN; IRAQ; ISRAEL; MIDDLE EAST; YEMENS, THE

VALESIO, PAOLO, Professor of Italian, Yale University; Author, *Between Italian and French: The Fine Semantics of Active Versus Passive:* LITERATURE—*Italian*

VAN RIPER, PAUL P., Professor and Head, Department of Political Science, Texas A&M University; Author, *History of the United States Civil Service* and *The American Federal Executive* and *Handbook of Practical Politics:* POSTAL SERVICE

VOGT, BILL, Senior Editor, *National Wildlife* and *International Wildlife* magazines; Author, *How to Build a Better Outdoors:* ENVIRONMENT

VOLSKY, GEORGE, Center for Advanced International Studies, University of Miami: CUBA

WALKER, JEWEL, Professor, Department of Theater, University of Wisconsin, Milwaukee: THEATER—*Mime*

WALL, JAMES M., Editor, *The Christian Century;* Author, *Church and Cinema* and *Three European Directors:* RELIGION—*Protestantism*

WATTERS, ELSIE M., Director of Research, The Tax Foundation, Inc.: TAXATION

WEEKS, JEANNE G., Member, American Society of Interior Designers; Coauthor, *Fabrics for Interiors:* INTERIOR DESIGN

WEISMAN, CELIA B., Professor, Wurzweiler School of Social Work, Yeshiva University; Director, Yeshiva University Gerontological Institute; Author, *The Future Is Now:* OLDER POPULATION

WEISS, JONATHAN M., Associate Professor of French, Department of Modern Languages, Colby College, Waterville, ME: LITERATURE—*Canadian: Quebec*

WEISS, PAULETTE, Popular Music Editor, *Stereo Review:* MUSIC—*Popular;* RECORDINGS

WENTZ, RICHARD E., Chairman, Religious Studies Department, Arizona State University; Author, *Saga of the American Soul:* RELIGION—*Survey, Far Eastern Religions*

WHEELER, JOHN ARCHIBALD, Ashbel Smith Professor and Director of the Center for Theoretical Physics, University of Texas, Austin; Author, *Einstein's Vision;* Recipient, Fermi Award, National Medal of Science: ALBERT EINSTEIN REMEMBERED

WHITNEY, DANIEL D., Senior Nuclear Engineer, Rancho Seco Nuclear Generating Station, Sacramento Municipal Utility District: ENERGY—*Three Mile Island and Nuclear Energy*

WHITNEY, DWIGHT, Chief, Hollywood Bureau, *TV Guide:* THE SITUATION COMEDY

WILLARD, F. NICHOLAS: JORDAN; LEBANON; SYRIA

WILLIAMS, DENNIS A., Associate Editor, *Newsweek:* ETHNIC GROUPS; OBITUARIES—*A. Philip Randolph*

WILLIAMS, ERNEST W., Professor of Transportation, Graduate School of Business, Columbia University; Author, *The Economics of Transportation and Logistics:* TRANSPORTATION

WILLIS, F. ROY, Professor of History, University of California, Davis; Author, *Italy Chooses Europe* and *France, Germany, and the New Europe:* BIOGRAPHY—*Simone Veil;* EUROPE; OBITUARIES—*Jean Monnet*

WOLF, WILLIAM, Film Critic, *Cue New York* Magazine; Author, *The Marx Brothers;* Coauthor, *The Landmark Films:* MOTION PICTURES; OBITUARIES—*Mary Pickford, John Wayne*

WOOD, JOHN W., Professor of Political Science, University of Oklahoma: OKLAHOMA

WOODS, GEORGE A., Children's Books Editor, *The New York Times;* Author, *Vibrations* and *Catch a Killer:* LITERATURE—*Children's*

YOUNGER, R. M., Author, *Australia and the Australians* and *Australia's Great River* and *Australia! Australia! March to Nationhood:* AUSTRALIA; KIRIBATI; SAINT LUCIA; SAINT VINCENT AND THE GRENADINES

ZABEL, ORVILLE H., Professor of History, Creighton University, Omaha: NEBRASKA

INDEX

Main article headings appear in this index as bold-faced capitals; subjects within articles appear as lower-case entries. Both the general references and the subentries should be consulted for maximum usefulness of this index. Illustrations are indexed herein. Cross references are to the entries in this index.

ALABAMA 94
Alabama, University of 470
ALASKA 95
Land Use 56
Petroleum 200
Alaska Pipeline: see Trans-
Alaska Pipeline System
Alawite Sect (Mus. rel.) 429,
488
ALBANIA 96
Statistical Data 573, 576
fol., 580
Yugoslavia 559
ALBERTA 96
Albuquerque, N.Mex.:
Illus. 203
Alcohol (chem.):
Gasohol 204, 339
Alcoholism:
Teenagers 443
Alevis (Mus. rel.) 429
Alexander, Lamar (Amer.
gov.) 498
Algae 410
ALGERIA 97, 87
Morocco 351
Statistical Data 573, 576,
577, 579, 580
Ali, Muhammad (Amer. athl.)
469
Alien (film) 357
Illus. 354
Alimony 94, 175, 297
Allagash River, Me. 320
All Digital Video Imaging Sys-
tem for Atmospheric Re-
search: see ADVISAR
Allelopathy (bot.) 143
Allen, Woody (Amer. writ.,
dir., act.) 356
Illus. 355
Alligator 211
All in the Family (TV series)
50
Illus. 23
Alonso, Dámaso (Sp. poet,
schol.) 317
Aluminum 578
Alvin (submersible vessel) 391
Ambassadors, U.S., List of
585
American Academy and Insti-
tute of Arts and Letters
Awards 415, 416
American Agricultural Move-
ment 283
American Airlines:
DC-10 Crash 512
American Ballet Theatre 187
American Broadcasting Com-
pany 494, 495
American Federation of Labor-
Congress of Industrial
Organizations 289
American Federation of Teach-
ers 192, 393
American Institute on Taiwan
489
American Library Association
303, 308
American Literature 305, 419
American Medical Association
328
American Motors Corporation
124, 125
American Numismatic Associa-
tion 176
American Petroleum Institute
534
American Telephone and Tele-
graph Company 359
Amin, Hafizullah (Afg. pres.)
84
Amin Dada, Idi (Ugandan
dict.) 86, 516
Libya 304
Tanzania 491
Amish (people) 398
Amnesty International:
Tunisia 514
Amniocentesis (med.) 327
Amos 'n' Andy (TV series):
Illus. 48
Amtrak 510, 514
Anderson, John (Amer. pol.)
531
Andreotti, Giulio (It. premier)
274, 276
Andrus, Cecil (Amer. pub.
offi.) 106
Anesthesia (med.):
Childbirth 327
Angelo Lauro (ship) 551
Anglim, Philip (Amer. act.)
500
Angoff, Charles (Amer. writ.,
prof.) 383

ANGOLA 98, 89, 90
Cuba 185
Statistical Data 573, 576
fol., 580
United Nations 526
Animal Behavior 567
Animal Feed:
Contamination 164, 338,
319
Animal Rights 566
Animals: see Livestock; Zool-
ogy
Antarctic 410
ANTHROPOLOGY 99
Antiballistic Missiles 9
Antibiotics 326
Antigua:
Statistical Data 573
Antimony 578
Antiques 108
Anti-Semitism 430
Anti-Smoking Legislation 329
Ants (insects) 566
Apocalypse Now (film) 353
Arab Deterrent Force 301, 302
Arab-Israeli Conflict 340
Austria 123
Egypt 196
Egyptian-Israeli Peace
Treaty 271, 340, 543
Jordan 282
Lebanon 301
Rumania 438
Saudi Arabia 440, 441
Syria 488
United Nations 525
USSR 521
Arab League 197, 282, 342,
514, 557
Arafat, Yasir (Pal. guerrilla
leader) 123, 302
Illus. 343
ARCHAEOLOGY 100
Archery 481
ARCHITECTURE 102
Prizes and Awards 415
Arctic 410
Arctic Ocean 230
ARGENTINA 105, 295
Automobiles 124
Literature 317
Pan American Games 461,
462
Statistical Data 573, 576,
577, 579, 580
ARIZONA 106
Tunnels 209
ARKANSAS 107
Arkansas, University of 470
Arms Control and Disarma-
ment:
Strategic Arms Limitation
Talks 6
United States 544
USSR 519
Arms Sales 345, 544
Egypt 197
Jordan 282
Kenya 285
Korea, South 287
Morocco 88, 351
Saudi Arabia 442
Thailand 499
Armstrong, Neil (Amer. astro-
naut):
Illus. 450
Arrington, Richard (Amer.
mayor) 94
ART 108
Canada 158
Great Britain 241
Investments 485
Museum of Modern Art 112
Photography 402
Photo-Murals 258
Prizes and Awards 415
Art Galleries: see Museums
and Galleries
Art Institute of Chicago, Ill.
110
Arts Council (Gt.Brit.) 241
Arzner, Dorothy (Amer. film
dir.) 383
Asbestos 347, 578
ASEAN: see Association of
Southeast Asian Nations
Ashe, Arthur (Amer. athl.)
480
ASIA 116
Refugees 118, 443
Steel 256
United States 544
USSR 520
Aspartame (artificial sweet-
ener) 221
Assad, Hafez al- (Syr. pres.)
488, 489

Assault (crime) 181
Association of Southeast Asian
Nations 93, 321, 442
Associations, List of 586
Astronauts 450
ASTRONOMY 121
Space Exploration 450 fol.
Atchafalaya River Basin, La.
319
Atherosclerosis (med.) 228
Atherton, Alfred (Amer. dipl.)
341
Atlanta, Ga. 230
Illus. 510
Atlanta Federal Penitentiary,
Ga. 414
Atlantic City, N.J. 368
Atmosphere 330, 331
Jupiter 454
Polar Research 410
Space Exploration 452
Atomic Weapons: see Nuclear
Weapons
Attica Prison, N.Y. 414
Atwood, Margaret (Can. au.)
310
Auctions:
Art 108
Coins 176
Race Horses 476
Audimeter 46
Austin, Tracy (Amer. athl.)
478
Illus. 479
AUSTRALIA 122
Agriculture 91, 92
Archaeology 100
Automobiles 124
Dams 209
Statistical Data 573, 576
fol.
AUSTRIA 123
Automobiles 124
International Trade and
Finance 263
Statistical Data 573, 576
fol.
AUTOMOBILES 124, 509, 529,
580
Business and Corporate Af-
fairs 147
Consumer Affairs 179
Industrial Review 256
Thefts 181
Auto Racing 463
Avco World Trophy (hockey)
474
Aviation: see Air Transporta-
tion
Awards: see Prizes and
Awards
Azerbaijanis (Turkic-speaking
people) 268

B

Baader-Meinhof Group (Ger.
terrorists) 182
Ba'ath Party (Arab pol.) 269
Backfire Bomber 11, 13
Bacteriology 339
Genetics 128
Badlands, reg., S.Dak. 449
Badminton 481
Baganda (Afr. people) 516
Bahamas 568
Pan American Games 462
Statistical Data 573
Bahrain 568
Statistical Data 573
Bahro, Rudolf (Ger. au.) 233
Baker, Howard (Amer. pol.)
531
BAKER, Russell (Amer. col-
umnist) 129
Bakhtiar, Shahpour (Iran. pol.
leader) 265
Bakr, Ahmed Hassan al- (Iraqi
pres.) 488
Balance of Payments:
Bolivia 142
Brazil 145
Great Britain 240
Hungary 247
Israel 342
Japan 277, 281
Kenya 285
Sudan 486
Switzerland 487
United States 260
Balanchine, George (Amer.
choreog.) 187, 188

Ball, Lucille (Amer. act.) 45
Illus. 49
Ballet: see Dance
Baltimore, Md. 323
Baltimore Colts (football team)
323
Baltimore Orioles (baseball
team) 323, 464
Bamboo (bot.) 143
Banabans (people) 285
BANGLADESH 125
India 253
Statistical Data 573, 576,
577, 580
BANKING 126, 537
Credit Cards 179, 180
Luxembourg 320
Bank Robberies 181
New York City 371
Barbados 568
Statistical Data 573
Barcelona, Spain:
Illus. 103
Barges 509
Barite 578
Barre, Raymond (Fr. prime
minis.) 222, 223, 225,
350
Barre, Siad (Somali pres.) 87
Barry, Marion (Amer. mayor):
Illus. 553
BART: see Bay Area Rapid
Transit
Barth, John (Amer. nov.) 305
Bartlett, Dewey F. (Amer.
pol.) 383
Baryshnikov, Mikhail (Russ.
dancer) 187
Illus. 21
Barzani, Mustafa al- (Kurd-
ish gen.) 383
Baseball 464
Stargell, Willie 137
Basketball 467
Basques (Eur. people) 223,
456
Bathurst, N.B., Can. 366
Battered Women 443
Battery 164
Bauxite 578
Bay Area Rapid Transit, Calif.
511
Bayh, Marvella (Amer. writer)
383
Bazargan, Mehdi (Iran. prime
minis.) 266
BBC: see British Broadcasting
Corporation
Beagle Channel Dispute, Arg.-
Chile 106
Beame, Abraham (Amer. may-
or) 371
Beef 91
Bee Gees (mus. group) 424
Illus. 415
Beer 580
Begin, Menahem (Isr. prime
minis.) 271, 272, 341
Illus. 67
BELGIUM 127
Automobiles 124
Statistical Data 573, 576
fol.
Zaire 560
Belize:
Pan American Games 462
Bell, Griffin (Amer. pub. offi.)
531
Bell System American Orches-
tras on Tour Program 359
Ben Bella, Ahmed (Alg. pol.)
98
Benin 86, 568
Statistical Data 573
Bennett, William R. (Can. pol.)
145
Bent, play (Sherman) 501
Berenson, Bernard (Amer. art
crit.) 108
Berg, Alban (Aus. comp.) 358
Bergland, Bob (Amer. pub.
offi.) 92
Illus. 91
Bering Sea 410
Berlin, Ger. 234
Berlinguer, Enrico (It. pol.)
274
Best Boy (film) 357
Best-Sellers (books) 419
Beta Phi Mu Award 302
Betting: see Gambling
Beverly Hillbillies, The (TV
series):
Illus. 47
Bezoar Stones 567
Bhutan 568
Statistical Data 573

H

J

K

Put The World At Your Fingertips . . .

ORDER THIS EXQUISITELY DETAILED LENOX GLOBE!

The world's never looked better! Why? Because this Lenox Globe — the most popular raised-relief model made by Replogle — is as stunning to look at as the living planet it represents.

Handsomely crafted and easy-to-use, the Lenox is the latest word in the state of the mapmaker's art — an ingenious marriage of classic, antique styling with clean, modern readability.

The Lenox is a giant 12-inch globe, beautifully inscribed with eye-catching "cartouches" and colorful compass "roses" . . . solidly-mounted on an elegantly sturdy, 18-inch Fruitwood stand . . . and covered with three dimensional "mountain ranges" children love to touch!

Five pounds light, the Lenox comes complete with a 32-page **STORY OF THE GLOBE** — a richly-illustrated, full-color handbook you and your whole family will refer to over and over again.

TO ORDER, simply send us your name and address, along with a check or money order for $29.95* to:

Grolier Yearbook, Inc.
Lenox Globe
Sherman Turnpike
Danbury, Connecticut 06816

*Please note: New York and Connecticut residents must add state sales tax.

THE LENOX GLOBE . . . by Replogle. Make it yours *today.*
(This offer good through May, 1981.)